THE JERUSALEM TALMUD

THIRD ORDER: NAŠIM
TRACTATE *KETUBOT*

SIXTH ORDER: TAHOROT
TRACTATE *NIDDAH*

STUDIA JUDAICA

FORSCHUNGEN ZUR WISSENSCHAFT DES JUDENTUMS

HERAUSGEGEBEN VON
E. L. EHRLICH UND G. STEMBERGER

BAND XXXIV

WALTER DE GRUYTER · BERLIN · NEW YORK

THE JERUSALEM TALMUD
תלמוד ירושלמי

THIRD ORDER: NAŠIM
סדר נשים
TRACTATE *KETUBOT*
מסכת כתובות

SIXTH ORDER: TAHOROT
סדר טהרות
TRACTATE *NIDDAH*
מסכת נדה

EDITION, TRANSLATION, AND COMMENTARY

BY

HEINRICH W. GUGGENHEIMER

WALTER DE GRUYTER · BERLIN · NEW YORK

ISBN 978-3-11-068122-2
e-ISBN (PDF) 978-3-11-091020-9

This volume is text- and page-identical with the hardback published in 2006.

Library of Congress Control Number: 2020942840

Bibliographic information published by the Deutsche Nationalbibliothek
The Deutsche Nationalbibliothek lists this publication in the
Deutsche Nationalbibliografie;
detailed bibliographic data are available on the Internet at http://dnb.dnb.de.

© 2020 Walter de Gruyter GmbH, Berlin/Boston

Printing and binding: CPI books GmbH, Leck

www.degruyter.com

Preface

The present volume is the eighth in this series of the Jerusalem Talmud, the third in a four volume edition, translation, and Commentary of the Third Order of this Talmud. It also contains an edition of the surviving fragment of Tractate *Niddah*, of the Sixth Order. The principles of the edition regarding text, vocalization, and Commentary have been spelled out in detail in the Introduction to the first volume. The text in this volume is based on the manuscript text of the Yerushalmi edited by the Academy of the Hebrew Language, Jerusalem 2001.

The text contains many passages which are paralleled in other Tractates of this Talmud. It is general knowledge that parallel passages in the Jerusalem Talmud are copies of one another. Since there are no parallel sources for Tractate *Ketubot* and only two Geniza fragments for Tractate *Niddah*, parallel passages are considered as parallel sources and a full list of variant readings is given in every case. These readings show that in fact parallel passages are to be considered witnesses to the same original text but it appears that a number of deviations cannot be explained as copyists' errors and that the scribe of the Leiden ms. copied different tractates from different mss. representing different histories of transmission and different stages of adaptation of Palestinian spelling (as represented by most Geniza fragments) to the Babylonian spelling with which the scribes were familiar.

The extensive Commentary is not based on emendations; where there is no evidence from manuscripts or early prints to correct evident scribal errors, the proposed correction is given in the Notes. As in the preceding volume, for each paragraph the folio and line numbers of the text in the Krotoschin edition are added. It should be remembered that these numbers may differ from the *editio princeps* by up to three lines. It seems to be important that a translation of the Yerushalmi be accompanied by the text, to permit the reader to compare the interpretation with other translations.

Again I wish to thank my wife, Dr. Eva Guggenheimer, who acted as critic, style editor, proof reader, and expert on the Latin and Greek vocabulary. Her own notes on some possible Latin and Greek etymologies are identified by (E. G.).

Contents

Introduction to Tractate Ketubot   1

Ketubot Chapter 1, בתולה
- Halakhah 1   9
- Halakhah 2   31
- Halakhah 3   41
- Halakhah 4   45
- Halahkah 5   50
- Halakhah 6   54
- Halakhah 7   57
- Halakhah 8   60
- Halakhah 9   63
- Halakhah 10   68

Ketubot Chapter 2, האשה שנתארמלה
- Halakhah 1   76
- Halakhah 2   83
- Halakhah 3   89
- Halakhah 4   94
- Halakhah 5   101
- Halakhah 6   105
- Halakhah 8   107

Halakhah 9	112
Halakhah 10	114
Halakhah 11	119

Ketubot Chapter 3, אילו נערות

Halakhah 1	127
Halakhah 2	145
Halakhah 3	147
Halakhah 4	149
Halakhah 5	153
Halakhah 6	156
Halakhah 7	161
Halakhah 8	164
Halakhah 9	165
Halakhah 10	170

Ketubot Chapter 4, נערה שנתפתחה

Halakhah 1	175
Halakhah 2	182
Halakhah 3	186
Halakhah 4	189
Halakhah 6	205
Halakhah7	209
Halakhah 8	211
Halakhah 9	224
Halakhah 11	226
Halakhah 12	229
Halakhah 13	233
Halakhah 14	236
Halakhah 15	239

Ketubot Chapter 5, אף על פי

Halakhah 1	242
Halakhah 2	251
Halakhah 3	255
Halakhah 4	260
Halakhah 5	266
Halakhah 6	272
Halakhah 8	278
Halakhah 10	285
Halakhah 11	292
Halakhah 12	293
Halakhah 13	295

Ketubot Chapter 6, מציאת האשה

Halakhah 1	300
Halakhah 2	305
Halakhah 3	307
Halakhah 4	310
Halakhah 5	314
Halakhah 6	317
Halakhah 7	322

Ketubot Chapter 7, המדיר

Halakhah 1	329
Halakhah 2	335
Halakhah 3	336
Halakhah 4	337
Halakhah 5	338
Halakhah 7	341
Halakhah 9	352
Halakhah 10	364
Halakhah 11	366

Ketubot Chapter 8, האשה שנפלו לה

Halakhah 1	370
Halakhah 2	373
Halakhah 3	376
Halakhah 4	378
Halakhah 5	380
Halakhah 6	383
Halakhah 7	384
Halakhah 8	385
Halakhah 9	387
Halakhah 10	389
Halakhah 11	394

Ketubot Chapter 9, הכותב לאשתו

Halakhah 1	401
Halakhah 2	420
Halakhah 3	423
Halakhah 4	426
Halakhah 5	428
Halakhah 6	434
Halakhah 7	436
Halakhah 8	444
Halakhah 9-10	447
Halakhah 12	452
Halakhah 12-13	457

Ketubot Chapter 10, מי שהיה נשוי

Halakhah 1	462
Halakhah 2	469
Halakhah 3	472
Halakhah 4	474
Halakhah 5	484

Halakhah 6	488

Ketubot Chapter 11, אלמנה
Halakhah 1	492
Halakhah 2	498
Halakhah 3	503
Halakhah 4	504
Halakhah 5	510
Halakhah 6	514
Halakhah 7	519

Ketubot Chapter 12, הנושא
Halakhah 1	526
Halakhah 2	530
Halakhah 3	533
Halakhah 4	549
Halakhah 5	550

Ketubot Chapter 13, שני דייני גזילות
Halakhah 1	555
Halakhah 2	563
Halakhah 3	569
Halakhah 4	575
Halakhah 5	582
Halakhah 6	584
Halakhah 7	586
Halakhah 8	589
Halakhah 9	591
Halakhah 10	594
Halakhah 11	596

CONTENTS

Introduction to Tractate Niddah	599

Niddah Chapter 1, שמי

Halakhah 1	601
Halakhah 3	615
Halakhah 4	619
Halakhah 5	627
Halakhah 6	635
Halakhah 7	640

Niddah Chapter 2, כל היד

Halakhah 1	647
Halakhah 2	653
Halakhah 3	655
Halakhah 4	661
Halakhah 5	664
Halakhah 6	667

Niddah Chapter 3, המפלת

Halakhah 1	677
Halakhah 2	679
Halakhah 3	690
Halakhah 4	695
Halakhah 5	706

Niddah Chapter 4, בנות כותים

Halakhah 1	713

Indices

Index of Biblical Quotations	715
Index of Talmudic Quotations	
Babylonian Talmud	716

Jerusalem Talmud	719
Mishnah and related texts	720
Tosephta	721
Midrashim	721
Rabbinical Literature	722
Index of Greek, Latin, and Hebrew words	722
Author Index	723
Subject Index	723

Introduction to Tractate Ketubot

The Tractate mostly deals with the monetary aspect of talmudic marital law. Its Babylonian equivalent is known as "miniature Talmud" since a mastery of this Tractate requires concurrent mastery not only of all aspects of marriage law (as given in Tractates *Yebamot*, *Giṭṭin*, and *Qidduŝin*) but also of torts and all aspects of civil law (contained in the three Gates of Tractate *Neziqin*) and of judicial oaths (from Tractate *Šebuot*). The same characterization can be applied to the Yerushalmi Tractate.

The word *ketubah* denotes the document which spells out the husband's obligations towards his wife. (There is a question whether to write *ketubah* or *ketubbah* for the Hebrew כְּתוּבָּה. It is clear that the word is spelled, and is pronounced, by all Jewish groups with ב to distinguish it from the feminine passive participle כְּתוּבָה, but it seems that universally the /b/ is treated as having *dagesh lene*. A duplication of *b* seems to be unwarranted.) The *ketubah* document contains several sections. The obligatory ones are: (1) a declaration that the bride, mentioned by name, has agreed to be married by the groom, also mentioned by name. (2) A promise by the groom of a *donatio propter nuptias*, to be paid upon termination of the marriage either by divorce or by the husband's death. The required minimum is two minas for a virgin, one mina for a widow.

The actual value of such a sum can be determined by Mishnah *Peah* 8:8 which states that a person who owns two minas in passive investments is precluded from applying for public charity. The minimum sum is always stated explicitly; the groom is free to obligate himself for additional sums[1]. (3) A summary statement of the mutual duties of the spouses. (4) A description and evaluation of the dowry brought by the bride, which becomes the husband's property for the duration of the marriage. Originally, in the times of the establishment of Jewish customs after the Babylonian exile, the husband pledged specific guarantees for dowry and donation. In Hasmonean times, this was changed to a general lien on all real property held by the husband[2]. (5) A declaration that the bride's rights in this document were irrevocably affirmed in the presence of two witnesses who signed the document.

The first Chapter states first the principle that the basic amount of the *ketubah* of a virgin is 200 *zuz*, two minas, and that of a non-virgin one mina. Since the second mina is *pretium pudicitiae*, there follow rules under which circumstances the husband can claim that his bride was not a virgin and he has the right of either to declare the marriage null and void

---

1   In modern Israeli *ketubot*, a sufficient amount in modern currency is pledged.

2   The specific pledge is found in Hellenic law in Egypt; the general lien on all property was Egyptian native practice. Cf. R. Taubenschlag, *The Law of Greco-Roman Egypt in the Light of the Papyri*, New York 1944, p. 94. In general, local laws are more relevant for Talmudic law than Roman law which in matters of personal relations superseded local customs in the East only in Christian times.

This section is missing in most modern *ketubot*, since the transfer of jurisdiction in money matters from rabbinic to State courts has reduced most *ketubot* in the Western world to meaningless pieces of paper.

or to reduce the *ketubah*. (Since Deut. 22:13-21, about the husband claiming his bride was not a virgin, deals with criminal law, it is clear that in rabbinic interpretation the entire paragraph has to be re-interpreted. Since the husband is married to his wife, he is barred from testifying for or against her as a relative. Criminal matters can be decided only by the testimony of two independent witnesses. Therefore, the paragraph presumes that the husband produces two witnesses to the adultery of his bride between preliminary and definitive marriage ceremonies.) It is clear that the husband has no claim if before the definitive marriage he had unchaperoned access to his fiancée. The second part of the Chapter is devoted to the weight given to testimony of the parties in absence of witnesses or documents in all kinds of civil suits.

The second Chapter starts with a case in which there is no *ketubah* document; what kind of proof is admitted for a claim of a divorcee or widow for full payment of a virgin's dower. The remainder of the Chapter is devoted to two principles of procedure in matters other than criminal law. The first is that *the mouth which forbade is the mouth which permits*; i. e., if a person testified to anything which is to his detriment and which was not known from another source, he must be believed if he testifies to another fact which neutralizes the detriment. The second is that while people cannot testify in their own behalf since everybody is related to himself and relatives cannot testify, two people can mutually testify to each other's benefit. The main application of that principle is to the rules of priesthood. A priest may not be married to a woman who had sexual relations with a man whom she could not legally marry. A woman raped by a Gentile cannot be married to a Cohen. But women who were kidnap victims together can testify for one another that they had not been raped. This then leads to a discussion of further rules for victims of kidnappings or wars.

The third Chapter deals with the fines and other payments imposed on rapists and seducers, whose payments are in biblical law tied to the "bride money of virgins", which is identified with the two minas of the basic *ketubah*. A close relative who rapes or seduces cannot be made to pay since for an act which is a capital crime the perpetrator cannot be made to pay even if he cannot be executed for lack of eye-witnesses. Whether a person who is punished by whipping can be made to pay is a matter of dispute. There are differences in law depending on the age of the victim, whether underage, adolescent, or adult. This leads to a discussion of *patria potestas* over the different categories of girls (there is no *materna potestas* in rabbinic law.) The rapist or seducer who confesses to his crime can be made to pay for the damage he caused but cannot be made to pay a fine since nobody (e. g., a thief) can be punished by a fine on his own confession.

The main topic of the fourth Chapter is the father's power over his underage or adolescent daughter, based on the biblical rules regarding a rapist and a seducer on one side and of the man falsely accusing his wife (whom he married when she was underage) of infidelity. Marriage emancipates a girl from her father's power. This leads to a discussion of the husband's power over and obligations towards his wife and children. The second part of the Chapter contains a list of obligations of the husband or his estate towards his wife and children which are independent of a written *ketubah*; they are implied by the fact that a marriage exists. If a wife is kidnapped, the husband has to ransom her. If she falls sick, he has to pay for her medical expenses. (For the widow, there is a difference in treatment of an acute or chronic illness.) In a polygamous marriage, if a wife dies before her husband, her sons will inherit their mother's *ketubah* claim. Daughters, who do not inherit if there are sons, have the right to be supported until they marry and to receive an appropriate dowry. The widow is given the choice either of remaining in her husband's house and being supported by his estate or to claim payment of her *ketubah* and leaving.

The fifth Chapter starts with a discussion of the value of a *ketubah*. Everybody agrees that there is no upper limit to the amount for which the groom can obligate himself in the *ketubah*, and that the basic amount must be two minas for the virgin and one mina for the previously married woman. There is an opinion that the bride may write a fake receipt, in fact reducing the basic amount. The opposing opinion holds that any marriage without full financial responsibility of the husband is immoral. A second topic is the way in which a non-priestly woman enters the priestly clan by marriage; the complications are uniquely the result of the rabbinic system of double marriage ceremonies, preliminary and definitive. The wife is obligated to keep house; there is a list of necessary duties which depend on the amount of dowry the bride brings with her; most authorities hold that even the richest heiress has to do some housekeeping, if only for her own mental health. Then follows a discussion of the marital duties; a husband's duty to satisfy his wife's sexual needs depend on his working life; it ranges from once every day for financiers to once in six months for sailors. If a wife refuses to sleep with her husband, he can go to court to reduce her *ketubah*; if the husband refuses to sleep with his wife, she can go to court to increase her discussion turns to details of other obligations the spouses have to one another.

The sixth Chapter starts with a discussion of the wife's earnings but most of the Chapter is devoted to the treatment of dowries and the obligations of the husband in exchange for receiving the dowry as working capital.

The seventh Chapter is devoted to cases in which one of the parties misbehaves and either the wife can force a divorce with full payment of the *ketubah,* or the husband can divorce without paying.

The eigth Chapter deals with property the wife inherits during the marriage. This is *paraphernalia* property, property outside the *ketubah,* of which the husband has power of administration but no property rights. The relevant rules are then extended to levirate marriages.

The ninth Chapter starts with the power of the contracting parties to live in a regime of separation of property. It then turns to the order of precedence between creditors, the widow, and heirs of an estate, and to rules covering the accountability to the heirs of a wife active in her husband's business, or one whose *ketubah* claim is not clear-cut.

The tenth Chapter essentially discusses bankruptcy cases, disguised as rules governing the liquidation of *ketubah* claims of wives of a polygamous husband whose estate is insufficient to pay all claims. The case of three wives with different *ketubah* amounts, all married at the same moment, presents an interesting mathematical problem; the rule implied by the Mishnah is one of the rare cases in which a Mishnah is rejected by both Talmudim without much discussion.

The eleventh Chapter treats the rights of a widow in dealing with her late husband's estate, and the rules of judicial liquidation sales. The twelfth Chapter first treats the case that a husband undertook certain obligations regarding his wife's daughters from a previous marriage and then returns to the widow's rights. The Halakhah for this part repeats a Halakhah in *Kilaim*.

The thirteenth and last Chapter contains different rules about money matters, some of them connected with marital law. The thread which connects the different subjects is that all theses rules are attributed to two judges active sometime during the Second Commonwealth. The last part of the Chapter returns to marital matters: the limited power of the husband to determine the marital domicile and the currency in which the *ketubah* has to be liquidated in case of change of domicile.

בתולה פרק ראשון

(fol. 24c) **משנה א**: בְּתוּלָה נִישֵּׂאת בַּיּוֹם הָרְבִיעִי וְאַלְמָנָה בַּיּוֹם הַחֲמִישִׁי שֶׁפַּעֲמַיִם בַּשַּׁבָּת בָּתֵּי דִינִין יוֹשְׁבִין בָּעֲיָירוֹת בְּיוֹם הַשֵּׁנִי וּבְיוֹם הַחֲמִישִׁי שֶׁאִם הָיָה לוֹ טַעֲנַת בְּתוּלִים הָיָה מַשְׁכִּים לְבֵית דִּין.

Mishnah 1: A virgin is married on Wednesday and a widow on Thursday, for in smaller towns court convenes two times per week, on Monday and Thursday, so if he has a complaint about virginity he can quickly go to court[1].

1   This reason, explored at length (and rejected) in the Halakhah, refers only to the marriage of the presumed virgin. For the widow, both Talmudim explain that the groom will have three days, the day of the wedding, Friday, and the Sabbath, to spend with his new wife. If he marries any other day, the groom might be expected to go to work the next day. In a metropolis one might expect to have the court available every working day.

(24d line 23) **הלכה א**: בְּתוּלָה נִישֵּׂאת בַּיּוֹם הָרְבִיעִי כול'. בַּר קַפָּרָא אָמַר. מִפְּנֵי שֶׁכָּתוּב בָּהּ בְּרָכָה. וַהֲלֹא אֵין כָּתוּב בְּרָכָה אֶלָּא בַּחֲמִישִׁי וּבַשִּׁישִׁי בִּלְבָד. בַּחֲמִישִׁי בָּעוֹפוֹת וּבַדָּגִים. בַּשִּׁישִׁי בְּאָדָם וְחַוָּה. אָמַר רִבִּי יוֹסֵי. טַעְמָא דְּבַר קַפָּרָא. רְבִיעִי אוֹר חֲמִישִׁי. חֲמִישִׁי אוֹר שִׁישִׁי. וַהֲלֹא כָתוּב בְּרָכָה בַּשְּׁבִיעִי. אֵין כָּתוּב בְּרָכָה בַּבְּרִיּוֹת אֶלָּא בַיּוֹם.

Halakhah 1: "A virgin is married on Wednesday," etc. Bar Qappara said, because a blessing is written there. But a blessing in only written on the Fifth and the Sixth days! On the Fifth for birds and fish[2], on the Sixth for Adam and Eve[3]. Rebbi Yose said, the reason of Bar Qappara is the Fourth, evening of the Fifth[4], and the Fifth, evening of the Sixth[5]. Is there not a blessing written also on Sabbath[6]? No blessing is written for creatures, only for the day.

2   The days of the week, which in Hebrew are simply numbered from 1 to 6, are identified with the Days of Creation. Fish and birds, created on the Fifth Day (Thursday) are blessed in Gen. 1:22.

3   Gen. 1:28.

4   A couple which marries on Wednesday will first sleep together in the following night. Since the Jewish day starts at nightfall, this already is Thursday; they immediately benefit of the blessing to be fruitful and multiply. In the Babli, 5a, this is a *baraita* in Bar Qappara's name.

5   In the Babli, 5a, the explanation of R. Yose is part of the *baraita* attributed to Bar Qappara.

6   Gen. 2:3.

(24d line 28) מִפְּנֵי שֶׁאֵין כָּתוּב בְּרָכָה בַּבְּרִיוֹת. הָא אִילוּ הֲוָה כָּתוּב בְּרָכָה בַּבְּרִיוֹת הָיְתָה נִישֵּׂאת בַּשַּׁבָּת. לֹא כֵן תַּנֵּי. לֹא יִבְעוֹל אָדָם בְּעִילָה כַּתְּחִילָּה בַּשַּׁבָּת מִפְּנֵי שֶׁהוּא עוֹשֶׂה חַבּוּרָה. מִפְּנֵי שֶׁאֲחֵרִים מַתִּירִין. אֶלָּא כָּאֲחֵרִים. מִפְּנֵי שֶׁאֲחֵרִים מַתִּירִין כְּלוּם אֲחֵרִים מַתִּירִין אֶלָּא בְשֶׁכָּנַס. שֶׁעַד שֶׁלֹּא כָנַס אֵינוֹ זַכַּאי לֹא בִמְצִיאָתָהּ וְלֹא בְמַעֲשֵׂה יָדֶיהָ וְלֹא בְהֶפֵר נְדָרֶיהָ. מִשֶּׁכָּנַס זַכַּאי בִּמְצִיאָתָהּ וּבְמַעֲשֵׂה יָדֶיהָ וּבְהֶפֵר נְדָרֶיהָ. אִם אוֹמֵר אַתְּ כֵּן נִמְצֵאתָהּ כְּקוֹנֶה קִנְיָין בַּשַּׁבָּת. אָמַר רִבִּי מָנָא. הָדָא אָֽמְרָה. אִילֵּין דִּכְנָסִין אַרְמְלָן צָרִיךְ לְכוֹנְסָהּ מִבְּעוֹד יוֹם. שֶׁלֹּא יְהֵא כְקוֹנֶה קִנְיָין בַּשַּׁבָּת.

Because no blessing is written for creatures? Could she have been married on the Sabbath if a blessing were written for creatures? But was it not stated[7]: "A man should not first have sexual relations[8] on the Sabbath, for he makes a wound." It must follow "others", for "others permit it.[9]" But "others" permit only when he is already married[10], for before he was married he had no right to what she finds, what she earns[11], and to dissolve her vows[12]. After he married her, he has the right to receive what she finds or earns, and to dissolve her vows. If you say so, he is like someone who acquires on the Sabbath[13]. Rebbi Mana said, this means that those who marry a widow[14] must take her in[15] when it is still daytime on Friday, that he should not be like someone who acquires on the Sabbath.

7   This *baraita* is stated in full in *Berakhot* 2:6 (5b l. 7), Note 261.

8   With his virgin bride.

9   This is part of the *baraita* text in *Berakhot*. In the Babli, *Ketubot* 6b, the opinion of "others" is ascribed to "the Sages" and practice is decided following them.

10   Meaning the final marriage ceremony in which the bride enters her husband's house, which consists of the recitation of the "Seven Benedictions" in the presence of at least ten witnesses (cf. Note 76) after which the couple is considered married in all respects by being alone together. This ceremony activates all monetary aspects of the marriage contract.

11   In addition, the woman acquires the right to all services the husband is obligated to deliver in return for his acquisition of her property rights.

12   Without needing her father's consent; cf. *Nedarim* Chapter 11.

13   Which is certainly forbidden by rabbinic standards, and, in the opinion of Isaiah, by biblical standards (*Is.* 58:13).

14   Who make the big wedding meal Friday night, to save the expenses of a separate Sabbath meal.

15   He must take her into his house before sunset to acquire his marital rights.

This sentence, which has no parallel in the Babli, is the source of an extensive rabbinic literature; cf. *Šulḥan 'Arukh Even Ha'ezer* 64:5. (In Tosafot, *Yoma* 13b, *s. v.* לחדא, the statement is quoted in the name of R. Ḥanina.) The question is whether the clause "to take her in", is different from "entering the *ḥuppah*" used to describe the final marriage ceremony of a virgin. From Medieval times, *ḥuppah* denotes the canopy, open on all sides, under which the pair stands for the recitation of the "Seven Benedictions". But there is no reason to assume that חוּפָּה originally meant anything but the totally covered bridal bedroom (*Ps.* 19:6), from חפה "to cover". There is no indication here that the rules of transfer of property rights are different for marriages of virgins and widows.

(24d line 35) רִבִּי לָעֶזֶר מַייתֵי לָהּ טַעַם דְּמַתְנִיתִין. שֶׁאִם הָיָה לוֹ טַעֲנַת בְּתוּלִים הָיָה מַשְׁכִּים לְבֵית דִּין. מַתְנִיתָא מְסַייְעָא לְרִבִּי לָעֶזֶר. מִן הַסַּכָּנָה וְהֵילָךְ נָהֲגוּ לָשֵׂאת בַּשְּׁלִישִׁי וְלֹא מִיחוּ בְיָדָן חֲכָמִים. בַּשֵּׁינִי אֵין שׁוֹמְעִין לוֹ. וְאִם מִפְּנֵי הָאוֹנֶס מוּתָּר. מִפְּנֵי הַכְּשָׁפִים. מַה בֵין שֵׁינִי לַשְּׁלִישִׁי. לֹא דוֹמָה מִשְׁתָּהֵא יוֹם אֶחָד לְמִשְׁתָּהֵא שְׁנֵי יָמִים. וְיִשְׁתָּהֵא שְׁנֵי יָמִים. שֶׁלֹּא יֶעֱרַב עָלָיו הַמֶּקַח. וְיֶעֱרַב עָלָיו הַמֶּקַח. לֵית יְכוֹל. דְּאָמַר רִבִּי אִילָא בְשֵׁם רִבִּי אֶלְעָזָר. מָצָא הַפֶּתַח פָּתוּחַ אָסוּר לְקַייְמָהּ מִשּׁוּם סְפֵק סוֹטָה. וְחָשׁ לוֹמַר שֶׁמָּא אֲנוּסָה הִיא. קוֹל יוֹצֵא לָאֲנוּסָה. וַאֲפִילוּ תָחוּשׁ לָהּ מִשּׁוּם אֲנוּסָה. לֹא סָפֵק אַחֵר. סָפֵק אֲנוּסָה סָפֵק פְּתוּחָה. מִדְּבַר תּוֹרָה לְהַחֲמִיר. אָמַר רִבִּי יוֹסֵי. וַאֲפִילוּ תָחוּשׁ לָהּ מִשּׁוּם אֲנוּסָה. שְׁתֵּי סְפֵיקוֹת. סָפֵק אֲנוּסָה סָפֵק פְּתוּחָה סָפֵק מִשֶּׁנִּתְאָרְסָה סָפֵק עַד שֶׁלֹּא תֵאָרֵס. שְׁתֵּי סְפֵיקוֹת מִדְּבַר תּוֹרָה לְהָקֵל.

Rebbi Eleazar explains the reason given in the Mishnah, that if he has a complaint about virginity he can quickly go to court[16]. A *baraita* supports Rebbi Eleazar: Since the time of danger[17] they used to marry on Tuesdays and the Sages did not object; about Monday one does not listen to him, but if it was because of a danger it is permitted, because of sorcery[18]. What is the difference between Monday and Tuesday? One who waits one day cannot be compared to one who waits two days. Why not let him wait two days? That his acquisition should not be sweet for him. Why should his acquisition not be sweet for him? One cannot tolerate it, since Rebbi Hila said in the name of Rebbi Eleazar, if he found the door open, he is forbidden to keep her because she might have been unfaithful[19]. Could we not suspect that she was raped[20]? A rape is public knowledge. And even if you suspect that she was raped, there is no other doubt[21]. There is a doubt whether she was raped or whether she was [willingly] opened[22]. From the words of the Torah one has to be stringent. Rebbi Yose said, if you suspect that she was raped, there are two doubts. There is a doubt whether she was raped or whether she was [willingly] opened; there is a doubt whether it happened after she was preliminarily married or before. From the words of the Torah, with two doubts one has to be lenient[23].

16   His explanation is given later, by R. Hila. He insists that the Mishnah does not refer only to the fact that if he married a girl supposed to be a virgin and he found her lacking virginity that he can divorce her without paying but he can claim "erroneous acquisition" and ask the court to void the marriage without bill of divorce.

17   Tosephta 1:1, Babli 3b. As S. Lieberman points out (*Tosefta ki-Fshutah* vol. 6, p. 187), "danger" always refers to the persecutions after the war of Bar Kokhba, when Jewish observances were forbidden and, therefore, marrying on Wednesday would have been a capital crime. (The Babli explains otherwise.)

18   If somebody is afraid that sorceresses will put a spell on him to make him impotent if he marries on a day known to be a day for marrying, one lets him marry on any other day.

19   Here סוטה means "unfaithful, deviant" in a general sense, not in the technical sense discussed in Tractate *Sotah*. R. Eleazar holds that the Mishnah does not only give the husband the right to complain about lack of virginity but obligates him to go to court to annul his marriage since nobody can stay married to an adulterous wife (Mishnah *Sotah* 5:1) and he presumes his bride was deflowered after she was preliminarily married to him, up to a year earlier. In the Babli, 8b/9a, the same argument is quoted in his name.

20   If a married woman is raped, the husband does not have to divorce her unless he is a Cohen.

21 In *editio princeps*: לֹא סָפֵק אֶחָד "is there not *only one* doubt?" It is a generally recognized principle in both Talmudim that a single doubt referring to biblical precepts has to be judged restrictively, a double doubt leniently. Cf *Yebamot* 7:2, Note 73; Babli *Beṣah* 3a.

22 If she was a willing partner to adultery. This only applies to a girl which has the status of adolescent since "the seduction of a minor is rape" (Babli *Yebamot* 33b).

23 The husband who claims that his bride was not a virgin is not obligated to divorce his wife against his will; R. Eleazar's interpretation of the Mishnah is rejected by R. Yose.

(24d line 47) קִידְּשָׁהּ בַּחוּפָּה לֵית לֵיהּ בְּאִילֵּין קְנָסַיָּיא. אָמְרִין. רִבִּי מַתַּנְיָה עֲבַד לִבְרַתֵּיהּ כֵּן.

If he performed the preliminary marriage in the bridal chamber, these strictures do not apply. They said that Rebbi Mattaniah acted thus for his daughter[24].

24 If the preliminary marriage (see *Peah* 6:2, Note 46) precedes the final marriage ceremony only by a few moments, the bride could not possibly have committed adultery and R. Eleazar's argument becomes pointless.

R. Mattaniah's procedure was adopted by all Jewish groups (except that the bridal chamber was transformed into a canopy, Note 15.) To separate the preliminary from the final marriage, one spends some time by publicly reading the marriage contract. However, it seems that the current procedure is not derived from any talmudic statement but is a consequence of the poverty of the remnants of the Jewish communities in Western Europe after the devastation of the First Crusade which did not allow most people to organize two festivities, one for the preliminary and a separate one for the definitive wedding; cf. I. Schepansky, תקנות בישראל, vol. 3, Jerusalem-NewYork 1992, pp. שע-שעא.

HALAKHAH 1   15

(24d line 49) עַל דַּעְתֵּיהּ דְּרִבִּי לָעְזָר בְּמָקוֹם שֶׁבָּתֵּי דִינִין יוֹשְׁבִין בְּכָל־יוֹם תִּינָשֵׂא בְּכָל־יוֹם. וּבְמָקוֹם שֶׁאֵין בָּתֵּי דִינִין יוֹשְׁבִין (בְּכָל־יוֹם) לֹא תִינָשֵׂא כָּל־עִיקָר. שֶׁלֹּא לַעֲקוֹר זְמַנּוֹ שֶׁלָּרְבִיעִי. וְיַעֲקוֹר זְמַנּוֹ שֶׁלָּרְבִיעִי. אַף הוּא אִית לֵיהּ כְּהָדָא דְתַנֵּי בַּר קַפָּרָא. בַּר קַפָּרָא אָמַר. מִפְּנֵי שֶׁכָּתוּב בָּהּ בְּרָכָה. וְתִינָשֵׂא בָּראשׁוֹן וְיַשְׁכִּים לְבֵית דִּין בַּשֵּׁינִי. אִית דְּבָעֵי מֵימָר. שֶׁלֹּא לַעֲקוֹר זְמַנּוֹ שֶׁלָּרְבִיעִי. וְאִית דְּבָעֵי מֵימַר כְּהָדָא דְתַנֵּי בַּר קַפָּרָא. דְּבַר קַפָּרָא אָמַר. מִפְּנֵי שֶׁכָּתוּב בָּהּ בְּרָכָה.

In the opinion of Rebbi Eleazar, could she be married any day at a place where courts are in session every day[25]? And at a place where there are no courts (every day)[26] could she never be married? One does not want to abolish the time of Wednesday[27]. Why does one not want to abolish the time of Wednesday? Because he[28] also accepts what Bar Qappara stated. Bar Qappara said, because a blessing is written there. Could she not be married on Sunday, that he might quickly go to court on Monday? Some want to say, not to abolish the time of Wednesday; some want to say, because of what Bar Qappara stated, for Bar Qappara said, because a blessing is written there[29].

25   In the Babli, 3a, (and at the end also in the Yerushalmi, cf. Note 66) this is accepted as a declarative sentence (subject to the condition that the groom spend three days to prepare the wedding feast.)

26   An erroneous corrector's addition (reproduced in *editio princeps*).

27   Nobody challenges the first statement in the Mishnah, even if they disagree with the meaning of the later part of that Mishnah.

28   R. Eleazar accepts that the Wednesday/Thursday combination is preferable over Sunday/Monday, even though local courts always also sit on Monday.

29   In the Babli, 3b, the reason of the rejection is that the groom has to spend three days to prepare the wedding feast.

(24d line 55) שָׁוִין שֶׁאֵינָהּ נִישֵּׂאת לֹא בְּעֶרֶב שַׁבָּת וְלֹא בְּמוֹצָאֵי שַׁבָּת. לֹא בְּעֶרֶב שַׁבָּת. מִפְּנֵי כְבוֹד שַׁבָּת. וְלֹא בְּמוֹצָאֵי שַׁבָּת. חֲבֶרַיָּיא אוֹמְרִין. מִפְּנֵי הַטּוֹרַח. רִבִּי יוֹסֵי אוֹמֵר. מִפְּנֵי כְבוֹד שַׁבָּת. מַתְנִיתָא מְסַיְּיעָא לַחֲבֶרַיָּיא. מִפְּנֵי מַה אָמְרוּ. בְּתוּלָה נִישֵּׂאת בַּיּוֹם הָרְבִיעִי. כְּדֵי שֶׁיְּהֵא אָדָם מַתְקִין צְרָכָיו שְׁלֹשָׁה יָמִים זֶה אַחַר זֶה.

One agrees that she should not be married either Friday or Saturday night. Not on Friday, for the honor of the Sabbath[30]. Not Saturday night: The colleagues say, because of the exertion; Rebbi Yose says, for the honor of the Sabbath[31]. A *baraita*[32] supports the colleagues: Why did they say, a virgin is married on Wednesday? That a man should prepare for his needs[33] three consecutive days.

30 That the wedding feast should not impinge on the observance of the Sabbath and the Sabbath meal. As noted above, the wedding of a widow, which proceeds without great fanfare, may be scheduled for Friday.

31 That he should not prepare on the Sabbath for the feast scheduled directly after nightfall; Babli 5a.

32 Babli 2a,3a,5a,7a. In the Tosephta, 1:1, this is given as an alternative to the reason explained in the Mishnah.

33 The wedding feast.

(24d line 55) רִבִּי בָּא בַּר בַּר כֹּהֵן אָמַר קוֹמֵי רִבִּי יוֹסֵי רִבִּי אָחָא בְּשֵׁם רִבִּי יַעֲקֹב בַּר אִידִי. אָסוּר לְאָדָם לִישָּׂא אִשָּׁה בְּעֶרֶב שַׁבָּת. הָדָא דְאַתְּ אָמַר לַעֲשׂוֹת סְעוּדַת אֵירוּסִין. הָא לָאֲרוֹס יְאָרֵס. שְׁמוּאֵל אָמַר. אֲפִילוּ בְתִשְׁעָה בְּאָב יְאָרֵס. שֶׁלֹּא יְקַדְּמֶנּוּ אַחֵר. מַחְלְפָה שִׁיטָתָא דִשְׁמוּאֵל. תַּמָּן הוּא אָמַר אֱלֹהִים מוֹשִׁיב יְחִידִים בַּיְתָה וגו' בַּמֹּאזְנַיִם לַעֲלוֹת הֵמָּה מֵהֶבֶל יָחַד. וּבַהֲהוּא אָמַר אָכֵין. אֶלָּא שֶׁלֹּא יְקַדְּמֶנּוּ אַחֵר בִּתְפִילָּה. וְאַף עַל פִּי כֵן לֹא קַיְימָה.

[34]Rebbi Abba bar Cohen said before Rebbi Yose: Rebbi Aḥa in the name of Rebbi Jacob bar Idi: A man may not [preliminarily] marry on a

Friday. That means, to make an engagement feast[35]. This implies that the preliminary marriage itself is permitted. Samuel says, even on the Ninth of Ab[36] a preliminary marriage is permitted, lest another forestall him. The argument of Samuel seems inverted. There[37], he says, "God puts singles in a house, etc.[38]," "To rise on scales; they all are of vapor![39]" And there, he says so[40]? That means, that he should not forestall him in prayer[41]. Even so, it would not be permanent[41].

34   The parallels are in *Beṣah* 5:2 (63, l. 64) and *Ta'aniot* 4:9 (69b, l. 50).

35   Since this would impinge on the Sabbath meal. It is in order to make the preliminary marriage on Friday and arrange the engagement feast as the Sabbath meal.

36   The anniversary of both destructions of the Temple, the most severe day of mourning in the Jewish calendar, where any exhibition of joy is frowned upon.

37   A similar argument in the Babli, *Mo'ed Qaṭan* 18b.

38   *Ps.* 68:7. The verse means that marriages are pre-ordained in Heaven. The verse is quoted in the name of R. Joḥanan in the Babli, *Soṭa* 2a and *Sanhedrin* 22a, to show that selecting the right mate is as difficult as the liberation of Israel from Egypt, the topic of the second half of the verse.

39   *Ps.* 62:1. In *Lev. rabba* 29(5), this verse is the topic of a sermon of R. Ḥiyya bar Abba in the name of R. Levi, that when the fetuses still are like vapor in their mothers' wombs, they already are joined together on Heaven's scales.

40   If marriages are pre-ordained, why should anybody be afraid that another man could snatch the bride preselected for him?

41   Another man may by his prayer cause the Heavenly decree to be changed.

42   In the Babli, Samuel tells a man that praying to change Heaven's decree leads to an early death of either groom or bride.

(24d line 66) רִבִּי חִזְקִיָה רִבִּי אָחָא בְּשֵׁם רִבִּי אַבָּהוּ אָמַר. אָסוּר לָדוּן דִּינֵי מָמוֹנוֹת בְּעֶרֶב שַׁבָּת. וְהָא מַתְנִיתָא פְּלִיגָא. לְפִיכָךְ אֵין דָּנִין לֹא בְּעֶרֶב שַׁבָּת

וְלֹא בְּעֶרֶב יוֹם טוֹב דִּינֵי נְפָשׁוֹת. הָא דִּינֵי מָמוֹנוֹת דָּנִין. וְתַנֵּי רִבִּי חִייָה כֵן. דָּנִין דִּינֵי מָמוֹנוֹת בְּעֶרֶב שַׁבָּת אֲבָל לֹא דִּינֵי נְפָשׁוֹת. כָּאן לַהֲלָכָה כָּאן לִדְבַר תּוֹרָה.

[43]Rebbi Ḥizqiah, Rebbi Aḥa, said in the name of Rebbi Abbahu: It is forbidden to judge money matters on Friday. Does not a Mishnah object[44]: "Therefore, one does not judge criminal matters on Friday or any day before a holiday"? Therefore, one judges money matters[45]! Also, Rebbi Ḥiyya stated thus: One judges money matters on Friday but not criminal matters. One is for practice, the other for Torah study[46].

43 The same text in *Beṣah* 5:2 (64 l. 59), Sanhedrin 4:6 (22b l. 17).

44 *Sanhedrin*, Mishnah 4:6: "In money matters, judgment can be rendered immediately. In criminal matters, the accused can be found innocent immediately, but he can be found guilty only the next day; therefore..." Since judgment may not be rendered on the Sabbath, the panel discussion cannot be held on Friday.

45 The prohibition is explicitly restricted to criminal matters.

46 In Sanhedrin: כָּאן לַהֲלָכָה כָּאן לְמַעֲשֶׂה "here for practice, there for action." It is declared practice not to judge money matters on Friday but if a court held a session on Friday its decisions are valid. In the Babli (*Baba Qama* 113a): One does not schedule court sessions on the eve of a Sabbath or holiday.

(24d line 70) רִבִּי יוֹנָה בְּשֵׁם רִבִּי קְרִיסְפָּא. בּוֹגֶרֶת כְּתָבִית פְּתוּחָה הִיא. הָדָא דְאַתְּ אָמַר. שֶׁלֹּא לְהַפְסִידָהּ מִכְּתוּבָּתָהּ. אֲבָל לְקַייְמָהּ אֵינוֹ רַשַּׁאי מִשּׁוּם סְפֵק סוֹטָה. וְאַתְייָא כַּיי דְּרִבִּי חֲנִינָא. דְּרִבִּי חֲנִינָא אָמַר. מַעֲשֶׂה בְּאִשָּׁה אַחַת שֶׁלֹּא נִמְצְאוּ לָהּ בְּתוּלִים. וּבָא מַעֲשֶׂה לִפְנֵי רִבִּי. אָמַר לָהּ. אֵיכָן הֵן. אָמְרָה לֵיהּ. מַעֲלוֹתָיו שֶׁלְּבֵית אַבָּא הָיוּ גְּבוֹהִין וְנָשְׁרוּ. וְהֶאֱמִינָהּ רִבִּי. הָדָא דְּתֵימַר שֶׁלֹּא לְהַפְסִידָהּ מִכְּתוּבָּתָהּ. אֲבָל לְקַייְמָהּ אֵינוֹ רַשַּׁאי מִשּׁוּם סְפֵק סוֹטָה. וְאַתְייָא כַּיי דְּתַנִּינָן תַּמָּן. בְּתוּלָה וְאַלְמָנָה גְּרוּשָׁה וַחֲלוּצָה מִן הָאֵירוּסִין כְּתוּבָּתָן מָאתַיִם

HALAKHAH 1

וְיֵשׁ לָהֶן טַעֲנַת בְּתוּלִים. הָדָא דְאַתְּ אָמַר. מִכְּתוּבַּת מָנֶה מָאתַיִם. אֲבָל לְקַיְּימָהּ אֵינוֹ רַשַּׁאי מִשּׁוּם סְפֵק סוֹטָה. וְאַתְיָיא כַּיי דְתַנִּינָן תַּמָּן. הָאוֹכֵל אֵצֶל חָמִיו בִּיהוּדָה שֶׁלֹּא בָּעֵדִים אֵינוֹ יָכוֹל לִטְעוֹן טַעֲנַת בְּתוּלִים מִפְּנֵי שֶׁהוּא מִתְיַיחֵד עִמָּהּ. הָדָא דָּמַר לִכְתוּבַּת מָנֶה מָאתַיִם. אֲבָל לְקַיְּימָהּ אֵינוֹ רַשַּׁאי מִשּׁוּם סְפֵק סוֹטָה. וְתַיְיא כַּיי דְתַנִּינָן. הַנּוֹשֵׂא אֶת הָאִשָּׁה וְלֹא מָצָא לָהּ בְּתוּלִים. וְהִיא אוֹמֶרֶת. מְשֶׁאֵירַסְתַּנִי נֶאֱנַסְתִּי וְנִסְתַּחֲפָה שָׂדָךְ. וְהוּא אוֹמֵר. לֹא כִּי אֶלָּא עַד שֶׁלֹּא אֵרַשְׂתִּיךְ. וְהָיָה מִקְחוֹ מֶקַח טָעוּת. הָדָא דָּמַר לִכְתוּבַּת מָנֶה מָאתַיִם. אֲבָל לְקַיְּימָהּ אֵינוֹ רַשַּׁאי מִשּׁוּם סְפֵק סוֹטָה. וְתַיְיא כַּיי דְתַנִּינָן תַּמָּן. הִיא אוֹמֶרֶת. מוּכַּת עֵץ אֲנִי. וְהוּא אוֹמֵר. לֹא כִּי אֶלָּא דְרוּסַת אִישׁ אַתְּ. הָדָא דְּתֵימַר לִכְתוּבַּת מָנֶה מָאתַיִם. אֲבָל לְקַיְּימָהּ אֵינוֹ רַשַּׁאי מִשּׁוּם סְפֵק סוֹטָה. וְכוּלְּהוֹן מִן הַהִיא דְּאָמַר רִבִּי הִילָא בְּשֵׁם רִבִּי אֶלְעָזָר. מָצָא הַפֶּתַח פָּתוּחַ אָסוּר לְקַיְּימָהּ מִשּׁוּם סְפֵק סוֹטָה.

Rebbi Jonah in the name of Rebbi Crispus: An adult woman is like an open amphora[47,48]. That means, not to let her lose her *ketubah*. But he is not permitted to keep her because she might have been unfaithful[19,49]. This also applies to what Rebbi Ḥanina said, since Rebbi Ḥanina said: It happened that a woman was found without virginity and the case came before Rebbi[50]. He said to her, where is it? She said, the stairs in my father's house were high and it was rubbed off. Rebbi believed her. That means, not to let her lose her *ketubah*. But he is not permitted to keep her because she might have been unfaithful. This[51] also applies to what we stated there[52]: "The *ketubah* sum of a virgin who is a widow, or a divorcee, or one who had received *ḥaliṣah,* after a preliminary marriage[53] is 200 [*zuz*], and they are subject to complaints about virginity." That means, referring to a *ketubah* sum of a mina or 200 [*zuz*][54]. But he is not permitted to keep her because she might have been unfaithful. This[51] also applies to what we stated there[55]: "One who eats unchaperoned at his father-in-law's in Judea cannot go to court about virginity since he was alone with her." That means, referring to a *ketubah* sum of a mina or 200 [*zuz*][54]. But he is not permitted to keep her because she might have been unfaithful[56]. This[51] also applies to what we stated[57]: "If somebody married a woman and found her not to be a virgin. She says, I was raped after the preliminary marriage and your field was flooded[58], but he says, no, it was before the preliminary marriage and my acquisition was in error,[59]" that refers to a *ketubah* sum of a mina or 200 [*zuz*]. But he is not permitted to keep her because she might have been unfaithful. This[51] also applies to what we stated[60]: "She says, I was injured by a piece of wood, but he says no, you were trampled on by a man," that refers to a *ketubah* sum of a mina or 200 [*zuz*]. But he is not permitted to keep her because she might have been unfaithful. All these cases are based on what Rebbi Hila said in the name of Rebbi Eleazar, if he found the door open, he is forbidden to keep her because she might have been unfaithful[19].

47   Once she is older than $12^1/_2$ years, her body is so soft that the rupture of the hymen may not be noticed. The court will not hear such a case.

48   In the quote in Tosaphot (9a, s. v. האומר): "an open wine amphora."

49   In the parallel case in the Babli, 9a, the argument acribed here to R. Yose (Notes 21-23) is used to restrict R. Eleazar's statement to the case of either a Cohen (who has to divorce his wife in case of rape) or a person who preliminarily married a girl aged less than 3 full years (who could not have had premarital sex). Note also the change of language: R. Hila in the name of R. Eleazar states that he *is forbidden* to keep her; here he *is not authorized* to keep her. As Rashi explains in the Babli, there one treats the case that the husband comes to court to report the case and is ready to be convinced if the proceedings clear

his wife. In the Yerushalmi one treats the case that the husband comes to complain convinced that his bride was unfaithful after the preliminary marriage. Then one follows the principle that if somebody is convinced that something is forbidden, one cannot permit it.

Since the husband is only subjectively forbidden to keep his wife who objectively may have been a virgin, he has to pay the full amount of her *ketubah* since obligations based on written contracts can be abolished only by a full proof of the guilt of the beneficiary.

50 In the Babli, 10b, a woman did not bleed when deflowered and Rabban Gamliel the elder accepted the fact that not to bleed was hereditary in her family and told the husband to enjoy his wife. In another case quoted there, Rebbi convinced the husband that he had not penetrated on his weddding night.

51 That the woman wins her case in money matters does not imply that the court tells the husband to keep her.

53 Mishnah 1:2. In all three cases the husband died before the *ḥuppah* ceremony and the women are presumed to be virgins.

54 The *ketubah* sum of a non-virgin is 100 *zuz*, called מָנֶה, a *mina* (1Mvâ = 100 Δραχμη, in contrast to the Babylonian מָנֶה *manē* = 60 *šeqel*).

55 Mishnah 1:5.

56 Even though the court will not hear a claim to annul the marriage because of missing virginity since the groom was alone, unchaperoned, with his preliminarily married wife, if he asserts that he did not sleep with her before the *ḥuppah* one tells him that he cannot keep his wife.

57 Mishnah 1:6.

58 If a farmer buys a field and after the property rights were transferred to him the field is flooded and unusable for that year, he has no regress on the seller. While it is true that her *ketubah* is only a mina since the *ketubah* is executed at the time of the final marriage, his acquisition of marital rights was at the preliminary marriage and, therefore, he cannot claim to have been lured by false pretenses and cannot annul the marriage without paying anything.

59 It is a question who has the burden of proof. For Rabban Gamliel and R. Eliezer, the husband has the burden of proof and if he cannot prove his assertion he has to pay. For R. Joshua, the wife has the burden of proof and if she cannot prove her case

the marriage is annulled and she gets nothing.

60 Mishnah 1:7. This case is completely parallel to the preceding one.

(25a line 20) עַל דַּעְתֵּיהּ דְּרִבִּי לָעְזָר בּוֹגֶרֶת אֵימָתַי הִיא נִשֵּׂאת. בְּתוּלָה מִן הַנִּישׂוּאִין אֵימָתַי הִיא נִשֵּׂאת. מוּכַּת עֵץ כְּרִבִּי מֵאִיר אֵימָתַי הִיא נִשֵּׂאת. נִישְׁמְאִינָהּ מִן הָדָא. אִם יֵשׁ עֵדִים שֶׁיָּצְאָת בְּהִינוּמָא. וְלָא אִדְּכַּר רְבִיעִי. הָדָא אָמְרָה דְלֵית רְבִיעִי כְּלוּם.

When is an adult married following Rebbi Eleazar[61]? When is a virgin after marriage married[62]? When is a woman injured by a piece of wood married following Rebbi Meïr[63]? Let us hear from the following[64]: "If there are witnesses that she went out in *hinuma*.[65]" Wednesday was not mentioned. This means that Wednesday does not mean anything[66].

61 Since it was stated that no claim of missing virginity is possible for adult girls, there is no need to have the wedding on Wednesdays.

62 If the husband died immediately after the final marriage ceremony, the widow is still a virgin but in her next marriage she can claim only the widow's mina for her *ketubah*, the same as a widow who is not a virgin. Therefore, for R. Eleazar there is no reason why she should marry on a Wednesday.

63 Mishnah 1:3. She can claim a virgin's *ketubah* but is not subject to a claim of missing virginity.

64 Mishnah 2:1.

65 A woman whose *ketubah* was lost who claims that she married as a virgin. If she can produce witnesses that ὑμέναια "wedding songs" were sung at her wedding, it is a proof that she married as a virgin (M. Sachs). Since wedding songs were prohibited after the wars of Bar Kokhba (*Soṭah* 9:13, Note 189), the word *hinuma* changed its meaning. In Babylonia it became "a veil" (2:1, 26a l. 71; Babli 17b), in Galilee φόρημα "a litter".

66 A marriage on Wednesday is no proof of virginity and a marriage on another day is no proof of non-virginity.

HALAKHAH 1   23

(25a line 23) וְאַלְמָנָה בַּיּוֹם הַחֲמִישִׁי. שֶׁאִם אוֹמֵר אַתְּ לוֹ בְּאֶחָד מִכָּל־יְמוֹת הַשָּׁנָה אַף הוּא מַשְׁכִּים וְיוֹצֵא לִמְלַכְתּוֹ. מִתּוֹךְ שֶׁאַתְּ אוֹמֵר לוֹ בַּחֲמִישִׁי בְשַׁבָּת אַף הוּא שָׂמֵחַ עִמָּהּ חֲמִישִׁי שִׁישִׁי וּשְׁבִיעִי.

"A widow [is married] on Thursday." For if you would let him [marry] any other day of the year, he would go to work the next morning. Since you tell him, on a Thursday, he enjoys himself with her on Thursday, Friday, and Sabbath[67].

67 The same argument, somewhat enlarged, in the Babli, 5a, and Tosephta, 1:1. From the Tosephta text it seems likely that one whould read - בְּאֶחָד מִכָּל יְמוֹת הַשַּׁבָּת "any other weekday". Since the husband has to spend time on Friday and buy provisions for the Sabbath, it is not worthwhile for him to go to work.

(25a line 23) מֹשֶׁה הִתְקִין שִׁבְעַת יְמֵי הַמִּשְׁתֶּה וְשִׁבְעַת יְמֵי הָאָבֶל וְלֹא הִתְקִין לָאַלְמָנָה כְלוּם. אַף עַל גַּב דְּתֵימַר. לֹא הִתְקִין לָאַלְמָנָה כְלוּם. טְעוּנָה בְרָכָה. מְבוֹעַז. דִּכְתִיב וַיִּקַּח בּוֹעַז עֲשָׂרָה אֲנָשִׁים מִזִּקְנֵי הָעִיר וַיֹּאמֶר שְׁבוּ פֹה וַיֵּשֵׁבוּ. אָמַר רִבִּי אֲלֶכְּסַנְדְּרִי. מִכָּאן שֶׁאֵין קָטָן רַשַּׁאי לֵישֵׁב עַד שֶׁיֹּאמַר לוֹ הַגָּדוֹל שֵׁב. אָמַר רִבִּי פִינְחָס. מִכָּן לַבַּיִת הַזֶּה שֶׁהֵן מְמַנִּין זְקֵנִים בְּבָתֵּי מִשְׁתְּיוֹת שֶׁלָּהֶן. אָמַר רִבִּי לֶעְזָר בֵּירִבִּי יוֹסֵי. מִכָּן לְבִרְכַּת חֲתָנִים שֶׁהִיא בַּעֲשָׂרָה. אָמַר רִבִּי יוּדָה בַּר פָּזִי. וְלֹא סוֹף דָּבָר בָּחוּר לִבְתוּלָה אֶלָּא אֲפִילוּ אַלְמוֹן לְאַלְמָנָה. מִבּוֹעַז שֶׁהָיָה אַלְמוֹן וְרוּת הָיְתָה אַלְמָנָה. וּכְתִיב וַתֵּהוֹם כָּל־הָעִיר עֲלֵיהֶם. וְאִיפְשָׁר כֵּן. כָּל־קַרְתָּא מִתְבַּהֲלָה בְּגִין נָעֳמִי עַל עֲלִיבְתָּא. אֶלָּא אִשְׁתּוֹ שֶׁל בּוֹעַז מֵתָה בְּאוֹתוֹ הַיּוֹם. עַד כָּל־עַמָּא גָמַל חַסְדָּא נִכְנְסָה רוּת עִם נָעֳמִי. וְנִמְצֵאת זוֹ יוֹצְאָת וְזוֹ נִכְנֶסֶת.

Moses instituted seven days of a marriage feast[68] and seven days of mourning[69], but he instituted nothing for the widow. Even though you say that he instituted nothing for the widow, she needs a benediction[70].

From Boaz, as it is written[71]: "And (Boaz)[72] took ten men of the city Elders and said, sit here, and they sat down." Rebbi Alexander said, [73]from here [one learns that] the lesser person is not permitted to sit down until the more important person[74] tells him to sit down. Rebbi Phineas said, from here [one learns that] this family[75] appoints Elders for their marriage feasts. Rebbi Eleazar ben Rebbi Yose said, from here [one learns that] the wedding blessing needs ten people [present][76]. Rebbi Jehudah bar Pazy said, not only a bachelor marrying a virgin, but also a widower marrying a widow, since Boaz was a widower and Ruth a widow, as it is written[77] "The entire city was in an uproar because of them." Is that possible that the entire town was in alarm because of the sorry state of Naomi? But Boaz's wife had died that very day and when all the people went to the burial, Ruth and Naomi entered. It turned out that when one left, the other entered.

68   The week-long wedding feast of Jacob and Leah, *Gen.* 29:27. But in the interpretation of Naḥmanides, the Yerushalmi refers to an oral tradition going back to Moses, without reference to biblical verses. Sforno sees in *Gen.* 29:21 a biblical justification for R. Mattaniah's procedure (Note 24). In *Yalquṭ Šim'oni* II, 70, in a note attributed to *Pirqe R. Eliezer* (not in the surviving text): "The seven days of a wedding feast we learned from Jacob and Simson (*Jud.* 14:12)."

69   The week-long mourning for Jacob, *Gen.* 50:10. Since this mourning was held before the burial, it cannot be the real paradigm for the rabbinic mourning period which starts after burial.

70   The "Seven Benedictions" without which the final marriage ceremony cannot be held. The same argument in the Babli, 7a, as an Amoraic statement.

71   *Ruth* 4:2.

72   Not in the biblical text, implied by *v.* 4:1; is also in *Ruth rabba* 4(7).

73   This and the following statements are also in *Ruth rabba* 4(7).

74   Since Boaz was of the family of

HALAKHAH 1

the princes of Judah, *Ruth* 4:21; cf. the author's Commentary to *Seder 'Olam* (Northvale NJ 1998), pp. 124-125.

75 The descendants of King David.

76 In contrast to the preliminary marriage ceremony which requires only the presence of two witnesses.

77 *Ruth* 1:19. The same argument in the Babli, *Baba batra* 91a; *Ruth rabba* 3(6).

(25a line 36) תַּנֵּי. אוֹמֵר בִּרְכַּת חֲתָנִים כָּל־שִׁבְעָה. [רְבִּי יִרְמְיָה סְבַר מֵימַר מַפְקִין כַּלָּתָה כָּל־שִׁבְעָה].[78] אֲמַר לֵיהּ רְבִּי יוֹסֵי. וְהָא תַנֵּי רְבִּי חִיָּיא. אוֹמֵר בִּרְכַּת אֲבֵלִים כָּל־שִׁבְעָה. מַפְקִין מִיתָא כָּל־שִׁבְעָה. מַאי כְדוֹן. מַה כָּאן מְנַחֵם עִמּוֹ אַף כָּאן מְשַׂמֵּחַ עִמּוֹ. מַה כָּאן מַזְכִּירִין אַף כָּאן מַזְכִּירִין.

It was stated: The marriage benedictions are said all seven days[79]. [Rebbi Jeremiah wanted to say that one re-enacts the marriage all seven days.[80]] Rebbi Yose said to him, but did not Rebbi Hiyya state: The benedictions of mourners[81] are said all seven days. Can you say that one buries the dead all seven days? How is that? Since here he consoles with him, so there he enjoys with him[82]; as here one remembers, so there one remembers[83].

78 Addition from the parallel text in *Megillah* 4:4 (75a l. 74), missing here in ms. and *editio princeps*.

79 In the Babli, 7b: One recites the marriage benedictions in the presence of 10 persons all seven days. In *Megillah*: "Neither the marriage benedictions nor the mourning benedictions are said all seven days." The following discussion shows that this cannot be the correct version.

80 How else could one recite the wedding benedictions?

81 The special version of Grace for the mourner.

82 Anytime visitors to a house of mourners bring food and eat with the mourners, they recite the special version of Grace; anytime visitors of a newlywed couple who participate in a festive meal append the seven wedding benedictions to Grace recited after the meal.

In *Megillah*, the positions of

"consoles" and "enjoys" are switched.

83 The topic of conversation in a house of mourning is the deceased; the topic of conversation with the newlyweds is the marriage ceremony.

(25a line 41) תַּנֵּי. אָמַר רִבִּי יוּדָה. בִּיהוּדָה בָּרִאשׁוֹנָה הָיוּ מַעֲמִידִין אוֹתָן שְׁנֵי שׁוּשְׁבִּינִין. אֶחָד מִשֶּׁל כַּלָּה וְאֶחָד מִשֶּׁלְּחָתָן. אַף עַל פִּי כֵן לֹא הָיוּ מַעֲמִידִין אוֹתָן אֶלָּא בִּשְׁעַת נִישּׂוּאִין. וּבְגָלִיל לֹא הָיוּ עוֹשִׂין כֵּן. בִּיהוּדָה בָּרִאשׁוֹנָה הָיוּ מְיַיחֲדִין חָתָן אֵצֶל הַכַּלָּה שָׁעָה כְּדֵי שֶׁיְּהֵא לִבּוֹ גַס בָּהּ. וּבְגָלִיל לֹא הָיוּ עוֹשִׂין כֵּן. בִּיהוּדָה בָּרִאשׁוֹנָה הָיוּ הַשּׁוּשְׁבִּינִין מְפַשְׁפְּשִׁין בִּמְקוֹם חָתָן וּבִמְקוֹם הַכַּלָּה. וּבְגָלִיל לֹא הָיוּ עוֹשִׂין כֵּן. יהוּדָה בָּרִאשׁוֹנָה הָיוּ הַשּׁוּשְׁבִּינִין יְשֵׁינִין בִּמְקוֹם חָתָן וּבִמְקוֹם כַּלָּה. וּבְגָלִיל לֹא הָיוּ עוֹשִׂין כֵּן. כָּל שֶׁלֹּא נָהַג כְּמִנְהַג זֶה אֵינוֹ יָכוֹל לִטְעוֹן טַעֲנַת בְּתוּלִים.

[84]It was stated: Rebbi Jehudah said, in Judea in earlier times they appointed two best men, one for the bride and one for the groom, but[85] they appointed them only for the wedding day. In contrast, this was not done in Galilee.

In Judea in earlier times one let the fiancé be alone with the fiancée for an hour so that he became familiar with her; in contrast, this was not done in Galilee[86].

In Judea in earlier times the best men were investigating the places of groom and bride; in contrast, this was not done in Galilee[87].

In Judea in earlier times the best men were sleeping in the room with groom and bride[88]; in contrast, this was not done in Galilee. Anybody who did not follow these rules[89] could not present a claim of missing virginity.

84 Slightly different version of this *baraita* are in the Babli, 12a, and the Tosephta, 1:4.

85 This is a hidden polemic against the formulation of the Tosephta, that the best men were appointed three days before the wedding day and conducted a common investigation of the bridal chamber, so that there was no place where the groom possibly could make a blood-stained cloth disappear in order to accuse the bride falsely of not being a virgin and also that the bride could not hide beforehand a blood-stained cloth in order to fake a non-existing virginity.

86 This practice is confirmed by Mishnah 1:5. As noted there, it is obvious that at a place where one lets the pair be alone together there can be no claim of virginity and no best men were appointed.

In the Babli, and it seems also in the Yerushalmi's discussion of R. Eleazar's position (Note 54), one assumes that at certain places in Judea one was very stringent and at others very lax. But it seems from Halakhah 1:5 that the radical change from appointing best men to letting the fiancé to be alone with the fiancée is not a matter of different localities but of different times (and the Yerushalmi's practice certainly does not follow R. Eliezer).

87 This paragraph belongs together with the first; it explains the roles of the best men.

88 After bride and groom had finished their first sexual relations, the best men were invited for the remainder of the night to make sure no evidence was removed or introduced.

89 In Jehudah, at a place where one did not let the pair be together unchaperoned.

(25a line 49) תַּמָּן תַּנִּינָן. כָּל־גֶּפֶן יֵשׁ בָּהּ יַיִן. וְשֶׁאֵין בָּהּ יַיִן טְרוּקְטֵי. רִבִּי יִרְמְיָה בָּעֵי. מֵעַתָּה אֵין טַעֲנַת בְּתוּלִים בְּרִבִּי יוּדָה. אָמַר רִבִּי יוֹסֵה. כָּל־גַּרְמָהּ אָמְרָה שֶׁיֵּשׁ טַעֲנַת בְּתוּלִים בְּרִבִּי יוּדָה. דְּתַנֵּי. אָמַר רִבִּי יוּדָה. בִּיהוּדָה בָרִאשׁוֹנָה הָיוּ מַעֲמִידִין שְׁנֵי שׁוּשְׁבִּינִין. אֶחָד מִשֶּׁלְּחָתָן וְאֶחָד מִשֶּׁלַּכַּלָּה. אַף עַל פִּי כֵן לֹא הָיוּ מַעֲמִידִין אֶלָּא בִשְׁעַת נִישּׂוּאִין. וּבְגָלִיל לֹא הָיוּ עוֹשִׂין כֵּן. עַד יְשִׁינִין בִּמְקוֹם חָתָן וּבְמָקוֹם כַּלָּה. וּבְגָלִיל לֹא הָיוּ עוֹשִׁין כֵּן. מַאי כְדוֹן. עָלֶיהָ לְהָבִיא רְאָיָה שֶׁהִיא מִמִּשְׁפַּחַת טְרוּקְטֵי.

There, we have stated[90]: "Every vine gives wine; if there is no wine it is dried up[91]." Rebbi Jeremiah asked: Does that mean that Rebbi Jehudah does not admit claims of missing virginity[92]? Rebbi Yose said, in itself it means that Rebbi Jehudah admits claims of missing virginity, as it was stated: Rebbi Jehudah said, in Judea in earlier times they appointed two best men, one for the groom and one for the bride, but they appointed them only for the wedding day. In contrast, this was not done in Galilee . . . they were sleeping in the room with groom and bride; in contrast, this was not done in Galilee. How is this? She has to bring proof that she comes from a family of dryness[93].

90 Mishnah *Niddah* 9:11, a statement of R. Jehudah.

91 Greek τρυγητής, from τρύγη, ἡ, "crop, vintage; dryness". It means that there are women who are congenitally unable to bleed. (In this and similar discussions it is always assumed that the causes of menstrual bleeding and bleeding when the hymen is torn are the same.)

92 Since he states that there are women who do not bleed when they are deflowered.

93 The proven absence of bleeding is prima facie evidence of non-virginity, open to medical explanation which preserves the fact and denies the inference.

(25a line 56) רִבִּי יִרְמְיָה סָבַר מֵימַר. מִנְהַג יְהוּדָה בַּגָּלִיל. אָמַר לֵיהּ רִבִּי יוֹסֵי. וְכִי מִנְהַג יְהוּדָה בַּגָּלִיל עֵדוּת תּוֹרָה הִיא. אֶלָּא מִנְהַג יְהוּדָה בִּיהוּדָה וּמִנְהַג גָּלִיל בַּגָּלִיל. מִכֵּיוָן דְּתֵימַר. אֵינָהּ עֵדוּת תּוֹרָה. לֹא יַעֲמֹד. אֶלָּא שֶׁלֹּא יִפְרְצוּ בְנוֹת יִשְׂרָאֵל בְּזִימָּה. אִם בִּשְׁבִיל שֶׁלֹּא יִפְרְצוּ בְנוֹת יִשְׂרָאֵל בְּזִימָּה אֲפִילוּ מַעֲמִיד לֹא יְהֵא נֶאֱמָן. רִבִּי יוֹסֵי בְּשֵׁם רִבִּי אִילָא. אֵין אָדָם עָשׂוּי לְהוֹצִיא יְצִיאוֹתָיו וּלְהוֹצִיא שֵׁם רַע עַל אִשְׁתּוֹ. אִם מִשּׁוּם שֶׁאֵין אָדָם עָשׂוּי לְהוֹצִיא יְצִיאוֹתָיו וּלְהוֹצִיא שֵׁם רַע עַל אִשְׁתּוֹ אֲפִילוּ אֲפִילוּ אֵינוֹ מַעֲמִיד יְהֵא נֶאֱמָן. אָמַר רִבִּי הִילָא. מִפְּנֵי חֶשַׁד אֶחָד מִפְּנֵי פָרוּץ אֶחָד. מָה אֲנָן קַיָּימִין. אִם

בְּשֶׁפִּישְׁפֵּשׁ וּמָצָא הֲרֵי מָצָא. אִם בְּשֶׁלֹּא מָצָא הֲרֵי פִּישְׁפֵּשׁ לֹא פִּישְׁפֵּשׁ. אֶלָּא כָּכִין אֲנָן קַיָּימִין. בְּשֶׁלֹּא פִּישְׁפֵּשׁ וּמָצָא. הִיא אוֹמֶרֶת. דַּם בְּתוּלִים הִיא. וְהוּא אוֹמֵר. לֹא כִּי אֶלָּא דַּם צִיפּוֹר הִיא. הוֹרַע כּוֹחוֹ שֶׁלֹּא נָהַג כְּמִנְהַג זֶה. הָדָא דְּתֵימַר. שֶׁלֹּא לְהַפְסִידָהּ מִכְּתוּבָּתָהּ. אֲבָל לְקַיְּימָהּ אֵינוֹ רַשַּׁאי מִשּׁוּם סְפֵק סוֹטָה. וְאַתְיָיא כַּיי דְּתַנִּינָן תַּמָּן. בְּתוּלָה וְאַלְמָנָה וכו'. וְכוּלְּהוֹן מִן הֲהֵין דְּאָמַר רִבִּי הִילָא בְּשֵׁם רִבִּי אֶלְעָזָר. מָצָא פֶּתַח פָּתוּחַ אָסוּר לְקַיְּימָהּ מִשּׁוּם סְפֵק סוֹטָה.

Rebbi Jeremiah was of the opinion to follow the standard of Judea in Galilee[94]. Rebbi Yose said to him, is the standard of Judea in Galilee a testimony by biblical standards[95]? No, [one follows] the standard of Judea in Judea and the standard of Galilee in Galilee. If you say, it is not testimony by biblical standards, why appoint them[96]? That the daughters of Israel should not become wanton in immorality. If it is that the daughters of Israel should not become wanton in immorality, even if one appoints, they should not be trustworthy! Rebbi Yose in the name of Rebbi Hila: A man would not go to all this expense in order to give his wife a bad reputation[97]. If it is that a man would not go to all this expense in order to give his wife a bad reputation, even if one does not appoint, he should be believed. Rebbi Hila said, because of one suspicion, because of one immoral person[98]. Where do we hold? If he investigated and found, he found[99]! If he did not find but investigated, did he not investigate[100]? But we deal with the case that he did not investigate and found[101]. She says, it is blood of virginity. He says no, it is a bird's blood. His case is damaged since he did not follow the procedures. [49]That means, not to let her lose her *ketubah*. But he is not permitted to keep her because she might have been unfaithful. It follows what we stated there[102]: "A virgin and a widow, etc." All these cases are based on what Rebbi Hila said in the name of Rebbi Eleazar, if he found the door open, he is forbidden to keep her because she might have been unfaithful[19].

94 Since at the end of the Tosephta R. Jehudah states that anybody not following the procedure of Judea cannnot claim absence of virginity, it seems that he denies to the people of Galilee the right to bring any such claim.

95 The assertion of R. Jeremiah is unreasonable since the procedure of certain places in Judea has no biblical basis.

96 If the testimony of the best men is not needed, why are they there?

97 Since the groom bears all expenses of the wedding feast, he would not do that if his intention was from the start to claim non-virginity and go for an annulment of the match. There are much cheaper ways to get a woman for one night. (In a different context, the same argument is made in the Babli, *Ketubot* 10a, *Yebamot* 107a, *Qiddušin* 45b.)

98 The entire set-up in certain regions in Judea is only because in a very few cases bad things do happen.

99 He is bound by the testimony of the best men that his wife was a virgin.

100 He can go to court and ask for annulment of the marriage. {R. Nissim Gerondi (שיטה לר״ן, ed. A. L. Feldman, Jerusalem 1997, col. 28), copied from R. Crescas, reads: "If he did not check and found, or his side checked but not her side."}

101 He claims that he could enter his (underage) wife without resistance and that, therefore, she could not have been a virgin. The Babli, 10b, dismisses such claims out of hand since (a) it might be possible to enter without rupturing the hymen and (b) any man making such a claim must have ample experience with women, virgins and non-virgins, so that he must be treated as an amoral person.

102 Mishnah 1:2, cf. Note 53.

(25a line 71) תַּנֵּי. טַעֲנַת בְּתוּלִים כָּל־שֶׁהֵן. מַעֲשֶׂה בְּאִשָּׁה אַחַת שֶׁלֹּא נִמְצָא לָהּ בְּתוּלִים אֶלָּא כְּעֵין הַחַרְדָּל וּבָאת לִפְנֵי רִבִּי יִשְׁמָעֵאל בֵּירִבִּי יוֹסֵי. אָמַר לָהּ. כְּמוֹתָךְ יַרְבּוּ בְיִשְׂרָאֵל. רבי זכריה חתניה דרבי לוי. מְקַלְקְלָהּ. בְּאִינְשֵׁי רָאוּיָה

HALAKHAH 2

לְסַמְיָה סַגִּי נְהוֹרָא. חֲבֵרַיָּה אָמְרֵי. מְקַנְתֵּר לָהּ. כָּל אִשָּׁה שֶׁדָּמֶיהָ מְעוּטִין וְלָדֶיהָ מְעוּטִין. רִבִּי יוֹסֵי אָמַר. מְקַלֵּס לָהּ. כָּל אִשָּׁה שֶׁדָּמֶיהָ מְעוּטִין אֵינָהּ מְצוּיָה לְטַמֵּא טַהֲרוֹת.

It was stated: The claim of virginity is based on any amount (of blood). It happened that for a certain woman nothing was found except for [a stain the size of] a mustard seed. She came before Rebbi Ismael ben Rebbi Yose, who said to her, there should be many like you in Israel. Rebbi Zachariah the son-in-law of Rebbi Levi: He cursed her[103], like people who, when they see a blind man, call him "much light". The colleagues said, he needled her, any woman with little blood has few children[104]. Rebbi Yose said, he praised her, any woman with little blood will not cause impurity to food prepared in purity[105].

103 As explained later, because she might not have children.
104 In the Babli, 10b, R. Meïr states the contrapositive: Any woman with much blood has many children.
105 In the Babli, 10b: She will not cause her husband any problems with the impurity of her period.

(fol. 24c) **משנה ב:** בְּתוּלָה כְּתוּבָּתָהּ מָאתַיִם וְאַלְמָנָה מָנֶה. בְּתוּלָה אַלְמָנָה גְרוּשָׁה וַחֲלוּצָה מִן הָאֵירוּסִין כְּתוּבָּתָן מָאתַיִם וְיֵשׁ לָהֶן טַעֲנַת בְּתוּלִים. הַגִּיּוֹרֶת וְהַשְּׁבוּיָה וְהַשִּׁפְחָה שֶׁנִּפְדּוּ שֶׁנִּשְׁתַּחְרְרוּ וְשֶׁנִּתְגַּיְּירוּ פְּחוּתוֹת מִבְּנוֹת שָׁלֹשׁ שָׁנִים וְיוֹם אֶחָד כְּתוּבָּתָן מָאתַיִם וְיֵשׁ לָהֶן טַעֲנַת בְּתוּלִים.

Mishnah 2: The *ketubah*[106] of a virgin is 200 and that of a widow one mina[107]. The *ketubah* of virgins who after a preliminary marriage[53] become widows, divorcees, or who received *ḥaliṣah*, is 200 and they are subject to a claim of non-virginity[108]. The *ketubah* of a proselyte, a prisoner, and a slave who were redeemed[109], freed[110], or converted[111] at less than three years and one day of age, is 200 and they are subject to a claim of non-virginity[108].

106 The minimum payable to the bride at the dissolution of the marriage either by divorce or by the husband's death. This does not exclude that the *ketubah* document may stipulate higher amounts.

107 100 *zuz*. The Mishnah remains noncommittal about the nature of the coin involved.

108 To invalidate the document if they are found not to be virgins.

109 It is assumed that a female kidnap victim will be raped as a matter of course. But a girl raped at age less than 3 years still is a virgin.

110 Since slaves can have guiltless sexual relations with Gentiles, it is assumed that they do have such relations.

111 There is no presumed minimal age for sexual activity of Gentiles. Therefore, a proselyte aged more than 3 years at conversion is presumed not to be virginal.

(25b line 1) **הלכה ב**: בְּתוּלָה כְּתוּבָּתָהּ מָאתַיִם וְאַלְמָנָה מָנָה. כול׳. חוּנָה בְּשֵׁם שְׁמוּאֵל. בְּשֶׁקֶל הַקּוֹדֶשׁ. רִבִּי בָּא בַר בִּינָא אָמַר. מַטְבֵּעַ יוֹצֵא. מַתְנִיתָא מְסַייְעָא לְרִבִּי בָּא בַר בִּינָא. וְחָמֵשׁ סְלָעִים שֶׁל בֵּן בְּמָנֶה צוֹרִי שְׁלֹשִׁים שֶׁל עֶבֶד חֲמִישִׁים שֶׁל אוֹנֵס וְשֶׁל מְפַתֶּה מֵאָה שֶׁל מוֹצִיא שֵׁם רַע כּוּלָּן בְּשֶׁקֶל הַקּוֹדֶשׁ בְּמָנֶה צוֹרִי. וְלֹא תַנָּא כְּתוּבַּת אִשָּׁה עִמָּהֶן. אָמַר רִבִּי אָבִין. כְּלוּם לָמְדוּ מִכְּתוּבַּת אִשָּׁה לֹא מֵאוֹנֵס וּמִמְּפַתֶּה. מִכֵּיוָן דְּתַנִּינָן. הָאוֹנֵס וְהַמְפַתֶּה. כְּמַאן דְּתַנָּא. כְּתוּבַּת אִשָּׁה עִמָּהֶן.

"The *ketubah* of a virgin is 200 and that of a widow one mina," etc. Huna in the name of Samuel: In the Temple *šeqel*[112]. Rebbi Abba bar Bina said, circulating coin[113]. A Mishnah supports Rebbi Abba bar Bina[114]: "The five tetradrachmas of the firstborn[115] are in Tyrian coinage, the 30 of the slave[116], the 50 of the rapist and the seducer[117], the 100 of the slanderer[118], are all computed in Temple *šeqels* in Tyrian coinage." A woman's *ketubah* is not stated with them. Rebbi Abin said, did they not learn the *ketubah* of a woman from the rapist and the seducer[119]? Since the rapist and the seducer are mentioned, it is as if women's *ketubah* was stated with them[120].

112 The Temple *šeqel* coins struck in Jerusalem during the first war with the Romans are silver coins weighing between 13.5 and 14.3 g. The corresponding Tyrian coinage is about 13.5 g. A Temple *šeqel* in Babylonian theory is twice the weight of a common *šeqel*, which is the name of the two-denar coin. This means that the Temple *šeqel* is equal, both in the Yerushalmi and in the Babli, to the Roman tetradrachma (סֶלַע), based on an unadulterated silver denar (drachma, זוז) of 3.4 g. Tyre ceased to mint coins between the reigns of Augustus and Septimius Severus, meaning that Tyrian coins in the Mishnaic period were unadulterated silver. Samuel requires that the *ketubah* be adjusted for the inflation caused by the debasement of the currency in circulation. It may be that he holds that the basic *ketubah* amount is a biblical requirement (cf. Halakhah 13:11).

113 The value of the *ketubah* has to be computed on the basis of the currency in circulation.

114 Mishnah *Bekhorot* 8:7; cf. Tosephta *Ketubot* 12:6.

115 The redemption of the firstborn, *Num.* 3:47, identifying the biblical *šeqel* as tetradrachma.

116 30 *šeqel* weregilt for the killing of another person's slave by one's ox, *Ex.* 21:32.

117 50 *šeqel* bride money paid by the rapist (*Deut.* 22:29) and, by inference, the seducer (*Ex.* 22:15-16) of a girl.

118 The fine imposed on a man wrongly accusing his wife of committing adultery during her preliminary marriage period, *Deut.* 22:19.

119 Since the 50 tetradrachmas due from the rapist and the seducer are exactly 200 denarii; either these 200 denarii are the "bride money" described in the verse *Ex.* 22:16 or at least they

are the inspiration for the rabbis to fixate the minimum *ketubah* at 200 *zuz*.

120 The Mishnah from *Bekhorot* does not prove anything.

(25b line 7) עַד כְּדוֹן בִּתוּלָה. אַלְמָנָה מַאי. אָמַר רַב חִינָנָא. דַּייָהּ לָאַלְמָנָה שֶׁתִּיטּוֹל מַחֲצִית בְּתוּלָה.

So far about a virgin. What about a widow? Rab Ḥinena said, it is enough for a widow that she take half of a virgin's portion[121].

121 Everybody agrees that the *ketubah* of a widow is a rabbinic institution.

(25b line 9) אָמַר רִבִּי חִייָה בַּר אָדָא. אֲפִילוּ נִיתְנֵי. כְּתוּבַּת אִשָּׁה עִמָּהֶן. לֵית כָּל־אִילֵּין רַבָּנִין פְּלִיגִין. רִבִּי חֲנַנְיָה וְרִבִּי יוֹנָתָן תְּרֵיהוֹן אָמְרִין. מַטְבֵּעַ יוֹצֵא. רִבִּי יְהוֹשֻׁעַ בֶּן לֵוִי אָמַר. מַטְבֵּעַ יוֹצֵא. רִבִּי יַעֲקֹב בַּר אָחָא רִבִּי אִימִּי רִבִּי שִׁמְעוֹן בֶּן לָקִישׁ בְּשֵׁם רִבִּי יוּדָן נְשִׂייָא. מַטְבֵּעַ יוֹצֵא. אָמַר רִבִּי יוֹחָנָן. סְלָעִים סְבֵירְרָנִיּוֹת מְהַגֵּנִיּוֹת יְרוּשַׁלְמִיּוֹת. אִילֵּין אָמְרִין אָכֵן וְאִילֵּין אָמְרִין אָכֵן. אֶלָּא אַף הוּא חָזַר וְסָבַר דִּכְוָותְהוֹן. וְלֵית כָּל־מִילַּייָא אָכֵן אִילֵּין אָמְרִין אָכֵן וְאִילֵּין אָמְרִין אָכֵן. הָא אַף הוּא חָזַר וְסָבַר דִּכְוָותְהוֹן.

Rebbi Ḥiyya bar Ada said, even if "a woman's *ketubah*" was stated with them[122], do not all these rabbis disagree? Rebbi Ḥananiah and Rebbi Jonathan both say, circulating[123] coin. Rebbi Joshua ben Levi said, circulating coin. Rebbi Jacob bar Aḥa, Rebbi Immi, Rebbi Simeon ben Laqish in the name of Rebbi Jehudah Neśia: Current coin. Rebbi Joḥanan said[124], good Severan tetradrachmas, Jerusalem ones[125]. These are saying so, those are saying otherwise[126]! But he[127] also changed his mind and thought like them. Are not always these saying so, those are saying otherwise[128]? Here, even he changed his mind and thought like them.

122 Even if the Mishnah did state that the *ketubah* of the virgin is a biblical institution, practice could not follow that Mishnah since all amoraic authorities hold that the *ketubah* is a purely rabbinic institution. The Babli (*Qiddušin* 10b) quotes Mishnah *Bekhorot* 8:7 with the addition that "all money due by rabbinic institutions is local coin", following R. Abba bar Bun. A similar statement underlies the text here.

123 This can be debased coin. However, if merchants refuse to accept debased silver coin but require to be paid in gold, it would not be possible to liquidate a *ketubah* debt in legal but not circulating coin.

124 The history of interpretation of this sentence is documented by D. Sperber, *Roman Palestine 200-400, Money & Prices*, Ramat Gan 1974, p. 223. I follow Sperber in identifying the coins referred to as those of Severus Alexander, whose Antiochene coins, following those of Elagabalus, earned the attribute of "good", returning to earlier standards after the debasement of the gold minting by Caracalla.

125 This must refer to the full weight Jerusalem Temple *šeqels* of the war against the Romans, not the copper coins of Aelia Capitolina. R. Joḥanan here holds with Samuel that the *ketubah* goes by biblical standards.

126 In general, R. Jonathan, R. Joshua ben Levi, and R. Joḥanan are the leading authorities; it is difficult to decide if they disagree.

127 R. Joḥanan changed his mind and agreed that the *ketubah* has to be satisfied by rabbinical standards.

128 The standing of the *ketubah* is no different from most other rabbinic institutions.

(25b line 15) אָתָא עוֹבְדָא קוֹמֵי דְרַבִּי חֲנִינָא. בְּאִשָּׁה שֶׁהָיְתָה כְּתוּבָּתָהּ פְּחוּתָה מִמָּאתַיִם זוּז. וְאָמַר. תִּיטוֹל מַה שֶׁכָּתַב לָהּ. אָמַר לְרַבִּי מָנָא. שֵׁב וַחֲתוֹם. אָמַר לֵיהּ. אַשְׁוֵי שִׁיטָתָךְ וּבָהּ חֲתוֹם. לֹא רַבִּי חִיָּיה דְּאָמַר בְּשֵׁם שְׁמוּאֵל. בְּשֶׁקֶל הַקּוֹדֶשׁ. רַבִּי אֲבוֹדְמָא דְצִיפּוֹרִי בְּשֵׁם רַבִּי חוּנָה. מִשֵּׁם וִיתּוּר. מֵעַתָּה אִשָּׁה שֶׁהָיְתָה כְּתוּבָּתָהּ פְּחוּתָה מִמָּאתַיִם טַטְמִין כְּתוּבָּתָהּ כְּדֵי שֶׁתִּיטוֹל בְּשֶׁקֶל הַקּוֹדֶשׁ. אָמְרֵי בְּשֵׁם רַבִּי חוּנָה. בְּמָקוֹם שֶׁאֵין כּוֹתְבִין כְּתוּבָּה. אֲבָל בְּמָקוֹם שֶׁכּוֹתְבִין כְּתוּבָּה מַה דּוּ מַפְקָא הִיא גוֹבָה. אָמַר רַבִּי יוֹחָנָן. וְתַנֵּי כֵן. חֵרֵשׁ שֶׁנָּשָׂא פִיקַחַת

אֵין לָהּ עָלָיו מְזוֹנוֹת וְלֹא כְּתוּבָּה. וְאִם מֵתָה הוּא יוֹרְשָׁהּ. שֶׁהִיא רֵצְתָה לָזוּק לוֹ נְכָסֶיהָ. וְהוּא לֹא רוֹצֶה לָזוּק לָהּ בִּנְכָסָיו. פִּיקֵחַ שֶׁנָּשָׂא חֵרֶשֶׁת יֵשׁ לָהּ עָלָיו מְזוֹנוֹת וּכְתוּבָּה. וְאִם מֵתָה אֵינוֹ יוֹרְשָׁהּ. שֶׁהוּא רוֹצֶה לָזוּק לָהּ נְכָסָיו וְהִיא לֹא רֵצְתָה לָזוּק לוֹ נְכָסֶיהָ. וְחֵרֶשֶׁת יֵשׁ לָהּ קְנִיִין וְיֵשׁ לָהּ כְּתוּבָּה. רִבִּי יִרְמְיָה בְשֵׁם רִבִּי לֶעְזָר. תִּיפְתָּר כְּשֶׁכְּנָסָהּ פִּיקַחַת כֵּנְסָהּ. רִבִּי יַעֲקֹב בַּר אָחָא בְשֵׁם רִבִּי לֶעְזָר. כְּשֶׁכְּנָסָהּ פִּיקַחַת וְנִתְחָרְשָׁה. מִכָּל־מָקוֹם לֹא פִיקַחַת כְּנָסָהּ. רִבִּי יַעֲקֹב בַּר אָחָא בְשֵׁם רִבִּי לֶעְזָר. תִּיפְתָּר שֶׁהָיְתָה חֵרֶשֶׁת וְנִתְפַּקְּחָה. כְּנָסָהּ פִּיקַחַת וְנִתְחָרְשָׁה. שֶׁלֹּא תֹאמַר. הוֹאִיל וְהָיְתָה חֵרֶשֶׁת תְּחִילָּה יֵשׁ לָהּ כְּתוּבָּה. לְפוּם כֵּן צָרִיךְ לְמֵימַר אֵין לָהּ. רִבִּי יוֹסֵי לֹא אָמַר כֵּן אֶלָּא כֵּן אָמַר אִילּוּ מִי שֶׁבָּא עַל הַחֵרֶשֶׁת שֶׁמָּא אֵין לָהּ קְנָס. וְכָל־שֶׁאֵין לָהּ קְנָס אֵין לָהּ כְּתוּבָּה. אָמַר רִבִּי יוּדָן. וְכִי בִקְנָס הַדָּבָר תָּלוּי. הֲרֵי בוֹגֶרֶת אֵין לָהּ קְנָס וּכְתוּבָּתָהּ מָאתַיִים. הֲרֵי בְתוּלָה מִן הַנִּישׂוּאִין יֵשׁ לָהּ קְנָס וּכְתוּבָּתָהּ מָנֶה.

There came a case before Rebbi Ḥanina of a woman whose *ketubah* was less than 200 *zuz*[129], and he said, she should take what he had written for her. He said to Rebbi Mana[130], sit down and sign. He answered, follow your argument and sign yourself, did not Rebbi Ḥiyya[131] say in the name of Samuel, by the Temple *šeqel*? Rebbi Eudaimon of Sepphoris in the name of Rebbi Ḥuna: Because of a renunciation[132]. Now, should a woman whose *ketubah* was for less than 200 [*zuz*] not hide her *ketubah* in order to collect by the Temple *šeqel*? They said in the name of Rebbi Ḥuna, at a place where one does not write a *ketubah*[133]. But at a place where one writes a *ketubah*, what she presents she collects. Rebbi Joḥanan said, it was stated thus: If a deaf-mute man married a hearing wife, she has no claim for support nor *ketubah*, but if she died, he inherits from her, for she wanted to connect him with her property, but he could not want to connect her with his property[134]. If a hearing male married a deaf-mute woman, she has a claim to support and *ketubah*, but if she died, he does not inherit, for he wanted to connect her with his property, but she could not want to connect him with her property. But can a deaf-mute woman acquire and have *ketubah*?[135] Rebbi Jeremiah in the name of Rebbi Eleazar, explain it that at the moment he married her, she was hearing. Rebbi Jacob bar Aḥa in the name of Rebbi Eleazar, he married her when she was hearing but she turned deaf-mute[136]. In any case, did he not marry her when she was hearing[137]? Rebbi Jacob bar Aḥa in the name of Rebbi Eleazar, explain it that she was deaf-mute and turned hearing; he married her when she was hearing and she turned deaf[138]. That you should not say, because at the start she was deaf-mute she has [no] *ketubah*, therefore it is necessary to say that she (does not have) [has][139]. Rebbi Yose does not say so, but since if one has sexual relations with a deaf-mute, is he not liable for a fine[140]? Only if there were no fine would there be no *ketubah*. Rebbi Yudan said, does that depend on a fine? Look, the adult woman[141] collects no fine but her *ketubah* is 200, the virgin after marriage collects a fine[142] but her *ketubah* is a mina[62]!

129 The rabbinic commentaries all explain that the *ketubah* was written for 200 (debased) silver denars, as R. Ḥanina lived in the first half of the third Century C.E., at the end of the Severan dynasty and the early military anarchy. It could also be that the document was written in terms of a foreign currency, Persian or other, which when translated into local currency turned out to be less than the statutory 200 *zuz*. In any case, it is clear that the *ketubah* did not amount to the value of 50 Temple *šeqel* when it became due.

130 R. Mana I.

131 This probably is a scribal error since R. Ḥiyya the Elder preceded Samuel and R. Ḥiyya bar Abba lived two generations later. One should read (Rav) Ḥuna, student of Samuel's contemporary Rav (Note 112).

132 Since the woman had agreed at the moment of marriage to be satisfied with the smaller amount. [In Mishnah 5:2, R. Meïr states that living with a woman without guaranteeing her the minimum support of the *ketubah* is immoral and cannot be tolerated. The Babli, 57a, decides that practice follows R. Meïr, against the opinion of R. Yose (usually the higher authority) that money matters between consenting adults are their private business. The Yerushalmi discusses R. Meïr's opinion in Halakhah 4:9 in a non-committal way; the discussion here shows that it accepts R. Yose's opinion as determining practice.]

133 It seems that there were places in Galilee where nobody could read or write. At such a place, the *ketubah* by default is 200 full weight silver denar. (A standard *ketubah*, as explained later, contains additions which exceed the legal minimum. Such additions are impossible if the *ketubah* is not written.)

134 One must assume that the deaf-mute is also illitterate since, if he could communicate in writing, he would be able to conduct business. If he cannot write, he cannot transact business, cf. *Yebamot*, Chapter 14. The woman who marries him can accept all financial consequences of marriage, but her husband is incompetent to do so. (Naturally, the question could be asked, how can an incompetent person inherit? The question is asked for the next statement; it could have been asked here. The Babli, *Yebamot* 113a, notes that if the husband is healed and becomes able to conduct business, the marriage ceremony has to be repeated.)

135 It is clear that the deaf-mute woman has a claim to support since she lives with her husband. The question is only, how can the deaf-mute woman acquire a claim to the *ketubah* that could be enforced against her husband's legal heirs, whose claim to the inheritance is biblical?

In contrast, the Babli, *Yebamot* 113a, holds that in this case of a deaf-mute bride her legal status is irrelevant; since the groom dedicated the *ketubah* money to her, the court will transfer it to her guardians. This must also be the theory of the Tosephta, 1:3, which prescribes 200 *zuz* for the virgin deaf-mute or insane bride.

136 The two statements in the name of R. Eleazar are identical in meaning.

137 The explanation cannot work: if the woman was competent when she married, she acquired all the rights of a married woman and her later loss of

138 She was deaf-mute before the marriage, she is deaf-mute now. But in between there was a period in which she could communicate with the outside world; she acquired all the rights of a married wife if the husband lived with her during her lucid period.

139 The words in parentheses are those of the ms.; the words in brackets are those of the *editio princeps*. Only the latter make sense.

140 The fines of the rapist and the seducer (Note 117) of an underage girl. The Tosephta (3:5) states that the deaf-mute has no claim to a fine. The existing mss. and the *editio princeps* of the Babli (36a) quote the Tosephta to the effect that she has a claim, but *Tosafot RID* quotes "she has no claim".

S. Lieberman concludes that the original version of the Babli (if there existed a uniform original version) cannot be reconstructed. He also accepts the emendation of M. Margalit: אִילוּ מִי שֶׁבָּא עַל הַחֲרֶשֶׁת שֶׁמָּא אִית לָהּ קְנָס. וְכָל־שֶׁאֵין לָהּ קְנָס אֵין לָהּ כְּתוּבָּה. "If one has sexual relations with a deaf-mute, would he be not liable for a fine? Since there is no fine there is no *ketubah*." Even though this changes only one letter in the text, one should hesitate to accept emendations of M. Margalit without very convincing reasons.

141 Who marries as a virgin.

142 If she still has not reached 12 years and 6 months of age. The argument of R. Yose is shown to be wrong.

(25b line 35) חֵרֵשׁ אוֹ שׁוֹטֶה שֶׁיְּכָנְסוּ פִּיקַחַת. אַף עַל פִּי שֶׁחָזַר הַחֵרֵשׁ וְנִתְפַּקֵּחַ שׁוֹטֶה וְנִשְׁתַּפָּה אֵין לָהּ כְּתוּבָּה. רָצָה לְקַיְימָהּ כְּתוּבָתָהּ מָנָה. רִבִּי לְעָזָר בְּשֵׁם רִבִּי חֲנִינָה. וְהוּא שֶׁבָּא עָלֶיהָ מִשֶּׁנִּתְפַּקַּח וּמִשֶּׁנִּשְׁתַּפָּה. אֲבָל אִם לֹא בָא עָלֶיהָ מִשֶּׁנִּתְפַּקַּח וּמִשֶּׁנִּשְׁתַּפָּה אֲפִילוּ כְּתוּבַת מָנָה אֵין לָהּ.

[143]"A deaf-mute or an insane male who were taken in[144] by a hearing woman. Even if the deaf-mute became hearing, or the insane sane, she has no *ketubah*. If he wants to keep her, her *ketubah* is one mina[145]." Rebbi Eleazar in the name of Rebbi Ḥanina: Only if he slept with her after he became hearing or sane. If he did not sleep with her after he became hearing or sane, she does not even have a *ketubah* of a mina[146].

143 Tosefta 1:3; a slightly different wording in the Babli, *Yebamot* 113a.
144 Married.
145 Even if at the start she was a virgin, now, at the moment her husband is legally able to contract a marriage, she is no virgin.
146 Since there never was a legal marriage.

(25b line 39) פְּחוּתוֹת מִבְּנוֹת שָׁלֹשׁ שָׁנִים וְיוֹם אֶחָד. רִבִּי יוֹסֵי בְשֵׁם רִבִּי חִייָה בַּר אַשִׁי רִבִּי יוֹנָה רַב חִייָה בַּר אַשִׁי בְשֵׁם רַב. לְמָה זֶה דוֹמֶה. לְעוֹשֶׂה גוּמָא בְבָשָׂר וְחוֹזֵר וּמִתְמַלֵּא. תַּנֵּי רִבִּי חִייָה. לְעוֹכֵר אֶת הָעַיִן וְחוֹזֶרֶת וְצוֹלֶלֶת. אָמַר רִבִּי יוֹסֵי. מַתְנִיתָא אָמְרָה כֵן. פְּחוּתוֹת מִיכָּן כְּנוֹתֵן אֶצְבַּע בָּעַיִן. אָמַר רִבִּי אָבוּן. אֶקְרָא לֵאלֹהִים עֶלְיוֹן לָאֵל גּוֹמֵר עָלַי. בַּת שָׁלֹשׁ שָׁנִים וְיוֹם אֶחָד וְנִמְלָכִין בֵּית דִּין לְעוֹבְרוֹ הַבְּתוּלִין חוֹזְרִין. וְאִם לָאו אֵין הַבְּתוּלִין חוֹזְרִין.

At less than three years and one day of age[147], Rebbi Yose in the name of [Rav] Ḥiyya bar Ashi, Rebbi Jonah, Rav Ḥiyya bar Ashi in the name of Rav: What is this like? One makes a dimple in the flesh which straightens out by itself. Rebbi Ḥiyya stated: Like one who muddies a source which becomes clear again. Rebbi Yose said, a Mishnah says so[148]: Younger than that, it is as if one puts a finger on an eye. [149]Rebbi Abun said: "I am calling to Almighty God, to the God who decides with me." If a girl is three years and one day old, if the Court decided to lengthen, her hymen repairs itself, otherwise her hymen does not repair itself.

147 This explains the statement of the Mishnah that girls violated less than three years of age are still virgins.
148 *Niddah* 5:4
149 From *Nedarim* 6:13, Notes 138-141. Variant readings: ונמלכין | נמלכו , אין הבתולין | אינן , הבתולין | בתולין .

HALAKHAH 3

(fol. 24c) **משנה ג:** הַגָּדוֹל שֶׁבָּא עַל הַקְּטַנָּה וְהַקָּטָן שֶׁבָּא עַל הַגְּדוֹלָה וּמוּכַּת עֵץ כְּתוּבָּתָן מָאתַיִם דִּבְרֵי רַבִּי מֵאִיר. וַחֲכָמִים אוֹמְרִים מוּכַּת עֵץ כְּתוּבָּתָהּ מָנֶה.

Mishnah 3: If an adult male had sexual relations with an underage girl[150], or an underage boy[150] with an adult female, or one injured by wood[151], their *ketubot* are 200 [*zuz*], the words of Rebbi Meïr. But the Sages say, the *ketubah* of one injured by wood is a mina.

150   Too young to marry.
151   Her hymen was split by an accident.

(25b line 45) **הלכה ג:** הַגָּדוֹל שֶׁבָּא עַל הַקְּטַנָּה כול'. אֵי זֶהוּ קָטָן וְאֵי זוּ קְטַנָּה. מִשּׁוּם רַבִּי יְהוּדָה בֶּן חַגְרָא אָמְרוּ. קָטָן פָּחוֹת מִבֶּן תֵּשַׁע שָׁנִים וְיוֹם אֶחָד וּקְטַנָּה פְּחוּתָה מִבַּת שָׁלֹשׁ שָׁנִים וְיוֹם אֶחָד. נִיחָא גָּדוֹל שֶׁבָּא עַל הַקְּטַנָּה הַבְּתוּלִין חוֹזְרִין. קָטָן שֶׁבָּא עַל הַקְּטַנָּה הַבְּתוּלִין חוֹזְרִין. קָטָן שֶׁבָּא עַל הַגְּדוֹלָה אֵין הַבְּתוּלִין חוֹזְרִין. אָמַר רַבִּי אָבִין. תִּפְתָּר שֶׁבָּא עָלֶיהָ שֶׁלֹּא כְּדַרְכָּהּ. אָמַר רַבִּי יוֹסֵי בֵּרַבִּי אָבִין. וַאֲפִילוּ תֵּימָא כְּדַרְכָּהּ. קָטָן בִּיאָתוֹ בִּיאָה. אֲבָל אֵין בּוֹ כֹּחַ לִיגַּע בַּסִּימָנִין. וְתַנֵּי כֵן. מַעֲשֶׂה שֶׁעִיבְּרָה וּבְתוּלֶיהָ קַיָּימִין.

"If an adult male had sexual relations with an underage girl," etc. What is an underage boy and what is an underage girl? They said in the name of Rebbi Jehudah ben Ḥagra, an underage boy is younger than nine years and one day[152], an underage girl is younger than three years and one day[147]. One understands that if an adult male had sexual relations with an underage girl, her hymen repairs itself. If an underage boy has sexual relations with an underage female, her hymen repairs itself. But if an underage boy has sexual relations with an adult female, her hymen does not repair itself![153] Rebbi Abin, explain it that he had relations with her without penetration[154]. Rebbi Yose ben Rebbi Abin said, you can even say that he had normal relations with her. The relations of an underage boy are relations but he does not have the force to damage her hymen[155]. It was stated thus: It happened that [an adult] became pregnant while her hymen was intact[156].

152 The sex act of a boy of 9 years and one day has legal consequences; cf. *Yebamot*, Mishnaiot 10:15-18; Chapter 3, Note 143. The sex act of a younger boy has no legal consequences.

153 How can she marry as a virgin?

154 There was no penetration.

155 This is a matter of dispute in the Babli, 11b.

156 The Babli, *Ḥagigah* 14b/15a, holds that an intact virgin might become pregnant in a bathtub from semen floating there.

(25b line 52) מֵיתִבִּין לְרִבִּי מֵאִיר. בְּתוּלִין אֵין כָּאן. וְתֵימַר כְּתוּבָּה מָאתַיִם. אָמַר לוֹן. וְכִי בִבְתוּלִין הַדָּבָר תָּלוּי. הֲרֵי בוֹגֶרֶת אֵין לָהּ בְּתוּלִים וּכְתוּבָּתָהּ מָאתַיִם. הֲרֵי בְּתוּלָה מִן הַנִּישׂוּאִין יֵשׁ לָהּ בְּתוּלֵיהֶן וּכְתוּבָּתָהּ מָנֶה. מַאי כְדוֹן. בּוֹגֶרֶת לֹא בָטַל חֵינָהּ. בְּתוּלָה מִן הַנִּישׂוּאִין בָּטַל חֵינָהּ. מַה פְלִיגִין. בְּמוּכַּת עֵץ. דְּרִבִּי מֵאִיר אוֹמֵר. לֹא בָטַל חֵינָהּ. וְרַבָּנִין אָמְרִין. בָּטַל חֵינָהּ.

They objected to Rebbi Meïr: There is no hymen[157] and you say, her *ketubah* is 200 [*zuz*]? He answered them, is that dependent on the hymen? But the adult has no hymen[47] and the *ketubah* is 100; the virgin widow has a hymen and her *ketubah* is a mina[158]! What is the reason? The adult still has all her grace[159]; the virgin widow has lost her grace. Where do they disagree? If she was injured by wood. Rebbi Meïr says, she did not lose her grace, but the rabbis say, she lost her grace.

157 Referring to the virgin whose hymen was ruptured in a mechanical accident.

158 Mishnah 4, about a girl whose husband dies in the *ḥuppah* after the recitation of the wedding benedictions.

159 The groom is willing to pay for a woman who never was with another male.

(25b line 57) מַה פְּלִיגִין. בְּתוּלָה הַנִּבְעֶלֶת מִן הַקָּטָן וּמִמִּי שֶׁאֵינוֹ אִישׁ כְּשֵׁירָה לִכְהוּנָה. תַּנֵּי רִבִּי חֲלַפְתָּא בֶּן שָׁאוּל. כְּשֵׁירָה אֲפִילוּ לְכֹהֵן גָּדוֹל.

Did they disagree that a virgin who had sexual relations with an underage boy[160] or with someone who is not a man[161] is enabled for the priesthood? Rebbi Halaphta ben Shaul said, she is enabled even for the High Priest[162].

160 This is a problem only for R. Eleazar who holds (*Yebamot* 6:5, Note 108; 7:5, Note 105; 13:1, Note 14) that sexual relations between unmarried partners are always harlotry which bars the female from marrying a priest. For all other authorities, there would only be a problem regarding the High Priest who may marry only a virgin.

161 Sexual relations of a woman with an animal is a capital crime if initiated by the woman. But it has no influence on her marital status.

162 In the Babli, *Yebamot* 59b, this is an Amoraic statement by Samuel.

(25b line 59) רִבִּי יִרְמְיָה וְרִבִּי אִמִּי מַקְשֵׁי. מַה בֵּינָה לְבֵין הַנִּבְעֶלֶת בְּאֶצְבַּע. אִילוּ הַנִּבְעֶלֶת בְּאֶצְבַּע שֶׁמָּא אֵינָהּ פְּסוּלָה לִכְהוּנָה. אָמַר רִבִּי חַגַּי. תִּיפְתָּר שֶׁבָּא עָלֶיהָ שֶׁלֹּא כְדַרְכָּהּ. בְּעָא רִבִּי חַגַּיי מֵיהַדֵּר בֵּיהּ. אָמַר לֵיהּ רִבִּי אַבָּא. לֹא תַהֲדוֹר בָּךְ. וְלָמָּה בְעָא רִבִּי חַגַּיי מֵיהַדֵּר בֵּיהּ. מִן הָדֵין דִּכְתִיב וְהוּא אִשָּׁה בִבְתוּלֶיהָ יִקָּח. עַד שֶׁתְּהֵא בְתוּלָה מִשְּׁנֵי צְדָדֶיהָ. וְדִכְוָותָהּ. בְּתוּלָה וְאִישׁ לֹא יְדָעָהּ. בְּתוּלָה כְדַרְכָּהּ. וְאִישׁ לֹא יְדָעָהּ שֶׁלֹּא כְדַרְכָּהּ. אָמַר רִבִּי יִצְחָק בֶּן אֶלְעָזָר. אֲפִילוּ בְיָדָיו לֹא תָבַע בָּהּ. שֶׁנֶּאֱמַר כִּי לֹא יָנוּחַ שֵׁבֶט הָרֶשַׁע עַל גּוֹרַל הַצַּדִּיקִים. מַה עֲבַד רִבִּי חַגַּיי עַד שֶׁלֹּא יַחֲזִיר בּוֹ. פָּתַר לָהּ בְּהֶעֱרָיָיה. וְלָמָּה לֵית רַב יוֹסֵף פָּתַר לֵיהּ בְּהֶעֱרָיָיה. אָמַר רִבִּי מָנָא. דְּהִיא צְרִיכָה לָהּ. רִבִּי יוֹסֵי בְּעָא. הֶעֱרָיָיה בִּזְכוּר מָהוּ. הֶעֱרָיָיה בִּבְהֵמָה מָהוּ. כַּד שָׁמַע רִבִּי יִרְמְיָה הָדָא דְרִבִּי חַגַּיי אָמַר. לֹא עַל הָדָא הֲוָה רִבִּי אִמִּי מַקְשֶׁה.

Rebbi Jeremiah and Rebbi Ammi asked[163]: What is the difference between her[164] and one who had sex with a finger[165]? Is the one who had sex with a finger not disabled for priesthood[166]? Rebbi Ḥaggai said, explain it that there was no penetration[167]. Rebbi Ḥaggai wanted to change his mind; Rebbi Abba said to him, do not change your mind. Why did Rebbi Ḥaggai want to change his mind? Because of the verse[168]: "But he shall marry a wife in her virginities," only if she is a virgin in both respects[169]. Similarly, "a virgin and no man had known her.[170]" A virgin, with respect to penetration. No man had known her, without penetration. Rebbi Isaac ben Eleazar said, [no man] ever had wanted to touch her hand, for it was said[171]: "The staff of evil shall not rest on the just's lot." Why did Rebbi Ḥaggai want to change his mind? He could explain it by "touching". Why does (Rav Yosef) [Rebbi Yasa][172] not explain it by "touching"? Rebbi Mana said, because it presented a problem for him: Rebbi Yasa asked: What is the legal status of "touching"[173] with a male? "Touching" with an animal? When Rebbi Jeremiah heard that of Rebbi Ḥaggai, he said, that was not Rebbi Ammi's problem[174].

163 The text is impossible as it stands. It must have been either "R. Jeremiah (fourth generation) said that R. Immi (second generation) asked" or "R. Yasa and R. Immi asked". The sequel would support both versions.

164 The woman whose hymen was impaired by a mechanical accident, who is declared eligible to marry a High Priest.

165 Either she or another person perforated her hymen with his finger in sexual activity without penetration by a penis.

166 The high priesthood. Only the High Priest is required to marry a virgin.

167 If the girl had sexual experience without any penetration, she will qualify for a virgin's *ketubah*.

168 *Lev.* 21:13, speaking of the high priest. The complicated expression אשׁה

בִּבְתוּלֶיהָ "a woman in her virginities" instead of simpy בְּתוּלָה "a virgin" calls for an explanation.

169 She must be a virgin without any sexual experience; cf. Babli *Yebamot* 59a.

170 *Gen.* 24:16; here again the double expression calls for an explanation. In *Gen. rabba* 60(5), the explanation is ascribed to R. Simeon ben Laqish.

171 *Ps.* 125:3. In *Gen. rabba* 60(5), this explanation is ascribed to R. Johanan.

172 Since the author here cannot be the fourth generation Babylonian Rav Joseph (bar Hiyya), most likely he is Rebbi Yasa (cf. Note 163).

173 The touching of the genitals of two persons, whether there was penetration or emission or not. "Touching" is the legal definition of the sex act both for marriage (cf. *Yebamot* 4:2, Note 59; Mishnah 6:1) and for criminal law (Mishnah *Keritut* 2:4; cf. *Sotah* 1:2, Notes 97,98). The same question is asked in *Qiddušin* 1:1 (59c l. 14).

174 That solution is too obvious not to have occured to R. Ammi, and it does not address his question which asks for the difference between a hymen split by mechanical means or by the girl's own finger. In both cases, no male was involved.

(fol. 24c) **משנה ד:** בְּתוּלָה אַלְמָנָה גְּרוּשָׁה וַחֲלוּצָה מִן הַנִּישׂוּאִין כְּתוּבָּתָן מָנָה וְאֵין לָהֶן טַעֲנַת בְּתוּלִים. הַגִּיּוֹרֶת וְהַשְּׁבוּיָה וְהַשִּׁפְחָה שֶׁנִּפְדּוּ אוֹ שֶׁנִּתְגַּיְּירוּ אוֹ שֶׁנִּשְׁתַּחְרְרוּ יְתֵירוֹת עַל שָׁלֹשׁ שָׁנִים וְיוֹם אֶחָד כְּתוּבָּתָן מָנָה וְאֵין לָהֶן טַעֲנַת בְּתוּלִים.

Mishnah 4: [175]For virgins who after a final marriage become widows, divorcees, or who received *halisah*[158], their *ketubah* is a mina and they are not subject to a claim of non-virginity. For a proselyte, a prisoner, and a slave who were redeemed, converted, or freed at more than three years and one day of age, their *ketubah* is a mina and they are not subject to a claim of non-virginity.

175 Cf. Mishnah 2, Notes 108-111.

(25b line 70) **הלכה ד**: בְּתוּלָה וְאַלְמָנָה גְרוּשָׁה מִן הַנִּישׂוּאִין כול'. אֵי זוֹ הִיא בְּתוּלָה מִן הַנִּישׂוּאִין. אָמַר רִבִּי יוֹחָנָן. כָּל־שֶׁנִּכְנְסָה לַחוּפָּה וְעֵידֶיהָ מְעִידִין אוֹתָהּ שֶׁלֹּא נִבְעֲלָה. אָמַר רִבִּי יוֹסֵי. הָדָא אֲמָרָה נָשָׂא אִשָּׁה בְחֶזְקַת בְּתוּלָה וְנִמְצֵאת בְּעוּלָה אֵין זֶה מֶקַח טָעוּת לְהַפְסִידָהּ מִכְּתוּבַּת מָנֶה. נָשָׂא אִשָּׁה בְחֶזְקַת שֶׁלֹּא זִינְתָה וְנִמְצֵאת שֶׁזִּינְתָה אֵין זֶה מֶקַח טָעוּת לְהַפְסִידָהּ מִכְּתוּבַּת מָנֶה.

Halakhah 4: "A virgin, a widow, a divorcee after final marriage," etc. Who is a virgin after marriage? Rebbi Johanan said, any who entered the bridal chamber but her witnesses testify that she had no sexual relations[176]. Rebbi Yose said, this implies that if a man married a woman under the presumption[177] that she was a virgin and she turned out not to be a virgin, that is not an erroneous acquisition to deprive her of the *ketubah* of a mina[178]. If a man married a woman under the presumption that she never had illegitimate sex and she turned out that she had illegitimate sex, that is not an erroneous acquisition to deprive her of the *ketubah* of a mina[179].

176 A different formulation of the same fact is in the Tosephta, 1:4, and the Babli, 11b.

177 *Hazaqah* "holding fast" is the presumption that a known *status quo ante* remains unchanged until a change in status has been observed. In the case here, the groom had the right to assume that his bride was still the virgin she had been at birth. If before the marriage he required special assurances that the bride was a virgin, that is not a case of presumption, and if she was not virginal he can claim acquisition in error and annulment of marriage and forfeit of *ketubah*.

178 In the case of the Mishnah there was a presumption of virginity but only a *ketubah* of one mina; this shows that the presumption does not exclude that the bride was not a virgin. In the Babli, 11b (13a), a statement of Rav

Sheshet; this might imply that "R. Yose" here is R. Yasa.

179 This is essentially the previous case since, if there are witnesses that the husband had not slept with her, any defect could have come only from illegitimate sexual activity.

(25b line 75) רִבִּי לֶעְזָר שָׁאַל. הַבָּא עַל שִׁפְחָה מְשׁוּחְרֶרֶת מָהוּ. נִישְׁמְעִינָהּ מִן הָדָא. יָכוֹל הַבָּא עַל שִׁפְחָא אֲרָמִית יְהֵא חַיָּיב. תַּלְמוּד לוֹמַר מָהֹר יִמְהָרֶנָּה לּוֹ לְאִשָּׁה. אֶת שֶׁיֵּשׁ לוֹ הֲוָיָיה בָהּ. יָצָא שִׁפְחָה אוֹ מִי שֶׁאֵין לוֹ הֲוָיָיה בָהּ. מִפְּנֵי שֶׁאֵין לוֹ בָהּ הֲוָיָה. הָא אִם בָּהּ לוֹ הֲוָיָיה בָהּ יֵשׁ לָהּ קְנָס. וְכָל־שֶׁיֵּשׁ לָהּ קְנָס יֵשׁ לָהּ כְּתוּבָּה. אָמַר רִבִּי יוּדָן. וְכִי בִקְנָס הַדָּבָר תָּלוּי. הֲרֵי בוֹגֶרֶת אֵין לָהּ קְנָס וּכְתוּבָּתָהּ מָאתַיִם. הֲרֵי בְתוּלָה מִן הַנִּישׂוּאִין יֵשׁ לָהּ קְנָס וּכְתוּבָּתָהּ מָנֶה. אָמַר רִבִּי זְעִירָא קוֹמֵי רִבִּי מָנָא. תִּיפְתָּר בְּשֶׁנִּתְגַּיְּירוּ אוֹ שֶׁנִּשְׁתַּחְרְרוּ פְּחוּתוֹת מִבְּנוֹת שָׁלֹשׁ שָׁנִים וְיוֹם אֶחָד. אָמַר לֵיהּ. אִם בְּשֶׁנִּתְגַּיְּירוּ אוֹ שֶׁנִּשְׁתַּחְרְרוּ פְּחוּתוֹת מִבְּנוֹת שָׁלֹשׁ שָׁנִים וְיוֹם אֶחָד כְּיִשְׂרָאֵל הֵן.

Rebbi Eleazar asked, what about a male who sleeps with a manumitted slave girl[180]? Let us hear from the following[181]: I could think that a male who sleeps with a Gentile slave has to pay[182]; the verse says[183]: "He shall take her as wife by the bride price." If he can marry her. This excludes the [gentile] slave (or any)[184] whom he cannot marry. Only because he cannot marry her! Therefore, if he can marry her[185], she collects the fine, and any who collects the fine has a *ketubah*. [186]Rebbi Yudan said, does that depend on a fine? Look, the adult[141] collects no fine but her *ketubah* is 200, the virgin after marriage collects a fine[142] but her *ketubah* is a mina[62]! Rebbi Ze'ira said before Rebbi Mana, explain it if she was converted or freed before she reached three years and one day. He said to him, any woman who was converted or manumitted before she reached three years and one day is like an Israel[187].

180 It seems that this is a rhetorical question since the *ketubah* of the freedwoman is determined in Mishnaiot 1:2,4 and her right to the fine imposed on the rapist or the seducer in 3:1,2. R. David Fraenckel emends מהו to מניין and reads the question as asking for the biblical source of the Mishnaiot mentioned.

181 A parallel text in Halakhah 3:1.

182 The fine imposed on a person raping or seducing an underage girl, cf. Note 117.

183 *Ex.* 22:15.

184 Reading ארמית for או מי of the text.

185 If she is freed and can contract a marriage.

186 From Halakhah 1:2.

187 Mishnaiot 1:2, 3:1 state clearly that in matters of marriage, girls becoming Jewish at a very young age are equal to those born Jewish [except for marriages with priests where practice follows *Ez.* 44:22; cf. *Bikkurim* 1:5 (Notes 89-99), Babli *Yebamot* 60b.]

(25c line 9) סוּמָה וְאַיְילוֹנִית יֵשׁ לָהֶן טַעֲנַת בְּתוּלִין. סוּמְכוֹס אָמַר מִשֵּׁם רִבִּי מֵאִיר. סוּמָה אֵין לָהּ טַעֲנַת בְּתוּלִים. וּמַה טַעֲמָא דְרִבִּי מֵאִיר. אֲנִי אוֹמֵר. מָצָא וְאִיבֵּד. מַה טַעֲמָא דְרַבָּנָן. יְכוֹלָה הִיא לְתוֹפְשׂוֹ. מָה עָבַד לָהּ רִבִּי מֵאִיר. יָכוֹל הוּא לִדְחוֹתָן בְּרוֹק.

The blind woman and the she-ram[188] are subject to claims of missing virginity. Symmachos said in the name of Rebbi Meïr that the blind woman is not subject to claims of missing virginity. What is Rebbi Meïr's reason? I say, he found [her to be a virgin] and destroyed [the evidence][189]. What is the rabbi's reason? She can catch him. What does Rebbi Meïr with this argument? He can cleanse it with spittle[190].

188 A woman without secondary female sex characteristics, presumed to be infertile; cf. *Yebamot* 1:1, Note 65.

189 Since the blind woman cannot see what her husband does, she cannot see to it that the traces of her hymeneal blood are not destroyed, leaving her without defenses in court. R. Meïr assumes that she prefers to have an untouchable mina as *ketubah* over having 200 *zuz* with a chance of being deprived of it by a cheating husband.

HALAKHAH 4

190 The Babli, 36a, connects the disagreement between R. Meïr and the rabbis to that of Rabban Gamliel and R. Joshua (Mishnaiot 1:8,9) whether her unsupported statement is credible or not. The rabbis follow Rabban Gamliel, R. Meïr follows R. Joshua. The Tosephta, 3:5, knows only of the rabbis' position.

(25c line 13) תַּנֵּי. טַעֲנַת בְּתוּלִים עַד שְׁלֹשִׁים יוֹם. דִּבְרֵי רִבִּי מֵאִיר. וַחֲכָמִים אוֹמְרִים. מִיָּד. מַה נָן קַיָּימִין. אִם בְּשֶׁבָּעַל. מִיָּד. אִם בְּשֶׁלֹּא בָעַל אֲפִילוּ לְאַחַר מִיכָּן עַד כַּמָּה. אֶלָּא כֵן אֲנָן קַיָּימִין בִּסְתָם. רִבִּי מֵאִיר אוֹמֵר. חֲזָקָה אָדָם מַעֲמִיד עַצְמוֹ שְׁלֹשִׁים יוֹם. וְרַבָּנִין אֲמְרִין. אֲפִילוּ יוֹם אֶחָד אֵין אָדָם מַעֲמִיד אֶת עַצְמוֹ. רִבִּי יִרְמְיָה בָּעָא. מָהוּ שֶׁיְּהֵא נֶאֱמָן לוֹמַר עַל דְּרִבִּי מֵאִיר. הֶעֱמַדְתִּי עַצְמִי שְׁלֹשִׁים יוֹם. כְּדֵי לַעֲשׂוֹת אֶת הַוָּלָד שְׁתוּקִי. נִשְׁמְעִינָהּ מִן הָדָא. הַיְבָמָה שֶׁאָמְרָה בְּתוֹךְ שְׁלֹשִׁים יוֹם. לֹא נִבְעַלְתִּי. כּוֹפִין אוֹתוֹ שֶׁיַּחֲלוֹץ לָהּ. לְאַחַר שְׁלֹשִׁים יוֹם מְבַקְשִׁים מִמֶּנּוּ שֶׁיַּחֲלוֹץ לָהּ. וְאָמַר רִבִּי לָעְזָר. דְּרִבִּי מֵאִיר הִיא. וְאָמַר רִבִּי לָעְזָר. לֹא שָׁנוּ אֶלָּא אֶצְלָהּ. הָא אֵצֶל צָרָתָהּ לֹא. כְּמַהּ דְּתֵימַר תַּמָּן. לֹא הַכֹּל מִמֶּנָּה לַחוֹב לְצָרָתָהּ. אַף הָכָא לֹא הַכֹּל מִמֶּנָּה לָחוֹב לִבְנָהּ.[191]

2 אם | ואם   3 לאחר מכן כמה | כמה   אומר | אמר   4-5 אפילו יום אחד אין אדם מעמיד את עצמו | אין אדם מעמיד אפילו יום אחד   5 בעא | בעי   6 כדי | בשביל   8 מבקשים | מבקשין   10 ממנה | ממנו   לבנה | לבנו

[192]It was stated: A claim of non-virginity may be brought within thirty days, the words of Rebbi Meïr. But the Sages say, immediately. Where do we hold? If he copulated, immediately. If he did not copulate, even after a longer delay. But we must deal with the case that it was not spelled out. Rebbi Meïr said, it is credible that a man may hold himself back for thirty days. But the Sages say, a man does not hold himself back even for one day. Rebbi Jeremiah asked: According to Rebbi Meïr, would a man be believed to assert that he held himself back for thirty days in order to make the child of unknown paternity? Let us hear from

the following: "If the sister-in-law claims within thirty days that she was not copulated with, one forces him to perform *halisah* with her. After thirty days, one asks him to perform *halisah* with her." And Rebbi Eleazar said, this is Rebbi Meïr's. And Rebbi Eleazar said, that refers only to her, but not to her co-wife. As you say there, she is not believed to damage her co-wife, so here, he is not believed to damage his son.

191 The queer spelling in the ms. was read in *editio princeps* as לא הכל ממנה לחוב לבנה "she is not believed to damage her son"!

192 This is from *Yebamot* 13:15, Notes 123-130; cf. Babli *Yebamot* 111b. The variant readings from *Yebamot* are indicated by י.

(fol. 24d) **משנה ה:** הָאוֹכֵל אֵצֶל חָמִיו בִּיהוּדָה שֶׁלֹּא בְעֵדִים אֵינוֹ יָכוֹל לִטְעוֹן טַעֲנַת בְּתוּלִים מִפְּנֵי שֶׁמִּתְיַחֵד עִמָּהּ. אֶחָד אַלְמָנַת יִשְׂרָאֵל וְאֶחָד אַלְמָנַת כֹּהֲנִים כְּתוּבָּתָן מָנֶה. בֵּית דִּין שֶׁלַּכֹּהֲנִים הָיוּ גּוֹבִין לַבְּתוּלָה אַרְבַּע מֵאוֹת זוּז וְלֹא מִיחוּ בְיָדָם חֲכָמִים.

Mishnah 5: If somebody eats at his father-in-law's in Judea without chaperones cannot claim missing virginity since he is alone with her[193]. Both for an Israel widow as a Cohanim widow[194] the *ketubah* is a mina. The court of priests collected 400 *zuz* for a virgin[195], to which the Sages did not object.

193 As the Halakhah makes clear, he is supposed to sleep with his fiancée.

194 The daughter of a Cohen, even if married to an Israel.

195 It is not clear whether this applies to marriages of daughters of Cohanim, or marriages of Cohanim, or both. Since this is generally accepted practice known to the groom at the

time he contracted the marriage, it is legal and can be enforced even if the original *ketubah* was lost.

(25c line 24) **הלכה ח**: הָאוֹכֵל אֵצֶל חָמִיו כול'. בָּרִאשׁוֹנָה גָזְרוּ שְׁמָד בִּיהוּדָה. שֶׁכֵּן מְסוֹרֶת לָהֶם מֵאֲבוֹתָם שֶׁיְּהוּדָה הָרַג אֶת עֵשָׂיו. דִּכְתִיב יָדְךָ בְּעוֹרֶף אוֹיְבֶיךָ. וְהָיוּ הוֹלְכִין וּמְשַׁעְבְּדִין בָּהֶן וְאוֹנְסִין אֶת בְּנוֹתֵיהֶן וְגָזְרוּ שֶׁיְּהֵא אִיסְטְרָטִיּוֹס בּוֹעֵל תְּחִילָּה. הִתְקִינוּ שֶׁיְּהֵא בַּעֲלָהּ בָּא עָלֶיהָ עוֹדָהּ בְּבֵית אָבִיהָ. שֶׁמִּתּוֹךְ שֶׁהִיא יוֹדַעַת שֶׁאֵימַת בַּעֲלָהּ עָלֶיהָ עוֹד הִיא נִגְרֶרֶת. מִכָּל־מָקוֹם אֵין סוֹפָהּ לְהִיבָּעֵל מֵאִיסְטְרָטִיּוֹס. אֲנוּסָה הִיא וַאֲנוּסָה מוּתֶּרֶת לִבְעְלָהּ. כֹּהֲנוֹת מָה הָיוּ עוֹשׂוֹת. מַטְמִינוֹת הָיוּ. וְיַטְמִינוּ אַף בְּנוֹת יִשְׂרָאֵל. קוֹל יוֹצֵא וּמַלְכוּתָא שָׁמְעָה וְאִילֵּין וְאִילֵּין מִתְעָרְבְבִין. מַה סִימָן הָיָה לָהֶן. קוֹל מַגְרוֹס בָּעִיר. מִשְׁתֶּה שָׁם מִשְׁתֶּה שָׁם. אוֹר הַנֵּר בִּבְרוֹר־חַיִל. שָׁבוּעַ בֶּן שָׁבוּעַ בֶּן. אַף עַל פִּי שֶׁבָּטַל הַשְּׁמָד הַמִּנְהַג לֹא בָטַל. כַּלָּתוֹ שֶׁלְּרַבִּי הוֹשַׁעְיָה נִכְנְסָה מְעוּבֶּרֶת.

Halakhah 5: "If somebody eats at his father-in-law's," etc. In earlier times[196] they decided on a persecution in Judea because they had a tradition from their forefathers that Jehudah had killed Esaw[197], as it is written[198]: "Your hand is on your enemies' neck." They went and enslaved them[199] and raped their daughters; they decided that a soldier[200] would have sex with her first. They decreed that her husband should come to her when still in her father's house[201]; for when she knows that her husband's fear is on her she is drawn after him[202]. But is she not in the end being used for sex by a soldier? She is raped, and a rape victim is permitted to her husband[203]. What did Cohanot do? They were hiding them. Why did they not also hide the daughters of Israel? That becomes talk[204] and the government hears it; then these and those will be taken together. What kind of a sign did they have? The talk of a cook[205] in town: There is a wedding meal, there is a wedding meal[206]; there is light in Beror-Ḥayil[207]: a week for a son, a week for a son. When the persecution ended, the custom did not end. Rebbi Hoshaia's[208] daughter-in-law was pregnant when she married definitively.

196 The only time when the Roman government could be supposed to act officially in the manner described was during Hadrian's persecution in the aftermath of the war of Bar Kokhba.

197 "Esaw" is a code name for Rome; e. g., *Eccl. rabba* to 5:7. The story that Jehudah killed Esaw when the latter wanted to kill Jacob at Isaac's funeral is in *Midraš Soḥer Ṭob* 18:32, mentioned in *Sifry Deut.* 348, quoted in *Yalquṭ Šim'ony* 162. In the tradition of the Babli, *Soṭa* 13a, Esaw was killed by Ḥushim ben Dan at Jacob's funeral.

198 *Gen.* 49:8.

199 After the war of Bar Kokhba, most of the Jewish population of Judea were sold as slaves.

200 Greek στρατιώτης. In the considerably toned down version of the Babli, 3b, it was only the general, ἡγεμών, who would exercise a *ius primae noctis* over girls married on Wednesdays.

201 After the preliminary marriage.

202 The commentaries and S. Lieberman emend נִגְרַרְתּ to נִגְדֶּרֶת "she is fenced in." This emendation has to be rejected since it is understandable that one should want the girl to be drawn to her husband and not to the soldier with whom she otherwise would have her first sexual experience.

203 *Sifry Num.* 7, based on *Num.* 5:13.

204 If everybody does it, it cannot be kept secret.

205 Greek μάγειρος, ὁ, "cook, butcher".

206 While in biblical Hebrew מִשְׁתֶּה is any festive meal, in rabbinic Hebrew the term is used exclusively for wedding festivities. Since one could not speak of weddings during the persecution, one spoke of the cook.

207 *Beror-Ḥayil* was the residence of Rabban Yoḥanan ben Zakkai after the first war with the Romans; it must have been in the imperial domain of Jabneh, in the plain. Lights were lit to indicate an invitation to attend a forbidden circumcision, just as the presence of a professional cook indicated a wedding.

208 He taught in Galilee 100 years after the Hadrianic persecution. His

family was from Judea, where his father still lived (*Niddah* 3:3, 50 c l. 71).

(25c line 35) תַּנֵּי. וְלָאַלְמָנָה מָאתַיִם. אֶחָד אַלְמָנַת יִשְׂרָאֵל וְאֶחָד אַלְמָנַת כֹּהֲנִים כְּסֵדֶר הַזֶּה. אָמַר רִבִּי יוֹסֵי. מִסְתַּבְּרָא בַּת כֹּהֵן לְיִשְׂרָאֵל תִּגְבֶּה. שֶׁשִּׁבְטָהּ גּוֹבֶה. בַּת יִשְׂרָאֵל לְכֹהֵן לֹא תִגְבֶּה. לָא מִסְתַּיְּיא דְסַלְקָא לִכְהוּנָתָא אֶלָּא דְתֵימַר תִּגְבֶּה. אָמַר רִבִּי מָנָא. לָא מִסְתַּבְּרָא דְלָא חֲלִיפִין. בַּת יִשְׂרָאֵל לְכֹהֵן תִּגְבֶּה דְּסַלְקָא לִכְהוּנָתָא. וּבַת כֹּהֵן לָא תִגְבֶּה דִנְחִיתָא מִן כְּהוּנָתָא. אָמַר רִבִּי יוֹסֵי בֵּירִבִּי אָבוּן. אַחַת זוֹ וְאַחַת זוֹ קְנָס קָנְסוּ בָהֶן כְּדֵי שֶׁיְּהֵא אָדָם מִידַּבַּק בְּשִׁבְטוֹ וּבְמִשְׁפַּחְתּוֹ.

It was stated: "And for a widow 200.[209]" This order applies both to a widow of an Israel[210] and a widow of a Cohen[211]. Rebbi Yose said, it is reasonable that the daughter of a Cohen should collect, for her tribe collects. The daughter of an Israel married to a Cohen should not collect; is it not sufficient that she rose to the priesthood that you say, she should collect? Rebbi Mana said, it is reasonable the other way. The daughter of an Israel married to a Cohen should collect for she rose to the priesthood; the daughter of a Cohen should not collect for she stepped down from the priesthood. Rebbi Yose bar Abun said, in both cases they demanded a fine so that everybody should cling to his tribe and family.

209 The court of Cohanim collected 200 *zuz* for a widow, against the explicit testimony of the Mishnah. In the opinion of the Babli, 12a/b, the priestly families tried to enforce this for their daughters but were forced to retract since nobody would take a widow for 200 *zuz* when he could get a virgin for the same price. The Babli also gives to non-priestly noble families the right to establish the higher tariff as default option for their daughters; the Yerushalmi considers this part of the Mishnah obsolete.

210 The daughter of a Cohen, widow of an Israel.

211 The daughter of an Israel, widow of a Cohen.

משנה ו: (fol. 24d) הַנּוֹשֵׂא אֶת הָאִשָּׁה וְלֹא מָצָא לָהּ בְּתוּלִים הִיא אוֹמֶרֶת מִשֶּׁאֵירַסְתַּנִי נֶאֱנַסְתִּי וְנִסְתַּפְּחָה שָׂדְהוּ וְהוּא אוֹמֵר לֹא כִּי אֶלָּא עַד שֶׁלֹּא אֵירַסְתִּיךְ וְהָיָה מִקְחִי מֶקַח טָעוּת. רַבָּן גַּמְלִיאֵל וְרַבִּי אֱלִיעֶזֶר אוֹמֵר נֶאֱמֶנֶת. רִבִּי יְהוֹשֻׁעַ אוֹמֵר לֹא מִפִּיהָ אָנוּ חַיִין אֶלָּא הֲרֵי זוֹ בְחֶזְקַת בְּעוּלָה עַד שֶׁלֹּא תִּתְאָרֵס וְהִיטְעַתּוֹ עַד שֶׁתָּבִיא רְאָיָה לִדְבָרֶיהָ.

Mishnah 6: Somebody married a woman and found that she was no virgin[212]. She says, I was raped after you had married me preliminarily, so your field was flooded[213]. He says not so, but it happened before I married you preliminarily; therefore, my acquisition was made in error. Rabban Gamliel and Rebbi Eliezer say, she is believed[214]. Rebbi Joshua said, we do not live off her mouth but there is a presumption that she had sexual relations before she was preliminarily married unless she provides proof of her statement[215].

212 The fact is not in dispute.
213 Cf. Note 58.
214 If neither of them has any corroborating evidence, her claim that she *certainly* was raped later is stronger than his assertion that *maybe* she was raped or had consensual sex earlier. If the husband wants to deny her claim, he has to provide evidence.
215 Since she claims a *ketubah* and he does not want to pay at all, she claims money and a claimant in a civil suit carries the burden of proof.

הלכה ו: (25c line 42) הַנּוֹשֵׂא אֶת הָאִשָּׁה וְלֹא מָצָא לָהּ בְּתוּלִים כול׳. רִבִּי יִרְמְיָה בָּעֵי. מֵעַתָּה אֵין טַעֲנַת בְּתוּלִים לֹא כְרַבָּן גַּמְלִיאֵל וּכְרִבִּי אֱלִיעֶזֶר אֶלָּא כְרִבִּי יְהוֹשֻׁעַ. וְחָזַר וְאָמַר. יֵשׁ טַעֲנַת בְּתוּלִים כְּרַבָּן גַּמְלִיאֵל וּכְרִבִּי אֱלִיעֶזֶר בְּשׁוֹתֶקֶת. וַאֲפִילוּ תֵּימֵר בִּמְדַבֶּרֶת. בְּאוֹמֶרֶת. מָצָא וְאִיבֵּד. וּתְהֵא נֶאֱמֶנֶת. לֵית יָכִיל. דְּאָמַר רִבִּי אִילָא בְּשֵׁם רִבִּי לָעְזָר. מָצָא פֶּתַח פָּתוּחַ אָסוּר לְקַיְימָהּ מִשּׁוּם סָפֵק

HALAKHAH 6

סוֹטָה. הָכָא אִיתְּמַר נֶאֱמֶנֶת. וְהָכָא אִיתְּמַר אֵינָהּ נֶאֱמֶנֶת. תַּמָּן שְׁנֵיהֶן מוֹדִין בְּשֶׁהַפֶּתַח פָּתוּחַ.

"Somebody married a woman and found that she was no virgin", etc. Rebbi Jeremiah asked: Does this mean that a claim of missing virginity is impossible following Rabban Gamliel and Rebbi Eliezer[216], only following Rebbi Joshua? He turned around and said, a claim of missing virginity is possible following Rabban Gamliel and Rebbi Eliezer, if she remains silent. And even if you say that she talks, if she said that he found her a virgin and destroyed the evidence. Why should she not be believed[217]? One cannot tolerate it, since Rebbi Hila said in the name of Rebbi Eleazar, if he found the door open, he is forbidden to keep her because she might have been unfaithful[19]. Here you say, she is believed. There, you say that she is not believed. In this case, both agree that the door was open[218].

216 If the court automatically has to side with the woman, how could the husband hope to be heard?

217 If she claims to have been a virgin at the time of the final marriage ceremony.

218 In the case of the Mishnah here, the facts are not in dispute, only their explanation is. It is possible to prefer an explanation presented as certain over a presumed argument. But if she denies not being a virgin, he has to assume that she is forbidden to him and, because he *thinks* her to be guilty, has to divorce her irrespective of the real facts behind the case.

(25c line 49) תַּמָּן תַּנִּינָן. הָיוּ בָהּ מוּמִין וְעוֹדָהּ בְּבֵית אָבִיהָ הָאָב צָרִיךְ לְהָבִיא רְאָיָה. רִבִּי לֶעְזָר שָׁאַל לְרִבִּי יוֹחָנָן. מַתְנִיתָא דְרַבָּן גַּמְלִיאֵל וְרִבִּי אֱלִיעֶזֶר דְּלֹא כְרִבִּי יְהוֹשֻׁעַ. אָמַר לֵיהּ. דִּבְרֵי הַכֹּל הִיא. שְׁנִייָא הִיא מוּמִין שֶׁדַּרְכָּן לְהִיוָּלֵד. אָמַר רִבִּי יוֹסֵי. מִקַּמָּא דְּנָן חֲמֵי רַבָּנָן מְדַמּוּ מוּמִין לִבְתוּלִין. אִילֵּין יָלְפִין מִן אִילֵּין וְאִילֵּין יָלְפִין מִן אִילֵּין. מוּמִין מִבְּתוּלִים. שֶׁאִם בָּא עָלֶיהָ עוֹדָהּ בְּבֵית

אָבִיהָ צָרִיךְ הָאָב לְהָבִיא רְאָיָיה. בְּתוּלִים מְמוּמִין. שֶׁאִם נוֹלְדוּ לָהּ מוּמִין סָפֵק מִשֶּׁנִּכְנְסָה לִרְשׁוּתוֹ סָפֵק עַד שֶׁלֹּא תִּיכָּנֵס לִרְשׁוּתוֹ הַבַּעַל צָרִיךְ לְהָבִיא רְאָיָיה. מִן אִילֵּין בְּתוּלִין. וּבְתוּלִין וְכִי בָטְלוּ לֹא בְּבֵית אָבִיהָ בָטְלוּ. וְאַתְּ אָמַר. הַבַּעַל צָרִיךְ לְהָבִיא רְאָיָיה. וָכָא הַבַּעַל צָרִיךְ לְהָבִיא רְאָיָיה.

There, we have stated[219]: "If she had bodily defects while still in her father's house, the father has to bring proof." Rebbi Eleazar asked Rebbi Johanan: Is this Mishnah from Rabban Gamliel and Rebbi Eliezer? Not from Rebbi Joshua[220]? He said to him, those are everybody's words. There is a difference because bodily defects have a way to appear[221]. Rebbi Yose said, formerly we saw rabbis who compared bodily defects to [defects of] virginity. These can be inferred from those and those can be inferred from these[222]. Bodily defects from claims of missing virginity: For if he slept with her in her father's house, the father has to provide proof[223]. Claims of missing virginity from bodily defects[224]: For if she developed bodily defects and there is a doubt whether it happened after she entered his domain or before she entered his domain, the husband has to provide proof, from claims of missing virginity. But if she lost her virginity, was it not in her father's house? Nevertheless, you say, the husband has to provide proof[225]; so here also, the husband has to provide proof.

219 Mishnah 7:8. The groom says that he never would have agreed to the marriage had he known that the bride had a bodily defect; his preliminary marriage was arranged under false pretenses; he wants to withdraw without paying. The father asserts that at the time of the preliminary marriage the bride was without defects, and that "the groom's field was flooded". If the disagreement surfaces before the final marriage, the burden of proof is on the father; after that, the burden of proof is on the husband.

HALAKHAH 7

220 Since R. Joshua puts the burden of proof on the wife in the Mishnah here; why is there no disagreement recorded there?

221 For problems that have to be expected, the person in control of the place where they happened is responsible. In Halakhah 7:8, it is stated that in the matter of very frequent defects, the husband can complain if at the start he had stipulated that the bride be free from even the most minute impairment.

222 Claims for annulment of the marriage because of bodily defects of the bride and because of missing virginity follow identical rules.

223 It really is the other way around; in this case the rule about a complaint about virginity is derived from that about defects. If the final marriage ceremony is held at the father's house, then in case of a blemish the burden of proof would have to be on the father; therefore, for the claim of missing virginity the father has to bring proof that his daughter either was a virgin at the moment of final marriage or lost her virginity in a manner which did not impair the validity of the marriage.

224 Again, this should be inverted: Rules for claims about blemishes derived from rules of complaints about virginity.

225 This follows only Rabban Gamliel and R. Eliezer; it is the only indication that practice should follow Rabban Gamliel (and not R. Joshua against R. Eliezer); this is stated explicitly in the Babli (12b). In the Mishnah here it is agreed that the loss of virginity occured in her father's house. But since the argument developed after the final marriage in the husband's house, the burden of proof is on the husband.

(fol. 24d) **משנה ז:** הִיא אוֹמֶרֶת מוּכַּת עֵץ אֲנִי וְהוּא אוֹמֵר לֹא כִּי אֶלָּא דְרוּסַת אִישׁ אַתְּ רַבָּן גַּמְלִיאֵל וְרִבִּי אֱלִיעֶזֶר אוֹמֵר נֶאֱמֶנֶת. רִבִּי יְהוֹשֻׁעַ אוֹמֵר לֹא מִפִּיהָ אָנוּ חַיִּין אֶלָּא הֲרֵי זוֹ בְחֶזְקַת דְּרוּסַת אִישׁ עַד שֶׁתָּבִיא רְאָיָיה לִדְבָרֶיהָ.

Mishnah 7: She says[226], I was injured by wood, but he says not so, you were trampled on by a man; Rabban Gamliel and Rebbi Eliezer say, she is believed[214]. Rebbi Joshua said, we do not live off her mouth but there is a presumption that she was trampled on by a man unless she provides proof of her statement[215].

226 This Mishnah is a continuation of the previous one; there is no doubt but that the bride was not an intact virgin.

(25c line 60) **הלכה ז**: הִיא אוֹמֶרֶת מוּכַּת עֵץ אֲנִי כול'. אָמַר רִבִּי לְעָזָר. דְּרִבִּי מֵאִיר הִיא. דְּרִבִּי מֵאִיר אָמַר. מוּכַּת עֵץ כְּתוּבָּתָהּ מָאתַיִם. אָמַר רִבִּי יוֹסֵי. וַהֲוֵינָן סָבְרִין מֵימַר. מַה פְּלִיגִין רִבִּי מֵאִיר וְאִילֵּין רַבָּנָן. בְּשֶׁכְּנָסָהּ בְּחֶזְקַת מוּכַּת עֵץ. אֲבָל אִם כְּנָסָהּ בְּחֶזְקַת בְּתוּלָה וְנִמְצֵאת מוּכַּת עֵץ אַף רִבִּי מֵאִיר מוֹדֶה. מִן מַה דְּתַנִּינָן. הִיא אוֹמֶרֶת. מוּכַּת עֵץ אֲנִי. וְהוּא אוֹמֵר. לֹא כִּי אֶלָּא דְּרוּסַת אִישׁ אַתְּ. הָדָא אָמְרָה. אֲפִילוּ כְּנָסָהּ בְּחֶזְקַת מוּכַּת עֵץ וְנִמְצֵאת מוּכַּת עֵץ הִיא מַחֲלוּקֶת. רִבִּי יִרְמְיָה בְּשֵׁם רִבִּי זְעִירָא לֹא אָמַר כֵּן אֶלָּא. הִיא אוֹמֶרֶת. מוּכַּת עֵץ אֲנִי וּכְתוּבָּתָהּ מָאתַיִם. וְהוּא אוֹמֵר. לֹא כִּי אֶלָּא דְּרוּסַת אִישׁ אַתְּ וְאֵין לָךְ עָלַי כְּלוּם. מָה אֲנַן קַיָּימִין. אִם בְּשֶׁכְּנָסָהּ בְּחֶזְקַת בְּתוּלָה וְנִמְצֵאת מוּכַּת עֵץ. אַף רִבִּי מֵאִיר מוֹדֶה. אִם בְּשֶׁכְּנָסָהּ בְּחֶזְקַת מוּכַּת עֵץ וְנִמְצֵאת מוּכַּת עֵץ נִיכָּר הוּא בְּפֶתַח פָּתוּחַ בֵּין בְּעֵץ בֵּין בְּאָדָם. רִבִּי הוּנָא בְּשֵׁם רִבִּי זְעִירָא לֹא אָמַר כֵּן אֶלָּא. הִיא אוֹמֶרֶת מוּכַּת עֵץ אֲנִי. כֵּן אַתְנֵיתִי עִמָּךְ. וְהוּא אוֹמֵר. לֹא כִּי אֶלָּא דְּרוּסַת אִישׁ אַתְּ. לֹא אַתְנֵיתִי עִמָּךְ כְּלוּם.

Halakhah 7: "She says, I was injured by wood," etc. Rebbi Eleazar said, that follows Rebbi Meïr, since Rebbi Meïr said the *ketubah* of one injured by wood is 200 [*zuz*][227]. Rebbi Yose said, we would think to say, when did Rebbi Meïr disagree with those rabbis? If he took her in assuming she was injured by wood. But if he took her in assuming she was a virgin and it turned out she was injured by wood, then even Rebbi Meïr agrees[228], since we have stated: "She says, I was injured by wood, but he says not so, you were trampled on by a man." That means, there is a disagreement even if he took her in assuming she was injured by wood[229] and she turned out to have been injured by wood.

Rebbi Jeremiah in the name of Rebbi Ze'ira did not say so, but: She says, I was injured by wood and my *ketubah* is 200 [*zuz*]. He says, it is not so, but you were trampled on by a man and you have no claim on me. What are we talking about? If he married her as a virgin and she turns out to have been injured by wood, Rebbi Meïr will agree[228]. If he married her as one injured by wood and she turns out to have been injured by wood, is there a recognizable difference in the opening of the door between wood or man[230]?

Rebbi Huna in the name of Rebbi Ze'ira did not say so, but: She says, I was injured by wood and so I stipulated with you, but he says, it is not so, but you were trampled on by a man and there was no stipulation between you and me[227].

227 In the Babli, 13a, R. Eleazar is reported that she claims 100 *zuz* as *ketubah* but he does not want to give anything. This is the position articulated by R. Huna here. R. Johanan holds that she claims 200 but he wants to give only 100.

228 If the husband was not informed of the facts when he signed the *ketubah*, R. Meïr agrees that he can sue to annul the contract.

229 There is agreement among all commentators that this should read: "if he took her in assuming she was a virgin." But if that were true, R. Jeremiah would say the same as R. Yose. In addition, we know that there is a difference of opinion between R. Meïr and the rabbis about the *ketubah* of one who claims to have been injured by wood.

230 In that case, the position of

Rabban Gamliel and R. Eliezer is preferable since she holds the contract in her hands and the burden of proof is on the party contesting a written contract (*Baba batra* 9:8, 17a l. 56).

(fol. 24d) **משנה ח**: רָאוּהָ מְדַבֶּרֶת עִם אֶחָד אָמְרוּ לָהּ מַה טִיבוֹ שֶׁלָּזֶה. אִישׁ פְּלוֹנִי וְכֹהֵן הוּא רַבָּן גַּמְלִיאֵל וְרִבִּי אֱלִיעֶזֶר אוֹמֵר נֶאֱמֶנֶת. רִבִּי יְהוֹשֻׁעַ אוֹמֵר לֹא מִפִּיהָ אָנוּ חַיִּין אֶלָּא הֲרֵי זוֹ בְחֶזְקַת בְּעוּלָה לְנָתִין וּלְמַמְזֵר עַד שֶׁתָּבִיא רְאָיָה לִדְבָרֶיהָ.

Mishnah 8: If she was seen speaking[231] to a man and one asked her, what kind of man is this? He is Mr. X, a Cohen; Rabban Gamliel and Rebbi Eliezer say, she is believed[232]. Rebbi Joshua said, we do not live off her mouth but there is a presumption that she was lying with a Gibeonite and a bastard unless she provides proof of her statement[233].

231 An unmarried woman was seen having an affair with an unknown person.

232 A single person engaging in sexual activity with a man whom she could marry is still permitted to marry a Cohen.

233 Bastards (children of adultery or incest punishable by death by the court or Heaven) are forbidden to marry into the congregation by biblical decree (cf. *Yebamot* 1:1, Note 29) and Gibeonites by tradition (cf. *Yebamot* 2:4, Note 72). Therefore, a woman sleeping with such a man is a זוֹנָה and forbidden to marry a Cohen (*Yebamot* 6:5, Note 100).

(25c line 73) **הלכה ח**: רָאוּהָ מְדַבֶּרֶת עִם אֶחָד כול׳. מָהוּ מְדַבֶּרֶת. נִבְעֶלֶת. וְלָמָּה תַּנִּינָן מְדַבֶּרֶת. לָשׁוֹן בָּקִי. רִבִּי אוֹמֵר נָקִי.

"If she was seen speaking to a man," etc. What is "speaking"? She had sexual relations[234]. Why did we state "speaking"? An expression for the knowing; Rebbi says, of purity.

234 In the Babli, 13a, this is the opinion of Rav Assi. His (Babylonian) contemporary Ze'iri explains that R. Joshua already disqualifies her from marrying into the priesthood if she had a rendez-vous with an unidentified person.

(25c line 75) רִבִּי יַעֲקֹב בַּר אָחָא בְּשֵׁם רִבִּי יֹאשִׁיָּה. הֲלָכָה כְּרַבָּן גַּמְלִיאֵל וּכְרִבִּי אֱלִיעֶזֶר מִשּׁוּם שְׁנַיִם שֶׁרַבּוּ עַל אֶחָד. רִבִּי יוֹסֵי בָּעֵי. אִם הֲלָכָה לָמָּה שְׁנַיִם. וְאִם שְׁנַיִם לָמָּה הֲלָכָה. מֵעַתָּה אֵין יִסְבּוֹר רִבִּי יוֹחָנָן כְּרִבִּי יְהוֹשֻׁעַ אֵין הֲלָכָה כְּרַבָּן גַּמְלִיאֵל וּכְרִבִּי אֱלִיעֶזֶר אֶלָּא כְּרִבִּי יְהוֹשֻׁעַ. מַאי כְּדוֹן. מִשּׁוּם עֵדוּת שֶׁהָאִשָּׁה כְּשֵׁירָה לָהּ. חָווֹן בָּעֵי מֵימַר. מַה פְּלִיגִין רִבִּי יְהוֹשֻׁעַ וְאִילֵּין רַבָּנִין. בִּמְקוֹם שֶׁרוֹב פְּסוּלִין. אֲבָל בִּמְקוֹם שֶׁרוֹב כְּשֵׁירִין אַף רִבִּי יְהוֹשֻׁעַ מוֹדֵי. אָתָא רִבִּי יַעֲקֹב בַּר אָחָא בְּשֵׁם רִבִּי יוֹחָנָן וְרִבִּי אִילָא בְּשֵׁם רִבִּי לֶעֱזָר. אֲפִילוּ בִּמְקוֹם שֶׁרוֹב כְּשֵׁירִין הִיא מַחֲלוֹקֶת. סָבַר רִבִּי יְהוֹשֻׁעַ. הַזְּנוּת רָצָה אַחַר הַפְּסוּלִים. אָמַר רִבִּי זְעִירָא. מַתְנִיתָא אֲמָרָהּ. אֲפִילוּ כְּשֵׁירִין מְזַנִּין. דְּתַנֵּי. אֲפִילוּ חָסִיד שֶׁבַּחֲסִידִים אֵין מְמַנִּין אוֹתוֹ אֶפִּיטְרוֹפּוֹס עַל עֲרָיוֹת.

Rebbi Jacob bar Aḥa in the name of Rebbi Joshia: Practice follows Rabban Gamliel and Rebbi Eliezer since two form a majority against one[235]. Rebbi Yose asked: If it is practice, why two? And if two, why practice[236]? Would that mean if Rebbi Joḥanan would hold with Rebbi Joshua that practice would not follow Rabban Gamliel and Rebbi Eliezer but Rebbi Joshua[237]? What about it? It is a testimony for which a woman in empowered[238]. They wanted to say, when does Rebbi Joshua disagree with these rabbis? At a place where most are disabling, but at a place where most are qualified, even Rebbi Joshua will agree[239]. There came Rebbi Jacob bar Aḥa in the name of Rebbi Joḥanan, Rebbi Hila in the name of Rebbi Eleazar: There is disagreement even at a place where most are qualified. Does Rebbi Joshua think that immorality runs after the disabling[240]? Rebbi Ze'ira said, a *baraita* stated that even qualified people whore, as it was stated: Even the most pious man cannot be appointed guardian for illicit sex[241].

235 Since R. Joshua is a higher authority than either Rabban Gamliel or R. Eliezer, the formulation of the Mishnah as a vote of 2 against 1 is to be read as endorsing the majority opinion.

236 "Practice" usually means "prior practice", going back for generations. In that case, the formulation of the Mishnah invites scrutiny whether it really supports a decision. In the Babli, 14a, the situation is resolved by the ruling that "practice follows Rabban Gamliel but one should act only if most people around that woman are qualified", see Note 239.

237 If the decision in the Mishnah is problematic a leading Amora, whose opinion would count for nothing against an anonymous Mishnah, could lend his weight to the opposite opinion.

238 In general, women can testify in court for matters of fact but not in law. But for the personal status of women, the testimony of women is accepted as it is from qualified men (*Yebamot* Chapter 15). The Babli concurs, 13b.

239 We have a principle that "it may be assumed *prima facie* that anybody who comes from a group belongs to the majority in that group" (Babli, 15a). In a town where most inhabitants are Gentile, or otherwise disqualified from marrying Jewish women, one would assume that the unidentified man sleeping with that woman was disqualified (siding with R. Joshua), but in a town where she could legally marry most of the men, he would be qualified (siding with Rabban Gamliel and R. Eliezer).

240 If only the disqualified engage in extramarital sex, the unidentified man does not come from the large group of city dwellers, most of whom are qualified, but from the small group of whorers, most of whom are disqualified. Then R. Joshua would be consistent and should be followed.

241 The formulation in the Babli (13b) and the Tosephta (1:6) is: "There does not exist a guardian against illicit sex." In Babli and Tosephta this belongs to R. Joshua's argument. For Greek ἐπίτροπος "guardian, administrator", cf. *Bikkurim* 1:5, N. 82.

HALAKHAH 9

(fol. 24d) **משנה ט:** הָיְתָה מְעוּבֶּרֶת וְאָמְרוּ לָהּ מַה טִיבוֹ שֶׁלְּעוּבָּר הַזֶּה. מֵאִישׁ פְּלוֹנִי וְכֹהֵן הוּא רַבָּן גַּמְלִיאֵל וְרִבִּי אֱלִיעֶזֶר אוֹמֵר נֶאֱמֶנֶת. רִבִּי יְהוֹשֻׁעַ אוֹמֵר לֹא מִפִּיהָ אָנוּ חַיִּין אֶלָּא הֲרֵי זוֹ בְחֶזְקַת מְעוּבֶּרֶת לְנָתִין וּלְמַמְזֵר עַד שֶׁתָּבִיא רְאָיָה לִדְבָרֶיהָ.

Mishnah 9: If she was pregnant and one asked her, what kind of fetus is this? He is from Mr. X, a Cohen; Rabban Gamliel and Rebbi Eliezer say, she is believed. Rebbi Joshua said, we do not live off her mouth but there is a presumption that she is pregnant from a Gibeonite or a bastard unless she provides proof of her statement.

(25d line 10) **הלכה ט:** הָיְתָה מְעוּבֶּרֶת כול'. אָמַר רִבִּי לֶעְזָר. הַכֹּל מוֹדִין בְּוָלָד שֶׁהוּא שְׁתוּקִי. וְתַנֵּי כֵן. בַּמֶּה דְבָרִים אֲמוּרִים. בְּעֵדוּת אִשָּׁה גוּפָהּ. אֲבָל בְּוָלָד הַכֹּל מוֹדִין שֶׁהוּא שְׁתוּקִי. אָמַר לֵיהּ רִבִּי יוֹחָנָן. שְׁתוּקִי סְתָם. מָצִינוּ שְׁתוּקִי כֹּהֵן גָּדוֹל. הֵיךְ עֲבִידָא. סִיעָה שֶׁל כֹּהֲנִים עוֹבֶרֶת וּפֵירֵשׁ אֶחָד מֵהֶן וּבָעַל. הֲרֵי מָצִינוּ שְׁתוּקִי כֹּהֵן גָּדוֹל.

"If she was pregnant," etc. Rebbi Eleazar said, everybody agrees that the child is of unknown paternity[242]. It was stated thus[243]: "Where was this said[244], for the testimony of the woman in her own behalf. But everybody agrees that the child is of unknown paternity." Rebbi Johanan said to him, simply of unknown paternity[245]! We find that a child of unknown paternity can be High Priest. How is this possible? A group of Cohanim was passing by, one of them came[246] and had sexual relations; it turns out that the child of unknown paternity can be High Priest[247].

242 In Mishnah *Qiddušin* 4:1, the child of unknown paternity is barred from intermarrying with qualified Jews and is permitted only marriage with proselytes, freedmen, bastards, Gibeonites, those of unknown paternity, and foundlings.

243 Tosephta 1:6; Babli 13b.

244 That the woman's testimony is accepted without corroboration.

245 Since the father is unknown, the child cannot inherit from him. The expression שְׁתוּקִי "silenced one" can be explained as "one silences him if he claims inheritance".

246 He was not identified by name but certainly was a Cohen.

247 The Babli, 13b, agrees that the child is qualified to marry in the congregation but denies that he is a Cohen, based on *Num.* 25:13: "A covenant of priesthood it shall be for him and his seed after him", from which it is inferred that only a Cohen's child which is recognized as his is a Cohen. In the case under discussion, the child "is silenced from claiming priesthood".

(25d line 15) אָמַר לֵיהּ רִבִּי לָעְזָר. הֲרֵי אַלְמָנַת עִיסָה הֲרֵי הִיא כְשֵׁירָה וּבִתָּהּ פְּסוּלָה. אָמַר לֵיהּ. כִּדְבְרֵי שֶׁהוּא מַכְשִׁיר בָּהּ מַכְשִׁיר בְּבִתָּהּ. אָמַר רִבִּי יַעֲקֹב בַּר אָחָא. לֹא אָמַר כִּדְבְרֵי שֶׁהוּא מַכְשִׁיר. הָא מִכְּלָל דְּאִית חוֹרָן פּוֹסֵל. מַנִּי מַכְשִׁיר. רִבִּי מֵאִיר. מַנִּי פוֹסֵל. רַבָּנָן. דְּתַנֵּי. אֵי זוֹ הִיא עִיסָה כְשֵׁירָה. כָּל־שֶׁאֵין בָּהּ לֹא חָלָל וְלֹא מַמְזֵר וְלֹא נָתִין. רִבִּי מֵאִיר אוֹמֵר. כָּל־שֶׁאֵין בָּהּ אַחַת מִכָּל־אֵילוּ בִּתָּהּ כְּשֵׁירָה לִכְהוּנָה. אֲבָל מִשְׁפָּחָה שֶׁנִּשְׁתַּקַּע בָּהּ פְּסוּל. רִבִּי מֵאִיר אוֹמֵר. בּוֹדֵק עַד אַרְבַּע אִימָהוֹת וּמַשִּׂיא. וַחֲכָמִים אוֹמְרִים. בּוֹדֵק לְעוֹלָם.

Rebbi Eleazar said to him: Is not the dough widow[248] qualified but her daughter is disqualified[249]? He said to him, whoever declares her to be qualified, declares her daughter to be qualified[250]. Rebbi Jacob bar Aḥa said, did he not say "whoever declares her to be qualified"? This implies that there is another who disqualifies! Who declares qualified? Rebbi Meïr. Who disqualifies? The rabbis. As we have stated[251]: What is qualified dough, anyone about whom there is [no suspicion of descent from] a desecrated, a bastard, or a Gibeonite. Rebbi Meïr says, the daughter of any woman not tainted with one of these is qualified for the priesthood. But about a family in which a disability had disappeared[252], Rebbi Meïr says he checks up to four mothers[253] and marries, but the Sages say, he checks forever[254].

248 As a dough is a mixture of several ingredients, so the dough widow is a mixture; she is a woman qualified for priesthood who was married to a husband with a questionable family background (one whose females are permitted to marry Israels but not Cohanim). The problem is that there is the knowledge that something was wrong in the marriages of that family but the exact nature of the defect is not known.

249 She carries the possible disabilities of the father's family.

250 If the daughter might be disqualified then the mother might be desecrated, i. e., her husband might have been the offspring many generations back of a union forbidden to Cohanim.

251 In the Tosephta (*Qiddušin* 5:2) and the Babli (14a; *Qiddušin* 4:4, 66a l.29), there is no mention of the desecrated, but there is the added category of "king's slaves", who were used by the king to run the state and, by their influence and riches, were able to marry Jewish women even if not manumitted. In Jewish tradition (Rashi 14a), Herod was a slave of the Hasmoneans.

In the Babli tradition (cf. *Otzar ha-Geonim* 8, *Ketubot*, הפירושים p. 12), the dough widow was a woman who had married a man possibly descending from a desecrated woman. This definition is reproduced by Rashi, 14a. The difference between the Galilean and Babylonian traditions was already highlighted by Rabbenu Hananel (*Otzar ha-Geonim* l. c., לקוטי פירוש רבינו חננאל p. 12).

252 The nature of the disability was no longer known.

253 These are really 8 mothers, spanning 3 to 4 generations, enumerated in Mishnah *Qiddušin* 4:4.

254 Until he finds the source of the trouble.

(25d line 22) רִבִּי יִרְמְיָה בְּשֵׁם רִבִּי זְעִירָא לֹא אֶלָּא כֵּן אָמַר רִבִּי לְעָזֶר שָׁאַל לְרִבִּי יוֹחָנָן. אַלְמָנַת עִיסָּה מָה הִיא. אָמַר לֵיהּ. כְּשֵׁירָה. בִּיתָּהּ מָה הִיא. אָמַר

לֵיהּ. כִּדְבָרֵי שֶׁהוּא מַכְשִׁיר בָּהּ מַכְשִׁיר בְּבִתָּהּ. הָוֵון בָּעֵיי מֵימַר. עַל דַּעְתֵּיהּ דְּרִבִּי לָעְזָר שְׁתוּקִי פָּסוּל. עַל דַּעְתֵּיהּ דְּרִבִּי יוֹחָנָן שְׁתוּקִי כָּשֵׁר. אַף רִבִּי יוֹחָנָן אִית לֵיהּ שְׁתוּקִי פָּסוּל. בְּשִׁיטָתוֹ הֱשִׁיבוֹ. בְּשִׁיטָתָךְ שֶׁאַתְּ אוֹמֵר. אַף שְׁתוּקִי סְתָם. מָצִינוּ שְׁתוּקִי כֹּהֵן גָּדוֹל. הֵיךְ עֲבִידָא. סִיעָה שֶׁל כֹּהֲנִים עוֹבֶרֶת וּפֵירֵשׁ אֶחָד מֵהֶן וּבָעַל. הֲרֵי מָצִינוּ שְׁתוּקִי כֹּהֵן גָּדוֹל.

Rebbi Jeremiah in the name of Rebbi Ze'ira had a different version: Rebbi Eleazar asked Rebbi Johanan, what is the rule about a dough widow[248]? He said to him, she is qualified. What about her daughter? He said to him, the one who declares her to be qualified, declares her daughter to be qualified[250]. They wanted to say, according to Rebbi Eleazar, a child of unknown paternity is disqualified[242]; according to Rebbi Johanan, a child of unknown paternity is qualified. Rebbi Johanan also holds that in some cases a child of unknown paternity is disqualified; he answered [Rebbi Eleazar] following the latter's reasoning: Since you reason that the child is simply of unknown paternity, we find that a child of unknown paternity can be High Priest! How is this possible? A group of Cohanim was passing by, one of them came[246] and had sexual relations; it turns out that the child of unknown paternity can be High Priest[247].

(25d line 30) מִילְתֵיהּ דְּרִבִּי זֵירָא אָמְרָה. שְׁתוּקִי כָּשֵׁר. רִבִּי זְעִירָא בְּעָא קוֹמֵי רִבִּי יוֹסֵי. אַף לְעִנְיָין מִשְׁפָּחָה כֵּן. אָמַר לֵיהּ. כֵּן אָמַר רִבִּי שִׁמְעוֹן בֶּן לָקִישׁ. תַּמָּן תַּנִּינָן לְעִנְיָין מִשְׁפָּחָה. בְּרַם הָכָא לְעִנְיָין קָדְשֵׁי הַגְּבוּל. מִילְתָא דְּרִבִּי שְׁמוּאֵל בַּר יִצְחָק. שְׁתוּקִי פָּסוּל. רִבִּי שְׁמוּאֵל בַּר רַב יִצְחָק בְּעָא. מֵעַתָּה אֵין שְׁתוּקִי כְרַבָּן גַּמְלִיאֵל וּכְרִבִּי אֱלִיעֶזֶר אֶלָּא כְּרִבִּי יְהוֹשֻׁעַ. חָזַר וְאָמַר. יֵשׁ שְׁתוּקִי כְּרַבָּן גַּמְלִיאֵל וּכְרִבִּי אֱלִיעֶזֶר בְּשׁוֹתֶקֶת. וַאֲפִילוּ תֵימַר בִּמְדַבֶּרֶת. בְּאוֹמֶרֶת. אֵינִי יוֹדַעַת.

HALAKHAH 9

The word of Rebbi Zera[255] implies that a child of unknown paternity is qualified, for Rebbi Ze'ira asked before Rebbi Yasa[256]: Is it the same for families[257]? He said to him, so says Rebbi Simeon ben Laqish: There, for families[258], but here for sanctified food in the country[259]. The word of Rebbi Samuel ben [Rav] Isaac implies that a child of unknown paternity is disqualified, for Rebbi Samuel ben Rav Isaac asked: Does this mean that a child of unknown paternity is does not exist following Rabban Gamliel and Rebbi Eliezer, only following Rebbi Joshua? He turned around and said, a child of unknown paternity is possible following Rabban Gamliel and Rebbi Eliezer, if she remains silent. And even if you say that she talks, if she said that she does not know[260].

255 This is the Babylonian spelling of Ze'ira.

256 It is clear that R. Ze'ira asked before his teacher R. Yasa, not before his student's student R. Yose.

257 In the Mishnah, Rabban Gamliel and R. Eliezer declare than one believes the woman if she says that her child is a Cohen's. Mishnah *Qiddušin* 4:1 excludes a child of unknown paternity from marrying most Jews. What is the relation of the two Mishnaiot?

258 If somebody looks after the purity of his blood line, he should follow the Mishnah in *Qiddušin*.

259 "Sanctified food in the country" is heave. The child is empowered to eat heave; this implies that he is qualified for certain aspects of the priesthood (on the model of the local priests in Josiah's reform, 2K. 23:9).

260 If the mother states that she does not know the identity of the child's father, the child doubtless is of unknown paternity.

(fol. 24d) **משנה י**: אָמַר רִבִּי יוֹסֵי מַעֲשֶׂה בְּתִינוֹקֶת שֶׁיֵּרְדָה לְמַלְאוֹת מַיִם מִן הָעַיִן וְנֶאֱנָסָה אָמַר רִבִּי יוֹחָנָן בֶּן נוּרִי אִם רוֹב אַנְשֵׁי הָעִיר מַשִּׂיאִין לַכְּהוּנָה הֲרֵי זוֹ תִינָשֵׂא לַכְּהוּנָה.

Mishnah 10: Rebbi Yose said: It happened that, when a girl was raped while she went to draw water from the spring, Rebbi Yoḥanan ben Nuri said: If most people of the town can marry into the priesthood then she can marry into the priesthood[261].

261 He confirms the principle explained in Note 239, that without proof to the contrary one may assume that an unidentified member of a group belongs to the majority in that group. Therefore, the girl was raped by a man whom she could have married without detriment to her status; the rape does not diminish her status.

(25d line 36) **הלכה י**: אָמַר רִבִּי יוֹסֵי מַעֲשֶׂה בְּתִינוֹקֶת כול׳. רַב יְהוּדָה בְשֵׁם רַב. כְּהָן קְרוֹנָה שֶׁלְצִיפּוֹרִין הֲוָה עוֹבְדָא.

Halakhah 10: "Rebbi Yose said: It happened," etc. Rav Jehudah in the name of Rav: That happened at the source[262] of Sepphoris.

262 Greek κρήνη "well, source" (in the Hebrew transliteration, read י for ו.) The translator of the LXX books of Kings uses the word for בְּרֵיכָה "pond".

In the Babli, 14b/15a, the statement is used in an argument that R. Joshua will agree with R. Yose only in this case when the rape happened at a place where not only the inhabitants of the city but all travelers congregate and it was known that at that point in time only qualified people travelled there. One cannot read the Babli's interpretation into the Yerushalmi text.

(25d line 38) רִבִּי יִרְמְיָה רִבִּי חָמָא בַר עוּקְבָא תְּרֵיהוֹן אָמְרֵי בְּשֵׁם רִבִּי חֲנִינָה בְּשֵׁם רִבִּי יַנַּאי. מוֹדֶה רִבִּי יְהוֹשֻׁעַ בָּאֲנוּסָה. רִבִּי חִזְקִיָּה רִבִּי אַבָּהוּ בְּשֵׁם רִבִּי יוֹחָנָן. מוֹדֶה רִבִּי יְהוֹשֻׁעַ בָּאֲנוּסָה. רַב חִיָּיה בַּר אַשִׁי אָמַר בְּשֵׁם רַב. הֲלָכָה

כְּרְבִּי יוֹסֵי שֶׁאָמַר מִשֵּׁם רִבִּי יוֹחָנָן בֶּן נוּרִי. רִבִּי זְעִירָא בְעָא קוֹמֵי רִבִּי יָסָא. הֵיךְ עָבְדִין עוֹבְדָא. אָמַר לֵיהּ. כְּרְבִּי יוֹסֵי. שֶׁאָמַר מִשֵּׁם רִבִּי יוֹחָנָן בֶּן נוּרִי.

Both Rebbi Jeremiah, Rebbi Ḥama bar Uqba, say in the name of Rebbi Ḥanina in the name of Rebbi Yannai: Rebbi Joshua agrees in the case of the rape victim[263]. Rebbi Ḥizqiah, Rebbi Abbahu in the name of Rebbi Joḥanan: Rebbi Joshua agrees in the case of the rape victim. Rav Ḥiyya bar Ashi said in the name of Rav: Practice follows Rebbi Yose who said in the name of Rebbi Yoḥanan ben Nuri. Rebbi Ze'ira asked before Rebbi Yasa: How does one act in a practical case? He said to him, following Rebbi Yose who spoke in the name of Rebbi Yoḥanan ben Nuri.

263 The Babli, 15a, disagrees and holds that R. Yose speaks of a very special case, that the rape occured on a market day when many קָרוֹנוֹת, carriages, came to Sepphoris and it was ascertained that both the majority of inhabitants of Sepphoris and the majority of foreign traders there were acceptable to marry into the priesthood, implying that R. Joshua agrees that no special proof is needed only in case (a) there are two groups and the majority of both is acceptable and (2) the woman was a victim, not a willing partner.

(25d line 43) אָמַר רִבִּי אִילָא בְשֵׁם רִבִּי יַנַּאי. תּוֹכָהּ שֶׁבְּצִיפּוֹרִין בָּעַל. רַבָּא בְשֵׁם רִבִּי יַנַּאי. רָאוּ אוֹתוֹ פּוֹרֵשׁ מִצִּיפּוֹרִין וּבַעַל חֲזָקָה שֶׁפּוֹסֵל שָׁם בָּעַל. פְּלַטְיָא מָהוּ. רִבִּי יִרְמְיָה בַּר וָא רִבִּי יוֹסֵי אוֹמֵר. בְּרוֹב. חֵיילֵיהּ דְּרִבִּי יִרְמְיָה מִן הָדָא. דָּמַר רִבִּי חִייָה בְשֵׁם רִבִּי יוֹחָנָן. מָבוֹי שֶׁכּוּלוֹ גוֹיִם וְיִשְׂרָאֵל אֶחָד דָּר בְּתוֹכוֹ וְנָפַל בְּתוֹכוֹ מַפּוֹלֶת מְפַקְּחִין עָלָיו בִּשְׁבִיל יִשְׂרָאֵל שָׁשָּׁם. וּפְלַטְיָא הוֹלְכִין אַחַר הָרוֹב. וּמָהוּ דְאָמַר רִבִּי בָּא בְשֵׁם רִבִּי יַנַּאי. רָאוּ אוֹתוֹ פּוֹרֵשׁ מִצִּיפּוֹרִין וּבוֹעֵל חֲזָקָה שֶׁפָּסוּל שָׁם בָּעַל. עַל דַּעְתֵּיהּ דְּרִבִּי יִרְמְיָה. וְהֵן שֶׁרָאוּ אוֹתוֹ פּוֹרֵשׁ מִן הַבָּתִּים. וְעַל דַּעְתֵּיהּ דְּרִבִּי יוֹסֵי. אֲפִילוּ בִּפְלַטְיָא. הָיְתָה צִיפּוֹרִין נְעוּלָה. רִבִּי יוֹסֵי אוֹמֵר. עַד שִׁיּוּכִיחַ. וְכָא רִבִּי יוֹסֵי אוֹמֵר. בְּרוֹב. חֵיילֵיהּ דְּרִבִּי יוֹסֵי מִן הָדָא.

דָּמַר רִבִּי זְעִירָא. רִבִּי (יוֹסֵי) [חִייָא]274 בְּשֵׁם רִבִּי יוֹחָנָן. נִתְחַלְפָה (פִּיתוֹ) [קוּפָתוֹ]274 אֶצֶל הַטּוֹחֵן. אִם הוּחְזָק עַם הָאָרֶץ לִהְיוֹת טוֹחֵן שָׁם בְּאוֹתוֹ הַיּוֹם חוֹשֵׁשׁ וְאִם לָאו אֵינוֹ חוֹשֵׁשׁ. מַה בֵּינָה וּלְסֵירָקֵי. לֹא כֵן תַּנֵּי סֵירָקִית שֶׁקְּיָתָה מִסְתַּפֶּקֶת יוֹם אֶחָד מִן הָאִיסוּר נַעֲשָׂה אוֹתוֹ הַיּוֹם הוֹכִיחַ לְכָל־הַיָּמִים. סֵירָקִית אִיפְשַׁר לָהּ שֶׁלֹּא לְהִסְתַּפֵּק. וָכָא אֲנִי אוֹמֵר. לֹא הוּחְזָק עַם הָאָרֶץ לִהְיוֹת טוֹחֵן שָׁם בְּאוֹתוֹ הַיּוֹם וְחוֹשֵׁשׁ. וָכָא אֲנִי אוֹמֵר. לֹא יָרַד הַפָּסוּל אֶלָּא לְמַלְאוֹת שָׁם בְּאוֹתוֹ הַיּוֹם וְחוֹשֵׁשׁ. וְהָא רִבִּי אִילָא בְּשֵׁם רִבִּי יַנַּאי אוֹמֵר. תּוּכָהּ שֶׁבְּצִיפּוֹרִין בָּעַל. וְהָא רִבִּי בָּא בְּשֵׁם רִבִּי יַנַּאי אוֹמֵר. רָאוּ אוֹתוֹ פּוֹרֵשׁ מִצִּיפּוֹרִין וּבוֹעֵל חֲזָקָה פָּסוּל שֶׁשָּׁם בָּעַל.

12 חושש | חושש. ד ויחוש   סירוקית | ד סירוקי   13 האיסור | ד האסור   סירוקית | ד סירוקי   14 וכא אני אומר | ד ברם הכא

Rebbi Hila said in the name of Rebbi Yannai: He cohabited with her inside of Sepphoris[264]. Rebbi Abba in the name of Rebbi Yannai: If he was seen coming out of Sepphoris and he cohabited, the presumption is that he disqualifies since he cohabited there[265]. What about a thoroughfare[266]? Rebbi[267] Jeremiah bar Abba, Rebbi Yose says: By a majority. The force of Rebbi[267] Jeremiah comes from the following which Rebbi Ḥiyya had said in the name of Rebbi Joḥanan: If a wall fell in a dead-end street populated by Gentiles, but where one Jew lived, one digs there[268] because of the Jew; but in a thoroughfare one follows the majority[269]. And what is the interpretation of what Rebbi Abba said in the name of Rebbi Yannai, if he was seen coming out of Sepphoris and he cohabited, the presumption is that he is disqualified since he cohabited there? In the opinion of Rebbi[267] Jeremiah, if one saw him coming out of a house[265]. In the opinion of Rebbi Yose, even in a thoroughfare[270]. If Sepphoris was locked[271]. Rebbi Yose says, until there is proof. But here[272], Rebbi Yose says, by a majority! The force of Rebbi Yose comes from the following, which Rebbi Ze'ira had said: [273]Rebbi [Ḥiyya] (Yose)[274] in the name of Rebbi Joḥanan: If his [box] (bread)[274] was exchanged at the miller's, if it was established that an *am haärez* gave [grain] to be milled there that day, he has to worry[275]; otherwise, he does not have to worry. Should he not worry? What is the difference between this and the Saracens? Was it not stated: "If a group of Saracens one day provisioned themselves from forbidden supplies[276], then that day becomes a proof for all days." It is impossible for Saracens not to supply themselves[277]. But here it was not established that the *am haärez* was milling there that day.[278] And here, I am saying that the disqualified person went to draw water only that day, and one has to worry. And here, Rebbi Hila said in the name of Rebbi Yannai: He cohabited with her inside of Sepphoris. And here, Rebbi Abba said in the name of Rebbi Yannai: If he was seen coming out of Sepphoris and he cohabited, the presumption is that he is disqualified since he cohabited there[279].

264 The scene described by the Babli (Note 263) is rejected; it is purely the question of the people of the place.

265 This is based on a statement attributed in the Babli (15a) to R. Ze'ira: Everything fixed in its place is judged as 50/50. Since the population of the town has fixed residences, if a person was seen coming from one of the houses, he cannot be considered to be from the qualified majority but one considers it only a 50% chance that he be qualified. In this case, R. Joḥanan ben Nuri will agree that the rape victim cannot marry a Cohen.

266 Greek πλατεῖα, cf. *Berakhot* 5:1, Note 56. The thoroughfare is government property even in the town.

267 This must be "Rav". He is the early Amora Rav Jeremiah bar Abba, presenting a tradition of R. Yose the Tanna. He might be one of the editors of R. Yose's *Seder 'Olam*; cf. the author's Introduction (pp. x-xi) to his

268   On the Sabbath, because for saving a life one violates all prohibitions of the Torah (except murder, incest and adultery, and idolatry).

269   One searches for victims only if the majority of the users are Jewish or at least known not to be idolators.

270   Since the thoroughfare is a Roman military road, it may be assumed that the majority of users are not qualified to marry Cohanim.

271   If the rape happened in the night, when the gates of Sepphoris are locked, by the argument of Note 265 there is no majority of qualified people and the rapist would have to be identified in order to permit his victim to marry into the priesthood.

272   In the Mishnah.

273   The following sentences are from *Demay* 3:4, Notes 93-96; the variant readings are noted ז. The problem is that a person who is careful about the laws of tithing brings his grain to a mill that also serves the *'am haäreṣ*, the person who can be presumed to have given heave but not tithes from his grain. If the miller switches batches, the observant is in trouble.

274   The words in brackets are from *Demay*, those in parentheses from *Ketubot*. The text from *Demay* seems preferable.

275   He has to tithe a second time under the rules of *demay*.

276   If the travelling Arabs buy once from unobservant Jews, one has to assume that they always do, and that the grain they sell is not exempt Gentile produce.

277   Since they are itinerant sellers they have to buy provisions all the time. But the farmer mills once for his entire season.

278   End of the quote from *Demay*. The quote establishes that there is a presumption that things go wrong, in our case that the rapist was from a family disqualified for the priesthood.

279   This conclusion differs from the position of the Babli (Note 263) but not by much: One can qualify the rape victim only if the gates of the city were not locked and the perpetrator was not seen coming from a fixed place; that the group from which he came was not composed of locals only (Note 265).

HALAKHAH 10

(25d line 62) וּבְנִמְצָא הוֹלְכִין אַחַר הָרוֹב. מִן קוּשְׁיַי מְדַמּוּ לָהּ רַבָּנִין לִשְׁרָצִים. דְּתַנֵּי. תֵּשַׁע צְפַרְדְּעִים שֶׁרֶץ אֶחָד בִּרְשׁוּת הַיָּחִיד וְנָגַע בְּאֶחָד מֵהֶן וְאֵין יָדוּעַ בְּאֵי זוּ נָגַע סְפֵיקוֹ טָמֵא. פֵּירַשׁ לִרְשׁוּת הָרַבִּים וְנָגַע סְפֵיקוֹ טָהוֹר. חָזַר לִרְשׁוּת הַיָּחִיד וְנָגַע סְפֵיקוֹ טָמֵא. וּלְנִמְצָא הַלֵּךְ אַחַר הָרוֹב. אָמַר רַב חִסְדָּא. וְלֹא מָצְאוּ כָל־אַנְשֵׁי חַיִל יְדֵיהֶם. אָמַר רִבִּי אִימִּי. בָּרוּךְ שֶׁבָּחַר בָּהֶם וּבְדִבְרֵיהֶם. עַד דְּאַתְּ מְדַמֵּי לָהּ לִרְשׁוּת הַיָּחִיד דְּמִיתָהּ לִרְשׁוּת הָרַבִּים. דְּתַנֵּי. תֵּשַׁע שְׁרָצִים וּצְפַרְדֵּעַ אֶחָד בֵּינֵיהֶן בִּרְשׁוּת הָרַבִּים וְנָגַע בְּאֶחָד מֵהֶן וְאֵין יָדוּעַ בְּאֵי זֶה מֵהֶן נָגַע סְפֵיקוֹ טָהוֹר. פֵּירַשׁ לִרְשׁוּת הַיָּחִיד וְנָגַע בּוֹ סְפֵיקוֹ טָמֵא. חָזַר לִרְשׁוּת הָרַבִּים וְנָגַע בּוֹ סְפֵיקוֹ טָהוֹר. וּלְנִמְצָא הַלֵּךְ אַחַר הָרוֹב. אָמַר רַב חִסְדָּא. וְלֹא מָצְאוּ כָל־אַנְשֵׁי חַיִל יְדֵיהֶם. אָמַר רִבִּי אִימִּי. בָּרוּךְ שֶׁבָּחַר בָּהֶם וּבְדִבְרֵיהֶן. קְרוֹנָה שֶׁלְּצִיפּוֹרִין לָאו רְשׁוּת הָרַבִּים הוּא. אָמַר רִבִּי יוֹסֵי. מִכֵּיוָן שֶׁשְּׁנֵיהֶן יְכוֹלִין לְהִתְיַיחֵד כְּמָאן דְּהוּא רְשׁוּת הַיָּחִיד.

"And everything found is judged by a majority."[280] In difficult cases the rabbis compare this[281] to crawling things[282], as it was stated[283]: "Nine frogs and one crawling thing[284] in a private domain[285], if somebody touched one of them and it is not known which one he touched, in doubt he is impure. If he transferred to the public domain and touched, in doubt he is pure. If he returned to the private domain and touched, in doubt he is impure. And for what is found one follows the majority." Rav Ḥisda said, no valiant person can find his hands[286]. Rebbi Immi said, praise to Him Who chose them[287] and their words; do not compare this[288] to a private domain but to the public domain! As it was stated: "Nine crawling things and one frog between them in the public domain, if somebody touched one of them and it is not known which one he touched, in doubt he is pure[289]. If he transferred to a private domain and touched, in doubt he is impure. If he returned to the public domain and touched, in doubt he is pure. And for what is found one follows the majority." Rav Ḥisda said, no valiant person can find his hands. Rebbi Immi said, praise to Him Who chose them and their words; is the spring of Sepphoris not public domain? Rebbi Yose said, since the two could be alone together it is treated as private domain[290].

280 This sentence does not really belong here but is an intrusion from the Tosephta quoted in the sequel. It is also quoted in the Babli, 15a, in the same context. What is meant here is that a find is pure if most things in town are pure, otherwise it is impure. In principle, this can also be applied to permitted or prohibited things: If 9 stores in town sell kosher meat and 1 non-kosher, then any meat found on the street can be considered as kosher (Rabban Simeon ben Gamliel disagrees, Tosephta *Tahorot* 6:1).

281 The status of the rape victim.

282 *Lev.* 11:29-30 contains a list of "crawling things", mostly reptiles, whose cadaver is a source of impurity. The only cadavers that produce impurity are those of crawling things and mammals.

283 A shorter version of this *baraita* is in the Babli 15a, *Niddah* 18a and Tosephta *Tahorot* 6:2.

284 They are all dead; the dead frogs do not carry impurity.

285 Questions of doubt in matters of ritual impurity must be resolved by a presumption of impurity in private domains and a presumption of purity in public domains; cf. *Soṭah* 1:2, Note 88.

286 This is not rational, since the place where the object was found should be of importance.

287 The Sages. A similar expression in the heading of the *baraita* of *Abot*.

288 The case of the raped girl whose disqualification would be a case of impurity.

289 Even against all probabilities.

290 The difference between public and private domains is not in the ownership but in accessibility. A cave in the public domain has the status of private domain. Rav Ḥisda is justified; this kind of argument is not relevant to explain the relation of Mishnah 10 to Mishnaiot 8,9.

(25d line 75) מַעֲשֶׂה בְּתִינוֹקֶת שֶׁרָאוּ אוֹתָהּ מוּשְׁלֶכֶת לְאִישְׁפָּה. אָתָא עוֹבְדָא קוֹמֵי רִבִּי יִשְׁמָעֵאל בֵּירְבִּי יוֹסֵי וְאָמַר. תִּיטָפֵל לְעִיסָה. רִבִּי יִרְמְיָה סָבַר מֵימַר. לְעִיסָה כְּשֵׁירָה. רִבִּי יִשְׁמָעֵאל בֵּירְבִּי יוֹסֵי חָלוּק עַל אָבִיו. אָמַר רִבִּי יוֹסֵי. וַאֲפִילוּ תֵימָא. לְעִיסָה פְּסוּלָה. לֵית רִבִּי יִשְׁמָעֵאל בֵּירְבִּי יוֹסֵי חָלוּק עַל אָבִיו. לָמָה. כְּשֵׁירִים מְזַנִּין וּפְסוּלִין מַשְׁלִיכִין.

It happened that a baby girl was noticed who had been thrown on a garbage heap. The case came before Rebbi Ismael ben Rebbi Yose, who said, she should be adjoined to dough[248,291]. Rebbi Jeremiah thought to say, to qualified dough, would Rebbi Ismael ben Rebbi Yose disagree with his father[292]? Rebbi Yose said, even if you say to disqualified dough, Rebbi Ismael ben Rebbi Yose would not disagree with his father. Why? While the qualified whore, only the disqualified throw away [293].

291 She should be adopted by a family of questionable status.

292 He said that in a town of mostly qualified families, the children are automatically qualified.

293 Therefore, that baby is from a group of mostly unqualified children.

האשה שנתארמלה פרק שיני

(fol. 26a) **משנה א:** הָאִשָּׁה שֶׁנִּתְאַרְמְלָה אוֹ שֶׁנִּתְגָּרְשָׁה הִיא אוֹמֶרֶת בְּתוּלָה נְשָׂאתַנִי וְהוּא אוֹמֵר לֹא כִּי אֶלָּא אַלְמָנָה נְשָׂאתִיךְ אִם יֵשׁ עֵדִים שֶׁיָּצְאָת בְּהִינוּמָא וְרֹאשָׁהּ פָּרוּעַ כְּתוּבָּתָהּ מָאתַיִם. רִבִּי יוֹחָנָן בֶּן בְּרוֹקָה אוֹמֵר אַף חִילוּק קְלָיוֹת רְאָיָיהּ.

Mishnah 1: If a woman became widowed or divorced and she claims[1] to have been married as a virgin, but he says not so, I married you as a widow, if there are witnesses that she went out in *hinuma*[2] or with uncovered hair[3], her *ketubah* is 200 [*zuz*]. Rebbi Johanan ben Beroqa says, the distribution of roasted kernels also is proof[4].

1 Either her *ketubah* is lost or, if she married at a place of illiterates, it never was written.
2 Cf. Chapter 1, Note 65; Chapter 2, Note 22.
3 A virgin will start covering her hair only at the wedding.
4 At his place, this was a sign of the wedding of a virgin.

(26a line 45) **הלכה א:** הָאִשָּׁה שֶׁנִּתְאַלְמְנָה כול'. נִיחָא שֶׁנִּתְגָּרְשָׁה. נִתְאַלְמְנָה. מִי עוֹרֵר. הַיּוֹרְשִׁין.

Halakhah 1: "If a woman became widowed," etc. We understand if she was divorced. If she became widowed, who opposes? The heirs[5].

5 Only the husband's descendants, and in their absence the husband's family, do inherit; *Num.* 27:6-11. The widow can claim only her *ketubah* (in the absence of a will).

(26a line 46) וְהַלֵּךְ אַחַר הָרוֹב וְרוֹב הַנִּישָׂאוֹת בְּתוּלוֹת נִישָׂאוֹת. אֱמוֹר מֵעַתָּה. בְּתוּלָה נִישֵׂאת. זֹאת אוֹמֶרֶת שֶׁלֹּא הִילְכוּ לְמִידַת הַדִּין וּלְמָמוֹן אַחַר הָרוֹב. תַּמָּן תַּנִּינָן. שׁוֹר שֶׁנָּגַח אֶת הַפָּרָה וְנִמְצָא עוּבָּרָהּ בְּצִידָהּ. וְכִי רוֹב הַפָּרוֹת מַפִּילוֹת. אֱמוֹר מֵעַתָּה. מֵחֲמַת נְגִיחָה הִפִּילָה. אָמַר רִבִּי אַבָּהוּ. זֹאת אוֹמֶרֶת שֶׁלֹּא הִילְכוּ לְמִידַת הַדִּין וּלְמָמוֹן אַחַר הָרוֹב. אָמַר רִבִּי אָבוּן. וּבְדָבָר אֶחָד הִילְכוּ לְמִידַת הַדִּין וּלְמָמוֹן אַחַר הָרוֹב. כְּהָדָא דְתַנֵּי רִבִּי אָחָא. גָּמָל שֶׁהָיָה אוֹחֵר בֵּין הַגְּמַלִּים וְנִמְצָא שָׁם אֶחָד מֵהֶן מֵת. חַיָּיב. אֲנִי אוֹמֵר. אוֹתוֹ שֶׁהָיָה אוֹחֵר נְשָׁכוֹ.

Should one follow the majority, and most women are married as virgins. Say then that she was married as a virgin[6]! This implies that in criminal cases and in money matters one does not apply a majority argument[7]. There[8], we have stated: "If an ox gored a cow and one finds her fetus beside her.[9]" Do most cows have miscarriages? Say therefore that the goring induced the miscarriage. Rebbi Abbahu said, this implies that in criminal cases and in money matters one does not apply a majority argument. Rebbi Abun[10] said, in one case they applied a majority argument, as Rebbi Aḥa stated: If a camel was in heat among camels and one finds one of them dead, I am saying that the one in heat bit it[11].

6 Why does the Mishnah put the burden of proof on the woman when there should be a presumption in her favor to require the husband or the heirs to prove their case.

7 Since the woman claims money, the burden of proof is on her; cf. Chapter 1, Note 215. The Babli agrees, *Baba Batra* 93a.

8 Mishnah *Baba Qama* 5:1.

9 If it cannot be ascertained whether the miscarriage was induced by the goring or preceded the goring, the ox's owner pays (by biblical decree, *Ex.* 21:35) half of the damage done to the cow but only a quarter of the value of the fetus. It is clear that the proven fact of the goring creates a presumption that the miscarriage was induced by it. This presumption is not

sufficient to force the owner of the ox to pay; the value of the fetus, had it grown to be a calf, is "money in dispute". Money in dispute for which there are no proofs either way is split evenly between the parties (Babli *Baba Meṣi'a* 2b). A similar text is in *Baba Qama* 5:1. The Babli, *Baba Qama* 46a, denies the designation as "money in dispute" and puts the burden of proof on the claimant, the injured party.

10   In *Baba Qama*, R. Yose.

11   In the Babli, *Baba Batra* 93a: It is known that the one in heat killed it. The Babli holds that this is not a case of majority but one of *prima facie* evidence: Proof that the camel was in heat implies proof that it did attack other males. Therefore, the owner of the camel in heat would have to prove that the attack by the male in heat on the male not in heat was not lethal.

(26a line 46) טְעָנוֹ מָנֶה וְכָפַר בּוֹ וְהֵבִיא עֵדִים שֶׁחַיָיב לוֹ חֲמִשִׁים. רִבִּי חִיָיה רִבָּא אוֹמֵר. נִשְׁבַּע עַל הַשְּׁאָר. רִבִּי יוֹחָנָן אוֹמֵר. אֵינוֹ נִשְׁבַּע עַל הַשְּׁאָר. מִשְׁנַיִם אוֹחֲזִין בְּטַלִית לָמַד רִבִּי חִיָיה רִבָּא. דְּתַנִינָן תַּמָּן. שְׁנַיִם אוֹחֲזִין בְּטַלִית. זֶה אוֹמֵר. אֲנִי מְצָאתִיהָ. וְזֶה אוֹמֵר. אֲנִי מְצָאתִיהָ. זֶה שְׁטוּפֵס בְּחֶצְיָיהּ כְּמֵבִיא עֵדִים שֶׁחֶצְיָיהּ שֶׁלּוֹ. וַהֲלָהּ אוֹמֵר. כּוּלָהּ שֶׁלִּי. וְזֶה שֶׁהוּא טוֹפֵס בְּחֶצְיָיהּ כְּמֵבִיא עֵדִים שֶׁחֶצְיָיהּ שֶׁלּוֹ. וַהֲלָהּ אוֹמֵר. כּוּלָהּ שֶׁלִּי. נִשְׁבַּע שֶׁאֵין כּוּלָהּ שֶׁלּוֹ. וְלֹא שְׁמִיעַ דָּמַר רִבִּי אִילָא בְּשֵׁם רִבִּי יוֹחָנָן. תְּקָנַת שְׁבוּעָה הִיא. שֶׁלֹּא יְהֵא אָדָם רוֹאֶה אֶת חֲבֵירוֹ בַּשּׁוּק וְאוֹמֵר לוֹ. טַלִּית שֶׁעָלֶיךָ שֶׁלִּי הוּא. בּוֹא וְחַלֵּק עִמִּי טַלִּיתָךְ. רִבִּי אָבִין בְּשֵׁם רַב. מוֹדֶה חֲבִיבִי בִּשְׁטָר. הֵיךְ עֲבִידָא. טְעָנוֹ מָנֶה וְכָפַר בּוֹ וְהוֹצִיא שְׁטָר שֶׁהוּא חַיָיב לוֹ חֲמִשִׁין. אֵין לוֹ אֶלָּא חֲמִשִׁין. וְאָמַר רִבִּי יוֹסֵי בֵּירִבִּי בּוּן. נִישְׁמְעִינָהּ מִן הָדָא. כֶּסֶף סִילְעִין דִּי אִינּוּן וְנִמְחֲקוּ אֵין פּוֹחֵת מִשְּׁנַיִם. מִכָּן וְאֵילָךְ הַמַּלְוֶה אוֹמֵר. חָמֵשׁ. וְהַלֹּוֶה אוֹמֵר. שָׁלֹשׁ. בֶּן עַזַּאי אוֹמֵר. הוֹאִיל וְהוֹדָה מִן הַטַּעֲנָה יִשָּׁבַע. וַחֲכָמִים אוֹמְרִים. אֵין הוֹדָאָה מִן הַטַּעֲנָה. מִפְּנֵי שֶׁאֵין הוֹדָאָה מִן הַטַּעֲנָה. וְהָא אִם הוֹדָיָיהּ מִן הַטַּעֲנָה חַיָיב. וְכָא לֹא כְמִי שֶׁהוֹדָיָיהּ מִן הַטַּעֲנָה הִיא. כָּל־עַמָּא מוֹדֵיי שֶׁהוּא חַיָיב לָהּ מְנֶה. וְהִיא כְּתוֹבַעַת בְּיָדוֹ מְנֶה אֶחָד וְהוּא אֵינוֹ מוֹדֶה לָהּ. הַמּוֹצִיא מֵחֲבֵירוֹ עָלָיו הָרְאָיָיה.

If somebody claimed a mina, the [defendant] denied it, and the [claimant] produced witnesses that the [defendant] owes him 50 [*zuz*]. The older Rebbi Ḥiyya said, [the defendant] has to swear about the remainder. Rebbi Joḥanan says, he does not have to swear[12]. The older Rebbi Ḥiyya learned it from two who are grabbing a toga, as we have stated there[13]: "Two are grabbing a toga, one says, I found it, and the other says, I found it." The one who grabs half of it is as if he brought witnesses that that half belongs to him. The other says, "it belongs to me entirely", and the fact that he grabs half of it is as if he brought witnesses that this half belongs to him. The one who says, "it belongs to me entirely", swears that not the entire [toga] is the other's. But he did not hear that Rebbi Hila said in the name of Rebbi Joḥanan[14] that this oath is a rabbinic institution, that a man should not see another in the market and tell him, the toga which you are wearing is mine, come and split your toga with me![15] Rebbi Abin in the name of Rav: My uncle[16] agrees in the case of a document. How is that? He claimed a mina, the [defendant] denied it, and the [claimant] produced a document that the [defendant] owed him 50 [*zuz*]. He has only fifty. And Rebbi Yose ben Rebbi Abun said, we can understand it from the following[17]: "'The amount of . . . tetradrachmas' and it was illegible, he owes no less than two." If it is more, if the lender says five but the borrower says three, Ben Azzay says since he partially agreed to the claim, he has to swear, but the Sages say, what he agreed to is not of the kind which was claimed[18]. Because it was not of the kind which was claimed! Therefore, if it were of the kind which was claimed, he would be obligated. And is it not here that the agreed sum was part of the claim[19]? Everybody agrees that he owes her a mina[20]. But she claims another mina from him, to which he does not agree. The burden of proof is on the claimant[21].

12 Following the principle that the defendant in a suit for money can by biblical law only be forced to swear if he admits that part of the claim is justified; based on *Ex.* 22:8, where the expression אֲשֶׁר יֹאמַר כִּי הוּא זֶה "if he agrees that this is so." In *Baba Meṣi'a* (1:1, 7d l. 24; Babli 3a) the reason of the older R. Ḥiyya is "that what he admits himself should not have greater force than the testimony of witnesses."

13 Mishnah *Baba Meṣi'a* 1:1. If two people come to court, each grabs half of a toga and asserts ownership of the entire piece because he found it, each of them has to swear that he owns no less than half of it (so the court should not force obvious perjury) and takes half of the piece since "it is money in dispute".

14 The student of the older R. Ḥiyya's son Ḥizqiah.

15 *Baba Meṣi'a* 1:1, 7d l. 33; Babli 3a; both in the name of R. Joḥanan. Rabbinic institutions do not imply anything for biblical law.

16 The older R. Ḥiyya, half-brother to both of Rav's parents.

17 Mishnah *Baba Batra* 10:2. If the amount of indebtedness is illegible, the use of the plural proves that the amount was at least two.

18 In *Baba Batra* 10:2 (by the editorial team of *Neziqin*, different from the editors of the rest of the Yerushalmi) and the Babli, *Baba Meṣi'a* 4b, the "Sages" are identified as R. Aqiba. In the Babli, Ben Azzai is replaced by R. Simeon ben Eleazar, 2 generations younger than Ben Azzai and R. Aqiba. In both sources, the reason of R. Aqiba is given that the borrower, in agreeing to pay more than he could be forced to by the existing document, is like a person returning what the other had lost, not directly answering the lender's claim.

19 In our Mishnah, why should the divorcing husband not be forced to swear that he does not have to pay 200 *zuz* even if there are no witnesses, since he agrees that he owes 100? (The heirs, not being able to swear, would have to pay.)

20 Since this amount is not in dispute, the husband cannot be considered as agreeing to part of the claim; no oath is due.

21 This is the standard formulation, Babli *Baba Qama* 46b.

בְּהֵינוּמָא (26a line 71). תַּמָּן. נָמְנוּמָא. רַבָּנִין דְּהָכָא אָמְרִין. פִּירְיוֹמָא.

HALAKHAH 1　　　　　　　　81

"In *hinuma*". There, a veil. The rabbis here say, a *phorema*[22].

22   As explained in Chapter 1, Note 65, originally a virgin was led to her husband's house with ὑμέναιοι "wedding songs". After the war of Bar Kokhba, when these songs were forbidden (*Soṭah* 9:13, Note 189), the word *hinuma* changed its meaning. In Babylonia it became "a veil" (Babli 17b), literally "a slumber cloth" from נום "to sleep", in Galilee φόρημα "that which is carried", i. e., "a litter".

(26a line 72) יוֹצְאָה וְרֹאשָׁהּ פָּרוּעַ. רִבִּי חִייָה בְשֵׁם רִבִּי יוֹחָנָן. בְּגִין אֵילוּ שֶׁיָּצְאוּ בְיוֹם הַכִּיפּוּרִים. וְרֹאשָׁהּ פָּרוּעַ וְעֵידֶיהָ מְעִידִין אוֹתָהּ שֶׁלֹּא נִבְעֲלָה. וְחָשׁ לוֹמַר. שֶׁמָּא בְתוּלָה מִן הַנִּישׂוּאִין הִיא. זֹאת אוֹמֶרֶת. בְּתוּלָה מִן הַנִּישׂוּאִין אֵינָהּ יוֹצְאָה וְרֹאשָׁהּ פָּרוּעַ. וְחָשׁ לוֹמַר. שֶׁמָּא מוּכַּת עֵץ הִיא. אֶלָּא כְרִבִּי מֵאִיר. דְּרִבִּי מֵאִיר אוֹמֵר. מוּכַּת עֵץ כְּתוּבָתָהּ מָאתַיִם. אָמַר רִבִּי יוֹחָנָן. לֹא חָשׁוּ לְדָבָר שֶׁאֵינוֹ מָצוּי.

"She went out with uncovered head." Rebbi Ḥiyya in the name of Rebbi Joḥanan, like those who went out on the Day of Atonement[23]. If she went out with uncovered head, the witnesses testify[24] that she had not been cohabitated with. Should one not worry that she was a virgin after final marriage? That means, a virgin after final marriage does not go out with uncovered head[25]. Should one not worry that she had been injured by wood? That must follow Rebbi Meïr, since Rebbi Meïr says[26] the *ketubah* of one injured by wood is 200 [*zuz*]. Rebbi Joḥanan said, they did not worry about infrequent occurrences[27].

23   The virgins of Jerusalem who went out to dance in the vineyards on the 15th of Ab and the Day of Atonement to find husbands (*Mishnah Ta'anit* 4:8).

24   To the fact that she had her head uncovered before the wedding.

25   As in German one says "under

die Haube kommen" ("to get under the bonnet") for "to be married", the widow who is a virgin is a lady, always wearing a hat, no longer a girl.

26 Mishnah 1:3.

27 Mishnah 2:1 does not contradict the position of the Sages in Mishnah 1:3. The Babli agrees in a different context, 16a.

(26b line 5) רִבִּי יוֹחָנָן בֶּן בְּרוֹקָה אוֹמֵר אַף חִילוּק קְלָיוֹת רְאָיָיה. וְחָשׁ לוֹמַר. שֶׁמָּא בְתוּלָה מִן הַנִּישׂוּאִין הִיא. זֹאת אוֹמֶרֶת. בְּתוּלָה מִן הַנִּישׂוּאִין אֵין לָהּ חִילוּק קְלָיוֹת. תַּנֵּי. אַבָּא שָׁאוּל אוֹמֵר. אַף מִי שֶׁהוֹלִיכוּ לְפָנֶיהָ חָבִית שֶׁלַּבְּסוֹרוֹת. וְחָשׁ לוֹמַר. שֶׁמָּא בְתוּלָה מִן הַנִּישׂוּאִין הִיא. זֹאת אוֹמֶרֶת. בְּתוּלָה מִן הַנִּישׂוּאִין אֵין לָהּ חָבִית שֶׁלַּבְּשׂוֹרוֹת.

"Rebbi Johanan ben Beroqa says, the distribution of roasted kernels also is proof." Should one not worry that she was a virgin after final marriage? That means, for a virgin after final marriage one does not distribute roasted kernels. It was stated[28]: Abba Shaul says, also if one brought before her an amphora of good news[29]. Should one not worry that she was a virgin after final marriage? That means, in front of a virgin after final marriage one does not bring an amphora of good news.

28 In the Babli, 16b, in an anonymous *baraita* it is stated that it was a sign of a virgin's wedding if one brought before her a cup of good news or danced at her wedding.

29 In the Babli, the "cup of good news" is explained as a cup of heave wine, since heave is called "beginning" (*Num.* 18:12), the bride also represents a beginning. It probably is difficult to have a full amphora of heave wine; so one might think of the "good news amphora" as one of new wine which is opened for the first time at the wedding, just as the bride will be "opened" after the wedding.

HALAKHAH 2   83

(fol. 26a) **משנה ב**: וּמוֹדֶה רִבִּי יְהוֹשֻׁעַ בְּאוֹמֵר לַחֲבֵירוֹ שָׂדֶה זוֹ שֶׁלְאָבִיךָ הָיְיתָה וּלְקַחְתִּיהָ מִמֶּנּוּ שֶׁהוּא נֶאֱמָן שֶׁהַפֶּה שֶׁאָסַר הוּא הַפֶּה שֶׁהִתִּיר. וְאִם יֵשׁ עֵדִים שֶׁהִיא שֶׁלְאָבִיו וְהוּא אוֹמֵר לְקַחְתִּיהָ מִמֶּנּוּ אֵינוֹ נֶאֱמָן.

Mishnah 2: Rebbi Joshua agrees[30] that if somebody says to another: "This field did belong to your father but I bought it from him," that he is trustworthy since the mouth which forbade is the mouth which permits. But if there are witnesses that it did belong to [the second man's] father and [the first] said, I bought it, he is not trustworthy[31].

30 Even though he held in Chapter 1 that uncorroborated statements are not admissible in court, he agrees that if the question would not arise had a person not pointed it out, the same person is empowered to remove the difficulty he himself created. This is the principle behind the following Mishnaiot of this Chapter.

31 If there are witnesses, even if they come to court after the first person explained the problem, the first person has to establish his claim following all rules of testimony.

(26b line 10) **הלכה ב**: וּמוֹדֶה רִבִּי יְהוֹשֻׁעַ כול'. מוֹדֵי רבי יהושע ואין פליג בקדמייתא.

Halakhah 2: "Rebbi Joshua agrees," etc. Rebbi Joshua agrees, but he does not disagree[32]? In the former.

32 No disagreement is mentioned in Mishnah 1. Why should it be noted that R. Joshua agrees in another case? The reference is to all Mishnaiot of Chapter 1 where he disagrees. The same explanation is in the Babli, 16a.

(26b line 11) אֵינוֹ נֶאֱמָן. בְּשֶׁלֹא אֲכָלָהּ שְׁנֵי חֲזָקָה. אֲבָל אִם אֲכָלָהּ שְׁנֵי חֲזָקָה נֶאֱמָן. בְּשֶׁלֹא מֵת אָבִיו מְתוּכָהּ. אֲבָל אִם מֵת אָבִיו מִתּוֹכָהּ אֲפִילוּ (לֹא)[33] אֲכָלָהּ שְׁנֵי חֲזָקָה [אֵינוֹ][34] נֶאֱמָן. כְּחָדָא. רְאוּבֵן אוֹכֵל שָׂדֶה בְחֶזְקַת שֶׁהִיא שֶׁלוֹ וְהֵבִיא שִׁמְעוֹן עֵדִים שֶׁמֵּת אָבִיו מִתּוֹכָהּ. מַפְקִין לָהּ מֵרְאוּבֵן וּמַחֲזִירִין לֵיהּ

לְשִׁמְעוֹן. חָזַר רְאוּבֵן וְהֵבִיא עֵדִים שֶׁלֹּא מֵת אָבִיו מִתּוֹכָהּ. אָמַר רִבִּי נַחְמָן בַּר יַעֲקֹב. אֲנָא אַפִּיקְתֵּיהּ מֵרְאוּבֵן אֲנָא מַחֲזִיר לֵיהּ לִירְאוּבֵן. רַבָּנִין דְּהָכָא סָבְרִין כֵּן. רַבָּנִן דְּתַמָּן אֱמְרִין. מִשָּׁעָה שֶׁיָּצְאָת עֵדוּת בְּרוּרָה יָצָאת. כֵּן רַבָּנָן דְּהָכָא אֱמְרִין. מִשָּׁעָה שֶׁנִּישֵּׂאת בְּעֵדוּת בְּרוּרָה נִישֵּׂאת. אָמַר רִבִּי יוֹסֵי. מוֹדוּ רַבָּנָן דְּתַמָּן שֶׁאִילוּ מִשָּׁעָה רִאשׁוֹנָה שְׁנַיִם אוֹמְרִים. מֵת אָבִיו מִתּוֹכָהּ. וּשְׁנַיִם אוֹמְרִים. לֹא מֵת מִתּוֹכָהּ. שֶׁהַשָּׂדֶה בְּחֶזְקַת רְאוּבֵן.

"He is not trustworthy" if he did not eat the years of legal claim[35] from it. But if he ate the years of legal claim from it, he is trustworthy if [the second person's] father did not die in possession. But if [the second person's] father died in possession, he is [not] trustworthy[36]. [37]As the following: Reuben ate from a field[38] claiming that it was his. Simeon brought witnesses that his father died in possession. One removes [the field] from Reuben and hands the title to Simeon. Reuben came back and brought witnesses that [Simeon's] father did not die in possession. Rebbi Naḥman ben Jacob[39] said, I took it from Reuben, I am returning it to Reuben[40]. That is what the rabbis here think. The rabbis there say, from the time it was removed, by clear testimony it was removed[41]. So the rabbis here say, from the time she married, by clear testimony she married[42]. Rebbi Yose said, the rabbis there agree that if during the first proceedings two [witnesses] say that his father died in possession and two say, he did not die in possession, Reuben's claim is upheld[43].

33 This word appears both in the ms. and *editio princeps*; it seems a copyist's error.

34 This word is missing in the ms. but appears in *editio princeps*.

35 If a person can prove three years of undisturbed possession of real estate and claims legal acquisition (by sale, inheritance, or gift), the court has to confirm him in possession since documents have to be kept only for three years.

36 The three years of undisturbed possession count only if the person from whom he acquired it was alive during these years since the heirs might not be knowledgeable enough of the details of the deceased's property to exercise their duty to object to the squatter's occupation.

37 Except for the last sentence, the following is Halakhah *Baba Batra* 3:4 in a different editing.

38 Undisturbed for 3 years.

39 He should be called Rav Nahman ben Jacob, in the Babli simply called Rav Nahman, chief judge and highest authority in money matters in Babylonia.

40 If there are two against two witnesses and all four testimonies hold up under cross examination, there is no testimony and Simeon has no claim. The identical statement appears in the Babli, *Baba Batra* 31b.

41 Since (*Deut.* 19:15) "by the testimony of two or three witnesses the case shall be confirmed", Reuben's witnesses cannot be accepted unless they prove that Simeon's witnesses were lying.

It is difficult to see who "the rabbis from there" are since Rab Nahman was the authority in Babylonia and the Babli (*loc. cit.*) decides explicitly that later claims are admissible in money matters.

42 This really belongs to the next paragraph, about a woman whose husband has disappeared and she remarried on the testimony of two witnesses that her husband had died; when two witnesses come and say he is alive, they are not listened to.

43 If during court proceedings there are contradictory statements, none of which can be shown to be false, there is no proof and the claim of legal possession cannot be denied.

(26b line 21) אָמַר רִבִּי יוֹחָנָן. וְתַנֵּי כֵן. שְׁנַיִם אוֹמְרִים מֵת. וּשְׁנַיִם אוֹמְרִים. לֹא מֵת. לֹא תִינָּשֵׂא. וְאִם נִישֵּׂאת לֹא תֵצֵא. שְׁנַיִם אוֹמְרִים. נִתְגָּרְשָׁה. וּשְׁנַיִם אוֹמְרִים. לֹא נִתְגָּרְשָׁה. לֹא תִינָּשֵׂא. וְאִם נִישֵּׂאת תֵּצֵא. תַּמָּן אָמְרִין. לֹא שַׁנְיָיה. הִיא מִיתָה הִיא גֵירוּשִׁין לֹא תִינָּשֵׂא. וְאִם נִישֵּׂאת לֹא תֵצֵא. עַל דַּעְתֵּיהוֹן דְּרַבָּנִין דְּתַמָּן נִיחָא. הִיא מִיתָה הִיא גֵירוּשִׁין. עַל דַּעְתֵּיהוֹן דְּרַבָּנִין דְּהָכָא מַה בֵין מִיתָה מַה בֵין גֵּירוּשִׁין. רִבִּי זְעִירָא אָמַר לָהּ סְתָם. רִבִּי חִייָה

בְּשֵׁם רַבִּי יוֹחָנָן. הַדַּעַת מַכְרַעַת בְּעֵידֵיי[44] מִיתָה. שָׁאִילוּ יָבוֹא הוּא מַכְחֵשׁ. אָמַר רַבִּי חִזְקִיָה. רַבָּנִין דְּתַמָּן כְּדַעְתֵּין. כַּמָּה דְּרַבָּנִין דְּתַמָּן אָמְרִים. בְּשָׁעָה שֶׁיָּצָאת בְּעֵידוּת בְּרוּרָה יָצָאת. כֵּן רַבָּנִין דְּהָכָא אָמְרִין. בְּשָׁעָה שֶׁנִּישָּׂאת בְּעֵידוּת בְּרוּרָה נִישָּׂאת. אָמַר רַבִּי יוֹסֵי. לֹא[45] מִסְתַּבְּרָא דְּלָא מִחְלְפָא שִׁיטָתִין דְּרַבָּנִין דְּתַמָּן. לֹא מוֹדוּ רַבָּנָן דְּתַמָּן שֶׁאִילוּ מִשָּׁעָה רִאשׁוֹנָה שְׁנַיִם אוֹמְרִים. מֵת אָבִיו מְתוּכָהּ. וּשְׁנַיִם אוֹמְרִים. לֹא מֵת אָבִיו מְתוּכָהּ. שֶׁהַשָּׂדֶה בְּחֶזְקַת רְאוּבֵן. אִילּוּ שְׁנַיִם אוֹמְרִים. נִתְגָּרְשָׁה וְנִשֵּׂאת. וּשְׁנַיִם אוֹמְרִים לֹא נִתְגָּרְשָׁה. לֹא תֵצֵא. יָאוּת. מַתְנִיתָא פְּלִיגָא עַל רַבִּי יוֹחָנָן. שְׁנַיִם אוֹמְרִים. נִתְקַדְּשָׁה. וּשְׁנַיִם אוֹמְרִים. לֹא נִתְקַדְּשָׁה. לֹא תִינָשֵׂא. וְאִם נִישֵּׂאת לֹא תֵצֵא. אָמַר רַבִּי הוֹשַׁעְיָה. פָּתַר לָהּ רַבִּי יוֹחָנָן. שְׁנַיִם אוֹמְרִים. נִתְגָּרְשָׁה. וּשְׁנַיִם אוֹמְרִים. לֹא נִתְגָּרְשָׁה. לֹא תִינָשֵׂא. וְאִם נִישֵּׂאת לֹא תֵצֵא. מַה בֵּינָהּ לְקַדְמִיתָא. תַּמָּן הוּחְזָקָה אֵשֶׁת אִישׁ בִּפְנֵי הַכֹּל. בְּרַם הָכָא לֹא הוּחְזָקָה אֵשֶׁת אִישׁ אֶלָּא בִּפְנֵי שְׁנַיִם. לִכְשֶׁיָּבוֹאוּ שְׁנַיִם וְיֹאמְרוּ. זֶה הוּא שֶׁקִּידֵּשׁ. מַתְנִיתָא פְּלִיגָא עַל רַבִּי יוֹחָנָן. שְׁנַיִם אוֹמְרִים. נִשְׁבֵּית וְהִיא טְהוֹרָה. וּשְׁנַיִם אוֹמְרִים. נִשְׁבֵּית וְהִיא טְמֵיאָה. לֹא תִינָשֵׂא. וְאִם נִישֵּׂאת לֹא תֵצֵא. אָמַר רַבִּי יוֹסֵי. מֵאַחַר שֶׁאִילּוּ אוֹמְרִים. טְהוֹרָה. וְאִילּוּ אוֹמְרִים. טְמֵיאָה. כְּמִי שֶׁאִילּוּ אוֹמְרִים. נִשְׁבֵּית. וְאִילּוּ אוֹמְרִים. לֹא נִשְׁבֵּית. וַאֲנָן חַיִּים מִפִּיהָ. שְׁנַיִם אוֹמְרִים נִתְקַדְּשָׁה. וּשְׁנַיִם אוֹמְרִים לֹא נִתְקַדְּשָׁה. רַבִּי יוֹנָה מְדַמֵּי לָהּ לַחֲלָבִין. אִילּוּ שְׁנַיִם אוֹמְרִים. פְּלוֹנִי אָכַל חֵלֶב. וּשְׁנַיִם אוֹמְרִים. לֹא אָכַל חֵלֶב. שֶׁמָּא אֵינוֹ מֵבִיא אָשָׁם תָּלוּי מְסֻפָּק. וְכָא יִתֵּן גֵּט מְסֻפָּק. אָמַר לֵיהּ רַבִּי יוֹסֵי. לֹא תְדַמִּינָהּ לַחֲלָבִין. שֶׁכֵּן אֲפִילוּ אָמַר. לְבֵי נוֹקְדֵּינִי. מֵבִיא אָשָׁם תָּלוּי. מַתְנִיתָא פְּלִיגָא עַל רַבִּי יוֹסֵי. שְׁנַיִם אוֹמְרִים. נִתְקַדְּשָׁה. וּשְׁנַיִם אוֹמְרִים. לֹא נִתְקַדְּשָׁה. לֹא תִינָשֵׂא. וְסוֹפָא פְּלִיגָא עַל רַבִּי יוֹנָה. אִם נִשֵּׂאת תֵּצֵא. אָמַר רַבִּי מָנָא. לֹא דְּרַבִּי יוֹסֵי אוֹמֵר. תִּינָשֵׂא. וְלֹא רַבִּי יוֹנָה אוֹמֵר. אִם נִשֵּׂאת תֵּצֵא. לֹא אָמַר אֶלָּא. לֹא תְדַמִּינָהּ לַחֲלָבִים. שֶׁאֲפִילוּ אָמַר. לְבֵי נוֹקְדֵּינִי. מֵבִיא אָשָׁם תָּלוּי.

19 זה הוא | י זהו 22-23 ואנן חיים | י ואנו חיין   26 נוקדני | י נוקריני 28
וסופא פליגא | י וסיפא פליג

⁴⁶Rebbi Joḥanan said, it was stated thus: "Two [witnesses] say he died, [later] two witnesses say, he did not die. She shall not remarry, but if she has remarried she should not leave. Two [witnesses] say she was divorced, [later] two witnesses say, she was not divorced. She shall not remarry; if she has remarried she must leave.⁴⁷" There, they say, it makes no difference; whether about death or divorce she should not leave. In the opinion of the rabbis there it is understandable, there is no difference between death and divorce. In the opinion of the rabbis here, what is the difference between death and divorce? Rebbi Ze'ira said it without attribution, Rebbi Ḥiyya in the name of Rebbi Joḥanan: It is reasonable to decide in the case of witnesses of death that if he returns he contradicts them. Rebbi Ḥizqiah said, the rabbis there stick to their opinion since the rabbis there say, when the [first] testimony was accepted, it was accepted as certain. So the rabbis here say, at the moment of her remarriage, she remarried based on certified testimony. Rebbi Yose said, it is reasonable that the rabbis there did not change their argument. Do the rabbis there not agree if two [witnesses] say, his father died while in possession, [and two say his father died while not in possession,] that the field is in Reuben's possession? Therefore, if two say, she was divorced and remarried, and two say she was not divorced, rightly she should not leave.

A *baraita* disagrees with Rebbi Joḥanan: "If two are saying, she was preliminarily married, and two are saying, she was not preliminarily married, she should not get married, but if she married she should not leave." Rebbi Hoshaia said, Rebbi Joḥanan may explain it as follows: "If two are saying, she was divorced, and two are saying, she was not divorced, she should not get married, but if she married she should not leave." What is the difference between this and the first case? There, she was considered a married woman in everybody's opinion. Here, she is considered a married woman only for two people. If two others came and identified the man who was betrothed to her.

A *baraita* disagrees with Rebbi Johanan: "If two are saying, she was kidnapped but is pure, and two are saying, she was kidnapped and is impure, she should not get married, but if she married she should not leave.[48]" Rebbi Yose said, since these say, she is pure, and those say, she is impure, it is as if two said, she was kidnapped, and two said, she was not kidnapped, and we depend on what she says.

If two are saying, she had been betrothed and two are saying she had not been betrothed. Rebbi Jonah compares that to fat. If two said, X ate fat, and two said, X did not eat fat, did he not have to bring a "hung" reparation sacrifice because of the doubt? Here, he should give a bill of divorce because of the doubt. Rebbi Yose said to him, do not compare this to fat, because even if he says my conscience bothers me, he brings a "hung" reparation sacrifice. A *baraita* disagrees with Rebbi Yose: If two are saying she had been betrothed and two are saying she had not been betrothed, she should not get married. The end disagrees with Rebbi Jonah: If she married she must leave. Rebbi Mana said, Rebbi Yose did not say that she may marry, nor did Rebbi Jonah say if she married she must leave, he said only, do not compare this to fat, because even if he says my conscience bothers me, he brings a "hung" reparation sacrifice.

44 Reading of the parallel in *Yebamot*. Reading here לִידֵי "on behalf of".

45 This word is not in *Yebamot*; it should be read since לא מסתברה דלא is a standard formula.

46 From *Yebamot* 10:4, explained in Notes 99-114. The variant readings are noted by י.

47 Tosephta *Yebamot* 14:1

48 A similar text in Tosephta *Ketubot* 2:2. The kidnap victim who was raped cannot marry a Cohen.

(fol. 26a) **משנה ג:** הָעֵדִים שֶׁאָמְרוּ כְּתָב יָדֵינוּ הוּא זֶה אֲבָל אֲנוּסִים הָיִינוּ קְטַנִּים הָיִינוּ פְּסוּלֵי עֵדוּת הָיִינוּ הֲרֵי אֵלּוּ נֶאֱמָנִין. וְאִם יֵשׁ עֵדִים שֶׁהוּא כְּתָב יָדָן אוֹ שֶׁהָיָה כְּתָב יָדָן יוֹצֵא מִמָּקוֹם אַחֵר אֵינָן נֶאֱמָנִין.

Mishnah 3: If witnesses said, this is our signature, but we were under duress, or underage, or disqualified[49], these are trustworthy[50]. But if there are witnesses to identify their signatures, or their signatures are confirmed from another document[51], they are not trustworthy.

49 If at the time they witnessed the document they lived off illegal or immoral earnings (e. g., as gamblers having no other employment, who cannot make money if the game is honest).

50 They have witnessed a document of indebtedness or transfer of property which ended up in court. The court must first establish that the document is genuine by certifying the signatures of the witnesses. If the witnesses were unknown to the court, their testimony qualifies the document as genuine. But since theirs is the mouth which permits the introduction of the document, their mouth can prohibit its introduction by claiming that their signatures were obtained illegally.

51 If the witnesses were unknown to the court but another document was presented carrying their signatures and certified by another court as genuine,

then the court judging the present document is empowered to certify their signatures by comparing them to the certified ones. Their mouth is not the one which permits; therefore, their mouth cannot prohibit.

(26b line 53) **הלכה ג**: הָעֵדִים שֶׁאָמְרוּ. כְּתַב יָדֵינוּ הוּא זֶה כול'. תַּנֵּי. וְכֵן הָעֵדִים שֶׁהֵעִידוּ בֵּין לְטַמֵּא בֵּין לְטַהֵר. בֵּין לְרַחֵק בֵּין לְקָרֵב. בֵּין לֶאֱסוֹר בֵּין לְהַתִּיר. בֵּין לִזְכוּת בֵּין לְחוֹבָה. עַד שֶׁלֹּא נֶחְקְרָה עֵדוּתָן בְּבֵית דִּין אָמְרוּ. מְבַדִּין הָיִינוּ. הֲרֵי אֵילוּ נֶאֱמָנִין. מִשֶּׁנֶּחְקְרָה עֵדוּתָן בְּבֵית דִּין אָמְרוּ. מְבַדִּין הָיִינוּ. אֵינָן נֶאֱמָנִין. רִבִּי שִׁמְעוֹן בֶּן לָקִישׁ אָמַר. עָשׂוּ הָעֵדִים הַחֲתוּמִין עַל הַשְּׁטָר כְּמִי שֶׁנֶּחְקְרָה עֵדוּתָן בְּבֵית דִּין. הֵן אוֹמְרִים. כְּתַב יָדֵינוּ הוּא זֶה. וַאֲחֵרִים אוֹמְרִים. כְּתַב יָדָן הוּא. תַּנֵּי רִבִּי חִייָה. לֹא מַעֲלִין וְלֹא מוֹרִידִין. אָמַר רִבִּי יוֹסֵי. מַתְנִיתִין אָמְרָה כֵן. אִם יֵשׁ עֵדִים שֶׁהוּא כְּתָב יָדָן אוֹ שֶׁהָיָה כְּתַב יָדָן יוֹצֵא מִמָּקוֹם אַחֵר אֵינָן נֶאֱמָנִין.

Halakhah 3: "If witnesses said, this is our signature," etc. It was stated[52]: And similarly, the witnesses who testified whether to declare impure or pure, or to remove or include, or to forbid or permit, or to obligate or absolve[53], if they say we did invent this[54] before their testimony was investigated by the court[55], they can be believed; after their testimony was investigated by the court, they are not trustworthy." Rebbi Simeon ben Laqish said, they considered witnesses who signed a document as if their testimony had been investigated by the court[56]. If they say, these are our signatures, and others say, these are their signatures, Rebbi Ḥiyya stated: Their [testimony] does not add and does not detract[57]. Rebbi Yose said, our Mishnah says so, "if there are witnesses to identify their signatures, or if their signatures are confirmed from another document[51], they are not trustworthy."

52 In slightly different wording in Tosephta *Ketubot* 2:1, *Sanhedrin* 6:5.

53 These testimonies are all about personal status. To declare impure or pure is the same as to exclude (bastards from marrying Jewish partners or desecrated females from marrying Cohanim) or to include them in the pool of eligible marriage partners. Similarly, to forbid marriages (because the woman is still married) or to permit, to impose a purification sacrifice for sinful marriage or to absolve. The parallel Tosephta in *Sanhedrin* must be interpreted to deal with money matters, to impose payment or to absolve from payment.

54 The text here is in doubt. The Erfurt ms. of the Tosephta reads מְבוּדִּין אָנוּ in both places, "we were made to lie"; this is the reading of many German and Italian medieval authorities in the Yerushalmi. The text of the ms. and *editio princeps* is also the text of the Vienna ms. of the Tosephta and most African, Spanish, and French authorities; cf. *Tosefta ki-Fshutah*, part 6, p. 199-200.

55 This does not necessarily mean investigation by cross-examination but indicates that identification of their signatures was accepted by the court; cf. *Tosefta ki-Fshutah*, part 6, p. 200-202.

56 Once the signatures have been accepted, the witnesses cannot change their stories since "no witness can testify twice in the same matter" (Babli 18b; *Bikkurim* 3:4, Note 72). The Babli agrees, 18b. Cf. also *Ševi'it* 10:5, Note 96.

57 Since their testimony is not needed, they do not have the power to modify the terms of the contract which they signed as witnesses.

(26b line 61) הֵן אוֹמְרִים. כְּתָב יָדֵינוּ הוּא. וַאֲחֵרִים אוֹמְרִים. אֵינוֹ כְּתָב יָדָם. אָמַר רִבִּי מָנָא. נַעֲשָׂה כִשְׁטָר שֶׁנִּקְרָא עָלָיו עִרְעֵר. אָמַר אַסִּי. וּבִלְבַד בִּשְׁטָר שֶׁנִּקְרָא עָלָיו עִרְעֵר וְנִתְקַיֵּים בְּבֵית דִּין. רִבִּי לֶעְזָר אָמַר. לֹא נִתְקַיֵּים בְּבֵית דִּין. אָמַר רִבִּי אִילָא. טַעֲמָא דְּרִבִּי לֶעְזָר. כֵּיוָן שֶׁהוּחְזְקוּ הָעֵדִים לִהְיוֹת חֲתוּמִין בִּשְׁטָר כְּמִי שֶׁנֶּחְקְרָה עֵדוּתָן בְּבֵית דִּין.

They say, these are our signatures, but others[58] say, not their signatures. Rebbi Mana said, that becomes a document which has been put under a cloud⁵⁹. Issi said, only if it had been put under a cloud but was confirmed by the court⁶⁰. Rebbi Eleazar said, if it was not confirmed by a court⁶¹. Rebbi Ila said, the reason of Rebbi Eleazar is, that after the witnesses were confirmed as the signatories of the document, it is as if their testimony had been investigated by the court.

58 Witnesses before the court.

59 A document signed by unidentified witnesses is worthless.

60 This refers to the statement of the Mishnah, that witnesses are not needed if "their signatures are confirmed from another document." He holds that signatures can be confirmed from other documents without asking the witnesses if there was a problem with the other document and it was confirmed by a court after due investigation. Since the signatures on a document whose validity is acknowledged by all parties do not have to be investigated, those signatures should not be used to validate documents in dispute. This opinion is quoted in the Babli, 19b, as tannaïtic. Later, 20a, in the name of R. Assi (Issi), it is interpreted to mean that one may use a document in dispute to validate other documents only if the first document was confirmed by a court, implying that an undisputed document can be used even if no court ever had given its opinion on it. This cannot be the meaning in the Yerushalmi.

61 Any document accepted by a court, after investigation or without, is valid to compare signatures.

(26b line 66) רַב חָנָה אָמַר. לְמֵידִין מִסֵּפֶר מוּגָּה. כְּגוֹן אִילֵּין דְּאָמְרִין. סַפְרוֹי דְאָסִי וּכְאִילֵּין אִיגְרָאתָא צְרִיכִין. אָמַר רבִּי יוֹסֵי בֵּירבִּי בּוּן. וּבִלְבַד שְׁלשָׁה שְׁטָרוֹת שֶׁלִּשְׁלשָׁה בְנֵי אָדָם.

Rav Ḥana said, one learns from a corrected scroll, like those who say, Issi's scribe⁶². From letters it is problematic⁶³. Rebbi Yose ben Rebbi Abun said, only from three documents in the hands of three people⁶⁴.

62 A document in the characteristic handwriting of a known scribe can be accepted, since that scribe would not be a party to a dishonest document.

63 Letters cannot directly be used to identify handwriting since it is known, from Geniza documents and Sephardic documents through the 18th Century, that people develop very intricate signatures that cannot be compared directly to their fluent writing in letters.

64 The Babli, 20a, accepts two documents in the hands of two people to verify signatures. It is explained that two documents in the hand of the same person are no help since just as he forged one document so he may have forged the other.

(line 68 26b) רַב חוּנָה בְּשֵׁם רַב. נֶאֱמָנִין הָעֵדִים לוֹמַר. שְׁטָר אֲמָנָה וּשְׁטָר פּוֹסִיטִיס הוּא. דְּרַב אָמַר. אָסוּר לַחְתּוֹם בִּשְׁטָר אֲמָנָה וּבִשְׁטָר פּוֹסִיטִיס. מַה וּפְלִיג. אָמְרֵי בְשֵׁם רַב. נֶאֱמָנִין הָעֵדִים לוֹמַר. שְׁטָר אֲמָנָה וּשְׁטָר פּוֹסִיטִיס הוּא. מִילְתָא דְרַב פְּלִינָא עַל מִילְתָא דְרַב. אָמַר רִבִּי חַגַּי. לֹא דְרַב אָמַר. אָסוּר לַחְתּוֹם אֶלָּא אָסוּר לְקַיֵּים. כְּהָדָא. אִם אָוֶן בְּיָדְךָ הַרְחִיקֵהוּ. זֶה שְׁטָר אֲמָנָה וּשְׁטָר פּוֹסִיטִיס. וְאַל תַּשְׁכֵּן בְּאוֹהָלֶיךָ עַוְלָה. זֶה שְׁטָר פָּרוּעַ.

Rav Huna in the name of Rav: The witnesses can be trusted if they say, that is a document given in good faith[65], or a document in trust[66]. But Rav said, it is forbidden to sign a document given in good faith, or a document in trust. Does this contradict what they say in the name of Rav, the witnesses can be trusted if they say, that is a document given in good faith, or a document in trust? One word of Rav contradicts a word of Rav! Rebbi Haggai said, Rav did not say it is forbidden to sign but it is forbidden to keep[67]. As the following[68], "if evil is in your hand, remove it," that is a document given in good faith, or a document in trust, "do not let injustice dwell in your house," that is a document of indebtedness which was paid[69].

65 A document of indebtedness while no debt exists, to be activated later if the debtor needs money, given in good faith that the lender will not use it unless there really will be a loan (naturally interest-free).

In a more general sense, a good faith document is a document covering eventualities which the parties expect never to happen. Such a document is not enforceable. Some rabbinic authorities hold that pre-nuptial agreements about eventual modalities of divorce are good faith documents since nobody marries with the idea of a divorce in mind.

66 Greek πίστις "trust, credit, credence" (in the *editio princeps* the spelling is פיסטיס; Musaphia reads פסטיס). A document which does not correspond to reality and is not intended ever to correspond to reality, but to make the holder appear richer than he really is.

67 The Babli, in the name of Amoraim of the last generation, disagrees and holds that it is forbidden to sign inactive documents and that witnesses who claim the documents were not meant to be used declare themselves to be sinners and, therefore, unacceptable as witnesses. But if they say that the debtor stated before them that he agreed to the document only under duress, they are to be believed.

68 *Job* 11:14. In the Babli, 19b, this is attributed to R. Joshua ben Levi.

69 It should be torn up rather than invalidated by a separate receipt.

(fol. 26a) **משנה ד:** זֶה אוֹמֵר זֶה כְּתָב יָדִי וְזֶה כְּתָב יָדוֹ שֶׁלַּחֲבֵירִי וְזֶה אוֹמֵר זֶה כְּתָב יָדִי וְזֶה כְּתָב יָדוֹ שֶׁלַּחֲבֵירִי הֲרֵי אֵילוּ נֶאֱמָנִין. זֶה אוֹמֵר זֶה כְּתָב יָדִי וְזֶה אוֹמֵר זֶה כְּתָב יָדִי צְרִיכִין שֶׁיִּצְטָרֵף עִמָּהֶן אַחֵר דִּבְרֵי רִבִּי. וַחֲכָמִים אוֹמְרִים אֵינָן צְרִיכִין שֶׁיִּצְטָרֵף עִמָּהֶן אַחֵר אֶלָּא נֶאֱמָן אָדָם לוֹמַר זֶה כְּתָב יָדִי.

Mishnah 4: If one says, this is my signature and that is my colleague's signature, and the other says, this is my signature and that is my colleague's signature, they are trustworthy[70]. If each of them says, that is my signature, each of them needs another with him, the words of Rebbi, but the Sages say, everybody is trustworthy to confirm his own signature[71].

70 There is a document before the court which should be certified and for that the court has to check whether the signatures of the two witnesses on the document are genuine. If each of the two witnesses testifies to the genuineness of both signatures, there are two witnesses for each signature and the document is validated. (While nobody can testify in his own behalf, here the witness testifies in behalf of the owner of the document.)

71 As the Halakhah explains, Rebbi requires that each signature on the document be certified by two witnesses but the Sages hold that only the contents of the document have to be certified by two witnesses.

(26b line 74) **הלכה ד**: זֶה אוֹמֵר זֶה כָתַב יָדִי כול׳. לָמָה נִצְרְכָה. לְרבִּי. אַף עַל גַּו דְּרבִּי אוֹמֵר. צְרִיכִין שֶׁיִּצְטָרֵף אַחֵר עִמָּהֶן. מוֹדֶה הוּא הָכָא שֶׁהֵן נֶאֱמָנִין.

Halakkhah 4: "If one says, this is my signature," etc. Why was this necessary? For Rebbi. Even though Rebbi says, each of them needs another with him, here he agrees that they are trustworthy[72].

72 He accepts cross validations since there are two witnesses for every signature.

(26b line 74) אָמַר רבִּי זְעִירָא. תַּנֵּי בִּכְתוּבוֹת דְּבֵית רַב. דִּבְרֵי רבִּי (לְעָזָר) עַל הַשְּׁטָר וְדִבְרֵי חֲכָמִים בְּמֵעִיד עַל הַמִּלְוָה.

Rebbi Ze'ira said: It was stated in Rav's *Ketubot*: The words of Rebbi (Eleazar)[73] that he testifies about the document, the words of the Sages that he testifies about the loan[71,74].

73 This is in the ms. and *editio princeps*, but does not fit the context. The correct text is in *Sefer Ha'iṭṭur* (vol. 1, 14b, Note 74): אָמַר רִבִּי זְעִירָא. דִּבְרֵי רִבִּי כְּמֵעִיד עַל הַשְּׁטָר וְדִבְרֵי חֲכָמִים כְּמֵעִיד עַל הַמִּלְוָה. This is the basis of the translation. However, since it leaves out the irrelevant information about Rav's *Ketubot*, it probably is not an exact copy of the Yerushalmi text.

74 The Babli agrees (after some discussion), 20b/21a.

(26c line 2) תַּנֵּי. כּוֹתֵב אָדָם עֵדוּתוֹ וּמְעִידָהּ אֲפִילוּ לְאַחַר כַּמָּה שָׁנִים. רַב חוּנָא אָמַר. וְהוּא שֶׁיְּהֵא זָכוּר עֵדוּתוֹ. רִבִּי יוֹחָנָן אָמַר. אֲפִילוּ שֶׁאֵינוֹ זָכוּר עִידוּתוֹ. וַתְיָיא דְרַב חוּנָה כְּרִבִּי וְרִבִּי יוֹחָנָן כְּרַבָּנִין.

It was stated: A person may write down his testimony and testify about it even some years later[75]. Rav Huna said, only if he remembers his testimony. Rebbi Johanan said, even if he does not remember his testimony. It turns out that Rav Huna follows Rebbi and Rebbi Johanan the Sages[76].

75 Babli 20a; Tosephta 2:1 (there, the wording is: even after 100 years.) The problem is that the verse (*Deut.* 19:15) requires that "anything be confirmed *by the mouth* of two or three witnesses." The disagreement of Rav Huna and R. Johanan is confirmed by the Babli, but not its explanation.

76 It is obvious that nobody has to refresh his memory in order to identify his signature, so the difference must be about testifying to the substance of the document. R. Johanan follows the Sages since his testimony about his signature certifies the document and any additional information is ancillary but for Rav Huna the testimony about the signature says nothing about the contents of the document; any additional testimony must be *by the mouth* of the witnesses and not by his writing. (The explanation of *Tosaphot* 20a, *s. v.* ורבי יוחנן, is difficult to accept.)

(26c line 4) רִבִּי זְעִירָא רַב חוּנָה בְּשֵׁם רַב. אֵין הוּא וְאַחֵר מִצְטָרְפִין עַל חֲתִימַת הָעֵד הַשֵּׁנִי. הֵיךְ עֲבִידָא. הָיָה אֶחָד מַכִּיר כְּתָב יָדוֹ וּכְתָב יָדוֹ שֶׁלַּחֲבֵירוֹ וְאֶחָד

HALAKHAH 4

אֵין אָדָם מַכִּירוֹ וַחֲבֵירוֹ מַכִּירוֹ. חֲבֵירוֹ מָה הוּא שֶׁיִּצְטָרֵף עִם אֶחָד מִן הַשׁוּק לְהָעִיד עָלָיו. הָדָא הוּא דָּמַר רִבִּי זְעִירָא רִבִּי הוּנָא בְּשֵׁם רַב. אֵין הוּא וְאַחֵר מִצְטָרְפִין עַל חֲתִימַת הָעֵד הַשֵּׁינִי. לֹא צוּרְכָה דְּלֹא כְּשֶׁהָיוּ שְׁנַיִם. אֶחָד הַכֹּל מַכִּירִין כְּתָב יָדוֹ וְאֶחָד אֵין אָדָם מַכִּירוֹ וַחֲבֵירוֹ מַכִּירוֹ. חֲבֵירוֹ מָה הוּא שֶׁיֵּעָשֶׂה כְּאֶחָד מִן הַשׁוּק לְהָעִיד עָלָיו. אִם אַתָּה אוֹמֵר כֵּן נִמְצֵאת הָעֵדוּת מִתְקַייֶּמֶת בְּעֵד אֶחָד. אָמַר רִבִּי יוּדָן. וְיֵאוֹת. אִילּוּ שְׁנַיִם שֶׁיָּצְאוּ מֵעִיר שֶׁרוּבָּהּ גּוֹיִם כְּגוֹן הָדָא סוּסִיתָא. אֶחָד הַכֹּל מַכִּירִין אוֹתוֹ שֶׁהוּא יִשְׂרָאֵל וְאֶחָד אֵין אָדָם מַכִּירוֹ חֲבֵירוֹ מַכִּירוֹ. מָהוּ שֶׁיֵּעָשֶׂה כְּאֶחָד מִן הַשׁוּק לְהָעִיד עָלָיו. אִם אוֹמֵר אַתְּ כֵּן לֹא נִמְצֵאת כָּל־הָעֵדוּת מִתְקַייֶּמֶת בְּעֵד אֶחָד. וְכָא נִמְצֵאת כָּל־הָעֵדוּת מִתְקַייֶּמֶת בְּעֵד אֶחָד.

Rebbi Ze'ira, Rav Huna, in the name of Rav: One witness and someone from the market place cannot together certify the signature of the second witness[77]. How is that? If one identified his own signature[78] and that of his colleague, but that second witness's signature was not known to anybody[79] except his colleague, may that colleague together with somebody from the market place[80] testify on that signature? That is what Rebbi Ze'ira, Rav Huna, said in the name of Rav: One witness and someone from the market cannot together certify the signature of the second witness. Another case where there are no two persons: The signature of one is known by everybody, but that second witness's signature is not known to anybody except his colleague. Can that colleague testify on his signature as if he were someone from the market place? If you say so, the entire testimony is confirmed by one witness. Rebbi Yudan said, that is correct. If two people come from a town that is mostly Gentile, like Hippos[81]. One is known by everybody as a Jew, but the other is not known by anybody except his companion. Can the latter be considered one from the market place to testify about him[82]? If you say so, the entire testimony would be confirmed by one witness[83]! And in the prior case, the entire testimony would be confirmed by one witness.

77 In the formulation of the Babli, 21a, one witness comes before the court but the other has died in the meantime. If the surviving witness were enabled to testify to his own signature and, with the help of an unrelated person, to that of the other witness, then 75% of the testimony would be from one witness (100% of his own half and 50% of the other half). But testimony of witnesses is acceptable only if both of them have equal validity.

The paragraph appears also in *Roš Haššanah* 2:1, 57d.

78 Which he is enabled to do by the Mishnah following the Sages.

79 In court.

80 I. e., unconnected with the court and the parties before the court.

81 On the mountain ridge overlooking the Eastern Shore of Lake Genezareth.

82 To establish a Jewish identity, one witness is enough since it is a testimony about Torah prohibitions.

83 If the two testify about a document executed in the city of Hippos, the second witness testifies only because he was enabled by the first. Therefore, the second witness cannot be considered to be independent of the first.

(26c line 18) רִבִּי חַגַּיי אָמַר רִבִּי זְעִירָא בָּעָא. עֵד אֶחָד בְּפֶה וְעֵד אֶחָד בִּשְׁטָר מַהוּ שֶׁיִּצְטָרְפוּ. עֵד אֶחָד בִּכְתָב כְּלוּם הוּא. לָכֵן צְרִיכָה. כְּשֶׁהָיוּ שְׁנַיִם. מָצְאוּ לְקַיֵּים כְּתַב יָדוֹ שֶׁלָּרִאשׁוֹן וְלֹא מָצְאוּ לְקַיֵּים כְּתַב יָדוֹ שֶׁלַּשֵּׁינִי. רִבִּי מָנָא בָּעָא. עֵד אֶחָד בִּכְתָב מַהוּ לְזוֹקְקוֹ לִשְׁבוּעָה. עֵד אֶחָד בִּכְתָב כְּלוּם הוּא. לָכֵן צְרִיכָה. כְּשֶׁהָיוּ שְׁנַיִם מָצְאוּ לְקַיֵּים כְּתַב יָדוֹ שֶׁלָּרִאשׁוֹן וְלֹא מָצְאוּ לְקַיֵּים כְּתַב יָדוֹ שֶׁלַּשֵּׁינִי. כְּהָדָא. אֵין מְקַבְּלִין מִן הָעֵדִים אֶלָּא אִם כֵּן רָאוּ שְׁנֵיהֶן כְּאַחַת. רִבִּי יְהוֹשֻׁעַ בֶּן קָרְחָה אוֹמֵר. אֲפִילוּ רָאוּ זֶה אַחַר זֶה. רִבִּי יִרְמְיָה רִבִּי שְׁמוּאֵל בַּר רַב יִצְחָק בְּשֵׁם רַב. מוֹדִין חֲכָמִים לְרִבִּי יְהוֹשֻׁעַ בֶּן קָרְחָה בְּעֵידֵי בְּכוֹרָה וּבְעֵידֵי חֲזָקָה.

Rebbi Haggai said that Rebbi Ze'ira asked: Can one witness testifying orally and one by a document be taken together? Is a single witness on a written document worth anything[84]? Therefore, his question was, if there are two. They managed to confirm the first signature but not the second[85]. Rebbi Mana asked, is one witness on a written document enough to force anybody to swear[86]? Is a single witness on a written document worth anything? Therefore, his question was, if there are two. They managed to confirm the first signature but not the second. [87]Parallel to it: One does not accept testimony from witnesses unless they had seen together. Rebbi Joshua ben Qorha says, even if they saw one after the other[88]. Rebbi Jeremiah, Rebbi Samuel bar Rav Isaac, in the name of Rav: The Sages agree with Rebbi Joshua ben Qorha for witnesses about primogeniture and rights of possession.

84 Mishnah *Baba batra* 10:2: A document signed by a single witness is invalid.

85 In the Babli, *Baba batra* 165a, this is a question, if one signature was confirmed from another document and one by oral testimony. It is resolved that the document is valid.

86 *Ex.* 22:9 decrees that in all money matters in dispute, "if there is one who says, he is the one" who owes money, there should be an oath. This is interpreted to mean that the claimant can force the defendant to swear if he can support his claim by a single witness but does not have the two witnesses necessary to force the defendant to pay.

87 From here to the end of the Halakhah, the text is from *Sotah* Chapter 1, Notes 46-71. The text here is from the hand of the corrector; the scribe of the ms. only notes גרש בהילכתא קדמיתא דסוטה כולה עד וכה "כל סימן וסימן צריך שני עדים One reads all this in the first Halakhah of *Sotah* up to 'and here, every single hair needs two witnesses'." There are several differences in the sequence of sentences in addition to systematic differences in spelling; it is clear that the corrector copied from a different

ms. which now is lost.

88   R. Joshua ben Qorḥa will accept the written testimony of one witness (of two on a document) combined with the oral one of another; the Sages will reject it except in the three cases stated here. The same disagreement in the Babli 26b, *Sanhedrin* 30b.

(26c line 26) רִבִּי בָּא בְשֵׁם רִבִּי יִרְמְיָה. אַף בְּעֵידֵי סִימָנִים כֵּן. מַה דָא פְּשִׁיטָא. בְּשֶׁזֶּה אוֹמֵר. רָאִיתִי שְׁתֵּי שְׂעָרוֹת בְּגַבּוֹ. וְזֶה אוֹמֵר. רָאִיתִי שְׁתֵּי שְׂעָרוֹת בְּגַבּוֹ. אֶחָד אוֹמֵר. רָאִיתִי שְׂעָרָה אַחַת בְּגַבּוֹ. וְאֶחָד אוֹמֵר. רָאִיתִי שְׂעָרָה אַחַת בִּכְרֵיסוֹ. לֹא כְלוּם. כָּל־שֶׁכֵּן גַּבּוֹ וְגַבּוֹ. שְׁנַיִם אוֹמְרִים. רָאִינוּ שְׂעָרָה אַחַת בְּגַבּוֹ. וּשְׁנַיִם אוֹמְרִים. רָאִינוּ שְׂעָרָה אַחַת בִּכְרֵיסוֹ. רִבִּי יוֹסֵי בֵּירְבִּי בּוּן וְרִבִּי הוֹשַׁעְיָה בְּרֵיהּ דְּרִבִּי שַׁמַּאי. חַד אָמַר. פָּסוּל. וְחָרְנָא אָמַר. כָּשֵׁר. מָן דָּמַר. פָּסוּל. כְּמֵעִיד עַל חֲצִי סִימָנִין. וּמָן דָּמַר. כָּשֵׁר. שֶׁמָּא נָשְׁרוּ. אֶחָד אוֹמֵר. רָאִיתִי שְׁתֵּי שְׂעָרוֹת בְּגַבּוֹ. וְאֶחָד אוֹמֵר. רָאִיתִי שְׁתֵּי שְׂעָרוֹת בִּכְרֵיסוֹ. רִבִּי בָּא אוֹמֵר. דִּבְרֵי הַכֹּל כָּשֵׁר. רִבִּי חַגַּי אוֹמֵר. דִּבְרֵי הַכֹּל פָּסוּל. רִבִּי יוֹסֵי אָמַר. בְּמַחֲלוֹקֶת. אָמַר רִבִּי יוֹסֵי לְרִבִּי חַגַּי. וְהָא רִבִּי יוּדָן סָבַר דִּכְוָתִי. אָמַר לֵיהּ. עַל דְּרַבְּיֵהּ אֲנָא פְלִיג לֹא כָל־שֶׁכֵּן עֲלָוֵיהּ. אָמַר רִבִּי מָנָא. יָאוּת אָמַר רִבִּי חַגַּי. אִלּוּ שְׁטָר שֶׁהוּא מְחוּתָם בְּאַרְבַּע חוֹתָמוֹת וְקָרָא עָלוּי עִרְעָר זֶה מֵעִיד עַל שְׁנַיִם וְזֶה מֵעִיד עַל שְׁנַיִם. שֶׁמָּא כְלוּם הוּא. וְאֵין כָּל־חֲתִימָה וַחֲתִימָה צְרִיכָה שְׁנֵי עֵדִים. וְכָה כָּל־סִימָן וְסִימָן צָרִיךְ שְׁנֵי עֵדִים. רִבִּי חֲנִינָא יָלִיף לָהּ מִשְּׁנֵי חֲזָקָה. אִלּוּ אֶחָד מֵעִידָהּ שֶׁאֲכָלָהּ שָׁנָה רִאשׁוֹנָה וּשְׁנִיָּה וּשְׁלִישִׁית וְאֶחָד מֵעִידָהּ שֶׁאֲכָלָהּ רְבִיעִית חֲמִישִׁית וְשִׁישִׁית שֶׁמָּא כְלוּם הוּא. וְאֵין כָּל־חֲזָקָה וַחֲזָקָה צְרִיכָה שְׁנֵי עֵדִים. וְכָה כָּל־סִימָן וְסִימָן צָרִיךְ שְׁנֵי עֵדִים.

[87]Rebbi Abba in the name of Rebbi Jeremiah. The same holds for testimony regarding signs. In that case, it is obvious if one says, I saw two hairs on his back and the other says, I saw two hairs on his back. If one says, I saw one hair on his back and the other says, I saw one hair on his belly, that is nothing; similarly on his back and on his back. If two say, we

saw one hair on his back and two others say, we saw one hair on his belly? Rebbi Yose ben Rebbi Abun and Rebbi Hoshaia ben Rebbi Shammai, one said, it is invalid, but the other said, it is valid. He who saysid it is invalid considers him as one who testifies to half a sign. He who said it is valid? Maybe they were rubbed off. One says, I saw two hairs on his back and one says, I saw two hairs on his belly. Rebbi Abba said, everybody agrees that this is valid [testimony]. Rebbi Haggai said, everybody agrees that this is invalid. Rebbi Yose said, this is in disagreement. Rebbi Yose said to Rebbi Haggai, does not Rebbi Yudan[89] follow my opinion? He answered, I am disagreeing with his teacher, so much more with him. Rebbi Mana said, Rebbi Haggai was correct. If a document was signed by four witnesses and it was disputed, if one person verified the signature of two [witnesses] and another that of the other two, is that worth anything? Does not every single signature need two witnesses? And here, every single hair needs two witnesses. Rebbi Hanania learns it from the years of possession. If one [witness] testified that he ate from the property the first, second, and third years and another [witness] testified that he ate from it the fourth, fifth, and sixth, is that worth anything[71]? Does not every single year need two witnesses? And here, ever single hair needs two witnesses.

89   The statement of R. Yudan is in   the text in *Soṭah*, missing here.

(fol. 26a) **משנה ח:** הָאִשָּׁה שֶׁאָמְרָה אֵשֶׁת אִישׁ הָיִיתִי וּגְרוּשָׁה אֲנִי נֶאֱמֶנֶת שֶׁהַפֶּה שֶׁאָסַר הוּא הַפֶּה שֶׁהִתִּיר. וְאִם יֵשׁ עֵדִים שֶׁהִיא אֵשֶׁת אִישׁ וְהִיא אוֹמֶרֶת גְּרוּשָׁה אֲנִי אֵינָהּ נֶאֱמֶנֶת.

Mishnah 5: If a woman said, I was married but I am divorced[90], she is to be trusted, since the mouth which forbade is the mouth which permits. But if there are witnesses that she is married and she says, I am divorced, she is not trustworthy[91].

90 She is new in the community and produces no divorce document.

91 If the witnesses know of her marriage but do not know of her divorce, she has to prove her assertion; in the meantime she is treated as legally married and cannot remarry.

(26c line 44) **הלכה ה**: הָאִשָּׁה שֶׁאָמְרָה אֵשֶׁת אִישׁ הָיִיתִי כול'. תַּנֵּי. אִם מִשֶּׁנִּישֵּׂאת בָּאוּ עֵדִים הֲרֵי זוֹ לֹא תֵצֵא. רַב חוּנָא וְרִבִּי חֲנִינָה תְּרֵיהוֹן אָמְרִין. לֹא סוֹף דָּבָר מִשֶּׁנִּישֵּׂאת אֶלָּא אֲפִילוּ הִתִּירוּהָ בֵּית דִּין לְהִינָּשֵׂא. כְּהָדָא. חָדָא אִיתְּיָא אֲתָת לְגַבֵּי רִבִּי יוֹחָנָן אָמְרָה לֵיהּ. אֵשֶׁת אִישׁ הָיִיתִי וּגְרוּשָׁה אֲנִי. וְהִתִּירוּהָ. מִן דְּנַפְקַת אָמְרִין לֵיהּ. רִבִּי. הֲרֵי עִידֶיהָ בְּלוֹד. אָמַר. כָּךְ אֲנִי אוֹמֵר. אֲפִילוּ עִידֶיהָ בקסוסנון תַּמְתִּין. אָמַר רִבִּי יוֹסֵי בַּר בּוּן. תְּרֵין עוּבְדִין הֲווֹן. אֶחָד אָמְרִין לֵיהּ. הֲרֵי עִידֶיהָ בְּלוֹד. וְאֶחָד אָמְרִין לֵיהּ. הֲרֵי עִידֶיהָ בְּקַסְרִין. וְכֵן הֲוָה. אֲמַר לוֹן. כָּךְ אוֹמֵר אֲנִי. אֲפִילוּ עִידֶיהָ בקסוסנון תַּמְתִּין.

Halakhah 5: "If a woman said, I was married," etc. It was stated: If the witnesses came after she remarried, she should not leave[92]. Rav Huna and Rebbi Hanina both say, not only after she remarried but even after the court authorized her to remarry[93]. As the following: A woman came to Rebbi Johanan and said to him, I was married but I am divorced, and he permitted her. After she left, they said to him, are not her witnesses at Lod[94]? He said, so I am saying: Should she wait even if her witnesses are at קסוסנון[95]? Rebbi Yose bar Rebbi Abun said, there were two cases. In one case, they said to him, are not her witnesses at Lod? In the other case, they said to him, are not her witnesses at Caesarea[96]? And so it was!

He said to them, so I am saying: Should she wait even if her witnesses are at קסוסנון?

92   Her second marriage should not be dissolved.

93   In the Babli, 23a, this is a statement of Samuel's father, of the generation of transition between Tannaïm and Amoraïm.

94   She said that she had been married at Lod. Therefore, it would be possible to check her out by sending for witnesses from Lod.

95   In the *editio princeps*, the spelling is קסוסנין. (Perhaps cf. Greek κασαυρεῖον, τό, also κασώριον, "brothel", with assimilation of σ from Greek ρ. The implication is that witnesses in any case would not be considered [E. G.].)

96   Caesarea Philippi, much closer to Tiberias than Lod in the South.

(26c line 52) רִבִּי יוּדָן בְּעָא. אֵשֶׁת אִישׁ הָיִיתִי וְנִתְגָּרַשְׁתִּי בְּמָקוֹם פְּלוֹנִי. וּבָאוּ שְׁנַיִם וְאָמְרוּ. לֹא נִתְגָּרְשָׁה אִשָּׁה בְּמָקוֹם פְּלוֹנִי. מַכְחִישִׁין הֵן אוֹתָהּ. רִבִּי יוֹסֵי בְּעָא. אָמְרָה. אֵשֶׁת אִישׁ הָיִיתִי וְנִתְגָּרַשְׁתִּי בְּמָקוֹם פְּלוֹנִי בְּאוֹתוֹ הַיּוֹם. וּבָאוּ וְאָמְרוּ. נִתְגָּרְשָׁה אִשָּׁה בְּמָקוֹם פְּלוֹנִי. וּבָאוּ שְׁנַיִם וְאָמְרוּ. לֹא נִתְגָּרְשָׁה אִשָּׁה בְּמָקוֹם פְּלוֹנִי. בְּהַכְחִישׁ עֵדוּת בְּתוֹךְ עֵדוּת אָנוּ כְּחַיִּין מִפִּיהָ.

Rebbi Yudan asked: "I had been married but I was divorced at place X"; if two [witnesses] come and say, no woman was divorced at place X, do they contradict her[97]? Rebbi Yose asked, if she said, I had been married but I was divorced at place X at a certain date," and two came and said, a woman was divorced at that place[98], but two [others] came and said, no woman was divorced at that place? That is a contradiction of the essence of the testimony; we live off her mouth.

97   No answer is given. The Babli (23a) notes, "'we did not see' is no proof." There are divorces done in privacy, and this kind of negative testimony is inadmissible. The reluctance of the Yerushalmi to decide

here is understandable; it may be that the correct spelling of the place in question had not been established and a divorce document is invalid if the names of the persons or of the place are incorrect. (For example, the Jewish community in Basel, Switzerland, was founded by Jews from Alsatia and until after 1918 all divorces were executed in old established Alsatian communities. When it was found necessary to perform divorces in Basel, the problem arose whether to write the name of the city as באזעל following the rules of Western Yiddish in which /a/ = א, /e/ = ע, or באזל since the /e/ is almost inaudible in local speech. The problem had to be settled by an outside expert in the writing of divorce documents.)

98 But they have no direct knowledge of the specific case in question.

(26c line 63) הַיוֹם אָמְרָה. אֵשֶׁת אִישׁ הָיִיתִי. וּלְמָחָר אָמְרָה. גְּרוּשָׁה אֲנִי. אָמְרִינָן לָהּ. אֶתְמוֹל אָמְרַתְּ אָכֵין וְיוֹם דֵּין אָכֵין. אָמְרָה לוֹן. מִפְּנֵי כַּת שֶׁלִּפְרִיצִים שֶׁהָיוּ בָאִין לְהִזְדַּוֵּוג לִי. רִבִּי אָבִין בְּשֵׁם רִבִּי אִילָא. מִכֵּיוָן שֶׁהֵבִיאָה מַתְלָא לִדְבָרֶיהָ נֶאֱמֶנֶת. כְּהָדָא. שְׁמוּאֵל בָּאָה אִיזְדְּקוּקֵי לְאִיתְּתֵיהּ. אָמְרָה לֵיהּ. טְמֵיאָה אֲנִי. לִמְחָר אָמְרָה לֵיהּ. טְהוֹרָה אֲנִי. אֲמַר לָהּ. אֶתְמוֹל אָמְרַתְּ טְמֵיאָה וְיוֹמָא דֵין טְהוֹרָה. אָמְרָה לֵיהּ. לָא הֲוָה בְחֵיילִי הַיי שַׁתָּא. אָתָא שָׁאַל לְרַב. אֲמַר לֵיהּ. מִכֵּיוָן שֶׁהֵבִיאָה מַתְלָא לִדְבָרֶיהָ נֶאֱמֶנֶת.

One day, she said, I am married. The next day, she said, I am divorced. We asked her, yesterday you said this, today you say otherwise? She said to them, because of a group of amoral people who wanted to start up with me[99]. Rebbi Abun in the name of Rebbi Ila: Since she provided an explanation for her words, she can be believed[100]. A similar case: Samuel wanted to sleep with his wife, but she said to him, I am impure[101]. The next day, she said, I am pure. He said to her, yesterday, you said impure, today pure? She said to him, I did not feel well enough at that moment. He came and asked Rav, who told him, since she provided an explanation for her words, she can be believed[102].

99 She needed the protection given in society to married women.

100 In the Babli, 22a, the case and its resolution is tannaïtic, attributed to the Sages of the court at Usha (probably under Antoninus Pius).

101 And therefore forbidden for an additional 10 days.

102 In the Babli, 22a/b, Samuel accepted the ruling for everybody except himself; cf. Tosaphot 22b, *s. v.* ואפילו.

(fol. 26a) **משנה ו:** הָאִשָּׁה שֶׁאָמְרָה נִשְׁבֵּיתִי וּטְהוֹרָה אֲנִי נֶאֱמֶנֶת שֶׁהַפֶּה שֶׁאָסַר הוּא הַפֶּה שֶׁהִתִּיר. וְאִם יֵשׁ עֵדִים שֶׁנִּשְׁבֵּית וְהִיא אוֹמֶרֶת טְהוֹרָה אֲנִי אֵינָהּ נֶאֱמֶנֶת. וְאִם מִשֶּׁנִּשֵּׂאת בָּאוּ עֵדִים לֹא תֵצֵא.

Mishnah 6: If a woman said, I was kidnapped[103] but I am pure, she is to be trusted, since the mouth which forbade is the mouth which permits. But if there are witnesses that she was kidnapped and she says, I am pure, she is not trustworthy. If the witnesses came after she was married, she should not leave[104].

103 Even if a woman is held for ransom, it is assumed that her Gentile kidnapper raped her and that, therefore, she is forbidden to marry a Cohen.

104 If she is married to a Cohen, he does not have to divorce her.

(26c line 70) **הלכה ו:** הָאִשָּׁה שֶׁאָמְרָה נִשְׁבֵּיתִי כוּל'. רַב חוּנָא אָמַר. לֹא סוֹף דָּבָר שֶׁנִּישֵּׂאת אֶלָּא אֲפִילוּ הִתִּירוּהָ בֵית דִּין לְהִינָּשֵׂא.

Halakhah 6: "If a woman said, I was kidnapped," etc. Rav Huna said, not only after she remarried but even after the court authorized her to remarry[93].

(26c line 71) נָשִׁים נִשְׁבּוּ לְשָׁם. אָתָא עוֹבְדָא קוֹמֵי אַבָּא בַר בָּא וְלֵוִי וּשְׁמוּאֵל אָמְרוּ. וּמָסְרוּ לָהֶן עֵדִים נִיסְקוּן לְאַרְעָא דְיִשְׂרָאֵל. אָמַר לֵיהּ. וּמָה נַעֲשָׂה לַיָּמִים הָרִאשׁוֹנִים שֶׁנִּתְיַיחֲדוּ. אָמַר לֵיהּ אַבָּא בַר בָּא. אִילּוּ הֲוַיִין בְּנָתָךְ כֵּן הָיִיתָה אוֹמֵר. וְאִישְׁתַּבְּבִיָין בְּנָתֵיהּ דִּשְׁמוּאֵל כִּשְׁגָנָה שֶׁיּוֹצָא מִלִּפְנֵי הַשַּׁלִּיט. כַּד סַלְקוֹן לְהָכָא סַלְקָן שָׁבְיָין עִמְּהוֹן. עֲלִין קוֹמֵי רִבִּי חֲנִינָה אוֹקְמִינָן שָׁבְיָין מִלְּבָר. אָמְרִין לֵיהּ. נִשְׁבֵּינוּ וּטְהוֹרוֹת אָנוּ. וְהִתִּירָן. מִן דְּנַפְקָן שְׁלָחוּן שָׁבְיָין עֲלֵין אָמַר. נִיכָּרוֹת אִילוּ שֶׁבְּנוֹת חָכָם הֵן. מִן דְּאִיתוּ דְּעִין מָאן הַוְיָן אָמְרִין לְשִׁמְעוֹן בַּר בָּא. אִיטְפַּל בִּקְרִיבָתָךְ. נְסַב לְקַדְמִיתָא וּמִיתַת. לְתִנְיָינָא וּמִיתַת. לָמָּה. בְּגִין דְּשָׁקְרוֹן. חַס וְשָׁלוֹם. לָא שָׁקְרוֹן. אֶלָּא מִן חַטָּאת דַּחֲנַנְיָה בֶּן אֲחִי רִבִּי יְהוֹשֻׁעַ שֶׁעִיבֵּר אֶת הַשָּׁנָה בְּחוּצָה לָאָרֶץ.

[105]Women were kidnapped and brought there[106]. The case came before Abba bar Abba[107], and Samuel. They ordered and gave them over to chaperones who were to return them to the Land of Israel. He[108] said to him[107]: What did we do for the earlier times when they were alone with them? Abba bar Abba said to him, would you say so if they were your daughters? Samuel's daughters were kidnapped, "like an error which comes from the ruler"[109]. When they were brought here, their kidnappers came with them. They came before Rebbi Ḥanina and left their kidnappers outside. They said to him, we were kidnapped but we are pure[110]. He permitted them. After they left, their kidnappers sent after them[111]. He said, it is obvious that these are the daughters of a Sage. When they came to know who they were, they said to Simeon bar Abba[112], take care of your relatives. He married the first one, but she died. The second one and she died. Why? Because they lied? God forbid, they did not lie. But because of the sin of Ḥanania, Rebbi Joshua's nephew, who intercalated the year outside the Land[113].

105 The entire Halakhah is reproduced in the Babli, 23a.

106 To Nahardea in Babylonia.

107 Samuel's father.

108 Samuel.

109 *Eccl.* 10:5. From the story of another daughter of Samuel, Rachel, who was kidnapped and raped during the destruction of Nahardea by a soldier of Odenathus who later converted and married her, it seems that one has to date this at 259 C.E., after Samuel's death.

110 Speaking Hebrew, they made it clear that they were educated.

111 To collect the redemption money from the Jewish community of Sepphoris.

112 A relative of Samuel and a Cohen.

113 He was the founder of the Academy of Nahardea and the ancestor of its leaders, Abba bar Abba and Samuel. He validly intercalated years during the war of Bar Kokhba but tried to hold on to his prerogative after the patriarchate was re-established; cf. *Nedarim* 6:13, Notes 118-129, Babli *Berakhot* 63a.

The last sentences of this paragraph have no parallel in the Babli.

(fol. 26a) **משנה ז**: שְׁתֵּי נָשִׁים שֶׁנִּשְׁבּוּ זֹאת אוֹמֶרֶת טְהוֹרָה אֲנִי וְזֹאת אוֹמֶרֶת טְהוֹרָה אֲנִי אֵינָן נֶאֱמָנוֹת. וּבִזְמַן שֶׁהֵן מְעִידוֹת זוֹ אֶת זוֹ נֶאֱמָנוֹת.

Mishnah 7: Two women who were kidnapped[114] and each one of them says I am pure, are not trustworthy. But if they testify one for the other they can be trusted[115].

114 This was known before the testimony.

115 In order to help kidnap victims, one admitted the testimony of a single witness. The Mishnah notes that this is true even if one would suspect that they do this in order to help one another.

משנה ח: וְכֵן שְׁנֵי אֲנָשִׁים. זֶה אוֹמֵר כֹּהֵן אֲנִי וְזֶה אוֹמֵר כֹּהֵן אֲנִי אֵינָן נֶאֱמָנִין. וּבִזְמַן שֶׁהֵן מְעִידִים זֶה אֶת זֶה נֶאֱמָנִים.

Mishnah 8: Similarly, if of two men each one says that he is a Cohen, the cannot be trusted. But if they testify for one another, they can be trusted[116].

116 This follows the opinion stated in the next Mishnah that the testimony of a single witness suffices to enable a person to receive heave and other gifts to the priesthood.

(26d line 1) **הלכה ח**: וְכֵן שְׁנֵי אֲנָשִׁים כול'. רִבִּי חִייָה בְּשֵׁם רִבִּי יוֹחָנָן. מַתְנִיתִין לְעִנְייָן קָדְשֵׁי הַגְּבוּל. אֲבָל לְעִנְייָן מִשְׁפָּחָה וּלְקוֹדְשֵׁי הַמִּזְבֵּחַ צָרִיךְ שְׁנֵי עֵדִים. וְהָא תַנֵּי. מַעֲלִין לִכְהוּנָּה לִלְוייָה לְיִשְׂרָאֵל עַל פִּי עֵד אֶחָד. נִיחָא לִכְהוּנָּה לִלְוייָה. לְיִשְׂרָאֵל וְלֹא לְעִנְייָן מִשְׁפָּחָה. לִיתֵּן לוֹ מַעֲשֵׂר עָנִי.

Halakhah 8: "Similarly, if of two men," etc. Rebbi Ḥiyya in the name of Rebbi Joḥanan: The Mishnah is valid for countryside sanctified food[117]. But for family matters and the sanctified food of the altar[118] one needs two witnesses. But was it not stated[119]: One raises to priesthood, levitic status, or Israel, by the testimony of one witness. One understands priesthood and levitic status. But the status of an Israel[120]? Is that not regarding family status[121]? To give him the tithe of the poor[122].

117 Heave and *Ḥallah*. In the Babli, 24a, that is a tannaïtic statement.

118 In fact, Mishnah *Qiddušin* 4:4 requires a check on the families of bride and groom for several generations to ascertain that no ancestor is a bastard or desecrated.

119 Tosephta 2:3. The Tosephta continues: But one demotes only on the testimony of two witnesses.

120 What privileges accrue only to an Israel?

121 This would imply that the family status of a Cohen as entitled to

serve in the Temple also could be proven by a single witness.

122 But family status depends on two witnesses. This means that, even if the Temple is rebuilt, it cannot be staffed until either seamless documentary proof is found for some priestly families that their direct ancestors served in the Temple and none of them in the intervening time married an unsuitable woman, or that the immortal Prophet Elijah comes to indicate which Cohanim pass muster.

(26d line 4) שְׁתֵּי חֲזָקוֹת לִכְהוּנָּה בָּאָרֶץ יִשְׂרָאֵל נְשִׂיאוּת כַּפַּיִם וְחִילוּק גְּרָנוֹת וּבְסוּרְיָה נְשִׂיאוּת כַּפַּיִם אֲבָל לֹא חִילוּק גְּרָנוֹת. עַד מָקוֹם שֶׁשְּׁלוּחֵי הַחוֹדֶשׁ מַגִּיעִין עַד נְמִרִין וּבָבֶל כְּסוּרְיָה. רַבִּי שִׁמְעוֹן בֶּן אֶלְעָזָר אוֹמֵר. אַף בָּאֲלַכְּסַנְדְּרִיאָה בְּשָׁעָה שֶׁבָּתֵּי דִּינָיו יוֹשְׁבִין שָׁם. תַּנֵּי רַבָּן שִׁמְעוֹן בֶּן גַּמְלִיאֵל. כְּשֵׁם שֶׁהַתְּרוּמָה חֲזָקָה לִכְהוּנָּה כָּךְ מַעֲשֵׂר רִאשׁוֹן חֲזָקָה לִכְהוּנָּה. וְהַחוֹלֵק עַל פִּי בֵית דִּין אֵינָהּ חֲזָקָה לִכְהוּנָּה. אֲנִי אוֹמֵר. תְּרוּמָה נָפְלָה לוֹ מֵאֲבִי אִמּוֹ כֹהֵן.

[123]"In the Land of Israel there are two legal claims to priestly status, the priestly blessings[124] and the distribution from the threshing floor[125]. In Syria[126], priestly blessings but not distribution from the threshing floor[127]. Up to the place where the messengers for the New Moon arrive, up to Nimerin[128]. Babylonia is like Syria. Rebbi Simeon ben Eleazar says, also in Alexandria in the time when regular courts are sitting there[129]. Rabban Simeon ben Gamliel stated: Just as heave establishes a legal claim to priesthood, so First Tithe establishes a legal claim to priesthood[130]. If somebody gives his heave to the court to distribute he has no legal claim to priesthood;" I am saying that the heave came to him from his mother's father, a Cohen.

123 Tosephta 3:1; most of it also in *Peah* 4:6; Babli *Ketubot* 25a, 26a.

124 If somebody is admitted to recite the priestly blessings in the synagogue, it must be that the rabbinic authority at that place found him

125 Since a point can be made that heave and *ḥallah* in the Land of Israel are biblical obligations, the rabbinic authorities would not empower a man to receive heave unless they checked his credentials.

126 The land ruled over by David outside the biblical borders of the Land; cf. *Peah* 7:6, Note 119.

127 Since heave cannot be a biblical obligation in Syria, nobody checks eligibility there.

128 A distance of 14 days' walk from Jerusalem, cf. Mishnah *Roš Haššanah* 1:3-4. (The place of Nimerin has not been determined, cf. *Ševi'it* 6:1, Note 50; it could be biblical *Bet Nimra* (*Jos.* 13:27) in the territory of the tribe of Gad in Gilead.)

129 As long as the Jews of Alexandria enjoyed a certain autonomy, before the revolt against Trajan.

130 In the Tosephta: "for Levitic status." The text of the Yerushalmi is also that of the Babli, 26a. It is appropriate for the Babli, which reserves the First Tithe to priests, against the biblical rules. It is not appropriate for the Yerushalmi which assigns tithes to the Levites, but to priests only in their quality of Levites (cf. *Ma'aśer Šeni* 5:5, Notes 88-89.) One has to assume a copyist's error; in the absence of parallel sources this cannot be confirmed.

(26d line 10) אָמַר רִבִּי יִשְׁמָעֵאל בֵּירִבִּי יוֹסֵי. מִיָּמַיי לֹא הֵעַדְתִּי עֵדוּת. וּפַעַם אַחַת הֵיעַדְתִּי וְהֶעֱלֵיתִי עֶבֶד לִכְהוּנָה. רִבִּי יִצְחָק חֲקוּלָה וְרִבִּי שִׁמְעוֹן בְּרִבִּי. חַד הֶעֱלָה אָח מִפִּי אָחִיו וְחָרְנָה הֶעֱלָה בֵן מִפִּי אָבִיו. חַד לִכְהוּנָה וְחַד לִלְוָיָה. חַד בַּר נַשׁ אֲתָא לְגַבֵּי דְרִבִּי אִילָא. אָמַר לֵיהּ. בְּנִי הוּא זֶה וְכֹהֵן הוּא. אָמַר לֵיהּ. בִּנְךָ הוּא וְאֵינוֹ כֹהֵן. אָמַר לֵיהּ רִבִּי חִייָה רוּבָּה. אִם מַאֲמִינוּ אַתְּ שֶׁהוּא בְנוֹ הַאֲמִינוֹ שֶׁהוּא כֹהֵן. וְאִם אֵין אַתְּ מַאֲמִינוּ שֶׁהוּא בְנוֹ אַל תַּאֲמִינוּ שֶׁהוּא כֹהֵן. אָמַר לוֹ. בְּנוֹ הוּא אֶלָּא אֲנִי אוֹמֵר. בֶּן גְּרוּשָׁה הוּא אוֹ בֶן חֲלוּצָה הוּא. אָמַר רִבִּי אָבִין. אָכֵין אָמַר לֵיהּ. אִם מַאֲמִינוּ אַתְּ שֶׁהוּא בְנוֹ הַאֲמִינוּ שֶׁהוּא כֹהֵן. וְאִם אֵין אַתְּ מַאֲמִינוּ שֶׁהוּא כֹהֵן אַל תַּאֲמִינוּ שֶׁהוּא בְנוֹ. וְיֵיעָשֶׂה כְּהַרְחֵק עֵדוּת וִיהֵא נֶאֱמָן עָלָיו. אָמַר לֵיהּ. בְּנוֹ הוּא אֶלָּא אֲנִי אוֹמֵר. בֶּן גְּרוּשָׁה וַחֲלוּצָה הוּא.

HALAKHAH 8

לֹא כֵן אָמְרוּ. רִבִּי יִצְחָק חֲקוּלָה וְרִבִּי שִׁמְעוֹן בֶּרְבִּי. חַד הֶעֱלָה אָח מִפִּי אָחִיו וְחָרָנָה הֶעֱלָה בֶּן מִפִּי אָבִיו. נֵימָא. מִשֶּׁהֶעֱלָה רִבִּי אָח מִפִּי אָחִיו. אֲפִילוּ תֵימָא בֶּן מִפִּי אָבִיו. לַלְוִיָּה.

Rebbi Ismael ben Rebbi Yose said, I never testified except once, when I raised a slave to priestly status[131]. Rebbi Isaac Ḥaqula and Rebbi Simeon ben Rebbi, one raised a brother on the testimony of his brother, the other a son on the testimony of his father; one to the priesthood, the other to levitic status[132]. A person came before Rebbi Hila[133]; he said to him, this is my son[134] and he is a Cohen. He answered him, he is your son but he is no Cohen[135]. Rebbi Ḥiyya the elder said to him, if you believe him that he is his son, believe him that he is a Cohen. If you do not believe him that he is his son, do not believe him that he is a Cohen. He answered, he is his son but I say that he is the son of a divorcee or one who had performed *haliṣah*[136]. Rebbi Abin said, so he said to him: If you believe him that he is his son, believe him that he is a Cohen. If you do not believe him that he is a Cohen, do not believe him that he is his son. In that case, he would be unrelated and trustworthy in his testimony![137] He answered, he is his son but I say that he is the son of a divorcee or one who had performed *haliṣah*. Did they not say, Rebbi Isaac Ḥaqula and Rebbi Simeon ben Rebbi, one raised a brother on the testimony of his brother, the other a son on the testimony of his father[138]? Let us say that Rebbi[139] elevated a brother on the testimony of his brother. You may even say, a son on the testimony of his father, to levitic status[140].

131 This disproves the Tosephta, that receiving heave is a sign of priestly status since all members of a Cohen's household, including his slaves, are entitled to eat heave. In the Babli, 28b, the problem is connected with a

dispute between R. Jehudah and R. Yose on whether a slave is entitled to receive heave from any person other than his master.

In the Babli, 28b, the story is transferred to his brother, R. Eleazar ben R. Yose, and is explained away.

132 The problems raised here are explained at the end of the paragraph. In the Babli, 25b, the actors are Rebbi and the elder R. Ḥiyya.

133 In the Babli, 25b, the discussion is theoretical and put into the mouths of Rebbi and the elder R. Ḥiyya. Here, it is reported as an actual case. There is something wrong with the tradition of names here. If the case was before R. Hila, the opponent must be R. Ḥiyya bar Abba, his fellow-student before R. Joḥanan. If the opponent is the elder R. Ḥiyya, the case must be before Rebbi.

134 From an extramarital relationship, otherwise he would not need confirmation as an heir by the court.

135 He is accorded all rights of inheritance (and cannot marry his close relatives from his father's side) but he cannot act as a priest.

136 Following R. Joshua in Chapter 1, the court is obligated to think the worst of an extramarital relationship unless proven wrong.

137 Since we said that one witness is enough to establish a title to priesthood, if the man is not his father, he could testify that the child is a Cohen (which by R. Ḥiyya's argument would make the man his father and disqualified from testifying.)

138 If the brother was a full brother, there is no problem. In the Babli, it was R. Ḥiyya who elevated a man to levitic status by the testimony of a (paternal half-)brother, since for Levites the status of the mother is irrelevant (as long as she is Jewish and not a bastard.)

139 It seems that a name is missing here under the influence of the Babli.

140 Cf. Note 128. In the Babli, the cases are switched.

(fol. 26a) **משנה ט**: רִבִּי יְהוּדָה אוֹמֵר אֵין מַעֲלִין לַכְּהוּנָּה עַל פִּי עֵד אֶחָד. אָמַר רִבִּי אֶלְעָזָר אֵימָתַי בְּמָקוֹם שֶׁיֵּשׁ עוֹרְרִין אֲבָל בְּמָקוֹם שֶׁאֵין עוֹרְרִין מַעֲלִין

לִכְהוּנָה עַל פִּי עֵד אֶחָד. רַבָּן שִׁמְעוֹן בֶּן גַּמְלִיאֵל אוֹמֵר מִשּׁוּם רַבִּי שִׁמְעוֹן בֶּן הַסְּגָן מַעֲלִין לַכְּהוּנָה עַל פִּי עֵד אֶחָד.

Mishnah 9: Rebbi Jehudah says, one does not elevate to the priesthood by the testimony of one witness. Rebbi Eleazar said, when is this? If there are protesters[141]; but if there are no protesters, one elevates to the priesthood by the testimony of one witness. Rabban Simeon ben Gamliel says in the name of Rebbi Simeon, the son of the second in command[142], that one elevates to the priesthood by the testimony of one witness.

141 They claim that the person's mother was disqualified to marry into the priesthood.
142 The executive officer of the Temple, who must have known the practice of the Temple Court which had to certify priests to be admitted to the service.

(26d line 24) **הלכה ט**: רַבִּי יְהוּדָה אוֹמֵר אֵין מַעֲלִין כול׳. רַבִּי חִיָּיה בְּשֵׁם רַבִּי יוֹחָנָן. אֵין עִרְעֵר פָּחוֹת מִשְּׁנַיִם. רַבִּי בּוּן בַּר חִיָּיה בְּעָא. מָה אֲנָן קַיָּימִין. אִם בְּשֶׁהֶעֱלוּ אוֹתוֹ בְּאֶחָד יוֹרִידוּ אוֹתוֹ בְּאֶחָד. וְאִם בְּשֶׁהֶעֱלוּ אוֹתוֹ בִּשְׁנַיִם אֲפִילוּ כַּמָּה לֹא יוֹרִידוּ אוֹתוֹ. אָמַר רַבִּי הוּנָה. אַתְיָיא כְרַבָּנִין דְּתַמָּן. בְּרַם כְּרַבָּנִין דְּהָכָא וּכְרַב נַחְמָן בַּר יַעֲקֹב. כְּשֵׁם שֶׁמַּעֲלִין אוֹתוֹ בִּשְׁנַיִם כָּךְ מוֹרִידִין אוֹתוֹ בִּשְׁנַיִם.

Halakhah 9: "Rebbi Jehudah says, one does not elevate," etc. Rebbi Hiyya in the name of Rebbi Johanan: A complaint needs at least two [plaintiffs][143]. Rebbi Abun bar Hiyya asked, how do we hold? If they elevated him on the testimony of one person, they should demote him on the testimony of one person. If they elevated him on the testimony of two persons, even if there are many [opposed] they should not demote him[144]! Rebbi Huna said, it follows the rabbis there[145]. But following the rabbis here and Rav Nahman bar Jacob[146], just as one elevates him on the testimony of two persons, one demotes him on the testimony of two persons.

143 Babli, 26a. The court will not listen to a claim that the person is the son of a disqualified mother unless confirmed by at least two independent witnesses.

144 Since two witnesses confirm a fact by biblical standards, they are as weighty as any number of witnesses.

145 Cf. Note 41; to cancel an action of the court, they require full testimony.

146 Note 39.

(fol. 26a) **משנה י**: הָאִשָּׁה שֶׁנֶּחְבְּשָׁה בִּידֵי גוֹיִם עַל יְדֵי מָמוֹן מוּתֶּרֶת לְבַעֲלָהּ עַל יְדֵי נְפָשׁוֹת אֲסוּרָה לְבַעֲלָהּ. עִיר שֶׁכְּבָשָׁהּ כַּרְקוֹם כָּל־הַכֹּהֲנוֹת שֶׁנִּמְצְאוּ בְתוֹכָהּ פְּסוּלוֹת וְאִם יֵשׁ עֵדִים אֲפִילוּ עֶבֶד אֲפִילוּ שִׁפְחָה הֲרֵי אֵילוּ נֶאֱמָנִין שֶׁאֵין אָדָם נֶאֱמָן עַל יְדֵי עַצְמוֹ. אָמַר רִבִּי זְכַרְיָה בֶּן הַקַּצָּב הַמָּעוֹן הַזֶּה לֹא זָזָה יָדָהּ מִיָּדִי מִשָּׁעָה שֶׁנִּכְנְסוּ הַגּוֹיִם לִירוּשָׁלֶם וְעַד שֶׁיָּצְאוּ. אָמְרוּ לוֹ אֵין אָדָם מֵעִיד עַל עַצְמוֹ.

Mishnah 10: A woman who was jailed by Gentiles, if because of money matters, she is permitted to her husband[147]; if because of criminal matters, she is prohibited to her husband[148]. If a city was conquered after a siege[149], all wives of priests in it are disqualified[150]; but if they have witnesses, even a slave, even a slave girl, those are trustworthy[151]; but[152] nobody is trustworthy about himself. Rebbi Zachariah, the son of the butcher[153], said, by the Temple! Her hand did not leave my hand from the moment the Gentiles entered Jerusalem until they left! They said to him, nobody testifies on his own behalf.

147 She is permitted to her Cohen husband since certainly she was not raped; the Gentiles who hold her for the payment of a debt would be afraid to have to pay the diminution of her value following a rape.

148 It is not clear whether this means that she is forbidden to her Cohen husband since she certainly would be raped, or even to her Israel husband since she would agree to sleep with one of her jailers who promised to save her.

149 Greek χαράκωμα "palisade".

150 Disqualified from eating heave and from living with their husbands.

151 The singular shows that a single witness is acceptable, even though first "witnesses" are mentioned.

152 This is one of the examples that שׁ may mean ו (cf. Mishnah *Beṣah* 1:2).

153 He was a Cohen.

(26d line 29) **הלכה י**: הָאִשָּׁה שֶׁנֶּחְבְּשָׁה בִּידֵי גוֹיִם כול׳. תַּמָּן תַּנֵּינָן. הֵעִיד רִבִּי יוֹסֵי הַכֹּהֵן וְרִבִּי זְכַרְיָה בֶּן הַקַּצָּב עַל תִּינוֹקֶת שֶׁהוּרְהֲנָה בְּאַשְׁקְלוֹן וְרִיחֲקוּהָ בְּנֵי מִשְׁפָּחָה. וְעֵידֶיהָ מְעִידִין אוֹתָהּ שֶׁלֹּא נִסְתְּרָה וְלֹא נִטְמָאָה. לְפִי שֶׁהָעֵדִים מְעִידִין אוֹתָהּ שֶׁלֹּא נִסְתְּרָה וְלֹא נִטְמָאָה. הָא אִם אֵין עֵידֶיהָ מְעִידִין אוֹתָהּ שֶׁלֹּא נִסְתְּרָה וְלֹא נִטְמָאָה לֹא. אָמַר רִבִּי לָעְזָר. שַׁנְיָיא הִיא בְּהֵירְהוֹן שֶׁהָרַבִּים נוֹהֲגִין לוֹ בְהֶתֵר.

Halakhah 10: "A woman who was jailed by Gentiles," etc. There, we have stated[154]: "Rebbi Yose the Cohen and Rebbi Zachariah the son of the butcher testified about a girl who was given as a pledge in Ascalon[155] and her family excluded her[156], but her witnesses testified that she never was in a secret place and was not impure." Because the witnesses testified that she never was in a secret place and was not impure; therefore, not if no witnesses testified that she never was in a secret place and was not impure[157]! Rebbi Eleazar said, there is a difference about a pledge, because many treat her as permitted[158].

154 Mishnah *Idiut* 8:2; quoted *in extenso* in the Babli, 26b/27a. The argument is about the part of the Mishnah not quoted here, that the Sages forced the family to accept her as marriageable by a Cohen.

155 That she could be sold as a slave if her parents did not pay their debt.

156 Declared her unfit to be married by a Cohen.

157 She was held for money, and according to the Mishnah should need no witnesses.

158 People assumed that ultimately she would be sold as a slave and, therefore, could be treated as such even beforehand. In the Babli, 27a, this explanation is offered by Rava (cf. Introduction to Tractate Yebamot, p. 6), but is rejected in that Talmud.

(26d line 35) עַל יְדֵי נְפָשׁוֹת אֲסוּרָה. רִבִּי יוּדָן בְּרֵיהּ דְּרַב חָמָא דִכְפַר תְּחֻמִין בְּשֵׁם חִזְקִיָּה. וְהוּא שֶׁנִּגְמַר דִּינָהּ לַהֲרִיגָה. רִבִּי יוֹחָנָן אָמַר. אֲפִילוּ לֹא נִגְמַר דִּינָהּ לַהֲרִיגָה. אָמְרִין בְּשֵׁם רִבִּי יוֹחָנָן. אֵשֶׁת לִיסְטִיס כְּלֵיסְטֵיס.

"If because of criminal matters she is prohibited." Rebbi Yudan the son of Rav Ḥama[159] from Kefar Teḥumim in the name of Ḥizqiah: Only if she was sentenced to death. Rebbi Joḥanan said, even if she was not sentenced to death[160]. They said in the name of Rebbi Joḥanan: A robber's wife is like a robber[161,162].

159 The title "Rav" is certainly suspect. He might be identical with Rebbi Ḥiyya from Kefar Teḥumim.

160 Their disagreement is confirmed

in the Babli, 27a.

161 Greek λῃστής.

162 In the Babli, this is Rav's opinion.

(26d line 38) אֵי זֶהוּ כַּרְקוֹם. רִבִּי בָּא בְּשֵׁם רַב חִיָּיה בַּר אַשִׁי. כְּגוֹן זוּגִין[163] וְשַׁלְשְׁלָיוֹת וּכְבָלִים וַאֲזִיקִים וְתַרְנְגוֹלִין וְאַפַּרְטוֹטוֹת מַקִּיפִין אֶת הָעִיר. וָמַר רִבִּי בָּא בְּשֵׁם רַב חָמָא בַּר אַשִׁי. מַעֲשֶׂה הָיָה וּבְרָחָה מִשָּׁם סוּמָה אַחַת. הָיָה שָׁם פִּירְצָה אַחַת מַצֶּלֶת אֶת הַכֹּל. הָיוּ שָׁם מַחְבּוּיִים צְרִיכָה. רִבִּי וְעִירָה רִבִּי בָּא בַּר

HALAKHAH 10

זַבְדָּא רִבִּי יִצְחָק בַּר חֲקוּלָה בְּשֵׁם רִבִּי יוּדָן נְשִׂיאָה. וּבִלְבַד בַּרְקוֹם שֶׁל אוֹתוֹ מַלְכוּת אֲבָל בַּרְקוֹם שֶׁלְּמַלְכוּת אַחֶרֶת כְּלֵיסְטֵיס הֵן.

What are palisades? Rebbi Abba in the name of Rav Ḥiyya bar Ashi: For examples if bells, chains, and ropes[164], and geese, and chickens and machinery[165] surround the town[166]. And Rebbi Abba in the name of Rav Ḥama[167] bar Ashi said, it happened that a blind woman was able to flee from there[168]. If there was one breach[169], it saves all. If there were hiding places, it is questionable[170]. Rebbi Ze'ira, Rebbi Abba bar Zavda, Rebbi Isaac bar Ḥaqula, in the name of Rebbi Yudan the prince: Only if there were palisades of that government[171]. But palisades from another government are like robbers.

163 From a parallel text in *Giṭṭin* 3:4 (45a l.4). The text here has the unexplained word דוגין.

164 Interpretation of Musaphia. The parallel text in *Giṭṭin* reads וְאִיסְטְרָטִיּוֹת *soldiery*.

165 In *Giṭṭin* כְּלָבִים "dogs". The same in the Babli, 27a.

166 The bells, geese, etc. shall make sure that nobody escapes.

167 Here certainly חמא is a mistake for חייה, cf. Note 159.

168 He questions the Mishnah. If a blind woman can escape a siege conducted so that nobody should escape, then everybody could escape and the fact that at the beginning of the siege the wife of a Cohen was in the town does not mean anything.

169 In the palisades surrounding the town.

170 It is undecided whether a woman can claim that she was in hiding and not a victim of the entering army.

171 The Mishnah speaks only of a revolt or a civil war, when the army is ordered to attack (and enslave) the civilian population. A conquering foreign army might plunder, but its soldiers are not under orders to rape all women. In the interpretation of Tosaphot (*s. v.* כאן), the same statement appears in the Babli, 27a, in the name of Ḥizqiah.

(26d line 44) וַאֲפִילוּ קָטָן. רִבִּי אִימִּי בְשֵׁם רִבִּי יְהוֹשֻׁעַ בֶּן לֵוִי. אֲפִילוּ קָטָן אֲפִילוּ קָרוֹב. אֲפִילוּ קָטָן וְקָרוֹב. נִישְׁמְעִינָהּ מִן הָדָא. חֲנַנְיָה קַרְתִּיסָיָה אִשְׁתַּבָּאי הוּא וּבְנֵיהּ וְאִיתְּתֵיהּ. אֲתוֹן לְגַבֵּי רִבִּי חֲנִינָה וְלָא קִבְּלוֹן. אֲתוֹן לְגַבֵּי רִבִּי יְהוֹשֻׁעַ בֶּן לֵוִי וְקִבְּלוֹן. הָדָא אָמְרָה אֲפִילוּ קָטָן וְקָרוֹב.

And even a minor. Rebbi Immi in the name of Rebbi Joshua ben Levi: Even a minor, even a relative. Even an underage relative? Let us hear from the following: Ḥananiah from Cartes[172] was kidnapped, he, his son, and his wife. They came before Rebbi Ḥanina who did not receive them. They came before Rebbi Joshua ben Levi who received them[173]. This implies, even an underage relative.

172 In the parallel in the Babli, 27b, the story is told by a R. Ḥanina from Carthage (or Carthagena).

173 He let the husband, a Cohen, stay married to his wife on the testimony of his own underage son.

The Babli disagrees, 27b, and admits the testimony of children and family slaves only if given spontaneously, without being asked; certainly not in the court of a rabbi.

(26d line 51) רִבִּי חִייָה בַּר יוֹסֵף שָׁלַח בָּתַר אִיתְּתֵיהּ. אָמַר. יִסְקוּן עִמָּהּ תְּלָתָא תַּלְמִידִין. שֶׁאִם יַפְנֶה אֶחָד מֵהֶן לְצוֹרְכוֹ תִּתְיָיחֵד עִם שְׁנַיִם. וְהָא תַּנִּינָן. מוֹסְרִין לוֹ שְׁנֵי תַלְמִידֵי חֲכָמִים שֶׁמָּא יָבוֹא עָלֶיהָ בַּדֶּרֶךְ. אָמַר רִבִּי אָבִין. וּבַעֲלָהּ. הֲרֵי שְׁלֹשָׁה. אַף הוּא שָׂכַר לָהּ בַּיִת וְהוּא מַעֲלֶה לָהּ מְזוֹנוֹת וְלֹא הָיָה מִתְיָיחֵד עִמָּהּ אֶלָּא בִּפְנֵי בָנֶיהָ. וְקָרָא עַל עַצְמוֹ הַפָּסוּק הַזֶּה יָגַעְתִּי בְאַנְחָתִי וּמְנוּחָה לֹא מָצָאתִי.

1 תלתא | ס תלת   2 מוסרין | ס ומוסרין   4 והוא | ס והיה

[173]Rebbi Ḥiyya bar Yosef sent after his wife. He said, three students should accompany her, so that if one has to absent himself for his needs, she should still be with two of them. But did we not state: "And they

give him two scholars to prevent him from sleeping with her on the trip"? Rebbi Abin said, with her husband that makes three.

[174]Also he rented a house for her and looked after her upkeep but was never alone with her except in the presence of her children. He applied to himself the verse[175]: "I exercised myself in my worry but found no rest".

173   This text is from *Soṭah* 1:3, Notes 162-164. It is copied here by mistake because of the next paragraph which refers to the Mishnah.

174   "He" is R. Zachariah, the son of the butcher, and "she" is his wife whom he refused to divorce but with whom he could not live.

175   *Jer.* 45:3.

(fol. 26a) **משנה יא:** וְאֵילוּ נֶאֱמָנִין לְהָעִיד בְּגוֹדְלָן מַה שֶׁרָאוּ בְקוּטְנָן. נֶאֱמָן אָדָם לוֹמַר זֶה כְּתָב יָדוֹ שֶׁלְאַבָּא וְזֶה כְּתָב יָדוֹ שֶׁלְרַבִּי וְזֶה כְּתָב יָדוֹ שֶׁלְאָחִי. זָכוּר הָיִיתִי בִּפְלוֹנִית שֶׁיָּצְתָה בְּהִינוּמָא וְרֹאשָׁהּ פָּרוּעַ וְשֶׁהָיָה אִישׁ פְּלוֹנִי יוֹצֵא מִבֵּית הַסֵּפֶר לִטְבּוֹל לֶאֱכוֹל בִּתְרוּמָה וְשֶׁהָיָה חוֹלֵק עִמָּנוּ עַל הַגּוֹרֶן וְהַמָּקוֹם הַזֶּה בֵּית הַפְּרָס וְעַד כָּאן הָיִינוּ בָּאִין בַּשַׁבָּת. אֲבָל אֵינוֹ נֶאֱמָן אָדָם לוֹמַר דֶּרֶךְ הָיָה לִפְלוֹנִי בַּמָּקוֹם הַזֶּה מַעֲמָד וּמִסְפֵּד הָיָה לִפְלוֹנִי בַּמָּקוֹם הַזֶּה.

Mishnah 11: In the following cases, one is trustworthy to testify as an adult about what one saw in one's minority. A man is trustworthy to say, this is my father's handwriting, my teacher's handwriting, my brother's handwriting[176]; I remember that this person went out in *hinuma*[22] and uncovered hair[177], or that this man left school to immerse himself to eat heave[178], or that he took his part with us on the threshing floor[179], or that this place is *bet happeras*[180], or this far we went on the Sabbath[181]. But a person is not trustworthy to say that X had a right of way at this place[182], or that X had a space for eulogies at this place.[183]

176 Even though a minor is not admitted as a witness in money matters, since he testifies only to the genuineness of the document, not about its monetary implications, he can be admitted. A similar text is in Tosephta 3:3.

177 The implication of the testimony is that the woman can collect a virgin's *ketubah*; but this is not the direct text of the testimony.

178 He is a Cohen and was taken by his father to learn how to eat heave in purity.

179 One Cohen testifies for another that he is a Cohen.

180 A "field of pieces" is a lot of which it is known that there had been a grave but which was ploughed over and, therefore, there might be pieces of human bones anywhere and the passage through this lot is forbidden to Cohanim.

181 To indicate the Sabbath boundary, 2000 cubits from the town. There may be implications for money matters, as noted in the Halakhah, if the town expanded or shrank in the meantime.

182 In that case, his testimony would directly transfer money's worth from one person to another.

183 Eulogies cannot be delivered in the graveyard; since the dead cannot deliver sermons, sermonizing there would be blasphemy since (*Pr.* 17:5) "he who mocks the poor insults his Maker". There were public places on the road from the town to the graveyard where eulogies were held; some families had their own spots for eulogies of their deceased. The right to hold these eulogies has monetary value.

[184](26d line 58) תַּנֵּי. וּבִלְבַד דְּבָרִים שֶׁהֵן רְגִילִין בָּהֶן. תַּנֵּי. וּבִלְבַד שֶׁיִּצְטָרֵף עִם אֲחֵרִים.

It was stated: Only these which they are used to[185]. It was stated: Only if they are supported by others[186].

| 184 Here starts Halakhah 11, even though in the ms. and *editio princeps* this title appears only towards the end.
185 The adult is restricted to testifying about the handwriting of his father, teacher, and brother which he | saw in his youth. He is not able to testify about other people's handwriting even if he saw it frequently.
186 The need for two witnesses is not waved. |
|---|---|

(26d line 59) וְחָשׁ לוֹמַר. שֶׁמָּא עֶבֶד הוּא. הָדָא מְסַייְעָא לְהָהִיא דָּמַר רִבִּי חָמָא בַּר עוּקְבָּא בְּשֵׁם רִבִּי יוֹסֵי בֶּרִבִּי חֲנִינָה. אָסוּר לָאָדָם לְלַמֵּד אֶת עַבְדּוֹ תּוֹרָה. לֹא כֵן אָמַר רִבִּי זְעִירָא בְשֵׁם רַב יִרְמְיָה. הָעֶבֶד עוֹלֶה מִשִּׁבְעָה קְרָיּוֹת. וַיְדַבֵּר עוֹלֶה מ[ג] פְּסוּקִים. תִּיפְתָּר שֶׁלָּמַד מֵאֵילָיו אוֹ שֶׁלִּמְּדוֹ רַבּוֹ כְּטָבִי. וְחָשׁ לוֹמַר. שֶׁמָּא עֶבֶד הוּא. מְסַייְעָא לְהָהִיא דְּתַנֵּי רִבִּי חִייָה. נָשִׁים וַעֲבָדִים אֵינָן חוֹלְקִין עַל הַגּוֹרֶן אֲבָל נוֹתְנִין לוֹ מַתְּנוֹת כְּהוּנָה וּלְוִייָה מִתּוֹךְ הַבַּיִת.

Should one not worry that he might be a slave[187]? This supports what Rebbi Ḥama bar Uqba said in the name of Rebbi Yose ben Rebbi Ḥanina[188]: It is forbidden for a man to teach Torah to his slave[189]. But did not Rebbi Ze'ira say in the name of Rav Jeremiah: A slave is counted as one of the seven readers[190]; *wayedabber* is counted as one of three verses[191]! Explain it, if he learned it by himself or his master taught him like Tebi[192].

Should one not worry that he might be a slave[193]? This supports what Rebbi Ḥiyya stated: Women[194] and slaves cannot share in the distribution on the threshing floor, but one gives them the gifts of priesthood and levitic status from the house[195].

| 187 May the child taken after school to be immersed to be purified for heave not be the slave of a Cohen who is entitled to eat it (*Lev.* 22:11)? | 188 In the Babli, 28a, in the name of R. Joshua ben Levi.
189 In contrast to the Greek and Roman world, the literate person was |
|---|---|

supposed to be free, not a slave.

190 On the Sabbath, he can be one of the seven people called to read in the Torah. If he is illiterate, how could he possibly read? The same argument in the Babli, 28b.

191 In any public Torah reading, three verses are the minimum. The short verse: "The Eternal spoke to Moses, saying" is a full verse and counted as one of the three; the rule also is stated in *Megillah* 21b.

This was the version written by the scribe. The corrector crossed out "3" and replaced it by "7"; followed in the *editio princeps*.

192 Rabban Gamliel's slave; cf. Mishnah *Berakhot* 2:8.

193 This refers to the testimony that the person was receiving heave on the threshing floor.

194 Since a Cohen's daughter loses her claim to heave upon marriage to a non-Cohen and the wife of a Cohen might lose it by divorce, they should not establish customary rights to receive heave directly from the farmer (Babli *Yoma* 10a).

195 Since they are entitled to eat. In all these cases, the Babli restricts the testimony to cases of rabbinic heave (other than heave of grain, wine, and olive oil in the Holy Land).

(26d line 66) מָהוּ לְהוֹצִיא מָמוֹן מִתּוֹךְ עֵדוּתָן. הֵיךְ עֲבִידָא. הָיוּ הַכֹּל יוֹדְעִין עַד שְׂדֵה רְאוּבֵן תְּחוּם שַׁבָּת. וּבָאוּ וְאָמְרוּ. עַד כָּאן הָיִינוּ בָּאִין בַּשַּׁבָּת. וְנִמְצֵאת הַשָּׂדֶה שֶׁלְּשִׁמְעוֹן. מָהוּ מֵפִיקְתָהּ מִן שִׁמְעוֹן וּמַחֲזַרְתָּהּ לִרְאוּבֵן.

May one act in money matters on their testimony[196]? How is that? If everybody knew that the Sabbath boundary was at Reuben's field; they came and said, this far we came on the Sabbath, and it turns out that this field is in Simeon's hand. May one take it from Simeon and return it to Reuben[197]?

196 For example, on the testimony about the Sabbath boundary in earlier times.

197 If Reuben claims ownership of the field but has no documents; Simeon also has no documents and does not claim to have bought it from Reuben. Neither this nor the following questions are answered.

HALAKHAH 11　　　　　　　　123

(26d line 69) מַהוּ שֶׁיְּהוּ נֶאֱמָנִין לוֹמַר. יוֹצְאִין הָיוּ לְלַקֵּט פַּגֵּי שְׁבִיעִית וְשָׁמַעְנוּ פְלוֹנִי מְמַלֵּל עַל פְּלוֹנִית אִשְׁתּוֹ. אִשָּׁה פְלוֹנִית מְמַלֶּלֶת עַל בָּנֶיהָ.

Would they be trustworthy to say, we went out to collect unripe figs in the sabbatical year and heard X talking about his wife Y, or woman Z talking about her children[198]?

198　The Mishnah gives the adult permission to tell from his youth to confirm another man in the priesthood. Is he also permitted to tell things that would bar a man from the priesthood or even from marrying in the congregation, such as Mr. X telling about the unfaithfulness of his wife, or a woman about the fact that some or all of her children are not her husband's?

(26d line 71) רִבִּי אָחָא רִבִּי שְׁמוּאֵל בָּעֵי. הוּזְּמוּ מָהוּ שֶׁיְּשַׁלְּמוּ. אוֹ יָבֹא כַיי דְּאָמַר רִבִּי בָּא רַב יְהוּדָה בְּשֵׁם שְׁמוּאֵל. אֵין לוֹמְדִין דָּבָר מִדָּבָר בְּעֵדִים זוֹמְמִין. וְכָא כֵן.

Rebbi Aḥa, Rebbi Samuel asked: If they were proven to be false witnesses[199], do they have to pay? [200]Or it might be, following what Rebbi Abba, Rav Jehudah[43], said in the name of Samuel: One does not infer one thing from another in the matter of false witnesses. And here it is so.

199　By biblical decree (*Deut.* 19:16-21), the punishment of a false witness is that he suffers the punishment that would have been imposed on the defendant had the testimony stood up in court. Since the entire Mishnah is interpreted to speak about money matters, the punishment in this case would be monetary. (In rabbinic theory, a witness can be proven false only if it is shown that his testimony is impossible, i. e., that he was not at the place he testifies about at the time in question.)

200　*Soṭah* 1:1, Note 44.

(26d line 73) תַּנֵּי. שֶׁאָכַלְנוּ בִּקְצִיצַת פְּלוֹנִי וּפְלוֹנִי. מָהוּ בִקְצִיצַת. בְּשָׁעָה שֶׁהָיָה אָדָם מוֹכֵר אֶת שָׂדֶה אֲחוּזָתוֹ הָיוּ קְרוֹבָיו מְמַלִּין חָבִיּוֹת קְלָיוֹת וֶאֱגוֹזִים וְשׁוֹבְרִין לִפְנֵי הַתִּינוֹקוֹת. וְהַתִּינוֹקוֹת מְלַקְטִין וְאוֹמְרִים. נִקְצַץ פְּלוֹנִי מֵאֲחוּזָתוֹ. וּבְשָׁעָה שֶׁהָיְתָה חוֹזֶרֶת לוֹ הָיוּ עוֹשִׂין לוֹ כֵן וְאוֹמְרִים. חָזַר פְּלוֹנִי לַאֲחוּזָתוֹ. אָמַר רִבִּי יוֹסֵי בֵּירִבִּי בּוּן. אַף מִי שֶׁהָיָה נוֹשֵׂא אִשָּׁה שֶׁאֵינָהּ הוֹגֶנֶת לוֹ קְרוֹבָיו מְמַלִּין חָבִיּוֹת קְלָיוֹת וֶאֱגוֹזִים וְשׁוֹבְרִין לִפְנֵי הַתִּינוֹקוֹת. וְהַתִּינוֹקוֹת מְלַקְטִין וְאוֹמְרִים. נִקְצַץ פְּלוֹנִי מִמִּשְׁפַּחְתּוֹ. וּבְשָׁעָה שֶׁהָיָה מְגָרְשָׁהּ הָיוּ עוֹשִׂין לוֹ כֵן וְאוֹמְרִים. חָזַר פְּלוֹנִי לְמִשְׁפַּחְתּוֹ.

It was stated[201]: "That we ate in **X** or **Y**'s clipping." What is clipping? If a man sold his inherited field, his relatives filled amphoras with roasted kernels and nuts and broke them before children. The children were collecting them and saying, **X** was clipped from his inheritance. When he bought it back, they were doing the same and saying, **X** returned to his inheritance. Rebbi Yose ben Rebbi Abun said, [202]also if a man married an unsuitable woman, his realtives filled amphoras with roasted kernels and nuts and broke them before children. The children were collecting them and saying, **X** was clipped from his family. Whe he divorced her, they were doing the same and saying, **X** returned to his family.

201 Tosephta 3:3.
202 Babli 38b. If a Cohen married a woman forbidden to him, his children would not be Cohanim and forbidden as marriage partners to the rest of the family. (Rabbinically, he himself would be barred from all priestly functions until he divorced the unsuitable wife.)

(26d line 81) **הלכה יא**: אֵילוּ נֶאֱמָנִין לְהָעִיד בְּגוֹדְלָן מַה שֶּׁרָאוּ בְקוֹטְנָן כּוֹל׳. אֵין נֶאֱמָנִין אֶלָּא בְגוֹדְלָן מַה שֶּׁרָאוּ בְקוֹטְנָן. הָא בְקוֹטְנָן לֹא. תַּמָּן תַּנִּינָן. נֶאֱמֶנֶת אִשָּׁה אוֹ קָטָן לוֹמַר. מִיכָּן יָצָא נָחִל. מְהַלֵּךְ לְתוֹךְ שָׂדֵהוּ וְנוֹטֵל אֶת

נְחִילוֹ. וְכָה הוּא אוֹמֵר כֵּן. רִבִּי אֲחָא רִבִּי חֲנַנְיָה בְּשֵׁם רִבִּי יוֹחָנָן. לֹא אָמַר רִבִּי יוֹחָנָן בֶּן בְּרוֹקָה אֶלָּא עַל נְחִיל שֶׁלַּדְּבוֹרִים שֶׁאֵין גְּזֵילוֹ דְבַר תּוֹרָה. תַּנֵּי רַב אוֹשַׁעְיָה. וּבִלְבַד בְּמַפְרִיחַ. אֲבָל בְּשׂוֹכוֹ לֹא. רִבִּי זְעִירָא בְּעָא קוֹמֵי רִבִּי מָנָא. לֹא מִסְתַּבְּרָא עַל אָתָר. הָא לְאַחַר זְמָן לֹא. אָמַר לֵיהּ. אַף אֲנָא סָבוּר כֵּן. וְתַנִּינָן. בַּמֶּה דְבָרִים אֲמוּרִים. שֶׁהֵעִידוּ בְּמַאֲמָרָן. אֲבָל יָצְאוּ וְחָזְרוּ אֲנִי אוֹמֵר. מִפְּנֵי יִרְאָה וּפִיתּוּי אָמְרוּ.

Halakhah 11: "In the following cases, one is trustworthy to testify as an adult about what he saw in his minority," etc. They are only trustworthy as adults[203] about what they saw as minors; therefore, not as minors! There[204], we have stated: "A woman or a minor are trustworthy when they said, from there a swarm of bees left. He then can enter another's field and take his swarm.[205]" And here, you say so? Rebbi Aḥa, Rebbi Ḥananiah in the name of Rebbi Joḥanan: Rebbi Joḥanan ben Beroqa said this only about a swarm of bees because taking it is not robbery by biblical standards[206]. Rav Oshaiah stated, only if it is swarming[207]. But not if it clings to a branch[208]. Rebbi Ze'ira asked before Rebbi Mana: Is that not reasonable only when it happens, but not after some time? He said to him, I agree. And we have stated: When is this said? When they testified to what they said[209]. But if they left and came back, I am saying that they speak out of fear or were seduced.

203 Otherwise, the Mishnah simply could have stated: "In the following cases, one is trustworthy to testify about what he saw in his minority."

204 Mishnah *Baba Qama* 10:2, a statement of R. Joḥanan ben Beroqa.

205 The beekeeper has permission to enter to retrieve his swarm but he has to pay for any damage he may cause.

206 In *Baba Qama* 10:2: "Because taking it is not robbery by stipulation." There, the stipulation is attributed to Joshua at the time of the distribution of

the Land. The moment the bees swarm, they really become ownerless. If the right of the beekeeper to the swarm which leaves his hive is by stipulation, then the testimony of a minor also can be accepted by stipulation; cf. 13:7, Note 110. The Babli (*Baba Qama* 114b) agrees.

207   Some commentators want to refer "swarming" to the minor; that he can testify only as a "swarming minor" (Babli *Berakhot* 47b), one for whom it is not clear whether he is a minor or an adult. That does not make sense, in particular because in the Yerushalmi (*Berakhot* 7:2, Note 66) he is simply called "doubtful".

208   *Sefer Ha'ittur* (part 2, p. 115a, Note 135) reads: אֲבָל בְּשָׁכֵן לֹא "but not when it is resting." The text of the ms. is preferable since (a) it is confirmed by the different editorship of *Baba Qama* and (b) the Mishnah continues with a dispute whether the beekeeper is entitled to cut off the tree branch on which the bees have settled (and then pay the tree's owner.)

209   *Sefer Ha'ittur* (*loc. cit.*) reads: בִּזְמַן שֶׁהָעֵדִים בְּמַעֲמָדָן "as long as the witnesses stand (before the court)." The text of the ms. is preferable since (a) by the general rules of procedure no witnesses can testify twice in the same matter (Note 56) and (b) the reference is to the Mishnah here which is interpreted to mean that they are only trustworthy in matters that have pecuniary implications if their testimony is taken as soon as they indicate that they have knowledge of the matter, but not if in the meantime they were subject to outside influences. The Babli (*Baba Qama* 114b) admits the testimony of the minor about the swarm of bees "if he speaks without being prompted."

אילו נערות פרק שלישי

(fol. 27a) **משנה א**: אֵילוּ נְעָרוֹת שֶׁיֵּשׁ לָהֶן קְנָס הַבָּא עַל הַמַּמְזֶרֶת וְעַל הַנְּתִינָה וְעַל הַכּוּתִית וְהַבָּא עַל הַגִּיּוֹרֶת וְעַל הַשְּׁבוּיָה וְעַל הַשִּׁפְחָה שֶׁנִּפְדּוּ וְשֶׁנִּתְגַּיְּירוּ וְשֶׁנִּשְׁתַּחְרְרוּ פְּחוּתוֹת מִבְּנוֹת שָׁלֹשׁ שָׁנִים וְיוֹם אֶחָד. הַבָּא עַל אֲחוֹתוֹ וְעַל אֲחוֹת אָבִיו וְעַל אֲחוֹת אִמּוֹ וְעַל אֲחוֹת אִשְׁתּוֹ וְעַל אֵשֶׁת אָחִיו וְעַל אֵשֶׁת אֲחִי אָבִיו וְעַל הַנִּדָּה יֵשׁ לָהֶן קְנָס אַף עַל פִּי שֶׁהֵן בְּהִיכָּרֵת אֵין בָּהֶן מִיתַת בֵּית דִּין.

Mishnah 1: The following adolescent girls[1] can claim a fine: From someone who has intercourse with a bastard girl[2], or a Gibeonite or a Samaritan girl, and one who comes to a female proselyte, a kidnap victim, or a slave girl who was redeemed, converted, or freed, at less than three years and one day of age[3]. Also from one who has intercourse with his sister, or his father's sister, or his mother's sister, or his wife's sister, or his brother's wife[4], or his paternal uncle's wife[5], or a menstruating girl; he has to pay the fine since it is not a capital crime[6] even though he is subject to extirpation.

1   The biblical law prescribes (*Deut*. 22:28-29) that the man raping נַעֲרָה בְּתוּלָה "a virgin adolescent girl" has to pay her father 50 šeqel and must marry her. In the corresponding law about the seducer of a virgin (*Ex*. 22:15) he has to pay if he does not marry the girl. In that paragraph, the adolescent is not mentioned; but since it is stated that the father has the right to withhold her from the seducer, it follows that the girl cannot be an adult; she must be underage or adolescent. An adolescent is a girl in the first 6 months after she grows two pubic hairs, cf. *Nedarim* Chapter 10, Note 1.

The age at which the fine can be claimed is the topic of Halakhah 3:9.

2   Obviously, one who rapes or seduces an eligible Jewish girl has to pay. The Mishnah enumerates only those categories where there might be an argument that he should not be required to pay. Each category is discussed in the Halakhah. A bastard is excluded from contracting a valid marriage in the native congregation in *Deut.* 23:3.

3   Cf. Mishnah 1:2.

4   If she was divorced or became a widow before the final marriage. The preliminary marriage activates all incest prohibitions implied by marriage.

5   But for a capital crime he does not pay since there cannot be two punishments for one crime. Extirpation is a divine punishment, outside the purview of a human court.

(27a line 46) **הלכה א:** אֵילוּ נְעָרוֹת כול׳. כְּתִיב וְלוֹ תִהְיֶה לְאִשָּׁה. אִשָּׁה שֶׁהִיא רְאוּיָה לוֹ. וּמַמְזֶרֶת הִיא רְאוּיָה לוֹ. רִבִּי שִׁמְעוֹן בֶּן לָקִישׁ אָמַר. כֶּסֶף יִשְׁקוֹל כְּמוֹהַר הַבְּתוּלוֹת. רִיבָּה כָאן בְּתוּלוֹת הַרְבֵּה. אָמַר רִבִּי זְעִירָא. אֵילוּ הָיָה כָתוּב בְּתוּלַת כְּמוֹהֲרִיּוֹת. לֵית כְּתִיב אֶלָא כְּמוֹהַר הַבְּתוּלוֹת. לֹא רִיבָּה אוֹתָן הַכָּתוּב אֶלָא לְמוֹהַר בִּלְבָד. וַיי דָא אֲמָרָה הָדָא. דְּתַנֵּי חִזְקִיָה. אִם מָאֵן יְמָאֵן אָבִיהָ. אֵין לִי אֶלָא שְׁמִיאָן אָבִיהָ. מְנַיִין שֶׁאִם יְמָאֲנוּ אֲפִילוּ מִן הַשָּׁמַיִם. תַּלְמוּד לוֹמַר מָאֵן יְמָאֵן מִכָּל־מָקוֹם. מֵעַתָּן הַבָּא עַל הַשִּׁפְחָה (לֹא)[6] יְהֵא לוֹ קְנָס. לֵית יְכִיל. דְּתַנֵּי. יָכוֹל הַבָּא עַל הַשִּׁפְחָה אֲרָמִית יְהֵא חַיָּיב. תַּלְמוּד לוֹמַר מָהֹר יִמְהָרֶנָּה לוֹ לְאִשָּׁה. אֶת שֶׁיֵּשׁ לוֹ הֲוָיָיה בָהּ. יָצְאַת שִׁפְחָה אֲרָמִית שֶׁאֵין לֹה הֲוָיָיה בָּהּ. הֲתִיבוּן. הֲרֵי אֲחוֹתוֹ אֵין לוֹ הֲוָיָיה בָהּ וְהוּא מְשַׁלֵּם קְנָס. שַׁנְיָיא הִיא שֶׁיֵּשׁ לָהּ הֲוָיָיה אֵצֶל אַחֵר. הֲרֵי בִתּוֹ יֵשׁ לָהּ הֲוָיָיה אֵצֶל אַחֵר וְאֵינוֹ מְשַׁלֵּם קְנָס. שַׁנְיָיה הִיא שֶׁהוּא מִתְחַיֵּיב בְּנַפְשׁוֹ. שֶׁכָּל־הַמִּתְחַיֵּיב בְּנַפְשׁוֹ אֵינוֹ מְשַׁלֵּם מָמוֹן.

Halakhah 1: "The following adolescent girls," etc. It is written[7]: "She should be his wife," one who can be his wife[8]. Can the bastard girl be his wife? Rebbi Simeon ben Laqish said, "he should weigh silver appropriate for the bride-price of virgins⁹", that added many virgins. Rebbi Ze'ira said, if it had said "virgin's brides-prices"; but it says only "appropriate for the bride-price of virgins"; the verse added them only for the bride-price¹⁰. But where was this said¹¹? As Ḥizqiah stated: "If refusing her father should refuse⁹," not only if her father refuses; from where even if from Heaven they refuse¹²? The verse says "refusing should refuse", in any case. But then a man who has intercourse with a slave girl should pay the fine! This is impossible, as it was stated: I could think that one who has intercourse with a Gentile slave-girl should be obligated, the verse says, "by bride-money he should take her as a wife to himself." Only one whom he can marry; this excludes the Gentile slave whom he cannot marry¹³. But he cannot marry his sister and he pays the fine! There is a difference since she can be married to others. But his daughter can be married to others and he does not pay the fine¹⁴! There is a difference since it is a capital crime and nobody who commits a capital crime pays money¹⁵.

6   This word is in the ms. and *editio princeps* but should be deleted.
7   *Deut.* 22:29, speaking of the rapist.
8   This argument will be used at the end of the paragraph to exclude the slave-girl from consideration since she cannot legally marry anybody. The bastard can legally marry a proselyte or another bastard (Mishnah *Qiddušin* 4:1). The inverse question could be asked if a bastard rapes a regular Jewish girl. The question is asked in the Babli, 29b.
9   *Ex.* 22:16, speaking of the seducer. In the Babli, 29b, R. Simeon ben Laqish argues differently.
10   It implies only that even a virgin disqualified in general still has a claim to a full *ketubah*; e. g., if a bastard girl marries a proselyte.
11   That the fine must be paid.
12   By a biblical prohibition.
13   While the Gentile slave-girl of a

Jewish owner becomes pseudo-Jewish by baptism in a *miqweh*, she would be able to contract a marriage only by manumission by which she would become a full-fledged proselyte. Cf. Halakhah 1:4, Notes 181-184.

14 Mishnah 3:2.

15 Even if he cannot be convicted because there were no two eye-witnesses to the act.

(27a line 59) נְתִינָה. אָמַר רִבִּי יוֹסֵי. נְתִינִים לֹא חָשׁוּ לָהֶם אֶלָּא מִשּׁוּם פְּסוּלֵי מִשְׁפָּחָה. אַף תֵּימַר. מִשּׁוּם פְּסוּלֵי עַבְדוּת. מֵעַתָּה הַבָּא עַל הַנְּתִינָה לֹא יִהְיֶה לוֹ קְנָס. וְתַנִּינָן. הַבָּא עַל הַנְּתִינָה יֶשׁ לוֹ קְנָס.

"The Gibeonite." Rebbi Yose said, they were worried about them only because of the detriment to the families[16]. Could you not say, because of the disability of slaves[17]? If that were true, one who cohabits with a Gibeonite would not be subject to a fine[18]; but we have stated: One who cohabits with a Gibeonite is subject to a fine[19].

16 Gibeonites are descendants of genuine proselytes; they are only excluded from intermarrying with Jews because they are considered undesirable. The extended discussion of the problem of Gibeonites is in *Qiddušin* 4:1.

17 Would the fact that the Gibeonites were "wood cutters and water drawers for the congregation" (*Jos.* 9:21) imply that they had servile status? Since nowhere in the Bible we hear that they were freed, their descendants then would still be slaves and unable to contract marriages.

18 Mishnah 3:2.

19 Therefore, even in the time of Joshua the Gibeonites were subordinate but not servile.

(27a line 62) כּוּתִית. אַתְיָא כְּמָאן דְּאָמַר. כּוּתִי כְּיִשְׂרָאֵל לְכָל־דָּבָר. בְּרַם כְּמָאן דְּאָמַר. כּוּתִי כְגוֹי. לֹא בְדָא. דְּאִיתְפַּלְּגוּן. כּוּתִי כְגוֹי. דִּבְרֵי רִבִּי. רַבָּן שִׁמְעוֹן בֶּן גַּמְלִיאֵל אוֹמֵר. כּוּתִי כְיִשְׂרָאֵל לְכָל דָּבָר. אֲפִילוּ תֵימָא. כּוּתִי כְגוֹי. כּוּתִים מִשּׁוּם מָה הֵן פְּסוּלִין. לֹא מִשּׁוּם גּוֹי וְעֶבֶד. גּוֹי וְעֶבֶד הַבָּא עַל בַּת יִשְׂרָאֵל

הַוְולָד מַמְזֵר. וּמַמְזֶרֶת יֵשׁ לָהּ קְנָס. לְחוּמָרִין אוֹ לְעִנְיָן מִשְׁפָּחָה אַתְּ עָבֵד לֵיהּ גּוֹי וְעֶבֶד הַבָּא עַל בַּת יִשְׂרָאֵל הַוְולָד מַמְזֵר. לְעִנְיָן קְנָס אַתְּ עָבֵד לֵיהּ כְּיִשְׂרָאֵל הַבָּא עַל הַגּוֹיָה הַוְולָד גּוֹי.

"A Samaritan." That follows him who said, a Samaritan is a like full Jew. But for him who says that a Samaritan is like a Gentile, it is not so. As they disagreed[20]: A Samaritan is like a Gentile, the words of Rebbi. Rabban Simeon ben Gamliel said, a Samaritan is like a Jew in every respect. Even if you say, a Samaritan is like a Gentile, why are Samaritans disqualified? Not because of a Gentile and a slave[21]? If a Gentile or a slave has intercourse with a Jewish woman, the child is a bastard[22]. But a bastard girl can claim a fine! For restrictions or family relations you consider him a Gentile or a slave who had intercourse with a Jewish woman; the child is a bastard. But for a fine you consider this as a Jew having intercourse with a Gentile woman, in which case the child is a Gentile[23].

20 Cf. *Demay* 3:4, Note 98; *Berakhot* 7:1, Note 59.

21 Since *2K*. 17, 24ff. clearly states that the settlers from Babylon, Kuta, etc. at the start were idolators; if they intermarried with the remainders of the Israelite populations there, their descendants all acquired the status of descendants of Gentiles (or slaves) from Israelite mothers.

22 This is the argument of R. Johanan and R. Simeon ben Laqish in *Yebamot* 7:6, Note 129; it is rejected there since the child of a Jewish woman from a Gentile, together with her mother, is disqualified from priesthood but not a bastard (Notes 130,131).

23 The separation from Samaritans is purely one of practice, with no theoretical basis, and disapproved of by the Mishnah. In the Babli, 29b/30a, the argument (attributed to R. Meïr) is rejected, in order not to reward a sinner (the rapist or seducer.)

(27a line 69) אָמַר רִבִּי יוֹסֵי בֵּירִבִּי חֲנִינָא. הָאוֹנֵס וְהַמְפַתֶּה אֶת הַיְתוֹמָה פָּטוּר. אָמַר רִבִּי בָּא בַּר מָמָל. מַחֲלוֹקֶת כְּרִבִּי יוֹסֵי הַגָּלִילִי. בְּרַם כְּרִבִּי עֲקִיבָה יֵשׁ לָהּ קְנָס וּקְנָסָהּ שֶׁלְּעַצְמָהּ. אָמַר רִבִּי יוֹסֵי. מַתְנִיתָא אָמְרָה פְחוּתוֹת מִבְּנוֹת שָׁלֹשׁ שָׁנִים וְיוֹם אֶחָד. וְלֹא כִיתוֹמָה הִיא. וְהָתַנֵּי. תַּחַת אֲשֶׁר עִינָהּ. לְרַבּוֹת אֶת הַיְתוֹמָה לִקְנָס. דִּבְרֵי רִבִּי יוֹסֵי הַגָּלִילִי. אָמַר רִבִּי אֲחַי. תִּיפְתָּר שֶׁבָּא עָלֶיהָ עַד שֶׁלֹּא מֵת אָבִיהָ וּמֵת אָבִיהָ. כְּבָר נִרְאָה לִיתֵּן לְאָבִיהָ.

Rebbi Yose ben Rebbi Ḥanina said, a man who rapes or seduces an orphan girl does not have to pay[24]. Rebbi Abba bar Mamal said, that is a disagreement, it follows Rebbi Yose the Galilean[25]. But following Rebbi Aqiba she can claim the fine and the fine becomes her property. Rebbi Yose said, the Mishnah said "at less than three years and one day of age," and is she not like an orphan[26]? And did we not state: "Because he raped her,[27]" that includes an orphan for a fine, the words of Rebbi Yose the Galilean? Rebbi Aḥai said, explain it that he had intercourse with her when her father was alive; when her father died, he already had the obligation to give to her father[28].

24 Since *Deut.* 22:29 states that "the man who had intercourse with her has to give her father 50 silver [šeqel]." This seems to negate the obligation if there is no father to collect the fine.

25 He holds in Mishnah 3:7 that an underage girl which was preliminarily married and then divorced as a virgin has no claim to the fine (since by the preliminary marriage she was emancipated from her father's power.) R. Aqiba holds that she can claim the fine for herself.

26 Neither the proselyte nor the freedwoman are under the authority of a father; nevertheless, the Mishnah gives them the right to claim the fine.

27 *Deut.* 22:29. In the Babli, 44b, and *Mekhilta dR. Ismael* (*Mišpaṭim* 17; ed. Horovitz-Rabin p. 309), the inference is from *Ex.* 22:16. In any case, R. Yose the Galilean seems to contradict himself.

28 For R. Yose the Galilean the fine belongs to the father's heirs.

HALAKHAH 1

(27b line 6) תַּמָּן תַּנִּינָן. הָאוֹכֵל תְּרוּמָה מֵזִיד מְשַׁלֵּם אֶת הַקֶּרֶן וְאֵינוֹ מְשַׁלֵּם אֶת הַחוֹמֶשׁ. וְתַנִּינָן. אֵילוּ הֵן הַלּוֹקִין. הָכָא אַתְּ אָמַר לוֹקֶה. וְכָא אַתְּ אָמַר. מְשַׁלֵּם. אָמַר רִבִּי יוֹחָנָן. לִצְדָדִין הִיא מַתְנִיתָה. אִם הִתְרוּ בוֹ לוֹקֶה. לֹא הִתְרוּ בוֹ מְשַׁלֵּם. סָבַר רִבִּי יוֹחָנָן לְמֵימַר. בִּמְקוֹם מַכּוֹת וְתַשְׁלוּמִין מְשַׁלֵּם וְאֵינוֹ לוֹקֶה. וְיִלְקֶה וִישַׁלֵּם. כְּדֵי רִשְׁעָתוֹ. מִשּׁוּם רִשְׁעָה אַחַת אַתָּה מְחַיְּיבוֹ וְאֵי אַתָּה מְחַיְּיבוֹ מִשּׁוּם שְׁתֵּי רְשָׁעִיּוֹת. וִישַׁלֵּם וְלֹא יִלְקֶה. בְּמִי שֶׁיֶּשׁ בּוֹ שְׁתֵּי רְשָׁעִיּוֹת הַכָּתוּב מְדַבֵּר וְהִפִּילוֹ הַשּׁוֹפֵט וְהִכָּהוּ לְפָנָיו כְּדֵי רִשְׁעָתוֹ בְּמִסְפָּר.

2 הלוקין | ת הלוקין והא תנינן אלו נערות   3 לא | ת אם לא   4 למימר | ת מימר
5 כדי | ת -   משום | ת (twice)   6 במי שיש בו | ת במחייבי

[29]There, we have stated: "If somebody eats heave intentionally, he pays the principal but not the fifth." And we have stated: "The following are flogged." Here you say, he is flogged, and there you say, he pays. Rebbi Johanan said, the Mishnah is two-sided: If he was cautioned, he is flogged; if he was not cautioned, he pays. Rebbi Johanan is of the opinion that in a case where there is flogging or restitution, when he pays he is not flogged. Why should he not be flogged and have to pay? (Deut. 25:2) "Corresponding to his guilt." You sentence him for one offence but you may not sentence him for two offences. The verse speaks of one who may incur two punishments (Deut. 25:2): "The judge shall have him laid down and flogged in his presence a number [of times] because of his guilt."

29 The parallel (with very minor deviations) to the remainder of the Halakhah is in *Terumot* 7:1, fully explained there in Notes 3-73, shortened also *Baba Qama* 7:2 (fol. 5d), *Makkot* 1:1 (fol. 31a); Babli *Ketubot* 32b, *Baba Qama* 36a, *Makkot* 7b, 13b. The variant readings from *Terumot* are noted ת.

(27b line 14) רִבִּי שִׁמְעוֹן בֶּן לָקִישׁ אָמַר. וַאֲפִילוּ לֹא הִתְרוּ אֵינוֹ מְשַׁלֵּם. מֵאַחַר שֶׁאִילוּ מַתְרִין בּוֹ לוֹקֶה. מַתְנִיתָא פְּלִיגָא עַל רִבִּי שִׁמְעוֹן בֶּן לָקִישׁ. הָאוֹכֵל תְּרוּמָה שׁוֹגֵג מְשַׁלֵּם אֶת הַקֶּרֶן וְחוֹמֶשׁ. וְאִלּוּ הִתְרוּ בּוֹ אֵינוֹ לוֹקֶה. פָּתַר לָהּ כְּרִבִּי מֵאִיר. דְּרִבִּי מֵאִיר אָמַר. לוֹקֶה וּמְשַׁלֵּם. מַתְנִיתָא פְלִיגָא עַל רִבִּי שִׁמְעוֹן בֶּן לָקִישׁ. דְּתַנִּינָן. אֵילוּ נְעָרוֹת שֶׁיֵּשׁ לָהֶן קְנָס. אִילוּ הִתְרוּ בּוֹ אֵינוֹ לוֹקֶה. פָּתַר לָהּ כְּרִבִּי מֵאִיר. דְּרִבִּי מֵאִיר אָמַר. לוֹקֶה וּמְשַׁלֵּם. רִבִּי אַבָּהוּ בְשֵׁם רִבִּי שִׁמְעוֹן בֶּן לָקִישׁ. מִן הַמּוֹצִיא שֵׁם רַע לָמַד רִבִּי מֵאִיר. וְיִסְּרוּ אוֹתוֹ מַכּוֹת. וְעָנְשׁוּ אוֹתוֹ מָמוֹן. רַבָּנִין אֱמְרִין לְחִידּוּשׁוֹ יָצָא הַמּוֹצִיא שֵׁם רַע. דָּבָר שֶׁהוּא יוֹצֵא בְחִידּוּשׁוֹ אֵין לוֹמְדִין מִמֶּנּוּ. לְפִי שֶׁבְּכָל־מָקוֹם אֵין אָדָם מִתְחַיֵּיב מִדִּיבּוּרוֹ. וְכָאן אָדָם מִתְחַיֵּיב מִדִּיבוּרוֹ. הוֹאִיל וְכֵן אִי אַתָּה לָמֵד מִמֶּנּוּ. דָּבָר אַחֵר. כָּאן אֵין אַתְּ לָמֵד מִמֶּנּוּ לֹא עוֹנְשִׁין וְלֹא מַכּוֹת. לֹא כֵן אָמַר רִבִּי אַבָּהוּ בְשֵׁם רִבִּי יוֹחָנָן. שׁוֹגֵג בְּחֵלֶב מֵזִיד בְּקָרְבָּן מַתְרִין בּוֹ לוֹקֶה וּמֵבִיא קָרְבָּן. וְכָא לוֹקֶה וּמְשַׁלֵּם. רִבִּי בּוּן בַּר חִייָה בְּשֵׁם רִבִּי שְׁמוּאֵל בַּר רַב יִצְחָק אָמַר כְּדֵי רִשְׁעָתוֹ. שְׁנֵי דְבָרִים מְסוּרִין לְבֵית דִּין. אַתְּ תּוֹפֵס אֶחָד מֵהֶן. יָצָא דָבָר שֶׁהוּא מָסוּר לַשָּׁמַיִם.

[30]Rebbi Simeon ben Laqish said, even if he was not cautioned should he not pay since when cautioned he would be flogged? A Mishnah disagrees with Rebbi Simeon ben Laqish: "If somebody eats heave in error, he pays principal and fifth[31]," but if he was cautioned, will he not be flogged? He explains it following Rebbi Meïr since Rebbi Meïr said, he is flogged and pays. A Mishnah disagrees with Rebbi Simeon ben Laqish, as we have stated: "The following adolescent girls can claim a fine," but if he was cautioned, will he not be flogged? He explains it following Rebbi Meïr since Rebbi Meïr said, he is flogged and pays. Rebbi Abbahu in the name of Rebbi Simeon ben Laqish: Rebbi Meïr learned from the calumniator. (*Deut.* 22:18) "They shall punish him," flogging; (*Deut.* 22:19) "and they shall fine him", money. But the rabbis say, [the law of] the calumniator is

separate because of its novelty; one cannot learn from a novelty! Because nowhere else will a person become guilty by speech, but here he becomes guilty by speech; therefore, nothing can be inferred.   Another explanation: one cannot transfer the rules of either payment or flogging. Did not Rebbi Abbahu say in the name of Rebbi Johanan: If he [eats] fat in error but is intentional about the sacrifice, if he was cautioned he will be flogged and has to bring a sacrifice? So here, he is flogged and he pays. Rebbi Abun bar Ḥiyya in the name of Rebbi Samuel bar Rav Isaac said, (*Deut.* 25:2) "Because of his guilt." If two possibilities are given to the court, one chooses one of them. This excludes matters in the power of Heaven.

30   The text in *Terumot* is close enough that the explanations given there are valid here, but the details of the texts differ too much to be presented as variant readings of one and the same text.

31   Mishnah *Terumot* 6:1.

(27b line 30) הַכֹּל מוֹדִין שֶׁאֵין מָמוֹן אֵצֶל מִיתָה. מִן הָדָא מַכֵּה בְהֵמָה יְשַׁלְּמֶנָּה וּמַכֵּה אָדָם יוּמָת. מַה מַכֵּה בְהֵמָה לֹא חִלַּקְתָּה בָּהּ בֵּין שׁוֹגֵג בֵּין מֵזִיד לְחַיְּיבוֹ מָמוֹן. אַף מַכֵּה אָדָם לֹא תַחֲלוֹק בּוֹ בֵּין שׁוֹגֵג לְמֵזִיד לְפוֹטְרוֹ מָמוֹן. מַה פְּלִיגִין בְּמָמוֹן אֵצֶל מַכּוֹת. רִבִּי יוֹחָנָן אָמַר. אֵין מָמוֹן אֵצֶל מִיתָה וְיֵשׁ מָמוֹן אֵצֶל מַכּוֹת. רִבִּי שִׁמְעוֹן בֶּן לָקִישׁ אוֹמֵר. כְּשֵׁם שֶׁאֵין מָמוֹן אֵצֶל מִיתָה כָּךְ אֵין מָמוֹן אֵצֶל מַכּוֹת.

1 מן הדא | ת דכתיב   2 לחייבו | ת לפטור   3 למזיד | ת בין מזיד   לפוטרו ממון | ת לפטור   במה | ת מה   5 ר' | ת ור'   אומר | ת אמר

Everybody agrees that there is no money payment in capital cases, as it is written (*Lev.* 24:21): "The slayer of an animal must pay for it but the slayer of a human shall be put to death." Just as you did not make a difference between unintentional and intentional action of a slayer of an animal to force him to pay money, so you should not make a difference between unintentional and intentional action of a slayer of a human to free him from paying money. Where do they differ? About money in a flogging case. Rebbi Joḥanan said, there is no money in a capital case but there is money in a flogging case, but Rebbi Simeon ben Laqish said, just as there is no money in a capital case so there is no money in a flogging case.

(27b line 36) רִבִּי אִמִּי בַּבְלָייָא בְשֵׁם רַבָּנִין דְּתַמָּן. טַעֲמָא דְּרִבִּי שִׁמְעוֹן בֶּן לָקִישׁ. רָשָׁע רָשָׁע. נֶאֱמַר רָשָׁע בִּמְחוּיְיבֵי מִיתָה וְנֶאֱמַר רָשָׁע בִּמְחוּיְיבֵי מַכּוֹת. מַה רָשָׁע שֶׁנֶּאֱמַר בִּמְחוּיְיבֵי מִיתוֹת בֵּית דִּין אֵין מָמוֹן אֵצֶל מִיתָה. אַף רָשָׁע שֶׁנֶּאֱמַר בִּמְחוּיְיבֵי מַכּוֹת אֵין מָמוֹן אֵצֶל מַכּוֹת.

2 מיתה | **ת** מיתות   3 בית דין | **ת** -

Rebbi Immi the Babylonian in the name of the rabbis from there: The reason of Rebbi Simeon ben Laqish is "criminal, criminal." "Criminal" is mentioned in capital cases, "criminal" is mentioned in cases of flogging. Just as for the criminal in capital cases there is no monetary fine, so for the criminal mentioned in flogging cases there is no monetary fine.

(27b line 40) נָתָן בַּר הוֹשַׁעְיָה אָמַר. כָּאן בְּנַעֲרָה כָּאן בְּבוֹגֶרֶת. נַעֲרָה יֵשׁ לָהּ קְנָס וְאֵין לָהּ מַכּוֹת. בּוֹגֶרֶת יֵשׁ לָהּ מַכּוֹת וְאֵין לָהּ קְנָס. וְאֵין לָהּ בּוֹשֶׁת וּפְגָם. רַבָּנִין דְּקֵיסָרִין אָמְרִין. תִּיפְתָּר שֶׁפִּיתְּתוֹ אוֹ שֶׁמְּחָלָה לוֹ. וְסָבַר נָתָן בַּר הוֹשַׁעְיָה. בִּמְקוֹם מַכּוֹת וְתַשְׁלוּמִין מְשַׁלֵּם וְאֵינוֹ לוֹקֶה. וְיִלְקֶה וִישַׁלֵּם. כְּדֵי רִשְׁעָתוֹ. מִשּׁוּם רִשְׁעָה אַחַת אַתָּה מְחַיְּיבוֹ וְאִי אַתָּה מְחַיְּיבוֹ מִשּׁוּם שְׁתֵּי רִשְׁעָיוֹת. וִישַׁלֵּם וְלֹא יִלְקֶה כְּעֵדִים זוֹמְמִין. כְּמָה דְתֵימַר תַּמָּן בְּעֵדִים זוֹמְמִין. מְשַׁלְּמִין וְאֵין לוֹקִין. וְכָא מְשַׁלֵּם וְאֵינוֹ לוֹקֶה. אָמַר רִבִּי יוֹנָה. טַעֲמָא דְּרִבִּי נָתָן בַּר הוֹשַׁעְיָה. כְּדֵי רִשְׁעָתוֹ. אֶת שֶׁמַּכּוֹתָיו יוֹצְאוֹת כְּדֵי רִשְׁעָתוֹ. יָצָא זֶה שֶׁאָמַר לוֹ עֲמוֹד וְשַׁלֵּם.

HALAKHAH 1

2 מכות | **ת** מכר   מכות | **ת** לא מכר   ואין לה | **ת** ולא   3 וסבר | **ת** סבר   4 במקום
| **ת** למקום   5 משום | **ת** - (twice)   5-6 וישלם ולא ילקה כעדים | **ת** מן עדים   6
כמה דתימר תמן בעדים | **ת** מה עדים   ואין | **ת** ואינן   7 וכא | **ת** אף הכא   יונה | **ת**
נתן   8 כדי רשעתו | **ת** והפילו השפט והכהו לפניו   רשעתו | **ת** רשעו

Nathan bar Hoshiah said, one speaks about an adolescent girl, the other about an adult woman. The adolescent has a fine but nobody is flogged for her; for the adult he is flogged but pays no fine, she cannot be sold; she has no claim for shame and blemish. The rabbis of Caesarea said, explain it that she seduced him or remitted [the fine] for him. Nathan bar Hoshaiah thinks that in a case of flogging and payment he pays but is not flogged. Why should he not be flogged and have to pay? (*Deut.* 25:2) "Because of his guilt." You sentence him for one offence but you may not sentence him for two offences. From perjured witnesses. Just as you say there, perjured witnesses pay but are not flogged, here also he pays and is not flogged. Rebbi Jonah said, the reason of Rebbi Nathan bar Hoshaiah: (*Deut.* 25:2): "For his evil deed." It refers to one whose flogging frees him from his guilt, excluding one who is told: get up and pay.

(27b line 49) מַתְנִיתִין פְּלִיגָא עַל רִבִּי שִׁמְעוֹן בֶּן לָקִישׁ. הָאוֹכֵל תְּרוּמָה מֵזִיד מְשַׁלֵּם אֶת הַקֶּרֶן וְאֵינוֹ מְשַׁלֵּם אֶת הַחוֹמֶשׁ. עַל דַּעְתֵּיהּ דְּנָתָן בַּר הוֹשַׁעְיָה דְּאָמַר. מְשַׁלֵּם. נִיחָא. עַל דַּעְתֵּיהּ דְּרִבִּי יוֹחָנָן דְּאָמַר. אִם הִתְרוּ בּוֹ לוֹקֶה וְאִם לֹא הִתְרוּ בּוֹ מְשַׁלֵּם. פָּתַר לָהּ מֵזִיד בְּ[לֹא][32] הַתְרָאָה. עַל דַּעְתֵּיהּ דְּרִבִּי שִׁמְעוֹן בֶּן לָקִישׁ לֹא שַׁנְיָיא. הִיא שׁוֹגֵג הִיא מֵזִיד. הִיא הִתְרוּ בּוֹ הִיא לֹא הִתְרוּ בּוֹ. פָּתַר לָהּ כְּרִבִּי מֵאִיר דְּאָמַר. לוֹקֶה וּמְשַׁלֵּם.

1. האוכל | **ת** והא תנינן האוכל   an entire sentence missing in *Ketubot*   2 משלם את הקרן ואינו משלם את החומש | **ת** -   דאמר | **ת** דו אמר   4 בהתראה | **ת** בלא התראה   5-6 | - **ת** סבר ר' שמעון בן לקיש

Our Mishnah disagrees with Rebbi Simeon ben Laqish! "If somebody eats heave intentionally he pays the principal but not the fifth." In the opinion of Nathan bar Hoshaiah who said he pays, it is understandable. In the opinion of Rebbi Joḥanan who said, if he was cautioned he is flogged, but if he was not cautioned he pays, he explains it as intentional without cautioning. In the opinion of Rebbi Simeon ben Laqish there is no difference between intentional and unintentional, between cautioned or not cautioned. He explains following Rebbi Meïr who says, he is flogged and he pays.

32 From the text in Terumot; missing here.

(27b line 55) אָמַר רִבִּי חֲנִינָה קוֹמֵי רִבִּי מָנָא. וַאֲפִילוּ יְסָבוֹר רִבִּי שִׁמְעוֹן בֶּן לָקִישׁ כְּדְמַתְנִיתֵין דְּרִבִּי מֵאִיר. קָרְיָיה דְּרִבִּי מֵאִיר. וְהָא כְתִיב אִישׁ כִּי יֹאכַל קוֹדֶשׁ בִּשְׁגָגָה. אֶלָּא מִיסְּבַּר סָבַר רִבִּי שִׁמְעוֹן בֶּן לָקִישׁ. חוֹמֶשׁ קָרְבָּן. וַאֲפִילוּ תֵּימַר. חוֹמֶשׁ קָרְבָּן. קֶרֶן קָרְבָּן. אָמַר רִבִּי יוּדָן בַּר שָׁלוֹם. מַתְנִיתִין אָמְרָה שֶׁהַקֶּרֶן קְנָס. דְּתַנִּינָן תַּמָּן אֵינוֹ מְשַׁלֵּם תְּרוּמָה אֶלָּא חוּלִין מְתוּקָּנִין וְהֵן נַעֲשִׂין תְּרוּמָה. אִילוּ מִמַּה שֶׁאָכַל הָיָה מְשַׁלֵּם נִיחָא. וְעוֹד מֵהָדָא דְּתַנֵּי. אָכַל תְּרוּמָה טְמִיאָה מְשַׁלֵּם חוּלִין טְהוֹרִין. וְאִם שִׁילֵּם חוּלִין טְמֵאִין יָצָא. וְלֹא דְמֵי עֵצִים הוּא חַיָּיב לוֹ. הָדָא אָמְרָה שֶׁהַקֶּרֶן קְנָס. כְּמָה דְּאַתְּ אָמַר קֶרֶן קְנָס. וְדִכְוָתָהּ חוֹמֶשׁ קְנָס. אֶלָּא רִבִּי שִׁמְעוֹן בֶּן לָקִישׁ כְּדַעְתֵּיהּ. כְּמָה דוּ אָמַר תַּמָּן. הַכֹּל הָיָה בִכְלָל לֹא תַעֲנֶה בְרֵעֲךָ עֵד שָׁקֶר. יָצָא וַעֲשִׂיתֶם לוֹ כַּאֲשֶׁר זָמַם לַעֲשׂוֹת לְאָחִיו. לֹא כֵּן שֶׁיְּשַׁלֵּם מָמוֹן. וְכָא הַכֹּל הָיוּ בִכְלָל וְכָל־זָר לֹא יֹאכַל קוֹדֶשׁ. יָצָא וְאִישׁ כִּי יֹאכַל קוֹדֶשׁ בִּשְׁגָגָה שֶׁיְּשַׁלֵּם מָמוֹן.

1 חנינה | ת חיננא   ואפילו | ת ואין   2 כדמתניתי' | ת כל מתנית'   3 שהחומש | ת חומש   4 תימר | ת יסבור   5 דתנינן תמן | ת דתנינן   6 ניחא | ת יאות   ועוד מהכא דתני | ת דתני כן   8 כמה דאת אמר | ת וכמה דתימר   אלא | ת אלא אמר   9 אמר | ת ר' שמעון בן לקיש אמר   10 יצא | ת יצא זה   11 לא שישלם | ת לחייבו וכא | ת והכא   12 שישלם | ת לחייבו

Rebbi Ḥinena said before Rebbi Mana: Even if Rebbi Simeon ben Laqish thought the entire Mishnaiot were Rebbi Meïr's, does the verse agree with Rebbi Meïr? Is it not written (*Lev.* 22:14): "If a person ate consecrated food in error"? But Rebbi Simeon ben Laqish must hold that the fifth is a sacrifice. But even if he holds that the fifth is a sacrifice, can the principal be a sacrifice? Rebbi Yudan bar Shalom said, the Mishnah declares that the principal is a fine, as we have stated: "He does not pay in heave but in totally profane food which is turned into heave." If he had to pay from what he ate, it would be fine. And it was stated: "If he ate impure heave, he has to pay in pure profane food, but if he paid in impure profane, he discharged his obligation." Does he not owe him the price of wood? That shows that the principal is a fine and since the principal is a fine, the fifth also is a fine. But Rebbi Simeon ben Laqish follows his own opinion. Just as Rebbi Simeon ben Laqish said, there, everybody was under the obligation of (*Ex.* 20:16) "Do not become a false witness against your neighbor", but this one was treated separately, (*Deut.* 19:19) "do to him what he intended to do to his brother", to pay money; also here, everybody was under the obligation of (*Lev.* 22:10) "no outsider shall eat holy [food]," but this one was treated separately, (*Lev.* 22:14) "if somebody should eat holy [food] in error," to pay money.

(27b line 67) וְתַנֵּי מוֹדִין חֲכָמִים לְרִבִּי מֵאִיר בְּגוֹנֵב תְּרוּמַת חֲבֵירוֹ וַאֲכָלָהּ שֶׁהוּא לוֹקֶה וּמְשַׁלֵּם. שֶׁכֵּן הָאוֹכֵל תְּרוּמָה לוֹקֶה. וְהָתַנֵּי מוֹדִין חֲכָמִים לְרִבִּי מֵאִיר בְּגוֹנֵב חֵלֶב חֲבֵירוֹ וַאֲכָלוֹ שֶׁלּוֹקֶה וּמְשַׁלֵּם. שֶׁכֵּן הָאוֹכֵל חֶלְבּוֹ לוֹקֶה. וְהָתַנֵּי הַחוֹסֵם אֶת הַפָּרָה מְשַׁלֵּם שֵׁשֶׁת קַבִּין לְפָרָה וְאַרְבָּעָה קַבִּין לַחֲמוֹר. שֶׁכֵּן הַחוֹסֵם פָּרָתוֹ לוֹקֶה. אָמַר רִבִּי יוֹסֵי. שֶׁכֵּן בִּמְחוּיָּיבֵי מִיתוֹת. גָּנַב תְּרוּמַת הַקּוֹדֶשׁ וַאֲכָלָהּ שֶׁהוּא לוֹקֶה וּמְשַׁלֵּם. מִכָּל־מָקוֹם הִפְסִידוֹ מָמוֹן.

1 ותני | ת׳ והתני   תרומת חבירו | ת׳ חלבו של חבירו ואכלה   2 תרומה | ת׳ חלב   3
חלב חבירו ואכלה | ת׳ תרומת חבירו   שלוקה | ת׳ שהוא לוקה   חלבו | ת׳ תרומתו   4
החוסם | ת׳ מודין חכמים לרבי מאיר שהחוסם   את הפרה | ת׳ פרתו של חבירו   משלם | ת׳
שהוא לוקה ומשלם   ארבעה | ת׳ ארבעת   5 הקודש | ת׳ הקדש   הפסידו | ת׳ הפסיד

Did we not state: The Sages admit to Rebbi Meïr that one who stole his neighbor's heave is flogged and has to pay since whoever eats heave is flogged. Did we not state: The Sages admit to Rebbi Meïr that one who stole his neighbor's fat is flogged and has to pay since whoever eats fat is flogged. Did we not state: The Sages admit to Rebbi Meïr that one who muzzled his neighbor's cow is flogged and has to pay six *qab* per cow and four *qab* for a donkey since whoever muzzles his cow is flogged. Rebbi Yose said, the same holds if death is the penalty. If he stole Temple heave and ate it, he is whipped and has to pay since in any case he caused monetary loss.

(27b line 74) אָמַר רִבִּי מָנָא קוֹמֵי רִבִּי יוֹסֵי. מֵעַתָּה הַבָּא עַל אֲחוֹתוֹ קְטַנָּה יִלְקֶה וִישַׁלֵּם. שֶׁכֵּן הַבָּא עַל אֲחוֹתוֹ בּוֹגֶרֶת לוֹקֶה. חָזַר וְאָמַר. גַּבֵּי אֲחוֹתוֹ חָל עָלָיו תַּשְׁלוּמִין וּמִיתָה כְּאַחַת. בְּרַם הָכָא. מִכֵּיוָן שֶׁחֲסָם נִתְחַיֵּיב מַכּוֹת. מִכָּן וְאֵילַךְ בְּתַשְׁלוּמִין. הֵתִיב רִבִּי עֶזְרָא קוֹמֵי רִבִּי מָנָא. הֲרֵי הַמֵּצִית גְּדִישׁוֹ שֶׁלַּחֲבֵירוֹ בַשַּׁבָּת. עַל שִׁיבּוֹלֶת הָרִאשׁוֹן חַיָּיב [מִיתָה]³³ מִכָּן וְהֵילַךְ לְתַשְׁלוּמִין. וְלֵית אָמַר כֵּן עַל כָּל־שִׁיבּוֹלֶת וְשִׁיבּוֹלֶת יֵשׁ בָּהּ הַתְרָיִית מִיתָה. וְכָא עַל כָּל־חֲסִימָה וַחֲסִימָה יֵשׁ בָּהּ הַתְרָיִית מַכּוֹת. תְּרֵין אֲמוֹרָאִין. רִבִּי יוֹסֵי בֵּי רִבִּי בּוּן אָמַר. חַד אָמַר. בְּחוֹסֵם בִּתְרוּמָה וּבְקָדָשִׁים. וְחָרְנָה אָמַר. בְּחוֹסֵם עַל יְדֵי שָׁלִיחַ. שָׁלִיחַ לוֹקֶה וְהוּא פָּטוּר. דָּם יֵחָשֵׁב לָאִישׁ הַהוּא וְלֹא לְשׁוּלְחָיו.

1 קטנה | ת׳ בוגרת   2 בוגרת | ת׳ קטנה   ומר | ת׳ ר׳ מנא ואמר   גבי אחותו | ת׳ תמן
3 תשלומין ומיתה | ת׳ מיתה ותשלומין   מיכון שחסם | ת׳ מהחסימה הראשונה   מכן | ת׳
ומכן   4 הרי | ת׳ -   5 על שיבולת הראשון | ת׳ משיבולת הראשונה   חייב מכות | ת׳
נתחייב מיתה   והילך | ת׳ ואילך   6 כן | ת׳ הכן אלא   התריית מיתה | ת׳ מכות והתריית

תשלומין | וכא | ת ואוף הכא   7 מכות | ת מכות והתריית תשלומין   ר1ת יוסי ביר' בון
אמר | ת אמר ר' יוסי ביר' בון   8 בקדשים | ת במוקדשין   9 לשולחיו | ת לשלוחיו

Rebbi Mana said before Rebbi Yose: If it is so, he who sleeps with his minor sister should be flogged and have to pay since if he sleeps with his adult sister he is flogged. He reversed himself and said, there death and payment fall on him simultaneously. But here, when he muzzled he is subject to flogging but only later for payment. Rebbi Ze'ira objected before Rebbi Mana: He who sets fire to his neighbor's grain stack on the Sabbath is subject to capital punishment from the first ear but only later for payment! One cannot say that because for every single ear there is cautioning for the death penalty. Here also, for every moment of muzzling there is cautioning for flogging. Rebbi Yose bar Abun said, two Amoraïm. One said, if he muzzled for heave which is Temple property. The other one said, if he muzzled through an agent. Then the agent is flogged and he is free (*Lev.* 17:4): "As a blood guilt it will be charged on *this* man," not on his employers.

33   Reading of the text in *Terumot*; here: מַכּוֹת "flogging".

(27c line 8) שׁוֹגֵג בִּתְרוּמָה וּמֵזִיד בְּחָמֵץ. שׁוֹגֵג בִּתְרוּמָה וּמֵזִיד בְּנָזִיר. שׁוֹגֵג בִּתְרוּמָה וּמֵזִיד בְּיוֹם הַכִּיפּוּרִים. אִין תִּפְתְּרִינָהּ בִּשְׁנֵי דְבָרִים נִיחָא. וְאִין תִּיפְתַּר בְּדָבָר אֶחָד מַחְלוֹקֶת רִבִּי יוֹחָנָן וְרִבִּי שִׁמְעוֹן בֶּן לָקִישׁ.

2 תפתרינה | ת נפתרינה   תפתר | ת נפתרינה

In error for heave and intentional for leavened, in error for heave and intentional for *nazir*, in error for heave and intentional for the Day of Atonement. If one explains it with two things, it is fine. If one explains it for one, this is the disagreement of Rebbi Johanan and Rebbi Simeon ben Laqish.

(27c line 11) תַּמָּן תַּנִּינָן. אֵין בֵּין שַׁבָּת לְיוֹם הַכִּיפּוּרִים אֶלָּא שֶׁזֶּה זְדוֹנוֹ בִּידֵי אָדָם וְזֶה זְדוֹנוֹ בְּהִיכָּרֵת. הָא בְּתַשְׁלוּמִין זֶה וְזֶה שָׁוִין. מַתְנִיתָא דְּרִבִּי נְחוֹנְיָיא בֶּן הַקָּנָה. דְּרִבִּי נְחוֹנְיָה בֶּן הַקָּנָה אוֹמֵר. יוֹם הַכִּיפּוּרִים כְּשַׁבָּת לְתַשְׁלוּמִין. רִבִּי שִׁמְעוֹן בֶּן מְנַסְיָא אוֹמֵר. מְחוּיָּבֵי כְרִיתוּת כִּמְחוּיָּבֵי מִיתוֹת בֵּית דִּין. מַה בֵּינֵיהוֹן. רִבִּי אָחָא בְשֵׁם רִבִּי אֲבִינָא. נַעֲרָה נִדָּה בֵּינֵיהוֹן. רִבִּי מָנָא אוֹמֵר. אַף אֲחוֹת אִשְׁתּוֹ בֵּינֵיהוֹן. עַל דַּעְתֵּיהּ דְּרִבִּי נְחוֹנְיָיא בֶּן הַקָּנָה. מַה שַׁבָּת אֵין לָהּ הֶיתֵּר אַחַר אִיסּוּרָהּ אַף יוֹם הַכִּיפּוּרִים אֵין לוֹ הֶיתֵּר אַחַר אִיסּוּרוֹ. וְאִילּוּ הוֹאִיל וְיֵשׁ לָהֶן הֶיתֵּר אַחַר אִיסּוּרָן מְשַׁלֵּם. עַל דַּעְתֵּיהּ דְּרִבִּי שִׁמְעוֹן בֶּן מְנַסְיָא מַה שַׁבָּת יֵשׁ בָּהּ כָּרֵת. אַף יוֹם הַכִּיפּוּרִים יֵשׁ בָּהּ כָּרֵת וְאִילּוּ הוֹאִיל וְאֵין בָּהֶן כָּרֵת מְשַׁלֵּם.

2 נחונייא | ת נחוניא   דר' | ת דתני ר'   ר' | ת ור'   4 מחוייבי | ת כמחוייבי   כמחייבי | ת כך חייבי   5 נערה | ת אמר נערה   מנא אומר | ת אמר ר' מנא   אף | ת אוף   7 אף יום | ת ויום   ואילו | ת וזו   8 לחן | ת לה   איסורין | ת איסורה   על דעתיה דר' | ת דר'   9 מה | ת אומר   ואילו | ת וזו   אין | ת יש   בהן | ת בו   10 משלם | ת אינו משלם

There, we have stated: "The only difference between the Sabbath and the Day of Atonement is that intentional infraction of the former is punished by the hands of man, but intentional infraction of the latter is punished by extirpation." Therefore, for payment both follow the same rules. This is by Rebbi Neḥoniah ben Haqanah since "Rebbi Neḥoniah ben Haqanah says, the Day of Atonement follows the rules of Sabbath for payment. But Rebbi Simeon ben Menassiah says those subject to extirpation equal those subject to capital punishment." What is between them? Rebbi Aḥa in the name of Rebbi Avina said, a menstruating adolescent girl is between them. Rebbi Mana said, also his wife's sister is between them. In the opinion of Rebbi Neḥoniah ben Haqanah, just as the Sabbath does not become permitted after its prohibition started; so the

Day of Atonement does not become permitted after its prohibition started. However, these may become permitted after their prohibition started, he has to pay. But Rebbi Simeon ben Menassiah said, extirpation applies to the Sabbath and the day of Atonement; extirpation does not apply to these, he has to pay.

(27c line 21) רִבִּי יוּדָה בַּר פָּזִי בְעָא. מַכּוֹת וְכָרֵת מַה אָמְרִין בָּהּ אִילֵּין תַּנָּיֵי. אָמַר רִבִּי יוֹסֵי. צְרִיכָה לְרַבָּנִין. רִבִּי יוֹנָה בְעָא. לָמָּה לֹא שָׁמַע לָהּ מִן הָדָא דְּתַנֵּי רִבִּי שִׁמְעוֹן בֶּן יוֹחַי. דְּתַנֵּי רִבִּי שִׁמְעוֹן בֶּן יוֹחַי. רִבִּי טַרְפוֹן אוֹמֵר. נֶאֱמַר כָּרֵת בְּשַׁבָּת וְנֶאֱמַר כָּרֵת בְּיוֹם הַכִּיפּוּרִים. מַה כָּרֵת שֶׁנֶּאֱמַר בְּשַׁבָּת אֵין מַכּוֹת אֵצֶל כָּרֵת אַף כָּרֵת שֶׁנֶּאֱמַר בְּיוֹם הַכִּיפּוּרִים אֵין מַכּוֹת אֵצֶל כָּרֵת. אָמַר רִבִּי מָנָא קוֹמֵי רִבִּי יוֹסֵי. מַה צְּרִיכָה. לֹא כְרִבִּי שִׁמְעוֹן בֶּן לָקִישׁ. בְּרַם כְּרִבִּי יוֹחָנָן. מַה מַכּוֹת אֵצֶל מִיתָה יֵשׁ לוֹ כָּל-שֶׁכֵּן מַכּוֹת אֵצֶל כָּרֵת. וְאִיתְפַּלְגוּן. הַשּׁוֹחֵט אוֹתוֹ וְאֶת בְּנוֹ לְשֵׁם עֲבוֹדָה זָרָה. רִבִּי יוֹחָנָן אָמַר. הִתְרוּ בוֹ מִשֵּׁם אוֹתוֹ וְאֶת בְּנוֹ לוֹקֶה. מִשֵּׁם עֲבוֹדָה זָרָה הָיָה נִסְקָל. רִבִּי שִׁמְעוֹן בֶּן לָקִישׁ אָמַר. אֲפִילוּ הִתְרוּ מִשֵּׁם אוֹתוֹ וְאֶת בְּנוֹ אֵינוֹ לוֹקֶה מֵאַחַר שֶׁאִילּוּ הִתְרוּ בוֹ מִשֵּׁם עֲבוֹדָה זָרָה הָיָה נִסְקָל. אָמַר לֵיהּ. אֲפִילוּ כְרִבִּי יוֹחָנָן צְרִיכָה לוֹ. תַּמָּן שְׁנֵי דְבָרִים. וְכָא דָּבָר אֶחָד.

1 מכות וכרת | ת לווין וכריתות   2 ר' יונה בעא | ת אמר ר' יונה   למה | ת ולמה   לח | ת ליה   4 שנאמר | ת האמור   אין מכות אצל כרת | ת אין ממון אצל מיתה אף כרת האמור ביום הכיפורים אין ממון אצל כרת   6 צריכה | ת צריכין   לא | ת ליה   7 מכות | ת ממון   ואיתפלגון | ת אמר ליה אף כר' יוחנן צריכה ליה איתפלגון   8 התרו | ת אם התרו   משם | ת לשום   9 משם | ת לשם   אפילו | ת ואפילו   10 התרו משם | ת התרו בו לשום   משם | ת לשם   11 אמר ליה אפילו כר' יוחנן צריכה לו תמן | ת הכא וכא | ת והכא

Rebbi Judah bar Pazi asked: What say these Tannaïm about whipping and extirpation? Rebbi Yose said, that is a problem for the rabbis. Rebbi Jonah said, why can we not understand it from what Rebbi Simeon ben

Iohai stated? As Rebbi Simeon ben Iohai stated: "Rebbi Țarphon says, extirpation was mentioned for the Sabbath and the Day of Atonement. Since for extirpation mentioned for the Sabbath there is no payment in a case involving the death penalty, so for extirpation mentioned for the Day of Atonement there is no payment in a case involving extirpation." Rebbi Mana said before Rebbi Yose: When do we need this? Not for Rebbi Simeon ben Laqish? But for Rebbi Johanan, if he admits flogging in death penalty cases, certainly flogging in extirpation cases, since they disagreed: If somebody slaughters [an animal] and its young for idolatrous purposes. Rebbi Johanan says, if he was cautioned about an animal and its young, he is flogged, about idolatry, he is stoned to death. Rebbi Simeon ben Laqish said, even if he was cautioned about an animal and its young, he is not flogged since he would be stoned to death had he been cautioned about idolatry. He said to him, we need it even for Rebbi Johanan! Here are two cases, there it is one case.

(27c line 32) עַל דַּעְתֵּיהּ דְּרַבִּי שִׁמְעוֹן בֶּן לָקִישׁ מַה אִיכָּא בֵּין אִילֵּין תַּנָּיֵי לְאִילֵּין רַבָּנִין. לָאוִין. לֹא כְרִיתוּת. רִבִּי יוּדָן אָמַר. הַבָּא עַל הַמַּמְזֶרֶת בֵּינֵיהוֹן. רִבִּי חֲנַנְיָה אָמַר. הַמֵּצִית גְּדִישׁוֹ שֶׁל חֲבֵירוֹ בְּיוֹם טוֹב[34] בֵּינֵיהוֹן. עַל דַּעְתִּין דְּאִילֵּין תַּנָּאֵי הוֹאִיל וְאֵין בָּהֶן כָּרֵת מְשַׁלֵּם. עַל דַּעְתִּין דְּרַבָּנִין דְּאִילּוּ הוֹאִיל וְיֵשׁ בָּהֶן מַכּוֹת אֵינוֹ מְשַׁלֵּם. מֵעַתָּה אִילּוּ נְעָרוֹת שֶׁיֵּשׁ לָהֶן קְנָס. דְּלָא כְרַבָּנִין. אָמַר רִבִּי מַתַּנְיָה. תִּפְתָּר דִּבְרֵי הַכֹּל בְּמַמְזֵר שֶׁבָּא עַל הַמַּמְזֶרֶת.

1 איכא | ת -   2 לאוין | ת ללאוין   כריתות | ת לכריתות   ר' יודן אמר | ת אמר ר' יודן הבא על הממזרת ביניהון | ת ר' שמעון בן לקיש דו אמר כר' מאיר דו אמר לוקה ומשלם 3 ר' חנניה אמר | ת אמר ר' חנניה   ביום הכיפורים | ת ביום טוב   על דעתין דעילין | ת אילין   4 הואיל | ת סברין מימר הואיל   על דעתין דרבנין דאילו | ת ואילין רבנין סברין מימר   ויש | ת יש   5 שיש להן קנס | ת -   6 תפתר דברי הכל בממזר שבא | ת בבא   . | ת ביניהון.

According to Rebbi Simeon ben Laqish, what is between these Tannaïm and those rabbis? Prohibitions without extirpation. Rebbi Judan said, he who sleeps with a bastard girl is between them. Rebbi Ḥananiah said, he who puts fire to the grain stack of his neighbor on a holiday is between them. These Tannaïm think, since there is no extirpation, he pays. Those rabbis think, since there is flogging he does not pay. But then "these are the adolescent girls who can claim a fine" cannot follow the rabbis! Rebbi Mattaniah said, explain it according to everybody if it refers to a bastard male who sleeps with a bastard girl.

34   Reading of the text in *Terumot*; here: יוֹם הַכִּיפּוּרִים "the Day of Atonement", whose desecration is punished by extirpation.

(27c line 38) וְאֵשֶׁת אָחִיו לָאו יְבִימְתּוֹ הִיא. אָמַר רִבִּי מַתַּנְיָה. תִּפְתָּר שֶׁהָיוּ לְאָחִיו בָּנִים וְאֵירַס אִשָּׁה וָמֵת וּבָא אָחִיו וַאֲנָסָהּ.

1 אמר ר' מתניה | ת - | שהיו | ת שמת אחיו וחיו | לאחיו | ת לו   2 אירס | ת ואירש

But is his brother's wife not his sister-in-law? Explain it that the man's brother had children and had performed the preliminary wedding with a woman when he died and [the surviving] brother came and raped her.

(fol. 27a) **משנה ב:** וְאֵילוּ שֶׁאֵין לָהֶן קְנָס. הַבָּא עַל הַגִּיּוֹרֶת וְעַל הַשְּׁבוּיָה וְעַל הַשִּׁפְחָה שֶׁנִּפְדּוּ וְשֶׁנִּתְגַּייְרוּ וְשֶׁנִּשְׁתַּחְרְרוּ יְתֵירוֹת עַל בְּנוֹת שָׁלֹשׁ שָׁנִים וְיוֹם אֶחָד. רִבִּי יְהוּדָה אוֹמֵר. שְׁבוּיָה שֶׁנִּיפְדֵּית הֲרֵי הִיא בִּקְדוּשָׁתָהּ אַף עַל פִּי שֶׁהִיא גְדוֹלָה.

Mishnah 2: The following cannot claim a fine: One who comes to a proselyte woman, a kidnap victim, or a slave girl who was redeemed, converted, or freed, at more than three years and one day of age[3]. Rebbi Jehudah says, the redeemed kidnap victim is in her holiness[35] even if she is an adult.

35 She is trustworthy if she asserts that she is a virgin.

(27c line 40) **הלכה ב:** אֵילוּ שֶׁאֵין לָהֶן קְנָס כול'. אָמַר רִבִּי יוֹחָנָן. לֹא רִיבָּה אוֹתָהּ רִבִּי יְהוּדָה אֶלָּא לִקְנָס. תַּנֵּי רִבִּי חִייָה. אַף לִכְתוּבַּת מָנָה מָאתַיִם. רִבִּי שִׁמְעוֹן בֶּן לָקִישׁ אָמַר. אַף לְהַאֲכִילָהּ תְּרוּמָה. עַל דַּעְתֵּיהּ דְּרִבִּי שִׁמְעוֹן בֶּן לָקִישׁ רִבִּי יוּדָה וְרִבִּי דוֹסָא שְׁנֵיהֶן אוֹמְרִים דָּבָר אֶחָד. דְּתַנִּינָן תַּמָּן. הַשְּׁבוּיָה אוֹכֶלֶת בִּתְרוּמָה. דִּבְרֵי רִבִּי דוֹסָא. אָתָא רִבִּי חֲנִינָה בְּשֵׁם רִבִּי שִׁמְעוֹן בֶּן לָקִישׁ הֲלָכָה כְרִבִּי דוֹסָא.

Halakhah 2: "The following cannot claim a fine," etc. Rebbi Johanan said, Rebbi Jehudah excepted the kidnap victim only for the fine[36]. Rebbi Hiyya stated: Also for the *ketubah* of a mina or 200 [*zuz*][37]. Rebbi Simeon ben Laqish said, even to let her eat heave. In the opinion of Rebbi Simeon ben Laqish[38], Rebbi Jehudah and Rebbi Dosa both said the same, as we have stated there[39]: The kidnap victim eats heave, the words of Rebbi Dosa. Rebbi Hanina[40] came in the name of Rebbi Simeon ben Laqish: Practice follows Rebbi Dosa[41].

36 But he accords her only the *ketubah* of one mina and forbids her to marry a Cohen.

37 Tosephta 3:4: "R. Jehudah says, a kidnapped underage Israel girl, even one 10 years old, remains in her holiness and her *ketubah* stays intact."

38 In the Babli, 36b, this is the opinion of R. Johanan.

39 Mishnah *Idiut* 3:6.

40 He should be R. Hinena, not R. Hanina the teacher of R. Simeon ben Laqish.

41 The Babli, 36b, which has to follow this ruling since it attributes it to R. Johanan, explains it away as

applying only to the fine, that a sinner should not get away with his crime, and for rabbinic heave; in all other respects one follows the anonymous majority.

(fol. 27a) **משנה ג:** הַבָּא עַל בִּתּוֹ עַל בַּת בִּתּוֹ עַל בַּת בְּנוֹ עַל בַּת אִשְׁתּוֹ עַל בַּת בְּנָהּ עַל בַּת בִּתָּהּ אֵין לָהֶן קְנָס מִפְּנֵי שֶׁהוּא מִתְחַיֵּיב בְּנַפְשׁוֹ שֶׁמִּיתָתוֹ בִּידֵי בֵית דִּין וְכָל־הַמִּתְחַיֵּיב בְּנַפְשׁוֹ אֵינוֹ מְשַׁלֵּם מָמוֹן שֶׁנֶּאֱמַר וְלֹא יִהְיֶה אָסוֹן עָנוֹשׁ יֵעָנֵשׁ.

Mishnah 3: The one who comes to his daughter, his granddaughter from his daughter or his son, his wife's daughter, his wife's granddaughter from her daughter or her son[42] does not pay the fine since he committed a capital crime and should be executed by the court; for anybody committing a capital crime[43] does not pay cash as it is said[44]: "If there is no case of murder, a fine shall be imposed."

42   These are the only cases among the incest prohibitions of *Lev.* 18,20 which are both capital crimes and may involve a virgin girl.

43   Even if he cannot be executed because of missing eyewitnesses to a due warning and the deed.

44   *Ex.* 21:22. The next verse reads: "But if it is a case of murder, you shall take life for life." This excludes the imposition of a fine in a murder trial.

(27c line 45) **הלכה ג:** הַבָּא עַל בִּתּוֹ כול'. אִילּוּ אַחֵר בָּא עָלֶיהָ קְנָסָהּ לָאו לְאָבִיהָ הוּא. תִּיפְתָּר שֶׁבָּא עָלֶיהָ עַד שֶׁלֹּא מֵת אָבִיהָ וּמֵת אָבִיהָ. כְּרִבִּי יוֹסֵי הַגְּלִילִי. בְּרַם כְּרִבִּי עֲקִיבָה יֵשׁ לָהּ קְנָס וּקְנָסָהּ שֶׁלְּעַצְמָהּ.

Halakha 3: "The one who comes to his daughter," etc. If another man had come to her, would the fine not be her father's[45]? Explain it that another man came to her before her father died and then her father died[46]. That follows Rebbi Yose the Galilean. But following Rebbi Aqiba, she collects a fine and the fine is hers[47].

45 Why does the Mishnah state in this case that he does not have to pay the fine because he committed a capital crime; in that particular case it is because he would have to pay the fine to himself.

46 If the girl was raped by a third person during her father's lifetime but the father died before he could collect the fine, the girl collects the fine for herself. But if she was raped by her father, she cannot claim the fine from the estate because the rape was a capital crime.

47 Their disagreement is in Mishnah 4; cf. also Note 25.

(27c line 48) רִבִּי יִרְמְיָה בְשֵׁם רִבִּי לָעָזָר. מִמַּשְׁמַע שֶׁנֶּאֱמַר וְלֹא יִהְיֶה אָסוֹן אֵינִי יוֹדֵעַ אִם יִהְיֶה אָסוֹן וְנָתַתָּ נֶפֶשׁ תַּחַת נָפֶשׁ. וּמַה תַלְמוּד לוֹמַר אִם יִהְיֶה אָסוֹן לְרַבּוֹת אֶת הַמֵּזִיד בְּהַתְרָיָיה. אָמַר רִבִּי יוֹסֵי. וְלָאו מַתְנִיתָא הִיא שֶׁכָּל־הַמִּתְחַיֵּב בְּנַפְשׁוֹ אֵינוֹ מְשַׁלֵּם מָמוֹן. דְּלָא אָתְיָא אֶלָּא בְשׁוֹגֵג. אָמַר חִזְקִיָה. עוֹד תַּנֵּי מַתְנִיתָא. מַכֵּה בְהֵמָה יְשַׁלְּמֶנָּה וּמַכֵּה אָדָם יוּמָת. מָה מַכֵּה בְהֵמָה לֹא חִלַּקְתָּה בּוֹ בֵּין שׁוֹגֵג בֵּין מֵזִיד לְחַיֵּיב מָמוֹן. אַף מַכֵּה אָדָם לֹא תַחֲלוֹק בּוֹ בֵּין שׁוֹגֵג בֵּין מֵזִיד לִפְטוֹר מָמוֹן.

Rebbi Jeremiah in the name of Rebbi Eleazar: We understand that, since it said[44] "if there is no case of murder, a fine shall be imposed", that if it is a case of murder, you shall take life for life? Why does the verse say, it is a case of murder? To add the case of premeditation and warning[48]. Rebbi Yose said, is that not a Mishnah, "for anybody committing a capital crime does not pay cash", that it deals not only with cases of error. [49]Hizqiah said, one states a *baraita*[50]: "The slayer of an animal must pay for it but the slayer of a human shall be put to death." Just as you did not make a difference between unintentional and intentional action of a slayer of an animal to force him to pay money, so you should not make a difference between unintentional and intentional action of a slayer of a human to free him from paying money.

48   Which is a case where a person actually could face execution.
49   Cf. fol. 27b, line 30; *Terumot* 7:1,

Notes 16,18; Babli 35a.
50   *Lev.* 24:21.

(fol. 27a) **משנה ד:** נַעֲרָה שֶׁנִּתְאָרְסָה אוֹ שֶׁנִּתְגָּרְשָׁה רִבִּי יוֹסֵי הַגְּלִילִי אוֹמֵר אֵין לָהּ קְנָס. רִבִּי עֲקִיבָה אוֹמֵר יֵשׁ לָהּ קְנָס וּקְנָסָהּ שֶׁל עַצְמָהּ.

Mishnah 4: If an adolescent girl had been preliminarily married but was divorced[51], Rebbi Yose the Galilean says she cannot collect the fine; Rebbi Aqiba says, she can collect the fine and it belongs to her.

51   If she was raped while still preliminarily married, it was a capital crime and she cannot collect the fine.

(27c line 55) **הלכה ד:** נַעֲרָה שֶׁנִּתְאָרְסָה כול'. מַה טַעֲמָא דְרִבִּי יוֹסֵי הַגָּלִילִי. אֲשֶׁר לֹא אוֹרָשָׂה.

Halakhah 4: "An adolescent girl who had been preliminarily married," etc. What is the reason of Rebbi Yose the Galilean? "Who was not preliminarily married.[52]"

52   In both the rules about the seducer (*Ex.* 22:15) and the rapist (*Deut.* 22:28) it is emphasized that the fine is due only for "a virgin who was not preliminarily married." Now the verse cannot mean "a virgin not currently preliminarily married" since it is obvious that seduction or rape of a

preliminarily married girl is a capital crime and, therefore, free from paying the fine and the mention of her status would be superfluous. R. Aqiba also agrees with this analysis of the verse (Babli 38a), only he reads it that for "a virgin who was not preliminarily married" the fine is payable to her father; otherwise it is payable to the girl whose preliminary marriage emancipated her from her father's power. The same argument is quoted in the Babli 38a, *Mekhilta dR. Ismael, Mišpaṭim, Neziqin* 17; a similar argument is *Sifry Deut.* 244. An argument strictly following R. Yose the Galilean is in *Mekhilta deR. Simeon ben Ioḥai Mišpaṭim*, pp. 207-208.

(27c line 56) עַד שֶׁלֹּא נִתְאָרְסָה נוֹתֵן לְאָבִיהָ. נִתְאָרְסָה נוֹתֵן לְעַצְמָהּ. עַל דַּעְתֵּיהּ דְּרִבִּי יוֹסֵי הַגָּלִילִי. נַעֲרָה נוֹתֵן לְאָבִיהָ. בּוֹגֶרֶת נוֹתֵן לְעַצְמָהּ. בְּתוּלָה נוֹתֵן לְאָבִיהָ. מוּכַּת עֵץ נוֹתֵן לְעַצְמָהּ. שַׁנְיָיא הִיא דִכְתִיב נַעֲרָה. נַעֲרָה וְלֹא בוֹגֶרֶת. בְּתוּלָה. בְּתוּלָה וְלֹא מוּכַּת עֵץ. לֵית כְּתִיב אֲשֶׁר לֹא אוֹרָשָׂה. אֲשֶׁר לֹא אוֹרָשָׂה מְלַמֵּד הַיְמִינָהּ לִגְזִירָה שָׁוָה. מַה תַּמָּן חֲמִשִּׁין אַף הָכָא חֲמִשִּׁין. וְלֵית לֵיהּ לְרִבִּי יוֹסֵי חֲמִשִּׁין. אִית לֵיהּ כֶּסֶף כֶּסֶף. מַה כֶּסֶף שֶׁנֶּאֱמַר לְהַלָּן חֲמִשִּׁין. אַף כָּאן חֲמִשִּׁין.

Before she was preliminarily married, he gives to her father; after she had been preliminarily married, he gives to herself[53]. In the opinion of Rebbi Yose the Galilean[54], if she is an adolescent, he gives to her father[55]; if she is an adult, does he give it to herself? If she is a virgin, he gives to her father; if she is injured by wood, does he give it to herself? It is different, because it is written "an adolescent", adolescent but not adult. "A virgin," a virgin not one injured by wood. Is it not written[52] "who was not preliminarily married," "who was not preliminarily married," to infer from there by an equal cut[56]? Since in one case it is 50, so in the other case it is 50[57]. Does Rebbi Yose[58] not have "50"? He has "silver, silver"[59]. Since "silver" written at one place is 50, so "silver" [written at the other place][57] also is 50.

53 This is R. Aqiba's opinion; a mention of R. Aqiba might have been omitted by the scribe; the statement is ascribed to R. Aqiba in the *Mekhilta*.

54 As shown at the end of the paragraph, this should read "R. Aqiba".

55 The rule for the rapist is formulated for "a virgin adolescent", when the payment of 50 pieces of silver is due to her father; in the rule for the seducer, only "a virgin" is mentioned, and payment of "bride money", due to the woman at the dissolution of the marriage. On the face of it, the rule for the seducer does not exclude an adult victim.

56 The second hermeneutical rule, that equal expressions in two different paragraphs lets one transfer rules from one paragraph to the other. A condition for the applicability of that rule is that the expressions should be "free", not needed to establish a rule. For R. Yose the Galilean, the expressions "who was not preliminarily married" are not free since they establish a nontrivial rule; they cannot be used to argue by "equal cut". But for R. Aqiba the expressions are essentially superfluous and can be used.

57 The amount of bride money is not stated in *Ex.* 22; it is taken from *Deut.* 22 to be 50 holy šeqel which in talmudic theory are 200 *zuz*.

58 Rebbi Yose the Galilean who cannot accept R. Aqiba's "equal cut" as valid.

59 In *Ex.* 22:16, "he shall weigh *silver*"; in *Deut.* 22:29 "50 *silver pieces*". The same argument is quoted in the Babli, 38b.

(27c line 63) בָּא עָלֶיהָ עַד שֶׁלֹּא נִתְאָרְסָה וְנִתְגָּרְשָׁה. לֵית מִילְתָא דְרִבִּי אַחַי אָמְרָה שֶׁהוּא נוֹתֵן. וְהָתַנֵּי תַּחַת אֲשֶׁר עִנָּהּ. לְרַבּוֹת אֶת הַיְתוֹמָה לִקְנָס. דִּבְרֵי רִבִּי יוֹסֵי הַגָּלִילִי. אָמַר רִבִּי אַחַי. תִּיפְתָּר שֶׁבָּא עָלֶיהָ עַד שֶׁלֹּא מֵת אָבִיהָ וּמֵת אָבִיהָ כְּבָר נִרְאֶה לִיתֵּן לְאָבִיהָ. הוּא בָא עָלֶיהָ עַד שֶׁלֹּא מֵת אָבִיהָ וּמֵת אָבִיהָ וְהוּא בָא עָלֶיהָ עַד שֶׁלֹּא נִתְאָרְסָה וְנִתְגָּרְשָׁה. רִבִּי זְעִירָא אָמַר רַב חִסְדָּא בְּעָא. בָּא עָלֶיהָ עַד שֶׁלֹּא נִישֵּׂאת וְנִישֵּׂאת. מִמַּה דְּתֵימַר תַּמָּן תַּחַת בַּעֲלָהּ הִיא הוּא נוֹתֵן לְאָבִיהָ. וְכָא תַּחַת בַּעֲלָהּ הִיא הוּא נוֹתֵן לְאָבִיהָ.

If he came to her before she was preliminarily married, then she was preliminarily married and divorced[60]. Does the statement of Rebbi Aḥai not imply that he pays? Did we not state: "For he had mistreated her,[61]" to include the orphan for the fine, the words of Rebbi Yose the Galilean[62]. Rebbi Aḥai said, explain it that he came to her before her father died; when subsequently her father died he already was obligated to give to her father[63]. One came to her before her father died and subsequently her father died; one came to her before she was preliminarily married, subsequently she was divorced[64]. Rebbi Ze'ira said that Rav Ḥisda asked: If one came to her before she was married and then she was married[65]? Since you say there, she is under her husband but he has to pay to her father, so in this case she is under her husband but he has to pay to her father.

60 Does R. Yose the Galilean require the rapist to pay even after his victim was preliminarily married?

61 *Deut.* 22:29. A reason is given for the punishment of the rapist; therefore, the punishment applies any time the reason applies.

62 In *Sifry Deut.* 245, R. Eliezer holds that this refers only to the rapist, for whom the reason is given, but not to the seducer, for whom the rules do not extend to the orphan. In the Babli, 44b, R. Yose the Galilean applies the same rule to the orphaned victim of the seducer by an argument reproduced in *Mekhilta dR. Ismael, Mišpaṭim, Neziqin* 17.

63 R. Yose the Galilean is not contradicting himself; he only exempts the rapist or seducer of the preliminarily married girl if the sexual act happened while the girl was no longer in the father's power. But if it happened earlier, even though the court proceedings had not started at the father's death or the girl's preliminary marriage, the obligation of rapist or seducer is not erased.

64 The two cases are parallel.

65 Who collects the fine if an adolescent was raped and then (both preliminarily and definitively) married before the rape was adjudicated in court?

משנה ה: הַמְפַתֶּה נוֹתֵן שְׁלשָׁה דְּבָרִים וְהָאוֹנֵס אַרְבָּעָה. הַמְפַתֶּה נוֹתֵן (fol. 27a)
בּוֹשֶׁת וּפְגָם וּקְנָס. מוֹסִיף עָלָיו הָאוֹנֵס שֶׁנּוֹתֵן אֶת הַצַּעַר וְהַמְפַתֶּה אֵינוֹ נוֹתֵן אֶת
הַצַּעַר. הָאוֹנֵס נוֹתֵן מִיָּד וְהַמְפַתֶּה לִכְשֶׁיּוֹצִיא. הָאוֹנֵס שׁוֹתֶה בַּעֲצִיצוֹ וְהַמְפַתֶּה
אִם רָצָא לְהוֹצִיא מוֹצִיא.

Mishnah 5: The seducer pays for three things and the rapist for four. The seducer pays for shame, diminution of value[66], and fine. The rapist in addition pays for suffering; the seducer does not pay for suffering. The rapist pays immediately, the seducer only if he divorces her[67]. The rapist drinks from his pot[68]; the seducer may divorce if he wishes.

66 The computation of payments for shame and diminution of value are explained in Mishnah 8. Usually, the diminution of value refers to the loss of virginity but, in the case of forcible rape, it may also include the consequences of bodily injury such as a scar or a broken bone.

67 The rapist's fine is formulated as a fine in *Deut.* 22:29. That verse, stipulating that the fine goes to the father, then decrees that the rapist has to marry his victim and is barred from ever divorcing her. In contrast, the payment of the seducer is formulated in *Ex.* 22:16 as payment of a virgin's *ketubah* in case of a divorce.

68 He has to marry her even if she is ugly and deformed.

(27c line 71) **הלכה ה**: הַמְפַתֶּה נוֹתֵן שָׁלשׁ כוּ'. וּדְלָא כְרַבִּי שִׁמְעוֹן. דְּרַבִּי שִׁמְעוֹן פָּטַר אֶת הָאוֹנֵס מִן הַצַּעַר. לְמָה זֶה דוֹמֶה. לְחוֹתֵךְ יַבֶּלֶת חֲבֵירוֹ וְעָתִיד לְחַתְּכָהּ. לְמָה זֶה דוֹמֶה. לְקוֹצֵץ נְטִיעוֹת חֲבֵירוֹ וְעָתִיד לְחַתְּכָן. אָמְרוּ לוֹ. אֵינוֹ דוֹמָה נִבְעֶלֶת בְּאוֹנֶס לַנִּבְעֶלֶת בְּרָצוֹן. לֹא דוֹמָה נִבְעֶלֶת בְּאַשְׁפָּה לַנִּבְעֶלֶת בְּחוּפָּה. מַה מְקַיֵּים רִבִּי שִׁמְעוֹן תַּחַת אֲשֶׁר עִנָּהּ. אָמְרֵי בְּשֵׁם רַב חִסְדָּא. תִּיפְתָּר בְּשֶׁבָּא עָלֶיהָ עַל הַקּוֹצִים.

Halakhah 5: "The seducer pays three," etc. This does not follow Rebbi Simeon, since Rebbi Simeon freed the rapist from paying for suffering[69].

To what can you compare this? To one who cuts somebody's wart when that one would have cut it himself in the future. To what can you compare this? To one who cuts somebody's trees when that one would have cut them himself in the future. They said to him, you cannot compare one who is deflowered by rape to one who is deflowered by consent; you cannot compare one who is deflowered on a dungheap to one who is deflowered in the bridal chamber! How does Rebbi Simeon interpret "because he mistreated her"? They said in the name of Rav Ḥisda, explain it that he raped her on thorns.

69 In the Babli, 39a, there is a short discussion on what the suffering is for which the rapist has to pay. In the opinion of Samuel, represented in the Yerushalmi by his student's student Rav Ḥisda, it is the suffering inflicted by the attack. This is rejected in the Babli, since R. Simeon could not have opposed that payment. The payment for suffering therefore is restricted in the Babli to payment for the pain caused by the rupture of the hymen. In contrast, the Yerushalmi starts out with assuming that the pain is that of the deflowering and ends up with embracing the point of view of Samuel.

(27d line 1) וְהַמְפַתֶּה לִכְשֶׁיּוֹצִיא. אָמַר רַב חִסְדָּא. בְּשֶׁלֹּא רָצָה לְקַיְּיֵם. אֲבָל אִם רָצָה לְקַיְּיֵם אֵינוֹ נוֹתֵן כְּלוּם. תַּנֵּי רִבִּי יִשְׁמָעֵאל. כֶּסֶף יִשְׁקוֹל כְּמוֹהַר הַבְּתוּלוֹת. מַגִּיד שֶׁהוּא עוֹשֶׂה אוֹתָן עָלָיו מוֹהַר. וְאֵין מוֹהַר אֶלָּא כְתוּבָּה. כְּמָה דְאַתְּ אָמַר הַרְבּוּ עָלַי מְאֹד מוֹהַר וּמַתָּן.

"The seducer only if he divorces her," etc. Rav Ḥisda said, if he does not want to keep her. But if he decides to keep her, he does not give anything. Rebbi Ismael stated: "He should weigh silver appropriate for the bride-price of virgins[9]", which indicates that his obligation is for him that of bride-price, and bride-price is the *ketubah*[70]; as it also says[71] "add for me much bride-price and gifts."

70 This implies that *all* his obligations are transformed into *ketubah* obligations due at the dissolution of the marriage; not only the 200 *zuz* basic fee but also the sums fixed for shame and diminution of value.

71 Gen. 34:12.

(27d line 4) רִבִּי אֶלְעָזָר שָׁאַל. בְּנוֹת אֲנוּסָה מַהוּ שֶׁיְהֵא לָהֶן בְּתָנַאי כְּתוּבָּה. פְּשִׁיטָא לִי בָאֲנוּסָה דְלֵית לָהּ בְּנִין דְּכְרִין. בִּמְפוּתָּה דְלֵית לָהּ בְּנִין דְּכְרִין. אִין תֵּימַר תְּרֵיהוֹן צְרִיכָה לֵהּ. נְשָׁאוֹל. בְּנוֹת אֲנוּסָה וּבְנוֹת מְפוּתָּה מַהוּ שֶׁיְהֵא לָהֶן בְּתָנַאי כְּתוּבָּה. הֵן דִּצְרִיכָה לִי כְּרַבָּנִין. הֵן דְּפָשִׁיטָא לֵיהּ כְּרִבִּי יוֹסֵי בֵּירִבִּי יְהוּדָה. דְּתַנֵּי. רִבִּי יוֹסֵי בֵּירִבִּי יְהוּדָה אוֹמֵר. הָאוֹנֵס נוֹתֵן כְּתוּבַּת מָנֶה.

Rebbi Eleazar asked: Do the daughters of the rape victim have the rights given by the *ketubah* stipulations[72]? It is clear to me that the rape victim has no [*ketubah*] of the male children, and that the seduced victim has no [*ketubah*] of the male children[73]. If you say that he questions in both cases, we could ask, do the daughters of the rape victim and the daughters of the seduced girl have the rights given by the *ketubah* stipulations? That is a problem following the rabbis[74], but it is obvious following Rebbi Yose ben Rebbi Jehudah; as it was stated: Rebbi Yose ben Rebbi Jehudah says, the rapist gives a mina as *ketubah*[75].

72 Mishnaiot 4:8-12 contain a number of stipulations which the courts will enforce whether or not they were written in the *ketubah* document. The one in question here (Mishnah 11) states that the daughters, who do not inherit in the presence of sons, will have to be fed and lodged from the inheritance until they marry (they have a lien on the inheritance which has to be satisfied before the sons, the heirs, can take any money from the inheritance.) Since R. Ismael stated in the preceding paragraph that the seducer has to write a virgin's *ketubah*, it is clear to him that *all* stipulations of Mishnaiot 4:8-12 apply to the future children of the seduced girl. The only problem is with the rape victim who, never facing divorce, does not have a

ketubah in the opinion of the rabbis who disagree with R. Yose ben R. Jehudah later in this paragraph. In the Babli, 54a, this question is also asked and similarly left unanswered. In practice, this is a negative answer since "the burden of proof is on the claimant" and in the absence of a rule the daughters cannot prove their claim.

73 The *ketubah* of male children (Mishnah 4:10) stipulates that if a man has sons from different wives, the amounts of the different *ketubot* are first taken from the inheritance and distributed among the sons of the wives; the remainder is then split evenly among the sons (except that an eventual male firstborn takes a double portion). The reason given for this stipulation is that fathers should be encouraged to give their daughters ample dowries which become part of the *ketubah* obligations of their husbands, to make them attractive to prospective suitors. Therefore, the stipulation is necessary to insure that the property remains in the possession of the direct descendants of the givers. But since the rape victim and the seduced girl are married by biblical decree, they cannot expect dowries.

74 And is unanswered.

75 In contrast to the seducer who writes the *ketubah* of a virgin for a minimal sum of 200 *zuz*, the rapist already paid the fine of 200 *zuz* to the girl's father. He therefore writes for his wife an additional *ketubah* of the non-virgin.

(fol. 27a) **משנה ו:** כֵּיצַד הוּא שׁוֹתֶה בַעֲצִיצוֹ. אֲפִילוּ הִיא חִיגֶּרֶת אֲפִילוּ הִיא סוּמָה וְאֲפִילוּ הִיא מוּכַּת שְׁחִין. נִמְצָא בָהּ דְּבַר זִימָה אוֹ שֶׁאֵינָהּ רְאוּיָה לָבוֹא בְיִשְׂרָאֵל אֵינוֹ רַשַּׁאי לְקַיְּימָהּ שֶׁנֶּאֱמַר וְלוֹ תִהְיֶה לְאִשָּׁה אִשָּׁה שֶׁהִיא רְאוּיָה לוֹ.

Mishnah 6: How does he[76] drink from his pot? Even if she is lame, even if she is blind, or even if she is afflicted with boils[77]. If a matter of immorality was found with her[78] or she could not marry in Israel[79], he may not keep here since it is written[80]: "She shall be his wife," a wife appropriate for him.

76 The rapist mentioned in Mishnah 5.
77 He has to marry her and is prohibited from divorcing her.
78 If she was found guilty of adultery or incest. In that case, the husband is not permitted to keep her.
79 If she was a bastard or a Gibeonite.
80 *Deut.* 22:29.

(27d line 10) **הלכה ו:** בְּאֵי זֶה צַד הוּא שׁוֹתֶה בַעֲצִיצוֹ כול׳. רִבִּי יִרְמְיָה רִבִּי חִייָה בְּשֵׁם רִבִּי שִׁמְעוֹן בֶּן לָקִישׁ. לֹא יֹאמַר וְלוֹ תִהְיֶה לְאִשָּׁה זֶה הַמּוֹצִיא שֵׁם רָע. שֶׁאֵינוֹ צָרִיךְ שֶׁכְּבָר הִיא תַּחַת יָדוֹ. וּמַה תַּלְמוּד לוֹמַר וְלוֹ תִהְיֶה לְאִשָּׁה. תְּלַמֵּד הֵימֶנּוּ לִגְזֵירָה שָׁוָה. מִתְדָּרֵשׁ וְלוֹ תִהְיֶה וְלוֹ תִהְיֶה. מַה וְלוֹ תִהְיֶה שֶׁנֶּאֱמַר לְהַלָּן אִשָּׁה שֶׁרְאוּיָה לוֹ אַף וְלוֹ תִהְיֶה שֶׁנֶּאֱמַר כָּאן אִשָּׁה הָרְאוּיָה לוֹ. אִי מַה לְהַלָּן אִשָּׁה הָרְאוּיָה לוֹ וּמְשַׁלֵּם קְנָס. אַף וְלוֹ תִהְיֶה שֶׁנֶּאֱמַר כָּאן אִשָּׁה הָרְאוּיָה לוֹ וּמְשַׁלֵּם קְנָס. רִבִּי זְעִירָא עוּלָא (בְּשֵׁם רִבִּי) יִשְׁמָעֵאל בְּשֵׁם רִבִּי אֶלְעָזָר. לֹא יֹאמַר וְלוֹ תִהְיֶה בְּמוֹצִיא שֵׁם רָע שֶׁאֵינוֹ צָרִיךְ כְּבָר הִיא תַּחַת יָדוֹ. מַה תַּלְמוּד לוֹמַר וְלוֹ תִהְיֶה לְאִשָּׁה. מְלַמֵּד הֵימֶנּוּ לִגְזֵירָה שָׁוָה. מִתְדָּרְשָׁהּ וְלוֹ תִהְיֶה וְלוֹ תִהְיֶה. מַה תִּהְיֶה שֶׁנֶּאֱמַר לְהַלָּן גֵּירֵשׁ אוֹמְרִים לוֹ שֶׁיַּחֲזִיר אַף וְלוֹ תִהְיֶה הָאָמוּר כָּאן גֵּירֵשׁ אוֹמְרִים לוֹ שֶׁיַּחֲזִיר. תַּנֵּי רִבִּי חִייָה. אֶחָד הָאוֹנֵס וְאֶחָד הַמּוֹצִיא שֵׁם רָע שֶׁגֵּירְשׁוּ כּוֹפִין אוֹתָן לְהַחֲזִיר. אִם הָיוּ כֹהֲנִים סוֹפְגִין אֶת הָאַרְבָּעִים.

Halakhah 6: "How does he drink from his pot," etc. Rebbi Jeremiah, Rebbi Ḥiyya, in the name of Rebbi Simeon ben Laqish: It should not have said "she shall be his wife" for the calumniator[81]; it is superfluous since she already is his! Why does the verse say, "she shall be his wife"? You should infer from this by an *equal cut*[82]. One has to infer from "she shall be his wife", "she shall be his"[83]. Since "she shall be his" which is said there means a wife appropriate for him, so "she shall be his" which is said here means a wife appropriate for him. Then since "she shall be his" which is said there means a wife appropriate for him and he pays the fine, so "she shall be his" which is said here means a wife appropriate for him and he pays the fine[84].

Rebbi Ze'ira, Ulla [ben][85] Ismael, in the name of Rebbi Eleazar: It should not have said "she shall be his wife" for the calumniator; it is superfluous since she already is his! Why does the verse say, "she shall be his wife"? You should infer from this by an *equal cut*. One has to infer from "she shall be his wife", "she shall be his". Since "she shall be" which is said there means that if he divorced her one tells him to take her back, so "she shall be his" which is said here means that if he divorced her one tells him to take her back.

Rebbi Ḥiyya stated[86]: "In the cases of both the rapist and the calumniator who divorced, one forces them to take back. If they were Cohanim they absorb the forty[87]."

81 The man who claims that his bride was not a virgin; *Deut.* 22:13-19. Since the verse treats this as accusing his wife of a capital crime, it must be that he accuses her of adultery while living in her parents' house but preliminarily married to. him. If he cannot prove the accusation, he is fined 100 pieces of silver (400 *zuz*) and "she shall be his wife; he cannot send her away all his days." Since he can only accuse her if she is his wife, the first clause of this sentence is superfluous.

It should be noted that since the husband is related to his wife, he is barred from testifying in court against her. *Deut.* 22:14 states only that he calumniates her and asserts that he did not find her a virgin. That would be a civil case, discussed in the first Chapter. To make this a criminal case, one must assume that the husband brought witnesses to the adultery. This is the standard rabbinic interpretation of the case.

Without invocation of the rule of *gezerah šawah*, *Sifry Deut.* 238 reads the verse as applying the rules of Mishnah 6 to the case of the calumniator.

82 Cf. Note 56. The preceding argument makes it clear that the

expression "she shall be his wife" is not needed for any inference; the application of the rule of *gezerah šawah* is legitimate.

83 Identical expressions in *Deut.* 22:19 (the calumniator) and 22:29 (the rapist).

84 Only the calumniator pays 100 pieces of silver, the rapist 50.

85 The Amora who is called Ulla in the Babli is always called Ulla ben Ismael in the Yerushalmi. That must be the reading here also. The text as written, Ulla in the name of R. Ismael (Tanna of the 2nd generation) in the name of R. Eleazar (Amora) does not make sense. Ulla's argument, in a very complicated formulation, is also in the Babli, *Makkot* 15a.

86 Tosephta 3:7.

87 Since a Cohen may not take back his divorcee, by divorcing her he committed a sin which cannot be repaired and "absorbs" 39 lashes (which are called 40 in *Deut.* 25:3).

(27d line 23) כְּחָדָא דְתַנֵּי. בְּעוּלַת בַּעַל. לְהָבִיא אֶת הַמְקַבֶּלֶת בַּעֲלָהּ בְּבֵית אָבִיהָ וְהִיא אֲרוּסָה וְהַבָּא אַחֲרָיו בְּחֶנֶק. וְלֹא סוֹף דָּבָר מִכְּדַרְכָּהּ אֶלָא אֲפִילוּ שֶׁלֹא כְדַרְכָּהּ. רִבִּי אַבָּהוּ בְּשֵׁם רִבִּי יוֹחָנָן. לְכֵן צְרִיכָה שֶׁלֹא כְדַרְכָּהּ. אֲפִילוּ תֵימָא מִכְּדַרְכָּהּ לָמָּה לִי בְּעֲלָהּ. אֲפִילוּ כַּיי דְתַנִּינָן תַּמָּן. בָּאוּ עָלֶיהָ שְׁנַיִם. הָרִאשׁוֹן בִּסְקִילָה וְהַשֵּׁינִי בְּחֶנֶק. נַעֲרָה מְאוֹרָסָה. בָּעוּ עָלֶיהָ עֲשָׂרָה שֶׁלֹא כְדַרְכָּהּ וְאֶחָד כְּדַרְכָּהּ כּוּלָן בִּסְקִילָה. כּוּלְּהוֹן כְּדַרְכָּהּ. הָרִאשׁוֹן בִּסְקִילָה וְהַשְּׁאָר בְּחֶנֶק. הֶעֱרוּ בָהּ עֲשָׂרָה בְּנֵי אָדָם וְאֶחָד גָּמַר אֶת הַבִּיאָה כּוּלְּהוֹן בִּסְקִילָה. כּוּלְהוֹן גָּמְרוּ אֶת הַבִּיאָה. הָרִאשׁוֹן בִּסְקִילָה וְהַשְּׁאָר בְּחֶנֶק. וּבִפְנוּיָה. בָּאוּ עָלֶיהָ עֲשָׂרָה שֶׁלֹא כְדַרְכָּהּ וְאֶחָד כְּדַרְכָּהּ כּוּלָם בִּקְנָס. כּוּלְּהוֹן כְּדַרְכָּהּ. הָרִאשׁוֹן בִּקְנָס וְהַשְּׁאָר פָּטוּר. בֵּירְרָהּ לָהּ אֶחָד מֵהֶן נִפְטְרוּ כּוּלָן מִלֹּא תַעֲשֶׂה. אָמְרָה. אִיפְשָׁר. בּוֹרֶרֶת וְחוֹזֶרֶת וּבוֹרֶרֶת. הָיָה נָשׂוּי אֶת אֲחוֹתָהּ כְּבָר נִפְטַר. מֵתָה כְּבָר נִפְטַר. מֵת אֵין כּוֹפִין אֶת הַיָּבָם.

As it was stated[88]: "Living married to a husband[89]," that includes one who had received her husband in her father's house while preliminarily married; the one who comes after him is strangled. Not only a regular intercourse but even perverse[90]. Rebbi Abbahu in the name of Rebbi Johanan; it is necessary to mention perverse intercourse for if it were regular, why mention her husband[91]? As we have stated: If she was raped by two men, the first is stoned, the second strangled[92].

The preliminarily married adolescent girl. If ten men came upon her perversely and then one regularly, they are all stoned[93]. If they all come upon her regularly, the first is stoned and the remainder strangled. If ten men "touched" her[94] and then one penetrated, they are all stoned. If they all penetrated, the first is stoned and the remainder strangled.

A single girl. If ten men came upon her perversely and then one regularly, they all pay the fine. If they all come upon her regularly, the first is stoned and the remainder is free[95]. If she chose one of them, the others were freed from the prohibition[96]. If she said, he[97] is impossible, she repeatedly chooses. If he was married to her sister, he already is freed[98]. If she died, he is freed. If he died, one does not force the levir[99].

88   *Sifry Deut.* 241; Tosephta *Sanhedrin* 10:10.

89   *Deut.* 22:22. While the man sleeping with a preliminarily married girl is stoned, the adulterer with a woman who had lived with her husband while preliminarily married is strangled; *Sifry Deut.* 241.

90   Perverse intercourse is one which leaves the woman a virgin but leads to sexual satisfaction.

91   As is implicit in the text here and made explicit in the Babli, *Qiddušin* 9b, the preliminarily married girl who had perverse relations with her husband is no longer a virgin in criminal law but any other man can remove her status of virgin only by penetration.

92   Speaking of the virgin preliminarily married girl *Deut.* 22:23-27. The second man sleeps with a married woman who is not a virgin, *Deut.* 22:22.

93   The same statement in slightly different formulations in the Babli,

Qiddušin 9b, Sanhedrin 66b, Yerushalmi Qiddušin 1:1 (fol. 58b); Tosephta Sanhedrin 10:9.

94 Their penises touched her genitals without injuring the hymen; cf. Yebamot 4:2, Note 59.

95 They are freed from the biblically imposed fine of the rapist; they still can be sued for claims of diminution of value and suffering.

96 This sentence clearly refers to the prior case that all the men raping her are liable for the fine. In that case, all of them are required to marry her and forbidden to divorce her. But since a woman cannot have more than one husband, she may choose one of them. The others then do not infringe on the prohibition to divorce her since they cannot marry her.

97 Her first choice among the rapists.

98 A man raping his wife's sister cannot marry her (Lev. 18:18). He pays but does not marry her.

99 If the childless rapist dies before he marries his victim, there is no obligation on the levir to marry her since the rape is no marriage; it only creates an obligation of marriage.

(fol. 27a) **משנה ז:** יְתוֹמָה שֶׁנִּתְאָרְסָה וְנִתְגָּרְשָׁה רִבִּי לְעָזָר אוֹמֵר הָאוֹנֵס חַיָּיב וְהַמְפַתֶּה פָּטוּר.

About an orphan girl who had been preliminarily married and was divorced[100], Rebbi Eleazar says that the rapist has to pay but the seducer does not[101].

100 This Mishnah follows R. Aqiba (Mishnah 3) who holds that the underage girl who is emancipated from her father's power either by her marriage arranged by the father or the father's death has the status of an orphan and collects the fine for herself.

101 What he has or does not have to pay is a matter of dispute in the Halakhah.

(27d line 36) **הלכה ז:** יְתוֹמָה שֶׁנִּתְאָרְסָה וְנִתְגָּרְשָׁה כול'. אָמַר רִבִּי יוֹחָנָן. אַתְיָא דְּרִבִּי אֶלְעָזָר בְּשִׁיטַת רִבִּי עֲקִיבָה רַבּוֹ. כְּמָה דְּרִבִּי עֲקִיבָה אָמַר. יֵשׁ לָהּ קְנָס וּקְנָסָהּ לְעַצְמָהּ. כֵּן אָמַר רִבִּי אֶלְעָזָר. יֵשׁ לָהּ קְנָס וּקְנָסָהּ שֶׁלְּעַצְמָהּ. מְעַתָּה אֲפִילוּ בִמְפוּתָּה. רִבִּי יִרְמְיָה אוֹמֵר בְּשֵׁם רִבִּי אֶלְעָזָר. תִּיפְתָּר שֶׁמָּחֲלָה לוֹ. וְיֵשׁ אָדָם מוֹחֵל דָּבָר שֶׁאֵינוֹ שֶׁלוֹ. פָּתַר לָהּ בִּיתוֹמָה. וְתַנֵּי דְּבֵית רִבִּי כֵן. הַיְתוֹמָה. רִבִּי אֶלְעָזָר אָמַר. הָאוֹנֵס חַיָּיב וְהַמְפַתֶּה פָּטוּר. וְיֵשׁ אָדָם מוֹחֵל דָּבָר שֶׁאֵינוֹ בִרְשׁוּתוֹ. נִישְׁמְעִינָהּ מִן הָדָא. דָּמַר רִבִּי בּוּן בַּר חִייָה בְּשֵׁם רִבִּי זְעוּרָה. קְנָס אֵין בּוֹ מִשָּׁעָה הָרִאשׁוֹנָה. דְּתַגִּינָן תַּמָּן. עָמְדָה בַדִּין עַד שֶׁלֹּא מֵת אָבִיהָ הֲרֵי הֵן שֶׁלָּאָב: מֵת הָאָב הֲרֵי הֵן שֶׁלָּאַחִין. אִם אוֹמֵר אַתְּ כֵּן קְנָס כֵּן הוּא מִשָּׁעָה הָרִאשׁוֹנָה. הֲרֵי הֵן שֶׁלָּאַחִין מִשָּׁעָה הָרִאשׁוֹנָה. רָבָא בְּשֵׁם רַב חִסְדָּא. בְּבוֹשֶׁת וּפְגָם הָדָא מַתְנִיתָא. דְּרִבִּי מָנָא אָמַר. מָהוּ. הָאוֹנֵס חַיָּיב וְהַמְפַתֶּה פָּטוּר מִן הַכֹּל. רִבִּי אָבִין אָמַר. שַׁמַּי בָּעֵי. מָהוּ הָאוֹנֵס חַיָּיב וְהַמְפַתֶּה פָּטוּר. הָאוֹנֵס חַיָּיב בַּכֹּל וְהַמְפַתֶּה פָּטוּר מִן הַבּוֹשֶׁת וּמִן הַפְּגָם וְחַיָּיב בִּקְנָס. וְהָא רִבִּי עֲקִיבָה. אוֹ. הָאוֹנֵס פָּטוּר מִן הַבּוֹשֶׁת וְחַיָּיב בִּקְנָס וְהַמְפַתֶּה פָּטוּר מִן הַכֹּל. הַהִיא דְּרִבִּי יוֹסֵי הַגְּלִילִי הוּא.

Halakhah 7: "About an orphan girl who had been preliminarily married and was divorced," etc. Rebbi Johanan said, it turns out that Rebbi Eleazar[102] follows the opinion of his teacher Rebbi Aqiba. Just as Rebbi Aqiba said that she can collect the fine and it belongs to her, so Rebbi Eleazar said that she can collect the fine and it belongs to her. Then also for a seduced one? Rebbi Jeremiah said in the name of Rebbi Eleazar[103], explain it that she remitted it to him[104]. Can anybody remit anthing that does not belong to him[105]? Explain it for an orphan; as it was stated in the House of Rebbi thus[106]: The orphan, Rebbi Eleazar said that the rapist has to pay her but the seducer does not. Can anybody remit something which is not in his possession? Let us hear from the following, as Rebbi Abun bar Ḥiyya said in the name of Rebbi Ze'ura: The fine is not due from the first moment on[107]. As we have stated there[108]: "If she came to court before her father died, [the payments due] belong to her father and if the father died they belong to the brothers." If you say that the fine is due from the first moment, it would belong to the brothers from the first moment[109]! Rebbi Abba in the name of Rav Ḥisda: The Mishnah deals with shame and diminution of value[110]. As Rebbi Mana said, how is it? The rapist is obligated for everything and the seducer is free from everything[111]. Rebbi Abin said, [Rebbi] Shammai asked: What does it mean that the rapist has to pay but the seducer does not? The rapist has to pay everything but the seducer is free [from paying] for shame and diminution of value but is obligated for the fine[112]. That is Rebbi Aqiba's. Or, the rapist is free [from paying] for shame and diminution of value but is obligated for the fine but the seducer is free from everything? That is Rebbi Yose the Galilean's[113].

102 Ben Shamua, the Tanna.

103 Bar Pada, the Amora.

104 Rashi and all of his followers explain that, since she legally is an adult, she slept with him of her own free will and the law will assume that in doing so she forgave him all payments due. The Babli, 40a, simply states that practice follows R. Eleazar without discussing the reason.

105 It seems that this Amora did not have "an orphan" in his Mishnah. He asks whether the consent of the minor has any legal consequences since the money is her father's and she has no possibility of depriving him of his claim.

106 This is our Mishnah. The text seems to indicate that this is a later edition of the Mishnah and that in the first Mishnah the orphan was not mentioned.

107 The question is whether the fine is due because of the seducer's illegal act, then it is due from the moment of the act and the seduced girl has the

possibility to forgive all monetary claims to her lover, or whether it is due only upon sentence by the court. In the latter case, forgiveness would need a conscious act by the seduced and, by the time the case comes to court, she could well have changed her mind and go after the money. Then there is no reason that the law should assume that she remitted all money claims to her seducer.

108 Mishnah 4:1.

109 The Mishnah states that the heirs have claim to the money only if the father had a claim, i. e., if the case came before the court during the father's lifetime. The Mishnah also asserts that the money belongs to the girl if the case came before the court after the father's death. If a claim had existed from the moment of the seduction, it should have been part of the inheritance. Therefore, there is no claim before the case came to court.

110 Since the monetary value of these claims depends on the determination of the court, they certainly do not exist from the time of the seduction.

111 This is the ruling accepted by the Babli, 40a.

112 Since she has no power to forgive the fine at the moment of the act, this claim still exists. But since she was a willing partner, she certainly will have forgiven him any payment for shame and diminution of value.

113 While it is difficult to understand why the rapist should not pay for the shame (since he will have to pay for the shame of an adult victim who has no fine), otherwise the ruling follows R. Yose the Galilean in Mishnah 4.

(fol. 27a) **משנה ח:** וְאֵי זֶהוּ הַבּוֹשֶׁת הַכֹּל לְפִי הַמְבַיֵּישׁ וְהַמִּתְבַּיֵּישׁ. פְּגָם רוֹאִין אוֹתָהּ כְּאִילּוּ הִיא שִׁפְחָה נִמְכֶּרֶת כַּמָּה הָיְתָה יָפָה וְכַמָּה הִיא יָפָה. קְנָס שָׁוֶה בְּכָל־אָדָם. וְכָל־שֶׁיֵּשׁ לוֹ קִיצְבָה מִן הַתּוֹרָה שָׁוֶה בְּכָל־אָדָם.

Mishnah 8: How much is shame worth? Everything depends on the offender and the offended[114]. For diminution of value one considers her as if she were a slave girl to be sold; how much would she have been worth before[115] and how much would she be worth now. The fine is equal for everybody since everything determined by the Torah is equal for everybody.

114 The amount is in the discretion of the court subject to the guidelines expressed here.

115 As a virgin.

(27d line 52) **הלכה ח:** אֵי זֶהוּ הַבּוֹשֶׁת. הַכֹּל לְפִי הַמְבַיֵּישׁ וְהַמִּתְבַּיֵּישׁ כול'. לֹא דוֹמֶה הַמְבַיֵּישׁ אֶת הַגָּדוֹל לַמְבַיֵּישׁ אֶת הַקָּטָן. לֹא דוֹמֶה מִתְבַּיֵּישׁ מִן הַגָּדוֹל לַמִּתְבַּיֵּישׁ מִן הַקָּטָן. בּוֹשֶׁת גָּדוֹל מְרוּבָּה וְנִזְקוֹ מְמוּעָט. בּוֹשֶׁת קָטָן מְמוּעָט וְנִזְקוֹ מְרוּבָּה.

Halakhah 8: "How much is shame worth? Everything depends on the offender and the offended," etc. One cannot compare one who is offended by a person of high standing to one offended by a person of low standing. The shame for a person of high standing is great but the injury he incurs is small. The shame for a person of low standing is small but the injury he incurs is great[116].

116 While the amount of damages is fixed in cases involving virgins, in the case an adult insults another adult, the injured party can sue for damages which have to be fixed following the principle stated here.

(fol. 27a) **משנה ט:** כָּל־מָקוֹם שֶׁיֵּשׁ מֶכֶר אֵין קְנָס וְכָל־מָקוֹם שֶׁיֵּשׁ קְנָס אֵין מֶכֶר. קְטַנָּה יֵשׁ לָהּ מֶכֶר וְאֵין לָהּ קְנָס. נַעֲרָה יֵשׁ לָהּ קְנָס וְאֵין לָהּ מֶכֶר. הַבּוֹגֶרֶת לֹא מֶכֶר וְלֹא קְנָס.

Mishnah 9: Anytime there is a sale there is no fine and anytime there is a fine there is no sale. The underage girl is subject to sale but not to fine; the adolescent can claim a fine but has no sale; the adult has neither fine nor sale[117].

117 It is generally agreed that a father can sell his daughter as a domestic slave only as long as she is a minor since the verse calls her "daughter" (*Ex*. 21:7) and in legal texts "son" and "daughter" are always interpreted to mean minors. This Tanna is of the opinion that the fine applies only to the adolescent since the victim is called "an adolescent virgin" in *Deut*. 22:28 (but in the case of the seducer she simply is called "a virgin".) It is agreed that the adult cannot claim a fine (she will be able to claim damages.)

(27d line 55) **הלכה ט:** כָּל־מָקוֹם שֶׁיֵּשׁ מֶכֶר כול׳. רִבִּי חִייָה בְּשֵׁם רִבִּי יוֹחָנָן. דְרִבִּי מֵאִיר הִיא. בְּרַם כְּרַבָּנִין יֵשׁ מֶכֶר וּקְנָס כְּאַחַת. כְּרִבִּי מֵאִיר. מִבַּת יוֹמָהּ וְעַד ג שָׁנִים וְיוֹם אֶחָד יֵשׁ לָהּ מֶכֶר וְאֵין לָהּ קְנָס. מִבַּת ג שָׁנִים וְיוֹם אֶחָד עַד שֶׁתִּבְגּוֹר יֵשׁ לָהּ קְנָס וְאֵין לָהּ מֶכֶר. הַבּוֹגֶרֶת לֹא מֶכֶר וְלֹא קְנָס. כְּרַבָּנִין. מִבַּת יוֹמָהּ וְעַד ג שָׁנִים וְיוֹם אֶחָד מֶכֶר וּקְנָס כְּאַחַת. מִבַּת ג שָׁנִים וְיוֹם אֶחָד עַד שֶׁתָּבִיא שְׁתֵּי שְׂעָרוֹת יֵשׁ לָהּ מֶכֶר וְאֵין לָהּ קְנָס. מִשֶּׁתָּבִיא שְׁתֵּי שְׂעָרוֹת עַד שֶׁתִּבְגּוֹר יֵשׁ לָהּ קְנָס וְאֵין לָהּ מֶכֶר. בּוֹגֶרֶת לֹא מֶכֶר וְלֹא קְנָס.

Halakhah 9: "Anytime there is a sale," etc. Rebbi Ḥiyya in the name of Rebbi Joḥanan: This is Rebbi Meïr's. But for the rabbis there can be sale and fine together. Following Rebbi Meïr: From one day old until the age of 3 years and one day there is sale but no fine. From the age of 3 years and one day until she becomes an adult there is a fine but no sale. The adult, neither sale nor fine[118]. Following the rabbis[119]: From one day old until the age of 3 years and one day there is sale and fine together.

From the age of 3 years and one day until she grows two pubic hairs there is sale but no fine. After she grows two pubic hairs until she becomes an adult[120] there is a fine but no sale. The adult, neither sale nor fine.

118 In the Bablylonian sources (Babli 40b, 29a; Tosephta 3:8), R. Meïr is reported to decree sale but no fine for a girl from the age of one day until adolescence, fine but no sale for the adolescent, and nothing for the adult. Since for a rape at age below three years the hymen is supposed to repair itself, there is no place for the fine at that age. The statement that a father cannot sell his daughter once she reaches the age of marriage, 3 years and one day, is found only here. In any case, the statement is purely theoretical since the institution of Hebrew slaves was not re-established on the return from Babylonia even though the girl was supposed to be sold in marriage.

119 In the Babylonian sources, the rabbis hold that a daughter can be sold until she becomes an adolescent and she can claim the fine starting at the age of 3 years and one day. As explained in the preceding Note, it does not seem reasonable to have a fine for the rape of a girl below the age of 3 years and one day. Therefore, it seems that the statements regarding girls below and above the age of 3 years and one day should be switched.

120 A period of 6 months.

(27d line 63) תַּמָּן תַּנִינָן. הַבָּא עַל נַעֲרָה מְאוֹרָסָה אֵינוֹ חַיָּיב עַד שֶׁתְּהֵא נַעֲרָה בְתוּלָה מְאוֹרָסָה בְּבֵית אָבִיהָ. בָּאוּ עָלֶיהָ שְׁנַיִם. הָרִאשׁוֹן בִּסְקִילָה וְהַשֵּׁינִי בְחֶנֶק. רִבִּי יָסָא בְשֵׁם רִבִּי יוֹחָנָן רִבִּי חִייָה בְשֵׁם רִבִּי לֶעְזָר. דְּרִבִּי מֵאִיר הִיא. בְּרַם כְּרַבָּנִין אֲפִילוּ [קְטַנָּה].[121] מַאי טַעֲמָא דְרִבִּי מֵאִיר. נַעַר חָסֵר כָּתוּב בַּפָּרָשָׁה. מַה מְקַיְימִין רַבָּנִין נַעַר. רִבִּי אַבָּהוּ אָמַר בְּשֵׁם רִבִּי שִׁמְעוֹן בֶּן לָקִישׁ. נַעֲרָה אַחַת שְׁלֵימָה כָּתוּב בַּפָּרָשָׁה. לִימְדָה עַל כָּל־הַפָּרָשָׁה שֶׁהִיא גְדוֹלָה. מָתִיב רִבִּי מֵאִיר לָרַבָּנִין. הֲרֵי הַמּוֹצִיא שֵׁם רַע הֲרֵי כָּתוּב בּוֹ נַעַר וְהִיא גְדוֹלָה. דְּאֵין הַקְּטַנָּה נִסְקֶלֶת. מַה עָבְדִין לָהּ רַבָּנָן. אָמַר רִבִּי אָבִין. תִּיפְתָּר שֶׁבָּא עָלֶיהָ דֶּרֶךְ זְכָרוּת.

4 גדולה | ן קטנה   מאי | ן מה   כתוב | ן אמור   5 רבנין | ן רבנן   6 כתוב | ן אמורה
לימדה | ן ולימדה   כל הפרשה | ן כל הפרשה כולה   7 כתוב בו | ן אין כתוב בו אלא
דאין | ן שאין   8 רבנן | ן רבניו

There[122], we have stated: "He who comes to a preliminarily married adolescent is guilty[123] only if she was an adolescent, virgin, preliminarily married, in her father's house[124]. If two came upon her, the first is stoned and the second strangled[125]." Rebbi Yasa in the name of Rebbi Joḥanan, Rebbi Ḥiyya in the name of Rebbi Eleazar: That is Rebbi Meïr's. But following the rabbis even if she is a minor. What is Rebbi Meïr's reason? "A lad" is written in the paragraph[126]. How do the rabbis explain "a lad"? Rebbi Abbahu said in the name of Rebbi Simeon ben Laqish: Once in the paragraph it is written "a young woman"; this teaches that in the entire paragraph she is an adult[127]. Rebbi Meïr objected to the rabbis: In the matter of the calumniator, "a lad" is written and she is an adult since a minor is not stoned[128]! What do the rabbis with this? Rebbi Abin said, explain it if he came to her as to a male[129].

121   From the text in *Sanhedrin*. Text here: גְדוֹלָה "an adult", which certainly is an error.
122   Mishnah *Sanhedrin* 7:15; Tosephta 10:8. From "Rebbi Yasa" to the end of the Halakhah, the text is also in *Sanhedrin* 7:14; the readings from there are noted ו
123   To be stoned, *Deut*. 22:24. The penalty for adultery (if the act is observed by two independent witnesses) is death by strangling.
124   As the Babli explains (*Sanhedrin* 66b), the law does not apply if the girl had been delivered to the husband's emissaries to be brought to his place for the final wedding.
125   Since she was no longer a virgin.
126   In the entire Pentateuch with the exception of *Deut*. 22:19, "girl" is written in the masculine form נער "a lad". R. Meïr takes this as a restriction that the rules apply only to the adolescent in the strict sense. The

rabbis take the spelling to mean that one deals with a girl that is not yet feminine, not yet sexually awakened. (Instead of postulating a unique Hebrew-Phoenician root נער III "youth", the rabbis probably derive נער from the root עור "to awake".)

127 *Deut.* 22:19; the case of the calumniator must deal also with the possibility that the wife is criminally responsible, as pointed out by R. Meïr. Therefore, נַעֲרָ in the context of sexual offenses must mean "underage and adolescent".

128 *Deut.* 22:21. An underage person is not criminally responsible; the seduction of a minor is statutory rape. If the criminal sanctions do not apply, why should the rest of the rules apply to an underage girl?

129 The rapist is punished even if he uses the נַעֲרָ as if she were a נַעַר without penetration.

(27d line 71) יַעֲקֹב בַּר בָּא בְעָא קוֹמֵי רַב. הַבָּא עַל הַקְטַנָּה מָהוּ. אָמַר לֵיהּ. בִּסְקִילָה. הַבָּא עַל הַבּוֹגֶרֶת מָהוּ. אָמַר לֵיהּ. אֲנִי אֶקְרָא נַעֲרָה וְלֹא בוֹגֶרֶת. וּקְרָא נַעֲרָה וְלֹא קְטַנָּה. תַּחַת אֲשֶׁר עִנָּהּ לְרַבּוֹת אֶת הַקְטַנָּה לִקְנָס. וּקְרָא תַּחַת אֲשֶׁר עִנָּהּ לְרַבּוֹת אֶת הַבּוֹגֶרֶת לִקְנָס. אָמַר רַב. אַף עַל גַּב דִּנְצָחֵיהּ יַעֲקֹב בְּדִינָה הֲלָכָה. הַבָּא עַל הַקְטַנָּה בִּסְקִילָה וְהִיא פְטוּרָה. רִבִּי אָבִין בְּשֵׁם שְׁמוּאֵל. וְלָמָּה. שָׁמַע לָהּ מִן הָדָא וּמֵת הָאִישׁ אֲשֶׁר שָׁכַב עִמָּהּ לְבַדּוֹ. וְכִי אֵין אָנוּ יוֹדְעִין שֶׁאֵין לַנַּעֲרָה חֵט מָוֶת. מַה תַּלְמוּד לוֹמַר וְלַנַּעֲרָה לֹא תַעֲשֶׂה דָבָר אֵין לַנַּעֲרָה חֵט מָוֶת. לְהָבִיא הַבָּא עַל הַקְטַנָּה מְאוֹרָסָה בִּסְקִילָה וְהִיא פְטוּרָה.

1 בר בא | ן בר אבא   3 תחת | ן ולית את מודה לי שהיא בקנס. אמר ליה תחת   4 דנצחיה | ן דנצחי   יעקב | ן ר' יעקב בר אבא   5 שמואל | ן ר' שמואל   שמע לה | ן לא פטר ליה   7 מה | ן מאי   8 חט | ן חטא   להביא | ן אלא מכאן   מאורסה | ן -

Jacob bar Abba asked before Rav: What is the law for him who comes to a minor[130]? He said to him, by stoning. What is the law for him who comes to an adult? He said to him, I am reading "an adolescent[131]", not an adult.[132] Read "an adolescent", not a minor! "'Because he mistreated her', that includes a minor for a fine", read 'because he mistreaded her',[131] that includes an adult for a fine! Rav said, even though Jacob won the logical argument, practice is that he who comes to a minor is [punished] by stoning but she is free. Rebbi Abin in the name of Samuel: Why? He understood it from the following[133]: "The man who had lain with her alone should die." Did we not know that "the girl has not committed a capital crime"? Then why does the verse say: "Do not do anything to the girl, the girl has not committed a capital crime"? That includes him who comes to a preliminarily married underage girl that he is stoned and she is free[134].

130   A preliminarily married underage girl, whether by seduction or rape.

131   In *Deut.* 22:29.

132   The man who commits adultery with an adult preliminarily married woman is punished for adultery, as if it were with a definitively married woman.

133   *Deut.* 22:26, speaking of the preliminarily married rape victim. It should be obvious that the rape victim is innocent; why does the verse have to emphasize this?

134   The verse is not written for the adolescent rape victim, whose innocence is obvious, but for the consenting underage girl who would have committed a capital crime had she been adolescent. But because of her age, her seduction was statutory rape and she is immune from any form of punishment.

(fol. 27a) **משנה י:** הָאוֹמֵר פִּיתִּיתִי אֶת בִּתּוֹ שֶׁלְּפְלוֹנִי מְשַׁלֵּם בּוֹשֶׁת וּפְגָם עַל פִּי עַצְמוֹ וְאֵינוֹ מְשַׁלֵּם קְנָס. הָאוֹמֵר גָּנַבְתִּי וְטָבַחְתִּי וּמָכַרְתִּי מְשַׁלֵּם אֶת הַקֶּרֶן עַל פִּי עַצְמוֹ וְאֵין מְשַׁלֵּם לֹא תַשְׁלוּמֵי כֶפֶל וְלֹא תַשְׁלוּמֵי אַרְבָּעָה וַחֲמִישָׁה. הֵמִית שׁוֹרִי אֶת פְּלוֹנִי אוֹ שׁוֹרוֹ שֶׁלְּפְלוֹנִי הֲרֵי זֶה מְשַׁלֵּם עַל פִּי עַצְמוֹ. הֵמִית שׁוֹרִי

עַבְדּוֹ שֶׁלִּפְלוֹנִי אֵינוֹ מְשַׁלֵּם עַל פִּי עַצְמוֹ. זֶה הַכְּלָל כָּל־הַמְשַׁלֵּם יוֹתֵר עַל מַה שֶּׁהִזִּיק אֵינוֹ מְשַׁלֵּם עַל פִּי עַצְמוֹ.

Mishnah 10: One who says, I seduced X's daughter, pays for shame and diminution of value on his own testimony but he does not pay the fine[135]. One who says, I stole and I slaughtered or sold, pays the value on his own testimony but neither double restitution nor four or five times[136]. My ox killed X or X's ox, he pays on his own testimony[137]. My ox killed X's slave, he does not pay on his own testimony[138]. This is the principle: Anybody who has to pay more than the damage he caused does not pay on his own testimony[139].

135 Payments for shame and diminution of value are civil claims and for civil claims "the admission of the debtor is worth 100 witnesses" (Tosephta *Baba Meṣi'a* 1:10; Babli *Baba Meṣi'a* 3b). But the fine is assessed in a criminal trial and confessions are inadmissible in criminal trials.

136 The criminal fine for stealing livestock is double the value if the animal is found alive, but four or five times its value if it was slaughtered or stolen (*Ex.* 22:2,3).

137 Restitution in civil law.

138 The payment is a fixed sum of 30 šeqel (*Ex.* 21:32) whose status is discussed in the Halakhah.

139 Since any excess payment has the character of a penalty.

(28a line 4) **הלכה י:** הָאוֹמֵר פִּיתִּיתִי אֶת בִּתּוֹ שֶׁלִּפְלוֹנִי כול׳. רִבִּי יִצְחָק שָׁאַל. מַהוּ שֶׁיְשַׁלֵּם דְּמֵי הַעֶבֶד מִפִּי עַצְמוֹ. מַה צְּרִיכָה לֵיהּ. כָּל־שְׁלֹשִׁים קְנָס אוֹ יוֹתֵר מִדָּמָיו קְנָס. אִין תֵּימַר. כָּל־שְׁלֹשִׁים קְנָס. [אֵין][140] מְשַׁלֵּם. אִין תֵּימַר. יוֹתֵר מִדָּמָיו קְנָס. (אֵינוֹ)[141] מְשַׁלֵּם. תַּמָּן תַּנִינָן. הֵמִית שׁוֹרְךָ אֶת עַבְדִּי. וְהוּא אוֹמֵר. לֹא הֵמִית. מַשְׁבִּיעֲךָ אֲנִי. וְאָמַר אָמֵן. [פָּטוּר].[142] אָמַר רִבִּי חַגַּיי קוֹמֵי רִבִּי יוֹסֵי. תִּיפְתָּר שֶׁהֵמִית עֶבֶד מוּכֶּה שְׁחִין. אָמַר לוֹ. אָמוּר דְּבַתְרָהּ. הֵמִית שׁוֹרְךָ אֶת בְּנִי. וְהוּא אוֹמֵר. לֹא הֵמִית. מַשְׁבִּיעֲךָ אֲנִי. וְאָמַר אָמֵן. חַיָּיב. וּפָתְרָהּ

בְּמוּכָּה שְׁחִין וִיהֵא פָטוּר. אָמַר רִבִּי חַגַּיי קוֹמֵי רִבִּי יוֹסֵי. תִּיפְתָּר כְּמָאן דָּמַר. וְנָתַן פִּדְיוֹן נַפְשׁוֹ. שֶׁלַּמַּזִּיק. אָמַר לֵיהּ. וְאִין כְּמָאן דְּאָמַר. וְנָתַן פִּדְיוֹן נַפְשׁוֹ. שֶׁלַּמַּזִּיק. כּוּלוֹ קְנָס. מָהוּ שֶׁיֹּאמְרוּ לוֹ. צֵא יְדֵי שָׁמַיִם. נִשְׁמְעִינָהּ מִן הָדָא. מַעֲשֶׂה בְרַבָּן גַּמְלִיאֵל שֶׁהִפִּיל שֵׁן טְבִי עַבְדוֹ. אָתָא גַּבֵּי דְרִבִּי יְהוֹשֻׁעַ. אָמַר לֵיהּ. טְבִי עַבְדִּי מָצָאתִי עִילָּה לְשַׁחְרְרוֹ. אָמַר לֵיהּ. וּמַה בְּיָדָךְ. וְאֵין קְנָסוֹת אֶלָּא בְּבֵית דִּין וּבְעֵדִים. וְיֹאמְרוּ לוֹ. צֵא יְדֵי שָׁמַיִם. הָדָא אָמְרָה שֶׁאֵין אוֹמְרִין לוֹ צֵא יְדֵי שָׁמַיִם. רִבִּי גַמְלִיאֵל בֵּירִבִּי אֲבִינָה בְעָא קוֹמֵי רִבִּי מָנָא. רַבָּן גַּמְלִיאֵל כְּמָאן דָּמַר. מוּתָּר לְשַׁחְרְרוֹ. אָמַר לֵיהּ. כָּל־גָּרְמָהּ אָמְרָה שֶׁאָסוּר לְשַׁחְרְרוֹ. דִּי לֹא כֵן הָיוּ לוֹ לְשַׁחְרֵר מִשָּׁעָה רִאשׁוֹנָה.

Halakhah 10: "One who says, I seduced X's daughter," etc. [143]Rebbi Isaac asked: Would he have to pay the slave's value on his own testimony? What is his problem? Are the entire 30 [šeqel][138] a fine or is only the excess over his value a fine? If you say, the entire 30 [šeqel] are a fine, he does not pay. If you say, the excess over his value is a fine, he pays[144]. There, we have stated[145]: "'Your ox killed my slave'! The other said, 'he did not kill'. 'I want you to swear' and he said 'Amen', he is free.[146]" Rebbi Haggai said before Rebbi Yose, explain it if he killed a slave afflicted with boils[147]. He said to him, what does it say afterwards[148]? "'Your ox killed my son'! The other said, 'he did not kill'. 'I want you to swear' and he said 'Amen', he is obligated.[149]" Why do you not explain it that he was afflicted with boils, then he would be free[150]. Rebbi Haggai said before Rebbi Yose, explain it following him who says "he shall pay the redemption of his person", the one's who caused the damage[151]. He said to him, if following him who says "he shall pay the redemption of his person", the one's who caused the damage, everything is a fine[152]. Can one say to him, be also in the clear with Heaven[153]? Let us hear from the following: It happened that Rabban Gamliel knocked out his slave Tebi's tooth[154]. He came to Rebbi Joshua[155] and said to him, I found a reason to free my slave Tebi. He said to him, what do you have in your hand? Fines can be imposed only by a court! Could they not say to him, do your duty before Heaven? That means one does not tell him, do your duty before Heaven! Rebbi Gamliel ben Avina[156] asked before Rebbi Mana: Does Rabban Gamliel follow him who said, it is permitted to manumit? He said to him, the story in itself implies that it is forbidden to manumit since, otherwise, he could have freed him immediately!

140 From the text in *Šebuot*, missing here.

141 Written in the text here, missing in *Šebuot*.

142 From the text in *Šebuot*, here חייב "he is obligated".

143 The entire Halakhah is part of a larger text in *Šebuot* 5:7.

144 The slave's market value.

145 Mishnah *Šebuot* 5:5. The topic of the Mishnah is the obligation to bring a purification sacrifice for a false oath (*Lev.* 5:4). The sacrifice is due for "an expression of the lips for worse or good", i. e., if the oath changes the situation as far as monetary obligations are concerned. If A was accused by B to have seduced B's daughter (when B has no witnesses to prove his claim) and A swore falsely, A is obligated for a sacrifice since by admitting guilt he would have had to pay for shame and diminution of value.

146 This Tanna assumes that the entire 30 šeqel to be paid for the slave are a fine which cannot be collected upon the confession of the guilty party. Therefore, the oath did not change the situation as far as monetary obligations are concerned and no purification sacrifice is possible.

147 If the slave could not be sold on the slave market, he has no value and certainly all of the 30 šeqel are a criminal fine and not due upon confession.

148 This is a *baraita*, not the continuation of the Mishnah.

149 Since he would have to pay damages upon agreeing that his ox did the damage, his false oath requires a

sacrifice.

150   If no damages were due.

151   *Ex.* 21:30: "If weregilt is imposed on him, he shall pay the redemption of his person, all that is imposed on him." The question is, to which person does "his person" refer? Is the weregilt assessed by the person killed or the owner of the ox? The question is discussed in *Baba Qama* Tosephta 4:7, Yerushalmi 4:7 (4c), Babli 27a, 40a; Babli *Makkot* 2b; *Mekhilta dR. Ismael Mišpaṭim* p. 285, *dR. Simeon bar Ioḥai* p. 182.

152   In that case there is no direct connection between the amount to be paid and the damage caused.

153   Is there a moral obligation to pay when there is no legal way to force payment?

154   A slave has to be freed if his owner injures one of his limbs (*Ex.* 21:26,27). On the other hand, there is an interpretation of *Lev.* 25:46 which reads the statement about Gentile slaves, "for ever you shall have them work for you" that manumission of Gentile slaves without a good reason is forbidden. In the Yerushalmi (*Yebamot* 11:6, Note 134) this interpretation is ascribed to R. Yose the Galilean, in the Babli to Rav Jehudah (*Berakhot* 47b) or R. Aqiba (*Soṭah* 3b). Another interpretation of the verse [Babli *Niddah* 47a; *Sifra Behar Parašah* 6(6)] insists that slaves can be used only for work, not sexual purposes.

155   The Babli, *Baba Qama* 74b/75a, reads the story as a ruling by R. Joshua that anybody who freed himself by confession from a fine cannot be fined even if later the fact is proven by two witnesses. It holds that Rabban Gamliel should have produced witnesses before talking informally to R. Joshua who even in a private setting could not forget about his position of president of the court.

156   Elsewhere, the name is Ininia (cf. *Peah* 1:1, Note 61).

נערה שנתפתתה פרק רביעי

(fol. 28a) **משנה א**: נַעֲרָה שֶׁנִּתְפַּתְּתָה בָּשְׁתָּהּ וּפְגָמָהּ וּקְנָסָהּ לְאָבִיהָ וְהַצַּעַר בִּתְפוּסָה. עָמְדָה בְבֵית דִּין עַד שֶׁלֹּא מֵת הָאָב הֲרֵי הֵן שֶׁלָּאָב. מֵת הָאָב הֲרֵי הֵן שֶׁלָּאַחִין. לֹא הִסְפִּיקָה לַעֲמוֹד בְּבֵית דִּין עַד שֶׁמֵּת הָאָב הֲרֵי הֵן שֶׁלְּעַצְמָהּ.

Mishnah 1: Payments for shame, diminution of value, and fine of a seduced adolescent girl belong to her father, as are payments for suffering for the victim of an attack. If she appeared in court during her father's lifetime, they are the father's; after the father's death they are the brothers'[1]. If she did not appear in court until after the father's death, they belong to herself[2].

---

1 The claim to the payments is established with the first appearance of the claimants before the court (today one would say with the filing of court papers.) This might be different from the Babli, whose Mishnah requires that there were actual court proceedings during the father's lifetime. Cf. also Chapter 3, Note 109. Once the claim is noted as the father's, upon the father's death it becomes part of the estate which is inherited by the male children. The inheritance of the brothers is subject to the claims of the daughters for sustenance and dowry. If there are only daughters, the daughters inherit.

2 Following R. Aqiba (Mishnah 3:4).

(28a line 69) **הלכה א**: נַעֲרָה שֶׁנִּתְפַּתְּתָה כול'. מָאן תַּנָּא נַעֲרָה. רִבִּי מֵאִיר. בְּרַם כְּרַבָּנִין אֲפִילוּ קְטַנָּה.

Halakhah 1: "A seduced adolescent girl," etc. Who stated "adolescent"? Rebbi Meïr. But following the rabbis, even an underage girl[3].

3   Cf. Halakhah 3:9; Babli 40b.

(28a line 70) וְהַצַּעַר בִּתְפוּסָה. בְּאָנוּסָה. וּדְלָא כְרִבִּי שִׁמְעוֹן. דְּרִבִּי שִׁמְעוֹן פּוֹטֵר אֶת הָאוֹנֵס מִן הַצַּעַר.

Halakhah 1: "Payments for suffering for the victim of an attack." The rape victim. This does not follow Rebbi Simeon since Rebbi Simeon frees the rapist from paying for suffering[4].

4   Cf. Halakhah 3:5.

(28b line 1) עַד כְּדוֹן דְּבָרִים הַבָּאִים מֵחְמַת הַבִּיאָה. חָבַל בָּהּ. סִימָּה אֶת עֵינָהּ. קָטַע אֶת יָדָהּ. שִׁיבֵּר אֶת רַגְלָהּ. לְמִי הוּא מְשַׁלֵּם לָהּ אוֹ לְאָבִיהָ. רִבִּי יוֹחָנָן אָמַר. נוֹתֵן לְאָבִיהָ. רִבִּי שִׁמְעוֹן בֶּן לָקִישׁ אָמַר. נוֹתֵן לְעַצְמָהּ. מִיסְבַּר סָבַר רִבִּי שִׁמְעוֹן בֶּן לָקִישׁ שֶׁמַּעֲשֵׂה יָדֶיהָ שֶׁלָּהּ עַד שֶׁתִּבְגּוֹר. רִבִּי יוֹחָנָן אָמַר. מִבּוּגְרָה וְאֵילָךְ. רִבִּי אָבִין בְּשֵׁם רִבִּי הִילָא. עַד שְׁעַת בּוּגְרָהּ פְּלִיגִין. אֲבָל מִבּוּגְרָה וְאֵילָךְ כָּל־עַמָא מוֹדֵיי שֶׁהֵן שֶׁלְעַצְמָהּ. מַתְנִיתָא מְסַייְעָא לְדֵין וּמַתְנִיתָא מְסַייְעָא לְדֵין. וּמַתְנִיתָא מְסַייְעָא לְרִבִּי יוֹחָנָן. הַחוֹבֵל בְּבִתּוֹ וּבְנוֹ שֶׁלַּחֲבֵירוֹ. שֶׁלְבְנוֹ יִתֵּן מִיָּד. וְשֶׁלְבִתּוֹ יַעֲשֶׂה בָהֶן סְגוּלָה. אָמַר רִבִּי יוּדָן אֲבוֹי דְרִבִּי יוּדָה אֲבוֹי דְרִבִּי מַתַּנְיָה. אִית מַתְנֵי. רֵישָׁא וְסֵיפָא מְסַייֵעַ לְרִבִּי שִׁמְעוֹן בֶּן לָקִישׁ. הַחוֹבֵל בְּבִתּוֹ קְטַנָּה נִיזְקָהּ שֶׁלָּהּ וּפָטוּר מִן הַבּוֹשֶׁת וּמִן הַפְּגָם. אֲחֵרִים שֶׁחִיבְּלוּ בָהּ נִיזְקָהּ שֶׁלָּהּ וְהַשְּׁאָר יַעֲשֶׂה בָהֶן סְגוּלָה וּבוֹשְׁתָּהּ וּפְגָמָהּ שֶׁלְאָבִיהָ.

So far payments that are consequences of sexual relations[5]. If somebody injured her, blinded one of her eyes, cut off one of her hands, broke one of her legs[6]? To whom does he pay, to her or to her father? Rebbi Johanan said, he pays to her father; Rebbi Simeon ben Laqish said, he pays to her. Rebbi Simeon ben Laqish is of the opinion that her earnings belong to her even before she becomes an adult. Rebbi Johanan says, only after she comes of age. Rebbi Abin in the name of Rebbi Hila: They disagree before she comes of age, but after she is an adult everybody agrees that all belongs to her. A *baraita* supports either one of them. A *baraita* supports Rebbi Johanan: If somebody injures somebody else's daughter or son, the payments for the son must be given immediately[7]; those for the daughter shall be held as property value[8,9]. Rebbi Yudan, the father of Rebbi Judah the father of Rebbi Mattaniah, said that some state it so that beginning and end support Rebbi Simeon ben Laqish: If somebody injures his own underage daughter, diminution of value belong to her and he is free from paying for shame and diminution of value[10]. If others injure her, diminution of values belong to her, the rest shall be transformed into property value[11], but payments for shame and diminution of value belong to her father.

5   Since biblical law allows a father to marry off his daughter and to pocket the money given for her preliminary marriage, and explicitly states that the father receives the fine imposed on the rapist, it is natural that the father should receive all benefits accruing to him from the fact that she is his underage female child. But since the text nowhere gives monetary rights deriving from male children to the father, the question is who receives payments which do not depend on the sex of the child. The Babli, *Baba Qama* 87a/b, states flatly that the father has no claims to sums due under laws which are independent of the sex of the injured party.

6   Mishnah *Baba Qama* 8:1 states that the person causing an injury is liable to pay for diminution of values (permament reduction of earning power), suffering, medical costs, lost earnings (earnings lost while disabled in treatment), and shame.

7   As always, "son" or "daughter"

means underage child. In the Babli, *Baba Qama* 87b, and the Tosephta, *Baba Qama* 9:8, the payment due the son is given in the form of a capital value which is transferred to the son on his reaching majority. Everybody agrees that the father has no claim to any sum due to his son.

8   In the *baraitot* of Babli and Tosephta: They belong to the father. This is then explained away as referring only to lost earnings since in the Babli everybody holds that all earnings of an underage daughter belong to the father.

9   In the opinion of R. David Fraenckel, the father collects the yield of the capital reserved for the daughter until she reaches adulthood and in this the *baraita* supports R. Joḥanan.

10   Since he collects payments for shame and diminution of value from the rapist, he collects all payments of this kind due to his underage daughter. If he is the guilty party, he is free since he would have to pay to himself. In Babli and Tosephta, he is never required to pay anything to his own underage children of either sex.

It is clear that in the case of the father attacking his own daughter, "diminution of value" must refer to damage done to her physical appearance, not defloration. Since sexual relations with one's daughter are a capital crime, no payment can be demanded (cf. Note 111, Chapter 3:1 Note 30, *Terumot* 7:1 Note 5 ff.)

11   In Tosephta *Baba Qama* 9:9 and the *baraita* in Babli *Baba Qama* 87b nothing is awarded to the father. This is then explained away as referring to children who no longer live at home. In the Yerushalmi, payments for shame and diminution of value belong to the father; of the others he collects the yield of the capital until the daughter reaches adulthood. The treatments in the two Talmudim have very few points in common even though they are based on almost identical tannaitic texts.

(28b line 13) מַה חֲמִית מֵימַר כֵּן. תַּנֵּי רִבִּי שִׁמְעוֹן בֶּן יוֹחַי. וְנָתַן לַנַּעֲרָה. וְנָתַן לַאֲבִי הַנַּעֲרָה. הָא כֵיצַד. עָמְדָה בַדִּין עַד שֶׁלֹּא מֵת אָבִיהָ אַשְׁכָּחַת אָמַר. וְנָתַן לַאֲבִי הַנַּעֲרָה. מֵת אָבִיהָ אַשְׁכָּחַת אָמַר. וְנָתַן לְעַצְמָהּ. עָמְדָה בַדִּין עַד שֶׁלֹּא בָגְרָה אַשְׁכָּחַת אָמַר. וְנָתַן לַאֲבִי הַנַּעֲרָה. מִשֶּׁבָּגְרָה אַשְׁכָּחַת אָמַר. וְנָתַן לְעַצְמָהּ.

HALAKHAH 1   179

What did you see to say so[12]? Rebbi Simeon ben Iohai stated: "He shall give to the girl; he shall give to the girl's father.[13]" How is this? If there were court proceedings[14] before her father died, you can say "he shall give to the girl's father"; after the father died you can say "he shall give to her". If there were court proceedings before she became an adult, you can say "he shall give to the girl's father"; after she became an adult[15] you can say "he shall give to her."

12 This refers to the Mishnah, that if the case came to court after the father's death the fine is not part of the inheritance but belongs to the girl even if she still is supported by the brothers and her earnings go to them.

13 The following is the interpretation of R. David Fraenckel. In the case of the calumniator it is written (*Deut.* 22:19): "[The court] shall fine him 100 pieces of silver and give them to the girl's father *because he calumniated a virgin of Israel*", stating first the fine and then the reason. But for the rapist it says (v. 29): "The man *who had lain with her* shall give 50 pieces of silver to the girl's father." Since the reason is stated immediately after the obligation to pay, it is inferred that the obligation to pay is independent of the availability of the father. Therefore, in the absence of a father, or if the girl is no longer in his *potestas*, one may disregard the mention of the father and read the verse as an obligation to pay the girl.

14 This quotes the language of the Babli Mishnah, cf. Note 1.

15 This refers to Mishnah 2.

(28b line 17) מְנָן אִילֵּין מִילַּיָּא. רִבִּי אַבָּהוּ בְשֵׁם רִבִּי יוֹחָנָן. וְהִתְנַחַלְתֶּם אוֹתָם לִבְנֵיכֶם אַחֲרֵיכֶם לָרֶשֶׁת אֲחֻזָּה. אוֹתָם לִבְנֵיכֶם. אֵין בְּנוֹתֵיכֶם לִבְנֵיכֶם. בִּקְנָס הַכָּתוּב מְדַבֵּר. תַּנֵּי רִבִּי חִייָה. אֵין לָהֶן לֹא בִקְנָסֵי הַבַּת וְלֹא בְּפִיתּוּיָהּ וְלֹא בַחֲבָלֶיהָ. קְנָס אֵימָתַי הוּא מִתְחַייֵב. רִבִּי יוֹנָה אָמַר. מִשָּׁעָה רִאשׁוֹנָה. רִבִּי יוֹסִי אָמַר. בְּסוֹף. מֵתִיב רִבִּי יוֹסִי לְרִבִּי יוֹנָה. עַל דַּעְתָּךְ דְּתֵימַר מִשָּׁעָה רִאשׁוֹנָה. וְהָא תַנִּינָן. עָמְדָה בְדִין עַד שֶׁלֹּא מֵת הָאָב הֲרֵי הֵן שֶׁלָּאָב. מֵת הָאָב הֲרֵי הֵן

שֶׁלָּאַחִין. אָמַר לֵיהּ. מָטִינְתָּהּ לְהַהִיא דְּתַנֵּי רִבִּי שִׁמְעוֹן בֶּן יוֹחַי. וְנָתַן לַנַּעֲרָה. וְנָתַן לַאֲבִי הַנַּעֲרָה. מְתִיב רִבִּי יוֹנָה לְרִבִּי יוֹסֵי. עַל דַּעְתָּךְ דְּתֵימַר בְּסוֹף. וְהָא תַנִּינָן. עָמְדָה בַדִּין עַד שֶׁלֹּא בָּגְרָה הֲרֵי הֵן שֶׁלָּאָב. מִשֶּׁבָּגְרָה הֲרֵי הֵן שֶׁלְּעַצְמָהּ. וּבוֹגֶרֶת יֵשׁ לָהּ קְנָס. אָמַר לֵיהּ. מָטִינְתָּהּ לְהַהִיא דְּתַנֵּי רִבִּי חִיָּיה. דְּתַנֵּי רִבִּי חִיָּיה. תַּחַת אֲשֶׁר עִנָּהּ. לָרַבּוֹת שֶׁהָיְתָה נַעֲרָה וּבָגְרָה. וְאַתְיָא אִילֵּין פְּלוּגְוָותָא כְּהָלֵין פְּלוּגְוָותָא. דְּתַנִינָן תַּמָּן. גָּנַב מִשֶׁלְּאָבִיב טָבַח וּמָכַר וְאַחַר כָּךְ מֵת מְשַׁלֵּם תַּשְׁלוּמֵי אַרְבָּעָה וַחֲמִשָׁה. מְתִיב רִבִּי יוֹסֵי לְרִבִּי חַגַּיי. עַל דַּעְתָּךְ דְּתֵימַר. בָּעֲמִידַת בֵּית דִּין הַדָּבָר תָּלוּי. נִיתְנֵי. גָּנַב מִשֶׁלְּאָבִיב טָבַח וּמָכַר בְּחַיֵּי אָבִיו. לֹא הִסְפִּיק לַעֲמוֹד בַּדִּין עַד שֶׁמֵּת אָבִיו מְשַׁלֵּם תַּשְׁלוּמֵי כָּפֶל. וְהֵן אָמַר. אַרְבָּעָה וַחֲמִשָׁה. בְּרַם הָכָא כָּל־עַמָּא מוֹדוּ שֶׁהֵן שֶׁלְּעַצְמָהּ. לָא צוּרְכָא דְּלָא לְמִי הוּא נוֹתֵן לְעַצְמָהּ. נוֹתֵן לְאָבִיהָ.

From where comes this[12]? Rebbi Abbahu in the name of Rebbi Joḥanan: "You shall give *them* as inheritance to your sons to inherit property," those to your sons and not your daughters to your sons; the verse speaks about the fine[16]. Rebbi Ḥiyya stated: They[17] have no right to the fines of the daughter nor to payments for seduction or injuries. When does the fine become due? Rebbi Jonah said, from the first moment[18]; Rebbi Yose said, at the end[19]. Rebbi Yose objected to Rebbi Jonah: Since you say, from the first moment, did we not state: "If there were court proceedings during her father's lifetime, [the payments] are the father's; after the father's death they are the brothers'[20]"? He said to him, that refers to what Rebbi Simeon ben Ioḥai stated, "He shall give to the girl; he shall give to the girl's father.[21]" Rebbi Jonah objected to Rebbi Yose. In your opinion, since you say, at the end, did we not state[22]: "If there were court proceedings before she became an adult, they are the father's; after she became an adult they belong to herself." Does an adult have a claim to a fine? He said to him, that refers to what Rebbi Ḥiyya stated, as Rebbi Ḥiyya stated: "Because he mistreated her," that includes if she was an adolescent and became an adult[23]. Does it turn out that this disagreement parallels another disagreement, as we have stated there[24]: "If he stole from his father, slaughtered or sold, and afterwards [his father] died, ..., he pays fourfold or fivefold[25]"? Rebbi Yose objected to Rebbi Ḥaggai[26]: In your opinion, since you say that it depends on the court proceedings, should one not state: If he stole from his father, slaughtered or sold during his father's lifetime but did not appear in court until after his father's death, he pays twofold[27]? But it says fourfold or fivefold! But here[28], everybody agrees that they belong to herself. The only problem is whether he has to pay to her or to her father.

16 In Babylonian sources, this is a tannaitic statement: *Ketubot* 43a, *Qidduŝin* 16b; *Sifra Behar Paraŝah* 6(5). The verse, *Lev.* 25:46, speaks of Gentile slaves. The main import of the verse is that slaves can be bought or inherited following the rules of real estate. As a side remark, it is stated that income due because of daughters does not become part of the estate.

17 The father's heirs.

18 The act of rape creates the obligation to pay the fine.

19 The judgment of the court creates the obligation to pay the fine.

20 If this is an argument of R. Yose against R. Jonah, the reference must be to the Mishnah in general and in particular to the last part, not quoted here, which gives the fine to the girl if court proceedings start after the father's death. If the fine was due from the moment of rape, it should be part of the estate.

21 Cf. Note 13. The exclusion of the fine from the estate is a biblical decree, independent of when the obligation starts.

22 An enlarged version of Mishnah 2.

23 It is not that an adult rape victim can claim a fine but the verse gives the adult the right to sue for what was done to her as an adolescent.

24 Mishnah *Baba Qama* 7:2.

25 The fine for stealing is double restitution; the fine for selling or slaughtering stolen livestock is fourfold or fivefold restitution. The Mishnah requires the thief to pay fourfold or fivefold to the estate (unless he is the sole heir); but if the obligation does not start with the act of larceny then the fine should depend on the relative times of selling/slaughtering and the father's death, as explained in the next sentence.

26 This should read: R. Haggai objected to R. Yose (who holds that any obligation starts only with the court's action.)

27 There is no doubt that he stole from the estate and has to make good. But since the injured party is no longer alive, according to R. Yose he should not have to pay the extra penalty for selling or slaughtering. The Babli, *Baba Qama* 71b, agrees with this reasoning.

28 The verses, in R. Simeon's interpretation, determine the obligation to pay a fine irrespective of the recipient of the fine. Therefore, the question of the start of the obligation is secondary.

(fol. 28a) **משנה ב:** עָמְדָה בְבֵית דִּין עַד שֶׁלֹּא בָגְרָה הֲרֵי הֵן שֶׁלָּאָב. מֵת הָאָב הֲרֵי הֵן שֶׁלָּאַחִין. לֹא הִסְפִּיקָה לַעֲמוֹד בְּבֵית דִּין עַד שֶׁבָּגְרָה הֲרֵי הֵן שֶׁלְּעַצְמָהּ. רִבִּי שִׁמְעוֹן אוֹמֵר אִם לֹא הִסְפִּיקָה לִגְבּוֹת עַד שֶׁמֵּת הָאָב הֲרֵי הֵן שֶׁלְּעַצְמָהּ. מַעֲשֵׂה יָדֶיהָ וּמְצִיאָתָהּ אַף עַל פִּי שֶׁלֹּא גָּבְתָה מֵת הָאָב הֲרֵי הֵן שֶׁלָּאַחִין.

Mishnah 2: If she did appear in court before she became an adult, [the payments] belong to her father, after the father's death, they belong to the brothers. If she did not appear in court before she became an adult, they belong to herself. Rebbi Simeon says, if she did not collect before the father died, they belong to herself[29]. Her earnings and what she finds, even if she had not collected [by the time] the father died, belong to the brothers[30].

29 R. Simeon holds that the father's rights start only with the delivery of the money as explained in the Halakhah (and the Babli, 42b). The anonymous majority hold that the payment ordered by the court can be enforced by foreclosure and therefore is ready money and part of the estate.

30 The earnings of an underage daughter belong to the father since even the money given for a preliminary marriage of an underage daughter is pocketed by her father (Mishnah 4:6). After the death of the father only uncollected earlier earnings go to the estate, not her later earnings. The situation is slightly paradoxical since the brothers are obligated to support their unmarried sister but the father has only a religious, not a legal duty to support his daughters (Halakhah 4:8).

(28b line 35) **הלכה ב**: עָמְדָה בְּבֵית דִּין עַד שֶׁלֹא בָגְרָה כול׳. תַּנֵּי רִבִּי שִׁמְעוֹן בֶּן יוֹחַי. וְנָתַן הָאִישׁ הַשּׁוֹכֵב עִמָּהּ לַאֲבִי הַנַּעֲרָה חֲמִשִׁים כָּסֶף. מְלַמֵּד שֶׁאֵין הָאָב זוֹכֶה אֶלָּא בִנְתִינָה. רִבִּי שִׁמְעוֹן אוֹמֵר. בַּמִּגְבָּה הַדָּבָר תָּלוּי. וְרַבָּנִין אוֹמְרִין. בַּעֲמִידַת בֵּית דִּין הַדָּבָר תָּלוּי. רִבִּי שִׁמְעוֹן עָבַד לָהּ כְּמַעֲשֵׂה בֵית דִּין וְרַבָּנִין עָבְדִין לָהּ כְּמִלְוָה. עַל דַּעְתֵּיהּ דְּרִבִּי שִׁמְעוֹן גּוֹבָה בְעֵידִית. עַל דַּעְתּוֹן דְּרַבָּנִין גּוֹבָה בְּבֵינוֹנִית. עַל דַּעְתֵּיהּ דְּרִבִּי שִׁמְעוֹן אֵין שְׁבִיעִית מְשַׁמְּטָתָהּ. עַל דַּעְתּוֹן דְּרַבָּנִין הַשְּׁבִיעִית מְשַׁמְּטָתָהּ. עַל דַּעְתֵּיהּ דְּרִבִּי שִׁמְעוֹן הַבְּכוֹר נוֹטֵל פִּי שְׁנַיִם. עַל דַּעְתּוֹן דְּרַבָּנִין אֵין הַבְּכוֹר נוֹטֵל פִּי שְׁנַיִם.

Halakhah 2: "If she did appear in court before she became an adult," etc. Rebbi Simeon ben Iohai stated: "The man who had lain with her shall give 50 silver pieces to the girl's father;" this teaches that the father acquires only by handing over[31]. Rebbi Simeon says, the matter depends on the collection, but the rabbis say, the matter depends on the court procedure. Rebbi Simeon treats it as court decrees[32] but the rabbis treat it as a loan[33]. In the opinion of Rebbi Simeon, he forecloses from the best land; in the opinion of the rabbis he forecloses from average land[34]. In the opinion of Rebbi Simeon, the Sabbatical year does not cancel the debt;

in the opinion of the rabbis the Sabbatical year cancels the debt[35]. In the opinion of Rebbi Simeon the firstborn takes a double portion; in the opinion of the rabbis the firstborn does not take a double portion[36].

31   In the Babli, 42b, this is an Amoraic interpretation of R. Simeon's position.

32   Money receivable because of a judicial decision is not counted as property to be part of the estate since in many cases the collection of such a judgment depends on the claimant swearing that his claim was not otherwise satisfied and the heirs cannot swear for their deceased father.

33   Outstanding documented loans are property and part of the estate since the debtor would have to prove his case if he claims that the loan had been repaid.

34   If the debtor is unable to pay cash and the creditor comes to foreclose real estate, Mishnah *Giṭṭin* 5:1 states that debts for torts are foreclosed from the most valuable real estate, loans from average, and a *ketubah* from the least valuable (R. Meïr says, from average.) The value is determined by the going rate for a unit of surface area.

35   Only private debts are cancelled by the Sabbatical year, not those created by court order nor those handed over to a court for collection; Mishnah *Ševi'it* 10:2. The details of the laws of the Sabbatical relating to this case are explained in *Ševi'it* 10:2, Note 69.

36   The law of inheritance of the firstborn (*Deut.* 21:17) states that the father has to give him a double portion (or $2/3$, assuming there are only two sons) "of everything that is found with him", meaning everything in actual possession at the time of death. Money due for an executable court order is money in possession; money due for an outstanding loan is not money in possession since it is subject to the uncertainties of a court proceeding if foreclosure is needed and the position of the firstborn is not privileged in regard to future income.

(28b line 42) רִבִּי זְעִירָא שָׁלַח לְרַב נַחְמָן בַּר יַעֲקֹב וּלְרִבִּי אִימִי בַּר פַּפִּי. מַעֲשֶׂה יְדֵי הַבַּת שֶׁלְמִי. אָמְרוּ לֵיהּ. שׁוֹקֵד אָמַר. לְעַצְמָהּ. מַנִּי שׁוֹקֵד. שְׁמוּאֵל. אָמַר

רִבִּי מַתָּנָה. בְּשֵׁם רִבִּי אֱמָרוּהָ וּמִדְרָשׁ אֱמָרוּהָ. וְהִתְנַחַלְתֶּם אוֹתָם לִבְנֵיכֶם אַחֲרֵיכֶם לָרֶשֶׁת אֲחוּזָה. אוֹתָם לִבְנֵיכֶם. אֵין בְּנוֹתֵיכֶם לִבְנֵיכֶם. בְּמַעֲשֵׂה יְדֵי הַבַּת הַכָּתוּב מְדַבֵּר. אָמַר רִבִּי יוּדָן. מַתְנִיתָא אָמְרָה כֵן מַעֲשֵׂה יָדֶיהָ וּמְצִיאָתָהּ אַף עַל פִּי שֶׁלֹּא גָבָת וּמֵת הָאָב הֲרֵי הֵן שֶׁלְּאַחִין. מַעֲשֵׂה שֶׁעָשְׂת בְּחַיֵּי הָאָב. אֲבָל עָשְׂת לְאַחַר מִיתַת הָאָב כָּל־עַמָּא מוֹדוּ שֶׁהֵן שֶׁלְּעַצְמָהּ.

[37]Rebbi Ze'ira sent to Rav Naḥman bar Jacob and Rebbi Immi bar Pappai[38]: Who owns the earnings of the daughter? They said to him, the diligent said, herself. Who is the diligent? Samuel! Rebbi Mattanah said, it was said in the name of Rebbi[39] as explanation of a verse: "You shall give *them* as inheritance to your sons to inherit property," those to your sons and not your daughters to your sons; the verse speaks about the earnings of the daughter[16].

Rebbi Yudan said, the Mishnah says so: "Her earnings and what she finds, even if she had not collected when the father died, belong to the brothers." Anything she earned during her father's lifetime. But what she earned after her father's death according to everybody is hers[40].

37   A slightly different version of the entire paragraph is in the Babli, 43b, where R. Ze'ira points out that the brothers have to support their sisters but do not receive their incomes.

38   In the Babli Rav Abime bar Pappai; cf. Note 262.

39   In the Babli: Rav.

40   If the heirs retained the right to the earnings of the underage daughters, the Mishnah would not have to emphasize that they retain the right to income earned but not collected. The same argument in the Babli, 43a.

משנה ג: הַמְאָרֵס אֶת בִּתּוֹ וְגֵירְשָׁהּ אֲרָסָהּ וְנִתְאַלְמְנָה כְּתוּבָּתָהּ שֶׁלּוֹ. (fol. 28a)
הִישִׂיאָהּ וְגֵירְשָׁהּ הִישִׂיאָהּ וְנִתְאַרְמְלָה כְּתוּבָּתָהּ שֶׁלָּהּ. רִבִּי יְהוּדָה אוֹמֵר.
הָרִאשׁוֹנָה שֶׁלָּאָב. אָמְרוּ לוֹ מִשֶּׁהִשִּׂיאָהּ אֵין לְאָבִיהָ רְשׁוּת בָּהּ.

Mishnah 3: If somebody gives his daughter in preliminary marriage and she was divorced, in preliminary marriage and she was widowed, the *ketubah* belongs to him[41]. If he gave her in definitive marriage and she was divorced, in definitive marriage and she was widowed, the *ketubah* belongs to her. Rebbi Jehudah says, the first *ketubah* is his. They said to him, from the moment he gave her in definitive marriage, he no longer has any power over her[42].

41 As long as his daughter lives in his house, she is his property. The question whether a preliminarily married woman has a *ketubah* is treated in Halakhah 5:1.

42 Even an underage girl is emancipated in civil law by marriage.

(28b line 50) **הלכה ג**: הַמְאָרֵס אֶת בִּתּוֹ כול'. אָמַר רִבִּי בּוּן בַּר חִייָה. טַעֲמָא דְרִבִּי יוּדָה כְּדֵי שֶׁיְּהֵא אָדָם מָצוּי לִיתֵּן לְבִתּוֹ בְּעַיִן יָפָה. רִבִּי יַעֲקֹב בַּר אָחָא בְּשֵׁם רִבִּי יִצְחָק. מַמּוֹצִיא שֵׁם רַע לָמַד רִבִּי מֵאִיר. וְהָתַנֵּי רִבִּי חִייָה. זִינְתָה וְעוֹדָהּ בְּבֵית אָבִיהָ מִשֶּׁבְּגָרָה הוֹצִיא עָלֶיהָ שֵׁם רַע. הוּא אֵינוֹ לוֹקֶה וְאֵינוֹ נוֹתֵן מֵאָה סֶלַע אֶלָּא הִיא אוֹ זוֹמְמֶיהָ מַקְדִּימִין לְבֵית הַסְּקִילָה. רִבִּי מָנָא בְּעָא קוֹמֵי רִבִּי יוֹסֵי. הַגַּע עַצְמָךְ. הוֹצִיא עָלֶיהָ שֵׁם רַע עוֹדָהּ נַעֲרָה וּבְגָרָה. אָמַר לֵיהּ. שָׁמַעְנוּ שְׁנוֹתֵן לְאָבִיהָ. אָמַר רִבִּי יִרְמְיָה קוֹמֵי רִבִּי זְעוּרָא. וְתַמְיָהּ אֲנִי הֵךְ רַבָּנִין מְדַמּוּ כְּתוּבָּה לִקְנָס. וְלֹא דָמֵי. דּוּ כְּתוּבָּה מִשָּׁעָה הָרִאשׁוֹנָה וּקְנָס בַּסּוֹף. וְאַתְּ אָמַר אָכֵן. אָמַר לֵיהּ. וּמִי יֹאמַר לָךְ. וַאֲפִילּוּ קְנָס מִשָּׁעָה הָרִאשׁוֹנָה הוּא. וְאָתְיָא דְרִבִּי מָנָא כְּרִבִּי יִרְמְיָה וּכְרִבִּי יוֹסֵי בַּר זְעִירָא.

Halakhah 3: "If somebody gives his daughter in preliminary marriage," etc. Rebbi Abun bar Ḥiyya said, the reason of Rebbi Jehudah is to encourage a man to give an ample dowry to his daughter[43]. Rebbi Jacob bar Aḥa in the name of Rebbi Isaac: Rebbi (Meïr)[44] learned from the calumniator[45]. Did not Rebbi Ḥiyya state: If she whored while in her father's house and he calumniated her[46] after she became an adult, he is not flogged[47] nor does he pay 100 tetradrachmas[48] but either she or the false witnesses are executed by stoning[49]? Rebbi Mana asked before Rebbi Yose: Think of it, if he calumniated her when she was an adolescent and now she is an adult? He said to him, we heard that he pays to her father[50]. Rebbi Jeremiah said before Rebbi Ze'ira: I am wondering how could the rabbis compare a *ketubah* to a fine when they are not comparable! For the *ketubah* is an obligation from the first hour[51] but the fine is only at the end[52]; and you say so? He said to him, who says that to you? Even the [obligation of the] fine is from the first moment[53]. It turns out that Rebbi Mana is like Rebbi Jeremiah and (like Rebbi Yose ben Ze'ira)[54].

43   This presupposes the earlier practice that the *ketubah* was written and the dowry given at the time of the preliminary marriage, in contrast to the later practice which postponed these transactions to the time of the definitive marriage. In that case, the dowry has to be returned at the dissolution of the preliminary marriage and it is clear that the father wants to have the dowry returned to him. {Many Jewish communities in the Middle Ages enacted rules which guaranteed the return of the dowry to the wife's family if the marriage was of short duration and/or there were no children; the best known being the rules of the community of Ṭulaiṭula (Toledo), *Šulḥan 'Arukh Even Ha'Ezer* §118.}

44   Since R. Meïr is not mentioned otherwise in this connection, it seems that this is a scribal mistake for R. Jehudah.

45   The calumniator accuses his definitively married wife, who is an

adolescent, of infidelity while preliminarily married. If his accusation is false, he pays the fine to the father, not to his wife. This shows that the father retains an interest in the money coming to his adolescent daughter even if she is definitively married. In the opinion of Maimonides (*More Nebukhim*, part 3, Chapter 49) and Nachmanides (Commentary to *Deut.* 22:19), the fine of the calumniator is 400 *zuz* since he wanted to steal from her the *ketubah* sum of 200 *zuz* by his accusation; as a thief he has to pay double restitution to the injured party. This supports R. Jehudah's contention that the father is the injured party. (Interpretation following R. Baruch Fränkel-Teomim.)

46 He is called a calumniator by the biblical text because he has to accuse his wife of adultery in front of the court, and for that he is punished if his accusation is not sustained. For the court to act on his accusation he has to produce two witnesses to the adultery since as husband he is his wife's relative and barred from acting as a witness for or against her.

47 The expression "they shall punish him" in *Deut.* 22:17 is interpreted to mean "they have him flogged."

48 In *Deut.* 22:18 it is written: They shall fine him 100 silver pieces and give them to the adolescent's father. If the girl is no longer an adolescent, the punishment does not apply.

49 The standard punishment for adultery by a preliminarily married adolescent, *Deut.* 22:24. If the witnesses for the husband are shown to be false (cf. Note 86), they are stoned since any false witness is punished by the sentence that would have been passed upon the accused if the testimony had been true.

50 As long as the accusation is made when the girl is an adolescent, the verse gives the money to the father.

51 The groom has to accept all obligations of the *ketubah* before a definitive marriage is possible.

52 The fine is due only upon sentencing.

53 He holds that the act of rape creates the obligation to pay the fine rather than the court's sentence.

54 This probably should read: וְרִבִּי יוֹסֵי כְּרִבִּי זְעִירָא. "and Rebbi Yose like Rebbi Ze'ira," that the obligation of the fine starts with the rape and, therefore, fine and *ketubah* are parallel institutions; the rules of the fine may inspire rules of *ketubah*.

(fol. 28a) **משנה ד:** הַגִּיוֹרֶת שֶׁנִּתְגַּיְּירָה בִתָּהּ עִמָּהּ וְזִינְתָה הֲרֵי זוֹ בְחֶנֶק אֵין לָהּ לֹא פֶתַח בֵּית הָאָב וְלֹא מֵאָה סֶלַע. הָיְתָה הוֹרָתָהּ שֶׁלֹּא בִקְדוּשָׁה וְלֵידָתָהּ בִּקְדוּשָׁה הֲרֵי זוֹ בִסְקִילָה אֵין לָהּ לֹא פֶתַח בֵּית הָאָב וְלֹא מֵאָה סֶלַע. הָיְתָה הוֹרָתָהּ וְלֵידָתָהּ בִּקְדוּשָׁה הֲרֵי הִיא כְּבַת יִשְׂרָאֵל לְכָל־דְּבָרֶיהָ. יֵשׁ לָהּ אָב וְאֵין לָהּ פֶּתַח בֵּית הָאָב יֵשׁ לָהּ פֶּתַח בֵּית הָאָב וְאֵין לָהּ אָב הֲרֵי זוֹ בִסְקִילָה. לֹא נֶאֱמַר פֶּתַח בֵּית הָאָב אֶלָּא לְמִצְוָה.

Mishnah 4: If a proselyte woman converted together with her daughter and the latter committed adultery[55], she is [executed] by strangling[56]; she has neither a door of her father's house[57] nor 100 tetradrachmas[58]. If she was conceived not in holiness but born in holiness[59], she is [executed] by stoning; she has neither a door to her father's house[60] nor 100 tetradrachmas. If she was conceived and born in holiness[61], she is a Jewish woman in all respects. If she[62] has a father but no door to her father's house[63], or a door to her father's house but no father[64], she is stoned since the door to her father's house was mentioned only as a commandment[65].

55   As a preliminarily married adolescent.

56   As any adulteress. The special rules of the preliminarily married adolescent are addressed to "a virgin of Israel". She may be a virgin, if she was converted before she reached the age of three years and a day, but she is not of Israel.

57   The adulterous preliminarily married adolescent is stoned there (*Deut.* 22:21).

58   If her husband had falsely accused her.

59   Her mother converted while pregnant.

60   Since her mother's relationship with her father was a relationship of Gentiles at the moment of conception, it is non-existent for Jewish law.

61   Her mother became pregnant after her conversion. Holiness is Judaism.

62   This now refers to Jewish

adolescents, rather than to proselytes. The sentence probably is the missing Mishnah 5.

63   Her father owns no house.

64   If her father died.

65   A biblical commandment only requires execution to the letter if it is characterized as either חוּקָה or תּוֹרָה.

(28b line 51) **הלכה ד**: הַגִּיוֹרֶת שֶׁנִּתְגַּיְיְרָה כול׳. כְּתִיב כִּי הוֹצִיא שֵׁם רָע עַל בְּתוּלַת יִשְׂרָאֵל. יָצְתָה זוֹ שֶׁאֵינָהּ מִיִּשְׂרָאֵל. כִּי הוֹצִיא שֵׁם רָע עַל בְּתוּלָה. לְרַבּוֹת אֶת הַגִּיוֹרֶת שֶׁהֲרָיָתָהּ הוֹרָתָהּ שֶׁלֹּא בִקְדוּשָׁה וְלֵידָתָהּ בִּקְדוּשָׁה תְּהֵא בִסְקִילָה. וְרִבָּהּ אוֹתָהּ לַקְּנָס. לֵית יְכִיל. וְתַנֵּי חִזְקִיָּה כֵן. מִמַּשְׁמָע שֶׁנֶּאֱמַר וּסְקָלוּהָ אֵין אָנוּ יוֹדְעִין שֶׁהִיא מֵתָה. מַה תַּלְמוּד לוֹמַר מֵתָה. אֶלָּא יֵשׁ לָךְ אַחֶרֶת שֶׁהִיא בִסְקִילָה וְהִיא פְטוּרָה. וְאֵי זוֹ זוֹ. זוֹ גִּיוֹרֶת שֶׁהָיְתָה הוֹרָתָהּ שֶׁלֹּא בִקְדוּשָׁה וְלֵידָתָהּ בִּקְדוּשָׁה שֶׁתְּהֵא בִסְקִילָה.

Halakhah 4: "If a proselyte woman converted," etc. It is written[66]: "For he calumniated a virgin of Israel". That excludes this one[67] who is not from Israel. "For he calumniated a virgin," to include the proselyte whose conception was not in holiness but her birth was in holiness, that she should be stoned. Why does one not add her for the fine[68]? You cannot do that; as Hizqiah stated[69]: We understand that it was said "they shall stone her[70]," does that not imply that she dies? Why does the verse say, "and she shall die"? But there must be another one who is stoned but (she)[71] [he] is free; who is that? That is the proselyte whose conception was not in holiness but who was born in holiness.

66   *Deut.* 22:19.

67   The girl not born Jewish.

68   The verse refers to the fine when she was falsely accused, not to her death when she was proven to be an adulteress.

69   In the Babli, 44b, that is a statement of R. Simeon ben Laqish.

70   *Deut.* 22:21, speaking of the girl proven to be an adulteress: "her town's people should stone her with stones that she dies."

71 This is the text of ms. and *editio princeps* but one has to read וְהוּא פָּטוּר for וְהִיא פְּטוּרָה. As the Babli argues, there must be one case which is added only for this kind of death penalty.

(28b line 68) כְּתִיב כִּי יִקַּח אִישׁ אִשָּׁה וּבָא עָלֶיהָ וּשְׂנֵאָהּ. לְעוֹלָם אֵינוֹ חַיָּיב עַד שֶׁיִּכְנוֹס וְיִבְעוֹל וְיִטְעוֹן טַעֲנַת בְּתוּלִים. וְשָׂם לָהּ עֲלִילוֹת דְּבָרִים. יָכוֹל אֲפִילוּ הִקְדִּיחָה לוֹ אֶת הַתַּבְשִׁיל. נֶאֱמַר כָּאן עֲלִילוֹת דְּבָרִים וּלְמַטָּן נֶאֱמַר עֲלִילוֹת דְּבָרִים. מַה עֲלִילוֹת דְּבָרִים לְמַטָּן זְנוּת אַף לְמַעֲלָן זְנוּת. אִי מַה עֲלִילוֹת דְּבָרִים שֶׁלְּמַטָּן מִמְּקוֹם בְּתוּלִין אַף כָּאן. מִנַּיִין אֲפִילוּ בָא עָלֶיהָ בִיאָה אַחֶרֶת. תַּלְמוּד לוֹמַר וְהוֹצִיא עָלֶיהָ שֵׁם רָע. מִכָּל־מָקוֹם. וְאָמַר אֶת הָאִשָּׁה הַזֹּאת לָקַחְתִּי וָאֶקְרַב אֵלֶיהָ. פְּרָט לְיִיעוּדִין. לָקַחְתִּי. פְּרָט לְשׁוֹמֶרֶת יָבָם. לָקַחְתִּי. פְּרָט לַאֲרוּסָה.

It is written[72]: "If a man takes a wife, comes to her, and hates her." He is not guilty unless he marries her definitively, has intercourse[73], and accuses her not to be a virgin. "He puts a libel on her"; I could think even if she spoiled a dish[74]? It says here "a libel" and it says later "a libel"[75]. Since "a libel" later implies whoring, so also here it means whoring. Since "a libel" later implies from the place of virginity, so also here? From where if he came upon her otherwise[76]? The verse says, "and he calumniates her", in any way. "He said, I took this wife[77] and came to her," that excludes assignations[78]; "I took", to exclude the one waiting for her levir[79]; "I took", to exclude the preliminarily married one[80].

72 *Deut.* 22:13 ff.
73 In the Babli, 46a, this interpretation is attributed to R. Eliezer ben Jacob, in *Sifry Deut.* 235, to R. Jehudah, as dissenting opinions.
74 Which according to the House of Hillel could be a cause for divorce, Mishnah *Giṭṭin* 9:10.
75 V. 14 reads: "He attacks her by libel and calumniates her, *and* he says, I took this woman, came to her and did not find her to be a virgin." One could

read this as meaning that the libel and the claim of missing virginity are two different actions by the husband. But v. 17 makes it clear that there is only one action: "He attacks her by libel, saying, I did not find your daughter to be a virgin." The same argument is in *Sifry Deut.*

76   He sets himself up for punishment even if during the first intercourse he did not penetrate. The Babli disagrees, 46a/b; *Sifry Deut.* agrees.

77   לָקַחְתִּי can be translated as: "I bought".

78   If a man buys somebody's underage daughter as an indentured servant (*Ex.* 21:7-11) he can later *assign* the price he paid for her as bride money either for himself or for his son and declare her preliminarily married without investing an additional penny in her. But since the money originally was given for her work as a servant, not for marriage, the husband cannot say "I bought her as a wife".

79   The levir did not give any money, his deceased brother did.

80   In this case, money was given but the marriage not consummated.

(28c line 1) לָקַחְתִּי. פְּרָט לְיִיעוּדִין. אָמַר רִבִּי יוֹנָה. אֲפִילוּ כְּמָאן דָּמַר. מִשָּׁעָה רִאשׁוֹנָה יָתֵן כֶּסֶף לְיִיעוּדִין. לָקַחְתִּי. פְּרָט לְשׁוֹמֶרֶת יָבָם. לֹא סוֹף דָּבָר כְּמִשְׁנָה הָרִאשׁוֹנָה שֶׁמִּצְוַת יִבּוּם קוֹדֶמֶת לְמִצְוַת חֲלִיצָה. אֶלָּא אֲפִילוּ כְּמִשְׁנָה אַחֲרוֹנָה שֶׁמִּצְוַת חֲלִיצָה קוֹדֶמֶת לְמִצְוַת יִיבּוּם. לָקַחְתִּי. פְּרָט לָאֲרוּסָה.

"I took", that excludes assignations[78]. Rebbi Jonah said, even following him who says that the money from the start was given for assignation[81]. "I took", to exclude the one waiting for her levir[79]; not only for the earlier teachings that the obligation of the levirate precedes that of *ḥaliṣah*, but even according to the later teachings that the obligation of *ḥaliṣah* precedes the obligation of levirate[82]. "I took", to exclude the preliminarily married one[80].

81   In *Qidduŝin* 1:2 (59b l. 40), Babli 19a, the only other places where the question is raised, only R. Yose ben R. Jehudah holds that the original money

was not given with the idea that eventually it would be used as bridesmoney. But everybody agrees that the verses *Ex.* 21:8-9 require a separate action of assignment which is distinct from the original acquisition; therefore, the marriage of the indentured servant is not a "buy".

82   Cf. *Yebamot* 12:7, Note 140; *Bekhorot* Mishnah 1:7.

(28c line 5) וָאֶקְרַב אֵלֶיהָ וְלֹא מָצָאתִי לָהּ בְּתוּלִים. וְחָשׁ לוֹמַר שֶׁמָּא מָצָא וְאִיבֵּד. שֶׁהֵבִיא הַבַּעַל עֵדִים שֶׁזִּינְתָה עוֹדָהּ בְּבֵית אָבִיהָ. וְאֵלֶּה בְּתוּלֵי בִתִּי. וְחָשׁ לוֹמַר שֶׁמָּא דַם צִיפּוֹר הוּא. שֶׁהֵבִיא הָאָב עֵדִים לְהָזִים עִידֵי הַבַּעַל. אָמַר רִבִּי יוֹסֵי בֵּירִבִּי בּוּן. הַפָּרָשָׁה הַזּוֹ יֵשׁ בָּהּ עֵדִים וְזוֹמְמֵיהֶן וְזוֹמְמֵי זוֹמְמֵיהֶן. הַבַּעַל אוֹמֵר. הֲרֵי עֵדִים שֶׁזִּנְתָה בְּבֵית אָבִיהָ. וְהֵבִיא הָאָב עֵדִים לְהָזִים עִידֵי הַבַּעַל. אָמַר רִבִּי יוֹסֵי בֵּירִבִּי בּוּן. הֵבִיא הָ[אָ]ב עֵדִים לְהָזִים עִידֵי הַבַּעַל. וְהֵבִיא הַבַּעַל עֵדִים לְהָזִים עִידֵי הָאָב. אִית תַּנָּיֵי תַּנֵּי. אִם אֱמֶת הָיָה הַדָּבָר הַזֶּה בְּשֶׁמָּצָא הָאָב עֵדִים לְהָזִים עִידֵי הַבַּעַל.

"I came to her and did not find her a virgin[83]." Should we not worry that he found and made disappear[84]? The husband brought witnesses that she committed adultery while in her father's house. "This is proof of my daughters virginity.[85]" Should we not worry that this is bird's blood? The father brought witnesses to prove perjury by the husband's witnesses[86]. Rebbi Yose ben Rebbi Abun said, in this paragraph there are witnesses, witnesses of perjury, and witnesses of perjury of the witnesses of perjury: The husband says, these are witnesses that she whored in her father's house. The father brought witnesses to prove perjury of the husband's witnesses. Rebbi Yose ben Rebbi Abun said: The father brought witnesses to prove perjury of the husband's witnesses. And the husband brought witnesses to prove perjury of the father's witnesses. Some Tannaïm state: "If this was true," that the father found witnesses to prove perjury of the husband's witnesses[87].

83 *Deut.* 22:14.

84 It is difficult to accept that the court should take the case simply on the husband's statement, in particular because the husband cannot be cross-examined as a witness since he is related to his wife and relatives are barred from being witnesses.

85 *Deut.* 22:17. The father also is barred from being a witness in a case involving his daughter.

86 The case is a regular criminal case to be adjudicated following all rules of criminal procedure; the only new feature is the punishment inflicted on the husband if his case is not sustained in court.

In talmudic law, there are unreliable witnesses and there are perjurers. If the story of the witnesses does not hold up under cross-examination, or if the witnesses's story is contradicted by equally trustworthy witnesses, the witnesses are unreliable and their testimony is not accepted as basis of a judgment. Perjury with its attendant penalties (*Deut.* 19:18-20) only is impossible testimony, i. e., that the opposing party produces witnesses to testify that the other witnesses could not possibly have seen what they testify to since they were at another place at the time they pretend to have seen certain things.

87 The penalties mentioned in this paragraph can only be imposed if the case is one of proven formal perjury.

(28c line 12) וּפָרְשׂוּ הַשִּׂמְלָה. הַכֹּל מָשָׁל. תַּנֵּי רִבִּי יִשְׁמְעֵאל. זֶה אֶחָד מִשְּׁלֹשָׁה מִקְרִיּוֹת שֶׁנֶּאֶמְרוּ בַתּוֹרָה בְּמָשָׁל. אִם יָקוּם וְהִתְהַלֵּךְ בַּחוּץ עַל מִשְׁעַנְתּוֹ וְנִקָּה הַמַּכֶּה. וְכִי עָלָת עַל דַּעְתָּךְ שֶׁיְּהֵא זֶה מְהַלֵּךְ בַּשּׁוּק וַחֲלָה נֶהֱרָג עַל יָדָיו. אֶלָּא מָהוּ עַל מִשְׁעַנְתּוֹ. עַל בּוּרְיוֹ. אִם זָרְחָה הַשֶּׁמֶשׁ עָלָיו דָּמִים לוֹ. וְכִי עָלָיו לְבַדּוֹ הַחַמָּה זוֹרַחַת. אֶלָּא מַה זְרִיחַת הַשֶּׁמֶשׁ מְיוּחֶדֶת שֶׁהִיא שָׁלוֹם לְכָל־בָּאֵי עוֹלָם. אַף זֶה בִּזְמַן שֶׁהוּא יוֹדֵעַ שֶׁהוּא שָׁלוֹם מִמֶּנּוּ וַהֲרָגוֹ הֲרֵי זֶה חַיָּיב.

"And they spread out the cloth.[88]" That is all simile. Rebbi Ismael stated: That is one of three verses in the Torah which have been written as simile[89]. "If he gets up and walks outside on his support, the one who hit him is not prosecuted.[90]" Could anybody think that one walks in the market and the other is executed because of him? But what is "on his support", in his health[91]. "If the sun shone on him, he has blood.[92]" Does the sun shine only on him? But just as the sun is particular that it brings peace to the entire world, so also this one, if one knows that [the other] is at peace with him and he kills him, he is guilty[93].

88   *Deut.* 22:17. It was proven that this sentence cannot mean what it says.
89   *Sifry Deut.* 237; in Finkelstein's opinion not of the original *Sifry* text. A slightly enlarged version is in *Sanhedrin* 8:8, 26c l. 6.
90   *Ex.* 21:19, speaking of a person who deliberatly injures another. *Mekhilta dR. Ismael Mišpaṭim* 6; *Mekhilta dR. Simeon ben Ioḥai* p. 174.
91   If the injured person regains his health but then has a relapse and dies, the person who injured him cannot be prosecuted for murder.

92   *Ex.* 22:2, speaking of a thief digging a tunnel under a house, who can be killed with impunity if found out since in the tunnel "he has no blood".
93   In the opinion of the Babli, *Sanhedrin* 72a/b, this can only be asserted of a father coming to steal from his son. In the opinion of the Yerushalmi (Note 89) it cannot be asserted of anybody. Cf. *Mekhilta dR. Ismael Mišpaṭim* 13; differently in *Mekhilta dR. Simeon ben Ioḥai* p. 192.

(28c line 19) תַּנֵּי. רִבִּי אֱלִיעֶזֶר בֶּן יַעֲקֹב אוֹמֵר. יֵאָמְרוּ הַדְּבָרִים כִּכְתָבָם. מָהוּ יֵאָמְרוּ הַדְּבָרִים כִּכְתָבָם. אָמַר רִבִּי יוֹסֵי בֵּירִבִּי בּוּן. לְעוֹלָם אֵינוֹ חַיָּיב עַד שֶׁיִּכְנוֹס וְיִבְעוֹל וְיִטְעוֹן טַעֲנַת בְּתוּלִים. וּפֵרְשׁוּ הַשִּׂמְלָה. לֹא סוֹף דָּבָר וּפֵרְשׁוּ הַשִּׂמְלָה. אֶלָּא עַד שֶׁיִּתְחַוְורוּ הַדְּבָרִים כַּשִּׂמְלָה. רִבִּי אַסִּי אָמַר. וּפֵרְשׁוּ הַשִּׂמְלָה. לְעוֹלָם אֵין הָעֵדִים נִסְקָלִין וְלֹא הַבַּעַל לוֹקֶה וְלֹא נוֹתֵן מֵאָה סֶלַע עַד שֶׁיֹּאמְרוּ. עִמָּנוּ הָיָה בְּמָקוֹם פְּלוֹנִי. וְהַבַּעַל שְׂכָרָן לְהָעִיד עֵדוּת שֶׁקֶר. אָמְרוּ. עִמָּנוּ הָיָה בְּמָקוֹם פְּלוֹנִי. וְלֹא אָמְרוּ. הַבַּעַל שְׂכָרָן לְהָעִיד עֵדוּת שֶׁקֶר. רִבִּי יוֹסֵי בֵּירִבִּי בּוּן רִבִּי יוֹחָנָן בְּשֵׁם רִבִּי שִׁמְעוֹן בֶּן לָקִישׁ. נֶאֱמַר כָּאן שׂוּמָה וְנֶאֱמַר לְהַלָּן שׂוּמָה. מַה שׂוּמָה שֶׁנֶּאֱמַר לְהַלָּן מָמוֹן אַף כָּאן מָמוֹן. וְהָתַנֵּי. לֹא אָמַר לָעֵדִים. בּוֹאוּ

וְהֵעִידוּנִי. אֶלָּא הֵן בָּאִין מֵאֵילֵיהֶן. הוּא אֵינוּ לוֹקֶה וְאֵינוּ נוֹתֵן מָאָה סֶלַע אֶלָּא אוֹ הִיא אוֹ זוֹמְמֶיהָ מַקְדִּימִין לְבֵית הַסְּקִילָה. מִפְּנֵי שֶׁלֹּא אָמַר. הָא אִם אָמַר. אֲפִילוּ לֹא שְׂכָרָן כְּמִי שֶׁשְּׂכָרָן. הֵבִיא הָאָב שְׁנֵי כִיתֵּי עֵדִים. אַחַת אוֹמֶרֶת. עִמָּנוּ הְיִיתֶם בְּמָקוֹם פְּלוֹנִי. וְאַחַת אוֹמֶרֶת. הַבַּעַל שְׂכָרָן לְהָעִיד עֵדוּת שֶׁקֶר. פְּשִׁיטָא אוֹתָן שֶׁאָמְרוּ. עִמָּנוּ הָיָה בְּמָקוֹם פְּלוֹנִי. נִסְקָלִין. וְאוֹתָן שֶׁאָמְרוּ. הַבַּעַל שְׂכָרָן לְהָעִיד עֵדוּת שֶׁקֶר. לוֹקִין וְנוֹתְנִין מֵאָה סֶלַע. אָמַר רִבִּי יוֹסֵי בֵּירִבִּי בּוּן. וְלֹא עַל יְדֵי אֵילּוּ וְלֹא עַל יְדֵי אֵילּוּ לוֹקִין וְנוֹתְנִין מֵאָה סֶלַע. אֶלָּא לוֹקִין מִשּׁוּם לֹא תַעֲנֶה בְרֵעֲךָ עֵד שָׁקֶר.

It was stated[94]: Rebbi Eliezer ben Jacob says, the words should be said as they are written. What means "the words should be said as they are written"? Rebbi Yose ben Rebbi Abun said, he is not guilty unless he marries her definitively, has intercourse[73], and accuses her not to be a virgin. "They spread the cloth[88]". Not that "they spread the cloth" but until the things become clear like a cloth[95]. Assi said, "they spread the cloth", the witnesses are not stoned, nor is the husband flogged and pays 100 tetradrachmas, until they say: you were with us at a certain place[96], and the husband hired them to testify falsely[97]. If they said, you were with us at a certain place, but they did not say, the husband hired them to testify falsely? Rebbi Yose ben Rebbi Abun, Rebbi Johanan in the name of Rebbi Simeon ben Laqish[98]: It is said here "putting", it is said there "putting". Since "putting" there means money, also "putting" here must mean money[99]. But did we not state: He did not say to the witnesses, come and testify in my case, but they came on their own, he is not flogged nor does he pay 100 tetradrachmas but either she or the false witnesses would be stoned[49,100]? Because he did not say. But if he said, even if he did not hire them it is as if he hired them[101]. If the father brought two groups of witnesses[102]. One side say, you were with us at a certain place. The other side say, the husband hired them to testify falsely. It is obvious that those who said, you were with us at a certain place, are stoned[103], and those who said, the husband hired them to testify falsely, are flogged and pay 100 tetradrachmas[104]. Rebbi Yose ben Rebbi Abun said, neither by these not by those are they flogged and pay 100 tetradrachmas[104], but they atre flogged because of "you shall not testify as a false witness against your fellow man.[106]"

94 Babli 46a, *Sifry Deut.* §237. In the interpretation of the Babli, R. Eliezer ben Jacob requires that the court hear testimony about virginal blood.

95 Usually, new cloth was simply bleached, not dyed. חִוֵּר really means "pale"; only in a derivative sense it means "logically consistent".

96 This is necessary to prove the witnesses guilty of perjury, cf. Note 86.

97 This is necessary to impose penalties on the husband.

98 This attribution seems most unlikely. Since the argument is quoted in the Babli, 46a, as a tannaitic statement attributed to R. Jehudah, it is more likely that the original text was: In the name of R. Simeon ben Iohai.

99 The argument is a little more explicit in the Babli. It is written here, "he puts a libel on her". It is written in *Ex.* 22:24: "you shall not charge interest to [the recipient of a loan]." From the principle that a word has only one meaning, one infers that the husband "puts" a libel on his wife by paying for it; then according to this opinion he cannot be punished unless he actually pays for the false testimony.

100 The Babli agrees, 46a.

101 This disagrees with the opinion given before. The husband must actively be involved in bringing the witnesses before the court but he does not have to pay them in order to become criminally liable. In general, a person who hires another to commit a crime (or simply induces him to commit a crime) cannot in general be prosecuted since "there is no agent for sin" (Babli *Qiddušin* 42b); exeptions to that rule must have a biblical basis.

102 Who then are proven to have

perjured themselves. (The Babli, *Sanhedrin* 9b, discusses only the simple case that the same witnesses testify both about the other witnesses and the husband's involvment.)

103 Since, if their testimony had been true, the husband's witnesses would have been stoned.

104 Since they testify to the involvement of the husband in the prosecution of his wife.

105 The husband is not flogged and does not have to pay if his witnesses tell the truth. Therefore, the witnesses who testify to his involvement in the recruiting of his witnesses are not the only cause of him being flogged and having to pay; without the other set of witnesses their testimony would have been irrelevant.

106 *Ex.* 20:17. The Babli disagrees, *Makkot* 2b, since "a prohibition violated without an action is not prosecutable" (cf. *Nedarim* 1:1, Note 2).

(28c line 36) רִבִּי בּוּן בַּר חִיָּיה בְּעָא קוֹמֵי רִבִּי זְעִירָא. הֵבִיא הָאָב עֵדִים לְהָזִים עֵידֵי הַבַּעַל. הוּזְמוּ עֵידֵי הָאָב. לוֹקֶה וְנוֹתֵן מֵאָה סֶלַע בִּשְׁלֹשָׁה וְהָעֵדִים נִסְקָלִין בְּעֶשְׂרִים וּשְׁלֹשָׁה. אָמַר לֵיהּ. אִילוּ לֹא הוּזְמוּ עֵידֵי הָאָב לֹא נִמְצָא הַבַּעַל לוֹקֶה וְנוֹתֵן מֵאָה סֶלַע בִּשְׁלֹשָׁה וְהָעֵדִים נִסְקָלִין בְּעֶשְׂרִים וּשְׁלֹשָׁה. סָבַר רִבִּי זְעִירָא. שְׁנֵי דִינִין הֵן. רִבִּי יִרְמְיָה בְּשֵׁם רִבִּי אַבָּהוּ. כּוּלּוֹ דִין אֶחָד הוּא. מַתְנִיתָא פְּלִיגָא עַל רִבִּי אַבָּהוּ. אֶל זִקְנֵי הָעִיר זֶה בֵית דִּין שֶׁלִּשְׁלֹשָׁה. הַשַּׁעְרָה זֶה בֵית דִּין שֶׁלְכ"ג. פָּתַר לָהּ כְּרִבִּי מֵאִיר. דְּרִבִּי מֵאִיר אוֹמֵר. לוֹקֶה וּמְשַׁלֵּם. תַּמָּן תַּנִּינָן. הָאוֹנֵס וְהַמְפַתֶּה וְהַמּוֹצִיא שֵׁם רַע בִּשְׁלֹשָׁה. דִּבְרֵי רִבִּי מֵאִיר. וַחֲכָמִים אוֹמְרִים. מוֹצִיא שֵׁם רַע בִּשְׁלֹשָׁה וְעֶשְׂרִים שֶׁיֵּשׁ בּוֹ דִינֵי נֶפֶשׁ. רִבִּי מָנָא אָמַר. בְּנַעֲרָה מְאוֹרָסָה פְּלִיגִין. רִבִּי מֵאִיר אוֹמֵר. מַפְסֶדֶת כְּתוּבָּתָהּ בִּשְׁלֹשָׁה וְנִסְקֶלֶת בִּשְׁלֹשָׁה וְעֶשְׂרִים. וַחֲכָמִים אוֹמְרִים. מָקוֹם שֶׁנִּסְקֶלֶת שָׁם הִיא מַפְסֶדֶת כְּתוּבָּתָהּ. אֲבָל בְּמוֹצִיא שֵׁם רַע כָּל־עַמָּא מוֹדוּ מָקוֹם שֶׁהָעֵדִים נִסְקָלִין שָׁם הַבַּעַל לוֹקֶה וְנוֹתֵן מֵאָה סֶלַע. אָמַר לֵיהּ רִבִּי יוֹסֵי בֵּירִבִּי בּוּן. אֵין דְּלָא תַנִּיתָהּ פְּלִיגָא. אֶלָּא בְּמוֹצִיא שֵׁם רַע פְּלִיגִין. רִבִּי מֵאִיר אוֹמֵר. לוֹקֶה וְנוֹתֵן מֵאָה סֶלַע בִּשְׁלֹשָׁה וְהָעֵדִים נִסְקָלִין בִּשְׁלֹשָׁה וְעֶשְׂרִים. וְרַבָּנִין אָמְרִין. מָקוֹם שֶׁהָעֵדִים נִסְקָלִין שָׁם הַבַּעַל לוֹקֶה וְנוֹתֵן מֵאָה סֶלַע. אֲבָל בְּנַעֲרָה מְאוֹרָסָה כָּל־עַמָּא מוֹדוּ מָקוֹם

שֶׁנִּסְקָלֶת שָׁם מַפְסֶדֶת כְּתוּבָּתָהּ. וְאָתְיָא דְרִבִּי יוֹסֵי בֵּירִבִּי בּוּן כְּרִבִּי זְעִירָא וּדְרִבִּי מָנָא כְּרִבִּי אַבָּהוּ.

Rebbi Abun bar Ḥiyya asked before Rebbi Ze'ira: If the father brought witnesses to prove the perjury of the husband's witnesses; but the father's witnesses were proven perjurers, is he flogged and pays 100 tetradrachmas by the judgment of three and the witnesses are stoned by the judgment of 23[107]? He said to him, if the father's witnesses are not proven perjurers, is not the husband flogged and pays 100 tetradrachmas by the judgment of three and the witnesses are stoned by the judgment of 23[108]? Rebbi Ze'ira is of the opinion that there are two different proceedings. Rebbi Jeremiah in the name of Rebbi Abbahu: There is only one proceeding[109]. A *baraita* disagrees with Rebbi Abbahu: "To the town's Elders", that is a court of three members; "to the gate", that is a court of 23[110]. He explains it following Rebbi Meïr, since Rebbi Meïr says that he is flogged and pays[111]. There[112], we have stated: "The seducer, the rapist, and the calumniator [are judged] by three [judges], the words of Rebbi Meïr; but the Sages say, the calumniator by 23 since it is a potential capital case.[113]" Rebbi Mana said, they disagree about the preliminarily married adolescent. Rebbi Meïr says, she loses her *ketubah* in a court of three and is stoned by a court of 23; but the Sages say, at the same place which sentences her to be stoned she loses her *ketubah*[114]. But in the case of the calumniator, everybody agrees that by the court in which the witnesses are stoned, the husband is flogged and pays 100 tetradrachmas. Rebbi Yose ben Rebbi Abun said to him, would they differ where it was not stated[115]? But they differ about the calumniator! Rebbi Meïr says, he is flogged and pays 100 tetradrachmas by the judgment of three and the witnesses are stoned by the judgment of 23; but the rabbis say, by the court in which the witnesses are stoned, the husband is flogged and pays 100 tetradrachmas. But by the case of the preliminarily married adolescent, everybody agrees that at the same place which sentences her to be stoned she loses her *ketubah*. [It turns out that Rebbi Yose ben Rebbi Abun follows Rebbi Ze'ira and Rebbi Mana [follows] Rebbi Abbahu][116].

107 Money matters are adjudicated in a court of 3 judges (Mishnah *Sanhedrin* 1:1), capital cases by a court of 23 (Mishnah 1:4). The anonymous majority hold that potential cases of flogging are adjudicated by a court of 3 (Mishnah 1:2). Therefore, flogging and payment of a fine can be imposed by the same court.

108 It is not necessary to discuss the case that the witnesses to perjury are found to be themselves perjurers; the same result can be obtained assuming the husband's witnesses are perjurers. Then also the husband's case is one of flogging and fine, in the competence of a small court, but that of the witnesses is a capital case which requires the large court.

In the Babli, *Sanhedrin* 8b, this is reported as the opinion of R. Ḥiyya bar Abin and the Babylonian Rava.

109 Since the husband can only be flogged and fined if the witnesses are stoned, the husband's case is an appendix to that of the witnesses.

110 This *baraita* is not found in other sources. The reference is to *Deut.* 22:15, where the girl's father is instructed to go "to the town's Elders, to the gate." The double determination is read as instruction to appear before two different courts.

111 Cf. Chapter 3:1, Note 30. He will agree that the two punishments of the husband are in the competence of one court. The Sages, who hold that in general the culprit who is flogged does not pay, must agree that the husband can only be flogged by the court which sentences the witnesses for perjury.

112 Mishnah *Sanhedrin* 1:1.

113 Since the wife has to be stoned if found to have committed adultery as a preliminarily married adolescent.

114 Since the husband can be freed from his obligations under the *ketubah* only if the wife is found guilty, a set-up

in which two courts could come to contradictory conclusions is impossible.
115 Mishnah *Sanhedrin* 1:1 states clearly that there is a disagreement in the case of the calumniator. If there were a disagreement in the case of the preliminarily married adolescent, it would have to be stated in the Mishnah.
116 Text of the Constantinople edition. Text of the ms. and *editio princeps*: וְאָתְיָא דְרִבִּי מָנָא כְּרִבִּי זְעִירָא

"Rebbi וְדִרְבִּי יוֹסֵי בֵּירִבִּי בּוּן כְּרִבִּי אַבָּהוּ Mana follows R. Ze'ira and R. Yose bar Abun follows R. Abbahu." It is possible to explain that version, in that R. Yose bar Abun was forced to invent the case that the witnesses for perjury were perjurers since in the case of the husband he follows R. Abbahu and that R. Mana, who in the main rule disagrees with R. Ze'ira, accepts his explanation that the *baraita* is R. Meïr's.

(28c line 56) לְעוֹלָם אֵין הַבַּעַל לוֹקֶה וְלֹא נוֹתֵן מֵאָה סֶלַע עַד שֶׁיִּסָּקְלוּ הָעֵדִים. קְנָס אֵימָתַי הוּא מִתְחַיֵּיב. רִבִּי יוֹנָה אָמַר. בְּסוֹף. רִבִּי יוֹסֵה אָמַר. מִשָּׁעָה רִאשׁוֹנָה. מְתִיב רִבִּי יוֹסֵי לְרִבִּי יוֹנָה. עַל דַּעְתָּךְ דְּתֵימַר. בְּסוֹף. לוֹקֶה וְנוֹתֵן מֵאָה סֶלַע בִּשְׁלֹשָׁה וְהָעֵדִים נִסְקָלִין בִּשְׁלֹשָׁה וְעֶשְׂרִים. אָמַר רִבִּי מָנָא. אֲפִילוּ עַל דְּרִבִּי יוֹסֵי דְּכִי אַתְיָיא מַקְשְׁיֵיהּ כְּמָאן דָּמַר. עֵדִים זוֹמְמִין צְרִיכִין הַתְרָיָיה. וְלֹא הִתְרָה בָהֶן לוֹקֶה וְנוֹתֵן מֵאָה סֶלַע בִּשְׁלֹשָׁה וְהָעֵדִים נִסְקָלִין בִּשְׁלֹשָׁה וְעֶשְׂרִים. אָמַר רִבִּי אַבָּמְרִי. מָאן דָּמַר דּוּ כֵן.

The husband is never flogged, nor does he pay 100 tetradrachmas, unless the witnesses are stoned[117]. When is he obligated for the fine? Rebbi Jonah said, at the end. Rebbi Yose said, from the first hour[118]. Rebbi Yose objected to Rebbi Jonah: In your opinion, since you say at the end, can he be flogged and made to pay 100 tetradrachmas by a court of three and the witnesses stoned by a court of 23[119]? Rebbi Mana said, even according to Rebbi Yose one could ask the question following him who holds that perjured witnesses need to be warned. If they did not warn them, is he flogged and made to pay 100 tetradrachmas by a court of three; are the witnesses stoned by a court of 23[120]? Rebbi Abbamari said, who is that who says so[121]?

117 Since only in this case is the husband's guilt established.

118 They switch their positions from Halakhah 1, in the case of the fine imposed on the rapist. "At the end" means after sentence is imposed, "the first hour" is the moment he falsely accuses his wife of adultery.

119 If the obligation of the fine is a consequence of the conviction of the witnesses, flogging and the fine should be mentioned after the sentence imposed on the witnesses and not before.

120 If the witnesses are shown to be perjurers but they cannot be punished because they were not warned of the consequences of perjury, the fact that they cannot be convicted frees the husband and, therefore, his obligation could not be from the first moment.

121 Nobody holds that witnesses need special warnings since they must be informed by the court about the importance of their testimony. The Babli agrees, 33a.

(28c line 63) רִבִּי יוֹסֵי בֵּירְבִּי חֲנִינָה. הָאוֹנֵס וְהַמְפַתֶּה אֶת הַיְתוֹמָה פָּטוּר. אָמַר רִבִּי בָּא בַר מָמָל. מַחֲלוֹקֶת כְּרִבִּי יוֹסֵי הַגָּלִילִי. בְּרַם כְּרִבִּי עֲקִיבָה יֵשׁ לָהּ קְנָס וּקְנָסָהּ שֶׁלְעַצְמָהּ. אָמַר רִבִּי יוֹסֵי. מַתְנִיתָא אָמְרָה כֵן. אֵין לָהּ פֶּתַח בֵּית אָב וְלֹא מֵאָה סֶלַע. וְלֹא כִיתוֹמָה הִיא. רִבִּי אִימִּי וְרִבִּי יְהוֹשֻׁעַ בֶּן לֵוִי תְּרֵיהוֹן אָמְרִין. הַמּוֹצִיא שֵׁם רַע עַל הַקְטַנָּה פָּטוּר. אָמַר רִבִּי הוֹשַׁעְיָה. וְיֵאוֹת. אִילוּ גְדוֹלָה שֶׁלֹּא הִתְרוּ בָהּ שֶׁמָּא כְלוּם הִיא. וּקְטַנָּה שֶׁהִתְרוּ בָהּ כִּגְדוֹלָה שֶׁלֹּא הִתְרוּ בָהּ.

Rebbi Yose ben Rebbi Ḥanina: One who rapes or seduces an orphan is free[122]. Rebbi Abba bar Mamal said, this is in dispute; following Rebbi Yose the Galilean. But following Rebbi Aqiba a fine is due, and the fine belongs to herself[123]. Rebbi Yose said, the Mishnah[124] says so: "She has neither a door to her father's house nor 100 tetradrachmas;" is she not like an orphan[125]? Rebbi Immi and Rebbi Joshua ben Levi both say, one who calumniates an underage girl is free[122]. Rebbi Hoshaiah said, that is correct. If she were an adult who was not warned, would there be any case[126]? And an underage girl who was warned is like an adult who was not warned[127].

122 He does not have to pay the criminal fine, but the payments enumerated in Mishnah 3:5 in civil law are still due.

123 Halakhah 3:4.

124 This now refers to Mishnah 5.

125 The Mishnah refers to the girl whose mother converted while pregnant with her, who legally has no father since by conversion her mother became a new person, unrelated to her prior existence.

126 Even the adolescent, who is an adult in criminal law, cannot be executed for adultery if at the moment of her adultery she was not duly warned in front of two witnesses that she would risk the death penalty if she went ahead with her adultery. It was stated before that the husband pays only if his witnesses are stoned. But his witnesses can be stoned only if the woman would be stoned had their testimony been true. If there are no witnesses to the warning, the witnesses to the adultery cannot cause her to be executed. Therefore, if these witnesses are found perjured, they cannot be stoned. Therefore, the husband cannot be flogged and fined.

127 A minor cannot be criminally liable. Since the underage wife could under no circumstances be stoned, the husband cannot possibly be flogged and fined. The same argument in the Babli, 44b.

(28c line 70) רִבִּי זְעִירָא רַב הַמְנוּנָא בְּשֵׁם רַב אָדָא בַּר אֲחָוָה. לְעוֹלָם אֵינָהּ מַקְדֶּמֶת לְבֵית הַסְּקִילָה עַד שֶׁתְּהֵא נַעֲרָה בִּשְׁעַת הוֹצָאָה. מַאי טַעְמָא. וְהוֹצִיאוּ הַנַּעֲרָה אֶל פֶּתַח בֵּית אָבִיהָ. וְהָא תַּנֵּי רִבִּי חִייָה. זִינַת עוֹדָהּ בְּבֵית אָבִיהָ וּמִשֶּׁבְּגָרָה הוֹצִיא עָלֶיהָ שֵׁם רַע. הוּא אֵינוֹ לוֹקֶה וְאֵינוֹ נוֹתֵן מֵאָה סָלַע. אֶלָּא אוֹ הִיא אוֹ זוֹמְמֶיהָ מַקְדִּימִין לְבֵית הַסְּקִילָה. מַתְנִיתָא פְּלִיגָא עַל רַב אָדָא בַּר

אֲחָוָה. מִי שֶׁנִּגְמַר דִּינוֹ וּבָרַח וְאַחַר כָּךְ הִקִּיף זְקַן הַתַּחְתּוֹן. תַּמָּן אַתְּ יָכִיל מֵימַר. וְהוֹצִיאוּ אֶת הַנַּעֲרָה שֶׁזִּינָת. אִית לָךְ מֵימַר הָכָא. וְהוֹצִיאוּ אוֹתוֹ אֶת הַבֵּן.

Rebbi Ze'ira, Rav Hamnuna in the name of Rav Ada bar Aḥawa: She cannot be executed unless she is an adolescent at the time of the execution. What is the reason? "They shall execute the adolescent at her father's door[128]." But did not Rebbi Ḥiyya state[46-49]: If she whored in her father's house and [the husband] calumniated her after she became an adult, he is not flogged nor does he pay 100 tetradrachmas but either she or the witnesses are executed by stoning. A Mishnah disagrees with Rav Ada bar Aḥawa: "If he escaped after being sentenced and then his pubic hair grew fully.[129]" There, you can say "they shall execute the adolescent" who whored; can you say here "they shall execute him", the son[130]?

128 *Deut.* 22:18-21.
129 Mishnah *Sanhedrin* 8:6, speaking of the unruly son, *Deut.* 21:18-21, who can be judged only if he is an adolescent, in the 6 months after he grew two pubic hairs before the pubic hair is fully grown. If he was sentenced as an adolescent, he can be executed as an adult.
130 *Deut.* 22:21 says only "they shall stone him", without indicating age.

(28d line 2) תַּנֵּי. נַעֲרָה מְאוֹרָסָה שֶׁזִּינָת סוֹקְלִין אוֹתָהּ עַל פֶּתַח בֵּית אָבִיהָ. אֵין לָהּ פֶּתַח בֵּית אָבִיהָ סוֹקְלִין אוֹתָהּ בִּמְקוֹם שֶׁזִּינָת. אִם הָיְתָה עִיר שֶׁל גּוֹיִם סוֹקְלִין אוֹתָהּ עַל פֶּתַח בֵּית דִּין. וְהָעוֹבֵד עֲבוֹדָה זָרָה סוֹקְלִין אוֹתוֹ בִּמְקוֹם שֶׁעָבַד. וְאִם הָיְתָה עִיר שֶׁלְּגוֹיִם סוֹקְלִין אוֹתוֹ עַל פֶּתַח בֵּית דִּין. וְהָתַנֵּי רִבִּי חִיָּיה. הוֹצֵא אֶת הַמְקַלֵּל מִחוּץ לַמַּחֲנֶה. מְלַמֵּד שֶׁבֵּית דִּין מִבִּפְנִים וּבֵית הַסְּקִילָה מִבַּחוּץ. אָמַר רִבִּי יוֹסֵי. שַׁנְיָיא הִיא. הוּא שַׁעַר שֶׁקִּילְקֵל בּוֹ הוּא שַׁעַר שֶׁנִּמְצָא בוֹ הוּא שַׁעַר שֶׁנִּידּוֹן בּוֹ הוּא שַׁעַר שֶׁנִּסְקַל בּוֹ. כִּי עָשְׂתָה נְבָלָה בְּיִשְׂרָאֵל.

HALAKHAH 6

נִבְלָה זוֹ כָּל־יִשְׂרָאֵל. שֶׁבָּא לִזְנוֹת בֵּית אָבִיהָ יָבוֹאוּ גִידוּלִים רָעִים שֶׁגִּדְּלוּ יִתְנַבְּלוּ הֵן וְגִידוּלָן.

It was stated[131]: One stones a preliminarily married adolescent girl who whored at her father's door. If she does not have a father's house's door one stones her where she whored. If it was a Gentile town one stones her at the court's door. Also, a person who practiced idolatry one stones at the place where he worshipped. If it was a Gentile town one stones him at the court's door. But did not Rebbi Ḥiyya state: "Take the blasphemer out from the encampment,[132]" this teaches that the court sits inside and the place of stoning is outside. Rebbi Yose said, there is a difference: The place where he went astray is the place where he was found, is the place where he was judged, is the place where he was stoned[133]. "For she did a foul deed in Israel." This one befouled all of Israel, for she came to whore in her father's house. The bad growth they grew shall come and foul up them and their growth.

131 Babli 45b; Tosephta *Sanhedrin* 10:10.
132 *Lev.* 24:14. The same statement in the Babli *Sanhedrin* 45b.
133 In the Babli, 45b, this is a tannaitic statement about *Deut.* 17:5, that the idolator has to be stoned "at your gates." In *Sifry Deut.* 148: "The gate where he was found, not the gate where he was judged."

משנה ו: (fol. 28a) הָאָב זַכַּאי בְּבִתּוֹ בְּקִידּוּשֶׁיהָ בַּכֶּסֶף בַּשְּׁטָר וּבַבִּיאָה וְזַכַּאי בִּמְצִיאָתָהּ וּבְמַעֲשֵׂה יָדֶיהָ וּבְהֶפֵר נְדָרֶיהָ וּמְקַבֵּל אֶת גִּיטָּהּ וְאֵינוּ אוֹכֵל פֵּירוֹת בְּחַיֶּיהָ. נִיסֵּית יָתֵר עָלָיו הַבַּעַל שֶׁאוֹכֵל פֵּירוֹת בְּחַיֶּיהָ וְחַיָּיב בִּמְזוֹנוֹתֶיהָ

בְּפִרְקוֹנָהּ וּבִקְבוּרָתָהּ. רִבִּי יְהוּדָה אוֹמֵר אֲפִילוּ עָנִי שֶׁבְּיִשְׂרָאֵל לֹא יִפְחוֹת לָהּ מִשְּׁנֵי חֲלִילִין וּמְקוֹנֶנֶת.

Mishnah 6: The father has the benefit to give his daughter[134] in preliminary marriage by money[135], contract[136], or intercourse[137]; he has the right to what she finds and to her earnings, to dissolve her vows[138], and to receive her bill of divorce[139], but cannot eat usufruct in her lifetime[140]. If she is definitively married, the husband in addition[141] eats usufruct in her lifetime[142] but is required to pay for her upkeep, her ransom[143], and her burial. Rebbi Jehudah says, even the poorest in Israel should not provide for her less than two flutes and one wailing woman.

134 As long as she is not an adult.
135 He can pocket the money.
136 He can make himself be paid for signing the marriage contract.
137 Mishnah *Qiddušin* 1:1 states that a woman can be preliminarily married either by money (given by the groom to his bride or her father) or by a contract (by which the groom signs his intention to marry his bride) or by intercourse (which has to be performed in front of two witnesses to be legally valid); the latter way is frowned upon in practice.

138 Cf. *Nedarim* Chapters 10-11.
139 As long as she is not definitively married.
140 If her mother is dead and she inherits from her maternal grandfather, all yield from that property is hers and has to be kept in trust for her. But if she dies unmarried, the father inherits from her.
141 In addition to what she finds and earns, and to dissolve her vows.
142 Of all property she brings into the marriage; cf. Chapter 8.
143 If she is kidnapped.

(28d line 11) **הלכה ו**: הָאָב זַכַּאי בְּבִתּוֹ כול׳. נִיחָא בַּכֶּסֶף וּבַשְּׁטָר הָאָב זַכַּאי. בַּבִּיאָה. תִּיפְתַּר שֶׁאָמַר לוֹ. לִכְשֶׁתִּקָּנֶה לִי בִיתָךְ יִהְיֶה לָךְ כֶּסֶף זֶה.

Halakhah 6: "The father has the benefit to give his daughter," etc. One understands that the father has a benefit from money or contract. By intercourse? Explain it that [the groom] said to [the father]: When your daughter becomes mine by intercourse, this money shall be your property.

(28d line 13) זָכַּאי בִּמְצִיאָתָהּ. רִבִּי זַכַּאי דְּאָלֶכְסַנְדְּרִיאָה מִישְׁאַל שָׁאַל. מְצִיאָה שֶׁנָּפְלָה לָהּ מֵחֲמַת שָׂדֶה מָה אַתְּ עָבֵד לָהּ בִּמְצִיאָה אוֹ בְּאוֹכֶלֶת פֵּירוֹת שָׁלָהּ. אֵין תַּעֲבְדִינָהּ בְּאוֹכֶלֶת פֵּירוֹת שָׁלָהּ.

"He has the right to what she finds." Rebbi Zakkai from Alexandria asked: How do you treat what she found on [her] field[144], as a find or as her usufruct? If you treat it as usufruct it is hers.[145].

144 A field which she inherited from her mother's side and to whose yield the father has no claim.

145 While R. Zakkai's question is not answered, the fact that only one interpretation is analyzed further seems to indicate that anything she finds on her field belongs to her.

(28d line 15) נִישֵּׂאת יוֹתֵר עָלָיו הַבַּעַל שֶׁאוֹכֵל פֵּירוֹת בְּחַיֶּיהָ. תְּקָנָה תִּיקְנוּ שֶׁיְּהֵא מְפַקֵּחַ עַל נִיכְסֵי אִשְׁתּוֹ וְאוֹכֵל. וְאוֹמֵר. אַף בָּאָב כֵּן. בְּלֹא כָךְ הָאָב מְפַקֵּחַ עַל נִיכְסֵי בִתּוֹ וְאוֹכֵל. חַייָב בִּמְזוֹנוֹתֶיהָ בְּפִרְקוֹנָהּ. תַּנֵּי. הַבַּעַל שֶׁאָמַר. אִי אֶפְשִׁי לֹא לוֹכַל וְלֹא לְפַקֵּחַ. אֵין שׁוֹמְעִין לוֹ. הָאָב שֶׁאָמַר. אֲנִי אוֹכֵל וּמְפַקֵּחַ. שׁוֹמְעִין לוֹ.

"If she is definitively married, the husband in addition eats usufruct in her lifetime," as a regulation they instituted that he should oversee his wife's property and eat from it. Is it also thus for the father? Without incentives the father overseas the daughter's property; should he eat? "He is required to pay for her upkeep and her ransom.[146]" It was stated: If the husband said, it is impossible for me to eat and to oversee, one does not listen to him[147]; but if the father said, I shall oversee if I can eat, one listens to him[148].

146 This is an unnecessary quote from the Mishnah; the text continues to refer to the wife's property.

147 Since this is a generally valid regulation, the court cannot relieve the husband from caring for his wife's property. (But the husband can cede the administration of the property to his wife by a private contract as long as no court is involved.)

148 The court may allow the father a reasonable fee for administering his underage daughter's property if this is to her advantage.

(28d line 20) וּבְקבוּרָתָהּ. תַּנֵּי. לֹא רָצָה הַבַּעַל לְקוֹבְרָהּ הָאָב קוֹבְרָהּ וּמוֹצִיא מִמֶּנּוּ בַּדִּין. אָמַר רִבִּי חַגַּיי. לֹא אָמְרוּ אֶלָּא הָאָב. הָא אַחֵר אֵינוֹ גוֹבֶה. רִבִּי יוֹסֵי אוֹמֵר. בֵּין אָב וּבֵין אַחֵר גּוֹבֶה. וַתְיָיאן אִילֵּין פְּלוּגָתָא. דְּתַנִּינָן תַּמָּן. וְחַיָּיב בִּמְזוֹנוֹתֶיהָ בְּפִרְקוֹנָהּ וּבִקְבוּרָתָהּ. אָמַר רִבִּי חַגַּיי. לֹא אָמְרוּ אֶלָּא אַחֵר הָא הָאָב גּוֹבֶה. רִבִּי יוֹסֵי אוֹמֵר. בֵּין אָב בֵּין אַחֵר אֵינוֹ גוֹבֶה. עַל דַּעְתֵּיהּ דְּרִבִּי חַגַּי בֵּין לִקְבוּרָהּ בֵּין לִמְזוֹנֵי הָאָב גּוֹבֶה אַחֵר אֵינוֹ גוֹבֶה. עַל דַּעְתֵּיהּ דְּרִבִּי יוֹסֵי. לִקְבוּרָהּ בֵּין אָב בֵּין אַחֵר גּוֹבֶה. שֶׁלֹּא עָלַת עַל דַּעַת שֶׁתְּהֵא אִשְׁתּוֹ מוּשְׁלֶכֶת לַכְּלָבִים. תַּנֵּי. כָּל־מָקוֹם שֶׁנָּהֲגוּ לְהַסְפִּיד מַסְפִּידִין.

"And her burial." It was stated: If the husband refused to bury her, the father buries her and recovers his expenses in court. Rebbi Ḥaggai said, they said only, the father. Therefore, a third party cannot recover. Rebbi Yose says, both the father and also a third party can recover. There is a parallel disagreement, as we have stated there: "He is required to pay for her upkeep, her ransom, and her burial.[149]" Rebbi Ḥaggai said, they said only, a third party. Therefore, the father can recover. Rebbi Yose says, neither the father nor a third party can recover. In the opinion of Rebbi Ḥaggai, both for burial and for upkeep the father can recover, a third party cannot recover. In the opinion of Rebbi Yose, for burial both the father and also a third party can recover because it is unthinkable that his wife should be thrown to the dogs[150]. It was stated[151]: At a place where it is customary to eulogize, one eulogizes.

149 The reference here really should be to Mishnah 13:2; the parallel to this paragraph, formulated in a slightly different way, is at the end of Halakhah 13:2. The essence of that Mishnah is that if the husband is absent without providing for his wife and a third party supports the wife without either having the wife sign a document that she recognizes the money for support as a loan, or being appointed her guardian by the court, he has no regress on the husband upon his return.

150 If the community buries her, they can recover the costs from the husband. The Babli, 47a, refers this to the husband: If somebody tells his heirs not to bury him, the community buries him and recovers the cost from the estate since one will not allow a man to have himself buried with taxpayers' money in order to increase his estate.

151 Tosephta 4:2, Semaḥot 14:7. The fee of the preacher who eulogizes the deceased can be recovered from the husband.

(fol. 28a) **משנה ז**: לְעוֹלָם הִיא בִּרְשׁוּת הָאָב עַד שֶׁתִּיכָּנֵס לִרְשׁוּת הַבַּעַל לַנִּישּׂוּאִין. מָסַר הָאָב לִשְׁלוּחֵי הַבַּעַל הֲרֵי הִיא בִּרְשׁוּת הַבַּעַל. הָלַךְ הָאָב עִם שְׁלוּחֵי הַבַּעַל אוֹ שֶׁהָלְכוּ שְׁלוּחֵי הָאָב עִם שְׁלוּחֵי הַבַּעַל הֲרֵי הִיא בִּרְשׁוּת הָאָב. מָסְרוּ שְׁלוּחֵי הָאָב לִשְׁלוּחֵי הַבַּעַל הֲרֵי הִיא בִּרְשׁוּת הַבַּעַל.

Mishnah 7: She always remains in the father's power[152] until she enters the husband's power for definitive marriage. If the father entrusted her to the husband's emissaries she is in the husband's power. If the father went with the husband's emissaries, or the father's emissaries went with the husband's emissaries, she is in the father's power. If the father's emissaries entrusted her to the husband's emissaries[153], she is in the husband's power.

152 For all the rights and duties enumerated in the preceding Mishnah.
153 Even though they will accompany the bride to the place of the nuptials and participate in them.

(28d line 29) **הלכה ז**: לְעוֹלָם הִיא בִּרְשׁוּת הָאָב כול'. לֹא סוֹף דָּבָר לַחוּפָּה אֶלָּא לַבַּיִת שֶׁיֵּשׁ לוֹ חוּפָּה. בְּעֵי דָא אָמְנוּתָא טְרִקִילִין וְקָיְטוֹן חוּפָּה וְקָיְטוֹן נִכְנְסָה לִטְרִיקְלִין. לְהָדָא מִילָא. רִבִּי לָעְזָר אָמַר. לְיוֹרְשָׁהּ. רִבִּי שִׁמְעוֹן בֶּן לָקִישׁ אָמַר. לְהָפֵר נְדָרֶיהָ. אָמַר רִבִּי זְעִירָא. אַף עַל גַּב דְּרִבִּי שִׁמְעוֹן בֶּן לָקִישׁ אָמַר. לְהָפֵר נְדָרֶיהָ. מוֹדֶה שֶׁאֵינוֹ מֵיפֵר לָהּ עַד שֶׁתִּיכָּנֵס לַחוּפָּה. אָמַר רִבִּי הוּנָא. מַתְנִיתָא מְסַיְיעָא לְרִבִּי שִׁמְעוֹן בֶּן לָקִישׁ. לִזְנוֹת בֵּית אָבִיהָ. פְּרָט שֶׁמָּסְרוּ שְׁלוּחֵי הָאָב לִשְׁלוּחֵי הַבַּעַל שֶׁלֹּא תְהֵא בִסְקִילָה אֶלָּא בְחֶנֶק.

"She always remains in the father's power," etc. Not only to the bridal chamber[154] but to a house where the bridal chamber is. In which way? A banquet hall[155] and a bedroom[156], the bridal chamber being the bedroom, and she entered the banquest hall. In which respect? Rebbi Eleazar said, to inherit from her[157]. Rebbi Simeon ben Laqish said, to dissolve her vows[158]. Rebbi Ze'ira said, even though Rebbi Simeon ben Laqish said, to dissolve her vows, he agrees that he does not actually dissolve them until she enters the bridal chamber. Rebbi Huna said, a *baraita*[159] supports Rebbi Simeon ben Laqish: "To whore in her father's house," that excludes the case that the father's emissaries entrusted her to the husband's emissaries, after which she[160] should not be stoned but strangled.

154 It seems that the original Yerushalmi Mishnah did not read "until she enters the husband's power for definitive marriage" but "until she enters the bridal chamber" with most Mishnah mss. and the Munich ms. of the Babli. S. Lieberman emphasizes on several occasions that it seems that the scribe of the Leiden ms. obtained the Mishnah text not from the Yerushalmi text he was copying but from a separate Mishnah ms.

155 Greek τρικλίνιον, cf. *Berakhot* 3:5, Note 229.

156 Greek κοιτών.

157 In the Babli, 48b, this is Samuel's opinion, that after the signing of the *ketubah* document, the husband's rights and obligations are activated not by the formal "seven benedictions" of the definitive marriage but by the bride entering the husband's power.

158 In the Babli, 48b, he is reported to hold that after this moment, if she is divorced or widowed before entering the bridal chamber, she legally becomes a divorcee or widow after definitive marriage. This parallels R. Ze'ira's interpretation here, that the husband acquires all rights even if he cannot exercise them yet.

159 A similar *baraita* is quoted in the Babli, 49a.

160 If now she should commit adultery before two witnesses after being duly warned that it would be a capital crime, she is treated as a definitively married woman, not as a preliminarily married adolescent.

(fol. 28a) **משנה ח**: הָאָב אֵינוֹ חַיָּב בִּמְזוֹנוֹת בִּתּוֹ. זֶה מִדְרָשׁ דָּרַשׁ רִבִּי אֶלְעָזָר בֶּן עֲזַרְיָה בַּכֶּרֶם בְּיַבְנֶה. הַבָּנִים יִירְשׁוּ וְהַבָּנוֹת יִיזוֹנוּ מַה הַבָּנִים אֵינָן יוֹרְשִׁין אֶלָּא לְאַחַר מִיתַת אֲבִיהֶן אַף הַבָּנוֹת אֵינָן נִזּוֹנוֹת אֶלָּא לְאַחַר מִיתַת אֲבִיהֶן.

Mishnah 8: The father is not obligated to support his daughter[161]. This inference did Rebbi Eleazar ben Azariah explain in the vineyard of Jabneh[162]: "The sons shall inherit and the daughters be supported.[163]" Since the sons do not inherit before their father's death, neither are the daughters supported before their father's death.

161 The *ketubah* contract with his wife does not force a father to feed his underage or adolescent daughter even though he has the right to receive her earnings.

162 The seat of the central rabbinic authority in the time between the two wars with the Romans.

183 The original Hebrew text of the ketubah stipulation quoted in Aramaic in Mishnah 12.

(28d line 36) **הלכה ח**: הָאָב אֵינוֹ חַיָּיב בִּמְזוֹנוֹת בִּתּוֹ כול׳. מִצְוָה לָזוּן אֶת הַבָּנוֹת אֵין צָרִיךְ לוֹמַר אֶת הַבָּנִים. רִבִּי יוֹחָנָן בֶּן בְּרוֹקָה אוֹמֵר. מִצְוָה לָזוּן אֶת הַבָּנוֹת. אִית תַּנָּיֵי תַנֵּי. הַבָּנִים עִיקָר. וְאִית תַּנָּיֵי תַנֵּי. הַבָּנוֹת עִיקָר. מָאן דָּמַר. הַבָּנִים עִיקָר. לְתַלְמוּד תּוֹרָה. וּמָאן דָּמַר. הַבָּנוֹת עִיקָר. שֶׁלֹּא יֵצְאוּ לְתַרְבּוּת רָעָה.

Halakhah 8: "The father is not obligated to support his daughter," etc. [184]It is meritorious to feed one's daughters, unnecessary to say this of sons. Rebbi Joḥanan ben Beroqa said, it is meritorious to feed one's daughters. Some Tannaim state, the sons are most important[185]. Some Tannaim state, the daughters are most important. He who says the sons are most important, for the study of Torah. He who says the daughters are most important, that they should not go outside for bad behavior[186].

184 Tosephta 4:8, Babli 49a. In these sources, and in the *editio princeps* corrected following the Babli, "R. Joḥanan ben Beroqa said, it is *obligatory* to feed one's daughters.
185 The Babli, 49a, identifies this Tanna as R. Meïr, the one who gives preference to the daughters as R. Jehudah, with the same reasoning as given here. In the Tosephta only the first opinion is given, anonymously.
186 That they should not be forced into prostitution.

(28d line 41) רִבִּי שִׁמְעוֹן בֶּן לָקִישׁ בְּשֵׁם רִבִּי יְהוּדָה בֶּן חֲנַנְיָה. נִמְנוּ בְאוּשָׁה שֶׁיְּהֵא אָדָם זָן אֶת בָּנָיו קְטַנִּים. אָמַר רִבִּי יוֹחָנָן. יוֹדְעִין אָנוּ מִי הָיָה בַּמִּנְיָין. עוּקְבָא אָתָא לְגַבֵּי רִבִּי יוֹחָנָן. אָמַר לֵיהּ. עוּקְבָא. זוּן בָּנֶיךָ. אָמַר לֵיהּ. מְנָן מָרִי. אָמַר לֵיהּ. עוּקְבָא רְשִׁיעָא. זוּן בָּנֶיךָ. אָמַר רִבִּי עוּלָה. מַתְנִיתָא אָמְרָה כֵן שֶׁיְּהֵא אָדָם זָן אֶת בָּנָיו קְטַנִּים. דְּתַנִּינָן תַּמָּן. אִם הָיְתָה מֵנִיקָה פּוֹחֲתִין לָהּ מִמַּעֲשֵׂה יָדֶיהָ וּמוֹסִיפִין לָהּ עַל מְזוֹנוֹתֶיהָ.

HALAKHAH 8

Rebbi Simeon ben Laqish in the name of Rebbi Jehudah ben Hananiah[187]: They voted at Usha[188] that a man has to feed his underage children. Rebbi Johanan said, we know who participated in that vote[189]. Uqba came before Rebbi Johanan[190] who said to him: Uqba, feed your children. He answered, Master, why[191]? He said to him: Evil Uqba, feed your children. Rebbi Ulla[192] said, a Mishnah[193] confirms that a man has to feed his underage children, since we have stated there: "If she is nursing, she has to work less and one adds to her food."

187 In the Babli, 49b, in *Peah* 1:1, Note 59, and eventually in the next paragraph, he is called R. Jehudah bar Hanina.

188 The temporary meeting place of the supreme religious authority in the aftermath of the war of Bar Kohkba; cf. *Peah* 1:1, Note 60.

189 They were important enough to accept their vote as judicial practice. (In today's practice of the Israeli Rabbinate, support is required to the end of the child's schooling.)

190 He was sued for child support by either his wife or the local overseer of charity who did not want to spend public funds on Uqba's children.

191 There is no biblical authority to force me to feed them.

192 Probably R. Hila (Ilaï), the tradent of R. Simeon ben Laqish's statements in the Babli, 49b.

193 Mishnah 5:13. The Mishnah shows that the husband has less revenue and more expenses because of the feeding of his baby.

(28d line 46) רִבִּי שִׁמְעוֹן בֶּן לָקִישׁ בְּשֵׁם רִבִּי יְהוּדָה בֶּן חֲנַנְיָה. נִמְנוּ בְאוּשָׁה בְּכוֹתֵב נְכָסָיו לְבָנָיו הוּא וְאִשְׁתּוֹ נִיזּוֹנִין מֵהֶן. בָּנָיו קְטַנִּים מָה הֵן. רִבִּי אַבָּהוּ בְּשֵׁם רִבִּי יוֹסֵי בֵּירִבִּי חֲנִינָה. וְאִית דְּאָמְרֵי לָהּ בְּשֵׁם רִבִּי יוּדָה בֶּן חֲנִינָה. הוּא וְאִשְׁתּוֹ וּבָנָיו קְטַנִּים נִיזּוֹנִין מֵהֶן. אַלְמָנָתוֹ מָהוּ. אָמַר רִבִּי זְעִירָא. אִתְּתָבַת וְלָא אִפְּרְשַׁת. אָמַר רִבִּי בָא בַּר מָמָל. אִתְּתָבַת וְאִפְּרְשַׁת. אָמַר רִבִּי בָא. נִרְאִין דְּבָרִים אִם הָיְתָה אוֹכֶלֶת בְּיָמֵי בַעֲלָהּ אוֹכֶלֶת. וְאִם לָאו אֵינָהּ אוֹכֶלֶת. לֹא

אָמַר אֶלָּא כּוֹתֵב. הָא מוֹכֵר לֹא. כָּתַב לְבָנָיו וּמָכַר לַאֲחֵרִם מָה הֵן מִסְתַּבְּרָה אָתָא. אָמַר רִבִּי חֲנִינָה. אֲנָא לֵית מַתַּת לֵיהּ אָתָא. רִבִּי מָנָא. לֹא מִסְתַּבְּרָה אַגְרִין לֵיהּ שַׁמָּשָׁא וּמְסַבִּין לֵיהּ אִיתָּא כְּמָה דוּ דְהִיא שַׁמְּשָׁא.

Rebbi Simeon ben Laqish in the name of Rebbi Jehudah ben Hananiah: They voted in Usha that if one writes all his property over to his sons, he and his wife are supported by them[194]. What is the situation of underage children? Rebbi Abbahu in the name of Rebbi Yose ben Rebbi Jehudah, but some say it in the name of Rebbi Judah ben Hanina: He, his wife and his underage children are supported by them[195]. What about his widow[196]? Rebbi Ze'ira said, this was asked but not resolved. Rebbi Abba bar Mamal said, it was asked and resolved, Rebbi Abba said, it seems reasonable that if she ate during her husband's lifetime then she eats; otherwise, she does not eat. It says only "if one writes"; that excludes the seller. If he wrote to his sons[197] and sold to others, what is here reasonable? Rebbi Hanina said, I would not give him anything. Rebbi Mana: Is it not reasonable that they hire him a servant and marry a wife to him so she should serve him[198]?

194 Even if the property be given unconditionally and immediately, it is a law promulgated at Usha that the sons have to care for their parents (Rashi, on Babli 49b).

195 The adult sons who inherited from their living parents.

196 She cannot collect her *ketubah* since her husband died without leaving an estate. Therefore, if the sons supported her during their father's lifetime, they must support his widow indefinitely.

197 The sons received only part of the estate; the remainder was sold to outsiders and the proceeds used up.

198 As a matter of honoring father and mother, not as a monetary obligation deriving from their partial inheritance.

(28d line 56) בְּנֵי בָנִים מָה הֵן. רִבִּי מָנָא אָמַר. [בְּנֵי בָנִים הֲרֵי הֵן כְּבָנִים. רִבִּי יוֹסֵי אָמַר. אֵין בְּנֵי בָנִים כְּבָנִים.]¹⁹⁹ רִבִּי יוֹסֵי בֵּירִבִּי בּוּן וְרִבִּי מַתַּנְיָה הֲווֹן יַתְבִין. סָבְרִין מֵימַר. הוּא בְּנֵי בָנִים שֶׁכָּן הוּא בָנִים שֶׁלְּהַלָּן. אָמַר לֵיהּ רִבִּי יוֹסֵי בֵּירִבִּי בּוּן. בְּנֵי בָנִים קָפְצָה עֲלֵיהֶן יְרוּשַׁת תּוֹרָה.

1 שכן הוא בנים שלהלן. אמר ליה | גי בני בנים הרי הן כבנים. רבי יוסי אמר. אין בני בנים כבנים   2 ר' יוסי ביר' בון | גי ר' שמואל בריה דר' יוסי ביר' בון   3 בנים | גי בני בנים   ליה | גי לון

²⁰⁰What is the situation of grandchildren? Rebbi Mana said, [grandchildren are like children. Rebbi Yose said, grandchildren are not like children.] Rebbi Yose ben Rebbi Ḥanina and Rebbi Mattaniah were sitting together. They wanted to say, the same situation applies to grandchildren here as there. Rebbi Yose ben Rebbi Ḥanina said to him, inheritance by biblical law jumped on grandchildren²⁰¹.

199 Text from the parallel *Giṭṭin* 5:3, line 64. The text here is unintelligible.

200 This paragraph, transmitted here in rudimentary form, is from *Giṭṭin* 5:4. The variant readings are indicated by גי. In this text, "here" means the text in *Giṭṭin*, "there" is a different setting in *Yebamot* 6:6 (Notes 115,116). The topic of the Mishnah in *Giṭṭin* is the enforcement of the *ketubah* contract for the support of a wife and her daughters; the question is whether the *ketubah* also covers granddaughters. Similarly, here the question is whether the rules of Usha require a man to feed his underage grandchildren (if they have no father or the father is incapacitated.) In *Yebamot*, the question is whether grandchildren count as much as children in the obligation "to be fruitful and multiply." The answer there is a qualified yes, while here and in *Giṭṭin* it is no.

201 In biblical obligations, grandchildren can be counted as children. But in rabbinic institutions involving monetary obligations, only what is specified counts.

(28d line 60) רִבִּי שִׁמְעוֹן בֶּן לָקִיש בְּשֵׁם רִבִּי יְהוּדָה בַּר חֲנִינָה. נִמְנוּ בְאוּשָׁה בְּמַקְפִּיד אֶת הַזָּקֵן וְהִכָּהוּ יִינָתֵן לוֹ בּוֹשְׁתּוֹ שָׁלֵם. מַעֲשֶׂה בְּאֶחָד שֶׁהִקְפִּיד אֶת הַזָּקֵן וְהִכָּהוּ וְנָתַן לוֹ בָשְׁתּוֹ מֻשְׁלָם. אָמְרֵי. רִבִּי יוּדָה בֶּן חֲנִינָה הֲוָה.

Rebbi Simeon ben Laqish in the name of Rebbi Jehudah bar Ḥaninah: They voted in Usha that one who insults an Elder or hits him has to indemnify him fully for his shame. It happened, that somebody who insulted an Elder and hit him had to indemnify him fully for his shame. They said, it happened to Rebbi Jehudah ben Ḥanina[202].

202 It is explained in *Baba Qama* 8:6 (6c) that the "full payment for shame" is one Roman *libra* of gold.

(28d line 63) רִבִּי שִׁמְעוֹן בֶּן לָקִיש בְּשֵׁם רִבִּי יְהוּדָה בֶּן חֲנִינָה. נִמְנוּ בְאוּשָׁה שֶׁיְּהֵא אָדָם מַפְרִיש חוֹמֶשׁ מִנְּכָסָיו לְמִצְוֹת. עַד אֵיכָן. רִבִּי יִרְמְיָה וְרִבִּי אַבָּא בַּר כַּהֲנָא חַד אָמַר עַד כְּדֵי תְרוּמָה וּתְרוּמַת מַעֲשֵׂר. וְחָרְנָא אָמַר. כַּבֵּד אֶת ייָ מֵהוֹנֶךָ. כְּמֵרֵאשִׁית כָּל־תְּבוּאָתֶךָ. רִבִּי נַמְלִיאֵל בַּר אִינְיָא בָּעֵי קוֹמֵי רִבִּי מָנָא. מַה חוֹמֶשׁ בְּכָל־שָׁנָה. גָּרַשׁ בְּהִילְכָתָא קַדְמִיָתָא דְפֵיאָה וְלֹא מוֹת. אֶלָּא שֶׁלֹּא יָמוּת לֶעָתִיד לָבוֹא.

[203]Rebbi Simeon bar Laqish said in the name of Rebbi Jehudah ben Ḥanina: They voted at Usha that a person may donate a fifth of his property for good deeds. How far down? Rebbi Jeremiah and Rebbi Abba bar Cahana; one said corresponding to *terumah* and the *terumah* of the tithe, the other said (*Prov.* 3:9): "Honor the Eternal with your property" . . . "corresponding to the first of all your yield"[204]. Rebbi Gamliel bar Ininia asked before Rebbi Mana: Does it mean one fifth every year? {One studies this in the first Halakhah of Peah.}[203] Will he not die[205]? But lest he die in the future.

203 This paragraph is essentially from *Peah* 1:1, Notes 58-64, as noted by the scribe when he stopped copying the entire paragraph. In the Babli, 50a.

204 In *Peah* it is clear that the inference is from the part of the verse which is not quoted here.

205 If every year he gives away one fifth of his property, soon he will have nothing. This part is formulated differently in *Peah*: A person is permitted to give to charity one fifth of his property once; from thereon in he is restricted to one fifth of his income lest he die of hunger in the future.

(28d line 69) רִבִּי לָעְזָר בֶּן עֲזַרְיָה עֲבַד לָהּ כְּתוּבָה מִמִּדְרָשׁ. שֶׁדְּרָשָׁהּ רִבִּי אֶלְעָזָר בֶּן עֲזַרְיָה. הַבָּנִים יִירְשׁוּ וְהַבָּנוֹת יָזוּנוּ. מַה הַבָּנִים אֵינָן יוֹרְשִׁין אֶלָּא לְאַחַר מִיתַת אֲבִיהֶן אַף הַבָּנוֹת לֹא יְזוּנוּ אֶלָּא לְאַחַר מִיתַת אֲבִיהֶן.

ממדרש | י מדרש לה | ו - דרש | י שדרשה אלעזר | י לעזר   3 לא יזונו | י אינן ניזונות

206Rebbi Eleazar ben Azariah insisted on interpreting the *ketubah*: Rebbi Eleazar ben Azariah explained: 'The sons shall inherit and the daughters shall be supported.' Since the sons can only inherit after their father's death, so the daughters can claim support only after their father's death.

206 From here to the end of the Halakhah the text essentially is from *Yebamot* 15:3, Notes 34-79 (whose readings are denoted by י); its Tannaïtic parts are paralleled in Tosephta *Ketubot* 4:9-13.

(28d line 72) דְּבֵית הֵלֵּל עָבְדִין לָהּ כְּתוּבָה מִדְרָשׁ. דָּרַשׁ הִלֵּל הַזָּקֵן לְשׁוֹן הֶדְיוֹט. כָּךְ הָיוּ כוֹתְבִין בְּאַלֶכְּסַנְדְרִיאָה שֶׁהָיָה אֶחָד מֵהֶן מְקַדֵּשׁ אִשָּׁה וַחֲבֵירוֹ חוֹטְפָהּ מִן הַשּׁוּק. וּכְשֶׁבָּא מַעֲשֶׂה לִפְנֵי חֲכָמִים בִּקְּשׁוּ לַעֲשׂוֹתָן מַמְזֵירִים. אָמַר לָהֶן הִלֵּל הַזָּקֵן. הוֹצִיאוּ כְּתוּבַת אִימּוֹתֵיכֶן. וְהוֹצִיאוּ כְּתוּבַת אִימּוֹתֵיהֶן וּמָצְאוּ כָתוּב בָּהֶן. לִכְשֶׁתִּיכָּנְסִי לְבֵיתִי תְּהוּיִין לִי לְאִינְתּוּ כְּדַת מֹשֶׁה וִיהוּדָאֵי.

1 דבית | י בית לה | ו -   כד | י -

The House of Hillel insist on interpretation of the *ketubah*. Hillel the Elder explained it, using the vernacular. In Alexandria they were writing that a man there became betrothed to a woman. Another man abducted her from a public place. When this came before the Sages, they intended to declare [the children] as bastards. Hillel the Elder told them, bring your mothers' *ketubah*. They brough their mothers' *ketubah*. They found written there: "When you enter my house you shall be my wife according to the laws of Moses and the Jews."

29a line 1) בֵּית שַׁמַּי עָבְדִין כְּתוּבָה מִדְרָשׁ. דְּבֵית שַׁמַּי דָּרְשֵׁי. בְּסֵפֶר כְּתוּבָתָהּ מְלַמֵּד. שֶׁהוּא כּוֹתֵב לָהּ. שֶׁאִם תִּינָשְׂאִי לְאַחֵר תִּיטְּלִי מַה שֶּׁכָּתוּב לֵיכִי. חָזְרוּ בֵית הִלֵּל לְהוֹרוֹת כְּדִבְרֵי בֵית שַׁמַּי.

1 דרשי | י דרשין   בספר | י מספר   נלמוד | י מלמד   2 ליכי | י ליך   3 כדברי בית | י כבית

The House of Shammai insist on interpretation of the *ketubah*. As the House of Shammai explain, the text of her *ketubah* document teaches, for he writes: "If you would be married to another man you shall take the amount I wrote for you." The House of Hillel reversed themselves and taught following the House of Shammai.

29a line 4) רִבִּי מֵאִיר עָבַד כְּתוּבָה מִדְרָשׁ. דָּרַשׁ רִבִּי מֵאִיר. הַמְקַבֵּל שָׂדֶה מֵחֲבֵירוֹ מִשֶּׁזָּכָה בָהּ (חֲבֵירוֹ)[207] שָׁמִין אוֹתָהּ כַּמָּה הִיא רְאוּיָה לַעֲשׂוֹת וְנוֹתֵן לוֹ. שֶׁהוּא כוֹתֵב לוֹ. אִם אוֹבִיר וְלֹא אַעֲבִיד אֲיַשֵּׁלֵם בְּמֵיטָבָא.

1 דרש | י דאמר   2 שזכה בו חבירו | י -   ונותן | י ונותנין   3 אישלם | י אשלם

Rebbi Meïr insists on interpreting the contract text. Rebbi Meir explained, if somebody accepts a field as a contractor, at the moment [he] accepts, one estimates how much it is expected to yield and he gives to [the owner]. Because the standard contract reads: "If I let it lie fallow and do not work on it, I shall pay as if from the best."

207 Not in the text in *Yebamot* and out of place here.

(29a line 7) רִבִּי יוּדָה עֲבַד כְּתוּבָה מִדְרָשׁ. דָּרַשׁ רִבִּי יוּדָה. אָדָם מֵבִיא עַל יְדֵי אִשְׁתּוֹ כָּל־קָרְבָּן שֶׁהִיא חַיֶּיבֶת. אֲפִילוּ אָכְלָה חֵלֶב אֲפִילוּ חִילְּלָה שַׁבָּת. וְכֵן הָיָה רִבִּי יוּדָה אוֹמֵר. פְּטָרָהּ אֵינוֹ חַיָּב בָּהּ. שֶׁכֵּן הִיא כוֹתֶבֶת לוֹ. וְאַחֲרָן דִּי אָתְיָין לִי עֲלָךְ מִן קֳדָמַת דְּנָא.

1 דרש | י תנו בשם   אדם מביא | י מביא הוא אדם   3 פטרה | י פוטרה   ואחרן | י ואוחרן   4 לי עלך | י לך

Rebbi Jehudah insists on interpreting the contract text. Rebbi Jehudah explained: A man brings for his wife any sacrifice she is obligated for, even if she ate suet or desecrated the Sabbath. Also, Rebbi Jehudah says, once he divorces her, he is no longer obligated for her, for she writes to him "any other obligations that may come to you from me from earlier times."

(29a line 11) רִבִּי יוֹסֵי עֲבַד כְּתוּבָה מִדְרָשׁ. דָּרַשׁ רִבִּי יוֹסֵי. מָקוֹם שֶׁנָּהֲגוּ לַעֲשׂוֹת כְּתוּבָה מִלְוָה גּוֹבָה אֶת הַכֹּל. לִכְפּוֹל אֵינָהּ גּוֹבָה אֶלָּא מֶחֱצָה. רִבִּי אֶלְעָזָר הַקַּפָּר עֲבַד כְּתוּבָה מִדְרָשׁ. דָּרַשׁ רִבִּי אֶלְעָזָר הַקַּפָּר. אֵין אָדָם רַשַּׁאי לִיקַּח בְּהֵמָה חַיָּה וְעוֹף כֵּן הִתְקִינוּ לָהֶן מְזוֹנוֹת. רִבִּי יְהוֹשֻׁעַ בֶּן קָרְחָה עֲבַד כְּתוּבָה מִדְרָשׁ. דָּרַשׁ רִבִּי יְהוֹשֻׁעַ בֶּן קָרְחָה. הַמַּלְוֶה אֶת חֲבֵירוֹ לֹא יְמַשְׁכְּנֶנּוּ אֶלָּא בְבֵית דִּין. לֹא יִכָּנֵס לְבֵיתוֹ לִיטּוֹל אֶת מַשְׁכּוֹנוֹ. שֶׁכֵּן הוּא כּוֹתֵב. תַּשְׁלוּמָהּ מִן נִכְסַיָּהּ דִּי אַתְיָין לִי וְדִי אַקְנָה לְקַבֵּל דְּנָה.

2 אלעזר | י לעזר   3 הקפר | י -   ערב כתובה מדרש. דרש ר' אלעזר הקפר | י אמר ליקח | י ליקח לו   5 דרש | י דאמר   6 אלא בבית דין | י יותר על חובו   שהוא | י שכן הוא   כותב | י כותב לו   7 תשלומה | י תשלומתה   נכסיה די אתיין לי ודי אקנה | י נכסיי דיאתיין ליידי דאקנה

Rebbi Yose insists on interpreting the contract text. Rebbi Yose explained: In a place where one treats the *ketubah* as a loan, she collects the entire amount. Where one doubles, she collects only half the amount.

Rebbi Eleazar the caper grower insists on interpreting the contract text. Rebbi Eleazar the caper grower explained: nobody is permitted to buy domesticated or wild animals or birds unless he has food prepared for them.

Rebbi Joshua ben Qorḥa insists on interpreting the contract text. Rebbi Joshua ben Qorḥa explained: a person lending money to another person should not take pledges except in court; he should not enter [the debtor's] house to take the pledge, for he writes to him: "It will be paid by the property that came to my hand that I shall acquire corresponding to this [sum]."208

208 In the text of *Yebamot*: "a person lending money to another person should not take pledges from him for more than the value of the loan since he writes for him: It will be paid . . ." That text should be considered the correct one since (a) it refers to the text of the contract and (b) the statement here is a biblical commandment (*Deut.* 24:10-11).

(29a line 18) רַב הוּנָא עֲבַד כְּתוּבָה מִדְרָשׁ. דָּרַשׁ רַב הוּנָא. הַבָּנִים יִירְשׁוּ וְהַבָּנוֹת יִזּוֹנוּ. מַה הַבָּנִים יוֹרְשִׁין מִן הַמִּטַּלְטְלִין אַף הַבָּנוֹת נִיזוֹנוֹת מִן הַמִּטַּלְטְלִין. שְׁמוּאֵל אָמַר. אֵין הַבָּנוֹת נִיזוֹנוֹת מִן הַמִּטַּלְטְלִין. מַתְנִיתָא מְסַייְעָא לִשְׁמוּאֵל. בְּנָן נוּקְבָּן דִיהַוּוֹן לֵיכִי מִינַּאי וְהַוְיָין יָתְבָן בְּבֵיתִי וּמִיתְזְנָן מִנִּיכְסַיי עַד דְּתִינַּסְּבוּן לְגוּבְרִין. וְתַגֵּי עֲלָהּ. מִן מְקַרְקְעֵי וְלֹא מִן מְטַלְטְלֵי. אָמַר רִבִּי בָּא בַּר בַּר זַבְדָּא. אַתְיָא דְרַב הוּנָא כְּרִבִּי וְדִשְׁמוּאֵל כְּרִבִּי שִׁמְעוֹן בֶּן אֶלְעָזָר. דְּתַנֵּי. אֶחָד נְכָסִים שֶׁיֵּשׁ לָהֶן אֲחֵרָיוּת וְאֶחָד נְכָסִים שֶׁאֵין לָהֶן אֲחֵרָיוּת נִפְרָעִין מֵהֶן לִמְזוֹן הָאִשָּׁה וְהַבָּנוֹת. דִּבְרֵי רִבִּי. רִבִּי שִׁמְעוֹן בֶּן אֶלְעָזָר אוֹמֵר.

נְכָסִים שֶׁיֵּשׁ לָהֶן אַחֲרָיוּת הַבָּנִים מוֹצִיאִין מִן הַבָּנִים וְהַבָּנוֹת מוֹצִיאוֹת מִן הַבָּנוֹת וְהַבָּנִים מִן הַבָּנוֹת וְהַבָּנוֹת מִן הַבָּנִים. וְשֶׁאֵין לָהֶן אַחֲרָיוּת הַבָּנִים מוֹצִיאִין מִן הַבָּנוֹת וְאֵין הַבָּנוֹת מוֹצִיאִין מִן הַבָּנִים. אָמְרֵי. חָזַר בֵּיהּ רַב הוּנָא. אָמְרִין. יֵאוּת. כְּתוּבָּה מִדְּבַר תּוֹרָה וּמְזוֹן הַבָּנוֹת מִדִּבְרֵיהֶן. וְדִבְרֵיהֶן עוֹקְרִין דְּבַר תּוֹרָה. אֶלָּא בְּכֶסֶף כְּתוּבַּת אִימָּן פְּלִיגִין. [אֲפִילוּ תֵימָא. בְּכֶסֶף כְּתוּבַּת אִימָּן פְּלִיגִין.] וְכֶסֶף כְּתוּבַּת אִימָּן לֹא קַרְקַע הוּא.

1 הונא | י חונא   5 עד דתינסבון לגוברין | י -   מן מקרקעי | י ממקרקעי   6 ודשמואל | י ור' שמואל   8 אלעזר | י לעזר   9 מוציאות | י -   11 אמרי | י אמרין ביה רב חונא | י בה רב חונא   14 [ ] | י -

Rav Huna insists on interpreting the contract text. Rav Huna explained: "The sons shall inherit but the daughters must be fed." Since the sons inherit movables, the daughters also are fed from movables. Samuel said, the daughters are not fed from movables. A Mishnah supports Samuel: "The female children you shall have from me shall dwell in my house and be supported from my property." It was stated on this: From real estate but not from movables. Rebbi Abba bar Zavda said: Rav Huna follows Rebbi and Samuel follows Rebbi Simeon ben Eleazar, as it was stated: "One uses both guaranteed property and non-guaranteed property for the support of the wife and the daughters, the words of Rebbi. Rebbi Simeon ben Eleazar says, guaranteed property may be taken by sons from sons, by daughters from daughters, by sons from daughters, and by daughters from sons. But non-guaranteed property may be taken by sons from daughters but not by daughters from sons." They said, Rav Huna reversed himself. They said, that was well done, *ketubah* is a biblical commandment but support of the daughters is from their words. May their words uproot a biblical commandment? It must be that they differ about the money contained in their mother's *ketubah*. [Even if you say, they differ about the money contained in their mother's *ketubah*.][209] But is the money stipulated in their mother's *ketubah* not also real estate[66]?

209 Inserted here by the corrector who prepared the *editio princeps*; missing in *Yebamot*.

(29a line 33) הַיּוֹרֵד לְנִכְסֵי אִשְׁתּוֹ וְנָתַן עֵינָיו בָּהּ לְגָרְשָׁהּ וְקָפַץ וְתָלַשׁ מִן הַקַּרְקַע הֲרֵי זֶה זָרִיז וְנִשְׂכָּר. הַיּוֹרֵד לְנִכְסֵי שְׁבוּיִין וְשָׁמַע עֲלֵיהֶן שֶׁהֵן מְמַשְׁמְשִׁין וּבָאִין וְקָפַץ וְתָלַשׁ מִן הַקַּרְקַע הֲרֵי זֶה זָרִיז וְנִשְׂכָּר. אִילּוּ הֵן נִכְסֵי שְׁבוּיִין. כָּל־שֶׁהָלַךְ אָבִיו אוֹ אָחִיו אוֹ אֶחָד מִכָּל־הַמּוֹרִישָׁן אוֹתוֹ לִמְדִינַת הַיָּם נִשְׁמַע עֲלֵיהֶן שֶׁמֵּתוּ וְיָרַד לְנַחֲלָה. אֲבָל נִכְסֵי נְטוּשִׁין מוֹצִיאִין מִיָּדוֹ. וְאִילּוּ הֵן נִכְסֵי נְטוּשִׁין. כָּל־שֶׁהָלַךְ אָבִיו אוֹ אֶחָד מִכָּל־הַמּוֹרִישָׁן אוֹתוֹ לִמְדִינַת הַיָּם וְלֹא שָׁמַע עֲלֵיהֶן שֶׁמֵּתוּ וְיָרַד לוֹ לְנַחֲלָה. אָמַר רַבָּן שִׁמְעוֹן בֶּן גַּמְלִיאֵל. שָׁמַעְתִּי הֵן שְׁבוּיִין הֵן נְטוּשִׁין. אֲבָל נִכְסֵי רְטוּשִׁין מוֹצִיאִין מִיָּדוֹ. וְאִילּוּ הֵן נִכְסֵי רְטוּשִׁין. כָּל־שֶׁהָלַךְ אָבִיו אוֹ אָחִיו אוֹ אֶחָד מִכָּל־הַמּוֹרִישָׁן אוֹתוֹ לִמְדִינַת הַיָּם וְאֵין יָדוּעַ הֵיכָן הֵם. שְׁמוּאֵל אָמַר. שָׁבוּי זֶה שֶׁיָּצָא שֶׁלֹּא לְדַעַת. שְׁאִילּוּ לְדַעַת יָצָא הָיָה מְצַוֵּיהוּ. נָטוּשׁ זֶה שֶׁיָּצָא לְדַעַת. תֵּידַע לָךְ שֶׁעֲיֵילָה הָיָה רוֹצֶה לְהַבְרִיחוֹ מִנְּכָסָיו. שֶׁהֲרֵי לְדַעַת יָצָא וְלֹא צִיוָּהוּ. רִבִּי בָּא רַב יְהוּדָה בְּשֵׁם שְׁמוּאֵל. הַמְטַלְטְלִין אֵין בָּהֶן מִשּׁוּם נִכְסֵי רְטוּשִׁין. רִבִּי יַעֲקֹב בַּר אָחָא בְּשֵׁם רַב. אִילֵּין דְּקַלַיָּא דְּבָבֶל דְּלָא צְרִיכִין מֶרְכָּבָה לֹא מִסְתַּבְּרָא מֵיעַבְדִּינָן כְּקָמָה עוֹמֶדֶת לִקְצוֹר וּגְפָנִים עוֹמְדוֹת לִבְצוֹר.

3 שבויין | • שבויים 4 נשמע | • ושמע 5 וירד | • וירד לו מוציאין | • מוציאין אותו 6 אביו | • אביו או אחיו 7-8 הן שבויין הן נטושין | • הוא שבויים הוא נטושים 10 הם | • הוא לדעת יצא | • יצא לדעת 12 ציווהו | • ציוחו ר' בא | • ר' אחא ר' בא 13 רב | • רב יהודה 14 עומדת לקצור | • עוברת לחקצר 15 עומדות לבצור | • עוברות להבצר

"If somebody who works his wife's property has the intention of divorcing her and goes and takes from the ground, he is quick and is rewarded. If somebody who works the property of prisoners heard that they prepare to return, goes and takes from the ground, he is quick and is rewarded. These are properties of prisoners: In any case where his father, brother, or any person from whom he might inherit, went overseas; it was heard that they died, and he went to work the inheritance. But property of abandoning persons one takes out of their hands. These are properties of abandoning persons: In any case where his father or any person from whom he might inherit went overseas, he did not hear that they died, but he went to work the inheritance. Rabban Simeon ben Gamliel said, I heard that there is no difference between prisoners and abandoning persons. But property of broken persons one takes out of their hands. These are properties of broken persons: In any case where his father, brother, or any person from whom he might inherit, went overseas, and his whereabouts are not known. Samuel says, the prisoner is one who left involuntarily. If he had left voluntarily he would have given him instructions. The abandoning person is one who left voluntarily. You should know that he had the intention of keeping [the relative] off his property since he left voluntarily and did not give him instructions. Rebbi Abba, Rav Jehudah in the name of Samuel: Movables do not fall under the rules of broken people. Rebbi Jacob bar Aḥa in the name of Rav[210]: [211]Those date palms of Babylonia which do not need grafting, is it not reasonable that we should treat them like standing grain ready to be harvested and grapes ready to be harvested?

210 In *Yebamot*, "Rav Jehudah". It is impossible to determine the original reading since R. Jacob bar Aḥa, a student of R. Joḥanan, was a great collector of the sayings of earlier authorities.

211 There are two sentences from *Yebamot* missing here which are needed to make sense of the statement. "Standing grain ready to be harvested and grapes ready to be harvested are movables [for the rules of broken people]. Rav Sheshet asked".

(fol. 28a) **משנה ט:** לֹא כָתַב לָהּ כְּתוּבָּה בְּתוּלָה גּוֹבָה מָאתַיִם וְאַלְמָנָה מָנֶה מִפְּנֵי שֶׁהוּא תְנָאי בֵּית דִּין. כָּתַב לָהּ שָׁוֶה מָנֶה תַּחַת מָאתַיִם זוּז וְלֹא כָתַב כָּל־נִיכְסִין דְּאִית לִי אַחֲרָאִין לִכְתוּבָּתִיךְ חַיָּיב שֶׁהוּא תְנָאי בֵּית דִּין.

Mishnah 9: If he did not write her a *ketubah*, a virgin collects 200 [*zuz*] and a widow 100, for this is a stipulation enforced by the court[212]. If he substituted something[213] valued at a mina for the 200 *zuz* and did not write "that all my property is guaranty for your *ketubah*," he still is obligated by it, for this is a stipulation enforced by the court[214].

212 The fact that there is a marriage creates the financial obligations of the husband even in the absence of a contract. This stipulation bars any *mut'a* marriage (temporary marriage for sexual pleasure only). A similar institution, ἄγραφος γάμος, "marriage without written contract," which nevertheless implied all monetary obligations of the husband towards his wife, was known in contemporary Egyptian native law; cf. R. Taubenschlag, *The Law of Greco-Roman Egypt in the Light of the Papyri*, New York 1944, Chapter IIB3.

213 In the Mishnah of the Babli: "A field." Since the lien of the *ketubah* is a mortgage (primarily or exclusively) on all the husband's property, it is reasonable to assume that in the Yerushalmi version likewise it is understood that a piece of real estate

was offered to satisfy the *ketubah* claims.

214 Therefore, all the stipulations mentioned in this and the following Mishnaiot are not written in *ketubah* contracts following the Babylonian style; the fact that a document is designated as *ketubah* makes these stipulations enforceable.

(29a line 50) **הלכה ט**: לֹא כָתַב לָהּ כְּתוּבָּה כול׳. מַתְנִיתָא דְּרִבִּי מֵאִיר. דְּרִבִּי מֵאִיר אָמַר. כָּל־הַפּוֹחֵת לִבְתוּלָה מִמָּאתַיִם וּלְאַלְמָנָה מִמָּנֶה הֲרֵי זוּ בְּעִילַת זְנוּת. לְמִי נִצְרְכָה. לְרִבִּי מֵאִיר. אַף עַל גַּב דְּרִבִּי מֵאִיר אוֹמֵר. שְׁטָר שֶׁאֵין בּוֹ אֲחֵרָיוּת נְכָסִין אֵינוֹ גוּבָה. מוֹדֶה הוּא הָכָא שֶׁהוּא גוּבָה.

Halakhah 9: "If he did not write her a *ketubah*," etc. The Mishnah is Rebbi Meïr's, since Rebbi Meïr said[214]: "Anybody who writes for a virgin less that 200 [*zuz*] or a mina for a widow engages in immoral intercourse.[215]" Who needs it[216]? Rebbi Meïr! Even though Rebbi Meïr says that any contract which does not contain an alienation clause[217] cannot be foreclosed, here he agrees that it can be foreclosed[218].

214 Mishnah 5:2; he is opposed by R. Jehudah who lets the woman agree to a reduction of the *ketubah* amount.

215 For R. Meïr, the existence of a marriage is proof of a responsibility of the husband or his estate for at least 200 or 100 *zuz*; that amount can therefore be foreclosed. A similar argument is in the Babli, 51a, where, however, the position is taken that R. Jehudah agrees that in the absence of evidence to the contrary the obligation of the husband's estate is 200 or 100 *zuz* but that by *written* agreement of the wife this obligation can be reduced.

216 The position of R. Meïr in Mishnah 5:2 does not yet explain why a document of indebtedness does not have to be produced in court.

217 R. Meïr holds that a loan document which is not a mortgage, i. e., does not contain a clause which states that in the case of nonpayment some of the debtor's property will be alienated to the creditor, cannot be enforced in court. In that he is opposed by R. Jehudah who holds that the absence of such a clause is a scribal error (Babli

51a/b; Mishnah *Baba Meṣi'a* 1:6).

218 The Babli, 51b, qualifies this statement that R. Meïr permits foreclosure only from real estate not otherwise pledged while the Yerushalmi will permit foreclosure from real estate pledged after the marriage was contracted (because the wife's lien cannot be removed.)

משנה י: לֹא כָתַב לָהּ אִם תִּשְׁתַּבְּיָין אֶפְרְקִינִיךְ וְאוֹתְבִינִיךְ לִי לְאִינְתּוּ וּבְכֹהֲנוֹת אַהֲדְרִינֵךְ לִמְדִינְתִּיךְ חַיָּיב שֶׁהוּא תְּנַאי בֵּית דִּין. (fol. 28a)

Mishnah 10: If he did not write her "if you are kidnapped I shall ransom you and bring you back as my wife," or for Cohens' wives "I shall return you to your country[219]," he is obligated,[220] for this is a stipulation enforced by the court.

משנה יא: נִשְׁבֵּית חַיָּיב לִפְדוֹתָהּ וְאִם אָמַר הֲרֵי גִיטָהּ וּכְתוּבָּתָהּ תִּפְדֶּה אֶת עַצְמָהּ אֵינוֹ רַשָּׁאי. לָקְתָה חַיָּיב לְרַפּוֹתָהּ. אָמַר הֲרֵי גִיטָהּ וּכְתוּבָּתָהּ תִּפְדֶּה אֶת עַצְמָהּ רַשָּׁאי.

Mishnah 11: If she was kidnapped he is obligated to ransom her. If he said, here is her divorce document and her *ketubah*, let her redeem herself; he is not allowed to do that[221]. If she was smitten[222], he is obligated to heal her. If he said, here is her divorce document and her *ketubah*, let her redeem[223] herself; he is allowed to do that[224].

219 Since she is forbidden to him as a probably rape victim, he has to divorce her and pay her *ketubah* in addition to the ransom he paid for her.

220 Even if the ransom will exceed the value of her *ketubah*.

221 He is not allowed (a) to cap possible ransom by the value of the *ketubah* and (b) to deduct the amount of the ransom from her *ketubah*.

222 If she became sick.

223 This probably is a scribal error.

In all other mss. (Babli and independent Mishnah mss.): תְּרַפֵּא "let her heal herself."

224 The explanation given for the rule is in Tosephta 4:5, that ongoing medical expenses are part of the upkeep promised in the *ketubah*. This means, as explained in the Halakhah, that medical costs which can be determined beforehand are not part of the husband's obligation but ongoing costs for chronic conditions are to be paid by the husband just like ongoing costs for food are his responsibility.

(29a line 54) **הלכה יא**: לֹא כָתַב לָהּ דְּאִין תִּשְׁתַּבְּיָין אֶפְרְקִינָּיךְ כוֹל׳. נִשְׁבֵּית חַיָּיב לִפְדּוֹתָהּ כוֹל׳. תַּנֵּי. יְבָמָה שֶׁנִּשְׁבֵּית אֵין הַיּוֹרְשִׁין חַיָּיבִין לִפְדּוֹתָהּ. רִבִּי חִייָה בַּר אָשִׁי בְּשֵׁם רַב. לֹא סוֹף דָּבָר בְּנִשְׁבֵּית בְּחַיֵּי בַעֲלָהּ אֶלָּא אֲפִילוּ שֶׁנִּשְׁבֵּית לְאַחַר מִיתַת הַבַּעַל אֵין הַיּוֹרְשִׁין חַיָּיבִין לִפְדּוֹתָהּ. רִבִּי חִייָה בַּר אָחָא. מַתְנִיתִין מְסַיִּיעָא לְרַב. וְאוֹתְבִינָךְ לִי לְאִינְתּוּ. אֵין כָּאן אִינְתּוּ.

"If he did not write her "if you are kidnapped I shall ransom you," etc. "If she was kidnapped he is obligated to ransom her," etc. It was stated[225]: If a sister-in-law[226] was kidnapped, the heirs do not have to ransom her. Rebbi[227] Ḥiyya bar Ashi in the name of Rav: Not only if she was kidnapped when her husband was still alive but even if she was kidnapped after the husband's death, the heirs do not have to ransom her. Rebbi Ḥiyya bar Aḥa[228]: The Mishnah supports Rav: "And bring you back as wife;" there is no "wife".

225 Tosephta 4:5.
226 The widow of a childless man who waits to be married in levirate. The Babli, 52a, reports the same rule for any widow.
227 This should be "Rav".

228 This name does not appear otherwise in the Talmudim. In the Babli, Rav reports his argument in the name of his uncle, the elder Rabbi Ḥiyya (bar Abba bar Aḥa Karsala).

(29a line 59) וּבַכְּהֲנוֹת אֲהַדְרִינָךְ לִמְדִינְתָּא. מָה. לִמְדִינְתָּהּ מַמָּשׁ. לְיִישּׁוּב.

"For Cohens' wives 'I shall return you to your country.'" Does this mean, exactly to her country? To a civilized place.²²⁹

229   To a Jewish community where he pays her the *ketubah* and where she can find a new husband.

(29a line 60) תַּנֵּי רַבָּן שִׁמְעוֹן בֶּן גַּמְלִיאֵל. כָּל־מַכָּה שֶׁיֵּשׁ לָהּ קִיצָה מִתְרַפָּה מִכְּתוּבָתָהּ. וְשֶׁאֵין לָהּ קִיצָה מִתְרַפְאָה מִן הַנְכָסִין. כְּהָדָא. חָדָא אִיתָא אֲתַת לְגַבֵּי רִבִּי יוֹחָנָן. אָמַר לָהּ. קְצַץ הוּא אֲסִייָךְ.²³⁰ אָמְרָה לֵיהּ. לָא. לֹא כֵן אָמַר רִבִּי חַגַּי בְּשֵׁם רִבִּי יְהוֹשֻׁעַ בֶּן לֵוִי. אַל תַּעַשׂ עַצְמָךְ כְּעוֹרְכֵי הַדַּייָנִין. שֶׁלֹּא לְגַלּוֹת לְיָחִיד אֶת דִּינוֹ. יָדַע הֲוָה בָהּ שֶׁהִיא כְשֵׁירָה.

²³¹Rabban Simeon ben Gamliel stated²³²: For any hurt which has a fixed medical fee, she is healed from her *ketubah*. If it does not have a fixed medical fee, she is healed from the estate²³³. As the following: A woman came to Rebbi Joḥanan. He asked her: Did your doctor give a fixed price? She said, no²³⁴. Did not Rebbi Aḥai say in the name of Rebbi Joshua ben Levi: "Do not turn yourself into an pleader²³⁵," that one shall not disclose the judgment to a party? He knew her to be honest²³⁶.

230   Reading of the quote in *Arukh*, s. v. ערך, and in (the differently formulated) parallel in *Baba Batra* 9:6, 17a l. 20. The ms. text reads: קְצָץ הוּא "Did he fix a price?" which was emended by the corrector who prepared the *editio princeps* into: קְצָץ הוּא אֲבִיד "if he [the doctor] fixed the price, it is lost [you have to pay yourself]." The emendation appears as a distortion of the text.

231   This paragraph refers to the statement about medical costs.
232   Tosephta 4:5; Babli, 52b.
233   If she is a widow who preferred to be sustained by the estate instead of collecting her *ketrubah* in cash.
234   He told her to insist the doctor be paid for each visit, not to give the treatment on an all-inclusive fixed price. In *Baba Batra* 9:6, 17a l. 20, the woman is identified as a relative of R.

Simeon ben Abba. In the Babli, 52b, R. Johanan is reported to have sided with the heirs, telling them to get an all-inclusive price from the doctor.

235 Mishnah *Abot* 1:8. It is unethical for a judge to dispense legal advice.

236 She would not change her behavior based on the information received from him.

(fol. 28a) **משנה יב:** לֹא כָתַב לָהּ בְּנִין דִּיכְרִין דְּיִהֲוֹן לֵיכִי מִינַאי אִינּוּן יְרתוּן כְּסַף כְּתוּבְתִּיךְ יָתֵר עַל חוּלָקְהוֹן דְּעִם אֲחֵיהוֹן חַיָּיב תְּנַיֵי בֵית דִּין.

Mishnah 12: If he did not write her "the male children you will have from me shall inherit the amount of your *ketubah* in addition to their part with their brothers[237]"; he is obligated, for this is a stipulation enforced by the court.

237 If the wife should die before the husband and the husband inherits from her then, if the husband dies, the sons of his several wives can first claim their mother's *ketubah* (the ≥200 *zuz* from the husband and all the dowry noted in the document) from the estate; only the remainder is divided between the sons (with an eventual first-born son taking two parts).

(29a line 65) **הלכה יב:** לֹא כָתַב לָהּ. בְּנִין דִּיכְרִין כול׳. הָדָא דְּאָמַר רִבִּי אַמִּי. כְּדֵי שֶׁיְּהֵא אָדָם מָצוּי לִיתֵּן לְבִתּוֹ בְּעַיִן יָפָה.

Halakhah 12: "If he did not write her "the male children," etc. That is what Rebbi Immi said, that a man should be disposed to give generously to his daughter[238].

238 If he knows that the dowry will remain the possession of his grandchildren, he will be more inclined to provide his daughter with a dowry. In the Babli, 52b, the explanation is ascribed to R. Johanan and the

recommended amount is 10% of the father's property.

The same statememt is also in Halakhah 10:2.

(29a line 66) תַּמָּן תַּנִּינָן. רִבִּי יוֹחָנָן בֶּן בְּרוֹקָה אוֹמֵר. אִם אָמַר עַל שֶׁרָאוּי לְיוֹרְשׁהּ דְּבָרָיו קַיָּימִין. וְעַל מִי שֶׁאֵין רָאוּי לְיוֹרְשָׁהּ אֵין דְּבָרָיו קַיָּימִין. אָמַר רִבִּי יוֹחָנָן. לֹא אָמַר בֶּן בְּרוֹקָה אֶלָּא עַל בֵּן בֵּין הַבָּנִים וְעַל (בַּת)²⁴¹ בֶּן בֵּין הַבָּנוֹת. בַּת בֵּין הָאָח לֹא. אָח בֵּין הַבָּנוֹת לֹא. רִבִּי יָסָא בְּשֵׁם רִבִּי יוֹחָנָן. מַעֲשֶׂה הָיָה וְהוֹרָה רִבִּי כְּרִבִּי יוֹחָנָן בֶּן בְּרוֹקָה. רִבִּי זְעִירָא רִבִּי יָסָא בְּשֵׁם רִבִּי יוֹחָנָן. רִבִּי שָׁאַל אֶת נָתָן הַבַּבְלִי. מַה טַעֲמָא אָמְרוּ. הֲלָכָה כְּרִבִּי יוֹחָנָן בֶּן בְּרוֹקָה. רִבִּי בָּא רִבִּי חִייָה בְּשֵׁם רִבִּי יוֹחָנָן. מַה טַעַם שָׁאַל אֶת נָתָן הַבַּבְלִי. מַה רָאוּ חֲכָמִים לוֹמַר. הֲלָכָה כְּרִבִּי יוֹחָנָן בֶּן בְּרוֹקָה. לֹא אַתְּ שֶׁשְּׁנִיתָהּ לָנוּ כֵּן יִרְתּוּן. (אָמַר לֵיהּ. יִטְלוּן תִּנְיַת. אֲתָא לְגַבֵּיהּ.) אָמַר לֵיהּ. לֵית כָּאן יִרְתּוּן אֶלָּא יִטְלוּן. אֲתָא לְגַבֵּי אַבוֹי אָמַר לֵיהּ. קִיפַּחְתָּהּ אֶת נָתָן הַבַּבְלִי. לֵית כָּאן יִטְלוּן אֶלָּא יִרְתּוּן. אָמַר רִבִּי יוֹסֵי בֵּירִבִּי בּוּן. אָכֵין אָמַר לֵיהּ. טָעִיתִי טָעוּת שֶׁשְּׁנִיתִי לָכֶם. לֵית כָּאן יִטְלוּן אֶלָּא יִרְתּוּן. אָמַר רִבִּי זְעִירָא. קַל הוּא בִּתְנַאי כְּתוּבָּה. לְפִי שֶׁבְּכָל־מָקוֹם אֵין אָדָם מְזַכֶּה אֶלָּא בִּכְתוּבָּה וְכָאן אֲפִילוּ בִּדְבָרִים. לְפִי שֶׁבְּכָל־מָקוֹם אֵין אָדָם מְזַכֶּה אֶלָּא לְמִי שֶׁהוּא בָּעוֹלָם וְכָאן לְמִי שֶׁאֵינוֹ בָּעוֹלָם. אָמַר רִבִּי יִרְמִיָה קוֹמֵי רִבִּי זְעִירָא. וְתַמִּיהָ אֲנָא אֵיךְ רַבָּנִין מְדַמּוּ כְּתוּבָּה לִירוּשָׁה. לֹא דָמֵי. דִּירוּשָׁה מִדְּבַר תּוֹרָה כְּתוּבָּה מִדִּבְרֵיהֶן וְתֵימַר אָכֵן. אֲפִילוּ תֵימַר כְּתוּבָּה מִדִּבְרֵי תוֹרָה לֹא מוֹדוּ בִּתְנָייֵ כְּתוּבָּה שֶׁהוּא מִדִּבְרֵיהֶן.

[239]There, we have stated[240]: "Rebbi Johanan ben Beroqa says, if he speaks about somebody who is a legal heir, his statements are valid, but about somebody who is not a legal heir, his statements are invalid." Rebbi Johanan said, Ben Beroqa spoke only about a son among sons or a (daughter)[241] son among daughters, not about a daughter and brother or a brother among daughters. Rebbi Yasa in the name of Rebbi Johanan: There was a case and Rebbi decided following Rebbi Johanan ben Beroqa.

HALAKHAH 12   231

Rebbi Ze'ira, Rebbi Yasa in the name of Rebbi Johanan: Rebbi asked Nathan the Babylonian, why did they say that practice follows Rebbi Johanan ben Beroqa? Rebbi Abba, Rebbi Hiyya in the name of Rebbi Johanan: What is the reason? He asked Nathan the Babylonian, why did the Sages say that practice follows Rebbi Johanan ben Beroqa[242]? Are you not the one who stated "shall inherit"? (He said to him, you stated "shall take"; he came to him)[243]. He said to him, there is no "shall inherit" but "shall take"[244]. When he came to his father, he said to him[245]: you disadvantaged Nathan the Bablylonian; there is no "shall take" but "shall inherit". Rebbi Yose ben Rebbi Abun said, this is what he told him: I made an error in what I taught you; there is no "shall take" but "shall inherit". Rebbi Ze'ira said, this is one of the leniencies of the *ketubah* stipulations. In general, a person can transfer rights only by a document; here even verbally. In general, a person cannot transfer rights to somebody not yet existing; here to the non-existing[246]. Rebbi Jeremiah said before Rebbi Ze'ira: I am wondering how the rabbis can compare *ketubah* to inheritance, for inheritance is a biblical law but *ketubah* is from their words[247]; how can one argue this? Even if you say that *ketubah* is a biblical law, do they not agree that the stipulations of the *ketubah* are from their words[248]?

239   A similar, but more tersely and clearly formulated text is in *Baba Batra* 8:6.

240   Mishnah *Baba Batra* 8:6. The biblical law of inheritance (*Num.* 27:8-11) states that inheritances should be distributed to the next of kin; it is implied that all persons of the same degree of relationship shall be treated equally (except for the rule of the firstborn. *Deut.* 21:15-17). In Mishnah 8:5, the anonymous majority states that a person may make a will in which he distributes his property unevenly. The

will will be valid if formulated in the language of gifts, invalid in the language of inheritance. In Mishnah 8:6, R. Joḥanan ben Beroqa states that even the language of gifts is acceptable if and only if the recipient is a legal heir directly in line; e. g., one son among many, but not a daughter in the presence of sons since daughters inherit only if there are no sons. If there are no sons, R. Joḥanan ben Beroqa will accept unequal distribution of the estate among the daughters. The Mishnah here is formulated following Ben Beroqa since it accepts unequal distribution of the estate even without writing (Babli *Baba Batra* 131a).

241 This was the first (correct) word written by the scribe who then (incorrectly) crossed it out and replaced it by "son" to produce a meaningless sentence.

242 Since the Mishnah in *Ketubot* is anonymous, it represents practice and it follows R. Joḥanan ben Beroqa. The Babli, *Baba Batra* 131a, presents the question in slightly different form and ends up by denying its validity. The Babli holds (seemingly against the Yerushalmi) that property rights based on a *ketubah* stipulation are strictly weaker than those mentioned in the *ketubah* contract in that they cannot be asserted against third parties.

243 The fragments of sentences in this parenthesis make no sense; they belong to nearby texts and the scribe seems to have been unsure about the order of the sentences. It is best to leave the parenthesis unexplained.

244 It is not quite clear whether this is Rebbi's or R. Nathan the Babylonian's statement. It changes the language of the Mishnah, that the woman's sons "shall take her *ketubah*", making the transaction one of a gift valid from the time of the marriage. Therefore, the rules of inheritance are irrelevant and there is no relation between the Mishnah here and Ben Beroqa's statement about wills. (Everybody agrees that by a gift "valid now but executed only after my death", a person can freely dispose of his assets without regard to biblical laws of inheritance.)

245 When Rebbi came to Rabban Simeon ben Gamliel, the latter affirmed the text of the Mishnah as the correct one.

246 At the date of the marriage, no sons are yet born. For everybody except R. Meïr, the unborn cannot be the recipient of a gift (other than through a guardian); the same argument is in the Babli, *loc. cit.*

247 *Ketubah* is purely a rabbinic institution (or better, a generally followed practice in post-exilic Judaism, inspired by but not derived from the biblical "bridal gift".) This is the opinion of Rabban Simeon ben Gamliel, cf. the last paragraph of this tractate.

Since the Mishnah text is Rabban Simeon ben Gamliel's, the question is relevant.

248 Therefore, there is no connection between the *ketubah* stipulations and the laws of inheritance.

(fol. 28a) **משנה יג:** בְּנָן נוּקְבָן דְּיֶהֶוְיָן לִיכִי מִינַאי אִינּוּן תְּהוֹן יָתְבָן בְּבֵיתִי וּמִתְזְנָן מִנִּכְסַי עַד דְּיִתְנַסְבָן לְגוּבְרִין חַיָּיב שֶׁהוּא תְנַאי בֵּית דִּין.

Mishnah 13: "The female children you will have by me shall live in my house and be supported by my estate until they are married to men"; he is obligated, for this is a stipulation enforced by the court.

(fol. 29b line 8) **הלכה יג:** בְּנָן נוּקְבָן דְּיֶהֶוְוָן לִיכֵי מִינַאי כּוּל׳. רַב חִסְדָּא אָמַר. בָּגְרוּ אִיבְּדוּ מְזוֹנוֹת. נִישְּׂאוּ אִיבְּדוּ פַּרְנָסָתָן. תַּנֵּי רִבִּי חִייָה. בָּגְרוּ לֹא נִשְּׂאוּ נִשְּׂאוּ לֹא בָגְרוּ. אִיבְּדוּ מְזוֹנוֹתָן וְלֹא אִיבְּדוּ פַּרְנָסָתָן. רִבִּי אָבִין בְּשֵׁם הִילָא. וּמוֹדִין לְהַד כְּהָדָא. אַלְמָנָה שֶׁהִיא תּוֹבַעַת מִן הַיּוֹרְשִׁין. הִיא אוֹמֶרֶת. לֹא נִתְקַבַּלְתִּי מִכְּתוּבָּתִי. וְהַיּוֹרְשִׁין אוֹמְרִין לָהּ. נִתְקַבַּלְתְּ כְּתוּבָּתָךְ. עַד שֶׁלֹּא נִישֵּׂאת הַיּוֹרְשִׁין צְרִיכִין לְהָבִיא רְאָייָה שֶׁנִּתְקַבְּלָה כְּתוּבָּתָהּ. נִישֵּׂאת עָלֶיהָ לְהָבִיא רְאָייָה שֶׁלֹּא נִתְקַבְּלָה כְּתוּבָּתָהּ. וְהָא תַנִּינָן. יְתוֹמָה שֶׁהִשִּׂיאָה אִמָּהּ אוֹ אָחִיהָ וְכָתְבוּ לָהּ מֵאָה וַחֲמִשִּׁים זוּז וְכוּלָּהּ הִיא מִשֶּׁתַּגְדִּיל לְהוֹצִיא מִיָּדָם. טַעְמָא דִקְטַנָּה. הָא גְדוֹלָה וִיתִּירָה. תִּיפְתָּר שֶׁנָּטְלָה מִקְצָת. לֹא כֵן אָמַר רִבִּי אֲבִינָה בְּשֵׁם רִבִּי אַסִּי. בְּכוֹר שֶׁחָלַק בְּפָשׁוּט חֲזָקָה וִיתֵּר. עוֹד הִיא שֶׁנָּטְלָה מִקְצָת. אָמַר רִבִּי יוֹסֵי בֵּירִבִּי בּוּן. לֹא נָטַל זֶה מִבְּכוֹרָתוֹ כְּלוּם. אָתָא עוֹבְדָא קוֹמֵי רִבִּי מָנָא וּבְעָא מֵיעֲבַד כְּהָדָא דְּרַב חִסְדָּא. אָמַר לֵיהּ רִבִּי חֲנַנְיָה. וְהָא תַּנֵּי רִבִּי חִייָה. בָּגְרוּ וְלֹא נִשְּׂאוּ נִשְּׂאוּ וְלֹא בָגְרוּ אִיבְּדוּ מְזוֹנוֹתָן וְלֹא אִיבְּדוּ

פַּרְנָסָתָן. אָמַר לֵיהּ. אֲנָא אֲמְרִי שְׁמוּעָה וְאַתְּ אֲמַרְתְּ מַתְנִיתָא. תִּבָּטֵל שְׁמוּעָה מֵיקַמֵּי מַתְנִיתָא.

Halakhah 13: ""The female children you will have by me," etc. Rav Hisda said, if they became adults, they lost the support[249]. If they married, they lost their dowries[250]. Rebbi Hiyya stated[251]: "If they became adults without being married or were married without being adults, they lost their support but not their dowries." Rebbi Abin in the name of Hila: They all agree on the following: If a widow sues the heirs, she says I did not receive my *ketubah*, but the heirs say you received your *ketubah*. Before she remarried, the burden of proof is on the heirs that she received her *ketubah*[252]. After she remarried, the burden of proof is on her that she had not received her *ketubah*[253]. But did we not state[254]: "If an orphan was married off by her mother or her brother and they wrote her [a dowry of] 150 *zuz*, after she grows up she can extract from them." The reason, because she was underage. Therefore, a grown up gave up her claim[255]. Explain it that she had received partial payment[256]. Did not Rebbi Avina say in the name of Rebbi[257] Assi: If a firstborn took as a simple [brother][258], this is *prima facie* evidence that he gave up his claim. Still, if she had received part payment. Rebbi Yose ben Rebbi Abun said, this one did not take anything from his primogeniture[259]. There came a case before Rebbi Mana, who wanted to act following Rav Hisda. Rebbi Hananiah said to him, did not Rebbi Hiyya state, "if they became adults without being married or were married without being adults, they lost their support but not their dowries"? He said to him: I quoted a tradition, you quoted a *baraita*. Let the tradition be disregarded before the *baraita*.

249 Since support for daughters is stipulated only until marriage, the support ends once the usual age for marriage, adolescence, has passed.

250 If after the father's death she did not claim her dowry at the moment of marriage, she is presumed to have renounced her right to a dowry which on average is 10% of the estate (cf. Halakhah 6:6). In the Tosephta, 4:17, this is the opinion of R. Simeon ben Eleazar.

251 Tosephta 4:17, opinion of the anonymous majority.

252 There is a parallel text in the Babli, 96a/b, but it deals with the case that the widow comes at the end of a year and claims not to have received support for the past year. There is no mention of *ketubah* in the Babli since it requires either that the widow present the *ketubah*, which will be torn up upon payment, or bring witnesses that she married at a place where routinely no *ketubah* is written; then she has to deliver a receipt.

253 Since all support by the estate stops upon remarriage of the widow, it would be a most unusual circumstance if the *ketubah* was not liquidated at that time.

254 Mishnah 6:6.

255 She is supposed to have renounced her claim if she did not request her dowry at the time of the marriage; the underage girl may wait until she becomes an adult able to act in legal matters.

256 If the quarrel is not about the entire amount of the *ketubah*, there can be no argument that the widow renounced her claim.

257 This must be Rav Assi, quoted in the Babli, *Baba Batra* 136a.

258 The ms. form בְּפָשׁוּט, in his quality of "simple" brother (i. e., taking only one portion in contrast to the firstborn's double share), is good rabbinic Hebrew style and does not have to be changed into כְּפָשׁוּט.

259 Therefore, the case of the firstborn is different from that of widow or orphan girl. In the Babli, *Baba Batra* 136a, this is very much in dispute since a dissenting opinion holds that the firstborn only lost his right to re-open past distributions but that he is not restrained from asserting his double claim in the future.

(fol. 28a) **משנה יד:** וְאַתְּ תְּהֵא יָתְבָא בְּבֵיתִי וּמִתְזַנָּה מִנִּכְסַיי כָּל־יְמֵי מֵייגַד אַרְמְלוּתִיךְ בְּבֵיתִי חַייָב שֶׁהוּא תְנָיי בֵּית דִּין.

Mishnah 14: "And you shall dwell in my house and be supported by my property during all of your widowhood"; he is obligated, for this is a stipulation enforced by the court.

(29b line 23) **הלכה יד:** וְאַתְּ תְּהֵא יָתְבָא בְּבֵיתִי. רָבִין בַּר חִייָה בְּעָא קוֹמֵי רִבִּי זְעִירָא. בָּא עָלֶיהָ עוֹדָהּ בְּבֵית אָבִיהָ. מֵעַכְשָׁיו נִתְקַייְמוּ בָהּ תְּנָאֵי כְּתוּבָּה אוֹ אֵינוֹ אֶלָּא דֶּרֶךְ נִישּׂוּאִין. רִבִּי בּוּן בַּר חִייָה בְּעָא קוֹמֵי רִבִּי זְעִירָא. מָחֲלָה לוֹ עַל כְּתוּבָּתָהּ מָהוּ. זְכוּתָהּ אָבְדָה זְכוּת בָּנֶיהָ לֹא אָבְדָה.

Halakhah 14: ""And you shall dwell in my house". Rebbi Abun bar Ḥiyya asked before Rebbi Ze'ira: If he slept with her when she still was in her father's house, did he then activate all *ketubah* stipulations or is that only by definitive marriage[260]? Rebbi Abun bar Ḥiyya asked before Rebbi Ze'ira: If she renounced her *ketubah,* what is the situation? She renounced her rights but not those of her children[261].

260 The question is not answered. In the Babli, 53a, it is stated that *ketubah* stipulations do not apply to the preliminarily married woman. This is obviously implied by the question raised here.

261 One could read this sentence as a question: She renounced her own rights (which she can do following R. Jehudah, Mishnah 5:2), but was she able to renounce those of her children? In the Babli, 53a, the question is answered in the positive: she renounced all rights. Under the influence of the Babli, the commentators chose the interpretation as a question.

(29b line 27) רִבִּי זְעִירָא שָׁאַל לְרַב נַחְמָן בַּר יַעֲקֹב וּלְרַב אֲבִימֵי בַּר פַּפֵּי. לֹא הָיָה שָׁם בַּיִת. אָמְרוּ לֵיהּ. הַיּוֹרְשִׁין שׂוֹכְרִין לָהּ בַּיִת. מִיכָּן וָהֵילַךְ הִיא אוֹמֶרֶת קַרְקַע וְהֵן אוֹמְרִין מָעוֹת. הַדִּין עִם הַיְתוֹמִים. כְּהָדָא. חָדָא אִיתָא הֲוָה פּוּרְנָהּ עֶשְׂרִין דֵּינָרִין. וַהֲוָה תַּמָּן חַד בַּיִת כְּרַב עֲשָׂרָה דֵּינָרִין. אֲתָא עוֹבְדָא קוֹמֵי רִבִּי חֲנִינָה. אָמַר. אוֹ יֵיבוֹן לָהּ בַּיְתָא אוֹ יֵבוֹן לָהּ עֶשְׂרִים דֵּינָרִין. אָמַר רִבִּי מָנָא. מִכֵּיוָן דְּלֵית בֵּיתָא טָב אֶלָּא עֶשְׂרִים כְּמָאן דְּלֵית לָהּ פּוּרְנָה אֶלָּא עֶשְׂרִים. מִיכָּן וָהֵילַךְ הִיא אוֹמֶרֶת קַרְקַע וְהֵן אוֹמְרִין מָעוֹת. הַדִּין עִם הַיְתוֹמִים.

[262]Rebbi Ze'ira asked Rav Naḥman bar Jacob and (Rebbi) Abime bar Pappai: What if there was no house? They said to him, the heirs rent a house for her. One concludes that if she says real estate and they say money, the law sides with the heirs. As the following: A woman's *ketubah* was twenty denars, and there was a house worth at most ten denars. The case came before Rebbi Ḥanina who said, either they give her a house or they give her twenty denars. Rebbi Mana said, since the house is not worth more than 20 it is as if her *ketubah* was only twenty. One concludes that if she says real estate and they say money, the law sides with the heirs.

262 This text is difficult in several places. There exists a version quoted and explained by *Rosh* (R. Asher ben Ieḥiel) which in itself is not without problems, see Note 267. As the reader will easily verify, the Aramaic portions of the text have been adapted to Babylonian spelling. Therefore, the text cannot serve as witness to the details of the text:

רִבִּי זְעִירָא שָׁלַח שָׁאִיל לְרַב נַחְמָן בַּר יַעֲקֹב וּלְרַב אֲבִימֵי בַּר פַּפָּא. לֹא הָיָה שָׁם בַּיִת מַאי. אָמְרוּ לֵיהּ. הַיּוֹרְשִׁין שׂוֹכְרִין לָהּ בַּיִת. מִיכָּן וְאֵילַךְ הִיא אוֹמֶרֶת קַרְקַע וְהֵם אוֹמְרִים מָעוֹת. הַדִּין עִם הַיְתוֹמִים. כְּהָדָא. חָדָא אִיתְּתָא הֲוָה פּוּרְנָהּ עֶשְׂרִין דֵּינָרִים. וַהֲוָה תַּמָּן חַד בַּיִת טָב עֲשָׂרָה דֵּינָרִין. אֲתָא עוֹבְדָא קוֹמֵי רִבִּי חֲנִינָה. אָמַר. אוֹ יְהָבוֹן לָהּ בַּיְתָא אוֹ יְהָבוֹן לָהּ עֶשְׂרִים דֵּינָרִין. אָמַר לֵיהּ רִבִּי מָנָא. מִכֵּיוָן דְּלֵית בֵּיתָא אֶלָּא בַּעֲשָׂרָה דֵּינָרִין כְּמָאן דְּלֵית לָהּ

פּוּרְנָה אֶלָּא בַּעֲשָׂרָה דֵינָרִין. מִיכָּן וָהֵילָךְ הִיא אוֹמֶרֶת קַרְקַע וְהֵן אוֹמְרִין מָעוֹת. הַדִּין עִם הַיְתוֹמִים.

Rebbi Ze'ira *sent to ask* Rav Naḥman bar Jacob and (Rebbi)[263] Abime bar Pappai: What if there was no house? They said to him, the heirs rent a house for her. One concludes[264] that if she says real estate and they say money, the law sides with the heirs. As the following: A woman's *ketubah*[265] was twenty denars[266], and there was a house worth at most ten denars. The case came before Rebbi Ḥanina who said, either they give her the house or they give her twenty[267] denars. Rebbi Mana said, since the house is not worth more than 10 it is as if her *ketubah* was only 10[268]. One concludes that if she says real estate and they say money, the law sides with the heirs.

The following is Rosh's explanation (Chapter 4, #29): "This is the explanation: What are the rules if there was no house there appropriate as a dwelling for the widow and the orphans together? They said to him, the orphans rent a house for her and if she says, real estate, i. e., 'I want to dwell in my husband's house', but they say money, 'we rent you an apartment but we want to dwell [in the house]', the law sides with the heirs since she has no property rights in the real estate, only an easement. Therefore, they can rent an apartment for her and they can dwell in that house. [And what we say that she has the right to continue living in her husband's dwelling (Mishnah 12:3), that is if the house is large enough for all but they want to move her to a lesser apartment.] In the case of that woman, whose *ketubah* was 20 denars and the only apartment in the estate was a house worth 10 denars (Note of *Qorban Nathanael*: insufficient to pay the *ketubah*), R. Ḥanina ruled that either they give her the house or they pay her 20 denars. On that, R. Mana(I) said that she should not take the real estate but that they could give her 10 denars since she has no property rights in the real estate, only an easement. Therefore also in general, since she has no property rights to the apartment, only a claim to be given one, they can move her out of the apartment and rent a different one for her.

263 This title is in error; it might be "Rav". In the Babli, he has no title.

264 This interpretation of מכאן ואילך as a technical term follows *Qorban Nathanael* (the standard commentary to Rosh), ad loc.

265 Greek φερνή "nuptual gift" used as synonym with *ketubah*, representing both the sum the husband gave from his side and the dowry which has to be returned at the dissolution of the marriage.

266 Gold denars, at the usual rate of 25 silver *zuzim* for one gold denar a total of 500 *zuz*.

267 In the version of the ms., supported by the quote in *RAN* (R. Nissim Gerondi, in his commentary on Alfasi, 20b in the Wilna ed.), R. Ḥanina tells the heirs either to give the widow (who probably is not their mother) the house to dwell in or to pay the *ketubah* in full, where R. Mana disagrees and holds, in accordance with the practice of the Babli, that the *ketubah* cannot be worth more than the real estate which guarantees it. In *Rosh*'s version, the entire discussion is only about the right of the widow to an apartment.

268 This sentence certainly is correct in *Rosh* and incorrect in the ms.

(fol. 28a) **משנה טו:** כָּךְ הָיוּ אַנְשֵׁי יְרוּשָׁלַיִם כּוֹתְבִין. אַנְשֵׁי הַגָּלִיל הָיוּ כוֹתְבִין כְּאַנְשֵׁי יְרוּשָׁלַיִם. אַנְשֵׁי יְהוּדָה הָיוּ כוֹתְבִין עַד שֶׁיִּרְצוּ הַיּוֹרְשִׁין לִיתֵּן לָהּ כְּתוּבָּה לְפִיכָךְ אִם רָצוּ הַיּוֹרְשִׁין נוֹתְנִין לָהּ כְּתוּבָּתָהּ וּפוֹטְרִין אוֹתָהּ.

Mishnah 15: This[269] is what the people of Jerusalem wrote. The people of Galilee wrote like the people of Jerusalem. The people of Judea wrote: "Until the heirs will want to pay her the *ketubah*." Therefore, if the heirs wish they can pay her the *ketubah* and send her away[270].

269 The stipulation of Mishnah 14.

270 Whereas in Jerusalem it was the widow's choice whether to claim housing and support or payment of the *ketubah*.

(fol. 29b line 35) **הלכה טו:** כָּךְ הָיוּ אַנְשֵׁי יְרוּשָׁלַיִם כּוֹתְבִין כול׳. אַנְשֵׁי הַגָּלִיל חָסוּ עַל כְּבוֹדָן וְלֹא חָסוּ עַל מָמוֹנָן. אַנְשֵׁי יְהוּדָה חָסוּ עַל מָמוֹנָן וְלֹא חָסוּ עַל

כְּבוֹדָן. רִבִּי חֲנַנְיָה בְּרֵיהּ דְּרִבִּי אַבָּהוּ. וְאִית דְּאָמְרֵי לָהּ בְּשֵׁם רִבִּי אַבָּהוּ. קֵיסָרִין כִּיהוּדָה וּשְׁאָר כָּל־הָאֲרָצוֹת כִּירוּשָׁלֵם.

Halakhah 15: "This is what the people of Jerusalem wrote," etc. The people of Galilee cared for their honor more than for their money[271]; the people of Judea cared for their money more than for their honor. Rebbi Hananiah the son of Rebbi Abbahu, and some say it in the name of Rebbi Abbahu: Caesarea[272] follows Judea and all other countries Jerusalem[273].

271 Since the widow can claim her *ketubah* unless she was supported by the estate for 25 years (Mishnah 12:4), it is clear that the heirs save money by immediately paying the *ketubah* in full. But certainly it is not honorable to evict the widow from her husband's home.

272 Caesarea Philippi, cf. *Berakhot* 2:1, Note 40.

273 The stipulation of Mishnah 14 is enforced everywhere except in R. Abbahu's town.

(fol. 29b line 39) חַד בַּר נָשׁ מִי דְמַךְ אָמַר. יֵיבוֹן לְאִיתְּתָא דְּהַהוּא גַּבְרָא פְרָגָא. אֲתָא עוֹבְדָא קוֹמֵי רִבִּי מָנָא אָמַר. יִתְקַיְימוּן דִּבְרֵי הַמֵּת. אָמַר לֵיהּ רִבִּי חֲנִינָה. וְיֵשׁ אָדָם מְבַטֵּל תְּנַאי כְּתוּבָּה בַּפֶּה. אָמַר לֵיהּ. אַנְתְּ אֲמָרַת אַתְּ מְנָא לָךְ. אָמַר לֵיהּ. וְלֹא בַּגָּלִיל אֲנָן קַיְימִין. וְסַבְרִינָן מֵימַר. אַנְשֵׁי הַגָּלִיל חָסוּ עַל כְּבוֹדָן לֹא עַל מָמוֹנָן.

A man said when he was dying: "This man's wife should be paid her *ketubah*.[275]" The case came before Rebbi Mana, who said, let the words of the deceased be confirmed[276]. Rebbi Hanina said to him: Can a person do away verbally with a *ketubah* stipulation[277]? He answered, since you are saying that, what is your reason? He said to him, are we not living in Galilee? And we are taught to say that the people of Galilee prefer their honor over their money[278].

275 He told his heirs to immediately pay the *ketubah* and not provide dwelling and sustenance for his widow.

276 It is a general principle that legal death-bed dispositions must be followed.

277 Since the *ketubah* stipulations are part of the marriage contract, they cannot be abrogated except by mutual consent, by a rider attached to the *ketubah* contract. There can be no unilateral abrogation of contractual obligations.

278 Since the wife at the time of marriage could expect that all *ketubah* stipulations were part of the contract; the dying husband's wish was illegal and could not be enforced.

אף על פי פרק חמישי

(fol. 29b) **משנה א**: אַף עַל פִּי שֶׁאָמְרוּ בְּתוּלָה גּוֹבָה מָאתַיִם וְאַלְמָנָה מָנֶה אִם רָצָא לְהוֹסִיף אֲפִילוּ מֵאָה מָנֶה יוֹסִיף. נִתְאַרְמְלָה אוֹ נִתְגָּרְשָׁה בֵּין מִן הָאֵירוּסִין בֵּין מִן הַנִּישׂוּאִין גּוֹבָה אֶת הַכֹּל. רִבִּי אֶלְעָזָר בֶּן עֲזַרְיָה אוֹמֵר. מִן הַנִּישׂוּאִין גּוֹבָה אֶת הַכֹּל מִן הָאֵירוּסִין בְּתוּלָה גּוֹבָה מָאתַיִם וְאַלְמָנָה מָנֶה שֶׁלֹא כָתַב לָהּ אֶלָּא עַל מְנָת לְכוֹנְסָהּ.

Mishnah 1: Even though they said that a virgin collects 200 [*zuz*] and a widow a mina, if he wants to add even 100 minas, he may add[1]. If she became widowed or divorced, whether preliminarily or definitively married, she collects everything. Rebbi Eleazar ben Azariah says, definitively married, she collects everything; preliminarily married a virgin collects 200 [*zuz*] and a widow a mina since he added only with the idea to bring her in[2].

1   The *ketubah* document is formulated to indicate that the husband obligates himself for 200/100 *zuz* by law; the additional sum he takes on himself must be spelled out separately.

2   Since the document was signed and witnessed beforehand and it is stated that the addition is invalid before the definitive wedding, the question arises when and how the addition becomes enforceable by law.

(29c line 29) **הלכה א**: אַף עַל פִּי שֶׁאָמְרוּ בְּתוּלָה גּוֹבָה מָאתַיִם כול׳. כְּמָה[3] הוּא מִתְחַיֵּיב לָהּ. לֹא כֵן רִבִּי יוֹחָנָן וְרִבִּי שִׁמְעוֹן בֶּן לָקִישׁ תְּרֵיהוֹן אָמְרִין. הַכּוֹתֵב שְׁטָר חוֹב עַל חֲבֵירוֹ בְּחֶזְקַת שֶׁהוּא חַיָּיב לוֹ וְנִמְצָא שֶׁאֵינוֹ חַיָּיב לִיתֵּן לוֹ. רוֹצֶה

הוּא לִיתֵּן כַּמָּה וְלָקְרוֹת חַתְנוֹ שֶׁלִפְלוֹנִי. עַד כְּדוֹן בְּשֶׁפָּסַק מִן הָאֵירוּסִין. פָּסַק מִן הַנִּישׂוּאִין. רוֹצֶה הוּא לִיתֵּן כַּמָּה בְּתַשְׁמִישָׁהּ שֶׁהוּא עָרֵב. עַד כְּדוֹן בְּשֶׁבָּעַל. לֹא בָעַל. רוֹצֶה הוּא לִיתֵּן כַּמָּה עַל קִנְיָינוֹ שֶׁהוֹסִיף. פָּסַק מִן הָאֵירוּסִין פָּסַק מִן הַנִּישׂוּאִין וְלָקְרוֹת חַתְנוֹ שֶׁלִפְלוֹנִי כְּבָר הוּא בִּרְאוּי. תַּשְׁמִישׁ אֵין בּוֹ. קִנְיָין לֹא הוֹסִיף. מִיכָּן רוֹצֶה הוּא לִיתֵּן כַּמָּה וְלֹא תַחֲזוֹר בָּהּ. וִיכוֹלָה הִיא. לֹא כֵן תַּנֵּי. הָאִישׁ אֵינוֹ מוֹצִיא אֶלָּא לִרְצוֹנוֹ. אָמַר רִבִּי אָבִין. מְעִיקָה הִיא לֵיהּ הוּא מְשַׁבֵּק לָהּ.

Halakhah 1: "Even though they said that a virgin collects 200," etc. How does he become indebted to her? Do not Rebbi Joḥanan and Rebbi Simeon ben Laqish both say, if somebody writes a debenture for another person under the assumption that he owes him and it turns out that he does not owe, [he does not have][4] to give to him! He wants to give much to be called X's son-in-law[5]. That is, if he decided this[6] at the time of the preliminary marriage. What if he decided this[6] at the time of the definitive marriage? He wants to give much for sexual relations with her, which are sweet[7]. That is if he slept with her. If he did not sleep with her? He wants to give much for the acquisition[8] he made. If he had decided at the preliminary marriage, at the definitive marriage, he already is called X's son-in-law, sexual relations are nothing new, there is no new acquisition; from thereon[9] he wants to give much that she should not change her mind[10]. But can she? Was it not stated[11] that "a man divorces only by his own will"? Rebbi Abin said, she makes his life miserable and he frees her[12].

3   In Halakhah 12:1 בְּמָה.
4   From the parallel text in Halakhah 12:1, required by the context.

If the addition is not valid for the woman who becomes a widow before her definitive wedding, why is the additional gift ever enforceable in court? Can the heirs not argue that the deceased never was obligated to pay the addition and, therefore, his estate is not required to pay?

5   The addition is payment for value received; this makes it an enforceable obligation.

6   To add to the obligatory amount of the *ketubah*.

7   Old German law knew of a similar gift, called *Morgengabe*, "gift on the morning (after the nuptials)"; Latin *dotalicium*. This is the only reason accepted by the Babli, 56a.

8   The marriage which is called "acquisition".

9   I. e., if the husband should add to the *ketubah* sum while married, what makes that addition enforceable?

10   But stay married to him.

11   Mishnah *Yebamot* 14:2. In strict talmudic law, divorce is a unilateral act by the husband though in cases of spousal abuse the court can force a divorce by punishing the husband "until he says, I want [to divorce]". Otherwise, the wife cannot force a divorce.

12   Nobody says that she needs a court to get a divorce.

(29c line 39) תַּנֵּי. כְּשֵׁם שֶׁהַבַּעַל פּוֹסֵק כָּךְ הָאָב פּוֹסֵק אֶלָּא שֶׁהַבַּעַל מְזַכֶּה בִּכְתָב וְהָאָב אֵינוֹ מְזַכֶּה אֶלָּא בִדְבָרִים. וּבִלְבַד דְּבָרִים שֶׁהֵן נִקְנִין בַּאֲמִירָה. הֵיךְ עֲבִידָא. גִּידוּל בְּשֵׁם רַב. כַּמָּה אַתָּה נוֹתֵן לִבְנְךָ. כָּךְ וְכָךְ. כַּמָּה אַתָּה נוֹתֵן לְבִתְּךָ. כָּךְ וְכָךְ. כֵּיוָן שֶׁקִּידְּשָׁהּ זָכַת בֵּין הַבָּנוֹת. אָמַר רִבִּי חִייָה בַּר יוֹסֵף. אַשְׁכָּח גִּידוּל רְבִיתָהּ נָמַר זְעִירְתָא. אֶלָּא כֵינִי. כַּמָּה אַתָּה נוֹתֵן לִבְנְךָ. כָּךְ וְכָךְ. כַּמָּה אַתָּה נוֹתֵן לְבִתְּךָ. כָּךְ וְכָךְ. כֵּיוָן שֶׁקִּידְּשָׁהּ זָכְתָה הַבַּת בֵּין הַבָּנוֹת וְהַבֵּן בֵּין הַבָּנִים. אָמַר רִבִּי זְעִירָא. וְהָדָא הִיא זְעִירְתָא. לֹא נִמְצָא קוֹנֶה אִשָּׁה בִּמְטַלְטְלִין בְּשָׁוֶה פְרוּטָה. וְאֵין אָדָם קוֹנֶה שְׁתֵּי נָשִׁים בְּשָׁוֶה פְרוּטָה. וּמַה בֵּין אֵין אָדָם קוֹנֶה קַרְקַע וְכַמָּה מִטַּלְטְלַיִן בְּשָׁוֶה פְרוּטָה. שֶׁכֵּן אָדָם קוֹנֶה שְׁתֵּי קַרְקָעוֹת בְּשָׁוֶה פְרוּטָה וְאֵין אָדָם קוֹנֶה שְׁתֵּי נָשִׁים בְּשָׁוֶה פְרוּטָה.

It was stated: Just as the husband decides[13], so the father decides[14]; only that the husband transfers rights in writing but the father only by speech, restricted to those things that can be acquired by speech[15]. What is that? Gidul in the name of Rav: How much are you giving to your son? Such and such. And how much are you giving to your daughter? Such and such. When he preliminarily married her[16], the daughter acquired among the daughters. Rebbi Hiyya bar Joseph said, Gidul found something large and said something small[17]! But it is as follows: How much are you giving to your son? Such and such. How much are you giving to your daughter? Such and such. When he preliminarily married her, the daughter acquired among the daughters and the son among the sons[18]. Rebbi Ze'ira said, is that something small? Does he not acquire a wife on top of movables with one *peruṭa*'s worth[19]? But nobody can acquire two wives with one *peruṭa*'s worth[20]! But cannot a person acquire real estate and several movables with one *peruṭa*'s worth[21]? For a person can acquire two pieces of real estate with one *peruṭa*'s worth, but nobody can acquire two wives with one *peruṭa*'s worth.

13 He may decide to give to his wife more than the legal minimum.

14 He decides to give his daughter a dowry. The daughters have a legal right to a dowry from the estate but not from the living father.

15 Dowries of daughters and endowments of sons are the only things that can be finalized by speech only; Babli 102a.

16 In the Babli, 102a: If the groom preliminarily married the bride immediately after the young couple was promised the money by their respective parents. The Yerushalmi has to be understood in this sense also.

17 By restricting the right of informal acquisition to the daughter.

18 This is the Babli's formulation of Rav Gidul's statement. "Among the daughters" means that if the father should die before the dowry was paid, its amount does not form part of the estate; the same holds for the son and the capital promised him.

19 The minimum amount a man has to give a woman for the preliminary marriage is one *peruṭah* (in the tradition of the House of Hillel; Mishnah *Qiddušin* 1:1). The *peruṭah* is

the smallest coin, about 2 g bronze, valued at $1/144$ or $1/192$ of a silver *denar* ($1/6$ or $1/8$ of the smallest Roman coin, the *as*). That coin disappeared with the Hasmonean kingdom; it remained as the smallest unit of value in legal theory. In rabbinic practice, *Šulḥan 'Arukh Even Ha'ezer* 27:10, the value of a *peruṭah* is half a grain of sterling silver (0.0324 g).

If the marriage of the couple is contracted by the respective parents, the groom acquires not only a wife but all that is promised him from both sides by giving one *peruṭah*. Since the *peruṭah* is the smallest unit of computation, the fact that one may acquire more than one thing with one *peruṭah* is not trivial and needs to be spelled out.

20 Mishnah *Qiddušin* 2:6. It is possible for a man to simultaneously preliminarily marry any number of women by giving something of value to one of them if she is empowered by the other women to receive the value on their behalf and if there is at least one *peruṭah* for each of them.

21 Real estate can be acquired by money and everything can be acquired with real estate (Mishnah *Qiddušin* 1:5); therefore, any number of things can be acquired by giving one *peruṭah* for real estate (cf. also *Peah*, Chapter 3, Notes 135 ff.).

(29c line 50) רִבִּי בָּא בַּר חִייָה בְשֵׁם רִבִּי יוֹחָנָן. כַּמָּה אַתָּה נוֹתֵן לִבְנָךְ. כָּךְ וְכָךְ. כַּמָּה אַתָּה נוֹתֵן לְבִתָּךְ. כָּךְ וְכָךְ. כֵּיוָן שֶׁקִּידְּשָׁהּ זֶכְתָה הַבַּת בֵּין הַבָּנוֹת וְהַבֵּן בֵּין הַבָּנִים. וּבִלְבַד מִן הַנִּישׂוּאִין הָרִאשׁוֹנִים. וַתְייָא כַּיי דָּמַר רִבִּי חֲנַנְיָא. הַמַּשִּׂיא אֶת בְּנוֹ בְבַיִת זָכָה בַּבַּיִת. וּבִלְבַד מִן הַנִּישׂוּאִין הָרִאשׁוֹנִים. תַּנֵּי רִבִּי הוֹשַׁעְיָה. זָכָת בַּמְטַלְטְלִין וְלֹא זָכָת בַּבַּיִת. וּפְלִיג. רִבִּי יִרְמִיָה בְשֵׁם רִבִּי אַבָּהוּ. תִּיפְתָּר שֶׁהָיָה אוֹצָרוֹ שֶׁלְּאָבִיב נָתוּן שָׁם. רִבִּי חִזְקִיָה בְשֵׁם רִבִּי יְהוֹשֻׁעַ בֶּן לֵוִי. לָכֵן צְרִיכָה. אֲפִילוּ שְׁאוּלִין מִן הַשּׁוּק. אָמַר רִבִּי אַבָּהוּ. אִם אָמַר לוֹ לִשְׁאֵילָה לֹא זָכָה בָהֶן. אָתָא עוֹבְדָא קוֹמֵי רִבִּי יַעֲקֹב בֵּירִבִּי בּוּן וְהוֹרֵי כְרִבִּי אַבָּהוּ. אָמַר רִבִּי זְעִירָא. עִיקָּרָא לֵית לָהּ תֵּימְלִיוֹסִים. וְרַבָּנִין בָּנִין וְסַלְקוֹן עֲלָהּ.

Rebbi Abba bar Ḥiyya in the name of Rebbi Joḥanan: "How much are you giving to your son? Such and such. How much are you giving to your daughter? Such and such. When he preliminarily married her, the daughter acquired among the daughters and the son among the sons," but only if it is a first marriage[22]. This follows what Rebbi Ḥanania said: If somebody definitively married off his son in a house, the latter acquired the house, but only if it is a first marriage[23]. Rebbi Hoshaia said, she[24] acquired movables but did not acquire the house. Do they disagree? Rebbi Jeremiah in the name of Rebbi Abbahu: Explain it that his father used it for storage[25]. Rebbi Ḥizqiah in the name of Rebbi Joshua ben Levi: It is needed in case what was stored was borrowed from the market. Rebbi Abbahu said, if he said it is loaned[26], he did not acquire it. There came a case before Rebbi Jacob ben Rebbi Abun and he instructed following Rebbi Abbahu. Rebbi Ze'ira said, essentialy this has no basis[27] but the rabbis build and add to it!

22   The waiver of the rules of acquisition explained in the previous paragraph applies only if it is the first marriage for both parties.

23   In the Babli, *Baba Batra* 144a, only if (1) the son was an adult, (2) marrying a virgin, (3) as his first wife, and (4) is the first of his children to be married. Since "house" usually means "one-room house", the father gives the house to be used by the pair as bridal chamber, with them staying there alone after all wedding guests have left.

24   Probably this sentence has to be formulated in the masculine.

25   While the newlyweds were living there alone, if the place was used as storage for produce, that is indication enough that it was intended only as a temporary dwelling place and R. Hanania will agree that the son did not acquire the house with the wife.

26   If the father tells his son that the house is a loan, not a gift, it is not a gift.

27   Greek θεμελίωσις, "basis". The acquisition of valuables by speech has no basis in the rabbinic legal system; nevertheless, it is subject to detailed rules. In the Babli, *loc. cit.*, this is called "practice lacking a reason".

(29c line 60) אִתְּ אָמַר. הָאָב פּוֹסֵק עַל יְדֵי בִתּוֹ אֲפִילוּ בוֹגֶרֶת. נִישְׁמְעִינָהּ מִן הָדָא. הָאָב פּוֹסֵק עַל יְדֵי בִתּוֹ וְלֹא אִשָּׁה עַל יְדֵי בִתָּהּ וְלֹא אָח עַל יְדֵי אֲחוֹתוֹ. שַׁנְיָיא הִיא אֲחוֹתוֹ בֵּין שֶׁהִיא נַעֲרָה בֵּין שֶׁהִיא בוֹגֶרֶת. וְכָא לֹא שַׁנְיָיא בֵּין שֶׁהִיא נַעֲרָה בֵּין שֶׁהִיא בוֹגֶרֶת. רִבִּי בָּא קַרְטִיגְנָא בָעָא. אֲפִילוּ אַחֵר. אָמְרִין. אֲפִילוּ בוֹגֶרֶת. אַחֵר. נִישְׁמְעִינָהּ מִן הָדָא. הָאָב פּוֹסֵק עַל יְדֵי בִתּוֹ. לֹא אִשָּׁה עַל יְדֵי בִתָּהּ. לֹא אָח עַל יְדֵי אֲחוֹתוֹ. כָּל־שֶׁכֵּן בּוֹגֶרֶת. אַף לְמִידַּת הַדִּין כֵּן. תֵּן בִּתְּךָ לִפְלוֹנִי וַאֲנִי אֶתֵּן לָךְ כָּךְ וְכָךְ. קַח שָׂדֶה פְלוֹנִית וַאֲנִי נוֹתֵן לָךְ כָּךְ וְכָךְ.

You say that the father decides for his daughter; even if she is an adult[28]? Let us hear from the following: The father decides for his daughter, but the mother does not decide for her daughter, nor the brother for his sister[29]. Is there a difference about his sister whether she is an adolescent or an adult? So here, there is no difference whether she is an adolescent or an adult[30]. Rebbi Abba from Carthage asked, even a third party? They said, even if she be an adult? A third party, let us hear from the following: The father decides for his daughter, but the mother does not decide for her daughter, nor the brother for his sister[31]. So much more for the adult. Also in money matters it is so: Give your daughter to X and I shall give you so-and-so much. Buy this field and I shall give you so-and-so much[32].

28 Is the promised dowry for an adult daughter due on a verbal promise if the daughter is already an adult, no longer in the father's power. Since the Babli (Note 23) requires the bride to be a virgin, it must deny the power of verbal acquisition to the adult daughter.

29 Reading of Alfassi (12:1,#384): "Neither the brother for his sister nor the mother for her daughter, even if she is underage." Mother and brother can give only in the legal forms, by money, document, or handing over.

30 Since the *baraita* formulates no age criterion, there is none.

31 If mother and brother are disqualified from informal giving, so are third parties.	32 If close relatives other than the father are excluded, then third parties in general are excluded.

(29c line 68) כֵּינֵי מַתְנִיתָא. שֶׁלֹּא הוֹסִיף לָהּ אֶלָּא בִּשְׁבִיל חִיבַּת לַיְלָה הָרִאשׁוֹן שֶׁבָּעַל. בָּעַל גֵּירְשָׁהּ וְהֶחֱזִירָהּ וַעֲדַיִין חִיבַּת לַיְלָה הָרִאשׁוֹן קַיֶּימֶת. בָּעַל מֵת וְנָפְלָה לִפְנֵי יָבָם עֲדַיִין חִיבַּת לַיְלָה הָרִאשׁוֹן קַיֶּימֶת. רִבִּי יַעֲקֹב בַּר אֲחָא רִבִּי אַלֶכְּסָא בְּשֵׁם חִזְקִיָּה. הֲלָכָה כְּרִבִּי אֶלְעָזָר בֶּן עֲזַרְיָה שֶׁאָמַר. נִתְאַלְמְנוּ אוֹ נִתְגָּרְשׁוּ מִן הָאֵירוּסִין גּוֹבָה מָאתַיִם. מִן הַנִּישּׂוּאִין גּוֹבָה אֶת הַכֹּל. רִבִּי חֲנַנְיָה אָמַר. הִילְכָתָא כְּרִבִּי אֶלְעָזָר בֶּן עֲזַרְיָה. אָמַר רִבִּי אַבַּיֵי. אָמְרוּ לְרִבִּי חֲנַנְיָה צֵא וּקְרָא. רִבִּי יוֹנָה רִבִּי זְעִירָא בְּשֵׁם רִבִּי יוֹנָתָן אָמַר. הֲלָכָה כְּרִבִּי אֶלְעָזָר בֶּן עֲזַרְיָה. רִבִּי יוֹסָה רִבִּי זְעִירָא בְּשֵׁם רִבִּי יוֹנָתָן אָמַר. אֵין הֲלָכָה כְּרִבִּי אֶלְעָזָר בֶּן עֲזַרְיָה. אָמַר רִבִּי יוֹסֵי. סִימָן הָיָה לָן דְּחִזְקִיָּה וְרִבִּי יוֹנָתָן שְׁנֵיהֶן אָמְרוּ דָבָר אֶחָד. דְּתַנֵּי. מִי שֶׁהָלַךְ בְּנוֹ לִמְדִינַת הַיָּם וְשָׁמַע עָלָיו שֶׁמֵּת וְעָמַד וְכָתַב כָּל־נְכָסָיו לְאַחֵר וְאַחַר כָּךְ בָּא בְנוֹ. מַתָּנָתוֹ קַיֶּימֶת. רִבִּי שִׁמְעוֹן בֶּן מְנַסְיָא אוֹמֵר. אֵין מַתָּנָתוֹ קַיֶּימֶת. שֶׁאִילּוּ הָיָה יוֹדֵעַ שֶׁבְּנוֹ קַיָּים לֹא הָיָה כוֹתְבָן. וְאָמַר רִבִּי יַעֲקֹב בַּר אֲחָא. הֲלָכָה כְּרִבִּי אֶלְעָזָר בֶּן עֲזַרְיָה. וְהִיא דְּרִבִּי אֶלְעָזָר בֶּן עֲזַרְיָה וְהִיא דְּרִבִּי שִׁמְעוֹן בֶּן מְנַסְיָא. וָמַר רִבִּי יַנַּאי. אָמְרוּ לְרִבִּי חֲנִינָה צֵא וּקְרָא. וְאָמַר רִבִּי יוֹסֵי בַּר זְעִירָה בְּשֵׁם רִבִּי יוֹנָתָן. אֵין הֲלָכָה כְּרִבִּי אֶלְעָזָר בֶּן עֲזַרְיָה. וְכֵן נְפַק עוֹבְדָא כְּרִבִּי אֶלְעָזָר בֶּן עֲזַרְיָה.

So is the Mishnah[33]: "Because he did only add for the love of the first night, when he had intercourse with her." If he slept with her, divorced her, and took her back[34], the love of the first night is still there. If he slept with her, died, and she became available to the levir, the love of the first night is still there[35]. Rebbi Jacob bar Aḥa, Rebbi Alexis in the name of Ḥizqiah: Practice follows Rebbi Eleazar ben Azariah who said, if they were divorced or widowed after a preliminary marriage she collects 200, after the definitive marriage she collects everything. Rebbi Ḥanania said, practice follows Rebbi Eleazar ben Azariah. Rebbi Abbai[36] said, they said to Rebbi Ḥanania, get outside to recite[37]. Rebbi Jonah, Rebbi Ze'ira in the name of Rebbi Jonathan said, practice follows Rebbi Eleazar ben Azariah. Rebbi Yosa, Rebbi Ze'ira[38] in the name of Rebbi Jonathan said, practice does not follow Rebbi Eleazar ben Azariah. Rebbi Yose said, we had a rule that Ḥizqiah and Rebbi Jonathan said the same thing. As it was stated[39]: If somebody's son went overseas and one heard that he died, [the father] went and wrote his property to somebody else, and after that, the son returned. The gift remains valid; Rebbi Simeon ben Menasia says that the gift is invalid since he would not have written the deed if he had known that his son was alive[40]. And Rebbi Jacob bar Aḥa said, practice follows Rebbi Eleazar ben Azariah, and the reason of Rebbi Eleazar ben Azariah is the reason of Rebbi Simeon ben Menasia[41]; and Rebbi Yannai said, they said to Rebbi Ḥanania, get outside to recite. And Rebbi Yose bar Ze'ira in the name of Rebbi Jonathan said, practice does not follow Rebbi Eleazar ben Azariah[42]. An actual case was judged according to Rebbi Eleazar ben Azariah[43].

33   This is a parapharase of the Mishnah, given also in the Babli, 56a. The problem of the Babli, whether the contract becomes valid by intercourse or by the possibility of intercourse, attributed there to the Galilean R. Abin, seems to have been decided in Galilee without great discussion. Cf. J. N. Epstein, מבוא לנוסח המשנה[2], p. 494, and Halakhah 2.

34   He took her back on the terms of the prior *ketubah* before he paid her for the divorce; he remains obligated for the entire sum.

35   Her claim to the entire sum is intact.

36   This name is unknown otherwise. The quote below and the parallel in the Babli (56a) show that one must read: R. Yannai.

37 In the Babli: Get out and recite your verse outside; a standard expression of disapproval.

38 The Amora quoted here cannot be R. Yose, the colleague of R. Jonah, who proves below that practice follows R. Eleazar ben Azariah. Therefore, the name quoted later, R. Yose bar Ze'ira (no relative of R. Ze'ira) seems to be the correct one, characterizing his statement as that of a very minor figure.

39 Tosephta 4:14, Babli *Baba Batra* 132a.

40 The deed is a will, executed now to become effective after the testator's death, and duly signed by two witnesses.

41 In the Babli, *loc. cit.*, Rav Naḥman, the great authority in matters of money and contracts, agrees.

42 His opinion is not counted against that of R. Jonah, head of the Academy.

43 The Babli agrees to the practice after an inconclusive debate, *Ketubot* 56a.

(fol. 29b) **משנה ב:** רִבִּי יְהוּדָה אוֹמֵר רָצָה כּוֹתֵב לִבְתוּלָה שְׁטָר שֶׁלְּמָאתַיִם וְהִיא כּוֹתֶבֶת הִתְקַבַּלְתִּי מִמָּךְ מָנֶה וּלְאַלְמָנָה מָנֶה וְהִיא כּוֹתֶבֶת הִתְקַבַּלְתִּי מִמָּךְ חֲמִשִּׁים זוּז. רִבִּי מֵאִיר אוֹמֵר. כָּל־הַפּוֹחֵת לִבְתוּלָה מִמָּאתַיִם וּלְאַלְמָנָה מִמֵּאָה הֲרֵי זוֹ בְעִילַת זְנוּת.

Mishnah 2: Rebbi Jehudah says, if he wants he writes for a virgin a contract of 200 [*zuz*] and she writes "I received 100 from you", or for a widow a mina and she writes "I received 50 from you.44" Rebbi Meïr says, anyone who diminishes [the *ketubah*] of a virgin below 200 or that of a widow below 100 is engaging in whoring copulation45.

44 Obviously the woman must agree to the smaller sum.

45 For him, the sums of 100/200 *zuz* are the absolute minimum. He admits that there are places where one does not write a *ketubah* document; this fact does not diminish the amount of *ketubah* due.

(29d line 11) **הלכה ב**: רִבִּי יְהוּדָה אוֹמֵר אִם רָצָה כּוֹתֵב כול'. מִיסְבַּר סָבַר רִבִּי יְהוּדָה. אֵין פּוֹחֲתִין לִבְתוּלָה מִמָּנֶה וּלְאַלְמָנָה מֵחֲמִשִּׁים זוּז. וְיִכְתּוֹב כֵּן מִשָּׁעָה רִאשׁוֹנָה. אֶלָּא בְּפוֹחֵת וְהוֹלֵךְ. וְיִכְתּוֹב. שֶׁנִּתְקַבַּלְתִּי מִמָּךְ כָּךְ וְכָךְ. אַשְׁכָּח תַּנֵּי בַּר קַפְּרָא. שֶׁנִּתְקַבַּלְתִּי מִמָּךְ כָּךְ וְכָךְ. אָמַר רִבִּי יוֹחָנָן. לֹא אָמַר רִבִּי יוּדָה אֶלָּא בְסוֹף. אֲבָל בַּתְּחִילָּה אַף רִבִּי יוּדָה מוֹדֶה. אֵין הוּא בַתְּחִילָּה וְאֵין הוּא בַסּוֹף. חֲבֵרַייָא בְשֵׁם רִבִּי יוֹחָנָן. עַל שֶׁלֹּא בָעַל וּמִשֶּׁבָּעַל. רִבִּי זְעִירָא בְשֵׁם רִבִּי יוֹחָנָן. עַד שֶׁלֹּא כָנַס וּמִשֶּׁכָּנַס. לֹא בָעַל וְגִירְשָׁהּ וְהֶחֱזִירָהּ הִיא כַּתְּחִילָּה הִיא בַסּוֹף.

Halakhah 2: "Rebbi Jehudah says, if he wants he writes," etc. Does Rebbi Jehudah think that the minimum for a virgin is a mina and for a widow 50 *zuz*[46]? Should he not write so from the start? But it must be a diminution afterwards[47]. Why can he not write that "I received from you such and such"? It was found that *bar Kappara* stated: "I received from you such and such[48]". Rebbi Joḥanan said: Rebbi Jehudah formulated this only for the end; but at the start, even Rebbi Jehudah agrees[47]. What is the beginning and what is the end? The colleagues in the name of R. Joḥanan: Before he had intercourse[49], and after he had intercourse. Rebbi Ze'ira in the name of R. Joḥanan: Before he took her in, and after he took her in[50]. If he did not have intercourse with her, divorced her, and took her in again; that is before and after[51].

46 Since those are the amounts he settles for.

47 R. Jehudah cannot alter the established practice that at the time of the wedding the amounts must be 200/100 *zuz*. The Babli disagrees (57a) in the name of Bar Qappara.

48 Any amount is possible if the wife agrees.

49 This is the definition of beginning.

50 "Taking in" is the ceremony of the definitive marriage; in this second version the wife can write a partial

receipt even before they sleep together.

In a different setting, the Babli (57a) quotes these two possibilities and in addition "beginning" as before the definitive marriage and "end" as after sexual relations. This is theoretical since the Babli decides that practice follows R. Meïr.

51 Since a woman divorced after the definitive marriage but before sexual relations can claim only a *ketubah* of a mina, it is at the end. But since she still is a virgin, it is the beginning. The definition of R. Ze'ira leads to the construction of a self-contradictory case; it should be rejected.

(29d line 19) וְאֵי זוֹ הִיא אִשָּׁה וְאֵי זוֹ הִיא פִּילֶגֶשׁ. רְבִּי מֵאִיר אוֹמֵר. אִשָּׁה יֵשׁ לָהּ כְּתוּבָה פִּילֶגֶשׁ אֵין לָהּ כְּתוּבָה. רְבִּי יוּדָה אוֹמֵר. אַחַת זוֹ וְאַחַת זוֹ יֵשׁ לָהּ כְּתוּבָה. אִשָּׁה יֵשׁ לָהּ כְּתוּבָה וּתְנָאֵי כְתוּבָה. פִּילֶגֶשׁ יֵשׁ לָהּ כְּתוּבָה וְאֵין לָהּ תְּנָאֵי כְתוּבָה. רְבִּי יוּדָה בְּשֵׁם רַב. זוֹ דִּבְרֵי רְבִּי מֵאִיר וְרְבִּי יְהוּדָה. אֲבָל דִּבְרֵי חֲכָמִים. נוֹשֵׂא אָדָם אִשָּׁה וּמַתְנֶה עִמָּהּ עַל מְנָת שֶׁלֹּא לְזוּנָהּ וּלְפַרְנְסָהּ. וְלֹא עוֹד אֶלָּא שֶׁתְּהֵא זוּנַתּוֹ וּמְפַרְנְסַתּוֹ וּמְלַמַּדְתּוֹ תוֹרָה. מַעֲשֶׂה בְּרְבִּי יְהוֹשֻׁעַ בְּנוֹ שֶׁל רְבִּי עֲקִיבָה שֶׁנָּשָׂא אִשָּׁה וְהִתְנָה שֶׁלֹּא לָזוּן וְשֶׁלֹּא לְפַרְנֵס. וְלֹא עוֹד אֶלָּא שֶׁתְּהֵא זוּנַתּוֹ וּמְפַרְנְסָתּוֹ וּמְלַמַּדְתּוֹ תוֹרָה. וְכֵיוָן שֶׁבָּאוּ שְׁנֵי רַעֲבוֹן וְחָלְקוּ הַנְּכָסִים בֵּינֵיהֶן הִתְחִילָה קוֹבֶלֶת עָלָיו לְחַכְמֵי יִשְׂרָאֵל. אָמַר לָהֶן. הִיא נֶאֱמֶנֶת עָלַי יוֹתֵר מִן הַכֹּל. אָמְרָה לָהֶן. בְּוַדַּאי כָּךְ הִתְנֵיתִי עִמּוֹ. אֵין אַחַר קִנְיָן כְּלוּם.

What is a wife and what is a concubine[52]? Rebbi Meïr says, a wife has a *ketubah*, a concubine has no *ketubah*[53]. Rebbi Jehudah says, both have a *ketubah*. A wife has a *ketubah* and the *ketubah* stipulations; a concubine has a *ketubah* but no *ketubah* stipulations[54]. Rav[55] Jehudah in the name of Rav: These are the opinions of Rebbi Meïr and Rebbi Jehudah. But the words of the Sages[56]: "A man may marry a woman and stipulate with her not to feed her and not to provide for her[57]. Not only that, but that she should feed and provide for him and teach him Torah[58]. It happened that

Rebbi Joshua, son of Rebbi Aqiba, married a woman and stipulated with her not to feed her and not to provide for her. Not only that, but that she should feed and provide for him and teach him Torah. But when years of famine came and they distributed the properties among themselves[59], she started complaining about him to the Sages of Israel. He[60] said to them, for me she is trustworthy more than anybody. She told them, it is true that thus I stipulated with him. [They said to her][61], nothing comes after acquisition[62]."

52 Since the institution of *pilegeš* does not exist in rabbinic practice, the question is of purely theoretical character, an inquiry into the essence of the biblical institution of legal concubine.

53 Since R. Meïr in the Mishnah forbids any marriage without a full *ketubah*, he must hold that a concubine is not married. This is the position of the Babli, *Sanhedrin* 21a, articulated by Rav. (For rabbinic practice in Medieval Spain, cf. Menaḥem ben Aaron ben Zeraḥ, צדה לדרך Part 3, Chapter 2.)

54 Since he permits any modification of the financial aspects of marriage by written mutual consent, he also admits a situation in which a female of lower social rank signs away her rights.

55 The context requires this translation.

56 Tosephta 4:7.

57 This Tosephta has two aspects. It implies that the institution of concubines has no place in rabbinic law but that the parties are free to decide on the material aspects of their marriage (while retaining the formal requirement of a *ketubah* of 200/100 zuz). It also recognizes that a woman of higher social standing can buy herself a husband on her terms. Cf. *Tosefta ki-Fshutah*, part 6, p. 244.

58 This may mean that she pays for him so he can go and study full time. However, R. Petaḥya of Regensburg reports that a daughter of the Gaon of Baghdad was a lecturer in his Academy, and the Yerushalmi looks approvingly on women's Torah study; cf. *Berakhot* 3:3, Note 137.

59 It is not clear what this means; it

could be that her family's property was distributed among the heirs and her part was no longer sufficient.

60   R. Aqiba's son said to the Sages.
61   Inserted from the Tosephta, not in the Yerushalmi text.
62   Since there are contracts written for the future, such as the *ketubah*, the execution of the contract alone does not make it valid or irrevocable. For this it needs an act of acquisition, exemplified by *Ruth* 4:7, where the acquirer (Boaz) takes his sandal and lets the seller (the redeemer) move it in front of witnesses. (In the Tosephta, the expression is קיצה "contract".) After acquisition, a contract can only be modified by a written rider agreed to by the parties.

(fol. 29b) **משנה ג:** נוֹתְנִין לִבְתוּלָה שְׁנֵים עָשָׂר חוֹדֶשׁ מִשֶּׁתְּבָעָהּ הַבַּעַל לְפַרְנֵס אֶת עַצְמָהּ. וּכְשֵׁם שֶׁנּוֹתְנִין לָאִשָּׁה כֵּן נוֹתְנִין לָאִישׁ לְפַרְנֵס אֶת עַצְמוֹ. וּלְאַלְמָנָה שְׁלֹשִׁים יוֹם. הִגִּיעַ זְמָן וְלֹא נִישְּׂאוּ אוֹכְלוֹת מִשֶּׁלּוֹ וְאוֹכְלוֹת בַּתְּרוּמָה. רִבִּי טַרְפוֹן אוֹמֵר נוֹתְנִין לָהּ הַכֹּל תְּרוּמָה. רִבִּי עֲקִיבָה אוֹמֵר מֶחֱצָה חוּלִין וּמֶחֱצָה תְּרוּמָה.

Mishnah 3: One gives a virgin twelve months from when the husband requested to marry her to provide for herself[63]. Just as one gives to the woman so one gives to the man to provide for himself[64]. And to a widow thirty days[65]. If the time has come and they are not definitively married, they eat from his [property] and may eat heave[66]. Rebbi Tarphon says, one gives her everything in heave. Rebbi Aqiba said, half profane and half heave[67].

63   To make her trousseau.
64   To look for a house and otherwise prepare for a family. The girl's family cannot force the husband into a definitive marriage before 12 months after the date of the preliminary

marriage.

65 Since she already has a trousseau.

66 If the prospective husband is a Cohen, the preliminary marriage is the act of acquisition. *Lev.* 22:11, speaking about heave, reads: "If a Cohen buy a person with his money, that person may eat it." Since the preliminary marriage is formally an acquisition by money, the bride can eat heave as soon as the groom is required to feed her. Therefore, if the delay of the wedding is his fault, the girl's family can require that he feed her after the statutory 12 months delay, and he can fulfill his obligation by providing her with heave (for which he did not pay) and which she must eat in levitic purity in her father's house.

67 As the Halakhah explains, a woman regularly has periods of impurity. R. Aqiba requires the groom to provide her with profane food for her periods of impurity; R. Tarphon, in the interpretation of the Babli, thinks that she can sell the heave and buy profane food for the money. This is a very problematic proposition since heave, for which the only possible buyers are other Cohanim, cannot fetch a price commensurate with that of profane food.

(29d line 31) **הלכה ג**: נוֹתְנִין לִבְתוּלָה שְׁנֵים עָשָׂר חוֹדֶשׁ. תַּנֵּי. הַבֶּגֶר בִּשָׁעָה שְׁנֵים עָשָׂר חוֹדֶשׁ. אָמַר רִבִּי הִילָא. תַּנֵּי תַמָּן. נוֹתְנִין לְבֶגֶר שְׁנֵים עָשָׂר חוֹדֶשׁ וְנוֹתְנִין לָהּ קִידּוּשִׁין. וּלְאַלְמָנָה שְׁלֹשִׁים יוֹם. תַּנִּינָן נוֹתְנִין לִבְתוּלָה שְׁנֵים עָשָׂר חוֹדֶשׁ וְאַתְּ אָמַר אָכֵין. רִבִּי אָבִין בְּשֵׁם רִבִּי הִילָא. לְאַחַר בּוֹגְרָהּ שְׁנֵים עָשָׂר חוֹדֶשׁ נוֹתְנִין לָהּ קִידּוּשִׁין שְׁלֹשִׁים יוֹם. עָשְׂתָה שְׁנֵים עָשָׂר חוֹדֶשׁ לִפְנֵי הָרִאשׁוֹן וְאַחַר כָּךְ בָּא הַשֵּׁנִי. אָמַר לָהּ. לֹא כְבָר הֵימַנְתִּי. יְכוֹלָה הִיא לוֹמַר. חִיבָּתוֹ עָלַי מִן הַבָּחוּר. הוּא אַלְמוֹן וְהִיא בְתוּלָה וְהוּא בָּעָא מֵיסָב. יְכוֹלָה הִיא לוֹמַר. חִיבָּתוֹ עָלַי מִן הַבָּחוּר. הוּא בָּחוּר וְהִיא אַלְמָנָה וְהִיא בָּעֲיָא מֵיסָב. יָכוֹל הוּא מֵימַר. חִיבָתָהּ עָלַי יוֹתֵר מִבְּתוּלָה. הִיא קְטַנָּה וְרוֹצָה לְהַגְדִּיל שׁוֹמְעִין לָהּ.

Halakhah 3: "One gives a virgin twelve months." It was stated[68]: Adulthood in its time is twelve months. Rebbi Hila said, state: One gives an adult twelve months and one gives her a preliminary wedding, and

HALAKHAH 3

thirty days to a widow. We have stated: "One gives a virgin twelve months," and you say so[69]? Rebbi Abin in the name of Rebbi Hila[70]: After she was an adult for twelve months one gives her the preliminary marriage and afterwards thirty days. If she spent twelve months for the first[71] and then the second one came. If he says to her, did you not wait already? She can say to him, I love you better than the young one[72]. He is a widower, she is a virgin, and he wants to definitively marry. She can say, I love you better than a bachelor[73]. If he is a bachelor and she a widow, and she wants to be definitively married. He can say, I love you better than a virgin[73]. If she is underage and wants to grow up one listens to her[74].

68 Similar texts are Tosephta 5:1, Babli 57b. It is difficult to know what "in its time" means. The Tosephta reads: "Adulthood is equivalent to a request [for marriage], twelve months." This means the same as the explanation in the Babli: "If a girl became preliminarily married after she was an adult for 12 months, one gives her 30 days as for a widow," since she had ample time to sew her trousseau. One can read the Yerushalmi in the same sense, that the time of reaching adulthood is as good as an engagement.

69 How can the time given between definitive and preliminary marriages be 30 days when it is 12 months?

70 This is the explanation in the Babli (cf. Note 68) where also the tannaitic text is close to unintelligible.

71 And for some reason, she was not married but divorced or widowed.

72 She has everything prepared but never used her trousseau. Her new fiancé wants to marry immediately and notes that she already has everything. She can say that her trousseau was good enough for the first, to whom she never was definitively married, but for him it will not be good enough and she needs more time to prepare more things. She cannot be forced be marry immediately.

73 The same kind of argument as in the preceding case. In each case,

neither party can be sued for breach of contract before the time allotted in the Mishnah has expired.

74 While the underage girl can be preliminarily married to a man by her father without her being asked, she cannot be definitively married against her will while underage. The formulation of the Babli (57b) is: One does not contract for an underage girl to be definitively married while underage but one may contract for an underage girl to be definitively married when reaching adulthood. That formulation does not require the underage girl to ask for the delay.

(29d line 42) הִגִּיעַ זְמָן וְלֹא נִישְׂאוּ אוֹכְלוֹת מִשֶּׁלּוֹ וְ[אֵינָם] אוֹכְלוֹת בַּתְּרוּמָה. מֵתוּ בַעֲלֵיהֶן אוֹכְלוֹת מִשֶּׁלּוֹ וְאוֹכְלוֹת בִּתְרוּמָה. אָמַר שְׁמוּאֵל אֲחֵי דְרִבִּי בְּרֶכְיָה. וְהוּא שֶׁשָּׁלֵם הַזְּמָן בָּרְבִיעִי. שֶׁשָּׁלֵם הַזְּמָן בַּשְּׁלִישִׁי בַּחֲמִישִׁי. רִבִּי חָמָא בַר עוּקְבָּא בְּשֵׁם רִבִּי יוֹסֵי בֵּירִבִּי חֲנִינָה וְלֵוִי תְּרֵיהוֹן אָמְרִין. נַעֲשָׂה כְמִי שֶׁחֲבָשׁוּהוּ סוֹפְרִים. אָמַר רִבִּי יְהוֹשֻׁעַ בֶּן לֵוִי. אִם הָיְתָה עִיכּוּבָהּ מֵחֲמָתוֹ נִיזּוֹנֶת מִשֶּׁלּוֹ.

When the time came and they were not definitively married, they eat from his property and [do not] eat heave. If the husbands died, they eat from his property and eat heave[75]. Samuel, the brother of Rebbi Berekhiah, said: Only if the time was up on a Wednesday[76]. What if the time was up on Tuesday or Thursday? Rebbi Ḥama bar Uqba in the name of Rebbi Yose ben Rebbi Ḥanina and Levi: Both say that he is as if the Sages had jailed him. Rebbi Joshua ben Levi said, if the delay is his fault, she is fed from his property[77].

75 The word in parenthesis is a correction by the scribe himself, in the wrong gender and probably at the wrong place. The sentence is quoted by *Tosafot*, 58a, s. v. זאפילו there it reads: הִגִּיעַ זְמָן וְלֹא נִישְׂאוּ אוֹ שֶׁמֵּתוּ בַעֲלֵיהֶן אוֹכְלוֹת מִשֶּׁלּוֹ וְאוֹכְלוֹת בִּתְרוּמָה. "When the time came and they were not definitively married or their husbands died, they eat from his property and eat heave." The next Mishnah will state that all this and the

connected difficulties are removed by later practice, that no woman married to a Cohen can eat from her husband's heave unless she is definitively married to him. The practice of the returnees from Babylonia probably should read: "When the time has come and they were not definitively married, they eat from his property and eat heave. If the husband died, they eat from his property and [do not] eat heave." The levir who is a Cohen cannot cause his prospective wife to eat heave since in contrast to his brother he has no preliminary marriage that could count as acquisition. A Cohen's widow can eat heave only if she remains a member of the priestly clan, i. e., if any descendants of her husband by her survive her husband's death. Vice versa, a Cohen's daughter married to an Israel can eat heave after her husband's death only if no descendants of her husband by her survive her husband's death.

76 "12 months after she was asked to marry" means that the virgin can request to be definitively married on the first Wednesday following the end of the twelfth month (Mishnah 1:1). Therefore, she cannot ask to be sustained by her husband before that Wednesday.

77 The court will uphold her claim to be paid back the money she spent on her own food only if the delay is the groom's fault.

(29d line 46) תַּנֵּי. רִבִּי טַרְפוֹן אוֹמֵר. נוֹתְנִין לָהּ הַכֹּל תְּרוּמָה. שֶׁהַתְּרוּמָה מְצוּיָה בְּכָל־מָקוֹם. רִבִּי עֲקִיבָה אוֹמֵר. מֶחֱצָה חוּלִּין וּמֶחֱצָה תְרוּמָה. שֶׁהַנָּשִׁים מְצוּיוֹת לְטַמֵּא טְהָרוֹת. תַּנֵּי. רַבָּן שִׁמְעוֹן בֶּן גַּמְלִיאֵל אוֹמֵר. כָּל־מָקוֹם שֶׁהִזְכִּיר תְּרוּמָה נוֹתְנִין לָהּ כִּפְלַיִים בְּחוּלִּין.

It was stated[78]: "Rebbi Ṭarphon says, one gives all heave to her, for heave is found everywhere. Rebbi Aqiba says, half profane [food] and half heave, for women frequently are impure for holy things.[79]" It was stated: "Rabban Simeon ben Gamliel says, any place, where heave is mentioned, one gives her twice the corresponding amount of profane [food][80].

78 Tosephta 5:1, Babli 58a, speaking of a Cohen's wife. It is to be noted that the complete rules of purity were fully observed for almost 200 years after the destruction of the Temple; cf. *Berakhot* 1:1, Note 3. If heave cannot be eaten, it has to be given in minute amounts ("1 kernel of grain frees an entire silo") and be destroyed; no wife can be fed with it.

79 Since she is not yet definitively married she can be presumed not to be pregnant; then she is impure every month during her menstrual period.

80 He agrees with R. Tarphon that she can be given all her food as heave but he holds that for her period of impurity she has to be given enough of the heave that she could sell a certain amount to Cohanim and buy profane food. Since there are few buyers, heave can be sold only at a large discount. Babylonian sources (Babli 58a and Tosephta) record a fourth opinion, by R. Jehudah ben Bathyra of Nisibis, that she is given $2/3$ of heave and $1/3$ in profane food, which should be enough for her total sustenance.

(fol. 29b) **משנה ד:** הַיָּבָם אֵינוֹ מַאֲכִיל בַּתְּרוּמָה. עָשְׂתָה שִׁשָּׁה חֳדָשִׁים בִּפְנֵי הַבַּעַל וְשִׁשָּׁה חֳדָשִׁים בִּפְנֵי הַיָּבָם וַאֲפִילוּ כּוּלָן בִּפְנֵי הַבַּעַל חָסֵר יוֹם אֶחָד בִּפְנֵי הַיָּבָם אוֹ כּוּלָן בִּפְנֵי הַיָּבָם חָסֵר יוֹם אֶחָד בִּפְנֵי הַבַּעַל אֵינוֹ אוֹכֶלֶת בַּתְּרוּמָה. זוֹ מִשְׁנָה רִאשׁוֹנָה. בֵּית דִּין שֶׁלְּאַחֲרֵיהֶן אָמְרוּ אֵין הָאִשָּׁה אוֹכֶלֶת בַּתְּרוּמָה עַד שֶׁתִּיכָּנֵס לַחוּפָּה.

Mishnah 4: The levir does not cause her to eat heave[81]. If she spent six months for her husband and six months for the levir, or even all the time for the husband except for one day for the levir[82], or all the time for the levir except for one day for the husband, she cannot eat heave. That is the earlier Mishnah[83]. The court in later times said that no woman eats heave unless she had been entering the bridal chamber[84].

HALAKHAH 4

81 Since he cannot acquire his sister-in-law otherwise than by sexual relations, after which she will be his wife in all respects, a woman engaged to be married by the levir is not part of his clan.

82 The moment a levir enters the picture, the earlier acquisition by the husband is suspended.

83 Both Mishnaiot 3 and 4.

84 The definitive marriage. For the original husband, no sexual act is required.

(29d line 50) **הלכה ד**: הַיָּבָם אֵינוֹ מַאֲכִיל בַּתְּרוּמָה כול׳. אָמַר רִבִּי יִרְמְיָה. תַּנֵּי תַמָּן. הַיְבָמָה כָּל־שְׁלֹשָׁה חֳדָשִׁים נִיזּוֹנֶת מִשֶּׁלְּבַעֲלָהּ. עָמַד יְבָמָהּ בַּדִּין וּבָרַח נִיזּוֹנֶת מִשֶּׁלּוֹ. חָלָה כְּמִי שֶׁבָּרַח דָּמֵי. וְהָלַךְ לוֹ לִמְדִינַת הַיָּם כְּמִי שֶׁבָּרַח. אַלְמָנָה שֶׁאָמְרָה. הֲרֵי אֲנִי מֵיגֶדֶת אַלְמְנוּתִי בְּבֵית בַּעֲלִי שׁוֹמְעִין לָהּ. רִבִּי יוֹסֵי בְּשֵׁם רִבִּי הִילָא. הָאוֹמֵר. אֵינִי חוֹלֵץ. כְּאִילּוּ אוֹמֵר. אֵינִי מְגָרֵשׁ. אָמַר רַב זַבְדָּא. הוֹרֵי רִבִּי יִצְחָק. הָאוֹמֵר. אֵינִי חוֹלֵץ. כְּאִילּוּ אוֹמֵר. אֵינִי מְגָרֵשׁ.

Halakhah 4: "The levir does not cause her to eat heave," etc. Rebbi Jeremiah said, we stated there: The sister-in-law is fed from her husband's estate all of the three months[85]. If her levir had come before the court[86] and fled, she is fed from his property[87]. If he became sick it is as if he had fled[88]. If he went overseas it is as if he had fled. If the widow said, I am bound in my widowhood to my husband's house, one listens to her[89]. Rebbi Yose in the name of Rebbi Hila: The one who says, I shall not give *ḥaliṣah*[90], is like the one who says, I shall not divorce. Rav Zabda said, Rebbi Isaac intructed that the one who says., I shall not give *ḥaliṣah*, is like the one who says, I shall not divorce.

85 The widow of a childless man cannot remarry or be freed by her levir to remarry until three months have passed since her husband's death and it has been ascertained that she is not pregnant, Mishnah *Yebamot* 4:11. Therefore she can claim her sustenance from her husband's estate like any

other widow. The same statement is in the Babli 107b, *Yebamot* 41b.

86   And he had agreed to marry his brother's widow in levirate, or to free her by *ḥaliṣah* after the end of the three months' waiting period.

87   Since he had taken responsibility for his sister-in-law, he cannot avoid his financial responsibility by his absence.

88   In the interpretation of Tosaphot, 107b, *s. v.* עמד, this rule does not apply if the levir is sick at the end of the three months and is unable to marry his sister-in-law at the first possible moment.

89   If she says that she has no desire to remarry, neither in levirate to her levir nor to any other man by *ḥaliṣah*, the heirs have to pay indefinitely for her upkeep in her husband's house.

90   He says that he wants to marry his sister-in-law; therefore, he becomes responsible for her upkeep immediately at the end of the three months' waiting period.

(29d line 56) עֲשָׂת שִׁשָּׁה חֳדָשִׁים בִּפְנֵי הַבַּעַל וְשִׁשָּׁה חֳדָשִׁים בִּפְנֵי הַיָּבָם אֵינוֹ אוֹכֶלֶת בַּתְּרוּמָה. וְלֹא סוֹף דָּבָר וֹ חֳדָשִׁים לִפְנֵי הַיָּבָם אֶלָּא אֲפִילוּ כּוּלָּם לִפְנֵי הַיָּבָם חָסֵר יוֹם אֶחָד אֵינוֹ אוֹכֶלֶת בַּתְּרוּמָה. מַתְנִיתִין לֹא כְמִשְׁנָה הָרִאשׁוֹנָה וְלֹא כְמִשְׁנָה הָאַחֲרוֹנָה אֶלָּא כְמִשְׁנָה הָאֶמְצָעִית. דְּתַנֵּי. בָּרִאשׁוֹנָה הָיוּ אוֹמְרִים. אֲרוּסָה בַת יִשְׂרָאֵל אוֹכֶלֶת בַּתְּרוּמָה. דַּהֲווֹן דָּרְשִׁין וְכֹהֵן כִּי יִקְנֶה נֶפֶשׁ קִנְיַן כַּסְפּוֹ. דְּלֹא כֵן מַה בֵּין קוֹנֶה אִשָּׁה וּבֵין קוֹנֶה שִׁפְחָה. חָזְרוּ לוֹמַר. לְאַחַר י'ב חוֹדֶשׁ לִכְשֶׁיִּתְחַיֵּיב בִּמְזוֹנוֹתֶיהָ. בֵּית דִּין שֶׁלְּאַחֲרוֹן אָמְרוּ. לְעוֹלָם אֵין הָאִשָּׁה אוֹכֶלֶת בַּתְּרוּמָה עַד שֶׁתִּיכָּנֵס לַחוּפָּה. וּכְבָר שָׁלַח רִבִּי יוֹחָנָן בֶּן בַּגְבַּג אֵצֶל רִבִּי יְהוּדָה בֶּן בָּתִירָה לִנְצִיבִין. אָמְרוּ מִשְּׁמוֹ שֶׁאֲרוּסָה בַת יִשְׂרָאֵל אוֹכֶלֶת בַּתְּרוּמָה. שָׁלַח אֶצְלוֹ וְאָמַר לוֹ. מוּחְזָק הָיִיתִי בָךְ שֶׁאַתָּה בָּקִי בְסִתְרֵי תוֹרָה. אֲפִילוּ לִדְרוֹשׁ בְּקַל וָחוֹמֶר אֵין אַתְּ יוֹדֵעַ. מַה אִם שִׁפְחָה כְנַעֲנִית שֶׁאֵין הַבִּיאָה קוֹנָה אוֹתָהּ לְהַאֲכִילָהּ בַּתְּרוּמָה הַכֶּסֶף קוֹנֶה אוֹתָהּ לְהַאֲכִילָהּ בַּתְּרוּמָה. אִשָּׁה שֶׁהַבִּיאָה קוֹנָה אוֹתָהּ לְהַאֲכִילָהּ בַּתְּרוּמָה אֵינוֹ דִּין שֶׁהַכֶּסֶף קוֹנֶה אוֹתָהּ לְהַאֲכִילָהּ בַּתְּרוּמָה. וּמָה אֶעֱשֶׂה וְהֵן אָמְרוּ. לְעוֹלָם אֵין הָאִשָּׁה אוֹכֶלֶת בַּתְּרוּמָה עַד שֶׁתִּיכָּנֵס לַחוּפָּה. וְסָמְכוּ לָהֶם מִקְרָא כְּמוֹ שֶׁנֶּאֱמַר כָּל־טָהוֹר בְּבֵיתְךָ יֹאכְלֶנָּה.

HALAKHAH 4 263

אָמַר רִבִּי יוּדָן. הֲרֵי זֶה קַל וָחוֹמֶר שֶׁיֵּשׁ עָלָיו תְּשׁוּבָה. דּוּ יָכִיל מֵימַר לֵיהּ. לֹא. אִם אָמַרְתָּ בְּשִׁפְחָה כְּנַעֲנִית שֶׁהִיא נִקְנֵית בַּחֲזָקָה תֹּאמַר בְּזוֹ שֶׁאֵינָהּ נִקְנֵית בַּחֲזָקָה. וְכָל־קַל וָחוֹמֶר שֶׁיֵּשׁ עָלָיו תְּשׁוּבָה בָּטֵל קַל וָחוֹמֶר.

"If she spent six months for her husband and six months for the levir, she cannot eat heave. Not only six months for the levir but even all the time for the levir except for one day, she cannot eat heave." The Mishna follows neither the earliest not the last Mishnah, but the intermediate development. As it was stated[91]: First, they were saying that a preliminarily married woman, daughter of an Israel, could eat heave, for they were explaining: "If a Cohen acquires a person, acquistion by money[92];" for what would be the difference between one who acquires a wife and one who acquires a slave girl[93]? They changed, to say: after twelve months, when he becomes responsible for her upkeep. The court of the later ones said: A woman never eats heave before she enters the bridal chamber[94]. [95]"Already Rebbi Joḥanan ben Bagbag sent to Rebbi Jehudah ben Bathyra[96] at Nisibis: They say in your name that the preliminarily married daughter of an Israel eats heave. He sent back the following: I had been convinced that you are knowledgeable in the secrets of the Torah, but you do not even know the rules *de minore ad majus*! Since money can acquire a Gentile slave girl to permit her to eat heave, but she cannot be acquired by sexual relations[97] to permit her to eat heave, whereas a wife can be acquired by sexual relations to permit her to eat heave[98], it is only logical that money can acquire a wife to permit her to eat heave! But what can I do? They said that no woman eats heave before she enters the bridal chamber," and they supported it by the verse[99]: "Every pure person in your household shall eat it." Rebbi

Yudan said, that is an argument *de minore ad majus* that can be reversed! Because he could say to him, since a Gentile slave girl can be acquired by active possession[100] to permit her to eat heave, what can you say about a wife who cannot be acquired by active possession? If an argument *de minore ad majus* can be reversed, the argument is invalid.

91 A similar statement is in Tosephta 5:1, where, however, the intermediate Mishnah is not mentioned. Cf. also *Terumot* 8:1, Note 9.

92 *Lev.* 22:11. The verse ends: "He shall eat [the Cohen's sacred food]". A parallel statement in the Babli, 57b.

93 The slave girl, by becoming the property of a Jew, is presumed to become Jewish by immersion in a *miqweh*. Then she has to follow all Jewish laws valid for women (only that, being unable to marry, she is permitted guiltless unmarried sex with everybody except Jewish men). By manumission she would become a full Jewish woman. While a Gentile cannot become impure by biblical standards, the immersion in the ritual bath makes her subject to all rules of purity. If her owner is a Cohen, she may eat his sacred food if in the appropriate state of ritual purity.

A wife is usually acquired in preliminary marriage, as far as criminal law is concerned, by a gift of money or its equivalent. The argument is shaky since one should mention that if the wife is acquired by a matrimonial contract or by sexual relations without a gift of money (Mishnah *Qiddušin* 1:1), there would be no reason to permit heave to the Israel woman preliminarily married to a Cohen. Nowhere do we find that the way the preliminary marriage is effected makes any difference.

94 Tosephta 5:1. However, the same Tosephta (and the Yerushalmi. *Yebamot* 4:12, Note197) mentions that in a famine, R. Tarphon (a Cohen) preliminarily married 300 women to give them access to sanctified food. This means that the "later Mishnah" has to be dated some time after the destruction of the Temple when, probably, the importance of heave for the income of Cohanim was rapidly diminishing.

95 Tosephta 5:1.

96 The leader of Babylonian Jewry in the first half of the 2nd Century C.E.

97 Being Gentile, she could be married to a Gentile by sexual relations. But sexual relations with her are forbidden to a Jew and, therefore, she cannot be acquired by a Jew through sexual relations either as a slave or a wife.

98 If preliminary and definitive marriage are enacted together in the bridal chamber without any gift of money, the woman is a wife and entitled to eat her husband's food by biblical standards.

99 *Num.* 18:11. The wife is part of the household only after the definitive marriage. The argument is rejected in *Sifry Num.* 117, since in. v. 13 a similar restriction is noted, "every pure person in your household shall eat it," and it is a generally accepted hermeneutical principle that "two consecutive restrictions mean a relaxation", in this case, that the wife may eat heave from the moment of the preliminary marriage. Therefore, the restriction to definitively married wives is purely rabbinical.

100 The word חזקה "grasping" can have two very different meanings. In legal arguments, it denotes a general assumption which generates *prima facie* evidence. In the law of real estate and slaves, it denotes the exercise of possession. For example, if an intestate person dies without heirs (e. g., a proselyte who failed to start a Jewish family), his property becomes ownerless and is up for grabs. Therefore, if somebody goes to the ownerless real estate and acts as proprietor, fencing in or harvesting a field or painting a house, he has acquired the piece of real estate by his action. Similarly, if somebody takes an ownerless slave from the estate and tells him to work on his orders, the work of the slave makes him the property of the person giving the orders. The work can be quite symbolical, such as carrying a stone for a short stretch, to qualify as חזקה and if the acquirer is a Cohen, the slave is qualified to eat heave. Therefore, the means of acquisition of slave girls and wives are only partially comparable; the ways of acquisition of a slave are not subordinated to those for a wife.

משנה ה: הַמַּקְדִּישׁ מַעֲשֵׂה יְדֵי אִשְׁתּוֹ הֲרֵי זוֹ עוֹשָׂה וְאוֹכֶלֶת. הַמּוֹתָר (fol. 29b) רִבִּי מֵאִיר אוֹמֵר הֶקְדֵּשׁ. רִבִּי יוֹחָנָן הַסַּנְדְּלָר אוֹמֵר חוּלִין.

Mishnah 5: If somebody dedicates his wife's earnings[101], she can work and sustain herself[102]. The excess, Rebbi Meïr says, is dedicated, Rebbi Johanan the Alexandrian says, it is profane[103].

101   He makes a vow that any benefit that will accrue to him from his wife's earnings shall be dedicated to some religious institution.

102   It is explained in Mishnah 6 how much a wife must work for her husband to be entitled to support. If the husband does not support her, she certainly is entitled to work and use her work for her own support. The husband cannot dedicate anything to which he has no right of possession.

103   He holds that nobody can dedicate anything before it exists; therefore the husband cannot dedicate his wife's future earnings: the vow is void.

(30a line 1) **הלכה ה:** הַמַּקְדִּישׁ מַעֲשֵׂה יְדֵי אִשְׁתּוֹ כול׳. רִבִּי מֵאִיר אוֹמֵר. הֶקְדֵּשׁ בְּשֶׁלּוֹ. וְרִבִּי יוֹחָנָן הַסַּנְדְּלָר אוֹמֵר. חוּלִין בְּשֶׁלּוֹ. רִבִּי שִׁמְעוֹן בֶּן לָקִישׁ אוֹמֵר. בְּמוֹתָר מֵה סְלָעִים פְּלִיגִין. תִּיפְתָּר בְּמַעֲלָה לָהּ מְזוֹנוֹת וְאֵינוֹ נוֹתֵן לָהּ מָעָה כֶסֶף לְצָרְכֶיהָ. וְנוֹתְנִין. אִם [אֵינוֹ][104] נוֹתְנִין לָהּ מָעָה כֶסֶף לְצָרְכֶיהָ מַעֲשֵׂה יָדֶיהָ שֶׁלָּהּ. רִבִּי יוֹחָנָן אָמַר. בְּמוֹתַר אַחַר מִיתָהּ פְּלִיגִין. דּוּ אָמַר לֵיהּ. בְּשֶׁאֵינוֹ מַעֲלֶה לָהּ מְזוֹנוֹת. אֲבָל אִם מַעֲלֶה לָהּ מְזוֹנוֹת דִּבְרֵי הַכֹּל קָדְשׁוּ. אָמַר רִבִּי זְעִירָא. תַּנֵּי תַמָּן מְסַיֵּיעַ לֵיהּ לְרִבִּי יוֹחָנָן. בַּמֶּה דְבָרִים אֲמוּרִים. בְּשֶׁאֵינוֹ מַעֲלֶה לָהּ מְזוֹנוֹת. אֲבָל אִם הָיָה מַעֲלֶה לָהּ מְזוֹנוֹת. דִּבְרֵי הַכֹּל קָדְשׁוּ. וְאֵין כָּל־מַה שֶּׁיֵּשׁ לָאִשָּׁה מְשׁוּעֲבָד לָאִישׁ לַאֲכִילַת פֵּירוֹת.

Halakhah 5: "If somebody dedicates his wife's earnings," etc. Rebbi Meïr says, it is sanctified as his property[105]. Rebbi Johanan the Alexandrian says, it is profane as his property[106]. [107]Rebbi Simeon ben Laqish said, they disagree about the excess over five tetradrachmas. He explains it in the case of one who supports his wife with food but does not give her an obolus for her needs[51], as we stated: "If he does not give her an obolus for her needs, what she earns is hers". Rebbi Joḥanan said, they disagree about the excess left after [the husband's] death; for he explains it if he does not support her with food. But if he supports her with food, everybody agrees that it became dedicated.[108] Rebbi Ze'ira said, what one states there[109] supports Rebbi Joḥanan: "When was this said? If he does not feed her. But if he feeds her, everybody agrees that it was sanctified." But is not everything a wife has subject to the husband's claim to its yield[110]?

104 From the text in *Nedarim* and the Mishnah, missing here.

105 Rebbi Meïr holds that a man means what he says (*Nazir* 2:1, 51d l. 16; Babli *Arakhin* 5a). Since he must agree with R. Joḥanan the Alexandrian and everybody else that nobody can dedicate anything that is not under his control, he will interpret the husband's vow not that he dedicates the future earnings of his wife but he dedicates her hands for what they will produce in the future. Since the hands do exist and the wife is required to work for him, the vow is valid.

106 Nobody can dedicate anything that is not under his control; the husband can appropriate his wife's work for himself as profane property.

107 The following text is from *Nedarim* 11:4, Notes 50-53. In the Babli, 57b, different but similarly sounding explanations are given in the names of the Babylonians Rav and Samuel.

108 End of the parallel in *Nedarim*.

109 In Babylonia. The *baraita* is not in the Babli.

110 In the absence of a written contract to the contrary, the husband is the administrator of the wife's property; he is paid for his efforts by the cash yield of the property (Mishnah 6:1). Therefore, while he has no property rights to his wife's excess earnings, by the *ketubah* he has a contractual interest in the increase of property generated by these earnings since such an increase could increase the cash yield which will be his.

Therefore, he should be an interested party and his vow should be recognized by both R. Meïr and R. Joḥanan the Alexandrian without restrictions. This argument is too far-fetched to merit an answer.

(30a line 9) רִבִּי שְׁמוּאֵל בַּר רַב יִצְחָק אָמַר. מַעֲשֵׂה יָדַיִם בֵּינֵיהֶן. רִבִּי מֵאִיר אוֹמֵר. מַעֲשֵׂה יָדַיִים רְאוּיִין לְקָדֵשׁ מִשָּׁעָה רִאשׁוֹנָה. רִבִּי יוֹחָנָן הַסַּנְדְּלָר אוֹמֵר. אֵין מַעֲשֵׂה יָדַיִם רְאוּיִים לְקָדֵשׁ מִשָּׁעָה רִאשׁוֹנָה. מַה שֶּׁאִירַשׁ מֵאַבָּא (הַיּוֹם)¹¹¹ מָכוּר לָךְ. מַה שֶּׁאַעֲלֶה בִמְצוּדָתִי הַיּוֹם מָכוּר לָךְ. דְּבָרָיו קַיָּימִין. רִבִּי אַבָּהוּ בְּשֵׁם רִבִּי יוֹחָנָן. בְּלֹוֶה לְתַכְרִיכֵי אָבִיו. וְהוּא שֶׁיְּהֵא חוֹלֶה אָבִיו אוֹ מְסוּכָּן. רִבִּי אַבָּהוּ בְּשֵׁם רִבִּי יוֹחָנָן. וְהוּא שֶׁיְּהֵא מְצוּדָה פְרוּסָה בְּפָנָיו. וְאָמַר רִבִּי אַבָּהוּ בְּשֵׁם רִבִּי יוֹחָנָן. אַף לְקוֹדֶשׁ לֹא קָדְשׁוּ. לָמָּה. מִפְּנֵי הַמַּחֲלוֹקֶת. רִבִּי מֵאִיר וְרִבִּי יוֹחָנָן הַסַּנְדְּלָר. אוֹמְרִים. שָׁנְיָיא הִיא הֶקְדֵּשׁ מְצוּדָה שֶׁאֵינָהּ מְצוּיָה. אָמַר רִבִּי יוֹסֵי לְרִבִּי יַעֲקֹב בַּר אָחָא. נְהִיר דַּהֲוֵיתוֹן אֳמְרִין אַתְּ וְרִבִּי יִרְמְיָה בְּשֵׁם רִבִּי שִׁמְעוֹן בֶּן לָקִישׁ. מָאן תַּנֵּי. הֶקְדֵּשׁ מְצוּדָה שֶׁאֵינָהּ מְצוּיָה. מַחֲלוֹקֶת רִבִּי מֵאִיר וְרִבִּי יוֹחָנָן הַסַּנְדְּלָר. הָיוּ רַעְיוֹן רַעְיוֹן אִית לֵיהּ לְרִבִּי שִׁמְעוֹן בֶּן לָקִישׁ.

Rebbi Samuel ben Rav Isaac said, [the status] of her earnings is between them. Rebbi Meïr says, the earnings are susceptible to be dedicated from the first moment; Rebbi Joḥanan the Alexandrian says, the earnings are not susceptible to be dedicated from the first moment¹¹². "What I shall inherit from my father (today) is sold to you, what I shall catch today in my trap is sold to you; his words are valid.¹¹³" Rebbi Abbahu in the name of Rebbi Joḥanan: If he takes out a loan for his father's burial shrouds, if his father was sick or in mortal danger¹¹⁴. Rebbi Abbahu in the name of Rebbi Joḥanan: Only if the trap was set¹¹⁵. And Rebbi Abbahu said in the name of Rebbi Joḥanan: But as a dedication it would not be sanctified. Why? Because of the disagreement of Rebbi Meïr and Rebbi Joḥanan the Alexandrian¹¹⁶. One could say, there is a difference about the dedication, because the trap is not usually successful[117]. Rebbi Yose said to Rebbi Jacob bar Aḥa: Do you remember that both you and Rebbi Jeremiah were saying in the name of Rebbi Simeon ben Laqish: Who stated about the dedication, because the trap is not usually successful? The disagreement of Rebbi Meïr and Rebbi Joḥanan the Alexandrian! Rebbi Simeon ben Laqish has many a thought[118].

111   A corrector's addition; it is found in all parallel texts, where it is necessary, but it is not clear whether the word is necessary here.

112   They cannot be dedicated before they exist.

113   Tosephta *Nedarim* 6:7, Babli *Baba Meṣi'a* 16a, *Mekhilta dR. Simeon bar Ioḥai* p. 212. In the last source, the text is a commentary on *Ex.* 22:24, which is read as: "If you extend a loan *of what you have with you* to a poor person," meaning that transactions cannot validly be made about nonexisting things (explanation by J. N. Epstein).

114   The transaction should be invalid as long as his father is still alive. The Babli, *loc. cit.*, concurs that this is a rabbinic exemption from the rules if necessary for his father's honor.

115   The selling of the expected catch is accepted as regular trading practice once the trap is set because the probability that there will be a catch is high. In the Babli, *Baba Meṣi'a* 16a/b, the transaction is validated only on an emergency basis, if otherwise the catcher would have nothing to eat. It seems that the Tosephta follows the Yerushalmi.

116   This fixes practice following R. Joḥanan the Alexandrian, that futures contracts in general cannot be enforced.. In the Babli, 59a, this is an explicit statement.

117   Even R. Meïr will agree that a contract of which both parties assume that it will not be realized is invalid. The technical term for such a contract is אַסְמַכְתָּא (Since few people used to marry with the idea that the marriage would end in divorce, some rabbinic authorities hold that pre-nuptial agreements about the consequences of a divorce are *asmakhta*; but cf. Note 226.)

118   The explanation that a

dedication of future earnings is invalid as *asmakhta* contradicts R. Simeon ben Laqish's explanation of the Mishnah, which describes a setting in which the husband has lost his rights to his wife's earnings. Why did he not explain the Mishnah simply because one cannot dedicate future earnings, the explanation accepted in the Babli? The answer is that he would agree to the Babli's explanation, except that he has another one in addition. Since the Mishnah can be explained in several ways consistent with his legal doctrines, he may choose different (parallel, not contradictory) doctrines in different situations.

(30a line 9) רִבִּי יִרְמְיָה בְּעָא. הַמַּקְדִּישׁ מַעֲשֵׂה יְדֵי עַבְדּוֹ וְהָיָה צַיָּיד מָהוּ. נִישְׁמְעִינָהּ מִן הָדָא. הַמַּקְדִּישׁ אֶת עַבְדּוֹ הוּא קוֹדֶשׁ וּמַעֲשֵׂה יָדָיו חוּלִין. מַעֲשֵׂה יְדֵי עַבְדּוֹ הוּא חוּלִין וּמַעֲשֵׂה יָדָיו הֶקְדֵּשׁ. אָמַר רִבִּי יוֹחָנָן. הַקּוֹטֵעַ יְדֵי עַבְדּוֹ שֶׁלַּחֲבֵירוֹ רַבּוֹ נוֹטֵל נִזְקוֹ צַעֲרוֹ בּוֹשְׁתּוֹ וּפִגְמוֹ וַהֲלָה יֵצֵא וְיִתְפַּרְנֵס בַּצְּדָקָה. וְהָא תַנֵּי. הַמַּקְדִּישׁ אֶת עַבְדּוֹ יוֹצֵא הוּא לְפַרְנָסָה מֵהוּ וְהַשְּׁאָר הֶקְדֵּשׁ. אָמַר רִבִּי בָּא בַּר מָמָל. לֹא עַל דַּעְתּוֹ שֶׁיָּמוּת. [ ] יוֹתֵר מִן הָעֲבָדִים. לֹא כֵן אָמַר רִבִּי יוֹחָנָן. הַקּוֹטֵעַ יְדֵי עַבְדּוֹ שֶׁלַּחֲבֵירוֹ רַבּוֹ נוֹטֵל נִזְקוֹ צַעֲרוֹ בּוֹשְׁתּוֹ וּפִגְמוֹ וַהֲלָה יֵצֵא וְיִתְפַּרְנֵס מִן הַצְּדָקָה. רַבָּנִין דְּקַיסָרִין בְּשֵׁם רִבִּי אָחָא. מְצוּוִין יִשְׂרָאֵל לְפַרְנֵס קִיטְעִין אֲפִילוּ עֲבָדִים. רִבִּי יוֹחָנָן כַּל־מַה דַּהֲוָה אָכִיל יְהִיב לְעַבְדֵּיהּ. וַהֲוָה קָרֵי עֲלוֹהִי הֲלֹא בַבֶּטֶן עוֹשֵׂנִי עָשָׂהוּ וַיְכוּנֶנּוּ בָּרֶחֶם אֶחָד.

Rebbi Jeremiah asked: If somebody dedicated his slave's earnings and the latter was a hunter, what are the rules[119]? Let us hear from the following: If somebody dedicates his slave, that one is dedicated but his earnings are profane[120]. His [slave's] earnings, he is profane and his earnings are dedicated[121]. [122]Rebbi Joḥanan said, if somebody cuts off the hands of another person's slave, that one's owner collects the payments for his injuries, his pain, his shame, and impairment but he shall go out and subsist on alms. Did we not state[123]: If somebody dedicates his slave, that one takes out his provisions but the remainder is dedicated[124]. Rebbi Abba bar Mamal said, nobody thinks that he should die[125]. [ ] more than for slaves[126]. Did not Rebbi Joḥanan say, if somebody cuts off the hands of another person's slave, that one's owner collects the payments for his damages, his pain, his shame, and impairment[127] but he shall go out and subsist on alms. The rabbis of Caesarea in the name of Rebbi Aḥa: Jews are obligated to care for amputees, even slaves.[128] Rebbi Joḥanan gave to his slave from everything he himself ate[129] and quoted for this[130]: "Did not his Maker make me in the belly and formed me likewise in a womb?"

119 If the owner expects the slave to feed himself from his catch.

120 The slave becomes Temple property, but he can use anything he catches or earns for himself without stealing dedicated property.

121 In this version, the slave cannot eat anything he catches because that immediately becomes Temple property, any profane use of which is larceny. The Tanna of this *baraita* seems to hold that an owner is not obligated to feed his slave.

122 This sentence is out of place and belongs to the discussion below.

123 Tosephta *'Arakhin* 3:8.

124 Even though the slave is not dedicated, since the owner is obligated to feed his slave one automatically interprets his dedication to mean that only the excess earnings over the slave's minimal needs are dedicated.

125 It remains open whether there is an obligation on the part of the owner to feed his slave but in any case, nobody thinks that the slave should suffer king Midas's fate that he could not eat anything that he made or earned.

126 The text is defective. The original text must have been similar to the parallel in *Baba Qama* 8:4 from a different editorial team: אָמַר רִבִּי אֲחָא. מְצֻוִּים יִשְׂרָאֵל לְפַרְנֵס בְּנֵי חוֹרִין יוֹתֵר מֵעֲבָדִים. "Rebbi Aḥa said, Jews are more obligated to provide for free persons than for slaves."

127 In *Baba Qama* 8:4 one adds: His medical costs. This means that the owner presents the bill for medical costs to the person causing the injury.

128 In *Baba Qama*: "R. Aḥa said,

Jews are more obligated to provide for amputated slaves than for whole ones." On that statement then comes the objection that R. Joḥanan shares his meat and wine with his slave.

129 His deeds do not follow his words that the owner has the right to let his slave be fed from charity. In *Baba Qama*, the answer is given that his rule is legal, his behavior moral.

130 *Job* 31:15, speaking of Job's slaves.

(fol. 29b) **משנה ו**: אֵילוּ מְלָאכוֹת שֶׁהָאִשָּׁה עוֹשָׂה לְבַעֲלָהּ טוֹחֶנֶת וְאוֹפָה וּמְכַבֶּסֶת מְבַשֶּׁלֶת וּמֵינִיקָה אֶת בְּנָהּ וּמַצַּעַת הַמִּיטָה וְעוֹשָׂה בַצֶּמֶר. הִכְנִיסָה לוֹ שִׁפְחָה אַחַת לֹא טוֹחֶנֶת וְלֹא אוֹפָה וְלֹא מְכַבֶּסֶת. שְׁתַּיִם אֵינָהּ מֵינִיקָה אֶת בְּנָהּ. שָׁלֹשׁ אֵינָהּ מַצַּעַת אֶת הַמִּיטָה וְאֵינָהּ עוֹשָׂה בַצֶּמֶר. אַרְבָּעָה יוֹשֶׁבֶת בַּקַּתֵּידְרָא. רִבִּי אֱלִיעֶזֶר אוֹמֵר אֲפִילוּ הִכְנִיסָה לוֹ מֵאָה שְׁפָחוֹת כּוֹפָהּ לַעֲשׂוֹת בַּצֶּמֶר שֶׁהַבַּטָּלָה מְבִיאָה לִידֵי זִמָּה.

Mishnah 6: These are the kinds of work a woman does for her husband: She grinds flour, bakes, launders, nurses her baby, makes his bed, and spins wool[131]. If she brought a slave girl with her[132], she does not have to grind flour, bake, and launder. Two, she does not have to nurse her baby. Three, she does not have to make his bed or spin wool. Four, she sits in a chair[133]. Rebbi Eliezer says, even if she brought him a hundred slave girls, he forces her to spin wool because indolence causes immorality.

131 The amount is determined in Mishnah 13.

132 As her dowry.

133 Greek καθέδρα "chair". "Sitting in a καθέδρα" means "sitting idle".

(30a line 32) **הלכה ו**: אֵילוּ מְלָאכוֹת שֶׁהָאִשָּׁה עוֹשָׂה לְבַעְלָהּ כול'. תַּנֵּי. שִׁבְעָא גוּפֵי מְלָאכוֹת מָנוּ וְהַשְּׁאָר לֹא צָרְכוּ חֲכָמִים לִמְנוֹתָן.

Halakhah 6: "These are the kinds of work a woman does for her husband," etc. It was stated[134]: Seven main labors did they enumerate; the rest the Sages did not need to specify[135].

134 Tosephta 5:4.
135 The Babli (61a) notes that the additional services, such as mixing the wine, a wife does even if otherwise she is "sitting in a chair".

(30a line 34) מֵינִיקָה אֶת בְּנָהּ. אָמַר רִבִּי חַגַּיי. לֹא אָמַר אֶלָּא בְּנָהּ. הָא תְאוֹמִים לֹא. וְלָמָּה אָמַר. בְּנָהּ. שֶׁלֹּא תֵנִיק בֶּן חֲבֵירָתָהּ. כְּהָדֵין דְּתַנֵּי. אֵין הָאִישׁ כּוֹפֵף אֶת אִשְׁתּוֹ שֶׁתֵּינִיק בְּנוֹ שֶׁלַּחֲבֵירוֹ וְלֹא הָאִשָּׁה כּוֹפָה אֶת בַּעְלָהּ שֶׁתֵּינִיק בֶּן חֲבֵירָתָהּ. נָדְרָה שֶׁלֹּא לְהָנִיק אֶת בְּנָהּ. בֵּית שַׁמַּי אוֹמְרִים. שׁוֹמְטִין אֶת הַדַּד מִתּוֹךְ פִּיו. וּבֵית הִלֵּל אוֹמְרִים. כּוֹפִין אוֹתָהּ. נִתְגָּרְשָׁה אֵין כּוֹפִין אוֹתָהּ. בַּמֶּה דְּבָרִים אֲמוּרִים. בִּזְמָן שֶׁאֵינוֹ מַכִּירָהּ. אֲבָל אִם הָיָה מַכִּירִין אוֹתָהּ כּוֹפִין אוֹתָהּ וְנוֹתְנִין לָהּ שְׂכָרָהּ שֶׁתֵּינִיק אֶת בְּנָהּ. כַּמָּה יְהֵא לוֹ וִיהֵא מַכִּירָהּ. רִבִּי יִרְמְיָה בְּשֵׁם רַב. שְׁלֹשָׁה חֳדָשִׁים. וַהֲוָה רִבִּי זְעִירָא מִסְתַּכֵּל בֵּיהּ. אָמַר לֵיהּ. מָה אַתְּ מִסְתַּכֵּל בִּיהּ. נֵימַר לָךְ מִן הַהִיא דִשְׁמוּאֵל. דְּאָמַר שְׁמוּאֵל. שְׁלֹשָׁה יָמִים. שְׁמוּאֵל כְּדַעְתֵּיהּ. שְׁמוּאֵל אָמַר. חַכִּים אֲנָא לְחַיָּיתָא דְיַלְדִּין לִי. רִבִּי יְהוֹשֻׁעַ בֶּן לֵוִי אָמַר. חַכִּים אֲנָא לְגָזוֹרָא דְגָזְרִין לִי. רִבִּי יוֹחָנָן אָמַר. חַכִּים אֲנָא לְנָשַׁיָּיא דְּצָבְתִין עִם אִימָּא.

"She nurses her baby." Rebbi Ḥaggai said, is says only "her baby," therefore not twins[136]. Why does it say "*her* baby"? As it was stated[137]: "A man cannot force his wife to nurse another man's child, nor can a woman force her husband to let her nurse another woman's child[138]. If she made a vow not to nurse her baby, the House of Shammai say that one removes the breast nipple from his mouth[139], but the House of Hillel say, one forces her[140]. If she was divorced[141], one cannot force her if [the baby] is not used to her, but if he is used to her one forces her[142] and pays her wages to nurse her baby." How old is the baby if he can be presumed to know her? Rebbi Jeremiah[143] in the name of Rav: Three months. But Rebbi Ze'ira was staring at him[144]. He asked him, why are you staring at me? Should I say to you following Samuel, since Samuel said, three days[145]? Samuel follows his opinion, since Samuel said, I recognized[146] the midwives who delivered me. Rebbi Joshua ben Levi said, I recognized the circumciser who circumcised me. Rebbi Johanan said, I recognized the women who kept my mother company.

136 The singular implies that the husband has to hire a wet-nurse for the second child. Alfassi (§274) quotes this rule in the name of R. Hanina.

137 Tosephta 5:5, in a different order; a partial quote in the Babli, 59b.

138 To earn money.

139 The reason of the House of Shammai is not stated. The Babli, 59b, conjectures that the vow is one "between her and him" and, therefore, it would be in the husband's power to annul the vow (cf. *Nedarim* Chapter 10). If he does not annul his wife's vow, he has to pay the wet-nurse.

140 They always hold that nobody can get rid of his obligations by a vow. The vow does not have to be annulled.

141 The obligation to nurse her baby ends with the divorce.

142 In Tosephta *Niddah* 2:5, the formulation is: If the baby recognizes his mother one may not give him to a wet-nurse since that would be a danger to his life.

143 In the Babli, this is attributed to Rav Jeremiah bar Abba, of Rav's Academy. Probably something is missing from the text since R. Jeremiah cannot really have addressed his teacher R. Ze'ira as "you".

144 "Staring at somebody" is always a sign of disapproval.

143 In the Babli, 60a, Samuel is quoted as refusing to set a time limit but to put the mother in a line-up with other women and see whether the baby recognizes her.

144 As a newborn.

HALAKHAH 6

(30a line 46) תַּנֵּי. יוֹנֵק הַתִּינוֹק וְהוֹלֵךְ עַד עֶשְׂרִים וְאַרְבָּעָה חֳדָשִׁים. מִיכָּן וָהֵילָךְ כְּיוֹנֵק שֶׁקֶץ. דִּבְרֵי רִבִּי אֱלִיעֶזֶר. וְרִבִּי יְהוֹשֻׁעַ אוֹמֵר. יוֹנֵק וְהוֹלֵךְ אֲפִילוּ אַרְבַּע וְחָמֵשׁ שָׁנִים. פֵּירַשׁ אֵין מַחֲזִירִין אוֹתוֹ. עַד אֵיכָן. רִבִּי יַעֲקֹב בַּר אָחָא רִבִּי יִרְמְיָה בְּשֵׁם רַב. מֵעֵת לָעֵת. רִבִּי חִזְקִיָּה רִבִּי אַבָּהוּ בְּשֵׁם רִבִּי יְהוֹשֻׁעַ בֶּן לֵוִי. שְׁלֹשָׁה יָמִים מֵעֵת לָעֵת. תַּנֵּי מֵעֵת לָעֵת. רִבִּי חִזְקִיָּה רַב. בַּמֶּה דְּבָרִים אֲמוּרִים. בִּזְמָן שֶׁפֵּירַשׁ מִתּוֹךְ בּוּרְיוֹ. אֲבָל אִם פֵּירַשׁ מִתּוֹךְ חוֹלְיוֹ מַחֲזִירִין אוֹתוֹ מִיָּד. בְּשֶׁאֵינוּ שֶׁלְּסַכָּנָה. אֲבָל אִם הָיָה שֶׁלְּסַכָּנָה אֲפִילוּ אַחַר כַּמָּה יָמִים מַחֲזִירִין אוֹתוֹ.

It was stated[147]: A baby suckles continuously until 24 months; after that he is as if an unclean creature would suckle, the words of Rebbi Eliezer. But Rebbi Joshua says, he suckles continuously even four or five years. If he stopped, one does not return him. How long? Rebbi Jacob bar Aha, Rebbi Jeremiah[148] in the name of Rav: From hour to hour[149]. Rebbi Ḥizqiah, Rebbi Abbahu in the name of Rebbi Joshua ben Levi: Three days from hour to hour[150]. It was stated: From hour to hour. Rebbi Hizqiyah, Rav: When has this been said? If he stopped while being healthy. But if he stopped because of sickness, one does return him. When there was no danger. But if it was because of danger, one returns him even after a number of days[151].

147 Tosephta *Niddah* 2:3, Babli 60a. In both these texts, one reads: If he stopped *after 24 months*, one does not return him. A parallel text in Yerushalmi *Niddah* 1:5, with a different tradition of names.

148 This reading is impossible since R. Jacob bar Aha is one generation before R. Jeremiah. One must read "Rav Jeremiah", the colleague and student of Rav.

149 From a certain hour one day to the same hour the next day, i. e., 24 hours.

150 In the Babli, 60a, this is attributed to the school of Samuel.

151 This argument is not mentioned in the Babli which, therefore, can be assumed to agree.

(30a line 53) הַכְנִיסָה. אָמַר רִבִּי שְׁמוּאֵל בַּר רַב יִצְחָק. לֹא סוֹף דָּבָר הִכְנִיסָה אֶלָּא אֲפִילוּ הִיא רְאוּיָה לְהַכְנִיס. כְּהָדָא דְתַנֵּי. אִשְׁתּוֹ עוֹלָה עִמּוֹ אֲבָל לֹא יוֹרֶדֶת עִמּוֹ. אַלְמָנָה וּבָנֶיהָ יוֹרְדִין אֲבָל לֹא עוֹלִין. הַפּוֹעֲלִין עוֹלִין אֲבָל לֹא יוֹרְדִין. הַבַּת לֹא עוֹלָה וְלֹא יוֹרֶדֶת. וְתַכְנִיס שִׁפְחָה לְכָל־הַדְּבָרִים. אָמַר רִבִּי חִייָה בַּר יוּדָה. מִפְּנֵי חַיִּיס שֶׁלַּשִּׁפְחָה. אָמַר רִבִּי בּוּן. עַל יְדֵי שֶׁהַדְּבָרִים הַלָּלוּ שֶׁלְּבִיזָּיוֹן לְפִיכָךְ תָּלוּ אוֹתָן בְּשִׁפְחָה. אָמַר רִבִּי יוּדָה בֵּירִבִּי בּוּן. שֶׁאֵין דֶּרֶךְ הָאִשָּׁה לִהְיוֹת יוֹשֶׁבֶת בְּטֵילָה בְּתוֹךְ בֵּיתוֹ. רַב הוּנָא אָמַר. אֲפִילוּ הִכְנִיסָה לוֹ מֵאָה שְׁפָחוֹת כּוֹפָהּ לַעֲשׂוֹת לוֹ דְבָרִים שֶׁלְּיָחִיד. מָהוּ דְבָרִים שֶׁלְּיָחִיד. סָכַת לוֹ אֶת גּוּפוֹ וּמְרְחֶצֶת לוֹ אֶת רַגְלָיו וּמוֹזֶגֶת לוֹ אֶת הַכּוֹס. לָמָּה. מִשּׁוּם שֶׁהִיא חַיֶּיבֶת לַעֲשׂוֹת לוֹ אוֹ מִשּׁוּם שֶׁאֵינָן רְאוּיִין לְהִשְׁתַּמֵּשׁ בְּשִׁפְחָה. מַה נָּפַק מִבֵּינֵיהוֹן. הִכְנִיסָה לוֹ עֲבָדִים. אִין תֵּימַר מִשּׁוּם שֶׁאֵין רְאוּיִין לְהִשְׁתַּמֵּשׁ בְּשִׁפְחָה הֲרֵי הִכְנִיסָה לוֹ עֲבָדִים. הֲוֵי לֵית טַעֲמָא מִשּׁוּם שֶׁהִיא חַיֶּיבֶת לוֹ. רִבִּי אֲבוּדַימֵי בְּצִפּוֹרִין בָּעֵי קוֹמֵי רִבִּי מָנָא. לֹא מִסְתַּבְּרָה מִשּׁוּם שֶׁהִיא חַיֶּיבֶת לוֹ. אָמַר לוֹ. אוֹף אֲנִי סָבַר כֵּן.

"If she brought". Rebbi Samuel bar Rav Isaac said, not only if she brought but even if she could have brought[152]. As it was stated: His wife ascends with him but does not descend with him[153]; a widow and her children descend but do not ascend[154]; workers ascend but do not descend[155]. The daughter neither ascends nor descends. Rebbi Ḥiyya bar Jehudah said, because one cares for the slave girl[156]. Rebbi Abun said, Because these labors are degrading, they are referred to as the slave girl's. Rebbi Judah ben Rebbi Abun said, because usually a woman does not sit aimlessly in her house[157]. Rav Huna said, even if she brought him 100 slave girls, he can force her to serve him with particular attention[158].

What are services with particular attention? She rubs his body, washes his feet, and mixes him the cup[159]. Why? Because she is obligated to do that, or because it is not appropriate to use a slave girl for these[160]? If you say because it is not appropriate to use a slave girl for these, here she brought him slaves[161]! It must be because she is obligated to do that. Rebbi Eudaimon in Sepphoris asked before Rebbi Mana: Is it not reasonable because she is obligated to do that? He said to him, that is what I am always thinking.

152 If her dowry is large enough to pay for a slave girl. In the Babli, 61a, this is a statement of R. Samuel ben Naḥmani.

153 This clause is also in the Babli (48a, 61a). It means that if the material circumstances of the husband improve, he has to provide for his wife according to his social standing; but if he loses money, he cannot reduce her standard of living below the level he provided for her at the time of the wedding.

154 They are supported from the estate and only have a claim to the lesser amount of the yield of the estate at the time of the husband's death or now. If the heirs improve the yield of the estate, the improvement is theirs (assuming zero inflation). Similarly, the claim of the daughters to a dowry is limited to 10% of the estate at the time of the father's death.

155 The standard contract for journeymen stipulates that the employer must feed the workers (Mishnah *Baba Meṣi'a* 7:1); he cannot reduce his contribution below the standard accepted at the beginning of the contract.

156 That she should not be overworked. It is difficult to see why the slave girl should be overworked with three types of work but the wife not with seven. In the Babli, 61a, this question is asked and the answer is that the slave girl also has to care for guests.

157 The other things, except grinding flour, baking, and washing, the wife does anyhow.

158 A similar statement is in the Babli, 61a.

159 In the Babli, "she mixes his cup,

makes his bed, and washes his face and feet."

160 These are intimate services; if a slave girl would perform those, the husband would start to sleep with her.

161 The Mishnah does not mention that she could have brought a male slave as dowry who could serve as the husband's valet, to free the wife from personal services.

(30a line 68) וְתָנֵי כֵן. כּוֹפָהּ לַעֲשׂוֹת בְּצֶמֶר אֲבָל לֹא בְּפִשְׁתָּן. מִפְּנֵי שֶׁהִיא מַסְרַחַת אֶת הַפֶּה וּמְשַׁלְבֶּקֶת אֶת הַשְּׂפָיוֹת.

It was stated so: He forces her to work[162] with wool, but not with flax since that causes bad breath and broadens the lips[163].

162 Following R. Eliezer.

163 In *Baba Meṣi'a* 1:5, it is stated in more general terms: He can force her to work with wool but not anything else (unless stipulated otherwise in the marriage contract) since the terms of a contractual relationship cannot be changed unilaterally. For the damage that spinning flax does to the lips, cf. the Brothers Grimm's fairy tale, *die drei Spinnerinnen*.

(fol. 29b) **משנה ז**: רַבָּן שִׁמְעוֹן בֶּן גַּמְלִיאֵל אוֹמֵר. אַף הַמַּדִּיר אֶת אִשְׁתּוֹ מִלַּעֲשׂוֹת מְלָאכָה יוֹצִיא וְיִתֵּן כְּתוּבָּה שֶׁהַבַּטָּלָה מְבִיאָה לִידֵי שְׁעָמוּם.

Mishnah 7: Rabban Simeon ben Gamliel says, also a man who by a vow forbids his wife to work must divorce her and pay her *ketubah*[164] since idleness induces mental illness.

משנה ח: הַמַּדִּיר אֶת אִשְׁתּוֹ מִתַּשְׁמִישׁ הַמִּטָּה בֵּית שַׁמַּאי אוֹמְרִים שְׁתֵּי שַׁבָּתוֹת. בֵּית הִילֵּל אוֹמְרִים שַׁבָּת אַחַת. הַתַּלְמִידִים יוֹצְאִין לְלִמּוּד תּוֹרָה שֶׁלֹּא בִּרְשׁוּת שְׁלֹשִׁים יוֹם. הַפּוֹעֲלִים שַׁבָּת אֶחָת. הָעוֹנָה הָאֲמוּרָה בַּתּוֹרָה הַטַּיָּילִין בְּכָל־יוֹם. הַפּוֹעֲלִין שְׁתַּיִם בַּשַּׁבָּת. הַחַמָּרִים אַחַת בַּשַּׁבָּת. הַגַּמָּלִין אַחַת לִשְׁלֹשִׁים יוֹם. הַסַּפָּנִין אַחַת לְשִׁשָּׁה חֳדָשִׁים דִּבְרֵי רִבִּי אֱלִיעֶזֶר.

Mishnah 8: If somebody by a vow bars his wife from sexual intercourse, the House of Shammai say two weeks, the House of Hillel say one week[165]. Students can go to study Torah for thirty days without permission[166]; journeymen one week[167]. The period mentioned in the Torah[168]: People who do not have to work every day[169], journeymen twice a week, donkey drivers once a week, camel drivers once in thirty days, sailors once in three months, the words of Rebbi Eliezer.

164 Since the divorce is his fault.

165 If he does not have his vow dissolved by that time, the wife can go to court and force a divorce with full payment of the *ketubah*.

166 Without asking his wife's permission if she married him knowing he was a student.

167 They can hire themselves out to work at another place where they cannot return to their homes every night.

168 *Ex.* 21:10, where it is spelled out that a man can take a second wife only if he does not reduce the amount of sexual activity with his first wife.

169 If a man marries a woman telling her that he is rich enough not to have to work, he is obligated to sleep with her every night and cannot later reduce this amount without the wife's consent. Similarly, a donkey driver engaged in local traffic, who is home every week, cannot change his profession to camel driver engaged in long distance caravan traffic without his wife's consent.

(30a line 71) **הלכה ח**: הַמַּדִּיר אֶת אִשְׁתּוֹ מִתַּשְׁמִישׁ הַמִּטָּה כול׳. בֵּית שַׁמַּי אוֹמְרִים. שְׁתֵּי שַׁבָּתוֹת כִּימֵי לֵידַת נְקֵיבָה. וּבֵית הִלֵּל אוֹמְרִים. שַׁבָּת אֶחָד כִּימֵי לֵידַת זָכָר אוֹ כִּימֵי נִדָּתָהּ.

Halakhah 8: "If somebody by a vow bars his wife from sexual intercourse," etc. [170]The House of Shammai say, two weeks as after the birth of a girl[171]. But the House of Hillel say one[172] week, as after the birth of a boy[173] or the days of her menstruation[174].

170 Tosephta 5:6.	in this context.
171 After the birth of a girl, the mother is forbidden intercourse for two weeks, *Lev.* 12:5. Since this is a normal occurrence in a marriage, the wife can be assumed to be able to live for two weeks without intercourse.	173 *Lev.* 12:2.
	174 *Lev.* 12:2, 15:19. Since a forced abstinence of seven days is routine in the marriage, it is reasonable to ask the wife to wait for 7 days before giving her the right to sue in court (the Babli's interpretation of the House of Hillel, 61b).
172 The masculine אֶחָד refers to שָׁבוּעַ "week", the intended meaning of שַׁבָּת	

(30a line 73) הַתַּלְמִידִים יוֹצְאִין לְתַלְמוּד תּוֹרָה שֶׁלֹּא בִרְשׁוּת בָּתֵּיהֶן שְׁלֹשִׁים יוֹם. הָא בִרְשׁוּת בָּתֵּיהֶן אֲפִילוּ כַמָּה. רִבִּי שְׁמוּאֵל בַּר נַחְמָן בְּשֵׁם רִבִּי יוֹנָתָן. וַיִּשְׁלָחֵם לְבָנוֹנָה עֲשֶׂרֶת אֲלָפִים לַחוֹדֶשׁ. אָמַר רִבִּי אָבִין. חִיבֵּב הַקָּדוֹשׁ בָּרוּךְ הוּא פְּרִיָּה וְרִבִיָּה יוֹתֵר מִבֵּית הַמִּקְדָּשׁ. מַאי טַעֲמָא. חוֹדֶשׁ יִהְיוּ בַלְּבָנוֹן וּשְׁנַיִם חֳדָשִׁים בְּבֵיתוֹ. רַב אָמַר. הַבָּאָה וְהַיּוֹצֵאת חוֹדֶשׁ בְּחוֹדֶשׁ לְכֹל חָדְשֵׁי הַשָּׁנָה.

"Students can go to study Torah for thirty days without *their wives*'[175] permission." Therefore, with permission even longer[176]. Rebbi Samuel bar Nahman in the name of Rebbi Johanan: "He sent them to the Libanon, ten thousand per month.[177]" Rebbi Abin said, the Holy One, praise to Him, preferred being fruitful and multiplying over the Temple. What is the reason? "One month they would be in Libanon, two months each in his house."[178] Rav said, "the one entering and the one leaving, month for month for all months of the year.[179]"

175 Addition to the Mishnah text.	for it and spend double the time with his wife.
176 The Babli agrees, 61b/62a.	
177 *1K.* 5:28.	179 *1Chr.* 27:1, speaking of all watches in the service of the king. The interpretation is that each watch served for six months each year, one
178 The Babli, 62a, is explicit that R. Johanan requires a student who leaves his house for study to make up	

HALAKHAH 8

month at a time. Rav will require a student to spend only one month with his wife for every month away. In the Babli, R. Johanan rejects this argument since the king's servants were well paid and absences for money-making purposes follow different rules.

(30b line 2) הָכָא אַתְּ אָמַר שַׁבָּת אֶחָד. וְכָא אַתְּ אָמַר פְּעָמַיִים בַּשַּׁבָּת. תַּנֵּי בַּר קַפְּרָא. הַפּוֹעֲלִין יוֹצְאִין לִמְלַאכְתָּן שֶׁלֹּא בִּרְשׁוּת בָּתֵּיהֶן שַׁבָּת אֶחָד.

Here you say, one week. But there, you say, twice a week[180]. Bar Qappara stated: "Journeymen can hire themselves out without their wives' permission for one week."[181]

180 The Mishnah permits journeymen to absent themselves for one week but requires them to sleep with their wives twice a week. How can the two statements be reconciled?

181 The agreement of the wife is taken for granted since she also lives off her husband's earnings. But if he is at home, she has the right to expect that he sleep with her twice a week.

(30b line 5) הָעוֹנָה הָאֲמוּרָה בַּתּוֹרָה. אִית תַּנָּיֵי תַנֵּי. שְׁאָר זֶה דֶּרֶךְ אֶרֶץ. עוֹנָה זֶה הַמָּזוֹן. אִית תַּנָּיֵי תַנֵּי. עוֹנָה זֶה דֶּרֶךְ אֶרֶץ. שְׁאָר זֶה הַמָּזוֹן. מָאן דָּמַר. שְׁאָר זֶה דֶּרֶךְ אֶרֶץ. אִישׁ אֶל כָּל־שְׁאֵר בְּשָׂרוֹ. עוֹנָה זֶה הַמָּזוֹן. וַיְעַנְּךָ וַיַּרְעִיבֶךָ. מָאן דָּמַר. שְׁאָר זֶה הַמָּזוֹן. וַיַּמְטֵר עֲלֵיהֶם כֶּעָפָר שְׁאֵר. עוֹנָה זֶה דֶּרֶךְ אֶרֶץ. אִם תְּעַנֶּה אֶת בְּנוֹתָיי. זֶה דֶּרֶךְ אֶרֶץ. רִבִּי לִיעֶזֶר בֶּן יַעֲקֹב פָּתַר קְרָייָה שְׁאֵרָהּ כְּסוּתָהּ. שֶׁתְּהֵא הַכְּסוּת לְפִי הַשְּׁאֵר. שֶׁלֹּא יִתֵּן לָהּ אֶת הַיַּלְדָּה לַזְּקֵינָה וְלֹא אֶת הַזְּקֵינָה לַיַּלְדָּה. כְּסוּתָהּ וְעוֹנָתָהּ. שֶׁתְּהֵא הַכְּסוּת לְפִי הָעוֹנָה. שֶׁלֹּא יִתֵּן שֶׁלַּקַּיִיץ בִּימוֹת הַגְּשָׁמִים וְלֹא שֶׁלַּגְּשָׁמִים בַּקַּיִיץ. מְנָא לֵיהּ מָזוֹן. מָה אִם דְּבָרִים שֶׁאֵין בָּהֶן קִיּוּם נֶפֶשׁ אֵינוֹ רַשַּׁאי לִמְנוֹעַ מִמֶּנָּה דְּבָרִים שֶׁהֵן קִיּוּם נֶפֶשׁ לֹא כָל־שֶׁכֵּן. מְנָא לָהּ עוֹנָה. מָה אִם דְּבָרִים עַד שֶׁלֹּא נִישֵּׂאת לְכָאן מִשָּׁעָה רִאשׁוֹנָה אֵינוֹ רַשַּׁאי לִמְנוֹעַ מִמֶּנָּה דְּבָרִים שֶׁנִּישֵּׂאת לְכָאן מִשָּׁעָה רִאשׁוֹנָה לֹא כָל־שֶׁכֵּן.

"The period mentioned in the Torah." [182]Some Tannaïm state[183]: שְׁאֵר that is intercourse; עוֹנָה that is food. Some Tannaïm state: עוֹנָה that is intercourse; שְׁאֵר that is food. He who said שְׁאֵר is intercourse: "No person to the שְׁאֵר of his flesh;[184]" עוֹנָה is food: "He fed you and made you hunger[185]". He who said שְׁאֵר is food: "He let rain on them שְׁאֵר like dust[186]"; עוֹנָה that is intercourse, "that you should not deprive my daughters,[187]" that refers to intercourse. Rebbi Eliezer ben Jacob explains the verse[188], "her flesh her garment", that her garment should fit her flesh, that he should not give a young woman clothes of an old woman nor an old woman clothes of a young one. "Her garment her season", that he should not give summer clothing for the rainy season nor that for the rainy season in summer. From where does he get food[189]? Since he is not permitted to withhold from her things that are not necessities of life[190], not so much more things that are necessities of life! From where does he get the obligation of periodic intercourse? Since he may not withhold from her things which do not constitute the main reason for marriage[190], so certainly he may not withhold the things which constitute the main reason for marriage!

182 In *Mekhilta dR. Ismael* (ed. Horovitz-Rabin p. 259), the first opinion is attributed to Rebbi, the second to R. Joshia; the explanation attributed here to R. Eliezer ben Jacob is there in the name of R. Jonathan. In the Babli, 47b, the first opinion is attributed to R. Eleazar or R. Eliezer, the second is anonymous; the *midrash* of R. Eliezer ben Jacob is given in his name, 48a. *Mekhilta dR. Simeon ben Ioḥai* follows the attributions of the Yerushalmi (pp. 167-168).

183 The problem is *Ex.* 21:9 which states that a man who takes an additional wife may not diminish שְׁאֵר, כְּסוּת, and עֹנָה of his first wife. The meaning of כְּסוּת "garment, covering" is clear but the meaning of the other two words is a matter of controversy. שְׁאֵר

means "flesh" but, as the verses quoted in support of different meanings show, it means both "meat" and "relative, one's flesh and blood." Note also in Accadic *šērum* "flesh", *š'r* (of a different etymology) "to go towards; to have sexual relations". The root שאר II has no connection with the usual שאר "to remain, be a remainder" (Arabic سار).

The problem with עִנָּה is that the verb ענה "to humiliate, inflict pain" in sexual context always means "to rape, to have forced intercourse" but in the verse here it has a positive meaning, the intercourse to which the wife is entitled. [Note that in Arabic, عنا means both "produce plants" (said of the earth) and "to be humiliated, captive" (from this المَوَاني "Moslem women").] From the positive meaning of עִנָּה in the verse comes the rabbinic-modern Hebrew עוֹנָה "season", used in the *midrash* of R. Eliezer ben Jacob.

184 *Lev.* 18:6: "No person to the שְׁאֵר of his flesh should come close, to uncover nakedness."

185 *Deut.* 8:3, usually translated as: "He *chastised you* and made you hunger before He fed you with the manna that neither you nor your fathers knew."

186 *Ps.* 78:27.

187 *Gen.* 31:50. "That you should not deprive my daughters nor take wives in addition to my daughters." In *Gen. rabba* 74(12), this verse is explained that (a) Bilha and Silpa also were Laban's daughters from slave women and (b) that Laban made Jacob swear that he would not deprive his daughters of intercourse during their lifetime nor take additional wives after their deaths.

188 He denies that there is a biblical command which fixes minimal amounts of sexual attention due wives. He explains *Ex.* 21:9 as exhortation rather than prescription, reading "her flesh, her garment, and her season he should not diminish".

189 How can he establish an obligation of the husband to feed his wife?

190 A new garment at least twice a year.

(30b line 17) מִמִּנְחָה שֶׁשָּׁלַח יַעֲקֹב אָבִינוּ לְעֵשָׂיו אָחִיו לָמַד רִבִּי אֱלִיעֶזֶר. שְׁשִׁילַח לוֹ כְּדֶרֶךְ הָאָרֶץ. עִזִּים מָאתַיִם וּתְיָישִׁים עֶשְׂרִים חַד לַעֲשָׂרָה. רְחֵלִים מָאתַיִם וְאֵילִים עֶשְׂרִים חַד לַעֲשָׂרָה. גְּמַלִּים מֵינִיקוֹת וּבְנֵיהֶם שְׁלֹשִׁים. אָמַר רִבִּי

בְּרָכְיָה. הֵן עַל יְדֵי שֶׁהוּא צָנוּעַ בְּתַשְׁמִישׁוֹ לְפִיכָךְ לֹא פִירְסְמוֹ הַכָּתוּב. פָּרוֹת
אַרְבָּעִים וּפָרִים עֲשָׂרָה. חַד לְאַרְבַּע. דְּאִינּוּן לָעֲיֵי. אֲתוֹנוֹת עֶשְׂרִים וַעְיָרִים
עֲשָׂרָה חַד לִתְרֵי. דְּאִינּוּן לָעֲיֵי.

Rebbi Eliezer[191] inferred from the gift which Jacob had sent to his brother Esaw, for he sent him according to copulations. "200 she-goats and 20 he-goats," one for ten; "200 ewes and 20 rams," one for ten[192]. "Nursing camels and their sons 30." Rebbi Berekhiah said, because it is decent in his sexual behavior did the verse not publicize[193]. "40 cows and ten bulls," one for four since they are tired[194]; "20 she-donkeys and ten he-donkeys," one for two since they are tired.

191 His list of prescribed minimal frequencies of intercourse is based on the occupation of the male. The same argument is given in *Gen. rabba* 76(6); it is reproduced in Rashi's Commentary to *Gen.* 32:15-16.

192 One male can satisfy 10 females since it has nothing to do except grazing and copulating.

193 In *Gen. rabba* 76(6), R. Berekhiah in the name of Rabban Simeon ben Gamliel implies that 30 males (בנאים "builders") accompanied the 30 females.

194 Cattle was used extensively for ploughing and drawing agricultural implements.

(30b line 22) רִבִּי יִרְמְיָה בְּעָא. אִילֵּין תַּלְמִידֵי חֲכָמִים לֹא מִסְתַּבְּרָא מֵיעַבְדִּינוֹן
בְּטֵילִין. אָמַר רִבִּי מָנָא. לֹא מִסְתַּבְּרָא דְּלָא כְּאַסְפּוֹן שֶׁהֵן יְגֵעִין יוֹתֵר. רַב
אָמַר. אוֹכֶלֶת עִמּוֹ מִלֵּילֵי שַׁבָּת לְלֵילֵי שַׁבָּת. בִּלְשׁוֹן נְקִיָּה.

Rebbi Jeremiah asked: Is it reasonable to consider scholars like those who do not work[195]? Rebbi Mana said, would it not be more reasonable to compare them to sailors[196] since they exert themselves harder? Rav said, "she eats with him every Friday night"[197], in clean language[198].

196 Who have to sleep with their wives only once every six months.

197 Mishnah 5:13. A man who does not live with his wife but supports her financially through an intermediary nevertheless has to sleep with her every Friday night (unless he actually is away as in the cases enumerated in the Mishnah). Therefore, the scholar has to sleep with his wife at least every Friday night.

198 "Eating" is a common metaphor for sexual relations; cf. *Gen.* 39:6, *Prov.* 30:20.

(fol. 29c) **משנה ט:** הַמּוֹרֶדֶת עַל בַּעֲלָהּ פּוֹחֲתִין לָהּ מִכְּתוּבָּתָהּ שִׁבְעָה דֵינָרִים בַּשַּׁבָּת. רְבִּי יְהוּדָה אוֹמֵר. שִׁבְעָה טְרָפָּעִיקִין.

Mishnah 9: If a woman revolts[199] against her husband, one[200] reduces her *ketubah* by seven denars a week; Rebbi Jehudah says, by seven *tropaïkes*[201].

משנה י: עַד אֵימָתַי הוּא פּוֹחֵת. עַד כְּנֶגֶד כְּתוּבָּתָהּ. רְבִּי יוֹסֵי אוֹמֵר. לְעוֹלָם הוּא פּוֹחֵת וְהוֹלֵךְ שֶׁמָּא תִיפּוֹל לָהּ יְרוּשָׁה מִמָּקוֹם אַחֵר יִגְבֶּה אוֹתָהּ מִמֶּנָּה. וְכֵן הַמּוֹרֵד עַל אִשְׁתּוֹ מוֹסִיפִין לָהּ עַל כְּתוּבָּתָהּ שְׁלֹשָׁה דֵינָרִין בַּשַּׁבָּת. רְבִּי יְהוּדָה אוֹמֵר. שְׁלֹשָׁה טְרָפָּעִיקִין.

Mishnah 10: For how long does one reduce? Up to the amount of her *ketubah*[202]. Rebbi Yose says, he continues to reduce[203], for maybe an inheritance will come to her from outside and he would be able to collect from it. Similarly, if the husband revolts against his wife, one adds to her *ketubah* three denars a week; Rebbi Jehudah says three *tropaïkes*.

199 While one could read the Mishnah as speaking of a woman refusing any of the work enumerated in Mishnah 6, from the Halakhah it seems that one speaks only of a woman refusing sexual relations with her husband. (This remains a matter of dispute in the Babli, 63a/b.)

200 The court, following the husband's complaint.

201 Late classical Greek τροπαϊκόν, τό, "a half denarius" defined in the Babli (64a) as στατήρ (name introduced by Alexander the Great for a gold coin but used in later antiquity for silver didrachmas of varying standards, i. e., half a *sela*.) The name τροπαϊκόν was given to coins depicting a trophy (τροπαίον); in the Roman Empire it was identified with the *victoriatus (nummus)*, a small silver coin stamped with the image of Victoria, goddess of victory; declared by Varro to be equal to the *quinarius argenteus*, one-half of a *denarius argenteus*. This is the meaning used here.

202 Then the court will force the husband to divorce his wife without payment of a *ketubah*.

203 The husband cannot be forced to divorce his wife.

(30b line 27) **הלכה י**: עַד אֵימָתַי הוּא פּוֹחֵת עַד כְּנֶגֶד כְּתוּבָּתָהּ כול'. הָכָא אַתְּ מַר שִׁבְעָה. וְהָכָא אַתְּ מַר שְׁלֹשָׁה. אָמַר רִבִּי יוֹסֵי בְּרִבִּי חֲנִינָא. הִיא עַל יְדֵי שֶׁהִיא חַיֶּיבֶת לוֹ שֶׁבַע הוּא פּוֹחֵת שֶׁבַע. וְהוּא עַל יְדֵי שֶׁהוּא חַיָּיב לָהּ שְׁלֹשָׁה הוּא מוֹסִיף לָהּ שְׁלֹשָׁה. הַגַּע עַצְמָךְ שֶׁהִכְנִיסָה לוֹ עֲבָדִים הֲרֵי אֵינָהּ חַיֶּיבֶת לוֹ כְּלוּם. הַגַּע עַצְמָךְ שֶׁהִתְנָה עִמָּהּ לֹא שְׁאֵר וְלֹא כְסוּת וְלֹא עוֹנָה הֲרֵי אֵינוֹ חַיָּיב לָהּ כְּלוּם. מַאי כְדוֹן. כֵּיי דָּמַר רִבִּי יוֹחָנָן. צַעֲרוֹ שֶׁלָּאִישׁ מְרוּבֶּה יוֹתֵר מִן הָאִשָּׁה. הָדָא הוּא דִכְתִיב וִיהִי כִּי הֵצִיקָה לוֹ בִדְבָרֶיהָ כָּל־הַיָּמִים וַתְּאַלְצֵהוּ. מַהוּ וַתְּאַלְצֵהוּ. אָמַר רִבִּי יִצְחָק בַּר לָעְזָר. שֶׁהָיְתָה שׁוֹמֶטֶת עַצְמָהּ מִתַּחְתָּיו. וַתִּקְצַר נַפְשׁוֹ לָמוּת. הוּא קָצְרָה נַפְשׁוֹ לָמוּת וְהִיא לֹא קָצְרָה נַפְשׁוֹ לָמוּת. וְיֵשׁ אוֹמְרִים. שֶׁהָיְתָה עוֹשָׂה צוֹרְכָהּ בְּאַחֵרִים. כָּל־שֶׁכֵּן דְּתָבַע. דְּאָמַר רִבִּי נַחְמָן בְּשֵׁם רִבִּי נַחְמָן. הָאֵבֶר הַזֶּה בָּאָדָם הַרְעִיבָתוֹ הִשְׂבִּעַתוֹ. הִשְׂבִּעָתוֹ הַרְעִיבָתוֹ.

Halakhah 10: "For how long does one reduce? Up to the amount of her *ketubah*", etc. [204]Here you say seven, and there you say three? Rebbi Yose ben Rebbi Ḥanina said, since she is obligated for seven[205], he deducts seven; he, since he is obligated for three[206], has to add three. Think of it, if she brought him slaves, she is not obligated for anything! Think of it, if he stipulated [that he is not obligated for] either *šěʿēr*, or dress, or *ʿonāh*[207], he is not obligated for anything! What is it? Following Rebbi Johanan, that the suffering of the male[208] is greater than that of the female. That is what is written[209]: "It was when she had nagged him day after day and pressured him." What means "and pressured him"? Rebbi Isaac ben Eleazar[210] said, that she slipped away from under him. "He felt badly, to die". *He* felt badly, ready to die, but she did not feel badly, to die. But some say that she fulfilled her needs with others. So much more she should have wanted[211], since Rebbi Nahman said in the name of Rebbi Nahman: This human limb, if you starved it you satisfied it, if you satisfied it you starved it.

204 A shortened version of the paragraph is in *Gen. rabba* 52(13), with most of the attribution of names omitted.

205 The 7 types of work enumerated in Mishnah 6.

206 The obligations enumerated in *Ex.* 21:9, whatever they mean.

207 While in general we hold (following R. Jehudah) that in money matters biblical rules are only default options which can be changed or eliminated by contract, in non-monetary matters one usually holds that biblical rules are prescriptive and cannot be abolished. The Yerushalmi here considers sexual intercourse a money matter since the Mishnah gives monetary value to the refusal of intercourse. This argument, which is against all principles of the Babli in the usual rabbinic interpretation, will be important for the last statement of the Halakhah.

In any case, the arguments given here show that the explanation cannot be the correct one (even though it is quoted by Tosaphot, 63a *s. v.* מותחין, as *the* opinion of the Yerushalmi. Tosaphot do not attribute the statement to R. Yose ben R. Hanina, even though the latter is also quoted in the Babli, 63a, representing the opinion that "revolting" refers to any of the mutual obligations in marriage). One must agree that the Mishnah speaks only of the case that one partner refuses sexual activity with the other. The Babli leaves the question open as to which interpretation is the correct one.

208 If deprived of sexual fulfillment.

209 *Jud.* 16:16, speaking of Delilah and Simson.

210 In the Babli, *Soṭah* 9b, in a slightly more graphic description, "R. Isaac in the name of Rebbi Ammi" or something similar.

211 This is a rather weak argument, that Delilah could not have slept with other men since then she would also have wanted to sleep more with Simson, in view of the enormous sum of money promised her by the Philistine princes. The argument of R. Naḥman in the name of a different R. Naḥman is in the Babli (*Sanhedrin* 107a) in the name of R. Jehudah.

(30b line 39) וּכְרַבִּי אֶלְעָזָר עַד כַּמָּה הוּא פּוֹחֵת. נִישְׁמְעִינָהּ מִן הָדָא. תַּנֵּי רַבִּי חִיָּיה. אֲרוּסָה וְחוֹלָה נִדָּה וְשׁוֹמֶרֶת יָבָם כּוֹתְבִין לָהּ אִיגֶּרֶת מֶרֶד עַל בַּעֲלָהּ. מָה אֲנַן קַיָּימִין. אִם בְּשֶׁמֶּרְדָה עָלָיו וְהִיא נִדָּה. הַתּוֹרָה הַמְרִדָּתָהּ עָלָיו. אֶלָּא כֵן אֲנַן קַיָּימִין. שֶׁמֶּרְדָה עָלָיו עַד שֶׁלֹּא בָּאָת נִידָּה בְּיָדָהּ וּבָאת לְנִידָּהּ. הֲרֵי אֵינָהּ רְאוּיָה לִמְרוֹד וְאַתְּ אָמַר כּוֹתְבִין וְכָא פּוֹחֵת. מַה מִיפָחוֹת מִפָּךְ פְּרָנוֹן דִּידָהּ. נִישְׁמְעִינָהּ מִן הָדָא. רַבִּי יוֹסֵי אוֹמֵר. לְעוֹלָם הוּא פּוֹחֵת וְהוֹלֵךְ. שֶׁמָּא תִפּוֹל לָהּ יְרוּשָׁה מִמָּקוֹם אַחֵר. וְיַחֲזוֹר וְיִגְבֶּה מִמֶּנָּה. לֹא אָמַר אֶלָּא יְרוּשָׁה. דָּבָר שֶׁאֵינוּ מָצוּי. הָדָא אָמְרָה לִפְחוֹת מִפָּךְ פְּרָנוֹן דִּידָהּ פּוֹחֵת. רַבִּי זְעִירָא בְּשֵׁם שְׁמוּאֵל. כּוֹתְבִין אִיגֶּרֶת מֶרֶד עַל אֲרוּסָה. וְאֵין כּוֹתְבִין אִיגֶּרֶת מֶרֶד עַל שׁוֹמֶרֶת יָבָם. וְהָתַנֵּי רַבִּי חִיָּיה. נִידָּה וְחוֹלָה אֲרוּסָה וְשׁוֹמֶרֶת יָבָם כּוֹתְבִין לָהּ אִיגֶּרֶת מֶרֶד עַל כְּתוּבָּתָהּ. כָּאן בְּמִשְׁנָה הָרִאשׁוֹנָה כָּאן בְּמִשְׁנָה הָאַחֲרוֹנָה. אָמַר רַבִּי יוֹסֵי בַּר בּוּן. אֲפִילוּ תֵימַר כָּאן כְּמִשְׁנָה אַחֲרוֹנָה. בֵּית דִּין שֶׁאַחֲרֵיהֶן. מַתִּירִין בָּהּ אַרְבַּע שַׁבָּתוֹת וְהִיא שׂוֹבֶרֶת כְּתוּבָּתָהּ וְיוֹצְאָה.

Following Rebbi Eliezer[212], how far can he deduct? Let us hear from the following[213]: Rebbi Ḥiyya stated: One writes a bill of rebellion for the husband[214] of a preliminarily married woman[215], or a sick one, a menstruating woman or one who is waiting for her levir. Where do we hold? If she rebelled against him when she was having her period, the Torah made her rebel against him[216]! But we must hold that she rebelled against him before she had her period and now she has it. At that moment she would not be able to rebel but you say one writes, therefore one also deducts[217]. From where does one deduct? From the additions to her *ketubah*[218]. Let us hear from the following: "Rebbi Yose says, he continues to reduce, for maybe an inheritance will come to her from outside and he would be able to collect from it." He mentioned only inheritance, which is infrequent. That means he deducts from the additions to he *ketubah*. [219]Rebbi Ze'ira in the name of Samuel: One writes a bill of rebellion for a preliminarily married woman, but one does not write a bill of rebellion for one who is waiting for her levir[220]. But did not Rebbi Hiyya state that one writes a bill of rebellion on the *ketubah* of a menstruating woman or a sick one, a preliminarily married woman or one who is waiting for her levir? There, according to the first Mishnah, here according to the later Mishnah[221]. Rebbi Yose bar Abun said, even if you say according to the later Mishnah, [222]"the later Court [instituted that] one warns her for four weeks, then she writes a receipt for her *ketubah* and leaves[223]."

212 Who in the Mishnah held the wife of a sailor to one sex act every six months. If she refuses sex with her husband, does she lose 7 denars every week or every six months?

213 In a somewhat different formulation, Tosephta 5:7, Babli 63a, 64a.

214 The expression על בעלה is uncommon. Although it can be explained as "for her husband's benefit", probably it is a copyist's error for על כתובתה mentioned in the quote of the Tosephta later in this paragraph.

215 Who now is forbidden to sleep with her husband but who made it clear that she will refuse sex with him when definitely married. The Babli, 63a, explains that she is inflicting pain on the husband since "one cannot compare one who has bread in his basket to one who has no bread in his basket", i. e., one who is assured of a sexual partner after time. The same argument is to be assumed for the woman being temporarily disabled by her period.

216 Since sexual relations with her are forbidden, *Lev.* 18:19.

217 Therefore, the sailor's wife loses money every week, not every three months.

218 Greek τά παράφερνα, "additions to the dowry which the bride brings". This corresponds to תּוֹסֶפֶת כְּתוּבָּה, the amounts the husband promises his wife for her dowry over and above the legal minimum of 200/100 *zuz* (cf. Mishnah 6:3). In this opinion, one forces the husband to divorce his wife after the additions to the dowry were written down.

219 From here on, a parallel but different text is in the Babli, 64a.

220 Since she always can receive *ḥaliṣah* and leave the family.

221 Mishnah *Bekhorot* 1:7, that in earlier times levirate marriage was preferred over *ḥaliṣah*, so that the woman refusing her levir was inflicting pain on him, but today *ḥaliṣah* is preferred and in refusing her levir the woman is acting correctly. Cf. *Yebamot* 12:7, Note 140.

222 Different formulations in Tosephta 5:6, Babli 63b.

223 I. e., she confirms in writing that her former husband does not owe her any money; then she can claim a bill of divorce from him.

(30b line 53) רִבִּי חֲנִינָה בְּשֵׁם רִבִּי יִשְׁמָעֵאל בֵּירִבִּי יֹסֵא. הַיּוֹצְאָה מִשּׁוּם שֵׁם רַע אֵין לָהּ בְּלָיוֹת. מוֹרֶדֶת יֵשׁ לָהּ. רִבִּי סִימוֹן בְּשֵׁם רִבִּי יְהוֹשֻׁעַ בֶּן לֵוִי. הַמּוֹרֶדֶת וְהַיּוֹצֵאת מִשּׁוּם שֵׁם רַע אֵין לָהּ לֹא מְזוֹנוֹת וְלֹא בְלָיוֹת.

Rebbi Ḥanina in the name of Rebbi Ismael ben Rebbi Yose: A wife who leaves because of a bad reputation[224] has no rags[225]; the rebellious one has rags. Rebbi Simon in the name of Rebbi Joshua ben Levi: The rebellious one and the one who leaves because of a bad reputation can claim neither sustenance nor rags.

224 A woman whom her husband divorces without paying the *ketubah* since he can produce evidence of unfaithfulness of his wife even though it does not add up to formal legal proof (which could be produced only by the testimony of two eye witnesses to the illicit copulation.)

225 If the value of the garments she brought into the marriage was determined and written into the *ketubah* document as monetary obligation of the husband. If the divorce is for cause, the husband does not have to pay. It is stated here that in this case, even if the garments still exist at the time of the divorce, the divorcee cannot take them; they remain the husband's property. The Babli, 101b, emphatically disagrees.

(30b line 53) אָמַר רִבִּי יוֹסֵה. אִילֵּין דְּכָתְבִין. אִין שְׂנָא אִין שְׂנָאת. תְּנָיֵי מָמוֹן. וּתְנָיִין קַייָמִין.

[226]Rebbi Yose said: Those who write: "If he hates, if she hates", that is a monetary condition and these conditions are valid[227].

226 This sentence has been discussed in great detail by M. A. Friedman, *Jewish Marriage in Palestine, A Cairo Geniza Study*, Tel-Aviv and New York 1980, vol. 1, Chapter V,A: The Wife's Right to Demand Termination of the Marriage, pp. 312-346.

The stipulation referred to is quoted in part in Halakhah 7:7, Note 96. The full text has been recovered by Friedman (*loc. cit.*, pp. 328-329) from Geniza *ketubot*: "If X, the groom, hates this Y, does not desire her, and wants to separate from her, he shall pay all that is written and specified in this marriage contract, completely. And if this Y hates this X, her husband, and desires to leave his home, she shall lose her *ketubah* money, and she shall not take anything but only that which she brought from her father's house and she shall go out by the mouth of the court (עַל פֶּם בֵּית דִּינָה) and with the consent of our masters, the Sages."

The sentence about the husband hating his wife does not bring anything new. The sentence about the wife hating the husband states first that the husband does not have to pay the promised *ketubah* sum, then that she takes the rags with her (following R.

Ismael ben R. Yose in the preceding paragraph), and, finally, that she is to be divorced "by the mouth of the court," i. e., that the court will direct the husband to divorce his wife. Even though biblical law, as interpreted by all Jewish sects, does grant the husband the exclusive power to divorce, to the exclusion of any right of the wife to force a divorce, R. Yose (the Amora) holds that if the divorce is forced as consequence of a monetary settlement, the stipulation regards monetary, not religious, obligations and is enforceable in court.

The essence of this prenuptial agreement, which allows a woman to buy her freedom from an intolerable marriage, was adopted in Babylonia by the Saboraim Rav Rabba and Mar Rav Huna as a *taqqanah*, a rabbinic ordinance, which instructed the husband to divorce his rebellious wife while granting him the monetary advantages of the Yerushalmi agreement. This ordinance was in fact disestablished by R. Asher ben Iehiel, *Rosh*, in the 14th Century, when he interpreted the rule as a recommendation, not obligatory on the husband. Cf. I. Szczepansky, The *Takkanot* of Israel, Jerusalem-New York; Vol. 3, Chapter 13 (1992) (Hebrew). The dependency of the Saboraïm on the Yerushalmi is studied by Dr. Eliahu Rahamim Ziani, רבנן סבוראי וכללי ההלכה, Haifa 1992.

227 In the Babli, this is asserted as R. Jehudah's opinion: *Qiddušin* 19b. In the Yerushalmi it is a generally accepted principle transmitted anonymously: Below 9:1 (32d l. 51); *Baba meṣi'a* 7:10 (11c l. 11), *Baba batra* 8:6 (16b l. 28), 8:8 (16c l. 37).

(fol. 29c) **משנה יא:** הַמַּשְׁרֶה אֶת אִשְׁתּוֹ עַל יְדֵי שָׁלִישׁ לֹא יִפְחוֹת לָהּ מִקַּבַּיִים חִיטִּין אוֹ מֵאַרְבָּעָה קַבִּין שְׂעוֹרִין. אָמַר רִבִּי יוֹסֵי לֹא פָּסַק לָהּ שְׂעוֹרִים אֶלָּא רִבִּי יִשְׁמָעֵאל שֶׁהָיָה סָמוּךְ לֶאֱדוֹם.

Mishnah 11: If somebody provides for his wife through a third party, he cannot give her less that two *qab*[228] of wheat or four *qab* of barley.

Rebbi Yose said, only Rebbi Ismael assigned her barley, becaused he lived in proximity of Idumea[229].

228 One sixth of a *seah*, about 2.17 liters. One speaks here of grain, delivered per week.

229 The Babli, 64b, reads this sentence as meaning that only R. Ismael requires that the quantity of barley be double that of wheat. There is no reason to assume this interpretation for the Yerushalmi; it seems that R. Yose forbids a husband to give his wife barley except in regions in which wheat is not cultivated.

(30b line 58) **הלכה יא:** הַמְפַרְנֵס אֶת אִשְׁתּוֹ עַל יְדֵי שָׁלִישׁ כול׳. מָהוּ סָמוּךְ לֶאֱדוֹם. לִדְרוֹמָהּ.

Halakhah 11: "If somebody provides for his wife through a third party," etc. What is "in proximity of Idumea"? In the South[230].

230 It is known that R. Ismael, the student of R. Joshua, lived in the South but it is not known what the definition of "South" is, whether in the mountains South of Hebron or in the Southern plain near Ascalon. He probably did not live in *Kefar Aziz*, cf. *Kilaim*, Chapter 6, Note 42. Idumea in Second Temple times was the Negev.

(fol. 29c) **משנה יב:** נוֹתֵן לָהּ חֲצִי קַב קִיטְנִית וַחֲצִי לוֹג שֶׁמֶן. וְקַב גְּרוֹגְרוֹת אוֹ מָנֶה דְבֵילָה וְאִם אֵין לוֹ פּוֹסֵק לְעוּמָּתָן פֵּירוֹת מִמָּקוֹם אַחֵר. וְנוֹתְנִין לָהּ מִטָּה וּמַפֵּץ וְאִם אֵין לוֹ מִיטָה מַפֵּץ מַחֲצֶלֶת. וְנוֹתְנִין לָהּ כִּפָּה לְרֹאשָׁהּ וַחֲגוֹר לְמָתְנֶיהָ וּמִנְעָל מִמּוֹעֵד לְמוֹעֵד. וְכֵלִים שֶׁלַּחֲמִשִּׁים זוּז מִשָּׁנָה לְשָׁנָה. וְאֵין נוֹתְנִין לָהּ לֹא חֲדָשִׁים בִּימוֹת הַחַמָּה וְלֹא שְׁחָקִים בִּימוֹת הַגְּשָׁמִים. אֲבָל נוֹתְנִין לָהּ כֵּלִים שֶׁלַּחֲמִשִּׁים זוּז בִּימוֹת הַגְּשָׁמִים וְהִיא מִתְכַּסָּה בְּלַאוֹתֵיהֶן בִּימוֹת הַחַמָּה וְהַשְּׁחָקִין שֶׁלָּהּ.

Mishnah 12: One gives her half a *qab* of legumes[231] and half a *qab* of oil[232], a *qab* of dried figs or a mina[233] of fig cake; if there are none available one finds her fruit from other places. Also one gives her a bed and a mat; if he has no bed, a mat and a rug[234]. Also, one gives her a cap for her head[235] and a belt for her loins, and shoes every holiday, and garments worth 50 tetradrachmas every year. One does not give her new ones in the summer or worn ones in the winter, but one gives her garments worth 50 tetradrachmas in the winter and she covers herself with the worn garments[236] in the summer; and the rags are hers[237].

231 Peas or beans.
232 Olive oil.
233 The *mina* as a weight is 60 *šeqel*.
234 To sleep on it.
235 Since a married woman may not be seen in public without a bonnet on her head. Bed, mat, cap, and belt are once-a-lifetime gifts.
236 Which in the meantime became summer weights by constant use.
237 The husband has no right to require her to hand over last year's used garments before giving her the new ones.

(30b line 59) **הלכה יב**: נוֹתֵן לָהּ חֲצִי קַב קִיטְנִית וַחֲצִי לוֹג שֶׁמֶן כול׳. אָמַר רִבִּי מָנָא. מָנֶה וְאַרְבַּע רִיטְלִין. נוֹתֵן לָהּ כַּר גֵּר וּפְתִילָה כּוֹס וְחָבִית וּקְדֵירָה. רִבִּי יוֹסֵי אָמַר. כַּר אֵין לָהּ. שֶׁאֵין נְשֵׁי הָעֲנִיִּים יְשֵׁינוֹת עַל הַכַּר. רִבִּי חִייָה בְשֵׁם רִבִּי יוֹחָנָן. הוֹתִירָה מְזוֹנוֹת שֶׁלָּהּ הוֹתִירָה בְלָיוֹת שֶׁלּוֹ הוֹתִירָה בְלָיוֹת שֶׁלָּהּ. הָדָא דְתֵימַר בְּאֵשֶׁת אִיש. אֲבָל בְּאַלְמָנָה בֵּין שֶׁהוֹתִירָה מְזוֹנוֹת בֵּין שֶׁהוֹתִירָה בְלָיוֹת שֶׁלָּהּ.

Halakhah 12: "One gives her half a *qab* of legumes and half a *qab* of oil," etc. Rebbi Mana said, a mina, i. e. four *riṭl*[238]. He gives her a pillow, a light[239] and wick, and an amphora, and a pot. Rebbi Yose said, she has no right to a pillow since the wives of poor men do not sleep on a pillow[240]. Rebbi Ḥiyya in the name of Rebbi Joḥanan: If she left over from her food, it is hers, if she left over rags they are his - if she left over rags they are hers[241]. That is, of a married woman. But for a widow, both her leftover food and her leftover rags are hers[242].

238   It is not known what these *riṭl* are. It is the consensus of the linguists that Syriac *raṭl*, Arabic *roṭl*, with the derived verb *rṭl* "to weigh by hand" is simply Greek λίτρα, a Roman pound of 12 oz. This also is Musaphia's explanation of *riṭl*; but a mina of 60 *seqalim* is about 2 *librae*. (In modern times, the weight of a *roṭl* varied from .45 kg in Egypt to 3.2 kg in Syria.) R. Mana states that the mina used here is 4 Roman lbs., 1.38 kg, or 100 "holy" *šeqel*. The translation follows S. Lieberman [*Tarbiz* 4 (1933), p. 377-378] who identifies ו as shorthand for הוא "this is".

239   A small clay vessel to be filled with oil.

240   Since the rules given here have to be generally valid, only the minimum amounts can be prescribed; the remainder is a matter of private contract between husband and wife. The rule is a matter of dispute in the Babli, 65a.

241   The text is unclear here between the scribe and the first corrector. The next sentence shows that both possibilities are valid; it was a matter of dispute between schools which alternative was chosen. The Babli disagrees with all the rules spelled out here, 65b.

242   Anything given by the heirs to the widow becomes the latter's unconditional property.

(fol. 29c) **משנה יג:** נוֹתְנִין לָהּ מָעָה כֶסֶף לְצָרְכֶיהָ וְאוֹכֶלֶת עִמָּהּ לֵילֵי שַׁבָּת. וְאִם אֵינוֹ נוֹתֵן לָהּ מָעָה כֶסֶף לְצָרְכֶיהָ מַעֲשֵׂה יָדֶיהָ שֶׁלָּהּ. וּמַה הִיא עוֹשָׂה לוֹ. מִשְׁקַל חָמֵשׁ סְלָעִים שְׁתִי בִּיהוּדָה שֶׁהֵן עֶשֶׂר סְלָעִים בַּגָּלִיל. אוֹ מִשְׁקַל עֶשֶׂר

סְלָעִים עֶרֶב בִּיהוּדָה שֶׁהֵן עֶשְׂרִים סְלָעִים בַּגָּלִיל. וְאִם הָיְתָה מֵינִיקָה פּוֹחֲתִין לָהּ מִמַּעֲשֵׂה יָדֶיהָ וּמוֹסִיפִין לָהּ עַל מְזוֹנוֹתֶיהָ. בַּמֶּה דְבָרִים אֲמוּרִים. בְּעָנִי שֶׁבְּיִשְׂרָאֵל. אֲבָל בַּמְכוּבָּד שֶׁבְּיִשְׂרָאֵל הַכֹּל לְפִי כְבוֹדוֹ.

Mishnah 13: One gives her a silver obolus for her needs and she eats with him Friday nights[198]. If he does not give her a silver obolus for her needs, she works for herself. And what does she work for him? In Judea, a weight of five tetradrachmas warp[243], which is ten tetradrachmas in Galilee, or in Judea the weight of ten tetradrachmas woof which are twenty tetradrachmas in Galilee. If she was nursing, one reduces the amount of her work and increases her food. When has this been said[244]? For the poorest man in Israel. But for the most honored one, everything commensurable with his honor[245].

243 She spins. The warp, being fixed under tension in the weaving frame, has to be spun much tighter than the woof.

244 For whom are the amounts mentioned in Mishnaiot 11-13 binding?

245 The wife would have standing in court if she complains about being treated shabbily.

(30b line 64) **הלכה יג**: נוֹתֵן לָהּ מָעָה כֶסֶף לְצָרְכֶיהָ וְאוֹכֶלֶת עִמָּה מְלֵילֵי שַׁבָּת לְלֵילֵי שַׁבָּת כול׳. דְּבָרִים אֲמוּרִים לָשׁוֹן נָקִי. שִׁמְעוֹן בַּר בָּא בְשֵׁם רִבִּי יוֹחָנָן. אֲכִילָה מַמָּשׁ. עַל דַּעְתֵּיהּ דְּרַב אוֹכֶלֶת מִשֶּׁלּוֹ. עַל דַּעְתֵּיהּ דְּרִבִּי יוֹחָנָן אוֹכֶלֶת מִשֶּׁלָּהּ.

Halakhah 13: "One gives her a silver obolus for her needs and she eats with him every Friday night," etc. The matters are formulated in clean language[246]. Simeon bar Abba in the name of Rebbi Joḥanan: Really eating[247]. In the opinion of Rav, she eats at his expense[248]; in the opinion of Rebbi Joḥanan she eats at her own expense.

246 This is the opinion of Rav at the end of Halakhah 8, Note 198. In the Babli, 65b, it is attributed to Rav Assi, the colleague of Rav (in many mss. and the *editio princeps* erroneously: Rav Ashi).

247 In the Babli, this opinion is attributed to Rav Naḥman, Samuel's student.

248 Since "eating" is meant as an euphemism for sexual intercourse, it implies in the context that she does not eat Friday nights from the food allotted her during the week.

(30b line 68) יַיִן אֵין לָהּ שֶׁאֵין עֲנִיּוֹת יִשְׂרָאֵל שׁוֹתוֹת יָיִן. וַעֲשִׁירוֹת שׁוֹתוֹת. וְהָתַנֵּי. מַעֲשֶׂה בְמָרְתָּא בַת בַּיְיתוֹס שֶׁפָּסְקוּ לָהּ חֲכָמִים סָאתַיִם יַיִן בְּכָל־יוֹם. וּבֵית דִּין פּוֹסְקִין יַיִן. אָמַר רִבִּי חִייָה בַר אָדָא. עַל שׁוּם זְנוּת יַיִן וְתִירוֹשׁ יִקַּח לֵב. וְהָא תַנִּינָן. אִם הָיְתָה מֵנִיקָה פּוֹחֲתִין לָהּ מִמַּעֲשֵׂה יָדֶיהָ וּמוֹסִיפִין לָהּ עַל מְזוֹנוֹתֶיהָ. מָהוּ מוֹסִיף. רִבִּי יְהוֹשֻׁעַ בֶּן לֵוִי אָמַר. יַיִן שֶׁהוּא מַרְבֶּה אֶת הֶחָלָב. רִבִּי חִזְקִיָּה רִבִּי אַבָּהוּ בְשֵׁם רִבִּי יוֹחָנָן. אַף לְתַבְשִׁילָהּ פָּסְקוּ. אַף עַל פִּי כֵן קִילְלָה אוֹתָן וְאָמְרָה לָהֶן. כָּךְ תִּתְּנוּ לִבְנוֹתֵיכֶם. אָמַר רִבִּי אָחָא. וְעָנִינוּ אַחֲרֶיהָ אָמֵן. אָמַר רִבִּי אֶלְעָזָר בַּר צָדוֹק. אֶרְאֶה בַּנֶּחָמָה אִם לֹא רְאִיתִיהָ מְלַקֶּטֶת שְׂעוֹרִים מִבֵּין טַלְפֵי סוּסִים בְּעַכּוֹ. וְקָרָאתִי עָלֶיהָ הַפָּסוּק הַזֶּה הָרַכָּה בָךְ וְהָעֲנוּגָה וגו'. אִם לֹא תֵדְעִי לָךְ הַיָּפָה בַּנָּשִׁים צְאִי לָךְ בְּעִיקְבֵי הַצֹּאן וגו'. וְהָתַנֵּי מַעֲשֶׂה בְמִרְיָם בִּתּוֹ שֶׁלְּשִׁמְעוֹן בֶּן גּוּרְיוֹן שֶׁפָּסְקוּ לָהּ חֲכָמִים בַּחֲמֵשׁ מֵאוֹת דֵּינָר קוּפָּה בְשָׁמִים בְּכָל־יוֹם וְלֹא הָיְתָה אֶלָּא שׁוֹמֶרֶת יָבָם. אַף עַל פִּי כֵן קִילְלָה אוֹתָן וְאָמְרָה לָהֶן. כָּךְ תִּתְּנוּ לִבְנוֹתֵיכֶם. אָמַר רִבִּי אָחָא. וְעָנִינוּ אַחֲרֶיהָ אָמֵן. אָמַר רִבִּי אֶלְעָזָר בַּר צָדוֹק. אֶרְאֶה בַּנֶּחָמָה אִם לֹא רְאִיתִיהָ קְשׁוּרָה בִשְׂעָרָהּ בְּזָנָב הַסּוּס בְּעַכּוֹ וְקָרָאתִי עָלֶיהָ הַפָּסוּק הַזֶּה הָרַכָּה בָךְ וְהָעֲנוּגָה כול'.

She has no claim to wine since poor Jewish women do not drink wine[249]. Do rich women drink? Did we not state: It happened that the Sages assigned to Martha bat Boethos[250] two *seʿah* of wine every day. How can the court assign wine[251]? Rebbi Ḥiyya bar Ada said, because of "Whoring, wine, and cider will destroy the mind.[252]" But did we not state:

"If she was nursing, one reduces the amount of her work and increases her food"? Rebbi Joshua ben Levi said wine, for it increases the milk[253]. Rebbi Ḥizqiah, Rebbi Abbahu in the name of Rebbi Joḥanan: Also[254] they assigned it for cooking[255]. Nevertheless, she cursed them and said to them, so you should give to your daughters. Rebbi Aḥa said, and we answered her, Amen[256]. Rebbi Eleazar ben Rebbi Zadoq said, I should not see consolation[257] if I did not see her collecting barley grains between horses' hooves at Acco. I quoted about her the verse: "The dainty one among you and the pampered, . . .[258]" "If you have no experience, most beautiful of women, go following the flock . . .[259]". But did we not state[260]: It happened that the Sages assigned to Miryam, the daughter of Simeon ben Gorion, a daily supply of perfume for 500 denar, when she was only waiting for her levir. Nevertheless, she cursed them and said to them, so you should give to your daughters. Rebbi Aḥa said, and we answered her, Amen. Rebbi Eleazar ben Rebbi Zadoq said, I should not see consolation if I did not see her bound with her hair to a horse's tail at Acco. I quoted about her the verse: "The dainty one among you and the pampered, . . .".

249 And the rules are written only for the poor; Tosephta 5:8; Babli 64b.

250 The paradigm of a rich widow; cf. *Yebamot* 6:4, Note 75.

251 Let a woman drink wine in the absence of a husband. The Babli, 65a, approves of not more than one cup of wine per meal.

252 *Hosea* 4:11. It is inferred that drinking wine induces sexual desires.

253 The same statement is in the Babli, 65b.

254 The original scribe wrote אין which by the first corrector was changed into אף One has to assume that the scribe intended אִין Babylonian Aramaic "yes"; in a Yerushalmi text this is a corruption.

255 If her food was cooked with wine there was no problem since

cooking eliminates the alcohol.

256 As confirmation.

257 Being part of an oath formula, the positive has a negative implication and vice versa. The implication is that the speaker would give up his share of paradise if what he says is not true.

258 *Deut.* 28:56, the chapter of curses.

259 *Cant.* 1:8. This verse has a positive interpretation in all Midrash sources.

260 The reliability of the tradition about Martha bat Boethos is questioned since a parallel tradition is reported about another woman. But it seems that both traditions are one and that Martha ("the lady") bat ("of the family of") Boethos is Miryam bat Simeon ben Boethos, cf. *Yebamot* 6:4, Note 75; Josephus *Antiquities* xv. 320 ff. In the Babli, 65a and 66b/67a (for the second story, Tosephta 5:9-10), both stories refer to one person, the widowed daughter-in-law of one Nikodaimon ben Gorion waiting for her levir; in the second story (in an intended contrast to the Yerushalmi) it is emphasized that nobody said "amen", (because the unhappiness of a childless widow cannot be compensated with money.)

מציאת האשה פרק ששי

(fol. 30c) **משנה א:** מְצִיאַת הָאִשָּׁה וּמַעֲשֵׂה יָדֶיהָ לְבַעֲלָהּ. וִירוּשָׁתָהּ הוּא אוֹכֵל פֵּירוֹת בְּחַיֶּיהָ. בּוֹשְׁתָּהּ וּפְגָמָהּ שֶׁלָּהּ. רִבִּי יְהוּדָה בֶּן בְּתֵירָה אוֹמֵר בִּזְמַן שֶׁבְּסֵתֶר לָהּ שְׁנֵי חֲלָקִים וְלוֹ אֶחָד וּבִזְמַן שֶׁבַּגָּלוּי לוֹ שְׁנֵי חֲלָקִים וְלָהּ אֶחָד. שֶׁלּוֹ יִנָּתֵן מִיָּד וְשֶׁלָּהּ יִלָּקַח בָּהֶן קַרְקַע וְהוּא אוֹכֵל פֵּירוֹת.

Mishnah 1: What a woman finds or makes with her hands belongs to her husband[1]. Of what she inherits he eats the yield during her lifetime[2]. [Payments she receives for] settlements for shame and diminution of value belong to her[3]; Rebbi Jehudah ben Bathyra says, in case it is covered[4], she receives two thirds and he one third; in case it is visible, he receives two thirds and she one third. His part shall be given immediately; her part shall be invested in real estate and he eats its yield.

1 As stated in Mishnah 4:6.

2 He is obligated to administer her property so it retains its value. For this, he is paid with the yield of the property. All these rules can be modified by prenuptial agreements.

3 If she is injured by a third party, Mishnah *Baba Qama* 8:1 states that the attacker has to pay for injury, pain, medical costs, lost earnings, and mental anguish. The expression "diminution of value" used here covers both injury (permanent impairment) and pain; "shame" is mental anguish. Since the husband has a claim to her handiwork, he also has a claim for payment for the time his wife is unable to work.

4 The wife's injury is covered by her clothing; then the husband's shame that he was unable to defend his wife is not so great. If the wife's injury is visible, the husband's loss of face is serious.

(30c line 38) **הלכה א**: מְצִיאַת הָאִשָּׁה וּמַעֲשֵׂה יָדֶיהָ לְבַעֲלָהּ כול׳. רִבִּי חִזְקִיָּה בְּשֵׁם רִבִּי אִימִּי. אִיתְפַּלְגוּן רִבִּי יוֹחָנָן וְרִבִּי שִׁמְעוֹן בֶּן לָקִישׁ. חַד אָמַר. דִּבְרֵי הַכֹּל. וְחָרְנָא אָמַר. בְּמַחֲלוֹקֶת. וְלָא יְדַעְנָא מָאן אֲמַר דָּא וּמָאן אֲמַר דָּא. מִסְתַּבְּרָא דְּרִבִּי שִׁמְעוֹן בֶּן לָקִישׁ הוּא דוּ אֲמַר. בְּמַחֲלוֹקֶת. דּוּ פָתַר לָהּ בְּמַעֲלֶה לָהּ מְזוֹנוֹת. וְאֵינוֹ נוֹתֵן לָהּ מָעָה כֶסֶף לְצָרְכֶיהָ. וְתַנִּינָן. וְאִם אֵינוֹ נוֹתֵן לָהּ מָעָה כֶּסֶף לְצָרְכֶיהָ מַעֲשֵׂה יָדֶיהָ שָׁלָּהּ. מַעֲשֵׂה יָדַיִם שֶׁהֵן כִּמְצִיאָה. אָתָא רִבִּי יַעֲקֹב בַּר אִימִּי בְּשֵׁם רִבִּי שִׁמְעוֹן בֶּן לָקִישׁ. דִּבְרֵי הַכֹּל הִיא. הֲוֵוי דַּעֲוָן דַּעֲוָן אִית לֵיהּ לְרִבִּי שִׁמְעוֹן בֶּן לָקִישׁ.

Halakhah 1: "What a woman finds or makes with her hands belongs to her husband," etc. Rebbi Ḥizqiah in the name of Rebbi Immi: Rebbi Joḥanan and Rebbi Simeon ben Laqish disagree: One said, this is everybody's opinion, the other said it is in dispute[5]. We do not know who said what. It is reasonable that Rebbi Simeon ben Laqish should be the one who said it is in dispute since he explained that [the husband] provides her with food but does not give her a silver obolus as pocket money[6], and we did state: "If he does not give her a silver obolus as pocket money, what she makes with her hands is hers." The work of her hands is parallel to what she finds. Rebbi Jacob bar Immi came in the name of Rebbi Simeon ben Laqish: It is everybody's opinion[7]. That means that Rebbi Simeon ben Laqish varies in his opinions[8].

5 Between R. Meïr and R. Joḥanan the Alexandrian who disagree in Mishnah 5:5 whether a man can dedicate his wife's work to Heaven.

6 Cf. Halakhah 5:5; *Nedarim* 11:4, Notes 51-55. R. Meïr holds that the obligatory work the wife does for her husband is for her silver obolus and what she does in addition is for her food. Therefore, if he does not provide her with pocket money, he has no right to her work and, similarly, to what she finds. For R. Joḥanan the Alexandrian, the work is for her food and the excess

for the pocket money. (This is where R. Joḥanan disagrees.) Therefore, the husband has the right to what she makes and finds.

7   What she finds belongs to her husband according to everybody, as explained in the next paragraph.

8   It seems that he taught different approaches to different students.

(30c line 45) לְמִי נִצְרְכָה. לְרִבִּי מֵאִיר. אַף עַל גַּב דְּלְרִבִּי מֵאִיר עָבִיד יַד הָעֶבֶד כְּיַד רַבּוֹ זָכַת אִשָּׁה זָכָה בַעֲלָהּ. מוֹדֶה שֶׁאֵין עָלֶיהָ אֶלָּא אוֹכֶלֶת פֵּירוֹת בִּלְבָד. תַּמָּן תַּנִּינָן. מְצִיאַת בְּנוֹ וּבִתּוֹ הַקְּטַנִּים וְעַבְדּוֹ וְשִׁפְחָתוֹ הַכְּנַעֲנִים וּמְצִיאַת אִשְׁתּוֹ הֲרֵי אֵילוּ שֶׁלּוֹ. שֶׁהוּא יָכוֹל לְשַׁנּוֹתָן לִמְלָאכָה אֶחֶרֶת. מַה טַעַם אָמְרִינָן. מְצִיאַת בְּנוֹ וּבִתּוֹ הַגְּדוֹלִים וְעַבְדּוֹ וְשִׁפְחָתוֹ הָעִבְרִים הֲרֵי אֵילוּ שֶׁלָּהֶן. שֶׁאֵינוֹ יָכוֹל לְשַׁנּוֹתָן לִמְלָאכָה אֶחֶרֶת. הֲתִיבוֹן. הֲרֵי אִשְׁתּוֹ אֵינוֹ יָכוֹל לְשַׁנּוֹתָהּ לִמְלָאכָה אֶחֶרֶת וְאַתְּ אָמַר. מְצִיאָתָהּ שֶׁלּוֹ. אָמַר רִבִּי יוֹחָנָן. טַעַם אַחֵר יֵשׁ בְּאִשָּׁה. מַהוּ טַעַם אַחֵר בְּאִשָּׁה. אָמַר רִבִּי חַגַּיי. מִפְּנֵי קְטָטָה. רִבִּי יוֹסֵי לֹא אָמַר כֵּן. אֶלָּא שֶׁלֹּא תְהֵא מַבְרַחַת מִשֶּׁלְבַעֲלָהּ וְאוֹמֶרֶת. מְצִיאָה מָצָאתִי. הַגַּע עַצְמָךְ שֶׁנְּתָנָן לָהּ אַחֵר מַתָּנָה. קוֹל יוֹצֵא לְמַתָּנָה וְאֵין קוֹל יוֹצֵא לִמְצִיאָה. הַגַּע עַצְמָךְ שֶׁמְּצָאָהּ בְּעֵדִים. זוֹ מִפְּנֵי זוֹ. אָמַר רִבִּי יוֹחָנָן. בְּשֶׁאֵין טְפוּלִין לַאֲבִיהֶן. אֲבָל אִם הָיוּ טְפוּלִין לַאֲבִיהֶן מְצִיאָתָן שֶׁלּוֹ.

For whom is it needed[9]? For Rebbi Meïr! Even though for Rebbi Meïr the hand of the slave is his master's hand[10] and if the wife acquired title the husband should have acquired it; he agrees that his rights over it[11] are restricted to the use of the yield. There, we have stated[12]: "The finds of his underage son and daughter or of his Canaanite slave[13] or slave-girl as well as his wife's find belong to him," for he can direct them to do other work. Why do we say: "The finds of his adult son and daughter or of his Hebrew slave[14] or slave-girl belong to them," because he cannot direct them to do other work[15]. But his wife he cannot direct to do other work[16] and you say that her find belongs to him! Rebbi Joḥanan said, there is another reason for his wife. What is the other reason for his wife? Rebbi Ḥaggai says, because of quarrel[17]. Rebbi Yose does not say so, but that she should not smuggle away[18] any of her husband's property and say, I found it. Think of it, if another person gave it to her as a gift[19]! A gift is public knowledge, a find is not public knowledge. Think of it, if she found it in the presence of witnesses! This because of that[20]. Rebbi Yoḥanan said, if they[21] are not dependent on their father. But if they are dependent on their father, their finds belong to him.

9   The clause in the Mishnah that the husband has only the usufruct of any inheritance coming to his wife during the marriage.

10   Similarly, R. Meïr holds that a wife cannot act legally except as her husband's representative. It would seem reasonable that a wife can retain separate property by prenuptial agreement (cf. *Yebamot* 7:1, Note 1), but for R. Meïr one would expect that a wife can only acquire an inheritance as representative for her husband. Therefore, it is essential that the Mishnah state that an inheritance becomes the wife's sole property for which the husband has to act as administrator. Cf. *Nedarim* 11:8, Note 70; *Ma'aser Šeni* 4:4, Note 95; Babli *Nedarim* 88b, *Qiddušin* 23b.

11   The inheritance.

12   Mishnah *Baba Meṣi'a* 1:5.

13   It is not required that the slave be Phoenician. Any non-Jewish slave who became semi-Jewish by circumcision (for a male) and immersion in a *miqweh* is called "Canaanite slave". In the theory of the Babli, the Canaanite slave's body is the property of his master; therefore, if the slave lifts a find to acquire it, it is legally his master whose hand took it.

14   While the rules for the treatment of Hebrew slaves (*Ex.* 21:1-11) are a frequent topic in the Talmudim, the subject is purely theoretical since the institution of Hebrew slavery disappeared with the end of the First Commonwealth. It is asserted that only the working capability of the slave is the master's, not his body. Therefore, if he lifts a find to acquire it, it is not the master's hand which lifts the find.

15   Obviously, the master can direct the Hebrew slave to perform any task he asks of him; but he cannot direct him not to use his hands for anything else.

16   In Chapter 5, an exhaustive list was given of work the husband can demand from his wife. The wife's body certainly is not her husband's property. Therefore, one does not understand why her find should be her husband's.

17   One has such a poor opinion of Jewish husbands that one is afraid he would be offended if the wife would not share her find with him [mentioned also in *Baba Meṣi'a* 1:5 (8a l. 15)]. This is the only explanation offered in the Babli, 96a; it is called "because of jealousy".

18   Meaning: stealing.

19   The gift can be given on condition that the husband have no right to it. Should the wife not be believed if she says she received a gift?

20   R. Yose will agree that in the case of a find in the presence of other people his reason is invalid. He holds that, nevertheless, the rabbinic decree giving the find to the husband stands because it would be impractical to admit exceptions.

21   This refers to the adult children to whom the Mishnah in *Baba Meṣi'a* assigns their finds. This is qualified; the Mishnah applies only if the children are financially independent. In the Babli, this is formulated that "they are not dependent on their father's table." Cf. *Peah* 4:6, Note 107; *Baba Meṣi'a* 1:5 (8a l.3); Babli *Baba Meṣi'a* 12b.

(30c line 57) הוֹרֵי רִבִּי יִצְחָק בְּהֵן דְּמַשְׁבִּיק אִינְתְּתֵיהּ וְלָא מְמָרֵק לָהּ פּוֹרְנָהּ. שֶׁהוּא מַעֲלֶה לָהּ מְזוֹנוֹת עַד שָׁעָה שֶׁהוּא מְמָרְקָהּ.

Rebbi Isaac instructed about one who had sent away his wife but not liquidated her *ketubah*[22], that he has to feed her until the time he liquidated it.

22   Greek φερνή "dowry". In Halakhah 7:7, the word is used in the meaning of *ketubah*, the document in which the value of the dowry was recorded. Therefore, it seems reasonable to read the text that R. Isaac

obligated the former husband to support his former wife until he had paid the last penny of everything he was obligated to by the *ketubah* document, not only until he had returned all her dowry.

(30c line 59) רִבִּי רְדִיפָה רִבִּי אָחָא בְּשֵׁם רִבִּי בּוּן בַּר כָּהֲנָא. דְּלָא מְחַסֵּר לָהּ. בְּסֵתֶר לָמָה הוּא נוֹטֵל. מִפְּנֵי צַעֲרוֹ שֶׁמִּצְטַעֵר עִמָּהּ.

Rebbi Redipha, Rebbi Aha, in the name of Rebbi Abun bar Cahana: Because he does not make her lose anything[23]. In secret[24], why does he take? Because of the pain he suffers with her.

23 This refers to the rules of R. Yehudah ben Bathyra who gives the husband part of the payment for shame and diminution of value. Why should the husband get part of the payment for shame? Since the payment is pure revenue for the recipient, not restitution, she still ends up having more than she did before her injury.

24 If the scars of her injury are not visible in public. The Babli, 66a, formulates: His wife is his body.

(fol. 30c) **משנה ב:** הַפּוֹסֵק מָעוֹת לַחֲתָנוֹ וּמֵת חֲתָנוֹ אָמְרוּ חֲכָמִים יָכוֹל הוּא שֶׁיֹּאמַר לְאָחִיךָ הָיִיתִי רוֹצֶה לִיתֵּן וְלָךְ אֵי אֶפְשִׁי לִיתֵּן.

Mishnah 2: If somebody decided[25] on money for his son-in-law and the son-in-law died[26], the Sages said that he can say[27], I was ready to give to your brother, but it is impossible for me to give to you.

25 He promised a fixed amount of dowry payable at the moment of the final marriage ceremony.

26 Between the preliminary and the final marriage ceremony.

27 To the levir who is scheduled to marry his daughter. This is intended to induce the levir to prefer *ḥaliṣah* to the levirate marriage.

(30c line 61) **הלכה ב**: הַפּוֹסֵק מָעוֹת לַחֲתָנוֹ וּמֵת חֲתָנוֹ כול'. וְלֹא דְבָרִים שֶׁהֵן קוֹנִין בַּאֲמִירָה הֵן. תַּנֵּי בַּר קַפָּרָא. פּוֹסֵק לְשֵׁם כְּתוּבָּה עַל מְנָת לבנים.[28] וְכֵינִי. הַפּוֹסֵק מָעוֹת לְבִתּוֹ קְטַנָּה כּוֹפִין אוֹתוֹ לִיתֵּן. הָא לִגְדוֹלָה לֹא. אָמַר רִבִּי אָבוּן. כּוֹפִין אוֹתוֹ לִיתֵּן גֵּט.

Halakhah 2: "If somebody decided on money for his son-in-law and the son-in-law died," etc. Are these not the things that are acquired by speech[29]? Bar Qappara stated: He promised the dowry on condition there be a marriage[30]. And it is so[31]: If somebody decided on money for his underage daughter, one forces him to give. But not for the adult one[32]? Rebbi Abun said, one forces [the groom] to give a bill of divorce[33].

28 This word, "for sons", does not make any sense in the context. With all commentators it seems necessary to read לכנוס "to marry definitively" with the easily explained changes ו - י, ב - נ.

29 As explained in Halakhah 5:1, Notes 16 ff., that promises made at the moment of the preliminary marriage are enforceable in court. Why can the levir not sue for his brother's property?

30 A promise of dowry becomes enforceable only after the definitive marriage ceremony.

31 This refers to Halakhah 13:5: If somebody promised a sum to his son-in-law at the moment of the preliminary wedding but went bankrupt before the final wedding, and the groom is not willing to proceed with the definitive marriage without the dowry being paid, the question is whether the girl can insist on either to be married or to be freed to marry somebody else. In Tosephta 13:4, it is stated: If somebody decided on money for his underage daughter but then went bankrupt, one forces him to give because one can give a minor benefit but not obligation. A similar text is in the Babli, 109 a. In all these texts, it is stated "one forces him", without an explanation whom one forces.

32 Is a promise of dowry for an adult daughter not enforceable?

33 If the daughter was a minor at the time of the preliminary marriage and then the father went bankrupt, the court will force the groom either to marry the girl without money or to free her by a bill of divorce since acts

of third parties to the detriment of minors are invalid and not enforceable in court. The same explanation is given in the Babli, 109a, by Rava, a frequent discussion partner of Ravin (= R. Abun.)

(fol. 30c) **משנה ג**: פָּסְקָה לִכְנוֹס לוֹ אֶלֶף דֵּינָר הוּא פוֹסֵק כְּנֶגְדוֹ בַּחֲמִשָּׁה עָשָׂר מָנֶה. כְּנֶגֶד הַשּׁוּם הוּא פוֹסֵק פָּחוֹת חוֹמֶשׁ. שׁוּם בְּמָנֶה וְשָׁוֶה מָנֶה אֵין לוֹ אֶלָּא מָנֶה. שׁוּם בְּמָנֶה הִיא נוֹתֶנֶת שְׁלֹשִׁים וְאֶחָד דֵּינָר. בְּאַרְבַּע מֵאוֹת הִיא נוֹתֶנֶת חֲמֵשׁ מֵאוֹת וּמַה שֶׁהֶחָתָן פּוֹסֵק הוּא פוֹסֵק פָּחוֹת חוֹמֶשׁ.

Mishnah 3: If she decided to bring him 1'000 denars, he decides as equivalent fifteen minas[34]. Corresponding to estimates he decides one-fifth less[35]. If it was appraised for a mina and it is worth a mina, he has only a mina[36]. For the estimate of a mina she gives him 31 [tetradrachmas and one][37] denar[38]. For 400 she gives 500, for what the groom decides, he decides one-fifth less.

34 If the dowry is in cash which the groom will use in his business, he has to obligate himself in the *ketubah* to return 150% of the capital at the dissolution of the marriage to account for his earnings from that capital.

35 As a matter of principle, any part of the dowry given in goods has to be capitalized at 80% of its estimated value at the time of marriage. Some commentators of the Babli explain that the 20% represent the depreciation of things in use; others explain that estimators have a tendency to inflate the values to make the bride appear richer than she is. Cf. Note 42.

36 If the rule of the preceding paragraph is not followed and the groom agrees to accept in the *ketubah* the full written value as value received, he cannot later complain and have the *ketubah* sum reduced.

37 In ms. and *editio princeps*, and in a few other mss., two words are missing. The corrected text reads:

שְׁלֹשִׁים וְאַחַת סֶלַע וְאֶחָד דֵּינָר. This text was translated. Cf. The Babylonian Talmud with Variant Readings, Tractate Kethubot vol. 2, ed. M. Herschler, Jerusalem 1977, p. קי-קיא,

Notes 54-55.

38   31·4 + 1 = 125; 0.8·125 = 100. For a value of 100 denars written in the *ketubah*, she has to deliver goods estimated at 125 denars.

(30c line 64) **הלכה ג**:   פָּסְקָה לִכְנוֹס לוֹ אֶלֶף דֵּינָר כול׳. מָה רָאוּ לוֹמַר בִּכְסָפִים אָחָד וּמֶחֱצָה וּבְשׁוּם פָּחוֹת חוֹמֶשׁ. אָמַר רִבִּי יוֹסֵי בֶּן חֲנִינָה. שָׁמִין דַעְתָּהּ שֶׁל אִשָּׁה שֶׁהִיא רוֹצָה לְבַלּוֹת אֶת כֵּילֶיהָ וְלִפְחוֹת אוֹתָן חוֹמֶשׁ. שָׁמִין דַעְתּוֹ שֶׁלָאִישׁ רוֹצֶה לִישָּׂא וְלִיתֵּן בָּהֶן וְלַעֲשׂוֹתָן בְּאֶחָד וּמֶחֱצָה. אָמַר רִבִּי יוֹסֶה. זֹאת אוֹמֶרֶת שֶׁאֵין אָדָם רַשַּׁאי לִמְכּוֹר כְּלֵי אִשְׁתּוֹ. דְּלְמָה. רִבִּי חִייָה וְרִבִּי יָסָא וְרִבִּי אִימִּי סָלְקוֹן לְשׁוּמָא דִבְרַתָּהּ דְּרִבִּי יוֹסֵי בֶּן חֲנִינָה. אָמְרִין לֵיהּ. פְּחוֹת חוֹמֶשׁ וְכוֹפֵל. אָמַר לוֹן. פּוֹחֵת חוֹמֶשׁ וְאֵינוֹ כוֹפֵל.

Halakhah 3: "If she decided to bring him 1'000 denars," etc. Why did they say for money, one and one half times, and for estimations less one fifth? Rebbi Yose ben Ḥanina said, one estimates the will of the woman that she wants to use her vessels[39] and depreciates them by a fifth. One estimates the will of the man to use it[40] in trade and to make them one and one half[41]. Rebbi Yose said, this implies[40] that nobody has the right to sell his wife's vessels. Example: Rebbi Ḥiyya, Rebbi Yasa, and Rebbi Immi went to appraise for Rebbi Yose ben Ḥanina's daughter. They said to [the groom]: Deduct a fifth and double[43]. He said to them, he[44] deducts a fifth and does not double.

39   כלי includes both garments and household vessels. Tosaphot (66a, *s. v.* פוחת) quotes the statement in the name of Samuel but in Alfasi the text is quoted as in the ms.

40   The cash received.
41   He expects to earn more than 50% from the dowry.
42   That garments and vessels are depreciated in the *ketubah* implies that

they are intended for permanent use. The husband's responsibility for them does not give him the right to dispose of them.

43   First he is told to deduct 20% to arrive at the real value of the dowry and then to double, to inflate the apparent value. This was a widespread practice in Babylonia and was proposed by the three Babylonian-born rabbis acting as appraisers. The device was rejected by the Palestinian groom. The subject is dealt with by M. A. Friedman (cf. Chapter 5, Note 226), vol. 1, pp. 296-298, where references to the large literature about the subject are given. Friedman notes that none of the Palestinian *ketubot* edited by him exhibit artificial inflation of the value of the dowry.

44   Meaning himself.

(30d line 4) שִׁמְעוֹן בַּר אַבָּא בְּשֵׁם רִבִּי יוֹחָנָן. הִכְנִיסָה לוֹ זָהָב בְּשָׁוְיוֹ. וְתַנֵּי כֵן. תַּקְשִׁיטִין לַעֲשׂוֹתָן דֵּינָרִין בְּאֶחָד וּמֶחֱצָה. דֵּינָרִין לַעֲשׂוֹתָן תַּקְשִׁיטִין בְּשָׁוְיֵיהֶן. רִבִּי אָחָא בַּר פַּפָּא בְּעָא קוֹמֵי רִבִּי אִימִּי. הִכְנִיסָה לוֹ בְהֵמָה. אָמַר לֵיהּ. בְּשָׁוְיָיהּ. הִכְנִיסָה לוֹ קַרְקַע. אָמַר לֵיהּ. בְּשָׁוְיָהּ. וְאֵינוֹ מִשְׂתַּכֵּר. וְגוּבָה קַרְקַע. אֵין לוֹ אֶלָּא אֲכִילַת פֵּירוֹת.

Simeon bar Abba in the name of Rebbi Johanan: If she brought him gold, at full value[45]. This was also stated[46]. Jewellery to be turned into denars[47], at the rate of one and one half. Denars to be turned into jewellery, at their full value. Rebbi Aḥa bar Pappos asked before Rebbi Immi: If she brought him an animal[48]? He said to him, at full value. If she brought him real estate: He said to him, at full value. But does he not gain from it[49]? But she collects the real estate, he has only the usufruct[50].

45   Gold jewellery does not depreciate when worn. The Babli, 67a, points out that under a government which depreciates its currency, gold coins have the status of jewellery, not of coin.

46   The Mishnah states that certain things in the dowry are accepted at full value.

47   This becomes the husband's

working capital.

48 Either cattle for agricultural work or goats for milk.

49 Why is real estate not evaluated at 150%?

50 Real estate, whether mortmain or paraphernalia, remains the wife's property of which the husband has the usufruct. Since at the dissolution of marriage the real estate returns to the wife, there is no need to increase its value in the *ketubah*. (Cf. *Yebamot* 7:1, Note 1.)

(fol. 30c) **משנה ד:** פָּסְקָה לְהַכְנִיס לוֹ כְסָפִים סְלָעָה כֶּסֶף נַעֲשֵׂית שִׁשָּׁה דִּינָר וְהֶחְתָן מְקַבֵּל עָלָיו עֲשָׂרָה דֵינָרִים לַקּוּפָּה לְכָל מָנֶה וּמָנֶה. רַבָּן שִׁמְעוֹן בֶּן גַּמְלִיאֵל אוֹמֵר הַכֹּל כְּמִנְהַג הַמְּדִינָה.

Mishnah 4: If she decided to bring him money, each tetradrachma is turned into six denars[51] and the groom engages himself for ten denars for the perfume box for each mina[52]; Rabban Simeon ben Gamliel says, all follows local custom.

51 This is 150%, as stated in the preceding Mishnah.

52 He will provide her with perfumes and accessories worth one tenth of the cash dowry.

(30d line 9) **הלכה ד:** פָּסְקָה לְהַכְנִיס לוֹ כְסָפִים כול'. פָּסְקָה לְהַכְנִיס לוֹ חֲמֵשׁ מֵאוֹת דֵּינָרִים שׁוּם עָשׂוּ אוֹתוֹ אַרְבַּע מֵאוֹת. לֹא עָשׂוּ כֵן אֶלָּא עָשׂוּ אוֹתוֹ אֶלֶף. אִם עָשׂוּ קִיצוּתָא גוֹבָה אֶת הַכֹּל וְאִם לָאו מִגְרַע חֲמִשָּׁה דֵינָרִים לְכָל סֶלַע וְאֵינוּ גוֹרֵעַ בַּתּוֹסֶפֶת. פָּסְקָה לְהַכְנִיס לוֹ חֲמֵשׁ מֵאוֹת דֵּינָרִים כְּסָפִים עוֹשֶׂה אוֹתָן שְׁבַע מֵאוֹת וּמֶחֱצָה. לֹא עָשׂוּ כֵן אֶלָּא עָשׂוּ אֶלֶף. אִם עָשׂוּ קִיצוּתָא גוֹבָה אֶת הַכֹּל. וְאִם לָאו מִגְרַע שִׁשָּׁה דִּינָר לְכָל סֶלַע וְאֵינוֹ גּוֹרֵעַ בַּתּוֹסֶפֶת. פָּסְקָה לְהַכְנִיס לוֹ אֶלֶף זוּז צָרִיךְ לַעֲשׂוֹתָן טוּ מָנֶה. לֹא עָשׂוּ כֵן אֶלָּא כָּתַב לָהּ שָׂדֶה שָׁוֶה בִּשְׁנַיִם

עֶשֶׂר מָנֶה תַּחַת אֶלֶף זוּז. אִם עָשְׂתָה קִיצּוּתָא גּוֹבָה אֶת הַכֹּל. וְאִם לָאו אֵין פּוֹחֲתִין לִבְתוּלָה מִמָּתַיִם וְלָאַלְמָנָה מִמָּנֶה. הָכָא אַתְּ מַר. מִיגְרַע. וְהָכָא אַתְּ מַר. אֵינוֹ מִיגְרַע. כָּאן בְּנָטְלָה מִקְצָת כָּאן בְּשֶׁלֹא נָטְלָה מִקְצָת. הָכָא אַתְּ מַר. נוֹגֵעַ בַּתּוֹסֶפֶת. וְהָכָא אַתְּ מַר. אֵינוּ נוֹגֵעַ בַּתּוֹסֶפֶת. תַּמָּן. הוֹסִיף וְלֹא פִיחֵת. בְּרַם הָכָא. פִּיחֵת וְלֹא הוֹסִיף. תַּנְיָא. בֵּין בַּשּׁוּם בֵּין בַּכְּסָפִים. בְּשׁוּם מַה לְפִי מַה שֶׁהוּא פּוֹחֵת לְפִי מַה שֶׁהוּא מוֹסִיף לְפִי מַה שֶׁהִיא מַכְנֶסֶת.

Halakhah 4: "If she decided to bring him money," etc. "If she decided to bring him 500 denars by appraisal, he makes it 400. If he did not do that but made it 1'000; if she made an agreement[53], she collects everything; if not, he deducts five denars for each tetradrachma, but he cannot touch the addition[54]. If she decided to bring him 500 denars in coin, he makes it 750[55]. If he did not do that but made them 1'000; if she made an agreement, she collects everything; if not, he deducts six denars for each tetradrachma[56], but he cannot touch the addition. If she decided to bring him 1'000 *zuz*, he must turn them into fifteen minas. If he did not do that but wrote over to her a field worth 12 minas in place of the 1'000 *zuz*[57]. If she made an agreement, she collects everything; if not[58], one does not decrease for a virgin to less than 200 and for a widow to less than a mina." Here, you say, he deducts. But there, you say, he does not deduct[59]. Here, if she invalidated part of it, there if she did not invalidate part of it[60]. Here, you say, he touches the addition but there, you say, he does not touch the addition[61]. Here, he added but did not subtract; there, he subtracted but did not add. It was stated: Both for appraisal and for coin[62]. Why for appraisal? Corresponding to what he subtracts, corresponding to what what he adds, corresponding to what she brings[63].

53 This meaning is conjectural, based on the meaning of קצצא in Syriac (cf. *Tosefta ki-Fshutah Ketubot* p. 245). In the commentary on the Tosephta which is parallel to the text here (6:6-7), S. Lieberman reads in the text נקיצותה "what she had decided", based on the Tosephta text (6:6), and explains that the woman takes all if she actually delivered what she had promised. But in the ms. it is clear that in the Yerushalmi the word ends in the definite article תא, and Lieberman's identification of Tosephta and Yerushalmi texts (pp. 278-279) cannot be accepted (or the ending תה in the Tosephta should be interpreted as תא). In the Babli, קִיצוּתָא is "a fixed date", קִיצוּתָא "a fixed price." The explanation given here is close to that proffered by R. Moses Margalit.

Since the groom doubled the original appraisal and deviated from the norm, acceptance of this deviation is valid only if explicitly endorsed either in the *ketubah* or in an accompanying document. In the *ketubot* published by A. M. Friedman, the sums are regularly acknowledged by the bride's representatives. It is to be assumed that in every case where one speaks of an agreement made "by the bride," it means an agreement signed by her father or in his absence another duly authorized member of her family.

54 This follows the Mishnah, for each 5 denars of appraised value, the husband (or his estate) is obligated only for 4 denars, one *sela*. But what he added over and above the appraised value is his irrevocable gift since in Galilee one did not routinely double the appraisals (cf. Note 41.) The widow collects from the estate 400 denars for the appraisal and 500 additional, for a total of 900.

55 As prescribed by the Mishnah.

56 If the amount actually given as dowry cannot be ascertained, the husband's estate is entitled to deduct 6 denars for every 4 in dispute. But the additional 250 denars have to be paid in full.

57 He offers only 1200 in place of the 1500 for which he was obligated by the rules. If the wife accepts this in writing, because she prefers 1200 in real estate to 1500 in silver coin whose silver content depends on the policies of the government, she takes everything that is written in the *ketubah*.

58 And the amount of her claim is in dispute.

59 In all cases except the last,

definitive rules are given as to how to compute the claim on the estate. Only in the last case can the entire dowry be lost.

60 Following the reading בבטלה conjectured by S. Lieberman (loc. cit. p. 279) instead of בנטלה, בְּבְטְלָה "she invalidated" instead of בְּנְטְלָה "she took".

61 In all cases except the last one, the estate has to pay the full amount of the addition over and above the value of the dowry. Only in the last case, there is no clause that protects the addition. By taking real estate for 1'200 *zuz* she renounced 300 *zuz* that would have come to her, putting the entire *ketubah* in question.

62 They follow the same rules.

63 All this needs confirmation by the parties in writing.

(30d line 24) כֵּינֵי מַתְנִיתָא. וְקוּפַת בְּשָׂמִים הַכֹּל מָנֶה. אָמַר רִבִּי יוֹחָנָן. עָשׂוּ הֲנָיַת בְּשָׂמִים כַּהֲנָיַת כְּסָפִים. אָמַר רִבִּי אָבִין. עָשׂוּ הֲנָיַת פִּרְיָה וְרִבְיָה כַּהֲנָיַת כְּסָפִים. כְּהָדָא. תַּלְמִידוֹי דְּרִבִּי יוֹסֵי סַלְקוּן לְקַדִּישִׁין אַשְׁכְּחִינוּן עֲרִירִין. אָמְרוֹן לוֹן. אַתְנִיתוּן בֵּינֵיכוֹן. אִם הִתְנֵיתֶם בֵּינֵיכֶם הֲרֵי יָפֶה וְאִם לָאו הַכֹּל כְּמִנְהַג הַמְּדִינָה.

So is the Mishnah: "And a perfume box for every mina[64]." Rebbi Johanan said, they made usufruct of perfumes like usufruct of money[65]. Rebbi Avin said, they made usufruct of procreation like usufruct of money[66]. As the following: The students of Rebbi Yose went to Qaddišin; they found them childless. They said to them: Did you stipulate between you? If you stipulated, it is fine[67]; otherwise everything follows the local custom.

64 The corrected text is not that of the Mishnah (and the Tosephta, 6:6), "ten denars *for* the perfume box for each mina" but "ten denars *and a* perfume box for each mina." Cf. J. N. Epstein, מבוא לנוסח המשנה² p. 494; תלמוד
קיב ,vol. 2, p. בבלי עם שינויי נוסחאות כתובות p. 277. תוספתא כפשוטה כתובות ;Note 25

One has to interpret הַכֹּל מָנֶה as לְכָל־מָנֶה. It is not necessary to change the text; cf. the author's *The Scholar's Haggadah*, Northvale 1995, p. 322.

65 It is not clear what is referred to. From the next sentence, it seems that the paragraph refers to the statement of Rabban Simeon ben Gamliel that in the absence of explicit written agreement, all monetary aspects are judged based on local customs. Spices and perfumes given as articles of trade have the status of money (are better than money in an inflationary environment, and still are equal to money after Diocletian's stabilization of the Roman currency.) In the Babli, 67a, this is restricted to Antiochene spices and perfumes (which, probably, were of guaranteed quality.)

66 The groom can be generous in the conditions of the *ketubah* since he or his children will inherit the money. It is left to local custom (in the Middle Ages mostly: local regulations) to deal with the disposition of the dowry if the couple remain childless; a clause which denies the husband the inheritance of his childless deceased wife is authorized by R. Yose and the end of Halakhah 9:1; cf. M. A. Friedman, *Jewish Marriage in Palestine*, vol. 1, VE, pp. 391-418.

67 The rule that the husband inherits from his wife, being a money matter, can be set aside by stipulation. The biblical root of the rule is not explicit; cf. *Sifry Deut.* 134.

משנה ח: הַמַּשִּׂיא אֶת בִּתּוֹ סְתָם לֹא יִפְחוֹת לָהּ מֵחֲמִשִּׁים זוּז. פָּסַק (fol. 30c) לְהַכְנִיס עֲרוּמָה לֹא יֹאמַר הַבַּעַל כְּשֶׁתָּבוֹא לְבֵיתִי אֲכַסֶּנָּה בִּכְסוּתִי אֶלָּא מְכַסָּהּ וְעוֹדָהּ בְּבֵית אָבִיהָ. וְכֵן הַמַּשִּׂיאִין אֶת הַיְתוֹמָה לֹא יִפְחֲתוּ לָהּ מֵחֲמִשִּׁים זוּז. אִם יֵשׁ בַּכִּיס מְפַרְנְסִין אוֹתָהּ לְפִי כְבוֹדָהּ.

Mishnah 5: If somebody marries off his daughter without mentioning particulars he should not give her less than 50 *zuz*[68] If he had decided to take her in naked[69] the husband should not say, if she comes to my house I shall clothe her in my garment, but he covers her when she still is in her father's house. Similarly, those who marry off an orphan girl[70] should not give her less that 50 *zuz*, and if money is available one provides for her according to her social standing[71].

68 As dowry. A person having a capital of 50 *zuz* (silver denars) as working capital is barred from taking welfare payments (Mishnah *Peah* 9:9).

69 As stated in Halakhah 6, some people have to come up with a large dowry to marry off their daughter but some can take money for giving away their daughter.

70 The overseers of charity can use public money and even impose a tax on the public to provide a minimal dowry for a fatherless girl. (It is really the mother and/or the brothers who *marry off* the girl but the overseers of charity *provide* the money.)

71 The overseers of charity cannot collect money to provide the girl with a dowry that would approximate what her father would have given had he lived, but if there already is money in the charity account they have the right to vote her more than 50 *zuz*.

(30d line 28) **הלכה ה**: הַמַּשִּׂיא אֶת בִּתּוֹ כול'. רְבִּי אַבָּא מָרִי אָחוֹי דְרְבִּי יוֹסֵי בָּעֵי. לֹא כֵן תַּנֵּי. מִנַּיִין אֲפִילוּ אָמַר. הֲרֵינִי עוֹמֵד עָרוֹם וּמְכַסָּהּ. אֵין אוֹמְרִים לוֹ שֶׁיַּעֲמוֹד עָרוֹם וִיכַסָּהּ אֶלָּא מְכַסָּהּ בְּרָאוּי לָהּ. תַּמָּן אוֹרְחָא דְּבַר נָשָׁא מֵימַר. הֲנֵי לִי מֵיקוֹם עַרְטִילַיי וּמְכַסְיָיא אִינְתְּתִי. בְּרַם הָכָא הִתְנָה עִמָּהּ מִתְּחִילָּה.

Halakhah 5: "If somebody marries off his daughter," etc. Rebbi Abba Mari, Rebbi Yose's brother, asked: Did we not state: From where that even if he said, I shall go naked but clothe her, one does not tell him to be naked and to clothe her but he clothes her according to her social standing[72]? There, it is the way of people to say, it is better for me to stand naked if only I cover my wife; but here it was a prior condition.

72 The intended text is probably close to Tosephta 6:7: If somebody marries off his daughter and contracted with his son-in-law that the latter should stand naked if only he provided her with clothes, one does not tell him

to stand naked in public but that he has to clothe her according to her standing. In the Tosephta, "standing naked" is a figure of speech; why should it be taken literally in the Mishnah?

(30d line 33) כֵּינִי מַתְנִיתָא. וְכֵן הַמְפַרְנְסִין אֶת הַיְתוֹמָה. אָמַר רִבִּי חִינְנָא. זֹאת אוֹמֶרֶת שֶׁאוֹמְרִין לַפַּרְנָסִים לְלָוֹות. דּוּ פָתַר לָהּ בְּשָׁאֵין בַּכִּיס לוֹוִין עַד חֲמִשִׁים. אֲבָל אִם יֵשׁ בַּכִּיס מוֹסִיף. אָמַר רִבִּי יוֹסֵי. זֹאת אוֹמֶרֶת שֶׁאֵין אוֹמְרִין לַפַּרְנָסִים לְלָוֹות. דּוּ פָתַר לָהּ בְּשֶׁיֵּשׁ בַּכִּיס. אֲבָל אִם אֵין בַּכִּיס פּוֹחֵת. כְּהָדָא. בְּיַלְדָּה אַחַת בְּיוֹמוֹי דְּרִבִּי אִמִּי. אָמַר. יִשְׁתַּבּוֹק לְמוֹעֲדָא. אָמַר לֵיהּ רִבִּי זְעִירָא. גְּרָמִית יִפְסוֹד. אֶלָּא יִתָּכוֹל. דְּמָרֵיהּ דְּמוֹעֲדָא קַיָּים. וַתְיָיא דְּרִבִּי חֲנִינָה כְּרִבִּי זְעוּרָה וּדְרִבִּי יוֹסֵי כְּרִבִּי אִימִּי.

So is the Mishnah: And so those who provide for the orphan girl[73]. Rebbi Ḥinena said, this means that one says to the overseers to take out a loan[70]. For he explains it, if nothing is in the wallet one takes out a loan up to fifty. But if there is money in the wallet, one may add. Rebbi Yose said, this means that one does not say to the overseers to take out a loan. For he explains if there is money in the wallet[74]. But if there is no money one diminishes. As the following, about a girl in the days of Rebbi Immi. He said, let it be held over for the holiday[75]. Rebbi Ze'ira said to him, you are causing a loss[76], but give everything, for the Lord of the holiday exists[77]. It turns out that Rebbi Ḥanina holds with Rebbi Ze'ira and Rebbi Yose with Rebbi Immi[78].

73 Cf. Note 68, parenthesis.

74 It seems that he does not accept the last sentence in his Mishnah text.

75 R. Immi did not want to give public funds for the dowry of an orphan girl because he needed the money to distribute to the poor for their holiday needs.

76 The orphan girl will not be able to marry.

77 Give her a dowry of what is available in the charity account and

God will see to it that money will be donated to charity for the holiday.
78 If R. Immi thought that the overseers of charity can take out loans, he would not have to worry about the holiday.

(fol. 30c) **משנה ו:** יְתוֹמָה שֶׁהִשִּׂיאַתָּה אִמָּה אוֹ אַחֶיהָ מִדַּעְתָּהּ וְכָתְבוּ לָהּ בְּמֵאָה אוֹ בַחֲמִשִּׁים זוּז יְכוֹלָה הִיא מִשֶּׁתַּגְדִּיל לְהוֹצִיא מִיָּדָן מַה שֶּׁרָאוּי לְהִינָּתֵן לָהּ. רִבִּי יְהוּדָה אוֹמֵר אִם הִשִּׂיא אֶת הַבַּת הָרִאשׁוֹנָה יִינָּתֵן לַשְּׁנִייָה כְּדֶרֶךְ שֶׁנָּתַן לָרִאשׁוֹנָה. וַחֲכָמִים אוֹמְרִים פְּעָמִים שֶׁאָדָם עָנִי וְהֶעֱשִׁיר אוֹ עָשִׁיר וְהֶעֱנִי אֶלָּא שָׁמִים אֶת הַנְּכָסִים וְנוֹתְנִין לָהּ.

Mishnah 6: If an orphan girl was married off by her mother or her brothers and they wrote her 100 or 50 *zuz*[79], after she becomes an adult she can claim from them what is appropriate to be given to her. Rebbi Jehudah says, if he married off his first daughter, the second should be given in the way the first had been given[80]. But the Sages say, sometimes it happens that a person was poor and became rich, or was rich and became poor. But one appraises the property and gives to her[81].

79 Less than what she could have expected, given her father's wealth.
80 If the father died before the second daughter was married, the second should get the percentage of the estate that the first got from the property.
81 The standard 10%. They will interpret "rich" and "poor" as feeling rich or poor, and giving his daughter more or less than the standard 10%.

(30d line 40) **הלכה ו:** יְתוֹמָה שֶׁהִשִּׂיאַתָּה אִמָּהּ אוֹ אַחֶיהָ כול׳. כֵּינִי מַתְנִיתָא. אִם הִשִּׂיאוּ אֶת הַבַּת הָרִאשׁוֹנָה יִינָּתֵן. דִּבְרֵי חֲכָמִים. שֶׁפְּעָמִים שֶׁאָדָם מַשִּׂיא אֶת בִּתּוֹ וְנוֹתֵן עָלֶיהָ מָעוֹת. וּפְעָמִים שֶׁאָדָם מַשִּׂיא אֶת בִּתּוֹ וְנוֹטֵל עָלֶיהָ מָעוֹת.

Halakhah 6: "If an orphan girl was married off by her mother or her brothers," etc. So is the Mishnah: If they married off the first one there should be given[82]. The words of the Sages: [83]"Sometimes a man marries off his daughter and spends money on her, and sometimes a man marries off his daughter and collects money for her."

82   This is the reading of a number of Mishnah mss., among them both the Cambridge and the Kaufmann mss. A number of mss., among them the Parma ms., read השיאה "she (the mother) married off" (*Babli with variant readings*, p. קלג). In this version, what the father did is not a precedent for his heirs but the heirs have to be consistent in the treatment of the daughters. (The text of the Mishnah here, in the Babli, and Tosephta 6:3 which refers to the father, is found in the Munich ms. of the Babli and the Mishnah mss. of the Maimonides tradition.) The arguments of J. N. Epstein (*loc. cit.* Note 62) who wants to disregard the change in number, cannot be sustained in view of the many Mishnah mss. confirming the Yerushalmi reading.

83   Tosephta 6:3.

(30d line 43) רִבִּי זְעִירָה שָׁאַל לְרַב נַחְמָן בַּר יַעֲקֹב וּלְרַב אַמִּי בַּר פַּפֵּי. מָאן תַּנָּא עישׂוּר נְכָסִים. אָמַר לוֹ רִבִּי זְעוּרָה בְּשֵׁם רַב יִרְמְיָה. עִישׂוּר נְכָסִים כְּרִבִּי. בְּעוֹן קוּמֵי רִבִּי. הֲרֵי שֶׁהָיוּ עֶשֶׂר נְקֵיבוֹת. וְכֵן אִם נָטְלָה הָרִאשׁוֹנָה עִישׂוּר נְכָסִים וְהַשְּׁנִייָה עִישׂוּר נְכָסִין. וְהַשְּׁלִישִׁית וְהָרְבִיעִית וְהַחֲמִישִׁית וְכֵן עַד הָעֲשִׂירִית. אֵין כֵּן לֹא נִשְׁתַּיֵּיר לְבֵן כְּלוּם. אָמַר לָהֶן. הָרִאשׁוֹנָה נוֹטֶלֶת עִישׂוּר נְכָסִין וְיוֹצְאָה וְהַשְּׁנִייָה נוֹטֶלֶת עִישׂוּר נְכָסִים מִן הַמִּשְׁתַּיֵּיר וְהַשְּׁלִישִׁית מִן הַמִּשְׁתַּיֵּיר וְהָרְבִיעִית מִן הַמִּשְׁתַּיֵּיר עַד הָעֲשִׂירִית מִן הַמִּשְׁתַּיֵּיר. נִמְצְאוּ הַבָּנוֹת נוֹטְלוֹת תְּרֵין חוּלְקִין פָּרָא צִיבְחָר. וְהַבֵּן נוֹטֵל חַד חוּלָק וְאוּף צִיבְחָר.

Rebbi Ze'ira asked Rav Naḥman bar Jacob and Rav Ammi bar Pappai, who is the Tanna of "a tenth of the estate"? Rebbi Ze'ura[84] said to him in the name of Rav Jeremiah: A tenth of the estate following Rebbi[85]. They asked before Rebbi: If there were ten daughters. Then if the first one took a tenth of the estate, the second took a tenth of the estate, the third, the fourth, the fifth, and so on up to the tenth, there is nothing left for the son! He said to them: The first one takes a tenth of the estate and leaves[86]; the second takes a tenth of the remainder, the third from what then is left, the fourth of what then is left, up to the tenth from what then is left. It turns out that the daughters take two thirds less a little, and the son takes one third plus a little[87].

84 He probably is the Amora called Ze'iri in the Babli.

85 This is an explicit Tosephta, 6:3: Rebbi says, each [daughter] takes a tenth of the estate. (Babli 68a, 52b, *Nedarim* 39b.)

86 The first one takes her part, the younger sisters get less than she did. This is also accepted in the Babli, 68a/b.

87 Let us assume that each daughter takes a part p from the estate. Let E_0 be the original estate, E_n the amount left after the n-th daughter took her part. Then

$$E_n = (1-p)E_{n-1} = (1-p)^n E_0.$$

In our case, $p = .1$, $n = 10$, we have $.9^{10} = .3487 = .3333 + .0154$. The last term is the "little bit" which the son takes above $1/3$ and the daughters combined take less than $2/3$. On the word פָּרָא "less than" and its possible derivations cf. E. and H. Guggenheimer, Notes on the Talmudic Vocabulary, *Lešōnēnū* 39(1975) pp. 59-62.

(30d line 52) הֲרֵי שֶׁהָיוּ שְׁתֵּי בָנוֹת וּבֵן אֶחָד. וְנָטְלָה הָרִאשׁוֹנָה עִישׂוּר נְכָסִים. לֹא הִסְפִּיקָה הַשְּׁנִייָה לִיטוֹל עִישׂוּר נְכָסִים עַד שֶׁמֵּת הַבֵּן. רִבִּי חֲנִינָה סָבַר מֵימַר. הַשְּׁנִייָה נוֹטֶלֶת עִישׂוּר נְכָסִים וְהַשְּׁאָר חוֹלְקוֹת אוֹתוֹ בְשָׁוֶה. אָמַר לֵיהּ רִבִּי יוֹחָנָן. תַּמָּן בְּשֶׁלֹּא הָיָה לְהִתְפַּרְנֵס. בְּרַם הָכָא תִּמְכּוֹר אֶת הַשְּׁאָר וְתִתְפַּרְנֵס מִמֶּנּוּ. רִבִּי טְבִי בְשֵׁם רִבִּי יֹאשִׁיָּה. טַעֲמָא דְּרִבִּי חֲנִינָה. אֵין מִן הַמְשׁוּעֲבָּדִין הוּא גוֹבָה לֹא כָּל־שֶׁכֵּן מִמַּה שֶׁלְּפָנֶיהָ. רִבִּי יוֹחָנָן כְּדַעְתֵּיהּ. דָּמַר רִבִּי זְעִירָא.

רִבִּי יוֹחָנָן לֹא גָבֵי. מָאן גָבֵי. רִבִּי חֲנִינָה [וְרִבִּי אִילָא][88] גָבֵי. רִבִּי יָסָא אִיתְפְּקַד גַּבֵּיהּ מְדַל דְּיַתְמִין וַהֲוָה תַּמָּן יַתְמִין בְּעָיָין מְפַרְנְסָא. אָעִיל עוֹבְדָא קוֹמֵי רִבִּי אֶלְעָזָר וְקוֹמֵי רִבִּי שִׁמְעוֹן בַּר יָקִים. אָמַר רִבִּי שִׁמְעוֹן בַּר יָקִים. לֹא מוּטָב שֶׁיִּתְפַּרְנְסוּ מִשֶּׁלְאֲבִיהֶן וְלֹא מִן הַצְּדָקָה. אָמַר לֵיהּ רִבִּי אֶלְעָזָר. דָּבָר שֶׁאִילּוּ יָבוֹא לִפְנֵי רַבּוֹתֵינוּ וְאֵין רַבּוֹתֵינוּ נוֹגְעִין וְאָנוּ עוֹשִׂין אוֹתוֹ מַעֲשֶׂה. אָמַר רִבִּי יוֹסֵי. אֲנָא יְהִיב לוֹן וְאִין קָמוֹן יַתְמֵי וְעָרוּן אֲנָא יְהִיב לוֹן. אֲפִילוּ כֵן חֲמוֹן וְלֹא עִירוֹן. רִבִּי זְעִירָא בְּעָא קוֹמֵי רִבִּי יוֹסֵי. הֵיךְ עָבְדִין עוֹבְדָה. אָמַר לֵיהּ. כְּרִבִּי חֲנִינָה. וְכֵן נְפַק עוֹבְדָא כְּרִבִּי חֲנִינָה. רִבִּי אָבוּן בְּשֵׁם רִבִּי הִילָא. רוֹאִין אֶת הַנְּכָסִים כְּאִילוּ חֲרֵיבִין.

[89]If there were two daughters and one son; the first one took a tenth of the estate, but the son died before the second could take her tenth[90]. Rebbi Ḥanina was of the opinion that the second takes a tenth of the estate and the rest they divide equally among themselves. Rebbi Joḥanan told him that in this case there was nothing else to provide for her, but here she may sell from the remainder and provide for herself[91]! Rebbi Tebi in the name of Rebbi Joshia: The reason of Rebbi Ḥanina: If she can collect from encumbered real estate, from what lies before her not so much more[92]? Rebbi Joḥanan sticks to his opinion, since Rebbi Ze'ira said that Rebbi Joḥanan does not collect[93]. Who collects? Rebbi Ḥanina [and Rebbi Hila] collect. Rebbi Yasa was appointed custodian of orphans' property[94]. There were orphan [girls] who asked to be provided for. He brought the case before Rebbi Eleazar and Rebbi Simeon bar Yaqim. Rebbi Simeon bar Yaqim said, is it not better to provide for them from their father's estate rather than from charity[95]? Rebbi Eleazar said to him: If such a case came before our teachers, our teachers would not touch it[96]; would we act? Rebbi Yose said, I shall give to them, and if some orphans

get up and complain, I would give it to them[97]. Even so, they saw and did not complain. Rebbi Ze'ira asked before Rebbi Yose: How do you decide in practical cases? He said to him, following Rebbi Ḥanina. And so an actual case was decided following Rebbi Ḥanina[98]. Rebbi Abun in the name of Rebbi Hila: One considers the estate as if it were dry[99].

88   From a similar text in *Giṭṭin* 5:3. Text here: לא גבי "He does not collect."
89   Parallel arguments are in the Babli 69a, *Giṭṭin* 51a.
90   The son died childless; then the two daughters inherit the estate.
91   In the Babli, R. Joḥanan holds that the second daughter gave up her claim for the extra 10% and takes 50% of the estate. According to R. Ḥanina, 45% go to the first daughter and 55% to the second.
92   He holds that providing a dowry for the daughters is a *ketubah* obligation and as such has the status of a mortgage. Therefore, in talmudic law (abolished by the Geonim in Babylonia after the Arab conquest and apparently never followed in the European provinces of the Roman empire) the claim for a dowry must be satisfied by real estate. If the father sold a piece of real estate and there is none left to satisfy the demand for dowry, the daughter can go to court to repossess the land and let the buyer be indemnified by the estate.
93   He refuses to grant repossession for claims to dowry.
94   Valuables, not real estate.
95   The underlying hypothesis here is that dowries from estates are given only from real estate. R. Simeon ben Yaqim holds that an estate rich in money but without real estate should provide for the daughters in money and not force them to apply to public charity for their dowry.
96   The Patriarch's court in his days could not decide whether dowries should be paid from real estate or movables; why should a lower court deal with the matter?
97   In a similar situation, he provided for the daughters from movables. But since he had no precedent, if the male orphans were to appeal the judgment, he would rescind it. Since there was no appeal, a precedent was created that dowries be given from movables. The Babli strongly disagrees, 69b.

98 To split the inheritance 55% / 45%, cf. Note 89.
99 The daughters cannot claim part of the yield of the estate for their dowry.

(fol. 30c) **משנה ז**: הַמַּשְׁלִישׁ מָעוֹת לְבִתּוֹ וְהִיא אוֹמֶרֶת נֶאֱמָן עָלַי בַּעֲלִי יַעֲשֶׂה שָׁלִישׁ מַה שֶׁהוּשְׁלַשׁ בְּיָדוֹ דִּבְרֵי רַבִּי מֵאִיר. רַבִּי יוֹסֵי אוֹמֵר וְכִי אֵינָהּ אֶלָּא שָׂדֶה אַחַת וְהִיא רוֹצָה לְמָכְרָהּ הֲרֵי הִיא מוֹכְרָהּ מֵעַכְשָׁיו. בַּמֶּה דְבָרִים אֲמוּרִים בִּגְדוֹלָה. אֲבָל בִּקְטַנָּה אֵין מַעֲשֵׂה קְטַנָּה כְּלוּם.

Mischnah 7: If somebody gives money in trust[100] for his daughter and she says, I am trusting my husband[101], the trustee should execute what he was entrusted with[102], the words of Rebbi Meïr. Rebbi Yose says, is it not only about a field? If she wants to sell it, can she not sell it now[103]? When has this been said? If she is an adult. But about a minor, no legal act of a minor is valid[104].

100 To buy some real estate for his daughter, after the giver's death.
101 She wants the money to be given to her husband that he could buy the piece of real estate for her.
102 And not hand over the money to the husband.
103 Could she not legally sell today the field that in the future will be bought for her by the trustee, to be the buyer's after the trustee will have delivered the field to her. Therefore, the trustee should follow the daughter's instructions.
104 R. Yose agrees that the instructions of an underage daughter should not be followed.

(30d line 68) **הלכה ז**: הַמַּשְׁלִישׁ מָעוֹת לְבִתּוֹ וְהִיא אוֹמֶרֶת נֶאֱמָן עָלַי בַּעֲלִי כול'. מַתְנִיתָא בְּפָסַק מִן הָאֵירוּסִין. אֲבָל אִם פָּסַק מִן הַנִּישׂוּאִין אַף רַבִּי מֵאִיר מוֹדֶה. הַשְּׁלִישׁ מִן הַנִּישׂוּאִין הִיא הַמַּחֲלוֹקֶת.

HALAKHAH 7

Halakhah 7: "If somebody gives money in trust for his daughter and she says, I am trusting my husband," etc. The Mishnah speaks of the case that he gave at the time of the preliminary marriage. But if he gave at the definitive marriage even Rebbi Meïr agrees[105] If he established the trust after the definitive marriage, that is the disagreement[106].

[105] Since the husband gets the income from the real estate after the definitive marriage, there is no reason why he should not be entrusted with buying the real estate. A similar argument is in the Babli, 69b, and an explicit text in Tosephta 6:9.

[106] If the father by his action shows that he does not trust his son-in-law, the trustee should not hand over the money. R. Yose holds that even in this case the daughter can sell her rights to that land any day of that year.

(30d line 71) הָאוֹמֵר תְּנוּ לְבָנַי שֶׁקֶל בַּשַּׁבָּת. וְהֵן רְאוּיִין לִיטוֹל סֶלַע. נוֹתְנִין לָהֶן סֶלַע. אַל תִּתְּנוּ לָהֶן אֶלָּא שֶׁקֶל. נוֹתְנִין לָהֶן שֶׁקֶל. וּלְמָזוֹן הָאִשָּׁה וְהַבָּנוֹת בֵּין שֶׁאָמַר. תְּנוּ. בֵּין שֶׁאָמַר. אַל תִּתְּנוּ. נוֹתְנִין לָהֶן שֶׁקֶל. תַּנֵּי. רַבָּן שִׁמְעוֹן בֶּן גַּמְלִיאֵל אוֹמֵר. מֵאִיר הָיָה אוֹמֵר. הָאוֹמֵר. תְּנוּ לְבָנַיי שֶׁקֶל בַּשַּׁבָּת. וְהֵן רְאוּיִין לִיטוֹל סֶלַע. נוֹתְנִין לָהֶן שֶׁקֶל וְהַשְּׁאָר מִתְפַּרְנֵס מִן הַצְּדָקָה. וַחֲכָמִים אוֹמְרִין. גּוֹבִין וְהוֹלְכִין עַד שֶׁיִּכְלוּ הַנְּכָסִים וְהַשְּׁאָר יִתְפַּרְנְסוּ מִן הַצְּדָקָה. אָמַר רבִי יוֹסֵי. הָדָא פְּשַׁטָה שְׁאִילְתָּא דְחִילְפַי. אָמְרֵי. אַיְיתְבוֹן עַל גֵּיף נַהֲרָא דְּלָא אַפִּיקַת מַתְנָיָיה דְּרִבִּי חִיָּיה רַבָּא מִן מַתְנִיתָא וְיַרְקוּנִי לַנַּהֲרָא. מָה הֲוָה מֵימַר. יַעֲשֶׂה שָׁלִישׁ מַה שֶׁהוּשְׁלַשׁ בְּיָדוֹ.

[107]"If somebody says[108], give my sons one *šeqel* per week and they need a tetradrachma, one gives them a tetradrachma[109]. Do not give them more than one *šeqel* per week, one gives them a *šeqel*. But for the support of the wife and the daughters, whether he says give or do not give, one gives them a *šeqel*[110]. It was stated: Rabban Simeon ben

Gamliel says, Meïr used to say, if somebody says, give my sons one *šeqel* per week and they need a tetradrachma, one gives them a *šeqel*, and for the remainder they should be provided for by charity[111]. But the Sages say, one takes continuously until the property is used up[112] and after that they should be provided by charity." Rebbi Yose said, that gives a simple example for Ḥilfai's question. He said, I shall sit on the river bank and if I cannot extract the teachings of the elder Rebbi Ḥiyya[113] from the Mishnah, throw me into the river. What could he say[114]? "The trustee should execute what he was entrusted with.[115]"

107 Tosephta 6:10; the first part also in the Babli, 69b.

106 In his will to the executors of his estate after his death.

109 If prices rise, since 2 *šeqalim*, 1 tetradrachma, comprise at least one *šeqel*.

110 All sources of the Tosephta read: "A tetradrachma." This reading is required since the widow and her daughters are fed by the *ketubah* contract and a will cannot modify a contractual obligation.

111 The executors are not empowered to deviate from the testator's instructions even if it means that the children have to apply to public welfare.

112 Nobody should be forced to apply for welfare if there is a possibility to avoid it.

113 The Tosephta. In the Babli, 69b, he is called Ilfa and it is explained that he objected to the use of *baraitot* and *tosephtot* in the study of Jewish law and was ready to jump into the sea if somebody could produce a *baraita* whose teachings he could not derive from the Mishnah. In the Babli, R. Yose's observation is Ḥilfai's own.

114 Where does he find justification for the position of R. Meïr that the executors of the will cannot deviate from their instructions even in case of necessity.

115 Even if it seems reasonable to follow the daughter's wishes.

(31a line 4) מֵתוּ יִירְשׁוּ אֲחֵרִים. לֹא כֵן אָמַר רִבִּי אַבָּהוּ בְּשֵׁם רִבִּי יוֹחָנָן. כָּל־הַלְּשׁוֹנוֹת אָדָם מְזַכֶּה חוּץ מִלְּשׁוֹן יְרוּשָׁה. לֵית כָּאן יִרְתּוּן אֶלָּא יִטְלוּן. רִבִּי זְעִירָא בְּעָא קוֹמֵי רִבִּי מָנָא. כָּאן בְּמַתָּנָה. אִיתְפַּלְּגוּן. כָּתַב כָּל־נְכָסָיו לִשְׁנֵי בְנֵי אָדָם כְּאַחַת. כָּתַב לָזֶה בִּלְשׁוֹן מַתָּנָה וּלְזֶה בִּלְשׁוֹן יְרוּשָׁה. אָמַר רִבִּי אֶלְעָזָר. מִכֵּיוָן שֶׁזָּכָה בּוֹ בלשון מַתָּנָה זָכָה זֶה בִּלְשׁוֹן יְרוּשָׁה. אָמַר רִבִּי יוֹחָנָן. נִרְאִין דְּבָרִים. בִּלְשׁוֹן מַתָּנָה זָכָה בִּלְשׁוֹן יְרוּשָׁה לֹא זָכָה. אָמַר רִבִּי פִּינְחָס. אָתָא עוֹבְדִין קוֹמֵי רִבִּי יִרְמְיָה. מִכֵּיוָן דְּרִבִּי לָעֲזָר אָמַר אוּלְפָן. וְרִבִּי יוֹחָנָן אָמַר נִרְאִין. הֲלָכָה כְּרִבִּי אֶלְעָזָר. אָמַר רִבִּי שְׁמוּאֵל. לֹא רִבִּי מֵאִיר אֲמָרָהּ. וְאֵינָן נִרְאוֹת. שְׁמַע כְּלוּם הִיא. לֹא כֵן אָמַר רִבִּי יוֹחָנָן בְּשֵׁם רִבִּי יָסָא. צֶמֶר בְּכוֹר שֶׁטְּרָפוֹ בָּטֵל בְּרוֹב. וְאִיתְּתֵיהּ רִבִּי חִייָה צִיפּוֹרַייָה קוֹמֵי רִבִּי אִימִּי. לִיטְרָא בִּשְׁמוֹנֶה. וְלֹא הוֹרֵי לֵיהּ. דָּמַר רִבִּי יָסָא. לֹא מַתְנִיתָא הִיא. הָאוֹרֵג מְלֹא הַסִּיט מִצֶּמֶר הַבְּכוֹר בַּבֶּגֶד יִדָּלֵק הַבֶּגֶד. וּמִשְּׂעַר הַנָּזִיר וּמִפֶּטֶר חֲמוֹר בַּשַּׂק יִדָּלֵק הַשַּׂק. הוֹרֵי מַתְנִיתָא פְּלִיגָא עַל רִבִּי יוֹחָנָן. כָּתַב בֵּין בַּתְּחִילָּה בֵּין בָּאֶמְצַע בֵּין בַּסּוֹף בִּלְשׁוֹן מַתָּנָה דְּבָרָיו קַייָמִין. תַּמָּן לָזֶה בִּלְשׁוֹן מַתָּנָה וּלְזֶה בִּלְשׁוֹן יְרוּשָׁה. בְּרַם הָכָא כָּל־אֶחָד וְאֶחָד בִּלְשׁוֹן מַתָּנָה כָּל־אֶחָד וְאֶחָד בִּלְשׁוֹן יְרוּשָׁה. רִבִּי חַגַּיי בְּעָא קוֹמֵי רִבִּי יוֹסֵי. וְאֵינוֹ חָב לַאֲחֵרִים. אָמַר לֵיהּ. בְּשֶׁאֵין שָׁם אַחִין. וְאֵינוֹ חָב לַאֲחֵי אָבִיו. רִבִּי חֲנַנְיָה בְּרֵיהּ דְּרִבִּי הִילֵּל. רוֹצֶה הוּא בְּתַקָּנַת בֵּיתוֹ יוֹתֵר מִקְּרוֹבָיו.

[116]"If they died, others should inherit." Did not Rebbi Abbahu say in the name of Rebbi Joḥanan: A person can transfer property rights in any language except with an expression of inheritance[117]? One does not have here "they shall inherit" but "they shall take"[118]. Rebbi Ze'ira asked before Rebbi Mana: Do they not differ here in matters of a gift? If somebody signed over[119] all his property to two persons at the same time; to one he wrote in the language of gift but to the other in the language of inheritance. Rebbi Eleazar said, since the one acquired in the language of

gift, the other one acquired in the language of inheritance[120]. Rebbi Johanan said, it seems that one did acquire in the language of gift but the other did not acquire in the language of inheritance[121] Rebbi Phineas said, there came a case before Rebbi Jeremiah: Practice follows Rebbi Eleazar since Rebbi Eleazar stated a docrine but Rebbi Johanan[122] said only "it seems". Rebbi Samuel said, but did not Rebbi Meïr say that and it does not seem reasonable; is that nothing[123]? [124]Did not Rebbi Johanan say in the name of Rebbi Assi[125]: Carded firstling wool becomes insignificant in a plurality[126]. Rebbi Hiyya the Sepphorean brought before Rebbi Ammi a pound in eight[127] but the latter refused to rule since had not Rebbi Assi said, is that not a Mishnah[128]? "If somebody weaves the length of a *siṭ* of firstling's wool in a cloth, the cloth must be burned, of hair of a *nazir* or firstling donkey in sackcloth, the sackcloth must be burned"? The following Mishnah disagrees with Rebbi Johanan: "If he wrote any expression of gift either at the start, or in the middle, or at the end, his instructions are valid.[129]" There, to one person in an expression of gift and to one an expression of inheritance. But here to each one both in the language of gift and the language of inheritance[130] Rebbi Haggai asked before Rebbi Yose: But does he not prejudice the rights of others[131]? He said to him, if there are no brothers. But does he not prejudice the rights of his paternal uncles? Rebbi Hanania the son of Rebbi Hillel: A person prefers the good of his house over his relatives[132].

116 This refers to a sentence in the Tosephta quoted in the preceding paragraph: "If he said, if they should die, others should inherit, then one gives them only a *šeqel*, whether he said to give, or not to give more." The fact that others have to be mentioned in the will proves that these are not the legal heirs to whom the inheritance would have been given had the testator

died intestate.

117 Since inheritance is defined in *Num.* 27:6-11 and transfer of property by inheritance is restricted to the paternal family. The last sentence in this paragraph will make clear that one supposes that the beneficiaries of the will are one or more sons-in-law whose wives are excluded by biblical law from the inheritance if there is a son at the time of the father's death, even if that only son should then die childless.

In Mishnah *Baba Batra* 8:5, R. Johanan ben Beroqa holds that a testamentary gift may be formulated in the language of inheritance if the recipient is a relative on the father's side who might be an heir if the other prospective heirs would die before him.

118 It is suggested that the (Hebrew) text of the Tosephta be explained (in Aramaic) to remove the objection.

119 In one document.

120 He holds that a document is either valid or invalid. Since the bequest by gift is valid, the entire document is valid. The same argument is in the Babli in greater detail, *Baba Batra* 129a.

121 The document is valid but the bequest of inheritance to a non-heir is not enforceable in court.

122 R. Eleazar gives a straight decision, implying that he learned this principle from his teachers. R. Johanan's statement seems to be tentative.

123 R. Johanan gives a definitive statement: R. Meïr's opinions in the Tosephta are rejected. Therefore, R. Jeremiah's argument is without base.

124 The next three sentences are from *'Orlah* 3:2, Notes 88-94.

125 This must be read with the text in *'Orlah*: Rebbi Assi (Yasa) in the name of R. Johanan; the latter is the teacher and the former the student.

126 A firstling sheep may not be shorn (*Deut.* 15:19). The wool is forbidden for usufruct but, in contrast to fruits from a tree less than three years old, the wool according to R. Johanan does not make everything forbidden if it is mixed with permitted fibers.

127 One pound of firstling wool mixed with eight pounds of wool from other sheep, and thoroughly mixed so that one cannot recognize the fibers coming from the firstling.

128 It is Mishnah *'Orlah* 3:3 but Mishnah 3:2 shows that it represents R. Meïr's minority opinion; therefore, it is not practice.

129 Mishnah *Baba Batra* 8:5. If somebody wrote a will in which either

he gave some property to a non-heir or he distributes his estate in unequal portions between the heirs, if he wrote either "*as a gift* this property is given to X" or "this property *as a gift* is given to X" or "this property is given to X *as a gift*", the gift is valid and can be collected by court order. This is the Babli's interpretation in *Baba Batra*. The Yerushalmi in *Baba Batra* does not discuss the meaning of the sentence. R. Eleazar could read the Mishnah as stating that a will is valid if it gives property to three people if to one of them at least it is given as gift (position of Rav Sheshet in the Babli, *loc. cit.* Note 118).

The Mishnah clearly implies that any of these instructions makes the entire will valid.

130 R. Joḥanan would agree that a document, in which some property is given as a gift and other property as inheritance to one and the same person, is valid. But if the recipients are two different people, the validity for one does not imply the validity for the other.

131 By naming his daughters and their husbands as heirs after his sons, does he not deprive his brothers of their biblical right of inheritance?

132 In order to execute the will of the deceased, the court has to enforce a will giving property to daughters and their husbands even against the testator's brothers.

המדיר פרק שביעי

(fol. 31a) **משנה א:** הַמַּדִּיר אֶת אִשְׁתּוֹ מִלֵּיהָנוֹת לוֹ עַד שְׁלֹשִׁים יוֹם יַעֲמִיד לָהּ פַּרְנָס. יוֹתֵר מִיכֵּן יוֹצִיא וְיִתֵּן כְּתוּבָּה. רִבִּי יְהוּדָה אוֹמֵר בְּיִשְׂרָאֵל חֹדֶשׁ אֶחָד יְקַיֵּים וּשְׁנַיִם יוֹצִיא וְיִתֵּן כְּתוּבָּה וּבַכֹּהֶנֶת שְׁנַיִם מְקַיֵּים וּשְׁלֹשָׁה יוֹצִיא וְיִתֵּן כְּתוּבָּה.

Mishnah 1: If somebody makes a vow that his wife should not have any usufruct from him[1], up to thirty days[2] he shall appoint a provider[3], more than that he has to divorce her and pay the *ketubah*. Rebbi Jehudah says, if he is an Israel[4], for one month he should keep her, for two he has to divorce her and pay the *ketubah*; in the case of the wife of a Cohen[5] for two months he should keep her, for three he has to divorce her and pay the *ketubah*.

1 Then he cannot fulfill his obligation to feed, clothe, and house his wife.

2 This can be read to mean that the wife cannot sue for divorce if the husband limits his vow to thirty days. But if his vow is unlimited, the wife can demand an immediate divorce. It might also mean that in no case can the wife sue unless the husband did not provide for her for at least 30 days.

3 Who provides for her from his own money and only later is repaid by the husband.

4 Who can remarry his divorcee if he found an Elder who dissolves his vow.

5 He is given more time to find a way to dissolve his vow since he never could remarry his divorcee, *Lev.* 21:7.

(31b line 2) **הלכה א**: הַמַּדִּיר אֶת אִשְׁתּוֹ מִלֵּיהָנוֹת לוֹ כול׳. תַּמָּן תַּנִּינָן. הַמַּדִּיר אֶת אִשְׁתּוֹ מִתַּשְׁמִישׁ הַמִּטָּה. וָכָא אַתְּ אָמַר הָכֵין. תַּמָּן בְּמַדִּירָהּ מִגּוּפוֹ. בְּרַם הָכָא בְּמַדִּירָהּ מִנְּכָסָיו. וְיֵשׁ אָדָם נוֹדֵר שֶׁלֹּא לִפְרוֹעַ אֶת חוֹבוֹ. אָמַר רִבִּי יוֹסֵי בֶּן חֲנִינָה. מִכֵּיוָן שֶׁהוּא עָתִיד לְגָרְשָׁהּ וְלִיתֵּן לָהּ כְּתוּבָּה וּלְמָעֵט מִמְּזוֹנוֹתֶיהָ כְּמִי שֶׁאֵין בּוֹ חוֹב. וּתְהֵא יוֹשֶׁבֶת וּמַמְתֶּנֶת. וְאִם גֵּירַשׁ הֲרֵי יָפֶה. וְאִם לָאו יַעֲלֶה לָהּ מְזוֹנוֹת. כְּמָאן דָּמַר. אֵין מְזוֹנוֹת הָאִשָּׁה מִדְּבַר תּוֹרָה. כְּהָדָא דְּתַנֵּי. אֵין בֵּית דִּין פּוֹסְקִין לְאִשָּׁה מְזוֹנוֹת מִדְּמֵי שְׁבִיעִית. אֲבָל נִיזּוֹנֶת הִיא אֶצֶל בַּעֲלָהּ בַּשְּׁבִיעִית. וְיַעֲשׂוּ אוֹתָהּ כְּפוֹעֵל שֶׁאֵינוֹ שָׁוֶה פְּרוּטָה. הָדָא אָמְרָה שֶׁאֵין עוֹשִׂין אוֹתוֹ כְּפוֹעֵל שֶׁאֵינוֹ שָׁוֶה פְּרוּטָה.

Halakhah 1: "If somebody makes a vow that his wife should not have any usufruct from him," etc. There[6], we have stated: "If somebody by a vow bars his wife from sexual intercourse," and here you say so? There, he makes a vow to separate her from his body[7], but here he makes a vow to separate her from his property. But can anybody make a vow not to pay his debt[8]? Rebbi Yose ben Ḥanina said, since in the future he will divorce her, pay her the *ketubah*, and stop her food supply, it is as if there was no debt[9]. Why could she not sit there and wait; if he divorced her everything would be in order, otherwise let him provide her with food[10]? It follows him who said that the wife's food is not from words of the Torah[11], as it was stated[12]: The court will not determine food for the wife from Sabbatical money, but she may be given Sabbatical produce to eat at her husband's[13]. Then should she not be considered as a worker not worth a *peruṭah*[14]? This proves that she is not considered as a worker not worth a *peruṭah*.

6 Mishnah 5:8. There, the House of Hillel already force the husband to divorce his wife after one week.

7 A vow not to sleep with his

wife is essentially a vow to terminate the marriage; a vow concerning money matters is not.

8   Why should the vow be valid if it infringes contractual rights of third parties? (Cf. *Introduction to Tractate Nedarim.*)

9   The Babli, 70a, notes that the partners in a marriage have the right to separate their incomes: The husband can renounce any benefit from his wife's work and not pay any of her expenses or the wife can renounce any support from her husband and keep all her earnings. But any of these possibilities presuppose mutual consent.

10   Since in Halakhah 5:8 the obligation of the husband to feed his wife was given a biblical basis, why should the husband's vow not simply be declared invalid and he be forced to feed his wife by a court order?

11   This and the next argument are explained in *Ma'serot* 3:1, Notes 11-13. Cf. also the argument of R. Eliezer ben Jacob in Halakhah 5:8 and the last sentence of Chapter 13.

12   Tosephta *Ševi'it* 5:22.

13   If the husband is away on a trip and the wife needs money to survive, she can sell some of the husband's property under the supervision of the court. She cannot sell Sabbatical produce since nobody may use such produce to pay his debts (and the wife's claim is a debt based on the *ketubah* document.) But if the husband is present, she may eat from his Sabbatical fruit since this fulfills the rabbinic ordinance to support the wife and is not counted as paying a debt.

14   This sentence may not belong here; it is copied from *Ma'serot*. An agricultural worker can eat untithed produce by biblical decree (*Deut.* 23:25-26). If his work is not worth any wages (not even the smallest Hasmonean coin), anything he eats is a gift and a gift may not be eaten untithed. But the wife is considered identical with her husband and anything he may eat she also may eat. Therefore, she may eat his Sabbatical produce in his house. But then the question arises why the wife cannot use Sabbatical money to buy Sabbatical produce for herself if her food supply is not her husband's contractual obligation.

(31b line 11) וְיַעֲמִיד פַּרְנָס. כְּהָדָא. אִישׁ פְּלוֹנִי מוּדָּר מִמֶּנִּי הֲנָייָה וְאֵינִי יוֹדֵעַ מָה אֶעֱשֶׂה. יַעֲמִיד פַּרְנָס. רְשׁוּת בְּיַד אִשָּׁה לוֹמַר. אִי אֶפְשִׁי לְהִתְפַּרְנֵס מֵאַחֵר אֶלָּא מִבַּעֲלִי. וְהָתַנִּינָן. הַמַּשְׁרֶה אֶת אִשְׁתּוֹ עַל יְדֵי שָׁלִישׁ. כָּאן בְּשֶׁקִּיבְּלָה עָלֶיהָ וְכָאן בְּשֶׁלֹּא קִיבְּלָה עָלֶיהָ. אִי בְּשֶׁלֹּא קִיבְּלָה עָלֶיהָ אֲפִילוּ יוֹם אֶחָד לֹא יַעֲמִיד. מְגַלְגֶּלֶת עִמּוֹ שְׁלֹשִׁים יוֹם שֶׁמָּא יִמְצָא פֶּתַח לְנִדְרוֹ. שְׁמוּאֵל אָמַר. בְּמַדִּירָהּ שְׁלֹשִׁים יוֹם. אֲבָל בְּמַדִּירָהּ לְעוֹלָם מִיָּד יוֹצִיא וְיִתֵּן כְּתוּבָּה. רִבִּי זְעִירָה רִבִּי אֲבִינָא בְּשֵׁם רַב. וַאֲפִילוּ בְּמַדִּירָהּ לְעוֹלָם מְגַלְגֶּלֶת עִמּוֹ שְׁלֹשִׁים יוֹם שֶׁמָּא יִמְצָא פֶּתַח לְנִדְרוֹ.

He could appoint a provider[15], as the following: "X is forbidden any profit from me by a vow and I do not know what to do." Let him appoint a provider[16]! A woman has the right to say, it is impossible for me to be provided for by anybody other than my husband. But did we not state[17]: "If somebody provides for his wife through a third party." There, if she accepted it; here, if she did not accept it. If she did not accept it[18] then he should not appoint even for one day! She continues with him for one month, perhaps he will find an opening for his vow[19]. Samuel says, if he vowed for thirty days. But if he vowed forever, he shall divorce immediately and pay the *ketubah*. Rebbi Ze'ira, Rebbi Avina in the name of Rav: Even if he vowed forever, she continues with him for one month, perhaps he will find an opening for his vow[20].

15 The Mishnah requires the husband to look for a provider but in fact he cannot appoint one since his vow prohibits him to provide for his wife through an agent. The only way the husband can fulfill his obligation is indicated by Mishnah *Nedarim* 4:8 (Notes 101,102) quoted here, in that he indicates to a third person that he is ready to repay that person after he has provided for his wife, in a way that the provider could not have recourse to the courts if the husband would not pay.

16 Why can the wife force a

divorce if she is provided for?
17   Mishnah 5:11. That Mishnah and the following give detailed instructions how a wife is provided for by an agent, giving the impression that this refers to a permanent arrangement. Why is this only accepted as very temporary in the Mishnah here?
18   This clause is an insert by the first corrector. The text is suspect since אי is Babylonian, for Galilean אין "if".
19   One requires a cooling-down period of one month to give the husband time to regret his vow and seek dissolution of the vow by an Elder.
20   In the Babli, 71a, the positions attributed to Samuel and Rav are switched.

(31b line 19) אִית תַּנָּיֵי תַנֵּי. שְׁלֹשִׁים יוֹם. אִית תַּנָּיֵי תַנֵּי. עַד שְׁלֹשִׁים. מָאן דָּמַר. שְׁלֹשִׁים. מְסַיֵּיעַ לְרַב. וּמָאן דָּמַר. עַד שְׁלֹשִׁים. מְסַיֵּיעַ לִשְׁמוּאֵל.

Some Tannaïm state: thirty days. Some Tannaïm state: up to thirty days[21]. He who says thirty days[22] supports Rav; he who says up to thirty days[23] supports Samuel.

21   All ms. sources (Mishnah, Tosephta 7:1, quotes in Yerushalmi and Babli) support the second version.
22   This is the minimum delay before the wife can go to court; therefore the husband certainly has to provide for 30 days.
23   The divorce proceedings should be finished by then and the full *ketubah* paid.

(31b line 21) רִבִּי יוֹסֵי אוֹמֵר. בַּכֹּהֲנוֹת פְּלִיגִין. יוֹתֵר מִיכֵּן יוֹצִיא וְיִתֵּן כְּתוּבָה. בְּסוֹף שָׁנַיִם. רִבִּי יְהוּדָה אוֹמֵר. בְּיִשְׂרָאֵל חֹדֶשׁ אֶחָד יְקַיֵּים. וּשְׁנַיִם יוֹצִיא וְיִתֵּן כְּתוּבָה. בְּסוֹף שָׁנַיִם. וּבַכֹּהֲנוֹת שְׁנַיִם יְקַיֵּים. שְׁלֹשָׁה יוֹצִיא וְיִתֵּן כְּתוּבָה. בִּתְחִילַת שָׁלֹשׁ. וְתַנֵּי פְּלִיג בְּסוֹף שְׁלֹשָׁה. דִּבְרֵי רִבִּי מֵאִיר. אָמַר לֵיהּ רִבִּי מָנָא. הֵן דְּלָא תַנִּיתָהּ פְּלִיגְנָא אַתְּ עֲבַד לֵיהּ פְּלִיגְנָא. אֶלָּא בְּיִשְׂרָאֵל פְּלִיגִין. יוֹתֵר מִיכֵּן יוֹצִיא וְיִתֵּן כְּתוּבָה. בִּתְחִילַת שָׁנַיִם. רִבִּי יוּדָה אוֹמֵר בְּיִשְׂרָאֵל חֹדֶשׁ אֶחָד יְקַיֵּים וּשְׁנַיִם יוֹצִיא וְיִתֵּן כְּתוּבָה. בִּתְחִילַת שָׁנַיִם. וּבַכֹּהֲנוֹת שְׁנַיִם יְקַיֵּים. שְׁלֹשָׁה יוֹצִיא וְיִתֵּן כְּתוּבָה. בְּסוֹף שְׁלֹשָׁה. וְתַנֵּי כֵן. בְּסוֹף שְׁלֹשָׁה דִּבְרֵי הַכֹּל.

Rebbi Yose said, they[24] differ about wives of Cohanim. "Beyond that he has to divorce her and pay the *ketubah*," at the end of the second [month][25]. "Rebbi Jehudah says, if he is an Israel, for one month he should keep her, for two he has to divorce her and pay the *ketubah*," at the end of the second [month]. "In the case of the wife of a Cohen for two months he should keep her, for three he has to divorce her and pay the *ketubah*," at the beginning of the third. And a disagreement was stated[26], at the end of three [months], the words of Rebbi Meïr. Rebbi Mana said to him, where no disagreement was stated, you introduce a disagreement. But they disagree if he is an Israel. "Beyond that he has to divorce her and pay the *ketubah*," at the beginning of the second [month]. "Rebbi Jehudah says, if he is an Israel, for one month he should keep her[27], for two he has to divorce her and pay the *ketubah*," at the beginning of the second. "In the case of the wife of a Cohen for two months he should keep her, for three he has to divorce her and pay the *ketubah*," at the end of three [months]. It was stated thus: At the end of three by everybody's opinion.

24 R. Jehudah and R. Meïr, the author of the anonymous Mishnah. In Tosephta 7:1 it is stated: "He should appoint a provider for up to 30 days, and for a Cohen's wife three months, the words of R. Meïr." At first glance, this seems to indicate that R. Jehudah permits the court to force the husband to divorce his wife immediately after the end of the second month but R. Meïr only after the end of the third.

25 Scheduling one month for the court proceedings.

26 In the Tosephta.

27 In a short month only 29 days, in opposition to R. Meïr who requires 30 days in every case (Babli 71a).

(fol. 31a) **משנה ב:** הַמַּדִּיר אֶת אִשְׁתּוֹ שֶׁלֹּא תִטְעוֹם בְּאֶחָד מִכָּל מִינֵי פֵּירוֹת יוֹצִיא וְיִתֵּן כְּתוּבָה. רִבִּי יְהוּדָה אוֹמֵר בְּיִשְׂרָאֵל חֹדֶשׁ אֶחָד יְקַיֵּים שְׁנַיִם יוֹצִיא וְיִתֵּן כְּתוּבָה. וּבַכֹּהֶנֶת שְׁנַיִם יְקַיֵּים שְׁלֹשָׁה יוֹצִיא וְיִתֵּן כְּתוּבָה.

Mishnah 2: If somebody causes[28] a vow of his wife that she should not taste any kind of fruits has to divorce her and pay the *ketubah*. Rebbi Jehudah says, if he is an Israel, for one month[29] he should keep her, for two he has to divorce her and pay the *ketubah*; in the case of the wife of a Cohen for two [months] he should keep her, for three he has to divorce her and pay the *ketubah*.

28 The Halakhah will explain how a husband can cause a wife's vow.	The reading "month" is found in a number of early medieval authors discussing the Babli.
29 Most mss. of the Babli and the Mishnah read "day" instead of "month".	

(31b line 29) **הלכה ב:** הַמַּדִּיר אֶת אִשְׁתּוֹ כול'. וְיֵשׁ אָדָם שֶׁמַּדִּיר אֶת חֲבֵירוֹ מֵחַיִּים. אֶלָּא בְּשֶׁנָּדְרָה אִשָּׁה וְשָׁמַע בַּעֲלָהּ וְאָמַר לָהּ. אִם תֹּאכְלִי מֵחֶפֶץ פְּלוֹנִי תְּהֵא אֲסוּרָה מִנְּכָסָיו. אָכְלָה מֵאוֹתוֹ הַחֵפֶץ וּתְהֵא אֲסוּרָה מִנְּכָסָיו. וְהָנֵי רֹאשָׁהּ דְּפִרְקָא. אֲבָל בְּשֶׁנָּדְרָה אִשְׁתּוֹ וְשָׁמַע בַּעֲלָהּ וְלֹא הֵפֶר לָהּ וּכְמָאן דָּמַר. הוּא נָתַן אֶצְבָּעוֹ בֵּין שִׁינֶיהָ יוֹצִיא וְיִתֵּן כְּתוּבָה. אָמַר רִבִּי חוּנָה. אֲפִילוּ כְמָאן דָּמַר. הִיא נָתְנָה אֶצְבָּעוֹ בֵּין שִׁינֶיהָ תֵּצֵא בְּלֹא כְתוּבָה. מוֹדֵי בְמַקְנִיטָהּ וְנַדְרָהּ.

Halakhah 2: "If somebody causes a vow of his wife," etc. Can anybody cause somebody else's vow during his lifetime? It must be that the wife made a vow, the husband heard it, and said to her: If you will eat from such and such, my property will be forbidden to you. If she ate from such and such, why should his property not be forbidden to her[30]? Is that not the case from the beginning of the chapter[31]? But if his wife made a vow, her husband was informed, and did not dissolve it, following him who says that he put his finger between her teeth[32], he has to divorce her and pay the *ketubah*. Rebbi Huna said, even he who said that she put his finger between her teeth, and should be divorced without *ketubah*, will agree[33] in case he provoked her to make the vow.

30 Since she is the cause.

31 He forbade his property to her. Why does the anonymous Tanna require a stay of 30 days in the first Mishnah but none in the second?

32 The question whether the husband is responsible for the consequences if he does not dissolve his wife's vows is in the last paragraph of *Nedarim*, 11:13, Notes 98-103. The image is that if he puts his finger between her teeth, he has only himself to blame if she bites. R. Meïr and R. Jehudah hold that he put his finger between her teeth; cf. also Babli 71a.

33 That he has to pay.

(fol. 31a) **משנה ג:** הַמַדִּיר אֶת אִשְׁתּוֹ שֶׁלֹּא תִתְקַשֵׁט בְּאֶחָד מִכָּל־הַמִּינִין יוֹצִיא וְיִתֵּן כְּתוּבָה. רִבִּי יוֹסֵי אוֹמֵר בָּעֲנִיוֹת שֶׁלֹּא נָתַן קִיצְבָה וּבָעֲשִׁירוֹת שְׁלֹשִׁים יוֹם.

Mishnah 3: If somebody causes a vow of his wife that she should not adorn herself with one of the kinds[34] has to divorce her and pay the *ketubah*. Rebbi Yose says, among the poor if he did not give a time limit, among the rich for thirty days.

34 Kinds of perfume. In modern Hebrew, only jewellery would be קישוט.

(31b line 36) **הלכה ג:** הַמַדִּיר אֶת אִשְׁתּוֹ שֶׁלֹּא תִתְקַשֵׁט כול'. רַב הוּנָא אָמַר. כֵּינֵי מַתְנִיתָא. בָּעֲנִיוֹת שֶׁלֹּא נָתַן קִיצְבָה. עוּלָא בַּר יִשְׁמָעֵאל אָמַר. בָּעֲנִיוֹת שֶׁלֹּא נָתַן קִיצְבָה. אֲבָל אִם נָתַן קִיצְבָה אֲפִילוּ עַד עֶשֶׂר שָׁנִים מוּתָּר. שֶׁאֵין שׁוֹעַל עָפָר פְּרִין מֵת. נָתַן בַּר הוֹשַׁעְיָה אָמַר רִבִּי יוֹחָנָן. חוּץ מִן הָרֶגֶל.

Halakhah 3: "If somebody causes a vow of his wife that she should not adorn herself," etc. Rav Huna said, so is the Mishnah[35]: "Among the poor if he did not give a time limit." Ulla bar Ismael said, among the poor if he did not give a time limit; but if he gave a time limit even if it were for ten years[36] it is permitted, for no fox dies if he gets dusty from his lair[37]. Nathan bar Hoshaiah said in the name of Rebbi Johanan: Except holidays[38].

---

35   J. N. Epstein, מבוא לנוסח המשנה[2], p. 474-475 conjectures that originally the Mishnah read: "if he set a time limit, he may keep her," and only Rav Huna changed the text to adapt it to the other Mishnaiot of this series. In any case, all mss. of Mishnah and Babli follow Rav Huna's reading.

36   In the Babli, 71b, this is R. Johanan's opinion.

37   This popular saying also occurs in a slightly different version in the Babli, 71b. If the husband himself smells badly, he will not be bothered by his wife's smells.

38   In the Babli, 71b, this is ascribed to Rav Hisda.

(fol. 31a) **משנה ד:** הַמַּדִּיר אֶת אִשְׁתּוֹ שֶׁלֹּא תֵלֵךְ לְבֵית אָבִיהָ בִּזְמַן שֶׁהֵן עִמָּהּ בָּעִיר חֹדֶשׁ אֶחָד יְקַיֵּים שְׁנַיִם יוֹצִיא וְיִתֵּן כְּתוּבָה. וּבִזְמַן שֶׁהֵן בְּעִיר אֲחֶרֶת רֶגֶל אֶחָד יְקַיֵּים שְׁנַיִם יוֹצִיא וְיִתֵּן כְּתוּבָה.

Mishnah 4: If somebody causes a vow of his wife that she should not go to her father's house, if they live in the same city she does, for one month he should keep her, for two he has to divorce her and pay the *ketubah*. If they live in another city, for one holiday he should keep her, for two he has to divorce her and pay the *ketubah*.

(31b line 40) **הלכה ד**: הַמַּדִּיר אֶת אִשְׁתּוֹ שֶׁלֹּא תֵלֵךְ לְבֵית אָבִיהָ כול'. אָמַר רִבִּי זְעִירָא. תַּנֵּי תַמָּן. הִדִּירָהּ שֶׁלֹּא תִרְחַצִּי בַמֶּרְחָץ. בַּכְּרָכִים שַׁבָּת אַחַת וּבַכְּפָרִים שְׁתֵּי שַׁבָּתוֹת. שֶׁלֹּא תִנְעֲלִי מַנְעָל. בַּכְּפָרִים שְׁלֹשָׁה חֳדָשִׁים וּבַכְּרָכִים מֵעֵת לְעֵת.

Halakhah 4: "If somebody causes a vow of his wife that she should not go to her father's house," etc. Rebbi Ze'ira said, they stated there[39]: If he made her make a vow that she should not wash in the bathhouse[40], in walled cities one week, in villages two weeks. That she should not wear shoes[41], in villages three months[42], in walled cities 24 hours.

39	In Babylonia.	42	Maimonides (*Hilkhot Iššut* 13:9)
40	The public thermal bath.		reads: Three days.
41	Only sandals.		

(31b line 43) רִבִּי יוֹחָנָן אָמַר. בְּרֶגֶל רְדוּפִין שָׁנוּ. אֵי זֶהוּ רֶגֶל הָרְדוּפִין. אָמַר רִבִּי יוֹסֵי בֵּירִבִּי בּוּן. זֶה רֶגֶל רִאשׁוֹן שֶׁאָבִיהָ רוֹדְפָהּ לְבֵית בַּעֲלָהּ.

Rebbi Johanan[43] said, they taught that about the pursueds' holiday. What is the pursueds' holiday? Rebbi Yose ben Rebbi Bun said, that is the first holiday[44] when her father drives her to her husband's house[45].

43	In the Babli, 71b, this is said in the name of Rabba bar Ulla with the concurrence of R. Johanan.	45	When it is customary for the newlywed to visit her family and the father sends her back to her husband's house.
44	After her final marriage.		

(fol. 31a) **משנה ה**: הַמַּדִּיר אֶת אִשְׁתּוֹ שֶׁלֹּא תֵלֵךְ לְבֵית הָאֵבֶל אוֹ לְבֵית הַמִּשְׁתֶּה יוֹצִיא וְיִתֵּן כְּתוּבָה מִפְּנֵי שֶׁנּוֹעֵל מִפָּנֶיהָ. וְאִם הָיָה טוֹעֵן מִשּׁוּם דָּבָר אַחֵר רַשָּׁאי. אִם אָמַר לָהּ שֶׁתֹּאמְרִי לִפְלוֹנִי מַה שֶׁאָמַרְתִּי לָךְ אוֹ שֶׁתְּהֵי מְמַלְאָה וּמְעָרָה לָאַשְׁפּוֹת יוֹצִיא וְיִתֵּן כְּתוּבָה.

Mishnah 5: [46]If somebody causes a vow of his wife that she should not pay condolence visits or go to weddings has to divorce her and pay the *ketubah*. But if he argues because of another reason, he is in his rights. If he said to her you should tell X what I said to you[47] or that she should fill [vessels] and pour them out on garbage heaps, he has to divorce her and pay the *ketubah*.

46 The entire Mishnah is explained in the Halakhah.
47 This is the text in the Yerushalmi and one Babli mss. In all other Talmud or Mishnah mss.: "What you said to me or what I said to you" (text in the Halakhah) or "what I said to you or you said to me".

(31b line 45) **הלכה ה**: הַמַּדִּיר אֶת אִשְׁתּוֹ שֶׁלֹּא תֵלֵךְ לְבֵית הָאֵבֶל כול׳. הַדִּירָהּ שֶׁלֹּא לְהַשְׁאִיל נָפָה וּכְבָרָה. יוֹצִיא וְיִתֵּן כְּתוּבָּה. מִפְּנֵי שֶׁהוּא מַשִּׂיאָהּ שֵׁם רַע בִּשְׁכֵינוֹתֶיהָ. וְכֵן הִיא שֶׁנָּדְרָה שֶׁלֹּא לְהַשְׁאִיל נָפָה וּכְבָרָה תֵּצֵא שֶׁלֹּא בִּכְתוּבָּה. מִפְּנֵי שֶׁהִיא מַשִּׂיאָתוֹ שֵׁם רַע בִּשְׁכֵינָיו. הַדִּירָהּ שֶׁלֹּא תֵלֵךְ לְבֵית הָאֵבֶל אוֹ לְבֵית הַמִּשְׁתֶּה יוֹצִיא וְיִתֵּן כְּתוּבָּה. שֶׁלְּמָחָר מֵתָהּ מוּטָל לְפָנֶיהָ וְאֵין בְּרִייָה מַשְׁגַּחַת עָלֶיהָ. וְכֵן הִיא שֶׁנָּדְרָה שֶׁלֹּא תֵלֵךְ לְבֵית הָאֵבֶל אוֹ לְבֵית הַמִּשְׁתֶּה תֵּצֵא שֶׁלֹּא בִּכְתוּבָּה. שֶׁלְּמָחָר מֵתוֹ מוּטָל לְפָנָיו וְאֵין בְּרִייָה מַשְׁגַּחַת עָלָיו. רִבִּי מֵאִיר אוֹמֵר מִשּׁוּם רִבִּי עֲקִיבָה רַבּוֹ. טוֹב לָלֶכֶת אֶל בֵּית הָאֵבֶל מִלֶּכֶת אֶל בֵּית הַמִּשְׁתֶּה בַּאֲשֶׁר הוּא סוֹף כָּל־הָאָדָם וְהַחַי יִתֵּן אֶל לִבּוֹ. מַה תַּלְמוּד לוֹמַר וְהַחַי יִתֵּן אֶל לִבּוֹ. אֶלָּא עָבַד דְּיַעֲבַדּוּן סְפוֹד דְּיִסְפְּדוּן קָבוֹר דְּיִקְבְּרוּן לְוַי דִּילְווּן.

Halakhah 5: "If somebody causes a vow of his wife that she should not pay condolence visits," etc. [48]"If he made her vow not to lend out fine and coarse sieves, he shall divorce her and pay the *ketubah*, since he gives her a bad reputation among her [female] neighbors. And so if she made a vow not to lend out fine and coarse sieves, she should leave without *ketubah* since she gives him a bad reputation among his [male] neighbors."

[49]"If he made her vow not to pay condolence visits or go to weddings, he shall divorce her and pay the *ketubah*, since tomorrow a relative of hers will die and nobody will take notice of her. And so if she made a vow not to pay condolence visits or go to weddings, she should leave without *ketubah* since tomorrow a relative of his will die and nobody will take notice of him." [50]"Rebbi Meïr is saying in the name of his teacher Rebbi Aqiba: 'It is better to pay condolence visits than to go to a wedding since the former is the end of every human, and the living should take notice.' Why does the verse say, 'and the living should take notice'? But do so they shall: eulogize so they should eulogize, bury so they should bury, accompany[51] so they should accompany."

48   In the Babli, 72a, and Tosephta 7:4: "fine and coarse sieves and portable ovens."

49   Babli, 72a. In Tosephta 7:5: She will die and nobody will care.

50   Similar but slightly different texts in Babli, 72a, and Tosephta 7:6 (*Eccl.* 7:6).

51   Accompany the coffin to the cemetery.

(31b line 56) אִם הָיָה טוֹעֵן מִשּׁוּם דָּבָר אַחֵר רַשָּׁאי. מִשּׁוּם שֵׁם רַע.

"If he argues because of another reason, he is in his rights," because of bad reputation[52].

52   If he objects only to certain visits where his wife is likely to meet persons of bad reputation who might seduce her.

(31b line 57) אָמַר לָהּ עַל מְנָת שֶׁתֹּאמְרִי לְאִישׁ פְּלוֹנִי מַה שֶּׁאָמַרְתְּ לִי. בְּיָחִיד. אוֹ שֶׁאָמַרְתִּי לָךְ. בְּיָחִיד. אוֹ שֶׁתְּהֵא מְמַלָּא וּמְעָרָה לָאַשְׁפּוֹת יוֹצִיא וְיִתֵּן כְּתוּבָּה. תַּמָּן אָמְרִין. כְּגוֹן מַעֲשֵׂה עֵר. וְרַבָּנִין דְּהָכָא אָמְרִין. דְּבָרִים שֶׁלְּבַטָּלָה.

"If he said to her I require that you tell Mr. X what you said to me," alone, "or I said to you", alone[53], "or that she should fill [vessels] and pour them out on garbage heaps, he has to divorce her and pay the *ketubah*.[54]" There[55], they say, like Er's action[56], but the rabbis here say, senseless things[57].

53 Private matters at the time of sex play; Tosephta 7:6. The formulation in the Babli 72a, "shameful matters" is ambiguous.

54 In the Tosephta: Because he does not treat her following the laws of Moses and Israel. The formula for the preliminary marriage is that the woman shall be married to the man "following the laws of Moses and Israel."

55 Babli 72a in the name of Samuel.

56 Which in Jewish tradition was identical to Onan's sin. He requires her to take contraceptive action; *Gen.* 38:7,9. Cf. *Gen. rabba* 85(5) where the expression is: He ploughed in the gardens and poured out on the garbage heaps.

57 In the words of the Babli, 72a, if she pours water out on the garbage heap "her neighbors would consider her insane."

משנה ו: (fol. 31a) וְאֵילוּ יוֹצְאוֹת שֶׁלֹּא בִכְתוּבָּה. הָעוֹבֶרֶת עַל דָּת מֹשֶׁה וִיהוּדִית. וְאֵי זוֹ הִיא דָּת מֹשֶׁה. מַאֲכִילָתוֹ שֶׁאֵינוֹ מְעוּשָׂר וּמְשַׁמְּשָׁתוֹ נִידָּה וְלֹא קוֹצָה לָהּ חַלָּה וְנוֹדֶרֶת וְאֵינָהּ מְקַיְּימֶת. וְאֵי זוֹ הִיא דָּת יְהוּדִית. יוֹצְאָה וְרֹאשָׁהּ פָּרוּעַ וְטוֹוָה בַשּׁוּק וּמְדַבֶּרֶת עִם כָּל־אָדָם. אַבָּא שָׁאוּל אוֹמֵר. אַף הַמְקַלֶּלֶת יוֹלְדָיו בְּפָנָיו. רִבִּי טַרְפוֹן אוֹמֵר אַף הַקּוֹלָנִית.

Mishnah 6: The following leave without *ketubah*: Any one violating the laws of Moses or Jews. What is the law of Moses? She feeds him what is not tithed, or makes him sleep with her when she is menstruating, or does not cut *hallah*[58], or makes vows which she does not keep. And what is the law of Jews: She leaves home with her hair in disorder[59], or spins in public[60], or speaks with everybody[61]. Abba Saul says, also one who curses his parents in his presence. Rebbi Tarphon says, also the big-voiced.

משנה ז: וְאֵי זוֹ הִיא קוֹלָנִית. לִכְשֶׁהִיא מְדַבֶּרֶת בְּתוֹךְ בֵּיתָהּ וּשְׁכֵינֶיהָ שׁוֹמְעִין קוֹלָהּ.

Mishnah 7: What is the big-voiced? Any who speaks inside her house and her neighbors hear her voice.

58   In all these cases, she causes him to commit a sin punishable by extirpation. One recommends to the husband to divorce her since "nobody should live with a snake in the same basket" [Babli 72a; Yerushalmi *Demai* 2:2 (Note 129; 22d l. 59)].

59   In both Talmudim, this is interpreted that she leaves home with her hair uncovered.

60   It seems that it was a common sign of a free woman engaged in prostitution to appear as if spinning in public (in the Babli, 72b, if she is spinning with a rose on her ear), in contrast to slave girls used as prostitutes who were exhibited naked in front of brothels.

61   This also could be interpreted as a way of soliciting.

(31b line 61) **הלכה ז**: וְאֵילוּ יוֹצְאוֹת שֶׁלֹּא בִּכְתוּבָה כול'. וְאֵי זוֹ הִיא הַקּוֹלָנִית כול'. וְכוּלְּהוֹן בְּעֵדִים. פְּלוֹנִי עִישֵּׂר. פְּלוֹנִי רָאָה כִיתְמָן. פְּלוֹנִי קָצָה חַלָּתָהּ. פְּלוֹנִי הִתִּיר אֶת נִדְרָהּ. בָּדְקוּן כּוּלְּהוֹן וְלָא אַשְׁכְּחוּן.

Halakhah 7: "The following leave without *ketubah*," etc. "What is the big-voiced," etc. And all with witnesses. "X tithed[62], X saw the stains[63], X cut her *hallah*[64], X permitted her vow." They checked and found it was not so.

62 The same argument in the Babli, 72a.

63 She said to her husband that she showed her stained underwear to a rabbi who decided that it was not menstrual blood. In the first Century C.E. it was a common usage of Jewish sects to accuse the adherents of other sects of sleeping with menstruating women. Pharisees accused Sadducees and Samaritans because they considered all genital discharges as menstrual (Mishnah *Niddah* 4:1) and Sadducees accused Pharisees because they do not consider all genital discharges as menstrual (Damascus Document A 5:7). Later practice eliminated the problem by observing both Pharisaic and Sadducee prohibitions. Pharisaic distinctions between pure and impure blood required women to consult rabbis about their discharges. It is not likely that this ever was widespread practice except for wives of Cohanim in whose household impurity had to be reduced to an absolute minimum. The disappearance of priestly purity in the second century C.E. probably put an end to that practice even though the fourth Century Babylonian Rava still claimed full knowledge of all relevant rules.

64 The heave to be taken from bread dough. It was common practice to have a professional baker prepare bread dough for private households and to take *ḥallah* from it; cf. Mishnah *Ḥallah* 1:7.

(31b line 64) מַאֲכִילָתוֹ שֶׁאֵינוֹ מְעוּשָׂר וּמְשַׁמַּשְׁתוֹ נִידָה וְלֹא קוֹצָה לָהּ חַלָּה וְנוֹדֶרֶת וְאֵינָהּ מְקַיֶּימֶת. נִיחָא כּוּלְּהוֹן דְּאִית לֵהּ בְּהוֹן. נוֹדֶרֶת וְאֵינָהּ מְקַיֶּימֶת מָה אִית לָהּ בְּהָדֵיהּ. יָכִיל מֵימַר. אֵי אֶפְשִׁי אִשָּׁה נַדְרָנִית שֶׁהִיא קוֹבֶרֶת אֶת בָּנֶיהָ. תַּנֵּי בְּשֵׁם רִבִּי יוּדָן. בַּעֲווֹן נְדָרִים הַבָּנִים מֵתִים. דִּכְתִיב לַשָּׁוְא הִכִּיתִי אֶת בְּנֵיכֶם.

"She feeds him what is not tithed, or makes him sleep with her when she is menstruating, or does not cut *ḥallah*, or makes vows which she does not keep." We understand all these because he is involved[65]. "She makes vows which she does not keep," what is his interest in this? He can say, I cannot live with a vowing wife because she buries her children. It was stated in the name of Rebbi Yudan[66]: Children die for the sin of vows, as it is written[67]: "For vain [vows] I smote your children.

65   In the first three cases, she leads him into sin.
66   Giṭṭin 4:3 (45c l. 63), Šabbat 5b l. 8; Babli 72a in the name of Rav Naḥman. Šabbat 32b in the name of Rav Naḥman bar Isaac (also thus in one Geniza ms. of Ketubot); in Yalquṭ Šim'oni Jer. #266 a different verse in the name of R. Nathan (anonymous in the Babli, 72a).
67   Jer. 2:30.

(31b line 64) וְרֹאשָׁהּ פָּרוּעַ. לֶחָצֵר אֲמָרוּ. קַל וָחוֹמֶר לְמָבוֹי. רִבִּי חִייָה בְשֵׁם רִבִּי יוֹחָנָן. הַיּוֹצְאָה בְקַפְּלָטִין שֶׁלָּהּ אֵין בָּהּ מִשּׁוּם רֹאשָׁהּ פָּרוּעַ. הָדָא דְתֵימַר לֶחָצֵר. אֲבָל לְמָבוֹי יֵשׁ בָּהּ מִשּׁוּם יוֹצְאָה וְרֹאשָׁהּ פָּרוּעַ. יֵשׁ חָצֵר שֶׁהוּא כְמָבוֹי וְיֵשׁ מָבוֹי שֶׁהוּא כְחָצֵר. חָצֵר שֶׁהָרַבִּים בּוֹקְעִין בְּתוֹכוֹ הֲרֵי הוּא כְמָבוֹי. וּמָבוֹי שֶׁאֵין הָרַבִּים בּוֹקְעִין בְּתוֹכוֹ הֲרֵי הוּא כְחָצֵר.

"With her hair in disorder." They said that for the courtyard[68]; so much more for the passageway[69]. Rebbi Ḥiyya in the name of Rebbi Joḥanan: If one goes out in her wig[70], she does not go out with her hair in disorder. That is, to the courtyard; if she does it in the passageway, she goes out with her hair in disorder. There exists a courtyard which is like a passageway and a passageway which is like a courtyard. A courtyard through which outsiders have broken[71] is like a passageway and a passageway through which no outsiders are breaking[72] is like a courtyard.

68   It is supposed that no house has a direct exit to the street but that a number of houses share a common courtyard from which one leaves to a passageway or a street.
69   A side street which is not a thoroughfare. It may be a dead-end street or not; it is public domain but

mainly used by the dwellers of courtyards opening to that side street.

70   The word was identified by Musaphia as Latin *capillitium*. But the meaning of that word as given in the dictionaries is not "wig" as asserted by Musaphia but "the hair" (collective). The meaning "false hair, wig" is found in Latin *capillamentum*. Cf. also the Latin adjective *capillatus, -a, -um* "having hair, with fine head of hair".

The parallel in the Babli, 72b, has קלתה which Rashi explains as a makeshift head cover formed by an inverted basket, which is declared as forbidden.

71   It has become a shortcut for outsiders.

72   A dead-end street used only by the inhabitants of its houses.

(31b line 73) אָבָּא שָׁאוּל אוֹמֵר. אַף הַמְקַלֶּלֶת אֶת וְלָדָיו לִפְנֵי יוֹלְדָיו. רִבִּי טַרְפוֹן אוֹמֵר אַף הַקּוֹלָנִית. אֵי זוֹ הִיא קוֹלָנִית. שְׁמוּאֵל אָמַר. כָּל־שֶׁהִיא מְדַבֶּרֶת וּשְׁכֵינוֹתֶיהָ שׁוֹמְעוֹת אוֹתָהּ. רַב אָמַר. כָּל־שֶׁקּוֹלָהּ הוֹלֶכֶת מִמִּטָּה לְמִטָּה בִּשְׁעַת תַּשְׁמִישׁ.

Abba Saul says, also one who curses their child in his parents' presence[73]. Rebbi Tarphon says, also the big-voiced. What is the big-voiced? Samuel says, any who speaks and her women neighbors hear her voice[74]. Rav says, any one whose voice is heard by other people from bed to bed during intercourse[75].

73   In the Babli, 72b, as Amoraic statement: One who curses his parents before his children.

74   Therefore, all his marital disagreements are immediately public knowledge.

75   The same statement is also in the Babli, 72b.

(31c line 1) תַּנֵּי רִבִּי חָנִין בְּשֵׁם רִבִּי שְׁמוּאֵל. אֶחָד נָשִׁים שֶׁאָמְרוּ. יֵשׁ לָהֶן כְּתוּבָּה. וְאֶחָד נָשִׁים שֶׁאָמְרוּ. יוֹצְאוֹת שֶׁלֹּא בִכְתוּבָּה. כְּגוֹן הַיְתוֹמָה וְהַשְּׁנִייָה וְהָאַיְילוֹנִית. לֹא שָׁנוּ אֶלָּא כְּתוּבַּת מָנֶה מָאתַיִים. אֶלָּא אֲפִילוּ הָיְתָה כְּתוּבָּה שֶׁלְאֶלֶף דִּינָר מְאַבֶּדֶת וְנוֹטֶלֶת בְּלָיוֹת מִמַּה שֶׁיֵּשׁ לְפָנֶיהָ. וְהַיּוֹצְאָה מִשּׁוּם שֵׁם רַע

אֵין לָהּ בְּלָיוֹת. מָהוּ נְסַב מִן הַפָּךְ פַּרְנוֹן דִּידָהּ. רִבִּי זְעִירָה אָמַר. נָסְבָה. רִבִּי הִילָא אָמַר. לֹא נָסְבָה. רִבִּי הִילָא עֲבַד לָהּ כְּמִיתָה. רִבִּי הִילָא רִבִּי יָסָא רִבִּי בָּא בַּר כֹּהֵן מַטֵּי בָהּ בְּשֵׁם רִבִּי חֲנִינָה בֶּן גַּמְלִיאֵל. אֶחָד נָשִׁים שֶׁאָמְרוּ. יוֹצְאוֹת שֶׁלֹּא בִכְתוּבָה. לֹא שָׁנוּ אֶלָּא כְּתוּבַת מָנֶא מָאתַיִים אֶלָּא אֲפִילוּ הָיְתָה כְּתוּבָתָהּ שֶׁלְאֶלֶף דֵּינָר מְאַבֶּדֶת. רִבִּי סִימוֹן אָמַר רִבִּי יוֹחָנָן. כָּל־הַמִּשְׁנָיוֹת מְחוּבָּרוֹת בְּמִשְׁנָה זוֹ. אָמַר רִבִּי מָנָא קוֹמֵי רִבִּי יָסָא. בְּהַיי דָא מַתְנִיתָא. בְּרִבִּי חָנִין דִּשְׁמוּאֵל. אָמַר לֵיהּ. דִּבְרֵי הַכֹּל הִיא. וְתַנֵּי רִבִּי חִייָה כֵן. נָשִׁים הַמַּעֲבִרוֹת עַל הַדָּת מְאַבְּדוֹת אֶת הַכֹּל.

[76]Rebbi Ḥanin stated in the name of Rebbi Samuel: Both for women about whom they said that they have *ketubah* as also those about whom they said they leave without *ketubah*, as the minor, the secondarily prohibited[77], and the she-ram, did they speak about a mina or 200 [*zuz*]? But even if the *ketubah* was a thousand denars[78], she loses[79], but she takes her existing rags[80]. But the one who leaves because of a bad reputation loses everything[81]. Can she take her paraphernalia[82]? Rebbi Ze'ira said, she takes. Rebbi Hila said, she does not take. Rebbi Hila, Rebbi Yasa, Rebbi Abba bar Cohen mention it in the name of Rebbi Ḥanina ben Gamliel: Both women about whom they said that they leave without *ketubah*, did they speak about the *ketubah* of a mina or 200 [*zuz*]? But even if the *ketubah* was a thousand denars, she loses[83]. Rebbi Simon said, Rebbi Joḥanan: All the Mishnaiot[84] are connected to this *baraita*. Rebbi Mana said before Rebbi Yasa: About which *baraita*? Of Rebbi Ḥanin from Samuel[85]? He said to him, it is everybody's opinion. And Rebbi Ḥiyya formulated so[86]: "Women who infringe upon the law lose everything.

76   This text seems to be in rather bad shape and the secondary sources are contradictory, Note 79.

77   Obviously one has to read in the first clause: have no *ketubah*. Somehow the text should accommodate several kinds of divorces.

The minor who is mentioned in this connection is an underage girl married off by her mother or brothers after her father's death whose marriage has no biblical validity and who can walk out of it without formality (cf. *Yebamot* 1:2, Note 118). Her repudiation of her husband annuls her marriage and with it her *ketubah* but it does not touch her property rights; both mortmain (*dos aestimata*) as also paraphernalia (*dos non aestimata*) must be returned to her (cf. *Yebamot* 7:1, Note 1).

Secondary prohibitions are rabbinically prohibited unions extending biblical prohibitions, usually for one additional generation (cf. *Yebamot* 2:4, Note 67). The rabbinate will force the husband to divorce his wife and, in order to scare away women from such marriages, will not enforce any payment of *ketubah*. But her property rights for mortmain and paraphernalia are not touched (and her children are legitimate.)

The she-ram (*Yebamot* 1:1, Note 65) is a woman exhibiting secondary male sex characterstics. She is presumed to be congenitally infertile; her marriage is considered invalid by biblical standards, and she will have difficulty collecting the *ketubah* but not recovering her property.

The statement as it stands now does not cover women who are divorced following Mishnah 6, who may not be able to recover their property.

78   Promised by the husband; this does not touch repayment of the dowry.

79   R. Nissim Gerondi (Commentary to Alfasi, 59b in the Wilna edition) reads: נָשִׁים שֶׁאָמְרוּ חֲכָמִים אֵין לָהֶן כְּתוּבָּה. כְּגוֹן הַיְתוֹמָה וְהַשְּׁנִיָּה וְהָאַיְילוֹנִית. לֹא שָׁנוּ אֶלָּא מִנָא מָאתַיִים. אֲבָל כְּתוּבָּה שֶׁלָּאֶלֶף דִּינָר נוֹטֶלֶת "Women about whom they said that they leave without *ketubah*, as the underage orphan, the secondarily prohibited, and the she-ram, they spoke only about a mina or 200 [*zuz*] But if the *ketubah* was a thousand denars, she takes it." As the commentators of the Babli explain, the obligatory *ketubah* must be lost since she leaves without *ketubah*; but any additional sums are voluntary gifts from the husband. The claim to such a voluntary gift can be lost only by criminal behavior of the wife, not by an inherent defect of the marriage

which was known to the husband at the time he made the promise.

Naḥmanides (*Sefer Hazzekhut*, in Alfasi, *loc. cit.*) reads: תָּנֵי רִבִּי חָנִין בְּרִבִּי שְׁמוּאֵל. נָשִׁים שֶׁאָמְרוּ אֵין לָהֶן כְּתוּבָּה יֵשׁ לָהֶן תּוֹסָפֶת. וּשֶׁאָמְרוּ יוֹצְאוֹת שֶׁלֹּא בִּכְתוּבָּה אֵין לָהֶן אֲפִילוּ תוֹסָפֶת. "Rebbi Ḥanin ben Rebbi Samuel stated: Women about whom they said they have no *ketubah*, receive the additions; but those about whom they said that they leave without *ketubah* do not even get the additions." Women who have no *ketubah* are those whose marriage was invalid from the start, e. g., the underage orphan, the secondarily prohibited, and the she-ram. They receive the voluntary additions as explained above. Women who leave without *ketubah* are those who are divorced because of their crimes; they lose also the husband's voluntary gift since they force the husband to divorce them.

Probably one should read in the text: "Rav Ḥanin (known as Rav's student) in the name of Samuel." This is consistent with the quote later in the paragraph.

80   Her used clothing; cf. Chapter 5, Notes 224-225.

81   Including mortmain, the dowry given to the husband as the latter's property subject to his obligation to return their value in the fixed amount stated in the *ketubah* document. Nothing is said about paraphernalia, the wife's separate property which is administered by her husband. The parallel statement of Samuel in the Babli, 101a, agrees that she loses the husband's additions above the minimal *ketubah* but is silent about mortmain.

82   This means her dowry as addition to the *ketubah*, including mortmain and paraphernalia in the literal sense.

83   This text does not make too much sense. Probably one should read something similar to the text of Tosephta 7:7: כָּל־אֵילוּ שֶׁאָמְרוּ. יוֹצְאוֹת שֶׁלֹּא בִכְתוּבָּה. לֹא שָׁנוּ אֶלָּא מָנֶא מָאתַיִים אֶלָּא אֲפִילוּ הָיְתָה כְּתוּבָּתָהּ שֶׁלְאֶלֶף דֵּינָר מְאַבֶּדֶת אֶת־הַכֹּל וְנוֹטֶלֶת בְּלָאיוֹת שֶׁמּוֹצָא לְפָנֶיהָ. "[Women] about whom they said that they leave without *ketubah*, they spoke not only about a mina or 200 [*zuz*], but even if the *ketubah* was a thousand denars, she loses everything, but she takes her used clothing.." The Tosephta can be quoted in support of R. Hila that she takes anything that clearly is her property at that moment (her personal effects and the paraphernalia proper) but the husband is not required to return her mortmain which has become

his property; her claim to it is voided.
84   All Mishnaiot on the topic why a women should be divorced.
85   Since this is clearly formulated as Amoraic opinion of a single person, it cannot be the central topic of a whole series of Mishnaiot.
86   Tosephta 7:7.

(31c line 14) רִבִּי לְעָזָר בְּשֵׁם רִבִּי חֲנִינָה. רָאוּ אוֹתָהּ חוֹגֶרֶת בְּסִינָר רוֹכֵל יוֹצֵא מִתּוֹךְ בֵּיתָהּ. כָּאוּר הַדָּבָר תֵּצֵא. רוֹק עַל גַּבֵּי מִיטָתָהּ. כָּאוּר הַדָּבָר תֵּצֵא. רוֹק עַל גַּבֵּי מִיטָתוֹ. כָּאוּר הַדָּבָר תֵּצֵא. סַנְדָּלוֹ לִפְנֵי מִיטָתָהּ. כָּאוּר הַדָּבָר תֵּצֵא. סַנְדָּלוֹ לִפְנֵי מִיטָתוֹ. כָּאוּר הַדָּבָר תֵּצֵא. שְׁנֵיהֶם יוֹצְאִין מִמָּקוֹם אָפֵל. כָּאוּר הַדָּבָר תֵּצֵא. מַעֲלִין זֶה אֶת זֶה מִן הַבּוֹר. כָּאוּר הַדָּבָר תֵּצֵא. שְׁנֵיהֶם טוֹפְחוֹת עַל יְרֵיכָהּ בַּמֶּרְחָץ. כָּאוּר הַדָּבָר תֵּצֵא. חֲנִינָה בַּר אִיקָא בְּשֵׁם רִבִּי יְהוּדָה. וְכוּלְּהוֹן אִם הֱבִיאָהּ רְאָיָיהּ לִדְבָרֶיהָ נֶאֱמֶנֶת. רַב אָדָא בַּר אֲחַוָה בְּשֵׁם רַב. מַעֲשֶׂה בָּא לִפְנֵי רִבִּי וָמַר. מַה בְּכָךְ. בְּעָיָין קוֹמוֹי. אֲפִילוּ רָאוּ אוֹתוֹ נוֹתֵן פִּיו עַל פִּיהָ שֶׁלָּהּ. אָמַר. כָּזֶה בָּאת מַעֲשֶׂה בְּאֶחָד שֶׁרָאוּ אוֹתוֹ נוֹתֵן פִּיו עַל פִּיהָ שֶׁלָּהּ. אָתָא עוֹבְדָא קוֹמֵי רִבִּי יוֹסֵי אָמַר. תִּיפּוּק בְּלֹא פֶּרֶן. וְהַוִין קְרִיבֶיהָ עָרְרִין וְאָמְרִין. אֵין שׁוֹטָה הִיא תֵּיפוּק בְּלֹא פֶּרֶן. וְאֵין לֵית שׁוֹטָה הִיא תֵּיסַב פֶּרֶן שְׁלֵים. אָמַר לוֹן רִבִּי מָנָא. אַייתוֹן פָּרְנָא נִיקְרִיגֵּיהּ. אַייתוֹן פָּרְנָהּ וְאַשְׁכְּחוּן כְּתוּב בְּגַוָּוהּ. אִין הָדָא פְּלָנִית תִּסְבֵּי לְהָדֵין פְּלוֹנִי בַּעֲלָהּ וְלָא תִצְבֵּי בְּשׁוּתָּפוּתֵיהּ תִּיהֲוֵי נָסְבָה פַּלְגוּת פֶּרֶן. אָמַר רִבִּי אָבוּן. מִכֵּיוָן שֶׁקִּיבְּלָה עָלֶיהָ שֶׁיִּתֵּן פִּיו עַל פִּיהָ שֶׁלָּהּ כְּמַאן דְּשַׂנְאַת לֵיהּ וְלֵית לָהּ אֶלָּא פַּלְגוּת פֶּרֶן. הִיא גּוֹ חוֹבָה וְהוּא גּוֹ חוֹבָה סוֹטָה. מְגַפְּפִין סוֹטָה. מְנַשְּׁקִין סוֹטָה. תַּרְעָה טְרִיד סוֹטָה. מוּנָף צְרִיכָה.

Rebbi Eleazar in the name of Rebbi Ḥanina[87]: If they saw her putting on her underpants[88] and the pedlar leaves her house, the thing is ugly, she should leave[89]. There is slime on her bed, the thing is ugly, she should leave. There is slime on his[90] bed, the thing is ugly, she should leave. His sandal is in front of her bed, the thing is ugly, she should leave. Her sandal is in front of his[90] bed, the thing is ugly, she should leave. Both leave the same dark place, the thing is ugly, she should leave. They lift one another from the cistern, the thing is ugly, she should leave. Both of them clap on her thighs in the bathhouse[91], the thing is ugly, she should leave. Ḥanina bar Iqa in the name of Rebbi Jehudah, in all these cases, if she brings an explanation for her behavior she is believed. Rav Ada bar Aḥawa in the name of Rav: A case came before Rebbi and he said, what of it[92]? They asked before him[93]: Even if they saw him putting his mouth on her mouth? He said, this did happen, that they saw a man[94] putting his mouth on her mouth. The case came befote Rebbi Yose, who said that she should leave without *ketubah*. Her relatives appealed the case and said, if she is deviant[95], she should leave without *ketubah*. If she is not deviant, she should take the entire *ketubah*. Rebbi Mana said to them, bring the *ketubah* that we may read it. They brought the *ketubah* and found written in it[96]: If this X marries this Y as her husband and should no longer desire his company, she shall take half the *ketubah* sum. Rebbi Abun said, since she agreed that he[94] should put his mouth on her mouth it is as if she hated him; she has only half the *ketubah*. She lies in his bosom[97] or he lies in her bosom, she is deviant[98]. If they embrace, she is deviant. If they kiss, she is deviant. If the door is locked, she is deviant. If it is blocked[99], that is a problem[100].

---

87 In the opinion of S. Abramson, the name should be Ze'ira ben Ḥanina, an Amora contemporary with rabbis Yose and Mana mentioned later in the text. Cf. בירורים, שרגא אברמסון, Sinai 89 (1981) pp. 118-121.

88 Cf. *Soṭah* 1:2, Note 115.

89 In the Babli, *Yebamot* 24b-25a, this and the following statements are by R. Ḥiyya (the elder) quoting the authority of Rebbi. In all these cases, where adultery is not proven by two witnesses to the act, one implies that the woman can be divorced without

payment of the *ketubah* since the acts describe a high probability of adultery, which is admissible proof in money matters and does not need prior warning.

90   The other man's.

91   Where everybody is naked. Mishnah 9 implies that the use of public thermal baths was separate by sex; then the reference would be to lesbian relationships which, while not forbidden (cf. *Yebamot* 8:6, Note 240) are generally classified as undesirable.

92   It seems to mean that Rebbi did not want to see the courts involved as long as the testimony did not amount to a legal proof. Some commentators of the Babli read the sentence as referring to the woman's explanation, that Rebbi would not accept any explanation except a legal disproof (cf. R. Yosef Ḥabiba, *Nimmuqe Yosef*, on Alfassi *Yebamot*, 6a in the Wilna edition.)

93   This seems to refer to the person mentioned at the head of this paragraph Note 87.

94   A man other than the husband.

95   A proven adulteress. Since there is no legal proof, she should take the entire *ketubah* amount if the husband divorces her.

A document in which כתובה and פרנה are used interchangeably was published by S, Asaph, *Tarbiz* 9(1938), #1, p. 25.

96   About this *ketubah* text which gives the wife the right to force a divorce in exchange for a predetermined financial reward for the husband, see the details in Note 226, Chapter 5.

97   For Aramaic חוּבָּה = Hebrew חיק, cf. *Targum Yerušalmi Ex.* 4:6,7. A less likely explanation would be "hideout", derived from the Hebrew root חבא "to hide". In the cases mentioned here, there are witnesses but the parties are fully clothed.

98   And may be divorced without claim to the *ketubah*.

99   Not locked, but some obstacle would have to be removed before a third party could enter the room.

100   The wife has not lost her right to sue for the *ketubah* amount but the outcome of the suit cannot be guaranteed.

(fol. 31a) **משנה ח:** הַמְקַדֵּשׁ אֶת הָאִשָּׁה עַל מְנָת שֶׁאֵין עָלֶיהָ נְדָרִים וְנִמְצְאוּ עָלֶיהָ נְדָרִים אֵינָהּ מְקוּדֶּשֶׁת. כְּנָסָהּ סְתָם וְנִמְצְאוּ עָלֶיהָ נְדָרִים תֵּצֵא שֶׁלֹּא בִכְתוּבָּה. עַל מְנָת שֶׁאֵין עָלֶיהָ מוּמִין וְנִמְצְאוּ בָהּ מוּמִין אֵינָהּ מְקוּדֶּשֶׁת. כְּנָסָהּ סְתָם וְנִמְצְאוּ בָהּ מוּמִין תֵּצֵא שֶׁלֹּא בִכְתוּבָּה. שֶׁכָּל־הַמּוּמִין הַפּוֹסְלִין בַּכֹּהֲנִים פּוֹסְלִין בַּנָּשִׁים.

Mishnah 8: If somebody performed the preliminary marriage with a woman on condition that she had no obligation of vows on her and it turned out that she had vows to fulfill, she is not preliminarily married[101]. If he married her definitively without inquiry[102] and she had vows to fulfill[103], she should leave without *ketubah*. If somebody performed the preliminary marriage with a woman on condition that she had no bodily defects and it turned out that she had bodily defects, she is not preliminarily married. If he married her definitively without inquiry and she had bodily defects, she should leave without *ketubah*; and[104] all defects which disqualify a priest[105] disqualify a woman.

משנה ט: הָיוּ בָהּ מוּמִין וְעוֹדָהּ בְּבֵית אָבִיהָ הָאָב צָרִיךְ לְהָבִיא רְאָיָה שֶׁמִּשֶּׁנִּתְאָרְסָה נוֹלְדוּ בָהּ מוּמִין אִילוּ וְנִסְתַּפְּחָה שָׂדֵהוּ. נִכְנְסָה לִרְשׁוּת הַבַּעַל הַבַּעַל צָרִיךְ לְהָבִיא רְאָיָה שֶׁעַד שֶׁלֹּא נִתְאָרְסָה הָיוּ בָהּ מוּמִין אִילוּ וְהָיָה מִקְחוֹ מֶקַח טָעוּת דִּבְרֵי רִבִּי מֵאִיר. וַחֲכָמִים אוֹמְרִים בַּמֶּה דְבָרִים אֲמוּרִים בְּמוּמִין שֶׁבַּסֵּתֶר אֲבָל בְּמוּמִין שֶׁבַּגָּלוּי אֵינוֹ יָכוֹל לִטְעוֹן. אִם יֵשׁ מֶרְחָץ עִמּוֹ בְּאוֹתָהּ הָעִיר אַף מוּמִין שֶׁבַּסֵּתֶר אֵינוֹ יָכוֹל לִטְעוֹן מִפְּנֵי שֶׁהוּא בוֹדְקָהּ בִּקְרוֹבוֹתָיו.

Mishnah 9: If she had bodily defects[106], as long as she is in her father's house, the father has to prove that the defects developed after she was preliminarily married and his field was swamped[107]; once she entered her husband's domain, the husband has to prove that she had the defects before the preliminary wedding so that his acquisition was in error[108], the words of Rebbi Meïr. But the Sages say, when was this said? For hidden defects, but he has no claim about visible defects[109], and if there is a public bathhouse in his town he has no claim for hidden defects since he checks her out through his female relatives.

101 No conditional contract is valid if the condition is not fulfilled at the moment the contract is activated.

102 Vows were not mentioned at all in the preparations for the preliminary marriage.

103 Of the kind she could expect that the husband would object to.

104 This is one of the cases where שֶׁ and וְ have the same meaning.

105 From Temple service; cf. *Lev.* 21:16-24; Mishnah *Bekhorot* 7.

106 The preliminarily married groom divorces her because of the defects and refuses to pay the *ketubah*. Is the burden of proof on the claimant (in this case the bride and her father) or on the person who wants to break the contract (the groom)? Since in money matters the burden of proof is both on the claimant and on the person who disputes the validity of a document, a way has to be found to reconcile the two conflicting rules. This Mishnah presupposes that the *ketubah* was written at the time of the preliminary marriage.

107 This agricultural simile is used generally to describe that an accident happened in the buyer's domain. If somebody buys a field and then finds out that is was recently flooded and became unusable for the current season, it is of the essence that the date of the flood be determined exactly to find out whether it was his bad luck or that he had been sold the field fraudulently. In the latter case he can recover the price paid in court.

108 The underlying principle is: There is a *prima facie* assumption that a defect happened where it was discovered.

109 Since he is not supposed to marry a woman he had not seen before the marriage.

(31c line 33) **הלכה ט:** הַמְקַדֵּשׁ אֶת הָאִשָּׁה עַל מְנָת שֶׁאֵין עָלֶיהָ נְדָרִים וְנִמְצְאוּ עָלֶיהָ נְדָרִים כול׳. הָיוּ בָהּ מוּמִין וְעוֹדָהּ בְּבֵית אָבִיהָ כול׳. תַּנִּינָן מוּמִין. בְּאֵילוּ נְדָרִים. אָמַר רִבִּי יוֹחָנָן בְּשֵׁם רִבִּי שִׁמְעוֹן בֶּן יוֹצָדָק. נָדְרָה שֶׁלֹּא לוֹכַל בָּשָׂר

וְשֶׁלֹּא לִשְׁתּוֹת יַיִן וְשֶׁלֹּא לִלְבּוֹשׁ בִּגְדֵי צִבְעוֹנִין. אָמַר רִבִּי זְעִירָא. כְּלֵי פִשְׁתָּן הַדַּקִּין הַבָּאִים מִבֵּית שָׁן כִּכְלֵי צִבְעוֹנִין הֵן. אָמַר רִבִּי יוֹסֵי. מַתְנִיתָא בְּשָׁאָמַר לָהּ. עַל מְנָת שֶׁאֵין עָלַיִךְ נְדָרִים. אֲבָל אִם אָמַר. עַל מְנָת שֶׁאֵין עָלַיִךְ כָּל נֶדֶר. אֲפִילוּ נֶדְרָה שֶׁלֹּא לוֹכַל חָרוּבִין נֶדֶר הוּא.

3-2 באילו נדרים. אמר | ק באילו נדרים אמרו   4 הדקין | ק הדקים   5 הבאין | ק הבאים   מבית שן | ק מבית שאן   6 אמר | ק אמר לה   עליך כל | ק ליך

Halakhah 9: "If somebody performed the preliminary marriage with a woman on condition that she had no obligation of vows on her," etc. "If she had bodily defects, as long as she is in her father's house," etc. We have stated defects. Which vows[110]? Rebbi Joḥanan said in the name of Rebbi Simeon ben Yoṣadaq: If she vowed not to eat, or not to drink wine, or not to wear dyed garments[111]. Rebbi Ze'ira said, the fine linen garments which come from Bet She'an have the status of dyed garments[112]. Rebbi Yose said, the Mishnah deals with the case that he said to her, "on condition that you have no obligation of vows on you." But if he said, "on condition that you have no obligation of *any* vow on you," then even if she made a vow not to eat carob fruit[113] it is a vow.

110 The Mishnah stated a criterion for defects which are serious enough for annulment of the marriage. Does there exist a similar criterion for vows? "Vows" without a qualifier are always "vows or oaths of prohibition for the purposes of mortification"; cf. Introduction to Tractate *Nedarim*. The entire Halakhah from here on is also Halakhah *Qiddušin 2:5*. The variant readings are noted ק.

111 Babli 72b, Tosephta 7:8. These vows either interfere with her ability to cook for her husband or they detract from his standing in the community if his wife appears in undyed woolen or linen garments used only by the poor.

112 These are bleached white; he asserts that bleaching is the equivalent of dying.

113 In which case nobody should care. A similar argument is ascribed to Rav Pappa in the Babli, 72b.

(31c line 39) הָלְכָה אֵצֶל הַזָּקֵן וְהִתִּיר לָהּ הֲרֵי זוֹ מְקוּדֶּשֶׁת. אֵצֶל הָרוֹפֵא וְרִיפְּאָהּ אֵינָהּ מְקוּדֶּשֶׁת. מַה בֵּין זָקֵן וּמַה בֵּין רוֹפֵא. זָקֵן עוֹקֵר אֶת הַנֶּדֶר מֵעִיקָרוֹ. רוֹפֵא אֵינוֹ מְרַפֵּא אֶלָּא מִיכָּן וּלְהַבָּא. אִית תַּנָּיֵי תַנֵּי. אֲפִילוּ הָלְכָה אֵצֶל הַזָּקֵן וְהִתִּיר לָהּ אֵינָהּ מְקוּדֶּשֶׁת. מַתְנִיתָא דְּרִבִּי אֶלְעָזָר. דְּתַנֵּי תַמָּן. אָמַר רִבִּי לְעָזָר. לֹא אָסְרוּ זֶה אֶלָּא מִפְּנֵי זֶה. מַה טַעְמָא דְּרִבִּי לְעָזָר. בְּדִין הָיָה נֶדֶר שֶׁהוּא צָרִיךְ חֲקִירַת חָכָם מִפְּנֵי נֶדֶר שֶׁאֵינוֹ צָרִיךְ חֲקִירַת חָכָם. אִית תַּנָּיֵי תַנֵּי. מוּתֶּרֶת לְהִינָּשֵׂא בְּלֹא גֵט. אִית תַּנָּיֵי תַנֵּי. אֲסוּרָה לְהִינָּשֵׂא בְּלֹא גֵט. הֲווֹן בְּעָיִין מֵימַר. מָאן דָּמַר. מוּתֶּרֶת לְהִינָּשֵׂא בְּלֹא גֵט. רִבִּי לְעָזָר. וּמָאן דָּמַר. אֲסוּרָה לְהִינָּשֵׂא בְּלֹא גֵט. רַבָּנִין. כּוּלָּהּ דְּרַבָּנִין. וּמָאן דָּמַר. מוּתֶּרֶת לְהִינָּשֵׂא בְּלֹא גֵט. שֶׁמִּתּוֹךְ שֶׁהִיא יוֹדַעַת שֶׁאִם הוֹלֶכֶת הִיא אֵצֶל זָקֵן וְהוּא מַתִּיר לָהּ אֶת נִדְרָהּ וְהִיא אֵינָהּ הוֹלֶכֶת. לְפוּם כֵּן מוּתֶּרֶת לְהִינָּשֵׂא בְּלֹא גֵט. וּמָאן דָּמַר. אֲסוּרָה לְהִינָּשֵׂא בְּלֹא גֵט. שֶׁלֹּא תֵלֵךְ אֵצֶל הַזָּקֵן וְיַתִּיר לָהּ אֶת נִדְרָהּ וְקִידּוּשִׁין חָלִין עָלֶיהָ לְמַפְרֵעַ וְנִמְצְעוּ בָנֶיהָ בָּאִין לִידֵי מַמְזֵרוּת. לְפוּם כֵּן אֲסוּרָה לְהִינָּשֵׂא בְּלֹא גֵט.

4 אלעזר | ק לעזר   דתני | ק דתנינן   5 לא אסרו זה אלא מפני זה. מה טעמא דר' לעזר | ק אמר ר' לעזר   נדר | ק אפי' נדר   - | ק חכם שהזקן עוקר את הנדר מעקרו. ולמה אסרו נדר שהוא צריך   9 דרבנין | ק רבנין   ומאן | ק מאן   11 ומאן דמר | ק מאי טע' דמאן דמר

[114]"If she went to an Elder and her dissolved her vow, she is preliminarily married. To a doctor and he healed her, she is not preliminarily married." [115]What is the difference between the Elder and the doctor? The elder uproots the vow from its start; the doctor heals only for the future. [116]Some Tannaïm state: Even if she went to an Elder and her dissolved her vow, she is not preliminarily married. The *baraita* follows Rebbi Eleazar, as we have stated there: "Rebbi Eleazar said, they forbade this only because of the other.[117]" What is the reason of Rebbi Eleazar? It would have been logical about a vow which has to be investigated by a Sage ... because a vow which does not have to be

investigated by a Sage[118]. Some Tannaïm state: She is allowed to marry[119] without a bill of divorce. Some Tannaïm state: She is forbidden to marry without a bill of divorce[120]. They wanted to say that he who says, she is allowed to marry without a bill of divorce, is Rebbi Eleazar[121], and he who says, she is forbidden to marry without a bill of divorce, are the rabbis[122]. Everything follows the rabbis. He who says, she is allowed to marry without a bill of divorce: Since she knows that if she went to an Elder, he would dissolve her vow, since she does not go therefore she can be married without a bill of divorce[123]. But he who says, she is forbidden to marry without a bill of divorce, that she should not go to an Elder[124] who would dissolve her vow, then the preliminary marriage would become retroactively valid for her and it would turn out that her children become bastards. Therefore she is forbidden to marry without a bill of divorce[125].

114 Tosephta 7:8; quoted in Babli 74b; also in Yerushalmi *Qiddušin* 2:5 (62c l. 66).

115 In the Babli (previous Note) this is quoted as a tannaïtic text.

116 The following text has a parallel with different emphasis in the Babli, *loc. cit.*

117 The reference is to Mishnah *Giṭṭin* 4:7 where it is stated that a man who divorces his wife because of her vows is never permitted to take her back. This is a rabbinic rule. R. Meïr holds that no remarriage is permitted in case of any vow that needs to be annulled by an Elder (cf. *Nedarim* Chapter 9). The reason is that one has to avoid a situation in which the divorcee marries another man and for him goes to an Elder to have him annul the vow. If the ex-husband says, "if I had known that her vow will be annulled, I would not have divorced her," he retroactively would annul the bill of divorce, make his ex-wife a bigamist and bastards of her children from the second husband. Therefore, one has to make clear to him that the divorce is final and irreversible, to prevent him from having second

thoughts. But if the cause of the divorce is an invalid vow, the divorce is not caused by the vow and the husband may remarry his divorcee (as long as she did not marry another man). R. Eleazar says that remarriage was forbidden in the second case because of the first one since it is obvious that the husband must be an ignoramus if he divorces his wife because of a vow which every competent scholar will immediately declare as invalid if asked about it ("a vow which does not have to be investigated by a Sage" because the Sage will declare it invalid at first sight.)

118 This text is clearly elliptic. There does not seem to be a lacuna, but rather the text is a reference to an extensive argument in *Giṭṭin* 4:7 (and a related text in *Qidduŝin* 2:5):אָמַר רִבִּי לָעְזָר. לֹא אָסְרוּ זֶה אֶלָּא מִפְּנֵי זֶה. בְּדִין הָיָה שֶׁאֲפִילוּ נֶדֶר שֶׁהוּא צָרִיךְ חֲקִירַת חָכָם יַחֲזִיר. שֶׁהַדָּקֵן עוֹקֵר אֶת הַנֶּדֶר מֵעִיקָרוֹ. מִפְּנֵי מָה אָסְרוּ נֶדֶר שֶׁאֵין צָרִיךְ חֲקִירַת חָכָם. מִפְּנֵי נֶדֶר שֶׁהוּא צָרִיךְ חֲקִירַת חָכָם. "Rebbi Eleazar said, they forbade this only because of the other. It would have been logical that even in the case of a vow which has to be investigated by a Sage he could take her back. For the Elder uproots the vow from the start. Why did they forbid a vow which does not have to be investigated by a Sage? Because of a vow which has to be investigated by a Sage."

119 The woman whose preliminary marriage has been declared invalid because of her vows may marry any other man without a divorce from the first.

120 This is also quoted in the Babli, *loc. cit.*

121 Who holds that all these prohibitions are only extreme precautions.

122 This position, rejected here, is the one adopted in the Babli. It seems that the Babli would reject the argument given for the permission to remarry as unreasonable (cf. R. Nissim Gerondi, *ad* Alfassi 35a.)

123 If she does not go to stay married to the first husband, one does not expect her to try to dissolve her vow for any other man.

124 Having used the vows to escape a marriage chosen for her when adolescent by her father, she might be expected to have the vow annulled as an adult for a man of her choice.

125 From her first husband, who in executing the divorce has to forswear any hope ever again to be married to her.

(31c line 54) רִבִּי שִׁמְעוֹן בֶּן לָקִישׁ אָמַר. מַתְנִיתָא אָמְרָה בְּשֶׁקִידְּשָׁהּ עַל תְּנַאי וּכְנָסָהּ סְתָם. אֲבָל אִם קִידְּשָׁהּ סְתָם וּכְנָסָהּ סְתָם יֵשׁ לָהּ כְּתוּבָּה. רִבִּי יוֹחָנָן אָמַר. אֲפִילוּ קִידְּשָׁהּ סְתָם וּכְנָסָהּ סְתָם אֵין לָהּ כְּתוּבָּה. אָמַר רִבִּי חִייָה בְשֵׁם רִבִּי יוֹחָנָן. וּצְרִיכָה מִמֶּנּוּ גֵט אֲפִילוּ קִידְּשָׁהּ עַל תְּנַיי וּכְנָסָהּ סְתָם. רִבִּי זְעִירָא בְעָא קוֹמֵי רִבִּי מָנָא. קִידְּשָׁהּ סְתָם וְגֵירְשָׁהּ מִן הָאֵירוּסִין מָה אָמַר בָּהּ רִבִּי שִׁמְעוֹן בֶּן לָקִישׁ. נִישְׁמְעִינָהּ מִן הָדָא. הָיוּ בָהּ מוּמִין וְעוֹדָהּ בְּבֵית אָבִיהָ הָאָב צָרִיךְ לְהָבִיא רְאָייָה. הָא אִם הֵבִיא הָאָב רְאָייָה יֵשׁ לָהּ כְּתוּבָּה. מַה חָמִית לְמֵימַר. בְּשֶׁקִידְּשָׁהּ סְתָם וְגֵירְשָׁהּ מִן הָאֵירוּסִין. מָה אֲנַן קַיָּימִין. מִן דְּבָתְרָהּ. בַּמֶּה דְּבָרִים אֲמוּרִים. בְּמוּמִין שֶׁבַּסֵּתֶר. אֲבָל בְּמוּמִין שֶׁבַּגָּלוּי אֵינוֹ יָכוֹל לִטְעוֹן. וְאֵין [בְּמַתְנָה][126] אַף בְּמוּמִין שֶׁבַּגָּלוּי טוֹעֵן. הָא אָמְרִין חֲבֵרַייָא קוֹמֵי רִבִּי יוֹסֵי. אֱמוֹר דְּבָתְרָהּ וּתְהֵא פְלִיגָא עַל רִבִּי שִׁמְעוֹן בֶּן לָקִישׁ. נִכְנְסָה לִרְשׁוּת הַבַּעַל הַבַּעַל צָרִיךְ לְהָבִיא רְאָייָה. הָא אִם הֵבִיא הַבַּעַל רְאָייָה אֵין לָהּ כְּתוּבָּה. וְהָּ רִבִּי שִׁמְעוֹן בֶּן לָקִישׁ. יֵשׁ לָהּ כְּתוּבָּה. רִבִּי כֹּהֵן בְּשֵׁם רַבָּנִין דְּקַיְסָרִין. מַתְנִיתָא בְּשֶׁכָּנַס וְלֹא בָעַל. מָאן דָּמַר רִבִּי שִׁמְעוֹן בֶּן לָקִישׁ בְּשֶׁכָּנַס וּבָעַל. אֲנִי אוֹמֵר. נִתְרַצֶּה לָהּ בִּבְעִילָהּ.

1 ר' שמעון | ק כנסה סתם. ר' שמעון   אמרה | ק -   3 אמר | ק ואמר   4 וכנסה סתם | ק וכנסה על תנאי   6 נישמעינה | ק בעא נישמעינה   7 האב | ק -   10 ואין | ק ואם במתנה   במומין שבגלוי טוען | ק מומין שבגלוי טוען הוא   הא | ק -   יוסי | ק יוסה   12 ראיה | ק ראייה   וחך | ק והיך   13 לקיש | ק לקיש אמר   14 דמר | ק דאמ'

Rebbi Simeon ben Laqish said, the Mishnah deals with the case that he married her preliminarily conditionally but definitively silently[127]. But if he married her preliminarily silently and definitively silently, she can claim her *ketubah*[128]. Rebbi Joḥanan said, even if he married her preliminarily silently and definitively silently, she has no *ketubah*[129]. Rebbi Ḥiyya in the name of Rebbi Joḥanan: But she needs a bill of divorce from him even if he married her preliminarily conditionally but definitively silently[130]. Rebbi Ze'ira asked before Rebbi Mana: In case he married her preliminarily silently and divorced her after the preliminary marriage, what does Rebbi Simeon ben Laqish say[131]? Let us hear from the following: "If she had bodily defects, as long as she is in her father's house, the father has to prove." This implies that if the father proved his case, she can claim her *ketubah*. What do you see to say, if he married her preliminarily silently and divorced her after the preliminary marriage! Where do we hold[132]? Since afterwards [it is stated]: "When was this said? For hidden defects, but he has no claim about visible defects." If he [made it conditional][126], could he not also claim for visible ones? But did not the colleagues say before Rebbi Yose: Should we say that the following statement disagrees with Rebbi Simeon ben Laqish? "Once she entered her husband's domain, the husband has to prove." This implies that if the husband proved his case[133], she has no claim to *ketubah*. But by the statement of Rebbi Simeon ban Laqish, she has a claim to *ketubah*. Rebbi Cohen in the name of the rabbis of Caesarea: The Mishnah deals with the case that he definitively married her but did not sleep with her; Rebbi Simeon ben Laqish speaks about the case that he definitively married her and slept with her; I am saying that she was acceptable to him since he took her to bed[134].

---

126 From the parallel in *Qiddušin*, missing here in ms. and *editio princeps*.

127 The Mishnah does not spell out what the connections are between preliminary and definitive marriage ceremonies. R. Simeon ben Laqish reads the Mishnah as one statement: If he stipulated for the preliminary marriage that the woman should be without vows or blemishes, if his condition is not met he can walk out of his commitment without further obligation. If he goes ahead with the definitive marriage, the marriage is

valid and can be dissolved only by a bill of divorce, but his original condition has not been withdrawn and, therefore, he does not have to pay.

128 This case has not been dealt with in the Mishnah; therefore the groom has no legal basis for refusing to pay the *ketubah* even if one agrees that he can divorce his wife for cause since he cannot be expected to live with a vowing or invalid wife. The Tosephta, 7:9, supports R. Simeon ben Laqish.

129 He holds that the two cases in the Mishnah, referring to preliminary and definitive marriages, are independent of one another. Therefore, anybody who finds his wife encumbered by vows or having bodily defects can divorce her without *ketubah*, even if the subject was never mentioned at the preliminary marriage.

130 Since the stipulation was not repeated at the definitive marriage, the fact of the definitive marriage retroactively validates the preliminary marriage that would have been invalid if the condition of the bride had been investigated by the groom. Therefore, the stipulation can refer only to money matters, not to the validity of the marriage and the marriage cannot simply be declared nonexistent.

In the Babli, 72b/73a, this is the position of Rav, disputed by Samuel. The Babli explains that Rav holds that if a man sleeps with a woman he shows that in his mind he is legally married (and the preliminary marriage is validated retroactively); Samuel does not attribute such pious thoughts to men.

131 If the *ketubah* was written for the preliminary marriage, does R. Simeon ben Laqish equate the signing of the *ketubah* document to a definitive marriage as far as money matters go?

132 This proves that the Mishnah must assume the preliminary marriage to have been unconditional.

133 Referring to an unconditional preliminary marriage.

134 He must have been aware of her bodily defect. The Mishnah treats the cases of vows and defects as completely parallel; one must therefore restrict the statement of R. Simeon ben Laqish to the case that the husband was aware of his wife's vows when he slept with her for the first time.

(31c line 69) שֶׁכָּל־הַמּוּמִין הַפּוֹסְלִין בַּכֹּהֲנִים פּוֹסְלִין בַּנָּשִׁים. הוֹסִיפוּ עֲלֵיהֶן בָּאִשָּׁה רֵיחַ הַפֶּה וְרֵיחַ הַזִּיעָא שׁוּמָא בָּהּ שָׂעֵר. רִבִּי אָמִי בַּר עוּקְבָּא בְשֵׁם

HALAKHAH 9

רִבִּי יוֹסֵי בַּר חֲנִינָה. בְּעוֹר הַפָּנִים שָׁנוּ. וְהָא תַּנִּינָן. בַּמֶּה דְּבָרִים אֲמוּרִים בְּמוּמִין שֶׁבַּסֵּתֶר אֲבָל בְּמוּמִין שֶׁבַּגָּלוּי אֵינוֹ יָכוֹל לִטְעוֹן. וְזֶה מִן הַמּוּמִין שֶׁבַּגָּלוּי הוּא. תִּיפְתָּר הִיא דְּמִטְמְרָא לָהּ תַּחַת קַלְסְתָיהּ[135] דְּרֹאשָׁה. תַּנֵּי. שׁוּמָא שֶׁיֵּשׁ לָהּ שֵׂיעָר בֵּין בִּגְדוֹלָה בֵּין בִּקְטַנָּה בֵּין בַּגּוּף בֵּין בַּפָּנִים הֲרֵי זֶה מוּם. וְשֶׁאֵין בָּהּ שֵׂיעָר. בְּפָנִים מוּם בַּגּוּף אֵינוֹ מוּם. בַּמֶּה דְּבָרִים אֲמוּרִים. בִּקְטַנָּה. אֲבָל בִּגְדוֹלָה בֵּין בַּגּוּף בֵּין בַּפָּנִים הֲרֵי זֶה מוּם. עַד כַּמָּה גְּדוֹלָה. רַבָּן שִׁמְעוֹן בֶּן גַּמְלִיאֵל אוֹמֵר. עַד כְּאִיסָּר הָאִיטַלְקִי. רִבִּי אֶלְעָזָר בַּר חֲנִינָה אָמַר. כְּגוֹן הָדֵין דֵּינָרָא קוּרְדַיָּינָא שִׁיעוּרוֹ כַּחֲצִי זָהָב כָּל־שֶׁהוּא. רִבִּי רְדִיפָה רִבִּי יוֹנָה רִבִּי יִרְמְיָה שָׁאִיל. אִשָּׁה קָרַחַת[136] שִׁיטָה שֶׁלְּשִׂיעָר מַקֶּפֶת מֵאוֹזֶן לָאוֹזֶן. בָּעֵיי מִשְׁמַע מִן הָדָא. הוֹסִיפוּ עֲלֵיהֶן בְּאִשָּׁה רֵיחַ הַפֶּה וְרֵיחַ הַזֵּיעָא שׁוּמָא שֶׁאֵין בָּהּ שֵׂיעָר. וְלֹא אַדְכְּרוּן קָרְחָה. סָבְרִין מֵימַר שֶׁאֵינָהּ מוּם. אָתָא רִבִּי שְׁמוּאֵל בְּרֵיהּ דְּרִבִּי יוֹסֵי בֵּירִבִּי בּוֹן. אָמַר רִבִּי נָסָא. מוּם הוּא. לֹא מַתְנֵי אֶלָּא. דָּבָר שֶׁהוּא כְּאוֹר בַּזֶּה וּבַזֶּה. מוּם בַּזֶּה וְאֵינוֹ מוּם בַּזֶּה. אֲבָל דָּבָר שֶׁהוּא נוֹי בַּזֶּה וּמוּם בַּזֶּה. כְּגוֹן הָדָא קָרַחַת. אַף עַל גַּב דְּהוּא מוּם לֹא תַּנִּיתָא. תֵּדַע לָךְ שֶׁהוּא כֵן. הֲרֵי זָקָן הֲרֵי נוֹי בָּאִישׁ וּמוּם בָּאִשָּׁה. יֶתֶר עֲלֵיהֶן בָּאִשָּׁה זָקָן. הֲרֵי דַּדִּים הֲרֵי נוֹי בָּאִשָּׁה וּמוּם בָּאִישׁ. וְלֹא תַּנִּינָן. יֶתֶר עֲלֵיהֶן בָּאִישׁ דַּדִּים.

3 בר | ק בן   והא תנינן | ק והתנינן   4 וזה | ק וזו לא   5 היא | ק בההיא   קלסתיה | ק קלוסיתה   6 לה | ק בה   בגדולה | ק גדולה   בקטנה | ק קטנה   8 כמה | ק כמה   היא   9 ר׳ אלעזר בר חנינה אמר | ק ר1 לעזר בשם ר׳ חנינה   11 שאיל | ק שאל   קרדוה | ק קרחת   שיטה | ק ושוטח   משמע | ק מישמעי׳   13 שאינה | ק שאינו   14 ר נסא | ק בשם ר1 ניסא   מתני | ק אתינן מיתני   כאור | ק כעור   15 ואינו | ק ואין   נוי | ק נויי   16 שהוא | ק שהיא   17,18 נוי | ק נויי   18 תנינן | ק תנינתה

"And all defects which disqualify a priest disqualify a woman. They added to them for women mouth odor, sweat odor, and a hairless mole.[137]" Rebbi Ammi bar Uqba in the name of Rebbi Yose ben Ḥanina: They taught this[138] about the skin of the face. But did we not state: "When was this said? For hidden defects, but he has no claim about visible defects," and this is of the visible defects! Explain it if she hid it under her headgear. It was stated: "A mole with hairs is a defect, whether it be large or small, whether it be on the body or on the face. Without a hair it is a defect on the face but not on the body. When has this been said? If it is small. But if it is large, it is a defect whether it be on the body or on the face. How big is large? Rabban Simeon ben Gamliel says, up to an Italic *as*[139]." Rebbi Eleazar bar Ḥanina said, for example such a Gordianic denar[140] his measure is half an ubiquitous gold piece[141]. Rebbi Radifa, Rebbi Jonah: Rebbi Jeremiah asked: A bald woman with a row of hair going from one ear to the other[142]? They wanted to understand it from the following: "They added to them for women mouth odor, sweat odor, and a hairless mole." They did not mention baldness. They wanted to conclude that it is not a defect. There came Rebbi Samuel the son of Rebbi Yose ben Rebbi Abun: Rebbi Nasa said, it is a defect. It is listed only if it is ugly for both sexes. But something which is beautiful in one sex but ugly in the other, like a bald pate, even though it is a defect it was not listed. You should know that this is so because a beard is beautiful for a man and a defect for a woman, and we did not state: In addition, for a woman a beard. There are breasts which are beautyiful for a woman and a defect for men, and we did not state: In addtion, for a man women's breasts[143].

135 The correct spelling is in *Qiddušin*: קולסיתה "her head gear".

136 This is the reading in *Qiddušin*. Here: קררוה which is incomprehensible. In the Babli, 75a, in a similar but not identical argument, the word כִּפָּה "cap" is used.

137 Tosephta 7:9, quoted in Babli 75a. Mishnah *Bekhorot* Chapter 6 enumerates the defects which make an animal unfit for the altar. Chapter 7 states that any defect making an animal

unfit will disqualify a Cohen from Temple service. In addition, a misshapen head will disqualify a priest, also a bald pate not bordered in the front by a line of hair from ear to ear.

138 The mole.

139 A rather large copper coin, abount an inch in diameter.

The *baraita* is quoted in the Babli, 75a; the following amoraic comment (and reduction in size) has no parallel there.

140 Minted by Gordianus III. Really a double denar, an *Antoninianus*, but whose weight was only $1/3$ larger than the simple denars minted by Gordianus I and II. Cf. D. Sperber, *Roman Palestine, 200-400, Money and Prices*, Ramat Gan 1974, pp. 39,226. Since the text here is confirmed by its parallel in *Qiddušin*, the different readings in הילכות טרפות לבני ארץ ישראל, תלפיות ח, 1963, pp. 324-5, do not refer to the text here.

141 This R. Eleazar bar Ḥanina is not mentioned again in the Talmudim. In *Qiddušin*, the quote is "R. Eleazar in the name of R. Ḥanina"; the latter lived under the last Severan emperors and the early military anarchy. The gold coin is an *aureus* of Septimius Severus or his successors.

142 Which is not a defect for a male, cf. Note 137.

143 No list is complete. In the Babli, oversized woman's breasts are listed as defect.

In *Qiddušin*, this is the end of the Halakhah.

(31d line 12) מַתְנִיתָא בְּמוּמִין שֶׁאֵין דַּרְכָּן לְהִוָּלֵד. אֲבָל בְּמוּמִין שֶׁדַּרְכָּן לְהִוָּלֵד אֲפִילוּ מִשֶּׁנִּכְנְסָה לִרְשׁוּת הַבַּעַל צָרִיךְ לְהָבִיא רְאָיָיה וְלוֹמַר. הִתְנֵיתִי עִמָּהּ.

The Mishnah deals with defects which do not spontaneously appear[144]. But about defects which spontaneously appear, the husband has to bring proof and say that he stipulated about them.

144 Defects that do not appear during the natural aging process. Without prior stipulation the husband cannot complain if his wife is not permanently youthful looking.

There is a possibility that this

paragraph refers to a statement similar to Tosephta 7:10: The Sages agree with R. Meïr (in Mishnah 8) that for defects which usually develop (in Nachmanides's opinion, birth defects or defects that develop in early childhood) the father has to bring proof even if she is in her husband's house (even if these are visible defects). In the opinion of the Babli, 77a, epilepsy is a hidden defect if the onset of an attack is preceded by signs which give the girl time to hide herself; it is a public defect if attacks come without warning.

(fol. 31a) **משנה י**: הָאִישׁ שֶׁנּוֹלְדוּ בוֹ מוּמִין אֵין כּוֹפִין אוֹתוֹ לְהוֹצִיא. אָמַר רַבָּן שִׁמְעוֹן בֶּן גַּמְלִיאֵל בָּמֶּה דְבָרִים אֲמוּרִים. בְּמוּמִין הַקְּטַנִּים אֲבָל בְּמוּמִין הַגְּדוֹלִים כּוֹפִין אוֹתוֹ לְהוֹצִיא.

Mishnah 10: If a man developed defects, one does not force him to divorce[145]. Rabban Simeon ben Gamliel said, when has this been said? For minor defects. But for major defects one forces him to divorce.

145 If the wife claims that she cannot live with such a man.

(31d line 15) **הלכה י**: הָאִישׁ שֶׁנּוֹלְדוּ בוֹ מוּמִין כול'. רַב יְהוּדָה בְּשֵׁם רַב. כֵּינִי מַתְנִיתָא. בְּשֶׁהָיוּ בוֹ. אֲבָל נוֹלְדוּ בוֹ כּוֹפִין אוֹתוֹ לְהוֹצִיא. רִבִּי בָּא בַּר כַּהֲנָא בְּשֵׁם רִבִּי יוֹחָנָן. הֲלָכָה כְּרַבָּן שִׁמְעוֹן בֶּן גַּמְלִיאֵל. אָתָא עוֹבְדָא קוֹמֵי רִבִּי יִרְמְיָה בְּכוֹפִיחַ וּבְפָפוֹ.[146] וְאַתְיָיא דְּרַב בְּשָׁאֵין בּוֹ. וּדְרַבָּן שִׁמְעוֹן בֶּן גַּמְלִיאֵל בְּשֶׁנּוֹלְדוּ בוֹ. אָמַר רִבִּי זְעִירָא. אַתְיָיא דְּרַבָּן שִׁמְעוֹן בֶּן גַּמְלִיאֵל כְּרִבִּי מֵאִיר. הֵיי דֵין רִבִּי מֵאִיר. בְּקַדְמָיָיא בְּאַחֲרַיָיא. אִין בְּקַדְמָיָיא עַד שֶׁיִּתְנֶה. אִין בְּאַחֲרַיָיא אֲפִילוּ הִתְנָה לֹא כְלוּם. אֶלָּא סָלְקַת מַתְנִיתָא כְּרַבָּן שִׁמְעוֹן בֶּן גַּמְלִיאֵל. וְאִילוּ כֵן כּוֹפִין אוֹתוֹ לְהוֹצִיא. כְּרַבָּנִין. נִישְׁמְעִינָהּ מִן הָדָא. רַבָּן שִׁמְעוֹן בֶּן גַּמְלִיאֵל אוֹמֵר. אִם הָיָה מוּם גָּדוֹל. כְּגוֹן סוֹמֵא בְּאַחַת מֵעֵינָיו קִיטֵּעַ בְּאַחַת מִיָּדָיו חִיגֵּר

בְּאַחַר מֵרַגְלָיו מִיָד יוֹצִיא וְיִתֵּן כְּתוּבָה. הָדָא אֲמְרָה. סָלְקַת מַתְנִיתָא כְּרַבָּן שִׁמְעוֹן בֶּן גַּמְלִיאֵל. וְאֵילוּ שֶׁכּוֹפִין אוֹתוֹ לְהוֹצִיא כְּרַבָּנִין.

Halakhah 10: "If a man developed defects," etc. Rav Jehudah in the name of Rav: So is the Mishnah, "if he had.[147]" But if they developed newly, one forces him to divorce[148]. Rebbi Abba bar Cahana in the name of Rebbi Joḥanan: Practice follows Rabban Simeon ben Gamliel[149]. There came a case before Rebbi Jeremiah about a *kopeaḥ*[150], and he forced him[151]. It turns out that following Rav[152] if he did not become so, following Rabban Simeon ben Gamliel if he became so. Rebbi Ze'ira said, Rabban Simeon ben Gamliel follows Rebbi Meïr. Which [statement of] Rebbi Meïr? The former or the later[153]? If the former, until she made a condition[154]. If the later, even if he made a condition it is nothing[155]. But this Mishnah turns out following Rabban Simeon ben Gamliel[156]; does "the following one forces to divorce" [follows] the rabbis[157]? Let us hear from the following[158]: "Rabban Simeon ben Gamliel says, if it was a major defect, e. g., blind in one eye, amputated of one of his hands, lame in one of his legs, immediately he shall divorce and pay the *ketubah*." This Mishnah turns out following Rabban Simeon ben Gamliel[156]; "the following one forces to divorce" [follows] the rabbis[159].

146 One has to read: וכפפו

147 In the Babli, 77a, Rav Jehudah reads that the defect "developed (after the marriage)" and Rav's son Ḥiyya reads "was (in existence at the time of marriage)".

148 This is Rav Jehudah's conclusion.

149 In the Babli, this is a statement of R. Abba bar Jacob in the name of R. Joḥanan, it is rejected by the Babylonian Amoraïm.

150 This is mentioned in Mishnah *Bekhorot* 7:6 as כיפח (in the Maimonides tradition of the Mishnah and oriental mss. of the Babli collected by R.

Beṣalel Ashkenazi) or קיפח. According to Rashi (*Bekhorot* 45b), he is overly tall but has soft bones so that he cannot walk straight. R. Beṣalel Ashkenazi (*Bekhorot* 45b, Note י) quotes one opinion that he is an epileptic.

151 To divorce his wife upon her demand.

152 I. e., in Rav's interpretation of the anonymous Tanna in the Mishnah.

153 The former statement is in Mishnah 9, that one assumes that the defect occured at the place it was detected. The later statement is that of Mishnah 11: a woman may claim that she married because she thought she could stand to live with a man having such a defect but she recognizes now that this is impossible for her.

154 If the reference were to Mishnah 9, one would require the woman to stipulate before the marriage that the man be free of defects. In that case, everybody agrees that she can force a divorce.

155 If he divulged his defect to his fiancee before the marriage, R. Meïr still will not force the woman to stay married if she finds the experience intolerable.

156 The entire Mishnah 10 is Rabban Simeon ben Gamliel's. (One usually reads Mishnaiot containing a statement "when has this been said" to be the text of the person who explains). Since he makes a distinction between small and large defects, he must speak of newly developed defects.

157 Does Mishnah 11 follow the rabbis in Rav's interpretation, dealing with pre-existing conditons?

158 Tosephta 7:9, Babli 77a; the language of the Tosephta is closer to the Yerushalmi.

159 Since the defects mentioned in the Mishnah are not on Rabban Simeon ben Gamliel's list.

(fol. 31a) **משנה יא:** וְאֵילוּ שֶׁכּוֹפִין אוֹתָן לְהוֹצִיא מוּכֵּי שְׁחִין וּבַעַל פּוֹלִיפוּס וְהַמְקַמֵּץ וְהַמְצָרֵף נְחוֹשֶׁת וְהַבּוּרְסִי בֵּין שֶׁהָיוּ בָם עַד שֶׁלֹּא נִישְׂאוּ וּבֵין מִשֶּׁנִּישְׂאוּ לָמְדוּ. וְעַל כּוּלָּן אָמַר רִבִּי מֵאִיר אַף עַל פִּי שֶׁהִתְנָה עִמָּהּ יְכוֹלָה הִיא שֶׁתֹּאמַר סְבוּרָה הָיִיתִי שֶׁאֲנִי יְכוֹלָה לְקַבֵּל עַכְשָׁיו אֵינִי יְכוֹלָה לְקַבֵּל. וַחֲכָמִים אוֹמְרִים מְקַבֶּלֶת הִיא עַל כָּרְחָהּ חוּץ מִמּוּכֵּה שְׁחִין מִפְּנֵי שֶׁמְּמִיקַתּוּ. מַעֲשֶׂה בְצִידוֹן

בְּבוּרְסִי אֶחָד שֵׁמֵת וְהָיָה לוֹ אַח בּוּרְסִי אָמְרוּ חֲכָמִים יְכוֹלָה הִיא שֶׁתֹּאמַר לְאָחִיךָ הָיִיתִי יְכוֹלָה לְקַבֵּל וְלָךְ אֵינִי יְכוֹלָה לְקַבֵּל.

Mishnah 11: The following one forces to divorce: Those smitten with boils, the one afflicted with a polyp[160], the dung collector[161], the brass refiner, and the tanner[162], whether they were in this before they married or they came to it after they married. For all of these says Rebbi Meïr that, even if he contracted with her[163], she can say "I thought that I could stand it, now I cannot stand it." But the Sages say, she is forced to stand it except for the one smitten with boils because she causes him consumption[164]. It happened in Sidon that a tanner died[165] who had a brother tanner; there the Sages said, she can say: "I could stand that in your brother, I cannot stand it in you."

160 Greek πολύπους "many-footed", a cancerous growth in the nose (according to the Babli, 77a, an evil smelling growth.)

161 He collects animal dung to sell to tanners; he smells badly.

162 All these have professions that impregnate them with bad smells which even with a bath cannot be removed.

163 He informed her of his impediment before the marriage.

164 In talmudic medical theory there are kinds of boils for which sexual activity is very detrimental.

165 He died childless; his widow can force her levir not to take her in levirate marriage and free her by *ḥaliṣah*.

(31d line 26) **הלכה יא**: אֵילוּ שֶׁכּוֹפִין אוֹתָן לְהוֹצִיא מוּכֵּי שְׁחִין כול׳. הַמְקַמֵּץ. זֶה הַמְקַמֵּץ צוֹאָה. וְיֵשׁ אוֹמְרִים. זֶה הַבּוּרְסִי. אָמַר רְבִּי זְעִירָא. מַתְנִיתָא אָמְרָה. זֶה הַמְקַמֵּץ צוֹאָה. דְּתָנִינָן וְהַמְקַמֵּץ הַבּוּרְסִי. וְצוֹרֵף נְחוֹשֶׁת. שְׁמוּאֵל אָמַר. מַתִּיךְ נְחוֹשֶׁת מֵעִיקָרוֹ.

KETUBOT CHAPTER SEVEN

Halakhah 11: "The following one forces to divorce: Those smitten with boils," etc. "The *meqammes*." This is the dung collector; but some say it is the tanner. Rebbi Ze'ira said, the Mishnah implies that this is the dung collector since we have stated: "The *meqammes* and the tanner."[166] "The brass refiner." Samuel said, that is the one who smelts brass from its ore[167].

166 The Babli, 77a, explains the problem away that in the opinion of the dissenting Tosephta (7:11) there are different kinds of tanners, smelling differently.

167 In the Babli, 77a, this is only one opinion; Rav disagrees and holds that he repairs metal pots.

(31d line 29) תַּנֵּי. אָמַר רַבָּן שִׁמְעוֹן בֶּן גַּמְלִיאֵל. פָּגַע בִּי זָקֵן אֶחָד מוּכֵּה שְׁחִין מִצִּיפּוֹרִין. אָמַר לִי. כֹּד מִינֵי שְׁחִין הֵן וְאֵין לָךְ קָשֶׁה מְכוּלָּם וְשֶׁהָאִשָּׁה רָעָה לוֹ אֶלָּא רָאתָן. רִבִּי שְׁמוּאֵל בַּר נַחְמָן בְּשֵׁם רִבִּי יוֹנָתָן. וּבוֹ לָקָה פַרְעֹה הָרָשָׁע. הָדָא הוּא דִכְתִיב וַיְנַגַּע י"י אֶת פַּרְעֹה נְגָעִים גְּדוֹלִים וְאֶת בֵּיתוֹ וגו'. אָמַר רִבִּי בֶּרֶכְיָה. עַל דְּטָלְמֵסָן לְמַגַּע בְּסַמָהּ דְּמַטְרוֹנָה. אַרְבָּעָה וְעֶשְׂרִים מִינֵי אֲרָזִים הֵן וּמְכוּלָּן לֹא פֵירַשׁ הַכָּתוּב אֶלָּא שֶׁבַע בִּלְבַד. הָדָא הוּא דִכְתִיב אֶתֵּן בַּמִּדְבָּר אֶרֶז שִׁיטָה וַהֲדַס וְעֵץ שָׁמֶן אָשִׂים בָּעֲרָבָה בְּרוֹשׁ תִּדְהָר וּתְאַשּׁוּר יַחְדָּיו. בְּרוֹשׁ בְּרָתָא. תִּדְהָר אִדְרָא. וּתְאַשּׁוּר פִּיקְסִינָה. הוֹסִיפוּ עֲלֵיהֶן. אַלּוֹנִים עַרְמוֹנִים אַלְמוֹגִים. אַלּוֹנִים בְּלוֹטִים. עַרְמוֹנִים דּוּלְבֵּי. אַלְמוּגִים אֲלָוִים.

It was stated[168]: "Rabban Simeon ben Gamliel said, I met an old man, smitten with boils, from Sepphoris. He told me, there are 24 kinds of boils; the worst one, and the one for which a woman is bad, is flowing boils[169]. Rebbi Samuel bar Naḥman in the name of Rebbi Jonathan: With the latter kind, the evil Pharao was smitten[170]; that is what is written[171]: "The Eternal smote Pharao and his house with great plagues," etc. [172]Rebbi Berekhia said: Because he dared to touch the matron's body.

There are 24 kinds of cedar[173], and from all of them the verse mentioned only seven. That is what is written[174]: "I shall give in the desert cedar, acacia, myrtle, and oil wood[175]; I put in the prairie *beroš, tidhar*, and *teaššur* together. *Beroš* is cypress; *tidhar* is *idra*[176]; *teaššur* is the box-tree[177]. They added to them[178] *'allonim, 'armonim,* and *'almogim. 'Allonim* are oaks, *'armonim* plane trees, *'almuggim* aloës.

168 Tosephta 7:11 [*Gen. rabba* 41(2)] in this version only the person afflicted with *ritan* is required to divorce his wife for medical reasons. Another version in the Babli, 77b [*Lev. rabba* 16(1)], requires all sufferers from boils to refrain from sexual activity.

169 Usually derived somehow from Greek ῥέω "to flow".

170 This is anonymous in *Gen. rabba* 41(2).

171 *Gen.* 12:17.

172 This is slightly distorted in *Gen. rabba* 41(2), correct in 52(14). It was read by H. Graetz as mixed Aramaic/Greek/Latin sentence: *dĕ*-ἐτόλμησεν *lĕmagga' ba*-σῶμα *dĕ*-matrona; where ἐτόλμησεν is aorist of τολμάω "to dare, to presume".

173 This is added here because of the number 24. In the Babli (*Roš Haššanah* 23a, *Sukkah* 37a, *Ta'anit* 25b, *Baba batra* 80b) there are only 10 kinds mentioned, the 10 explained here, with sometimes different and multiple identifications. The original text seems to be in *Gen. rabba* 15(2): "R. Samuel ben Naḥman in the name of Rebbi Jonathan: There are 24 kinds of cedar but only 7 are of the best kind."

174 *Is.* 41:19.

175 In the Babli identified as the balsamum shrub.

176 This Aramaic word for a tree has not been identified. In the Babli identified as ג̇ל "teak".

177 Greek πύξινον "box-tree".

178 This expression is out of place here; it belongs to the tannaïtic tradition reported in the Babli that there are 10 kinds of cedar, with three added to the seven mentioned by Isaiah.

האשה פרק שמיני

(fol. 31d) **משנה א**: הָאִשָּׁה שֶׁנָּפְלוּ לָהּ נְכָסִים עַד שֶׁלֹּא תִתְאָרֵס מוֹדִים בֵּית שַׁמַּאי וּבֵית הִלֵּל שֶׁאִם מוֹכֶרֶת וְנוֹתֶנֶת קַיָּים. נָפְלוּ לָהּ מִשֶּׁנִּתְאָרְסָה בֵּית שַׁמַּאי אוֹמְרִים תִּמְכּוֹר וּבֵית הִלֵּל אוֹמְרִים לֹא תִמְכּוֹר. אִילוּ וְאִילוּ מוֹדִין שֶׁאִם מָכְרָה וְנָתְנָה קַיָּים. אָמַר רבי יְהוּדָה. אָמְרוּ לִפְנֵי רַבָּן גַּמְלִיאֵל. הוֹאִיל וְזָכָה בָאִשָּׁה לֹא יִזְכֶּה בַנְּכָסִים. אָמַר לָהֶם עַל הַחֲדָשִׁים אָנוּ בוֹשִׁין אֶלָּא שֶׁאַתֶּם מְגַלְגְּלִין עָלֵינוּ אֶת הַיְשָׁנִים.

Mishnah 1: If a woman inherited property before she became preliminarily married, the Houses of Shammai and Hillel agree that if she sells or gives it away it is valid[1]. If she inherited after she became preliminarily married, the House of Shammai say she may sell[2], the House of Hillel say she should not sell, but both of them agree that if she sold or gave it away it is valid. Rebbi Jehudah said: They said before Rabban Gamliel: If he obtained the right to the woman[3], should he not also acquire the right to the property? He said to them, are we not ashamed about the new [properties][4] and you want to burden us with the old ones[5]?

1   If she is an unmarried adult, she is fully capable of acting and does not need any male guardian or representative. "Properties" without further qualifications are real estate.

2   Up to the time of the definitive marriage. At the definitive marriage the husband becomes the administrator of the properties and receives their yield; he has no say in the matter before that date. Everybody agrees that after the definitive marriage the wife can sell only through her husband (unless a separation of property was

stipulated before the definitive marriage. Since these are money matters, they are all subject to modification by the contracting parties.)

3   Since the preliminary marriage makes the bride a married woman in all aspects of criminal law, should the husband not also have acquired a say in her properties.

4   Properties she inherits after the final wedding ceremony, of which Mishnah 2 decrees that the husband can veto her sale. It seems not reasonable that the secondary interest of the husband in the yield of the properties should override the primary property rights of the wife in her inheritance.

5   The properties inherited before the final wedding date

(32a line 16) **הלכה א:** הָאִשָּׁה שֶׁנָּפְלוּ לָהּ נְכָסִים כול׳. כִּינִי מַתְנִיתָא. עַד שֶׁלֹּא נִתְאָרְסָה. מַה בֵּין עַד שֶׁלֹּא נִתְאָרְסָה מַה בֵּין מִשֶּׁנִּתְאָרְסָה. עַד שֶׁלֹּא נִתְאָרְסָה לִזְכוּתָהּ נָפְלוּ. מִשֶּׁנִּתְאָרְסָה לִזְכוּתָהּ וְלִזְכוּתוֹ נָפְלוּ.

Halakhah 1: "If a woman inherited property," etc. So is the Mishnah: Before she was preliminarily married[6]. What is the difference between before she was preliminarily married and after she was preliminarily married? Before she was preliminarily married, it fell to her; after she was preliminarily married it fell to her and him[7].

6   There seems to be no difference in meaning between t-reflexive *hitpa'el* and n-reflexive *niph'al*. J. N. Epstein (*loc. cit.* Chapter 5, Note 33, p. 474) sees in this sentence only the introduction to the following question since in all quotes of the Mishnah in other parts of the Yerushalmi the formulation of the Mishnah is used.

7   The Babli, 78a, has a slightly more careful formulation, that after the preliminary marriage the husband *might have* an interest.

(32a line 19) רִבִּי פִּינְחָס בְּעָא קוֹמֵי רִבִּי יוֹסֵי. וְלָמָּה לֹא תַנִּיתָהּ מְקוּלֵּי בֵית שַׁמַּי וּמֵחוּמְרֵי בֵית הִלֵּל. אָמַר לֵיהּ. לָא אֲתִינָן מִיתְנֵי אֶלָּא דָּבָר חָמוּר מִשְּׁנֵי

צְדָדִין וְקַל מִשְּׁנֵי צְדָדִין. בְּרַם הָכָא חוֹמֶר הוּא מִצַּד אֶחָד וְקַל מִצַּד אֶחָד. וְהָא תַגִּינָן. בֵּית שַׁמַּי אוֹמְרִין. הֶבְקֵר לָעֲנִיִּים. הֲרֵי הוּא קַל לָעֲנִיִּים וְחוֹמֶר הוּא לְבַעַל הַבַּיִת. וְתַגִּיתָהּ. אָמַר לֵיהּ. קַל הוּא לָעֲנִיִּים וְאֵינוֹ חוֹמֶר לְבַעַל הַבַּיִת. שֶׁמִּדַּעְתּוֹ הֶבְקִירוֹ. אָמַר לֵיהּ. וְהָא תַגִּינָן. הָעוֹמֶר שֶׁהוּא סָמוּךְ לְגָפָה וּלְגָדִישׁ וּלְבָקָר וּלְכֵלִים וּשְׁכָחוֹ. הֲרֵי הוּא קַל לְבַעַל הַבַּיִת וְחוֹמֶר הוּא לָעֲנִיִּים. אָמַר לֵיהּ. קַל הוּא לְבַעַל הַבַּיִת וְאֵינוֹ חוֹמֶר לָעֲנִיִּים. שֶׁאֲדַיִין לֹא זָכוּ בוֹ. וֶאֱמוֹר אוּף הָכָא. קַל הוּא לָאִשָּׁה וְאֵינוֹ חוֹמֶר לְבַעַל. שֶׁאֲדַיִין לֹא זָכָה בָהּ. אָמַר לֵיהּ. מִכֵּיוָן שֶׁקִּדְּשָׁהּ לִזְכוּתָהּ וְלִזְכוּתוֹ נָפְלוּ.

1 תניתה | פ תנינתה   2 חמור | פ שהוא חומר   3-4 והא תנינן | פ והתנינן   4 לעניים | פ לעניים הבקר   5 אמר ליה. קל | פ קל   6 הבקירו | פ הובקרו   העומר | פ עומר   8 בו | פ בהן   9 לבעל | פ לבעל הבית.

⁸Rebbi Phineas asked before Rebbi Yose, why did we not state it with the leniencies of the House of Shammai and the stringencies of the House of Hillel? He said to him, the Mishnaiot apply only to circumstances that are either stringent on both sides or lenient on both sides. But here it is a stringency on one side and a leniency on the other side. But did we not state: "The House of Shammai say, property abandoned to the poor [is abandoned]?" Is this not lenient for the poor and stringent for the householder, and it was stated! He said to him, it is lenient for the poor and not stringent for the householder, since he intentionally abandoned it. He said to him, did we not state: "If the sheaf that was near a closure, a stack, cattle, or vessels was forgotten," is this not lenient for the householder and stringent for the poor, and it was stated! He said to him, it is lenient for the householder but not stringent for the poor, because they did not acquire it yet. You may also say here, it is lenient for the woman and not stringent for the husband since he did not yet acquire property rights to it. He said to him, since he became betrothed to her, the inheritance fell to both of them.

(32a line 29) אָמַר רִבִּי יוּדָא. אָמְרוּ לִפְנֵי רַבָּן גַּמְלִיאֵל. הוֹאִיל וְהָאֲרוּסָה אִשְׁתּוֹ הִיא וְהַנְּשׂוּאָה אִשְׁתּוֹ הִיא. מַה זֶה מִכְרָהּ בָּטֵל אַף זֶה מִכְרָהּ בָּטֵל. אָמַר לָהֶן בַּחֲדָשִׁים אָנוּ בוֹשִׁים אֶלָּא שֶׁאַתֶּם מְגַלְגְּלִין חֲדָשִׁים עַל הַיְשָׁנִים. אֵילוּ הֵן הַחֲדָשִׁים. מִשֶּׁנִּישֵּׂאת. וְאֵילוּ הֵן הַיְשָׁנִים. עַד שֶׁלֹּא נִישֵּׂאת וְנִישֵּׂאת.

2 היא | פ - (2 times)   זה | פ זו (2 times)   לחן | פ ליה   3 חדשים על | פ עמנו על

Rebbi Jehudah said, they argued before Rabban Gamliel: Because preliminarily married she is his wife and definitively married she is his wife; just as the sale by the latter is void, the sale by the former also should be void. He said to them, we are ashamed of the new ones, now you want to roll the new on over the old ones! The new ones, after the definitive marriage; the old ones before the definitive marriage, when she was married in the second ceremony.

8 From here to the end of the Halakhah, the text is from *Peah* 6:2, explained there in Notes 45-55 (variants פ).

(fol. 31d) **משנה ב:** נָפְלוּ לָהּ נְכָסִים מִשֶּׁנִּישֵּׂאת אֵילוּ וָאֵילוּ מוֹדִין שֶׁאִם מָכְרָה וְנָתְנָה שֶׁהַבַּעַל מוֹצִיא מִיַּד הַלְּקוֹחוֹת. עַד שֶׁלֹּא נִשֵּׂאת וְנִשֵּׂאת רַבָּן גַּמְלִיאֵל אוֹמֵר אִם מָכְרָה וְנָתְנָה קַיָּמִים. אָמַר רִבִּי חֲנִינָה בֶּן עֲקִיבָה אָמְרוּ לִפְנֵי רַבָּן גַּמְלִיאֵל הוֹאִיל וְזָכָה בָאִשָּׁה לֹא זָכָה בַנְּכָסִים. אָמַר לָהֶם עַל הַחֲדָשִׁים אָנוּ בוֹשִׁים אֶלָּא שֶׁאַתֶּם מְגַלְגְּלִין עָלֵינוּ אֶת הַיְשָׁנִים.

Mishnah 2: If she inherited property[9] after she was definitively married, both agree[10] that if she sold or gave away the husband retrieves from the hand of the buyers[11]. [If she interited] before she was definitively married[12] and [sold] after she was definitively married,

Rabban Gamliel said if she sold or gave away it is valid[13]. Rebbi Ḥanina ben Aqiba[14] said, they said before Rabban Gamliel: If he obtained the right to the woman, did he not also acquire the right to the property[15]? He said to them, are we not ashamed about the new [properties][4], and you want to burden us with the old ones[5]?

9   This word is in the text of the Mishnah, not in the quote in the Halakhah nor in any other known Mishnah or Talmud ms. This supports S. Lieberman's opinion that the copyist of the Leiden ms. took the Mishnah text from a ms. different from the Talmud ms. before him.

10   The Houses of Shammai and Hillel.

11   In the absence of a contract to the contrary, the husband has the administration of the wife's paraphernalia and receives their yield. This means that at the moment the wife acquires title to the property, the husband acquires title to its yield. Therefore, he can go to court and invalidate the real estate transaction which was done without his concurrence.

12   Even after she was preliminarily married; therefore this property does not become part of her dowry proper (mortmain) but remains the wife's separate property as paraphernalia (*Yebamot* 7, Note 1).

13   Since she could have sold before the final marriage, as stated in Mishnah 1, the husband has no acquired rights in the property.

14   This name appears also in the Munich ms. and the Soncino print of the Babli. In most other sources: Aqabia.

15   Since with the act of definitive marriage he acquires his wife's mortmain properties, why are his rights over her paraphernalia properties not likewise absolute?

(32a line 33) **הלכה ב:** נָפְלוּ לָהּ מִשֶּׁנִּשֵּׂאת כול'. אֲנָן תַּנִּינָן. מוֹכֶרֶת וְנוֹתֶנֶת וְקַיָּים. תַּנֵּי רִבִּי חִייָה. לֹא תִמְכּוֹר וְלֹא תִתֵּן. וְאִם מָכְרָה וְנָתְנָה קַיָּים. אָמַר רִבִּי חֲנִינָה בֶּן עֲקִיבָה. לֹא כֵן הֵשִׁיבָן רַבָּן גַּמְלִיאֵל. אֶלָּא כֵן הֵשִׁיבָן. לֹא. אִם אֲמַרְתֶּם בָּאֲרוּסָה שֶׁאֵינוֹ זַכַּאי לֹא בִמְצִיאָתָהּ וְלֹא בְמַעֲשֵׂה יָדֶיהָ וְלֹא בְהֶפֵר

נְדָרֶיהָ. תּאמַר בִּנְשׂוּאָה שֶׁהוּא זַכַּאי בִּמְצִיאָתָהּ וּבְמַעֲשֵׂה יָדֶיהָ וּבְהֵפֶר נְדָרֶיהָ. אָמְרוּ לוֹ. הֲרֵי עַד שֶׁלֹּא נִשֵּׂאת וְנִשֵּׂאת תּוֹכִיחַ. שֶׁהוּא זַכַּאי בִּמְצִיאָתָהּ וּבְמַעֲשֵׂה יָדֶיהָ וּבְהֵפֶר נְדָרֶיהָ. וְאַתְּ מוֹדֶה לָנוּ שֶׁלֹּא תִמְכּוֹר וְלֹא תִתֵּן. אָמַר לָהֶן. כָּךְ אֲנִי מוֹדֶה לָכֶם שֶׁלֹּא תִמְכּוֹר וְלֹא תִתֵּן וְאִם מָכְרָה וְנָתְנָה מִכְרָהּ קַייָם. אָתָא עוֹבְדָא קוֹמֵי רִבִּי אִמִּי. אָמַר. לֹא רַבָּן גַּמְלִיאֵל יְחִידִי הוּא. לֹא סָמְכוּן עֲלוֹי. מַתְנִיתָא מְסַייְעָא לֵיהּ וּפְלִיג עֲלוֹי. רַבּוֹתֵינוּ חָזְרוּ נִמְנוּ וְהוֹרוּ בִּנְכָסִים שֶׁנָּפְלוּ לָהּ עַד שֶׁלֹּא נִישֵּׂאת וְנִישֵּׂאת שֶׁלֹּא תִמְכּוֹר וְלֹא תִתֵּן. וְאִם מָכְרָה וְנָתְנָה מִכְרָהּ בָּטֵל. פְּלִיגָא עֲלוֹי מִכְרָהּ בָּטֵל. מְסַייְעָא לֵיהּ רַבּוֹתֵינוּ חָזְרוּ הוֹרוּ וְנִמְנוּ. שֶׁעַד שֶׁלֹּא נִמְנוּ לֹא הָיוּ חוֹלְקִין עֲלוֹי.

Halakhah 2: "If she inherited after she was definitively married," etc. We did state: She[16] may sell or give away and it is valid. Rebbi Ḥiyya stated: She should not sell or give away, but if she sold or gave away it is valid. [17]"Rebbi Ḥanina ben Aqiba said, that is not what Rabban Gamliel gave as answer, but the following was his argument: No, if you have an argument about a preliminarily married one, where he has rights neither to what she finds, nor to her handiwork, nor to dissolve her vows[18], what can you say about a definitively married one where he has rights to what she finds, to her handiwork, and to dissolve her vows? Let the proof be the case of one who [inherited] before the definitive marriage and then was definitively married, in which case he has rights to what she finds, to her handiwork, and to dissolve her vows, and you admit to us that she should not sell or give away. He said to them, I agree that she should not sell or give away, but if she sold or gave away it is valid.." There came a case before Rebbi Immi. He said, is not Rabban Gamliel's an isolated opinion? One cannot rely on it. A *baraita* supports him[19] and disagrees with him: [20]"Our teachers took up the case again, voted, and instructed about property which she inherited before the definitive marriage and then was definitively married, that she should not sell or give away, and if she sold or gave away it is invalid." It disagrees[21] that the sale is invalid. It agrees that our teachers took up the case again, instructed, and voted. Before they voted, they did not disagree with him[22].

16 She inherited real estate before her definitive wedding.

17 Tosephta 8:1, Babli 78b. In both of these sources the text seems to be more correct: The argument is inverted. If the husband has property rights after the definitive marriage, what does this prove for the preliminary?

18 He has joint rights to dissolve the vows of the adolescent preliminarily married girl; Mishnah *Nedarim* 10:1. He has no rights to dissolve the vows of his adult preliminarily married wife.

19 Rabban Gamliel. The argument of R. Immi is faulty but his conclusion correct.

20 Tosephta 7:1, Babli 78b.

21 With Rabban Gamliel.

22 In his time, Rabban Gamliel represented the majority opinion; his rule was invalidated by a later generation.

(fol. 31d) **משנה ג:** רִבִּי שִׁמְעוֹן חוֹלֵק בֵּין נְכָסִים לִנְכָסִים. נְכָסִים הַיְדוּעִים לַבַּעַל לֹא תִמְכּוֹר וְאִם מָכְרָה וְנָתְנָה בָּטֵל. וְשֶׁאֵינָן יְדוּעִים לַבַּעַל לֹא תִמְכּוֹר וְאִם מָכְרָה וְנָתְנָה קַיָּים.

Mishnah 3: Rebbi Simeon differentiates between properties: Properties known to the husband she shall not sell and if she sold or gave away it is invalid[23]. Those unknown to the husband she shall not sell but if she sold or gave away it is valid.

23 Since this is not practice, neither Talmud gives a reason. According to the Tosephta (8:1), the husband can claim that he married her only because of the property he knew was coming to her and that, therefore, the validity of the marriage depends on his getting his hands on that property.

(32a line 47) **הלכה ג:** רִבִּי שִׁמְעוֹן חוֹלֵק בֵּין נְכָסִין לִנְכָסִין כול׳. אָמַר רִבִּי יוֹחָנָן. נְכָסִים הַיְדוּעִים לַבַּעַל. אֵילוּ הַקַּרְקָעוֹת. וְשָׁאֵינָן יְדוּעִין לַבַּעַל. אֵילוּ מִטַלְטְלִין. רִבִּי יוֹסֵי בֶּן חֲנִינָא אָמַר. נְכָסִים הַיְדוּעִין לַבַּעַל. אֵלוּ שֶׁנָּפְלוּ לָהּ בִּרְשׁוּת הַבַּעַל. וְשָׁאֵינָם יְדוּעִים לַבַּעַל. אֵילוּ שֶׁנָּפְלוּ לָהּ וּבַעֲלָהּ נָתוּן בִּמְדִינַת הַיָּם. מַתְנִיתָא מְסַיְּיעָא לְרִבִּי יוֹסֵי בֶּן חֲנִינָה. אֵילוּ הֵן נְכָסִין שֶׁאֵינָן יְדוּעִין לַבַּעַל. אֵילוּ שֶׁנָּפְלוּ לָהּ וּבַעֲלָהּ נָתוּן בִּמְדִינַת הַיָּם.

Halakhah 3: "Rebbi Simeon differentiates between properties," etc. Rebbi Johanan[24] said, properties known to the husband are real estate, those not known to the husband are movables. Rebbi Yose ben Hanina said, properties known to the husband are those she inherited in the presence of the husband, those not known to the husband are those she inherited while her husband was overseas[25]. A *baraita* supports Rebbi Yose ben Hanina: The following are properties not known to the husband, what she inherited while her husband was overseas.

24 In the Babli, 78b, this is attributed to R. Yose ben R. Hanina.

25 In the Babli, 78a, R. Johanan holds that all properties discussed here are real estate; but properties unknown to the husband are what she inherits overseas. Since the husband cannot administer these properties, he cannot object to his wife's selling the properties, turning them into money.

(fol. 31d) **משנה ד:** נָפְלוּ לָהּ כְּסָפִים יִלָּקַח בָּהֶן קַרְקַע וְהוּא אוֹכֵל פֵּירוֹת. פֵּירוֹת הַתְּלוּשִׁין מִן הַקַּרְקַע יִלָּקַח בָּהֶן קַרְקַע וְהוּא אוֹכֵל פֵּירוֹת. פֵּירוֹת הַמְחוּבָּרִין אָמַר רִבִּי מֵאִיר שָׁמִין אוֹתָן כַּמָּה הֵן יָפִין בַּפֵּירוֹת וְכַמָּה הֵן יָפִין בְּלֹא פֵּירוֹת וּמוֹתָר יִלָּקַח בָּהֶן קַרְקַע וְהוּא אוֹכֵל פֵּירוֹת. וַחֲכָמִים אוֹמְרִים הַמְחוּבָּרִין לַקַּרְקַע שֶׁלּוֹ וְהַתְּלוּשִׁין מִן הַקַּרְקַע שֶׁלָּהּ וְיִלָּקַח בָּהֶן קַרְקַע וְהוּא אוֹכֵל פֵּירוֹת.

Mishnah 4: If she inherited money; real estate should be bought[26] with it and he eats its yield. For produce cut from the ground, real estate should be bought and he eats its yield; with produce connected to the ground, Rebbi Meïr says one has to estimate how much the property[27] is worth with produce and how much without, for the difference real estate should be bought[28] and he eats its yield. But the Sages say, standing produce is his[29], cut it is hers; real estate should be bought from it and he eats its yield.

26 Since it is the husband's duty to preserve his wife's property. In the economic environment of the later Roman Empire, real estate was the only investment guaranteed to keep its value (investments appropriate for the guardian of widows and orphans). Simce the husband is required to pay for all her needs, she has no direct use for the cash she inherited.

27 The field in which the crop is standing.

28 Since R. Meïr holds that a crop is yield only if it grew under his care.

29 Since it is yield.

(32a line 53) **הלכה ד:** נָפְלוּ לָהּ כְּסָפִים יִלָּקַח בָּהֶן קַרְקַע כול'. אָמַר רִבִּי יִרְמְיָה. דְּרִבִּי מֵאִיר הִיא. דְּרִבִּי מֵאִיר עֲבַד מְחוּבָּרִין כִּתְלוּשִׁין. אָמַר רִבִּי יוֹסֵי. וְלֹא שְׁמִיעַ דָּמַר רִבִּי יוֹסֵי בֶּן חֲנִינָה. לֹא אָמַר רִבִּי מֵאִיר אֶלָּא בְקָמָה הָעוֹמֶדֶת לְהִיקָּצֵר וּגְפָנִים עוֹמְדוֹת לְהִיבָּצֵר. הָא שַׁחַת לֹא. בְּרַם הָכָא אֲפִילוּ שַׁחַת. רִבִּי יִרְמְיָה בְעָא. מִחְלְפָא שִׁיטָתֵיהּ דְּרִבִּי מֵאִיר. תַּמָּן לָא עֲבַד מְחוּבָּרִין כִּתְלוּשִׁין וְהָכָא עֲבַד מְחוּבָּרִין כִּתְלוּשִׁין. אָמַר רִבִּי יוֹחָנָן. לֹא דְּרִבִּי מֵאִיר עֲבַד מְחוּבָּרִין

כִּתְלוּשִׁין. אֶלָּא אִם אַתָּה רוֹאֶה קָמָה קְצוּרָה אַתְּ מְיַפֶּה כֹּחָהּ שֶׁל אִשָּׁה. שָׂדֶה שֶׁלֹּא נִזְרְעָה אַתְּ מְיַפֶּה כֹּחָהּ שֶׁלָּאִישׁ. מִסָּפֵק שָׁמִין אוֹתָהּ כַּמָּה הָיְתָה יָפָה עַד שֶׁלֹּא נִזְרְעָה וְכַמָּה הִיא יָפָא מִשֶּׁנִּזְרְעָה. עַד שֶׁלֹּא נִזְרְעָה הִיא טָבָה תְּרֵין דִּינָרִין. מִשֶּׁנִּזְרְעָה הִיא יָפָה חַד דֵּינָר. אוֹתוֹ הַדֵּינָר יִלָּקַח בּוֹ קַרְקַע וְהוּא אוֹכֵל פֵּירוֹת.

Halakhah 4: "If she inherited money; real estate should be bought," etc. Rebbi Jeremiah said, this is Rebbi Meïr's opinion since Rebbi Meïr considers standing [produce] as if it were cut[30]. Rebbi Yose said, he did not hear that Rebbi Yose ben Ḥanina said, Rebbi Meïr said this only for standing grain ready to be harvested and grapes ready to be harvested; therefore not unripe produce[31]. But here[32], even unripe produce. Rebbi Jeremiah[33] asked, are not the arguments of Rebbi Meïr contradictory? There[34], he did not consider standing [produce] as if it were cut, but here[32] he considers standing [produce] as if it were cut. Rebbi Joḥanan said, Rebbi Meïr does not consider standing [produce] as if it were cut. But if you see cut grain, you empower the woman[35]; if you see an unseeded field[36], you empower the man. In case of doubt you estimate how much it is worth unseeded and how much seeded. If before it was seeded it was worth (two denars)[37] and when it was seeded (one denar), with that denar real estate should be bought and he reaps its yield.

30 This refers to Mishnah *Ševuot* 6:6. In rabbinic interpretation, *Ex.* 22:8 defines when an oath is required by the court: "About any criminal matter, about an ox, a donkey, a sheep, a garment, or anything lost, *if he agrees that this is it*, the suit shall be heard by the judges . . ." This is read to mean that an oath is needed if the defendant agrees that the plaintiff has a case but that he owes less than what is being claimed (cf. *Mekhilta dR. Ismael, Mišpaṭim* 15). The part of the claim in dispute is what the claimant considers criminal withholding of his property by the defendant. If the defendant rejects

the entire claim, the claimant has to prove his case by witnesses or documents; if the defendant admits part of the claim the claimant can request that he swear not to owe more. But since the examples given in the verse are all about movables, it is concluded that claims of real estate cannot be resolved by an oath (Mishnah *Ševuot* 6:5). On that, R. Meïr states that "some things are on the ground but are not real estate". The example given is that the claim is "I handed over to you (to harvest and make wine from) ten vines full of fruit" but the defendant claims "there were ony five." In that case, R. Meïr requires the defendant to swear but the Sages hold that anything connected to the ground is like real estate.

Since the produce on the field is considered as the wife's capital, not the husband's produce, R. Jeremiah infers that the Mishnah does not represent practice since it follows R. Meïr in a case in which the majority disagrees.

31   Cf. *Yebamot* 15:3, Note 79; Babli *Ševuot* 43a.

32   The case of the wife's inheritance is not restricted to ripe produce.

33   This attribution is impossible. Rebbi Jeremiah cannot ask a question answered by his teacher's teacher's teacher R. Johanan. It might be Rav Jeremiah, one generation before R. Johanan.

34   In Mishnah *Ševuot* 6:6.

35   Cut grain is as good as coin for an inheritance.

36   This has to be tended; the husband will reap the fruits.

37   Obviously, the numbers have to be switched since 1 < 2.

משנה ה: רִבִּי שִׁמְעוֹן אוֹמֵר מָקוֹם שֶׁיִיפָּה כוֹחוֹ בִּכְנִיסָתָהּ הוֹרַע כּוֹחוֹ (fol. 31d) בִּיצִיאָתָהּ מָקוֹם שֶׁהוֹרַע כּוֹחוֹ בִּכְנִיסָתָהּ יִיפָּה כוֹחוֹ בִּיצִיאָתָהּ . הַמְחוּבָּרִין לַקַּרְקַע בִּכְנִיסָתָהּ שֶׁלוֹ וּבִיצִיאָתָהּ שֶׁלָּהּ וְהַתְּלוּשִׁין מִן הַקַּרְקַע בִּכְנִיסָתָהּ שֶׁלָּהּ וּבִיצִיאָתָהּ שֶׁלוֹ.

Mishnah 5: Rebbi Simeon says, in the circumstances where he was empowered at her entrance he was disabled at her exit, and in the circumstances where he was disabled at her entrance he was empowered at her exit. What was connected to the ground at her entrance is his and at her exit is hers, what was cut from the ground at her entrance is hers and at her exit is his[38].

38 He follows the Sages in the previous Mishnah that produce she brings into the marriage as capital and real estate is given over to his administration. He adds that at a divorce (if she exits the marriage) he has to deliver the field as is at the moment the bill of divorce is delivered, with all the grain standing if it was not cut before the divorce but that all produce harvested before the moment of divorce is his; cf. *Yebamot* 15:5, Notes 67-68.

(32a line 64) **הלכה ה:** רבי שמעון אומר מקום שֶׁיִּיפָּה כוחו כול'. אַתְּ אָמַר. בִּכְנִיסָתָהּ שֶׁלֹּא מְכָרָה אוֹתָן אֵינָן מְכוּרִין. נְתָנָתָן לְאָרִיס הוּא מְשַׁתֵּפָה מִמֶּנּוּ. עָשָׂת אוֹתָן בִּיכּוּרִים לֹא קָדְשׁוּ. אַתְּ אָמַר. בִּמְצִיאָתָהּ[39] שֶׁלָּה מָכַר אוֹתָן אֵינָן מְכוּרִין. נְתָנָתָן לְאָרִיס הוּא מְשַׁתֵּפָה מִמֶּנּוּ. עָשָׂת אוֹתָן בִּיכּוּרִים. תַּפְלוּגְתָא דְרָבִי יוֹחָנָן וְרַבִּי שִׁמְעוֹן בֶּן לָקִישׁ. דְּאִתְפַּלְגוּן. וְשָׂמַחְתָּ בְּכָל־הַטּוֹב אֲשֶׁר נָתַן לְךָ יי אֱלֹהֶיךָ וּלְבֵיתֶךָ. מְלַמֵּד שֶׁאָדָם[40] מֵבִיא בִיכּוּרִים מִנִּכְסֵי אִשְׁתּוֹ. רַבִּי שִׁמְעוֹן בֶּן לָקִישׁ אָמַר. לְאַחַר מִיתָה. הָא בְחַיִּים לֹא. אָמַר רַבִּי יוֹחָנָן. לֹא שַׁנְיָיא. הִיא בְחַיִּים הִיא לְאַחַר מִיתָה. רַבִּי שִׁמְעוֹן בֶּן לָקִישׁ כְּדַעְתֵּיהּ. דְּאָמַר אֵין אָדָם יוֹרֵשׁ אֶת אִשְׁתּוֹ מִדְּבַר תּוֹרָה. עַל דַּעְתֵּיהּ דְּרָבִּי שִׁמְעוֹן בֶּן לָקִישׁ לֹא קִידְּשׁוּ. עַל דַּעְתֵּיהּ דְּרָבִי יוֹחָנָן קִידְּשׁוּ וּפָקְעַת מִינַּיְיהוּ קְדוּשָּׁתָן.

"Rebbi Simeon says, in the circumstances where he was empowered," etc. You say, at her entrance they are his: If she sold them they are not sold, if she gave them to a sharecropper he has the reward from it[41], if she dedicated them as First Fruits they are not dedicated[42]. You say, at her exit they are hers, if he sold them they are not sold, if he gave them to a sharecropper she has the reward from it, if he dedicated them as First Fruits, this is the disagreement of Rebbi Joḥanan and Rebbi Simeon ben Laqish, since they disagreed: [43](*Deut.* 26:11): 'You shall enjoy all the good things that the Eternal, your God, gave to you and your house.' This teaches that a person brings First Fruits from his wife's property." Rebbi Simeon ben Laqish said, after her death but not during her lifetime. Rebbi Joḥanan said, there is no difference, during her lifetime and after her death. Rebbi Simeon ben Laqish follows his own opinion since he said, a person does not inherit from his wife as a biblical rule[44]. In the opinion of Rebbi Simeon ben Laqish it never was dedicated. In the opinion of Rebbi Joḥanan it is dedicated and the holiness is removed[45].

39 One has to read: ביציאתה "at her exit" instead of במציאתה "on the occasion of her finding."

40 This is the text of the parallel in *Bikkurim*. Text here: שאין אדם "for no person".

41 The text may mean: He takes it away from him. In the first interpretation, the standing crop given to the sharecropper is counted as part of the latter's compensation.

42 Since nobody can dedicate anything which is not his property and not in his possession.

43 The next few sentences are from *Bikkurim* 1:6, Notes 119-121. Cf. *Sifry Deut.* #301.

44 This is the common Sadducee-Karaite opinion that the wife is never mentioned in *Num.* 27:7-11 (only that the children inherit from their mother, *Num.* 36:3). In the Babli, *Giṭṭin* 47b, it is supposed that R. Simeon ben Laqish accepts that the wife is mentioned obliquely in *Num.* 27:11 and his disagreement with R. Joḥanan is about a technicality; the opinion attributed here to R. Simeon ben Laqish is attributed in the Babli, 84a, to Rav. In *Bekhorot* 52b, it is asserted without dissent that the husband's right of inheritance is biblical. (Maimonides,

Hilkhot Nahalot 6:8, asserts that the husband's right of inheritance from his wife is only rabbinic practice.)

45 If the First Fruits were dedicated during the marriage then the act of divorce removes the husband's ownership and with it the dedication.

(fol. 31d) **משנה ו:** נָפְלוּ לָהּ עֲבָדִים וּשְׁפָחוֹת זְקֵנִים יִמָּכְרוּ וְיִלָּקַח בָּהֶן קַרְקַע וְהוּא אוֹכֵל פֵּירוֹת. רַבָּן שִׁמְעוֹן בֶּן גַּמְלִיאֵל אוֹמֵר לֹא תִמְכּוֹר מִפְּנֵי שֶׁהֵן שְׁבָח בֵּית אָבִיהָ.

Mishnah 6: If she inherited old male and female slaves, they should be sold and real estate bought with the proceeds, of which he eats the yield. Rabban Simeon ben Gamliel says, she does not have to sell[46] because they are the glory of her father's house.

46 He cannot sell her family's slaves against her will.

(32b line 3) **הלכה ו:** נָפְלוּ לָהּ עֲבָדִים וּשְׁפָחוֹת כול׳. מַתְנִיתָא בְּשֶׁאֵינָן עוֹשִׂין כְּדֵי טִפְּלָתָן. אֲבָל אִם הָיוּ עוֹשִׂין כְּדֵי טִפְּלָתָן לֹא תִמְכּוֹר. שֶׁעֲדַיִּין כְּבוֹד בֵּית אָבִיהָ קַיָּים.

Halakhah 6: "If she inherited male and female slaves," etc. The Mishnah speaks of those who do not work enough[47] for their upkeep. But if they work enough for their upkeep, she does not have to sell[48] because the glory of her father's house still exists.

47 As Tosaphot notes (79b, *s. v.* והרי), if they cannot work at all they cannot be sold.

48 Even according to the anonymous Tanna.

משנה ז: נָפְלוּ לָהּ זֵיתִים וּגְפָנִים זְקֵנִים יִמָּכְרוּ לְעֵצִים וְיִלָּקַח בָּהֶן (fol. 31d) קַרְקַע וְהוּא אוֹכֵל פֵּירוֹת. רִבִּי יְהוּדָה אוֹמֵר לֹא תִמְכּוֹר מִפְּנֵי שֶׁהֵן שֶׁבַח בֵּית אָבִיהָ.

Mishnah 7: If she inherited old vines or olive trees, they should be sold for their wood and real estate bought with the proceeds, of which he eats the yield. Rebbi Jehudah[49] says, she does not have to sell[46] because they are the glory of her father's house.

(32b line 6) **הלכה ז:** נָפְלוּ לָהּ זֵיתִים וּגְפָנִים כול׳. רַב אָבוּן בְּשֵׁם רַבָּנִין דְּתַמָּן. מַתְנִיתָא בְּשֶׁנָּפְלוּ לָהּ זֵיתִים וְלֹא קַרְקָעוֹ. גְּפָנִים וְלֹא קַרְקָעוֹ. אֲבָל אִם נָפְלוּ לָהּ זֵיתִים וְקַרְקָעוֹ גְּפָנִים וְקַרְקָעוֹ לֹא תִקּוֹץ. שֶׁעֲדַיִין שֶׁבַח בֵּית אָבִיהָ קַיָּים. וְרַבָּנִין דְּהָכָא אָמְרִין. אֲפִילוּ נָפְלוּ לָהּ זֵיתִים וְקַרְקָעוֹ גְּפָנִים וְקַרְקָעוֹ. לֹא דְמֵי בֵית זֵיתָא דְּנָפְלוּ וְלֹא דְמֵי בֵית כַּרְמָא דְּנָפְלוּ. מַתְנִיתָא מְסַייְעָא לְרַבָּנִין דְּתַמָּן. כַּרְמָא אֲנִי מוֹכֵר לָךְ. אַף עַל פִּי שֶׁאֵין בּוֹ גְפָנִים הֲרֵי זֶה מָכוּר. שֶׁלֹּא מָכַר לוֹ אֶלָּא שְׁמוֹ. פַּרְדֵּיסָא אֲנִי מוֹכֵר לָךְ. אַף עַל פִּי שֶׁאֵין בּוֹ אִילָנוֹת הֲרֵי זֶה מָכוּר. שֶׁלֹּא מָכַר לוֹ אֶלָּא שְׁמוֹ.

Halakhah 7: "If she inherited old vines or olive trees," etc. Rav Abun in the name of the rabbis there[50]: The Mishnah deals with the case that she inherited olive trees but not their ground, vines but not their ground[51]. But if she inherited olive trees with their ground, vines with their ground, she does not have to sell since her father's house's glory still exists[52]. But the rabbis here say, even if she inherited olive trees with their ground, vines with their ground, did she not inherit the value of the olive grove, did she not inherit the value of the vineyard? A *baraita*[53] supports the rabbis there: "'I am selling you the vineyard', this is a valid sale even if there are no vines since he sells him [the real estate] by description[54]. 'I am selling you the grove', this is a valid sale even if there are no trees since he sells him [the real estate] by description."

49 It seems that Alfassi reads "Rabban Simeon ben Gamliel", with the Munich ms. of the Babli (38b in the Wilna edition.)
50 According to the Babli, 79b, these Babylonian rabbis are Rav Cahana in the name of Rav.
51 Therefore, if one waits until the trees have died, all value from the inheritance is lost.
52 On condition that the orchard or the vineyard be generally known as "her father's orchard or vineyard."
53 The remainder of this paragraph is from *Ma'serot* 2:5, Notes 107,108. The quote is from Tosephta *Baba Batra* 6:18, Babli *Baba Batra* 7a, *Baba Meṣi'a* 104a.
54 If the lot was popularly known as "vineyard" or "olive grove".

(fol. 31d) **משנה ח:** הַמּוֹצִיא יְצִיאוֹת עַל נִכְסֵי אִשְׁתּוֹ הוֹצִיא הַרְבֵּה וְאָכַל קִמְעָא קִמְעָא וְאָכַל הַרְבֵּה מַה שֶׁהוֹצִיא הוֹצִיא וּמַה שֶׁאָכַל אָכָל. הוֹצִיא וְלֹא אָכַל יִשָּׁבַע כַּמָּה הוֹצִיא וְיִטּוֹל.

Mishnah 8: If somebody invests in his wife's properties[55], if he invested much but it yielded little, or he invested little but it yielded much, what he invested he invested and what it yielded it yielded[56]. If he invested and had no yield, he shall swear how much he invested and get repaid[57].

55 The paraphernalia properties which in case of a divorce have to be returned to the wife.
56 He has no claim to be repaid for the excess of his investment over his gain.
57 If he divorced his wife before he had *any* income from his investment, he can ask to be repaid.

(32b line 14) **הלכה ח:** הַמּוֹצִיא יְצִיאוֹת עַל נִכְסֵי אִשְׁתּוֹ כול'. רִבִּי בָּא בְשֵׁם רַב חִייָה בַּר אַשִׁי. אֲפִילוּ לֹא אָכַל אֶלָּא מְלֹא חוֹתָלָא. אַסִּי אָמַר. וְהוּא

שֶׁתְּהֵא הוֹצָאָה יְתֵירָה עַל הַשְׁבָח. אֲבָל אִם הַשְׁבָח יָתֵר עַל הַהוֹצָאָה נוֹתֵן לוֹ אֶת הַשְׁבָח. מַתְנִיתָא פְּלִיגָא עַל אַסִּי. וְכוּלְהֹם שָׁמִין לָהּ בְּעָרִיס.[58] מַתְנִיתָא פְּלִיגָא בִּנְטִיעָה. מָאן דָּמַר אַסִּי בְּבִנְיָין. מַתְנִיתָא פְּלִיגָא בִּנְטִיעָה. עַל כֵּן אָמַר רִבִּי בָּא בְּשֵׁם רַב חִייָה בַּר אַשִׁי. אֲפִילוּ לֹא אָכַל אֶלָּא מְלֹא חוּתְלָא. אָמַר לֵיהּ. כָּאן בְּשֶׁאָכַל. כָּאן בְּשֶׁלֹּא אָכַל.

Halakhah 8: "If somebody invests in his wife's properties," etc. Rebbi Abba[59] in the name of Rav Ḥiyya bar Ashi: Even if he ate only one basket of dates. Assi[60] said, that is, if the investment is greater than the increase in value. But if the increase in value is greater than the investment, one gives him the increase in value[61]. A *baraita* disagrees[62] with Assi: "In all cases[63] one evaluates it as for a sharecropper." The *baraita* disagrees about planting; what Assi said was about a building. The *baraita* disagrees about planting, is that what Rebbi Abba said in the name of Rav Ḥiyya bar Ashi: Even if he ate only one basket of dates[64]. He said to him, in one case if he ate, in the other if he did not eat.

58 It seems that one has to read בְּעָרִיס (this is the word translated).
59 In the Babli, 80a, he says "one date cake".
60 It seems that he is the Babylonian, colleague of Rav; identified correctly in the Munich ms. of the Babli, 80a.
61 In the Babli, 80a, two interpretations are given for Assi's statement but in both of them, the husband is restricted to restitution of the amount he spent.

62 Tosephta 8:3; Babli *Baba Meṣi'a* 39a.
63 Any person who has to return property to its rightful owner, including the husband who divorces his wife and has to return her paraphernalia properties in kind. If he returns a field before it is ripe, he can claim to be paid for his work only as sharecropper.
64 Which is much less than the sharecropper's part.

(fol. 31d) **משנה ט:** שׁוֹמֶרֶת יָבָם שֶׁנָּפְלוּ לָהּ נְכָסִים מוֹדִין בֵּית שַׁמַּאי וּבֵית הִלֵּל שֶׁאִם מוֹכֶרֶת וְנוֹתֶנֶת קַיָּים. מֵתָה מַה יֵּעָשֶׂה בִכְתוּבָתָהּ וּבִנְכָסִים הַנִּכְנָסִין וְהַיּוֹצְאִין עִמָּהּ. בֵּית שַׁמַּאי אוֹמְרִים יַחֲלוֹקוּ יוֹרְשֵׁי הַבַּעַל עִם יוֹרְשֵׁי הָאָב. וּבֵית הִלֵּל אוֹמְרִים נְכָסִים בְּחֶזְקָתָן וּכְתוּבָה בְּחֶזְקַת יוֹרְשֵׁי הַבַּעַל וּנְכָסִים הַנִּכְנָסִין וְהַיּוֹצְאִין עִמָּהּ בְּחֶזְקַת יוֹרְשֵׁי הָאָב.

Mishnah 9: [65]If a woman waiting for her levir inherited property, the House of Shammai and the House of Hillel agree that if she sells or gives away it is valid. If she died, what shall be done with her *ketubah* and the properties which enter and leave with her? The House of Shammai say, the husband's and the father's heirs shall split it. But the House of Hillel say, the properties are in the hands of the holders; the *ketubah* in the hands of the husband's heirs and the properties which enter and leave with her in the hands of the father's heirs.

65   Mishnah and Halakhah are also   84-95 (variants noted י).
Yebamot 4:3, explained there in Notes

(32b line 22) **הלכה ט:** שׁוֹמֶרֶת יָבָם שֶׁנָּפְלוּ לָהּ נְכָסִים כול׳. הָכָא אַתְּ מַר. מוֹכֶרֶת וְנוֹתֶנֶת וְקַיָּים. וְהָכָא אַתְּ מַר. יַחֲלֹקוּ יוֹרְשֵׁי הַבַּעַל עִם יוֹרְשֵׁי הָאָב. אָמַר רִבִּי יוֹסֵי בֶּן חֲנִינָה. אִין דְּאַתְּ אָמַר מוֹכֶרֶת וְנוֹתֶנֶת וְקַיָּים. בְּשֶׁנָּפְלוּ לָהּ עַד שֶׁלֹּא נַעֲשֵׂית שׁוֹמֶרֶת יָבָם. וְהֵן דְּאַתְּ אָמַר. יַחֲלֹקוּ יוֹרְשֵׁי הַבַּעַל עִם יוֹרְשֵׁי הָאָב. בְּשֶׁנָּפְלוּ לָהּ מִשֶּׁנַּעֲשֵׂית שׁוֹמֶרֶת יָבָם. וְנָפְלוּ לָהּ עַד שֶׁנַּעֲשֵׂית שׁוֹמֶרֶת יָבָם וְעָשׂוּ פֵירוֹת מִשֶּׁנַּעֲשֵׂית שׁוֹמֶרֶת יָבָם כְּמוֹ שֶׁנָּפְלוּ לָהּ מִשֶּׁנַּעֲשֵׂית שׁוֹמֶרֶת יָבָם. אָמַר רִבִּי זְעִירָא. הָכֵן יָבָם צְרִיכָא לְבֵית שַׁמַּי. כְּבַעַל הוּא אוֹ אֵינוֹ כְּבַעַל. אִם הוּא כְּבַעַל יוֹרֵשׁ אֶת הַכֹּל. אִם אֵינוֹ כְּבַעַל לֹא יוֹרֵשׁ כְּלוּם. מִסָּפֵק יַחֲלֹקוּ יוֹרְשֵׁי הַבַּעַל עִם יוֹרְשֵׁי הָאָב. דְּבֵית הִלֵּל פְּשִׁיטָא לוֹן שֶׁהוּא כְּבַעַל וְיוֹרֵשׁ אֶת הַכֹּל. שֶׁכֵּן אֲפִילוּ אָח אֵין לוֹ עָלֶיהָ אֶלָּא אֲכִילַת פֵּירוֹת בִּלְבָד.

1 מר | י אמר   2 וקיים. | י וקיים. מתה מה יעשה בכתובתה.   מר | י אמר   3 בשנפלו | י כשנפלו   4 נעשית | י היתה   והן | י והא   5 ונפלו | י נפלו   שנעשית | י שלא נעשית   7 לבית | י דבית   7-8 אם הוא כבעל | י אין כבעל הוא   9 דבית | י בית לון שהוא | י ליה   10 אח | י אחיו

Halakhah 9: "If property came to a woman waiting for her levir," etc. Here, you say "she may sell or give away and it is valid." And you also say "the husband's heirs should split with her father's heirs!" Rebbi Yose ben Ḥanina said, when do you say "she may sell or give away and it is valid"? If they came to her before she became a woman waiting for her levir. When do you say "the husband's heirs should split with her father's heirs"? If they came to her after she became a woman waiting for her levir. If they came to her before she became a woman waiting for her levir and produced revenue after she became a woman waiting for her levir, [that revenue is as if] they came to her after she became a woman waiting for her levir. Rebbi Ze'ira said, the levir in this situation is a problem for the House of Shammai. If he is a husband, he inherits everything. If he is not a husband, he inherits nothing. Because of the doubt, "the husband's heirs should split with her father's heirs." For the House of Hillel it is obvious that he is a husband and inherits everything. For even his brother had only the usufruct.

(32b line 33) תַּנֵּי רבִּי הוֹשַׁעְיָה. יוֹרְשֶׁיהָ הַיּוֹרְבָתָהּ כְּתוּבָתָהּ חַיָּיבִין בִּקְבוּרָתָהּ. אָמַר רבִּי יוֹסֵי. אִי לָאו דְּתַנִּיתָהּ רבִּי הוֹשַׁעְיָה הֲוָת צְרִיכָה לָן מֵאַחַר שֶׁאֵין לָהּ כְּתוּבָה אֵין לָהּ קְבוּרָה. וְקַשְׁיָא. אִילוּ אִשָּׁה שֶׁאֵין לָהּ כְּתוּבָה שֶׁמָּא אֵין לָהּ קְבוּרָה. אִשָּׁה אַף עַל פִּי שֶׁאֵין לָהּ כְּתוּבָה יֵשׁ לָהּ קְבוּרָה. בְּרַם הָכָא. אִם יֵשׁ לָהּ כְּתוּבָה יֵשׁ לָהּ קְבוּרָה. וְאִם אֵין לָהּ כְּתוּבָה אֵין לָהּ קְבוּרָה.

1 יורשיח | י יירשו   2 אי לאו | י אילולי

Rebbi Hoshaia stated: Her heirs, those who inherit her *ketubah* are obliged to bury her. Rebbi Yose said, if Rebbi Hoshaia had not stated this, we would have had a problem. If she had no *ketubah*, do they not have to bury her? This is difficult. If a woman has no *ketubah*, does she not have to be buried? A wife, even if she has no *ketubah*, must be buried. This one, if she has a *ketubah*, is entitled to burial costs. But here, if she does not have a *ketubah*, she is not entitled to burial costs.

(fol. 32a) **משנה י:** הִנִּיחַ לוֹ אָחִיו מָעוֹת יִלָּקַח בָּהֶן קַרְקַע וְהוּא אוֹכֵל פֵּירוֹת. פֵּירוֹת הַתְּלוּשִׁין מִן הַקַּרְקַע יִלָּקַח בָּהֶן קַרְקַע וְהוּא אוֹכֵל פֵּירוֹת. פֵּירוֹת הַמְחוּבָּרִין בַּקַּרְקַע אָמַר רִבִּי מֵאִיר שָׁמִין אוֹתָן כַּמָּה הֵן יָפִין בַּפֵּירוֹת וְכַמָּה הֵן יָפִין בְּלֹא פֵּירוֹת וְהַמּוֹתָר יִלָּקַח בָּהֶן קַרְקַע וְהוּא אוֹכֵל פֵּירוֹת. וַחֲכָמִים אוֹמְרִים הַמְחוּבָּרִים לַקַּרְקַע שֶׁלּוֹ וְהַתְּלוּשִׁין מִן הַקַּרְקַע כָּל הַקּוֹדֵם זָכָה בָּהֶן. קָדַם הוּא זָכָה קֶדְמָה הִיא יִלָּקַח בָּהֶן קַרְקַע וְהוּא אוֹכֵל פֵּירוֹת. כְּנָסָהּ הֲרֵי הִיא כְּאִשְׁתּוֹ לְכָל־דָּבָר וּבִלְבַד שֶׁתְּהֵא כְתוּבָּתָהּ עַל נִכְסֵי בַעֲלָהּ הָרִאשׁוֹן.

Mishnah 10: If his brother left money, real estate should be bought with it and he eats its yield[66]. [67]For produce cut from the ground, real estate should be bought and he eats its yield; connected to the ground, Rebbi Meïr says one has to estimate how much it is worth with produce and how much without, for the difference real estate should be bought and he eats its yield. But the Sages say, standing produce is his[68], cut it is up for grabs[69]. If he[70] took possession first, it is his; if she took possession first[71], real estate should be bought for the proceeds and he eats its yield. [72]If he married her, she is his wife in every respect[73] except that her *ketubah* is a lien on the property of her first husband.

66   Since the first husband's inheritance is mortgaged to his widow as security for her *ketubah*, it is not available to the brother who marries the widow without due safeguards.

67   These rules follow Mishnah 4.

68   The Halakhah and the Babli (82a) change the text of the Mishnah and require: "are hers" for the same reason given for money left by her husband.

69   This applies only if one follows the Mishnah that a *ketubah* is guaranteed only by real estate. The author of this part of the Mishnah must hold that the statement about money left was R. Meïr's who holds that a *ketubah* can be guaranteed and paid for by movables.

70   The levir as heir of his brother. It is clear that a person without claim (i. e., other than the widow, a brother, or a creditor) has no right to the produce.

71   It becomes property coming to the wife after the wedding, i. e., paraphernalia property.

72   This is Mishnah *Yebamot* 4:4, Note 96.

73   He can divorce and remarry her; Halakhah *Yebamot* 4:4, Notes 97-100.

(32b line 39) **הלכה י:** הִנִּיחַ אָחִיו מָעוֹת כול'. רִבִּי אַבָּהוּ בְּשֵׁם רִבִּי יוֹחָנָן. לָכֵן צְרִיכָא בְּמוּפְקָדִים אֶצְלוֹ. שֶׁלֹּא תֹאמַר. הוֹאִיל וַאֲנִי הוּא הַיּוֹרֵשׁ שֶׁלִּי הֵן.

Halakhah 10: "If his brother left money," etc. Rebbi Abbahu in the name of Rebbi Joḥanan: It is necessary, if the money was deposited with him[74], that you would not let him say, since I am the heir it is mine.

74   Since the Mishnah states at the end that the *ketubah* in a levirate marriage is guaranteed by the estate and Mishnah 11 states that all the property is under this lien, it seems superfluous to note that cash left by the first husband cannot be spent by the levir. Then it is noted that it is necessary to state that money deposited with the levir has to be accounted for and separated for the wife's *ketubah*. In the Babli, 81b, this is an explicit *baraita*.

(32b line 41) רִבִּי אַבָּהוּ בְּשֵׁם רִבִּי יוֹחָנָן. לֵית כָּאן שֶׁלּוּ אֶלָּא. לְהָיֵי דָא מִילָא שְׁאִם קָדַם הַיּוֹרֵשׁ וְתָפַס מוֹצִיאִין מִיָּדוֹ. אַף בְּבַעַל חוֹב כֵּן. לֹא כֵן תַּנֵּי. יוֹרֵשׁ וּבַעַל חוֹב שֶׁקָּדַם אֶחָד מֵהֶן וְתָפַס מוֹצִיאִין מִיָּדוֹ. אָמַר רִבִּי אָחָא בַּר עוּלָּא. נִישְׁמָעִינָהּ מִן הָדָא. הִקְדִּישׁ תִּשְׁעִים מָנֶה וְהָיָה חוֹבוֹ מֵאָה מָנֶה מוֹסִיף עוֹד דֵּינָר וּפוֹדֶה נְכָסִים הַלָּלוּ. וְלֹא סוֹף דָּבָר דֵּינָר אֶלָּא אֲפִילוּ כָּל־שֶׁהוּא. שֶׁלֹּא יְהֵא הֶקְדֵּשׁ נִרְאֶה יוֹצֵא בְּלֹא פִדְיוֹן. רִבִּי אַבָּהוּ בְּשֵׁם רִבִּי יוֹחָנָן. מוֹעֲלִין מְעִילָה גְמוּרָה. וְקַשְׁיָא. אִם מוֹעֲלִין בָּהּ מְעִילָה גְמוּרָה יְהֵא נִפְדֶּה בְּשָׁוֶה. אִם אֵינוּ נִפְדֶּה בְּשָׁוֶה לֹא יִמְעֲלוּ בוֹ מְעִילָה גְמוּרָה. מָה אֲנָן קַיָּימִין. אִם בִּמְחוּבָּר לַקַּרְקַע. וְכִי יֵשׁ מְעִילָה בַּקַּרְקַע. אֶלָּא כֵן אֲנָן קַיָּימִין בְּקָמָה. מֵאַחַר שֶׁאִלּוּ עָבַר הַגּוּבָּר וְתָפַס [אֵין]⁷⁵ מוֹצִיאִין מִיָּדוֹ. הוּא גִיזְבָּר הוּא יוֹרֵשׁ. מַה גִיזְבָּר עָבַר הַגּוּבָּר וְתָפַס אֵין מוֹצִיאִין מִיָּדוֹ. אַף יוֹרֵשׁ עָבַר הַיּוֹרֵשׁ וְתָפַס אֵין מוֹצִיאִין מִיָּדוֹ. רִבִּי שְׁמוּאֵל רִבִּי אַבָּהוּ בְּשֵׁם רִבִּי יוֹחָנָן. אַף בְּשׁוֹר כֵּן. אִית לָךְ מֵימַר. שׁוֹר קַרְקַע. רִבִּי תַּנְחוּם בַּר מָרִי בְּשֵׁם רִבִּי יוֹסֵי. שׁוֹר עָשׂוּ אוֹתוֹ כְהֶקְדֵּשׁ שֶׁהִזִּיל. הָכָא אַתְּ אָמַר. מוֹצִיאִין מִיָּדוֹ. וְכָא אַתְּ אָמַר. אֵין מוֹצִיאִין מִיָּדוֹ. לְפִי שֶׁהִיְרְעָתָהּ כּוֹחָהּ שֶׁלְּאִשָּׁה שֶׁלֹּא תְהֵא כְתוּבָּתָהּ אֶלָּא עַל נִכְסֵי בַעֲלָהּ הָרִאשׁוֹן יִיפִּיתָהּ כּוֹחָהּ בַּדָּבָר הַזֶּה שְׁאִם קָדַם הַיּוֹרֵשׁ וְתָפַס מוֹצִיאִין מִיָּדוֹ. וְתַגֵּי כֵן. אִילָנוֹת וּקְצָצוֹת זְקֵינִים וּנְעָרִים מוֹצִיאִים מִיָּדָן.

Rebbi Abbahu in the name of Rebbi Johanan: One does not say "his"⁷⁶ but [ ]⁷⁷. In which respect? In case the heir took it⁷⁸, one removes it from his hand. Does one have the same rule for the creditor? Was it not stated: If either the heir or the creditor took it, one takes it from their hands⁷⁹? Rebbi Aha bar Ulla said, let us hear from the following: "If he dedicated 90 minas but his debt was 100 minas, [the creditor] adds another denar and redeems these properties.⁸⁰" Not necessarily a denar, but anything, that a dedication should not be seen to be profanated without redemption⁸¹. Rebbi Abbahu in the name of Rebbi Johanan: One would be guilty of complete larceny[82]. That is difficult. If one would be guilty of complete larceny, should if not be redeemed for its full value? If it can be redeemed for less than its full value, one should not be guilty of complete larceny! What are we talking about? If it is connected to the ground, can there be larceny about real estate[83]? But we talk about standing grain[84]. Since if the administrator[85] misbehaved and took it, one does not take it from his hand; the administrator and the heir follow the same rule[86]. Also if the heir misbehaved and took it, one does not take it from his hand. Rebbi Samuel, Rebbi Abbahu in the name of Rebbi Joḥanan: The same rule holds for an ox. Can you say that an ox is real estate[87]? Rebbi Tanḥum bar Mari in the name of Rebbi Yose: They made the rules for an ox parallel those of dedications that lost their value[88]. Here, you say one takes it from his hand, but there you say, one does not take it from his hand[89]. Since you diminished the woman's power in that her *ketubah* is a lien only on the properties of her first husband, you strengthened her power in this matter that if the heir came and took it, one removes it from his hand. It was stated thus: Trees and cutting, old or young, one removes from their hands.

75 This sentence has several corrections in the ms. It seems that the scribe first wrote שֶׁאִין עָבַד הַגִּזְבָּר וְתָפַס אֵין מוֹצִיאִין מִיָדוֹ "if the administrator acted and took it, one does not take it from him." This is a correct sentence but unvocalized it is misleading because of the simultaneous use of Aramaic אין "if" and Hebrew אין "not". Therefore, the scribe crossed out the first אין and replaced it by לו, read לו "if" which the corrector then completed (somewhat redundantly) to אילו The scribe also changed עבד "acted" to עבר "acted wrongly" and crossed out (mistakenly) the second אין The best version is the original text.

76 Since the widow's *ketubah* is guaranteed by her first husband's estate, there is no reason why the

standing grain should go to the levir. If the husband had lived, it would have been his, but it could not be the levir's before the latter actually married the widow. One has to correct the Mishnah to *hers* from *his*. This argument is R. Simeon ben Laqish's in the Babli, 82a.

77 The word "hers" is missing in ms. and *editio princeps*; it is understood in the text.

78 If the levir harvested the grain without crediting it to the widow's *ketubah* fund, she can go to court and have him acquire real estate for the corresponding amount.

79 The same statement is quoted in Halakhah 9:3; there the scribe wrote: "one does not remove from their hands", but the first corrector crossed out "not". In both cases, the context implies that the scribe's original text is the correct one. Since the heir does not have a claim on the standing grain, the heir's creditor does not have one either.

80 It is stated repeatedly in the Babli (*Yebamot* 46a,66b; *Giṭṭin* 40b; *Ketubot* 59b, *Nedarim* 86b; *Baba Qama* 90a) that dedications to the Temple break contracts. This rule is not mentioned in the Yerushalmi and the latter's position in this matter is not known. In Rashi's interpretation, only dedications to the altar break contracts, not dedications which are purely monetary gifts to Temple or charity. Therefore, that principle does not apply here in any case.

The text is Mishnah *'Arakhin* 6:2. There it is stated that if somebody dedicates his encumbered property, neither can the wife collect her *ketubah* nor a creditor his claim from Temple property which must first be redeemed. Then it is stated that if the creditor's claim is at least equal to the appraised value of the property, he may lend another denar to the debtor and force him to redeem it to be able to foreclose the now secular property.

81 This is a generally accepted principle; Babli *Arakhin* 32b, *Pesaḥim* 31a. The redemption is purely symbolical since the debtor did not have the right to injure the creditor's claim by dedication; therefore, the dedication is invalid.

82 *Me'ilah* is larceny with Temple property which requires restitution in the amount of 125% and a sacrifice; *Lev.* 5:14-16. R. Joḥanan implies that a person using the dedicated property for his personal advantage before it was redeemed is obligated for a sacrifice. On the other hand, it is sinful to offer unnecessary sacrifices which would be

"profane animals in the Temple courtyard." If the sacrifice is valid then the dedication must be valid and could not be undone by a token amount but would require appraisal by a Cohen (*Lev.* 27:11-14).

83 *Lev.* 5:14 restricts *me'ilah* to "the Eternal's holy things", which excludes real estate.

84 This is not subject to *me'ilah* when standing but will be subject once it is cut.

85 The Temple's chief financial officer. Since the dedication was invalid when made for the field, he should not have cut the grain. But once it was cut, it becomes legitimate Temple property and can be sold for the Temple's upkeep.

86 This does *not* mean that the levir can take the standing grain, cut it, and keep it, but that the heir's standing vis-à-vis the creditor is like the administrator's vis-à-vis the creditor. Since the creditor's lien is on the real estate, it cannot cover the grain once it is cut and made movable. (Cf. the commentary *RYDBZ ad loc.* in the Wilna ed., and the novellae of *Rashba*, *Gittin* 40b, end.)

87 Since the ox is movable, the dedication should be absolute.

88 This is a rabbinical rule to protect the holders of chattel mortgages.

89 This is the main question of this paragraph: Since the heir can cut the grain to the detriment of the lienholder, why can he not cut the grain to the detriment of the widow who also is a lienholder?

(fol. 32a) **משנה יא:** לֹא יֹאמַר לָהּ הֲרֵי כְּתוּבָּתֵיךְ מוּנַחַת עַל הַשּׁוּלְחָן אֶלָּא כָּל־נְכָסַיי אַחֲרָאִין לִכְתוּבָּתֵיךְ. גֵּירְשָׁהּ אֵין לָהּ כְּתוּבָּה. הֶחֱזִירָהּ הֲרֵי הִיא כְּכָל־הַנָּשִׁים וְיֵשׁ לָהּ כְּתוּבָּה.

Mishnah 11: He[90] should not say to her "here your *ketubah* is lying on the table" but "all my properties are pledged for your *ketubah*." If he divorced her, she has no *ketubah*-lien[91]. If he took her back, she is like all women who have a *ketubah*[92].

90 The levir who marries his sister-in-law and whose brother's inheritance is much larger than his wife's *ketubah* cannot split the inheritance, reserve the amount necessary for the *ketubah* in a separate account, and use the remainder for his business. If he wants to commingle the inheritance with his own properties for his working capital, he has to pledge all his properties for her *ketubah*.

91 After he paid her, he has unlimited use of the remainder of his brother's inheritance.

92 This is explained in the Halakhah.

(32b line 60) **הלכה יא:** לֹא יֹאמַר לָהּ הֲרֵי כְּתוּבָתֵיךְ כול׳. כֵּיצַד הוּא עוֹשֶׂה. כּוֹנֵס וּמְגָרֵשׁ וּמַחֲזִיר וְהִיא שׁוֹבֶרֶת לוֹ כְּתוּבָתָהּ. אָמַר רְבִּי יוֹסֵה. לִצְדָדִין הִיא מַתְנִיתָא. אוֹ שׁוֹבֶרֶת לוֹ כְּתוּבָתָהּ. רִבִּי זְעִירָא בְשֵׁם רַב הַמְנוּנָא. כְּנָסָהּ וְגֵירְשָׁהּ וְהֶחֱזִירָהּ. אִם חִידֵּשׁ לָהּ כְּתוּבָה כְּתוּבָתָהּ עַל נְכָסָיו. וְאִם לָאו כְּתוּבָתָהּ עַל נִיכְסֵי בַּעֲלָהּ הָרִאשׁוֹן. רִבִּי יוֹסֵי בֵּירִבִּי בּוּן בְּשֵׁם רַב חִסְדָּא. מַתְנִיתָא אָמְרָה כֵן. הַמְגָרֵשׁ אֶת הָאִשָּׁה וְהֶחֱזִירָהּ עַל מְנָת כְּתוּבָתָהּ הָרִאשׁוֹנָה הֶחֱזִירָהּ. סוֹף דָּבָר עַד שֶׁיִּכְנוֹס וִיגָרֵשׁ וְיַחֲזִיר. דְּרַבָּא אָתָא מֵימַר לָהּ. אֲפִילוּ כְּנָסָהּ וְגֵירְשָׁהּ וְהֶחֱזִירָהּ. אִם חִידֵּשׁ לָהּ כְּתוּבָה כְּתוּבָתָהּ עַל נְכָסָיו. וְאִם לָאו כְּתוּבָתָהּ עַל נִיכְסֵי בַּעֲלָהּ הָרִאשׁוֹן.

2 שוברת לו | י שוכרת לו על   3 שוברת לו | י שוכרת לו על   5 רבי בון | י אמר   7 דבר | י -   - | יכנוס | י יכניס   דרבא | י דרובא   8 כתובתה | י -

Halakhah 11: 93"He should not say to her 'here is your *ketubah*'", etc. What does he do? "He marries her, he may divorce her and take her back, and she writes him a receipt for her *ketubah*." Rebbi Yose said, the *baraita* has two possibilities. "Or she writes him a receipt for her *ketubah*." Rebbi Ze'ira in the name of Rav Hamnuna: If he married her, divorced her, and took her back, if he wrote her a new *ketubah*, the lien is on his property; otherwise, it is on the property of her first husband. Rebbi Yose ben Rebbi Abun said in the name of Rav Hisda, a Mishnah said so: "For he who takes back his wife, takes her back under the terms of her first *ketubah*[99]." In the end, if he married her, divorced her, and took her back? He tells you something new. Even if he married her, divorced her, and took her back, if he wrote her a new *ketubah*, the lien is on his property; otherwise, it is on the property of her first husband.

(32b line 69) רִבִּי זְעִירָא בְשֵׁם רַב הַמְנוּנָא אָמַר. אֲרוּסָה שֶׁמֵּתָה אֵין לָהּ כְּתוּבָּה. שֶׁלֹּא הוּתְרָה לְהִינָּשֵׂא לַשּׁוּק. שֶׁלֹּא תֹאמַר. יֵעָשֶׂה כְּמִי שֶׁגֵּירַשׁ וִיהֵא לָהּ כְּתוּבָּה. לְפוּם כָּךְ צָרִיךְ מֵימַר אֵין לָהּ כְּתוּבָּה.

1 זעירא | י זעורא   2 לה | י ליה

Rebbi Ze'ira in the name of Rav Hamnuna said: A betrothed woman who died does not have a *ketubah* since she was not permitted to marry outside. That you should not say [the case] should be considered as if he divorced her and she should have a *ketubah*; therefore it was necessary to say that she does not have a *ketubah*.

93 These two paragraphs constitute Halakhah 4:4 in *Yebamot*, explained there in Notes 97-101.

(32b line 72) בָּרִאשׁוֹנָה הָיְתָה כְּתוּבָּתָהּ מוּנַחַת כְּתוּבָּתָהּ אֵצֶל אֲבוֹתֶיהָ וְהָיְתָה קַלָּה בְעֵינָיו לְגָרְשָׁהּ. וְחָזְרוּ וְהִתְקִינוּ שֶׁתְּהֵא כְּתוּבָּתָהּ אֵצֶל בַּעֲלָהּ. אַף עַל פִּי כֵן הָיְתָה קַלָּה בְעֵינָיו לְגָרְשָׁהּ. וְחָזְרוּ וְהִתְקִינוּ שֶׁיְּהֵא אָדָם לוֹקֵחַ בִּכְתוּבַּת אִשְׁתּוֹ כּוֹסוֹת וּקְעָרוֹת וְתַמְחוּיִין. הָדָא הִיא דְתַנִּינָן. לֹא יֹאמַר לָהּ הֲרֵי כְתוּבָּתֵיךְ מוּנַחַת עַל הַשּׁוּלְחָן. אֶלָּא כָּל־נְכָסָיו אַחֲרָאִין לִכְתוּבָּתָהּ. וְחָזְרוּ וְהִתְקִינוּ שֶׁיְּהֵא אָדָם נוֹשֵׂא וְנוֹתֵן בִּכְתוּבַּת אִשְׁתּוֹ. שֶׁמִּתּוֹךְ שֶׁאָדָם נוֹשֵׂא וְנוֹתֵן בִּכְתוּבַּת אִשְׁתּוֹ וְהוּא מְאַבְּדָהּ הִיא קָשָׁה בְעֵינָיו לְגָרְשָׁהּ.

[94]In earlier times, her *ketubah* was deposited with her family; then it was easy for him to divorce her. They then instituted that her *ketubah*

had to be deposited with her husband[95]; even so it was easy for him to divorce her. Then they instituted that a man should buy with his wife's *ketubah* cups, plates, and bowls; that is what we did state: "He should not say to her 'here your *ketubah* is lying on the table' but all his properties are pledged for her *ketubah*." Finally they instituted that a person should use his wife's *ketubah* in business, then because he uses his wife's *ketubah* in his business dealings he loses track of it and it becomes difficult for him to divorce her.

94 A different version is in the Babli, 82b. It starts with a statement that women did not want to marry because their *ketubah* was unsecured and not privileged against the heirs.

95 In the Babli: With her father-in-law. Since the money was ready, there was no difficulty in finding the money for a divorce.

(32c line 3) וְהוּא הִתְקִין שִׁמְעוֹן בֶּן שָׁטַח שְׁלֹשָׁה דְבָרִים. שֶׁיְּהֵא אָדָם נוֹשֵׂא וְנוֹתֵן בִּכְתוּבַּת אִשְׁתּוֹ. וְשֶׁיְּהוּ הַתִּינוּקוֹת הוֹלְכִין לְבֵית הַסֵּפֶר. וְהוּא הִתְקִין טוּמְאָה לִכְלֵי זְכוּכִית. לֹא כֵן אָמַר רִבִּי זְעִירָא רִבִּי אֲבוּנָא בְּשֵׁם רַב יִרְמְיָה. יוֹסֵי בֶן יוֹעֶזֶר אִישׁ צְרֵידָה וְיוֹסֵי בֶן יוֹחָנָן אִישׁ יְרוּשָׁלֵם גָּזְרוּ טוּמְאָה עַל אֶרֶץ הָעַמִּים וְעַל כְּלֵי זְכוּכִית. רִבִּי יוֹסֵי אָמַר. רִבִּי יְהוּדָה בַּר טַבַּי. רִבִּי יוֹנָה אָמַר. יְהוּדָה בַּר טַבַּי וְשִׁמְעוֹן בֶּן שָׁטַח גָּזְרוּ טוּמְאָה עַל כְּלֵי מַתָּכוֹת וְהִלֵּל וְשַׁמַּי גָּזְרוּ עַל טַהֲרַת יָדָיִם. רִבִּי יוֹסֵי בֵּי רִבִּי בּוּן בְּשֵׁם רִבִּי לֵוִי. כָּךְ הָיְתָה הֲלָכָה בְּיָדָם וּשְׁכָחוּהָ. וְעָמְדוּ הַשְּׁנַיִים וְהִסְכִּימוּ עַל דַּעַת הָרִאשׁוֹנִים. לְלַמְּדָךָ. כָּל־דָּבָר שֶׁבֵּית דִּין נוֹתְנִין אֶת נַפְשָׁם עָלָיו סוֹף שֶׁהוּא מִתְקַיֵּים בְּיָדָם כְּמָה שֶׁנֶּאֱמַר לְמשֶׁה מִסִּינַי. וְאַתְיָיא כָּמָאן דְּאָמַר רִבִּי מָנָא כִּי לֹא דָבָר רֵק הוּא מִכֶּם כִּי הוּא חַיֵּיכֶם. וְאִם רֵק הוּא. מִכֶּם. לָמָּה. שֶׁאֵין אַתֶּם יְגֵיעִין בּוֹ. כִּי הוּא חַיֵּיכֶם. אֵימָתַי הוּא חַיֵּיכֶם בְּשָׁעָה שֶׁאַתֶּם יְגֵעִין בּוֹ.

7 ר' לוי | ש לוי   9 את נפשם | ש נפשם   סוף | ש סופו   10 כמאן | ש כיי   כי הוא חייכם | ש -   11 הוא | ש היא (2 times)

Simeon ben Sheṭaḥ decreed three things[96]: That a person should use his wife's *ketubah* in his business dealings. And that children have to go to school[97]. Also, he decreed impurity for glass ware[98]. But did not Rebbi Ze'ira, Rebbi Abuna say in the name of Rav Jeremiah: Yose ben Yo'ezer from Ṣereda and Yose ben Joḥanan[99] from Jerusalem decreed impurity for Gentile lands[100] and glass ware; Rebbi Yose said, Rebbi Jehudah bar Ṭabbai[101]? Rebbi Jonah said, Jehudah bar Ṭabbai and Simeon ben Sheṭaḥ decreed on metal vessels[102]; Hillel and Shammai decreed on the purity of hands[103]. [104]Rebbi Yose ben Rebbi Abun in the name of Levi: That was the current practice; they forgot it[105], but the later ones got up and agreed to the opinion of the earlier ones to teach you that everything the Court insists on will come to be in the end just as Moses was told on Sinai; as Rebbi Mana said (*Deut.* 32:47): "For it is not an empty word, from you," if it is empty it is from you because you do not exert yourself about it. "Because it is your life," when is it your life? At the time that you exert yourself!

96 In the Babli, *Šabbat* 14b, he is credited only with the institution of the *ketubah* and a decree about impurity of metal vessels (Note 102). "The institution of the *ketubah*" probably means the formulation of the *ketubah* as a contract, which was unnecessary as long as the sum due was paid, or at least earmarked, as bride money. His decrees can be dated to the reign of his sister Shlomzion (Salome), widow of Alexander Yannai, 79-69 B.C.E.

97 In the Babli, *Baba batra* 21a, universal mandatory schooling is attributed to the post-Herodian High Priest Joshua ben Gamla. The Babli also notes that before Joshua ben Gamla's time there was organized higher instruction only for youths 16 years and older. This cannot refer to Simeon ben Sheṭaḥ's institution reported in the Yerushalmi since by no stretch of the imagination can a 16 year old teenager be called תינוק

98 Biblical impurity applies only to kinds of vessels and implements mentioned in the rules of impurity: earthenware and metal (*Lev.* 6:21), leather and textiles (*Lev.* 13:49), bone and wood (*Num.* 31:20). Other vessels cannot become impure; to this fact one attributes the great number of stone vessels found on archeological sites of the Second Temple period. (Similarly intrinsically pure vessels made of cow dung have not survived for the archeological record.) The impurity of glass vessels, unknown to Moses, is purely rabbinical. One has to take the information that the impurity of glass ware "was decreed" by the head of the Synhedrion with a grain of salt. Most probably, he simply codified the rules which were popularly observed before, when the Pharisees obtained the leadership in the state. The reasons given in the Babli *Šabbat* 16a/b for the rules are inconsistent since the rules, derived from popular observance without any scriptural basis, are inconsistent as a mixture of two different sets of rules. Glass vessels are compared to earthenware vessels since the former are made from sand, the latter from clay. They are also compared to metal vessels since if broken they can be melted down and made into new vessels.

99 The heads of the pre-Maccabean Ḥassidim sect; cf. *Gen. rabba* 65(18).

100 Here also, a long-standing popular observance (cf. *Amos* 7:17) was codified which attributed to the earth of Gentile lands (within or without the Holy Land) the impurity of rotting human bodies.

101 The co-head with Simeon ben Sheṭaḥ in the leadership of the Pharisees under Shlomzion.

102 The possible impurity of metal vessels is biblical (Note 98). Following the Babli *Šabbat* 16b, what they decreed was that metal impure by the impurity of the dead should not become pure by being melted down, but only by sprinkling with water containing ashes of the red cow. The political background of this decision (which seems to contradict biblical rules, *Num.* 31:22-23) and the reliability of the Babli in this respect is difficult to establish.

103 They codified the rules that hands which were not all the time consciously guarded from impurity after being washed are impure in the second degree and, therefore, impart impurity to fluids, heave, and sacrifices but not to solid profane food (cf.

Demay 2:3, Notes 136-137; Babli *Šabbat* 14b).

104 From here to the end of the Chapter, the text is from *Ševi'it* 1:7, following Note 55 (variants noted ᴡ).

105 There was no rule-making authority in the time between the two Yoses and Simeon ben Sheṭaḥ and Jehudah ben Ṭabbai.

הכותב פרק תשיעי

(fol. 32c) **משנה א:** הַכּוֹתֵב לְאִשְׁתּוֹ דִּין וּדְבָרִים אֵין לִי בִנְכָסַיִיךְ הֲרֵי זֶה אוֹכֵל פֵּירוֹת וְאִם מֵתָה יוֹרְשָׁהּ. אִם כֵּן לָמָּה כָתַב לָהּ דִּין וּדְבָרִים אֵין לִי בִנְכָסַיִיךְ שֶׁאִם מָכְרָה וְנָתְנָה קַיָּים. כָּתַב לָהּ דִּין וּדְבָרִים אֵין לִי עָלַיִיךְ וּבְפֵירוֹתֵיהֶן הֲרֵי זֶה אֵינוֹ אוֹכֵל פֵּירוֹת בְּחַיֶּיהָ וְאִם מֵתָה יוֹרְשָׁהּ. רִבִּי יְהוּדָה אוֹמֵר לְעוֹלָם הוּא אוֹכֵל פֵּירֵי פֵירוֹת עַד שֶׁיִּכְתּוֹב לָהּ דִּין וּדְבָרִים אֵין לִי בִנְכָסַיִיךְ וּבְפֵירוֹתֵיהֶן וּבְפֵירֵי פֵירוֹתֵיהֶן עַד עוֹלָם. כָּתַב לָהּ דִּין וּדְבָרִים אֵין לִי בִנְכָסַיִיךְ וּבְפֵירוֹתֵיהֶן וּבְפֵירֵי פֵירוֹתֵיהֶן בְּחַיַּיִךְ וּבְמוֹתֵךְ אֵינוֹ אוֹכֵל פֵּירוֹת בְּחַיֶּיהָ וְאִם מֵתָה אֵינוֹ יוֹרְשָׁהּ. רַבָּן שִׁמְעוֹן בֶּן גַּמְלִיאֵל אוֹמֵר מֵתָה יוֹרְשָׁהּ מִפְּנֵי שֶׁהִתְנָה עַל מַה שֶּׁכָּתוּב בַּתּוֹרָה וְכָל־הַמַּתְנֶה עַל מַה שֶּׁכָּתוּב בַּתּוֹרָה תְּנָאוֹ בָּטֵל.

Mishnah 1: If somebody writes to his wife[1]: "I shall have nothing to do with your properties," he receives their revenues and if she should die, he inherits from her. In this case, why did he write "I shall have nothing to do with your properties"? If she sold or gave away, it is valid. If he wrote to her: "I shall have nothing to do with your properties, nor with their revenues," he does not receive their revenues during her lifetime but if she should die, he inherits from her. Rebbi Jehudah says, he continues to receive the investment results of her revenues[2] unless he writes: "I shall have nothing to do with your properties, nor with their revenues, nor with revenues derived from revenues, without limits[3]." If he wrote "I shall have nothing to do with your properties, nor with their revenues, nor with revenues derived from revenues during your lifetime and after your death," he does not receive the revenues during her lifetime and does not inherit from her after her death. Rabban Simeon ben Gamliel says, if she dies, he should inherit from her since he made a condition contradicting what is written in the Torah[4], and anybody's condition contradicting what is written in the Torah is invalid[5].

1 After the preliminary but before the definitive marriage, when he does not yet have the administration of her properties.

2 If the wife invests some or all of the revenue from her holdings, these new holdings are not referred to in the renunciation. They represent new paraphernalia and as such their administration is the husband's, who receives their yield.

3 I. e., even the yield of the k-th re-investment of prior yields, $k = 1,2,...$, is excluded by this contract.

4 Since in rabbinic interpretation (disputed by Sadducees/Karaites) the husband inherits from his wife but the wife not from her husband; cf. Babli *Baba batra* 111b, *Sifry Num.* 134. In the opinion of R. Ismael, this cannot be established from the pentateuchal law of inheritance (*Num.* 27:7-11) but from the books of *Josua*, 34:33, and *1Chr.* 2:22. According to R. Aqiba, the husband's right of inheritance follows by twisting the text of *Num.* 27:11.

5 As a general principle, this is Mishnaiot *Baba meṣi'a* 7:14, *Baba batra* 8:5. Quoted in *Peah* 6:10 (Note 159), *Giṭṭin* 9:1 (50a 1.48), *Qiddušin* 1:2 (59c l.40), *Baba meṣi'a* 7:10 (11c 1.11); Babli 56a/b, 83b, 84a, and 7 other quotes.

As far as money matters go, his opinion is that of a minority of one; cf. Chapter 5, Note 207. He will agree that in matters of revenues, whose assignment to the husband is purely rabbinic usage, there are no restrictions in the freedom to contract.

(32d, line 6) **הלכה א:** הַכּוֹתֵב לְאִשְׁתּוֹ דִּין וּדְבָרִים אֵין לִי בִּנְכָסַיִיךְ כול'. רִבִּי יוֹחָנָן בְּשֵׁם רִבִּי יַנַּיי. בְּשֶׁלֹּא כָנַס. אֲבָל אִם כָּנַס אֵין אָדָם מְאַבֵּד אֶת זְכוּתוֹ בְּלָשׁוֹן הַזֶּה. אָמַר רִבִּי יוֹסֵי בֵּירִבִּי בּוּן. מִילְתֵיהּ דְּרִבִּי חִייָה. הָאוֹמֵר. יָדַיי מְסוּלָּקוֹת מִן הַשָּׂדֶה הַזּוֹ וְרַגְלַיי מְסוּלָּקוֹת מִן הַשָּׂדֶה הַזּוֹ. לֹא אָמַר וְלֹא כְלוּם.

אָמַר רִבִּי אָבוּן בַּר חִיָּיה קוֹמֵי רִבִּי זְעִירָא. מַתְנִיתָא אָמְרָה כֵן שֶׁאֵין אָדָם מְאַבֵּד אֶת זְכוּתוֹ בְּלָשׁוֹן הַזֶּה. דְּתַנִינָן תַּמָּן. מִי שֶׁהָיָה נָשׂוּי שְׁתֵּי נָשִׁים וּמָכַר אֶת שָׂדֵהוּ וְכָתְבָה הָרִאשׁוֹנָה לַלּוֹקֵחַ. דִּין וּדְבָרִים אֵין לִי עִמָּךְ. הַשְּׁנִיָּה מוֹצִיאָה מִיַּד הַלּוֹקֵחַ. הָא הָרִאשׁוֹנָה לֹא. אָמַר לֵיהּ. כָּל־גַּרְמָהּ אָמְרָה שֶׁאֵין אָדָם מְאַבֵּד אֶת זְכוּתוֹ בְּלָשׁוֹן הַזֶּה. אֶלָּא כָאן אֲפִילוּ הַשְּׁנִיָּיה לֹא תוֹצִיא מִיַּד הָרִאשׁוֹנָה. וְלָמָּה אֵין הָרִאשׁוֹנָה מוֹצִיאָה מִיַּד הַלּוֹקֵחַ. שֶׁכֵּן הִיא כוֹתֶבֶת לוֹ. כָּל־עֲרֶר שֶׁיֵּשׁ לִי בְּשָׂדֶה זוֹ אַל יְהִי לִי עִמָּךְ כְּלוּם.

Halakhah 1: "If somebody writes to his wife[1]: "I shall have nothing to do with your properties," etc. Rebbi Johanan in the name of Rebbi Yannai: If he did not take her in[6]. But if he took her in, nobody can lose his rights by these expressions[7]. Rebbi Yose ben Rebbi Abun said, this is the word of Rebbi Hiyya: He who says that "my hands are removed from this field, my feet are removed from this field[8]," did not say anything. Rebbi Abun bar Hiyya asked before Rebbi Ze'ira: Does a Mishnah imply that nobody can lose his rights by these expressions? Did we not state there[9]: "If somebody was married to two wives when he sold a field[10] and the first one wrote for the buyer: I have no claims on you[11], the second[12] one can take it away from the buyer's hands," this implies, not the first one. He said to him, that text itself implies that nobody can lose his rights by these expressions, but here the second wife cannot take anything away from the first[13], and why can the first one not take it away from the buyer's hands? For she writes to him: For any complaint I shall have regarding this field, I shall have nothing against you[14].

6 The language quoted in the Mishnah is appropriate if the husband renounces his right to acquire the administration of his wife's property. This must be done before the definitive marriage. The Babli agrees, also in the

name of R. Yannai (83a).

7   Since he did acquire the right of administration by the definitive marriage, a contract executed after this moment would have to contain language of transfer of rights (by gift or sale) to be legally actionable.

In *Giṭṭin* 8:1 (49b l. 30 ff.) it is stated that the husband can deliver a bill of divorce to his wife by depositing it on her paraphernalia property only if previously he had validly renounced his rights to the income produced by that property because the right to income is an ownership right.

8   If he tells his wife that he does not want to take care of her properties, this has no legal consequences since he is obligated to work for her. The only way he can remove his obligation is by a formal transfer of his right to her as a gift.

The Babli (83a, 95a; *Giṭṭin* 77a; *Baba batra* 43a, 49a; *Keritut* 24b) notes that even between strangers such a formula would not transfer property rights.

9   Mishnah 10:6.

10   The field is mortgaged to both *ketubot*; if he dies and there is not enough money in his estate to satisfy the claims of both wives, the wives can reclaim the field from the buyer since their lien precedes his title.

11   She agrees with the sale and promises not to sue the buyer.

12   She was no party to the transaction. If her claim to *ketubah* is not satisfied, she can repossess the field.

13   The second wife by her action does not diminish the claim of the first to the property.

14   All the first wife agreed to was not to sue the buyer. This prevents her from going to court but has no influence on her rights vis-à-vis others. It is stated in Mishnah 10:1 that the *ketubah* of a first wife has precedence over that of a second wife. Therefore, if the second wife recovers the field from the buyer, the first one may sue the second for the unsatisfied part of her own *ketubah*. Therefore, the first wife did not transfer any property rights by her statement to the buyer.

(32d, line 17) כָּתַב לָהּ וְכָתַבְתָּהּ לוֹ. כְּשֵׁם שֶׁאֵינוֹ מְאַבֵּד זְכוּתוֹ כָּךְ אִשָּׁה אֵינָהּ מְאַבֶּדֶת זְכוּתָהּ. כָּתַב לָהּ מִן הָאֵירוּסִין וּמִן הַנִּישׂוּאִין. פְּלוּגְתָּא דְּבֵית שַׁמַּי וּבֵית הִלֵּל. עַל דַּעְתּוֹן דְּבֵית שַׁמַּי תִּמְכּוֹר. עַל דַּעְתּוֹן דְּבֵית הִלֵּל לֹא תִמְכּוֹר.

If he wrote for her and she wrote for him[15]. Just as he did not lose his rights so she did not lose her rights[16]. If he wrote to her "from preliminary and definitive marriage"[17], that is the disagreement between the Houses of Shammai and Hillel[18]. In the opinion of the House of Shammai she shall sell[19]; in the opinion of the House of Hillel she should not sell[20].

15 She wrote him the same text he wrote her, that "she has nothing to do with his properties."

16 If she becomes a widow or divorcee, she is not prevented from claiming his real estate as payment for her *ketubah*.

17 "I shall have nothing to do with your properties, from preliminary and definitive marriage." The question is, why did he mention preliminary marriage which gives him no rights of administration?

18 In Mishnah 8:1.

19 Since the House of Shammai give the wife the right to sell any inheritance she received while preliminarity married, the mention of the preliminary with the definitive marriage can only mean that the husband invites his wife to dispose of her property after definitive marriage as if it were only after preliminary marriage.

20 Mishnaiot 8:1, 9:1 give only legal standing to the wife's sales after the fact; they do not invite the wife to sell without her husband's consent. For the House of Hillel, the husband mentions his disinterest in her properties after the preliminary marriage in order to give her the right to dispose of her properties without asking him, against the opinion of the House of Hillel. But this does not imply that after the definitive marriage he does not want to be asked, following Mishnah 9:1.

(32d, line 20) רִבִּי יִרְמְיָה בְעָא קוֹמֵי רִבִּי זְעִירָא. כָּתַב לָהּ. דִּין וּדְבָרִים אֵין לִי בִּנְכָסַיִיךְ. וְנָפְלוּ לָהּ לְאַחַר מִיכֶּן. מָהוּ. וְיֵשׁ אָדָם מַתְנֶה עַל דָּבָר שֶׁאֵינוּ. אָמַר רִבִּי בּוּן בַּר חִייָה קוֹמֵי רִבִּי זְעִירָא. מִזְּכוּתוֹ אַתְּ לָמֵד חִיּוּבוֹ. אֶלָּא לֹא כָתַב לָהּ שְׁנִייָה [הִיא] אֵין לוֹ אֲכִילַת פֵּירוֹת. הֲוֵי מִזְּכוּתוֹ אַתְּ לָמֵד חִיּוּבוֹ. רִבִּי לֵוִי

בַּר חַיָּיתָא בְעָא. כָּתַב לָהּ. דִּין וּדְבָרִים אֵין לִי בִנְכָסַיִיךְ הָעֲתִידִין לִיפּוֹל לִיךְ. מַה הִן. וְיֵשׁ אָדָם מַתְנֶה עַל דָּבָר שֶׁאֵינוֹ בָעוֹלָם.

[21] Rebbi Jeremiah asked before Rebbi Ze'ira: If he wrote to her: "I shall have nothing to do with your properties," and she inherited properties afterwards, what is the rule[22]? Can a person put a condition on something not in existence[23]? Rebbi Abun bar Ḥiyya said before Rebbi Ze'ira: From his rights you can infer his obligations. If he had not written to her, would it make any difference, would he not receive its yield[24]? That means, from his rights you can infer his obligations. Rebbi Levi bar Ḥaita asked: If he wrote to her: "I shall have nothing to do with your properties which you shall inherit in the future," what is the rule? Can a person put a condition on something not in existence[25,26]?

21 There are many different interpretations of this paragraph, detailed by R. Jehudah Rosanes in his Commentary מִשְׁנֶה לַמֶּלֶךְ to Maimonides, *Hilkhot Iššut* 23:1. The following explanation is simply one which seems reasonable to the author.

22 This question is very elliptic. It is not obvious whether the document was written before or after the definitive marriage and whether the inheritance was foreseeable or not. If the document was written before the definitive marriage and the wife was in line for the inheritance, there is no reason why the husband's renunciation of his rights would not be valid since that essentially is the case of the Mishnah. In addition, it is the right of any person not to accept an inheritance. Therefore, in view of the answer given, it seems that one speaks of an inheritance which was unexpected, that at the moment of preliminary marriage the wife was not a probable recipient of the inheritance but that later some prospective heirs died which made the wife the next surviving kin. Since such an occurrence is not foreseeable, no contracts can be concluded about them. If the document was executed after the definitive marriage, it would require an additional statement in which the

husband cedes his rights to future yield to his wife.

23 For example, in talmudic law a farmer cannot write a futures contract on his grain harvest before his seed has sprouted. Similarly, no contract can be written covering unexpected inheritances.

24 Since the *ketubah* contract gives the husband the right to the yield of any future properties coming to his wife during their marriage, whether foreseen or not, it follows that he can deprive himself of his right to yield, whether foreseen or not.

25 If the succinct language proposed by R. Jeremiah is invalid, the more explicit language of R. Levi is also invalid. The objection of R. Abun bar Ḥiyya is irrelevant as far as a separate contract is concerned. But certainly it would be possible for the husband to renounce his right to yield in the *ketubah* document itself, since what he acquires by the *ketubah* he can renounce in the *ketubah*. In that case, his wife's hand in acquiring estates never was his hand and she does not need his renunciation.

26 In *Nazir* 2:5 (52b l. 41), the question is asked about a vow to pay for somebody's *nazir* sacrifices if a person will make a *nazir* vow in the future, an act over which the maker of the original vow has no control. The original vow is declared void since the text proposed by R. Levi ben Ḥaita is also void.

(32d, line 27) מָכְרָה פֵּירוֹת מְחוּבָּרִין לְקַרְקַע. רִבִּי אָחָא אָמַר. כְּמוֹכֶרֶת פֵּירוֹת תְּלוּשִׁין. אָמַר רִבִּי יוֹסֵי. בְּמוֹכֶרֶת אֶחָד מֵעֲשָׂרָה בַּקַּרְקַע. רִבִּי זְעוּרָא רַב יְהוּדָה בְּשֵׁם רַב. הַכּוֹתֵב שָׂדֶה מַתָּנָה לְאִשְׁתּוֹ אֵינָהּ מוֹכֶרֶת פֵּירוֹת. אָמַר רִבִּי זְעִירָא. מַתְנִיתָא אָמְרָה כֵן. אִילּוּ הֵן פֵּירֵי פֵירוֹת. מוֹכֵר פֵּירוֹת וְלוֹקֵחַ קַרְקַע וְהוּא אוֹכֵל פֵּירוֹת. רִבִּי אִמִּי בְעָא. אִילּוּ אַחֵר כָּתַב לָהּ יֵשׁ לוֹ אֲכִילַת פֵּירוֹת. הוּא שֶׁכָּתַב לָהּ לֹא כָל־שֶׁכֵּן. לֹא אָמַר אֶלָּא כוֹתֵב. אֲבָל מוֹכֵר לֹא. מַה בֵּין כּוֹתֵב מַה בֵּין מוֹכֵר. עוּלָא הָיָה רוֹצֶה לְהַבְרִיחַ מְזוֹנוֹת מִן הָאִשָּׁה.

If she sold produce connected to the ground[27]: Rav Aḥa said, as if she sold harvested [produce][28]; Rebbi Yose said, as if she sold a tenth of the ground[29]. Rebbi Ze'ira, Rav Jehudah in the name of Rav: If somebody writes a field over to his wife, she cannot sell the produce[30]. Rebbi Ze'ira said, a *baraita* says so[31] "What are revenues derived from revenues? He sells the produce, buys real estate, and eats its revenue[32]." Rebbi Immi asked: If another person had written [real estate] over to her, would he[33] not receive the revenue? If he himself wrote, not so much more[34]![35] He said only "wrote over", but not "sold"[36]. What is the difference between one who writes and one who sells? He tried to find a reason to hide food from the wife[37].

27 This refers to the statement in the Mishnah that the wife's sale is valid if the husband had written that he had nothing to do with her properties. Since he retains the right to the revenue, she certainly cannot sell harvested produce which is her husband's property. May she sell produce still standing?

28 The sale is invalid.

29 The sale is valid.

30 Since the field becomes paraphernalia property, he retains the right to its yield.

31 Tosephta 9:2, Babli 83b.

32 Since the field bought with the sale price of the produce becomes the wife's property, the revenue from revenue is revenue from the wife's paraphernalia given to her by her husband and belongs to the husband. This is the case mentioned by Rav.

33 The husband.

34 Why do we need Rav's statement in this case?

35 The preceding text is quoted in a slightly different form by Rosh (9:1):

רִבִּי זְעִירָא רַב יְהוּדָה בְּשֵׁם רַב. הַכּוֹתֵב שָׂדֶה מַתָּנָה לְאִשְׁתּוֹ אֵין לוֹ אֲכִילַת פֵּירוֹת. אָמַר רִבִּי מַתָּנָה. מַתְנִיתָא לֹא אָמְרָה כֵן. אֵלּוּ הֵן פֵּירֵי פֵּירוֹת. מוֹכֵר פֵּירוֹת וְיִלָּקַח בָּהֶן קַרְקַע וְהוּא אוֹכֵל פֵּירוֹת. לָאו כְּכוֹתֵב שָׂדֶה מַתָּנָה לְאִשְׁתּוֹ הוּא וְאַתְּ אָמַרְתְּ אֵין לוֹ לֹא פֵּירוֹת וְלֹא פֵּירֵי פֵּירוֹת. רִבִּי אִמִּי בָּעָא. אִילּוּ אַחֵר כָּתַב לָהּ יֵשׁ לוֹ אֲכִילַת פֵּירוֹת. הוּא כָּתַב לָהּ לֹא כָּל־שֶׁכֵּן.

Rebbi Ze'ira, Rav Jehudah in the name of Rav: If somebody writes a field over to his wife, *he has no claim to its yield*. Rebbi *Mattanah* said, a baraita *does not say so:* "What are revenues derived from revenues? He sells the produce, real estate *should be bought from the proceeds*, and he eats its revenue." *Is that not as if he wrote a field over to his wife, and you say, he has neither revenue nor revenue from revenue!* Rebbi Immi asked: If another person had written [real estate] over to her, would he not receive the revenue? If he himself wrote, not so much more?

The *baraita* refers to the Mishnah, regarding property which the wife inherits during her marriage. Then the question is raised why does the husband eat the yield of property coming from others but not from his own gift. But in this version, the questions of R. Mattanah and R. Immi duplicate one another. The text of Rosh seems to be a contamination of the current and the following paragraphs.

The passive voice, real estate *should be bought*, is that of our Tosephta text, in contrast to the quotes from both Talmudim in which *he* buys the real estate. In that version, the investment decision is not the husband's.

36   If the husband sold a field to his wife, he cannot claim the yield. The Babli, *Baba batra,* 51b, also decides that the husband eats the yield of the field sold but not the one given as a gift.

37   He gives the field to his wife that she should sustain herself from its yield and he would no longer have to care for her; for this purpose it is obvious that he does not want to take the yield.

(32d, line 34) נִיחָא עַל דַּעְתֵּיהּ דְּרַבִּי יוּדָה בְּשֶׁכָּתַב. דִּין וּדְבָרִים אֵין לִי בְּנִכְסַיְיךְ וּבְפֵירוֹת. אֵין לוֹ אֲכִילַת פֵּירוֹת. אֲפִילוּ כָתַב. דִּין וּדְבָרִים אֵין לִי בְשָׂדֶה זוֹ וּבְפֵירוֹתֶיהָ. אֵין לוֹ אֲכִילַת פֵּירוֹת. נִיחָא עַל דַּעְתֵּיהּ דְּרַבָּנִין בְּשֶׁכָּתַב. דִּין וּדְבָרִים אֵין לִי בְשָׂדֶה זוֹ וּבְפֵירוֹתֶיהָ. יֵשׁ לוֹ אֲכִילַת פֵּירוֹת. אֲפִילוּ כָתַב. דִּין וּדְבָרִים אֵין לִי בְּנִכְסַיְיךְ וּבְפֵירוֹתֵיהֶן. יֵשׁ לוֹ אֲכִילַת פֵּירוֹת. נִישְׁמְעִינָהּ מִן הָדָא. דָּמַר רַב זְעִירָא רַב יְהוּדָה בְּשֵׁם רַב. הַכּוֹתֵב שָׂדֶה מַתָּנָה לְאִשְׁתּוֹ אֵין לוֹ אֲכִילַת פֵּירוֹת. אָמַר רִבִּי זְעוּרָא. מַתְנִיתָא אֲמָרָה כֵן. וְאִילּוּ הֵן פֵּירֵי פֵירוֹת. מוֹכֵר פֵּירוֹת וְלוֹקֵחַ קַרְקַע וְאוֹכֵל פֵּירוֹת. מִכֵּיוָן שֶׁכָּתַב. דִּין וּדְבָרִים אֵין לִי בְּנִכְסַיְיךְ וּבְפֵירוֹתֵיהֶן. לֹא כְּכוֹתֵב שָׂדֶה מַתָּנָה לְאִשְׁתּוֹ הוּא. אַתְּ אָמַר. לֹא פֵירוֹת וְלֹא פֵּירֵי פֵירוֹת. הֲוֵי לֹא שַׁנְיָיא. עַל דַּעְתֵּיהּ דְּרַבִּי יוּדָה בְּשֶׁכָּתַב. דִּין וּדְבָרִים אֵין לִי עַל שָׂדֶה זוֹ וּבְפֵירוֹתֵיהֶן. בְּשֶׁכָּתַב. דִּין וּדְבָרִים אֵין לִי בְּנִכְסַיְיךְ

וּבְפֵירוֹתֵיהֶן. אֵין לוֹ אֲכִילַת פֵּירוֹת. וְדִכְוָותֵיהּ לְרַבָּנָן לֹא שַׁנְיָיא. בֵּין שֶׁכָּתַב. דִּין וּדְבָרִים אֵין לִי בְּנִכְסַיִיךְ וּבְפֵירוֹתֵיהֶן. בֵּין שֶׁכָּתַב. דִּין וּדְבָרִים אֵין לִי בַּשָּׂדֶה זוֹ וּבְפֵירוֹתֵיהֶן. יֵשׁ לוֹ אֲכִילַת פֵּירוֹת.

It is reasonable according to Rebbi Jehudah, if he wrote: "I shall have nothing to do with your properties and the revenues," that he cannot take the revenues. Even if he wrote: "I shall have nothing to do with this field and its yield," he cannot eat its yield[38]. It is reasonable according to the rabbis; if he wrote: "I shall have nothing to do with this field and its yield," can he eat its yield? Even if he wrote, "I shall have nothing to do with your properties and its yields," can he eat its yield?[39] Let us hear from the following, as Rebbi Ze'ira, Rav Jehudah said in the name of Rav: If somebody writes a field over to his wife, he has no right to its yield[40]. Rebbi Ze'ira said, a *baraita* says so[31] "What are revenues derived from revenues? He sells the produce[41], buys real estate, and eats its revenue." Since he wrote, "I shall have nothing to do with your properties and their yields," is that not as if he wrote a field over to his wife, and you say, he has neither revenue nor revenue from revenue! That means, there is no difference in the opinion of Rebbi Jehudah whether he wrote "I shall have nothing to do with this field and its yield," or he wrote "I shall have nothing to do with your properties and their revenues," he cannot take any revenue[42]. Similarly, for the rabbis it makes no difference whether he wrote "I shall have nothing to do with your properties and their revenues," or he wrote "I shall have nothing to do with this field and its yield," he can take its yield[43].

38 The statements are trivial since in the Mishnah both the rabbis and R. Jehudah agree that the husband has no right to the yields; their disgreement is

whether the yield of any money saved from the revenues reverts to the husband or not.

39 The answer should be a trivial "no" since the rabbis assign to the wife even the compound yield which R. Jehudah gives to the husband.

40 It is obvious that he has no right to the yield which he disclaimed. It is claimed here also that he has no investment power over the part of the yield which his wife does not spend on herself; this explains why he has no right to revenues derived from revenues saved.

41 Since he sells but not she, the Tanna of the *baraita* holds that the husband has investment power over the yield revenue which he cannot take for himself. (Cf. Note 35, last paragraph.)

42 According to R. Jehudah, the wife alone has investment powers for the savings part of the yield, but the husband has the right to the investment yield if not disavowed explicitly.

43 While he has no right to the yield from investments, he has the investment power unless explicitly disclaimed.

(32d, line 48) רִבִּי יִרְמְיָה בְשֵׁם רַב. הֲלָכָה כְּרַבָּן שִׁמְעוֹן בֶּן גַּמְלִיאֵל. אֲבָל לֹא לְעִנְיָין דְּבָרִים. הֲלָכָה כְּרַבָּן שִׁמְעוֹן בֶּן גַּמְלִיאֵל דְּאָמַר. אִם מֵתָה יְרוֹשָׁתָהּ. אֲבָל דְּבָרִים שֶׁהִתְנָה עַל מַה שֶׁכָּתוּב בַּתּוֹרָה. וְכָל־הַמַּתְנֶה עַל מַה שֶׁכָּתוּב בַּתּוֹרָה תְּנָאוֹ בָטֵל. בִּתְנָאֵי גוּף. אֲבָל בִּתְנָאֵי מָמוֹן תְּנָאוֹ קַיָּים. וְזֶה תְּנַאי מָמוֹן הוּא. וְלָמָּה אָמְרוּ. תְּנָאוֹ בָטֵל. שֶׁבְּסוֹף הוּא זָכָה בָּהֶן. רִבִּי אִימִּי בְשֵׁם רִבִּי יוֹחָנָן. בְּדִין הָיָה שֶׁאִם מָכְרָה וְנָתְנָה שֶׁיְּהֵא מִכְרָהּ קַיָּים. שֶׁבְּסוֹף הוּא זוֹכֶה בָּהֶן. וְלָמָּה אָמְרוּ בָטֵל. שֶׁלֹּא תְהֵא אִשָּׁה מוֹכֶרֶת נְכָסִים שֶׁלְּבַעֲלָהּ וְאוֹמֶרֶת. שֶׁלִּי הֵן.

Rav[44] Jeremiah in the name of Rav: Practice follows Rabban Simeon ben Gamliel[45], but not in the matter of words[46]. Practice follows Rabban Simeon ben Gamliel for he said, if she dies he inherits from her, but in matters of words, "since he made a condition contradicting what is written in the Torah, and anybody's condition contradicting what is written in the Torah is invalid," in personal matters. But in money matters, one's stipulations are valid[47] and that is a money matter! Why did we say that the condition is invalid? Because in the end he acquired it[48]. Rebbi Immi in the name of Rebbi Joḥanan: The law should have been that if she[49] sold or gave it away it should be valid, for [the buyer] acquired it. Why did they say it is invalid? That a wife should not sell her husband's property and say, it is mine[50].

44 This is the correct text from the parallel in *Baba batra* 8:6 (from a different editorial team). *Rav* Jeremiah was a contemporary of Rav, *Rebbi* Jeremiah lived about 100 years later.

45 This also is Rav's position in the Babli, 83b, but with a reasoning diametrically opposed to that of the Yerushalmi.

46 Rosh has a slightly different text:

רִבִּי יִרְמְיָה בְּשֵׁם רַב. הָלָכָה כְּרַבָּן שִׁמְעוֹן בֶּן גַּמְלִיאֵל. שֶׁאִם מֵתָה יְרוּשְׁתָהּ אֲבָל לֹא לְעִנְיָין דְּבָרָיו שֶׁאָמַר מִפְּנֵי שֶׁהִתְנָה עַל מַה שֶׁכָּתוּב בַּתּוֹרָה. וְכָל־הַמַּתְנֶה עַל מַה שֶׁכָּתוּב בַּתּוֹרָה תְּנָאוֹ בָּטֵל. בִּתְנָאֵי גּוּף. וְהָכָא בִּתְנָאֵי מָמוֹן אָנוּ קַיָּימִין. וְלָמָּה אָמְרוּ תְּנָאוֹ בָּטֵל. שֶׁבְּסוֹף הוּא זָכָה בָּהֶן.

Rav Jeremiah in the name of Rav: Practice follows Rabban Simeon ben Gamliel, *that* if she dies he inherits from her, but *not because of his* words, "since he made a condition contradicting what is written in the Torah, and anybody's condition contradicting what is written in the Torah is invalid," in personal matters. But here we deal with money matters! *Why did they say that the condition is invalid?* Because in the end he acquired it.

47 A generally agreed principle in the Yerushalmi, cf. *Qiddušin* 1:2 (59c l.43), *Baba meṣi'a* 7:10 (11c l.11); in the Babli accepted with reservations in the name of R. Jehudah, 57a.

48 In *Baba batra* 8:6, the reason is given that practice follows R. Joḥanan ben Baroqa who holds that wills can be written only in favor of people who could be heirs (if a number of closer relatives had died.) Then the law of inheritance is compulsory and falls under the category of personal matters.

49 The definitively married wife

HALAKHAH 1

should retain the right of disposal of her paraphernalia property since she retains sole ownership.

She could claim that mortmain property was really hers to dispose of.

(32d, line 55) רִבִּי [יוֹסְטִינִי][51] הֲוָה לֵיהּ עוֹבְדָא וּשְׁאִיל לְרַבָּנִין. אֲמָרִין לֵיהּ. פּוּק מִנְכָסֶיךָ. שָׁאַל לְרִבִּי שִׁמְעוֹן בֶּן לָקִישׁ. אֲמַר לֵיהּ. עוּל בִּנְכָסֶיךָ. רִבִּי יִרְמְיָה בָּעָא קוֹמֵי רִבִּי זְעִירָא. הֵיי לוֹן רַבָּנִין. הָא רַב הָא רִבִּי יוֹחָנָן הָא רִבִּי שִׁמְעוֹן בֶּן לָקִישׁ. אֲמַר לֵיהּ. רַבָּנִין דְּרִבִּי יוֹסְטִינָה.

Rebbi Justinus had a case[52] and he asked the rabbis who told him, leave you properties[53]. He asked Rebbi Simeon ben Laqish, who told him, enter your properties[54]. Rebbi Jeremiah asked before Rebbi Ze'ira: Who are those rabbis? What about Rav[55], Rebbi Joḥanan[56], and Rebbi Simeon ben Laqish? He said to him, Rebbi Justinus's rabbis[57].

51 From the parallel in *Baba batra* 8:6. The reading here is יוּסטחא which is inconsistent with the second mention of the name. (Both *Juste* and *Justine* probably are provincial forms of *Justus, Justinus* (E.G.).)

52 He had an agreement with his wife that she was the sole administrator of her properties, also after [his] death. Unexpectedly, the wife died before he did.

53 He had no right to inherit from his wife.

54 He confirmed him as his wife's heir, acting as an appeals judge.

55 Declaring that practice follows Rabban Simeon ben Gamliel.

56 Holding in *Baba batra* (Note 48) that the basic provisions of the biblical law of inheritance are a matter of persons, not money.

57 The local court whose rulings were overturned.

(32d, line 59) בְּעוֹן קוֹמֵי רִבִּי יוֹחָנָן. מֵתָה מִי יוֹרְשָׁהּ. אֵלֶּין. דִּבְרֵי חֲכָמִים. אֶחֶיהָ יוֹרְשִׁין אוֹתָהּ.

They asked before Rebbi Joḥanan: Following the Sages, if she died who inherits from her[58]? Those, her brothers, inherit from her[59].

58 The Mishnah only states that if the husband had renounced his rights, he could not inherit from his wife living and dead. It does not state who inherits.

59 Here family certainly inherit from her but there seems to be no reason why they should not inherit as if she had been unmarried. The version in *Baba batra* 8:6 is more intelligible: Rebbi Joḥanan said, her father inherits from her [and after his death] her brothers inherit from her.

(32d, line 60) רִבִּי יִרְמְיָה בְּעָא קוֹמֵי רִבִּי זְעוּרָא. הָאַחִין שֶׁחָלְקוּ אַלְמָנָה נִיזוֹנֶת מִשֶּׁלָּהֶן. שֶׁלֹּא תֹאמַר. יֵעָשׂוּ כְּמוֹ שֶׁמָּכְרוּ וְלֹא תְהֵא נִיזוֹנֶת מִשֶּׁלָּהֶן. פְּשִׁיטָא. מָכְרוּ שֶׁלָּהֶן מָכְרוּ.

Rebbi Jeremiah asked before Rebbi Ze'ira: If the brothers divided [the inheritance], the widow is supported by them[60]. For you should not say, they should be considered as if they had sold the properties and the widow would not be supported by these, since it is obvious that if they sold, they sold their own property[61].

60 As stated in Mishnah 4:12, the widow has the option not to take the *ketubah* money but to live in her deceased husband's house and be supported by his estate. While the *ketubah* proper is a lien on the real estate, the widow's (and her daughters') support is not. This means that the brothers may divide the inheritance while their father's widow is still living.

61 And the widow has no regress on the buyer if the husband's heirs do not fulfill their duty towards her. The Babli (e. g., *Baba batra* 107a) strongly disagrees and holds that brothers who divided an inheritance are like buyers from one another but that they are liable in common for the debts of the estate.

(32d line 62) רִבִּי יִרְמְיָה בְּעָא קוֹמֵי רִבִּי אַבָּהוּ. כְּתִיב אִם יִהְיֶה הַיּוֹבֵל לִבְנֵי יִשְׂרָאֵל. בְּשָׁעָה שֶׁהַיּוֹבֵל נוֹהֵג הַנְחָלוֹת חוֹזְרוֹת וּבְשָׁעָה שֶׁאֵין הַיּוֹבֵל נוֹהֵג אֵין הַנְחָלוֹת חוֹזְרוֹת. אַדְּרַבָּה. אָתָא מֵימַר לָךְ. אֲפִילוּ בְּשָׁעָה שֶׁהַיּוֹבֵל נוֹהֵג וְהַנְחָלוֹת חוֹזְרוֹת יְרוּשַׁת תּוֹרָה אֵינָהּ חוֹזֶרֶת.

Rebbi Ze'ira asked before Rebbi Abbahu: It is written[62]: "If the Jubilee will happen for the Children of Israel." If the institution of the Jubilee exists[63], inheritances return; if the institution of the Jubilee does not exist, inheritances do not return[64]. It is the opposite way, it comes to tell you that even if the institution of the Jubilee exists and inheritances return, inheritance by biblical law does not return[65]!

62   *Num.* 36:4. The argument of the tribe of Manasseh is that if Salpaad's five daughters (representing most of the Cisjordanian tribe) would marry outside the tribe, their territory would be inherited by their husband's tribes and be lost to Manasseh.

63   I. e., as long as the 12 tribes were living on their ancestral lands.

64   From the moment that the tribes of Gad and Reuben were deported by the Assyrians, in all other parts of Canaan the land no longer had to be returned to its original owners by the buyers in the Jubilee year. Cf. *Ševi'it* 1:1, Note 7.

65   While the verse does not directly prove that the wife's property is inherited by her husband, it certainly implies that it is given to her sons as ancestral lands.

(32d, line 66) רִבִּי הִלֵּל בַּר פָּזִי בְּעָא קוֹמֵי רִבִּי יוֹסֵי. מָכַר הוּא וּמֵתָה הִיא. אָמַר לוֹ. מִכְרֹ"ה בָּטֵל. לְבֵן שֶׁמָּכַר בְּחַיֵּי אָבִיו וּמֵת אָבִיו. מָכְרָה הִיא וּמֵת הוּא. אָמַר לֵיהּ. מִכְרָהּ קַיָּים. לְאָב שֶׁמָּכַר בְּחַיֵּי בְנוֹ וּמֵת בְּנוֹ. רִבִּי חִיָּיה בַּר מַרְיָיא בְּעָא קוֹמֵי רִבִּי יוֹנָה. מָכְרָה לְבַעֲלָהּ מַהוּ. אָמַר לֵיהּ. מִדְּאָמַר חִזְקִיָּה. הֲלָכָה כְרִבִּי (יוּדָה). הָדָא אֲמְרָה מִכְרָהּ מָכֵר. תַּנֵּי. הָאוֹמֵר. יִנָּתְנוּ נְכָסַיי לִפְלוֹנִי. מֵת פְּלוֹנִי לִפְלוֹנִי. [מֵת פְּלוֹנִי לִפְלוֹנִי.][66] מֵת הָרִאשׁוֹן יִנָּתְנוּ לַשֵּׁנִי. מֵת הַשֵּׁנִי

יִינָתְנוּ לַשְּׁלִישִׁי. מֵת הַשֵּׁנִי בְחַיֵּי הָרִאשׁוֹן. מִכֵּיוָן שֶׁלֹּא זָכָה בָהֶן הַשֵּׁנִי לֹא זָכָה בָהֶן הַשְּׁלִישִׁי. אָמַר לֵיהּ. כָּךְ פֵּירֵשׁ רִבִּי הוֹשַׁעְיָה אֲבִי הַמִּשְׁנָה. אַחֲרָיו לִפְלוֹנִי וְאַחֲרָיו לִפְלוֹנִי. אִילּוּ אָמַר. מֵת הַשְּׁלִישִׁי בְחַיֵּי הַשֵּׁנִי. מִכֵּיוָן שֶׁלֹּא זָכָה בָהֶן הַשֵּׁנִי לֹא זָכוּ הַיּוֹרְשִׁין יְאוּת אַשְׁכָּחַת אֱמָר. אַחֲרָיו לִפְלוֹנִי אַחֲרָיו לִפְלוֹנִי. תַּנֵּי. הָרִאשׁוֹן מוֹכֵר קַרְקַע וְלוֹקֵחַ פֵּירוֹת דִּבְרֵי רִבִּי. רַבָּן שִׁמְעוֹן בֶּן גַּמְלִיאֵל אוֹמֵר. אֵין לוֹ אֶלָּא אֲכִילַת פֵּירוֹת בִּלְבַד. חִזְקִיָּה אָמַר. הֲלָכָה כְרִבִּי. אָמַר רִבִּי מָנָא. מִן מָה דְּאָמַר חִזְקִיָּה. הֲלָכָה כְרִבִּי. הָדָא אָמְרָה שֶׁאֵין נוֹתְנִין לוֹ כְּמַתְּנַת שְׁכִיב מְרַע. הָכָא אָמַר רִבִּי מָנָא קוֹמֵי רִבִּי יוֹסֵי. וְהָדָא אִשָּׁה מִכֵּיוָן שֶׁמְּזוֹנוֹתֶיהָ עַל בַּעֲלָהּ לֹא כְּמַתְּנַת שְׁכִיב מְרַע הִיא. אָמַר לֵיהּ. מְזוֹנוֹתֶיהָ עַל בַּעֲלָהּ בְּרָאוּי לָהּ. מַאֲכָל מֶשַׁח וּמֶלַח. וְהִיא בָעֵינָא מְזַבְּנָה וּמֵיכַל תַּרְנוּגְלִין. הָדָא אָמְרָה שֶׁאִם בִּקֵּשׁ הָרִאשׁוֹן מְזַבְּנָה וּמֵיכַל תַּרְנוּגְלִין יִזְבַּן. אָמַר רִבִּי יַעֲקֹב בַּר אָחָא. תַּנֵּי תַמָּן. קְבוּרָהּ כִּמְזוֹנוֹתֶיהָ. כְּמָה דְּאַתְּ אֱמַר תַּמָּן. מוֹכֵר קַרְקַע וְלוֹקֵחַ מְזוֹנוֹת. אַף הָכָא. מוֹכֵר קַרְקַע וְלוֹקֵחַ קְבוּרָה.

[67]Rebbi Hillel bar Pazi asked before Rebbi Yose: If he sold and then she died[68]? He said to him, his sale[69] is invalid; it is as if a son sold during his father's lifetime and then the father died[70]. If she sold and then he died[71]? He said to him, her sale is valid; it is as if a father sold during his son's lifetime and then the son died[72]. Rebbi Ḥiyya bar Marius asked before Rebbi Jonah: What is the situation if she sold to her husband? He said, since Ḥizqiah said, practice follows Rebbi Judah[73], this implies that her sale is a sale[74]. It was stated[75]: "If somebody says, my property should be given to X, if X died to Y, [if Y died to Z][76]. If the first one died the properties should be given to the second, if the second died they should be given to the third. If the second one died during the first's lifetime; since the second never acquired them, the third cannot acquire them[77]." He said to him, so did Rebbi Hoshaia[78], the father of the

Mishnah, explain: After him to X, after him to Y; it is as if stated: if the third died during the second's lifetime, since the second one did not acquire his heirs cannot acquire, one really could say: After him to X, after him to Y[79]. It was stated: "Rebbi says, the first one may sell the real estate and buy movables. Rabban Simeon ben Gamliel says, he has only the usufruct.[75,80]" Ḥizqiah said, practice follows Rebbi. Rebbi Mana said, since Ḥizqiah said, practice follows Rebbi, that implies that he cannot dispose of it by a death-bed will[81]. So said Rebbi Mana[82] before Rebbi Yose: Since this woman's upkeep is her husband's responsibility, is it not like a gift of sick persons[83]? He said to him, her upkeep is what is necessary for her: food, oil, and salt. But she wants to sell and buy chickens[84]. This means that if the first one wanted to sell and buy chickens, he may sell[85]. Rebbi Jacob bar Aḥa said, her burial is equal to her upkeep. Since you said there[86], he may sell real estate and buy food, so he may sell real estate and buy a burial.

66 Added from *Baba batra* 8:9 (16c l.20) (Tosephta *Baba batra* 8:4), missing here in ms. and *editio princeps*; cf. Note 76.

67 The first sentences are quoted by Naḥmanides in 'ה מלחמות (in the Wilna edition of Alfassi, *Yebamot* 22a).

68 The husband sold of his wife's paraphernalia property during her lifetime. Since he was not the owner, he could not sell; the sale is void even when he becomes the heir.

69 Naḥmanides writes מכרו; that may have been a correct ms. or it may be his (obvious) correction of the text. In these details, a medieval quote is not a witness to the text.

70 While a son can legally sell his right of inheritance to a speculator (who would take the risk that the son might die before the father and his investment become worthless), the son cannot sell his father's property before his father's death; such a sale is void even after the son becomes the heir.

71 She sold of her paraphernalia

properties, of which she is the owner, and her husband died during her lifetime. She sold irregularly since her husband had the administration of her properties during his lifetime but after her husband's death the sale is valid.

72 The father is not required to inconvenience himself to leave his properties for his heirs.

73 The reference is not to R. Jehudah (bar Illaï) mentioned in the Mishnah but to Rebbi, R. Jehudah ben Rabban Simeon, quoted in the *baraita* later in this paragraph.

74 As explained at length later, the temporary owner is a total owner and may sell at will. The question why she would want to sell is addressed below.

75 A similar text in Tosephta *Baba batra* 8:4 (fragmentary), Yerushalmi *Baba batra* 8:9 (16c l.19); Babli *Baba batra* 136b/137a (cf. R. Rabbinowicz, דקדוקי סופרים בבא בתרא p. 374, Note ח).

76 This clause appears in all texts mentioned in the preceding Note; it is necessary to introduce the third beneficiary of the will.

77 In the language of the Babli: If the second died while the first is alive, the properties should return to the first's legal heirs (in Yerushalmi *Baba batra*: to the testator's legal heirs).

78 In the Babli (*Baba batra* 136b), he is called "Rav Hoshaia in Babylonia".

79 As the Babli explains in the name of Rav Hoshaia, for him there is a difference between "it should be given to X, then to Y, then to Z" and "you should inherit, after you Y, after him Z." In the first case, the properties are given in usufruct but have to be preserved. In the second case, the properties are given in possession; the owner receives title. The only claim the successor has is to the real estate which still is in the preceding heir's hand at his death; Y cannot complain if X sells the properties. This is made clear in the following *baraita*.

80 In the Babli, the position of Rabban Simeon ben Gamliel is modified to mean that a sale is a breach of trust but not that it is void. Since a *baraita* which forces the Babli to its conclusion is not mentioned in the Yerushalmi, one has to assume that in its opinion for Rabban Simeon ben Gamliel there is no difference in the language of the will; in any case in which a succession of heirs is noted only usufruct is transferred and any sale of real estate is void.

81 In *Baba batra*, the text reads: "R. Yannai said, Rebbi agrees that he cannot dispose of it by a death-bed will. R. Johanan said, not even as a gift

between the living." The statement of R. Mana (I)/R. Yannai simply means that X, the first heir, cannot give the properties away in a will since the will becomes active only after X's death and at that moment the real estate is already Y's property (as explained in the Babli, *loc. cit.*). R. Joḥanan's statement is explained by R. Eliahu Fulda, that X may *sell* for his own needs because he is the owner, but he cannot *give away* since the original will prescribes that after X it *must be given to* Y.

82 R. Mana II.

83 Why should the wife have the power to sell the real estate whose proceeds go to her husband? Is it not that she received the properties on condition that after her, they should be given to her husband or children?

84 She may sell for expenses which the husband is not required to cover.

85 X may sell real estate only for his personal needs but the definition of personal need has to be very generous.

86 In the Tosephta from *Baba batra*. The wife may also sell some of her property and buy herself a burial plot (which, if used, becomes forbidden for all usufruct.)

(33a, line 13) אָמַר רִבִּי יוֹסֵי. וְאִילֵין דְּכָתְבִין. אִין מִיתַת דְּלָא בְנִין יְהֵא מִדְלָהּ חֲזַר לְבֵית אָבִיהָ. תְּנָאִי מָמוֹן הוּא וּתְנָאוֹ קַיָּים.

Rebbi Yose said: Those who write "if she should die childless, her property should return to her father's family" write a monetary condition which is a valid condition[87].

87 If the wife should die childless, both her mortmain and her paraphernalia properties return to her father's family. This text (and its ramifications in medieval rabbinic literature) has been studied by M. A. Friedman, *Jewish Marriage in Palestine* (cf. Chapter 5, Note 226), vol. 1, Chapter VE, pp. 391-418.

(fol. 32c) **משנה ב:** מִי שֶׁמֵּת וְהִנִּיחַ אִשְׁתּוֹ וּבַעַל חוֹב וְיוֹרְשִׁין וְהָיָה לוֹ פִּיקָדוֹן אוֹ מִלְוָה בְּיַד אֲחֵרִים רִבִּי טַרְפוֹן אוֹמֵר יִנָּתְנוּ לַכּוֹשֵׁל שֶׁבָּהֶן. רִבִּי עֲקִיבָה אוֹמֵר אֵין מְרַחֲמִין בַּדִּין אֶלָּא יִנָּתְנוּ לַיּוֹרְשִׁין שֶׁכּוּלָּן צְרִיכִין שְׁבוּעָה וְאֵין הַיּוֹרְשִׁין צְרִיכִין שְׁבוּעָה.

Mishnah 2: If somebody died and left his wife, a creditor[88], and heirs, and he was owed a deposit or a debt by a third party[89], Rebbi Ṭarphon says, these should be given to the weakest among them. Rebbi Aqiba says, one does not show mercy in law! But these should be given to the heirs for all others have to swear[90], only the heirs do not have to swear[91].

88 Who is secured by a mortgage lien on the deceased person's real estate.

89 Since a deposit is unsecured movable property, also the debt due to the deceased is presumed to be unsecured movable property.

90 The widow who wants to receive her *ketubah* in cash (instead of being supported by the heirs for the rest of her life) has to swear that she did not receive anything during her husband's lifetime. The creditor has to swear that his claim was not satisfied.

91 Since as movable property the deposit or debt was not mortgaged, it becomes the heirs' free property at the moment of death of the bequeather.

(33a, line 15) **הלכה ב:** מִי שֶׁמֵּת וְהִנִּיחַ אִשָּׁה כול׳. רִבִּי יוֹסֵי בַּר חֲנִינָה אָמַר. לַכּוֹשֵׁל שֶׁבִּרְאָיוֹתָיו. כְּגוֹן מַלְוֶה בְעֵדִים וּמַלְוֶה בִשְׁטָר יִנָּתְנוּ לְמַלְוֶה בְעֵדִים. רִבִּי יוֹחָנָן אָמַר. לַכּוֹשֵׁל בְּגוּפוֹ. הַגַּע עַצְמָךְ הוּא עָתִיר. כְּגוֹן אִילֵּין דְּבַר אַנְדְּרָאי. אָמַר רִבִּי אָחָא. לַכּוֹשֵׁל בְּגוּפוֹ וְעָנִי. כְּחָדָא. קְרִיבְתֵּיהּ דְּרִבִּי שְׁמוּאֵל בַּר אַבָּא יְהָבוּ לֵיהּ מִשּׁוּם כּוֹשֵׁל. אַייתֵי רִבִּי שִׁמְעוֹן בֶּן לָקִישׁ עַבְדּוֹי דְּרִבִּי יוּדָן נְשִׂייָא וַאֲפִיק מִינֵּיהּ. רִבִּי יוֹחָנָן הֲוָה מִיסְתַּמֵּיךְ עַל רִבִּי שִׁמְעוֹן בַּר אַבָּא. אָמַר לֵיהּ. מַה נַּעֲשָׂה בְּאוֹתָהּ הָעֲנִייָה. אָמַר לֵיהּ. אַייתֵי רִבִּי שִׁמְעוֹן בֶּן לָקִישׁ עַבְדּוֹי דְּרִבִּי יוּדָן נְשִׂייָא וַאֲפִיק מִינָּהּ. וְיָפֶה נַעֲשָׂה. אָמַר רִבִּי יִרְמְיָה קוֹמֵי רִבִּי זְעִירָא. אִי נֹאמַר. רִבִּי יוֹחָנָן כְּדַעְתֵּיהּ וְרִבִּי שִׁמְעוֹן כְּדַעְתֵּיהּ. דְּאִיתְפַּלְגוּן. הַכֹּל מוֹדִין

שֶׁאִם טָעוּ בְּשִׁיקוּל הַדַּעַת שֶׁאֵין מַחֲזִירִין. מִדִּבְרֵי תוֹרָה מַחֲזִירִין. מַה פְּלִיגִין. בְּטָעוּת מִשְׁנָה. שֶׁרְבִּי יוֹחָנָן אָמַר. בְּטָעוּת מִשְׁנָה שִׁיקוּל הַדַּעַת. רִבִּי שִׁמְעוֹן בֶּן לָקִישׁ אָמַר. טָעוּת מִשְׁנָה דְּבַר תּוֹרָה. הִיא טָעוּת מִשְׁנָה הִיא טָעוּת זְקֵינִים.

Halakhah 2: "If somebody died and left a wife," etc. Rebbi Yose ben Hanina said, the weakest in his claim[92]. For example, one lent before witnesses, the other lent on a mortgage document; it should be given to the one who lent before witnesses. Rebbi Johanan said, the weakest in his body[93]. Think about it, if he is rich[94], like those of the family Andreas. Rebbi Aha said, the weakest in his body and poor[95]. As the following: They gave to a relative of Rebbi Samuel bar Abba as the weakest[96]. Rebbi Simeon ben Laqish brought slaves of Rebbi Jehuda the Prince[97] and took it away from her. Rebbi Johanan was leaning on Rebbi Simeon bar Abba and said, what was done with that poor woman? He said to him, Rebbi Simeon ben Laqish brought slaves of Rebbi Jehuda the Prince and took it away from her. Was he justified in doing this[98]? Rebbi Jeremiah asked before Rebbi Ze'ira: Should we say that Rebbi Johanan follows his doctrine and Rebbi Simeon ben Laqish his own? Since they disagree: Everybody agrees that if they[99] err in arguments, one does not reverse. In the words of the Torah[100], one reverses. Where do they disagree? If one errs in a Mishnah, for Rebbi Johanan says, an error in Mishnah is like an error in arguments, but Rebbi Simeon ben Laqish says, an error in Mishnah is like an error in words of the Torah[101]. What is said of the Mishnah is also said of words of the Elders[102].

92 In the Babli according to Rashi, the creditor of a lower ranked mortgage; according to Alfasi any creditor because he can collect only if he proves his claim. The claim of a person giving money before witnesses

is very weak since he loses his money if both the borrower and his witnesses die.

93 The same statements are in the Babli, 84a. There, R. Joḥanan says explicitly that it should be given to the widow; his argument is buttressed by a *baraita*.

94 If the creditor is rich, even if he lent without a mortgage he does not need special protection.

95 The woman has precedence only if she is poor.

96 It is to be assumed that by the middle of the Third Century the common practice was to prefer R. Aqiba's opinion over that of any of his colleagues. Nevertheless, there was a court which followed R. Ṭarphon in the interpretation of R. Joḥanan. [In the opinion of *Rosh* (cf. Note 102), the Gaonic decree that all *ketubot* have to be satisfied by movables changed practice in the Mishnah from R. Aqiba to R. Ṭarphon.]

97 As head of the Patriarch's court, he ordered the *familiares* of the Patriarch to seize what he considered assigned by an erring court.

98 R. Joḥanan holds that the Patriarch's appeals court erred in reversing the lower court's decision. It is also mentioned in the Babli, 84b, that R. Simeon ben Laqish considers following R. Ṭarphon a reversible error.

99 A lower court whose judgment was appealed to the Patriarch's court. If it is a matter of weighing the evidence, the ruling of the lower court has to stand.

100 An error that even schoolchildren can detect.

101 R. Joḥanan's position in this matter is not mentioned in the Babli; the opposing view is quoted as universally accepted in the name of Rav Sheshet and Rav Assi, *Sanhedrin* 6b.

101 In the Babli, *loc. cit.*, Rav Pappa accepts as non-reversible error only a judicial argument rejected by the appeals court but which does not contradict existing precedents.

(33a, line 28) הַגַּע עַצְמָךְ שֶׁפְּטוּרִין מִן הַשְּׁבוּעָה. זוֹ תוֹרָה וְזוֹ אֵינָהּ תּוֹרָה.

Think of it, if they were exempt from swearing[102]? One is biblical[103], the other is not biblical.

102 In *Sefer Ha-iṭṭur* I, 23b (Note 16), followed by *Rosh* 9:2, the reading is "הַגַּע עַצְמְךָ שֶׁפְּטָרוֹ מִן הַשְּׁבוּעָה" "Think of it, if *he exempted them* from swearing", i. e., the debtor agreed to a clause in the mortgage contract which exempted the creditor from swearing to his heirs. In the version of the ms., there are additional cases when the creditor is by law exempted from swearing; for example, if the due date is later than the debtor's death (then the debt certainly was not paid) or if the debtor before his death acknowledged the debt.

103 Possession by the heirs is automatic by biblical law; all others have to prove their claims in court.

(fol. 32c) **משנה ג:** הִנִּיחַ פֵּירוֹת הַתְּלוּשִׁין מִן הַקַּרְקַע כָּל הַקּוֹדֵם בָּהֶן זָכָה. זָכְתָה הָאִשָּׁה יוֹתֵר מִכְּתוּבָּתָהּ וּבַעַל חוֹב יוֹתֵר עַל חוֹבוֹ. הַמּוֹתָר רִבִּי טַרְפוֹן אוֹמֵר יִנָּתְנוּ לַכּוֹשֵׁל שֶׁבָּהֶן. רִבִּי עֲקִיבָה אוֹמֵר אֵין מְרַחֲמִין בַּדִּין אֶלָּא יִנָּתְנוּ לַיּוֹרְשִׁין שֶׁכּוּלָּן צְרִיכִין שְׁבוּעָה וְאֵין הַיּוֹרְשִׁין צְרִיכִין שְׁבוּעָה.

Mishnah 3: If he left produce taken from the ground[104], the one who takes them first[105] acquires them. If the widow acquired more than her *ketubah* sum, or the creditor more than his claim, the remainder, Rebbi Ṭarphon says, should be given to the weakest among them[106]. Rebbi Aqiba says, one does not show mercy in law! But it should be given to the heirs since all others have to swear, only the heirs do not have to swear.

104 Or any other movables not in the actual possession of the deceased.

105 On condition that he have a legal claim on the estate, as widow or creditors do.

106 The excess over the claim has to be assigned by the court. A detailed study of the divergent interpretations of this Mishnah in Yerushalmi and Babli was made by I. Francus, שיטת הבבלי והירושלמי בתפיסת מטלטלין לגביית בתובה, *Sinai* 86 (1979/1980), 136-148.

(33a, line 29) **הלכה ג:** הִנִּיחַ פֵּירוֹת תְּלוּשִׁין כול'. רַב וְרִבִּי שִׁמְעוֹן בֶּן לָקִישׁ תְּרֵיהוֹן אָמְרִין. בִּצְבוּרִין בְּסוּרְקִי. אֲבָל אִם צְבָרָן בְּבֵיתוֹ זָכָה לוֹ בֵּיתוֹ. רִבִּי יוֹחָנָן אָמַר. וַאֲפִילוּ צְבוּרִין בְּבֵיתוֹ לֹא זָכָה לוֹ בֵּיתוֹ. דַּהֲוָה סָבַר דְּאִינּוּן דִּידֵהּ וְלֵית אִינּוּן דִּידֵהּ. וַאֲתֵי בַּעַל הַבַּיִת זָכָה בְּפֵירוֹתָיו בַּשְּׁבִיעִית. רִבִּי יִרְמְיָה סָבַר מֵימַר. מִשֶּׁיִּתְּנֵם לְתוֹךְ כֵּילָיו. אָמַר רִבִּי יוֹסֵי. אֲפִילוּ נְתָנָן לְתוֹךְ כֵּילָיו לֹא זָכָה בָּהֶן. דַּהֲוָה סָבַר מֵימַר דְּאִינּוּן דִּידֵהּ וְלֵית אִינּוּן דִּידֵהּ.

Halakhah 3: "If he left produce taken[107]," etc. Both Rav and Rebbi Simeon ben Laqish say, if they were collected at a trading place[108]. But if somebody collected it in his house, his house acquired for him. Rebbi Johanan said, even if he collected it in his house, his house did not acquire for him. For he thinks that they are his but they are not his. Does from this follow how the owner acquires his produce[109] in a Sabbatical year? Rebbi Jeremiah wanted to say, from the moment he put them into his vessel. Rebbi Yose said, even if he put them into his vessel he did not acquire, for he thinks that they are his but they are not his[110].

107 In this and the preceding Mishnah, the Mishnah text differs in a few details from the common reading of most Mishnaiot but the text quoted in the Halakhah is the standard Mishnah text.

108 "A place of Saracens." The problem discussed here is quite different from that discussed in the Babli, 84b, by the same authors. In the Yerushalmi, it is supposed that the acquirer removes the produce from the public place since it is obvious that it would not be his when left in the public place. But if the produce was already in a place belonging to the claimant, according to Rav and R. Simeon ben Laqish "a person's courtyard acquires for him automatically" (Babli *Baba meṣi'a* 10b). For R. Johanan, "a person's courtyard acquires for him only by a conscious act." Therefore, in a situation where an unlearned person could think that anything in a private domain to which the owner has a claim is automatically

his, we may assume that the conscious act of acquisition is missing. This argument assumes that the first part of the Mishnah is everybody's opinion and the difference between R. Tarphon and R. Aqiba refers only to the excess.

In the Babli, the entire first part of the Mishnah is considered R. Tarphon's and everybody agrees that "a person's courtyard acquires for him automatically"; cf. Note 106.

109 The ripe produce is ownerless by biblical decree. Naturally, the owner of the property has the same right to take it as does everybody else. Anybody but the owner acquires simply by taking. How does the owner acquire, that taking from him would be theft?

110 He can acquire only by a) putting the produce into his vessel and b) declaring that it is his.

(33a, line 35) הִיא אַרְמַלְתָּא תְּפָסַת אַמְהָתָא. אֲתָא עוֹבְדָא קוֹמֵי רִבִּי יִצְחָק. אָמַר. תְּפָסַת תְּפָסַת. רִבִּי אִימִי מַפִּיק מִינָהּ. דְּהִיא סָבְרָה דִּידָהּ וְלֵית אִינּוּן דִּידָהּ. כְּהָדָא. אִילֵּין בְּנֵי שַׁמַּי דִּדְמָךְ אֲבוּהוֹן שְׁבַק לָהֶן אֲבוּהוֹן עֵז. אָתָא מָרֵי חוֹבָה וּנְסָתַהּ. אֲתָא עוֹבְדָא קוֹמֵי רִבִּי אַבָּהוּ וְאָמַר. דִּידֵהּ נְסַב. לֹא כֵן תַּנֵּי. יוֹרֵשׁ וּבַעַל חוֹב שֶׁקָּדַם מֵהֶן אֶחָד וְתָפַס [אֵין] מוֹצִיאִין מִיָּדוֹ. דַּהֲווֹן סָבְרִין דְּאִינּוּן דִּידְהוֹן וְלֵית אִינּוּן דִּידְהוֹן. אָמַר רִבִּי יַעֲקֹב בַּר זַבְדִּי. מוֹדֶה רִבִּי אַבָּהוּ שֶׁאִם מְכָרוּהָ אוֹ מַשְׁכְּנוּהָ אוֹ טִילְטְלוּהָ מִמָּקוֹם לְמָקוֹם וְאַחַר כָּךְ בָּא בַּעַל חוֹב וְתָפַס מוֹצִיאִין מִיָּדוֹ.

That widow took a slave girl[111]. The case came before Rebbi Isaac who said, what she took, she took. Rebbi Immi took her away, for she thought that she was hers but she was not hers[112]. A similar case: The father of the sons of Shammai died and bequeathed a goat to them. The creditor came and took it. The case came before Rebbi Abbahu who said, he took his own property. Did we not state that if either an heir or a creditor came and took, one does [not][113] remove from his hand; for they thought they were theirs but they were not theirs. Rebbi Jacob bar Zabdi said, Rebbi Abbahu agrees that if they[114] sold it, or gave it as a pledge, or moved it to another place, if then the creditor came and took it one removes it from his possession.

111 She took her as a servant from her husband's estate as part payment of her *ketubah*. The case is also quoted in *Qiddušin* 1:3 in the discussion whether slaves are acquired under the rules of movables or of real estate.

112 If the widow could not point to an act of acquisition, the fact that the girl served her when she was a wife and continued to serve her when she was a widow does not make her the widow's peoperty.

113 This word was written by the scribe; it was deleted by the first corrector and, therefore, is missing in *editio princeps*. But the partial quote in Halakhah 8:10 proves that the original text was correct.

114 The creditor can take an unsecured part of the debtor's estate only if the heirs did not act as owners. The moment they acted as owners, and the father had not told them to liquidate his debts, the debtor can make himself paid only through regular foreclosure procedures in court.

(33a, line 43) הַגַּע עַצְמָךְ שֶׁפְּטוּרִין מִן הַשְּׁבוּעָה. זוֹ תוֹרָה וְזוֹ אֵינָהּ תּוֹרָה.

Think of it, if they were exempt from swearing[102]? One is biblical[103], the other is not biblical.

(fol. 32c) **משנה ד:** הַמּוֹשִׁיב אֶת אִשְׁתּוֹ חֶנְוָנִית אוֹ שֶׁמִּינָהּ אֲפִיטְרוֹפְיָא הֲרֵי זֶה מַשְׁבִּיעָהּ כָּל־זְמָן שֶׁיִּרְצֶה. רִבִּי אֱלִיעֶזֶר אוֹמֵר אֲפִילוּ עַל פִּילְכָהּ וְעַל עִיסָתָהּ.

Mishnah 4: If somebody engages his wife as grocer or appoints her as steward[115], he can make her swear any time he wants[116]. Rebbi Eliezer says, even about her distaff and her dough[117].

115 To administer his properties. The word is the feminine form to masc. Greek ἐπίτροπος; cf. Mishnah *Bikkurim* 1:5.

116 That her accounts are honest.

117 R. Eliezer disagrees with the anonymous Tanna and holds that the husband can make his wife swear that she did not take anything for herself from any domestic work she performed for him. (The Babli, 86b, is unsure whether R. Eliezer disagrees with the anonymous Tanna or holds that if the wife handles large sums of money, the husband can also make her swear on minutiae. In the latter version, the rabbis hold that a wife would rather want a divorce than be married to such a nitpicker.)

(33a, line 44) **הלכה ד:** הַמוֹשִׁיב אֶת אִשְׁתּוֹ חֶנְוָנִית כול'. יָאוּת אָמַר רִבִּי לִיעֶזֶר. מַה טַעֲמוֹן דְּרַבָּנִין. אִם אוֹמֵר אַתְּ כֵּן אֵין שָׁלוֹם בְּתוֹךְ בֵּיתוֹ לְעוֹלָם. שִׁיבְּרָה אֶת הַכֵּלִים מַה אַתְּ עָבַד לָהּ. כְּשׁוֹמֶרֶת חִנָּם אוֹ כְשׁוֹמֶרֶת שָׂכָר. מִסְתַּבְּרָה מֵיעַבְדִּינָהּ כְּשׁוֹמֶרֶת שָׂכָר. אָמְרִין. אֲפִילוּ כְשׁוֹמֶרֶת חִנָּם אֵינָהּ. אִם אוֹמֵר אַתְּ כֵּן אֵין שָׁלוֹם בְּתוֹךְ בֵּיתוֹ לְעוֹלָם.

Halakhah 4: "If somebody engages his wife as grocer," etc. Is Rebbi Eliezer not correct? What is the rabbis' reason[118]? If you say so, there never would be peace in his house. If she broke vessels[119], is she responsible as an unpaid or a paid trustee[120]? It would be reasonable to consider her a paid trustee. They said, she is not even an unpaid trustee, for if you say so, there never would be peace in his house[121].

118 Why do the rabbis permit the husband to make his wife swear only if she is entrusted with large sums of money? What is the difference between a business account and household money? In the Babli, 86b, the rabbis hold that a man who cannot trust his wife with household money should divorce her since "nobody lives with a snake in the same basket."

119 In the course of regular household duties.

120 The legal categories are defined in terms of shepherds, to agree with

the biblical verses. Mishnah *Baba meṣi'a* 7:8, *Šebuot* 8:1: "There are four kinds of responsible people: Unpaid and paid watchmen, the borrower and the lessee. The unpaid watchman swears about everything (which is missing or broken, that it is not by his fault); the borrower pays for everything; the paid trustee and the lessee swear about broken, robbed, or dead (animals) and pay for what was lost or stolen (for if an animal is lost or stolen it is their fault since it was not guarded correctly.)"

If the wife were an unpaid trustee, she would have to pay for the damage unless she can swear that it was not her fault. The same holds for the paid trustee except that she would have to pay for inattention.

121   The wife never pays for broken dishes.

(fol. 32c) **משנה ה:** כָּתַב לָהּ נֶדֶר וּשְׁבוּעָה אֵין לִי עָלַיִךְ אֵינוֹ יָכוֹל לְהַשְׁבִּיעָהּ אֲבָל מַשְׁבִּיעַ הוּא אֶת הַיּוֹרְשִׁין וְאֶת הַבָּאִין בִּרְשׁוּתָהּ. שְׁבוּעָה אֵין לִי עָלַיִךְ וְעַל יוֹרְשַׁיִךְ וְעַל הַבָּאִין בִּרְשׁוּתֵיךְ הוּא אֵינוֹ יָכוֹל לְהַשְׁבִּיעָהּ לֹא אוֹתָהּ וְלֹא אֶת יוֹרְשֶׁיהָ וְלֹא אֶת הַבָּאִין בִּרְשׁוּתָהּ אֲבָל יוֹרְשִׁין מַשְׁבִּיעִין אוֹתָהּ וְאֶת יוֹרְשֶׁיהָ וְאֶת הַבָּאִין בִּרְשׁוּתָהּ.

Mishnah 5: If he wrote to her[122]: "I have no vow or oath against you," he cannot make her swear, but he can ask an oath from the heirs[123] or her business associates[124]. "I have no oath against you, or your heirs, or your business associates," he cannot ask an oath from her, or her heirs, or her business associates, but the heirs[125] can ask an oath from her, or her heirs, or her business associates.

122   This continues Mishnah 4. If the wife refuses to conduct a business or a stewardship for him if he does not believe her accounts and will require her to swear, all depends on the language of the contract between

husband and wife. This Mishnah is really one together with Mishnah 6.

123 If she died, he can make her sons swear who will inherit her *ketubah* (Mishnah 4:10) or eventually her family if she was childless (Note 87). This "oath of heirs" is "that our mother did not tell us that the *ketubah* was paid, or that money of hers was due to others, etc."

124 They can swear that none of the husband's money is in their hands.

125 The husband's heirs, after the husband's death.

(33a, line 50) **הלכה ח:** כָּתַב לָהּ: נֶדֶר וּשְׁבוּעָה אֵין לִי עָלַיִךְ כול׳. רִבִּי יוֹנָה וְרִבִּי יוֹסֵה תְּרֵיהוֹן אָמְרִין. לֹא סוֹף דָּבָר בִּנְכָסִים שֶׁנִּשְׁתַּלְּטָה בָהֶן בְּחַיֵּי בַעְלָהּ. אֶלָּא אֲפִילוּ בִנְכָסִים שֶׁנִּשְׁתַּלְּטָה בָהֶן לְאַחַר מִיתַת הַבַּעַל אֵין הַיּוֹרְשִׁין מַשְׁבִּיעִין אוֹתָהּ.

Halakhah 5: "If he wrote to her: "I have no vow or oath against you," etc. Rebbi Jonah and Rebbi Yose both say, not only about properties over which she exercised control during her husband's lifetime but even about properties over which she exercised control after her husband's death are the heirs prevented from making her swear[126].

126 This paragraph is in the wrong place; it refers to Mishnah 6 where the husband exempts the wife and her heirs from any oath imposed by him and his heirs. In that case the wife is exempted as long as she acts within the powers entrusted to her by her husband.

(33a, line 53) תַּמָּן תַּנִּינָן. הַשּׁוֹכֵר פָּרָה מֵחֲבֵירוֹ וְהִשְׁאִילָהּ לְאַחֵר וּמֵתָה כְּדַרְכָּהּ יִשָּׁבַע הַשּׂוֹכֵר שֶׁמֵּתָה כְּדַרְכָּהּ וְהַשּׁוֹאֵל יְשַׁלֵּם לַשּׂוֹכֵר. רִבִּי הִילָא בְשֵׁם רִבִּי יַנַּאי. וְהוּא שֶׁנָּתַן לוֹ רְשׁוּת לְהַשְׁאִיל לַאֲחֵרִים. וְתַנֵּי רִבִּי חִייָה כֵן. אֵין הַשּׁוֹאֵל רַשַּׁאי לְהַשְׁאִיל וְלֹא הַשּׂוֹכֵר רַשַּׁאי לְהַשְׂכִּיר וְלֹא הַשּׁוֹאֵל רַשַּׁאי לְהַשְׂכִּיר וְלֹא הַשּׂוֹכֵר רַשַּׁאי לְהַשְׁאִיל. וְלֹא מִי שֶׁהוּפְקַד אֶצְלוֹ רַשַּׁאי לְהַפְקִיד אֵצֶל אַחֵר אֶלָּא אִם כֵּן נָטְלוּ רְשׁוּת מֵהַבְּעָלִים. וְכוּלָּן שֶׁשִּׁינּוּ אֶת שְׁמוֹתֵיהֶן שֶׁלֹּא מִדַּעַת הַבְּעָלִים חַיָּיבִין.

וְהַשּׁוֹאֵל לֹא אֲפִילוּ לֹא שִׁינָה חַיָּיב. אֶלָּא בְּגִין דְּתַנִּינָן. מַתָּנָה שׁוֹמֵר חִנָּם לִהְיוֹת פָּטוּר מִן הַשְּׁבוּעָה וְהַשּׁוֹאֵל לִהְיוֹת פָּטוּר מִלְּשַׁלֵּם. וְאָתָא מֵימַר לָךְ שֶׁאַף עַל פִּי שֶׁהִתְנָה עִמּוֹ שֶׁהוּא פָּטוּר שֶׁהוּא חַיָּיב. בִּיקֵּשׁ לְהַשְׁבִּיעַ אֶת הַשּׁוֹאֵל. נִישְׁמְעִינָהּ מִן הָדָא. כָּתַב לָהּ. נֶדֶר וּשְׁבוּעָה אֵין לִי עָלַיִיךְ. אֵינוֹ יָכוֹל לְהַשְׁבִּיעָהּ. אֲבָל מַשְׁבִּיעַ הוּא אֶת יוֹרְשֶׁיהָ וְאֶת הַבָּאִים בִּרְשׁוּתָהּ. הָדָא אָמְרָה שֶׁאִם בִּקְּשׁוּ לְהַשְׁבִּיעַ אֶת הַשּׁוֹאֵל הוּא מַשְׁבִּיעוֹ. הָדָא יָלְפָה מִן הַהִיא וְהַהִיא יָלְפָה מִן הָדָא. הָדָא יָלְפָה מִן הַהִיא. שֶׁאִם בִּקֵּשׁ לְהַשְׁבִּיעַ אֶת הַשּׁוֹאֵל מַשְׁבִּיעוֹ. וְהַהִיא יָלְפָה מִן הָדָא. שֶׁאִם בִּקֵּשׁ לְהַשְׁבִּיעַ אֶת הָאִשָּׁה (שֶׁלֹּא)[127] מַשְׁבִּיעָהּ. אָמַר רִבִּי חֲנִינָה. לָא צוֹרְכַת מֵילַף הָדָא מִן הַהִיא. וּמַה צּוֹרְכָה תֵּילַף הַהִיא מִן הָדָא. כַּיי דְּמַר רִבִּי הִילָא בְּשֵׁם רִבִּי יַנַּאי. וְהוּא שֶׁנָּתַן לוֹ רְשׁוּת לְהַשְׁאִיל. וְהָכָא. וְהוּא שֶׁנָּתַן לָהּ רְשׁוּת שֶׁיִּהְיוּ בָנֶיהָ אֶפִּיטְרוֹפִים. אָמַר רִבִּי יוֹסֵי. עָרוּךְ לְהַעֲלוֹת לוֹ שָׂכָר כָּל־זְמָן שֶׁהִיא שְׁכוּרָה אֶצְלוֹ. רִבִּי זְעוּרָה שָׁאַל לְרִבִּי אֲבוּנָא. שֶׁאָלוּהָ הַבְּעָלִים וָמֵתָה. אָמַר לֵיהּ. כֵּן אֲנָן אָמְרִין. אֲכָלוּהוּ. אָמַר רִבִּי יוֹסֵי בַּר אָבוּן. אָכְלוּ שֶׁלָּהֶן אָכְלוּ. רִבִּי זְעוּרָה בְעָא קוֹמֵי רִבִּי יָסָא. הֵיךְ עֲבָדִין עוֹבְדָא. אָמַר לֵיהּ. תְּרֵיי כָּלְקַבֵּל אַרְבָּעָה וְלָא עָבְדִין עוֹבְדָא כְסוּגְיָיא. תְּרֵיי קַבֵּל תְּרֵיי אִינּוּן. רִבִּי לָעְזָר תַּלְמִידֵיהּ דְּרִבִּי חִייָה רוּבָּה. רִבִּי יוֹחָנָן תַּלְמִידֵיהּ דְּרִבִּי יַנַּאי.

2 הילא | ק אילא   3 לאחרים | ק אבל אם לא נתן לו רשות להשאיל לא בדא.   6 את שמותיהן | ק -   7 והשואל | ק ושואל   דתנינן | ק דתנינין תמן   8 מן השבועה | ק משבועה   ואתא | ק אתא   שאע״פ שהתנה | ק אפי׳ שהתנה   9 שהוא חייב | ק חייב   נישמעינה | ק נשבע   11-12 בקשו להשביע את השואל הוא | ק ביקש את השואל שהוא   12-13 הדה ילפא מן ההיא וההיא ילפא מן הדא. הדא ילפא מן ההיא.   שאם בקש להשביע את השואל משביעו | ק -   14 שלא | ק שהוא   15 צורכת | ק צריכה   כורכה תילף | ק צריכה מילף   17 והוא | ק -   -   אפיטרופים | ק אפיטרופין   יוסי | ק יוסה   18 זעורה | ק זעירא (2 times)   אבונא | ק אבינא   19 אמרין | ק קיימין   אכלוהו | ק אפי׳ אכלוה   20 בר אבון | ק ביר׳ אבין   אכלו שלהן | ק שלחן   21 ולא | ק לא   22 רובה | ק רבא

[128]There[129], we have stated: "If somebody leases a cow from another person and lends it to a third party; if it died naturally, the lessee has to swear that it died naturally[130] and the borrower has to pay to the lessee.[131]" Rebbi Hila in the name of Rebbi Yannai: Only if he gave permission to lend to others[132]. Also Rebbi Ḥiyya stated thus[133]: "The borrower cannot lend, nor the lessee lease, nor the borrower lease, nor the lessee lend, nor the trustee give to another unless they received permission from the owners. And all who changed the titles without the owners' knowledge are liable. But the borrower is liable even if he did not change." But it is because we stated[134]: "An unpaid watchman can stipulate to be exempt from an oath and the borrower may stipulate that he not have to pay." This means that even if he stipulated to be exempt that he is obligated[135]. What if he wanted to let the borrower swear[136]? Let us hear from the following: "If he wrote to her: 'I have no vow or oath against you,' he cannot make her swear, but he can ask an oath from the heirs or her business associates." This implies that if he[137] wanted to make the borrower swear, he can force him to swear. The first case teaches about the second and the second about the first[138]. The first case teaches about the second, that if he wanted to make the borrower swear, he can force him to swear. The second case teaches about the first, that if he wants to force the wife to swear, that he can make her swear[139]. Rebbi Ḥanina said, it is not necessary to derive the first case from the second, and what does one learn for the second case from the first? Following what Rebbi Hila said in the name of Rebbi Yannai: Only if he gave permission to lend to others. And here, only if he gave permission to let her sons be stewards[140]. Rebbi Yose said, he has to pay the lease all

the time it is leased to him[141]. Rebbi Ze'ira asked Rebbi Abuna: If the owners borrowed it and it died[142]? He said to him, in that case we say, they ate it. Rebbi Yose bar Abun said, if they ate it, they ate their own property[143]. Rebbi Ze'ira asked before Rebbi Yasa: How does one act[144]? He said to him, there are two[146] against four; one does not act following the argument. He said to him, they are two against two! Rebbi Eleazar is the elder Rebbi Ḥiyya's student; Rebbi Joḥanan is Rebbi Yannai's student[147].

127 This word is not in the primary *Qiddušin* text.

128 This entire paragraph is from *Qiddušin* 1:4, fol. 60b. Since at the end it treats a question from there which was not introduced here, it is clear that the text here is secondary.

129 Mishnah *Baba meṣi'a* 3:3.

130 Since the lessee does not have to pay for acts of God; Note 120.

131 The borrower has to pay for every defect that develops; Note 120. Agreed to in the Babli, *Baba meṣi'a* 29b. In 96b, this is a matter of dispute; the Tanna R. Yose holds there that the borrower pays the original owners.

132 Otherwise the lessee violates the terms of his lease and becomes liable for every defect which develops. In the Babli, *Baba meṣi'a* 36a, this is a matter of dispute which is decided (36b) in conformity with the Yerushalmi.

133 Tosephta *Baba meṣi'a* 3:1 (the first sentence only), also quoted in *Baba meṣi'a* 3:3 (9a l.51).

134 Mishnah *Baba meṣi'a* 7:13.

135 If he deviated from the original terms; even if he later subleased with permission (unless he explicitly requested immunity also for the later change.)

136 Can the original owner of the cow go to court against the borrower from the lessee to have him swear that the cow died a natural death and, if the borrower refuses to swear, collect the value of the cow from the lessee, or can the borrower claim that he is involved only with the lessee and is immune to suits from third parties?

137 The original owner, since the borrower is a business associate of his lessee.

138 The first Mishnah *Ketubot* 9:5 and the second *Baba Meṣi'a* 3:3 with its Tosephta can be combined.

139 Cf. Note 127; *editio princeps* reads here "that he cannot make her swear." But the text is very clear, the fact that the husband freed his wife from having to swear about her fiduciary duties does not absolve her from responsibility and having to swear if she deviated from the framework of these duties.

140 The wife can appoint others to fulfill part of her duties (in the example given, her adult sons from a prior marriage) only with her husband's explicit agreement; they have to swear unless especially exempted (interpretation of Tosaphot 86b, *s. v.* נדר; *Sefer Ha'iṭṭur* 23a, Note ג)

141 This refers back to Mishnah *Baba meṣi'a* 3:1. Even if the original owner gave permission to the lessee to lend out his cow, the lessee is responsible for paying his lease the whole time the cow is in the hands of the non-paying borrower.

142 Is this true even if the original owners borrowed it back?

143 In that case, the lessee does not have to pay.

144 This refers to the problem dealt with in *Qiddušin* 60b l. 48: Rav Jehudah sent to R. Eleazar: A person having responsibility who handed it over to another (and something happened, who is responsible)? He said to him, the first one has to pay. Rebbi Joḥanan said, the second one has to pay; Rebbi Simeon ben Laqish said, the second one has to pay. (The following argument shows that one has to read that R. Joḥanan holds the first one has to pay.) In *Qiddušin* there follows the discussion of this paragraph, which shows that R. Yannai and R. Ḥiyya (the Elder) both agree with R. Eleazar and R. Joḥanan.

The Babli, *Baba qama* 11b, attributes to R. Eleazar the opinion that the first one is free from paying if he did not have to pay under the original arrangement; in practice it is decided that the first one always has to pay unless the original owner agreed to the new arrangements.

145 R. Simeon ben Laqish and Rav Jehudah. The latter would not have asked if he agreed with the Tosephta of which he certainly was cognizant.

146 The quote should have been: R. Eleazar says in the name of the Elder R. Ḥiyya, R. Joḥanan says in the name of R. Yannai (which is the quote of the latter in *Baba qama* 115a.)

משנה ו: נֶדֶר וּשְׁבוּעָה אֵין לִי לֹא לִי וְלֹא לְיוֹרְשַׁיי וְלֹא לַבָּאִים (fol. 32c) בִּרְשׁוּתִי עָלַיִךְ וְעַל יוֹרְשַׁיִךְ וְעַל הַבָּאִין בִּרְשׁוּתֵיךְ הֲרֵי זֶה אֵינוֹ יָכוֹל לְהַשְׁבִּיעָהּ לֹא הוּא וְלֹא יוֹרְשִׁין וְלֹא הַבָּאִין בִּרְשׁוּתוֹ לֹא אוֹתָהּ וְלֹא אֶת יוֹרְשֶׁיהָ וְלֹא אֶת הַבָּאִים לִרְשׁוּתָהּ

Mishnah 6: "I have no vow or oath against you, neither I, nor my heirs, nor my business associates, against you, or your heirs, or your business associates," he cannot ask an oath from her, neither he, nor the heirs, nor the business associates, from her, or her heirs, or her business associates.

הלכה ו: נֶדֶר וּשְׁבוּעָה אֵין לִי וּלְיוֹרְשַׁיי כול'. אָמַר רַבִּי יוֹנָה. וְהִיא (33b, line 2) שֶׁעָשָׂת אֶפִּיטְרוֹפָּא בְּחַיֵּי בַעֲלָהּ. אֲבָל אִם עָשָׂת אֶפִּיטְרוֹפָּא לְאַחַר מִיתַת הַבַּעַל אֵין הַיּוֹרְשִׁין מַשְׁבִּיעִין אוֹתָהּ. דּוּ מַתְנִיתָא. לֹא עָשָׂת אֶפִּיטְרוֹפָּא אֵין הַיּוֹרְשִׁין מַשְׁבִּיעִין אוֹתָהּ. אִם עָשָׂת אֶפִּיטְרוֹפָּא הַיּוֹרְשִׁין מַשְׁבִּיעִין אוֹתָהּ לְעָתִיד לָבוֹא. וְאֵין מַשְׁבִּיעִין אוֹתָהּ לְשֶׁעָבַר. אֵיזֶהוּ לְשֶׁעָבַר. מִשְּׁעַת מִיתָה עַד שְׁעַת קְבוּרָה. וְאָמַר רַבִּי יוֹסֵי. אֲפִילוּ עֲשָׂאָהּ אֶפִּטְרָפוֹס לְאַחַר מִיתַת בַּעֲלָהּ אֵין הַיּוֹרְשִׁין מַשְׁבִּיעִין אוֹתָהּ. וְהָא תַנִּינָן לֹא עֲשָׂתָהּ אֶפִּטְרָפוֹס אֵין הַיּוֹרְשִׁין מַשְׁבִּיעִין אוֹתָהּ. אִם עָשָׂת אֶפִּיטְרוֹפָּא הַיּוֹרְשִׁין מַשְׁבִּיעִין אוֹתָהּ לְעָתִיד לָבוֹא וְאֵין מַשְׁבִּיעִין אוֹתָהּ לְשֶׁעָבַר. פָּתַר לָהּ עַל רֹאשָׁהּ. וְאֵין עַל רֹאשָׁהּ כְּהָדָא. רַבִּי יוֹנָה וְרַבִּי יוֹסֵי תְּרֵיהוֹן אָמְרִין. לֹא סוֹף דָּבָר בִּנְכָסִים שֶׁנִּשְׁתַּלְּטָה בָּהֶן בְּחַיֵּי בַעֲלָהּ אֶלָּא אֲפִילוּ נְכָסִים שֶׁנִּשְׁתַּלְּטָה בָּהֶן לְאַחַר מִיתַת הַבַּעַל אֵין הַיּוֹרְשִׁין מַשְׁבִּיעִין אוֹתָהּ. פָּתַר לָהּ מִשְּׁעַת מִיתָה עַד שְׁעַת קְבוּרָה. דָּמַר רַבִּי אַבָּהוּ בְּשֵׁם רַבִּי יוֹחָנָן. מִשְּׁעַת מִיתָה עַד שְׁעַת קְבוּרָה אֵין הַיּוֹרְשִׁין מַשְׁבִּיעִין אוֹתָהּ. תַּנֵּי בַּר קַפָּרָא. שֶׁלֹּא תְהֵא מַנִּיחָתוֹ וְהוֹלֶכֶת לְבֵית אָבִיהָ.

Halakhah 6: ""I have no vow or oath against you," etc. [147] Rebbi Jonah said, only if she was made a steward during her husband's lifetime. But if she was appointed as a steward after her husband's death, the heirs can(not)[148] make her swear. That is the Mishnah: if she was not appointed a steward, the heirs cannot make her swear[149]. If she was appointed a steward, the heirs can make her swear for the future[150], but they cannot make her swear about the past. What is "about the past"? From the time of death to the time of burial[151]. And Rebbi Yose said, even if he appointed her as steward after her husband's death, the heirs can make her swear[152]. But did we not state[153]: "If he did not appoint her as steward, the heirs cannot make her swear. If he appointed her as steward, the heirs can make her swear for the future but cannot make her swear for the past." He explains it about the first case[154]. But if it is about the first case, Rebbi Jonah and Rebbi Yose both say, not only about property over which she had control during her husband's lifetime but even about property over which she acquired control after her husband's death the heirs cannot make her swear. Explain it, from the time of death to the time of burial. For Rebbi Abbahu said in the name of Rebbi Johanan: The heirs cannot make her swear from the time of death to the time of burial[155]. Bar Qappara stated: That she should not abandon him and leave for her family[156].

147 A lengthy discussion of this text is in R. Bezalel Ashkenazi, שיטה מקובצת כתובות (reprint Tel Aviv, n/d) p. 221 a/b. However, probably the text is not based on an original ms. since it is Babylonized, remarkable for such a careful author.

148 Probably this should be deleted since the husband cannot give her immunity if he appoints her as testamentary executor unless he makes the appointment valid "one hour before my death".

149 If she is not the executor of her husband's will and the husband had freed her from swearing about what she had overseen for him, the heirs cannot ask for an accounting of the past.

150 Since they now are the owners

and cannot be bound by their father's dispositions.

151 As explained at the end, it is not desirable that the widow should hand over the estate to the heirs before her husband's burial. Therefore, before the burial she is the husband's agent and not the heirs'. The Babli agrees, 87a.

152 Probably some addition is missing such as "only for the future". The entire sentence is a corrector's addition.

153 Mishnah 7, speaking of a woman who was freed by her husband from the obligation to swear, who resigned her stewardship at the time of her husband's burial.

154 Even in the case of Mishnah 5, the widow cannot be made to swear about the expenses of the funeral. The Babli agrees, 87a.

155 It is possible to explain this statement as a new paragraph, referring to Mishnah 7: Even a woman who was not appointed as steward, or whose stewardship ceased with her husband's death, and who was not granted exemption from swearing, cannot be made to account under oath for the expenses of her husband's burial.

156 The heirs, the beneficiaries of the estate, have the duty to bury the husband. It would be very bad for the reputation of the family if the widow would return to her own family before the burial because she fears to be accused by the heirs that she spent too much money on her husband's burial. Therefore, she is prevented from resigning her stewardship before the burial and, in exchange, is freed from having to provide an accounting of the burial costs under oath.

משנה ז: הָלְכָה מִקֶּבֶר בַּעֲלָהּ לְבֵית אָבִיהָ אוֹ שֶׁחָזְרָה לְבֵית חָמִיהָ וְלֹא נַעֲשֵׂית אֲפִיטְרוֹפָּא אֵין הַיּוֹרְשִׁין מַשְׁבִּיעִין אוֹתָהּ. וְאִם נַעֲשֵׂית אֲפִיטְרוֹפָּא הַיּוֹרְשִׁין מַשְׁבִּיעִין אוֹתָהּ לְעָתִיד לָבוֹא וְאֵין מַשְׁבִּיעִין אוֹתָהּ לְשֶׁעָבַר. (fol. 32c)

Mishnah 7: If she went from her husband's grave to her family[157], or she remained in her in-law's family[158] but was not appointed as steward, the heirs cannot make her swear. But if she was appointed as steward, the heirs can make her swear for the future[150], but they cannot make her swear about the past[155].

157 Then she requires that the full *ketubah* be paid to her immediately on the basis of the *ketubah* document which is as good as a mortgage coming due.

158 She prefers not to collect her *ketubah* but to be supported by her husband's family for the foreseeable future; cf. Mishnaiot 12:3-4.

(fol. 32c) **משנה ח:** הַפּוֹגֶמֶת כְּתוּבָּיָהּ לֹא תִיפָּרַע אֶלָּא בִשְׁבוּעָה. עֵד אֶחָד מֵעִידָהּ שֶׁהִיא פְרוּעָה לֹא תִיפָּרַע אֶלָּא בִשְׁבוּעָה. מִנִּיכְסֵי יְתוֹמִים וּמִנְּכָסִים מְשׁוּעְבָּדִין וְשֶׁלֹּא בְּפָנָיו לֹא תִיפָּרַע אֶלָּא בִשְׁבוּעָה.

Mishnah 8: If she had compromised her *ketubah*[159], she shall not be able to collect without an oath[160]. If one witness[161] testifies that [the *ketubah*] was paid, she shall not be able to collect without an oath. From orphans' property[162], or from encumbered property[163], in his[164] absence she shall not be able to collect without an oath.

159 She had signed a receipt for part of the *ketubah*, as explained in the next Mishnah.

160 She can collect the remainder of the *ketubah* only in a court proceeding in which she will have to swear to the amount of the *ketubah* which still is unpaid.

161 A single witness cannot legally prove anything (*Deut.* 19:15). That rule is stated for criminal proceedings. In money matters, it is a rabbinic institution that the testimony of a single witness creates a presumption that he testified truthfully. The opposing party therefore either has to produce a witness who contradicts the first, or she can swear that her claim is not satisfied.

162 Since the heirs are not usually cognizant of all business dealings between their deceased father and his

wife (who might not be their mother), she has to swear that she did not receive any valuables on account of the *ketubah*.

163   If the husband sold real estate after the date of his wedding, the sale did not remove the *ketubah* lien on the property. If the *ketubah* cannot be paid by the estate, the widow has regress on the buyer. Clearly, the buyer can require the widow to swear for the same reason the heirs of the estate can.

164   If the husband sends his wife a bill of divorce from abroad, the court handling the delivery of the bill of divorce to the wife will require her to swear that no part of the *ketubah* had been paid before overseeing the payment of the *ketubah*.

The Mishnah is repeated in *Šebuot* 7:7.

(33b, line 18) **הלכה ז:** הָלְכָה מִקֶּבֶר בַּעֲלָהּ לְבֵית אָבִיהָ כול'. אָמַר רִבִּי זְעוּרָה. כְּעֵין שְׁבוּעַת תּוֹרָה יָרְדָה לָהֶן. כְּתוּבָּה הוּחְזְקָה בְיָדָהּ לִגְבוֹת. כְּמִי שֶׁגָּבָה. וְהוּא כָתוּב עִם הַשְּׁטָר שֶׁלְּמָאתַיִם פָּרוּעַ. וְהִיא אוֹמֶרֶת מָנָה. לֹא תִיפָּרַע אֶלָּא בִשְׁבוּעָה.

Halakhah 7   "If she went from her husband's grave to her family," etc.[165] Rebbi Ze'ura said, this came down in the manner of a biblical oath. The *ketubah* is acknowledged in her hand for collection; it is as if collected. But since with the document of 200 there is an acknowledgment of payment and she says, one mina [is due to her], she cannot be paid without an oath[166].

165   This quote has nothing to do with the Halakhah which discusses only Mishnah 8.

166   He discusses the first case of the Mishnah, if she had compromised the *ketubah* by signing a receipt for partial payment without specifying the amount. The basic biblical text is *Ex.* 22:8: "About any guilty behavior, about an ox, or a sheep, or a garment, or anything lost, if he agrees that this is it, the case of the two parties shall come before *Elohim*." This is explained as follows (*Mekhilta dR. Ismael*, ed. Horovitz-Rabin p. 301; *Mekhilta dR. Simeon bar Iohai* ed. Epstein-Melamed

p. 203; Babli *Baba Qama* 107a, *Baba Meṣi'a* 5a,98a): The paragraph speaks in vv. 6-7 about a person who holds another's property without being paid for his services, who will not have to pay if the property is stolen and the holder never used it for his own purposes. Then v. 8 continues about *any* behavior implying monetary obligation, i. e., any monetary claim of one person against another, and requires first that the object of the claim be well defined (an ox, a sheep, etc.) and that the defendant of the suit agree that "this is it", i. e., that there is a case, then there shall be a trial before a judge acting as *Elohim*, as a representative of God as judge. *In praxi* this means that if the claimant cannot prove his case by witnesses or documents, the defendant can free himself from paying by swearing while holding a copy of the Torah and being subject to all the rules of judicial oaths. But if the claim is for one thing (e. g., an ox) and the defendant agrees only that something else is owed to the claimant (e. g., a sheep), or if the defendant disputes the entire claim, he cannot be forced to swear and the claimant loses his case.

R. Ze'ura notes that the case of the damaged *ketubah* has most of the features of a case requiring an oath by biblical standards, even though it seems otherwise since the divorced wife claims the remainder of the *ketubah* but the husband claims that all was paid. For that he argues that everybody knows that a *ketubah* becomes payable at the moment of divorce. Therefore, the husband is considered to have paid the *ketubah* sum and now he requests to get his money back, and the ex-wife disputes part of his claim. (In the opinion of the Babli, *Šebuot* 48b, 81a, this is held only by the House of Shammai; cf. Note 178.) There are two points why the case does not fit the framework of *Ex.* 22:8: The person who swears a biblical oath does not have to pay, but in the case under discussion the wife swears in order to collect money. This is by rabbinic tradition. Second, since the *ketubah* is a mortgage lien (or: in talmudic times was a mortgage lien), the suit is about real estate and real estate claims cannot be settled by oaths (Mishnah *Šebuot* 6:5). This argument is explicit in the Babli, 87b, where the place of R. Ze'ura is taken by (the slightly younger) Rami bar Ḥama.

KETUBOT CHAPTER NINE

(33b, line 22) תַּנֵּי הַפּוֹגֶמֶת. לֹא הַפּוֹחֶתֶת כְּתוּבָּתָהּ. כֵּיצַד. הָיְתָה כְּתוּבָּתָהּ מָאתַיִם וְהִיא אוֹמֶרֶת מָנֶה. נִפְרַעַת שֶׁלֹּא בִשְׁבוּעָה. מַה בֵּין פּוֹגֶמֶת וּמַה בֵּין פּוֹחֶתֶת. אָמַר רִבִּי חֲנִינָה. פּוֹגֶמֶת בָּא מַשָּׂא וּמַתָּן בֵּינֹתַיִים. פּוֹחֶתֶת לֹא בָא מַשָּׂא וּמַתָּן בֵּינֹתַיִים.

It was stated "compromised". Not that she reduced her *ketubah*[167]. If her *ketubah* was 200 but she claims a mina, she is paid without an oath[168]. What is the difference between one who compromises and one who claims less? Rebbi Ḥanina said, if she compromises there was a transaction between them[169]; if she claims less there was no transaction between them[170].

167 This statement is quoted in *Šebuot* 7:7 (38a l. 25), *Sanhedrin* 8:6 (26b l. 49); Babli 87b.

168 In the Babli, this is made more explicit: If her *ketubah* was 1000 *zuz*, the husband claims that it was paid but he has no receipt, the divorced wife states that she received nothing but that her claim was only a mina, this is *not* conceding part of the husband's claim (cf. Note 166) and she collects without an oath. It seems that the Yerushalmi would agree to that interpretation.

On documents which show that 200 *zuz* written in the *ketubah* might mean 100 *zuz* in actual money (and the standards by which the value of a *zuz* is determined), cf. M. A. Friedman, *loc. cit.* Note 87.

169 Therefore, the oath is required if only to protect creditors with claims against the estate.

170 At least, there is no presumption of any transactions between her and her husband regarding her *ketubah* during her marriage. Therefore, anybody claiming that there was such a transaction in order to impose an oath on the widow would have to prove his case in court.

(33b, line 22) רִבִּי יִרְמְיָה בָּעָא. כְּמָה דְאַתְּ אָמַר תַּמָּן. עֵד אֶחָד מֵעִידָהּ שֶׁהִיא פְרוּעָה לֹא תִיפָּרַע אֶלָּא בִשְׁבוּעָה. וְדִכְוָתָהּ. וְעֵד אֶחָד מֵעִידָהּ שֶׁהִיא פְחוּתָה

לֹא תִפְחוֹת אֶלָּא בִשְׁבוּעָה. אָמַר רִבִּי יוֹסֵי. בְּשָׁעָה שֶׁעֵד אֶחָד מְעִידָהּ שֶׁהִיא פְחוּתָה בְעֵד[171] אֶחָד מַכְחִישׁ אֶת שְׁנַיִם. וְאֵין עֵד אֶחָד מַכְחִישׁ אֶת שְׁנָיִם.

Rebbi Jeremiah asked: Since we stated there: "If one witness testifies that [the *ketubah*] was paid, she shall not be able to collect without an oath," should it be similar that if one witness testifies that [the *ketubah*] was reduced, she shall not be able to collect the reduced sum without an oath? Rebbi Yose said, at the moment that one witness testifies that the amount should be reduced, he is like a single witness who contradicts the testimony of two [witnesses][172] but no single witness can contradict the testimony of two[173].

171 This should be read as בְּעֵד, already corrected in *editio princeps*. The text in *Sanhedrin* 8:6 is formulated differently.

172 The two witnesses who signed the *ketubah* document.

173 There can never be an oath imposed for a lesser claim in the settlement of a *ketubah* since the preceding paragraph dealt with the case of no witnesses and there can be no oath if there are two witnesses.

(33b, line 30) תַּנֵּי. יוֹרֵשׁ שֶׁפָּגַם אָבִיו שְׁטַר חוֹבוֹ הַבֵּן גּוֹבָה שֶׁלֹּא בִשְׁבוּעָה. בְּזֶה יָפָה כֹּחַ הַבֵּן מִכֹּחַ הָאָב. שֶׁהַבֵּן גּוֹבָה שֶׁלֹּא בִשְׁבוּעָה. וְאָב אֵינוֹ גּוֹבָה אֶלָּא בִשְׁבוּעָה. אָמַר רִבִּי אֶלְעָזָר. וְנִשְׁבַּע שְׁבוּעַת יוֹרֵשׁ. שֶׁלֹּא פָּקַדְנוּ אַבָּא. שֶׁלֹּא אָמַר לָנוּ אַבָּא. שֶׁלֹּא מָצִינוּ שְׁטָר בֵּין שְׁטָרוֹתָיו שֶׁלְּאַבָּא שֶׁשְּׁטָר זֶה פָּרוּעַ. רִבִּי הוֹשַׁעְיָה בְעָא. מַתְנִיתָא דְבֵית שַׁמַּי. דְּבֵית שַׁמַּי אוֹמְרִים. נוֹטֶלֶת כְּתוּבָּתָהּ וְלֹא שׁוֹתָה. אָמַר רִבִּי יוֹסֵי. תַּמָּן טַעֲמוֹן דְּבֵית שַׁמַּי. הָבִיאוּ בַעֲלִי וַאֲנִי שׁוֹתָה. בְּרַם הָכָא. בְּדִין הָיָה אֲפִילוּ אָבִיו לֹא יִשָּׁבַע. תַּקָּנָה תִּיקְנוּ בּוֹ שֶׁיִּשָּׁבַע. בּוֹ תִּיקְנוּ. בִּבְנוֹ לֹא תִּיקְנוּ. כֵּיוָן שֶׁמֵּת הֶעֱמִדְתָּהּ אֶת בְּנוֹ עַל דִּין תּוֹרָה.

It was stated: If an heir's father held a compromised promissory note, the son collects without swearing[174]. In that the son's power is greater than the father's, since the son collects without swearing while the father can collect only by swearing[175]. Rebbi Eleazar said[176], nevertheless he has to execute an heir's oath, "that our father did not charge us, that our father did not tell us, that we did not find a document among our father's documents that this note was paid.[177]" Rebbi Hoshaia asked, does the *baraita*[178] follow the House of Shammai? For the House of Shammai say, "she collects her *ketubah* and does not drink."[179] Rebbi Yose said, there the reason of the House of Shammai is: Bring my husband and I shall drink[180]! But here, it would be in order that even his father would not have to swear. They instituted a rule that he has to swear[181]. They instituted that for him, but not for his son[182]. When he died, you put his son on the biblical rule.

174 If the father had indicated that a certain part of the note was paid, and both the lender and the borrower had died, the lender's son collects the remainder from the borrower's son without swearing that no more than the sum indicated had been paid (assuming that the borrower's son cannot produce a document or witnesses that more had been paid than was claimed), since he could not collect if he had to swear that he was 100% sure that his claim was in the correct amount.

175 If the borrower had died.

176 The same statement in the Babli, *Šebuot* 48a. It is in the heirs' power to swear that *according to their best knowledge* the claim is justified.

177 Mishnah *Šebuot* 7:7.

178 The one mentioned at the start of this paragraph, and also the Mishnah (cf. Note 166).

179 Mishnah *Soṭah* 4:3, about a woman whose husband, having no witnesses, formally accused her of adultery but died before he could bring her to the Temple for the cleansing ceremony. Since the verse requires the presence of the husband at the Temple ceremony (Yerushalmi *Soṭah*, p. 180, Note 14), the woman is prevented from clearing her name. The House of Hillel hold that she cannot collect her *ketubah* since she cannot prove her

innocence to the heirs (*loc. cit.* p. 185, Note 38) based on the general principle that "the burden of proof is on the claimant." Since the House of Shammai also agree to that principle, it must follow that for them the *ketubah* is as good as paid and the heirs are the claimants who want to have the money back but who cannot prove their case. This shows that for the House of Shammai the *ketubah* is the widow's property from the moment of the husband's death.

180 The preceding argument is invalid. The House of Shammai may not hold that the *ketubah* is the widow's property from the moment of the husband's death, but they hold that if the woman was ready to clear her name, any impediment which is not her fault cannot be held against her. The House of Hillel hold that the heirs do not have to pay her *ketubah;* since she brought the problem on herself by being seen with another man after having been duly warned by her husband in front of two witnesses; she cannot collect except by successfully clearing her name. The problem is discussed in similar terms in *Soṭah* 4:1, Notes 13-16.

181 His oath is a purely rabbinic institution for the prevention of fraud. Since it is rabbinic, it cannot be enforced if it would prevent anybody from collecting what is rightfully his.

182 Meaning, it could not be instituted as a burden on his son.

(33b, line 34) נִתְחַיֵּיב אָבִיו שְׁבוּעָה בְּבֵית דִּין וּמֵת אֵין בְּנוֹ גוֹבֶה. דְּל כֵּן מָה אֲנָן אָמְרִין. וְיֵשׁ אָדָם מוֹרִישׁ שְׁבוּעָתוֹ לִבְנוֹ. אָמַר רִבִּי אָבִין. אַתְּ אָמַרְתְּ. פְּגַם אָבִיו שְׁטָרוֹ בְּבֵית דִּין אֵין בְּנוֹ גוֹבֶה. רַב חִסְדָּא בְּעָא. בְּגִין דַּהֲלַךְ אִילֵּין תַּרְתֵּי פְּסִיעָתָא הוּא מַפְסִיד. אִילּוּ פְגָמוֹ חוּץ לְבֵית דִּין אַתְּ אָמַר. גּוֹבֶה. מִפְּנֵי שֶׁפְּגָמוֹ בְּבֵית דִּין אַתְּ אָמַר. אֵינוֹ גוֹבֶה.

If a father became obligated to swear in court[183] and died, his son cannot collect. If it were otherwise, what could we say? Can a man let his son inherit an obligation to swear[184]? Rebbi Avin said, you mean, if a man compromised his document in court, his son cannot collect. Rav Ḥisda asked: Because he walked those two steps, he loses? If he compromised it outside the court, he collects. Because he compromised it in court, he cannot collect[185]?

183 The context shows that the oath is a rabbinic one imposed on the person who wants to collect money.

184 Since he lacks the knowledge about the details of his father's business transactions, he can only swear a disclaimer of knowledge (Note 177) but not the required positive statement.

In the Babli, *Šebuot* 48a, this is a common formal statement by Rav and Samuel, not an obvious fact.

185 In the Babli, *Šebuot* 48a, R. Eleazar holds (with Rav Ḥisda here) that the heirs swear the heir's oath (Note 177) in any case. R. Abin's statement is rejected.

(33b, line 43) **הלכה ח:** הַפּוֹגֶמֶת כְּתוּבָּיָהּ לֹא תִפָּרַע אֶלָא בִשְׁבוּעָה כּוּל. אָמַר רִבִּי יוֹחָנָן בְּשֵׁם רִבִּי יַנַּאי. אֵין פּוֹרְעִין מִנִּכְסֵי יְתוֹמִים אֶלָא בִשְׁטָר שֶׁהָרִבִּית אוֹכֶלֶת בּוֹ. וְיֵשׁ אוֹמְרִים. אַף לִכְתוּבַת אִשָׁה. אָמַר רִבִּי יַנַּאי. מִפְּנֵי מְזוֹנוֹת. אָמַר רִבִּי מַתַּנְיָה. מָאן חָשׁ לִמְזוֹנוֹת. רִבִּי שִׁמְעוֹן. דְּרִבִּי שִׁמְעוֹן אוֹמֵר. בְּמִגְבָּה הַדָּבָר תָּלוּי. מַאי כְדוֹן. מִפְּנֵי חִינָא. מִפְּנֵי[185] שֶׁיְּהוּ הַכֹּל קוֹפְצִין עָלֶיהָ לִישָׂאֲנָהּ. וְיֵשׁ אוֹמְרִים. אַף לִגְזֵילָה וְלִנְזִיקִין. אָמַר רִבִּי יוֹסֵי. אַף אָנָן נַמִּי תַּנִּינָן תַּרְתֵּיהוֹן. לִגְזֵילָה מִן הָדָא. אִם הָיָה דָבָר שֶׁיֵּשׁ לוֹ אַחֲרָיוּת חַיָּיב לְשַׁלֵּם. לִנְזִיקִין מִן הָדָא. אֵין נִפְרָעִין מִנִּכְסֵי יְתוֹמִין אֶלָא מִן הַזִּיבּוּרִית. כֵּינֵי מַתְנִיתָא. אֵין נִפְרָעִין מִנִּכְסֵי יְתוֹמִין לִנְזִיקִין אֶלָא מִן הַזִּיבּוּרִית. וְהָא תַנֵּי. עָמַד הַבֵּן תַּחַת הָאָב הַנִּיזָּקִין שָׁמִין בָּעֵדִית[186] וּבַעֲלֵי הַחוֹב בַּבֵּינוֹנִית וּכְתוּבַת אִשָׁה בַּזִּיבּוּרִית. אָמַר רִבִּי יוֹסֵי בֵּירִבִּי בּוּן. כָּאן בְּיָתוֹם גָּדוֹל. כָּאן בְּיָתוֹם קָטוֹן.

1 אמר | ש -   2 פורעין | גי ש נפרעין   יתומים | גי ש יתומין קטנים   בשטר שהרבית | ש בשרבית   3 ויש אומרים | ש ר' נתן אומר   אימי | גי ינאי ש מנא   4 מתניה | גי מתנייה ש מתנייא   חש | ש חייש   אומ' | גי אמ'   5 מפני | ש משום   מפני | גי ש כדי   6 יוסי | גי יוסי ביר' בון   אנן נמי תנונן | ש נן תנינן   7 מן חדא | ש מחכא (2 times)   היה | גי יהיה   לו | ש בו   חייב | גי חייבין   8 מניכסי יתומין | גי מן הנכסים

HALAKHAH 8   445

שליתומין ש מניכסי יתומין קטנים   9 יתומין | גי יתומים ש יתומין קטנים   והא תני |
גי ש והתני   עמד | ש יעמוד   10 בעדית | גי ש להן בעידית   בעלי | ש שבעל   החוב |
ש חוב   וכתובת | ש וכתבת   11 כָּאן בְּיָתוֹם גָּדוֹל. כָּאן בְּיָתוֹם קָטוֹן | ש תיפתר דברי
הכל בהדא דייתיקי

Halakhah 8: "If she had compromised her *ketubah*, she shall not be able to collect without an oath," etc.   [187]Rebbi Johanan said in the name of Rebbi Yannai: One pays from an orphan's property only a document on which interest is due[188], and some say[189], also a woman's *ketubah*. Rebbi Yannai said, because of her sustenance. Rebbi Mattaniah said, who is worried about sustenance? Rebbi Simeon! Since Rebbi Simeon said, it depends on the collection[190]. What about it? For attraction, that everybody should jump to marry her[191]. Some say, also for robbery and torts[192]. Rebbi Yose said, we stated both of these. Robbery from the following: "If it was mortgageable, he has to pay.[193]" For torts from the following[194]: "One pays from an orphan's property only from the least valuable.[195]" So is the Mishnah: One pays for torts from an orphan's property only from the least valuable[196]. But was it not stated: If the son took his father's place, one estimates torts from the most valuable land, creditors from average quality, and a woman's *ketubah* from the least valuable[197]. Rebbi Yose ben Rebbi Abun said, here[197] about an adult orphan, there about an underage orphan.

185   This awkward expression seems to be a scribal error induced by the preceding word. In the parallels *Šebuot* 7:9, *Gittin* 5:3 (and *Arukh s. v.* חן) the idiomatic כדי שיהו is used.

186   The vocalization is from the ms., characteristic for Italian/Ashkenazic texts which almost never write *qamas*.

187   The Halakhah is repeated in *Gittin* 5:3, *Šebuot* 7:9.

188   To preserve the orphan's property. In the Babli, *'Arakhin* 22a, this opinion is ascribed to Rav Assi.

189   In the almost parallel text in

Šebuot 7:9, this is attributed to R. Nathan [who is called "some say" in the Babli (*Horaiot* 13b)]; in the Babli (*loc. cit.*) it, together with R. Yannai's explanation, appears in R. Johanan's name.

190 Mishnah 11:2 states that a married woman, for whose upkeep the husband is responsible, and whose husband does not fulfill his support duty, may sell from the estate without court supervision. The same holds for the estate after the husband's death as long as the *ketubah* was not paid. R. Simeon grants this right only to the definitively married woman and the wife who becomes a widow after definitive marriage, but not to the preliminarily married who cannot claim support but only *ketubah* if widowed or divorced. Mishnah 11:1 gives the estate the right to the widow's earnings in exchange for the support; it is held that R. Simeon thinks that, in general, the amount needed for her support is greater than her prospective earnings (Babli *loc. cit.*).

191 Since in those times a single woman had few possibilities of earning a living, if the heirs were not her children she needed the *ketubah* as dowry to attract a new husband.

192 If the father had been found guilty of robbery or causing damage but died before he paid the sums assessed by the court.

193 Mishnah *Baba Qama* 10:1: "If somebody robbed and used the proceeds to feed his children, [if the father died] they do not have to pay. But if it was mortgageable [real estate], they have to pay."

194 Mishnah *Gittin* 5:2.

195 An estate's real estate holdings are classified by their values per unit of area. It is assumed that the higher the unit value, the easier it is to sell the property. The debtor in general will try to satisfy his obligations with real estate of the lowest quality. The property which per unit area is valued highest is called עִידִית "elite", the average בֵּינוֹנִית "medium", and the lowest זִיבּוּרִית "stony field". These categories are not absolute; they refer to the holdings of an individual.

196 This statement was not discussed by J. N. Epstein in his treatment of כֵּינֵי מַתְנִיתָא (cf. Note 199). The statement should not be considered as emendation. A simple reading of the text will require that the statement apply to all cases in which an orphan's real estate is to be alienated. In the opinion of both Talmudim (*Gittin* 5:1, Babli 48b-50a; *Baba meṣi'a* 9:14, 12b l.

11) rabbinic practice demands that tort judgments have to be satisfied by best quality, financial debts by medium quality, and *ketubah* by lowest quality. In the opinion of most authorities, biblical law requires only minimal quality for the settlement of financial obligations. The rabbinic upgrading was a necessity to make it easier for people to get a loan. Since this argument is irrelevant for orphans, one does not need the Mishnah to know that mortgage debts paid by an estate are settled by low quality real estate. Where the Mishnah is really needed is payment for torts for which (*Ex.* 22:4) "the best of his fields or the best of his vineyards" are required. The statement therefore should be read: One pays *even for torts* from an orphan's property only from the least valuable; cf. *Tosaphot* 84a, *s. v.* לכתובת אשה.

197 The rules for the adult heir are the same as they would have been for the bequeather.

(fol. 32c) **משנה ט:** הַפּוֹגֶמֶת כְּתוּבָּתָהּ כֵּיצַד. הָיְתָה כְתוּבָּתָהּ אֶלֶף זוּז וְאָמַר לָהּ הִתְקַבַּלְתְּ כְּתוּבָּתֵיךְ וְהִיא אוֹמֶרֶת לֹא הִתְקַבַּלְתִּי אֶלָּא מָנֶה לֹא תִפָּרַע אֶלָּא בִשְׁבוּעָה.

Mishnah 9: If she had compromised her *ketubah*, how is that? If her *ketubah* was 1'000 *zuz* and he said to her, you received your *ketubah*, but she says, I received only one mina, she shall not be able to collect without an oath.

משנה י: עֵד אֶחָד מְעִידָהּ שֶׁהִיא פְרוּעָה כֵּיצַד. הָיְתָה כְתוּבָּתָהּ אֶלֶף זוּז וְאָמַר לָהּ הִתְקַבַּלְתְּ כְּתוּבָּתֵיךְ וְהִיא אוֹמֶרֶת לֹא הִתְקַבַּלְתִּי וְעֵד אֶחָד מְעִידָהּ שֶׁהִיא פְרוּעָה לֹא תִפָּרַע אֶלָּא בִשְׁבוּעָה.

Mishnah 10: If one witness testifies that [the *ketubah*] was paid, how is that? If her *ketubah* was 1'000 *zuz* and he said to her, you received your ketubah, but she says, I received nothing, and one witness testifies that [the ketubah] was paid, she shall not be able to collect without an oath.

משנה יא: מִנְּכָסִים הַמְשׁוּעְבָּדִים כֵּיצַד. מָכַר נְכָסָיו לַאֲחֵרִים וְהִיא נִפְרַעַת מִן הַלָּקוֹחוֹת לֹא תִפָּרַע אֶלָּא בִשְׁבוּעָה. מִנִּכְסֵי יְתוֹמִים כֵּיצַד. מֵת וְהִנִּיחַ נְכָסָיו לִיתוֹמִים וְהִיא נִפְרַעַת מִן הַיְתוֹמִים לֹא תִפָּרַע אֶלָּא בִשְׁבוּעָה. שֶׁלֹּא בְּפָנָיו כֵּיצַד. הָלַךְ לוֹ לִמְדִינַת הַיָּם וְהִיא נִפְרַעַת שֶׁלֹּא בְּפָנָיו לֹא תִיפָּרַע אֶלָּא בִשְׁבוּעָה. רִבִּי שִׁמְעוֹן אוֹמֵר כָּל־זְמַן שֶׁתּוֹבַעַת כְּתוּבָּתָהּ הַיּוֹרְשִׁין מַשְׁבִּיעִין אוֹתָהּ. אֵינָהּ תּוֹבַעַת כְּתוּבָּתָהּ אֵין הַיּוֹרְשִׁין מַשְׁבִּיעִין אוֹתָהּ.

Mishnah 11: From encumbered property, how is that? If he sold his real estate to others and she collects from the buyers, she shall not be able to collect without an oath. From orphans' property, how is that? If he died and left his estate to the orphans, if she is paid out by the orphans she shall not be able to collect without an oath. Not in his presence, how is that? If he went overseas[164] and she collects in his absence, she shall not be able to collect without an oath. Rebbi Simeon says, any time she asks for her *ketubah*, the heirs can require an oath from her. If she does not ask for her *ketubah*, the heirs cannot require an oath from her[198].

198 If the widow prefers to be supported by the estate for an unlimited period, the heirs can never ask for an oath that she did not receive part payment of the *ketubah* (which would disqualify her from being supported) during her husband's lifetime. But if she asks for her *ketubah*, they do not have to pay unless she swears, even if her husband had freed her from any obligation to swear. R. Simeon disagrees with Mishnaiot 5,6.

(33b, line 56) **הלכה ט-י:** הַפּוֹגֶמֶת כְּתוּבָּתָהּ כֵּיצַד. הָיְתָה כְּתוּבָּתָהּ אֶלֶף זוּז כול'. וְעֵד אֶחָד מְעִידָהּ שֶׁהִיא פְרוּעָה כול'. כֵּינֵי מַתְנִיתָא. וְשֶׁלֹּא בְּפָנָיו לֹא תִיפָּרַע אֶלָּא בִשְׁבוּעָה.

HALAKHAH 9-10

Halakhah 9-10: "If she had compromised her *ketubah*, how is that? If her *ketubah* was 1'000 *zuz*," etc. "If one witness testifies that [the *ketubah*] was paid," etc. So is the Mishnah[199]: "If she collects in his absence, she shall not be able to collect without an oath."

---

199   J. N. Epstein, ²מבוא לנוסח המשנה p. 475 notes that this כיני מאתניתא is not an emendation but simply a quote from the third Mishnah which belongs to this Halakhah.

(33b, line 58) וְהַנִּפְרַעַת שֶׁלֹּא בְּפָנָיו לֹא תִפָּרַע אֶלָּא בִּשְׁבוּעָה. וְנִפְרָעִין מֵאָדָם שֶׁלֹּא בְּפָנָיו. אָמַר רְבִּי יִרְמְיָה. תִּיפָּתַר בִּשְׁטָר שֶׁהָרִבִּית אוֹכֶלֶת בּוֹ. וּבֵית דִּין גּוֹבִין רִיבִּית. תִּיפָּתַר שֶׁעָרַב לוֹ מִן הַגּוֹי.

וְהַנִּפְרַעַת שֶׁלֹּא בְּפָנָיו לֹא תִפָּרַע אֶלָּא בִּשְׁבוּעָה. וְנִפְרָעִין מֵאָדָם שֶׁלֹּא בְּפָנָיו. אָמַר רְבִּי יִרְמְיָה. תִּיפָּתַר בִּשְׁרִיבִּית אוֹכֶלֶת בּוֹ. וּבֵית דִּין גּוֹבִין רִיבִּית. תִּיפָּתַר בְּעָרַב לוֹ מִגּוֹי.

"If she collects in his absence, she shall not be able to collect without an oath.[200]" Can one collect from a person in his absence[201]? Rebbi Jeremiah says, explain it about a contract for which interest is due[202]. Would the court collect interest[203]? Explain it that it was guaranteed for a Gentile[204].

---

200   The Halakhah (after the introductory paragraph) appears also in *Šebuot* 7:7; it seems to be closer to the original form. That text for the main section is given here in smaller type; it is taken as basis of the translation, with the deviations from the text in *Ketubot* noted in the Commentary.

The quote from the Mishnah is not in *Šebuot* since the Mishnah there deals with creditors in general, not only the divorcee or widow. Since the text from *Šebuot* has all the characteristics of being the original, the discussion of the Halakhah refers to contracts in general, not only to *ketubot*.

201   It is a general principle in Jewish law that זָכִין לָאָדָם שֶׁלֹּא בְּפָנָיו וְאֵין חָבִין לוֹ אֶלָּא בְּפָנָיו "one may benefit a person without his knowledge but one

may not obligate him without his knowledge," Mishnah *Gittin* 1:6. Since a *ketubah,* and also a loan document in general, is executed as a lien on all of the debtor's properties, not on a specified piece of real estate, it cannot be foreclosed without court proceedings in the presence of the debtor or his representative.

202 In that case the court will act for the benefit of the debtor if this satisfies the creditor.

203 Since taking interest among Jews is forbidden, the court will not enforce any interest clause in a contract.

204 If the Jewish defendant is sued as guarantor for a Gentile from whom the Jewish creditor may take interest legally, the court will recognize the contract as valid.

(33b, line 60) כְּחָדָא אַלֶכְסָא. אָמַר לוֹ רִבִּי מָנָא. אֲנַן עָבְדִין טָבוֹת סַגִיא מִינְכוֹן. אֲנַן כָּתְבִין דִין מוּגְמָרִין. אִין אָתָא טָבָאוֹת. וְאִין לָא אֲנַן מַחְלְטִין נִיכְסַיָּיא. אָמַר לֵיהּ. אַף אֲנַן עָבְדִין כֵּן. אֲנַן מְשַׁלְחִין בַּתְרֵיהּ תְּלָת אִיגְרִין. אִין אָתָא הָא טָבָאוֹת. וְאִין לָא אֲנַן מַחְלְטִין נִיכְסַיָּיא. אָמַר לֵיהּ. הַגַּע עַצְמָךְ דַּהֲוָה בְאֶתָר רְחִיק. אֲנַן מְשַׁלְחִין בַּתְרֵיהּ תְּלָת אִיגְרִין. חָדָא גְוָא תַלְתִּין וְחָדָא גַן תַּלְתִּין וְחָדָא גַן תַּלְתִּין. אִין אָתָא הָא טָבָאוֹת. וְאִילָא אֲנַן מַחְלְטִין נִיכְסַיָּיא. אָמַר רִבִּי מַתַּנְיָה. וְהוּא שֶׁעָמַד בַּדִּין וּבָרַח. אֲבָל אִם לֹא עָמַד בַּדִּין וּבָרַח לֵית כָּאן מַחְלְטִין אֶלָּא מַכְרְזִין.

לֵיכְסָא אָמַר קוֹמֵי רִבִּי מָנָא. אֲנַן עָבְדִין טָבוֹת סַגִין מִינְכוֹן. אֲנַן מְשַׁלְחִין דְיָאטִיגְמָטִין.206 אִין אָתָא הָא טָבוֹת. וְאִין לָא אָתָא אֲנַן מַחְלְטִין נִיכְסוֹי. אָמַר לֵיהּ. אוּף אֲנַן עָבְדִין כֵּן. מַכְרְזִינָן ל' יוֹמִין. אִין אָתָא טָבוֹת. וְאִילָא מַחְלְטִינָן נִיכְסוֹי. אָמַר לֵיהּ. הַגַּע עַצְמָךְ דַּהֲוָה בָזְוֵי רְחִיקֵי. אָמַר לֵיהּ. אֲנַן מְשַׁלְחִין ג' אִיגְרָן. חָדָא גַן ל' יוֹמִין. וְחָדָא גַן ל' יוֹמִין. וְחָדָא גַן ל' יוֹמִין. אִין אָתָא הָא טָבוֹת. וְאִילָא מַחְלְטִינָן נִיכְסוֹי. אָמַר רִבִּי חֲנִינָה. וְשֶׁעָמַד בַּדִּין וּבָרַח. אֲבָל אִם לֹא עָמַד בַּדִּין לָא מַחְלְטִינָן אֶלָּא מַכְרְזִינָן.

Alexis said before Rebbi Mana: We act much better than you do[205]. We send edicts[206]. If he[207] comes, it is good. If he does not come, we irrevocably give away his properties. He answered him, we also act in this way, we have the herald announce for thirty days[208]. If he comes, it is good. If he does not come, we irrevocably give away his properties. He said to him, think of it, if he was in distant corners. He said to him, we send three letters, one after thirty days, one after the next thirty days, and one after the next thirty days[209]. If he comes, it is good. If he does not come, we irrevocably give away his properties. Rebbi Ḥanina[210] said, that is, if he was present at the trial and then fled[211]. But if he was not present at the trial, we[212] cannot irrevocably give away, but only announce.

205 In the *Ketubot* text, R. Mana speaks to the Gentile Alexis. In that text it is not always clear who is the speaker.

206 Greek διατάγματα; in Roman praxis referring to edicts of the emperor or the provincial prefect. The corresponding Aramaic word דִּין מוּגְמָרִין in the *Ketubot* text, if it is not simply a corruption, means "judgment that cannot be appealed." Since the prefect also was the chief judge of the province, there is really no difference between the Roman administrative edict and the Jewish court's letter of summons.

207 The debtor who refuses to appear in court for foreclosure proceedings.

208 The verb כרז "to announce" is formed from Greek κῆρυξ "herald". Public announcements were usually made Mondays and Thursdays, the market days.

209 This was Roman practice in Egypt, cf. R. Taubenschlag, *The Law of Graeco-Roman Egypt in the Light of the Papyri*, New York 1944, p. 383. In Jewish Babylonia, the person who did not obey the first summons was put in the ban (Babli, 88a; against *Tosafot s. v.* ורבא).

210 In *Ketubot*: R. Mattaniah.

211 Once the validity of a claim has been established in court, the execution of the court order may proceed in the absence of the debtor.

212 In *Ketubot*: "they" (third person).

אַשְׁכָּחַת אֲמַר. חָנָן וְרִבִּי שִׁמְעוֹן אֲמָרוּ דָבָר אֶחָד. כְּמָה דְּמַר (רבי)(33b, line 69)
חָנָן. לֹא תִשָּׁבַע אֶלָּא בְסוֹף. כֵּן רִבִּי שִׁמְעוֹן אָמַר. לֹא תִשָּׁבַע אֶלָּא בְסוֹף. כְּמָא
דְאַתְּ אֲמַר. הֲלָכָה כְחָנָן. וְהָכָא הֲלָכָה כְרִבִּי שִׁמְעוֹן.

You find that one may say that Hanan[213] and Rebbi Simeon said the same thing[214]. Just as Hanan said, she shall swear only at the end, so Rebbi Simeon says, she shall swear only at the end. Just as you say, practice follows Hanan[215], so here practice follows Rebbi Simeon[216].

213 Mishnah 13:1. If a man travelled overseas and his wife asks permission from the court to sell of his property for her upkeep, Hanan says that she can sell and only swears at the end, if either the husband returns or notice of his death is received, that she did not retain any of the husband's property over and above the amount she was entitled to. Hanan's opponents also require her to swear before permission is granted by the court.

214 He admits the widow's oath only if she demands her *ketubah*. The Babli, 88b, rejects this statement and finds other cases to which R. Simeon may refer. It therefore also rejects the conclusion (Note 216) reached here.

215 Mishnah 13:1, on the highest authority of R. Joshua.

216 By inference from the decision of Hanan.

(fol. 32c) **משנה יב:** הוֹצִיאָה גֵט וְאֵין עִמּוֹ כְתוּבָּתָהּ גּוֹבָה כְתוּבָּתָהּ. כְּתוּבָּה וְאֵין עִמָּהּ גֵּט הִיא אוֹמֶרֶת אָבַד גִּיטִי וְהוּא אוֹמֵר אָבַד שׁוֹבְרִי וְכֵן בַּעַל חוֹב שֶׁהוֹצִיא שְׁטָר חוֹב וְאֵין עִמּוֹ פְּרוֹזְבּוֹל הֲרֵי אִילּוּ לֹא יִפָּרֵעוּ. רַבָּן שִׁמְעוֹן בֶּן גַּמְלִיאֵל אוֹמֵר מִן הַסַּכָּנָה וְאֵילָךְ אִשָּׁה גּוֹבָה בְּלֹא גֵט וּבַעַל חוֹב גּוֹבָה שֶׁלֹּא בִפְרוֹזְבּוֹל.

Mishnah 12: If she produced her bill of divorce without a *ketubah*, she collects her *ketubah*[217]. A *ketubah* without the bill of divorce when she says, I lost my bill of divorce but he says, I lost my receipt; similarly, the holder of an instrument of debt not accompanied by a *prozbol*[218]; these shall not be paid. Rabban Simeon ben Gamliel says, since the times of the persecution[219], a woman collects without the bill of divorce and the creditor collects without *prozbol*.

217 The obligatory minimum amount of the *ketubah* due the divorcee. She has to sign a receipt or the bill of divorce has to be torn up to prevent her from collecting again in another court.

218 If the debt documented in the instrument runs beyond a Sabbatical year, the debt is cancelled unless secured by a *prozbol*; cf. *Ševi'it* 10:3 ff., pp. 650 ff.

219 The Hadrianic decrees in Palestine in the aftermath of the war of Bar Kokhba when all Jewish ritual was prohibited. In those times, the *prozbol* and the distinctively Jewish bill of divorce had to be torn up as soon as they had been delivered. After the decrees were lifted in the reign of Antoninus Pius, the *status quo ante* was not restored. The fact of a divorce could be established by witnesses; the existence of a *prozbol* was assumed.

הלכה יא: (33b, line 71) מִנְכָסִים הַמְשׁוּעְבָּדִים כֵּיצַד. רַבִּי חִייָה בְּשֵׁם רַבִּי יוֹחָנָן. הַקּוֹרֵא עֲרֵר עַל מַעֲשֵׂה בֵית דִּין לֹא הַכֹּל הֵימֶינוּ. אָמַר לֵיהּ רַבִּי חִייָה בַּר אַבָּא. וְלֹא מַתְנִיתָא הִיא. הוֹצִיאָהּ גֵּט וְאֵין עִמּוֹ כְּתוּבָּה גּוֹבָה כְּתוּבָּתָהּ. אָמַר לֵיהּ רַבִּי יוֹחָנָן. בְּבִלְיָיא. מָן דִּגְלִית לָךְ חַסְפָּא מִן מַרְגָּלִיתָא אַתְּ אָמַר לִי. וְלֹא מַתְנִיתָא הִיא. רַב אָמַר. בְּמָקוֹם שֶׁאֵין כּוֹתְבִין שְׁטָר כְּתוּבָּה. אֲבָל בְּמָקוֹם שֶׁכּוֹתְבִין שְׁטָר כְּתוּבָּה מַה דְּהִיא מַפְקָה הִיא גוֹבָה. חָזַר וְאָמַר. אֲפִילוּ בְּמָקוֹם שֶׁכּוֹתְבִין כְּתוּבָּה גּוֹבָה הִיא. מָן רַב חֲיֵילֵהּ מַתְבָה יְתִיב. הָתִיב רִבִּי יוֹסֵי. וְהָא תַנֵּי. גּוֹבָה גִיטָּהּ וּמַטְמֶנֶת כְּתוּבָּתָהּ וְחוֹזֶרֶת וְגוֹבָה. אֵין שָׁם בֵּית דִּין. בְּאִינּוּן רְמְתוּן.[220] וְאֵין שָׁם עֵדִים. הָבוּ. בְּשֶׁהָלְכוּ לָהֶם לִמְדִינַת הַיָּם. אֵין שָׁם אוֹמוֹלוֹגִייָה. וְלֵית רַב אוֹמוֹלוֹגִייָה. אִית רַב אוֹמוֹלוֹגִייָה. כָּהֵן דָּמַר. אבר ברטסין[221] עֲבַד חוֹרָן. אִית לֵיהּ כְּהַהִיא דַּאֲמַר. אִי אֲבַד פְּרוּנֶה עֲבַד חוֹרָן.

הָתִיב רִבִּי בָּא. דְּהָא תַנֵּי. גּוּבָה בְגִיטָּהּ וּמַטְמֶנֶת כְּתוּבָתָהּ וּמִמְתֶּנֶת עַד שֶׁיָּמוּת וְחוֹזֶרֶת וְגוּבָה. אָמַר לֵיהּ רִבִּי יוֹסֵי בֵּירִבִּי בּוּן. וְלֹא עָלֶיהָ לְהָבִיא רְאָיָיה שֶׁהָיְיתָה מְשַׁמַּשְׁתּוֹ עַד שֶׁמֵּת.

Halakhah 11: "From encumbered property, how is that?" Rebbi Ḥiyya in the name of Rebbi Joḥanan: If somebody disputes a court document, he is not trustworthy[222]. Rebbi Ḥiyya bar Abba[223] said to him: Is that not the Mishnah? "If she produced her bill of divorce without a *ketubah*, she collects her *ketubah*[224]"! Rebbi Joḥanan said to him: Babylonian, after I removed the clay from the pearl, you say to me: Is that not the Mishnah? Rav said, at a place where one does not write a *ketubah*. But at a place where one writes a *ketubah*, what she produces she collects[225]. He changed his mind and said, she collects even at a place where one writes a *ketubah*[226]; let anyone powerful object to this! Rebbi Yose objected: Was it not stated: She might collect on her divorce document, hide her *ketubah*, and collect a second time[227]? If those died. Are there not witnesses[228]? Bring them! They went overseas. Is there not an agreement[230]? Is there no registrar of agreements? There is a registrar of agreements; as you say, if a document is lost, one writes a replacement[231]. This is what one says, if the *ketubah* was lost, one writes a new one[231]. Rebbi Abba objected: Was it not stated, she might collect on her divorce document, hide her *ketubah*, wait until he dies, and collect a second time[232]? Rebbi Yose bar Abun said to him: Would she not have to prove that she lived with him until he died?

220 The consensus of all commentators is to read דמתון.
221 The consensus of all commentators is to read אבד פרטסין.
222 A document made in one court will be accepted by another court as

valid.

223 He is the same R. Ḥiyya who stated the thesis; it is recounted how he was convinced to attribute the statement to R. Joḥanan.

224 Since the bill of divorce is a court document but the *ketubah* a private one, the court document which proves her status as a divorcee is enough to have another court direct that she be paid the divorce settlement. If divorce and payment were handled by the same court, she would not have to present anything.

225 This is all part of R. Joḥanan's argument, that the Mishnah does not prove anything since Rav gave it an interpretation which has nothing to do with the divorce bill being a court document. Rav declares that there are places where one would not write a *ketubah* if the amount stipulated in it did not exceed the legal minimum. Since legally required terms do not have to be written in the *ketubah* (Mishnaiot 4:7-12), the amount itself does not have to be written (4:7) for the marriage to be legal.

226 R. Joḥanan asserts that Rav in the end did agree with him. The Babli disagrees, 89a, and asserts that Rav restricts the Mishnah to cases in which no *ketubah* was written; R. Joḥanan's opinion there is attributed to Samuel.

227 A similar text is in the Babli, 16b. This must be part of a *baraita* which explains the precautions necessary to prevent that the same claim could be presented in different jurisdictions.

228 In case no receipt was written or the document presented for payment was shredded.

230 Greek ὁμολογία "consensus", a joint statement of payor and payee.

231 The fact that it is a replacement has to be stated in the new document. Therefore, the new document cannot be used fraudulently as an original.

232 From the heirs, as a widow.

(33c, line 10) רִבִּי זְעִירָא רִבִּי אֲבוּנָה בְּשֵׁם רַב. בִּמְקוֹם שֶׁכּוֹתְבִין שְׁטָר כְּתוּבָה. הוּא אוֹמֵר. כָּתַבְתִּי. וְהִיא אוֹמֶרֶת. לֹא כָתַבְתָּ. עָלֶיהָ לְהָבִיא רְאָיָיה שֶׁלֹּא כָתַב. וּבִמְקוֹם שֶׁאֵין כּוֹתְבִין שְׁטָר כְּתוּבָה וְהוּא אוֹמֵר. כָּתַבְתִּי. וְהִיא אוֹמֶרֶת. לֹא כָתַבְתָּ. עָלָיו לְהָבִיא רְאָיָיה שֶׁכָּתַב.

Rebbi Ze'ira, Rebbi Abuna in the name of Rav: At a place where one writes *ketubah* documents, if he says I wrote, but she says you did not write, the burden of proof is on her to prove that he did not write. But at a place where one does not write *ketubah* documents, if he says I wrote, but she says you did not write, the burden of proof is on him to prove that he wrote[233].

233 In the Babli, 89a, this is an inference of Rav Anan from a statement of Samuel. Local usage is always *prima facie* evidence in questions of existence of documents.

(33c, line 14) רִבִּי חִייָה בַּר אַבָּא אַשְׁכַּח פְּרוֹזְבּוֹלָא דְּרִבִּי יוֹנָתָן וַהֲוָה פָּרֵי מִיתַּן לֵיהּ. אָמַר לֵיהּ. לֵית אֲנָא צְרִיךְ לֵיהּ. וְתַנֵּי כֵן. נֶאֱמָן הַמַּלְוֶה לוֹמַר. שְׁטָר זֶה פְּרַעְתִּיו וּקְרַעְתִּיו. רִבִּי יִרְמְיָה בְּשֵׁם רִבִּי חִייָה. מַתְנִיתָא אָמְרָה כֵן. מִן הַסַּכָּנָה וְאֵילָךְ אִשָּׁה גּוֹבָה בְּלֹא גֵט וּבַעַל חוֹב גּוֹבֶה שֶׁלֹּא בִּפְרוֹזְבּוֹל. וְאֶיפְשַׁר כֵּן. לֹא פְרַעְתִּיו וּקְרַעְתִּיו. וְהָכָא פְּרַעְתִּיו וּקְרַעְתִּיו.

Rebbi Ḥiyya bar Abba found Rebbi Jonathan's *prozbol* and ran to give it to him[234]. He said to him, I do not need it[235], as it was stated: The creditor can be believed if he says, I discarded this document[236] and tore it up. Rebbi Jeremiah in the name of Rebbi Ḥiyya: The Mishnah says so: "Since the times of the persecution, a woman collects without the bill of divorce and the creditor collects without *prozbol*." Is that not impossible? I tore it without discarding[237]? Here, I discarded and tore it[238].

234 Since R. Ḥiyya is two generations younger than R. Jonathan, this must have been a very young R. Ḥiyya bar Abba.
235 In the Babli, *Giṭṭin* 37b, this is a statement of Rav Naḥman, that Rabban Simeon ben Gamliel's elimination of the requirement to produce a bill of divorce or *prozbol* is permanent.
236 The *prozbol*.

237 He cannot possibly ask for payment if he does not claim to have had a *prozbol* to discard.

238 This includes the claim that a *prozbol* was in existence when needed.

(fol. 32c) **משנה יג:** שְׁנֵי גִטִּין וּשְׁנֵי כְתוּבוֹת גּוֹבָה שְׁתֵּי כְתוּבוֹת. שְׁתֵּי כְתוּבוֹת וְגֵט אֶחָד אוֹ כְתוּבָּה וּשְׁנֵי גִטִּין אוֹ כְתוּבָּה וְגֵט וּמִיתָה אֵינָהּ גּוֹבָה אֶלָּא כְתוּבָּה אַחַת שֶׁהַמְגָרֵשׁ אֶת אִשְׁתּוֹ וּמַחֲזִירָהּ עַל מְנָת כְּתוּבָּה הָרִאשׁוֹנָה הֶחֱזִירָהּ. קָטָן שֶׁהִשִּׂיאוֹ אָבִיו כְּתוּבָּתָהּ קַיֶּימֶת שֶׁעַל מְנָת כֵּן קִיְּימָהּ. גֵּר שֶׁנִּתְגַּיֵּיר וְאִשְׁתּוֹ עִמּוֹ כְּתוּבָּתָהּ קַיֶּימֶת שֶׁעַל מְנָת כֵּן קִיְּימָהּ.

Mishnah 13: Two bills of divorce and two *ketubot*, she collects two *ketubot*[239]. Two *ketubot* and one bill of divorce, or one *ketubah* and two bills of divorce, or one *ketubah*, and a bill of divorce, and death; she collects only one *ketubah* since a person who divorces his wife and takes her back, takes her back on the basis of her prior *ketubah*[240]. If a minor was married off by his father, [his wife's] *ketubah* is valid since he kept her by that understanding[241]. If a proselyte converted together with his wife, her *ketubah* is valid since he kept her by that understanding[242].

239 She was twice married and twice divorced from the same man. After the first divorce, she did not collect her *ketubah*. When he married her the second time, he wrote her a new *ketubah* (which he did not have to do, as explained in the Mishnah.) Then the new *ketubah* is a new obligation, additional to the old one, not superseding it.

240 Without documentary proof to the contrary, a man married twice to the same woman is presumed to owe only one *ketubah*.

241 A minor cannot legally take on obligations. The *ketubah* becomes only valid at the moment the minor becomes an adult and stays married to his wife.

242 The rabbinic court will enforce all obligations the groom had undertaken for his bride in Gentile law.

(33c, line 19) **הלכה יב-יג:** הוֹצִיאָה גֵט וְאֵין עִמּוֹ כְּתוּבָּתָהּ גּוֹבָה כְּתוּבָּתָהּ כול'. שְׁנֵי גִיטִין וּשְׁתֵּי כְתוּבּוֹת כול'. וְהוּא שֶׁיְּהֵא הַגֵּט יוֹצֵא מִכְּתוּבָּה לִכְתוּבָּה. עַד כְּדוֹן בְּשָׁווֹת. הָיָה בְזוֹ מָנֶה וּבְזוֹ מָאתַיִם. רַב הוּנָא וְרַב יִרְמְיָה וְרַב חִסְדָּא. חַד אָמַר. גּוֹבָה בָּרִאשׁוֹנָה. וָחֳרָנָה אָמַר. גּוֹבָה בִשְׁנִייָה. וְהַתּוֹסֶפֶת גּוֹבָה מִן זְמַנָּהּ שֶׁלַּשְׁנִייָה.

Halakhah 12-13: "If she produced her bill of divorce without a *ketubah*, she collects her *ketubah*," etc. "Two bills of divorce and two *ketubot*," etc. But only if the bill of divorce is dated between the two *ketubot*[243]. So far if they are equal. If one was for a mina, the other for 200 [*zuz*][244]? Rav Huna and Rav Jeremiah[245] and Rav Ḥisda. One said, she collects the first one. The other said, she collects the second one and the excess[246] she collects from the date of the second.

243 Otherwise the second *ketubah* was only intended to replace the first which was thought to be lost; a similar argument is in the Babli, 90a.

244 This refers to the second case, that the divorcee presents two *ketubot* and one bill of divorce. If the amounts are equal, the second bill replaces the first. If they are unequal, they cannot replace one another.

245 Probably it should read: Rav Huna in the name of Rav Jeremiah; otherwise, the name of a first generation Amora should not appear between the names of two second generation Amoraim.

246 Even if the first *ketubah* should be larger, it now is a lien on the husband's real estate only from the date of the second. Any real estate sold between the dates of the two *ketubot* cannot be taken by the divorcee. In the Babli, 43b, Rav Huna states that if she only claims the smaller amount she collects from the date of the first *ketubah*, otherwise from the time of the second.

(33c, line 24) אָמַר רִבִּי חֲנַנְיָה קוֹמֵי רִבִּי מָנָא. לֵית הָדָא אָמְרָה. הָהֵן דְּיָזִיף מִן חַבְרֵיהּ וְחָזַר וְיָזִיף מִינֵיהּ צָרִיךְ מֵימַר. לְבַד מִן כַּרְטוֹסָא קַדְמַייָא דְאִית לִי גַבָּךְ. אוֹרְחָא דְאִיתְּתָא מֵימַר. אֲבַד פְּוּרְנָהּ עֲבִיד חוֹרָן. אֶלָּא כִּי אוֹרְחָא דְּבַר נַשׁ מֵימַר. אֲבַד כַּרְטִיסוֹ עֲבַד חוֹרָן. אֶלָּא כִּי אִיפְשָׁר יוֹדֵי לֵיהּ.

Rebbi Ḥanaiah said before Rebbi Mana: Does this not mean that if a person borrows from another, and then he borrows again, he has to declare "in addition to the first paper you have on me"[247]? It is frequent that a woman says, my *ketubah* is lost, write me another[248]. Is it frequent that a man say, my paper is lost, write me another[249]? But it is possible that he should declare for him[250].

247 Would two commercial contracts be considered under the same rules as *ketubot*?
248 The husband would have to oblige, leaving the wife with two documents.
249 The debtor does not have to oblige; if he agrees in order to retain the possibility of future loans, the new contract will certainly be written so that the prior contract would be invalidated.
250 Instead of writing in the contract, the debtor could declare his multiple indebtedness in front of witnesses.

(33c, line 28) רִבִּי יוּדָן בַּר שִׁיקְלִי אֲעִיל עוֹבְדָא קוֹמֵי רִבִּי יוֹסֵי. לֹא כֵן אָמַר רִבִּי אַבָּהוּ בְּשֵׁם רִבִּי יוֹחָנָן. שְׁטַר שֶׁלָּוָה בוֹ וּפְרָעוֹ אַל יִלְוֶה בּוֹ בְּאוֹתוֹ הַיּוֹם. אָמַר לֵיהּ. כָּאן בִּשְׁפָרְעוֹ. כָּאן בְּשֶׁלֹּא פְרָעוֹ. תַּנֵּי רִבִּי חָנָן קוֹמֵי רִבִּי הִילָא. תְּרֵין אֲמוֹרִין. חַד אָמַר. לִכְתוּבָה אֲבָל לֹא לִתְנָאִין. וְחָרָנָה אָמַר. בֵּין לִכְתוּבָה בֵּין לִתְנָאִין.

Rebbi Yudan from Sicily[251] brought this case[252] before Rebbi Yose: Did not Rebbi Abbahu[253] say in the name of Rebbi Joḥanan: Nobody should use a paper on which he borrowed and paid the loan back to take out another loan on the same day²⁵⁴? He said to him, here if he had paid back, there if he did not pay back²⁵⁵. ²⁵⁶Rebbi Ḥanin stated before Rebbi Hila: Two Amoraïm, one said for *ketubah* but not for individual stipulations, the other said, both for *ketubah* and for individual stipulations.

251 Or, "son of Sicinius" (E. G.).

252 The statement that a man remarrying his divorcee can do that on the basis of the prior *ketubah*.

253 In the Babli, *Baba Meṣi'a* 17a, R. Assi (Yasa) in the name of R. Johanan.

254 If the loan was paid back the day it was taken out (otherwise the paper would be predated and invalid). The reason given in the Babli is that the rights given by the borrower to the lender by handing over the contract to the lender were annulled by the repayment and cannot be resurrected.

255 Obviously, if the *ketubah* was paid after the divorce, at the remarriage the husband has to execute a new *ketubah*. The Mishnah refers only to the case that the husband prefers to remarry instead of paying up.

256 This text is quoted in *Demay* 6:3, Notes 88-89. It refers to the validity of the *ketubah* for the remarried divorcee. From the Babli, 90a, one might be led to read this statement as belonging to the next paragraph, about the *ketubah* of a minor's wife, but this does not fit the interpretation given the statement in *Demay*.

(33c, line 31) נִיחָא גֵּר. קָטָן. וְקָטָן מְגָרֵשׁ. אָמַר רִבִּי חַגַּיי. קִייַמְתִּיהּ כַּיי דָּמַר רִבִּי לָעְזָר בְּשֵׁם רִבִּי חֲנִינָה. וְהוּא שֶׁבָּא עָלֶיהָ מִשֶּׁנִּתְפַּקֵּחַ וּמִשֶּׁנִּשְׁתַּפָּה. וְכָא הוּא שֶׁבָּא עָלֶיהָ מִשֶׁהִגְדִּיל.

One understands a proselyte²⁵⁷. A minor²⁵⁸? Can a minor divorce²⁵⁹? Rebbi Ḥaggai said, I explained it following what Rebbi Eleazar said in the name of Rebbi Ḥanina: Only if he slept with her when he regained sight or became sane mentally[260]. And here, if he slept with her after he reached adulthood.

257 He contracted the marriage as an adult. His conversion cannot invalidate his contractual obligations.

258 He cannot enter into valid contracts. If he dies, how can his wife enforce her claims against the minor's heirs whose rights are biblical?

259 Since a minor cannot act in law, he cannot divorce his wife and her *ketubah* cannot become due.

260 In Chapter 1, Note 146. The wife of a deaf-mute or insane man can collect a *ketubah* only if for some period she lived with him while he was legally competent. At that time, their marital relations validate the contract.

מי שהיה נשוי נשוי פרק עשירי

משנה א: (fol. 33c) מִי שֶׁהָיָה נָשׂוּי שְׁתֵּי נָשִׁים וָמֵת הָרִאשׁוֹנָה קוֹדֶמֶת לַשְּׁנִיָּיה. יוֹרְשֵׁי הָרִאשׁוֹנָה קוֹדְמִין לְיוֹרְשֵׁי הַשְּׁנִיָּיה. נָשָׂא אֶת הָרִאשׁוֹנָה וָמֵתָה נָשָׂה אֶת הַשְּׁנִיָּיה וּמֵת הוּא. שְׁנִיָּיה וְיוֹרְשֶׁיהָ קוֹדְמִין לְיוֹרְשֵׁי הָרִאשׁוֹנָה.

Mishnah 1: If somebody was married to two women when he died, the first one[1] precedes the second[2], and the heirs of the first precede the heirs of the second[3]. If the first one he had married died[4], then he married the second one and he himself died, the second and her heirs[5] precede the heirs of the first.

1 The wife whose *ketubah* is dated earlier.

2 Since a *ketubah* is a mortgage lien, the holder of the earlier mortgage has the right to foreclose any real estate before the holder of the later mortgage may foreclose. The rules of this Chapter are in essence rules of privileged creditors in bankruptcy proceedings since they become irrelevant if the estate is large enough to satisfy everybody.

3 If the wives die before they have collected their respective *ketubot*, the heirs collect these from the estate (Mishnah 4:10).

4 The husband then inherits his deceased wife's property; only after his death can the first wife's children claim her *ketubah* as inheritance.

5 The widow is a mortgage holder, a creditor of the estate; the first wife's children are heirs. The heirs can lay their hands on the estate only after all outstanding obligations are paid. If the widow dies before she is paid, her claim passes to her heirs.

הלכה א: מִי שֶׁהָיָה נָשׂוּי שְׁתֵּי נָשִׁים כול'. מַתְנִיתָא לְעִנְיָין כְּתוּבָּה. (33d line 2) אֲבָל לְעִנְיָין מְזוֹנוֹת שְׁתֵּיהֶן שָׁווֹת. כְּתוּבָּה וּקְבוּרָה מִי קוֹדֵם. כְּתוּבָּה וּמִלְוָה בְּעֵדִים מִי קוֹדֵם. כְּתוּבָּה וּפַרְנָסַת בָּנוֹת מִי קוֹדֵם. מָאן דְּאָמַר. גּוֹבִין פַּרְנָסָה מִן הַמְשׁוּעְבָּדִין. פַּרְנָסַת בָּנוֹת קוֹדֶמֶת. וּמָאן דְּאָמַר. אֵין גּוֹבִין פַּרְנָסָה מִן הַמְשׁוּעְבָּדִין. אֵין פַּרְנָסַת בָּנוֹת קוֹדֶמֶת.

Halakhah 1: "If somebody was married to two women," etc. The Mishnah refers to *ketubah*, but for sustenance both are equal[6]. Between *ketubah* and burial, what has precedence[7]? Between *ketubah* and a loan attested to by witnesses, what has precedence[8]? Between *ketubah* and daughters' dowry, what has precedence? For him who says[9], one collects for dowry from mortgaged property, daughters' dowry has precedence. But for him who says, one does not collect for dowry from mortgaged property, daughters' dowry does not have precedence.

6 If both widows prefer not to receive their *ketubah* but to be sustained by the estate, they have to be treated equally. The statement is also in Tosephta 10:1.

7 The estate is only sufficient either for the expenses of the man's burial or his widow's *ketubah*. The question is not answered, maybe because it never arose in practice. Since the deceased has to be buried before questions about payment are asked, it seems that the burial is charged to public welfare.

8 For R. Tarphon in Mishnaiot 9:2-3, the creditor has precedence since he depends on the testimony of witnesses who might die but the widow depends on the written *ketubah*.

9 R. Ḥanina in Halakhah 6:6, against R. Joḥanan (Notes 93, 96-97). The disagreement is also quoted in 13:3 (36a l. 15).

(33d line 7) לֹא אָמַר אֶלָּא מֵתָה. הָא נִתְגָּרְשָׁה כְּבַעַל חוֹב הִיא. כְּהָדָא דְּתַנֵּי. נָשָׂא אִשָּׁה וְכָתַב לָהּ כְּתוּבָּה. גֵּירְשָׁהּ וְלֹא נָתַן לָהּ כְּתוּבָּה. נָשָׂא אַחֶרֶת וְכָתַב לָהּ

כְּתוּבָה. הֶחֱזִיר אֶת הָרִאשׁוֹנָה וְכָתַב לָהּ כְּתוּבָה עַל כְּתוּבָּתָהּ הָרִאשׁוֹנָה. שֶׁהָרִאשׁוֹנָה קוֹדֶמֶת לַשְּׁנִיָּיה וְיוֹרְשֶׁיהָ. וְהַשְּׁנִיָּיה וְיוֹרְשֶׁהָ קוֹדְמִין לְיוֹרְשֵׁי הָרִאשׁוֹנָה.

It says only, "she died". Therefore, if she was divorced, her status is that of a creditor[10]. As it was stated[11]: "He married a woman and wrote her a *ketubah*. He divorced her but did not pay the *ketubah*. He married another woman and wrote her a *ketubah*. He took back the first one and wrote her a *ketubah* in addition to the first *ketubah*[12]. The [second *ketubah*] of the first [wife] has precedence over that of the second [wife] and her heirs, and the second [wife] and her heirs have precedence over the heirs of the first.[13]"

10 If the first one was divorced, her claim has preference over the claims of the second and her heirs.

11 Tosephta 10:1.

12 Then the husband died and his estate is not sufficient to satisfy all three *ketubot*.

13 That text is elliptic but its meaning is clear; it is not necessary to assume that the original text was that of the Tosephta and was shortened in transmission. The Tosephta reads: "The first *ketubah* of the first [wife] has precedence over the second and her heirs; the second and her heirs have precedence over the second *ketubah* of the first." Any prior document has precedence over any later one.

(33d line 11) אָמַר בֶּן עַזַּאי. יוֹרְשֵׁי הָרִאשׁוֹנָה אוֹמְרִים לְיוֹרְשֵׁי הַשְּׁנִיָּיה. אִם כְּבַעַל חוֹב אַתֶּם טְלוּ אֶת שֶׁלָּכֶם וּצְאוּ. וְאִם לָאו אָנוּ וְאַתֶּם נַחֲלוֹק בְּשָׁוֶה. אָמַר לוֹ רִבִּי עֲקִיבָה. בְּנֵי שְׁנִיָּיה קָפְצָה עֲלֵיהֶן יְרוּשַׁת תּוֹרָה וְנוֹטְלִין כְּתוּבַּת אִמָּן וְחוֹזְרִין וְחוֹלְקִין. רִבִּי מָנָא אָמַר. בְּשֶׁיֵּשׁ שָׁם דֵּינָר יָתֵר נֶחְלְקוּ. אֲבָל אִם אֵין שָׁם דֵּינָר יָתֵר אַף רִבִּי עֲקִיבָה יוֹדֶה לְבֶן נַנָּס שֶׁאִילּוּ וְאִילּוּ חוֹלְקִין בְּשָׁוֶה. אָמַר לֵיהּ רִבִּי יוֹסֵי בֵּירִבִּי בּוּן. הַךְ דְּלָא תַנִּיתָא פְּלִיגְנָא אַתְּ עֲבַד לֵיהּ פְּלִיגְנָא. אֶלָּא בִּשְׁאֵין שָׁם יָתֵר דֵּינָר נֶחְלְקוּ. אֲבָל אִם יֵשׁ שָׁם יָתֵר דֵּינָר אַף בֶּן נַנָּס יוֹדֵי לְרִבִּי

עֲקִיבָה. בְּנֵי שְׁנִייָה קָפְצָה עֲלֵיהֶן יְרוּשַׁת תּוֹרָה וְנוֹטְלִין כְּתוּבַּת אִמָּן וְחוֹזְרִין וְחוֹלְקִין.

Ben Azay[14] says[15], the heirs of the first say to the heirs of the second: If you are creditors, take what is yours and leave[16]; otherwise let us split evenly between yourselves and us[17]. Rebbi Aqiba said to him: Biblical inheritance "jumped" on the sons of the second; they take their mother's *ketubah* and come back to split[18]. Rebbi Mana[19] said, they disagree if there is an excess denar[20]. But if there is no excess denar, even Rebbi Aqiba will agree with Ben Nanas[14] that both parties split evenly[21]. Rebbi Yose ben Rebbi Abun said to him, a situation which was stated without disagreement you turn into a disagreement. They must disagree if there is no excess denar. But if there is an excess denar even Ben Nanas[14] agrees with Rebbi Aqiba that biblical inheritance "jumped" on the sons of the second; they take their mother's *ketubah* and come back to split[18].

14 Later in the discussion, the author is called Ben Nanas in ms., *editio princeps*, and all ms. sources of the Babli, 90b. However, in the Constantinople edition with the commentary of Joshua Benvenist, the name is Ben Azay in both occurrences. Ben Nanas is mentioned in Mishnah 5.

15 This refers to the second case in the Mishnah, where the first wife died and the second becomes a widow. In that case, the husband inherited the first wife's property; the first wife's children have claim to inherit their mother's *ketubah* only by rabbinic institution, cf. Mishnah 4:10, whereas the widow (or her children in her stead) has a contractual claim on the estate. If the estate is larger than the sum of the two *ketubot* by at least "one excess denar", there is no problem. All children can inherit their mother's *ketubah* and part of the remainder. But if the estate is not sufficient and payment of the "*ketubah* of male children" instituted in 4:10 would eliminate biblical inheritance rules, the question is whether rabbinic inheritance can or cannot supersede biblical inheritance (which would treat

all children equally except that a male firstborn counts for two.)

16 The rabbinic institution of "*ketubah* of male children" eliminates the biblical laws of inheritance. The sons of the second wife take their mother's *ketubah* as inheritance from their mother, not their father; what remains of the estate is taken by the sons of the first wife as "*ketubah* of male children". In Tosephta 10:1, this is presented as anonymous rule: "If there is an excess denar, both parties take their mothers' *ketubot* and the remainder is split evenly; if there is no excess denar, the second wife or her heirs take her *ketubah* and the remainder is divided evenly.

17 If the sons of the second wife want to deprive the sons of the first of their "*ketubah* of male children", they lose their own *ketubah* and everybody becomes an heir in biblical law. Since this would be to the detriment of the sons of the second wife, the first alternative is operative.

18 The sons of the second wife take their mother's *ketubah* under the rules of creditors and the remainder is biblical inheritance split among all sons since rabbinic inheritance decrees cannot eliminate biblical rules if the estate is too small.

19 R. Mana II, contemporary of R. Yose ben R. Abun.

20 It is very difficult to accept that the second marriage invalidates the "*ketubah* of male children" of the first marriage.

21 It is equally difficult to accept that the *ketubah* of the second has the status of a creditor's claim only for the widow but not for their heirs. Since the argument of R. Yose ben R. Abun is reasonable, there seems to be no possibility to claim a copyist's corruption.

(33d line 20) וְהַחוֹב מְמָעֵט. וְדִכְוָותָהּ. וְהַחוֹב מַרְבֶּה. הֵיךְ עֲבִידָא. הָיָה שָׁם שָׂדֶה וְהִיא עֲתִידָה לַחֲזוֹר בַּיּוֹבֵל אַתְּ רוֹאֶה אוֹתָן כְּאִילוּ.

Debts diminish and, equally, debts add[22]. How is this? If there was a field which in the future would return in the jubilee year, you consider it virtual[23] [property].

22 In determining whether an estate is larger than the sum of the *ketubot* due, one deducts debts payable by the estate and adds debts due to it. The Babli agrees, 90b.

23 The example is purely theoretical since the institution of the jubilee disappeared under the Israelite monarchy; cf. Introduction to Tractate Ševi'it. The practical implication is that the "*ketubah* of male children" is due even if the estate reaches the required size only by counting contracts far into the future.

(33d line 22) הֵיךְ עֲבִידָא. קִידֵּשׁ רָחֵל וְכָנַס לֵאָה וְחָזַר וְכָנַס רָחֵל. עַל דַּעְתִּין דְּרַבָּנִין רָחֵל קוֹדֶמֶת. וְעַל דַּעְתֵּיהּ דְּרִבִּי אֶלְעָזָר בֶּן עֲזַרְיָה לֹא קוֹדָמֶת. אוֹמְרִים. אַף רִבִּי לָעְזָר מוֹדֵי. מֵאַחַר שֶׁחָזַר וְכָנַס רָחֵל קוֹדֶמֶת. לְמָה זֶה דוֹמֶה. לְאֶחָד שֶׁלָּוָה מֵחֲבֵירוֹ וְאָמַר לוֹ. אִם לֹא הֶחֱזַרְתִּי לָךְ מִיכָּן עַד י'ב חוֹדֶשׁ יְהִיוּ כָל־נְכָסַיי מְשׁוּעְבָּדִים לָךְ. הִגִּיעַ י'ב חוֹדֶשׁ וְלֹא הֶחֱזִיר נִשְׁתַּעְבְּדוּ הַנְּכָסִים מִכָּן וְלָבָא. אֲבָל אִם אָמַר לוֹ. לֹא יְהוּ נְכָסַיי מְשׁוּעְבָּדִים לָךְ אֶלָּא לְאַחַר י'ב חוֹדֶשׁ. לֹא נִשְׁתַּעְבֵּד אֶלָּא לְאַחַר י'ב חוֹדֶשׁ. יָמִים שֶׁבֵּנְתַיִים תַּפְלוּגְתָּא דְּרִבִּי מֵאִיר וְרַבָּנִין. עַל דַּעְתֵּיהּ דְּרִבִּי מֵאִיר בִּשְׁטָר נִתְחַיְּיבוּ הַנְּכָסִים. עַל דַּעְתִּין דְּרַבָּנִין בַּכֶּסֶף נִתְחַיְּיבוּ.

How is that[24]? If he preliminarily married Rachel, definitively married Leah[25], and only then definitively married Rachel. In the opinion of the rabbis, Rachel has precedence; in the opinion of Rebbi Eleazar ben Azariah she does not have precedence[26]. They say, even Rebbi Eleazar will agree that since in the end he definitively married Rachel, Rachel has precedence[27]. To what can this be compared? To one who took out a loan from another person and said to him, if I have not paid it back by twelve months, all my properties shall be mortgaged to you. If the twelfth month arrived and he has not paid back, his properties become mortgaged from that moment on[28]. But if he said, all my properties shall be mortgaged to you *only* after twelve months, they become mortgaged only after twelve months. The status of the days in between[29] is in dispute between Rebbi Meïr and the rabbis[30]. In Rebbi Meïr's opinion, the properties became pledged by the document[31]. In the rabbis' opinion, the properties became pledged by the money[32].

24 This sentence does not refer to anything; it seems to be a copyist's error.

25 By combining preliminary and definitive marriage (cf. Chapter 1, Note 24).

26 In Mishnah 5:1, R. Eleazar ben Azariah holds that a *ketubah* becomes executable only after definitive marriage; therefore, Leah's *ketubah* in effect should predate Rachel's even though Rachel's was executed earlier, at the time of her preliminary wedding. For the rabbis, the date of the contract is the determining factor.

27 R. Eleazar ben Azariah agrees that if both contracts are executable, the dates of the contracts determine precedence. He only holds that before definitive marriage the contract is not executable.

28 The moment of the loan. If the debtor had sold any real estate in the meantime, the creditor can have regress on it since the contract predates the sale even if it becomes executable only later.

29 The days between the signing of the contract and the end of 12 months when the contract becomes executable.

30 There are many disputes between R. Meïr and the other rabbis and it is a matter of conjecture to which dispute this refers. R. Moses Margalit points to a *baraita* quoted in the Babli *Baba meṣi'a* 13b, in which R. Meïr states that a loan contract allows regress on alienated property only if this was stated in the contract; but the rabbis hold that such regress is a matter of law and does not have to be stated explicitly.

31 The alienation clause becomes activated only after 12 months; it cannot apply to properties sold during these months.

32 The moment the loan money changed hands, the alienation clause became executable whether written or not.

(fol. 33c) **משנה ב:** מִי שֶׁהָיָה נָשׂוּי לִשְׁתֵּי נָשִׁים וָמֵתוּ וְאַחַר כָּךְ מֵת הוּא וְהַיְתוֹמִים מְבַקְשִׁים כְּתוּבַּת אִמּוֹתֵיהֶן וְאֵין שָׁם אֶלָּא כְדֵי שְׁתֵּי כְתוּבּוֹת חוֹלְקִין בְּשָׁוֶה. הָיָה שָׁם מוֹתָר דֵּינָר אִילּוּ נוֹטְלִין כְּתוּבַּת אִמָּן וְאִילּוּ נוֹטְלִין כְּתוּבַּת אִמָּן. וְאִם אָמְרוּ הַיְתוֹמִים אֲנַחְנוּ מַעֲלִים עַל נִכְסֵי אָבִינוּ יָפֶה דֵּנָר כְּדֵי שֶׁיִּטְּלוּ כְתוּבַּת אִמָּן אֵין שׁוֹמְעִין לָהֶן אֶלָּא שָׁמִין אֶת הַנְּכָסִים בְּבֵית דִּין.

Mishnah 2: If somebody was married to two women who both died, and then he died, and the orphans demand their mothers' *ketubot*, if [the estate] is sufficient only for both *ketubot* they split evenly[33]. If there was an excess denar, these take their mother's *ketubah* and those take their mother's *ketubah*[34]. If the orphans say[35], we accept the properties of our father for the value of an extra denar in order to take their mother's *ketubah*; one does not listen to them but one appraises the properties in court.

33 If there are *n* sons, the estate is divided into *n* equal parts. If one of the children is a male firstborn, the estate is divided into *n*+1 parts and the firstborn takes two. If there are no sons, only *n* daughters, the estate is divided into *n* equal parts.

34 The remainder is split evenly between the heirs.

35 If the *ketubot* were unequal, the sons of the mother with the larger *ketubah* would be interested to receive the *ketubah* rather than the inheritance. Similarly, if the *ketubot* were equal but one wife had few sons, the other many, the few sons would gain if they could split their mother's *ketubah* between them and not have to share with their many halfbrothers. These are willing to take some property at an inflated value in order to receive more than the other woman's sons.

(33d line 30) **הלכה ב:** מִי שֶׁהָיָה נָשׂוּי לִשְׁתֵּי נָשִׁים כול'. הָדָא הִיא דָּמַר רִבִּי אִימִּי. כְּדֵי שֶׁיְּהֵא אָדָם מָצוּי לִיתֵּן לְבִתּוֹ בְעַיִן יָפָה. מֵאַתָּה אֲפִילוּ אֵין שָׁם יָתֵר דֵּינָר. אָמַר רִבִּי אָבוּן. בְּשָׁעָה שֶׁאַתְּ יָכוֹל לְקַיֵּים דִּבְרֵיהֶן וְדִבְרֵי תוֹרָה אַתְּ

מְקַיְּים דִּבְרֵיהֶן וְדִבְרֵי תוֹרָה. בְּשָׁעָה שֶׁאַתְּ אֵין יָכוֹל לְקַיֵּים דִּבְרֵיהֶן וּלְקַיֵּים דִּבְרֵי תוֹרָה אַתְּ מְבַטֵּל דִּבְרֵיהֶן וּמְקַיֵּים דִּבְרֵי תוֹרָה.

Halakhah 2: "If somebody was married to two women," etc. That refers to what Rebbi Immi said, that a man should be induced to give generously to his daughter[36]. If that is so, then even if there is no excess denar[37]? Rebbi Abun said, in case you can uphold their words with the words of the Torah, you uphold their words with the words of the Torah[38]. But in case you cannot uphold their words with the words of the Torah, you disregard their words and uphold the words of the Torah.

36   Halakhah 4:12, Note 238.
37   If the "*ketubah* of male children" was instituted so that people would increase their daughters' dowries in the knowledge that the money will be transferred to their grandchildren, it does not seem reasonable to restrict the rules to sufficiently large estates.

38   If the estate is large enough, one can distribute the "*ketubah* of male children" and still have an estate which is distributed according to biblical law (*Num.* 27:6-11). Cf. M. A. Friedman, *Jewish Marriage in Palestine*, Tel Aviv 1980, vol. I, pp. 381 ff.

(33d line 35) רִבִּי יוּדָה בַּר פָּזִי בְּשֵׁם רִבִּי יוֹסֵי בֶּן חֲנִינָה. מֵת אֶחָד מִן הָאַחִין כּוּלְּהוֹן חוֹלְקִין בְּשָׁוֶה. אָמַר רִבִּי מָנָא. לָכֵן צְרִיכָה בְּשֶׁלֹּא חִלְקוּ. שֶׁלֹּא תֹאמַר. יֵעֲשֶׂה כְּמִי שֶׁאֵינוֹ כָן וְתִירָשֶׁנּוּ בִתּוֹ. הָיָה שָׁם בְּכוֹר. אַתְּ אָמַר. הַבְּכוֹר נוֹטֵל פִּי שְׁנַיִם. מָהוּ נוֹטֵל. פִּי שְׁנַיִם בְּבֵתוֹ אוֹ פִּי שְׁנַיִם בְּכָל הָאַחִים. תַּנֵּי רִבִּי הוֹשַׁעְיָה. הָיוּ שָׁם שְׁתֵּי כִיתֵּי בָנוֹת כּוּלְּהוֹן חוֹלְקוֹת בְּשָׁוֶה. הָיָה שָׁם בְּכוֹר אַתְּ אָמַר. הַבְּכוֹר נוֹטֵל פִּי שְׁנַיִם. מָהוּ נוֹטֵל פִּי שְׁנַיִם. נוֹטֵל פִּי שְׁנַיִם בְּבֵתוֹ אוֹ פִּי שְׁנַיִם בְּכָל הַכְּתוּבּוֹת.

Rebbi Judah bar Pazi in the name of Rebbi Yose ben Ḥanina: If one of the brothers died, they all split evenly[39]. Rebbi Mana said, that is necessary if they did not yet divide the estate. You should not say that he should be considered nonexistent and his house should inherit from him[40]. If there was a (male) firstborn, you say the firstborn takes a double portion[41]. What does he take? A double portion among his house or among all brothers[42]? Rebbi Hoshaia stated: If there were two groups of daughters, they all split evenly[43]. If there was a firstborn, you say the firstborn takes a double portion. What does he take? A double portion among his house or among all *ketubot*?[44]

39 If he dies without issue, all his paternal brothers inherit from him.

40 If the estate had been distributed by the time of his death, this would be a simple case of inheritance; in the absence of children his maternal brothers would inherit. But if the estate was not yet distributed, the question is whether the heirs are considered to have acquired their part at the moment of their father's death or whether they acquire only at the time of the actual distribution. Clearly, for the part of the estate which is distributed under biblical law, all surviving full and halfbrothers inherit equally. But for the "*ketubah* of male children", in the second case, only the maternal brothers share his part, while in the first they all share. R. Mana states here that an inheritance is acquired at the time of death of the bequeather. In the Babli, *Baba batra* 107a, this latter opinion is attributed to Rav; Samuel holds that "brothers at the distribution of the estate have the status of buyers from one another", i. e., their status is determined only at the time of distribution. Since the Babli follows Samuel in money matters, it will deny R. Mana's assertion.

41 *Deut.* 21:16-17. In that example, the firstborn takes $2/3$ since there are only two sons.

42 Is the "*ketubah* of male children" of the other wife exempt from the biblical rule of the firstborn?

43 Mishnah 4:10 refers only to male children. If all children are female, they each receive an equal share of the estate.

44 It is not clear why this question is repeated since R. Hoshaia does not deal with sons at all and a female firstborn has no special rights.

(33d line 42) מֵאֵמָתַי שָׁמִין לָהֶן. תַּלְמִידוֹי דְּרִבִּי מָנָא אָמְרִין. בְּסוֹף. אָמַר לוֹן רִבִּי יוֹסֵי בֵּירִבִּי בּוּן. לָא אַתּוּן דְּאָמְרִין בְּשֵׁם רבנין.[45] לְכוֹן צְרִיכָא בְּשָׁלֹא חִלְּקוּ. אֲבָל מִשָּׁעָה רִאשׁוֹנָה שנײם[46] לָהֶן.

At which point in time does one appraise? The students of Rebbi Mana say, at the end[47]. Rebbi Yose ben Rebbi Abun said to them, are you not those who speak in the name of your teacher, "that is necessary if they did not yet divide the estate"[48]? But one assesses from the first moment[49]!

45 Probably one should read רבכון, i. e., רַבְּכוֹן "your teacher" (R. Mana) instead of רַבָּנִין "the rabbis".
46 Almost certainly this should be שמים "one assesses".
47 At the time of distribution.
48 If the share of each son in the "*ketubah* of male sons" is determined at the moment of their father's death, the value of the estate must be determined at that moment since the "*ketubah* of male sons" depends on that value.
49 The moment of the father's death. This is asserted in the Babli, 91a/b, by Rav Naḥman, the highest authority in money matters. In his opinion, the status of the estate is not connected with the point in time at which the heirs take possession of their inheritance.

(fol. 33c) **משנה ג**: הָיוּ שָׁם נְכָסִים בָּרָאוּי אֵינָן כִּבְמוּחְזָק. רִבִּי שִׁמְעוֹן אוֹמֵר אַף עַל פִּי שֶׁיֵּשׁ שָׁם נְכָסִים שֶׁאֵין לָהֶן אַחֲרָיוּת אֵינוֹ כְלוּם עַד שֶׁיִּהְיוּ שָׁם נְכָסִים שֶׁיֵּשׁ לָהֶן אַחֲרָיוּת יוֹתֵר עַל שְׁתֵּי כְתוּבּוֹת דֵּינָר.

Mishnah 3: If the estate contained expected property, it does not have the status of property in actual possession[50]. Rebbi Simeon says, even if there was no mortgageable property[51], it does not count unless there is mortgageable property[52] in the value of at least a denar more than the two *ketubot*.

50 If the expected inheritance from a grandfather would bring the father's estate over the limit for distribution of the "*ketubah* of male sons", it cannot be counted until it becomes due. Similarly, the double portion of a male firstborn is restricted to "all that is present with him" at his father's death (*Deut*. 21:17); the firstborn has no special rights to any inheritance from other members of their family coming to the sons after the father's death.

51 Movables.

52 Real estate. R. Simeon holds that a *ketubah* is a mortgage lien and, therefore, cannot be satisfied by movable property.

(33d line 44) **הלכה ג**: הָיוּ שָׁם נְכָסִים בָּרָאוּי כּוּל׳. רִבִּי מָנָא אָמַר. בְּעִיקַּר שְׁתֵּי כְתוּבּוֹת פְּלִיגִין. רִבִּי שִׁמְעוֹן אוֹמֵר. קַרְקַע. וְרַבָּנִין אָמְרִין. מִטַלְטְלִין. בְּאוֹתָהּ הַדֵּינָר כָּל־עַמָּא מוֹדֵיי שֶׁהוּא מִטַלְטֵל. רִבִּי יוֹסֵי בֵּירִבִּי בּוּן אָמַר. כָּל־עַמָּא מוֹדֵיי בְּעִיקַּר שְׁתֵּי כְתוּבוֹת שֶׁהֵן קַרְקַע. מַה פְּלִיגִין. בְּאוֹתוֹ דֵינָר. רִבִּי שִׁמְעוֹן אוֹמֵר. קַרְקַע. וְרַבָּנִין אָמְרִין. מִטַלְטְלִין. רִבִּי בָּא בַּר זַבְדָּא בְּשֵׁם רַב. בְּרַם נָהֲגוּ בְסוּרְיָא לִהְיוֹת גּוֹבִין מִן הַנְּחוֹשֶׁת וּמִן הַצּוּעוֹת. רִבִּי אַבָּהוּ בְּשֵׁם רִבִּי יוֹחָנָן. וּבִלְבַד מִן הַצּוּעוֹת שֶׁבְּאוֹתוֹ הַלַּיְלָה. רַב שְׁמוּאֵל בַּר נַחְמָן בְּשֵׁם רִבִּי יוֹחָנָן. נָהֲגוּ הָעָם בַּעֲרָבִיָּיא לִהְיוֹת גּוֹבָה מִן הַבּוֹשֶׁם וּמִן הַגְּמָלִים. וְדִכְוָותָהּ. בִּלְבַד מִן הַבּוֹשֶׂם שֶׁבְּאוֹתוֹ הַלַּיְלָה. אַרְמַלְתָּא דְּרִבִּי חוּנָה גָבִי לָהּ מִן הַמִּטַלְטְלִין כְּמִנְהַג מְקוֹמָהּ.

Halakhah 3: "If the estate contained expected property," etc. Rebbi Mana said, they disagree about the basic claim of the two *ketubot*[53]. Rebbi Simeon says, real estate, but the rabbis say, movables. But for the excess denar everybody agrees that it is movable. Rebbi Yose ben Rebbi Abun said, everybody agrees about the basic claim of the two *ketubot* that it must be real estate. Where do they disagree? About the excess denar, where Rebbi Simeon says, real estate, but the rabbis say, movables. Rebbi Abba bar Zavda in the name of Rav: But in Syria they routinely collect from bronze and bedspreads[54]. Rebbi Abbahu in the name of Rebbi Johanan: Only from bedspreads of that night[55]. Rav Samuel bar Nahman in the name of Rebbi Johanan: The people in Arabia routinely collect from camels and spices[56]. Similarly, only from spices of that night[57]? Rebbi Huna's widow collected from movables following her place's custom[58].

53   It is not totally clear what "the basic claim of the *ketubah*" means. Is it only the required 100/200 *zuz* or is it that amount plus any dowry which became the husband's property, to exclude any sum the husband wrote into the *ketubah* in excess of minimum and dowry? The second version is preferred by the classical commentators.

54   Articles of trade, at places were Jews were not traditionally land owners.

55   He wants to restrict the recovery of the *ketubah* to the articles of the dowry brought by the bride.

56   Since they are bedouin traders, they do not possess any real estate; their equivalent of real estate are camels (affirmed in the Babli, 67a, by the same authors); their object of trade is spices.

57   Since it would be nonsensical to require the spices brought by the bride to be available to the widow; the condition about bedspreads is also nonsensical.

58   The famous Gaonic decree that *ketubot* be paid from movables is nothing but an application of the Yerushalmi rule that local conditions overrule general statements.

(fol. 33c) **משנה ד**: מִי שֶׁהָיָה נָשׂוּי שָׁלֹשׁ נָשִׁים וָמֵת כְּתוּבָּתָהּ שֶׁלָּזוֹ מָנֶה וְשֶׁלָּזוֹ מָאתַיִם וְשֶׁלָּזוֹ שְׁלֹשׁ מֵאוֹת וְאֵין שָׁם אֶלָּא מָנֶה חוֹלְקוֹת בְּשָׁוֶה. הָיוּ שָׁם מָאתַיִם שֶׁלְּמָנֶה נוֹטֶלֶת חֲמִשִּׁים שֶׁלְּמָתַיִם וְשֶׁלִּשְׁלֹשׁ מֵאוֹת שְׁלֹשָׁה שְׁלֹשָׁה שֶׁלְּזָהָב. הָיוּ

שָׁם שָׁלֹשׁ מֵאוֹת שֶׁלְּמָנָה נוֹטֶלֶת חֲמִשִּׁים וְשֶׁלְּמָתַיִם מָנֶה וְשֶׁלִּשְׁלֹשׁ מֵאוֹת שִׁשָּׁה שֶׁלְּזָהָב. וְכֵן שְׁלֹשָׁה שֶׁהִיטִילוּ לַכִּיס פָּחֲתוּ אוֹ הוֹתִירוּ כָּךְ הֵן חוֹלְקִין.

Mishnah 4: If somebody was married to three women when he died, the *ketubah* of one was a mina[59], of the other one 200, and of the other one 300. If the estate is only 100, they divide equally. If it was 200, the one who claims a mina takes 50, and those who claim 200 and 300 each take three gold denars[60]. If it was 300, the one who claims a mina takes 50, the one who claims 200 takes a mina[59], and the one who claims 300 takes six gold denars[60]. Similarly, if three who invested together lost or gained they would split in this manner[61,62].

[59] 100 *zuz*.

[60] 1 gold denar was worth 25 silver denars. 3 gold denars equal 75 *zuz*, 6 gold denars 150 *zuz*.

[61] This refers to the proportional distribution of the last case. Loss and gain of a stock company are distributed per share.

[62] This Mishnah poses difficult problems. First, it deals with a scenario that cannot arise since Mishnah 1 stated that a *ketubah* which precedes in time has to be satisfied from the estate before the later *ketubah* can be claimed. Therefore, the case of the Mishnah presupposes that the husband married three woman simultaneously. While this is possible in theory, it is excluded in practice. The problem is a practical one if applied to the case that the amount available in bankruptcy proceedings is not sufficient to cover all claims of equal rank.

At first glance, it seems that the Mishnah is inconsistent, applying three different rules to three different cases. Since the Mishnah must guide the judge to correctly apportion payment of claims c_1, c_2, c_3 if the available amount $a < c_1 + c_2 + c_3$, for all a between 0 and $c_1 + c_2 + c_3$, it is obvious that the Mishnah has to be explained by one single consistent formula or algorithm. In addition, the algorithm must be applicable to any number n of claims.

In the tenth Century, Saadya Gaon suceeded in reducing the number of different rules employed in the Mishnah to two (*Oṣar Hageonim*

Ketubot p. 310). A complete discussion of the Geonic treatment of the Mishnah was given by I. Francus, שיטת הגאונים בפירוש משנה ובריתא, סיני פכו-פכז (תשס-תשסא) קצה-ריב (M. H. Katzenellenbogen Memorial Volume).

The first complete solution of the problem of finding a uniform rule for all three cases was given by R. J. Aumann and M. Maschler, Game Theoretic Analysis of a Bankruptcy Problem from the Talmud, *J. Econom. Theory* **36**(1985) 195-213. In the framework of the theory of cooperative games, the authors show that the distribution of the Mishnah corresponds to the *nucleolus* strategy in game theory. Using only elementary mathematics, a single distribution formula covering all cases was given by M. Balinski in: Quelle équité, *Pour la science* **311** (September 2003) 82-87; What is Just? *Am. Math. MONTHLY* **112**(2005), 502-511. While these authors succeed in explaining the Mishnah in itself, they do not explain the interpretation given to the Mishnah by the Talmudim. Nor do they explain why in both Talmudim the Mishnah is rejected out of hand. The explanation of the Babli is in language close to the Yerushalmi but translated into mathematical formulas the results are quite different; in both Talmudim the proposed explanation results in a procedure which is not monotone; i. e., it is possible that if the available amount a is increased, the payouts for some claimants are decreased. The solutions both of Aumann/Maschler and Balinski are monotone, increasing with a.

Balinski shows that the Mishnah can be understood in terms of a different distribution problem in Mishnah *Baba meṣi'a* 1:1, as indicated by Alfasi (*Ketubot* 10, 51b in the Wilna ed.). Since this problem is also the basis of the arguments in both Talmudim, Balinski's method is explained first. In *Baba meṣi'a* there are two claimants for an amount of 1. The first claims it all, the second claims $1/2$. Both claims are of the same status. Then the first is awarded $3/4$, the second $1/4$. While the claims are in ratio 2:1, the awards are in ratio 3:1. The reason given is the rule ascribed to Symmachos, a student of R. Meïr, that "money in doubt is split evenly" [Babli *Baba meṣi'a* 2b, *Baba qama* 35b; Yerushalmi *Baba meṣi'a* 8:5 (11d l. 18); cf. Chapter 2, Notes 9 ff.]. Since the second claimant asks only for $1/2$, the other half is awarded to the first claimant. The first half is in doubt; therefore it is split evenly between the two parties, resulting in the awards mentioned.

In order to arrive at a mathematical formulation, assume that n claims c_i are advanced,

$$c_1 < c_2 < \ldots < c_n.$$

If several claims were identical they would be consolidated into a single claim and the award split evenly between the participants. For any amount a available for distribution, the payout for claimant i is $p_i(a)$,

$$p_1(a) + p_2(a) + \ldots + p_n(a) = a.$$

We also introduce the sum of the claims, $S = c_1 + c_2 + \ldots + c_n$ and $M = S/2$. For $n = 2$, Symmachos's argument determines the payouts uniquely:

If $a \leq c_1$, the entire sum is in dispute,

$$p_1(a) = p_2(a) = a/2.$$

Therefore, $p_1(c_1) = p_2(c_1) = c_1/2$.

If $c_1 < a \leq c_2$, the amount $a - c_1$ belongs to claimant 2 and

$$p_1(a) = c_1/2,$$
$$p_2(a) = a-c_1+c_1/2 = a-c_1/2,$$

and $p_1(c_2) = c_1/2$, $p_2(c_2) = c_2-c_1/2$.

If $c_2 < a$, both claimants have equal rights to the excess over c_2,

$$p_1(a) = c_1/2 + (a - c_2)/2$$
$$p_2(a) = c_2-c_1/2+(a-c_2)/2 = (a+c_2-c_1)/2.$$

If $a = c_2+c_1 = S$, all claims are satisfied in full. Using the function $\min(x,y) =$ smaller of x or y, Balinski did express the formulas given above by

(1) $p_i(a) = \min(c_i/2, \lambda)$ where λ is chosen so that $p_1(a) + p_2(a) = a$; $i = 1,2$.

An inspection of the formulas shows that the distribution is symmetric about the middle value of the claims:

(2) $p_i(M-x) + p_i(M+x) = c_i$.

This means that the distribution for $M \leq a \leq S$ is determined if it is determined for $0 \leq a \leq M$. In the Mishnah here, it should be sufficient to indicate the distribution up to an estate of 300 if the sum of claims is 600. But the generalization of the procedure for $n = 2$ to $n > 2$ is not trivial. As Balinski points out, an arbitrary distribution function which yields the given values for $a = c_i$ and satisfies (2) is compatible with the Mishnah. His own solution is to postulate (1) for $i = 1, \ldots n$. Then (2) is satisfied and the distribution is monotone. For example,
$\{p_1(400), p_2(400), p_3(400)\} =$
$\{100-p_1(200), 200-p_2(200), 300-p_3(200)\}$
$= \{50, 125, 225\}$.

The problem with this solution, as with most other solutions proposed in the last 1000 years, is that the Talmudim take another view. The solution of the Babli is easily described as a recursive computational procedure. We assume that $p_1(a), \ldots, p_{i-1}(a)$ have been determined; leaving an amount a_i

to be distributed. We determine $p_i(a_i)$. If $c_i \geq a_i$, $p_j(a_i) = a_i/(n-i)$ for $j = i, \ldots n$. Otherwise, all claims larger than c_i are consolidated into one claim $C_i = c_{i+1} + \ldots + c_n$ and $p_i(a_i)$ is the payout assigned to claimant #i in the two-person distribution problem for claims c_i, C_i and amount a_i. The fictitious second claimant then receives $P_i(a_i) = a_{i+1}$ and the process continues.

In the example of the Mishnah, $c_1 = 100$, $c_2 = 200$, $c_3 = 300$. For $a = 100$, by the first alternative $p_j(100) = 100/3$ for all j. For $a = 200$, $c_1 = 100$, $C_1 = 400$. Therefore, 100 is assigned to the second party and 100 is split evenly. This yields $p_1(200) = 50$, $P_1(200) = 150$. Since $200 > 150$, the latter amount is split evenly, resulting in $p_2(200) = p_3(200) = 75$. For $a = 300$, one sees that $p_1(300) = 50$, $P_1(300) = 250$; $p_2(300) = 100 = 200/2$, $p_3(300) = 50 + 200/2 = 150$. This explains the numbers stated in the Mishnah, but what about $a = 101$? In that case, $p_1(101) = 50$, $P_1(101) = 51$; $p_2(101) = p_3(101) = 51/2 = 25.5$. This clearly is unacceptable; the procedure of the Mishnah has to be rejected.

The explanation of the Yerushalmi (cf. Note 69) is not so clearly stated but it seems to be the following: The procedure also is recursive. If $c_i \geq a_i$, $p_j(a_i) = a_i/(n-i)$ for $j = i, \ldots n$. Otherwise, one considers all two-person problems between claimants i and $i+1, \ldots, n$. *In praxi*, this means that one has only to split between c_i and c_n. If $c_i < a_i < c_n$ then $p_i(a_i) = c_i/2$. If $c_n < a_i$ then write $a_i = c_n + \delta$. Claims n and i overlap to the amount $c_i - \delta$. This means that

$$p_i(a_i) = \delta + (c_i - \delta)/2 = (c_i + \delta)/2.$$

For $a \leq M$, the numbers obtained for Babli and Yerushalmi coincide; the Yerushalmi's method also is not monotone. The results for $a > M$ disagree. For example, for the data of Mishnah 4, the Yerushalmi gives $p_1(400)=100$, $p_2(400)=100$, $p_3(400)=200$ while the Babli gives $p_1(400)=50$, $P_1(400)=350$; $p_2(400)=100$, $p_3(400)=250$.

(33d line 54) **הלכה ד**: מִי שֶׁהָיָה נָשׂוּי שָׁלֹשׁ נָשִׁים כול'. שְׁמוּאֵל אָמַר שׁוּחְדָּא דְדַיָּינֵי. לִשְׁנֵי שְׁטָרוֹת שֶׁיָּצְאוּ עַל שָׂדֶה אַחַת אֵי זֶה מֵהֶן שֶׁיִּרְצוּ בֵית דִּין לְהַחֲלִיט מַחֲלִיטִין. מַתְנִיתָא פְלִיגָא עַל שְׁמוּאֵל. אֵין שָׁם אֶלָּא מָנֶה חוֹלְקוֹת בְּשָׁוֶה. לֹא שׁוּחְדָּא דְדַיָּינֵי אִיתְאָמְרַת. וְהָא תַגִּי. הַיּוֹרְשִׁין שֶׁיָּרְשׁוּ שְׁטַר חוֹב הַבְּכוֹר נוֹטֵל

פִּי שָׁנִים. עוֹד יָצָא עֲלֵיהֶן שְׁטַר חוֹב הַבְּכוֹר נוֹתֵן פִּי שְׁנַיִם. עוֹד הִיא לְשׁוּחְדָא דְדַיָּינֵי אִיתְאָמְרַת. רִבִּי אָבִין בְּשֵׁם שְׁמוּאֵל. לֹא שַׁנְיָיא. בֵּין שְׁנֵי שְׁטָרוֹת שֶׁיָּצְאוּ עַל שָׂדֶה אַחַת בֵּין שְׁטָר אֶחָד שֶׁיָּצָא עַל שְׁנֵי שָׂדוֹת אֵי זֶה מֵהֶן שֶׁיִּרְצוּ בֵית דִּין מַחֲלִיטִין.

Halakhah 4: "If somebody was married to three women," etc. Samuel said, sharpness of the judges[63]. As in the case of two mortgages written on one field, to whom the court wants to hand it over in possession they hand it over[64]. The Mishnah disagrees with Samuel: "If the estate is only 100, they divide equally.[65]" Was this said for the sharpness of the judges[66]? And did we not state: If the heirs inherited an instrument of indebtedness, the male firstborn takes a double portion[67]; and if an instrument of indebtedness was presented to them, the male firstborn pays a double portion. Was this said for the sharpness of the judges[68]? Rebbi Abin in the name of Samuel: There is no difference, whether two mortgages were written on one field or one mortgage was written on two fields, on whom the court decide they hand it over in possession.

63   Samuel seems to indicate that the court has to investigate and choose the method of distribution which seems most appropriate for the case before them, to whom to give real estate and to whom money or securities.

The translation of שוחדא is tentative. In the Babli, the word appears as שודא which either is derived from the Aramaic root שדי "to throw" (interpreted to mean that the court may "throw" the properties to the party it feels has the best claim) or it is identical with Galilean שוחדא because of the disappearance of ע in Babylonian speech. I am proposing to derive שוחדא from Arabic شحذ "to sharpen (a knife)", Mishnaic Hebrew שחז.

64   If the field is too small to be useful as property if divided up. The holder of the second mortgage (assuming both were written on the same day) has to be indemnified with

money; this is Samuel's position in Babli 94a.

65 Does this not indicate that all three women have to be treated exactly equally?

66 The Mishnah speaks only about the value, not about the mode of distribution.

67 Since a documented claim is as good as collected, such a document is counted as ready money, not as future claim (cf. Note 50). In Babli *Baba batra* 124a and in Tosephta *Bekhorot* 6:17 the firstborn is given the right to refuse a double portion of secured future claims and then not pay double part of future secured claims against the estate.

68 This is not a case that allows of judicial discretion.

(33d line 62) שְׁמוּאֵל אָמַר. בְּמַרְשׁוּת זֶה אֶת זוֹ. בְּשֶׁהִרְשְׁתָה הַשְּׁלִישִׁית אֶת הַשְּׁנִיָּיה לָדוּן עִם הָרִאשׁוֹנָה. אָמְרָה לָהּ. לֹא מָנֶה אִית לָךְ. סַב חַמְשִׁין וְאֵיזַל לָךְ.

Samuel said, if they empower one another[69]. If the third empowered the second to deal with the first. She said to her, is not a mina due to you[70]? Take 50 and leave!

69 To deal separately with the co-wife claiming the smallest amount. In the Babli, 93a, Samuel explains that the second wife empowered the third to represent her also; cf. Note 62. Unless all parties agree to the procedure, the estate has to be distributed proportional to the claims. It is difficult to see why all parties should agree; the procedure of the Mishnah is eliminated from practical use.

70 If the amount available is larger than a mina, the first has to split the mina only with one co-wife.

(33d line 64) וְכֵן שְׁלֹשָׁה שֶׁהִטִּילוּ לַכִּיס פָּחֲתוּ אוֹ הוֹתִירוּ כָּךְ הֵן חוֹלְקִין. אָמַר רִבִּי אֶלְעָזָר. הָדָא דְּאַתְּ אָמַר בְּשֶׁהָיְתָה הַסֶּלַע חֲסֵירָה אוֹ יְתֵירָה. אֲבָל לְשָׂכָר וּלְהֶפְסֵד כּוּלְּהוֹן חוֹלְקִין בְּשָׁוֶה. וְקַשְׁיָא. הָהֵן יְהַב מְאָה דֵינָרִין וְהָהֵן יְהַב עֲשָׂרָה. וְאַתְּ אָמַר אָכֵן. חֲבֵרַיָּיא אָמְרִין. יָכוֹל הוּא מֵימַר לֵיהּ. עַל יְדֵי מְנָיַי סָלְקַת

פְּרַגְמַטְיָא. עַד כְּדוֹן רְהַטַּת[71] פְּרַגְמַטְיָיא זְעֵירָא. הֲוָת פְּרַגְמַטְיָיא רוֹבָה. אָמַר רִבִּי אָבִין בַּר חִייָה. יָכוֹל הוּא מֵימַר לֵיהּ. עַד דְּאַתְּ מַזְבִּין חַד זְמָן אֲנָא מַזְבִּין עֲשָׂרָה זְמָנִים. עַד כְּדוֹן בְּמָקוֹם קָרוֹב. בְּמָקוֹם רָחוֹק. אָמַר רִבִּי הִילָא. יָכוֹל הוּא מֵימַר לֵיהּ. עַד דְּאַתְּ אָזִיל וַאֲתִי חַד זְמָן אֲנָא אָזִיל וַאֲתִי עֲשָׂרָה זְמָנִים. תַּמָּן תַּנִּינָן. חָזַר וְנָגַח שׁוֹר אֶחָד שָׁוֶה מָאתַיִם הָאַחֲרוֹן נוֹטֵל מָנֶה וְשֶׁלְּפָנָיו חֲמִשִּׁים זוּז וּשְׁנַיִם הָרִאשׁוֹנִים דִּינָר זָהָב. רִבִּי שְׁמוּאֵל בְּשֵׁם רִבִּי [זְעֵירָא].[72] וְכֵן לַשָּׂכָר. אָמַר רִבִּי יוֹסֵי. דְּרִבִּי זְעֵירָא פְּלִיגָא עַל דְּרִבִּי אֶלְעָזָר. רִבִּי מָנָא אָמַר קוֹמֵי רִבִּי יוּדָן. לֹא מוֹדֵי רִבִּי לָעְזָר שֶׁאִם הִתְנוּ בֵּינֵיהֶן שָׁוֶה נוֹטֵל לְפִי כִיסוֹ וְזֶה נוֹטֵל לְפִי כִיסוֹ. שְׁוָרִים כְּמוּתָנִים הֵן. חָזַר וְאָמְרָהּ קוֹמֵי רִבִּי יוֹסֵי. אָמַר לֵיהּ. בְּפֵירוּשׁ פְּלִיגִין. רִבִּי לָעְזָר אָמַר. סְתָמָּן חוֹלְקִין בְּשָׁוֶה. רִבִּי זֵירָא אָמַר. סְתָמָּן זֶה נוֹטֵל לְפִי כִיסוֹ וְזֶה נוֹטֵל לְפִי כִיסוֹ.

"Similarly, if three who invested together lost or gained they would split in this manner." [73]Rebbi Eleazar said: You say that in case the tetradrachma lost or added value. But for earnings or losses they split evenly[74]. That is difficult! One gave 100 denars and the other gave ten, and you say so? The colleagues say, he may say to him, by my contribution the merchandise rose. So far, if they ran after little merchandise[75]. If there was much merchandise? Rebbi Abun bar Hiyya said, he may say to him, by the time you sold one piece, I am selling ten. That is, at a nearby place. If it was far away? Rebbi Hila said, he may say to him, by the time you go and return once, I am going and returning ten times. There[76], we have stated: "If [the ox] gored an ox worth 200, the last one takes 100, the one before him 50, and the two first ones a gold denar." Rebbi Samuel in the name of Rebbi [Ze'ira]: The same holds for earnings[77]. Rebbi Yose said, the statement of Rebbi Ze'ira disagrees with Rebbi Eleazar. Rebbi Mana said before Rebbi Yudan: Does Rebbi Eleazar not agree if they contracted between themselves that each can take according to his contribution[78]? Oxen are as if contracted. He turned around and said, they disagree explicitly: Rebbi Eleazar said, if nothing was said, they split evenly; Rebbi Ze'ira said, if nothing was said, each takes according to his contribution[79].

71 Instead of this word "was running", *Sefer Ha'ittur* 42a reads הֲוָת "it was". The reading of the ms. may be confirmed as *lectio difficilior*.

72 The name is missing in the ms., it was added from the parallel in *Baba qama*, supported by *Sefer Ha'ittur* 42a,

as required from the text below.

73 This paragraph has a differently worded parallel in *Baba qama* 4:1 (by a different editorial team) which explains the somewhat cryptic wording here:

וְכֵן שְׁלֹשָׁה שֶׁהִיטִילוּ לַכִּיס פָּחֲתוּ אוֹ הוֹתִירוּ כָּךְ הֵן חוֹלְקִין. אָמַר רִבִּי בּוּן. נִרְאִין דְּבָרִים אִם נָטְלוּ מַרְגָּלִית. דְּיָכוֹל מֵימַר לֵיהּ אִילּוּלֵי עֲשַׂרְתָּא דִינָרַיי לֹא הֲוִיתָה מְזַבִּין כְּלוּם. אֲבָל דָּבָר שֶׁדַּרְכּוֹ לַחֲלֶק מְבִיאִין לְאָמְצַע וְחוֹלְקִין. אָמַר רִבִּי לְעָזָר וַאֲפִילוּ דָּבָר שֶׁדַּרְכּוֹ לַחֲלָק. דְּיָכִיל מֵימַר לֵיהּ אַתְּ פְּרַגְמַטְיָא דִידָךְ סַגִּין וְאַתְּ מַנְעָא מַזְבְּנִתָּא. אֲנָא פְרַגְמַטְיָא דִידִי קָלִיל וַאֲנָא חָפַךְ וּמִתְהַפֵּךְ בְּדִידִי וּמַטִּי בָהּ. עַד כְּדוֹן בְּשֶׁהָייְתָה פְרַגְמַטְייוֹ נְתוּנָה כָאן. הָייְתָה פְרַגְמַטְייוֹ נְתוּנָה בְרוֹמִי. דְּיָכִיל מֵימַר לֵיהּ. עַד דְּאַתְּ סָלִיק לְרוֹמִי אֲנָא חָפֵךְ וּמִתְהַפֵּךְ בְּדִידִי וּמַטִּי בָהּ. תַּמָּן תְּנִינָן. הָאַחֲרוֹן נוֹטֵל מָנָה וְשֶׁלְּפָנָיו חֲמִשִּׁים זוּז וּשְׁנַיִם הָרִאשׁוֹנִים דִּינָרֵי זָהָב. רִבִּי שְׁמוּאֵל בְּשֵׁם רִבִּי זְעִירָא. וְכֵן לְשָׂכָר. אָמַר רִבִּי יוֹסֵי. הָדָא דְּרִבִּי זֵירָא פְלִיגָא עַל דְּרִבִּי לְעָזָר. אָמַר רִבִּי מָנֵי. קַשְׁייָתָהּ קוֹמֵי רִבִּי יוּדָן. אָמַר לִי. לֹא מוֹדֶה רִבִּי לְעָזָר שֶׁאִם הִתְנוּ בֵינֵיהֶן שֶׁזֶּה נוֹטֵל לְפִי כִיסוֹ וְזֶה נוֹטֵל לְפִי כִיסוֹ. שְׁטָרִים כְּמוּתְנִים הֵן. חָזַר וְאָמְרָהּ קוֹמֵי רִבִּי יוֹסֵי. אָמַר לֵיהּ. בְּפֵירוּשׁ פְּלִיגֵי. רִבִּי לְעָזָר אָמַר. סְתָמָן חוֹלְקִין בְּשָׁוֶה. רִבִּי זְעִירָא אָמַר. סְתָמָן זֶה נוֹטֵל לְפִי כִיסוֹ וְזֶה נוֹטֵל לְפִי כִיסוֹ.

"Similarly, if three who invested together lost or gained they would split in this manner." Rebbi Abun said, the statement looks reasonable if they bought a precious stone because he can say to him, without my ten denars you could not have bought anything. But anything that usually is split (smaller units that can be bought with less capital) one adds together and splits (proportionally to the capital invested). Rebbi Eleazar says, even things that usually are split [are divided evenly], because he can say to him, you have a lot of merchandise and you have difficulty selling it. I have little merchandise and turn it over rapidly and make as much as you do. So far if his merchandise was here. What if his merchandise was in Rome? He can say to him, by the time you went to Rome, I turn mine over rapidly and make as much as you do.

There, we have stated: "If [the ox] gored an ox worth 200, the last one takes 100, the one before him 50, and the two first ones a gold denar." Rebbi Samuel in the name of Rebbi Ze'ira: The same holds for earnings. Rebbi Yose said, the statement of Rebbi Ze'ira disagrees with Rebbi Eleazar. Rebbi Mani said, *I asked this* before Rebbi Yudan. *He said to me:* does Rebbi Eleazar not agree if they contracted between themselves that each can take according to his contribution? Oxen are as if contracted. He turned around and said *this before Rebbi Yose, who answered him,* they disagree explicitly: Rebbi Eleazar said, if nothing was said, they split evenly; Rebbi Ze'ira said, if nothing was said, each takes according to his contribution. {This paragraph is a direct quote from *Ketubot* since the quote from "there" refers to here, *Baba qama* 4:1}.

74 Only results of financial operations are split per share. Results of personal effort by the shareholders are split evenly; they are *socii pro aequa parte* of Justinian's legislation.

75 Expensive items, as explained in the parallel text.

76 Mishnah *Baba qama* 4:1. *Ex.* 21:35 decrees that if an ox kills another ox, the owner of the attacking animal and the owner of the victim become co-owners of both the living and the dead animal. If the attacking ox attacks another one before it can be slaughtered, its co-owners now become co-owners with the owner of the second victim. The case quoted in the Mishnah is about an ox worth 200 *zuz* which attacks three oxen, each of which was worth 200 *zuz* but whose carcasses are not worth anything after the attack. Then the owner of the ox which was killed last takes half the combined value of the attacker and its victim as prescribed in the verse, 100 *zuz*. The owner of the second ox has a claim of 50% of the value of the combined value of the attacker and its victim. But since only 100 *zuz* remain of the value of the attacker and the victim is not worth anything, the second owner gets only 50 *zuz*. By the

same argument, the owner of the first ox gets 25 *zuz*, the same amount as the owner of the attacker retains.

77 R. Ze'ira interprets the Mishnah in *Baba qama* that in the company created by the attacking ox, the owner of the third victim contributed 200, the owner of the second 100, the owners of the first and of the attacker 50 each, and 50% of the value was lost as prescribed in the verse. Therefore, the Mishnah precribes proportional appropriations for a case which is not a financial operation; the Mishnah in *Ketubot* can be interpreted that in a company, all gains and losses have to be distributed in proportion to the capital invested.

78 Since in money matters, biblical law is not prescriptive.

79 Since R. Ze'ira is the later and higher authority, the Yerushalmi decides that all distributions must be proportional. The Babli, 93b, quotes the opinion attributed here to R. Eleazar in the name of Samuel as interpreted by Rav Hamnuna, it clearly decides that all distributions must be split equally.

(fol. 33c) **משנה ה**: מִי שֶׁהָיָה נָשׂוּי אַרְבַּע נָשִׁים וָמֵת הָרִאשׁוֹנָה קוֹדֶמֶת לַשְּׁנִיָּיה וּשְׁנִיָּיה לַשְּׁלִישִׁית וּשְׁלִישִׁית לָרְבִיעִית. הָרִאשׁוֹנָה נִשְׁבַּעַת לַשְּׁנִיָּיה וּשְׁנִיָּיה לַשְּׁלִישִׁית וּשְׁלִישִׁית לָרְבִיעִית וְהָרְבִיעִית נִפְרַעַת שֶׁלֹּא בִשְׁבוּעָה. אָמַר בֶּן נַנָּס וְכִי מִפְּנֵי שֶׁהִיא אַחֲרוֹנָה נִשְׂכָּרֶת אַף הִיא לֹא תִפָּרַע אֶלָּא בִשְׁבוּעָה. הָיוּ כוּלָּן יוֹצְאוֹת בְּיוֹם אֶחָד כָּל־הַקּוֹדֶמֶת לַחֲבֵירָתָהּ אֲפִילוּ שָׁעָה אַחַת זָכְתָה. וְכָךְ הָיוּ כּוֹתְבִין בִּירוּשָׁלֵם שָׁעוֹת. הָיוּ כוּלָּן יוֹצְאוֹת בְּשָׁעָה אַחַת וְאֵין שָׁם אֶלָּא מָנֶה חוֹלְקוֹת בְּשָׁוֶה.

Mishnah 5: If somebody was married to four women when he died, the first one[1] precedes the second[2], the second the third, and the third the fourth. The first one swears to the second[80], the second to the third, and the third to the fourth; the fourth is paid out without an oath[81]. Ben

Nanas said, should she be preferred because she is the last one? She also should be paid only after an oath[82]. If all [*ketubot*] were executed on the same day, one who precedes another one even if only by an hour has acquired [precedence]; therefore in Jerusalem one used to note hours[83]. If [the documents] were all executed at the same hour and there is only one mina, they split evenly[84].

[80] She has to swear that during their husband's lifetime she did not receive any downpayment on the *ketubah*, so that she is fully entitled to the sum she is receiving from the executors of the estate. The second wife can demand this oath because every penny the first one receives dimishes her chances of being fully paid by the remaining estate.

[81] No oath is due to any co-wife since all had been paid in full; she might have to swear to the heirs.

[82] There is a possibility that the prior wives might be disadvantaged if the fourth is paid too much: If any *ketubah* was satisfied by transfer of title of a field that turned out to be mortgaged and was repossessed by the lender, that wife then has regress on the remainder of the estate and, therefore, has a vital interest that the fourth wife not be paid too much. The Babli, 94a, has some additional reasons for Ben Nanas's opinion.

[83] Not only the date but also the hour of the signing of a contract were written into the document.

[84] As already noted in Mishnah 4.

(34a line 5) **הלכה ח**: מִי שֶׁהָיָה נָשׂוּי אַרְבַּע נָשִׁים כול'. רִבִּי אֲבוּנָא בְשֵׁם רִבִּי שְׁמוּאֵל. כִּדְבָרֵי בֶּן נַנָּס לְשִׁטָר אֶחָד שֶׁיָּצָא עַל (הָאִשָּׁה) לְקוּחוֹת כּוּלְהוֹן חוֹלְקִין בְּשָׁוֶה. אָמַר רִבִּי עֲקִיבָה קוֹמֵי רִבִּי מָנָא. לֵית הָדָא פְלִיגָא עַל רִבִּי שְׁמוּאֵל. דִּשְׁמוּאֵל אָמַר שׁוּחָדָא דְדַיָּינֵי. לִשְׁנֵי שְׁטָרוֹת שֶׁיָּצְאוּ עַל שָׂדֶה אַחַת. לְאֵי זֶה מֵהֶן שֶׁיִּרְצֶה לְהַחֲלִיט מַחֲלִיטִין. וְכָא הוּא אָמַר אָכֵין. לֹא בִשְׁתֵּי שְׁטָרוֹת דִּילְמָא בִשְׁטָר אֶחָד. וְכָא בִשְׁטָר אֶחָד אֲנָן קַיָּימִין. וְלָא שְׁמִיעַ דָּמַר רִבִּי אָבִין בְּשֵׁם שְׁמוּאֵל. לֹא שַׁנְיָיא. בֵּין שְׁנֵי שְׁטָרוֹת שֶׁיָּצְאוּ עַל שְׁנֵי שָׂדוֹת וּבֵין שְׁנֵי

שְׁטָרוֹת שֶׁיָּצְאוּ עַל שָׂדֶה אֶחָד. אֵי זֶה מֵהֶן שֶׁיִּרְצוּ בֵּית דִּין לְהַחֲלִיט מַחֲלִיטִין. הִנְהִיג רִבִּי בְּאַרְנוֹנָא וּבְגוּלְגּוֹלֶת וּבָאֲנָפוֹרוֹת כְּהָדָא דְּבֶן נַנָּס.

Halakhah 5: "If somebody was married to four women when he died," etc. Rebbi Abuna in the name of Rebbi Samuel: Following Ben Nanas, if one document was produced against (the wife) buyers, they all divide evenly[85]. Rebbi Aqiba[86] said before Rebbi Mana: Does this not disagree with Rebbi Samuel, since Samuel said, sharpness of the judges[63]? As in the case of two mortgages written on one field, to whom they want to hand it over in possession they hand it over[64]. And here, he says so[87]? Not with two mortgages, what about one[88]? He did not hear what Rebbi Abin said in the name of Samuel: There is no difference, whether two mortgages were written on two fields or two mortgages were written on one field[89], to whom the court decide they hand it over in possession. Rebbi instituted that one follows Ben Nanas in matters of *annona*[90], head taxes, and real estate taxes[91].

85   This sentence makes no sense; the word האשה clearly is wrong. In the absence of parallel sources, the exact wording cannot be reconstrued. The consensus of the commentators is that one must read approximately: "if one document was produced against [several] buyers, they all divide evenly". The deceased husband had taken a loan which cannot be satisfied by a single property; if the mortgage document is presented after the wives' *ketubot* were satisfied, they all have to contribute equally to the satisfaction of the mortgage.

Clearly, the title "Rebbi" given to Samuel here is misplaced. A similar statement is attributed to Samuel in the Babli, 94a.

86   This seems to be a scribal error.

87   Should the court not direct the claimant to one field, with the other buyers contributing money?

88   In his opinion, the case of one claimant against multiple owners is not covered by Samuel's original statement.

89 It seems that the deviation of this quote from the original in Halakhah 4 is a scribal error, but this cannot be proved. Samuel's statement can easily be applied to our case of a single document covering a multiplicity of real estate.

90 Latin *annona*, the prestations in kind required by the Roman army in the provinces; cf. *Peah* 1, Note 85. It is not clear what the relationship is between the statement of Ben Nanas and the collection of taxes. Since the tax was imposed on the community to be repartitioned by the local person responsible, the latter could impose an oath on the tax payer that he declared his situation honestly.

91 Greek ἀναφορά "report, listing". In the opinion of A. Gulak, this is the yearly tax which people paid who had the right to farm imperial domains in perpetuity; cf. S. Lieberman, תוספתא כפשוטה מעשר שני, p. 710.

(34a line 15) כְּהָדָא. קְרֵיבִין דְּרִבִּי יוֹסֵי זְבָנִין חַקְלָוָן מִן אִילֵין דְּבַר תַּפְקָן. אָזְלוּן אִינּוּן דְּבַר תַּפְקָן וְנָסְבִין לְהוֹן נָשִׁין. אֲתוֹן בָּעֵי מִתְגָּרְיָיא בִּקְרִיבֵי דְּרִבִּי יוֹסֵי. אָמַר לוֹן רִבִּי מָנָא. אֲנָא יָדַע כַּד זְבַנְתּוּן אִילֵין חַקְלָוָותָא לֹא הֲווֹן אִילֵין שְׁקִיעַיָּא קֳדָמֵיכוֹן.

As the following[92]. Relatives of Rebbi Yose bought fields from the family of Bar Tapqan. Those from the family of Bar Tapqan went and married women, and gave them *šeqi'in*[93]. They came and wanted to attack the relatives of Rebbi Yose[94]. Rebbi Mana said to them: I know that at the moment at which you bought these fields, these *šeqi'in* were not before you[95].

92 This paragraph refers to the Mishnah which states that the date of a document determines its status in foreclosure proceedings. The word שקיעין as designation of a document appears only in this paragraph. Since שקע means "to sink, to go down", it is reasonable to assume that שקיעין are mortgages on real estate the usufruct of which is given to the creditor to reduce the amount due and finally to retire the mortgage. This is called

מַשְׁכַּנְתָּא דְסוּרָא "Suran mortgage" in the Babli (*Baba meṣi'a* 67b, 110a; *Baba batra* 35b, 38a), and corresponds, in the interest-charging Gentile environment, to the ἀντίχρησις of the Digests (20,1,11,1) and the Egyptian papyri (P. Gron. 11), "substitution of usufruct for interest".

It seems that the men gave their brides documents on the fields they had sold which were predated before the date of the sale.

94 To take the usufruct of the fields for a fixed number of years.

95 A predated document is invalid.

(fol. 33c) **משנה ו**: מִי שֶׁהָיָה נָשׂוּי שְׁתֵּי נָשִׁים וּמָכַר אֶת שָׂדֵהוּ וְכָתְבָה הָרִאשׁוֹנָה לַלּוֹקֵחַ דִּין וּדְבָרִים אֵין לִי עִמָּךְ הַשְּׁנִיָּה מוֹצִיאָה מִן הַלּוֹקֵחַ וְהָרִאשׁוֹנָה מִן הַשְּׁנִיָּה וְהַלּוֹקֵחַ מִן הָרִאשׁוֹנָה וְחוֹזְרוֹת חָלִילָה עַד שֶׁיַּעֲשׂוּ פְשָׁרָה בֵּינֵיהֶן. וְכֵן בַּעַל חוֹב וְכֵן אִשָּׁה בַּעֲלַת חוֹב.

Mishnah 6: If somebody was married to two wives when he sold his field and the first wife wrote to the buyers "I have no claims against you", the second takes from the buyer, the first from the second, and the buyer from the first[96]; they go on in circles until they compromise between them. The same holds for a creditor[97] and a woman who is a creditor[98].

96 If the husband died and his estate did not suffice to satisfy the second wife's *ketubah*, she can have regress on the field since she did not sign away her rights. Since the first wife's *ketubah* has to be satisfied before the second wife has any claim, the first can take the field which by the action of the second was no longer the buyer's property but becomes part of the estate. But since the first had given up any claim to that field, the buyer can claim it back from the first. Therefore, all three claimants are forced to agree to a compromise to have *any* use of the property.

97 If a loan was given in the value of two fields which the borrower then

sold, and the creditor wrote to the second buyer that he would not exercise his rights against him; if the loan is foreclosed, the creditor can take the first field; the first buyer can indemnify himself by taking the second field; the creditor can take it from the first buyer but the second buyer can reclaim it from the creditor, etc.

98 An only wife whose *ketubah* was secured by two fields which were sold by her husband, and who wrote to the second buyer that she would not exercise her claim against him. In the last two cases it is necessary that the renunciation be for the second buyer since if it were for the first, the second would have no regress on the first.

(34a line 19) **הלכה ו**: מִי שֶׁהָיָה נָשׂוּי שְׁתֵּי נָשִׁים כול'. אָמַר רִבִּי יוֹסֵי. הָדָא אָמְרָה. חָהֵן דְּיָזִיף מִן תְּרֵין בְּנֵי נָשׁ. אֲתָא תִנְיָינָא אֲמַר לֵיהּ. קוּמֵי פּוֹשְׁרִין. אֲמַר לֵיהּ. וְלֵית סוֹפֵיהּ דְּקַדְמָיָיא מִשְׁמַע וּמֵיתֵי מִיטְרוֹף. יָכִיל מֵימַר לֵיהּ. פּוֹשְׁרִין. וְאִין טָרַף טָרַף. פִּישֵׁר מִן.[100] חֲזָקָה שֶׁהָרִאשׁוֹן בָּא וְטוֹרֵף. פִּישֵׁר מִן הָרִאשׁוֹן. אָמַר רִבִּי פִּינְחָס. אֲתָא עוֹבְדָא קוֹמֵי רִבִּי יִרְמְיָה וְאָמַר. פִּישֵׁר. אָמַר רִבִּי יוֹסֵי. וְלֹא כָתַב. דְּאִיקְנֵי. לֹא אַתְיָיא אֶלָּא בְּיוֹרֵשׁ. אָמַר רִבִּי חֲנִינָה. אֲפִילוּ בְּבַעַל חוֹב. אַתְיָיא הִיא בְּהַהִיא דְּלָא כְתִיב. כָּל־דְּאִיקְנֵי. אוֹ שֶׁאָמַר לֵיהּ. אַל יְהֵא לָךְ פֵּירָעוֹן אֶלָּא מִזֶּה. אָמַר רַב מַתַּנְיָיה. אַתְיָיא כְּמַאן דָּמַר. לִכְתוּבָּה אֲבָל לֹא לִתְנָיִין. בְּרַם כְּמַאן דָּמַר. בֵּין לִכְתוּבָּה בֵּין לִתְנָיִין. הָא חֲזִירָה.

Halakhah 6: "If somebody was married to two wives," etc. Rebbi Yose said, this means that if somebody borrowed from two persons and the second comes and says to him, get up and let us settle[99], and [the borrower] says, will not in the end the first hear of it and come to foreclose, he [the second lender] may say let us settle, and if he forecloses, he forecloses. If he settled[100], one may assume that the first will come and foreclose. If he settled with the first[101], Rebbi Phineas said, such a case came before Rebbi Jeremiah who said, he settled[102]. Rebbi Yose said, did he not write "what I shall acquire"[103]? It happens only with an heir[104]. Rebbi Ḥanina said, even with a creditor it can happen if he did not write "anything I shall acquire", or if he said, "you shall not be paid except from this.[105]" Rav Mattaniah said, this follows him who said, for *ketubah* but not for stipulations[106]. But for him who said, for *ketubah* and for stipulations, does it not return?

99   He realizes that the borrower is not in a position to repay the entire loan. Since his loan is an essentially unsecured second mortgage, he can settle with the borrower to receive part of the mortgaged property. Even if the secured first mortgage giver will in the end foreclose, the second has the usufruct in the meantime and will have saved something.

100   In the text, either מן is superfluous or a word is missing and it should read מן השני.

101   The first, secured, mortgage holder settled with the borrower and in the foreclosing took only part of the field while he could have taken all of it. The question now is whether the piece of land is remaining in the borrower's hand or if it was assumed to be foreclosed and then returned to the borrower. In the second case, the borrower took possession after the date of the second mortgage and the second lender has no regress. In the first case, the second lender may foreclose.

102   The second lender may not foreclose.

103   If the loan contract stipulated that all the borrower's present and future real estate holdings are mortgaged, there should be no difference in the status of the property left after a compromise with the first mortgage holder.

104   If the future clause really was in the contract, the second mortgage holder can foreclose from the original borrower. But if the borrower died and the heir settled with the holder of the first mortgage, the remaining land was acquired by the heir, not the borrower, and is not subject to the second mortgage.

105   If the mortgage was written on a specific piece of land, the lender cannot foreclose anything else.

106   The court stipulations required

for any *ketubah* as enumerated in Chapter 4, in particular the "*ketubah* of male sons". Whether this stipulation can be satisfied by foreclosure is discussed in the Babli, 55a, and the Yerushalmi, *Baba batra* 8:6 (16b l.23). The answer is positive in the Yerushalmi, negative in the Babli. For the Yerushalmi, the renunciation by the mother of her claim against the buyer is not valid for her heirs; they are free to foreclose in any case.

אלמנה ניזונת פרק אחד עשר

(fol. 34a) **משנה א**: אַלְמָנָה נִיזוֹנֶת מִינִּכְסֵי יְתוֹמִים מַעֲשֵׂה יָדֶיהָ שֶׁלָּהֶן וְאֵין חַיָּיבִין בִּקְבוּרָתָהּ. יוֹרְשֶׁיהָ הַיּוֹרְשִׁים כְּתוּבָּתָהּ חַיָּיבִין בִּקְבוּרָתָהּ.

Mishnah 1: If a widow is supported by the orphans' property[1], she has to work for them but they are not obligated to bury her[2]. Her heirs, the heirs of her *ketubah*, are obligated to bury her.

1 The widow who chose to be supported by the estate (as explained in Mishnah 4:12) rather than taking her *ketubah*.

2 If they are not her heirs, she has to keep house for them anyway. The husband whose wife dies before him must bury her since he is the heir of her property. If she died childless after her husband, the heirs of her side of the family have to bury her. Similarly, if she sold her future rights to a *ketubah* and died after her husband, the speculator who bought her *ketubah* has to bury her (cf. Note 57 and S. Lieberman, תוספתא כפשוטה כתובות p. 329).

(34a, line 55) **הלכה א**: אַלְמָנָה נִיזוֹנֶת מִינִּכְסֵי יְתוֹמִים כול'. רַב יְהוּדָה בְשֵׁם שְׁמוּאֵל רִבִּי אַבָּהוּ בְשֵׁם רִבִּי יוֹחָנָן. מְצִיאָתָהּ שֶׁלָּהּ. הוֹתִירָה מְזוֹנוֹת. אֵשֶׁת אִישׁ שֶׁמְּצִיאָתָהּ שֶׁלּוֹ הוֹתִירָה מְזוֹנוֹת שֶׁלּוֹ. אַלְמָנָה שֶׁמְּצִיאָתָהּ שֶׁלָּהּ הוֹתִירָה מְזוֹנוֹת שֶׁלָּהּ. הוֹתִירָה בְלָיוֹת שֶׁלָּהּ. מָה אִם אֵשֶׁת אִישׁ שֶׁהוֹתִירָה מְזוֹנוֹת שֶׁלּוֹ. הוֹתִירָה בְלָיוֹת שֶׁלָּהּ. אַלְמָנָה שֶׁהוֹתִירָה מְזוֹנוֹת שֶׁלָּהּ. הוֹתִירָה בְלָיוֹת לֹא כָל־שֶׁכֵּן. תַּמָּן צְרִיכָא לוֹן לְנִידָתָהּ. אַף הָכָא צְרִיכָא לוֹן לְנִידָתָהּ.

HALAKHAH 1

Halakhah 1: "If a widow is supported by the orphans' property," etc. Rav Jehudah in the name of Samuel[3], Rebbi Abbahu in the name of Rebbi Joḥanan: What she finds belongs to herself. If she had sustenance left over? Since her finds belong to her husband, the married woman's leftover sustenance belongs to her husband[4]. Since a widow's finds belong to herself, her leftover sustenance belongs to herself. Her worn-out clothing belongs to her[5]. Since even a married woman, whose leftover sustenance belongs to her husband, keeps her worn-out clothing to herself, the widow, whose leftover food belongs to herself, her worn-out clothing so much more! There, she needs them for the time of her period. Here also, she needs them for the time of her period[6].

---

3 He is the author of the same statement in the Babli, 96a.

4 A *baraita* in the Babli, 65b. (In *Nazir* 24b it is explained that the husband's property is the household money which she did not spend on food, rather than actual food she saved when being on a diet. The editing of *Nazir* seemingly is different from that of most Babli Tractates.)

5 A *baraita* in the Babli, 65b, rejected there.

6 A woman never has worn-out clothes since she always has occasion to wear rags. The Babli rejects this argument since in the absence of her husband she does not need a wardrobe of second rate dresses; she can wear real rags.

(34a, line 61) רִבִּי אִימִּי בְשֵׁם רִבִּי יוֹסֵי בֶּן חֲנִינָה. אַף הִיא אֵינָהּ עוֹשָׂה אוֹתָן דְּבָרִים שֶׁלְּיִיחוּד. מַה הֵן דְּבָרִים שֶׁלְּיִיחוּד. סָכָה לְהוֹן אֶת גּוּפָן וּמְרַחֶצֶת לְהוֹן אֶת פְּנֵיהֶן וּמוֹזֶגֶת לְהוֹן אֶת הַכּוֹס.

Rebbi Immi in the name of Rebbi Yose ben Ḥanina: Also she does not perform for them services of intimacy. What are services of intimacy? She rubs their bodies, washes their faces, or mixes their cup[7].

7   A slightly different list is in the Babli, 96a, also in the name of R. Yose ben Ḥanina. It is understood that the heirs have the right to expect from her all services a wife does for her husband, except those that are preliminaries to sexual relations.

(34a, line 64) וּמוֹסִיפִין לָהּ עַל מְזוֹנוֹתֶיהָ. אֵשֶׁת אִישׁ אֵין לָהּ יַיִן. אַלְמָנָה יֵשׁ לָהּ יַיִן. אֵשֶׁת אִישׁ שֶׁאָמְרָה. יֵצְאוּ מַעֲשֵׂה יָדַיי לִמְזוֹנוֹתַיי. אֵין שׁוֹמְעִין לָהּ. אַלְמָנָה שֶׁאָמְרָה. יֵצְאוּ מַעֲשֵׂה יָדַיי לִמְזוֹנוֹתַיי. שׁוֹמְעִין לָהּ.

One adds to her sustenance: A married woman has no wine[8], a widow has wine. If a married woman said, my earnings should be counted against my sustenance, one does not listen to her[9]; if a widow said, my earnings should be counted against my sustenance, one listens to her[10].

8   Cf. Chapter 5, Note 251.
9   She keeps all of her earnings and the husband does not have to pay for her (he still has to provide for her lodging.) The Babli emphatically permits such an arrangement by the wife's initiative (58b, 70a, 82b, 107b; *Baba qama* 40b; *Baba meṣi'a* 49b), i. e., against the husband's will. Since this is a money matter, the Yerushalmi will accept it in case of mutual agreement.
10 Even against the heirs' opposition.

(34a, line 66) רַב אָמַר. הַמֵּת אָמַר. אַל תְּקַבְּרוּנִי. נִקְבַּר בְּצִדְקָה. רִבִּי אִימִּי בְעָא. וְכִי עָלַת עַל דַּעְתָּךְ שֶׁיְּהוּ אֲחֵרִים מִתְפַּרְנְסִין מִשֶּׁלּוֹ וְהוּא נִקְבַּר בְּצִדְקָה. מַתְנִיתָא פְּלִיגָא עַל רַב. יוֹרְשֶׁיהָ הַיּוֹרְשִׁין כְּתוּבָּתָהּ חַייָבִין בִּקְבוּרָתָהּ. פָּתַר לָהּ בְּשֶׁיָּרְשׁוּ קַרְקַע. כְּהָדָא דְתַגִּי. הִנִּיחַ עֲבָדִים וּשְׁפָחוֹת וּשְׁטָרוֹת וּמְטַלְטְלִין. כָּל־הַקּוֹדֵם בָּהֶן זָכָה וַהֲלָהּ נִקְבַּר בְּצִדְקָה. מִפְּנֵי שֶׁקְּדָמָם וְתָפַס. הָא אִם לֹא קָדַם וְתָפַס מוֹצִיאִין מִיָּדוֹ. פָּתַר לֵיהּ בְּאוֹמֵר. קִבְרוּנִי. כְּהָדָא דְּאָמַר רִבִּי יוֹסֵי בְשֵׁם רַבָּנִין. נִקְבַּר הַמֵּת וְלֹא אָמַר. קִבְרוּנִי. אַף עַל פִּי שֶׁקָּדְמוּ אֲחֵרִים וְתָפְשׂוּ מוֹצִיאִין מִיָּדָן. בְּשֶׁתָּפְסוּ קַרְקַע. וְהָא דְאַתְּ אָמַר. מוֹצִיאִין מִיָּדָן. בְּשֶׁתָּפַס

קַרְקַע. אֲבָל בְּשֶׁתָּפְסוּ מְטַלְטְלִין אֵין מוֹצִיאִין מִיָּדָן. אֲבָל בְּמִלְוָה בְעֵדִים. בְּמִלְוָה בִשְׁטָר בֵּין שֶׁתָּפְסוּ קַרְקַע בֵּין שֶׁתָּפְסוּ מְטַלְטְלִין אֵין מוֹצִיאִין מִיָּדָן. דְּאָמַר רִבִּי אַבָּא בַּר רַב הוּנָא. עָשׂוּ דִבְרֵי שְׁכִיב מְרַע כִּבְרִיא שֶׁכָּתַב וְנָתַן. וְהוּא שֶׁמֵּת מֵאוֹתוֹ הַחוֹלִי. הָא הִבְרִיא לֹא. וּבִמְסַיֵּים וְאוֹמֵר. תְּנוּ שָׂדֶה פְלוֹנִית לִפְלוֹנִי. אָמַר. תְּנוּ שָׂדֶה פְלוֹנִית לִפְלוֹנִי. כְּמִי שֶׁסִּיֵּים. אוֹ עַד שֶׁיֹּאמַר. חֶצְיָיהּ בַּצָּפוֹן וְחֶצְיָיהּ בַּדָּרוֹם. רִבִּי יוּדָן בָּעֵי. אָמַר שָׂרְפוּנִי וְעַבְדוּ בִי עֲבוֹדָה וּתְנוּ חֲצִי שָׂדֶה פְלוֹנִית לִפְלוֹנִי. אִם אֵין שׂוֹרְפִין אֵין נוֹתְנִין. רִבִּי חַגַּיי בָּעָא. שְׁכִיב מְרַע שֶׁאָמַר. זָנוּנוּ בְנוֹתַיי. בְּלֹא כָךְ אֵין בְּנוֹתָיו נִיזוֹנוֹת. לֹא צוֹרְכָא דְלֹא. מָהוּ שֶׁיִּזּוֹנוּ מִן הַמְשׁוּעְבָּדִין וּמָהוּ שֶׁיִּזּוֹנוּ מִן הַמִּטַּלְטְלִין. רִבִּי יוּדָן בְּרַח לְנָוֵי אָתָא עוֹבָדָה קוֹמֵי רִבִּי יוֹסֵי. שְׁכִיב מְרַע שֶׁאָמַר. יִנָּתְנוּ אוֹתִיּוֹתָיו לִפְלוֹנִי. אָמַר לֵיהּ. אֵין שְׁכִיב מְרַע מְזַכֶּה אֶלָּא בִדְבָרִים שֶׁהֵן נִקְנִין אוֹ בִשְׁטָר אוֹ בִמְשִׁיכָה. וְאִילוּ נִקְנִין בִּמְשִׁיכָה וּבִשְׁטָר. כְּהָדָא דְתַנֵּי. סְפִינָה נִקְנֵית בִּמְשִׁיכָה. דִּבְרֵי הַכֹּל. רִבִּי נָתָן אוֹמֵר. סְפִינָה וְאוֹתִיּוֹת נִקְנִין בִּמְשִׁיכָה וּבִשְׁטָר. כָּתַב וְלֹא מָשַׁךְ מָשַׁךְ וְלֹא כָתַב לֹא עָשָׂה כְלוּם עַד שֶׁיִּכְתּוֹב וְיִמְשׁוֹךְ.

Rav said, if a dying person said, do not bury me, he is buried as a charge on public charity. Rebbi Immi asked, how could one think that others are provided for by his property and he is buried as a charge on public charity[11]? The Mishnah disagrees with Rav: "Her heirs, the heirs of her *ketubah*, are obligated to bury her.[12]" Explain it, if they inherited real estate[13]. As it was stated[14]: "If he left male and female slaves, mortgages, and movables, anybody[15] who takes them first acquires them and[16] he shall be buried by public charity." Because he took it first[17]. Therefore, if he did not take it first one removes from his hand. Explain it, if he said, bury me[18]. As Rebbi Yose said in the name of the rabbis: If a dead person was buried who had not said "bury me", even though others came and took [of his property] one removes from their hands. If they took real estate. In fact, what you say, one removes from their hands, if they took real estate. But if they took movables, one does not remove from their hands, if it was a loan by witnesses[19]. But for a documented loan, whether they took real estate or movables one does not[20] remove from their hands. For[21] Rebbi Abba, the son of Rav Huna, said[22]: They made the words of a bedridden person equal to those of a healthy person who wrote and delivered[23]. But only if he died from that illness, not if he recovered. And if he was explicit and said, give field X to Y. If he said, give field X to Y[24]? Is it as if he was explicit or only if he said, the Northern half, the Southern half?[25] Rebbi Yudan asked: If he said, burn me by pagan rites and give half of field X to Y. Since they do not burn, do they give?[26] Rebbi Haggai asked: A sick person who said, my daughters shall be supported. Would the daughters not be supported anyway[27]? No, it is necessary, for otherwise would they be supported from pledged real estate or would they be supported from movables[28]? Rebbi Yudan [   ][29] there came a case before Rebbi Yose about a bedridden person who had said, my documents shall be given to X. He said to him, the bedridden can only transfer property which is acquired either by a document *or* by taking hold[30]. But these are acquired by a document *and* by taking hold. As it was stated[31]: "A ship is acquired by taking hold in the opinion of everybody. Rebbi Nathan says a ship and documents are acquired by a document *and* by taking hold. [32]If he wrote and did not take hold, or took hold without writing [a transfer document] he did not do anything unless he both writes and takes hold."

11 This is the unanimous opinion of the Babli.

12 This is an obligation independent of the wishes of the

deceased.

13   Since usually a *ketubah* is payable in real estate.

14   A similar text in Tosephta 9:3.

15   Anybody with a claim sustainable in court, the widow for her *ketubah* or a creditor.

16   If nothing is left of his estate.

17   If the estate already had disappeared before the burial.

18   If the deceased had requested a burial before he died, the burial expenses are privileged.

19   In this case, time is of the essence since any one of the witnesses could die anytime. But real estate can be foreclosed only by a regular court procedure.

20   It seems that this is a scribal error and one should read: מוציאין "one does remove". Since the claim is documented, there is no need for the creditor to resort to self-help.

21   This is an unnecessary word; R. Abba explains general principles about the legal standing of death-bed requests.

22   In the Babli (*Baba batra* 152a, 175a; *Giṭṭin* 13a, 15a) this is an undisputed statement of Rav Naḥman.

23   The legal forms of a valid gift.

24   It seems that one has to read: Give field X to Y and Z. It is understood that each one gets half a field but the method of subdivision of the field was not indicated.

25   No answer is given since it is clear that the bequest cannot be enforced against the legal heirs; the burden of proof being on the claimants, who would have to prove in court that the method of division is that intended by the donor; this is impossible after the latter's death.

26   Since the first half of the request is clearly illegal, can the second half be legal?

27   Since daughters' right to sustenance is a standard condition of the *ketubah* (Mishnah 4:11), what did the mention of the daughters add to their rights?

28   At places where the *ketubah* could be taken only in real estate, the daughters could be supported only by real estate.

29   The words בָּרַח לְנוֹי "he fled to beauty" do not make sense here.

30   By bodily possession.

31   Tosephta *Qiddušin* 1:7.

32   This last sentence is not in the Tosephta or in the Babli (*Baba batra* 76a); R. Yose's ruling is rejected by Rav Naḥman (Note 22) who validates the transfer of documents by death-bed declaration.

(fol. 34a) **משנה ב**: אַלְמָנָה בֵּין מִן הָאֵירוּסִין בֵּין מִן הַנִּישׂוּאִין מוֹכֶרֶת שֶׁלֹּא בְּבֵית דִּין. רִבִּי שִׁמְעוֹן אוֹמֵר מִן הַנִּישׂוּאִין מוֹכֶרֶת שֶׁלֹּא בְּבֵית דִּין מִן הָאֵירוּסִין לֹא תִמְכּוֹר אֶלָּא בְּבֵית דִּין מִפְּנֵי שֶׁאֵין לָהּ מְזוֹנוֹת וְכָל־שֶׁאֵין לָהּ מְזוֹנוֹת לֹא תִמְכּוֹר אֶלָּא בְּבֵית דִּין.

Mishnah 2: A widow, whether after preliminary or definitive marriage, may sell without court supervision[33]. Rebbi Simeon says, after definitive marriage she may sell without court supervision; after preliminary marriage, she may sell only under court supervision since she has no sustenance and any person who has no claim to sustenance may sell only under court supervision.

33 The woman who becomes a widow before her definitive wedding may have a claim to *ketubah*; the widow after definitive marriage has a choice of either taking her *ketubah* or being sustained by the estate. Both Talmudim explain that nobody will want his family's honor compromised by forcing his widow into court; therefore, it is understood that he wrote the *ketubah* with the idea that it should be liquidated, if possible, in private.

(34b, line 24) **הלכה ב**: אַלְמָנָה בֵּין מִן הָאֵירוּסִין בֵּין מִן הַנִּישׂוּאִין כול׳. מִיסְבַּר סָבַר רִבִּי שִׁמְעוֹן. בִּמְזוֹנוֹת הַדָּבָר תָּלוּי. פָּסַק לָזוּן מִן הָאֵירוּסִין מוֹכֶרֶת שֶׁלֹּא בְּבֵית דִּין. פָּסַק לָזוּן מִן הַנִּישׂוּאִין לֹא תִמְכּוֹר אֶלָּא בְּבֵית דִּין. דִּבְרֵי חֲכָמִים. רִבִּי אָחָא רִבִּי חִינְּנָא בְּשֵׁם רִבִּי יוֹחָנָן. חַס הוּא אָדָם עַל כְּבוֹד אַלְמָנָתוֹ בֵּין מִן הָאֵירוּסִין בֵּין מִן הַנִּישׂוּאִין.

Halakhah 2: "A widow, whether after preliminary or definitive marriage," etc. Rebbi Simeon is of the opinion that everything depends on sustenance. If he had agreed to sustain her after preliminary marriage, she may sell without court supervision If he had agreed to sustain her after definitive marriage, she may sell only under court supervision[34]. The words of the Sages? Rebbi Aḥa, Rebbi Ḥinena in the name of Rebbi Joḥanan: A person is concerned for his widow's dignity[35] whether after preliminary or after definitive marriage.

34 If she is widowed before definitive marriage.
35 That she should not have to appear before an all-male court. This is also R. Joḥanan's opinion in the Babli, 97b, where it is not the only explanation.

(34b, line 29) רַב יְהוּדָה בְּשֵׁם שְׁמוּאֵל. הַמּוֹחֶלֶת כְּתוּבָּתָהּ לִיתוֹמִים נִיזוֹנֶת מִשֶּׁלָּהֶן. וְקַשְׁיָא. אִילוּ אִשָּׁה שֶׁאֵין לָהּ כְּתוּבָּה שֶׁמָּא אֵין לָהּ מְזוֹנוֹת. אִשָּׁה שֶׁאֵין לָהּ כְּתוּבָּה יֵשׁ לָהּ מְזוֹנוֹת. בְּרַם הָכָא לֹא דַּיָּיךְ שֶׁמְּחָלָה לִיתוֹמִין כְּתוּבָתָהּ אֶלָּא שֶׁאַתָּה מְבַקֵּשׁ לְהַבְרִיחָהּ מִמְּזוֹנוֹתֶיהָ.

Rav Jehudah in the name of Samuel: The one who renounced her *ketubah* in favor of the orphans is sustained by them. This is difficult. If there were a woman without *ketubah*[36], does she not have claim to sustenance? A woman without *ketubah* has claim to sustenance[37]. But here is it not enough that she renounced her *ketubah* in favor of the orphans, that you want to cheat her of her sustenance?

36 Cf. Mishnah 5:2; it is a matter of dispute whether a woman may donate her *ketubah* to her husband.
37 Since she is entitled to sustenance for the work she does in keeping house. The problem could not arise before the husband's death (hinted at in Babli 53a).

Many commentators want to emend the text; these emendations have to be rejected since the text as it stands is quoted in *Sefer Ha'iṭṭur* vol. 2, 32d, at Note 23.

(34b, line 32) רַב יְהוּדָה בְּשֵׁם רַב. הַתּוֹבַעַת כְּתוּבָתָהּ בְּבֵית דִּין אִיבְּדָה מְזוֹנוֹתֶיהָ. אָמַר רִבִּי יוֹסֵי. וּבִלְבַד מִן הַשּׁוֹפִי. הָא מֵאוֹנֶס לֹא. כְּהָדָא אַרְמַלְתָּא דְּרִבִּי אַבְדִּימוֹס דְּמוֹזְבָה. אָמְרוּ לָיהּ. רִבִּי בָּא בַר כֹּהֵן בְּעֵי לֵיהּ. תֶּבְעָה פְּרָנָהּ. אוֹבְדַת מְזוֹנוֹתֶיהָ. מִן דְּאִיתְיָדְעִין מִילַיָּיא אַעֲלוּן עוֹבְדָא קוֹמֵי רִבִּי יוֹסֵי. וְחָזְרָה לִמְזוֹנָה.

Rav Jehudah in the name of Rav[38]: If she requested her *ketubah* in court[39], she lost her claim to sustenance[40]. Rebbi Yose said, but only from a clear mind; not if forced. As in the case of the widow of Rebbi Eudaimon from Mozva to whom they[41] said, Rebbi Abba bar Cohen wants you. She requested her *ketubah* and lost her sustenance. After the matter became known[42], it was brought before Rebbi Yose and she returned to her sustenance.

38 In the Babli (*Ketubot* 54a, *Gittin* 25a, *Arakhin* 22a): Samuel.

39 Not if the request is made in private.

40 Since the widow is entitled either to be paid her *ketubah* or to be sustained by the estate.

41 The heirs informed her falsely that a rabbi of reputation wanted to marry her.

42 Fraudulent information by an interested party is counted as forced deal for the victim.

(34b, line 37) רִבִּי אֶלְעָזָר בְּשֵׁם רִבִּי יוֹסֵי בֶּן זִמְרָא. אַלְמָנָה שֶׁעָשְׂתָה שְׁנַיִם שְׁלֹשָׁה חֳדָשִׁים שֶׁלֹּא לִתְבּוֹעַ מְזוֹנוֹתֶיהָ אָבְדָה מְזוֹנוֹתֶיהָ דְּאֵינוּן תַּלְתֵּי יַרְחַיָּיא. בְּשֶׁלֹּא לִלְווֹת. אֲבָל אִם לָוְתָה גּוֹבָה. בְּשֶׁאֵין בְּיָדֶיהָ מַשְׁכּוֹן. אֲבָל אִם יֵשׁ בְּיָדֶיהָ מַשְׁכּוֹן אֲפִילּוּ לֹא לָוְתָה גּוֹבָה. רִבִּי יָסָא בְּשֵׁם רִבִּי יוֹחָנָן. זוֹ הִיא שֶׁאָמְרוּ. בַּתְּחִילָּה מוֹכְרִין מָזוֹן שְׁנֵים עָשָׂר חוֹדֶשׁ. וְנוֹתְנִין לָהּ מָזוֹן לְיוֹם. בְּסוֹף לְיוֹם הֵן אֲמָרִים. נָתְנוּ. וְהִיא אוֹמֶרֶת. לֹא נָטַלְתִּי. יָבוֹא כְּהָדָא. דָּמַר רִבִּי אַבָּהוּ בְּשֵׁם רִבִּי יוֹחָנָן. לוֹוָה מִמֶּנָּה יֹ"ב אֶלֶף לְשָׁנָה לִהְיוֹת מַעֲלֶה לָהּ מְדִינָר זָהָב לַחוֹדֶשׁ. פְּשִׁיטָא

חוֹדֶשׁ הָרִאשׁוֹן נָתַן וְחוֹדֶשׁ הָאַחֲרוֹן לֹא נָתַן. יָמִים שֶׁבְּנְתַיִים זוֹ הִיא שֶׁאָמְרוּ. הָא בַּתְּחִילָּה לֹא.

Rebbi Eleazar in the name of Rebbi Yose ben Zimra: A widow who lived two or three months without asking for sustenance, loses the sustenance of these three months[43]. That is, if she did not take a loan. But if she took out a loan, she collects. If there is no pledge in her hand. But if she has a pledge in her hand, she collects even if she did not take a loan[44]. Rebbi Yasa in the name of Rebbi Johanan: That is what they said, at the start one sells for sustenance of twelve months but one gives her sustenance for 30 days[45]. If at the end of thirty days they say, we gave, but she says, I did not receive[46], it would be similar to what Rebbi Abbahu said in the name of Rebbi Johanan: If one took a loan of 12'000 for a year in order to repay one gold denar[47] per month. It is obvious that he gave for the first month[48] and did not give for the last[49]. About the days in between they said, not at the start[50].

43 In the Babli, 97a, "two or three years".

44 Any action she takes earlier to show that she is aware of her claim validates the claim later.

45 If the widow goes to court to sell from the estate's real estate, it cannot be sold in small portions. One therefore sells to cover her sustenance for twelve months but the moneys are delivered to her in monthly installments since, as explained in the next paragraph, money delivered to the widow for her sustenance cannot be taken back (even if she remarries).

In the Babli, 97a, the time frame for which one sells is a matter of dispute.

46 Who carries the burden of proof? Is it the widow because she is the claimant, or is the *ketubah* considered as if collected in the widow's hand and the heirs want to deprive her of it and have to bring proof?

47 Under the Augustan monetary system, a gold denar was worth 25

silver denars. The present statement must have been formulated during the inflation of the Military Anarchy when the debased "silver" denars had even lost their name. In *Ma'aser Šeni* 4:1 (Notes 23,24) there is mention of an *aureus* worth 2'000. Cf. D. Sperber, *Roman Palestine 200-400, Money & Prices*, 1974, Chapter II.

48   Since this was due at the beginning of the contract, it may be presumed that payment was made. In this case, the burden of proof is on the recipient.

49   Since nobody can be presumed to pay before due date; if the payor claims to have paid before that day, the burden of proof is on him.

50   While in general in disputes about the fulfillment of contracts the burden of proof is on the claimant, in matters of payments to the widow the burden of proof is on the payor except for the first installment.

(34b, line 46) אָתָא רִבִּי אַבָּהוּ בְשֵׁם רִבִּי יוֹחָנָן. בַּתְּחִילָּה מוֹכְרִין מָזוֹן י'ב חוֹדֶשׁ וְנוֹתְנִין לָהּ מָזוֹן ל' יוֹם. וְיִמְכְּרוּ מָזוֹן שְׁנֵים עָשָׂר חוֹדֶשׁ. שֶׁלֹּא לְהוֹרַע כֹּחָהּ שֶׁל אִשָּׁה. וְיִתְּנוּ לָהּ מָזוֹן שְׁלֹשִׁים יוֹם. אִם אוֹמֵר אַתְּ כֵּן נִמְצֵאתָה חָב לִיתוֹמִים. כְּהָדָא דְתַנֵּי. אַלְמָנָה שֶׁתָּפְסָה אֲפִילוּ אֶלֶף זוּז לִמְזוֹנוֹתֶיהָ אֵין מוֹצִיאִין מִיָּדָהּ. מָהוּ מֵימַר לָהּ. הֲוִי מַה בְּיָדָיךְ. תַּלְמִידוֹי דְּרִבִּי מָנָא אָמְרִין לָהּ. הֲוִי מַה בְּיָדָיךְ. אָמַר לוֹן רִבִּי יוֹסֵי בֵּירִבִּי בּוּן. מִכֵּיוָן שֶׁהִיא עֲתִידָה לְהִישָּׁבַע בַּסּוֹף אֲפִילוּ מַה בְּיָדָיךְ אָמְרִין לָהּ. תְּהִי.

Rebbi Abbahu quoted in the name of Rebbi Johanan[51]: At the start one sells for sustenance of twelve months but one gives her sustenance for 30 days. Why should they sell for the sustenance of 12 months? Not to disadvantage the woman[52]. Why do they give her sustenance for 30 days? If you said otherwise, you would act in detriment of the orphans, as it was stated[53]: If a widow took possession even of 1'000 *zuz* for her sustenance, one does not take it away from her. What could one say to her? "Show[54] what is in your hands![55]" The students of Rebbi Mana said to her, "show what is in your hands." Rebbi Yose ben Rebbi Abun said to them, since in the end she will have to swear about anything in her hands⁵⁶, one says to her, let it be so.

51 Quoted in the preceding paragraph in the name of R. Yasa, Note 45. אתא here corresponds to גופא in the Babli as back reference.

52 She does not have to run after her sustenance every month.

53 A similar *baraita* is quoted in the Babli, 96a.

54 Reading הוי as equivalent of Babylonian חוי.

55 One might think that she can collect for next month's sustenance only after having accounted for the expenses of the past, reducing next month's payment by the amount not spent in the preceding.

56 If in the end she decides to take her *ketubah*, she has to deliver an accounting about any estate property in her hands.

(fol. 34a) **משנה ג**: מָכְרָה כְתוּבָּתָהּ אוֹ מִקְצָתָהּ נָתְנָה כְתוּבָּתָהּ לְאַחֵר אוֹ מִקְצָתָהּ לֹא תִמְכּוֹר אֶת הַשְּׁאָר אֶלָּא בְּבֵית דִּין. וַחֲכָמִים אוֹמְרִים מוֹכֶרֶת הִיא אֲפִילוּ אַרְבָּעָה וַחֲמִשָּׁה פְעָמִים. וּמוֹכֶרֶת לִמְזוֹנוֹת שֶׁלֹּא בְּבֵית דִּין וְכוֹתֶבֶת לִמְזוֹנוֹת מָכַרְתִּי. וּגְרוּשָׁה לֹא תִמְכּוֹר אֶלָּא בְּבֵית דִּין.

Mishnah 3: If she sold⁵⁷ her *ketubah* entirely or partially, or donated her *ketubah* to another, entirely or partially, she cannot sell the remainder except under court supervision⁵⁸. But the Sages say, she may sell even four or five times⁵⁹, and may sell for sustenance without court supervision but writes in the document that "I sold for sustenance." A divorcee may sell only under court supervision⁶⁰.

57 She sells her future right to the sum promised her in the *ketubah* to a speculator who assumes the risk that she might die before her husband and

the *ketubah* become void.

58 This belongs to R. Simeon's statement from the preceding Mishnah.

59 She may sell small portions of the *ketubah* without damaging her powers.

60 The divorcee can sell her former husband's property only if he sent her the bill of divorce from far away. In that case, the court supervision is justified to preserve the estate.

The Babli explains that the husband does not care if his divorcee has to apply to the court to collect her dues. The Yerushalmi rejects this argument in the second paragraph.

(34b, line 53) **הלכה ג**: מָכְרָה כְתוּבָתָהּ אוֹ מִקְצָתָהּ כול'. תַּנֵּי. מוֹכֶרֶת וְכוֹתֶבֶת אֵילוּ לִכְתוּבָּה וְאֵילוּ לִמְזוֹנוֹת. דִּבְרֵי רִבִּי יְהוּדָה. רִבִּי יוֹסֵי אוֹמֵר. מוֹכֶרֶת וְכוֹתֶבֶת סְתָם. וּבְזוֹ כֹּחָהּ מְיוּפֶּה. בָּאת מִלְוֶה בָעֵדִים. אוֹמֶרֶת. לִמְזוֹנוֹת מָכַרְתִּי. בָּאת מִלְוֶה בִשְׁטָר. אוֹמֶרֶת. לִכְתוּבָּה מָכַרְתִּי. וַאֲפִילוּ בָּאת מִלְוֶה בָעֵדִים מוֹכֶרֶת לִמְזוֹנוֹת וְחוֹזֶרֶת וְטוֹרֶפֶת לְשֵׁם כְּתוּבָּה. וְלָא אָמְרִין לָהּ. הֲוֵי זְבְנַיִיךְ. תִּיפְתָּר שֶׁהוֹקִיר הַמֶּקַח.

Halakhah 3: "If she sold her *ketubah* entirely or partially," etc. It was stated[61]: "She sells and writes 'this I sold for *ketubah*' and 'this I sold for sustenance,' the words of Rebbi Jehudah. Rebbi Yose said, she sells and writes non-specifically; in this she is empowered." If a loan before witnesses [comes due], she says, I sold for sustenance[62]. If a loan by contract [comes due], she says, I sold for my *ketubah*[63]. And even if a loan before witnesses [comes due], she sells for sustenance and turns around and forecloses it for her *ketubah*; could one not say to her, show your sale[64]? Explain it, if the object increased in value[65].

61 Tosephta 11:1; Babli 96b.

62 If the loan was executed after the date of her marriage, she can claim that the real estate is mortgaged to her *ketubah*. If there is no unincumbered real estate, the creditor is prevented

from foreclosing. A verbal loan executed before witnesses cannot be used to foreclose property sold after the loan was made.

63   If no real estate is left in the estate, the creditor cannot foreclose from the buyers if his contract was dated later than her *ketubah*.

64   In the first case (Note 62), could not the amount of the sale and its circumstances inform a competent appraiser whether it was for sustenance or *ketubah*? Since a sale for sustenance is a sale on credit, to be paid over a 12 months' period, should it not bring a premium price?

65   And today it is impossible to determine the fair value at the time of sale.

(34b, line 59) רִבִּי יַעֲקֹב בַּר אָחָא בְּשֵׁם רִבִּי יוֹחָנָן רִבִּי הִילָא בְּשֵׁם רִבִּי לֶעְזָר. כְּשֵׁם שֶׁאָדָם חַס עַל כְּבוֹד אַלְמָנָתוֹ כָּךְ חַס עַל כְּבוֹד גְּרוּשָׁתוֹ. דְּאָמַר רִבִּי יַעֲקֹב בַּר אָחָא בְּשֵׁם רִבִּי לֶעְזָר. מִבְּשָׁרְךָ לֹא תִתְעַלָּם זוֹ גְרוּשָׁתוֹ. אִיתְּתֵיהּ דְּרִבִּי יוֹסֵי הַגְּלִילִי הֲוַת מֵעִיקָה לֵיהּ סַגִּין. סְלִיק רִבִּי לֶעְזָר בֶּן עֲזַרְיָה לְגַבֵּיהּ. אֲמַר לֵיהּ. רִבִּי. שִׁיבְקָהּ. דְּלֵית הִיא דְאִיקָרְךָ. אֲמַר לֵיהּ. פּוֹרְנָהּ רַב עֲלוֹי. אֲמַר לֵיהּ. אֲנָא יְהִיב לָךְ פָּרְנָהּ וְשָׁבְקָהּ. יְהַב לָהּ פָּרְנָהּ וְשָׁבְקָהּ. אָזְלָה וּנְסִיבַת לְטַסוֹרָא דְקַרְתָּא. אִתְנְחַת מִן נִיכְסוֹי וְאִיתְעֲבִיד כְּסַגִּיא נְהוֹרָא וַהֲוַת מְחַזְּרָה לֵיהּ עַל כָּל־קַרְתָּא וּמַדְבְּרָא לֵיהּ. חַד זְמַן חֲזַרְתֵּיהּ עַל כָּל־קַרְתָּא וְלֹא אִיתְיְיהַב לֵיהּ כְּלוּם. אֲמַר לָהּ. לֵית הָכָא שְׁכוּנָה חוֹרִין. אָמְרָה לֵיהּ. אִית הָכָא שְׁכוּנָה דִמְשַׁבְּקִי. וְלֵית בְּחֵיילִי עַיִל לֵהּ לְתַמָּן. שָׁרֵי חָבִיט לָהּ. עֲבַר רִבִּי יוֹסֵי הַגְּלִילִי וְשָׁמַע קַלּוֹן מִתְבַּזַּיֵּי בְּשׁוּקָא. נָסְבוֹן וִיהָבוֹן בְּגוֹ חַד בֵּיתָא מִן דִּידֵיהּ וַהֲוָה מַסִּיק לוֹן מְזוֹנִין כָּל־יוֹמִין דַּהֲווֹן בַּחֲיִין. עַל שֵׁם וּמִבְּשָׂרְךָ לֹא תִתְעַלָּם זוֹ גְרוּשָׁתוֹ. אֲפִילוּ כֵן אַצִּיתוֹן קָלוֹי בַּלַּיְלְיָא וְשָׁמְעִין קוֹלָהּ אָמְרָה. לֹא הֲוָה טָב דַּיָּיהּ צַעֲרָהּ לְבַר מִן גּוּפָהּ וְלֹא לְגוֹ גוּפָהּ.

Rebbi Jacob bar Aḥa in the name of Rebbi Joḥanan, Rebbi Hila in the name of Rebbi Eleazar: Just as a man is concerned about his widow's honor so he has to be concerned about his divorcee's honor[66], as [67]Rebbi

Jacob bar Aḥa said in the name of Rebbi Eleazar, "do not hide yourself from your flesh"[68], that refers to one's divorcee. Rebbi Yose the Galilean's wife[69] did mistreat him badly. Rebbi Eleazar ben Azariah went to him and told him, rabbi, send her away, for she does not treat you with the honor due to you. He said to him, her *ketubah* is too large for me. He said to him, I shall give you the *ketubah* and send her away. He gave him the *ketubah* and he divorced her. She went and married the city treasurer[70]. That one lost his property and became blind. She took him around the town and led him. Once they went around the entire town and nobody gave him anything. He said to her, is there not another neighborhood? She said to him, there is the neighborhood of my divorcer; it is beyond my powers to bring you there. He started hitting her. Rebbi Yose the Galilean passed by and heard them demeaning one another in public. He took them, brought them to one of his houses, and provided them with food all the days of their lives, because "do not hide yourself from your flesh", that refers to one's divorcee[71]. Nevertheless they quarelled loudly in the night and her voice was heard saying, the pain she suffered outside her body was easier to bear than that inside her body[72].

66 This disagrees with the Mishnah.

67 From here on, more wordy parallels are in *Gen. rabba* 17(3), *Lev. rabba* 34(14); *Yalquṭ Šim'oni Torah* #23, 665, *Is.* #492; it is hinted at in *Tanna dBe Eliahu rabba* 27.

68 *Is.* 58:7.

69 In *Gen. rabba* she is referred to as his niece, his sister's daughter, whom to marry is considered meritorious by Pharisees based on *Is.* 58:7 (but sinful by Sadducees, *CD* V 7-10).

70 Musaphia identifies the word טסורא with Greek θησαυριστής "collector". The parallel words in the Midrashim seem to be corrupted.

71 Here end the parallels.

72 She preferred being beaten by her current husband to the mental pain inflicted on her by her ex-husband's generosity.

משנה ד: אַלְמָנָה שֶׁהָיְתָה כְתוּבָּתָהּ מָאתַיִם וּמָכְרָה שָׁוֶה מָנֶה בְּמָאתַיִם (fol. 34a)
אוֹ שָׁוֶה מָאתַיִם בְּמָנֶה נִתְקַבְּלָה כְתוּבָּתָהּ. הָיְתָה כְתוּבָּתָהּ מָנֶה וּמָכְרָה שָׁוֶה
מָנֶה וְדֵינָר בְּמָנֶה מִכְרָהּ בָּטֵל. אֲפִילוּ הִיא אוֹמֶרֶת אֲנִי אַחֲזִיר אֶת הַדֵּינָר
לַיּוֹרְשִׁין מִכְרָהּ בָּטֵל.

Mishnah 4: If a widow's *ketubah* was 200 and she sold[73] either the worth of a mina for 200[74] or the worth of 200 for a mina[75], her *ketubah* was paid. If her *ketubah* was for a mina and she sold the worth of a mina and a denar for a mina, her sale is void[76]. Even if she says, I shall return the denar to the heirs, her sale is void[77].

73 She sold her husband's property not under the supervision of the court.
74 She received what was due her.
75 It is her fault if she had sold too cheaply; from the estate she received real estate in the valuie of her *ketubah*. While she was within her rights to sell the property, she could have chosen the process of judicial appraisal which would have shielded her against any claims by the heirs or their guardians.
76 Since she had the right only to sell for the payment of her *ketubah*, any excess is an unauthorized sale and invalidates the entire transaction.
77 An unauthorized transaction cannot be validated after the fact.

הלכה ד: אַלְמָנָה שֶׁהָיְתָה כְתוּבָּתָהּ מָאתַיִם כול'. נִיחָא שָׁוֶה מָנֶה (34b, line 74)
בְּמָאתַיִם אוֹ שָׁוֶה מָאתַיִם בְּמָנֶה. מִכָּל־מָקוֹם הֲרֵי מַפְסִידָה אֶת הַיְתוֹמִין בְּמָנֶה
בְּשָׁוֶה מָנֶה בְּמָאתַיִם אֵין סוֹפוֹ לַחֲזוֹר מִשּׁוּם מִקַּח טָעוּת. תִּיפְתָּר שֶׁהוֹקִיר
הַמֶּקַח. אָמַר רִבִּי אָבִין. הָדָא מְסַייְעָא לְרִבִּי שִׁמְעוֹן בֶּן לָקִישׁ. דְּרִבִּי שִׁמְעוֹן בֶּן

לָקִישׁ אָמַר. אֵין לְמִקַּח הוֹנָיָיה לְעוֹלָם. אָמַר רִבִּי יוֹחָנָן. אִם הָיָה הַמִּקָּח מוּפְלָג יֵשׁ לוֹ הוֹנָיָיה. מַתְנִיתָא פְּלִיגָא עַל רִבִּי יוֹחָנָן. אֵילוּ דְבָרִים שֶׁאֵין לָהֶן הוֹנָיָיה. הָעֲבָדִים וְהַשְּׁטָרוֹת וְהַקַּרְקָעוֹת וְהַהֶקְדֵּישׁוֹת. פָּתַר לָהּ. וּבִלְבַד דָּבָר שֶׁאֵינוּ מוּפְלָג. פָּדָה שָׁוֶה מָנָא בְּמָאתַיִם. רִבִּי יוֹחָנָן אָמַר. אֵינוּ פָדוּי. וְרִבִּי שִׁמְעוֹן בֶּן לָקִישׁ אָמַר. פָּדוּי. מַתְנִיתָא פְּלִיגָא עַל רִבִּי יוֹחָנָן. אָמַר. טַלִּית זֶה תַּחַת חֲמוֹר זֶה. יָצָא לְחוּלִין. וְסֵיפָא פְּלִיגָא עַל רִבִּי שִׁמְעוֹן בֶּן לָקִישׁ. צָרִיךְ לְהֵיעָשׂוֹת דָּמִים. אָמַר רִבִּי יוֹסֵה. כָּל־גַּרְמָהּ אֲמְרָה שֶׁהוּא צָרִיךְ לְהֵיעָשׂוֹת דָּמִים. מַה פְּלִיגִין. לְהָבִיא מְעִילָה. רִבִּי יוֹחָנָן אָמַר. מֵבִיא קָרְבָּן מְעִילָה. וְרִבִּי שִׁמְעוֹן בֶּן לָקִישׁ אָמַר. אֵינוּ מֵבִיא קָרְבַּן מְעִילָה.

Halakhah 4: "If a widow's *ketubah* was 200," etc. We understand worth a mina for 200[78] or worth 200 for a mina. In any case, she made the orphans lose a mina[79]. [If it was worth] a mina [and she sold it] for 200, would the sale not be invalidated as erroneous buy[80]? Explain it that the property increased in value[81]. Rebbi Abin said, this supports Rebbi Simeon ben Laqish, since Rebbi Simeon ben Laqish said, real estate buys are never under the laws of overcharging. Rebbi Johanan said, if the transaction was excessive, it comes under the law of overcharging. The Mishnah[82] disagrees with Rebbi Johanan: "The following do not fall under the laws of overcharging: Slaves, securities, real estate, and redemptions[83]." He explains it, unless it was excessive[84]. If he redeemed[85] what was worth a mina by 200, Rebbi Johanan said, it is not redeemed, but Rebbi Simeon ben Laqish said, it is redeemed[86]. A *baraita* disagrees with Rebbi Johanan: If he said, this toga instead of this donkey, the latter becomes profane[87]. And its end disagrees with Rebbi Simeon ben Laqish: It is necessary to compute the value[88]. Rebbi Yose said, the *baraita* itself implies that it is necessary to compute the value. Where do they disagree?

To bring [a sacrifice to atone for] larceny[89]. Rebbi Joḥanan said, he has to bring a sacrifice for larceny; Rebbi Simeon ben Laqish said, he does not have to bring a sacrifice for larceny.

78 The Babli, 98 ab, does not hold that it is trivial that the widow is not rewarded for getting such a good deal; it concludes that an agent by his office is always required to look for the best possible deal and the widow sells as an agent for the estate.

79 That she receives only 100 *zuz* for her *ketubah* if she sells real estate too cheaply is not a matter of the laws of *ketubah* but of torts in general; the person who causes damage has to pay for it.

80 *Lev.* 25:14: "If you sell a sale to you neighbor or buy from your neighbor's hand, do not overcharge one another." Rabbinic interpretation holds that an overcharge of a sixth, $16^2/_3\%$, entitles the injured party to rescind the transaction.

81 And the fair value on the date of transaction can no longer be determined.

82 *Baba meṣi'a* 4:9.

83 Real estate is excluded in *Lev.* 25:14 since it is not bought "from his hand"; slaves are excluded since they are traded under the rules of real estate; securities are excluded since what one buys "from the neighbor's hand" is the paper, but what is intended are the rights given by the paper and these are immaterial. The Temple is excluded in its transactions since it is not "a neighbor" (Babli *Baba meṣi'a* 56b).

84 He holds that any transaction is void in which the profit margin is 100% of the fair value. Tosaphot (*s. v.* אלמנה, 98a) find the same opinion expressed by Rav Naḥman in the Babli, *Baba meṣi'a* 57a.

85 He had donated something (other than a sacrificial animal) to the Temple. The redemption rules are based on *Lev.* 27:11-25.

86 The standard commentators agree to switch the places of "mina" and "200 *zuz*". Since the Yerushalmi never quotes Samuel's statement in the Babli (*Baba meṣi'a* 57a and 7 other instances) that a redemption of dedicated items worth a mina by a *peruṭa* is valid (i. e., in ratio 19200 : 1), there is no reason to assume that there should be any difference in the rules

for overpaying or underpaying.

87 He substitutes a toga for the dedicated donkey (which is redeemable since it is not a sacrificial animal) and presumably the donkey is worth at least two togas.

88 It is a biblical requirement that dedications can be redeemed only after their value has been determined (*Lev.* 27:12). The presumption is that the statement means not only that the value has to be determined but also that it has to be paid in full.

89 Unauthorized use of Temple property is sinful and has to be atoned for by a special sacrifice (*Lev.* 5:14-16). If the redemption of the donkey was valid, no sacrifice is due for using the donkey even if there remains the additional obligation to make up the difference in price between toga and donkey. If the redemption is invalid because the difference in price between the dedicated and the substitute values is too large, a sacrifice is due. The Babli, *Baba meṣi'a* 57a/b, is not quite sure to whom to attribute which opinion in this dispute.

(fol. 34a) **משנה ח:** רַבָּן שִׁמְעוֹן בֶּן גַּמְלִיאֵל אוֹמֵר לְעוֹלָם מִכְרָהּ קַיָּים עַד שֶׁתְּהֵא שָׁם כְּדֵי שֶׁתְּשַׁיֵּיר בַּשָּׂדֶה בַּת תִּשְׁעַת קַבִּים וּבַגִּנָּה בַּת חֲצִי קַב. וּכְדִבְרֵי רַבִּי עֲקִיבָה בֵּית רוֹבַע. הָיְתָה כְתוּבָּתָהּ אַרְבַּע מֵאוֹת זוּז וּמָכְרָה לָזֶה בְמָנֶה וְלָזֶה בְמָנֶה וְלָזֶה בְמָנֶה וְלָאַחֲרוֹן יָפֶה מָנֶה וְדִינָר בְּמָנֶה שֶׁלָּאַחֲרוֹן בָּטֵל וְשֶׁלְּכוּלָּן מִכְרָן קַיָּים.

Mishnah 5: Rabban Simeon ben Gamliel says, her sale is valid[90] unless there would have been left a field [for sowing] nine *qab*[91], and in a garden[92] half a *qab*, or following the words of Rebbi Aqiba, a fourth. If her *ketubah* was 400 *zuz*[93] and she sold to one person worth 100, to a second 100, to a third 100, and to the last the value of a mina and a denar for a mina, the last transaction is invalid but all others are valid.

90 This Mishnah is the direct continuation of the preceding one; in most Mishnah mss. it is part of Mishnah 4. Rabban Simeon ben Gamliel holds that the sale, about which the heirs claim that the widow sold too cheaply, is valid if the field which would have remained in the heirs' hands would not have qualified as an independent piece of agricultural real estate. Mishnah *Baba batra* 1:10 gives minimal measures for different kinds of real estate; if these measures are not reached, the real estate cannot be subdivided. Therefore, if the parcel, which the heirs claim should not have been sold, would be one that could not be sold under the rules of *Baba batra*, the widow cannot be faulted if she gave it away essentially for free; it is not a case of over- or undercharging.

91 The standard unit for agricultural land is *bet se'ah*, a plot of land on which in normal practice of extensive agriculture one would sow one *se'ah* of seed grain, which by tradition is fixed at 2500 square cubits (cf. *Peah* 2:1, Note 31). One *se'ah* equals 6 *qab*; the field of 9 *qab* then is 3750 square cubits. In the opinion of R. Jehudah, half of this area is a tradeable field.

92 A garden is intensively worked, irrigated property. The area for half a *qab* would then be $2500:12 = 208\ 1/3$ square cubits, and a quarter *qab* $104\ 1/6$.

93 This sentence refers back to Mishnah 4, and is not only Rabban Simeon ben Gamliel's. If one of several connected transactions is declared invalid, the others are not affected.

(34c, line 12) **הלכה ה**: רַבָּן שִׁמְעוֹן בֶּן גַּמְלִיאֵל אוֹמֵר לְעוֹלָם מִכְרָהּ קַיָּים כול'. עַד כְּדוֹן בְּשֶׁמְּכָרוּהָ לָהֶן בְּאַרְבַּע שְׁטָרוֹת. מְכָרָהּ לָהֶן בִּשְׁטָר אֶחָד תַּפְלוּגְתָּא דְרַבִּי יוֹחָנָן וְרַבִּי שִׁמְעוֹן בֶּן לָקִישׁ. דְּאִיתְפַּלְגוּן. כָּתַב כָּל־נְכָסָיו לִשְׁנֵי בְנֵי אָדָם כְּאַחַת וְהָיוּ הָעֵדִים כְּשֵׁרִין לָזֶה וּפְסוּלִין לָזֶה. רַבִּי הִילָא בְּשֵׁם רַבִּי יָסָא. אִיתְפַּלְגוּן רַבִּי יוֹחָנָן וְרַבִּי שִׁמְעוֹן בֶּן לָקִישׁ. חַד אָמַר. מֵאַחַר שֶׁהֵן פְּסוּלִין לָזֶה פְּסוּלִין לָזֶה. וְחָרָנָה אָמַר. כְּשֵׁירִין לָזֶה וּפְסוּלִין לָזֶה. רַבִּי מָנָא לֹא מְפָרֵשׁ. רַבִּי אָבִין מְפָרֵשׁ. רַבִּי יוֹחָנָן אָמַר. מֵאַחַר שֶׁהֵן פְּסוּלִין לָזֶה פְּסוּלִין לָזֶה. וְרַבִּי שִׁמְעוֹן בֶּן לָקִישׁ אָמַר. כְּשֵׁירִין לָזֶה וּפְסוּלִין לָזֶה. אָמַר רַבִּי לֶעֲזָר. מַתְנִיתָא מְסַיְיעָא לְרַבִּי יוֹחָנָן. מָה הַשְּׁנַיִם נִמְצָא אֶחָד מֵהֶן קָרוֹב אוֹ פָסוּל עֵידוּתָן

בְּטִילָה. אַף הַשָּׁלֹשָׁה נִמְצָא אֶחָד מֵהֶן קָרוֹב אוֹ פָּסוּל עֵידוּתָן בְּטִילָה. מִנַּיִין אֲפִילוּ מֵאָה. תַּלְמוּד לוֹמַר עֵידִים. רִבִּי יַעֲקֹב בַּר אָחָא אָמַר. אִיתְפַּלְגוּן רִבִּי חֲנַנְיָה חַבְרִין דְּרַבָּנִין וְרַבָּנִין. חַד אָמַר. יָאוּת אָמַר רִבִּי לֶעְזָר. וְחָרְנָה אָמַר. לֹא אָמַר רִבִּי לֶעְזָר יָאוּת. מָאן דָּמַר. יָאוּת אָמַר רִבִּי לֶעְזָר. נַעֲשִׂית עֵדוּת אֶחָד מֵאִישׁ אֶחָד. וּמָאן דָּמַר. לֹא אָמַר רִבִּי לֶעְזָר יָאוּת. נַעֲשִׂית כִּשְׁתֵּי כִיתֵּי עֵדוּת כְּשֵׁירִין לָזֶה וּפְסוּלִין לָזֶה.

4 העדים | גי עדים   הילא | גי אילא   בשם ר' | מ אמר   יסא | גי אמי מ -   7 אבין |
מ אבון   לעזר | גי אלעזר   9 עיידותן | גי מ עדותן (2 times)   מניין . . . עיידים | גי -
11 עיידים | מ עדים   12 חברין | מ חברון   13 לעזר יאות | גי לעזר   לעזר | גי
אלעזר   14-13 עדות אחד מאיש אחד | גי עדות אחת ובאיש אחד כעדות שבטלה
מקצתה בטלה כולה   מ עידות אחת וכהתרייה אחת. וכל עדות שבטלה מקצתה בטלה
כולה   14 נעשית | גי נעשה   עדות | גי מ עדים

Halakhah 5: "Rabban Simeon ben Gamliel says, her sale is valid," etc. That is, if she sold them in four contracts[94]. If she sold them in one contract, there is disagreement between Rebbi Johanan and Rebbi Simeon ben Laqish, as they disagreed[95]: If somebody wrote all his property over to two persons in one document[96] and the testimony of the witnesses was valid for one but invalid for the other[97]. Rebbi Hila in the name of Rebbi Yasa: Rebbi Johanan and Rebbi Simeon ben Laqish disagreed; one said, since it is invalid for one it is invalid for the other, but the other said, it is valid for one and invalid for the other. Rebbi Mana did not specify; Rebbi Abin specified: Rebbi Johanan said, since it is invalid for one it is invalid for the other[98]; but Rebbi Simeon ben Laqish said, it is valid for one and invalid for the other[99]. Rebbi Elazar said, a Mishnah[100] supports Rebbi Johanan: "Since testimony of two [witnesses] is invalid if one of them turns out to be related or disqualified, so also of three [witnesses] it is invalid if one of them turns out to be related or disqualified. From where even 100? The verse[101] says, 'witnesses'". Rebbi Jacob bar Aha said, Rebbi Hananiah the colleague of the rabbis and the rabbis disagree. One says, the argument of Rebbi Eleazar is correct, but the other says, the argument of Rebbi Eleazar is not correct. For him who says, the argument of Rebbi Eleazar is correct, it is as if there was one testimony about one person. For him who says, the argument of Rebbi Eleazar is not correct, it is as if two groups of witnesses came, valid for one and disqualified for the other[102].

94 The Halakhah deals only with the last case mentioned in the Mishnah, that the widow overstepped her authority only in part of the sale of property. If the legal and illegal contracts were executed separately, there is no reason to invalidate the earlier contracts because of the (necessarily last) invalid contract.

95 The same text is in *Giṭṭin* 1:1 (43a l. 54) וג and *Makkot* 1:16 (31b l. 26) מ; it is quoted in Alfasi *Makkot* 1, #1063 and discussed by his commentators R. Nissim Gerondi and Nahmanides.

96 His will.

97 Relatives are not admitted as witnesses even in civil proceedings.

98 He holds that testimony, even if in writing, is one whole; either it is valid or invalid. If it is invalid in one case, it must be invalid in general.

99 The testimony has to be separated from its application. If the witnesses are known not to be felons, their testimony is valid. In the case of a relative, it is not applicable.

100 *Makkot* 1:12. *Deut.* 17:6 reads: "By the testimony of two witnesses or three witnesses the guilty person shall be condemned to death; he cannot be condemned by the testimony of a single witness." The question is raised, if two witnesses are sufficient, why are three mentioned? The answer given in the Mishnah is that the since two witnesses are both disqualified if one of them is disqualified (in which case the remaining witness becomes a single witness), a group of three (or 100) witnesses who all testify to exactly the same effect is disqualified if one of them is disqualified. The witnesses signing a document necessarily all

testify to exactly the same facts. (Alfassi #1062 notes that the Geonim restrict the Mishnah to criminal cases.)

101 *Deut.* 17:6.

102 Since practice is not decided either way, the legal heirs can successfully attack the validity of the will, and the guardians of the orphans the validity of the entire sale by the widow.

(fol. 34a) **משנה ו:** שׁוּם הַדַּיָּינִין שֶׁפָּחֲת שְׁתוּת אוֹ הוֹתִיר שְׁתוּת מִכְרָן בָּטֵל. רַבָּן שִׁמְעוֹן בֶּן גַּמְלִיאֵל אוֹמֵר מִכְרָן קַיָּים אִם כֵּן מַה כֹּחַ בֵּית דִּין יָפֶה. אֲבָל אִם עָשׂוּ אִיגֶּרֶת בִּיקוֹרֶת אֲפִילוּ מָכְרוּ שָׁוֶה מָנֶה בְּמָאתַיִם אוֹ שָׁוֶה מָאתַיִם בְּמָנֶה מִכְרָן קַיָּים.

Mishnah 6: If the judges estimated one sixth too little or too much, their sale is invalid[103]. Rabban Simeon ben Gamliel says, their sale is valid[104]; otherwise, what is the court's power worth? But if they offered public tender[105], even if they sold either the worth of a mina for 200 or the worth of 200 for a mina, their sale is valid.

103 Since any overcharging of at least one sixth empowers the injured party to annul the transaction.

104 If they followed the rules of public sales detailed in Tractate *Arakhin*.

105 They made a written public announcement of a public sale and invited tenders and then sold to the highest bidder. The actual bids received are the best estimate of the value of real estate and override expert testimony as to the intrinsic value of the land.

Following Rashi, אִיגֶּרֶת בִּיקוֹרֶת is a circular inviting people to visit (בִּיקוּר) the property and make their offers.

(34c, line 28) **הלכה ו:** שׁוּם הַדַּיָּינִין שֶׁפָּחַת שְׁתוּת אוֹ הוֹסִיף שְׁתוּת כול'. כְּמָה דְּאַתְּ אָמַר בְּהֶדְיוֹט. בְּקַרְקַע עַד שְׁלִישׁ. בְּמִטַּלְטְלִין עַד שְׁתוּת. וְדִכְוָותָהּ בְּהֶקְדֵּשׁ. בְּקַרְקַע עַד שְׁתוּת וּבְמִטַּלְטְלִין עַד יב. תַּמָּן תַּנִּינָן. שׁוּם הַיְתוֹמִים שְׁלֹשִׁים יוֹם. שׁוּם הֶקְדֵּשׁ שִׁשִּׁים יוֹם. וּמַכְרִיזִין בַּבּוֹקֶר וּבָעֶרֶב. וְלָמָּה שְׁלֹשִׁים. כְּדֵי לְיַיפּוֹת כּוֹחָן שֶׁלִּיתוֹמִים. וְיַכְרִיזוּ יוֹתֵר. עַד שְׁלֹשִׁים יוֹם אַתְּ מְיַפֶּה כּוֹחָן. מִיכָּן וְאֵילַךְ אַתְּ מְרִיעַ כּוֹחָן. וֶאֱמוֹר אַף בְּהֶקְדֵּשׁ כֵּן. שַׁנְיָיא הִיא הֶקְדֵּשׁ. שֶׁאַתְּ תּוֹפֵס רִאשׁוֹן רִאשׁוֹן. וְיַכְרִיזוּ לְעוֹלָם. דַּייּוֹ לְהֶקְדֵּשׁ שֶׁיְּהֵא כִפְלַיִים בְּהֶדְיוֹט. אָמַר רִבִּי יוּדָן. מִן מַה דְּאַתְּ אָמַר. שַׁנְיָיא הִיא הֶקְדֵּשׁ שֶׁאַתְּ תּוֹפֵס רִאשׁוֹן רִאשׁוֹן. הָדָא אָמְרָה שֶׁאִם אָמְרוּ יִמְצָאוּ שׁוּמָן שֶׁאֵין מַחֲזִירִין וּמַחְלִיטִין.

Halakhah 6: "If the judges estimated one sixth too little or too much," etc. As you say for a private person, in real estate up to one third[106], in movables up to one sixth[80]. And similarly, for Temple property, in real estate up to one sixth, in movables up to [one in] twelve[107]. There[108], we have stated: "The estimation for orphans is thirty days, the estimation for Temple property sixty days, and one publicly announces mornings and evenings[109]." And why thirty? In order to empower the orphans. Why should they not announce longer? Up to thirty days you empower the orphans, more than that you diminish their power[110]. Why do you not say that for Temple property? Temple property is different because each offer made is firm[111]. Then they should announce forever! If suffices for the Temple that it should be twice that of a private person. Rebbi Yudan said, since you say that Temple property is different because each offer made is firm, this implies that if they find their estimation they do not continue but close the deal[112].

106 R. Joḥanan was reported to say in Halakhah 4 that in real estate the deviation must be 100%. This is interpreted here to mean than the

overcharge cannot be more than 100% of the undercharge, 150% *vs*. 50%, giving a ratio of 3 to 1 (*Pnei Mosheh*)..

107 For redemption of property dedicated to the Temple, all terms are halved or doubled to the advantage of the Temple as exemplified in the Mishnah, next Note.

108 *Arakhin* 6:1; cf. Tosephta *Ketubot* 11:3.

109 The court's herald announces the sale twice daily in public.

110 In less than 30 days one is not sure that all potential buyers hear of the sale; a shorter period would diminish the number of bidders. If the process is drawn out too long, people lose interest and one diminishes the number of buyers.

111 Each offer made to the Temple administration obliges the bidder to act on his bid until he is notified that he was released from his obligation because a higher bid was accepted. The Temple does not have to worry that it would lose bidders in a drawn out process.

112 If the administration had decided on an adequate price, the first bidder meeting this price can immediately be given possession and the public announcements stopped, since the Temple will get its full price. The sixty day period is a possibility, not a necessity.

(34c, line 38) וּמַכְרִיזִין בַּבּוֹקֶר וּבָעֶרֶב. בִּיצִיאַת פּוֹעֲלִים וּבְהַכְנָסַת פּוֹעֲלִים. וְאוֹמֵר שָׂדֶה וְסִימָנֶיהָ. אָמַר רִבִּי יוֹסֵי. בְּשֶׁלֹא מָצְאוּ שׁוּמָן מַחֲלִיטִין. דּוּ מַתְנִיתָא. שׁוּם הַדַּיָּינִים שֶׁפָּחַת שְׁתוּת אוֹ הוֹתִיר שְׁתוּת מִכְרָן בָּטֵל. מִפְּנֵי שֶׁפָּחֲתוּ אוֹ הוֹתִירוּ. אֲבָל מָצְאוּ שׁוּמָן מַחֲלִיטִין. אָמַר רִבִּי חֲנַנְיָה קוֹמֵי רִבִּי מָנָא. מַה חֲמִית מֵימַר. בְּשֶׁלֹא הוּכְרְזוּ אֲנָן קַיָּימִין. מִן דְּבַתְרָהּ. אֶלָּא אִם כֵּן עָשׂוּ אִיגֶּרֶת בִּיקּוֹרֶת. מָהוּ אִיגֶּרֶת בִּיקּוֹרֶת. רִבִּי יְהוּדָה בַּר פָּזִי אָמַר. אַכְרָזָה.

"And one announces mornings and evenings," at the time when [agricultural] workers go out or come back, and he mentions the field and its description[113]. Rebbi Yose said, if they do not get their estimated price[114], they can conclude the sale. Is that the Mishnah, "if the judges estimated one sixth too little or too much, their sale is invalid"? Because they sold too low or too high, but if they found their estimate they close the deal[115]. Rebbi Ḥananiah said before Rebbi Mana: What can you say, we deal with the case that they did not announce in public[116]! From what is said afterwards: "Except if they offered public tender." What is public tender? Rebbi Jehudah bar Pazi said, announcement[117].

113 Babli *Arakhin* 21b. As explained there, the landlord can then tell his workers to look up the property offered and to report back in the evening.

114 After the 30 days of public announcement. (The Babli in the end substitutes 8 weeks of announcement on market days for the 30 days of daily announcement.)

115 Even before the 30 days are up.

116 The disagreement between the rabbis and Rabban Simeon ben Gamliel is only in the absence of a public tender.

117 Quoted by Rashi in his commentary to the Mishnah.

(34c, line 44) עוּלָא בַּר יִשְׁמָעֵאל אָמַר. עֲבָדִים שֶׁלֹּא יִבְרְחוּ. וּשְׁטָרוֹת וּמִטַּלְטְלִין שֶׁלֹּא יִגָּנֵבוּ. רִבִּי בָּא בַּר כֹּהֵן בְּעָא קוֹמֵי רִבִּי יוֹסֵי. לֵית הָדָא אָמְרָה שֶׁהָעֶבֶד נִפְדֶּה בִשְׁלֹשָׁה. אָמַר לֵיהּ. אִין. וְהָתַנִּינָן. וּבְקַרְקָעוֹת תִּשְׁעָה וְכֹהֵן. וְאָדָם כְּיוֹצֵא בָהֶן. אָמַר לֵיהּ. אָדָם שֶׁכֵּן בֶּן חוֹרִין הוּא.

1 בר | מ בר'   ושטרות | מ שטרות ס השטרות   ומטלטלין | מ ומיטלטלין ס והמטלטלין
2 יגנבו | מ ייגנבו   יוסי | מ יוסה   שהעבד נפדה | מ שהעבדים נפדים ס שהעבדים נפדין
3 אין | ס אכין   4 שכן | מ דהכא ס דכא

[118]Ulla bar Ismael said, slaves lest they flee, securities and movables lest they be stolen[119]. Rebbi Abba bar Cohen asked before Rebbi Yose: Does this not imply that a slave is redeemed in front of three people[120]? He answered him, yes. He said to him, but did we not state[121]: "Real estate[122] nine persons and a Cohen, and a human[123] by the same rule"? He answered him, the human here is a free person.

118 This paragraph is also in *Megillah* 4:4 (75b l. 22), noted ם, and *Sanhedrin* 1:3 (19b l.6), noted ט. The origin is in *Sanhedrin* since only there one finds the *baraita* which is explained by Ulla: "The following are not subject to public tender: Slaves, securities, and movables."

119 Since the owner has to be mentioned, thieves would be informed that it is worth while to break into that house.

120 If a slave was dedicated to the Temple and then redeemed by his owner, this should be a private procedure.

121 Mishnah *Sanhedrin* 1:3, determining the number of jurors in judicial cases.

122 Real estate dedicated to the Temple and redeemed following the rules of *Lev.* 27:22-23.

123 A person who dedicates his own worth and finds it impossible to give the prescribed value; *Lev.* 27:8. In both cases, the Cohen's determination has to be made in public; the definition of "public knowledge" is "known by at least 10 people."

(34c, line 48) חֲנַנְיָה בַּר שִׁילְמְיָה בְּשֵׁם רַב. אָתָא עוֹבְדָא קוֹמֵי רִבִּי. בְּעָא מֵיעֲבַד כְּרַבָּנָן. אָמַר לוֹ רִבִּי אֶלְעָזָר בֶּן פְּרָטָא בֶּן בְּנוֹ שֶׁל רִבִּי אֶלְעָזָר בֶּן פְּרָטָא. לֹא כֵן לִימַּדְתָּנוּ בְשֵׁם זְקֵינֶיךָ. אֶלָּא אִם כֵּן עָשׂוּ אִיגֶּרֶת בִּיקוּרֶת. וְקִיבְּלָהּ. וְחָזַר בֵּיהּ וַעֲבַד כְּרַבָּן שִׁמְעוֹן בֶּן גַּמְלִיאֵל.

[124]Hananiah bar Šelemiah in the name of Rav: A case came before Rebbi, who wanted to act following the rabbis[125]. Rebbi Eleazar ben Proteus, the grandson of Rebbi Eleazar ben Proteus[126], said to him: Did you not teach us in your old man's[127] name, "except if they offered public tender"[128]? He accepted it; Rebbi changed his mind and acted following Rabban Simeon ben Gamliel.

124 With slight changes in names this is quoted in the Babli, 100a.

125 A case was appealed to him, in which the local court had sold property, deviating more than a sixth from the appraised value. He wanted to annul the sale.

126 Who can be dated to the first

half of the Second Century.
127 For זקיניך as "your father" cf. S. Lieberman, תיקוני ירושלמי *Tarbiz* 4(1933), p. 378.
128 In this interpretation, the last sentence of the Mishnah is Rabban Simeon's and is disputed by the rabbis. This disagrees with the findings above, Note 116. In the Babli, the entire case dealt with a sale without public announcement which Rebbi refrained from annulling.

(fol. 34a) **משנה ז:** הַיְתוֹמָה וְהַשְּׁנִיָּיה וְהָאַיְילוֹנִית אֵין לָהֶן כְּתוּבָה וְלֹא פֵירוֹת וְלֹא מְזוֹנוֹת וְלֹא בְלָאוֹת. וְאִם מִתְּחִילָּה נְשָׂאָהּ לְשֵׁם אַיְילוֹנִית יֵשׁ לָהּ כְּתוּבָה. אַלְמָנָה לְכֹהֵן גָּדוֹל גְּרוּשָׁה וַחֲלוּצָה לְכֹהֵן הֶדְיוֹט מַמְזֶרֶת וּנְתִינָה לְיִשְׂרָאֵל בַּת יִשְׂרָאֵל לְנָתִין וּלְמַמְזֵר יֵשׁ לָהֶן כְּתוּבָה.

Mishnah 7: Neither the orphan[129], nor the secondarily prohibited[130], nor the she-ram[131] may claim *ketubah*, or usufruct[132], or sustenance, or depreciation[133]. But if he married her from the start as a she-ram, she has claim to her *ketubah*[134]. A widow [married] to the High Priest[135], a divorcee or one who had received *ḥaliṣah* to a common priest[136], a bastard or Gibeonite girl to an Israel, an Israel girl married to a bastard or Gibeonite[137], have claim to *ketubah*.

129 The orphaned underage girl who was married off by her mother or brothers, who repudiated her husband before reaching adulthood (cf. *Yebamot* 1:2, Note 118). By walking out, she showed the marriage to be non-existent (*Yebamot* Mishnah 13:4).

In all Babli mss. and in all Mishnah mss. of the Babylonian tradition, instead of "the orphan" one reads outright הַמְמָאֶנֶת "the repudiating". Cf. *The Babylonian Talmud with Variant Readings, Kethuboth II*, p. תיד, Note 59. The Yerushalmi version must have been the original one since the Babli, 100b, discusses whether the Mishnah implies that no minor can claim a *ketubah*.

130 She is her husband's relative but not a close one; her marriage is valid by biblical standards but considered incestuous by rabbinical rules; *Yebamot* 2:4, Note 67. But since the marriage is valid by biblical standards, her children are not bastards. She is denied a *ketubah* in order to induce her to refuse the marriage from the start.

131 The infertile female who lacks secondary female sex characteristics; cf. *Yebamot* 1:1, Note 65. If she was married underage and failed to become an adult physically, the husband may claim that he entered the marriage thinking that she was fully female and that, therefore, the marriage transaction was in error and invalid.

132 The husband does not have to return the usufruct he had from her dowry during the existence of the marriage.

133 He is not responsible to replace depreciated goods brought as her dowry.

134 Not only *ketubah*, but all other payments due to the divorcee or widow, since the marriage certainly was valid.

135 The High Priest is forbidden to marry her (*Lev.* 21:14); she is not forbidden to marry him but she is barred from eating sanctified food and her children are desecrated from the priesthood. By biblical decree, she and her children are desecrated. This is punishment. Her marriage is biblically valid; there is no rabbinic reason to deny her the *ketubah* and the benefits accruing automatically to a wife.

136 He is forbidden to marry her (*Lev.* 21:7); she is not forbidden to marry him but she is barred from eating sanctified food and her children are desecrated from the priesthood.

137 The bastard is forbidden by biblical law to marry an Israelite girl (*Deut.* 23:3, cf. *Yebamot* 1:5 Note 176; 4:15 Note 211), the Gibeonite by an old popular tradition ascribed to King David (*Yebamot* 2:4, Note 72). By Mishnah *Qiddušin* 3:14, in both cases the children inherit the status of the partner with the lower status.

(34c, line 52) **הלכה ז**: הַיְתוֹמָה וְהַשְּׁנִיָּה וְהָאַיְלוֹנִית כול'. נִיחָא שְׁנִיָּיה אַיְלוֹנִית. יְתוֹמָה. וִיתוֹמָה אֵין לָהּ כְּתוּבָּה. רִבִּי חִזְקִיָה רִבִּי אַבָּהוּ בְּשֵׁם רִבִּי יוֹחָנָן. תִּיפְתָּר בִּיתוֹמָה שֶׁמֵּיאֵינָה. רבִּי אַייבוֹ בַּר נַגְרִי רִבִּי אִימִי. כְּשֵׁם שֶׁקָּנְסוּ

בָּהּ כָּךְ קָנְסוּ בוֹ. לֵיי דֶה מִילָה. שֶׁאִם קִידְּשָׁהּ בְּלִיטְרָא שֶׁלְּזָהָב שֶׁהוּא מְאַבֵּד אֶת הַכֹּל.

Halakhah 7: "Neither the orphan girl, nor the secondarily prohibited, nor the she-ram," etc. One understands the secondarily prohibited and the she-ram. The orphan? Does an orphan not have *ketubah*? Rebbi Ḥizqiah, Rebbi Abbahu in the name of Rebbi Joḥanan: Explain it for an orphan who repudiated[129]. Rebbi Ayvo bar Naggari, Rebbi Immi: Just as they fined her, so they fined him. In which respect? That if he preliminarily married her by [giving her] a pound of gold, he loses it all.

(34c, line 56) וְלֹא פֵירוֹת. אָמַר רְבִּי יִרְמְיָה. שֶׁאֵין לוֹ עָלֶיהָ אֶלָּא אֲכִילַת פֵּירוֹת בִּלְבַד. תַּנֵּי רְבִּי יוֹסֵי צַיְידָנַיָּיא קוֹמֵי רְבִּי יִרְמְיָה וּפָלִיג עַל רְבִּי יִרְמְיָה. וְזַכַּאי בִּמְצִיאָתָהּ וּבְמַעֲשֶׂה יָדֶיהָ וּבְהֶפֵר נְדָרֶיהָ. מַהוּ לֹא פֵירוֹת. שֶׁאֵינָהּ יְכוֹלָה לְהוֹצִיא מִמֶּנּוּ אֲכִילַת פֵּירוֹת שֶׁאָכַל.

2 ציידנייא | • ציידנייה   לא | • ולא

[138]"No usufruct." Rebbi Jeremiah said, that he has from her only the usufruct. Rebbi Yose the Sidonian stated before Rebbi Jeremiah, in disagreement with Rebbi Jeremiah: "He has the right to what she finds and earns, and to dissolve her vows." What means "no usufruct"? That she cannot reclaim from him the usufruct he had [from her property].

138 From here to the end of the Halakhah, this is Halakhah *Yebamot* 9:4, variant readings noted י, explained there in Notes 31-53.

(34c, line 60) אָמַר רְבִּי יוֹסֵי. בְּכָל־שָׁעָה הֲוָה רְבִּי הִילָא רְבִּי אָמַר לִי. תְּנִי מַתְנִיתָךְ. יוֹרְשָׁהּ וּמִיטַּמֵּא לָהּ. וְתַנִּי רְבִּי חִייָא כֵן. מְטַמֵּא הוּא אָדָם לְאִשְׁתּוֹ כְשֵׁירָה. וְאֵינוֹ מִיטַמֵּא לְאִשְׁתּוֹ פְּסוּלָה.

1 יוֹסִי | י יוֹסה   בכל | י כל   הוה | י הויא   ר' הילא רבי | י ר' הילא   2 ר' חייא | י -
3 לאשתו | י באשתו (2 times)   כשירה | י הכשירה

Rebbi Yose said: All the time my teacher Rebbi Hila told me, state in your *baraita* that he inherits from her and defiles himself for her. We have also stated so: A man defiles himself for his qualified wife but does not become defiled for his disqualified wife.

(34c, line 56) רִבִּי רְאוּבֵן בְּעָא קוֹמֵי רִבִּי מָנָא. עַבְדֵי שְׁנִיּוֹת מַהוּ שֶׁיֹּאכְלוּ בִתְרוּמָה. אָמַר לֵיהּ. שְׁתוֹק וְיָפָה לָךְ. הִיא אוֹכֶלֶת וַעֲבָדֶיהָ אֵינָן אוֹכְלִין.

1 ראובן | י אבון[139]   שנייות | י שניות

Rebbi Reuben asked before Rebbi Mana: May the slaves of a secondarily forbidden [wife] eat heave? He said to him, be quiet, it is better for you. She eats but her slaves do not eat.

139 It is impossible to decide between the two versions; R. Reuben could have asked R. Mana I and R. Abun II R. Mana II.

(34c, line 64) תַּמָּן תַּנִּינָן. גֵּט הַמְעוּשֶׂה בְיִשְׂרָאֵל כָּשֵׁר וּבַגּוֹיִם פָּסוּל. שְׁמוּאֵל אָמַר. פָּסוּל וּפוֹסֵל בִּכְהוּנָה. שְׁמוּאֵל אָמַר. אֵין מְעַשִׂין אֶלָּא כְּגוֹן אַלְמָנָה לְכֹהֵן גָּדוֹל. גְּרוּשָׁה וַחֲלוּצָה לְכֹהֵן הֶדְיוֹט. וְהָא תַּנִּינָן. שְׁנִיּוֹת. לָא בְגִין דָּא אָמַר שְׁמוּאֵל. וְהָא תַּנִּינָן. הַמַּדִּיר אֶת אִשְׁתּוֹ מִלֵּיהָנוֹת לוֹ. עַד שְׁלֹשִׁים יוֹם יַעֲמִיד פַּרְנָס. יוֹתֵר מִכֵּן יוֹצִיא וְיִתֵּן כְּתוּבָּה. שָׁמַעְנוּ שֶׁהוּא מוֹצִיא. שָׁמַעְנוּ שֶׁכּוֹפִין.

1 המעושה | י מעושה   2 בכהונה | י לכהונה   - | י ומר שמואל. אכרזון בקרויכון פסול ופוסל בכהונה. שמואל אמר. אין מעשין אלא פוסלין   4 דא | י -   מכן | י מיכן
6 שכופין | י כופין

There, we have stated: "A forced bill of divorce is valid in Israel[41]; it is invalid from Gentiles.[42]" Samuel said, it is invalid and disqualifies for the priesthood. Samuel said, one does not force, only disqualify. Samuel said, one does not force except for example a widow married to a High Priest, a divorcee or one freed by *ḥaliṣah* for a simple priest. But did we not state: "Secondarily forbidden"? Did he not say "for example"? But did we not state: "A person who by a vow forbids his wife to have any usufruct from him, up to 30 days he shall appoint a caretaker; after 30 days he shall divorce her and pay *ketubah*"! We heard that he shall divorce; did we hear that one forces him?

(34c, line 69) מַה בֵּין אֵילוּ לָאֵילוּ. אֵילוּ עַל יְדֵי שֶׁהֵן דִּבְרֵי תוֹרָה דִּבְרֵי תוֹרָה צְרִיכִין חִיזּוּק. לְפִיכָךְ יֵשׁ לָהּ כְּתוּבָה. וְאֵילוּ עַל יְדֵי שֶׁהֵן דִּבְרֵי סוֹפְרִין וְדִבְרֵי סוֹפְרִין צְרִיכִין חִיזּוּק. לְפִיכָךְ אֵין לָהּ כְּתוּבָה. אִית דְּבָעֵי מֵימַר. אֵילוּ עַל יְדֵי שֶׁקְּנָסָן בְּיָדָן וּבְיַד הַוָּלָד וְלֹא קְנָסוּ בָּהֶן דָּבָר אַחֵר. לְפִיכָךְ יֵשׁ לָהּ כְּתוּבָה. וְאֵילוּ עַל יְדֵי שֶׁאֵין קְנָסָן בְּיָדָן וּבְיַד הַוָּלָד וְקָנְסוּ בָּהֶן דָּבָר אַחֵר. לְפִיכָךְ אֵין לָהּ כְּתוּבָה. מַה נְפִיק מִן בֵּינֵיהוֹן. הַמַּחֲזִיר גְּרוּשָׁתוֹ מִשֶּׁנִּיסֵּית. מָאן דָּמַר. אֵילוּ עַל יְדֵי שֶׁהֵן דִּבְרֵי תוֹרָה. וְזוֹ הוֹאִיל וְהוּא דְבַר תּוֹרָה לְפִיכָךְ יֵשׁ לָהּ כְּתוּבָה. וּמָאן דָּמַר. אֵילוּ עַל יְדֵי שֶׁקְּנָסָן בְּיָדָן וּבְיַד הַוָּלָד. וְזוֹ הוֹאִיל וְאֵין קְנָסָהּ בְּיָדוֹ וּבְיַד הַוָּלָד לְפִיכָךְ אֵין לָהּ כְּתוּבָה.

1 תורה | י תורה ואין   לה | י להן   (all occurrences) 6 נפיק | י נפק   גרושתו | י את גרושתו   7 משניסית | י משנישאת   דמר | י דאמר   8 ומאן דמר | י ואית דבעי מימר   9 וזו | י וזה

What is the difference between these and those? Since these are words of the Torah and the words of the Torah [do not][140] need support, therefore they have *ketubah*. Those, because they are words of the Sopherim and the words of the Sopherim need support, therefore they do not have *ketubah*. Some want to say since these are punished together with the child, they did not fine them, therefore they have *ketubah*. Those, since they are not punished together with the child, they fined them, therefore they do not have *ketubah*. What is the difference between them? He who remarried his divorced wife after she had remarried. For him who says since these are words of the Torah, and this case is a word of the Torah, therefore she has *ketubah*. For him who says since these are punished together with the child, this one, since neither she nor the child is punished, therefore, she has no *ketubah*.

140 Missing in *Ketubot*; considered a scribal error since it is implied by the later quote.

(34d, line 3) רִבִּי יַעֲקֹב בַּר אָחָא אָמַר. רִבִּי זְעִירָא וְרִבִּי הִילָא תְּרֵיהוֹן אָמְרִין. בִּמְזוֹנוֹת פְּלִיגִין. רִבִּי יוֹחָנָן אָמַר. יֵשׁ לָהּ מְזוֹנוֹת. אָמַר לֵיהּ רִבִּי אֱלִיעֶזֶר. אוֹמְרִים לוֹ.¹⁶¹ הוֹצִיא. וְאַתְּ אָמַר אָכֵין. הוּא בָעֵי מֵימַר. מָן דָּמַר. כְּתוּבָּה פְּלִיגִין. רִבִּי יוֹחָנָן אָמַר. יֵשׁ לָהּ תְּנָאֵי כְתוּבָּה. אָמַר לֵיהּ רִבִּי אֶלְעָזָר. כָּל־עַמָּא מוֹדֵי שֶׁאֵין לָהּ מְזוֹנוֹת. בְּיוֹרְשֶׁיהָ קָנְסוּ. כָּל־שֶׁכֵּן בָּהּ. מָאן דָּמַר. פְּלִיגִין. בִּמְזוֹנוֹת. הָא בִּתְנַאי כְתוּבָּה לֹא. בָּהּ קָנְסוּ. לֹא קָנְסוּ בְּיוֹרְשֶׁיהָ.

1 זעירא | י זעירה   2 אליעזר | י לעזר   3 לו | י לה   אכין | י הכין   הוא | י הוון   בעי | י בעיין   מימר | י מימר כן   4 בתנאי | י בתניי   ר' יוחנן ... ר' אלעזר | י -   5 כל שכן | י לא כל שכן   6 מאן | י ומאן   פליגין במזונות | י במזונות פליגין   בתניי | י בתניי   בה | י למה. בה   לא | י ולא

Rebbi Jacob bar Aḥa said that Rebbi Zeʿira and Rebbi Hila say that they differ about sustenance. Rebbi Joḥanan said, she may demand sustenance. Rebbi Eleazar said to him, one says to him, divorce her! And you say so? They wanted to say, for him who says they differ about the conditions attached to a *ketubah*, Rebbi Joḥanan said, she has the *ketubah* stipulations. Rebbi Eleazar said to him, everybody agrees that she cannot claim support since they even punished her heirs, so much more herself. But for him who says that they differ about sustenance, it follows that they do not differ about the stipulations of a *ketubah*. They fined her, but did not fine her heirs.

הנושא את האשה פרק שנים עשר

(fol. 34d) **משנה א**: הַנּוֹשֵׂא אֶת הָאִשָּׁה וּפָסְקָה עִמּוֹ כְּדֵי שֶׁיָּזוּן אֶת בִּתָּהּ חָמֵשׁ שָׁנִים חַיָּיב לְזוּנָהּ חָמֵשׁ שָׁנִים. נִישֵּׂאת לְאַחֵר וּפָסְקָה עִמּוֹ כְּדֵי שֶׁיָּזוּן אֶת בִּתָּהּ חָמֵשׁ שָׁנִים חַיָּיב לְזוּנָהּ חָמֵשׁ שָׁנִים. לֹא יֹאמַר הָרִאשׁוֹן לִכְשֶׁתָּבֹא אֶצְלִי אֲזוּנָהּ אֶלָּא מוֹלִיךְ לָהּ מְזוֹנוֹתֶיהָ לַמָּקוֹם שֶׁהִיא. וְכֵן לֹא יֹאמְרוּ שְׁנֵיהֶן הֲרֵי אָנוּ זָנִין אוֹתָהּ כְּאֶחָד אֶלָּא אֶחָד זָנָהּ וְאֶחָד נוֹתֵן לָהּ דְּמֵי מְזוֹנוֹת.

Mishnah 1: If somebody marries a woman and contracts with her to sustain her daughter[1] for five years, he is obligated to sustain her for five years[2]. If [the mother] was married[3] to another man who contracted with her to sustain her daughter for five years, he is obligated to sustain her for five years. The first one cannot say, if she will come to live with me I shall sustain her, but he has to bring her support to her place[4]. Similarly, the two cannot say we shall support her in common, but one of them sustains her and the other gives the money equivalent to her sustenance.

1   From a prior marriage.

2   Even if he divorces her mother before the end of the five years, since his obligation is towards the daughter, and obligations towards minors cannot be renegotiated.

3   During the five years from her marriage to the first.

4   Who is with her mother, in the second husband's house.

(34d line 32) **הלכה א**: הַנּוֹשֵׂא אֶת הָאִשָּׁה וּפָסְקָה עִמּוֹ כול'. בַּמֶּה הוּא מִתְחַיֵּיב לָהּ. לֹא כֵן רִבִּי יוֹחָנָן וְרִבִּי שִׁמְעוֹן בֶּן לָקִישׁ תְּרֵיהוֹן אָמְרִין. הַכּוֹתֵב שְׁטַר חוֹב עַל חֲבֵירוֹ בְּחֶזְקַת שֶׁהוּא חַיָּיב לוֹ וְנִמְצָא שֶׁאֵינוֹ חַיָּיב לוֹ אֵינוֹ חַיָּיב לִיתֵּן לוֹ.

רִבִּי שִׁמְעוֹן בֶּן לָקִישׁ אָמַר. עָשׂוּ אוֹתָהּ כְּתוֹסֶפֶת כְּתוּבָּה. וְיִתֵּן בְּסוֹף. עָשׂוּ אוֹתָהּ כְּקִידּוּשֵׁי אִשָּׁה. וְיִתֵּן מֵשָּׁעָה הָרִאשׁוֹנָה. עָשׂוּ אוֹתָהּ כִּמְקַדֵּשׁ אֶת הָאִשָּׁה עַל מְנָת לִיתֵּן לָהּ יֹ"ב דֵּינָר זָהָב בַּשָּׁנָה לִהְיוֹת מַעֲלֶה לָהּ מִדֵּינָר זָהָב לַחוֹדֶשׁ.

Halakhah 1: " If somebody marries a woman and had contracted with her," etc. How does he become indebted to her[5]? Do not Rebbi Joḥanan[6] and Rebbi Simeon ben Laqish both say, if somebody writes a debenture for another person under the assumption that he owes him and it turns out that he does not owe, he does not have to give to him[7]! Rebbi Simeon ben Laqish said, they gave it the status of an addition to the *ketubah*[8]. Then he should have to pay in the end[9]! They gave it the status of the gift for a woman's preliminary marriage[10]. Then he should pay up front[11]! They treated it as when one marries a woman preliminarily by promising to give her twelve silver denars within one year by delivering one silver denar's worth every month[12].

5   Since obviously the intention of the groom was to feed the daughter with her mother in his house; if he had known that he would divorce the mother before the daughter reached marriageable age he would not have agreed to these terms. Can he not claim now that he entered the obligation in error?

6   In the Babli, 101b, he is reported to hold that an obligation entered into voluntarily cannot be repealed, as pointed out by Tosaphot, 102a *s. v.* אליבא.

7   Cf. Chapter 5, Halakhah 1.

8   A voluntary addition by the groom to the minimal amounts of the *ketubah*, which is protected by all privileges given to the *ketubah*.

9   Not at the end of five years but at the end of the marriage, when the entire *ketubah* becomes due immediately. But the Mishnah lets him pay off his obligation for the remainder of the five years.

10   This is an awkward formulation of the answer given to the question in the Babli (102a): The mother acquires the rights for her daughter under the special rules for acquisition by the

children of sums promised by the respective parents when they decide on the marriage pact, cf. 5:1 (Notes 15,16), 6:2 (Note 29). The acquisition of rights by mother and daughter as a consequence of the oral promise of the groom.

11 Anything promised for preliminary marriage has to be delivered at the preliminary marriage.

12 The husband delivers by taking the daughter to live in his house together with her mother.

(34d line 38) תַּנֵּי. זָנָהּ חָמֵשׁ שָׁנִים הָרִאשׁוֹנִים בֵּין בְּיוֹקֶר בֵּין בְּזוֹל. הָיוּ בְיוֹקֶר וְהֵזִילוּ. אִם הוּא גָרִים נוֹתֵן בְּיוֹקֶר. וְאִם הִיא גָרְמָה נוֹתֵן בְּזוֹל. הָיוּ בְזוֹל וְהוֹקִירוּ. בֵּין שֶׁהוּא גָרַם בֵּין שֶׁהִיא גָרְמָה נוֹתֵן בְּזוֹל. הָדָא הִיא. הַבַּת לֹא עוֹלָה וְלֹא יוֹרֶדֶת.

It was stated: He supports her the first five years, whether in inflation or in deflation. If [living expenses] were high and became low, if he was the cause[13], he pays the high rate, if she was the cause, he pays the low rate. If they were low and became high, whether he was the cause or she was the cause, he pays the low rate[14]. That is, "the daughter neither ascends nor descends.[15]"

13 If he divorced the girl's mother by his own initiative before the end of the contracted years.

14 He obligated himself only for living expenses which were the going rate at the time the contract was signed.

15 Cf. Chapter 5:6, Note 154.

(34d line 42) תַּמָּן תַּנִּינָן. בְּנָן נוּקְבָן דְּיִהְוְיָן לִיכִי מִינַּאי אִינּוּן תְּהוֹן יָתְבָן בְּבֵיתִי וּמִתְזְנָן מִנִּכְסַיי. וְתַנֵּי עֲלָהּ. וּמִתְכַּסְּיָין בִּכְסוּתִי. מַעֲשֶׂה יְדֵי הַבַּת שֶׁל מִי. נִישְׁמְעִינָהּ מִן הָדָא. נִישֵּׂאת. הַבַּעַל חַיָּיב בִּמְזוֹנוֹתֶיהָ וְהֵן נוֹתְנִין לָהּ דְּמֵי מְזוֹנוֹת. הָדָא אָמְרָה. זָנָהּ וּמַעֲשֶׂה יָדֶיהָ שֶׁלְּבַעֲלָהּ. אָמַר רַבִּי יוֹסֵי. הָדָא אָמְרָה. פָּסַק לָזוּן כַּלָּתוֹ זָנָהּ וּמַעֲשֶׂה יָדֶיהָ שֶׁלִּבְנוֹ. הוּא רוֹצֶה שֶׁתָּבוֹא אֶצְלוֹ וְהִיא אֵינָהּ רוֹצָה.

הַדִּין עִמָּהּ. דְּתַנִּינָן. וְהֵן נוֹתְנִין לָהּ דְּמֵי מְזוֹנוֹת. חָלַת כְּמִי שֶׁנִּישֵׂאת. מֵתָה כְּמִי שֶׁנִּישֵׂאת. מֵתָה כְּבָר מֵתָה.

There[16], we have stated: "The female children you will have by me shall live in my house and be supported by my estate," and it was stated about this: They will be clothed with garments supplied by me[17]. For whom does the daughter work? Let us hear from the following[18]: "The husband has to sustain her and they pay the cost of her sustenance." This means, he feeds her but she works for her husband[19]. Rebbi Yose[20] said, this means that if somebody had agreed to sustain his daughter-in-law, he has to sustain her, but she works for his son. If he wants her to be with him[21] but she does not want to, the law is with her, as we have stated: "They pay the cost of her sustenance." If she fell ill, it is as if she had married. If she died, is it as if she had married[22]? If she died, she already is dead[23].

16 Mishnah 4:13.

17 One should not interpret מזונות narrowly as "food" but more generally as "sustenance" (but excluding rent.)

18 Mishnah 12:2, about the wife's daughter who marries while her mother's (ex-)husbands continue to support her.

19 And if the daughter is still unmarried, she works for herself.

20 Rosh (Chapter 12, #1) reads: Rebbi Assi; this means that he read here דְּבֵי יָסָא, an unlikely reading.

21 The daughter of his divorcee, in the case that her mother did not remarry.

22 Is the husband's obligation one that the wife's daughter's heirs can collect?

23 The obligation ends with the daughter's death. In the Babli, *Baba batra* 140a, this is considered to be obvious.

KETUBOT CHAPTER TWELVE

(fol. 34d) **משנה ב**: נִיסֵּית הַבַּת הַבַּעַל חַיָּיב בִּמְזוֹנוֹתֶיהָ וְ[הֵן][24] נוֹתְנִין לָהּ דְּמֵי מְזוֹנוֹת. מֵתוּ בְּנוֹתֵיהֶן נִזּוֹנוֹת מִנְּכָסִים בְּנֵי חוֹרִין וְהִיא נִזּוֹנֶת מִנְּכָסִים מְשׁוּעְבָּדִים מִפְּנֵי שֶׁהִיא כְּבַעֲלַת חוֹב. הַפִּיקְחִים הָיוּ כוֹתְבִין עַל מְנָת שֶׁאָזוּן אֶת בִּתֵּךְ חָמֵשׁ שָׁנִים כָּל־זְמַן שֶׁאַתְּ עִמִּי.

Mishnah 2: If the daughter[25] married, the husband has to sustain her and they pay the cost of her sustenance. If they died[26], their daughters are supported from unincumbered property but she is supported from mortgaged property since her status is that of a creditor[27]. The intelligent ones did write: On condition that I support your daughter for five years the entire time you are with me[28].

24 In the ms: ואין "they do not." This is an obvious scribal error which has been corrected from the quote in Halakhah 1.
25 The one mentioned in Mishnah 1.
26 The mother's husband and/or ex-husband.
27 Her claim is that of her mother's *ketubah*.
28 Then the daughter's claim is terminated if either the mother is divorced or the mother or the husband died.

(34d line 49) **הלכה ב**: נִיסֵּית הַבַּת. הַבַּעַל חַיָּיב בִּמְזוֹנוֹתֶיהָ כול׳. תַּנֵּיי כְּתוּבָה שֶׁכְּתָבוֹ בִשְׁטָר. רִבִּי יַעֲקֹב בַּר אָחָא אָמַר. אִיתְפַּלְּגוֹן רִבִּי יוֹחָנָן וְרִבִּי שִׁמְעוֹן בֶּן לָקִישׁ. רִבִּי יוֹחָנָן אָמַר. לְחִיזּוּק כְּתָבָן. וְרִבִּי שִׁמְעוֹן בֶּן לָקִישׁ אָמַר. לִגְבּוֹת מִן הַמְשׁוּעְבָּדִים כְּתָבָן. רִבִּי יִרְמְיָה מַחֲלִיף שְׁמוּעָתָהּ. אָמַר רבי יוּדָן. מַתְנִיתָא מְסַייְּעָא לְמָאן דָּמַר. לְחִיזּוּק כְּתָבָן. דְּתַגִּינָן תַּמָּן. אֵין מוֹצִיאִין לַאֲכִילַת פֵּירוֹת וּלְשֶׁבַח קַרְקָעוֹת וּלְמְזוֹן הָאִשָּׁה וְהַבָּנוֹת מִנְּכָסִים הַמְשׁוּעְבָּדִים מִפְּנֵי תִּיקּוּן הָעוֹלָם. לֹא בִשְׁטָר. אַף הָכָא בִשְׁטָר. אָמַר רִבִּי חֲנַנְיָה. מִפְּנֵי שֶׁהִיא כְּבַעֲלַת חוֹב. לֹא בִשְׁטָר. אַף הָכָא בִשְׁטָר.

Halakhah 2: "If the daughter married, the husband has to sustain her," etc. What is the status of the *ketubah* stipulations if he wrote them in the document[29]? Rebbi Jacob bar Aha said, Rebbi Johanan and Rebbi Simeon ben Laqish disagree. Rebbi Johanan said, he wrote them for emphasis[30]; Rebbi Simeon ben Laqish said, he wrote them to collect from encumbered property. Rebbi Jeremiah switched the traditions[31]. Rebbi Yudan said, a Mishnah supports him who said, he wrote them for emphasis, since we stated there[32]: "One does not foreclose from mortgaged property to indemnify for produce or investment[33], or sustenance of widow and daughters[34], in order not to impede the economy." Are [the first categories] not based on a document? Here also based on the document[35]. Rebbi Hanania said, "since her status is that of a creditor"! Is that not based on a document? Here also based on the document[36].

---

29   All the stipulations enumerated in Mishnaiot 4:7 ff. are enforceable even if they are not written in the *ketubah*. What is the legal difference between a *ketubah* in which the stipulations are explicit and one in which they are implicit?

30   Without legal consequences. (In Rashi's interpretation of the Babli, 102b, Rav Ashi agrees.)

31   He switched the attributions to R. Johanan and R. Simeon ben Laqish. Therefore, the discussion proceeds without referring to names.

32   Mishnah *Gittin* 5:3.

33   If somebody sold a field, the title to which was later disputed and the court awarded the title to another person who then takes the field away from the buyer. The innocent buyer then has regress on the fraudulent seller. Real estate is always sold with a title guarantee; therefore the value of the field can be taken from the seller's mortgaged property (depending on the time of sale). But both the value of the standing crop which the buyer lost, and the value of the investments the buyer made in the property cannot be recovered from mortgaged property. The main difference is that the privileged amount, the value of the

field, is a well-defined sum written in the sales contract, whereas the rest are open-ended obligations which cannot be foreseen and whose inclusion in the causes for foreclosure would bring all real estate transactions to a halt.

34 These also are open-ended obligations which cannot be estimated beforehand; they cannot be enforced against mortgage holders, in contrast to the *ketubah* sum which is well-defined.

35 Since the regress of the buyer on the fraudulent seller is based on the sales contract, and it turns out that only part of the claim can be satisfied by foreclosure, it shows that the *ketubah* document also has parts which have the status of certificates of indebtedness and other parts which cannot be enforced by foreclosure.

36 The wife's daughter's claim is also based on her mother's *ketubah* document and is enforceable as a creditor's claim but her mother's own claim to sustenance as a widow is based on the same document and not thus enforceable.

(34d line 57) מֵתָה אֵינָהּ עִמָּהּ. נִתְגָּרְשָׁה אֵין עִמָּהּ. הֶחֱזִירָהּ. מָאן דְּאָמַר. לִכְתוּבָּה אֲבָל לֹא לִתְנָאִין תַּנֵּי. מָאן דְּאָמַר. בֵּין לִכְתוּבָּה בֵּין לִתְנָאִין. מַה חֲנֵי. הַפִּיקְחִים הָיוּ כוֹתְבִין. עַל מְנָת שֶׁאֲנִי זָן אֶת בִּתֵּךְ חָמֵשׁ שָׁנִים כָּל־זְמַן שֶׁאַתְּ עִמִּי. וְתַנֵּי עֲלָהּ. וּבִלְבָד מִן הַנִּישּׂוּאִין הָרִאשׁוֹנִים. וְאָתְיָיא כַּיי דָּמַר רִבִּי חֲנִינָה. הַמֵּשִׂיא אֶת בְּנוֹ בַּבַּיִת זָכָה בַּבַּיִת. וּבִלְבָד מִן הַנִּישּׂוּאִין הָרִאשׁוֹנִים.

If she dies she is not with him[37]. If she was divorced she is not with him. If he took her back[38]? One says, this was stated for the *ketubah* but not for the stipulations; one says, both for the *ketubah* and the stipulations, which opinion is valid[39]? "The intelligent ones did write: On condition that I support your daughter for five years the entire time you are with me;" on that it was stated: Only for the first marriage[40]. This parallels what Rebbi Ḥanina said, if somebody marries off his son in a house, the latter acquires the house, but only for a first marriage[41].

37 This refers to the stipulation of the "intelligent" who limit their liability.

38 Without writing a new *ketubah* document, as authorized in Mishnah 9:13 (Note 240).

39 R. Nissim Gerondi (commentary on the Mishnah) has a smoother text: מָאן דְּאָמַר. לִכְתוּבָּה אֲבָל לֹא לִתְנָאִין הָכָא נָמֵי. מָאן דְּאָמַר. בֵּין לִכְתוּבָּה בֵּין לִתְנָאִין. הָכָא נָמֵי. "Following the one who says, this was stated for the *ketubah* but not for the stipulations, it is clear; following the one who says, both for the *ketubah* and the stipulations, it is clear." But since הָכָא נָמֵי is purely Babylonian style, his text is a paraphrase, not a variant reading.

40 Even if in general stipulations are re-instated with remarriage, this particular condition has been permanently terminated by the divorce. It could only be re-instated by a separate document.

41 He gives them a house to live in alone during their wedding week; cf. 5:1 Note 23 (Babli 144a). For the Babli, there would be no parallel since there, R. Ḥanina assigns the house only to the oldest son who marries a virgin, and a woman with a daughter by another man is not a virgin.

(fol. 34d) **משנה ג:** אַלְמָנָה שֶׁאָמְרָה אֵי אֶפְשִׁי לָזוּז מִבֵּית בַּעֲלִי אֵין הַיּוֹרְשִׁין יְכוֹלִין לוֹמַר לָהּ לְכִי לְבֵית אָבִיךְ וְאָנוּ זָנִין אוֹתָךְ שָׁם. אֶלָּא זָנִין אוֹתָהּ וְנוֹתְנִין לָהּ מָדוֹר לְפִי כְבוֹדָהּ.

Mishnah 3: If the widow said, I cannot move from my husband's house, the heirs cannot say to her, go to your father's house and we shall support you there, but they support her and give her a dwelling commensurate with her honor.

The following Halakhah in its entirety is Halakhah *Kilaim* 9:4 (Notes 70-136). The ms. readings from *Kilaim* are printed in Frank-Rühl typeface in the variant readings.

(34d line 62) **הלכה ג**: אַלְמָנָה שֶׁאָמְרָה אֵי אֶפְשִׁי לָזוּז מִבֵּית בַּעֲלִי כול׳. כְּתִיב בַּמֵּתִים חָפְשִׁי כֵּיוָן שֶׁמֵּת אָדָם נַעֲשֶׂה חָפְשִׁי מִן הַמִּצְוֹת.

2 שמת אדם | שאדם מת

Halakhah 3: "If the widow said, I cannot move from my husband's house," etc. It is written (*Ps.* 88:6): "Among the dead is freedom." When a person dies he becomes free from the Commandments.

(34d line 64) רִבִּי צִינָה שְׁלֹשָׁה דְבָרִים בִּשְׁעַת פְּטִירָתוֹ. אַל תָּזוּז אַלְמָנָתִי מִבֵּיתִי. וְאַל תִּסְפְּדוּנִי בָעֲיָירוֹת. וּמִי שֶׁנִּיטַפַּל בִּי בְחַיַּי יְטַפֵּל בִּי בְמוֹתִי. אַל תָּזוּז אַלְמָנָתִי מִבֵּיתִי. אִי אֶפְשִׁי לָזוּז מִבֵּית בַּעֲלִי. אַלְמָנָה שֶׁאָמְרָה. וְלֹא מַתְנִיתָא הִיא. אָמַר רִבִּי דוֹסָא. דְּלָא יֵימְרוּן לָהּ. בֵּיתָהּ דִּנְשׁוֹוָתָהּ הוּא מְשׁוּעֲבָד הוּא לִנְשׁוֹוָתָהּ. אָמַר רִבִּי לְעָזָר בֶּן יוֹסֵי. כְּהָדָא דִּתְנֵּי. דָּרָה בַּבַּיִת כְּשֵׁם שֶׁהָיְתָה דָּרָה וּבַעֲלָהּ נָתוּן בִּמְדִינַת הַיָּם. וּמִשְׁתַּמֵּשׁ בִּכְלֵי כֶסֶף וּבִכְלֵי זָהָב כְּשֵׁם שֶׁהָיְתָה מִשְׁתַּמֶּשֶׁת וּבַעֲלָהּ נָתוּן בִּמְדִינַת הַיָּם. וְנִיזוֹנֶת כְּשֵׁם שֶׁהָיְתָה נִיזוֹנֶת וּבַעֲלָהּ נָתוּן בִּמְדִינַת הַיָּם. וְאַל תִּסְפְּדוּנִי בָעֲיָירוֹת. מִפְּנֵי הַמַּחֲלוֹקֶת. וּמִי שֶׁנִּיטַפַּל בִּי בְחַיַּי יְטַפֵּל בִּי בְמוֹתִי. אָמַר רִבִּי חֲנַנְיָה דְצִיפּוֹרִין. כְּגוֹן יוֹסֵף אֶפְרָתִי. יוֹסֵה חֵפְנִי. רִבִּי חִזְקִיָּה מוֹסִיף. אַל תַּרְבּוּ עָלַי תַּכְרִיכִין. וּתְהֵא אֲרוֹנִי נְקוּבָה לָאָרֶץ. מִילְּתָא אָמְרָה בְּסָדִין אֶחָד נִקְבַּר רִבִּי. דְּרִבִּי אָמַר. כַּמָּה דְּבַר אִינָשׁ אָזִיל הוּא אָתֵי. וְרַבָּנִין אָמְרִין. כַּמָּה דְּבַר נָשׁ אָזִיל הוּא אָתֵי. תַּנֵּי בְּשֵׁם רִבִּי נָתָן. כְּסוּת הַיּוֹרֶדֶת עִם אָדָם לִשְׁאוֹל הִיא בָּאָה עִמּוֹ. מַאי טַעְמָא. תִּתְהַפֵּךְ כְּחוֹמֶר חוֹתָם וְיִתְיַצְּבוּ כְּמוֹ לְבוּשׁ. אַנְטוֹלִינוֹס שָׁאַל לְרִבִּי. מַהוּ הָדֵין דִּכְתִיב תִּתְהַפֵּךְ כְּחוֹמֶר חוֹתָם. אָמַר לֵיהּ. מִי שֶׁהוּא מֵבִיא אֶת הַדּוֹר הוּא מַלְבִּישׁוֹ.

1 פטירתו | פטירתו מן העולם   3 ולא | ולאו   4 דוסא | דרוסא   דנשוותא | דנשיותא
5 ר' לעזר בן יוסי | ר' לעזר בר יוסה   בבית | בבתים   שהיתה דרה | (2 times)
שהיתה דרה בהן   6 ומשתמש | ומשתמשת   9 יוסף אפרתי | יוסי אפרתי   יוסה חיפני |
יוסף חפנים   10 לארץ | בארץ   11 אמרה | אמרים   נקבר | הוא נקבר   כמה | לא כמה
אזיל | אזל (2 times)   13 מאי | מה   14 מהו הדין דכתיב | מהו

Rebbi commanded three things on his death-bed: My widow should not move from my house; do not eulogize me in small towns; and he who served me during my lifetime should also serve me in death. "My widow should not move from my house," is that not a Mishnah? "The widow who said, I cannot possibly move from my husband's house . . ." Rebbi Dositheos said, that they should not say, this is the house of the patriarchate and must serve the patriarchate. Rebbi Eleazar bar Yose said, as we have stated: "She lives in the houses just as she lived while her husband was overseas, she uses silver and gold vessels just as she used to while her husband was overseas, she is fed just as she was fed while her husband was overseas." "Do not eulogize me in small towns" because of the quarrels. "He who served me during my lifetime should also serve me in death;" Rebbi Hananiah from Sepphoris said, for example Yose Ephrati and Joseph from Haifa. Rebbi Hizqiah added, do not use many shrouds on me and let my coffin have holes at the bottom. These words say that Rebbi was buried in a single shroud since Rebbi said, not as a man left, he will come. But the rabbis say, just as a man left, he will come. It was stated in the name of Rebbi Nathan: The garment that went with a person to the grave will come back with him. What is the reason? (*Job* 38:14) "The seal turns itself around like clay, they appear in dress." Antoninus asked Rebbi, what is the meaning of what is written: "The seal turns itself around like clay?" He said to him, He Who brings the generation clothes it.

(35a line 14) רִבִּי יוֹחָנָן מְפַקֵּד. אַלְבְּשׁוּנִי בּוֹרְדִיקָא לָא חִיוְרִין וְלָא אוּכְמִין. אִין קָמִית בֵּינֵי צַדִּיקַיָּא לָא נִבְהָת. אִין קָמִית בֵּינֵי רְשִׁיעַיָּיא לָא נִבְהִית. רִבִּי

יֹאשִׁיָּא פְּקִיד. אַלְבְּשׁוּנִי חִיוָרִין חֲפוּתִין. אָמְרוּ לֵיהּ. וּמַה אַתְּ טָב מִן רַבָּךְ. אָמַר לוֹן. וּמַה אֲנָא בְהִית בְּעוֹבְדַּאי. רִבִּי יִרְמְיָה מְפַקֵּד. אַלְבְּשׁוּנִי חִיוָרִין חֲפוּתִין. אַלְבְּשׁוּנִי דִּנְסָרַיי. וְהָווּן מְסָנַאיי בְּרַגְלַיי וְחוּטְרָא בְּיָדַיי וִיהָבוּנִי עַל סִיטְרָא. אִין אֲתֵי מְשִׁיחָא וַאֲנָא מְעָתָד.

1 אלבשוני	מלבשוני	בורדיקא	בורדייקא	חיורין	חיוורין	2 רשייעיא	רשיעיא
נבהית	גבהת	3 פקיד	מפקד	חפותין	חפיתין	אמרו	אמרין	4 בעובדאי	בעבדאי
חיורין חפותין	חיוורין חפיתין	דנסריי	בנסריי	והוון מסאניי	יהבון מסנא	5 ואנא	אנא

Rebbi Joḥanan commanded: Dress me in beige, neither white nor black. If I rise among the just I shall not be ashamed, if I rise among the wicked I shall not be ashamed. Rebbi Joshia commanded: Dress me in clean white. They said to him, in what are you better than your teacher? He said to them, why should I be ashamed of my deeds? Rebbi Jeremiah commanded: Dress me in clean white, dress me in my socks, put my shoes on my feet and a walking stick in my hand, lay me on my side; when the Messiah comes I shall be ready.

(35a line 20) צִיפּוֹרָיַיא אָמְרִין. מָאן דַּאֲמַר לָן דְּמִיךְ רִבִּי, אֲנָן קָטְלִין לֵיהּ. אֲדִיק לוֹן בַּר קַפָּרָא. רֵישֵׁיהּ מְכַסֵּי מָאנוֹי מְבַזְּעִין. אָמַר לוֹן. יְצוֹקִים וְאַרְאֵלִּים תְּפוּסִין בַּלּוּחוֹת הַבְּרִית וְגָבְרָה יָדָן שֶׁלְּאַרְאֵלִים וְחָטְפוּ אֶת הַלּוּחוֹת. אָמְרוּ לֵיהּ. דְּמָךְ רִבִּי. אָמַר לוֹן. אַתּוּן אֲמַרְתּוּן. וְקָרְעוּן. וַאֲזַל קָלָא דְּקַרְעַיי לְגוֹ פִּתְחָא מַהֲלָךְ תְּלָתָא מִילִין.

| 1 ציפורייא | ציפריא | דמיך רבי | רבי דמך | 32 בלוחות | בלוחות הברית | 4 אמרו |
| אמרין | ואזיל | ואזל | 5 לגו פתחא | לגופתחא |

The people from Sepphoris said: We shall kill anybody who tells us that Rebbi died. Bar Qappara associated with them, his head covered and his garments torn. He said to them: Earthlings and angels held the Tablets of the Covenant; the angels were stronger and they took away the

Tablets. They said to him: Rebbi died. He said to them: You said it. They tore their clothes and the sound of the tearing was heard from the gate to a distance of three *mil*.

(35a line 25) רִבִּי נָתָן בְּשֵׁם רִבִּי מָנָא. מַעֲשֵׂה נִיסִּים נַעֲשׂוּ בְּאוֹתוֹ הַיּוֹם. עֶרֶב שַׁבָּת הָיָה וְנִכְנְסוּ כָּל־הָעֲיָירוֹת לְהַסְפִּידוֹ. וְאִישְּׁרוֹנֵיהּ תְּמַנֵּי עֶשְׂרֵה (בניסן) [כְּנִישָׁן] וְאַחְתּוּנֵיהּ לְבֵית שָׁרָיי. וְתָלַת לוֹן יוֹמָא עַד שֶׁהָיָה כָּל־אֶחָד וְאֶחָד מַגִּיעַ לְבֵיתוֹ וּמְמַלֵּא לוֹ חָבִית שֶׁלְּמַיִם וּמַדְלִיק אֶת הַנֵּר. כֵּיוָן שֶׁשָּׁקְעָה הַחַמָּה קָרָא הַגֶּבֶר. שָׁרְיָין מְצִיקִין. אָמְרִין. דִּילְמָא דְחַלְלִינָן שַׁבָּתָא. וְאָתַת בַּת קוֹל וְאָמְרָה לוֹן. כָּל־מִי שֶׁלֹּא נִתְעַצֵּל בְּהֶסְפֵּידוֹ שֶׁלְּרִבִּי יְהֵא מְבוּשָּׂר לְחַיֵּי הָעוֹלָם הַבָּא בַּר מִן קַצְרָא. כֵּיוָן דִּשְׁמַע כֵּן סָלִיק לְאִיגְרָא וּטְלַק גַּרְמֵיהּ וּמִית. נָפְקַת בְּרַת קָלָא וְאָמְרַת וַאֲפִילּוּ קַצְרָא.

1 נתן | נחמן   ניסים | ניסין   2 היה | הייתה   ונכנסו | ונתכנסו   ואישרוניה | ואשרוניה בניסן (!!) | כנישן   4 ומדליק | ומדליק לו   5 שרייין | שרון   ואתת | יצאה   6 לון | להן   לחיי | מחיי   בר מן | חוץ מן   7 סליק | סלק ליה   ברת קלא | בת קלא   8 ואמרת | ואמרה

Rebbi Naḥman in the name of Rebbi Mana: Miracles happened that day. It was Sabbath eve and all the surrounding towns came together to eulogize him. They made him [Rebbi] rest in eighteen synagogues until they brought him to his resting place but the day extended for them until each one had time to get to his house, fill an amphora of water, and light the candles. When the sun set, the rooster crowed[86]. They were anxious and said, maybe we did desecrate the Sabbath? There came a voice and said to them, every one who was not lazy for the eulogies of Rebbi shall be announced for the life of the Future World, except the fuller[87]. When the latter heard this, he climbed on the roof, threw himself down, and died. There came a voice and said, including the fuller.

(35a line 33) רִבִּי הֲוָה יָתֵיב לֵיהּ בְּצִיפּוֹרִין שִׁבְעָה עָשָׂר שָׁנִין. וְקָרָא עַל גַּרְמֵיהּ וַיְחִי יַעֲקֹב בְּאֶרֶץ מִצְרַיִם שְׁבַע עֶשְׂרֵה שָׁנָה. וַיְחִי יְהוּדָה בְּצִיפּוֹרִין שְׁבַע עֶשְׂרֵה שָׁנִין. וּמִין גּוֹבֵּיהֶן עֲבַד תְּלַת עֶשְׂרֵה שְׁנִין חֲשִׁישׁ שִׁנּוּי. אָמַר רִבִּי יוֹסֵי בֵּי רִבִּי בּוּן. כָּל־אוֹתָן שְׁלֹשׁ עֶשְׂרֵה שָׁנָה לֹא מֵתָה חַיָּה בְּאֶרֶץ יִשְׂרָאֵל וְלֹא הִפִּילָה עוּבָּרָה בְּאֶרֶץ יִשְׂרָאֵל. וְלָמָּה חֲשִׁישׁ שִׁנּוּי. חַד זְמָן עֲבַר. חָמָא חַד עִינָּל מִתְנְכֵיס. גָּעָה וְאָמְרָה לֵיהּ. רִבִּי. שֵׁיזְבִי. אֲמַר לֵיהּ. לְכָךְ נוֹצֵרְתָּה. וּבְסוֹף הֵיךְ אִינְשְׁמָת. חֲמִתּוֹן אִין קְטָלוּן חָדָא קַן דְּעַכְבָּרִין. אֲמַר לוֹן. אַרְפּוּנוֹן. וְרַחֲמָיו עַל כָּל־מַעֲשָׂיו כְּתִיב.

1 שבעה עשר | שבע עשרה   3 שנין | שנה   גוביחן | גוביהין   חשיש שינוי | חשש בשינוי
6 מתנכיס | מנכס   נוצרתה | נוצרת   היך | איך   7 אין קטלון | קטלין   חדא | חד   אמר לון | אמר

Rebbi dwelt in Sepphoris seventeen years and applied to himself (*Gen.* 47:28): "Jacob lived in Egypt seventeen years," Jehudah lived in Sepphoris seventeen years. Of these he suffered from toothache for thirteen years. {Rebbi Yose ben Rebbi Abun said, all these thirteen years no woman lying-in died in the Land of Israel and no pregnant woman had a miscarriage in the Land of Israel.} Why did he have a toothache? Once he saw a calf to be slaughtered when it bellowed and said to him, Rebbi, save me! He said to it, for that you were created. At the end, how was he healed? He saw them killing a burrow of rats. He said to them, let them live, it is written (*Ps.* 145:9) "His mercy extends to all His creatures."

(35a line 41) רִבִּי הֲוָה עִינְוָון סַגִּין. וְהֲוָה אֲמַר. כָּל־מַה דְּיֵימַר לִי בַּר נָשָׁא אֲנָא עֲבִיד. חוּץ מִמַּה שֶׁעָשׂוּ זִקְנֵי בְּתֵירָא לִזְקֵנִי. דְּשָׁרוֹן גַּרְמוֹן וּמְנוֹנֵיהּ. אִין סָלֵיק רַב הוּנָא רֵישׁ גָּלוּתָא לְהָכָא אֲנָא מוֹתֵיב לְעֵיל מִינַּיי. דְּהוּא מִן יְהוּדָה וַאֲנָא מִבִּנְיָמִין. דְּהוּא מִן דִּכְרַיָּיא וַאֲנָא מִן נוּקְבְתָא. חַד זְמָן אֲעַל רִבִּי חִייָה רַבָּא לְגַבֵּיהּ. אֲמָרוּ לֵיהּ. הָא רַב הוּנָא לְכָאן. נִתְכַּרְכְּמוּ פָּנָיו שֶׁלְּרִבִּי. אֲמָרוּ לֵיהּ.

HALAKHAH 3

אֲרוֹנוֹ הוּא. אֲמַר לֵיהּ פּוּק חֲמֵי מַה בָּעֵי לְכָאן. נְפַק וְלָא אַשְׁכַּח בַּר נָשׁ. וְיָדַע דְּהוּא כָּעֵיס עֲלוֹי. עֲבַד דְּלָא עֲלִיל לְגַבֵּיהּ תַּלְתִּין יוֹמִין. אֲמַר רִבִּי יוֹסֵי בֵּירִבִּי בּוּן. כִּי אִתּוֹן תְּלִיתִיתֵי יוֹמַיָּא יָלִיף רִבִּי מִינֵּיהּ כָּל־כְּלָלָה דְּאוֹרָיְיתָא. בְּסוֹף תְּלַת עֲשְׂרֵה שַׁנְיָא וּתְלַתִּיתֵי יוֹמַיָּא אָעַל אֱלָיָּהוּ לְגַבֵּיהּ בִּדְמוּת רִבִּי חִיָּיה רַבָּה. אֲמַר לֵיהּ. מָה מָרִי עֲבִיד. אֲמַר לֵיהּ. חַד שִׁינָּא מְעִיקָה לִי. אֲמַר לֵיהּ. חֲמֵי לִי. וְחָמֵי לֵיהּ. וִיהַב אֶצְבְּעָתֵיהּ עֲלוֹי וְאִינְּשָׁמַתּ. לְמַחָר אָעַל רִבִּי חִיָּיה רַבָּה לְגַבֵּיהּ. אֲמַר לֵיהּ. מָה רִבִּי עֲבִיד. הַיי שִׁינָּךְ מָה הִיא עֲבִידָא. אֲמַר לֵיהּ. מִן הַהִיא שַׁעֲתָא דִיהַבְתְּ אֶצְבְּעָךְ עֲלָהּ אִינְּשָׁמַת. בְּאוֹתָהּ שָׁעָה אָמַר. אִי לָכֶם חַיּוֹת שֶׁבְּאֶרֶץ יִשְׂרָאֵל. אִי לָכֶם עוּבָּרוֹת שֶׁבְּאֶרֶץ יִשְׂרָאֵל. אָמַר. לָא הֲוֵינָא אֲנָא. מִן הַהִיא שַׁעֲתָא שָׁרֵי רִבִּי עֲבַד לֵיהּ אִיקָר. כַּד הֲוָה עֲלִיל לְבֵית וַעֲדָא הֲוָה אֲמַר. יִכָּנֵס רִבִּי חִיָּיה רַבָּה לִפְנִים מִמֶּנִּי. אֲמַר לֵיהּ רִבִּי יִשְׁמָעֵאל בֵּי רִבִּי יוֹסֵי לִפְנִים מִמֶּנִּי. אָמַר לוֹ. חַס וְשָׁלוֹם. אֶלָּא רִבִּי חִיָּא רַבָּה לִפְנִים וְרִבִּי יִשְׁמָעֵאל בֵּי רִבִּי יוֹסֵי לְפָנַי וְלִפְנִים. רִבִּי הֲוָא מַתְנֵי שְׁבָחֵיהּ דְּרִבִּי חִיָּיה רַבָּה קוֹמֵי רִבִּי יִשְׁמָעֵאל בֵּי רִבִּי יוֹסֵי. חַד זְמַן חֲמֵי גּוּ בָּנֵי וְלָא אִיתְכְּנַע מִן קוֹמוֹי. [אֲמַר לֵיהּ אֲהַנוּ דְאַתְּ מַתְנֵי שְׁבָחֵיהּ. אֲמַר לֵיהּ. מָה עֲבַד לָךְ. אֲמַר לֵיהּ חֲמָתֵיהּ גּוּ בָּנֵי וְלָא אִיתְכְּנַע מִן קוֹמוֹי.] אֲמַר לֵיהּ. לָמָּה עֲבַדְתְּ כֵּן. אֲמַר לֵיהּ. יֵיתֵי עָלַי דְּאֵין סְחִית לָא יָדָעִית. בְּהַהִיא שַׁעֲתָא אַשְׁגִּרִית עֵינַיי בְּכָל־סֵפֶר תְּהִילִים אֲגָדָה. מִן הַהִיא שַׁעֲתָא מָסַר לֵיהּ שְׁנֵי תַלְמִידִין דִּיהַלְכוּן עִימֵּיהּ גּוּ סַכַּנְתָּא.

1 עינוון | ענוון   2 ומנוניה | מנשי איתי   3 מותיב לעיל מיניה | מותיב ליה לעיל מיניה
4 דכרייא | דכריי   רבא | רובא   4 אמרו | אמר   לכאן | לבר   אמרו | אמר   6 הוא | הוא
בא   חמי מה בעי לכאן | וחמי מאן בעי לך לבר   ופק | ונפק   7 בירבי | בר   כי אתון
תליתיתי יומיא יליף רבי מיניה כל כללא דאוריתא | כל אינון תלתתוי יומיא יליף רב מיניה ככלי
דאורייתא   8-9 בסוף תלת עשר שנייא ותלתיתי יומיא | לסוף תלת עשרה שניא ותלתתוי
יומיא   9 רבה | רובה   10 שינא | שיניי   חמי לי | חמי לה לי   11 וחמי ליה | וחמי לה
ליה   עלוי | עלה   רבה | רובה   12 רבי עביד | עביד רבי   חיי | האי   13 אצבעך |
אצבעתך   אמר | אמר ליה   14 לא הוינא אנא | אנא לא הוינא   15 שרי ר' עביד ליה
איקר | נהיג ביה ביקר   16 רבי חייה רבה לפנים ממני | רבי חייא רובה לפנים   ליה | לו
17 חיא רבה | חייא רובה   18 לפני ולפנים | לפני לפנים   רבה | רובה   The text 19-21
in brackets is missing in *Ketubot*   23 גו סכנתא | בגין סכותא

Rebbi was very meek and said, all a man might ask from me I am ready to do, except what the Elders of Bathyra did for my ancestor: they divested themselves and appointed him. If Rav Huna, the Head of the Diaspora, came here I would let him sit higher than myself since he is from the tribe of Judah and I am from Benjamin, he is from the male line and I am from the female. Once, the elder Rebbi Hiyya visited him and said, Rav Huna is outside. The face of Rebbi became saffron-colored. He [R. Hiyya] said to him, it is his coffin. He [Rebbi] said to him, go outside and look who wants you there. He stepped outside and did not find anybody; he understood that he [Rebbi] was angry with him. He did not visit him again for thirty days. Rebbi Yose bar Abun said, in those thirty days did Rav learn from him [R. Hiyya] the principles of Torah. At the end of thirteen years and thirty days, Elijah visited him [Rebbi] in the likeness of the older Rebbi Hiyya. He said to him, how does my lord feel? He said to him, one tooth hurts me. He said to him, show it to me. He showed it to him, he put his finger on it and it was healed. The next day, the older Rebbi Hiyya came to him and asked him, how does Rebbi feel, what is with that tooth? He said to him, from the moment that you put your finger on it, it was healed. At that moment, he said, woe on you, lying-in women of the Land of Israel, woe on you, pregnant women of the Land of Israel! He [R. Hiyya] said to him, that was not me. From that moment on, he [Rebbi] treated him with honor.

When he [Rebbi] went to the assembly hall, he said, may the older Rebbi Hiyya come inside. Rebbi Ismael ben Rebbi Yose asked, closer than me? He said, beware! The older Rebbi Hiyya inside, and Rebbi Ismael ben Rebbi Yose innermost. Rebbi used to state the praises of the older

HALAKHAH 3

Rebbi Ḥiyya before Rebbi Ismael ben Rebbi Yose. {Once, he [R. Ismael ben R. Yose] saw him [R. Ḥiyya] in the bathhouse and he did not show him reverence. He [R. Ismael ben R. Yose] said to him [Rebbi], is that the one of whom you state praises? He said, what did he do to you? He said, I saw him in the bathhouse and he did not show me reverence.} He [Rebbi] said to him [R. Ḥiyya], why did you do that? He said to him, so much should come over me if I realized that I was washing myself, at that time my eyes were occupied with the allegorical interpretation of the entire book of Psalms. From that moment on, he [Rebbi] appointed two students to accompany him [R. Ḥiyya] because of the danger.

(35a line 63) דְּרבִּי יָסָא צָם תְּמָנֵיי צוֹמִין לְמֶיחְמֵי רַבִּי חִיָּיה רַבָּה. וּבְסוֹפָא חָמָא דָרְגִין דִּידֵיהּ וּכְהַן גְּנֵי גַּבּוֹי. וּכְאָן תֵּימַר. הָנָא רַבִּי יָסָא בַּר נַשׁ זְעִירָא. חַד גַּדְלַיי אֲתָא לְקַמֵּיהּ דְּרַבִּי יוֹחָנָן. אָמַר לֵיהּ. חָמִית בְּחֵילְמִי דִּרְקִיעַ נָפַל וְחַד מִן תַּלְמִידָךְ סְמִיךְ לֵיהּ. אָמַר לֵיהּ. חַכִּים אַתְּ לֵיהּ. אָמַר לֵיהּ. מִן אֲנָא חָמֵי לֵיהּ אֲנָא חַכַּם לֵיהּ. וַעֲבַר כָּל־תַּלְמִידוֹי קוֹמוֹי וְחַכַּם לְרַבִּי יָסָה. רַבִּי שִׁמְעוֹן בֶּן לָקִישׁ צָם תְּלַת מָאתָן צוֹמִין לְמֶיחְמֵי רַבִּי חִיָּיה רוֹבָה וְלָא חָמְתֵיהּ. וּבְסוֹפָא שָׁרֵי מִצְטַעֵר. אָמַר. מַה הֲוָה לָעֵי בְאוֹרַיְתָא סַגִּין מִינַּיי. אָמְרִין לֵיהּ. רִיבֵּץ תּוֹרָה בְיִשְׂרָאֵל יוֹתֵר מִמָּךְ. וְלֹא עוֹד אֶלָּא דַהֲוָה גְּלֵי. אֲמַר לוֹן. וַאֲנָא לֹא הֲוִינָא גְּלֵי. אָמְרִין לֵיהּ. אַתְּ הֲוִיתָה גְּלֵי מֵילַף. וְהוּא הֲוָה גְּלֵי מַלְפָא.

1 דרבי יסא | רבי יוסי   צומין | יומין   רבה | רובה   ובסופה | ולסופה   2 דרגין ידיה
וכהן גני גבוי | ורגזן ידיה וכהו עינוי   וכאן תימר | ואין תימר   הוה ר' יסא | דהוה ר' יוסי
זעירא | זעיר   3 גלדיי | גרדיי   לקמיה דר' | לגבי ר'   4-3 מן תלמידך | מתלמידך   4
סמך סמיך   חכם | וחכים   מן | אין   5 ועבר | עבר   וחכם | וחכים   יסה | יוסה   6
מאתן | מאוון   שרי | שרא   7 אמרין | אמרו   8 ואנא לא | ולא

Rebbi Yasa fasted eighty days to see the old Rebbi Ḥiyya. In the end, he saw his bier and him sleeping on it. If you say that Rebbi Assi was an insignificant person, one tanner came to Rebbi Joḥanan and said, I saw the sky falling but one of your students supported it. He asked him, could you recognize him? He said, if I would see him, I would recognize him. He made all his students pass before him [the tanner], and he recognized Rebbi Assi. Rebbi Simeon ben Laqish fasted three hundred fasts to see the old Rebbi Ḥiyya but did not see him. In the end, he started to feel badly and said, did he study Torah more than I did? They said to him, he spread Torah more than you did and in addition he went into exile. He said to them, did I not also go into exile? They said to him, you went into exile to study, he went into exile to teach.

(35a line 72) כַּד דְּמָךְ רַב הוּנָא רֵישׁ גָּלוּתָא אַסְקוּנֵיהּ לְהָכָא. אָמְרִין אָן אֲנָן יָהֲבִין לֵיהּ נֵיהֲבֵיהּ גַּבֵּי רִבִּי חִיָּיה דְּהוּא מִן דִּידְהוֹן. אָמְרִין. מָאן עָלִיל יָהַב לֵיהּ תַּמָּן. אָמַר רִבִּי חַגַּיי. אֲנָא עָלִיל יְהַב לֵיהּ תַּמָּן. אָמְרוּ לֵיהּ. עֵילָא אַתְּ בָּעֵי. דְּאַתְּ גְּבַר סַב. וְאַתְּ בָּעֵי מֵיעוֹל לָךְ מֵיתַב תַּמָּן. אֲמַר לוֹן. יָבוֹן מְשִׁיחָא בְּרִיגְלוֹי וְאֵין עֲנִיַּת אַתּוּן גָּרְשִׁין לִי. וְאַשְׁכַּח תְּלַת דָּנִין. יְהוּדָה בְּנֵי אַחֲרֵיךְ. וְאֵין עוֹד. חִזְקִיָּה בְּנֵי אַחֲרֵיךְ. וְאֵין עוֹד. אַחֲרֵיךְ יוֹסֵף בֶּן יִשְׂרָאֵל. וְאֵין עוֹד. תָּלָה עֵינוֹי מִסְתַּכְּלָה. אֲמַר לֵיהּ. אֲמִיךְ אֲפִיךְ. אֲמַר רִבִּי חִיָּיה רַבָּה יְהוּדָה בְּרֵיהּ. וּפִישׁ לְרַב חוּנָה יָתִיב לֵיהּ. וְלָא קְבִיל עֲלוֹי מָתִיב לֵיהּ. אָמְרִין. כְּמָא דְּלָא קְבִיל עֲלוֹי מָתִיב לֵיהּ כֵּן זַרְעִיָּיתֵיהּ לָא פְּסִיקָא לְעוֹלָם. וְיָצָא מִשָּׁם בֶּן שְׁמוֹנִים שָׁנָה וְנִכְפְּלוּ לוֹ שָׁנָיו.

1 אמרין | אמר   אין | אן   2 ניהביה | ניתיניה   חייה | חייה רובה   דידהון | דידהו   עליל | בעי   יהב ליה תמן | מיהב ליה   3 תמן | -   עילה | עילתא   4 לך מיתב | מיתב לך   יבון | יהבון   משיחא | משיחתא   בריגלוי | ברגליי   5 לי | -   ואשכח | אעל ואשכח   7 אמר | איתאמר   אמיך אפיך | אפיך אפיך   8 אמר רבי חייה שבח יהודה בריה | שמע קליה דרבי חייה רבא אמר לרב יהודה בריה   ופיש | נפיש   8 כמא | כמה   9 זרעייתיה | זרעיתיה   בן | והיה בן

When Rav Huna, the Head of the Diaspora, died they brought him here. They said, where shall we put him? They said, let us put him next to Rebbi Ḥiyya the elder for he is one of them. They said, who might want to bring him there? Rebbi Ḥaggai said, I shall go up to put him there. They said to him, you are looking for a pretext, for you are an old man and you want to go to rest there yourself. He said to them, put some string on my feet and when I shall be weak you pull. He went in and found the three arguing. "Jehudah my son, after you, and no more. Ḥizqiah my son, after you, and no more. Joseph ben Israel, after you, and no more." He [R. Ḥaggai] lifted his eyes to look, it was said to him lower [your eyes], turn around. Rebbi Ḥiyya the elder [who said to] his son Jehudah, make space for Rav Ḥuna that he may rest there. But [Rav Ḥuna] did not accept this. They said, since he did not accept that one made space for him, so his descendants will never end. He [R. Ḥaggai] exited from there eighty years old and his years were doubled.

(35b line 6) כְּתִיב וּנְשָׂאתָנִי מִמִּצְרַיִם וּקְבַרְתַּנִי בִּקְבוּרָתָם. יַעֲקֹב כָּל־חֵן דְּהוּא מַה הוּא מְנַבֵּי. רִבִּי לָעֲזָר אָמַר דְּבָרִים בְּגַב. רִבִּי יְהוֹשֻׁעַ בֶּן לֵוִי אָמַר דְּבָרִים בְּגַב. רִבִּי חֲנִינָא אָמַר דְּבָרִים בְּגַב. מַהוּ דְּבָרִים בְּגַב. רִבִּי שִׁמְעוֹן בֶּן לָקִישׁ אָמַר. אֶתְהַלֵךְ לִפְנֵי יי בְּאַרְצוֹת הַחַיִּים. וַהֲלֹא אֵין אַרְצוֹת הַחַיִּים אֶלָּא צוֹר וְקֵיסָרִין וַחֲבֵרוֹתֵיהָ. תַּמָּן כּוּלָּא תַּמָּן שָׂבַע. רִבִּי שִׁמְעוֹן בֶּן לָקִישׁ בְּשֵׁם בַּר קַפָּרָא. אֶרֶץ שֶׁמֵּיתֶיהָ חַיִּים תְּחִילָּה לִימוֹת הַמָּשִׁיחַ. מַה טַעֲמָא. נוֹתֵן נְשָׁמָה לָעָם עָלֶיהָ. מֵעַתָּה רַבּוֹתֵינוּ שֶׁבְּבָבֶל הִפְסִידוּ. אָמַר רִבִּי סִימַאי. הַקָּדוֹשׁ בָּרוּךְ הוּא מְחַלֵּךְ לִפְנֵיהֶן אֶל הָאָרֶץ וְהֵן מִתְגַּלְגְּלִין כְּנוֹדוֹת. וְכֵיוָן שֶׁמַּגִּיעִין לָאָרֶץ יִשְׂרָאֵל נַפְשׁוֹתֵיהֶן עִמָּהֶן. מַה טַעֲמָא. וְהֵבֵאתִי אֶתְכֶם אֶל אַדְמַתְכֶם וְנָתַתִּי רוּחִי בָּכֶם וִחְיִיתֶם.

2 מנכבי | מנכי   יהושע בן לוי | חנינא   3 חנינא | יהושע בן לוי   4-5 צור וקיסרין | צור וחבירותיה וקיסרין   כולה | זולה   שבע | שובעא   6 חיים | חיין   מה טעמא | ומה טעם
7 מעתה | אלא מעתה   שבבבל | שבגולה   סימאי | סימיי   7-8 הקב״ה מהלך לפניהן אל

הארץ | מרעיד הקב״ה לפניהן את הארץ   8 שמגיעין | שהן מגיעין   9 נפשותיהן עמהן | נפשן חוזרות עליהן   מה טעמא | ומה טעם   והבאתי אתכם אל אדמתכם | והנחתי אתכם על אדמת ישראל

It is written (*Gen.* 47:30): "You shall carry me from Egypt and bury me in their burial place." What would Jacob lose at any place he would prophesy? Rebbi Eleazar gave an inner reason, Rebbi Joshua ben Levi gave an inner reason, Rebbi Ḥanina gave an inner reason. What is the inner reason? Rebbi Simeon ben Laqish said, (*Ps.* 116:9) "I will walk before the Eternal in the Land of Life." But the lands of life are only Tyre and its surroundings and Caesarea (maritima) and its surroundings; there is cheap (food), there is plenty. Rebbi Simeon ben Laqish in the name of Bar Qappara, the Land whose dead will live again in the days of the Messiah. What is the reason? (*Is.* 42:9) "He gives soul to the people on it." That would mean that our teachers in Babylonia would lose out! Rebbi Simai said, the Holy One, praised be He, walks before them and they roll like wine barrels. When they arrive in the Land of Israel their souls are with them. What is the reason? (*Ez.* 36:24) "I shall bring you to your soil," (37:14) "give My spirit into you, and you will live."

(35b line 16) רִבִּי בְּרֶכְיָה שָׁאַל לְרִבִּי חֶלְבּוֹ. רִבִּי חֶלְבּוֹ שָׁאַל לְרִבִּי אִימִּי. רִבִּי אִימִּי שָׁאַל לְרִבִּי אֶלְעָזָר. רִבִּי לָעְזָר לְרִבִּי חֲנִינָה. וְאִית דְּאָמְרִין. רִבִּי חֲנִינָה שָׁאַל לְרִבִּי יְהוֹשֻׁעַ. וַאֲפִילוּ כְגוֹן יָרָבְעָם וַחֲבֵירָיו. אָמַר לֵיהּ. גָּפְרִית וָמֶלַח שְׂרֵיפָה כָל־אַרְצָהּ. אָמַר רִבִּי בְּרֶכְיָה. מַה הֵין דְּשָׁאִיל לְהוֹן לֹא שְׁמַעִינָן מִינַּהּ כְּלוּם. מַהוּ כְדוֹן. כֵּיוָן שֶׁנִּשְׂרְפָה אֶרֶץ יִשְׂרָאֵל נַעֲשֶׂה בָהֶן מִדַּת הַדִּין. תַּנֵּי בְשֵׁם רִבִּי יוּדָה. שֶׁבַע שָׁנִים עָשְׂתָה אֶרֶץ יִשְׂרָאֵל נִשְׂרָפָה. הָדָא הוּא דִכְתִיב וְהִגְבִּיר בְּרִית לָרַבִּים שָׁבוּעַ אֶחָד. שתים שֶׁבָּהּ מַה הָיוּ עוֹשִׂין. מַטְלִיּוֹת מַטְלִיּוֹת וְקָיְתָה נִשְׂרָפֶת.

HALAKHAH 3   545

3 ואפילו | אפילו   4 דשאל | דשאיל   להון | להון והן שאל להן   5 מהו | מיי   6 יודה |
יהודה   6 עשתה | עשת   נשרפה | נשרפת   7 שתים | כותים

Rebbi Berekhiah asked Rebbi Ḥelbo. Rebbi Ḥelbo asked Rebbi Immi. Rebbi Immi asked Rebbi Eleazar. Rebbi Eleazar asked Rebbi Ḥanina, some say Rebbi Ḥanina asked Rebbi Joshua: Even those like Jeroboam and his kind? He said to him, (*Deut.* 29:22) "Sulphur and salt, conflagration throughout the country." Rebbi Berekhiah said, one asked the other and we understand nothing from it. What does it mean? Since the Land of Israel was burned, judgment was executed on it. We have stated in the name of Rebbi Jehudah: Seven years was the Land of Israel burned; that is what is written (*Dan.* 9:27) "The Covenant overtook the public for one week." What did the secondaries in it do? Pieces, pieces and it was burned.

(35b line 24) כְּתִיב וְאַתָּה פַשְׁחוּר וְכָל יוֹשְׁבֵי בֵיתֶךָ תֵּלְכוּ בַשֶּׁבִי. וּבָבֶל תָּבוֹא וְשָׁם תָּמוּת וְשָׁמָּה תִּקָּבֵר. רִבִּי אַבָּא אָמַר. רִבִּי חֶלְבּוֹ וְרִבִּי חָמָא בַּר חֲנִינָה. חַד אָמַר. מֵת שָׁם וְנִקְבַּר שָׁם וְיֵשׁ בְּיָדוֹ שְׁתַּיִם. מֵת שָׁם וְנִקְבַּר כָּאן יֵשׁ בְּיָדוֹ אַחַת. וְחָרָנָה אָמַר. קְבוּרָה מְכַפֶּרֶת עַל מִיתָה שֶׁלָּהֶן.

1 תבוא | תבא   2 ושמה | ושם   אבא | אבא בר זמינא   חנינה | חנינא   3 ויש | יש   4 קבורה | קבורה שבכאן

It is written (*Jer.* 20:6-7): "But you, Pashḥur, and all inhabitants of your house will go into captivity. You will come to Babylon, die there, and be buried there." Rebbi Abba [bar Zemina] said, Rebbi Ḥelbo and Rebbi Ḥama bar Ḥanina. One of them said, if somebody dies there and is buried there, he has two [detriments] in hand. If he dies there and is buried here, he has one [detriment] in hand. The other one said, burial atones for their death.

(35b line 28) רִבִּי יוֹנָה בְּשֵׁם רִבִּי חָמָא בַּר חֲנִינָא. רִיגְלוֹי דְּבַר נַשׁ אִינּוּן מוֹבְלִין יָתֵיהּ כָּל־הֶן דְּמִתְבְּעֵי. כְּתִיב וַיֹּאמֶר לִי מִי יְפַתֶּה אֶת אַחְאָב וְיַעַל וְיִפֹּל בְּרָמוֹת גִּלְעָד. וְיָמוּת בְּתוֹךְ בֵּיתוֹ לֹא תַמָּן. אֱלִיחוֹרֶף וַאֲחִיָּה תְּרֵין אִיסְקְרִיטוֹרֵי דִשְׁלֹמֹה. חָמָא מַלְאַךְ מוֹתָא מִסְתַּכֵּל בּוֹן וַחֲרוּק בְּשִׁינָיו. אָמַר מִילָּה וִיהָבוֹן בַּחֲלָלָה. אֲזַל וּנְסַבְהוֹן מִן תַּמָּן. אֲתָא גְּחִיךְ קָם לֵיהּ קִיבְלֵיהּ. אֲמַר לֵיהּ. הַהִיא שַׁעֲתָא הֲוָת אַחְרוֹק בְּשִׁינוֹי. וּכְדוֹן אַתְּ גָּחִיךְ. אֲמַר לֵיהּ. אֲמַר לִי רַחֲמָנָא דְּנַסַּב לֶאֱלִיחוֹרֶף וַאֲחִיָּה מִן גּוֹא חֲלָלָה. וְאָמְרִית. מָאן יָהֵיב לִי אִילֵין לְהוֹן דִּשְׁלִיחִית מִינְסִיבֵינָין וִיהַב בְּלִיבָּךְ לְמֶיעֲבַד כֵּן בְּגִין דְּנַעֲבִיד שְׁלִיחוּת. אֲזַל וְאִיטְפַּל בְּהוֹן מִן תַּמָּן. תְּרֵין בְּנוֹי דְּרִבִּי רְאוּבֵן בַּר אִיסְטְרוֹבִילְיָה תַּלְמִידוֹי דְּרִבִּי. חָמָא מַלְאַךְ מוֹתָא מִסְתַּכֵּל בּוֹן וַחֲרִיק בְּשִׁינוֹי. אֲמַר. נִיגְלִינּוֹן לִדְרוֹמָא. שֶׁמָּא שֶׁהַגָּלוּת מְכַפֶּרֶת. אֲזַל וְנַסְתּוֹן מִתַּמָּן.

1 חנינא | חנינה   כש | נשא   אינון מובלין יתיה כל הן דמתבעי | ערבתיה למיקמתיה כל הן דהוא מתבעי   2 ויאמר לי | -   3 בתוך ביתו | בביתו   לא תמן | ולא תמן   איסקריטורי | איסקבטיריי   4 וחרוק בשיניו | וחריק בשינוי   5 חללה | חללא   אתא גחיך קם ליה | אתא קאים גחיך ליה   קיבליה | לקבליה   6 הוות אחרון בשינוי | הויתה איחרון בשינייך גחיך | גחיך לן   7 דנסב | דינסב   מן גוא | מן   מאן | מי   7-8 להון דשלחית מינסיבינין | להן דאישתלחית מיסביניין   8 שליחות | שליחותי   9 בהון | בון   מן | זמן   תרין בנוי | תרי ברויי   10 מלאך מותא | מאלכא דמותא   אמר | ואמר   11 שהגלות | הגלות

Rebbi Jonah in the name of Rebbi Ḥama bar Ḥanina: A human's feet bring him to where he is wanted. It is written (*1K.* 22:20) "The Eternal said, who will seduce Ahab that he should go and fall in Ramot Gilead?" Might he not die in his house rather than there? Eliḥoref and Aḥiah were two of Solomon's secretaries. He [Solomon] saw the Angel of Death looking at them and grinding his teeth. He said a word and put them into space. He [the Angel of Death] went and took them from there, then he came laughing before him [Solomon]. He said to him, just before you were grinding your teeth and now you are laughing at us? He said to him, the Merciful told me to take Eliḥoref and Aḥiah from space and I was wondering who would put them there where I was sent to take them; He put it into your mind to do so that I could complete my mission. I went and dealt with them there. The two sons of Rebbi Reuben ben Strobilos were students of Rebbi. He [Rebbi] saw the Angel of Death looking at them and grinding his teeth and said, let us exile them to the South, maybe the exile atones. He [the angel of death] went and took them from there.

(35b line 34) עֲלַלָא נְחוּתָה הֲוָה. אִידְמִיךְ תַּמָּן. שָׁרֵי בְּכִי. אָמְרִין לֵיהּ. מַה לָךְ בְּכִי. אִין מַסְקוּן לָךְ. אָמַר לוֹן. וּמָה הֲנָיָיה אִית לִי. וַאֲנָא מוֹבַד מַרְגְּלִיתִי גּוֹא אַרְעָא מְסָאבְתָא. לֹא דָמֵי הַפּוֹלְטָהּ לְחֵיק אִמּוֹ לַפּוֹלְטָהּ בְּחֵיק נָכְרִיָּה. רִבִּי מֵאִיר אִידְמִיךְ לֵיהּ בְּאַסִּייָא. אָמְרִין לִבְנֵי אַרְעָא דְּיִשְׂרָאֵל דִּי דָא מְשִׁיחְכוֹן דִּידְכוֹן. וַאֲפִילוּ כֵן אָמַר לוֹן. יְהַבוּן עַרְסִי עַל גֵּיף יַמָּא. דִּכְתִיב כִּי הוּא עַל יַמִּים יְסָדָהּ וְעַל נְהָרוֹת יְכוֹנְנֶיהָ.

1 עללה | עולא   נחותה | נחותא   אידמיך | אדמך   לך | את   2 אין | אנא   מסקון לך | מסקין לך לארעא דישראל   אית לי | לי   גוא | גו   3 דמי | דומה   לחיק אמו | בחיק אמו   4 אידמיך | הוה אידמיך ליה   אמרין | אמר אמורין   די דא | הא   5 ואפילו | אפילו

Ulla was an emigrant. He was dying there and started to cry. They said to him, why are you crying? We shall bring you [to the Land of Israel]. He said to them, how does this help me? I am losing my pearl in an impure land. One cannot compare one who expires in the bosom of his mother to one who expires in the bosom of a strange woman. Rebbi Meïr was dying in Assos. He said, tell the people of the Land of Israel, there is your Messiah. With all that, he said to put his bier on the cape since it is written (*Ps.* 24:2): "For He founded it on seas, based it on rivers."

(35b line 45) שִׁבְעָה יַמִּים סוֹבְבִין אֶרֶץ יִשְׂרָאֵל. יַמָּא רַבָּא. יַמָּא דְטִיבֶּרְיָא. יַמָּא דְכוּכְבוּ. יַמָּא דְמִילְחָא יַמָּא דְחִילָתָא. יַמָּא דְשִׁילְחָת. יַמָּא דְאַיפַּמְיָיא. וְהָא אִיכָּא יַמָּא דְחָמְץ. דִּיקְלֵיטְיָנוּס הִקְוְוה נְהוֹרוֹת וַעֲשָׂאוֹ. כְּתִיב וְנִשְׁקָפָה עַל פְּנֵי הַיְשִׁימוֹן. אָמַר רִבִּי חִייָה בַּר אַבָּא. כָּל־מִי שֶׁהוּא עוֹלֶה לְהַר הַיְשִׁימוֹן וְרָאָה כְּמִין כְּבָרָה קְטַנָּה בְּיַם טִיבֶּרְיָא זוּ הִיא בְּאֵרָהּ שֶׁל מִרְיָם. אָמַר רִבִּי יוֹחָנָן בַּר מָרָה. שַׁעֲרִנְהוּ רַבָּנָן וְהָא הִיא מְכוּוָּנָא כָּל־קֳבֵל תַּרְעָא מְצִיעָיָא דִכְנִישְׁתָּא עַתִּיקְתָא דְּים דּוּטְגִין.

1 ארץ | את ארץ   2 דכוכבו | דסמכו   דחילתא | דחולתא   דשילחת | דשליית   איפמייא | אפמיא   3 דיקליטינוס | דוקליטיאנוס   הקוה | הקוה   ונשקפה | הנשקפה   4 חייה בר אבא | חייא בירייא   הישימון | ישימון   וראה | ומצא   5 קטנה | -   בארה | בורה   5-6 בר מרה | -   6 שערינהו | שערונה   רבנן | רבנין   קבל | קביל

"Seven seas surround the Land of Israel: The ocean, lake Tiberias, lake *Samkho*, the salt sea, lake Ḥolata, lake Sheliat, lake Apamea." But does there not also exist the lake of Ḥomṣ? Diocletian dammed up rivers and created it. It is written (*Num.* 21:20): "Looking down on the desert." Rebbi Ḥiyya bar Abba said, if one ascends the desert mountain one finds the likeness of a sieve in lake Tiberias, that is the well of Miryam. Rebbi Joḥanan bar Mara said, the rabbis estimated it and it is assessed opposite the middle gate of the old synagogue of *Imdvtgyn*.

(35b line 51) דְּבַרְבִּי בַּר קִירְיָא וְרִבִּי לֶעְזָר הֲווֹן מְטַיְילִין בְּאִיסְטַרִין. רָאוּ אֲרוֹנוֹת שֶׁהֵן בָּאִין מֵחוּצָה לָאָרֶץ לָאָרֶץ. אָמַר רִבִּי בַּר קִירְיָא לְרִבִּי לֶעְזָר. מַה הוֹעִילוּ אֵילוּ. אֲנִי קוֹרֵא עֲלֵיהֶם וְנַחֲלָתִי שַׂמְתֶּם לְתוֹעֵבָה בְּחַיֵּיכֶם. וַתָּבוֹאוּ וַתְּטַמְּאוּ אֶת אַרְצִי בְּמִיתַתְכֶם. אָמַר לֵיהּ. כֵּיוָן שֶׁמַּגִּיעִין לְאֶרֶץ יִשְׂרָאֵל הָיוּ נוֹטְלִין גּוּשׁ עָפָר וּמַנִּיחִין עַל אֲרוֹנָן. דִכְתִיב וְכִפֶּר אַדְמָתוֹ עַמּוֹ.

1 דרב׳ בר קיריא | דר׳ ברקיריא   2 שהן | שהין   בר קיריא | ברקיריא   4 במיתתכם | במותתכם   שמגיעין | שהן מגיעין   היו | הן

Rebbi Bar Qiria and Rebbi Eleazar were taking a walk on the road when they saw coffins being brought into the Land from abroad. Rebbi Bar Qiria said to Rebbi Eleazar: What good is that going to do them? I am reading for them (*Jer.* 2:7) "My inheritance your considered an abomination" during your lifetime, "you came and made My Land impure[135]" in your death. He said to him, when they arrive in the Land, one takes a lump of earth and puts it on the coffin, as it is written (*Deut.* 32:43) "His earth atones for His people."

(fol. 34d) **משנה ד**: אָמְרָה אֵי אֶפְשִׁי לָזוּז מִבֵּית אַבָּא וְכוֹלִים הַיּוֹרְשִׁין לוֹמַר לָהּ אִם אַתְּ אֶצְלֵנוּ יֵשׁ לָךְ מְזוֹנוֹת וְאִם אַתְּ אֶצְלֵנוּ אֵין לָךְ מְזוֹנוֹת. אִם הָיְתָה טוֹעֶנֶת מִפְּנֵי שֶׁהִיא יַלְדָּה וְהֵן יְלָדִים נוֹתְנִים לָהּ מְזוֹנוֹת וְהִיא בְּבֵית אָבִיהָ.

Mishnah 4: If she[42] said, I cannot possibly move from my father's house, the heirs can tell her: If you are with us, you are provided with sustenance, but if you are not with us, you are not provided with sustenance[43]. If she argues because she is young and they are young[44], one provides her with sustenance while she is in her father's house.

42 The widow.	44 As the Halakhah explains, if they lived together, people would start to talk that she was sleeping with her stepsons.
43 If she does not want to keep house for them, she has to claim her *ketubah*.	

(33b line 56) **הלכה ד**: אָמְרָה אֵי אֶפְשִׁי לָזוּז מִבֵּית אַבָּא כול'. אִם הָיְתָה טוֹעֶנֶת מִפְּנֵי שֶׁהִיא יַלְדָּה וְהֵן יְלָדִים. מִשּׁוּם שֵׁם רַע.

Halakhah 4: "If she said, I cannot possibly move from my father's house," etc. "If she argues because she is young and they are young," to avoid a bad reputation.

(fol. 34d) **משנה ה**: כָּל־זְמַן שֶׁהִיא בְּבֵית אָבִיהָ גּוֹבָה כְתוּבָּתָהּ לְעוֹלָם. כָּל־זְמַן שֶׁהִיא בְּבֵית בַּעֲלָהּ גּוֹבָה כְתוּבָּתָהּ עַד עֶשְׂרִים וְחָמֵשׁ שָׁנִים שֶׁיֵּשׁ בְּעֶשְׂרִים וְחָמֵשׁ שָׁנִים שֶׁתַּעֲשֶׂה טוֹבָה כְּנֶגֶד כְּתוּבָּתָהּ דִּבְרֵי רִבִּי מֵאִיר שֶׁאָמַר מִשּׁוּם רַבָּן שִׁמְעוֹן בֶּן גַּמְלִיאֵל. וַחֲכָמִים אוֹמְרִים כָּל־זְמַן שֶׁהִיא בְּבֵית בַּעֲלָהּ גּוֹבָה כְתוּבָּתָהּ לְעוֹלָם. כָּל־זְמַן שֶׁהִיא בְּבֵית אָבִיהָ גּוֹבָה כְתוּבָּתָהּ עַד עֶשְׂרִים וְחָמֵשׁ שָׁנִים. מֵתָה יוֹרְשֶׁיהָ מוֹכְרִין כְּתוּבָּתָהּ עַד עֶשְׂרִים וְחָמֵשׁ שָׁנִים.

Mishnah 5: All the time she lives in her father's house, she always can collect her *ketubah*[45]; if she she lives in her husband's house, she can collect her *ketubah* for 25 years, for in 25 years she will have received benefits in the value of her *ketubah*, the words of Rebbi Meïr who spoke in the name of Rabban Simeon ben Gamliel. But the Sages say, all the time she lives in her husband's house, she always can collect her *ketubah*[46]; if she lives in her father's house, she can collect her *ketubah* for 25 years[47]. If she died, her heirs can sell[48] her *ketubah* for up to 25 years.

45 Since she was not sustained by the estate.

46 Since she has to keep house for the heirs, her sustenance is payment for her services and cannot be counted against her *ketubah*.

47 Since she is not supported by the estate and has no connection with the heirs, one may assume that she has decided not to claim the *ketubah*; this is a statute of limitation for claims.

48 This reading is found in the

Yerushalmi and two other Mishnah mss., as well as the *editio princeps* of the Tosephta (12:3). In the Halakhah it is quoted in the form of the Mishnah of the Babli and the great majority of Mishnah mss. and both Tosephta mss: מזכירין "they mention". This refers to the rule explained in the second paragraph of the Halakhah, that any mention of the *ketubah* to the heirs stops the statute of limitations and begins a new period of 25 years. Therefore, it is even possible to sustain the reading of the Mishnah, that her heirs can sell her claim within 25 years since the notification of the stake of the claim to the heirs automatically starts a new period of 25 years.

(35b line 57) **הלכה ו**: כָּל־זְמַן שֶׁהִיא בְּבֵית אָבִיהָ כול׳. בִּטוֹבָה שֶׁעָשׂוּ לָהּ שֶׁנֶּחְלְטוּ נִיכְסֶיהָ בְּחַיֵּי בַעֲלָהּ עַד עֶשְׂרִים וְחָמֵשׁ שָׁנָה מָחֲלָה כְּתוּבָּיָהּ. רַב חִיָּיה בַּר אַשִׁי בְּשֵׁם רַב חִיָּיה בָּעָא קוֹמֵי רִבִּי לָא. מִסְתַּבְּרָה בְּאִשָּׁה שֶׁאֵין לָהּ כְּתוּבָּה. אֲבָל בְּאִשָּׁה שֶׁיֵּשׁ לָהּ כְּתוּבָּה גּוֹבָה לְעוֹלָם. אָמַר לֵהּ. דְּרוּבָּה אָתָא מֵימַר לָהּ. אֲפִילוּ אִשָּׁה שֶׁיֵּשׁ לָהּ כְּתוּבָּה אֵינָהּ גּוֹבָה אֶלָּא עַד עֶשְׂרִים וְחָמֵשׁ שָׁנָה. מִילְתָא דְרִבִּי אֶלְעָזָר אָמְרָה. בַּעַל חוֹב גּוֹבֶה לְעוֹלָם. לֹא אָמַר אֶלָּא בַּעַל חוֹב. אֲבָל אִשָּׁה אֵינָהּ גּוֹבָה אֶלָּא עַד עֶשְׂרִים וְחָמֵשׁ שָׁנָה. אָמַר רִבִּי אָבִין. לֹא מִסְתַּבְּרָה אֶלָּא בְּאִשָּׁה שֶׁאֵין לָהּ מְזוֹנוֹת. אֲבָל בְּאִשָּׁה שֶׁיֵּשׁ לָהּ מְזוֹנוֹת אֲנִי אוֹמֵר. מִפְּנֵי מְזוֹנוֹתֶיהָ לֹא תָבְעָה.

Halakhah 6: "All the time she lives in her father's house," etc. For the good she received; her properties became delivered[49] during her husband's lifetime and after 25 years she gave up the claim to her *ketubah*. Rav Ḥiyya bar Ashi in the name of Rav Ḥiyya asked before Rebbi La: One understands for a woman who has no *ketubah*. But should a woman who has a *ketubah* not be able to collect forever? He answered him, it tells you more: Even a woman who has a *ketubah* collects only up to 25 years[50]. The statement of Rebbi Eleazar says[51], the creditor collects forever. He said only, "the creditor"; but a woman can collect only up to

25 years. Rebbi Abin said, this is reasonable only for a woman who is not being supported. But for a woman who is being supported, I say that she did not claim it because of her support[51].

49   In rabbinic Hebrew, חלט means not only "to parboil" but also "making a final decision". Neither meaning fits the context here. It seems that the word is Arabic خلط "to mix something with something else", meaning that her dowry was mixed with her husband's property all the time.

50   In the Babli, 104b, Rav Naḥman decides with Rav Ḥiyya bar Ashi that the limitation imposed by the Mishnah refers only to a widow who has no *ketubah* document to present to the court.

51   Tosephta 12:3 notes that the creditor (who is secured by a mortgage document) can foreclose forever, after the description of the difference between R. Meïr and the Sages, and a remark that R. Ismael sets the time limit at 30 years. (The first law enacted in the Roman Empire to set a time limit on the collection of debts seems to have been Theodosius II's *praescriptio triginta annorum* of 424 C.E.). The (anonymous) Tosephta is ascribed here to one of the Tannaïm named R. Eleazar.

51   Therefore, her claim is not subject to a time limit. The Babli agrees, 104b.

(35b line 66) אָמַר רִבִּי יוֹסֵי בֵּירִבִּי בּוּן. סוֹף דָּבָר עַד שֶׁתִּתְבַּע. אֲפִילוּ כֵן הִזְכִּירָה. דְּתַנִּינָן תַּמָּן. מֵתָה יוֹרְשֶׁיהָ מַזְכִּירִין כְּתוּבָּתָהּ עַד כ״ה שָׁנָה. דְּרוּבָה אָתָא מֵימַר לָךְ. אֲפִילוּ עָשְׂתָ כ״ה שָׁנִים חָסֵר יוֹם אֶחָד וְלֹא תָבְעָה וְאַחַר כָּךְ תָּבְעָה נוֹתְנִין לָהּ עוֹד כ״ה שָׁנָה.

Rebbi Yose ben Rebbi Abun said, not only that she claims, but even if she mentions [her claims], as we have stated there[52]: "If she died, her heirs can mention her *ketubah* for up to 25 years." He tells you more: Even if she let 25 years minus one day go by before claiming, and then claimed, one gives her another 25 years[53].

HALAKHAH 5

52 Since this refers to the Mishnah of this Halakhah, "there" is out of place. Probably the Mishnah is correct as given and the quote here refers to a text similar to Tosephta 12:3.

53 The claim does not necessarily have to be a claim for payment but may be a reminder that the claim exists. This is sufficient to start a new period of limitation. The Babli agrees, 104 a/b, but in connection with the rule that a documented *ketubah* is not subject to a statute of limitations; cf. Note 50.

(35b line 70) רִבִּי סִימוֹן בְּשֵׁם רִבִּי יְהוֹשֻׁעַ בֶּן לֵוִי. לֹא שָׁנוּ אֶלָּא כְתוּבַּת מָנֶה מָאתַיִם. אֲבָל כְּתוּבַת אֶלֶף דֵּינָר גּוֹבָה לְעוֹלָם. אָתָא רִבִּי אַבָּהוּ בְּשֵׁם רִבִּי יוֹחָנָן. אֲפִילוּ כְתוּבָּתָהּ שֶׁלְּאֶלֶף דֵּינָר אֵינָהּ גּוֹבָה אֶלָּא עַד כ״ה שָׁנָה. וְאַתְיָין אִילֵּין פְּלוּגְוָתָא כְּהֵילֵין פְּלוּגְוָתָא. דְּתַנִּינָן תַּמָּן. הַנִּיזָּקִין שָׁמִין לָהֶן בְּעֵידִית. וּבַעַל חוֹב בְּבֵינוֹנִית. וּכְתוּבַּת אִשָּׁה בְּזִיבּוּרִית. אָמַר לֵיהּ רִבִּי יִרְמְיָה. לֹא שָׁנוּ אֶלָּא מָנֶה מָאתַיִם. אֲבָל כְתוּבָּה שֶׁלְּאֶלֶף דֵּינָר גּוֹבָה בְּבֵינוֹנִית. וְאָמַר רִבִּי יוֹסֵי. וְאֲפִילוּ כְתוּבָּתָהּ אֶלֶף דֵּינָר אֵינָהּ גּוֹבָה אֶלָּא מִן הַזִּיבּוּרִית. וְאַתְיָיא דְּרִבִּי יוֹסֵי כְּרִבִּי יוֹחָנָן וְרִבִּי יִרְמְיָה כְּרִבִּי יְהוֹשֻׁעַ בֶּן לֵוִי. דְּתַנִּינָן תַּמָּן. הַכּוֹתֵב נְכָסָיו לְבָנָיו. כָּתַב לְאִשְׁתּוֹ קַרְקַע כָּל־שֶׁהוּא אִיבֵּד כְּתוּבָּתָהּ. דְּרַב אָמַר. בִּמְזַכָּה עַל יָדֶיהָ. וּשְׁמוּאֵל אָמַר. בִּמְחַלֵּק לְפָנֶיהָ. רִבִּי יוֹסֵי בֶּן חֲנִינָה אָמַר. מְקוּלֵּי כְתוּבָּה שָׁנוּ. אָמַר רִבִּי בָּא. טַעֲמָא דְּרִבִּי יוֹסֵי בֶּן חֲנִינָה. לֹא סוֹף דָּבָר כְּתוּבַּת מָנֶה מָאתַיִם אֶלָּא אֲפִילוּ כְתוּבָּתָהּ אֶלֶף דֵּינָר. מְקוּלֵּי כְתוּבָּה שָׁנוּ.

Rebbi Simon in the name of Rebbi Joshua ben Levi: One stated this only for the *ketubah* of a mina or 200 [zuz][54]. But a *ketubah* of 1'000 denar[55] she collects forever[56]. Rebbi Abbahu quoted in the name of Rebbi Joḥanan: Even a *ketubah* of 1'000 denar she can collect only up to 25 years. This disagreement parallels the following disagreement, as was stated there: "Torts are estimated from choice land, creditor's claims from average, and a woman's *ketubah* from the least valuable.[57]" Rebbi Jeremiah said to him, this was stated only for the *ketubah* of a mina or

200 [*zuz*], but a *ketubah* of 1'000 denar is evaluated in terms of average quality land[56]. But Rebbi Yose said, even a *ketubah* of 1'000 denar she collects only from the least valuable land. It turns out that Rebbi Yose follows Rebbi Joḥanan and Rebbi Jeremiah Rebbi Joshua ben Levi. As we have stated there[58]: "If somebody signs over his property to his sons and signs over some real estate to his wife, she lost her claim to *ketubah*." [59]Rav said, if he lets them acquire through her. Samuel says, if he distributes in her presence. Rebbi Yose ben Ḥanina said, they stated here a relaxation of the laws of *ketubah*. Rebbi Abba said, the reason of Rebbi Yose ben Ḥanina is that it applies not only to a *ketubah* of a mina or two hundred, but even regarding a *ketubah* of one thousand denar they proclaimed a relaxation of the laws of *ketubah*.

54 The amount the husband has to promise from his own money.

55 The greatest part of which is represented by the dowry, her own family's contribution.

56 Mortmain dowry is secured by a general mortgage on the husband's properties; there seems to be no reason to treat this mortgage differently from the mortgage executed for a third party lender.

57 Mishnah *Giṭṭin* 5:1. Since mortgages were usually not written on specific parcels, there are general rules governing foreclosures if the debtor cannot pay cash. The categories mentioned here are explained in Chapter 9, Note 195.

58 Mishnah *Peah* 3:9, Note 151.

59 This text is a slightly shortened version of a text in *Peah* 3:9, explained there in Notes 182-189.

שני דייני גזילות פרק שלשה עשר

משנה א: (fol. 35c) שְׁנֵי דַיָּינֵי גְזֵילוֹת הָיוּ בִירוּשָׁלֵם אַדְמוֹן וְחָנָן בֶּן אַבְשָׁלוֹם. חָנָן אוֹמֵר שְׁנֵי דְבָרִים אַדְמוֹן אוֹמֵר שִׁבְעָה. מִי שֶׁהָלַךְ לוֹ לִמְדִינַת הַיָּם וְאִשְׁתּוֹ תּוֹבַעַת מְזוֹנוֹת חָנָן אָמַר תִּישָּׁבַע בַּסּוֹף וְלֹא תִישָּׁבַע בַּתְּחִילָה. נֶחְלְקוּ עָלָיו בְּנֵי כֹהֲנִים גְּדוֹלִים וְאָמְרוּ תִּישָּׁבַע בַּתְּחִילָה וּבַסּוֹף. אָמַר רִבִּי דוֹסָא בֶּן הַרְכִּינָס כְּדִבְרֵיהֶן. אָמַר רַבָּן יוֹחָנָן בֶּן זַכַּאי יָפֶה אָמַר חָנָן לֹא תִישָּׁבַע אֶלָּא לַבַּסּוֹף.

Mishnah 1: Two robbery[1] judges were in Jerusalem, Admon and Ḥanan ben Absalom. Ḥanan said two things and Admon seven[2]. If somebody went overseas and his wife now is demanding sustenance[3], Ḥanan says that she is made to swear in the end[4]. The High Priests' sons disagreed with him and said, she is made to swear in the beginning[5] and in the end; Rebbi Dosa ben Hyrkanos endorsed their statement. Rabban Joḥanan ben Zakkai said, Ḥanan said correctly that she is made to swear only in the end.

1   In most sources of the Babli גזירות. Probably this is simply a case of change of liquids. It is stated in *Šeqalim* 4:3 that the judges in criminal law were paid from the Temple taxes.

2   All recorded statements of Admon and Ḥanan refer to civil law; the count refers only to those statements which were disputed by the High Priest's sons. It is possible that the latter represented Sadducee practice.

3   She goes to court to obtain permission to sell from her husband's real estate. She claims either that the husband did not provide her with household money before he left or that he stayed overseas longer than

intended and that her household money is now exhausted.

4   Either news is received that her husband died and she requests her *ketubah* or her husband returns and claims that she sold too much of his property. In both cases she has to provide an accounting and swear that nothing of her husband's money remains in her hand.

5   The court should not grant her permission to sell her husband's property unless she swears that all her claims are true.

(35c line 54) **הלכה א**: שְׁנֵי דַיָּינֵי גְזֵילוֹת הָיוּ בִּירוּשָׁלֵם כול'. לֹא כֵן אָמַר רִבִּי פִּינְחָס בְּשֵׁם רִבִּי הוֹשַׁעְיָה. אַרְבַּע מֵאוֹת וְשִׁשִּׁים בָּתֵּי כְנֵסִיּוֹת הָיוּ בִּירוּשָׁלֵם וְכָל־אַחַת וְאַחַת הָיָה לָהּ בֵּית סֵפֶר וּבֵית תַּלְמוּד. בֵּית סֵפֶר לְמִקְרָא וּבֵית תַּלְמוּד לַמִּשְׁנָה. וְאֵילוּ הֵם מְמוּנִּין עַל הַגֶּזֶל. לְלַמְּדָךְ שֶׁכָּל מִי שֶׁהוּא סִפְּקָה בְיָדוֹ לִמְחוֹת וְאֵינוֹ מַמְחֶה קַלְקָלָה תְלוּיָה בּוֹ. תַּנֵּי בְשֵׁם רִבִּי נָתָן. אַף נָחוּם הַמָּדִי הָיָה עִמְּהֶן. עַל דַּעְתֵּיהּ דְּרִבִּי נָתָן שְׁלֹשָׁה דַיָּינֵי גְזֵילוֹת הָיוּ בִירוּשָׁלֵם.

Halakhah 1: "Two robbery judges were in Jerusalem," etc. Did not Rebbi Phineas say in the name of Rebbi Hoshaia: 469 synagogues were in Jerusalem and each one of them had a Book house and a study house; the Book house for Scripture and the study house for Mishnah[6]? But these two were appointed for robberies; to teach you that if anybody has the power to intervene, if he does not exercise his power the misconduct is attributed to him[7]. It was stated in the name of Rebbi Nathan: Naḥum the Mede also was with them[8]. In Rebbi Nathan's opinion, three robbery judges were in Jerusalem.

6   Since every "study house" was a law school, it is obvious that Jerusalem had more than two judges.

The statement of R. Phineas is also in *Megillah* 3:1 (73d 28), Thr. rabbati 2:2, *Introduction* #12; in *Ta'anit* 4, (69a 13) the number of schools is put at 500 in the name of Rabban Simeon ben Gamliel. In the Babli, 105a, the number is 394.

7   The other judges were for civil cases. Those appointed to watch over public order are personally held responsible; therefore these judges are remembered by name. In the Babli, 105a, it is asserted that judges in a criminal court can be paid, in contrast to civil judges.

8   In the Babli, 105a, this tradition is denied.

(35c line 60) רִבִּי חִזְקִיָּה בְּשֵׁם רִבִּי אֲחָא. רִבִּי הָיָה דוֹרֵשׁ ג מִקְרָיּוֹת לְשָׁבַח. וַתֵּשֶׁב בְּפֶתַח עֵינָיִם. וְאֶיפְשָׁר כֵּן. אֲפִילוּ זוֹנָה שֶׁבַּזּוֹנוֹת אֵינָהּ עוֹשָׂה כֵן. אֶלָּא שֶׁתָּלַת עֵינֶיהָ לַפֶּתַח שֶׁכָּל־עֵינַיִם מְצַפּוֹת לוֹ. אָמְרָה לְפָנָיו. רִבּוֹנוֹ שֶׁלְעוֹלָם. אַל אֵצֵא רֵיקָם מִבַּיִת זֶה. דָּבָר אַחֵר. וַתֵּשֶׁב בְּפֶתַח עֵינָיִם. שֶׁפָּתְחָה לוֹ הָעֵינָיִם וְאָמְרָה לוֹ. פְּנוּיָה אֲנִי וּטְהוֹרָה אֲנִי. וְעָלִי זָקֵן מְאֹד וגו'. אֶת אֲשֶׁר יִשְׁכְּבוּן. יַשְׁכִּיבוּן כְּתִיב. אָמַר רִבִּי. שֶׁהָיוּ הַנָּשִׁים מְבִיאוֹת קִינֵּיהֶן לִיטַהֵר לְבַעֲלֵיהֶן וְהָיוּ מַשְׁהִין אוֹתָן. וּמַעֲלֶה עֲלֵיהֶן הַכָּתוּב כְּאִילוּ הֵן שׁוֹכְבִין עִמָּן. אָמַר רִבִּי תַנְחוּמָא. הָדָא הִיא דּוּ מְקַנְתֵּר לוֹן. לָמָּה תִבְעֲטוּ בְּזִבְחִי וּבְמִנְחָתִי. אֵין תֵּימַר. עֲבִירָה חֲמוּרָה יֵשׁ כָּאן. מַבְרִיחָן מִן הַחֲמוּרָה וּמְקַנְתְּרָן בַּקַּלָּה. וְלֹא הָלְכוּ בָנָיו בִּדְרָכָיו. שֶׁהָיוּ נוֹטְלִין מַעֲשֵׂר וְדָנִין. אָמַר רִבִּי בְּרֶכְיָה. מַבְרַכְתָּא הָיְתָה עוֹבֶרֶת וְהָיוּ מְנִיחִין צוֹרְכֵי יִשְׂרָאֵל וְעוֹסְקִין בְּפַרְגְּמַטְיָא.

1 מקרייות | ס מקראות   3 רבונו שלעולם | ס רבון כל העולמים   4 מבית זה | ס מן הבית הזה   ותשב | ס -   5 שפתחה | ס שפיתחה   ואמרה | ס שאמרה   6 אמר רבי | ס -   7 ליטהר | ס לטהר   ומעלה עליהן הכתוב | ס הקדוש ברוך הוא מעלה עליהן עמן | ס אותן   8 הדא | ס חרי   תבעטו | ס תבעתון

[9]Rebbi Ḥizqiya in the name of Rebbi Aḥa: Rebbi used to explain three verses for praise. "She sat at the entrance to the double spring." Is this possible? Even the most brazen whore would not do that. But she lifted her eyes to the door to which all hope is directed; she said before Him: Master of the universe, do not let me leave this house empty. Another explanation: "She sat at the entrance to the double spring;" she opened his eyes and told him, I am single and pure[14].

"And Eli was very old; . . . , that they slept with.[15]" It is written "they bedded them[16]". Rebbi said, the women were bringing their nests[17] to become purified for their husbands and they were deferring the sacrifices; the verse counts it as if they had slept with them. Rebbi Tanḥuma said, that is what he scolds them for: "Why do you disregard my slaughter sacrifice and my flour sacrifice?" Could he remove them from the serious sin and scold them for the simple one?

"His sons did not walk in his ways," that they were taking tithe and judging. Rebbi Berekhiah said, a camel caravan was passing by, they neglected public needs and dealt in merchandise.

9 This text is also in *Soṭah* 1:4, l. 66 f., Notes 198-208. The variant readings from there are indicated by ס. To the sources indicated there one may add *Gen. rabba* 85(8) (in the name of R. Immi.)

(35d line 3) מַעֲשֶׂה בְרַבִּי יִשְׁמָעֵאל שֶׁפָּסַק מְזוֹנוֹת לְאִשָּׁה בְשׁוּקֵי בְצִיפּוֹרִי. מַה בְשׁוּקֵי מְשׁוּקֵי. שָׁמַע רַבִּי וָמַר. מָאן אֲמַר לֵיהּ שֶׁלֹּא שִׁילַח לָהּ. מָאן אָמַר לִי שֶׁלֹּא הִנִּיחַ לָהּ. עָבְרִין יָדְעִין. רִבִּי הִילָא אָמַר. רִבִּי בָּעֵי. מִיסְבַּר סָבַר רִבִּי דְּלֵית מַתְנִיתָא בְּאֵשֶׁת אִישׁ אֶלָּא בְאַלְמָנָה. אָמַר. שְׁמוּאֵל וְרִבִּי שִׁמְעוֹן בֶּן לָקִישׁ תְּרֵיהוֹן אָמְרִין. בְּאַלְמָנָה הִיא מַתְנִיתָא. אָמַר רִבִּי אָבִין. תַּנֵּי דְבֵית רִבִּי כֵן. מִי שֶׁיָּצָא לִמְדִינַת הַיָּם וְאִשְׁתּוֹ תוֹבַעַת מְזוֹנוֹת. הֲוֹון בְּעֵי מֵימַר. מָאן דָּמַר. בְּאֵשֶׁת אִישׁ הִיא מַתְנִיתָא. כַּתְּחִילָּה שֶׁלֹּא שִׁילַח לָהּ. בַּסּוֹף שֶׁלֹּא הִטְמִינָה וְשֶׁלֹּא הֱעֱרִימָה. מָאן דָּמַר. בְּאַלְמָנָה הִיא מַתְנִיתָא. כַּתְּחִילָּה שֶׁלֹּא הִנִּיחַ לָהּ. בַּסּוֹף שֶׁלֹּא הִטְמִינָה וְשֶׁלֹּא הֱעֱרִימָה. אָמַר שְׁמוּאֵל אַחְוָה דְרִבִּי בְּרֶכְיָה. בְּשֶׁלֹּא מָחֲלָה לִיתוֹמִין עַל כְּתוּבָּתָהּ.

It happened that Rebbi Ismael allotted sustenance to a woman in the markets of Sepphoris[10]. What means "in the markets"[11]? From the markets. Rebbi heard this and said, who told him that he[12] did not send her? Who told me that he did not leave for her[13]? Do the passers-by know? Rebbi Hila said, this is what Rebbi asked: Rebbi is of the opinion that the Mishnah does not speak of a married woman but of a widow[14]. He said, Samuel[15] and Rebbi Simeon ben Laqish both say, the Mishnah deals with a widow. It was stated in the House of Rebbi thus: "If somebody left[16] for overseas and his wife demands sustenance." They wanted to say, for him who says, the Mishnah speaks of a married woman, "in the beginning"[17] that he did not send her, "in the end" that she did not put aside and did not act dishonestly. For him who says, the Mishnah speaks of a widow, "in the beginning" that he did not leave for her[18], "in the end" that she did not put aside and did not act dishonestly. Samuel, Rebbi Berekhiah's brother, said, that she did not renounce her *ketubah* in the orphans' favor[19].

10 In the Babli, 107b, this is R. Abin's version of what happened. Both in the Babli and here, "R. Ismael" cannot refer to the Tanna R. Ismael who lived in the South two generations earlier; the reference must be to R. Ismael ben R. Yose, the contemporary of Rebbi.

11 Could the woman get permission to sell her husband's property through an informal talk in the market? This would contradict all rules of judicial procedure.

12 The absent husband.

13 That the husband provided his wife with enough money to cover her expenses until his return.

14 The courts will not intervene in the monetary affairs of married couples. After the husband's death, the liquidation of the husband's estate is a legitimate object of the court's attention.

15 This is confirmed in the Babli, 107a, but rejected as practice, 107b.

16 Our Mishnah reads "if somebody *went* overseas", i. e., with the intent to return. In this version, the court will intervene in behalf of the married woman. But "if somebody *left for* overseas", i. e., emigrated permanently, then the Mishnah only deals either

with an abandoned wife or a widow, but not with a wife who expects her husband to return.

17   The oath required in the opinion of the High Priests' sons.

18   Before the husband left on his trip.

19   The initial oath required by the High Priests' sons does not refer to the amount of money she needs, since this can all be settled by the accounting she has to deliver under oath in the end. She has to swear at the beginning that in principle she is entitled to sustenance, since a widow who renounces her claim to *ketubah* at the same time also renounces her claim to sustenance.

(35d line 13) הֲרֵי שֶׁיָּצָא הוּא וְאִשְׁתּוֹ לִמְדִינַת הַיָּם וּבָאָת וְאָמְרָה. מֵת בַּעֲלִי. תִּזּוֹן וְתִיטוֹל כְּתוּבָּתָהּ. גֵּירְשַׁנִי בַעֲלִי. תִּזּוֹן מִכְּתוּבָּתָהּ. מַה נַּפְשָׁךְ. אִם הִיא אֵשֶׁת אִישׁ מִשֶּׁלְּבַעֲלָהּ הִיא נִיזוֹנֶת. אִם אֵינָהּ אֵשֶׁת אִישׁ מִכְּתוּבָּתָהּ הִיא נִיזוֹנֶת. הֲרֵי מִשֶּׁבָּא מִמְּדִינַת הַיָּם וְאִשְׁתּוֹ תּוֹבַעַת מְזוֹנוֹת וְאָמַר. יֵצְאוּ מַעֲשֵׂה יָדֶיהָ בִּמְזוֹנוֹתֶיהָ. שׁוֹמְעִין לוֹ. וְאִם פָּסְקוּ בֵית דִּין מַה שֶּׁפָּסְקוּ פָּסְקוּ. רִבִּי יִרְמְיָה אָמַר. בְּשֶׁאֵין מַעֲשֵׂה יָדֶיהָ כְּדֵי מְזוֹנוֹת. כְּהָדָא שׁוֹמְעִין לוֹ. כְּמָאן דָּמַר. אֵין מְזוֹנוֹת לְאִשָּׁה מִדְּבַר תּוֹרָה. כְּהָדָא דְּתַנֵּי. אֵין בֵּית דִּין פּוֹסְקִין לְאִשָּׁה מְזוֹנוֹת מִדְּמֵי שְׁבִיעִית. אֲבָל נִיזוֹנֶת הִיא עִם בַּעֲלָהּ בַּשְּׁבִיעִית. רִבִּי יוֹסֵי אוֹמֵר. בְּשֶׁיֵּשׁ מַעֲשֵׂה יָדֶיהָ כְּדֵי מְזוֹנָהּ. כְּהָדָא מַה שֶּׁפָּסְקוּ פָּסְקוּ. תִּיפְתָּר בְּשֶׁפָּסְקוּ יָתֵר.

[20]If somebody together with his wife left for overseas, then she returns and says, my husband died, she shall be supported and collect her *ketubah*[21]. My husband divorced me[22], she shall be supported from her *ketubah* since, as you take it, if she be a married woman, she must be supported from her husband's; if she is no longer a married woman[23], she can be supported from her *ketubah*[24]. [25]"If somebody returns from overseas and his wife requests support[26] but he says, let her earnings cover her sustenance, one listens to him[27]. But if the court had allotted, what they allotted, they have allotted[28]." Rebbi Jeremiah said, if her

earnings are not enough for her support[29]. In this case, does one listen to him[30]? Following him who says, there is no support for the wife in biblical law, as we have stated: "The court will not determine food for a wife from Sabbatical money, but she may be given Sabbatical produce to eat at her husband's."[31] Rebbi Yose says, if her earnings are sufficient for her support[32]. In that case, why what they allotted, they have allotted? Explain it, if they allotted excess.

20 This *baraita* is also discussed in the Babli, 107b.

21 Since Mishnah *Yebamot* 15:1 states that in this case the widow may remarry without proof of the husband's death, she certainly must be believed regarding the monetary implications of her husband's death.

22 In this case she is not permitted to remarry unless she proves the fact of her divorce either by a court document or by witnesses. Since her word alone is not accepted in criminal law, it cannot be accepted in civil law.

23 But she really is divorced.

24 If her husband's death later becomes known, she can collect only the amount of her *ketubah* minus the amounts already taken for her sustenance (Interpretation of the Babli).

25 Tosephta 12:4; Babli 107a.

26 His wife took out a loan under the supervision of the court and now the wife requests him to repay the loan.

27 He can request her to repay the loan from her own earnings. In the interpretation of R. Nissim Gerondi (Alfasi # 389), the husband has to pay the wife's debt beforehand and then can recover from her earnings.

28 If the court had empowered her to sell of the husband's property, he cannot require her to buy it back.

29 He explains the Tosephta in case that the earnings of the wife were not sufficient to cover her expenses; therefore the court was justified in giving her permission to sell and their order has to stand.

30 In this case, why should the husband be able to refuse to pay for his wife's borrowing.

31 *Ma'serot* 3:1, Notes 11-12. The marriage contract explicitly notes that the husband will "work for, honor,

feed, and provide for" his bride "in the manner of Jewish husbands." The language seems to imply that this is a contract following rabbinic guidelines; this is the position of Nachmanides and R. Asher ben Ieḥiel (*Rosh Ketubot* Chap. 13, Sec. 6.) Maimonides holds that nevertheless the obligation is biblical, *Hilkhot Iššut* 12:2.

The wife may not sell Sabbatical produce for her needs since Sabbatical produce may not be used to pay debts of any kind. But if the husband is present, she may eat of his Sabbatical fruits; since his obligation to feed his wife is only rabbinical, this is not considered paying his debts with Sabbatical produce.

32   He explains that the Tosephta is applicable even if the wife earns enough and does not have to go hungry in her husband's absence. Since by the *ketubah* contract the wife is entitled to live as well in her husband's absence as in his presence, the court is entitled to grant her money to make up the difference.

(35d line 23) הֲרֵי שֶׁהָיָה נָתוּן בִּמְדִינַת הַיָּם וְאָמַר. יִנָּתְנוּ אֵילּוּ לְבָנָיו. בְּנוֹתָיו בִּכְלָל. אִם (בַּשְּׁבִיעִית)[33] [בִּשְׁעַת מִיתָא] אָמַר. יִנָּתְנוּ אֵילּוּ לְבָנָיו. אֵין בְּנוֹתָיו בִּכְלָל.

If somebody was overseas and said, certain things should be given to his sons, his daughters are included[34]. If he said that when he was dying, certain things should be given to his sons, his daughters are not included[35].

33   The text in parentheses, "in the Sabbatical year", is the ms. text. The text in brackets, "when he was dying" is that of the quote by Alfasi *Baba batra* #887. However, there the text is different: מי ששלח ממדינת הים ואמר ינתנו אלו לבני בנותיו בכלל ואם אמר בשעת מיתה אלו לבני אין הבנות בכלל. "If somebody *sent from* overseas and said, certain things should be given to *my* sons, his daughters are included. If he said that when he was dying, certain things should be given to my sons, his daughters are not included." While the ms. text is corrupt and the translation follows Alfasi, the hybrid ms.-Alfasi text cannot really be considered as representing the original.

34 For gifts between the living, people make no distinction between sons and daughters. Following the general linguistic rule that for mixed genders the masculine is used (in educated speech), בנים can mean both "sons" and "children".

35 Death-bed instructions are to be interpreted as referring to inheritance. Since in biblical law daughters do not inherit in the presence of sons, daughters are not included in the absence of specific instructions (cf. Mishnah 4:8).

(35d line 25) רִבִּי זְעִירָא רַב חֲנַנְאֵל בְּשֵׁם רַב רִבִּי זְעִירָא בְּשֵׁם אַבָּא בַּר יִרְמְיָה. שְׁנֵי דְבָרִים אָמַר חָנָן הֲלָכָה כְיוֹצֵא בוֹ. שִׁבְעָה דְבָרִים אָמַר אַדְמוֹן אֵין הֲלָכָה כְיוֹצֵא בוֹ. רִבִּי בָּא בַּר זַבְדָא בְּשֵׁם רִבִּי יִצְחָק בַּר חֲקוּלָה. בְּכָל־מָקוֹם שֶׁשָּׁנִינוּ אָמַר רַבָּן גַּמְלִיאֵל. רוֹאֶה אֲנִי אֶת דִּבְרֵי אַדְמוֹן הֲלָכָה כְיוֹצֵא בוֹ.

Rebbi Ze'ira, Rav Ḥananel in the name of Rav; Rebbi Ze'ira in the name of Abba bar Jeremiah: Practice follows Ḥanan in his two statements; practice does not follow Admon in his seven statements. Rebbi Abba bar Zavda in the name of Rebbi Isaac bar Ḥaqula: In every case in which Rabban Simeon ben Gamliel said, I am convinced by Admon's statement, practice follows him[36,37].

36 Similar statements are in the Babli, 109a.

37 Only three of Admon's sayings are accepted in practice.

(fol. 35c) **משנה ב:** מִי שֶׁהָלַךְ לִמְדִינַת הַיָּם וְעָמַד אֶחָד וּפִירְנֵס אֶת אִשְׁתּוֹ חָנָן אָמַר אִיבֵּד אֶת מְעוֹתָיו. נֶחְלְקוּ עָלָיו בְּנֵי כֹהֲנִים גְּדוֹלִים וְאָמְרוּ יִשָּׁבַע כַּמָּה הוֹצִיא וְיִטּוֹל. אָמַר רִבִּי דּוֹסָא בֶּן הַרְכִּינָס כְּדִבְרֵיהֶן. אָמַר רַבָּן יוֹחָנָן בֶּן זַכַּאי יָפָה אָמַר חָנָן הִנִּיחַ מְעוֹתָיו עַל קֶרֶן הַצְּבִי.

Mishnah 2: If somebody went overseas and another person provided for his wife[38], Ḥanan says, he lost his money. The High Priests' sons disagreed with him and said, let him swear on what he expended, that she shall collect; Rebbi Dosa ben Hyrkanos endorsed their statement. Rabban Joḥanan ben Zakkai said, Ḥanan said correctly that he put his money on a deer's antler[39].

38 The other person neither was appointed by the husband to provide for his wife, nor did the wife sign that she received his support as a loan, to be repaid at her husband's return.

39 The deer runs away and sheds his antlers every year; a person who puts his money on a deer's antlers is declaring it ownerless.

(35d line 54) **הלכה ב**: מִי שֶׁהָלַךְ לוֹ לִמְדִינַת הַיָּם כול׳. [40]רִבִּי בָּא בַּר מָמָל בָּעֵי. הַפּוֹרֵעַ שְׁטַר חוֹבוֹ לַחֲבֵירוֹ שֶׁלֹּא מִדַּעְתּוֹ. תַּפְלוּגְתָּא דְחָנָן וּבְנֵי כֹהֲנִים גְּדוֹלִים. אָמַר רִבִּי יוֹסֵי. טַעֲמוֹן דִּבְנֵי כֹהֲנִים גְּדוֹלִים. תַּמָּן לֹא עָלְתָה עַל דַּעְתּוֹ שֶׁתָּמוּת אִשְׁתּוֹ בְּרָעָב. בְּרַם הָכָא מְפַיֵּיס הֲוֵינָא לֵיהּ וְהוּא מְחִיל לִי. הַגַּע בְּעַצְמָךְ דַּהֲוָה גְבֵיהּ מַשְׁכּוֹן. מְפַיֵּיס הֲוֵינָא לֵיהּ וְהוּא יְהַב לִי מַשְׁכּוֹנִי. עַד כְּדוֹן בְּבַעַל חוֹב שֶׁאֵינוֹ דוֹחֵק. וַאֲפִילוּ בְּבַעַל חוֹב שֶׁהוּא דוֹחֵק. שְׁמָעִינָן מִן הָדָא. וְשׁוֹקֵל אֶת שִׁקְלוֹ. וְלֹא שָׁקַל אֵין מְמַשְׁכְּנִין אוֹתוֹ. הָדָא אָמְרָה. וַאֲפִילוּ בְּבַעַל חוֹב שֶׁהוּא דוֹחֵק. תֵּדַע לָךְ שֶׁהוּא כֵן. דְּתַנִּינָן. וּמַקְרִיב עָלָיו קִינֵּי זָבִין וְקִינֵּי זָבוֹת קִינֵּי יוֹלְדוֹת חַטָּאוֹת וַאֲשָׁמוֹת. לֹא בִּשְׁלֹא נָתַן לְתוֹךְ יָדוֹ כְּלוּם. [וְכָא בְּשֶׁלֹּא יַכְנִס לְתוֹךְ יָדָיו כְּלוּם.][41]

2 לחבירו | ג שלחבירו   3 טעמון | ג טעמא   עלתה | ג עלת   דעתו | ג דעתן   4-3 שתמות אשתו | ג שימות עבדו   4 מחיל | ג מוחל   בעצמך | ג עצמך   6 שהוא דוחק | ג סדוחק   שמעינן | ג נישמעינה   7-6 ושוקל את שקלו. ולא שקל אין ממשכנין אותו | ג - 7 הָדָא אָמְרָה. וַאֲפִילוּ בְּבַעַל חוֹב שֶׁהוּא דוֹחֵק | ג -   8 וקיני | ג קיני   לא | ג -

HALAKHAH 2

Halakhah 2: "If somebody went overseas," etc. Rebbi Abba bar Mamal asked: If somebody pays off somebody else's debt without the latter's knowledge, is that the disagreement of Ḥanan and the High Priests' sons[21]? Rebbi Yose said, there the reason of the High Priest's sons is that he would not expect his wife to starve. But here, [the debtor could say:] "I could negotiate with him and he would forgive some." Think of it, if [the loan] was on a pledge! "I could negotiate with him and he would return my pledge." So far about a creditor who does not push [for repayment]. Even for a creditor who pushes, we can hear from the following: "He may give his *šeqel*." If somebody does not pay his *šeqel*, does one not take a pledge from him? This says, even for a creditor who pushes. You should know that this is so, as we have stated: "He can bring for him nests for males or females suffering from genital discharges, nests for childbirth, purification and reparation offerings" since nothing of these comes to [the other person's] hand. And here also, that nothing should come into his hand.

---

40 This and the following paragraphs are from *Nedarim* 4:2, explained there in Notes 20-44. Variant readings from there are denoted by ג.

The present paragraph refers there to Notes 20-26. The Mishnah in *Nedarim* explains what a person can do for someone else about whom he has vowed that he should not have any usufruct from him. According to Ḥanan, a person in that situation could support the other's wife in his absence since he has no legal right to recoup his money.

41 Sentence missing in the *Ketubot* text.

(35d, line 39) רִבִּי יְהוֹשֻׁעַ בֶּן לֵוִי אָמַר. אֵין לָךְ נִתְפָּס עַל חֲבֵירוֹ וְחַיָּיב לִיתֶּן לוֹ אֶלָא בְּאַרְנוֹן וּבְגוּלְגּוֹלֶת. רַב אָמַר. כָּל־הַנִּתְפָּס עַל חֲבֵירוֹ חַיָּיב לִיתֶּן לוֹ.

חַיְילֵיהּ דְּרַב מִן הָדָא. הַגּוֹזֵל שָׂדֶה וּנְטָלוּהָ מֵצִיקִין. וְלֹא שָׁמַע מַה דְּאָמַר רִבִּי יוֹחָנָן. קְנָס קָנְסוּ בְּגוֹזְלָן. רִבִּי אָבִין בָּעֵי. וְהֵן דַּהֲוָה רַבָּה. רִבִּי יוֹסֵי בֵּירִבִּי בּוּן וְרִבִּי חִייָה בַּר לוּלְיָינִי. תְּרֵיהוֹן בְּשֵׁם שְׁמוּאֵל אָמְרֵי. חַד אָמַר. כְּאָרְנוֹן וּכְגוּלְגּוֹלֶת. וְחָרְנָה אָמַר. אֵינָהּ כְּאָרְנוֹן וּכְגוּלְגּוֹלֶת.

1 אמר | ג אומר   2 נתפס | ג נתפס   3 ליתן לו | ג לו   מציקין | ג מסיקין   ולא | ג לא   מה | ג -   4 גוזלן | ג גזלן   וההן דהוה רבה | ג דהוה רביה   5 שמואל אמרי | ג רבי שמואל

Rebbi Joshua ben Levi says, nobody is held responsible for his neighbor except for *annona* and head-tax. Rav said, anything for which one is held responsible for one's neighbor has to be repaid. The strength of Rav is from the following: "He who appropriated a field and oppressors took it." He did not hear that Rebbi Johanan said, they exacted a fine from a robber. Rebbi Abin asked, what is greater? Rebbi Yose ben Rebbi Abun, and Rebbi Hiyya ben Julianus both said in the name of Samuel; one said, it is like *annona* and head-tax; the other said, it is not like *annona* and head-tax.

(35d, line 45) תַּמָּן תַּנִּינָן. מְרַפְּאֵהוּ רִיפּוּי נֶפֶשׁ אֲבָל לֹא רִפּוּי מָמוֹן. רִבִּי יְהוּדָה וְרִבִּי יוֹסֵי. חַד אָמַר. כָּאן בִּמְדִירָה מִגּוּפוֹ וְכָאן בִּמְדִירָה מִנְּכָסָיו. וְחָרְנָה אָמַר. כָּאן בְּשֶׁיֵּשׁ לוֹ מִי יְרַפְּאֶנּוּ וְכָאן בְּשֶׁאֵין לוֹ מִי יְרַפְּאֶנּוּ. אִם מִי שֶׁיֵּשׁ לוֹ מִי יְרַפְּאֶנּוּ אֲפִילוּ רְפוּאַת נֶפֶשׁ לֹא יְרַפְּאֶנּוּ. שֶׁלֹּא מִן הַכֹּל אָדָם זוֹכֶה לְהִתְרַפּוֹת.

1 ריפוי | ג רפואה   (2 times)   2 יהודה | ג יודה   3 מי שיש | ג בשיש   4-3 ירפאנו | ג שירפאנו   (3 times)   4 שלא מן הכל | ג שלא מכל

There, we have stated: "He heals him in the sense of personal healing but not in the sense of financial healing." Rebbi Judan and Rebbi Yose. One of them said, here if the vow refers to his body, there if the vow refers to his property. But the other said, here if he has somebody else who can heal him, there if there is nobody else who can heal him. If he has somebody else who can heal him, he should not be able to heal him personally! Not by everybody is a person successfully healed.

(35d, line 49) וְלֹא נִיכְסֵי הַמַּחֲזִיר הֵן שֶׁהֵן אֲסוּרִין לְבַעַל הַפָּרָה. עוּלָּא בַּר יִשְׁמָעֵאל בְּשֵׁם רִבִּי יִצְחָק. כְּשֶׁהָיוּ נְכָסָיו שֶׁלָּזֶה אֲסוּרִין עַל זֶה וּנְכָסָיו שֶׁלָּזֶה אֲסוּרִין עַל זֶה.

2 נכסיו שלזה | נ ניכסי זה   ונכסיו שלזה | נ ונכסי זה

Is not the property of the finder forbidden to the owner of the cow? Ulla bar Ismael in the name of Rebbi Isaac: If each man's property was forbidden to the other.

(35d, line 52) מָאן תַּנָּא תִּפּוֹל הֲנָיָיה לְהֶקְדֵּשׁ. רִבִּי מֵאִיר. דְּרִבִּי מֵאִיר אוֹמֵר. מוֹעֲלִין בָּאִסּוּרוֹת. רִבִּי אָבוּן בַּר חִייָה בָּעֵי. נָדַר מִן הַכִּיכָּר מַהוּ לְחַמֵּם בּוֹ אֶת יָדָיו. נִישְׁמְעִינָהּ מִן הָדָא. אָמַר. הַכִּכָּר הַזֶּה הֶקְדֵּשׁ. אֲכָלוֹ בֵּין הוּא בֵּין אַחֵר מָעַל. לְפִיכָךְ יֵשׁ לוֹ פִדְיוֹן. אִם אָמַר. הֲרֵי זֶה עָלַי. אֲכָלוֹ מָעַל בּוֹ בְּטוֹבַת הֲנָיָיה. דִּבְרֵי רִבִּי מֵאִיר. אֲחֵרִים לֹא מָעֲלוּ. לְפִיכָךְ אֵין לוֹ פִדְיוֹן. לֹא אָמַר אֶלָּא אֲכָלוֹ. הָא לְחַמֵּם בּוֹ אֶת יָדָיו מוּתָּר. תַּלְמִידוֹי דְּרִבִּי יוֹנָה בְּשֵׁם רִבִּי בּוּן בַּר חִייָה. כֵּינִי בָאוֹמֵר. לֹא אוֹכְלֶינָּהּ וְלֹא אַטְעֲמֶינָּהּ. לֹא אָסְרוּ עָלָיו אֶלָּא לַאֲכִילָה. עַד כְּדוֹן צְרִיכָה נָדַר מִן הַכִּיכָּר מַהוּ לְחַמֵּם בּוֹ אֶת יָדָיו.

2 אסורות | נ איסרות   אבון | נ בון   הככר | נ ככר   3 הככר הזה | נ ככר זה   4 זה |
נ הוא   6 תלמידוי | נ תלמידוהי   7 אטעמינו | נ אטעמנו   8 הככר | נ ככר

Who is the Tanna of "the gain should be given to the sacred fund"? Rebbi Meïr! For Rebbi Meïr said, one commits sacrilege with prohibitions. Rebbi Abun bar Ḥiyya asked: If somebody made a vow [to forbid] a loaf to himself, can he use it to warm his hands? Let us hear from the following: "If he said, this loaf shall be dedicated, if he or another person ate it, they committed sacrilege; therefore, it can be redeemed. But if he said, it is for me [as if dedicated], if he ate it he committed sacrilege on goodwill but others would not commit sacrilege." He said only, if he ate it. Therefore, to warm his hands is permitted. The students of Rebbi Jonah in the name of Rebbi Abun bar Ḥiyya: That is if he said I shall not eat it nor taste it; if he forbade only eating to himself. But the question was, if somebody made a vow [to forbid] a loaf to himself, can he use it to warm his hands?

(35d, line 60) דְּתַנֵּי. מִי שֶׁהָלַךְ לִמְדִינַת הַיָּם וְעָמַד אֶחָד וּפִירְנֵס אֶת אִשְׁתּוֹ. אָמַר רִבִּי חַגַּיי. לֹא אָמַר אֶלָּא אַחֵר. הָא הָאָב גּוֹבֶה. רִבִּי יוֹסֵי אוֹמֵר. בֵּין אָב בֵּין אַחֵר אֵינוֹ גּוֹבֶה. וְאַתְיָין אִילֵּין פְּלוּגְוָתָא כְּהַלֵּין פְּלוּגְוָתָא. דְּתַנִּינָן תַּמָּן. וְזַכַּאי בִּמְצִיאָתָהּ וּבְמַעֲשֵׂה יָדֶיהָ וּבְהֶפֵר נְדָרֶיהָ וּמְקַבֵּל גִּיטָהּ וְאֵינוֹ אוֹכֵל פֵּירוֹת בְּחַיֶּיהָ. וְחַיָּיב בִּמְזוֹנוֹתֶיהָ וּבְפִרְקוֹנָהּ וּבִקְבוּרָתָהּ. אָמַר רִבִּי חַגַּיי. לֹא אָמְרוּ אֶלָּא הָאָב. הָא אַחֵר אֵינוֹ גּוֹבֶה. רִבִּי יוֹסֵי אוֹמֵר. בֵּין אָב בֵּין אַחֵר גּוֹבֶה. עַל דַּעְתֵּיהּ דְּרִבִּי חַגַּיי. בֵּין לִקְבוּרָה בֵּין לִמְזוֹנוֹת הָאָב גּוֹבֶה אַחֵר אֵינוֹ גּוֹבֶה. עַל דַּעְתֵּיהּ דְּרִבִּי יוֹסֵי. לִקְבוּרָה בֵּין אָב בֵּין אַחֵר גּוֹבֶה. שֶׁלֹּא עָלַת עַל דַּעַת שֶׁתְּהֵא אִשְׁתּוֹ מוּשְׁלַחַת לַכְּלָבִים. וּבִמְזוֹנוֹת בֵּין אָב בֵּין אַחֵר אֵינוֹ גּוֹבֶה.

[42]As it was stated: "If somebody went overseas and another person provided for his wife." Rebbi Ḥaggai said, they said only, another. Therefore, the father[43] can recover. Rebbi Yose says, neither the father nor a third party can recover. There is a parallel disagreement, as we have stated there[44]: "He[45] has the right to what she finds and to her earnings, to dissolve her vows, and to receive her bill of divorce, but cannot eat usufruct in her lifetime... He[46] is required to pay for her

upkeep, her ransom, and her burial." Rebbi Haggai said, they said only, the father[47]. Therefore, a third party cannot recover[48]. Rebbi Yose says, both the father or a third party can recover. In the opinion of Rebbi Haggai, both for burial as for upkeep the father can recover, a third party cannot recover. In the opinion of Rebbi Yose, for burial both the father and also a third party can recover because it is unthinkable that his wife should be thrown to the dogs. For sustenance, neither the father nor a third party can recover[49].

42 A slightly different parallel to this paragraph is in Halakhah 4:6, Notes 149-150.
43 Who was responsible for her sustenance before her marriage; Mishnah 4:6.
44 Mishnah 4:6, Notes 138-140.
45 The father of an underage girl.
46 The husband after marriage.

47 This refers to the *baraita* stated at the start of the parallel paragraph in 4:6: "If the husband refused to bury her, the father buries her and recovers his expenses in court."
48 Burial expenses for an unrelated woman.
49 Unless given as a loan or by a court-appointed guardian.

(fol. 35c) **משנה ג:** אַדְמוֹן אָמַר שִׁבְעָה. מִי שֶׁמֵּת וְהִנִּיחַ בָּנִים וּבָנוֹת בִּזְמַן שֶׁהַנְּכָסִים מְרוּבִּין הַבָּנִים יוֹרְשִׁים וְהַבָּנוֹת יִזּוֹנוּ. נְכָסִים מוּעָטִים הַבָּנוֹת יִזּוֹנוּ וְהַבָּנִים יִשְׁאֲלוּ עַל הַפְּתָחִים. אַדְמוֹן אוֹמֵר. בִּשְׁבִיל שֶׁאֲנִי זָכָר הִפְסַדְתִּי. אָמַר רַבָּן שִׁמְעוֹן בֶּן גַּמְלִיאֵל רוֹאֶה אֲנִי אֶת דִּבְרֵי אַדְמוֹן.

Mishnah 3: Admon promulgated seven [rules]. If somebody dies and is survived by sons and daughters. If the estate is large, the sons inherit and the daughters will be sustained[50]. If the estate is small[51], the daughters shall be sustained and the sons shall go begging. Admon said, because I am a male, shall I lose? Rabban Simeon ben Gamliel said, I am convinced by Admon's statement[52].

50   From the estate.
51   If the entire estate is needed to sustain the daughters until they marry.

52   All underage children are sustained together.

(35d line 70) **הלכה ג**: אַדְמוֹן אָמַר שִׁבְעָה כול׳. כַּמָּה הֵן נְכָסִים מְרוּבִּין. רִבִּי זְעוּרָה רַב יְהוּדָה בְּשֵׁם רַב. כְּדֵי שֶׁיְּהֵא שָׁם מָזוֹן שְׁנֵים עָשָׂר חוֹדֶשׁ לְאֵילוּ וּלְאֵילוּ. שָׁמַע שְׁמוּאֵל וָמַר. זוֹ דִבְרֵי רַבָּן גַּמְלִיאֵל בְּרִבִּי. אֲבָל חֲכָמִים אוֹמְרִים. עַד שֶׁיִּבָּגוּרוּ אוֹ עַד שֶׁיִּנָּשְׂאוּ. בְּעוֹן קוֹמֵי רִבִּי יוֹסֵי. אַתְּ מַה שָׁמַעְתְּ מִן רִבִּי יוֹחָנָן. אָמַר לוֹן. נְפָרֵשׁ מִילֵּיהוֹן דְּרַבָּנִין מִן מִילֵּיהוֹן. נָתָן בַּר הוֹשַׁעְיָה בְּעָא קוֹמֵי רִבִּי יוֹחָנָן. הָיָה שָׁם מָזוֹן יֹ״ב חוֹדֶשׁ וְנִתְמָעֲטוּ הַנְּכָסִים. אָמַר לֵיהּ. מִכֵּיוָן שֶׁהִתְחִילוּ הַיְתוֹמִין לִהְיוֹת אוֹכְלִין בְּהֶיתֵר אוֹכְלִין וְהוֹלְכִין עַד שֶׁתִּיכְלֶה פְּרוּטָה הָאַחֲרוֹנָה.

Halakhah 3: "Admon promulgated seven [rules]," etc. [53]How large is a large estate? Rebbi Ze'ura, Rav Jehudah in the name of Rav: That there should be twelve months of sustenance for all of them[54]. Samuel heard this and said, this is the opinion of Rabban Gamliel ben Rebbi[55], but the Sages say, until they[56] reach adulthood or are married. They asked before Rebbi Yose[57], what did you hear from Rebbi Johanan? He said to them, let us explain the words of the Sages by their words! Nathan bar Hoshaia asked before Rebbi Johanan, if there was sustenance for twelve months but the estate diminished in value? He answered him, since the heirs[58] started to eat with permission, they continue to eat until the last coin is gone.

53 Most of this Halakhah is found in *Baba batra* 9:1, in a somewhat different formulation.
54 Sons and daughters together.
55 Gamliel III.
56 The daughters, who have to be supported until either they marry or reach adulthood.
57 This probably should read "R. Yasa" since R. Yose lived three generations after R. Joḥanan. In *Baba batra*, the person who was asked is R. Ḥiyya bar Abba, R. Joḥanan's successor as head of the Academy.
58 The sons. He follows the majority opinion in the Mishnah that only the daughters are supported by a small estate, but he follows Rabban Gamliel III in the definition of a large estate. Practice almost always follows R. Joḥanan.

(36a line 1) מֵאֵימָתַי שָׁמִין לָהֶן. רְבִּי מָנָא אָמַר. שָׁמִין לָהֶן בַּסּוֹף. אָמַר לֵיהּ רִבִּי חֲנִינָה. מִלֵּיהוֹן דְּרַבָּנִין לֹא שָׁמְעִין לָךְ. דְּנָתָן בַּר הוֹשַׁעְיָה בָּעָא קוֹמֵי רִבִּי יוֹחָנָן. הָיָה שָׁם מָזוֹן י̇ב̇ חוֹדֶשׁ וְנִתְמָעֲטוּ הַנְּכָסִים. אָמַר לִי. מִכֵּיוָן שֶׁהִתְחִילוּ הַיְּתוֹמִים לִהְיוֹת אוֹכְלִין בְּהֶיתֵר אוֹכְלִין וְהוֹלְכִין עַד שֶׁתִּיכָלֶה פְּרוּטָה הָאַחֲרוֹנָה. אֶלָּא מִשָּׁעָה רִאשׁוֹנָה שָׁמִין לָהֶן. רַב חִסְדַּאי בָּעֵי. הָיָה שָׁם מָזוֹן שְׁנֵים עָשָׂר חוֹדֶשׁ וְהוֹקִירוּ הַנְּכָסִים. נִשְׁמְעִינָה מִן הָדָא. דְּאָמַר רִבִּי חֲנִינָה רִבִּי יָסָא בְּשֵׁם רִבִּי יוֹחָנָן. עָמְדוּ הַיְּתוֹמִין וּמָכְרוּ שֶׁלָּהֶן מָכְרוּ. וְכָא הוֹקִירוּ שֶׁלָּהֶן הוֹקִירוּ. לֹא הָיָה שָׁם מָזוֹן י̇ב̇ חוֹדֶשׁ מַהוּ שֶׁיֹּאמְרוּ בָנִים לְבָנוֹת. טְלוּ אֶת שֶׁלָּכֶם וּצְאוּ. אָמַר רִבִּי אַבָּא מָהוּ. מַתְנִיתָא אָמְרָה שֶׁאֵין אוֹמְרִין לָהֶן. דְּתַנִּינָן תַּמָּן. אִם אָמְרוּ הַיְּתוֹמִין. הֲרֵי אָנוּ מַעֲלִין עַל נִכְסֵי אָבִינוּ יוֹתֵר דִּינָר. כְּדֵי שֶׁיִּטְלוּ כְתוּבַּת אִמָּן. אֵין שׁוֹמְעִין לָהֶן אֶלָּא שָׁמִין אֶת הַנְּכָסִים בְּבֵית דִּין.

When does one appraise for them? Rebbi Mana said, one appraises at the end[59]. Rebbi Ḥanina said to him, the words of the rabbis imply that one does not listen to you, for Nathan bar Hoshaia asked before Rebbi Joḥanan, if there was sustenance for twelve months but the estate diminished in value? He answered him, since the heirs started to eat with permission, they continue to eat until the last coin is gone! Therefore, one appraises at the start[60]. Rav Ḥisda asked: If there was sustenance for twelve months and then the property increased in value[61]? Let us hear from the following, for Rebbi Ḥanina, Rebbi Yasa[62] said in the name of Rebbi Joḥanan: If the heirs sold, they sold from their own property[63]. So here, if it increased in value, their property value increased[64]. If the estate was not sufficient for twelve months' sustenance, may the sons say to the daughters, take what is yours and leave[65]! Rebbi Abba said, is that a question? The Mishnah says that they cannot say so to them, as we have stated there[66]: "If the orphans say, we accept the properties of our father for the value of an extra denar in order to take their mother's *ketubah*; one does not listen to them but one appraises the properties in court."

59 At the end of 12 months.

60 The only valid appraisal is one made immediately after the father's death.

61 Can the daughters claim part of the value by which the estate has increased over the appraisal?

62 In *Baba batra*, the statement is in the name of "the Babylonian R. Ammi", i. e., R. Immi, the constant companion of R. Yasa.

63 If the male heirs sold real estate from a small estate, their sale is valid since they are the heirs in biblical law; the rights of the daughters are purely contractual. While the widow can take the real estate away from the buyer for her *ketubah* as prior mortgage holder, the daughters cannot since their claim was created only at their father's death, when the sons already were legal owners of the property.

The same statement by R. Assi (= Yasa) in the name of R. Joḥanan is in the Babli, 103a.

64 The daughters cannot acquire any rights to the inheritance which they did not have immediately upon their father's death.

65 If there was more than enough to sustain the daughters but not enough for daughters and sons together, can the sons pay the daughters and take the remainder as inheritance?

66 Mishnah 10:2.

(36a line 13) כְּמָה דְאַתְּ אָמַר. חוּץ מִכְּתוּבָתָהּ חוּץ מִקְבוּרָתָהּ חוּץ מִמִּלְוָה בְעֵדִים חוּץ מִמִּלְוָה בִשְׁטָר. חוּץ מִפַּרְנָסַת בָּנוֹת. מָאן דְּאָמַר. גּוֹבִין פַּרְנָסָה מִן הַמְשׁוּעְבָּדִים. פַּרְנָסַת בָּנוֹת קוֹדֶמֶת. וּמָאן דְּאָמַר. אֵין גּוֹבִין פַּרְנָסָה מִן הַמְשׁוּעְבָּדִים. אֵין פַּרְנָסַת בָּנוֹת קוֹדֶמֶת. נִישְׁמְעִינָהּ מִן הָדָא. אַלְמָנָה וּבָנִים שְׁנֵיהֶן שָׁוִין. אַלְמָנָה וּבָנוֹת שְׁתֵּיהֶן שָׁוֹת. אֵין אַלְמָנָה דוֹחָה אֶת הַבָּנִים וְאֵין אַלְמָנָה דוֹחָה אֶת הַבָּנוֹת. הֵיךְ עֲבִידָא. הָיָה שָׁם מָזוֹן יֹ"ב חוֹדֶשׁ וְאַלְמָנָה לָזוּן. הָדָא הִיא. פְּעָמִים שֶׁאַלְמָנָה דוֹחָה אֶת הַבָּנִים עַל יְדֵי הַבָּנוֹת. כְּשֵׁם שֶׁהִיא דוֹחָה אֶת הַבָּנִים עַל יְדֵי הַבָּנוֹת כֵּן תִּדְחֶה אוֹתָן עַל יְדֵי הַבָּנִים. רְאוּיָה הִיא לִתְבּוֹעַ כְּתוּבָתָהּ וּלְאַבֵּד מְזוֹנוֹתֶיהָ.

As you say, after deduction for her *ketubah*, after deduction of burial costs, after deduction of loans by witnesses or by contract[67]. After deduction for daughters' dowries? For him[68] who says, one forecloses from mortgaged property for daughters' dowries, the dowries are privileged. For him who says, one does not foreclose from mortgaged property for daughters' dowries, the dowries are not privileged. Let us hear from the following[69]: The widow and the sons are of equal rank[70]. The widow and the daughters are of equal rank. The widow does not push the sons aside and the widow does not push the daughters aside. How is that? If there was enough for 12 months sustenance and a widow to sustain[71]. That explains that sometimes the widow pushes out the sons by means of the daughters. Just as she pushes out the sons by means of the daughters, should she not push them out by means of the sons[72]? She might claim her *ketubah* and lose her right to sustenance[73].

67 The value of the estate is computed only after all liens and debts have been deducted.

68 In Halakhah 6:6, R. Ḥanina holds that daughters' dowries are privileged, R. Joḥanan that they are not privileged.

One would assume that practice would follow R. Joḥanan, but in *Baba batra* daughters' dowries are listed together with the *ketubah* and outstanding loans as diminishing the free portion of the estate used to determine whether it is "small" or "large".

69   This does not refer to any discussion; it introduces a new topic.

70   If the widow decides not to claim her *ketubah*, her claim of support by the estate is of equal weight with that of sons and daughters.

71   If there was just enough to sustain sons and daughters for 12 months but the widow also claims sustenance, then widow and daughters are sustained and the sons do not get anything.

72   This text does not make much sense. The text in *Baba batra* is in worse shape, but the original meaning can be gleaned from it even if the original text is lost irretrievably: פְּעָמִים שֶׁאַלְמָנָה דוֹחָה אֶת הַבָּנוֹת עַל יְדֵי הַבָּנִים. כְּשֵׁם שֶׁהָאַלְמָנָה דוֹחָה לְבָנוֹת עַל יְדֵי בָנִים כֵּן תִּדְחֶה אלמָנָה לבָנִים. "Sometimes the widow pushes out the daughters by means of the sons. Just as the widow pushes out the daughters by means of the sons, should she not push the sons out?" Since clearly here the roles of "sons" and "daughters" are exchanged, the question is whether the widow's sustenance should not preempt the daughters' if the estate is not sufficient for all of them.

73   Her claim to sustenance is conditional; it cannot override the claim of the daughters which is absolute. The Babli disagrees, 43a, and declares that the claim of the widow precedes that of the daughter.

(36a line 23) וְהַבָּנִים יִשְׁאֲלוּ עַל הַפְּתָחִים. אִית תַּנָּיֵי תַּגֵּי. יִשָּׁעֲנוּ. מָאן דְּאָמַר יִשָּׁעֲנוּ. וְהִשָּׁעֲנוּ עַל הָעֵץ. מָאן דְּאָמַר. יִשְׁאֲלוּ עַל הַפְּתָחִים. וְנוֹעַ יָנוּעוּ בָנָיו וְשָׁאֵלוּ וְדָרְשׁוּ מֵחָרְבוֹתֵיהֶם.

"The sons shall go begging." Some Tannaïm state, "shall support themselves.[74]" He who says "shall support themselves", "make yourselves comfortable under the tree.[75]" He who says, "go begging", "may his children wander about begging, asking out of their ruins.[76]"

74 In *Baba batra*, the Escurial ms. has a third reading יסחרו "shall go around."	75 Gen. 18:4. The text reads וְהִשָּׁעֲנוּ תַּחַת הָעֵץ.	
	76 *Ps.* 109:10.	

(35d line 25) רַב זְעִירָא רַב חֲנַנְאֵל בְּשֵׁם רַב זְעִירָא בְּשֵׁם אַבָּא בַּר יִרְמְיָה. שְׁנֵי דְבָרִים אָמַר חָנָן הֲלָכָה כְיוֹצֵא בוֹ. שִׁבְעָה דְבָרִים אָמַר אַדְמוֹן אֵין הֲלָכָה כְיוֹצֵא בוֹ. רִבִּי בָּא בַּר זַבְדָּא בְּשֵׁם רִבִּי יִצְחָק בַּר חֲקוּלָה. בְּכָל־מָקוֹם שֶׁשָּׁנִינוּ אָמַר רַבָּן גַּמְלִיאֵל. רוֹאֶה אֲנִי אֶת דִּבְרֵי אַדְמוֹן. הֲלָכָה כְיוֹצֵא בוֹ.

Rav Ze'ira, Rav Ḥananel in the name of Rav; Ze'ira in the name of Abba bar Jeremiah: Ḥanan made two statements, practice follows him; Admon made seven statements, practice does not follow him. Rebbi Abba bar Zavda in the name of Rebbi Isaac bar Ḥaqula: In every case in which Rabban Simeon ben Gamliel said, I am convinced by Admon's statement, practice follows him[77].

77 Except for small syntactical changes, this paragraph is identical with the one at the end of Halakhah 1, Notes 36, 37.

(fol. 35c) **משנה ד:** הַטּוֹעֵן אֶת חֲבֵירוֹ כַּדֵּי שֶׁמֶן וְהוֹדָה בְקַנְקַנִּים אַדְמוֹן אוֹמֵר הוֹאִיל וְהוֹדָה בְמִקְצַת הַטַּעֲנָה יִשָּׁבַע וַחֲכָמִים אוֹמְרִים אֵין זוֹ הוֹדָאָה מִמִּין הַטַּעֲנָה. אָמַר רַבָּן גַּמְלִיאֵל. רוֹאֶה אֲנִי אֶת דִּבְרֵי אַדְמוֹן.

Mishnah 4: If somebody sues another for amphoras of oil, and the defendant admits [that he owes him] vessels, Admon says, since he admitted part of the claim he is made to swear, but the Sages say, what he admitted was not of the kind that was claimed[78]. Rabban Simeon ben Gamliel said, I am convinced by Admon's statement,

78 If neither party has proof but the defendant admits to part of the claim, it is rabbinic interpretation (Mishnah *Šebuot* 6:1) of *Ex.* 22:8 that the defendant has to swear that he does not owe more than he admitted. In Admon's interpretation, a claim for amphoras of oil is a claim for oil and the vessels in which it is contained, but for the Sages it is simply a claim for a certain standard measure of oil; if ownership of the vessels is also claimed, it would have to be stated explicitly. This Mishnah is repeated as part of Mishnah *Šebuot* 6:3, in a series of explanations of what means "agreeing to part of the claim."

(36a line 31) **הלכה ד**: הַטּוֹעֵן אֶת חֲבֵירוֹ כַּדֵּי שֶׁמֶן כול'. מַתְנִיתָא בְשֶׁטוֹעֲנוֹ חִטִּים וְהוֹדָה לוֹ בִשְׂעוֹרִים. אֲבָל אִם טְעָנוֹ שְׁנֵי מִינִין וְהוֹדָה לוֹ בְּאֶחָד מֵהֶן דִּבְרֵי הַכֹּל פָּטוּר.

Text in *Ketubot*	Text in *Šebuot*
רִבִּי אִימִּי בְשֵׁם רִבִּי יוֹחָנָן. מַתְנִיתָא בְשֶׁטְּעָנוֹ חִטִּים וְהוֹדָה לוֹ בִשְׂעוֹרִים. אֲבָל אִם טְעָנוֹ שְׁנֵי מִינִין וְהוֹדָה לוֹ בְּאֶחָד מֵהֶן דִּבְרֵי הַכֹּל פָּטוּר. וְלָמָּה תַּנִּינָן. רַבָּן גַּמְלִיאֵל מְחַיֵּיב. בָּא לְהוֹדִיעָךְ כֹּחַ רַבָּן גַּמְלִיאֵל עַד הֵיכָן הוּא מְחַיֵּיב. רִבִּי אַבָּהוּ כְּהָדָא דְרִבִּי אִימִּי. רִבִּי שִׁמְעוֹן בֶּן לָקִישׁ אָמַר. מַתְנִיתָא בְשֶׁטְּעָנוֹ חִטִּים וְהוֹדָה לוֹ בִשְׂעוֹרִים. אֲבָל טְעָנוֹ שְׁנֵי מִינִין וְהוֹדָה לוֹ בְּאֶחָד מֵהֶן דִּבְרֵי הַכֹּל חַיָּיב. רַב כְּרִבִּי שִׁמְעוֹן בֶּן לָקִישׁ. חַד בַּר נַשׁ אֲזַל בָּעֵי מֵידוֹן עִם חַבְרֵיהּ קוֹמֵי רַב. שָׁרֵי מִיטְעַן עִימֵּיהּ שְׂעָרִין חִטִּין	רִבִּי אִמִּי בְּשֵׁם רִבִּי יוֹחָנָן. מַתְנִיתָא בְּטַעֲנוֹ חִטִּים וְהוֹדָה לוֹ בִשְׂעוֹרִים. אֲבָל טְעָנוֹ שְׁנֵי מִינִין וְהוֹדָה לוֹ בְּאֶחָד מֵהֶן דִּבְרֵי הַכֹּל פָּטוּר. אָמַר רִבִּי אַבָּהוּ בְּהָדָא דְרִבִּי אִמִּי. מַאי דָא דְתַנִּינָן. רַבָּן גַּמְלִיאֵל מְחַיֵּיב. בָּא לְהוֹדִיעָךְ כֹּחַ רַבָּן גַּמְלִיאֵל עַד הֵיכָן מְחַיֵּיב. רִבִּי חִיָּיה בְשֵׁם רִבִּי יוֹחָנָן. לֹא סוֹף דָּבָר בְּטַעֲנוֹ חִטִּים וְהוֹדָה לוֹ בִשְׂעוֹרִים. אֲבָל אִם טְעָנוֹ שְׁנֵי מִינִין וְהוֹדָה לוֹ בְּאֶחָד מֵהֶן דִּבְרֵי חֲכָמִים פָּטוּר. רִבִּי שִׁמְעוֹן בֶּן לָקִישׁ אָמַר. לֹא יְהֵא דָבָר בְּשֶׁטְּעָנוֹ שְׁנֵי מִינִין וְהוֹדָה לוֹ בְּאֶחָד מֵהֶן. אֲבָל אִם טְעָנוֹ חִטִּים וְהוֹדָה לוֹ בִשְׂעוֹרִים דִּבְרֵי הַכֹּל חַיָּיב.

כְּהָדָא דְּרִבִּי שִׁמְעוֹן בֶּן לָקִישׁ. חַד בַּר נָשׁ אֲזַל בָּעֵי מֵידוֹן קֳמֵי רַב דַּהֲוָה מַטְעוֹן לְחַבְרֵיהּ חִטִּין שְׂעוֹרִין וְכוּסְמִין. אָמַר לֵיהּ רַב. הַמְתֵּן עַד דְּיִגַּלְגֵּל עֲלָךְ כָּל־דְּבָעֵי וּבְסוֹפָא תִּישְׁתְּבַע עַל כּוּלָן. אָמַר רִבִּי אַבָּהוּ. כָּךְ מֵשִׁיב רִבִּי שִׁמְעוֹן בֶּן לָקִישׁ לְרִבִּי יוֹחָנָן. עַל דַּעְתָּךְ דְּתֵימַר. טְעָנוֹ שְׁנֵי מִינִין וְהוֹדָה לוֹ בְּאֶחָד מֵהֶן דִּבְרֵי חֲכָמִים פָּטוּר. וְהָתַנִּינָן. טְעָנוֹ חִטִּים וְקַרְקָעוֹת וְהוֹדָה לוֹ בַּכֵּלִים וְכָפַר בַּקַּרְקָעוֹת. בַּקַּרְקָעוֹת וְכָפַר בַּכֵּלִים. כֵּלִים וְכֵלִים חַיָּיב. כֵּלִים וְקַרְקָעוֹת לֹא כָל־שֶׁכֵּן. אָמַר לֵיהּ. לְזוּקְקוֹ שְׁבוּעָה דוּ מַתְנִיתָא. שֶׁהַנְּכָסִים שֶׁיֵּשׁ לָהֶן אַחֲרָיוּת זוֹקְקִין אֶת הַנְּכָסִים שֶׁאֵין לָהֶן אַחֲרָיוּת לִישָּׁבַע עֲלֵיהֶן. וַאֲפִילוּ עַל דְּרִבִּי שִׁמְעוֹן בֶּן לָקִישׁ לֵית הִיא פְּלִיגָא. דְּתַנִּינָן. הַטּוֹעֵן לַחֲבֵירוֹ כַּדֵּי שֶׁמֶן וְהוֹדָה לוֹ בְּקַנְקַנִּים. מַה נָּן קַיָּימִין. אִם בְּשֶׁטְּעָנוֹ קַנְקַנִּים וְשֶׁמֶן. כָּל־עַמָּא מוֹדֵיי שֶׁיֵּשׁ הוֹדָיָיה מֵהַטַּעֲנָה. אִם בְּשֶׁטְּעָנוֹ קַנְקַנִּין וְלֹא הוֹדָה בַשֶּׁמֶן. כָּל־עַמָּא מוֹדֵיי שֶׁאֵין הוֹדָיָיה מֵהַטַּעֲנָה. רִבִּי זְעִירָא רִבִּי אַבָּהוּ בְּשֵׁם שְׁמוּאֵל. בְּשֶׁטְּעָנוֹ קַנְקַנִּים שֶׁמֶן. אָהֵן אָמַר. קַנְקַנִּים וְלֹא שֶׁמֶן. וְאָהֵן אָמַר. שֶׁמֶן וְלֹא קַנְקַנִּים. נִיחָא קַנְקַנִּים וְלֹא שֶׁמֶן. שֶׁמֶן

כּוּסְמִין. אֲמַר לֵיהּ רַב. כָּל־מַה דְּאַתְּ יָכִיל מְגַלְגְּלָה עֲלוֹי גַלְגֵּל וּבְסוֹפָא הוּא מִישְׁתְּבַע לָךְ חֲדָא עַל כּוּלְּהוֹן. אָמַר רִבִּי אַבָּהוּ. כָּךְ מֵשִׁיב רִבִּי שִׁמְעוֹן בֶּן לָקִישׁ אֶת רִבִּי יוֹחָנָן. עַל דַּעְתָּךְ דְּאַתְּ אָמַר. טְעָנוֹ שְׁנֵי מִינִין וְהוֹדָה לוֹ בְּאֶחָד מֵהֶן דִּבְרֵי הַכֹּל פָּטוּר. וְהָא תַנִּינָן. טְעָנוֹ כֵלִים וְקַרְקָעוֹת. הוֹדָה בַכֵּלִים וְכָפַר בַּקַּרְקָעוֹת. בַּקַּרְקָעוֹת וְכָפַר בַּכֵּלִים. אִם כֵּלִים בַּכֵּלִים הוּא חַיָּיב כֵּלִים בַּקַּרְקָעוֹת לֹא כָל־שֶׁכֵּן. מָה עֲבַד לָהּ. דּוּ פָּתַר לֵיהּ לְזוֹקְקוֹ שְׁבוּעָה. וְהָתַנִּינָן. הַטּוֹעֵן אֶת חֲבֵירוֹ כַּדֵּי שֶׁמֶן וְהוֹדָה לוֹ בְקַנְקַנִּים. מָה אֲנָן קַיָּימִין. אִם בְּשֶׁטְּעָנוֹ קַנְקַנִּים וְשֶׁמֶן וְהוֹדָה לוֹ בְאַחַת מֵהֶן. כָּל־עַמָּא מוֹדֵיי שֶׁהוּא מִן הַטַּעֲנָה. וְאִם בְּשֶׁטְּעָנוֹ שֶׁמֶן וְהוֹדָה לוֹ בְקַנְקַנִּים. כָּל־עַמָּא מוֹדֵיי שֶׁאֵין הוֹדָיָיה מִן הַטַּעֲנָה. רִבִּי זְעִירָא רִבִּי אֲבוּנָא בְּשֵׁם רַב. בְּשֶׁטְּעָנוֹ קַנְקַנֵּי שֶׁמֶן הִיא מַתְנִיתָא. הָהֵן מִילִּין וְהָהֵן אֲמַר רֵיקָנִין. נִיחָא קַנְקַנִּים וְלֹא שֶׁמֶן. שֶׁמֶן וְלֹא קַנְקַנִּים. רִבִּי אֶלְעָזָר בְּשֵׁם רִבִּי אָבוּן מַפִּיק לִשָּׁנָה מַחְצִין דְּמָשַׁח. וְלֵית סוֹפֵיהּ מִשְׁאֲלָה. בַּהֲהוּא דְנִשְׁתַּתֵּק.

וְלֹא קַנְקַנִּים. רִבִּי לְעָזָר בְּשֵׁם רִבִּי אָבִין מַפִּיק לִישָׁנָה מֵחֲצִין דְּמָשַׁח. וְיִשְׁאָלוּנֵיהּ. בָּהוּא דְּאִישְׁתַּתֵּק.

Halakhah 4: "If somebody sues another for amphoras of oil," etc. The Mishnah, if he sued him for wheat and he admitted barley; but if he sued him for two kinds and he admitted one of them, according to everybody he is free[79].

Text in *Ketubot*.

Rebbi Immi in the name of Rebbi Joḥanan: The Mishnah, if he sued him for wheat and he admitted barley; but if he sued him for two kinds and he admitted one of them, according to everybody he is free[80]. And why did we state: "Rabban Gamliel obligates him"? This comes to tell you the power of Rabban Gamliel, how far he obligates people. Rebbi Abbahu [supported] that of Rebbi Immi. Rebbi Simeon ben Laqish says, the Mishnah, if he sued him for wheat and he admitted barley; but if he sued him for two kinds and he admitted one of them, according to everybody he is obligated[81]. Rav

Text in *Šebuot*.

Rebbi Immi in the name of Rebbi Joḥanan: The Mishnah, if he sued him for wheat and he admitted barley; but if he sued him for two kinds and he admitted one of them, according to everybody he is free. Rebbi Abbahu [following] that of Rebbi Immi, why did we state: "Rabban Gamliel obligates him"? This comes to tell you the power of Rabban Gamliel, how far he obligates people. *Rebbi Ḥiyya in the name of Rebbi Joḥanan: not only if he sued him for wheat and he admitted barley; but if he sued him for two kinds and he admitted one of them, according to everybody he is free*[87]. Rebbi Simeon ben Laqish followed Rebbi Simeon ben Laqish: A person went with another to court before Rav. He started claiming from him barley, wheat and spelt. Rav told him, charge him with anything you have to charge, and in the end he will swear one oath about everything. Rebbi Abbahu said, so argued Rebbi Simeon ben Laqish against Rebbi Joḥanan: In your opinion, since you say that if he sued him for two kinds and he admitted one of them, according to everybody he is free, did we not state[82] "if he sued him for vessels and real estate; if he admitted the vessels and denied the real estate, the real estate and denied the vessels"? If he is obligated for vessels about vessels, not so much more vessels for real estate[83]? What does he do with it? He explains it, to transfer an oath to him. But did we not state: If somebody sues another for amphoras of oil, and the defendant said, it is only if he sued him for two kinds and he admitted one of them, but if he sued him for wheat and he admitted barley according to everybody he is obligated. Following Rebbi Simeon ben Laqish: A person went to court before Rav. When he claimed from another wheat, barley, and spelt. Rav told him, wait until he charged you with anything he has to charge, and in the end you will swear one oath about everything. Rebbi Abbahu said, so argued Rebbi Simeon ben Laqish against Rebbi Joḥanan. In your opinion, since you say that if he sued him for two kinds and he admitted one of them, according to *the Sages* he is free, did we not state "if he sued him for vessels and real estate; if he admitted the vessels and denied the real estate, the real estate and denied the vessels"? For vessels about vessels he is obligated, not so much more vessels for real estate? He answered him, to transfer an oath to him *by the following Mishnah:*

admits [that he owes him] vessels'"? How do we hold? If he sued him for vessels and oil, and he admitted one of them, everybody agrees that this refers to the claim. But if he sued him for oil and he admitted vessels, everybody agrees that what he admitted does not refer to the claim, for Rebbi Ze'ira, Rebbi Abuna said in the name of Rav: The Mishnah deals with the case that he sued for vessels full of oil; the ones are full, the others empty[84]. One understands vessels but not oil. Oil but not vessels? Rebbi Eleazar in the name of Rebbi Abun formulates it as oil bucket[85]. Can one not ask him in the end[86]? If he lost his speech.

"For mortgageable property transfers an oath on not mortgageable property to swear about."[88] *This does not even disagree with Rebbi Simeon ben Laqish.* But did we not state: If somebody sues another for amphoras of oil, and the defendant admits [that he owes him] vessels"? How do we hold? If he sued him for vessels and oil, and he admitted one of them, everybody agrees that this refers to the claim. But if he sued him for vessels and he did not admit oil, everybody agrees that what he admitted does not refer to the claim. Rebbi Ze'ira, Rebbi Abuna said in the name of *Samuel*: If he sued for vessels full of oil; one said vessels but not oil, the other said oil but not vessels[89]. Rebbi Eleazar in the name of Rebbi Abin formulates it as oil bucket. Can one not ask him? About one who lost his speech.

79 Except for this sentence, which is redundant since it is repeated in the Mishnah with attribution of authorship, the Halakhah is a not quite complete copy of Halakhah *Šebuot* 6:3. Since the deviations between the two texts are

not easily described as variant readings, both texts are given here side by side. It is seen that the basis of discussion is Mishnah *Šebuot* 6:6, not *Ketubot* 13:4. The major additions and changes in the *Šebuot* text are indicated by *italics* in the translation.

80 The Mishnah referred to is *Šebuot* 6:3 which states that if the claim was for wheat but the defendant admits an obligation for barley, the admission is not relevant for the claim and the defendant does not have to swear, except that Rabban Gamliel holds that *any* admission by the defendant obligates the latter to swear. This sentence is followed by a copy of the Mishnah here, detailing the difference between Admon and the majority about claims for oil with or without the containers. It is now claimed in the name of R. Joḥanan that if a claim is put forward for two unrelated items, the admission in full of liability for one item does not induce an obligation on the defendant to swear if he denies all liability for the second claim since the two claims, while stated together before the court and treated at the same time, really constitute two separate suits. This opinion is quoted in the name of R. Ḥiyya bar Abba in the name of R. Joḥanan in the *Šebuot* text and in the Babli, 108b; it is explicitly rejected in the name of R. Joḥanan in the Babli *Šebuot* 40a where R. Joḥanan, Rav Naḥman and Samuel are quoted as stating that any claims which form one suit have to be treated as one common claim. The inconsistency of the Babli was recognized by the early commentators.

81 The opinion of R. Simeon ben Laqish and Rav quoted here is that of R. Joḥanan and Samuel in Babli *Šebuot* 40a; cf. the preceding Note. The Babli, *loc. cit.*, implies that R. Simeon ben Laqish's opinion in the matter is unknown.

82 This is the next sentence in Mishnah *Šebuot* 6:3. The Mishnah states that if one suit contains claims that have to be adjudicated following different rules of procedure, they cannot be consolidated and have to be treated separately. Since claims for real estate cannot be resolved by taking oaths (Mishnah *Šebuot* 6:5), if the claim was for movables and real estate, an admission by the defendant either of the claim for movables in full or for the claim for real estate either partially or in full cannot trigger an obligation to swear.

83 The last statement of Mishnah

Šebuot 6:3: A partial admission about movables triggers an obligation to swear about movables and real estate; a partial admission about real estate does not trigger an obligation to swear. As explained in this Mishnah, also Mishnah *Qiddušin* 1:5, and quoted in the *Šebuot* text, an obligation to swear about movables induces an obligation to swear about real estate.

84   See the *Šebuot* text for an intelligible version of this statement.

85   If the claim is not for storage vessels but for those used to draw oil from a large container.

86   The disagreement between Admon and the rabbis is not one that is frequently going to happen in practice.

Since the problem is one of semantics, does a claim for amphoras of oil imply separate claims for amphoras and the oil that fills them or is "amphora of oil" simply a technical term denoting a standard volume for which contracts of delivery are made? Any judge asked in such a matter will ask the parties to clarify the meaning of their statements and then it will be obvious whether the defendant accepted part of the claim or not. The difference in the interpretation could only arise if one of the parties cannot be asked, either if a party dies or if he loses his speech.

87   Cf. Note 80.

88   Cf. Note 83.

89   Cf. Note 84.

(fol. 35c) **משנה ה:** הַפּוֹסֵק מָעוֹת לַחֲתָנוֹ וּפָשַׁט לוֹ אֶת הָרֶגֶל תְּהֵא יוֹשֶׁבֶת עַד שֶׁתַּלְבִּין רֹאשָׁהּ. אַדְמוֹן אוֹמֵר אִילּוּ אֲנִי פָּסַקְתִּי לְעַצְמִי אֱהֵא יוֹשֶׁבֶת עַד שֶׁתַּלְבִּין רֹאשִׁי. אַבָּא פָּסַק עָלַי מָה אֲנִי יְכוֹלָה לַעֲשׂוֹת אוֹ כְנוֹס אוֹ פְּטוֹר. אָמַר רַבָּן גַּמְלִיאֵל. רוֹאֶה אֲנִי אֶת דִּבְרֵי אַדְמוֹן.

Mishnah 5: If somebody obligates himself about money for his son-in-law[90] but then goes bankrupt[91], she must wait until her hair grows white[92]. Admon says: "If I had obligated myself, I would have to wait until my hair grows white. My father obligated himself, what can I do?

Marry definitively or divorce!" Rabban Simeon ben Gamliel said, I am convinced by Admon's statement.

90 At the time of the preliminary marriage, the father signed a promise to deliver a dowry in a fixed amount before the definitive wedding date.

91 This is the meaning of the term in medieval rabbinic and modern Hebrew. "He stretched his foot" might also mean that he ran away; he cannot be found to be asked to fulfill his promise.

92 The bride, being preliminarily married, cannot marry any other man. Since the father did not fulfill his obligation, she cannot sue the groom either for a definitive wedding or for support after 12 months from the preliminary wedding.

(36a line 53) **הלכה ה**: הַפּוֹסֵק מָעוֹת לַחֲתָנוֹ וכול׳. מַתְנִיתָא בְּשֶׁפָּסַק בְּמַעֲמָדָהּ. אֲבָל אִם לֹא פָּסַק בְּמַעֲמָדָהּ. אַף רַבָּנִין מוֹדֵיי.

Halakhah 5: "If somebody obligates himself about money for his son-in-law," etc. The Mishnah [deals with the case] that he obligated himself in her presence. But if he obligated himself not in her presence, even the rabbis will agree[93].

93 While one may give a person a benefit without his knowledge, one cannot impose an obligation on him without his knowledge (Mishnah *Giṭṭin* 1:6). This implies in particular that a preliminarily married underage girl, whose father has promised money but has not paid, can always force a divorce once she reaches adulthood and is able to act in her own behalf. (The Babli, 109a, and Tosephta 12:4 hold that the court will intervene on behalf of a minor whose father does not pay and whose groom does not want to marry without money.)

(36a line 53) תַּנֵּי. אָמַר רִבִּי יוֹסֵי בֵּירִבִּי יְהוּדָה. לֹא נֶחֱלַק אַדְמוֹן וַחֲכָמִים עַל הַפּוֹסֵק מָעוֹת לַחֲתָנוֹ וּפָשַׁט לוֹ אֶת הָרֶגֶל תְּהֵא יוֹשֶׁבֶת עַד שֶׁיַּלְבִּין אֶת רֹאשָׁהּ. וְעַל מַה נֶחֱלָקוּ. עַל שֶׁפִּסְקָה לְעַצְמָהּ. אַדְמוֹן אוֹמֵר. יְכוֹלָה הִיא שֶׁתֹּאמַר. סְבוּרָה הָיִיתִי שֶׁאַבָּא רוֹצֶה לִיתֵּן וְעַכְשָׁיו אַבָּא אֵינוֹ רוֹצֶה לִיתֵּן. מָה אֲנִי יְכוֹלָה לַעֲשׂוֹת. אוֹ כְנוֹס אוֹ פְטוֹר. אָמַר רַבָּן גַּמְלִיאֵל. רוֹאֶה אֲנִי אֶת דִּבְרֵי אַדְמוֹן.

It was stated[94]: Rebbi Yose ben Rebbi Jehudah said, Admon and the rabbis did not disagree about one for whom the father had promised money but went bankrupt that she may sit until her hair grows white. Where did they disagree? If she promised herself. Admon says, she might say, "I was of the opinion that my father wants to give, but now my father does not want to give[95], what can I do? Marry definitively or divorce!" Rabban Simeon ben Gamliel said, I am convinced by Admon's statement.

94 Tosephta 12:4, Babli 108b.
95 The legal basis for the annulment of the preliminary marriage is the fact that the usual (but not unique) way of executing the marriage is a commercial transaction in which the groom buys the bride's agreement to the marriage by giving her an object of value (such as a gold ring.) The bride now claims that, if the groom does not want to marry her definitively as is, the transaction is invalid as מֶקַח טָעוּת "a commercial transaction entered into in error." Since the marriage is no real commercial transaction, it can be dissolved only by a divorce.

(fol. 35c) **משנה ו:** הָעוֹרֵר עַל הַשָּׂדֶה וְהוּא חָתוּם עָלֶיהָ בְּעֵד אַדְמוֹן אוֹמֵר הַשֵּׁנִי נוֹחַ לִי וְהָרִאשׁוֹן קָשֶׁה מִמֶּנּוּ וַחֲכָמִים אוֹמְרִים אִיבַּד אֶת זְכוּתוֹ. עֲשָׂאָהּ סִימָן לְאַחֵר אִיבַּד אֶת זְכוּתוֹ.

Mishnah 6: If somebody protests about a field when he himself had signed as a witness[96], Admon says: "The second one fits me, the first one was harder"[97]; but the Sages say, he lost his right [of appeal][98]. If he made [the field] a marker for another, he lost his right[99].

96 A goes to court to claim ownership of a parcel to which B holds title, and the contract by which B holds the land was signed by A as a witness to the sale.

97 Admon says that a person can argue in court that he put his signature on a fraudulent contract without declaring himself a criminal by explaining what he did. In the case in question he argues that the seller was a violent person who would have injured him had he claimed his property from him but that the buyer was a civilized person whom he could sue in court; therefore, it was in A's interest to sign the fraudulent document.

98 By testifying in writing that the transaction was legitimate, he is prevented from changing his testimony. This is a general principle, "after he spoke (as a witness, cross-examined in court), he cannot come back and speak again (in the same case)", cf. Halakhah 2:3, Notes 52-53. One has to assume here that the witness's signature had been confirmed in court.

99 If A himself executed a contract in which he described a parcel as being "bounded by B's field", he cannot later claim that the field was not B's. In this case, Admon will agree with the Sages.

(36b line 1) **הלכה ו**: הָעוֹרֵר עַל הַשָּׂדֶה כול'. וְלֹא סוֹף דָּבָר בְּשֶׁעֲשָׂאָהּ סִימָן לְאַחֵר. אֶלָּא אֲפִילוּ עָשָׂה אַחֵר לְאַחֵר מִכֵּיוָן שֶׁהוּא חָתוּם עָלֶיהָ אִיבַּד אֶת זְכוּתוֹ.

Halakhah 6: "If somebody protests about a field," etc. Not only if he himself made it a marker for another [field], but even if a third person made it for a fourth, when he signed as a witness, he lost his right[100].

100 C wrote a sales contract in which he sold a parcel to D and describing the adjacent properties mentioned the field in dispute as B's

field. If A signs as a witness on that contract, he cannot claim title to B's field since, as noted by the Babli, 109a, witnesses never sign a document without reading it first.

(fol. 35c) **משנה ז**: מִי שֶׁהָלַךְ לוֹ לִמְדִינַת הַיָּם וְאָבְדָה דֶרֶךְ שָׂדֵהוּ אַדְמוֹן אוֹמֵר יֵלֵךְ עָלֶיהָ בַּקְּצָרָה וַחֲכָמִים אוֹמְרִים יִקְנֶה לוֹ דֶרֶךְ בְּמֵאָה מָנֶה אוֹ יִפְרַח בָּאֲוִיר.

Mishnah 7: If somebody went overseas and lost the way to his field[101], Admon says, he shall go the shortest way[102] but the Sages say, he has to buy a right of access for a hundred minas[103] or fly through the air.

101 He left for a long time and left his field untended. In the meantime, the neighbors ploughed their field and in time incorporated the boundary strip by which the farmer reached his field into their fields. Upon his return, he did not find any witnesses who could testify to where his access path had been located.

102 Since it is obvious that there had been an access path.

103 Since "the burden of proof is on the claimant", if he wants to take away a strip of land from any of the current owners, he must prove his case.

(36b line 1) **הלכה ז**: מִי שֶׁהָלַךְ לוֹ לִמְדִינַת הַיָּם כול'. רִבִּי יוֹסֵי בֶּן חֲנִינָה אָמַר. הַטּוֹעֵן בִּרְאָיוֹתָיו. מִילְתֵיהּ אָמְרָה. וְהֵן שֶׁיְּהוּ אַרְבָּעָה מַקִּיפִין אוֹתוֹ. שְׁמוּאֵל אָמַר. אֲפִילוּ אֶחָד מַקִּיפוֹ מִכָּל־צַד. תָּנֵי יְהוֹשֻׁעַ. הֲרֵי שֶׁהָיָה טוֹעֶה בַּכְּרָמִים וּבַשָּׂדוֹת. מְקַדֵּד וְיוֹצֵא עַד שֶׁהוּא מַגִּיעַ לַדֶּרֶךְ אוֹ עַד שֶׁהוּא מַגִּיעַ לְבֵיתוֹ. אֲפִילוּ שָׂדֶה מְלֵיאָה כְּרָמִים. שֶׁעַל מְנָת כֵּן הִנְחִיל יְהוֹשֻׁעַ לְיִשְׂרָאֵל אֶת הָאָרֶץ. תָּנֵי יְהוֹשֻׁעַ לָצֵאת. שֶׁמָּא לְהִיכָּנֵס. תָּנֵי יְהוֹשֻׁעַ בְּגוּפוֹ. שֶׁמָּא בְּפָרָתוֹ. אָמַר רִבִּי יוֹסֵי. פָּרָה דַּרְכָּהּ לַחֲזוֹר. נְחִיל שֶׁלִּדְבוֹרִים עַל יְדֵי שֶׁאֵין דַּרְכּוֹ לַחֲזוֹר עָשׂוּ אוֹתוֹ כְּגוּפוֹ.

Halakhah 7: "If somebody went overseas," etc. Rebbi Yose ben Hanina said, if he sues with reasons[104]. This means, only if four [owners] surround him[105]. Samuel says, even if one surrounds him on all sides[106]. Joshua's stipulation[106]! "If he was lost in vineyards or fields, he crosses[107] and leaves until he reaches a road to his house, even a plot full of vineyards, for this is one of the conditions under which Joshua distributed the Land to Israel."[108] Joshua stated this to leave, maybe to enter? Joshua stipulated for a person, perhaps for his cow[109]? Rebbi Yose said, his cow usually returns; since a swarm of bees does not usually return, they treated it as if it were his body[110].

104 Admon gives the returnee a right of ingress if he can proof that he had a way and only its location is in doubt. The Sages require him to buy his right of way even if he can prove that he had one, as long as he cannot locate it.

105 In his interpretation, the returnee cannot reclaim his lost right of way if he cannot be sure from whom to claim. R. Yose ben Hanina would give him a right-of-way if all four adjacent fields belonged to the same person; in that case, the proof that a right-of-way existed should be sufficient.

106 As the Babli explains, Samuel agrees that the single owner of the four surrounding fields must give the returnee access to his field if he already had been the owner when the returnee left, since then certainly the owner of the surrounding fields took the lost path illegally. But if there were several owners when the returnee left, the current owner can claim that the returnee's suit must be directed against that prior owner who had taken over his earlier path, not against the buyer. If it is not known who in that case was the owner who incorporated the returnee's right-of-way into his property, the returnee cannot identify that owner, and loses his claim. The Babli, 109b, presents similar arguments in the name of other authors.

106 Ten categories of public use of private land are attributed to Biblical Joshua, attached as liens to the original distribution of land; cf. *Kilaim* 2:5,

Note 73, *Baba batra* 5:1 (15a l. 7); Bablí *Baba qama* 80b.

107   One of the meanings of Arabic ڤ. If somebody is lost in vegetation, he may cross growing fields and orchards until he regains his orientation.

108   If the person who lost his way can cross other peoples' fields, why can the returnee whose path was lost not cross into his field?

109   A path to the field is worthless if the field cannot be ploughed because the cattle to draw the plough cannot enter.

110   The beekeeper can enter another person's private domain to catch the swarm which left his hive; cf. 2:11, Notes 204-205.

(36b line 10) אָמַר רִבִּי יִרְמְיָה. אַדְמוֹן וְרִבִּי עֲקִיבָה שְׁנֵיהֶם אָמְרוּ דָבָר אֶחָד. דְּתַנִּינָן תַּמָּן. מְכָרָן לְאַחֵר. רִבִּי עֲקִיבָה אוֹמֵר. אֵינוֹ צָרִיךְ לִיקַּח לוֹ דֶּרֶךְ. וַחֲכָמִים אוֹמְרִים. צָרִיךְ לִיקַּח לוֹ דֶּרֶךְ. וְלֹא שָׁמַע דְּאָמַר רִבִּי הִילָא רִבִּי יָסָא בְּשֵׁם רִבִּי יוֹחָנָן. בִּסְתָם חֲלוּקִין. מָא אֲנָן קַייָמִין. אִם דָּבָר בָּרִיא שֶׁיֵּשׁ לוֹ דֶּרֶךְ כָּל־עַמָּא מוֹדֵיי שֶׁאֵין צָרִיךְ לִיקַּח לוֹ דֶּרֶךְ. וְאִם דָּבָר בָּרִיא שֶׁאֵין לוֹ דֶּרֶךְ כָּל־עַמָּא מוֹדֵיי שֶׁהוּא צָרִיךְ לִיקַּח לוֹ דֶּרֶךְ. אֶלָּא כֵן אֲנָן קַייָמִין. בִּסְתָם. רִבִּי עֲקִיבָה אוֹמֵר. אֵינוֹ צָרִיךְ לִיקַּח דֶּרֶךְ. וְרַבָּנִין אוֹמְרִין. יֵשׁ לוֹ דֶּרֶךְ. וְכָא אֲפִילוּ דָּבָר בָּרִיא יֵשׁ לוֹ דֶּרֶךְ כָּל־עַמָּא מוֹדֵיי שֶׁהוּא צָרִיךְ לִיקַּח לוֹ דֶּרֶךְ.

[111]Rebbi Jeremiah said, both Admon and Rebbi Aqiba said the same thing, as we have stated there[112]: "If he sold them to another person, Rebbi Aqiba said, he does not have to buy access, but the Sages say, he has to buy access." He had not heard that Rebbi Hila said, Rebbi Yasa in the name of Rebbi Johanan: They disagree when nothing was mentioned[113]. Where do we hold? If it is obvious that access was included[114], everybody agrees that he does not have to pay for access. If it is obvious that access was not included[115], everybody agrees that he has to pay for access. But we must hold that nothing was mentioned. Then

Rebbi Aqiba said, he does not have to buy access, but the rabbis say, he has to buy access. But in the case here, even while it is clear that he had access, everybody[116] agrees that he has to pay for access.

111 In a slightly different formulation, this paragraph is also in *Baba batra* 4:2.

112 Mishnah *Baba batra* 4:2. The Mishnah belongs to a series of statements about commercial contracts. If somebody sold cisterns in his backyard to a third party, R. Aqiba holds that nobody buys anything which he cannot use; therefore, it is understood that the seller, by offering the cisterns for sale, did also offer access to them. But the Sages hold that people also buy real estate for speculation and, therefore, the sale covers only what is explicitly stated in the sales contract and nothing more.

113 The sales contract does not mention access.

114 If the right of access to the property was mentioned in the contract.

115 It is not necessary that access was excluded, it suffices if the contract states that *only* cisterns are sold.

116 This is not everybody; everybody except Admon. The question in *Ketubot* is not one of interpretation of commercial contracts but of enforcing a claim if it is not known against whom the claim could be enforced.

(fol. 35c) **משנה ח:** הַמּוֹצִיא שְׁטָר חוֹב עַל חֲבֵירוֹ וְהַלָּה הוֹצִיא שֶׁמָּכַר לוֹ אֶת הַשָּׂדֶה אַדְמוֹן אוֹמֵר אִילּוּ חַיָּיב הָיִיתִי לָךְ הָיָה לָךְ לְהִיפָּרַע אֶת שֶׁלָּךְ כְּשֶׁמָּכַרְתָּ לִי אֶת הַשָּׂדֶה וַחֲכָמִים אוֹמְרִים זֶה הָיָה פִיקֵּחַ שֶׁמָּכַר לוֹ אֶת הַקַּרְקַע מִפְּנֵי שֶׁהוּא יָכוֹל לְמַשְׁכְּנוֹ.

Mishnah 8: If somebody produces a promissory note on another person who in his turn produces a document that [the creditor] sold him a field[117], Admon says, "if I really owed you, you should have collected what is yours when you sold me the field[118];" but the Sages say, that one was smart when he sold him real estate because he can take it as a pledge[119].

117 The field was sold after the note had become due.
118 The debtor can claim the debt documented in the I.O.U was forgiven since the creditor sold him something for the money which was due to him.
119 If the original mortgage stated that all present and future holdings of the debtor are pledged and the creditor was afraid the debtor would not pay, he seduced the latter into parting with his money by offering him real estate. If the debtor then does not pay, the creditor can take the real estate back and end up both with his money and his original property.

(36b line 19) **הלכה ח**: הַמּוֹצִיא שְׁטָר חוֹב עַל חֲבֵירוֹ כול'. רִבִּי יוֹנָה אוֹמֵר. בְּיָפָה בְכָךְ. רִבִּי יוֹסֵי אוֹמֵר. בְּשֶׁאֵינוֹ יָפָה בְכָךְ. הַגַּע עַצְמָךְ דַּהֲוָה לֵיהּ קַרְקַע. יָכִיל הוּא מֵימַר לֵיהּ. קַרְקַע טָב אֲנָא בְעֵי. הַגַּע עַצְמָךְ דַּהֲוָה לֵיהּ קַרְקַע טָב. יָכִיל הוּא מֵימַר לֵיהּ. דִּידִי אֲנָא בְעֵי. וְלֹא עוֹד אֶלָּא יָכִיל הוּא מֵימַר לֵיהּ. לֵית בְּחֵיילִי טְעִין טִרְחוֹתְהוֹן דִּתְרֵיי.

Halakhah 8: "If somebody produces a promissory note on another person," etc. Rebbi Jonah says, if it is worth it[120]; Rebbi Yose says, even if it is not worth it[121]. Think of it, if he had real estate[122]! He can say to him, I want good real estate[123]. Think of it, if he had good real estate[124]! He can say to him, I want mine. In addition, he can say to him, to care for two parcels overtaxes my powers[125].

120 The Sages' argument in the Mishnah is good only if the sale of real estate covers the entire amount due.
121 Even if the creditor cannot recover the entire amount of the bad debt, even partial recovery is better than nothing at all.
122 If the debtor had real estate and the I.O.U. was already secured as a mortgage.

123 The argument is not detailed since a creditor can claim only to be paid by real estate of average quality (Chapter 9, Note 195; Chapter 12, Note 57). The argument given here makes sense only if one assumes with the following statement that the creditor can take back his own property.

124 If the debtor already had real estate which would satisfy all demands of a creditor. [R. Nissim Gerondi (commentary to Alfasi) reads: "If he had no good real estate", i. e. if the creditor did not have real estate worth while for such a transaction.]

125 If he had to foreclose another parcel, he would have to work two fields. If he manages to foreclose his own, he has cash and only one field to work.

(fol. 35c) **משנה ט:** שְׁנַיִם שֶׁהוֹצִיאוּ שְׁטָר חוֹב זֶה עַל זֶה אַדְמוֹן אוֹמֵר אִילּוּ חַיָּיב הָיִיתִי לָךְ כֵּיצַד אַתָּה לוֹוֶה מִמֶּנִּי. וַחֲכָמִים אוֹמְרִים זֶה גּוֹבֶה שְׁטָר חוֹבוֹ וְזֶה גּוֹבֶה שְׁטָר חוֹבוֹ.

Mishnah 9: If two people mutually produced promissory notes of one on the other, Admon says: "If I owed you, how come you borrowed from me?"[126] But the Sages say, each collects the amount of his note.

126 The one whose note is dated later claims that his own indebtedness was paid off even though he has no receipt in his possession, since the other party could have taken its money back instead of taking out a loan.

(36b line 24) **הלכה ט:** שְׁנַיִם שֶׁהוֹצִיאוּ שְׁטָר חוֹב זֶה עַל זֶה כול׳. זֶה לָוָה מִזֶּה מָנֶא וְזֶה לָוָה מִזֶּה מָאתַיִם. רַב הוּנָא אָמַר. אִתְפַּלְגוּן רַב נַחְמָן בַּר יַעֲקֹב וְרַב שֵׁשֶׁת. חַד אָמַר. יוֹצִיא מָנֶה כְּנֶגֶד מָנֶה. וְחָרָנָה אָמַר. זֶה גּוֹבֶה שְׁטָר חוֹבוֹ וְזֶה גּוֹבֶה שְׁטָר חוֹבוֹ. מָאן דְּאָמַר. יוֹצִיא מָנֶה כְּנֶגֶד מָנֶה. יְלִיף לָהּ מִשְּׁוָורִים תַּמִּים שֶׁחָבְלוּ זֶה בָּזֶה מְשַׁלְּמִים בַּמּוֹתָר חֲצִי נֶזֶק. מָאן דְּאָמַר. זֶה גּוֹבֶה שְׁטָר חוֹבוֹ וְזֶה

גּוֹבֶה שְׁטַר חוֹבוֹ. יָלִיף לָהּ מֵרַבָּנִין וְאַדְמוֹן. דְּרַבָּנִין וְאַדְמוֹן מוֹדֵי שֶׁיּוֹצִיא מָנֶה כְנֶגֶד מָנֶה. אֶלָּא בְגִין דְּתַנֵּינָן. אַדְמוֹן אוֹמֵר. אִילוּ חַיָּיב הָיִיתִי לָךְ כֵּיצַד אַתָּה לֹוֶה מִמֶּנִּי. לְפִיכָךְ צָרִיךְ מֵימַר. זֶה גּוֹבֶה שְׁטַר חוֹבוֹ וְזֶה גּוֹבֶה שְׁטַר חוֹבוֹ. מָחַל שֶׁלְּמָאתַיִם בְּמָנֶה וְשֶׁלְּמָנֶה לֹא מָחַל. מָאן דְּאָמַר. יוֹצִיא מָנֶה כְנֶגֶד מָנֶה. שֶׁכְּבָר יָצָא מָנֶה כְנֶגֶד מָנֶה. וּמָאן דְּאָמַר. זֶה גּוֹבֶה שְׁטַר חוֹבוֹ וְזֶה גּוֹבֶה שְׁטַר חוֹבוֹ. אוֹתוֹ שֶׁמָּחַל אֵינוֹ גוֹבֶה וְאוֹתוֹ שֶׁלֹּא מָחַל גּוֹבֶה. כָּתַב שֶׁלְּמָאתַיִם בִּשְׁטָר וְשֶׁלְּמָנֶה לֹא כָתַב. מָאן דְּאָמַר. יוֹצִיא מָנֶה כְנֶגֶד מָנֶה. שֶׁכְּבָר יָצָא מָנֶה כְנֶגֶד מָנֶה. וּמָאן דְּאָמַר. זֶה גּוֹבֶה שְׁטַר חוֹבוֹ וְזֶה גּוֹבֶה שְׁטַר חוֹבוֹ. אוֹתוֹ שֶׁכָּתַב גּוֹבֶה וְאוֹתוֹ שֶׁלֹּא כָתַב אֵינוֹ גוֹבֶה.

Halakhah 9: "If two people mutually produced promissory notes of one on the other," etc. If one borrowed a mina from the other, but the other borrowed from him 200 [*zuz*]. Rav Huna said, Rav Naḥman bar Jacob and Rab Sheshet disagree. One says, one counts one mina against the other mina, but the other says, each one collects the amount of his note[127]. He who says, one counts one mina against the other mina, learns it from tame oxen who injured one another, where half of the excess damage is paid[128]. He who says, each one collects the amount of his note, learns it from the Sages and Admon[129]. Can the Sages and Admon not agree that one counts one mina against the other mina? Because we have stated: Admon says: "If I owed you, how come you borrowed from me?" Therefore it was necessary to say, each one collects the amount of his note[130]. If the holder of the note of 200 forgave a mina, but the holder of the note of a mina did not forgive. For him who says, one counts one mina against the other mina, already one mina against the other mina was counted[131]. But for him who says, each one collects the amount of his note, then what he forgave he cannot collect but what was not forgiven he can collect. If the note for 200 was written in a document but the loan for a mina was not written. For him who says, one counts one mina against the other mina, already one mina against the other mina was counted. But for him who says, each one collects the amount of his note, the holder of the written note can collect but the recipient of the oral promise cannot collect[132].

127 In the Babli, 110a, Rav Naḥman is identified as holding that each one collects the amount of his note, Rav Sheshet that one counts mina against mina. Rav Naḥman's opinion is then restricted to the case that neither of the parties has money to satisfy his obligation and that the average quality of their respective real estate holdings is unequal. This means that in the Babli, Rav Naḥman agrees with Rav Sheshet except in the case where such a mutual accounting would be to the detriment of one party. This interpretation is excluded by the Yerushalmi's examples at the end of this paragraph.

128 If a steer which has no history of injuring other animals gores another steer, *Ex.* 21:35 requires the owner of the animal to pay half of the damages caused by his steer. If two such steers fight with one another and injure one another, Mishnah *Baba qama* 3:9 prescribes that money changes hands only for the amount for which one injury was estimated to be larger than the other. Since the fighting steers create obligations for their owners, it is seen that mutual obligations can be counted one against the other.

129 Most commentators want to correct the text from מֵרַבָּנִין וְאַדְמוֹן to מֵרַבָּנִין דְּאַדְמוֹן "the rabbis opposing Admon." But since מֵרַבָּנִין וְאַדְמוֹן can be interpreted as "the rabbis in their discussion with Admon", the readings of ms. and *editio princeps* can be upheld as *lectio difficilior*.

130 It is not necessary to read the Mishnah as prescribing that the notes have to be paid in cash and cannot be liquidated by accounting. Since Admon would allow one of the note holders to contest the other note without producing a receipt, all the rabbis say is that nobody can claim that a valid note was paid unless he produces a

receipt.

131 No money changes hands since the two notes cancel one another out.

132 If one loan was given as a mortgage but the other as a loan before witnesses, the mortgage can be foreclosed from any property the debtor had but the loan before witnesses could be foreclosed only from property not otherwise encumbered. If there are any other mortgages outstanding on the debtor's property, the holder of the loan before witnesses cannot foreclose.

(fol. 35c) **משנה י:** שָׁלֹשׁ אֲרָצוֹת לַנִּישׂוּאִין יְהוּדָה וְעֵבֶר הַיַּרְדֵּן וְהַגָּלִיל. אֵין מוֹצִיאִין מֵעִיר לְעִיר וּמִכְּרַךְ לִכְרַךְ. אֲבָל בְּאוֹתָהּ הָאָרֶץ מוֹצִיאִין מֵעִיר לְעִיר וּמִכְּרַךְ לִכְרַךְ אֲבָל לֹא מֵעִיר לִכְרַךְ וְלֹא מִכְּרַךְ לְעִיר. מוֹצִיאִין מִנָּוֶה הָרַע לְנָוֶה הַיָּפֶה אֲבָל לֹא מִנָּוֶה הַיָּפֶה לְנָוֶה הָרַע. רַבָּן שִׁמְעוֹן בֶּן גַּמְלִיאֵל אוֹמֵר אַף לֹא מִנָּוֶה הָרַע לְנָוֶה הַיָּפֶה מִפְּנֵי שֶׁהַנָּוֶה הַיָּפֶה בּוֹדֵק.

Mishnah 10: There are three districts for marriage, Judea, Transjordan[133], and Galilee. One does not move[134] from one village to another village and from one walled city[135] to another walled city, except that in one district one moves from one village to another village and from one walled city to another walled city, but not from a village to a walled city or from a walled city to a village. One moves from a bad neighborhood to a better one but not from a better one to a worse one. Rabban Simeon ben Gamliel says, not even from a bad neighborhood to a better one, because the better neighborhood tests[136].

133 Cf. *Ševi'it* 9:2, Note 39. These districts are considered separate entities.

134 The husband who married without stipulating that he has the right to determine the place of residence at will cannot force his wife to move, except within her own district to

HALAKHAH 10

another place of approximately the same size.

135 Cf. *Berakhot* 9:5, Note 216.

136 A radical change of circumstances can cause medical problems.

(36b line 39) **הלכה י**: שָׁלֹשׁ אֲרָצוֹת לַנִּשּׂוּאִין יְהוּדָה וְעֵבֶר הַיַּרְדֵּן וְהַגָּלִיל כול'. מַתְנִיתָא בְּשֶׁהָיָה בִיהוּדָה וְנָשָׂא אִשָּׁה מִגָּלִיל. בַּגָּלִיל וְנָשָׂא אִשָּׁה מִיהוּדָה. אֲבָל אִם הָיָה מִיהוּדָה וְנָשָׂא אִשָּׁה מִיהוּדָה. בַּגָּלִיל וְנָשָׂא אִשָּׁה מִגָּלִיל. כּוֹפִין אוֹתָהּ לָצֵאת. אֲנִי פְלוֹנִי שֶׁמִּיהוּדָה וְנָשָׂא אִשָּׁה מִיהוּדָה כּוֹפִין אוֹתָהּ לָצֵאת. מִגָּלִיל אֵין כּוֹפִין אוֹתָהּ לָצֵאת. אֲנִי פְלוֹנִי שֶׁמִּגָּלִיל וְנָשָׂא אִשָּׁה מִגָּלִיל כּוֹפִין אוֹתָהּ לָצֵאת. מִיהוּדָה אֵין כּוֹפִין אוֹתָהּ לָצֵאת. תַּנֵּי. מוֹצִיאִין מֵעִיר שֶׁרוּבָּהּ גּוֹיִם לְעִיר שֶׁכּוּלָהּ יִשְׂרָאֵל. אֲבָל לֹא מֵעִיר שֶׁכּוּלָהּ יִשְׂרָאֵל לְעִיר שֶׁרוּבָּהּ גּוֹיִם.

"There are three districts for marriage, Judea, Transjordan, and Galilee.," etc. The Mishnah[137] refers to the case that he was from Judea and married a woman in Galilee[138], or from Galilee and married a woman in Judea. But if he was from Judea and married in Judea[139], or from Galilee and married in Galilee, one forces her to move. [140]"'I, X, am from Judea and married a woman in Judea,' one forces her to move, 'in Galilee' one does not force her to move. 'I, X, am from Galilee and married a woman in Galilee,' one forces her to move, 'in Judea' one does not force her to move. One moves from a mostly Gentile village to a totally Jewish village but not from a totally Jewish village to a mostly Gentile village.[141]"

137 The first sentence, which states that the husband cannot force his wife to move with him to a different district.

138 Without pre-nuptual agreement it is understood that the woman stays in the district where she married.

139 If the woman from Galilee came to Judea to be married, she cannot force her husband to live with her in

Galilee but must live with him in Judea.

140 Tosephta 12:5. They used to write in the *ketubah* the place of origin of the groom and the place of the wedding, in order not to leave any doubt in which district the husband could dwell without his wife being able to object.

141 In the Tosephta: "One moves from a mostly Gentile village to a mostly Jewish village but not from a mostly Jewish village to a mostly Gentile village." In Babylonia there were no totally Jewish villages.

(47 line 36b) וּמְנַיִין שֶׁהַנָּוֶה הַיָּפָה בּוֹדֵק. רִבִּי לֵוִי בְּשֵׁם רִבִּי חָמָא בְּשֵׁם חֲנִינָה. פֶּן תִּדְבָּקַנִי הָרָעָה וָמַתִּי. בַּמִּשְׁרָה וְסָמַךְ לְהָרָה וְאַתְּ אָמַר אָכֵין. אֶלָּא מִכָּאן שֶׁהַנָּוֶה הַיָּפָה בּוֹדֵק.

And from where that a better neighborhood tests[142]? Rebbi Levi in the name of Rebbi Ḥama in the name of Ḥanina: "That disaster should not cling to me and I die.[143]" He was in the plain and was directed to the mountains, and you say so? But from here that a better neighborhood tests!

142 That more healthy surroundings can cause problems.

143 *Gen.* 19:19, Lot speaking to the angels who had told him to move to the mountains to escape the destruction of Sodom. The climate in the Moabite mountains is much healthier that in the plain of the Dead Sea.

A slightly expanded version is in *Gen. rabba* 50(20) by R. Berekhia in the name of R. Levi. The Babli, 110b, quotes a verse of Sirach to the same effect.

(fol. 35c) **משנה יא:** הַכֹּל מַעֲלִין לְאֶרֶץ יִשְׂרָאֵל וְאֵין הַכֹּל מוֹצִיאִין. הַכֹּל מַעֲלִין לִירוּשָׁלֵם וְאֵין הַכֹּל מוֹצִיאִין. אֶחָד הָאֲנָשִׁים וְאֶחָד הַנָּשִׁים. כֵּיצַד נָשָׂא אִשָּׁה

בְּאֶרֶץ יִשְׂרָאֵל וְגֵרְשָׁהּ בְּאֶרֶץ יִשְׂרָאֵל נוֹתֵן לָהּ מִמָּעוֹת אֶרֶץ יִשְׂרָאֵל. נָשָׂא אִשָּׁה בְּאֶרֶץ יִשְׂרָאֵל וְגֵרְשָׁהּ בְּקַפּוֹדְקִייָה נוֹתֵן לָהּ מִמָּעוֹת אֶרֶץ יִשְׂרָאֵל. נָשָׂא אִשָּׁה בְּקַפּוֹדְקִייָה וְגֵרְשָׁהּ בְּאֶרֶץ יִשְׂרָאֵל נוֹתֵן לָהּ מִמָּעוֹת אֶרֶץ יִשְׂרָאֵל. רַבָּן שִׁמְעוֹן בֶּן גַּמְלִיאֵל אוֹמֵר מִמָּעוֹת קַפּוֹדְקִייָה. נָשָׂא אִשָּׁה בְּקַפּוֹדְקִייָה וְגֵרְשָׁהּ בְּקַפּוֹדְקִייָה נוֹתֵן לָהּ מִמָּעוֹת קַפּוֹדְקִייָה.

Mishnah 11: Everybody moves to the Land of Israel but not everybody leaves[144]. Everybody moves to Jerusalem but not everybody leaves. How is this[145]? If he married a woman in the Land of Israel and divorced her in the Land of Israel, he pays her in coin of the Land of Israel[146]. If he married a woman in the Land of Israel and divorced her in Kappadokia, he pays her in coin of the Land of Israel. If he married a woman in Kappadokia and divorced her in the Land of Israel, he pays her in coin of the Land of Israel[147]; Rabban Simeon ben Gamliel says, in coin of Kappadokia. If he married a woman in Kappadokia and divorced her in Kappadokia, he pays her in coin of Kappadokia[146].

144 As explained in the Halakhah, if one part of the family wants to emigrate to the Land of Israel, the other has to follow.

145 This word is not in the Babli; it is found in all Yerushalmi Mishnah mss. and Maimonides's autograph Mishnah. It implies that the preference given to the coin of the Land of Israel is a consequence of the first part of the Mishnah..

146 This is unproblematic; since *ketubah* and bill of divorce were executed in the same country, it is clear that the sum stipulated in the *ketubah*, whose payment was triggered by the bill of divorce, has to be settled in the coin of the country.

147 It is pointed out in the Babli that in terms of contract law, the two statements contradict one another. If he married in Israel and had to pay in coins of Israel, it implies that the *ketubah* determines the currency. But if he married in Kappadokia and had to pay in coins of Israel, it implies that

the bill of divorce, the trigger of the payment, determines the currency. (In the Babli, 101b, and the Tosephta, 12:6, Rabban Simeon ben Gamliel states that the place of executing the *ketubah* determines its currency.) The Babli, 110b, concludes that, since the Persian coins current in Kappadokia are better than the debased Roman coins in Israel, the obligation of the *ketubah* is a rabbinic institution and the possibility of paying with debased coin was part of the institution. The Yerushalmi (also Tosephta, 12:6) will argue that the Jewish coins of Israel, not the Roman coins, are meant and, therefore, the Mishnah proclaims a stringency which can only be explained by giving the *ketubah* biblical status.

(36b line 50) **הלכה יא**: הַכֹּל מַעֲלִין כול'. הוּא רוֹצֶה לַעֲלוֹת לְאֶרֶץ יִשְׂרָאֵל וְהִיא אֵינָהּ רוֹצָה כּוֹפִין אוֹתָהּ לַעֲלוֹת. הִיא רוֹצָה וְהוּא אֵינוֹ רוֹצֶה אֵין כּוֹפִין אוֹתוֹ לַעֲלוֹת. הוּא רוֹצֶה לַעֲלוֹת לִירוּשָׁלֵם וְהִיא אֵינָהּ רוֹצָה כּוֹפִין אוֹתָהּ לַעֲלוֹת. הִיא רוֹצָה וְהוּא אֵינוֹ רוֹצֶה אֵין כּוֹפִין אוֹתוֹ לַעֲלוֹת. הוּא רוֹצֶה לָצֵאת לְחוּצָה לָאָרֶץ וְהִיא אֵינָהּ רוֹצָה אֵין כּוֹפִין אוֹתָהּ לָצֵאת. הִיא רוֹצָה וְהוּא אֵינוֹ רוֹצֶה כּוֹפִין אוֹתָהּ שֶׁלֹּא לָצֵאת.

Halakhah 11: "Everybody moves," etc. If he wants to move to the Land of Israel but she does not, one forces her to move[148]. If she wants but he does not, one does not force him to move[149]. If he wants to move to Jerusalem but she does not, one forces her to move. If she wants but he does not, one does not force him to move[150]. If he wants to leave the Land of Israel but she does not, one does not force her to leave. If she wants to leave but he does not, one forces her not to leave.

148 In the Babylonian texts, Babli 110b and Tosephta 10:5, it is explained that "forcing" means that the refusing party is the guilty party in the ensuing divorce.

149 In Babli and Tosephta: "One forces him".

150 The sentences about Jerusalem are missing in Babli and Tosephta.

HALAKHAH 11

(36b line 50) נָתֵן לָהּ מִמָּעוֹת אֶרֶץ יִשְׂרָאֵל. הָדָא אֶמְרָה. שֶׁמַּטְבֵּעַ אֶרֶץ יִשְׂרָאֵל יָפֶה מִכָּל־הָאֲרָצוֹת. הָדָא מְסַיִּיעָא לְמָאן דְּאָמַר. כְּתוּבַת אִשָּׁה מִדִּבְרֵי תוֹרָה. וּדְלֹא כְרַבָּן שִׁמְעוֹן בֶּן גַּמְלִיאֵל. דְּתַנֵּי. רַבָּן שִׁמְעוֹן בֶּן גַּמְלִיאֵל אוֹמֵר. אֵין כְּתוּבַת אִשָּׁה אֶלָּא מִדִּבְרֵי סוֹפְרִים.

"He pays her in coin of the Land of Israel." This implies that the coins of the land of Israel are the best of all countries[151]. This supports him who says that a woman's *ketubah* is from the words of the Torah[152], against Rabban Simeon ben Gamliel, as it was stated[153]: Rabban Simeon ben Gamliel says, a woman's *ketubah* is only an institution of the *Soferim*[154].

151 Since Palestine had no imperial mint in Talmudic times, this cannot refer to Roman coins in circulation, which were coins *in* the Land but not *of* the Land. It must refer to the minting standards of the two revolts whose Jewish coins were intended to be used for the Temple tax and as such were of full weight, i. e. the "holy sheqel". This also must be the meaning of the statement in the Tosephta 12:6, cf. S. Lieberman, תוספתא כפשוטה כתובות p. 389.

152 Because it has to be paid in terms of biblical coin standards.

153 Babli 10a, in a first version. In the second version and in 110b, he is reported to consider *ketubah* a biblical obligation. In *Mekhilta dR. Simeon bar Iohai* p. 209, a Babylonian compilation in the opinion of J. N. Epstein, Rabban Simeon ben Gamliel is quoted as saying that *ketubah* has no fixed sum from the Torah; i. e., the institution is biblical, "the *mohar* of virgins", but the amount and all details are rabbinical.

The Babli follows the saboraic rule that practice always follows Rabban Simeon ben Gamliel in the Mishnah; a principle not known to the Yerushalmi and certainly rejected here. Cf. also 1:2, Notes 112-120, 4:8 (29a l. 30), 4:12 Note 248; *Yebamot* 7:2 Note 63, 15:3 Note 63. For biblical status of *ketubah*, *Mekhilta dR. Ismael, Mišpaṭim* 17 (p. 308, ed. Horovitz-Rabin).

154 I. e., dating from Ezra and/or his successors.

Introduction to Tractate Niddah

Tractate *Niddah* is the only one from the Seventh Order of the Mishnah, *Ṭahorot*, "purities", detailing the rules of impurity, which is treated in the Babylonian Talmud. In the Yerushalmi, only a fragment has survived, consisting of the first three Chapters and a few lines of the fourth. The theme of the Tractate is the impurity of a menstruating woman (*Lev.* 15:19-24) and of the woman after childbirth (*Lev.* 12:1-8). Connected with this impurity is the prohibition of sexual relations with menstruating women and those having given birth (*Lev.* 18:19).

The first two Chapters deal mostly with the effect of menstruation on the preparation of food in ritual purity. These rules seem vastly to exceed the biblical rules on which they are based. On the other hand, it is a pharisaic-rabbinic peculiarity that not all genital discharges imply impurity; the second Chapter contains a discussion of the impure discharges. It is known from the Damascus document that Sadducees regarded all genital discharges as impure.

The third Chapter is a collection of precepts on how to deal with stillbirths and fetal malformations.

שמי אומר פרק ראשון

(fol. 48d) **משנה א:** שַׁמַּי אוֹמֵר כָּל־הַנָּשִׁים דַּיָּין שַׁעְתָּן. הִלֵּל אוֹמֵר מִפְּקִידָה לִפְקִידָה אֲפִילוּ לְיָמִים הַרְבֵּה. וַחֲכָמִים אוֹמְרִים לֹא כְדִבְרֵי זֶה וְלֹא כְדִבְרֵי זֶה אֶלָּא מֵעֵת לְעֵת מְמַעֶטֶת עַל יַד מִפְּקִידָה לִפְקִידָה. וּמִפְּקִידָה לִפְקִידָה מְמַעֶטֶת עַל יַד מֵעֵת לְעֵת.

Mishnah 1: Shammai says, every woman's timing is exact[1]; Hillel says, from checking to checking[2], even if that is a long time. But the Sages say following neither of them but for checking to checking to be reduced by 24 hours, and from 24 hours to be reduced by checking[3].

משנה ב: כָּל־אִשָּׁה שֶׁיֵּשׁ לָהּ וֶסֶת דַּיָּיהּ שַׁעְתָּהּ. וְהַמְשַׁמֶּשֶׁת בְּעֵדִים הֲרֵי זוֹ כִּפְקִידָה וּמְמַעֶטֶת עַל יַד מֵעֵת לְעֵת וְעַל יַד מִפְּקִידָה לִפְקִידָה.

Mishnah 2: Every woman with a regular period[4] follows her exact timing; and if one has intercourse with cloths[5], this counts as checking and is reduced by 24 hours and by checking.

---

1 A menstruating woman is impure and imparts original impurity to anything she sits on (*Lev.* 15:19-23). While impurity of food is not mentioned in these verses, it is taken for granted that if she imparts impurity to implements that do not easily become impure, certainly she imparts impurity to food which easily becomes impure. The impurity is defined (v. 19) by "blood is flowing from her flesh". Shammai holds that a woman notices exactly when her period starts; therefore any food she touches after the onset of her period is impure but anything she had touched before is pure.

2 Hillel holds that blood drops

can separate from the uterine wall without necessarily flowing out of the vagina. For him, all food a woman touched between the last time she checked herself thoroughly and the noticed onset of her period are retroactively declared possibly impure.

3   For them, a woman with a regular period does not have to worry about retroactive impurity (Mishnah 2). If she has no regular period, she is expected to check herself from time to time but the retroactive impurity cannot extend to more than 24 hours; the interval of impurity is the smaller of 24 hours and the time from the last thorough check.

4   Latin *svetum*, corresponding to Hebrew אורח "regularity"; cf. E. and H. Guggenheimer, Notes on the Talmudic Vocabulary 8-11, *Lešonenu* 37 (1973), 105-112.

5   After intercourse (according to Rashi: before and after intercourse) she wipes herself with a clean cloth which can be inspected the next morning. The connection of the word עדים to the biblical *hapax* in *Is.* 64:5 is due to Qimḥi; according to Rashi (*Is.* 64:5), the biblical word is an Aramaism and means "to be discarded". In *Niddah*, Rashi seems to to read עד "a witness".

(48d line 28) **הלכה א:** שַׁמַּי אוֹמֵר. כָּל־הַנָּשִׁים דַּיָּין שְׁעָתָּן כול׳. מָהוּ דַּיָּין שְׁעָתָן. שְׁאֵינָן מְטַמּוֹת טַהֲרוֹת לְמַפְרֵעַ. וַחֲכָמִים אוֹמְרִים לֹא כְדִבְרֵי זֶה וְלֹא כְדִבְרֵי זֶה. לֹא כְשַׁמַּאי שֶׁלֹּא נָתַן סְיָיג לִדְבָרָיו וְלֹא כְהִלֵּל שֶׁהִפְלִיג עַל מִדּוֹתָיו. אֶלָּא מֵעֵת לְעֵת מְמַעֶטֶת עַל יַד מִפְּקִידָה לִפְקִידָה וּמִפְּקִידָה לִפְקִידָה מְמַעֶטֶת עַל יַד מֵעֵת לְעֵת. כֵּיצַד מֵעֵת לְעֵת מְמַעֶטֶת עַל יַד מִפְּקִידָה לִפְקִידָה. בָּדְקָה עַצְמָהּ בְּשֵׁינִי בְּשַׁבָּת וְרָאֲת בַּחֲמִשִׁי בְּשַׁבָּת אֵין טָמֵא אֶלָּא עַד מֵעֵת לְעֵת דְּאַרְבָּעְתָּא. כֵּיצַד מִפְּקִידָה לִפְקִידָה מְמַעֶטֶת עַל יַד מֵעֵת לְעֵת. בָּדְקָה בְּשַׁחֲרִית וְרָאֲת בְּמִנְחָה אֵן טָמֵא אֶלָּא עַד שַׁחֲרִית.

"Shammai says, every woman's timing is exact," etc. What means, "their timing is exact"? They do not retroactively impart impurity to food prepared in purity. "But the Sages say following neither of them," not following Shammai who imposed no restriction, and not like Hillel who went overboard. "But for checking to checking it is reduced by 24 hours, and from 24 hours is reduced by checking." How is checking to checking reduced by 24 hours? If she checked herself on Tuesday and saw blood on Thursday, [her food] is impure only from the same time on Wednesday. How is 24 hours reduced by checking? If she checked herself out in the morning and saw in the afternoon, it is impure only starting from the morning[6].

6   A slightly longer version is in Babli, 4b, and Tosefta 1:1-2.

(48d line 36) תַּמָּן תַּנִּינָן. הַשֶּׁרֶץ שֶׁנִּמְצָא בְּמָבוֹי מְטַמֵּא לְמַפְרֵעַ. רִבִּי אִמִּי בָּעֵי. מַתְנִיתָא דְּלֹא כְשַׁמַּי. אָמַר רִבִּי יוֹסֵי. אִין לֵית הוּא כְשַׁמַּי אֲפִילוּ כְהִלֵּל לֵית הִיא. וְלֹא מוֹדֶה הִלֵּל בְּמָבוֹי שֶׁהוּא מִתְכַּבֵּד וְשֶׁטֶף שֶׁלְּגְשָׁמִים עוֹבֵר בּוֹ שֶׁהוּא טָהוֹר. שַׁמַּי אוֹמֵר. הָדָא אִשָּׁה עַל יְדֵי שֶׁהִיא רְגִילָה בְּמֵי רַגְלַיִם עָשׂוּ אוֹתָהּ כְּמָבוֹי שֶׁהוּא מִתְכַּבֵּד וְשֶׁטֶף שֶׁלְּגְשָׁמִים עוֹבֵר בּוֹ וְהוּא טָהוֹר.

There[7], we have stated: "A [dead] crawling animal[8] found in a dead-end alley[9] causes impurity retroactively[10]. Rebbi Immi asked, does this Mishnah not disagree with Shammai? Rebbi Yose[11] said, this is true, it does not follow Shammai, but even Hillel it does not follow. Does Hillel not agree that a dead-end alley which was swept or inundated by a rainstorm[12] is pure? Shammai says, since this woman regularly urinates[13], she is like a dead-end alley which was swept or inundated by a rainstorm and is pure[14].

7   Mishnah *Niddah* 7:2.

8   Eight animals, reptiles, rats, and moles are enumerated in *Lev.* 11:29-38. In death, they are original sources of severe impurity.

9   A dead-end alley bordered on both sides by walls, either the back walls of houses or the walls of courtyards. One enters the houses of the alley through the courtyards. While the dead-end alley is public domain, it is not subject to all the rules

of public domains since it is used only by its inhabitants and their visitors. It can be turned into a private domain as far as the rules of the Sabbath are concerned (this is the topic of Tractate *Erubin*). It is a private domain for the rules of impurity, meaning that a doubt of impurity has to treated as presumptive impurity; cf. *Soṭah* 1:2, Note 88.

10   The Mishnah continues: "up to the time it was swept (with a broom)." If any food was transported through the alley, one assumes that the bearer touched the dead crawling thing, became impure, and transferred that impurity to the food he was carrying. One assumes that sweeping the alley with a broom cleans it, but one fears that the animal died very soon after the alley was swept. Therefore, it seems that impurity in a dead-end alley follows Hillel's rules.

11   It would seem that one has to read: R. Yasa, R. Immi's companion.

12   In this case, nobody checked but one assumes that the rain swept everything away. This case appears neither in the Mishnah nor in the Tosephta (6:12).

13   She would notice any blood at that time.

14   Shammai's position is the most rational one. It presumes that the Mishnah speaks of an alley which is swept regularly (Babli 56a/b). In the Babli, 3a, Hillel denies that a woman will check herself for blood when urinating.

(48d line 42) עַד כְּדוֹן בְּשֶׁבְּדָקָה וּמְצָתָה נָגוּב. בְּדָקָה וּמְצָתָה טָהוֹר. רִבִּי אִמִּי בְּשֵׁם רַב רִבִּי בָּא בְּשֵׁם רַב יְהוּדָה. בְּדָקָה וּמְצָתָה טָהוֹר אֲסוּרָה לְבֵיתָהּ עַד שֶׁיִּתְנַגֵּב מַעְיָינָהּ. חַד רִבִּי טוֹבִי אָמַר בְּשֵׁם רִבִּי אַבָּהוּ. אֲסוּרָה לְבֵיתָהּ עַד מֵעֵת לְעֵת. אָמַר רִבִּי יַעֲקֹב בַּר אָחָא. כַּד סְלִיקִית לְהָכָא שְׁמָעִית מִן כָּל־רַבָּנָן. מוּתֶּרֶת לְבֵיתָהּ מִיָּד. הֲווֹן בָּעֵיי מֵימַר. מָאן דָּמַר. מוּתֶּרֶת לְבֵיתָהּ. מִפְּקִידָהּ הוּא לְמָעֵט מֵעֵת לְעֵת. וּמָאן דָּמַר. אֲסוּרָה לְבֵיתָהּ. אֵינָהּ כִּפְקִידָהּ לְמָעֵט מֵעֵת לְעֵת. וַאֲפִילוּ כְמָאן דָּמַר. אֲסוּרָה לְבֵיתָהּ. כִּפְקִידָהּ הִיא לְמָעֵט מֵעֵת לְעֵת. וְלָמָּה הִיא אֲסוּרָה לְבֵיתָהּ. שֶׁמִּתּוֹךְ שֶׁהִיא מִתְרַגֶּלֶת בְּדָמִים טְהוֹרִין הִיא מִתְרַגֶּלֶת בְּדָמִים טְמֵאִין.

So far if she checked and found herself dry[15]. If she checked and found herself pure[16]? Rebbi Immi in the name of Rav, Rebbi Abba in the name of Rav Jehudah: If she checked and found herself pure she is forbidden to her husband until her [blood's] source dries up[17]. One Rebbi Tobi said in the name of Rebbi Abbahu, she is forbidden to her house for 24 hours. Rebbi Jacob bar Aḥa said, when I[18] immigrated here, I heard from all rabbis that she is immediately permitted to her husband[19]. They wanted to say that for him who says, she is permitted to her husband, this is a check which diminishes from 24 hours[20], but for him who says, she is forbidden to her husband, it is not counted as a check which diminishes from 24 hours[21]. But even for him who says, she is forbidden to her husband, it is counted as a check which diminishes from 24 hours[22]. Why is she forbidden to her husband? Because she is used to pure blood, she might get used to impure blood[23].

15 No discharge whatsoever.

16 She found a discharge from her body but it was of a kind declared pure in Mishnah 2:6. The existence of pure genital discharges is Pharisaic doctrine, absolutely denied by all Sadducee sources known to us; cf. the Damascus Document CD 5:7, Mishnah 4:2.

17 This is the standard Babylonian doctrine, culminating in the Babli (66a) in R. Ze'ira's doctrine, which accepts the Sadducee doctrine that all discharges are impure and, in order to avoid the consequences of this doctrine which are unacceptable in Pharisaic practice, treats every menstrual discharge as a continuing non-menstrual discharge (*Lev.* 15:25-30), which requires an additional seven days before purity may be achieved. Babylonian practice accepts the distinction between pure and impure discharges only for the rules of impurity, which were irrelevant in Babylonia, but not for those of marital relations.

18 A Babylonian immigrating into Palestine.

19 Since the determination of the character of blood as pure or impure is

in the domain of competence of a rabbi, it follows that the woman who claims her blood to be pure has to show her blood to a rabbi. It is not to be assumed that any woman did that unless her household was run on the rules of ritual purity, i. e., a family of Cohanim or of "fellows" (cf. Introduction to Tractate *Demay*).

20 All the food she prepares remains pure.

21 If she later has an impure discharge, the food becomes retroactively impure.

22 There is no reason to make the status of the check depend on its outcome.

23 Once she is used to the looks of the pure discharge, she might decide herself about the quality of her discharge and wrongly qualify impure for pure. The prohibition of marital relations in this case is purely rabbinical; it has no biblical source.

(48d line 51) בְּדְקָה וּמָצְאָה סָפֵק. פְּשִׁיטָה אֵינָהּ כִּפְקִידָה לְמָעֵט מֵעֵת לְעֵת. הוּא עַצְמוֹ מָהוּ שֶׁיִּטָּמֵא מִסָּפֵק. נִשְׁמְעִינָהּ מִן הָדָא. טוּמְטוּם וְאַנְדְּרוֹגִינָס שֶׁרָאוּ דַּיָּין שָׁעֲתָן. מָא אַתְּ שְׁמַע מִינָהּ. אָמַר רִבִּי יוֹסֵי. טוּמְטוּם וְאַנְדְּרוֹגִינָס סָפֵק וּמֵעֵת לְעֵת סָפֵק וְאֵין סָפֵק לְסָפֵק. וָכָא. רְאִייָתָהּ סָפֵק וּמֵעֵת לְעֵת סָפֵק וְאֵין סָפֵק לְסָפֵק.

If she checked herself and found it a doubtful case[24]. It is obvious that it is not counted as a check to diminish from 24 hours[25]. Itself[26], would it be impure because of doubt? Let us hear from the following: "A sexless[27] or a hermaphrodite[28] who had a discharge follow their exact timing." What do you infer from this? Rebbi Yose said, a sexless or a hermaphrodite represent a doubt, 24 hours represent a doubt, and a doubt is not superimposed on a doubt[29]. So here, whether she had a discharge[30] represents a doubt, 24 hours represent a doubt, and a doubt is not superimposed on a doubt.

24 If it cannot be decided whether the discharge is pure or impure. (This is the explanation of R. Moses Margalit. It is somewhat difficult to accept since

(a) in matters of biblical prohibitions a doubt has to be resolved in a restrictive way and (b) this is a matter of impurity in a private domain and has to be declared impure; cf. Note 9, *Soṭah* 1:2 Note 88. Therefore, it seems more likely that it cannot be determined whether there was any discharge.)

25 If later this was followed by a genuine discharge, the previous doubt was resolved and food retroactively became impure for 24 hours.

26 The blood according to R. Moses Margalit, or alternatively the cloth used for the check.

27 Tosephta 1:3. The sexless has neither penis nor vagina, cf. *Yebamot* 8:6, Note 226. He could be a male with an ingrown penis. It is difficult to see how he could have a female genital discharge.

28 He has penis, testicles, breasts and vagina; if he has a discharge, its status is in doubt since if he is a male, the vaginal discharge is irrelevant. Cf. *Yebamot* 8:6, Notes 224,225,236,237,242.

29 In the Babli, this is called סְפֵק סְפֵיקָא "a doubt superimposed on a doubt" (*Qiddušin* 75a); a prohibition in such a case would be disregarded. Cf. *Ketubot* 1:1 Note 23, *Yebamot* 16:1, last line.

30 R. Moses Margalit would translate: "The nature of her discharge is in doubt".

(48d line 56) הוּנָא בַּר חִיָּיא אָמַר. מֵעֵת לְעֵת שֶׁאָמְרוּ לַקֳּדָשִׁים אֲבָל לֹא לְטָהֳרוֹת. הָתִיב רַב חִסְדָּא. וְהָתַנֵּי. מַעֲשֶׂה בְרִיבָה אַחַת בְּעַייתְלוֹ שֶׁהִפְסִיקָה לָהּ שָׁלֹשׁ עוֹנוֹת וְלֹא רָעֵת כָּךְ רָאֵת. וּבָא מַעֲשֶׂה לִפְנֵי חֲכָמִים וְאָמְרוּ. דַּיָּיהּ שָׁעָתָהּ. וְכִי יֵשׁ קָדָשִׁים בְּעַייתְלוֹ. אֶלָּא בְּשֶׁנַּעֲשׂוּ לְטָהֳרַת הַקּוֹדֶשׁ. וְלֹא כְחוּלִּין הֵן. תִּיפְתָּר שֶׁנַּעֲשׂוּ לְטָהֳרַת מֵי חַטָּאת. שֶׁמֵּי חַטָּאת חֲמוּרִין מִן הַקּוֹדֶשׁ.

2 בריבה | תו בריבה אחת   בעייתלו | ב בהיתלו תו בחיתלות   לה שלש | ג שלשת 3 ולא | ג לא   4 תפתר שנעשו | ג בשנעשו

[31]Huna bar Ḥiyya[32] said, the 24 hours which were quoted refer to sacrifices but not to pure food[33]. Rav Ḥisda objected, was it not stated[34]: "It happened with a girl in Aitlo[35] that she missed for three periods and then had a period. When the case came before the Sages, they said that

her timing is exact." Are there sacrifices in Aitlo? But it must be food prepared in the purity of sacrifices[36]! Is that not really profane food[37]? Explain it if it was prepared in the purity of purifying water[38], since purifying water has more restrictive rules than sacrifices.

31 From here on, a Geniza fragment is available; its readings are denoted by א. For the quotations from a Tosephta, the Babli is denoted by ב, the Tosephta edited by Zuckermandel by ית

32 In the Babli, 4a, he is identified as Rav Huna. This is the only place in which his patronymic is given.

33 He denies the applicability of the Mishnah after the destruction of the Temple. Since the only sanctified food available after the destruction of the Temple was heave, the entire discussion becomes academic.

34 Tosephta 1:9, Babli 9b.

35 The vocalization is not known; the Babylonian tradition is different; the place has not been identified. But in any case it is impossible to prepare sacrifices outside of Jerusalem since living animals cannot become impure and the material for flour, wine, and oil sacrifices was controlled by the Temple.

In Babli and Tosephta it is stated that the impurity in effect should have been retroactive, that the ruling as given fits only extraordinary circumstances. One may assume that the Yerushalmi refers to a similar text and that Rav Hisda the Babylonian's question really refers to this, that under normal circumstances the impurity of a menstruating woman without regular period should act retroactively on food prepared in purity outside of Jerusalem.

36 Profane food, eaten by people who insist that they adhere to strict standards of purity. While most of these, called "fellows", observed the standards of heave (which recognizes three degrees of derivative impurity, cf. Introduction to Tractate *Demay*, p. 349; *Demay* 2:2, Note 137), some people adhered to standards of sacrifices which recognized four degrees (Mishnah *Tahorot* 2:5).

37 Mishnah *Tahorot* 2:8 decrees that profane food prepared according to the standards of sacrifices is still profane, admitting only two degrees of derivative impurity. A minority

opinion admits three degrees, but certainly not four. This may be a polemic against followers of sects similar to that of Qumran, whose MMT text seems to prescribe the purity of sacrifices for all members of the group of the select few.

38 The water to which ashes from the red cow were added and which purified from the impurity of the dead. This water had to be guarded even from touching sacrificial food, Mishnah *Parah* 10:6. The ashes were available in Palestine a long time after the destruction of the Temple, cf. *Berakhot* 1:1, Note 3; it was not impossible for a priestly family to preserve the rules of this purifying process.

(48d line 61) תַּנֵּי. מֵעֵת לְעֵת שֶׁאָמְרוּ תּוֹלִין אֲבָל לֹא שׂוֹרְפִין. וַהֲוָה רִבִּי זְעִירָא חֲדִי בָהּ. אַשְׁכַּח תַּנֵּי. הָרוֹאָה כֶתֶם מְטַמֵּא לְמַפְרֵעַ. וּמָה הִיא מְטַמְאָה. הָאוֹכְלִין וְהַמַּשְׁקִין וְהַמִּשְׁכָּבוֹת וְהַמּוֹשָׁבוֹת. וּמְקוּלְקֶלֶת לְמִנְיָינָהּ וּמְטַמֵּא אֶת בּוֹעֲלָהּ לְמַפְרֵעַ. הָרוֹאָה דָם מְטַמֵּא לְמַפְרֵעַ. וּמָה הִיא מְטַמֵּא. הָאוֹכְלִין וְהַמַּשְׁקִין וְהַמִּשְׁכָּבוֹת וְהַמּוֹשָׁבוֹת. וְאֵינָהּ מְקוּלְקֶלֶת לְמִנְיָינָהּ וְאֵינָהּ מְטַמֵּא אֶת בּוֹעֲלָהּ לְמַפְרֵעַ. רִבִּי עֲקִיבָה אוֹמֵר. מְטַמֵּא אֶת בּוֹעֲלָהּ לְמַפְרֵעַ. וְזֶה וָזֶה תּוֹלִין אֲבָל לֹא שׂוֹרְפִין. תַּמָּן אֲמָרִין. מֵעֵת לְעֵת שֶׁאָמְרוּ מְשַׁכְבָהּ כְּמַגָּעָהּ. מָה. כְּבוֹעֵל נִדָּה וְאֵינוֹ מְטַמֵּא בְהֵיסֵט וְאֵינוֹ מְטַמֵּא בִּכְלִי חֶרֶשׂ. אַשְׁכַּח תַּנֵּי. מְטַמֵּא כְלִי חֶרֶשׂ בְּהֵיסֵט. מֵעֵת לְעֵת שֶׁאָמְרוּ. מַגָּעָהּ בִּרְשׁוּת הָרַבִּים מַהוּ. נִישְׁמְעִינָהּ מִן הָדָא. מְעוּבֶּרֶת וּמֵנִיקָה טְהוֹרוֹת לְבַעֲלֵיהֶן. וְכֵן אִשָּׁה שֶׁיֵּשׁ לָהּ וֶסֶת. וּשְׁאָר כָּל־הַנָּשִׁים טְהוֹרוֹת בְּבִיאָה וּמְטַמְאוֹת בְּמַגָּע. הָדָא אֲמְרָה. וַדַּאי מַגָּעָהּ בִּרְשׁוּת הָרַבִּים טָמֵא.

39¹ והוה ‖ ג והווה   ר' זעירא ‖ ג ר' זעורה (all occurrences)   2 מטמאה ‖ ג מטמא   2,4 האכלין והמשקין ‖ ג אכלין ומשקין   5 מקולקלת ‖ ג מקלקלת   7 תמן אמרין ‖ ג   תני   8 בהיסט ‖ ג בהסט   בכלי חרש ‖ ג כלי (all occurrences)   11 ודאי ‖ ג ודיי   12 הרבים ‖ ג הרבין

It was stated: For the 24 hours which were stated, one suspends but one does not burn[40]. Rebbi Ze'ira enjoyed this [because] he found stated[41]: "A woman who detects a stain[42] makes impure retroactively[43].

What does she make impure? Food, and drinks, and seats, and beds[44]; her count is in disorder[45], and she makes her sex partner impure retroactively[46]. A woman who detects blood makes impure retroactively[47]. What does she make impure? Food, and drinks, and seats, and beds; her count is not in disorder[48], and she does not make her sex partner impure retroactively. Rebbi Aqiba says, she makes her sex partner impure retroactively. In both cases[49], one suspends but one does not burn." There[50], they say: For the 24 hours which were stated, her bed is like her touch[51]. How? Like one who sleeps with a menstruating woman[52] who does not make impure by moving[53] and does not make clay vessels impure. It was found stated: He makes clay vessels impure by moving[54]. For the 24 hours which were stated, what is the status of what she touches in the public domain[55]? Let us hear from the following[56]: Pregnant and nursing women are pure for their husbands[57], as is a woman with a regular period[58]. And all other women[59] are pure for sexual relations but impure in their touch[60]. That means, what she certainly touched in the public domain is impure.

39 All variant readings are from the Geniza fragment. Mostly they just represent Galilean spelling.

40 If heave was declared "impure" because a woman had handled it within 24 hours of her menstrual impurity, it cannot be burned as impure heave since the declaration was purely precautionary; the woman might have been impure when touching the heave. Since it is forbidden to destroy pure sanctified food, that heave neither can be destroyed, for perhaps it is pure, nor be used, for perhaps it is impure. It has to be left unused until it spoils, is no longer food, and automatically loses its sanctified status.

41 Tosephta 9:6,5; Babli 6a, both in slightly different formulation.

42 She detects a blood stain on her garment. This is proof that she bled sometime but she does not know when.

43 The retroactivity extends all the time back until either the time when the woman had checked herself or the garment had been washed.

44 By *Lev.* 15:20-23, any seat or couch used by a menstruating woman becomes a source of original impurity. The impurity of food is not mentioned in the verses; it is only secondary (cf. Note 36). The original impurity of beds and seats induced retroactively is also asserted in the Babli, 5b.

45 By tradition, denied by Sadducees, there are 11 days after the end of seven days of a menstrual period in which no new menses are possible, in which any bloody discharge cannot be menstrual but must follow the rules of *zava*. But if the start of the period is unknown, the count is impossible and any discharge triggers a seven day menstrual period.

46 Since her impurity was unknown to her.

47 In Tosephta and Babli: For 24 hours. The Yerushalmi probably assumes the validity of the Sages' statement in Mishnah 1.

48 She counts from the moment she notices the discharge.

49 Stain or blood.

50 In Babylonia. This statement is missing in the Geniza text.

51 Since her touch creates only derivative impurity, her seat and bed also do not become sources of original impurity.

52 *Lev.* 15:24 declares the man and his seat or bedding as impure but refrains from declaring seat and bedding as sources of original impurity.

53 *Lev.* 15:6 is interpreted that the male sufferer of gonorrhea imparts impurity to anything he moves, even if he never touches it. By biblical standards, a clay vessel cannot become impure by being touched from the outside; it becomes impure only by an original impurity inside its cavity. If a clay vessel has a cover fastened to it, it also cannot become impure by the impurity of the dead. But if either a (male or female) sufferer from gonorrhea or a menstruating woman indirectly moves a clay vessel, for example moving a wooden plank (in itself impervious to impurity) on which there is a closed clay vessel, that vessel and its contents become impure.

54 In the Tosephta (Note 41) this is asserted for both cases of menstrual impurity. The *baraita* quoted here disproves the earlier statement which denied the possibility of impurity by moving.

55 A general rule states that a

doubt about matters of impurity in a public domain can be disregarded (cf. Note 9). The question is, if a woman had certainly touched something in the public domain within 24 hours of her menstruation, is this counted as a doubt or not?

56   A related text in Tosephta 3:8.

57   They are not supposed to menstruate.

58   Except close to her time.

59   Excluding pre-puberty girls and post-menopausal women. There are not many women left in this category of "others".

60   Since at any time they could induce retroactive impurity.

(49a line 12) רִבִּי יוּדָן בָּעֵי. בָּדְקָה חֲלוּקָהּ בְּשַׁחֲרִית וּמְצָתָהּ טָהוֹר. וּבְמִנְחָה וּמָצְאת עָלָיו כֶּתֶם. פְּשִׁיטָא חֲלוּקָהּ אֵינוֹ טָמֵא אֶלָּא עַד שְׁעַת בְּדִיקָה. גּוּפָהּ מָהוּ שֶׁיְּהֵא טָמֵא מֵעֵת לְעֵת. כְּלוּם אַתְּ מְטַמֵּא גוּפָהּ אֶלָּא מַחֲמַת חֲלוּקָהּ. חֲלוּקָהּ אֵינוֹ טָמֵא אֶלָּא עַד שְׁעַת בְּדִיקָה וְגוּפָהּ טָמֵא מֵעֵת לְעֵת.

1 טהור | ג טהורה   2 ומצאת | ג ומצאתה   כתם | ג -

Rebbi Yudan asked: She checked her garment in the morning and found it pure, in the afternoon and found a stain on it. It is obvious that her garment is retroactively impure only after the time of her checking. Is her body impure for retroactive 24 hours? Does one not declare her body to be impure only because of her garment? Her garment is retroactively impure only after the time of her checking; her body should retroactively be impure for 24 hours[61]?

61   The 24 hour rule is never mentioned in connection with stains.

(49a line 16) וְהַמְשַׁמֶּשֶׁת בָּעֵדִים הֲרֵי זוֹ כַפְּקִידָה. הֵיךְ עֲבִידָא. בָּדְקָה עַצְמָהּ בְּשַׁחֲרִית וְשִׁמְשָׁה בְּעֵד בַּחֲצוֹת וְרָאֲת בְּמִנְחָה אֵין טָמֵא אֶלָּא עַד שְׁעַת תַּשְׁמִישׁ. לֵוִי אָמַר. בְּעֵד שֶׁלְּאַחַר תַּשְׁמִישׁ הִיא מַתְנִיתָא. אֲבָל בְּעֵד שֶׁלִּפְנֵי הַתַּשְׁמִישׁ הֲמוּמָה הִיא לְבֵיתָהּ וְאֵינָהּ בּוֹדֶקֶת יָפֶה. רִבִּי אָבוּן בְּשֵׁם רִבִּי זְעִירָא. בְּעֵד

שֶׁלִּפְנֵי תַשְׁמִישׁ הִיא מַתְנִיתָא. אֲבָל בְּעַד שֶׁלְּאַחַר הַתַּשְׁמִישׁ דִּיחָה הִיא מַחֲמַת שִׁכְבַת זָרַע.

3 מתניתא | ג מתניתה (all occurrences)

"And if one has intercourse with cloths, this counts as checking." How is that? If she checked herself in the morning, had intercourse with a cloth at noontime, and saw [blood] in the afternoon, she is impure only from after the time of intercourse. Levi said, the Mishnah speaks of a cloth used after intercourse, but for a cloth used before intercourse she would be impatient for her mate and not check thorougly. Rebbi Abun in the name of Rebbi Ze'ira, the Mishnah speaks of a cloth used before intercourse, but a cloth used after intercourse is faded because of semen[62].

62 The Babli, 5a, requires both checks.

(fol. 48d) **משנה ג:** כֵּיצַד דַּיָּיהּ שָׁעָתָהּ. הָיְתָה יוֹשֶׁבֶת בַּמִּטָּה וַעֲסוּקָה בְּטָהֳרוֹת פֵּירְשָׁה וְרָאֲתָה דָם הִיא טְמֵיאָה וְכוּלָּן טְהוֹרוֹת. אַף עַל פִּי שֶׁאָמְרוּ טְמֵיאָה מֵעֵת לְעֵת אֵינָהּ מוֹנָה אֶלָּא מִשָּׁעָה שֶׁרָאֲתָה. רִבִּי אֱלִיעֶזֶר אוֹמֵר אַרְבַּע נָשִׁים דַּיָּין שָׁעָתָן בְּתוּלָה וּמְעוּבֶּרֶת וּמֵינִיקָה וּזְקֵינָה אָמַר רִבִּי יְהוֹשֻׁעַ אֲנִי לֹא שָׁמַעְתִּי אֶלָּא בְתוּלָה אֲבָל הֲלָכָה כְּרִבִּי אֱלִיעֶזֶר.

Mishnah 3: How is her timing exact[63]? If she was sitting on a bed occupied with pure food, if she left [the bed] and saw blood, she is impure but all the food is pure. Even though they said, she is retroactively impure for 24 hours[64], she counts only from the moment she saw. Rebbi Eliezer says, the timings of four kinds of women are exact: a virgin[65], and a pregnant woman, and a nursing one, and a post-menopausal. Rebbi

Joshua said, I heard only about the virgin, but practice follows Rebbi Eliezer.

63 The woman with a regular period, who may prepare pure food until close to the time of her period.

64 The woman without an established period.

65 As explained in the next Mishnah, this is a young girl who never had a period, independent of any sexual activities she might have had.

(49a line 22) **הלכה ג**: אָמַר רִבִּי יְהוֹשֻׁעַ אֲנִי לֹא שָׁמַעְתִּי אֶלָּא בְתוּלָה. אֲבָל הֲלָכָה כְּרִבִּי לִיעֶזֶר. אֵין אוֹמְרִין מִי שֶׁלֹּא רָאָה אֶת הַלְּבָנָה יָבוֹא וְיָעִיד. אֶלָּא אוֹמְרִין. מִי שֶׁרָאָה אֶת הַלְּבָנָה יָבוֹא וְיָעִיד. אַתָּה לֹא שָׁמַעְתָּ אֲנִי שָׁמַעְתִּי. כָּל-יָמִים שֶׁהָיָה רִבִּי לִיעֶזֶר קַיָּים הֲיָתָה הֲלָכָה כְּרִבִּי יְהוֹשֻׁעַ. מִשֶּׁמֵּת רִבִּי לִיעֶזֶר הִנְהִיג רִבִּי יְהוֹשֻׁעַ הֲלָכָה כְּרִבִּי לִיעֶזֶר. אִם בְּשֶׁשָּׁמַע רִבִּי לִיעֶזֶר מִפִּי אֶחָד וְרִבִּי יְהוֹשֻׁעַ מִפִּי שְׁנַיִם בֵּין בַּחַיִּים בֵּין לְאַחַר מִיתָה תְּהֵא הֲלָכָה כְּרִבִּי יְהוֹשֻׁעַ. וְאִם בְּשֶׁשָּׁמַע רִבִּי יְהוֹשֻׁעַ מִפִּי אֶחָד וְרִבִּי לִיעֶזֶר מִפִּי שְׁנַיִם בֵּין בַּחַיִּים בֵּין לְאַחַר מִיתָה תְּהֵא הֲלָכָה כְּרִבִּי לִיעֶזֶר. כְּהָדָא דְתַנֵּי. אֶחָד אוֹמֵר. שָׁמַעְתִּי מִפִּי שְׁנַיִם. וּשְׁנַיִם אוֹמְרִין. שָׁמַעֲנוּ מִפִּי אֶחָד. יִיפֶּה כֹחַ הָאֶחָד שֶׁשָּׁמַע מִפִּי שְׁנַיִם מִכֹּחַ הַשְּׁנַיִם שֶׁשָּׁמְעוּ מִפִּי אֶחָד. אֶלָּא כֵן אֲנָן קַיָּימִין. בְּשָׁוִין. זֶה שָׁמַע מִפִּי אֶחָד וְזֶה שָׁמַע מִפִּי אֶחָד. זֶה שָׁמַע מִפִּי שְׁנַיִם וְזֶה שָׁמַע מִפִּי שְׁנַיִם. בְּחַיָּיו לֹא רָאָה דַעְתּוֹ. לְאַחַר מִיתָתוֹ רָאָה דַעְתּוֹ. מַה חַמִּית מֵימַר. בְּשֶׁרָאָה דַעְתּוֹ. כְּהָדָא דְתַנֵּי. אַרְבַּע נָשִׁים שֶׁאָמְרוּ חֲכָמִים. דַּיָּין שְׁעָתָן. כִּתְמָן טָמֵא לְמַפְרֵעַ חוּץ מִתִּינוֹקֶת שֶׁלֹּא הִגִּיעַ זְמַנָּהּ לִרְאוֹת מִפְּנֵי שֶׁאֵין לָהּ כְּתָמִין. דִּבְרֵי רִבִּי מֵאִיר. וַחֲכָמִים אוֹמְרִים. אַרְבַּע נָשִׁים שֶׁאָמְרוּ חֲכָמִים. דַּיָּין שְׁעָתָן. כִּתְמָן טָמֵא לְמַפְרֵעַ. אֲבָל תִּינוֹקֶת שֶׁהִגִּיעַ זְמַנָּהּ לִרְאוֹת כְּתָמָהּ כִּרְאִייָתָהּ. מַה רְאִייָתָהּ דַּיָּיהּ שְׁעָתָהּ אַף כִּתְמָהּ דַּיָּיהּ שְׁעָתָהּ. אָמַר רִבִּי יַנַּאי. מִפְּנֵי שֶׁשִּׁירְפָּהּ מָצוּי. וּמָה שֶׁזֶּה שֶׁסִּירְפָּהּ מָצוּי אַתְּ אָמַר. דַּיָּיהּ שְׁעָתָהּ. אִילּוּ שֶׁאֵין שִׁירְפָּן מָצוּי לֹא כָּל-שֶׁכֵּן. מִיכָּן שֶׁרָאָה דַעְתּוֹ.

3 שמעת | ג שמעתה   שמעתי | ג הוא ששמעתי   4 היתה | ג הייתה   5 הלכה | ג
שתהא הלכה   נן | ג אנן   6 מפי שנים | ג שמע מפי שנים   7 בששמע | ג כששמע
9 ייפה | ג יפה   10-11 שמע | ג ששמע (4 times)   12 חמית | ג חמת   13 כהדא | ג
כהדה   נשים | ג נשין   טמא | ג מטמא (2 times)   14 זמנה | ג זמנן   כתמין | ג כתם
15 וחכמים אומרים ארבע נשים שאמרו חכמים | ג ארבעה נשים אמרו חכמים   16
שהגיע | ג שלא הגיע   17 ינאי | ג ינייי   שירפה | ג סופה   18 סירפה | ג סופה   את
אמר | ג אתמר   שירפן | ג סופן

"Rebbi Joshua said, I heard only about the virgin, but practice follows Rebbi Eliezer." One does not say, somebody who did not see the new moon should come and testify[66], but one says, if somebody saw the new moon, he should come and testify[67]. You did not hear, I heard. All during Rebbi Eliezer's lifetime, practice followed Rebbi Joshua[68]. After Rebbi Eliezer's death, Rebbi Joshua introduced practice following Rebbi Eliezer. Where do we hold? If Rebbi Eliezer heard from one [authority] but Rebbi Joshua from two, practice should follow Rebbi Joshua whether [Rebbi Eliezer] was alive or dead. But if Rebbi Joshua heard from one [authority] but Rebbi Eliezer from two, practice should follow Rebbi Eliezer whether he was alive or dead. As it was stated: One says, I heard from two [authorities] and two say, we heard from one, the power of the one who heard from two is greater than that of two who heard from one[69]. But we must hold either that either one heard from one or that either one heard from two. During his[70] lifetime he[71] was not convinced of his opinion, after he[70] died he[71] became convinced of his[70] opinion. What did he[71] see to say that he[71] became convinced of his[70] opinion? As it was stated: The stains of all four categories of women, about whom the Sages said that their timings are exact, cause retroactive impurity except for a girl who is too young to menstruate, for that one has no stains[72], the words of Rebbi Meïr. But the Sages say, for all four categories of women about whom the Sages said that their timings are exact, their stains cause retroactive impurity except for a girl about to start to menstruate[73], for her stains start with her menstruation. Since if she sees blood her timing is exact, so also for her stain her timing. Rebbi Yannai said, because her sap[74] is frequent. If the timing of one whose sap is frequent is exact, the others whose sap is not so frequent so much more! By this reason he[71] became convinced of his[70] opinion.

66   To testify that he saw the new moon, to proclaim a new month.

67   In the language of the Mishnah (*Idiut* 2:2): "'We did not see' is no proof;" neither is 'we did not hear'.

68   Since R. Eliezer did not accept majority votes in religious practice, he was put in the ban and R. Joshua was the undisputed authority. After R. Eliezer's death, practice could follow his opinion without creating the danger of a schism.

69   The translation follows the Geniza text which reads יָפֶה כֹּחַ "the power is greater" rather than the Leiden ms. יִיפֶּה כֹּחַ "(an unknown subject) empowered". The principle is mentioned in Mishnah *Idiut* 5:7.

70   R. Eliezer.

71   R. Joshua.

72   The rules of stains do not apply to her. The Babli has a different version, 5a, and defines the onset of menstruation as the earlier of either the growth of two pubic hairs or 12 years of age.

73   The reading of the Leiden ms. seems superior to Geniza ms., "too young to menstruate".

74   שְׂרָף is tree sap. It is an appropriate image for body fluids before the discovery of the circulation of blood. There would have been reason to make the impurity of the girl in puberty retroactive. Since R. Joshua agrees that in her case there is no retroactivity, there is no reason to extend retroactivity to the other three cases.

HALAKHAH 4

משנה ד: אֵי זוֹ הִיא בְתוּלָה. כָּל שֶׁלֹּא רָאֲתָה דָם מִיָּמֶיהָ אַף עַל פִּי(fol. 48d) נְשׂוּאָה. מְעוּבֶּרֶת מִשֶּׁיִּוָּדַע עוּבָּרָהּ. מֵינִיקָה עַד שֶׁתִּגְמוֹל אֶת בְּנָהּ. נָתְנָה בְנָהּ לְמֵינִיקָה וּגְמָלַתּוּ אוֹ שֶׁמֵּת רִבִּי מֵאִיר אוֹמֵר מְטַמְּאָה מֵעֵת לְעֵת. וַחֲכָמִים אוֹמְרִים דַּיָּהּ שָׁעֲתָהּ.

Mishnah 4: What is a virgin? Any female who never saw blood, even if she was married. Pregnant, once the fetus is recognizable. Nursing, until she weans her child[75]. If she gave her child to a wet-nurse or weaned him, Rebbi Meïr says she causes retroactive impurity for 24 hours but the Sages say, her timing is exact[76].

75 24 months after birth, cf. *Soṭah* 4:4, Note 57.   76 The entire 24 months.

(49a line 42) **הלכה ד**: אֵי זוֹ הִיא בְתוּלָה. כָּל כו'. כֵּן הִיא מַתְנִיתָא. כָּל־שֶׁלֹּא רָאֲתָה דַם נִידָּה מִיָּמֶיהָ וְאַף עַל פִּי נְשׂוּאָה. בְּתוּלָה לְדָמִים אָמְרוּ. אֲבָל לֹא בְתוּלָה לִבְתוּלִים. פְּעָמִים שֶׁהִיא בְתוּלָה לְדָמִים וְאֵינָהּ בְתוּלָה לִבְתוּלִים. פְּעָמִים שֶׁהִיא בְתוּלָה לִבְתוּלִים וְאֵינָהּ בְתוּלָה לְדָמִים. בְּתוּלָה לְדָמִים בְּשֶׁרָאֲתָה וְאַחַר כָּךְ נִישֵּׂאת. בְּתוּלָה לִבְתוּלִים בְּשֶׁנִּישֵּׂאת וְאַחַר כָּךְ רָאֲתָה.

1 כן היא | ג כיני   מתניתא | ג מתניתה   2 נידה | ג נדה   נשואה | ג נשו   בתולה | ג אם בתולה   לדמים | ג לדמין   (all occurrences)   3 בתולים | ג בתולין   (all occurrences)

Halakhah 4: "What is a virgin? Any one," etc. So is the Mishnah: Any one who never did menstruate; they spoke of one virginal for blood, not one virginal for sexual relations. Sometimes she is virginal for blood and not virginal for sexual relations, sometimes she is virginal for sexual relations and not virginal for blood. She is virginal for blood if she started to menstruate before marrying; she is virginal for sexual relations if she married before menstruating.

(49a line 47) תַּנֵּי. שָׁלֹשׁ בְּתוּלוֹת הֵן. בְּתוּלַת אָדָם בְּתוּלַת שִׁקְמָה וּבְתוּלַת הָאָרֶץ. בְּתוּלַת אָדָם כָּל־שֶׁלֹּא נִבְעֲלָה מִיָּמֶיהָ. בְּתוּלַת שִׁקְמָה כָּל־שֶׁלֹּא נִקְצְצָה מִיָּמֶיהָ. בְּתוּלַת הָאָרֶץ כָּל־שֶׁלֹּא נֶחֱרַץ בָּהּ מִיָּמֶיהָ. רַבָּן שִׁמְעוֹן בֶּן גַּמְלִיאֵל אוֹמֵר. כָּל־שֶׁאֵין בָּהּ חֶרֶץ.

It was stated[77]: "There are three virgins: a human virgin, a virgin sycamore, and virgin soil. A human virgin, who never had intercourse. A virgin sycamore, which never was cut[78]. Virgin soil, which never was ploughed[79]; Rabban Simeon ben Gamliel says, which has no groove[80,81]."

77 Midrash *Samuel* 26:2; Tosephta *Ševi'it* 3:10, in a different order which is followed also in Babli *Niddah* 8b. This *baraita* somehow negates the Mishnah which transfers to name of "virgin" to the pre-menstrual girl.

78 Sycamores were planted not for their fruits but to produce logs for buildings. The sycamore can be cut and from the stump a new (and larger) tree will grow; cf. *Ševi'it* 4:5, Note 71.

79 Really: on which never any grooves had been made, referring to the furrows.

80 If no signs of agricultural activity are visible on the soil. In Babylonia the צ of חָרֵץ (which in Babylonian and modern Hebrew would be חָרִיץ) was heard as ס, resulting in חֶרֶס, חֶרֶשׂ "potsherd". Therefore, the Babylonian texts (and Midrash *Samuel*) declare as virgin any soil on which no potsherds are found (which would prove human activity at the place).

81 Here ends the first Geniza fragment of this Tractate.

(49a line 51) וַאֲפִילוּ נִישֵׂאת וַאֲפִילוּ עִיבְּרָה וַאֲפִילוּ מֵינִיקָה וַאֲפִילוּ שׁוֹפַעַת כָּל־שִׁבְעָה לְזָכָר וְכָל־אַרְבָּעָה עָשָׂר לִנְקֵיבָה. וּקְסָמָא בְיָדֶיהָ. בְּשָׁעָה שֶׁהוּא זָכָר שִׁבְעָה. וּבְשָׁעָה שֶׁהִיא נְקֵיבָה יוּ״ד. וְהִיא שֶׁהִפְסִיקָה דָם טוֹהַר. כְּהָדָא דְתַנֵּי. הִפְסִיקָה דָם טוֹהַר וְלֹא רָאֲתָה כָּךְ וְאַחַר כָּךְ רָאֲתָה. וּבָא מַעֲשֶׂה לִפְנֵי חֲכָמִים וְאָמְרוּ. דַּיָּיהּ שָׁעֲתָהּ. עַל דַּעְתֵּיהּ דְּרַב דְּהוּא אָמַר. מַעְיָין אֶחָד הוּא אֶלָּא שֶׁהַתּוֹרָה טִיהֲרָה אוֹתוֹ. נִיחָא. עַל דַּעְתֵּיהּ דְּרִבִּי יַנַּאי דּוּ אָמַר. מַעְיָין אֶחָד הוּא אֶלָּא

שֶׁהוּא מְשַׁתֶּנֶה. יָאוּת. עַל דַּעְתֵּיהּ דְּלֵוִי דְהוּא אָמַר. שְׁנֵי מַעְיָינוֹת הֵן. אֲפִילוּ לֹא הִפְסִיקָה דַם טוֹהַר תְּהֵא דַיָּיהּ שָׁעָתָהּ. אָמַר רִבִּי מָנָא. טַעֲמֵיהּ דְּלֵוִי. שֶׁמִּתּוֹךְ שֶׁהִיא מִתְרַגֶּלֶת בְּדָמִים טְהוֹרִין הִיא מִתְרַגֶּלֶת בְּדָמִים טְמֵאִין. אָמַר רִבִּי יוֹסֵי בֵּירִבִּי בּוּן. יָכִיל לֵוִי פָּתַר לָהּ מִן הָדָא דְתַנֵּינָן. רִבִּי יוֹסֵי אוֹמֵר. מְעוּבֶּרֶת וּמֵינִיקָה שֶׁעָבְרוּ עֲלֵיהֶן שָׁל'שׁ עוֹנוֹת דַּיָּין שָׁעָתָן. וְתַנֵּי עֲלָהּ. יְמֵי עִיבּוּרָהּ וִימֵי מֵינִיקוּתָהּ מִצְטָרְפִין לְשָׁל'שׁ עוֹנוֹת. דְּהוּא סָבַר. מַעְיָין אֶחָד הוּא.

"Even if she was married,[82]" even if pregnant, even if nursing, and even if she was bleeding all seven [days] for a boy or all fourteen for a girl[83]. Does she have a charm in her hand[84]? After [the birth of] a boy seven [days], after a girl fourteen, but only if she stopped during her period of purity. As it was stated: If she stopped during her period of purity and had no discharge, but later she had a discharge; this case came before the Sages who said that her timing was exact[85]. In Rav's opinion, who says that all is one source but the Torah purified it, it is understandable[86]. In Rebbi Yannai's opinion, who says that all is one source but it changes, it is in order[87]. In Levi's opinion, who says that there are two sources, should not her timing be exact even if she does not stop during her period of purity[88]? Rebbi Mana said, the reason of Levi is that since she became used to pure blood, she might become used to impure blood[89]. Rebbi Yose ben Rebbi Abun said, Levi can explain what we have stated[90]: "Rebbi Yose said, the timing of a pregnant or a nursing woman who had stopped for three periods is exact." On that it was stated[91]: The days of her pregnancy and her nursing add up to three periods. Can he think that there is only one source?

82 This refers to the Mishnah which enumerates the women whose impurity is not retroactive, in particular the girl having a baby

without ever having menstruated.

83   Lev. 15:25 creates a special category, *zavah*, for a woman whose discharge of blood is prolonged "many days after her menstrual period", who is subject to more complicated rules of cleansing. Since "days" must mean a minimum of two days, "many days" must mean at least three days (by the hermeneutic principle of definiteness, cf. H. Guggenheimer, Logical Problems in Jewish Tradition, in: *Confrontations with Judaism*, Ph. Longworth, ed., Blond, London 1966, pp. 174-175). Now it is stated here that bleeding after childbirth cannot induce a status of *zavah* since (1) the time span of 7 days after the birth of a boy and 14 after that of a girl are defined as "menstrual impurity" and (2) this is followed by a *period of purity* of 33 days (for a boy) or 66 (for a girl) in which no discharge has any implication for impurity (*Lev.* 12:4-5). Therefore, the only way a birth is followed by a status of *zavah* would be if the bloody discharges persist all through the period of purity.

84   This is a little pedantic about the formulation of the text, from which one might infer that the pregnancy already determines the length of the period of impurity. The text is then elaborated to indicate that this period is determined only at the time of delivery.

85   The status of the "blood virgin" is not changed by pregnancy and all the bleeding necessarily connected with giving birth.

86   Here starts the discussion of the condition that the discharges stop sometime during the period of purity. Rav holds that the blood lost during childbirth and the menstrual blood are of equal character; the period of purity is a biblical decree whose reason is unknown but a continuation of the discharge beyond this period shows that menstrual blood is flowing for "many days". (Everybody agrees that prolonged flow before the actual delivery creates a status of *zavah*.) Therefore, a retention of the status of "blood virgin" necessitates the cessation of discharge during the period of purity (or even earlier). Rav's opinion is detailed in the Babli, 11a, 35b.

87   This opinion is not reported in the Babli. The only difference to Rav's opinion is theoretical, that the biblical decree of the period of purity has a biological explanation.

88   His opinion is also discussed in the Babli, 11a and 35b. He holds that the blood lost in childbirth is different in nature from menstrual blood. Then

it is difficult to see why menstrual virginity should depend on a cessation of childbirth discharges during the period of purity.

89 Levi also subscribes to the cessation rule, but only as one of purely rabbinic character. Since she is used to discharges, she does not react to a menstrual discharge with the speed necessary to avoid retroactive contamination.

90 Mishnah 1:5.

91 Tosephta 1:10: "R. Yose and R. Simeon say that the timing of a pregnant or a nursing woman is not exact unless there passed three periods (without menstruation); the days of her pregnancy and those of her nursing are added together." It is clear that pregnancy and nursing cannot be counted together if the blood lost in childbirth is of menstrual character. Therefore, the Tosephta and the similar *baraita* quoted in the text are intelligible for Levi, not for Rav.

(49a line 63) עַד כַּמָּה הוּא הַכָּרַת הָעוּבָּר. סוּמְכוֹס אָמַר מִשּׁוּם רִבִּי מֵאִיר. עַד שְׁלֹשָׁה חֳדָשִׁים וגו'. אַף עַל פִּי שֶׁאֵין רְאָיָיה לַדָּבָר זֵיכֶר לַדָּבָר שֶׁנֶּאֱמַר וַיְהִי כְּמִשְׁלֹשׁ חֳדָשִׁים. אָמַר רִבִּי יוּדָן. אֲפִילוּ מְעוּבֶּרֶת רוּחַ. הָרִינוּ חַלְנוּ כְּמוֹ יָלַדְנוּ רוּחַ. תַּהֲרוּ חֲשַׁשׁ תֵּלְדוּ קַשׁ וגו'. רִבִּי זְעִירָא רִבִּי בָּא בַּר זוּטְרָא רִבִּי חֲנִינָה בְּשֵׁם רִבִּי חִייָה רוּבָּה. אֲפִילוּ רוּבּוֹ שֶׁלָּרִאשׁוֹן וְרוּבּוֹ שֶׁלָּאַחֲרוֹן וְהָאֶמְצָעִי שָׁלֵם. אַסִּי אָמַר. תִּשְׁעִים יוֹם שְׁלֵמִין. וּשְׁמוּאֵל אָמַר. הֵן וְעִיבּוּרֵיהֶן. אָתָא עוֹבְדָא קוֹמֵי רַבָּנָן דְּתַמָּן וְלָא יָדְעִין אִם שְׁלֹשָׁה עָשָׂר מִן הָרִאשׁוֹן וְשִׁבְעָא עָשָׂר מִן הָאַחֲרוֹן. אוֹ שִׁבְעָא עָשָׂר מִן הָרִאשׁוֹן וּשְׁלֹשָׁה עָשָׂר מִן הָאַחֲרוֹן וַחֲמִשָּׁה שְׁלֵמִין בָּאֶמְצַע. וּבִקְשׁוּ לִיגַּע בַּוְּלָד מִשּׁוּם סָפֵק מַמְזֵירוּת. אָמַר לוֹן רַב נַחְמָן בַּר יַעֲקֹב. כְּהָדֵין עוֹבְדָא אָתָא קוֹמֵי אַבָּה בַּר בָּא וְאַכְשֵׁר. וְאַבָּא בַּר בָּא פַּלִּיג עַל שְׁמוּאֵל בְּרֵיהּ. אָמַר רִבִּי בָּא. שַׁנְייָא הִיא הַכָּרַת הָעוּבָּר שַׁנְייָא הִיא לֵידָתוֹ. הַכָּרַת הָעוּבָּר לַחֳדָשִׁים שְׁלֵמִין וְלֵידָתוֹ לֶחֳדָשִׁים מְקוּטָעִין. תַּמָּן תַּנֵּינָן. כַּמָּה הִיא קִשּׁוּיָיהּ. רִבִּי מֵאִיר אוֹמֵר. אֲפִילוּ אַרְבָּעִים וַחֲמִשִּׁים יוֹם. רִבִּי יְהוּדָה אוֹמֵר. דַּיָּיהּ חוֹדְשָׁהּ. רִבִּי יוֹסֵי וְרִבִּי שִׁמְעוֹן אוֹמְרִים. אֵין קִישּׁוּי יוֹתֵר מִשְׁתֵּי שַׁבָּתוֹת. רִבִּי יוֹסֵי בְּשֵׁם רִבִּי בָּא. זֹאת אוֹמֶרֶת שֶׁהָאִשָּׁה יוֹלֶדֶת לַחֳדָשִׁים

מְקוּטָעִין. דְּלֹא כֵן נִיתְנֵי שְׁלֹשִׁים יוֹם. רִבִּי יוֹסֵי בֵּירְבִּי בּוּן בְּשֵׁם שְׁמוּאֵל זֹאת אוֹמֶרֶת שֶׁהָאִשָּׁה יוֹלֶדֶת לַחֲדָשִׁים שְׁלֵימִין. דְּתַנִינָן דַּיָּיהּ חָדְשָׁהּ.

1 כמה הוא | יכמה   3 אמר | יאומר   4 וגו' | י -   רבי חנינה | יאמר רבי חנינה
6 אסי | ירבי אסי   ועיבוריהן | יעיבוריהן   10 כהדין | יבההין   ואבא בר בא | י
אבא בר ווא   11 ר' בא | י רבא   13 קישוייה | יקישויה   וחמשים | יחמשים
יהודה | ייודה   14 יוסי | יוסה   15 בא | יווא   16 יוסי | יוסה   שמואל | י
רבי ווא

[92]How long is it until a pregnancy is recognized? Symmachos said in the name of Rebbi Meïr: After three months. Even though it is no proof, there is a hint: "It was after about three months, etc." Rebbi Yudan said, even for a phantom pregnancy, "we were pregnant, we were sick, as if we gave birth to wind," "get pregnant with dry grass, give birth to straw", etc. Rebbi Ze'ira, Rebbi Abba bar Zuṭra said, Rebbi Ḥanina in the name of the Great Rebbi Ḥiyya: Even most of the first, most of the last, and the middle one complete. Assi said, a full 90 days. Samuel said, they in their fulness. A case came before the rabbis there; we do not know if thirteen of the first and seventeen of the last or seventeen of the first and thirteen of the last, and five complete ones in the middle; they wanted to touch the child because of a doubt of bastardy. Rav Naḥman bar Jacob told them, such a case came before Abba bar Abba and he declared it acceptable. Does Abba bar Abba disagree with his son Samuel? Rebbi Abba said, there is a difference between recognizing a pregnancy and giving birth. A pregnancy is recognized after full months, a birth can happen after fractional months. There, we have stated: "How long can labor be? Rebbi Meïr said, even 40 to 50 days. Rebbi Jehudah said, her month is sufficient. Rebbi Yose and Rebbi Simeon say, no labor lasts longer than two weeks." Rebbi Yose in the name of Rebbi Abba: This implies that a

woman gives birth after fractional months. Since otherwise one should have stated "thirty days". Rebbi Yose ben Rebbi Abun in the name of Samuel: This implies that a woman gives birth after full months. Since we have stated: "Her month is sufficient."

92 From here to the end of the Halakhah, the text parallels *Yebamot* 4:11, Notes 130-155.

(49b line 7) רִבִּי יוּדָן בָּעֵי. סוֹף דָּבָר עַד שֶׁתֵּלֵד. לֹא אֲפִילוּ הִפִּילָה.

Rebbi Yudan asked: Does this hold until she gives birth? No, even if she had a miscarriage.

(49b line 8) אָמַר רִבִּי מָנָא. שְׁמָעִית בְּשֵׁם שְׁמוּאֵל. הִיא הַכָּרַת הָעוּבָּר הִיא לֵידָתוֹ. וְלֵית אֲנָא יְדַע מִן מַה שְׁמָעֵת. אָמַר רִבִּי בָּא בַּר כֹּהֵן קוֹמֵי רִבִּי יוֹסֵי. רִבִּי יִרְמְיָה אֲמָרָהּ. אָמַר לֵיהּ רִבִּי חִזְקִיָּה. לֹא אֲמָרָהּ רִבִּי יִרְמְיָה. וְאִיקְפִּיד רִבִּי יוֹסֵי לְקִיבְלֵיהּ. אָמַר. אִילוּ יְהוֹשֻׁעַ שֶׁהָיָה קָשׁוּר לְמֹשֶׁה לֹא הֲוָה אָמַר כֵּן וְהוּא אָמַר כֵּן. חָזַר וְאָמַר. אִין. אֲמָרָהּ. אֶלָּא כְּאִינֵּשׁ דְּשָׁמַע מִילָּה וּמַקְשֵׁי עֲלָהּ. וְאַבָּא בַּר בָּא פַּלִיג עַל שְׁמוּאֵל בְּרֵיהּ. רִבִּי בְּרֶכְיָה בְשֵׁם שְׁמוּאֵל. לְעוֹלָם אֵין הָאִשָּׁה יוֹלֶדֶת אוֹ לְמָאתַיִם וְשִׁבְעִים וְאֶחָד אוֹ לְמָאתַיִם וְשִׁבְעִים וּשְׁנַיִם אוֹ לְמָאתַיִם וְשִׁבְעִים וּשְׁלֹשָׁה אוֹ לְמָאתַיִם וְשִׁבְעִים וְאַרְבָּעָה. אָמַר לֵיהּ רִבִּי מָנָא. מְנָן שָׁמַע רִבִּי הָדָא מִילְּתָא. אָמַר לֵיהּ. מִן רִבִּי בָּא. מְחִלְפָא שִׁיטָתֵיהּ דְּרִבִּי בָּא. תַּמָּן הוּא אָמַר. שַׁנְיָיא הִיא הַכָּרַת הָעוּבָּר שַׁנְיָיא הִיא לֵידָתוֹ. וְהָכָא הוּא אָמַר הָכֵין. רִבִּי אַבָּא בַּר זוּטְרָא מִשְּׁמוּאֵל. כָּל־שֶׁהוּא בְהַרְבָּה הֲרֵי הוּא בְאַרְבַּע.

4 אמר | י אמר ליה   אילו | י שכן אפילו   5 והוא אמר | י ואת אומרה   אמרה | י דאמרה   6 עלה | י עליה   בא | י ווא   10 הוא אמר | י אמר   12 ארבע | י ארבה
(the text here is corrupt)

Rebbi Mana said, I heard in the name of Samuel that there is no difference between recognizing a pregnancy and giving birth, but I do not remember from whom I heard this. Rebbi Abba bar Cohen said before Rebbi Yose, Rebbi Jeremiah said this. Rebbi Ḥizqyah said to him, Rebbi Jeremiah did not say this; Rebbi Yose was offended by him. He said to him: Even Joshua who was bound to Moses would not have said so, but you said so! He checked himself and said, it is true that he said that but as a person who quotes something and questions it; does Abba bar Abba disagree with his son Samuel? Rebbi Berekhiah in the name of Samuel: A woman gives birth only either after 271, 272, 273, or 274 days. Rebbi Mana said to him, from whom did the rabbi hear this? He said to him, from Rebbi Abba. The position of Rebbi Abba seems inverted. There, he says, there is a difference between recognizing a pregnancy and giving birth, and here, he says so? Rebbi Abba bar Zuṭra in the name of Samuel: Everything which is "many" is 273.

(49b line 19) רַב חִייָה בַּר אַשִׁי הֲוָה יָתִיב קוֹמֵי דְרַב. חֲמִיתֵיהּ מִיבָעֵת. אָמַר לֵיהּ. מַהוּ כֵן. אָמַר לֵיהּ. חֲמָרְתִּי מְעַבְּרָה וְהִיא בְּעָיָיא מֵילַד וַאֲנָא בָּעֵי מִרְבַּעְתָּהּ דְּלָא תִצְטַגֵּן. אָמַר לֵיהּ. אֵימָתַי עָלָה עָלֶיהָ הַזָּכָר. אָמַר לֵיהּ. בְּיוֹם פְּלָן. וְחָשַׁב אָמַר לֵיהּ. בְּעָיָיא הִיא עַד כְּדוֹן. וְתַגֵּי כֵן. הַפּוֹחֶתֶת אֵינָהּ פּוֹחֶתֶת מִימוֹת הַלְּבָנָה. וְהַמּוֹסֶפֶת אֵינָהּ מוֹסֶפֶת עַל יְמוֹת הַחַמָּה. מִילְּתֵיהּ דְּרַבִּי יְהוֹשֻׁעַ פְּלִיגָא דָּמַר רִבִּי יְהוֹשֻׁעַ בֶּן לֵוִי. בָּקוֹרֶת שֶׁלְּאַנְטוֹנִינוֹס הָיְתָה עוֹבֶרֶת וְהִרְבִּיעוּ שֶׁלְּבֵית רִבִּי מִמֶּנָּה שְׁזוּרִין. וְיֵשׁ מֵהֶן שֶׁיָּלְדוּ עַכְשָׁיו. וְיֵשׁ מֵהֶן שֶׁיָּלְדוּ לְאַחַר זְמָן. כָּאן בִּבְהֶמָה טְמֵיאָה כָּאן בִּבְהֵמָה טְהוֹרָה. וְהָכְתִיב הֲיָדַעְתָּ עֵת לֶדֶת יַעֲלֵי סָלַע חוֹלֵל אַיָּלוֹת תִּשְׁמוֹר. תִּסְפּוֹר יְרָחִים תְּמַלֶּאנָה וְיָדַעְתָּ עֵת לִדְתָּנָה. אָמַר לֵיהּ. חַיָּה טְהוֹרָה כִּבְהֵמָה טְמֵאָה.

1 מיבעת | י מבעית   2 בעייא | י בעיה   3 דלא | י עד דלא   תצטנן | י תצנן   4
בעייא | י בעיה   הפוחתת | י חמרתא הפוחתת   6 - | י בן לוי   דמר | י דאמר
שלאנטונינוס | י שלמלכות   היתה עוברת | י עיברה   7 והרביעו | י והרביעי   שזורין)
(a corruption | י שוורים   8 טמיאה | י טהורה | י טהורה | י טמיאה   9 חולל
איילות תשמור | י -   תספר | י תספור   10 אמר ליה | י הידעת עת לדת

Rav Ḥiyya bar Ashi was sitting before Rav who saw him disturbed. He said to him, what is the matter? He said to him, my female donkey is pregnant and will give birth; then I have to get her to copulate before she is out of heat. He said to him, when did the male mount her? He said, on day X. He calculated and said, she still has some time until then. It was stated so: A quick one does not need less than the days of the moon and one who is late is not later than the days of the sun. The words of Rebbi Joshua disagree, since Rebbi Joshua ben Levi said, the cattle herd of Antoninus passed by and those of the house of Rebbi took bulls from them to copulate. Some cows gave birth soon and some of them later. Here it is about an impure animal, there about a pure animal. But is it not written, "do you know the time the mountain goats will give birth, watch the birthing of gazelles," "count months, make them complete, you will know the time of their giving birth." He told him: A pure wild animal is like a domestic impure animal.

(fol. 48d) **משנה ה:** אֵי זוֹ הִיא זְקֵינָה. כָּל־שֶׁעָבְרוּ עָלֶיהָ שָׁלֹשׁ עוֹנוֹת סָמוּךְ לְזִקְנָתָהּ. רִבִּי לְעָזָר אוֹמֵר כָּל־אִשָּׁה שֶׁעָבְרוּ עָלֶיהָ שָׁלֹשׁ עוֹנוֹת דַּיָּיהּ שָׁעָתָהּ. רִבִּי יוֹסֵי אוֹמֵר. מְעוּבֶּרֶת וּמֵינִיקָה שֶׁעָבְרוּ עֲלֵיהֶן שָׁלֹשׁ עוֹנוֹת דַּיָּין שָׁעָתָן.

Mishnah 5: What is an old woman? Any who missed three periods when she became old. Rebbi Eliezer says, the timing of *any* woman who misses three periods is exact. Rebbi Yose said, the timing of a pregnant or a nursing woman who had stopped for three periods is exact.

הלכה ה: אֵי זוֹ הִיא זְקֵינָה כול׳. רִבִּי מֵאִיר אוֹמֵר. מַחֲמַת (fol. 49b line 28) הֶחָלָב הַדָּמִים מִסְתַּלְּקִין. רִבִּי יוֹסֵי אוֹמֵר. מַחֲמַת הַצַּעַר הַדָּמִים מִסְתַּלְּקִין. אַשְׁכָּחַת אָמַר קוּלָּת וְחוּמְרַת עַל דְּרִבִּי מֵאִיר קַלַּת וְחוּמְרַת עַל דְּרִבִּי יוֹסֵי. קוּלַּת עַל דְּרִבִּי מֵאִיר. שֶׁאִם הָיָה מוֹשֵׁךְ וְיוֹנֵק אַרְבַּע אוֹ חָמֵשׁ שָׁנִים דַּיָּיהּ שָׁעָתָהּ. וְחוּמְרַת. שֶׁאִם נָתְנָה בְנָהּ לְמֵינִיקָה וּגְמָלַתּוּ וָמֵת מִטַּמָּא מֵעֵת לְעֵת. וְקוּלַּת עַל רִבִּי יוֹסֵי. שֶׁאִם נָתְנָה בְנָהּ לְמֵינִיקָה וּגְמָלַתּוּ וָמֵת דַּיָּיהּ שָׁעָתָהּ. וְחוּמְרַת. שֶׁאִם הָיָה מוֹשֵׁךְ וְיוֹנֵק אַרְבַּע אוֹ חָמֵשׁ שָׁנִים אָסוּר עַד כֹּד חוֹדֶשׁ. וְהָא רִבִּי מֵאִיר אָמַר. מְטַמָּא מֵעֵת לְעֵת. מָה. מִיַּד אוֹ לִכְשֶׁיִּפְסוֹק הַתִּינוֹק וְאֵינוּ יָכוֹל לַחֲזוֹר. נִישְׁמְעִינָהּ מִן הָדָא. יוֹנֵק הוּא הַתִּינוֹק וְהוֹלֵךְ עַד כֹּד חֹדֶשׁ שְׁלֵימִין. מִיכָּן וְהֵילָךְ כְּיוֹנֵק שֶׁקֶץ. דִּבְרֵי רִבִּי אֱלִיעֶזֶר. רִבִּי יְהוֹשֻׁעַ אוֹמֵר. יוֹנֵק הוּא הַתִּינוֹק וְהוֹלֵךְ עַד אַרְבַּע אוֹ חָמֵשׁ שָׁנִים וּמוּתָּר. פֵּירַשׁ אֵין מַחֲזִירִין אוֹתוֹ. עַד אֵיכָן. רִבִּי יַעֲקֹב בַּר אָחָא רִבִּי חִייָה בְשֵׁם רִבִּי יוֹחָנָן. עַד מֵעֵת לְעֵת. רִבִּי חִזְקִיָּה רִבִּי אַבָּהוּ בְשֵׁם רִבִּי שִׁמְעוֹן בֶּן לָקִישׁ. עַד שְׁלֹשָׁה יָמִים מֵעֵת לְעֵת. בַּמֶּה דְבָרִים אֲמוּרִים. בִּזְמַן שֶׁפֵּירַשׁ מִתּוֹךְ בּוּרְיָיו. אֲבָל אִם פֵּירַשׁ מִתּוֹךְ חוּלְיָיו מַחֲזִירִין אוֹתוֹ מִיָּד. וּבְתִינוֹק שֶׁאֵינוֹ שֶׁל סַכָּנָה. אֲבָל בְּתִינוֹק שֶׁהוּא שֶׁל סַכָּנָה אֲפִילוּ לְאַחַר כַּמָּה מַחֲזִירִין אוֹתוֹ מִיָּד.

9 הוא | כ - חדש שלימין | כ חדשים   10 רבי | כ ורבי   11 ומותר | כ -   12 ר' חייה בשם ר' יוחנן | כ ר' ירמיה בשם רב   13 ר' שמעון בן לקיש | כ ר' יהושע בן לוי   14 ברייו | כ בוריו   15 ובתינוק שאינו | כ ובשאינו   של סכנה | כ שלסכנה (2 times) בתינוק שהוא | כ אם היה   16 כמה | כ כמה ימים

Halakhah 5: "What is an old woman," etc. Rebbi Meïr says, the blood disappears because of the milk[93]. Rebbi Yose says, the blood disappears because of the pain[94]. You find a leniency and a stringency following Rebbi Meïr, and a leniency and a stringency following Rebbi Yose. A leniency following Rebbi Meïr, for if the baby was continuing to suckle for four ot five years, her timing continues exact[95]. And a stringency, if she handed her child to a wet-nurse or it died, she [makes impure] for 24 hours. A leniency for Rebbi Yose, for if she handed her child to a wet-nurse or it died, her timing is exact[96]. And a stringency, for if the baby was continuing to suckle for four ot five years, it is forbidden after 24 months[97]. But did not Rebbi Meïr say, she makes impure for 24 hours? When[98]? Immediately or if the baby stops and cannot start again? Let us hear from the following[99]: "A baby can nurse until 24 complete months, after that it is as if an abomination suckled, the words of Rebbi Eliezer. Rebbi Joshua said, a baby can nurse even four or five years; this is permitted. If he stopped, one cannot return him." How long? Rebbi Jacob bar Aha, Rebbi Hiyya in the name of Rebbi Johanan: up to 24 hours. Rebbi Hizqiah, Rebbi Abbahu in the name of Rebbi Simeon ben Laqish, up to three times 24 hours. When was this said? If he stopped when healthy. But if he stopped because of sickness, one can return him immediately. And for a baby which was not in danger[100]. But a baby who was in danger one can return him immediately even after a longer time.

93 In the Babli, 9a, "the blood is turned into milk".

94 In the Babli, 9a, R. Yose, R. Simeon, and R. Jehudah hold that "her limbs are in disorder and do not return to their natural shape before 24 months."

95 Babli 9a, Tosephta 2:1.

96 Up to 24 months after giving birth.

97 The text is influenced by the following discussion over the length of

the nursing period. R. Yose holds that the timing of a nursing woman is exact only up to 24 months; Babli 9a, Tosephta 2:1.

98   After stopping to nurse, when do the rules for the mother change from exact timing to retroactive impurity?

99   Tosephta 2:3, Babli *Ketubot* 60a; Yerushalmi *Ketubot* 5:6 (Notes 147-151)

in a slightly different version as seen from the variant readings denoted by ב. One may assume that the rich landlord R. Eliezer presents the rule usual in his moneyed circle and the poor charcoal burner R. Joshua those of the poor, who had no money for baby food and could use the implied contraception provided by nursing.

100   Danger to his life.

(49b line 45) זְקֵינָה. אֵי זוֹ הִיא זְקֵינָה. רִבִּי שִׁמְעוֹן בֶּן לָקִישׁ אָמַר. כָּל־שֶׁקּוֹרִין אוֹתָהּ אִימָא וְאֵינָהּ מַקְפֶּדֶת. וּבְדַעְתָּהּ הַדָּבָר תָּלוּי. אָמַר רִבִּי אָבִין כָּל־שֶׁהִיא רְאוּיָה לְהִיקָרוֹת אִימָא.

"An old woman." Who is an old woman? Rebbi Simeon ben Laqish said, any person whom one calls "mother" and she is not offended[101]. Does that depend on her opinion? Rebbi Abun said, any who should be called "mother"[102].

101   A similar opinion in the Babli, 9a/b. "Mother" is the obvious translation but the meaning is that of German *Mütterlein* "little mother", for which I did not find a concise English translation. Similar, אַבָּא in the next paragraph is *Väterlein* "little father".

102   Quoted in Tosaphot 9b, *s. v.* כל.

(49b line 48) תַּנֵּי. הָעֲבָדִים וְהַשְּׁפָחוֹת אֵין קוֹרִין אוֹתָן אַבָּא פְלוֹנִי אִימָא פְלוֹנִית. שֶׁלְּבֵית רַבָּן גַּמְלִיאֵל הָיוּ קוֹרִין לְעַבְדֵּיהֶן וּלְשִׁפְחוֹתֵיהֶן אַבָּא טָבִי וְאִמָּא טָבִיתָא.

It was stated[103]: One does not call male or female slaves "little father X" or "little mother Y". In the house of Rabban Gamliel they used to call their male and female slaves "little father Tabi" and "little mother Tabitha".

103 Šemaḥot 1:13; quoted in the Babli, *Berakhot* 16b. The quote is placed here because of the mention of אימא As noted by H. L. Fleischer in Levy's Dictionary *s. v.* טביתא, Acts 9:36 relates that a woman whose Aramaic name was Tabitha was called in Greek Δορκάς "gazelle, hind"; the names Tabi, Tabitha are the Aramaic nouns טָבְיָא "gazelle, hart", טָבִיתָא "gazelle, hind",

translations of Hebrew צְבִי (m.), צְבִיָּה (f., woman's name *2Chr.* 24:1). Fleischer insists that طِيبَة, صَبِيَّة "girl" (טביה, צביה) never means "servant girl" in classical Arabic. The occurrence of a name with its translation for the same person is a general phenomenon; cf. E. und H. Guggenheimer, *Etymologisches Lexikon der jüdischen Familiennamen.* München 1996, pp. xxvii-xxviii.

(49b line 50) תַּנֵּי רִבִּי הוֹשַׁעְיָה. יָלְדָה וְאַחַר כָּךְ נִתְגַּיְּירָה אֵין לָהּ דַּם טוֹהַר. אָמַר רִבִּי יוֹסֵי. וְיָאוּת. אִילוּלֵי דְּתַנִּיתָהּ רִבִּי הוֹשַׁעְיָה הֲוַת צְרִיכָה לוֹ. מֵאַחַר שֶׁאֵין לָהּ דָּמִים טְמֵאִין אֵין לָהּ דָּמִים טְהוֹרִין. תַּנֵּי. הַגִּיּוֹרֶת וְהַשְּׁבוּיָה וְהַשִּׁפְחָה שֶׁנִּפְדּוּ וְשֶׁנִּתְגַּיְּירוּ וְשֶׁנִּשְׁתַּחְרְרוּ צְרִיכוֹת לְהַמְתִּין שְׁלֹשָׁה חֳדָשִׁים. דִּבְרֵי רִבִּי יוּדָה. רִבִּי יוֹסֵי אוֹמֵר. אֵינָן צְרִיכוֹת לְהַמְתִּין שְׁלֹשָׁה חֳדָשִׁים. וּבְדָמִים. רִבִּי יוּדָה אוֹמֵר. דַּיָּיה שָׁעָתָהּ. רִבִּי יוֹסֵי אוֹמֵר. מְטַמֵּא מֵעֵת לָעֵת. אָמַר רִבִּי. נִרְאִין דִּבְרֵי רִבִּי יוֹסֵי בְּדָמִים וְדִבְרֵי רִבִּי יוּדָה בְּוָלָד. וְרִבִּי חִייָה בְּשֵׁם רִבִּי יוֹחָנָן הֲלָכָה כְּרִבִּי יוֹסֵי. דְּלֹא כֵן בָּעֵא קוֹמֵי רִבִּי יוֹסֵי. דְּלֹא כֵן מַה אֲנַן אֲמְרִין. רִבִּי יוּדָה וְרִבִּי יוֹסֵי אֵין הֲלָכָה כְּרִבִּי יוֹסֵי. אֶלָּא בְּגִין דָּמַר רִבִּי. נִרְאִין לֹא כֵן אָמַר רִבִּי בָּא בְּשֵׁם רִבִּי זְעִירָה. כָּל־מָקוֹם שֶׁשָּׁנָה רִבִּי. נִרְאִין. עֲדַיִין הַמַּחֲלוֹקֶת בִּמְקוֹמָהּ. חוּץ מִן הָעִיגּוּל שֶׁלַּדְּבֵילָה. דְּאָהֵן מוֹדֵי לְאָהֵן וְאָהֵן מוֹדֵי לְאָהֵן. אָמַר רִבִּי יוֹסֵי. קַשִּׁיתָהּ קוֹמֵי רִבִּי חֲנִינָה בְּרֵיהּ דְּרִבִּי אַבָּהוּ. וַאֲפִילוּ דָּבָר בָּרִיא שֶׁנִּבְעֲלוּ. אָמַר לֵיהּ. וּסְתָם גּוֹיוֹת לֹא כִּבְעוּלוֹת הֵן.

3 תני | א תני ר' חייה   5 שלשה חדשים | א י -   6 דייה שעתה | א מטמא מעת י מטמא מעת לעת   מטמא מעת לעת | א י דייה שעתה   7 יוסי | א יהודה   י יודה   יודה | א י יוסי   ור' חייה בשם ר' יוחנן הלכה כר' יוסי. ר' בא בר כהן בעא קומי ר' יוסי | א י א' ר' חנינה בתיה דר' אבהו (א אבהוא) אבא הוה ליה עובדא ושלח שאל (א ושאל) לר' חייה ול' יוסה ולר' אימי והורון ליה כר' יוסי בולד (י בולד)   9 דמר | א י דאמר

10 זעירה | י זעורה   11 מן העיגול | א י מעיגול   אהיין | א י דין (4 times)   12
קשיתה | י קשייתא   13 ליה | י לו

Rebbi Hoshaia stated: If [a woman] gave birth and then converted, she has no period of purity. Rebbi Yose said, this is correct. If Rebbi Hoshaia had not stated this, would it have been a problem for us? Since she has no period of impurity[104], she cannot have a period of purity. [105]It was stated: The proselyte, the captive, and the slave woman who were redeemed, or converted, or freed, have to wait three months, the words of Rebbi Judah. Rebbi Yose says, they do not have to wait. Their blood, Rebbi Jehudah says, is timed exactly; Rebbi Yose says, it makes impure 24 hours retroactively. Rebbi said, the words of Rebbi Yose are reasonable for the blood, and the words of Rebbi Judah for the child. But Rebbi Ḥiyya in the name of Rebbi Yoḥanan, practice follows Rebbi Yose. Rebbi Abba bar Cohen asked before Rebbi Yose: For if it were not so, what could we say? Between Rebbi Jehudah and Rebbi Yose, practice does not follow Rebbi Yose? But because Rebbi said, "they are reasonable". Did not Rebbi Abba say in the name of Rebbi Ze'ira, every time Rebbi taught "they are reasonable", the disagreement is unresolved except in the case of the fig cake where each party to the controversy accepts the opposition's argument. Rebbi Yose said, I stated a difficulty before Rebbi Ḥanina ben Rebbi Abbahu: Even if it is certain that they had sex? He said to him, is a normal Gentile not like one who had sex?

104 Living Gentiles cannot be impure by biblical standards; all their impurity is rabbinical. The biblical status of the impurity of Gentile corpses is a matter of dispute. Since the period of purity follows the period of impurity caused by birthing, the fact that the woman was still a Gentile when giving birth eliminates the period of impurity and with it the period of

purity.

105 From here to the end of the paragraph, the text (with some significant changes) is from *Yebamot* 4:11, Notes 167-171. In the variant readings, the Leiden ms. of *Yebamot* is noted by י, the Ashkenazic ms. fragments [*Qobez al yad* XII (XXII)] by א.

(49b line 63) רִבִּי לְעָזֶר אוֹמֵר. כָּל־אִשָּׁה שֶׁעָבְרוּ עָלֶיהָ שָׁלֹשׁ עוֹנוֹת דַּיָּיהּ שָׁעֲתָהּ. וְתַנֵּי עֲלָהּ. אָמְרוּ לוֹ. לֹא אָמְרוּ חֲכָמִים אֶלָּא זְקֵינָה. וְהָתַנֵּי. אָמַר רִבִּי לְעָזֶר. מַעֲשֶׂה בְרִיבָה אַחַת בְּעֵייתְלוֹ שֶׁהִפְסִיקָה לָהּ שָׁלֹשׁ עוֹנוֹת וְלֹא רָעַת וְאַחַר כָּךְ רָאַת. וּבָא מַעֲשֶׂה לִפְנֵי חֲכָמִים וְאָמְרוּ. דַּיָּיהּ שָׁעֲתָהּ. אָמְרוּ לוֹ. קָטָן הָיִיתָ. וְאֵין עֵדוּת לְקָטָן. פַּעַם אַחַת הוֹרָה רִבִּי כְּרִבִּי לְעֶזֶר וְהָיָה מִצְטָעֵר. אָמַר רִבִּי מָנָא קוֹמֵי רִבִּי יוֹסֵי. אִיתָא חֲמֵי. בְּשָׁעָה שֶׁהוֹרָה כְּקוּלֵּי רִבִּי מֵאִיר וּכְקוּלֵּי רִבִּי יוֹסֵי לֹא הָיָה מִצְטָעֵר וְכָאן הָיָה מִצְטָעֵר. אָמַר לֵיהּ. תַּמָּן יְחִידִין אִינּוּן. אִית לָךְ מֵימַר. נִצְרְפָה דַעְתּוֹ עִם רִבִּי מֵאִיר וְרָבוּ עַל רִבִּי יוֹסֵי. נִצְרְפָה דַעְתּוֹ עִם רִבִּי יוֹסֵי וְרָבוּ עַל רִבִּי מֵאִיר. אִית לָךְ מֵימַר הָכָא. נִצְרְפָה דַעְתּוֹ עִם רִבִּי לְעֶזֶר וְרָבוּ עַל חֲכָמִים. וְלֹא עוֹד אֶלָּא דְתַנֵּי עֲלָהּ. אָמְרוּ לוֹ. הוֹרָיַית שָׁעָה הָיְתָה.

"Rebbi Eliezer says, the timing of *any* woman who misses three periods is exact." But we stated on this: They said to him, the Sages said this only for the old woman. But did we not state[34]: "Rebbi Eliezer said, it happened with a girl in Aitlo[35] that she missed for three periods and then had a period. When the case came before the Sages, they said that her timing was exact." They said to him, you were underage, and an underage boy cannot testify[106]. Once did Rebbi decide to follow Rebbi Eliezer and he regretted it[107]. Rebbi Mana said before Rebbi Yose: Come and see, when he instructed following the leniencies of Rebbi Meïr and Rebbi Yose[108], he did not regret it, but in this case he regretted? He said to him, there we deal with isolated opinions[109]. You can say, we add his[110] opinion to that of Rebbi Meïr to form a plurality against Rebbi Yose, and we add his opinion to that of Rebbi Yose to form a plurality against Rebbi Meïr; can you say here that we add his opinion to that of Rebbi Eliezer to form a plurality against the Sages? And in addition, it was stated on this[111]: "It was an emergency decision."

106 In general, an adult cannot testify to what he saw when he was underage. A small number of exceptions is listed in Mishnah *Ketubot* 2:10.

107 Also mentioned in the Babli, 6a, 9b, *Erubin* 46a. In the Babli, Rebbi is quoted as saying that one may follow R. Eliezer in emergencies.

108 As explained in the next Halakhah, he followed R. Meïr against R. Yose in matters of impurity of a pregnant woman and R. Yose against R. Meïr in matters of impurity of a nursing woman.

109 No opinion of the anonymous majority was recorded.

110 Rebbi's own; while he lived one generation later, his standing is high enough that he may be counted with the students of R. Aqiba to decide matters.

111 In Tosephta 1:9, this is the answer which the majority gives to R. Eliezer about the ruling for the girl from Aitlo.

(49b line 74) רִבִּי יוֹסֵי אוֹמֵר. מְעוּבֶּרֶת וּמֵינִיקָה שֶׁעָבְרוּ עֲלֵיהֶן שָׁלֹשׁ עוֹנוֹת דַּיָּין שְׁעָתָן. וְתַנֵּי עֲלָהּ. יְמֵי עִיבּוּרָהּ וִימֵי מֵנִיקוּתָהּ מִצְטָרְפִין לְשָׁלֹשׁ עוֹנוֹת. דּוּ סָבַר מַעְיָין אֶחָד הוּא.

[90]"Rebbi Yose said, the timing of a pregnant or a nursing woman who had stopped for three periods is exact." On that it was stated[91]: The days of her pregnancy and her nursing add up to three periods. Can he think that there is only one source?

HALAKHAH 6

(fol. 48d) **משנה ו**: בַּמָּה אָמְרוּ דַּיָּיהּ שָׁעֲתָהּ. בִּרְאִיָּיה הָרִאשׁוֹנָה אֲבָל בִּשְׁנִיָּיה מְטַמְּאָה מֵעֵת לְעֵת. וְאִם רָאֲתָה הָרִאשׁוֹנָה מֵאוֹנֶס אַף הַשְּׁנִיָּיה דַּיָּיהּ שָׁעֲתָהּ.

Mishnah 6: Under which circumstances did they say that her timing is exact[112]? If she sees [blood] for the first time. But the second time she retroactively makes impure for 24 hours[113]. But if the first time she saw because of outside force[114], also the second time her timing is exact.

112 For the adolescent girl or the menopausal woman.
113 Her timing will be exact again if for three consecutive periods she counted exactly the same number of days between two periods. "Impure for 24 hours" naturally means "impure for the lesser of either 24 hours or the time of her last check", as stated in Mishnah 1.
114 If either she suffered great mental shock or was forced to extraordinary physical exertion.

(fol. 49b line 3) **הלכה ו**: בַּמָּה אָמְרוּ. דַּיָּיהּ שָׁעֲתָהּ כול׳. שְׁמוּאֵל אָמַר. לֹא שָׁנוּ אֶלָּא בְתוּלָה וּזְקֵינָה. אֲבָל מְעוּבֶּרֶת וּמֵינִיקָה נוֹתְנִין לָהּ כָּל־יְמֵי עִיבּוּרָהּ וְכָל־יְמֵי מֵינִיקוּתָהּ. רַב וְרִבִּי יוֹחָנָן תְּרֵיהוֹן אָמְרִין. הִיא בְתוּלָה הִיא זְקֵינָה הִיא מְעוּבֶּרֶת הִיא מֵינִיקָה. אָמַר רִבִּי זְעִירָא. אַתְיָיא דְרַב וּדְרִבִּי יוֹחָנָן כְּרִבִּי חֲנִינָה וְכוּלְּהוֹן פְּלִיגִין עַל שִׁיטָתֵיהּ דִּשְׁמוּאֵל. דָּמַר רִבִּי לָעְזָר בְּשֵׁם רִבִּי חֲנִינָה. פַּעַם אַחַת הוֹרָה רִבִּי כְּקוּלֵּי רִבִּי מֵאִיר וּכְקוּלֵּי רִבִּי יוֹסֵי. הֵיךְ עֲבִידָא. הוּכַּר עוּבָּרָהּ וְאַחַר כָּךְ רָאֲתָה. רִבִּי מֵאִיר אוֹמֵר. דַּיָּיהּ שָׁעֲתָהּ. רִבִּי יוֹסֵי אוֹמֵר. מְטַמֵּא מֵעֵת לְעֵת. רָאֲת רְאִיּוֹת הַרְבֵּה וְהִפְסִיקָה שָׁלֹשׁ עוֹנוֹת וְאַחַר כָּךְ רָאֲת. רִבִּי מֵאִיר אוֹמֵר. מְטַמֵּא מֵעֵת לְעֵת. רִבִּי יוֹסֵי אוֹמֵר. דַּיָּיהּ שָׁעֲתָהּ. וְאִם אוֹמֵר אַתְּ. נוֹתְנִין לָהּ כָּל־יְמֵי עִיבּוּרָהּ וְכָל־יְמֵי מֵינִיקוּתָהּ. לָמָּה לִי כְקוּלֵּי רִבִּי יוֹסֵי. הָדָא דְרִבִּי מֵאִיר קְלִילָא מִדְּרִבִּי יוֹסֵי. אָמַר רִבִּי מָנָא קוֹמֵי רִבִּי יוֹסֵי. אוֹ נֵימַר רִבִּי מֵאִיר וְרִבִּי יוֹסֵי דְחָלָב. אָמַר לֵיהּ. בְּפֵירוּשׁ הָכֵין אִיתְאָמְרַת.

Halakhah 6: "Under which circumstances did they say that her timing is exact," etc. Samuel said, they taught only about a virgin and an old woman. But to a pregnant or nursing woman they give all during preganncy and nursing time. Both Rav and Rebbi Johanan say, the rules are identical for virgin, post-menopausal, pregnant, or nursing woman[115]. Rebbi Ze'ira said, Rav and Rebbi Johanan parallel Rebbi Hanina's and they all disagree with Samuel's opinion, since Rebbi Eleazar said in the name of Rebbi Hanina: Once Rebbi instructed following the leniencies both of Rebbi Meïr and of Rebbi Yose. How was this? If the fetus was noticed and after that she bled, Rebbi Meïr says, her timing is exact; Rebbi Yose says, she retroactively makes impure for 24 hours. If she then[116] bled frequently, interrupted for three periods, and then bled, Rebbi Meïr says, she retroactively makes impure for 24 hours; Rebbi Yose says, her timing is exact. If you say, one gives her all the time during pregnancy, why would we need Rebbi Yose's leniency[117]? Is not that of Rebbi Meïr less weighty than that of Rebbi Yose[118]? Rebbi Mana said before Rebbi Yose[119]: Might we say, following Rebbi Meïr and Rebbi Yose of milk[120]? He said to him, it was said so explicitly[121].

115 Samuel's and Rav's opinions are reported similarly in the Babli, 10b. There, R. Johanan is reported to join Samuel's opinion, that pregnant and nursing women never induce retroactive impurity.

116 While pregnant.

117 R. Yose's leniency is a stringency for Samuel who would not require an interruption of three periods or almost three months.

118 The leniency of R. Meïr which Rebbi followed is simply that of Mishnah 4; it alone would never have to be mentioned.

119 The late Amora.

120 In Halakhah 5, Note 93 ff.

121 That it referred to the status of a pregnant woman.

HALAKHAH 6

(fol. 49b line 16) עַד כְּדוֹן בְּתִינוֹקֶת שֶׁהִגִּיעַ זְמַנָּהּ לִרְאוֹת. תִּינוֹקֶת שֶׁלֹא הִגִּיעַ זְמַנָּהּ לִרְאוֹת וְרָאֲתָה רְאִיּוֹת. רְאִיָּיה רִאשׁוֹנָה דַּיָּיהּ שָׁעָתָהּ. שְׁנִיָּיה דַּיָּיהּ שָׁעָתָהּ. שְׁלִישִׁית דַּיָּיהּ שָׁעָתָהּ. מִיכָּן וְהֵילַךְ מְטַמֵּא מֵעֵת לְעֵת. רִבִּי יִרְמְיָה בְּשֵׁם רַב. שְׁלִישִׁית עַצְמָהּ מְטַמֵּא מֵעֵת לְעֵת. זְקֵינָה שֶׁהִפְסִיקָה שָׁלֹשׁ עוֹנוֹת דַּיָּיהּ שָׁעָתָהּ. חָזְרָה וְהִפְסִיקָה שָׁלֹשׁ עוֹנוֹת וְאַחַר כָּךְ רָאֲת דַּיָּיהּ שָׁעָתָהּ. בְּשֶׁלֹא כְוֶונָה מַחֲמַת הַוֶוסֶת. בְּשֶׁפָּתְחָה אוֹ הוֹתִירָה. שֶׁאִילּוּ כְּוִינָה נִקְבְּעָה וַסְתָּהּ.

So far for a girl who reached the age of puberty. "If a girl did not reach the age of puberty but started menstruating? For the first bleeding, her timing is exact. For the second bleeding, her timing is exact. For the third bleeding, her timing is exact; after that it will retroactively impart impurity for 24 hours." Rav[122] Jeremiah in the name of Rav: At the third time itself it will retroactively impart impurity for 24 hours[123]. [124]"The timing of an old woman who had stopped for three periods is exact. If she then interrupted for three periods and then bled, her timing is exact. If she again interrupted for three periods and then bled, her timing is exact. If the interruption was not exact the same period; if it was less or more. But if it was exactly the same time, she established a [new] period[125]."

122 For historical reasons, the title has to be corrected.
123 This is the reading of the *baraita* in all Babylonian sources; Babli 9b, Tosephta 1:8.
124 Babli 9b, Tosephta 1:11.
125 And her timing is exact according to Mishnah 2.

(fol. 49b line 22) רִבִּי יוּדָן בָּעֵי. רָאֲת רְאִיָּיה רִאשׁוֹנָה וּשְׁנִיָּיה וְהִפְסִיקָה שָׁלֹשׁ עוֹנוֹת וְלֹא רָאֲת וְאַחַר כָּךְ רָאֲת. כְּוֶוסֶת אֲרוּכָה הִיא שֶׁתְּטַמֵּא מֵעֵת לְעֵת. אוֹ כְהֶפְסֵק עוֹנָה הִיא שֶׁתְּהֵא דַּיָּיהּ שָׁעָתָהּ. אָמַר לֵיהּ רִבִּי יוֹסֵי. מַה עִם בְּשָׁעָה שֶׁעֲשִׂיתָהּ כִּבְדָמִין אַתְּ אָמַר. דַּיָּיהּ שָׁעָתָהּ. כָּאן שֶׁלֹּא עֲשִׂיתָהּ כִּבְדָמִין לֹא

כָּל־שֶׁכֵּן. אָמַר לֵיהּ. וְאִין כֵּינִי אֲפִילוּ רָאָת רְאִייָה אַחַת לֹא תְטַמֵּא מֵעֵת לְעֵת עַד שֶׁתִּרְאֶה שָׁלֹשׁ אַחַר הַפְסָקָה. אָמַר לֵיהּ. דַּמְיָיא לְוֶסֶת אֲרוּכָה.

Rebbi Yudan asked: If she[126] bled a first and a second time and then interrupted for three periods before she bled again. Is that like one long regular period and she would retroactively impart impurity for 24 hours[127] or like an interruption[128] so that her timing would be exact? Rebbi Yose said to him, if at a time you considered her as ready to bleed you[129] said that her timing was exact, in this case when you do not consider her as ready to bleed[130], not so much more? He answered him: If that is so, even if she saw only once she should not retroactively impart impurity for 24 hours until she bled three times after that interruption! He agreed[131] that it is like one long regular period.

126 The girl who is too young to be menstruating.

127 As required by Tosephta 1:8.

128 Since for a menopausal woman any interruption of three periods without bleeding creates a new situation, Mishnah 5.

129 For her second period.

130 Since she did not reach puberty, the interruption of three periods will show that the earlier bleeding was not menstrual.

131 R. Yose retracted his earlier statement and agreed that at the third menstrual period she retroactively imparts impurity.

(fol. 49b line 29) כַּמָּה עוֹנָה נוֹתְנִין לָהּ. עוֹנָה בֵינוֹנִית. רִבִּי שִׁמְעוֹן בֶּן לָקִישׁ בְּשֵׁם רִבִּי יוּדָן נְשִׂייָא. נוֹתְנִין לָהּ עוֹנָה בֵינוֹנִית שְׁלֹשִׁים יוֹם. וְיִתְּנוּ לָהּ עוֹנָה. מֵאַחַר שֶׁלֹּא נִתְבָּרְרָה בְדָמִים אֵין לָהּ עוֹנָה. וּמַהוּ שֶׁיְּהֵא לָהּ כְּתָמִין. חִזְקִיָּה אָמַר. מֵאַחַר שֶׁעֲשִׂיתָהּ כְּכַד מַיִם יֵשׁ לָהּ כְּתָמִין. שְׁמוּאֵל אָמַר. אֲפִילוּ כָּל־הַסַּדִּין כּוּלוֹ מָלֵא טִיפִּין שֶׁלְּדָם אֵין לָהּ כְּתָמִין. רִבִּי יוֹחָנָן בְּשֵׁם רִבִּי יַנַּאי. אֲפִילוּ רָאָת מֵאָה פַעַם אֵין לָהּ כְּתָמִין. עַד אֵיכָן. עַד שֶׁתָּבוֹא לִימֵי הַנְּעוּרִים. וְאֵילוּ הֵן יְמֵי הַנְּעוּרִים. מִשֶּׁתָּבִיא שְׁתֵּי שְׂעָרוֹת. רִבִּי בָּא רִבִּי חִייָה רִבִּי יוֹחָנָן

בְּשֵׁם רִבִּי שִׁמְעוֹן בֶּן יוֹצָדָק. רוֹקָהּ טָהוֹר. מִדְרָסָהּ טָהוֹר. מַגָּעָהּ בִּרְשׁוּת הָרַבִּים טָהוֹר. סָבְרִין מֵימַר. מֵעֵת לְעֵת.

What is the period that is counted for her[132]? An average period[133]. Rebbi Simeon ben Laqish in the name of Rebbi Yudan Neśia[134]: One gives her 30 days as average period. Can she not have a personal period? Since it cannot be verified by blood, she has no period. Should she [become impure] by stains[135]? Hizqiah said, since you made her a full water pitcher[136], she has stains. Samuel[136] said, even if the entire bedsheet is full of drops of blood she has no stains. Rebbi Johanan in the name of Rebbi Yannai: Even if she bled a hundred times, she has no stains[137]. How long? Until she reaches the age of puberty. What is the age of puberty? When she grows two pubic hairs[138]. Rebbi Abba, Rebbi Hiyya, Rebbi Johanan in the name of Rebbi Simeon ben Yoṣadaq: Her spittle is pure, what she sits on is pure, what she touches in the public domain is pure[139]. They interpreted this: no 24 hours[140].

132 While the paragraph speaks of the pre-pubescent girl, the same question could be asked for the post-menopausal woman since for both Mishnah and Tosephta speak of "periods" while by the nature of things they have no period.

133 Of an adult woman of child-bearing age.

134 The same statement in the Babli, 9b.

135 Since an adult woman is impure if she detects a stain on her underwear even if she is unaware of any discharge, Note 42.

136 Her bleeding is like water overflowing from a full pitcher; therefore, minimal discharges indicated by a stain should not be excluded.

136 The medical authority denies any menstrual blood before puberty (execpt possibly at birth).

137 In the Babli, 10a, Hizqiah's opinion is reported as it is here, but R. Johanan's opposing view is restricted to a girl who had no more than one

episode of bleeding.

138 Cf. *Soṭah* 1:1, Note 61; *Yebamot* 1:2, Note 142.

139 None of the impurities associated with the menstruating woman or the *zavah* (cf. Notes 42, 44, 55) are applicable to the pre-pubescent girl.

140 None of the rules of retroactive impurity can apply to a young girl.

(fol. 48d) **משנה ז**: אַף עַל פִּי שֶׁאָמְרוּ דַּיָּהּ שָׁעָתָהּ צְרִיכָה לִהְיוֹת בּוֹדֶקֶת חוּץ מִן הַנִּדָּה וְהַיּוֹשֶׁבֶת לְדַם טוֹהַר. וְהַמְשַׁמֶּשֶׁת בָּעֵדִים חוּץ מִן הַיּוֹשֶׁבֶת עַל דַּם טוֹהַר וּבְתוּלָה שֶׁדָּמֶיהָ טְהוֹרִין. וּפְעָמִים שֶׁהִיא צְרִיכָה לִהְיוֹת בּוֹדֶקֶת בְּשַׁחֲרִית וּבֵין הַשְּׁמָשׁוֹת וּבְשָׁעָה שֶׁהִיא עוֹבֶרֶת לְשַׁמֵּשׁ אֶת בֵּיתָהּ. יְתֵירוֹת עֲלֵיהֶן הַכֹּהֲנוֹת בְּשָׁעָה שֶׁהֵן אוֹכְלוֹת בַּתְּרוּמָה. רִבִּי יְהוּדָה אוֹמֵר אַף בְּשָׁעַת עָבְרָתָן מִלֶּאֱכוֹל תְּרוּמָה.

Mishnah 7: Even though they said that their timing was exact[141], she has to check herself[142], except for the menstruating[143] and one in her period of purity[83]; even one who has intercourse with cloths[5,144] except one in her period of purity and a virgin[145] whose blood is pure. Twice she has to check herself, morning[146] and evening[147], and when she goes to have intercourse[148]. In addition, wives of Cohanim when they go to eat heave[149]. Rebbi Jehudah says, also when they stop eating heave[150].

141 The women enumerated in Mishnaiot 2 and 3.

142 If she prepares food in ritual purity.

143 The menstruating woman for seven days cannot prepare pure food. In the period of purity, a woman cannot become impure by any genital discharge.

144 She is pure for her husband and if she checks herself in the evening and finds herself pure she can be certain that the food she prepared during the preceding day is pure; but

for the next morning she still needs to check herself.

145 A "blood virgin" who can be married and even have children.

146 If she prepared pure food during the preceding night.

147 To justify the food she prepared during the preceding day.

148 This is necessary only if she regularly prepares pure food.

149 They have to be sure that they are pure when they eat sanctified food.

150 If there is any leftover food, they have to check themselves to be sure that it remained pure and usable.

(fol. 49b line 38) **הלכה ז**: אַף עַל פִּי שֶׁאָמְרוּ דַּיָּיהּ שָׁעָתָהּ כול׳. כֵּינִי מַתְנִיתָא. חוּץ מִן הַנִּידָה שֶׁלֹא הִפְסִיקָה לָהּ טַהֲרָה. וְהַמְשַׁמֶּשֶׁת בָּעֵדִים. כֵּינִי מַתְנִיתָא. צְרִיכָה שֶׁתְּשַׁמֵּשׁ בָּעֵדִים. וּבְתוּלָה שֶׁדָּמֶיהָ טְהוֹרִין. כֵּינִי מַתְנִיתָא. תִּינוֹקֶת שֶׁלֹּא הִגִּיעַ זְמַנָּהּ לִרְאוֹת וְנִשֵּׂאת.

Halakhah 7: "Even though they said that their timing was exact," etc. So is the Mishnah: Except for the menstruating woman whose period was not interrupted by purity[151]. "Even one who has intercourse with cloths," so is the Mishnah: She is required to have intercourse with cloths[152]. "And a virgin whose blood is pure," so is the Mishnah: A girl who has not reached puberty but was married[153].

151 During the prescribed seven days of impurity.

152 וְהַמְשַׁמֶּשֶׁת is corrected into וּמְשַׁמֶּשֶׁת. This correction is found in those modern printed Mishnah editions which are not based on mss.

153 An extensive discussion of this paragraph with variant readings from Mishnah and Babli mss. is in J. N. Epstein, מבוא לנוסח המשנה[2], Jerusalem-Tel Aviv 1964, pp. 483-485.

(fol. 49b line 42) שְׁמוּאֵל אָמַר. לַיְלָה וְיוֹם עוֹנָה. וּמִקְצָת עוֹנָה כְּכוּלָּהּ. הִפְסִיקָה וְאַחַר כָּךְ רָאֲתָה טְמֵיאָה. שִׁינַּת מַרְאֶה דָּמֶיהָ טְמֵיאָה. אָמַר רִבִּי זְעִירָה. בְּשֶׁלֹּא שִׁינַּת מֵחֲמַת הַתַּשְׁמִישׁ. אֲבָל אִם שִׁינַּת מֵחֲמַת הַתַּשְׁמִישׁ טְהוֹרָה. אָמַר רִבִּי

יוֹסֵי. וּמַתְנִיתָא אָמְרָה כֵן. וּבְתוּלָה שֶׁדָּמֶיהָ טְהוֹרִין. הָדָא אָמְרָה. שִׁינַת מַחֲמַת הַתַּשְׁמִישׁ טְהוֹרָה. וְאִם אוֹמֵר אַתְּ. שִׁינַת מַחֲמַת הַתַּשְׁמִישׁ תְּהֵא טְמֵאָה. וּתְשַׁמֵּשׁ בְּעֵד. שֶׁמָּא תְשַׁנֶּה מַחֲמַת הַתַּשְׁמִישׁ וּתְהֵא טְמֵיאָה.

Samuel said, a night and a day form a period, and part of a period is as if it were the entire period[154]. "If she ceased and then bled again, she is impure"[155]. If the look of the blood changed, she is impure. Rebbi Ze'ira said, if it did not change because of intercourse[156]. But if it changed because of intercourse, she is pure. Rebbi Yose said, the Mishnah says so, "a virgin whose blood is pure." That implies, if it changed because of intercourse, she is pure. Since if you said, if it changed because of intercourse she is impure, let her have intercourse with a cloth, maybe it would change because of intercourse and she would be impure[157]!

154 This refers to the case of a girl who was married after she reached puberty. In Mishnah 10:1, it is stated that the House of Shammai permit only the first intercourse which deflowers her, because the blood she loses as a consequence is considered as if it were menstrual blood. In the Mishnah and in Tosephta 9:8, the House of Hillel is reported to permit intercourse the entire first night. In the Tosephta (quoted in the Babli, 65a), Rabban Simeon ben Gamliel says "one gives her a full period, half a day and the night", meaning the first night and the following morning. In the *baraita* known to Samuel, the statement simply must have been "one gives her a full period," and he explains that a full period is night and day but that part of the day (until midday) is already counted as the entire day and after that, for the remainder of the wedding week, the bride is forbidden to the husband as if she were menstruating.

155 In Tosephta 9:7 it is explained that if a girl had not reached puberty when she was married, the wound from deflowering had healed, and she was able to have intercourse without bleeding, if then she bleeds for any reason she is impure as menstruating. That is the meaning of the small excerpt quoted here.

156 The first part of Tosephta 9:8 states: "If the look of the blood was changed she is impure as menstruating." R. Ze'ira disputes this reading and holds that if the blood is mingled with semen, it is obvious that she is injured by the intercourse; she remains pure until for the first time she bleeds not in connection with intercourse.

157 The argument goes as follows: The Mishnah here states that a prepuberty girl does not have to check herself when she works on pure food, and she does not have to check herself when she sleeps with her husband. If she could be impure by bleeding during intercourse, she should be prevented from working with pure food unless she checked herself after each intercourse. Since she is not prevented, if follows that she cannot be held to be menstruating unless either she reached puberty or she once bled in a way not connected with intercourse.

(fol. 49b line 48) פְּעָמִים שֶׁהִיא צְרִיכָה לִהְיוֹת בּוֹדֶקֶת כול'. אָמַר רִבִּי יוֹסֵי בִּירִבִּי בּוּן. כְּנֶגֶד שְׁנֵי פְעָמִים שֶׁהַיּוֹם מִשְׁתַּנֶּה עַל הַבְּרִיוֹת.

"Twice she has to check herself," etc. Rebbi Yose ben Rebbi Bun said, corresponding to the two times in which the day changes for creatures[158].

158 From darkness to light and from light to darkness. The rule is purely one of convention, not intrinsic to the situation.

(fol. 49b line 50) רִבִּי לָעֳזָר בְּשֵׁם רִבִּי הוֹשַׁעְיָה. כָּל־מָקוֹם שֶׁאָמְרוּ חֲכָמִים. בַּעֲלָהּ חַיָּיב בְּקָרְבָּן כְּנֶגְדָּהּ בְּטַהֲרוֹת טְמֵאוֹת. בַּעֲלָהּ פָּטוּר מִן הַקָּרְבָּן כְּנֶגְדָּהּ בְּטַהֲרוֹת טְהוֹרוֹת. בַּעֲלָהּ סָפֵק בְּקָרְבָּן כְּנֶגְדָּהּ בְּטַהֲרוֹת תְּלוּיוֹת. רִבִּי שְׁמוּאֵל בַּר רַב יִצְחָק בָּעֵי. אִילּוּ זָקֵן וְיֶלֶד שֶׁהָיוּ מְהַלְּכִין בִּטְרִיקְלִין. לֹא דָבָר בָּרִיא שֶׁהַזָּקֵן מְשַׁמֵּשׁ תְּחִילָּה. הָא אִם יֶלֶד בָּא וּמַטְעֵי בֵיהּ. רִבִּי אָבוּן בְּשֵׁם רִבִּי יוּדָן. אֲנִי אוֹמֵר. שָׁם הָיָה. בִּיאָה הִיא שֶׁהִיא סוֹתֶמֶת. בְּרַם הָכָא. אִילּוּ הֲוָה שָׁם מִי מְעַכְּבוֹ שֶׁלֹּא לָצֵאת. מַתְנִיתָא פְלִיגָא עַל רִבִּי הוֹשַׁעְיָה. פֵּירְשָׁה וְרָאָת הִיא טְמֵיאָה וְכוּפָּן טְהוֹרוֹת. מַתְנִיתָא פְלִיגָא עַל בַּר פְּדָיָה. רִבִּי יוּדָה אוֹמֵר. אַף בִּשְׁעַת עֲבָרָתָן מִלֶּאֱכוֹל בַּתְּרוּמָה. לֵיידָא מִילָּה. לֹא שֶׁאִם תֵּרָאֶה תְּהֵא מְטַמְּאָה

לְמַפְרֵעַ. אָמַר רִבִּי עֶזְרָא קוֹמֵי רִבִּי מָנָא. תִּיפְתָּר בְּאִשָּׁה שֶׁאֵין לָהּ וֶסֶת. אָמַר לֵיהּ. כֵּן אָמַר רִבִּי יוֹסִי רִבִּי. כָּל־מַה דַּאֲנָן קַייָמִין הָכָא בְּאִשָּׁה שֶׁיֵשׁ לָהּ וֶסֶת אֲנָן קַייָמִין. אָמַר רִבִּי יוֹסִי בֵּירִבִּי בּוּן. סָלְקַת מַתְנִיתָא. עַד כָּאן בְּאִשָּׁה שֶׁיֵשׁ לָהּ וֶסֶת. מִכָּן וְאֵילַךְ. בְּאִשָּׁה שֶׁאֵין לָהּ וֶסֶת. וַאֲפִילוּ תֵימַר. לֹא סָלְקַת מַתְנִיתָא. אֶלָּא כָּל־מַה דַּאֲנָן קַייָמִין הָכָא בְּאִשָּׁה שֶׁיֵשׁ לָהּ וֶסֶת אֲנָן קַייָמִין. וּמָה עֲבִיד לָהּ בַּר פְּדָיָה. חֲלוּקִין עַל רִבִּי יוּדָה.

Rebbi Eleazar in the name of Rebbi Hoshaia: In every situation in which the Sages said that her husband would be obligated for a sacrifice, pure food became impure; her husband would be exempt from a sacrifice, pure food remains pure; her husband would have to bring a sacrifice for a doubt, pure food is in limbo[159]. Rebbi Samuel bar Rav Isaac asked: If an old man and a child walk in a dining room, does the old man not enter first? But the child can come and make a fool of him[160]. Rebbi Abun in the name of Rebbi Yudan: I say, it was here but the intercourse stopped it from leaving; but there, what hindered it to leave[161]? The Mishnah[162] disagrees with Rebbi Hoshaiah: "If she left [the bed] and saw blood, she is impure but all the food is pure." The Mishnah disagrees with Bar Pedaiah[159]: "Rebbi Jehudah says, also when they stop eating heave." Why? Not that if she would bleed, the food should not retroactively become impure[163]? Rebbi Ezra said before Rebbi Mana: Explain it for a woman who has no regular period[164]. He said to him, so says my teacher Rebbi Yose: All that is described here is about a woman who has a regular period. Rebbi Yose ben Rebbi Abun said, the Mishnah rises[165]: Up to this point [it speaks] about a woman who has a regular period; from there on about a woman who has no regular period. But even if you say that the Mishnah does not rise[166], and we deal only with a woman who has a regular period, where does Bar Pedaiah hold? One differs with Rebbi Jehudah.

159 In the Babli 60b (and later in this paragraph in the Yerushalmi) this is attributed to Bar Pada or Pedaiah. Rashi explains the text:

A woman was occupied with pure food and noticed she was bleeding; since if that were to happen during intercourse her husband would have to bring a purification sacrifice (for a sin committed inadvertently), we assume that the blood was already there when she was touching the pure food, the food is certainly impure and has to be burned. But if only a short time after she was finished with the food she noticed it, since if she did notice blood a short time *after* intercourse her husband would have to bring an expiation sacrifice (not knowing whether a sin has been committed, cf. *Bikkurim* 2:9 Note 162), the food can neither be used nor burned. If the woman detected the blood after a longer interval, the husband is in the clear and the food is pure.

160 This simile is slightly pornographic. The dining hall is the woman's womb, the old man the penis, and the child menstrual blood. Even though the penis closes the entrance, the blood can sneak out before the penis leaves. The implication is that even in the case in which the husband only would be obligated for the expiation sacrifice, the food should be declared impure and be burned.

161 The argument in the preceding simile does not apply; a woman working in the kitchen is not to be compared to a woman during intercourse. In the first case, blood will flow out immediately under the action of gravity; in the second case she is lying down and her vagina is closed by the man's penis.

162 Mishnah 1:3. This refers to a case which, when occurring immediately after intercourse, would obligate the husband for an expiation sacrifice. Nevertheless, the food remains pure if the woman has a regular, predictable, period. (In the Babli, R. Hoshaia is reported to oppose the opinion ascribed to him in the present paragraph and to hold that in all cases other that direct touch by an impure person, pure food is held in limbo. This also is denied by the

Mishnah quoted.)

163 R. Jehudah's opinion can only be explained in the case that he requires a verification to avoid retroactive impurity even where the husband would be free from any obligation of sacrifice if there remains the possibility of retroactive impurity. But Bar Pedaiah asserts that in the latter case there is no retroactive impurity!

164 Following Mishnah 1.

165 The Mishnah has two parts; R. Jehudah does not address the same situation as does the anonymous majority; one cannot infer that he represents a minority opinion.

166 The Mishnah assumes a uniform background; R. Jehudah's opinion is that of a minority.

כל היד פרק שיני

(fol. 49c) **משנה א:** כָּל־הַיָד הַמַּרְבָּה לבדוק בַּנָשִׁים מְשׁוּבַּחַת וּבָאֲנָשִׁים תִּיקָּצֵץ. הַחֵרֶשֶׁת וְהַשׁוֹטָה וְהַסוֹמָה וְשֶׁנִּטְרְפָה דַעְתָּהּ אִם יֵשׁ לָהֶן פִּיקְחוֹת מַתְקִינוֹת אוֹתָן וְאוֹכְלוֹת בַּתְּרוּמָה. דֶּרֶךְ בְּנוֹת יִשְׂרָאֵל מְשַׁמְשׁוֹת בְּעֵדִים אֶחָד לוֹ וְאֶחָד לָהּ וְהַצְנוּעוֹת מַתְקִינוֹת לָהֶן שְׁלִישִׁית אֶחָד לְהַתְקִין אֶת הַבַּיִת.

Mishnah 1: Every hand which checks frequently[1] is praiseworthy[2] for women but should be cut off for men[3]. If an insane woman, or a blind, or a mentally disturbed[4] have sane[5] women friends, they can put them in order[6] so they can eat heave[7]. It is the way of Jewish women to have intercourse with cloths, one for him and one for her[8], and the religious ones prepare a third to put their house in order[9].

1 To check for genital emissions.
2 Since she minimizes impurity of foods.
3 Since it will arouse the man sexually.
4 The insane is permanently mentally disabled; the mentally disturbed is ill temporarily.
5 Depending on the context, פיקח can mean either "sane" or "seeing"; here it means both.
6 They can check them out and certify that they are not menstruating.
7 If they are members of a Cohen's household.
8 If they are preparing their food in purity and are required to check themselves at least twice a day, so they can wipe themselves after intercourse and inspect the cloths the next morning to be sure no blood appears on any cloth.
9 Since the requirement was already stated in Halakhah 1:7 that a woman engaged in preparing pure food has to check herself before intercourse, the question arises in the Halakhah what this Mishnah adds to Mishnah 1:7.

(49d line 22) **הלכה א:** כָּל־הַיָּד הַמַּרְבָּה לִבְדּוֹק בַּנָּשִׁים מְשׁוּבַּחַת כול׳. כֵּינֵי מַתְנִיתָא. כָּל־הַמַּרְבֶּה לִיתֵּן יָדוֹ עַל עֵינוֹ מַרְבֶּה לְהוֹצִיא דִמְעָה. רִבִּי טַרְפוֹן אוֹמֵר. תִּיקָּצֵץ עַל טִיבּוּרוֹ. אָמְרוּ לוֹ. וַהֲרֵי כְרֵיסוֹ נִבְקַעַת. אָמַר לָהֶן. לְכָךְ אֲנִי אָמַרְתִּי. שְׁמוֹתוֹ שֶׁלָּזֶה יָפִין לוֹ מֵחַיָּיו. חֲבֵרַיָּיא אָמְרִין. רִבִּי טַרְפוֹן מְקַלְּלוֹ קְלָלָה שֶׁהִיא נוֹגַעַת בְּגוּפוֹ. אָמַר רִבִּי יוֹסֵי. לֹא בָא אֶלָּא לְפָרֵשׁ שֶׁאָסוּר לְמַשְׁמֵשׁ מִן הַטִּיבּוּר וּלְמַטָּן. הָדָא דְתֵימַר לְעִנְיָין שִׁכְבַת זֶרַע. אֲבָל לְעִנְיָין זִיבָה כָּל־הַמַּרְבָּה לִבְדּוֹק מֵחֲבֵירוֹ מְשׁוּבָּח מֵחֲבֵירוֹ.

Halakhah 1: "Every hand which checks frequently is praiseworthy for women," etc. So is the *baraita*[10]: "Any one who frequently puts his hand on his eye will frequently have tears. Rebbi Ṭarphon says, it should be cut off on his navel. One said to him, does that not split open his belly? He said to them, that is what I said, for such a person's death is better than his life." The colleagues say, Rebbi Ṭarphon curses him in his body. Rebbi Yose said, he only explains that it is forbidden to manipulate lower than the navel. "That is, in the matter of semen. But in a case of gonorrhea, every hand which checks more frequently than another is more praiseworthy than the other.[11]"

---

10 A similar text is quoted piecewise in the Babli, 13a/b. A continuous text is in Tosephta 2:8: "Every hand which checks frequently is praiseworthy for women but should be cut off for men; Rebbi Ṭarphon says, it should be cut off on his navel. One said to him, does that not split open his belly? He said to them, that is what I said, to what can this be compared? To one who forcefully puts his hand on his eye who will have tears. When has this been said? In the matter of semen. But in a case of gonorrhea, every hand which checks more frequently than another is more praiseworthy than the other."

11 An exact check is necessary to determine the duration of his impurity and the correct way of purification once the patient is healed.

(49d line 29) צְנוּעוֹת הָיוּ בוֹדְקוֹת עַל כָּל־חָבִית וְחָבִית וְעַל כָּל־כִּכָּר וְכִכָּר. מַעֲשֶׂה בְּטַבִּיתָא שִׁפְחָתוֹ שֶׁלְּרַבָּן גַּמְלִיאֵל שֶׁהָיְתָה מַכְתֶּפֶת יֵינוֹת לִנְסָכִין וְהָיְתָה בּוֹדֶקֶת עַל כָּל־חָבִית וְחָבִית. אָמְרָה לוֹ. רַבִּי. רָאִיתִי כֶתֶם. וְנִזְדְּעְזַע רַבָּן גַּמְלִיאֵל. אָמְרָה לוֹ. בּוֹדֶקֶת הָיִיתִי עַל כָּל־חָבִית וְחָבִית וְלֹא נִטְמֵיתִי אֶלָּא עַל חָבִית זוֹ בִּלְבַד.

The religious women were checking themselves out for every amphora and every loaf. [12]It happened that Tabitha, the slave girl of Rabban Gamliel, was carrying wine for libations and checked herself for every amphora. She said to him, my master, I detected a stain. Rabban Gamliel started. She said to him, I was checking myself for every amphora and was impure only for that amphora.

12   A similar story appears in the Babli, 6b, where Rabban Gamliel had to rule that only the last amphora was impure. Rabban Gamliel here is clearly Gamliel I, Hillel's grandson, since libations are possible only in the Temple. The Babli has great trouble with the story because it identifies the master as Gamliel II of Jabne.

(49d line 34) אָמְרוּן בְּשֵׁם רְבִּי יַנַּאי. אֵין כָּן סוֹמָה. וְקָמַת. אָמְרוּן בְּשֵׁם רְבִּי יוֹסֵי בְּרְבִּי חֲנִינָה. אֵין כָּן סוֹמָה. וְקָמַת. רְבִּי אִילָא רְבִּי יוֹסֵי בֶּן חֲנִינָה בְּשֵׁם דְּבֵית רְבִּי יַנַּאי. אֵין כָּן סוֹמָה.

They said in Rabbi Yannai's name: There is no blind woman. Does this hold up? They said in Rabbi Yose ben Rebbi Hanina's name: There is no blind woman. Does this hold up? Rebbi Ila, Rabbi Yose ben Hanina, in the name of the House of Rebbi Yannai: There is no blind woman[13].

13   One has to omit the reference to a blind woman in the Mishnah. It seems that there was opposition to this statement and it was accepted only on the authority of R. Ilai. The Babli, 13b, quotes the statement in R. Yose ben R.

Hanina's name and explains that a blind woman can check herself and show the cloth to a seeing friend. While she needs help, she acts on her own and does not have to be certified.

(49d line 36) אָמַר רִבִּי יַנַּאי. אַף הָרִאשׁוֹנָה נִקְרֵאת צְנוּעָה. תַּנִּינָן צְרִיכוֹת בּוֹדְקוֹת. וְאַתְּ אָמַר הָכֵין. אָמַר רִבִּי אִילָא. לְהוֹדִיעָךְ שֶׁכָּל־מִי שֶׁהוּא מְקַיֵּים דִּבְרֵי חֲכָמִים נִקְרָא צָנוּעַ.

Rebbi Yannai said, the first one[14] also is called religious. We have stated "they have to check themselves", and you say so[15]? Rebbi Ila said, to tell you that everybody who keeps the directives of the rabbis is called religious[16].

14 The woman working on pure food mentioned in Mishnah 1:7 who is required to check herself before intercourse.

15 In Mishnah 1:7, the checking is stated as a requirement. In Mishnah 2:1, a similar statement appears as an act of special piety. It is impossible to explain Mishnah 2:1 as dealing with a woman not occupied with pure food since Mishnah 2:3 very clearly states that all women are permitted to their husbands without any checking.

16 The Babli, 12a, quotes the explanation attributed here to R. Ila in the name of R. Immi and rejects it since a person who does not follow the rabbis' directives is called evil. Rava explains there that the religious women take a new piece of textile for every check whereas others use the same piece repeatedly.

(49d line 38) רִבִּי יִרְמְיָה בְּשֵׁם רַב. בְּדָקָה בְיָד שֶׁאֵינָהּ בְּדוּקָה אוֹ שֶׁהִטְטִיח גּוּפָהּ לְבֵית תּוּרְפָּהּ חֶזְקַת הַגּוּף כְּבָדוּק הוּא. אָמַר רִבִּי זְעִירָא. מַתְנִיתָא אָמְרָה כֵן. נִמְצָא עַל שֶׁלּוֹ טְמֵאִין וְחַיָּיבִין בְּקָרְבָּן. לֹא שֶׁכָּל־הַגּוּף בְּחֶזְקַת בָּדוּק. אָמַר רִבִּי חֲנִינָה. תִּיפְתָּר שֶׁבְּדָקָק. וְאִיקְפַד רִבִּי זְעִירָא. אָמַר. וְדַרְכוֹ לְכֵן. רִבִּי זְעִירָה בְּשֵׁם רַב יִרְמְיָה. עַד כְּגְרִיס הִיא תוֹלָה. יוֹתֵר מִכֵּן צָרִיךְ מַתְלָא. אָמְרִין. חָזַר בּוֹ רַב יִרְמְיָה. אָמְרִין. כַּד שָׁמַע מִילֵּיהוֹן דְּרַבָּנָן חָזַר בֵּיהּ. רִבִּי מְשַׁבַּח לְרִבִּי

חָמָא אָבוֹי דְּרִבִּי הוֹשַׁעְיָה קוֹמֵי רִבִּי יִשְׁמָעֵאל בֵּירִבִּי יוֹסֵי. רִבִּי חָמָא אָבוֹי דְּרִבִּי הוֹשַׁעְיָה בָּעָא קוֹמֵי רִבִּי יִשְׁמָעֵאל בֵּירִבִּי יוֹסֵי. בָּדְקָה בְיָד שֶׁאֵינָהּ בְּדוּקָה אוֹ שֶׁהִטִּיחַ גּוּפָהּ לְבֵית תּוֹרְפָהּ. אָמַר לֵיהּ. כְּדִבְרֵי מִי אַתְּ שׁוֹאֲלֵינִי. כְּדִבְרֵי הָרַב כְּדִבְרֵי הַתַּלְמִיד. אָמַר לֵיהּ. אַבָּא אָמַר כֶּתֶם. וְרִבִּי אָמַר רְאִייָה. אָמַר לֵיהּ. דֵּין הוּא דְּאַתְּ מְשַׁבַּח בֵּיהּ. אָמַר רִבִּי זְעִירָה. הַנֵּי לְבַר נָשׁ מִישְׁמוֹע טַעֲמֵיהּ דְרַבֵּיהּ.

Rebbi Jeremiah[17] in the name of Rav: If she checked herself with an unchecked hand[18] or if she hit hard with her body on her genitals[19], the presumption is that her body was checked. Rebbi Ze'ira said, the Mishnah[20] says so: "If it was found on his [cloth], they are impure and obligated for a sacrifice.[21]" Does that not mean that there is a presumption that the body was checked? Rebbi Ḥanina said, explain it if he had checked himself. Rebbi Ze'ira was offended. Do people do that[22]? Rebbi Ze'ira in the name of Rav Jeremiah: Up to a broken bean she hangs it, more than that its needs an explanation[23]. They said, Rav Jeremiah retracted this. They said, he retracted it when he was informed of the words of the rabbis[24]. Rebbi praised Rebbi Ḥama, the father of Rebbi Hoshaiah, before Rebbi Ismael ben Rebbi Yose. Rebbi Ḥama, the father of Rebbi Hoshaiah, asked before Rebbi Ismael ben Rebbi Yose: If she checked herself with an unchecked hand or if she hit hard with her body on her genitals? He said to him, according to him are you asking me? Following the teacher or following the student? My father[25] said, a stain[26]. But Rebbi said, an episode of bleeding[27]. He said to him: That is the one of whom you are proud[28]? Rebbi Ze'ira said, it profits a man to learn his own teacher's reasons[29].

17 Later in the Halakhah he correctly is called Rav Jeremiah (bar Abba).

18 An unwashed hand which might have blood on it from other sources.

19 The expression is elliptic and uses the masculine for the feminine. If the woman sat down hard, or hit herself with a hard object on the outer genitals, and now there are blood drops found there. Rav declares her impure as menstruating since one has to assume that any blood found came from the body at the time it was found, and that her body, including her hand, was free of blood drops beforehand.

20 Mishnah 2:2.

21 If the next morning there was nothing on her cloth but a bloodstain was found on his, it is assumed that both their bodies were clean at the start of intercourse and that, therefore, the bloodstain had to come from her.

22 Nobody checks himself out like that.

23 This statement seems to be elliptic and should read: If the stain is smaller than a broken bean, one may presume it is the blood of a louse or flea. If the stain is larger, it comes from menstrual blood unless there is an explicit explanation, i. e., a known source of the blood. Yerushalmi מחלא is the same as Babylonian אמחלא "an explanation" (etymologically: a peg to hang on.)

24 In the following story.

25 R. Yose, Rebbi's teacher. In the Babli, 14a, R. Yose's opinion is credited to R. Ḥiyya (the Elder).

26 Which creates a doubt that it be menstrual blood.

27 A case of certain menstrual bleeding.

28 The reaction is unintelligible here. It is explained in the Babli, 14b, where R. Ḥama's question was about the situation discussed in the next paragraph and where R. Ḥama insisted to hear Rabbi's opinion, not that of R. Yose (R. Ismael's father and Rebbi's teacher), about which R. Ismael was offended.

29 R. Ḥama's question was justified (but he could have asked in a more diplomatic way.)

(49d line 51) בָּדְקָה וְהִנִּיחָתוֹ בְּקֻפְצָה שֶׁל זְכוּכִית. רִבִּי חִייָה אוֹמֵר. כֶּתֶם. וְרִבִּי אוֹמֵר. רְאִייָה. הָתִיב רִבִּי חִייָה לְרִבִּי. וְאַתְּ אֵין אַתְּ נוֹתֵן לָהּ מִיתְלָא. אָמַר

רִבִּי בּוּן בַּר חִייָה. טַעֲמָא דְרִבִּי. דֶּרֶךְ קְפָצִיּוֹת בְּדוּקוֹת מִן הַשְּׁרָצִים וְאֵינָן בְּדוּקוֹת מִן הַמַּאֲכוֹלֶת. עַד כְּגְרִיס הִיא תוֹלָה. יוֹתֵר מִכֵּן בַּמָּה יֵשׁ לִתְלוֹת בָּהּ.

If she checked[30] and deposited it in a glass box, Rebbi Hiyya said, a stain; Rebbi said, an episode of bleeding. Rebbi Hiyya objected to Rebbi: Do you not give her the possibility of an explanation? Rebbi Abun bar Hiyya said, Rebbi's reason is that a box is safe from crawling things, it is not safe from lice[31]. Up to the size of a broken bean she explains it; if it is larger, by what can it be explained?

30 She wiped herself with a cloth and put it away for inspection later when it was found stained.

31 Which might have been on the cloth. The size of a squeezed louse is the upper limit of a stain which may be explained away.

(fol. 49d) **משנה ב:** נִמְצָא עַל שֶׁלּוֹ טְמֵאִין וְחַיָּיבִין בְּקָרְבָּן. נִמְצָא עַל שֶׁלָּהּ אַוְתֵיאוֹס טְמֵאִין וְחַיָּיבִין בְּקָרְבָּן. נִמְצָא עַל שֶׁלָּהּ לְאַחַר זְמָן טְמֵאִין בְּסָפֵק וּפְטוּרִין מִן הַקָּרְבָּן.

Mishnah 2: If [a stain] is found on his [cloth][32], they are impure and obligated for a sacrifice[33]. If it is found on hers immediately[34], they are impure and obligated for a sacrifice. If it is found on hers later[35], they are possibly impure but free from the duty of a sacrifice.

32 Irrespective of when it was inspected, blood on his cloth is evidence of her menstrual blood.

33 If the Temple is rebuilt in their lifetime, they have to bring a purification sacrifice to atone for a sin committed inadvertently.

34 Greek εὐθέως "immediately".

35 She cleansed herself later when there was no possibility to determine whether she bled during or after intercourse.

NIDDAH CHAPTER TWO

(49d line 55) **הלכה ב:** נִמְצָא עַל שֶׁלּוֹ טְמֵאִין כול'. וְתַנֵּי עֲלָהּ. בֵּין הֱיוֹתִיאוֹס בֵּין שֶׁלֹּא הֱיוֹתְיוֹס נִמְצָא עַל שֶׁלּוֹ.

Halakhah 2: "If [a stain] is found on his [cloth]," etc. It was stated in this regard: If it is found on his, whether immediately or not immediately[36].

36 Unless he has an open wound on his penis, the bloodstain can only come from her; he is unlikely to have a bloody discharge.

(49d line 57) הֱיוֹתִיאוֹס טְמֵאִין. הֱיוֹתִיאוֹס לְקִינּוּחַ אָמְרוּ וְאֵין הֱיוֹתִיאוֹס לִבְדִיקָה. רַב הוּנָא אָמַר. כְּדֵי שֶׁתְּקַנֵּחַ פִּי הַבַּיִת מִבַּחוּץ אֲבָל לֹא מַה שֶּׁבַּחֲדָרִין וְלֹא מַה שֶּׁבַּסְּדָקִין. בְּעוֹן קוֹמֵי רַב נַחְמָן בַּר יַעֲקֹב. מַהוּ שֶׁתְּהֵא צְרִיכָה בְדִיקָה בְּתוֹךְ כְּדֵי הֱיוֹתִיאוֹס. אָמַר רִבִּי בָא. אִם אוֹמֵר אַתְּ שֶׁתְּהֵא צְרִיכָה בְדִיקָה בְּתוֹךְ כְּדֵי הֱיוֹתִיאוֹס בָּטֵל הֱיוֹתִיאוֹס. אָמַר רִבִּי יוֹסֵי בֵּירִבִּי בּוּן. אִם אוֹמֵר אַתְּ שֶׁתְּהֵא צְרִיכָה בְדִיקָה בְּתוֹךְ כְּדֵי הֱיוֹתִיאוֹס וְלֹא כִפְקִידָה הִיא לְמָעֵט מֵעֵת לְעֵת. וְתַנִּינָן. הַפְּקִידָה הִיא מְמַעֶטֶת מֵעֵת לְעֵת. אָמַר רִבִּי יוֹסֵי בֵּירִבִּי בּוּן. מָשָׁל לְשַׁמָּשׁ וְעֵד שֶׁהָיוּ עוֹמְדִין אַחַר הַשְּׁקוֹף. יָצָא הַשַּׁמָּשׁ וְנִכְנַס הָעֵד זֶה הֱיוֹתִיאוֹס.

"Immediately, they are impure." They said immediately for wiping, not for examination[37]. Rav Huna said, that she should wipe the face of the house from the outside, but not what is in the rooms nor in the crevices[38]. They asked before Rav Naḥman bar Jacob: Should she not examine it immediately? Rebbi Abba said, if you say that she should examine it immediately, you abolish immediacy[39]. Rebbi Yose ben Rebbi Abun said, if you say that she should examine it immediately, is that not checking, to be reduced from 24 hours, as we have stated: Checking reduces from 24 hours?[40] Rebbi Yose ben Rebbi Abun said, as an example, if the beadle and a witness were standing at the lintel. When the beadle comes out and the witness enters, that is "immediately"[41].

37 That should be done later in a leisurely fashion.

38 The woman is the house, the face of the house is the opening of the vagina; the rooms are the inner genitals, the crevices the folds of her skin.

39 You would have to extend the duration of "immediately".

40 Since the only purpose of the cloths is to let the woman check herself before she goes to work on pure food the next time, nothing could be gained by requiring an immediate inspection of her cloth.

41 A witness waits outside the courtroom to be called. The definition of "immediate" is the time required for the beadle to appear, to motion the witness to enter, and the witness to enter the courtroom. The same criterion is quoted in the Babli, 12a, 14b.

(49d line 66) וּפְטוּרִין מִן הַקָּרְבָּן. וּפְטוּרִין מִן הַחַטָּאת וְחַיָּיוִין בְּאָשָׁם תָּלוּי.

"They are free from the duty of a sacrifice." They are free from a purification sacrifice but are obligated for an expiation sacrifice[42].

42 Required when it is unknown whether a sin has been committed; cf. Chapter 1, Note 139. The same statement is in the Babli, 14 b and *Keritut* 17b.

(fol. 49d) **משנה ג:** אֵיזֶהוּ לְאַחַר זְמָן. כְּדֵי שֶׁתֵּרֵד מִן הַמִּיטָה וְתָדִיחַ אֶת פָּנֶיהָ וְאַחַר כָּךְ מְטַמֵּא מֵעֵת לְעֵת וְאֵינָהּ מְטַמָּא אֶת בּוֹעֲלָהּ. רַבִּי עֲקִיבָה אוֹמֵר מְטַמֵּא אֶת בּוֹעֲלָהּ. וּמוֹדִין חֲכָמִים לְרַבִּי עֲקִיבָה בָּרוֹאָה כֶּתֶם שֶׁהִיא מְטַמֵּא אֶת בּוֹעֲלָהּ. כָּל־הַנָּשִׁים בְּחֶזְקַת טַהֲרָה לְבַעֲלֵיהֶן. הַבָּאִין מִן הַדֶּרֶךְ נְשֵׁיהֶן לָהֶן בְּחֶזְקַת טַהֲרָה. בֵּית שַׁמַּאי אוֹמְרִים צְרִיכָה שְׁנֵי עִידִים עַל כָּל־תַּשְׁמִישׁ וְתַשְׁמִישׁ אוֹ תְשַׁמֵּשׁ לְאוֹר הַנֵּר. בֵּית הִלֵּל אוֹמְרִים דַּיָּיהּ בִּשְׁנֵי עִידִים כָּל־הַלַּיְלָה.

Mishnah 3: What is "later"[43]? That she should leave her bed and wipe her face[44]. After that time[45] she would retroactively make impure for 24 hours but does not make her sex partner impure; Rebbi Aqiba says, she makes her sex partner impure. The Sages agree with Rebbi Aqiba that one who finds a stain makes her sex partner impure[46]. All women are presumed pure for their husbands[47]. The wives of men coming from a trip are presumed pure. The House of Shammai say, she needs two cloths for each intercourse or she should have sex by candle light[48]. The House of Hillel say, two cloths for the entire night suffice.

43 Mentioned in Mishnah 2; Note 35.
44 Her outer genitals.
45 If she waits longer and then finds blood on her cloth.
46 A red stain found on her garment, even if it is not proven that it is a blood-stain.
47 Unless they tell them explicitly that they are impure.
48 This refers back to Mishnah 1. If a woman has to use cloths to check herself because of her occupation with pure food, the Hause of Shammai require that she use a separate cloth for each sex act, even if she examines them only the next morning, or, if she has only one cloth, that she examine it between any two sex acts. The House of Hillel admit repeated use of a single cloth for the entire night.

(49d line 67) **הלכה ג**: אֵיזֶהוּ לְאַחַר זְמָן כול׳. אָמַר רִבִּי יוֹסֵי בֵּירִבִּי בּוּן. אֵין זֶה אַחַר זְמָן אֶלָּא אַחַר אַחַר זְמָן. וְאֵיזֶהוּ לְאַחַר זְמָן. כְּדֵי שֶׁיִּפְשׁוֹט אֶת יָדָהּ וְתִיטוֹל אֶת הָעֵד מִתַּחַת הַכָּר. אֲבָל אַחַר אַחַר זְמָן בַּעֲלָהּ טָהוֹר.

Halakhah 3: "What is 'later'," etc. Rebbi Yose ben Rebbi Abun said, that is not later but after later. What is later? That she can stretch out her arm and take the cloth from under the bedsheet. But after later, her husband is pure[49].

49 The Sages disagree with R. Aqiba in the situation described in the Mishnah, that a stain is found after the woman left her bed to check herself. But in the situation described by R. Yose ben R. Abun the Sages will agree with R. Aqiba that both are impure. In the Babli, 14b, and the Tosephta, 3:6, the statement of R. Yose ben R. Abun is attributed to the Tanna R. Eleazar ben R. Sadoq (II), of R. Aqiba's generation.

(49d line 69) רִבִּי לֶעְזָר בְּשֵׁם רַב. דִּבְרֵי חֲכָמִים שֶׁהֵן בְּשִׁיטַת רִבִּי מֵאִיר. רִבִּי יוֹחָנָן אָמַר. חֲכָמִים מַמָּשׁ. מַאי כְדוֹן. חַבְרַייָא בְשֵׁם רִבִּי יוֹחָנָן. נֵילַף הָדָא דְרַבָּנָן מִן דְּרִבִּי עֲקִיבָה. כְּמַה דְרִבִּי עֲקִיבָה אוֹמֵר. מְטַמֵּא אֶת בּוֹעֲלָהּ וְאֵינָהּ מְקוּלְקֶלֶת לְמִנְייָנָהּ. כֵּן רַבָּנָן אָמְרִין. מְטַמֵּא אֶת בּוֹעֲלָהּ וְאֵינָהּ מְקוּלְקֶלֶת לְמִנְייָנָהּ.

Rebbi Eleazar in the name of Rav: The words of those Sages who follow the method of Rebbi Meïr[50]. Rebbi Johanan said, really the Sages[51]. How is that? The colleagues in the name of Rebbi Johanan: We shall infer the point of view of the Sages from that of Rebbi Aqiba. Just as Rebbi Aqiba says, she makes her sex partner impure retroactively but her count is not in disorder[52], so the Sages say, she makes her sex partner impure retroactively but her count is not in disorder[53].

50 The source which attributes the power to impart retroactive impurity to stains found on a garment (Chapter 1, Note 42) is attributed to R. Meïr. Rav thinks that if the Sages follow R. Aqiba in extending impurity to the sex partner in case a stain was found, they also must hold that the impurity is retroactive for 24 hours.

51 They deny retroactive impurity caused by stains.

52 Chapter 1, Note 45.

53 If the count is not in disorder, i. e., the 8th day after the onset of menstruation is well defined, then the onset is well defined and there is no place for retroactive impurity.

(50a line 4) אַבָּא בַּר יִרְמְיָה כַּהֲנָא בְשֵׁם שְׁמוּאֵל. כָּל־אִשָּׁה שֶׁאֵין לָהּ וֶסֶת אֲסוּרָה לְבֵיתָהּ עַד שֶׁתִּבְדּוֹק. וְהָתַנִּינָן. כָּל־הַנָּשִׁים בְּחֶזְקַת טַהֲרָה לְבַעֲלֵיהֶן. פָּתַר לָהּ. בַּבָּאִין מִן הַדֶּרֶךְ. וְהָתַנִּנָן. הַבָּאִין מִן הַדֶּרֶךְ נְשֵׁיהֶם לָהֶם בְּחֶזְקַת טַהֲרָה. אָמַר רִבִּי בּוּן בַּר חִיָּיה. תִּיפָּתַר שֶׁבָּא וּמְצָאָהּ עֵירָה. וְהָתַנֵּי. בֵּין שֶׁמְּצָאָהּ עֵירָה בֵּין צָאָהּ יְשֵׁינָה. אָמַר רִבִּי בָּא. תִּיפָּתַר שֶׁהִנִּיחָהּ בְּחֶזְקַת טַהֲרָה. כַּמָּה עוֹנָה נוֹתְנִין לָהּ. רִבִּי שִׁמְעוֹן בֶּן לָקִישׁ אָמַר. נוֹתְנִין לָהּ עוֹנָה בֵּינוֹנִית שְׁלֹשִׁים יוֹם. אָמַר רִבִּי יוֹחָנָן. שׁוֹנֶה אֲנִי אֲפִילוּ לְאַחַר שָׁלֹשׁ שָׁנִים מוּתָּר. וּבִלְבַד בְּאִשָּׁה שֶׁיֵּשׁ לָהּ וֶסֶת. אָמַר רִבִּי אַבָּהוּ. וְהִיא שֶׁשָּׁהָת אַחַר וַסְתָּהּ שִׁבְעַת יָמִים. וְחָשׁ לוֹמַר. שֶׁמָּא לֹא טָבְלָה. אָמַר רִבִּי חֲנִינָא. זֹאת אוֹמֶרֶת שֶׁאָסוּר לְאִשָּׁה לִשְׁהוֹת בְּטוּמְאָתָהּ. שְׁמוּאֵל בַּר אַבָּא בָעֵי. אֲפִילוּ דָּבָר בָּרִיא שֶׁיָּלְדָה. אָמַר רִבִּי יוֹסֵי. כָּךְ אָנוּ אוֹמְרִים. אֲפִילוּ נִטְמֵאת. אֶלָּא כֵּיוָן שֶׁיָּלְדָה בְּטָלָה חֶזְקָתָהּ. אַף הָכָא. כֵּיוָן שֶׁטִּימְאָת בָּטְלָה חֶזְקָתָהּ.

Abba bar Jeremiah, Cahana in the name of Samuel: Any woman without a definite period is forbidden to her house unless she checked herself[54]. But did we not state: "All women are presumed pure for their husbands." He explains it, for those who come from a trip. But did we not state: "The wives of men coming from a trip are presumed pure"? Rebbi Abun bar Ḥiyya said, explain it if he came and found her awake[55]. But was it not stated: Whether he found her awake or found her sleeping. Rebbi Abba said, explain it if he left her in a state of purity[56]. {What is the period that is counted for her? Rebbi Simeon ben Laqish said: One gives her 30 days as average period.}[57] Rebbi Joḥanan said, I am stating that it is permitted even after three years, but only for a woman who has a regular period[58]. Rebbi Abbahu said, only if it was seven days after the onset of her period[59]. Are you not worried that maybe she did not immerse herself[60]? Rebbi Ḥanina said, that means that it is forbidden for

HALAKHAH 3   659

a woman to stay in her impurity. Samuel bar Abba asked: Even if it was certain that she had given birth[61]? Rebbi Yose said, so we are saying, even if she became impure. But since her prior state was invalidated when she gave birth, so her prior state was invalidated when she became impure[62].

54 In the Babli, 54b, this is restricted to women preparing pure food. But the present paragraph seems to speak of women in general. Her house is her husband.

55 It is understood that she would inform him if she were forbidden to him.

56 One may assume that a prior state continues until one is appraised of a change. In the Babli 11b (Tosephta 3:8), this is a Tannaïtic statement; it is accepted as operative (16b) while in the Yerushalmi it is rejected at the end (Note 62).

57 It does not seem that this belongs here; it is an echo from Chapter 1, Note 132. It seems clear that if the wife has a regular period, the husband has to use *that* period to compute whether his wife is pure or impure at the time of his return, not any theoretical average.

58 Whose husband can compute in advance her days of purity. Then there is no question anymore of assuming the wife to be pure by her prior status of purity but of prior length of the period which may be assumed to remain unchanged. This is also the interpretation given R. Johanan's statement in the Babli, 15b.

59 Since the biblical days of impurity are 7, irrespective of the length of the menstruation.

60 And remain impure since her husband is away. This argument proves that in this paragraph one does not speak about a woman engaged in preparing pure food; if she prepared impure food her only reason for immersing herself in a *miqweh* would be to be able to sleep with her husband.

61 In that case, the prior regular period has ceased to exist and the woman has to establish a new period after she finishes nursing her baby. Even if she reestablishes a regular period of the same length, in most cases its position in the month will change. A prior knowledge cannot be

used when it is known to be obsolete. In the Babli, 15b, he addresses his question to R. Abba.

62 It is obvious that the computation based on the prior period cannot be used after it is known that the woman has given birth. Then it is also clear that if for any reason whatsoever the continuation of the regular period is in doubt, there can be no computation. The explanation given by R. Abba earlier in this paragraph is shown to be invalid since the woman is certain to have become impure by the time of her regular period and, therefore, has no presumption of purity. The only way to admit R. Joḥanan's statement is one based on the computation of pure days when there is no known change in the wife's regular period.

(50a line 17) בֵּית שַׁמַּאי אוֹמְרִים. צְרִיכָה שְׁנֵי עֵדִים עַל כָּל־תַּשְׁמִישׁ וְתַשְׁמִישׁ אוֹ תְשַׁמֵּשׁ לְאוֹר הַנֵּר. וְלֹא כֵן תַּנֵּי. הַמְשַׁמֵּשׁ מִיטָּתוֹ לְאוֹר הַנֵּר הֲרֵי זֶה מְגוּנֶּה. כֵּינֵי מַתְנִיתָא. תְּשַׁמֵּשׁ וְתִבְדוֹק לְאוֹר הַנֵּר. רִבִּי זְעִירָה רַב חִיָּיה בַּר אַשִׁי בְּשֵׁם רַב. שִׁימְּשָׁה בְעַד אֲסוּרָה לְבֵיתָהּ. אָמַר רִבִּי זְעִירָא. בְּשָׁעָה שֶׁהוֹכִיחָהּ קַיָּים מוּתֶּרֶת וּבְשָׁעָה שֶׁאֵין הוֹכִיחָהּ קַיָּים לֹא כָל־שֶׁכֵּן. אָמַר רִבִּי יוֹסֵי. תַּמָּן אַתְּ יָכוֹל לַעֲמוֹד עָלָיו. בְּרַם הָכָא אֵין אַתְּ יָכוֹל לַעֲמוֹד עָלָיו.

"The House of Shammai say, she needs two cloths for each intercourse or she should have sex by candle light." But was it not stated: The person who engages in sex by light is blameworthy[63]? So is the Mishnah: She may have sex[64] and [then] check by candle light. Rebbi Ze'ira, Rav Ḥiyya bar Ashi in the name of Rav: If she had intercourse using a cloth, she is forbidden to her house[65]. Rebbi Ze'ira said, if her proof exists, she is permitted; if there is no proof, not so much more[66]? Rebbi Yose said, there, you can determine the facts; here, you cannot determine the facts[67].

63 Also quoted in the Babli, 16b.
64 In the dark. The Babli takes the Mishnah as it is written.

65 She is working with pure food and, therefore, is cleansing herself after intercourse. If in the morning

(following the House of Hillel) the cloth cannot be found, she is declared impure until she checks herself out a second time.

66   A woman who does not work with pure food can have sex without checking herself with a cloth and is always presumed pure unless known to be impure. Why should a woman using a cloth be in a worse position than one who does not use it?

67   If she already has to use a cloth, that cloth must be of use. The use is to confirm her status of purity. If the status cannot be confirmed because the cloth was lost, why should her status of purity be confirmed?

(fol. 49d) **משנה ד:** מָשָׁל מָשְׁלוּ חֲכָמִים בָּאִשָּׁה. הַחֶדֶר וְהַפְּרוֹזְדוֹד וְהָעֲלִיָּה. דַּם הַחֶדֶר טְמֵאִים. נִמְצָא בַּפְּרוֹזְדוֹד סְפֵיקוֹ טָמֵא מִפְּנֵי שֶׁחֶזְקָתוֹ מִן הַמָּקוֹר.

Mishnah 4: The Sages gave a simile about a woman's anatomy: The room[68], the anteroom[69], and the upper floor[70]. The blood from the room is impure. If it is found in the anteroom it is impure even in the case of a doubt since it is presumed to come from the source[71].

68   The uterus.
69   The vagina. The Babli version is פְּרוֹזְדוֹר. Cf. Greek πρόθυρον "front door; porch", also πρόσοδος "approach, onset; sexual intercourse".
70   The ovary. The Fallopian tubes leading from the ovary to the uterus in the Babli are called לוּל "staircase, chicken coop".
71   The walls of the room. The implication is that blood originating in the ovary or the tubes is pure.

(50a line 23) **הלכה ד:** מָשָׁל מָשְׁלוּ חֲכָמִים בָּאִשָּׁה כול׳. כֵּינִי מַתְנִיתָא. דַּם הַחֶדֶר טָמֵא וְדַם עֲלִיָּיה טָהוֹר. רַב יְהוּדָה בְּשֵׁם שְׁמוּאֵל. הַחֶדֶר לִפְנִים מִן הַפְּרוֹזְדוֹד וְהָעֲלִיָּיה נְתוּנָה עַל גַּבֵּי חֲצִי הַפְּרוֹזְדוֹד וּפִיתְחָהּ שֶׁלָּעֲלִיָּיה פָּתוּחַ לַפְּרוֹזְדוֹד. רַב נַחְמָן בַּר רַב יִצְחָק שָׁאַל לְרַב חוּנָא. מַתְנִיתָא בְּשֶׁנִּמְצָא

מִפְתַּח הָעֲלִיָּה וְלִפְנִים. אָמַר לֵיהּ. אִם בְּשֶׁנִּמְצָא מִפְתַּח הָעֲלִיָּה וְלִפְנִים בְּוַדַּאי הִיא. אֶלָּא כֵּן אֲנָן קַיָּימִין. בְּשֶׁנִּמְצָא מִפְתַּח הָעֲלִיָּה וְלַחוּץ. מִילֵּיהוֹן דְּרַבָּנָן פְּלִיגִין. דָּמַר רִבִּי יוֹחָנָן. שְׁלֹשָׁה הֵן שֶׁהֵן כְּסָפֵק וְעָשׂוּ אוֹתָן כְּוַדַּאי. וְאֵילּוּ הֵן. הַמַּפֶּלֶת יָד חֲתוּכָה וְרֶגֶל חֲתוּכָה. וְשִׁילְיָא. וְדָם הַנִּמְצָא בִּפְרוֹזְדוֹד. מָה אֲנָן קַיָּימִין. אִם בְּשֶׁנִּמְצָא מִפְתַּח הָעֲלִיָּה וְלִפְנִים כְּוַדַּאי הִיא. אֶלָּא כֵּן אֲנָן קַיָּימִין. בְּשֶׁנִּמְצָא מִפְתַּח הָעֲלִיָּה וְלַחוּץ. רִבִּי אַבָּא בְּרֵיהּ דְּרִבִּי פַּפִּי בְּעָא קוֹמֵי רִבִּי יוֹסֵי. תְּנִינָן כַּמָּה סְפֵיקוֹת וְאַתְּ אָמַר הָכֵין. אָמַר לֵיהּ מַה דָּמַר רִבִּי יוֹחָנָן בְּאִשָּׁה.

Halakhah 4: "The Sages gave a simile about a woman's anatomy," etc. So is the Mishnah: The blood from the room is impure but the blood from the upper floor is pure[72]. Rav Jehudah in the name of Samuel: The room is inwards from the anteroom; the upper floor is over the room up to the middle of the anteroom, the door of the upper floor opens to the anteroom[73]. Rav Naḥman bar Rav Isaac asked Rav Huna: Does the Mishnah [deal with the case that blood was found] inwards of the door of the upper floor[74]? He said to him, if it was found inwards of the door of the upper floor it is certainly [impure]. But we deal with the case that it was found outwards from the door of the upper floor[75]. The words of the rabbis disagree, since Rebbi Joḥanan said, three are like a doubt but they treated them as certain, viz., the following: A woman who has a miscarriage in the form of a cut-off hand or cut-off foot[76], or a placenta[77], and blood found in the anteroom[78]. What are we speaking of? If it was found inwards of the door of the upper floor it is certainly [impure]. But we must deal with the case that it was found outwards from the door of the upper floor. Rebbi Abba the son of Rebbi Pappaios asked before Rebbi Yose: We have stated many doubts[79] and you say so? He said to him, Rebbi Joḥanan spoke only of a woman[80].

72 The second part of the Mishnah would be superfluous if all blood in the genital apparatus were impure.

73 It is not known what is the source of anatomical knowledge in Babylonian medical schools. The anatomy of Palestinian authors seems to be derived from lost Roman sources; it is reported (Babli 30b, Tosephta 4:17) that the slave girls who had helped with Cleopatra's suicide were delivered to Roman doctors who made them pregnant and then killed them in various stages of pregnancy to study the development of the fetus.

In the Babli, 17b, the statement is credited to the school of Rav Huna.

74 Does the presumption of impurity of the blood presuppose proof that it is unlikely to come from the tubes?

75 Therefore, the blood is treated as probably, but not certainly, impure. If the woman touched heave, the heave would be in limbo, could not be used nor be burned before it spoils.

76 Mishnah 3:1. If the miscarriage produces something that does not look at all like a human fetus, one might think that it was questionable whether there really had been a pregnancy and there should be no pure period but this is treated like a birth and the woman becomes impure (as for a female) and subsequently pure (as for a male).

77 An empty placenta is treated as sign of a birth even if it was not preceded by any child, Mishnah 3:4.

78 The case of the Mishnah here. According to R. Johanan, heave becomes certainly impure and has to be burned immediately. In the Babli, 17b, the disagreement between the Babylonian Rav Huna and the Galilean R. Johanan is quoted as one between the Babylonian Rav Qaṭina (a colleague of Rav Huna) and the Galilean R. Ḥiyya (the Elder).

79 There are many more Mishnaiot (partially enumerated in the Babli, 18a) in which cases of impurity are resolved by rabbinic rules without all the facts being known which would allow a factual determination. Why does R. Johanan count only three?

80 The same answer in the Babli, 18a.

(fol. 49d) **משנה ה:** חֲמִשָּׁה דָמִים טְמֵאִים בָּאִשָּׁה הָאָדוֹם וְהַשָּׁחוֹר וּכְקֶרֶן כַּרְכּוֹם וּכְמֵימֵי אֲדָמָה וְכַמֶּזֶג. בֵּית שַׁמַּאי אוֹמְרִים אַף כְּמֵי תִלְתָּן וּכְמֵימֵי בָּשָׂר צָלִי וּבֵית הֻלֵּל מְטַהֲרִין. הַיָּרוֹק עֲקַבְיָה בֶּן מַהֲלַלְאֵל מְטַמֵּא וַחֲכָמִים מְטַהֲרִים. אָמַר רִבִּי מֵאִיר אִם אֵינוֹ מְטַמֵּא מִשּׁוּם כֶּתֶם מְטַמֵּא מִשּׁוּם מַשְׁקֶה. רִבִּי יוֹסֵי אוֹמֵר לֹא כָךְ וְלֹא כָךְ.

Mishnah 5: Five kinds of blood are impure from a woman: Red, black, like saffron stigma[81], and like earth water[82], and like mixed wine[83]. The Hause of Shammai say, also like fenugreek water[84] and like roast beef juice, but the House of Hillel declare these pure. The green[85] Aqabia ben Mahalalel declares impure but the Sages declare it pure. Rebbi Meïr said, if it does not cause impurity as a stain, it causes impurity as a body fluid[86]. Rebbi Yose says, neither one nor the other.

81 Which has the shape of a horn, קרן.
82 Reddish ochre.
83 Red wine mixed with water.
84 Water in which fenugreek seeds were steeped.
85 Yellowish green, the color of an *etrog* (*citrus medica*).
86 The body fluids (blood, urine) of a menstruating woman are sources of original impurity.

(50a line 35) **הלכה ה:** חֲמִשָּׁה דָמִים טְמֵאִים בָּאִשָּׁה כול'. רַב וְרִבִּי יוֹחָנָן תְּרֵיהוֹן אָמְרִין. אַרְבָּעָה דָמִים הֵן. אָדוֹם הוּא שֶׁהוּא לוֹקֶה וְנַעֲשָׂה שָׁחוֹר. שְׁמוּאֵל אָמַר. שָׁחוֹר בָּא מִכּוּלָּן. מְנַיִין לַחֲמִשָּׁה דָמִים טְמֵאִים מִן הַתּוֹרָה. אָמַר רִבִּי יְהוֹשֻׁעַ בֶּן לֵוִי. וְהִיא גִילְתָהּ אֶת מְקוֹר דָּמֶיהָ. וְטָהֲרָה מִמְּקוֹר דָּמֶיהָ. דָּם יִהְיֶה זוֹבָהּ בִּבְשָׂרָהּ. וְהָא וְאִשָּׁה כִּי יָזוּב זוֹב דָּמָהּ מִינְהוֹן הוּא. אֶלָּא שֶׁבָּא עָלֶיהָ בִּימֵי זִיבָתָהּ וְעָשָׂה אוֹתָהּ זִיבָה. וּמְנַיִין שֶׁיֵּשׁ דָּמִים טְמֵאִין וְיֵשׁ דָּמִים טְהוֹרִין. רִבִּי חָמָא בַּר יוֹסֵף בְּשֵׁם רִבִּי הוֹשַׁעֲיָא. כְּתִיב כִּי יִפָּלֵא מִמְּךָ דָבָר לְמִשְׁפָּט בֵּין דָּם לְדָם אֵין כְּתִיב כָּאן אֶלָּא בֵּין דָּם לְדָם. מִיכָּן שֶׁיֵּשׁ דָּמִים טְמֵאִין וְיֵשׁ דָּמִים טְהוֹרִין.

Halakhah 5: "Five kinds of blood are impure from a woman," etc. Rav and Rebbi Joḥanan both say that there are four kinds of blood. The red one oxydizes and becomes black[87]. Samuel said, black comes from all of them. From where that there are five kinds of blood impure by the Torah? Rebbi Joshua ben Levi said, "she uncovered the source of her bloods[88]," "she shall be purified from the source of her bloods,[89]" "blood will be the excretion of her genitals.[90]" But "a woman whose excretion of blood flows"[91] is also there! That only comes to her in the days of her excessive flow to turn her into a *zavah*[92]. From where that there is impure and pure blood? Rebbi Ḥama ben Joseph in the name of Rebbi Hoshaiah[93]: It is written: "If something in the law is too difficult for you;" then it is not written "whether blood and blood" but "between blood and blood"[94], that shows that there is impure and pure blood[95].

---

87 In the Babli, 19a, 20a, this is a statement of R. Ḥanina supported by a Tannaïtic statement. Samuel's statement is ascribed there to Rami bar Abba, a student of Rav Huna.

88 *Lev.* 20:18.

89 *Lev.* 12:7.

90 *Lev.* 15:19. This verse is not quoted in the Babli, 19a, since only four kinds of blood have to be established. Also, that verse is needed to establish the fact that a menstruating woman is impure; in the hermeneutics of the Babli it cannot be used to establish details of the rule. The other two verses mention the blood as a kind of side remark; they can be used to establish the details. The argument is that in both verses the plural is used; an indefinite plural always means 2 (cf. H. Guggenheimer, *Logical Problems in Jewish Tradition*; cf. Chapter 1, Note 83), and 2+2 = 4.

91 *Lev.* 15:25.

92 The verse deals with a different subject, with blood that is not menstrual.

93 Quoted in the Babli, 19a, in the names of the same authors.

94 *Deut.* 17:8.

95 That there are cases of impurity of blood which need a judicial determination.

(50a line 45) בֵּית שַׁמַּאי אוֹמְרִים אַף כְּימֵי תִלְתָּן וּכְמֵימֵי בָשָׂר צָלִי. הֲרֵי שִׁבְעָה. דּוֹמִין הֵן לְמֵימֵי אֲדָמָה. רִבִּי יוֹסֵי בְשֵׁם רַב חֲבֵרַיָּיא בְשֵׁם רִבִּי יוֹחָנָן. לֹא טִימֵּא רִבִּי מֵאִיר אֶלָּא שֶׁנָּגַע בּוֹ עֲקִיבָה. וִיטַמֵּא כְּימֵי תִלְתָּן וּכְמֵימֵי בָשָׂר צָלִי שֶׁנָּגְעוּ בָהֶן בֵּית שַׁמַּי. אוֹמְרִין הֵן. דּוֹמִים לְמֵימֵי אֲדָמָה. דָּם טָהוֹר מַכְשִׁיר. דָּם טָמֵא אֵינוֹ מַכְשִׁיר.

"The Hause of Shammai say, also like fenugreek water and like roast beef juice." That makes seven[96]. They are similar to earth water[97]. Rebbi Yose in the name of Rav, the colleagues in the name of Rebbi Joḥanan: Rebbi Meïr did not declare impure, only Aqabia mentioned it[98]. Then it also should bring impurity like fenugreek water and like roast beef juice which were mentioned by the House of Shammai! These are similar to earth water[99]. Pure blood prepares for impurity, impure blood does not prepare[100].

96 The preceding paragraph established that there can be only five kinds.

97 Not counted separately.

98 As explained in Tractate *Demay,* Chapter 2, Notes 136, 137, 141, dry harvested produce remains impervious to impurity as long as it remains dry. But if it is wetted by human body fluids, it becomes susceptible to impurity. R. Meïr agrees that green discharge is not menstrual blood and therefore not impure in itself, but as a body fluid it will have the power to prepare dry food for impurity. R. Yose objects since a green discharge is not blood and only blood, breast milk, sweat, spittle, semen, and urine are the body fluids which prepare for impurity.

99 Therefore, the House of Hillel will agree that they can prepare for impurity.

100 This is a minority opinion of R. Eleazar ben Azariah, Mishnah *Makhširin* 6:5. According to the majority opinion, in general what prepares does not make impure but menstrual blood prepares and transfers impurity at the same moment. For this opinion, one would translate: "Impure blood does not need preparation."

משנה ו: אֵי זֶהוּ הָאָדוֹם כְּדַם הַמַּכָּה. הַשָּׁחוֹר כְּחֶרֶת. דִּיהֵא מִיכֵּן (fol. 49d) טָהוֹר. וּכְקֶרֶן כַּרְכּוֹם כַּבָּרוּר שֶׁבּוֹ. וּכְמֵימֵי אֲדָמָה מִבִּקְעַת בֵּית כֶּרֶם וּמֵצִיף מַיִם. וְכַמֶּזֶג שְׁנֵי חֲלָקִים מַיִם וְאֶחָד יַיִן מִן הַיַּיִן הַשָּׁרוֹנִי.

Mishnah 6: How is red? Like blood from a wound. Black, like ink-stone[101]; lighter than that is pure. Like saffron stigma, like the uniformly colored part of it[102]. Like earth water, from the valley of Bet Kerem[103] on which water was poured. And like mixed wine, two parts water for one part Sharon wine.

101 Ink is made by scraping of flakes and dissolving them in water.

102 Which is reddish, not yellow.

103 Near Jerusalem, from where the stones for the Temple were quarried (Mishnah *Middot* 3:4).

הלכה ו: אֵי זֶהוּ הָאָדוֹם כול'. רִבִּי יַעֲקֹב בַּר אָחָא רִבִּי עוּלָא (50a line 50) דְקַיְסָרִין בְּשֵׁם רִבִּי חֲנִינָה רִבִּי בָּא בְּשֵׁם רִבִּי שִׁמְעוֹן בֶּן מְנַסְיָא. כְּדַם הַמַּכָּה שֶׁלָּקַת וְשִׁינָּת. אָמַר רִבִּי יַעֲקֹב בַּר סוֹסַיי קוֹמֵי רִבִּי יוֹסֵי. וּמַתְנִיתָא אָמְרָה כֵן. אָדוֹם כְּדַם הַמַּכָּה. רִבִּי יִצְחָק בַּר נַחְמָן וְרִבִּי אַבְדּוּמָא דְמִן חֵיפָא הֲווֹן יָתְבִין. אָתָא חַד בַּר נַשׁ. אָמַר רִבִּי יִצְחָק בַּר נַחְמָן לְרִבִּי אַבְדּוּמָא. קָרוֹב הוּא זֶה לָבֹא לְדַם נִידָּה. מַה וּפְלִיג. שָׁאִילוּ יָשְׁנָה הֲוָה כְדַם הַנִּידָה.

Halakhah 6: "How is red," etc. Rebbi Jacob bar Aha, Rebbi Ulla from Caesarea in the name of Rebbi Ḥanina; Rebbi Abba in the name of Rebbi Simeon ben Menasia: Like blood of a wound which was hit a second time. Rebbi Jacob bar Sosai said before Rebbi Yose: The Mishnah implies this, "red like blood from a wound.[104]" Rebbi Isaac bar Naḥman and Rebbi Eudaimon from Haifa were sitting together when a man passed by them[105]. Rebbi Isaac bar Naḥman said to Rebbi Eudaimon from Haifa: That one is close to produce blood of a menstruating woman. Does he disagree? If he would be hit a second time, it would be like menstrual blood.

104 Blood coming from a pre-existing wound. In the Babli, 19b, many different characterizations are given and one of them is "blood from a wound on the small finger of an unmarried teenager which had healed and opened a second time." Such a string of conditions is characteristic for the Babli which wants to make sure that these criteria are never used *in praxi*.

105 It seems that he had an open wound.

(50a line 56) וְהַשָּׁחוֹר כְּחֶרֶת. כֵּיצַד הוּא עוֹשֶׂה. רִבִּי בָּא בְשֵׁם רַב יְהוּדָה. נוֹטֵל אֶת הַחֶרֶת וְנוֹתֵן עַל גַּבֵּי עוֹר לָבָן. רִבִּי יוֹסֵי בֵּירִבִּי בּוּן אָמַר. עַל גַּבֵּי עוֹר צָבוּעַ. רִבִּי זְעִירָא בְשֵׁם רַבָּנָן. שָׁחוֹר כְּעוֹרֵב שָׁחוֹר כְּעָנָב שָׁחוֹר כְּזֶפֶת טָהוֹר. חֲבֵרַיָּיא בְשֵׁם רִבִּי יוֹחָנָן. שָׁחוֹר כְּדִיוֹ טָהוֹר. רִבִּי אַמִי בְשֵׁם רִבִּי יוֹחָנָן. כְּפִילְיוֹן שֶׁלָּרֹאשׁ הַבָּא מִמְּדִינַת הַיָּם טָמֵא. רִבִּי זְעִירָא בְּעָא קוֹמֵי רִבִּי אַמִי. כָּל־הַלֵּין מִילַיָּיא לְעוֹבְדָא. אָמַר לֵיהּ. אִין. רִבִּי שִׁמְעוֹן בֶּן לָקִישׁ אָמַר. כּוּלְּהוֹן דִּיהֵא מִיכֵּן טָהוֹר. עָמוֹק מִיכֵּן טָמֵא. רִבִּי יוֹחָנָן אָמַר. כּוּלְּהוֹן דִּיהֵא מִיכֵּן טָהוֹר. עָמוֹק מִיכֵּן טָהוֹר חוּץ מִשָּׁחוֹר. מַתְנִיתָא מְסַיְּיעָא לְרִבִּי יוֹחָנָן. דְּתַנִינָן. וְהַשָּׁחוֹר כְּחֶרֶת טָמֵא. דִּיהֵא מִכֵּן טָהוֹר. הָא עָמוֹק מִכֵּן טָמֵא. לֹא אֲמָרִינָן אֶלָּא שָׁחוֹר. הָא כּוּלְּהוֹן אֲפִילוּ עֲמוּקִין מִיכֵּן טְהוֹרִין. קַרְתֵּיהּ דְּרַב יְהוּדָה כְּרִבִּי שִׁמְעוֹן בֶּן לָקִישׁ. וְרַב יְהוּדָה כְּרִבִּי יוֹחָנָן. תַּנֵּי בַּר קַפָּרָא וּמְסַיֵּיעַ לְרִבִּי שִׁמְעוֹן בֶּן לָקִישׁ וְלָא עָבְדִין עוֹבְדָא דִכְוָותֵיהּ. דְּרִבִּי חֲנִינָה מָזִיג מֶזֶג לְבַר קַפָּרָא. אָמַר לֵיהּ. כְּזֶה מָהוּ. אָמַר לֵיהּ. טָמֵא. אַדְהִיתֵיהּ. אָמַר לֵיהּ. טָהוֹר. אָמַר לֵיהּ. יְהֵא שְׁלָמָא לְנַבְרָא דְטָעָה בְּפוּמֵיהּ וְלֹא טָעָה בְּעַיְינוֹי. הֲווֹן בְּעָיֵי מֵימַר. מָאן דָּמַר. טָהוֹר. בְּמִצְחָחַ. וּמָאן דָּמַר. טָמֵא. בְּשֶׁאֵינוֹ מִצְחָחַ. נִישְׁמְעִינָהּ מִן הָדָא. מַעֲשֶׂה בְאִשָּׁה אַחַת מִשְּׁלְבֵית רִבִּי שֶׁהָיְתָה רוֹאָה דָמִים שְׁחוֹרִין. אָתָא עוֹבְדָא קוֹמֵי רִבִּי יַעֲקֹב בַּר זַבְדִּי וְקוֹמֵי רִבִּי יִצְחָק בַּר טַבְלַיי וּבָקְשׁוּ לְטַמוֹתָהּ. אָמַר לוֹן רִבִּי חֶלְבּוֹ. כֵּן אָמַר רַב חוּנָא בְשֵׁם רַב. שָׁחוֹר מַקְדִּיר טָהוֹר. מִצְחֶחַ טָמֵא. לֹא אָמַר אֶלָּא שָׁחוֹר. הָא כּוּלְּהוֹן אֲפִילוּ מִצְחָחִין טְהוֹרִין.

"And black, like ink-stone." How do you check that? Rebbi Abba in the name of Rav Jehudah: One takes the ink-stone and puts in on white leather[106]. Rebbi Yose ben Rebbi Abun said, on colored leather[107]. Rebbi Ze'ira in the name of the rabbis: Black like a raven, black like a grape berry, black like asphalt are pure. The colleagues in the name of Rebbi Johanan: Black like liquid ink is pure[108]. Rebbi Immi in the name of Rebbi Johanan: Like a felt hat imported from overseas is impure. Rebbi Ze'ira asked before Rebbi Immi: Are all these facts to be acted upon? He answered him, yes. Rebbi Simeon ben Laqish said, all of them, if they are lighter than the standard they are pure, darker than the standard impure[109]. Rebbi Johanan said, all of them, if they are lighter than the standard they are pure, darker than the standard pure except for black[110]. The Mishnah supports Rebbi Johanan, as we have stated: "And black like ink-stone is impure, lighter than that is pure." Therefore, darker than that is impure, but only black was mentioned in that connection. Therefore, all others, even if they are darker than the standards, are pure. The town of Rav Jehudah followed Rebbi Simeon ben Laqish but Rav Jehudah himself followed Rebbi Johanan. Bar Qappara stated a support for Rebbi Simeon ben Laqish[109] but one does not follow him in practice, since Rebbi Hanina mixed wine for Bar Qappara and asked him, if it is like that, what is its status? He answered, impure. He lightened it, then he answered, pure. He said to him, peace shall be on him who erred with his mouth but not with his eyes[111]. They wanted to say that he who says pure, refers to when it was polished[112]. But he who says impure, if it is not polished. Let us hear from the following: It happened that a woman from the Patriarchate had a discharge of black blood. The case came before Rebbi

Jacob bar Zabdi and Rebbi Isaac bar Tabelai; they wanted to declare her impure. Rebbi Helbo told them: So says Rav Huna in the name of Rav: Black which penetrates[113] is pure, that which polishes is impure. He said that only about black. Therefore, all others are pure even if they polish[114].

106 On a white background to make the black appear deeper. In the Babli, 20a, Samuel requires a white cloth.

107 To make the black appear more muted.

108 In the Babli, 20a, liquid ink and grape are classified as impure by Samuel, asphalt and raven as pure by R. Eleazar.

109 Tosephta 3:11. In the Babli, 20a, this is the position of Ulla and Bar Qappara (who is mentioned in the same sense later in this paragraph); the latter explicitly excludes the looks of mixed wine from this rule. The question is whether the list of shades given in the Mishnah is to be taken as limit of what is impure or is an exact description.

110 In the Babli, 20a, this is a definite minority opinion ascribed tentatively to Rebbi Immi (bar Abba). It is not mentioned in the Tosephta.

111 In the Babli, 20a, the same story is told with R. Hanina praising Bar Qappara who sticks to his teachings since he had exempted mixed wine from his general rule. In the Yerushalmi he is praised for following in practice what two generations later would be the teachings of R. Johanan while formulating support for what would be the position of R. Simeon ben Laqish.

112 If it forms a shiny crust.

113 The blood colors any textile but the stain never reflects light.

114 And do not exactly represent any of the colors described in the Mishnah.

(502 line 2) וּכְקֶרֶן כַּרְכּוֹם כַּבָּרוּר שֶׁבּוֹ. כָּלַח וְלֹא כְיָבֵשׁ. כָּעֶלְיוֹן וְלֹא כַתַּחְתּוֹן. בְּרוּאֶה אֶת הַצֵּל וְלֹא בְרוּאֶה אֶת הַחַמָּה. רִבִּי אַבָּהוּ אַייְתֵי קוֹמֵי רִבִּי לְעָזָר בְּאִילֵּין קוֹזְקַזְתְּחוֹן. אָמַר לֵיהּ. כְּבָר דָּהוּ מַרְאָיו. רִבִּי יַעֲקֹב בַּר זַבְדִּי אַייְתֵי

HALAKHAH 6

קוֹמֵי רִבִּי אַבָּהוּ דַּם שָׂעִיר בְּאָדוֹם. וְדַם דָּגִים בְּשָׁחוֹר. אֲמַר לֵיהּ. כְּבָר דָּהוּא מַרְאָיו.

"Like saffron stigma, like the uniformly colored part of it." Moist, not dried[115]. From the upper part, not the lower[116]. From the part in the shadow, not exposed to the sun. Rebbi Abbahu brought before Rebbi Eleazar[117] in cupper's vessels. He said to him, its looks already are dimmed. Rebbi Jacob bar Zavdi brought before Rebbi Abbahu goat's blood as [example of] red, fish blood as [example of] black. He said to him, its looks already are dimmed[118]

115 Agreed to in the Babli, 20a, and in Tosephta 3:11.	117 He brought him blood to examine, probably in a glass vessel.
116 Put in doubt in the Babli, 20a; confirmed in Tosephta 3:11.	118 The color of blood can be judged only when it is fresh.

(502 line 7) וּכְמֵימֵי אֲדָמָה מִבִּקְעַת בֵּית כֶּרֶם מֵיצֵף מַיִם. רִבִּי חֲנִינָה וְרִבִּי יוֹנָתָן תְּרֵיהוֹן אָמְרִין. מֵיצֵף מַיִם עַל גַּבֵּי מַטְלֵית.

"Like earth water, from the valley of Bet Kerem on which water was poured." Rebbi Ḥanina and Rebbi Jonathan both say one pours the water on a piece of cloth[119].

119 One checks the color remaining on the cloth. In the Babli, 20a, R.	Ḥanina is reported having used dry ochre; cf. Note 130.

(502 line 9) וְכַמֶּזֶג. אַבָּא בַּר חָנָה בְּשֵׁם רִבִּי יוֹחָנָן. כּוֹס מָזוּג נִרְאֶה מִבַּחוּץ. הֲווֹן בָּעֵיי מֵימַר. כְּגוֹן אִילֵּין כַּסַּיָּיא טִיבֶּרְיָיאָה. אָמַר רִבִּי אַבְדּוּמָא דְצִיפּוֹרִין קוֹמֵי רִבִּי מָנָא. כְּגוֹן הָדָא פִּיַּילִיתָא שֶׁאֵינָהּ עוֹשָׂה צֵל לִכְתָלֶיהָ. שְׁמוּאֵל אָמַר. כָּל־מִי שֶׁאֵינוֹ יוֹדֵעַ לִרְאוֹת דָּמִים טְהוֹרִין לֹא יִרְאֶה דָּמִים טְמֵאִין. רַב אָמַר. עַד שֶׁיְּהֵא בָקִי בָּהֶן וּבִשְׁמוֹתֵיהֶן. מִילְּתֵיהּ דְּרִבִּי יוֹחָנָן אָמְרָה כֵן. כָּל־דָּמִים

טְהוֹרִין אֲנִי יוֹדֵעַ וְכָל־דָּמִים טְמֵאִים אֲנִי יוֹדֵעַ. אִם טָהוֹר שֶׁבָּאָדוֹם הוּא. הוּא טָמֵא שֶׁכְּמֵימֵי אֲדָמָה. מָאן דְּלָא יְדַע הָא לָא יְדַע חֲמֵי. וְעוֹד מִן הָדָא דְּתַנֵּי. יְצָלְלוּ וְלֹא יַעֲכָרוּ. רִבִּי חֲנִינָה עֲכַר. אָמְרוּן קוֹמֵי רִבִּי יוֹחָנָן. רִבִּי חֲנִינָה עֲכַר וְאַתְּ לָא עֲכַר. אָמַר לוֹן. רִבִּי חֲנִינָה שָׁתֵי עוֹתִיק. רִבִּי יוֹחָנָן לֹא שָׁתֵי עוֹתִיק. רִבִּי חֲנִינָה שָׁתֵי עוֹתִיק דְּעוֹתְקָן. אָמַר רִבִּי הוֹשַׁעְיָה. מִן בְּגִין דְּרִבִּי חֲנִינָה עֵינֵיהּ שְׁבִיעָה בְּעוֹבְדֵיָּיהּ אֲפִילוּ עָכוּר לֹא פְסָלֵיהּ. רִבִּי שַׁמַּי בְּשֵׁם רִבִּי אָחָא. רִבִּי חֲנִינָה מְשַׁעֵר בְּגוּשׁ שֶׁלַּאֲדָמָה. רִבִּי אָבוּן רִבִּי שַׁמַּי בְּשֵׁם רִבִּי אָחָא. מִן בְּגִין דַּאֲנָן יָדְעִין דְּרִבִּי חֲנִינָה כָּשֵׁר בְּגִין כֵּן אֲנָן סָמְכִין עֲלוֹי. רִבִּי חֲנִינָה הֲוָה שָׁרֵי בְּצִיפּוֹרִין וַהֲווֹן אָתַאי קוֹמוֹי עוֹבְדִין וּמַפֵּק מִן תַּרְתֵּין זִימְנִין. וַהֲווֹן רִבִּי יוֹחָנָן וְרִבִּי שִׁמְעוֹן בֶּן לָקִישׁ שַׁרְיָין תַּמָּן וְלָא הֲוָה מְצָרֵף לוֹן עִמֵּיהּ. אָמְרִין. חֲכִים הוּא הַהוּא סָבָּא דְּפַרְזְלוֹי חֲרִיפִין. חַד זְמָן צְרָפוֹן עִמֵּיהּ. אָמְרִין. מַה חָמָא רִבִּי מַשְׁגַּח עֲלֵינָן יוֹמָא דֵין. אָמַר לוֹן. יֵיתֵי עָלַי אִם לֹא כָל־מַעֲשֶׂה וּמַעֲשֶׂה שֶׁהָיִיתִי מוֹצִיא אִם לֹא שְׁמַעְתִּי אוֹתוֹ מֵרִבִּי לַהֲלָכָה כִּשְׂעָרוֹת רֹאשִׁי. וּלְמַעֲשֶׂה שְׁלֹשָׁה פְעָמִים. וְהֵן עוֹבְדָא לֹא אָתָא קוֹמֵי רִבִּי אֶלָּא תְּרֵין זִימְנִין. מִן בְּגִין כֵּן צְרִיפַתְכוֹן עִמִּי.

"And like mixed wine." Abba bar Ḥana[120] in the name of Rebbi Joḥanan: As one sees a cup of mixed wine from the outside. They wanted to say, in a Tiberian cup. Rebbi Eudaimon from Sepphoris said before Rebbi Mana: As in a small phial[121] whose walls do not cast a shadow[122]. Samuel said, anybody who has no experience in seeing kinds of pure blood should not judge kinds of impure blood[123]. Rav said, only if he is competent about them and their names[124]. The words of Rebbi Joḥanan say so: I know all kinds of pure blood and of impure blood. The pure is the most red; the impure is like earth water. "If he has no experience[125]," therefore, if he has experience he can judge it. In addition, from what we have stated[126]: clear but not turbid. Rebbi Ḥanina used it turbid[127]. They said before Rebbi Johanan: Rebbi Hanina uses it turbid, but you said, not turbid. He said to them, Rebbi Hanina drinks old [wine], Rebbi Johanan does not drink old [wine], Rebbi Hanina drinks oldest [wine][128]. Rebbi Hoshaiah said: Since Rebbi Hoshaiah's eye is full of happenings[129], even turbid is not disqualified for him. Rebbi Shammai in the name of Rebbi Aha: Rebbi Hanina estimated with a lump of earth[130]. Rebbi Abun, Rebbi Shammai in the name of Rebbi Aha: Since we know that Rebbi Hanina is competent, do we follow his precedents[131]? Rebbi Hanina was living in Sepphoris, they brought cases before him and he decided on the basis of three precedents. Rebbi Johanan and Rebbi Simeon ben Laqish were there but he did not invite them to sit with him[132]. They said, the old man is a Sage since his irons are sharp[133]! Once he invited them to sit with him. They said, for what reason do you take notice of us this time? He said, so should come over me[134] if I had not heard every single case from Rebbi in theory as many times as there are hairs on my head, and in a practical way three times; but the present case did come before Rebbi only twice. Therefore, I adjoined you with me.

120   It seems rather that this should be R. Abba bar bar Hana, known as student of R. Johanan, and not his father Rav Abba bar Hana, nephew of R. Hiyya the Elder.
121   Diminutive of פַּיָילִי, Greek φιάλη, Latin *phiala*, "phial, saucer".
122   In a colorless glass phial (Rashi 21a), cf. Babli 21a.
123   He wants to restrict the authority to deliver an opinion on purity or impurity of blood to surgeons like himself.
124   An academically trained medical expert.
125   A quote from Samuel's statement.
126   Referring to the "earth water", paint made from ochre earth. In the Tosephta (3:11) the opposite is stated: One checks the color only if the water is turbid (i. e., if the entire fluid has a

uniform color), not if it is clear (if the ochre has separated and settled on the bottom.)

127 Confirmed in the Babli, 20a.

128 R. Ḥanina, of the generation of R. Joḥanan's teachers, had old traditions. In the Babli, 20b, R. Joḥanan complains that he never had training in judging kinds of blood because R. Ḥanina (a medical man) was so competent that he handled all cases by himself. This agrees with the story told here.

129 He has seen so many cases that he can use shortcuts to quickly come to a decision.

130 He did not have to dissolve it in water; confirmed by the Babli, 20a.

131 People with less competence have to follow the rules painstakingly.

132 There were young rabbis there but the Chief Rabbi kept them out of the decision process. R. Joḥanan himself said that he moved to Tiberias since he would never have amounted to much in Sepphoris because of R. Ḥanina's dominance.

133 His iron knife is sharp; i. e., he has no difficulty to decide. The Hebrew word for "judicial decision" is פְּסָק "what is cut off", a translation of Latin *decisio*, from *caedo* "to cut".

134 An oath inviting disaster if he was lying.

(502 line 30) רִבִּי יִצְחָק בַּר נַחְמָן יְלִיף מִן רִבִּי לְעָזָר דָּמִים טְהוֹרִין. הָא דָמִים טְמֵיאִין לֹא. וְלֹא כֵן אָמַר רִבִּי יִצְחָק בַּר נַחְמָן לְרִבִּי אֲבְדּוֹמָא דְחֵיפָא. קָרוֹב הוּא זֶה לָבוֹא לְדַם נִידָה. אֶלָּא מָאן דְּיָלִיף הָדֵין מִנֵּהּ יָלִיף הָדֵין. יִצְחָק בַּר יוֹנָתָן וְרַב הוּנָא הֲוֹון יְתִיבִין. אֲתַת חָדָא אִיתָּא וּשְׁאַלְתּוֹן. אָמַר לָהּ יִצְחָק בַּר יוֹנָתָן. חֲמִיתֵי עָטִיר מִנֵּיהּ. אָמַר לֵיהּ רַב הוּנָא. כֵּן אָמַר רַב. מִן דְּאָתֵי קוֹמֵיךְ הוֹרֵי. אָמַר רִבִּי יַעֲקֹב בַּר אָחָא בְּשֵׁם רִבִּי שִׁמְעוֹן בַּר אַבָּא. כַּמָּה קוּפִין דְּעוֹבָדִין הֲוָה אָתֵי קוֹמֵי רִבִּי חֲנִינָה וּמָה דַהֲוָה אָתֵי קוֹמוֹי הֲוָה אָמַר.

Rebbi Isaac bar Naḥman learned from Rebbi Eleazar the kinds of pure blood. Does this mean, not the impure kinds? But did not Rebbi Isaac bar Naḥman say to Rebbi Eudaimon from Haifa[135]: That one is close to produce blood of a menstruating woman[136]? But one who learns one kind, learns at the same time the other kind. Isaac bar Jonathan and Rav

Huna were sitting together when a woman came and asked them[137]. Isaac bar Jonathan said to her, did you see it more smoky than that[138]? Rav Huna said to him, so says Rav: Instruct according to what comes before you[139]! Rebbi Jacob bar Aḥa said in the name of Rebbi Simeon bar Abba: A number of chests full of problems came before Rebbi Ḥanina and about what came before him, he did pronounce[140].

135 Earlier, Note 105.
136 This shows that he was an expert in the matter of impure blood.
137 Showed them a blood stain.
138 Whether the stain originally was darker.
139 One has to decide according to the evidence produced. In the Babli, 20b, the formulation is: The judge has only what his eyes are seeing.
140 The "problems" were stained garments. He never investigated whether the stains had changed color in the meantime.

(502 line 38) מַהוּ לִרְאוֹת כְּתָמִים בַּלַּיְלָה. רִבִּי רָאָה בַּלַּיְלָה וְטִימֵּא. אָמַר. שׁוּבְקְתֵיהּ לְצַפְרָא. רָאָה בַּיּוֹם וְטִיהֵר. אָמַר. גְּדוֹלִים הֵן דִּבְרֵי חֲכָמִים שֶׁאָמְרוּ. אֵין רוֹאִין כְּתָמִים בַּלַּיְלָה. אָמַר. שׁוּבְקְתֵיהּ לְרַמְשָׁא. רָאָה בַּלַּיְלָה וְטִיהֵר. אָמַר. וְלֹא אֲנִי הוּא שֶׁטָּעִיתִי הוּא הוּא שְׁדִיחֶה.

May one review stains at night? [141]Rebbi reviewed at night and declared impure. He said, let it stay until morning. He reviewed at daylight and declared pure. He said, great are the words of the Sages who said, one does not review stains at night[142]. He said, let it stay until the evening. He reviewed at night and found pure. He said, I did not make a mistake[143]; that one faded!

(502 line 42) רָאָת עַל הַכָּר מָהוּ שֶׁתְּהֵא נֶאֱמֶנֶת לוֹמַר. כָּזֶה רָאִיתִי אוֹ כָזֶה. רִבִּי בָּא בְשֵׁם רַב יְהוּדָה רִבִּי חֶלְבּוֹ רִבִּי חִיָּיה בְשֵׁם רִבִּי יוֹחָנָן. רָאָת עַל הַכָּר נֶאֱמֶנֶת לוֹמַר. כָּזֶה רָאִיתִי אוֹ כָזֶה. וְתַנֵּי כֵן. נֶאֱמֶנֶת. יָכוֹל כְּשֵׁם שֶׁהִיא מַרְאָה מַרְאֵה כְתָמָהּ כֵּן תְּהֵא מַרְאָה מַרְאוֹת נְגָעִים. תַּלְמוּד לוֹמַר וְהוּבָא אֶל אַהֲרֹן הַכֹּהֵן אוֹ אֶל אֶחָד מִבָּנָיו הַכֹּהֲנִים.

If she saw on the bedsheet, is she trustworthy if she says, it looked like such and such? Rebbi Abba in the name of Rav Jehudah; Rebbi Ḥelbo, Rebbi Ḥiyya in the name of Rebbi Joḥanan: if she saw on the bedsheet, she is trustworthy if she says, it looked like such and such. It was stated so: She is trustworthy[144]. I could think that in the same way she shows the looks of her stain so she shows the looks of skin disease, the verse says[145]: "He shall be brought to Aaron the priest or to one of his descendants, the priests."

141 The same story in a different version is in the Babli, 20b.

142 Quoted also in the Babli, *Megillah* 14a.

143 One reviews stains at the first possible moment, even at night.

144 Such a *baraita* is also quoted in the Babli, 20b.

145 *Lev.* 13:2. Skin disease can be judged only by examining the patient personally, not by description.

המפלת פרק שלישי

(fol. 50b) **משנה א:** הַמַּפֶּלֶת חֲתִיכָה אִם יֵשׁ עִמָּהּ דָּם טְמֵאָה וְאִם לָאו טְהוֹרָה. רִבִּי יְהוּדָה אוֹמֵר בֵּין כָּךְ וּבֵין כָּךְ טְמֵאָה.

Mishnah 1: If a woman has a miscarriage in the form of a lump[1]; if this was accompanied by blood she is impure[2], otherwise she is pure. Rebbi Jehudah says, in any case she is impure.

1 Not anything recognizable as a human fetus.	2 Impure as menstruating, not as giving birth.

(50c line 2) **הלכה א:** הַמַּפֶּלֶת חֲתִיכָה כול׳. רַבָּנָן אֲמְרִין. מָקוֹר הוּא שֶׁהוּא מְגַדֵּל חֲתִיכָה. רִבִּי יוּדָה אוֹמֵר. דָּם הוּא שֶׁהוּא קָרוּשׁ וְנַעֲשָׂה חֲתִיכָה.

Halakhah 1: "If a woman has a miscarriage in the form of a lump," etc. The Sages say, the uterus grows the lump[3]. Rebbi Jehudah says, blood congealed and was formed into a lump[4].

3 The miscarriage is neither a birth nor menstruation; it cannot be classified with anything implying impurity.	4 Since any blood seeping from the walls of the uterus is a source of impurity, the fact of the discharge is proof of impurity.

(50c line 3) אָמַר רִבִּי יוֹחָנָן. לֹא טִימֵּא רִבִּי יוּדָה אֶלָּא כְגוֹן אַרְבָּעָה מִינֵי דָמִים. רִבִּי יַעֲקֹב בַּר אָחָא רִבִּי שִׁמְעוֹן בָּר בָּא בְשֵׁם רִבִּי יוֹסֵי בֵּירִבִּי נְהוֹרַיי. הֲלָכָה כְרִבִּי יוּדָה. שָׁמַע רִבִּי לְעָזָר וָמַר. אֵינִי מְקַבֵּל עָלַי אֶת הַדָּבָר הַזֶּה. שְׁמוּאֵל אָמַר. הֲלָכָה כְרִבִּי יוּדָה. אָמַר רִבִּי זְעִירָה. לֹא דוּ אָמַר. הֲלָכָה כְרִבִּי יוּדָה.

אֶלָּא דּוּ חֲמֵי רַבָּנָן נְהִגִין כְּרַבִּי יְהוּדָה. רִבִּי יוֹחָנָן בְּשֵׁם רִבִּי שִׁמְעוֹן בֶּן יוֹחַי. קוֹרְעָהּ. וְאִם נִמְצָא בָהּ דָּם אָגוּר טְמֵאָה וְאִם לָאו טְהוֹרָה. תַּנָּא רִבִּי לִיעֶזֶר בֶּן יַעֲקֹב וּפְלִיגָא עַל רִבִּי שִׁמְעוֹן בֶּן יוֹחַי. דָּם יִהְיֶה זוֹבָהּ בִּבְשָׂרָהּ. לֹא מַה שֶּׁבִּשְׁפִיר וְלֹא מַה שֶּׁבַּחֲתִיכָה.

Rebbi Johanan said, Rebbi Jehudah declared impure only in the color of the four kinds of blood[5]. Rebbi Jacob bar Aha, Rebbi Simeon bar Abba, in the name of Rebbi Yose bar Nehorai: Practice follows Rebbi Jehudah. Rebbi Eleazar heard that and said, I do not accept this. Samuel said, practice follows Rebbi Jehudah. Rebbi Ze'ira said, he did not say that practice follows Rebbi Jehudah but he saw that the rabbis are used to follow Rebbi Jehudah[6]. Rebbi Johanan in the name of Rebbi Simeon bar Iohai: One tears it open. If one finds blood collected there, she is impure, otherwise she is pure[7]. Rebbi Eliezer ben Jacob stated, disagreeing with Rebbi Simeon ben Iohai: "Blood would be her flow from her genitals,[8]" not what is in the amnion nor in a lump[9].

5 In the Babli, 21a, R. Johanan is reported to hold that even the Sages agree that a lump in the color of the four types recognized as impure blood (taking red and black together) makes the woman impure; for him the disagreement between the Sages and R. Jehudah refers only to lumps that do not look like blood. R. Johanan's opinion as quoted here is ascribed in the Babli to Rav Jehudah in the name of Samuel.

6 There is no principle involved that practice should follow R. Jehudah; he only stated what he recognized as usual among Babylonian rabbis.

7 In the Babli, 21b, this is a tannaïtic statement of Symmachos attributed to R. Meïr.

8 Lev. 15:19.

9 In the Babli, 21b, this is an amoraic statement attributed to R. Ze'ira. The explanation of the verse in *Sifra Meṣora' Parašah* 4(4) is rejected by R. Ze'ira in the Babli, 21b, and by R. Simeon (ben Iohai) in *Sifra*.

(fol. 50b) **משנה ב:** הַמַּפֶּלֶת כְּמִין קְלִיפָּה כְּמִין שַׂעֲרָה כְּמִין עָפָר כְּמִין יַבְחוּשִׁין אֲדוּמִין תַּטִּיל לַמַּיִם אִם נִימּוֹחוּ טְמֵיאָה. הַמַּפֶּלֶת כְּמִין דָּגִים חֲגָבִים שְׁקָצִים וּרְמָשִׂים אִם יֵשׁ עִמָּהֶן דָּם טְמֵאָה וְאִם לָאו טְהוֹרָה. הַמַּפֶּלֶת כְּמִין בְּהֵמָה חַיָּה וָעוֹף בֵּין טְמֵאִין בֵּין טְהוֹרִין אִם זָכָר תֵּשֵׁב לַזָּכָר וְאִם נְקֵיבָה תֵּשֵׁב לַנְּקֵיבָה וְאִם אֵין יָדוּעַ תֵּשֵׁב לַזָּכָר וְלַנְּקֵיבָה דִּבְרֵי רִבִּי מֵאִיר. וַחֲכָמִים אוֹמְרִים כָּל־שֶׁאֵין בּוֹ מְצוּרַת הָאָדָם אֵינוֹ וְלָד.

Mishnah 2: If a woman miscarried the form of a membrane, a hair, dust, or red mosquitoes, it should be soaked in water; if it dissolves she is impure[10]. If a woman miscarried the form of fishes, grasshoppers, abominable or crawling things; if this was accompanied by bleeding she is impure[11], otherwise pure. If a woman miscarried the form of a domestic or wild animal, or bird, whether pure or impure, if it is a male she should observe the days of a male birth[12], if a female of female births[13], if it cannot be determined then of both males and females[14], the words of Rebbi Meïr. But the Sages say, anything which has no human form is no child[15].

10   Everybody agrees that these are congealed masses of blood if they dissolve in water; there is menstrual blood but no birth.

11   Following the rules of menstruation.

12   Seven days of impurity followed by 33 days of purity.

13   14 days of impurity followed by 66 days of purity.

14   14 days of impurity as of a female followed by 26 days of purity (the 33 of a male minus 7 days assigned to the impurity of a female birth).

15   If there was bleeding, she is impure as menstruating, otherwise she remains pure.

(50c line 11) **הלכה ב:** הַמַּפֶּלֶת כְּמִין חֲתִיכָה כול׳. רִבִּי חֲנִינָה בְּשֵׁם רִבִּי שִׁמְעוֹן בֶּן לָקִישׁ. תַּטִּיל לְפוֹשְׁרִין. וְהִתְנִינָן. הַמַּפֶּלֶת כְּמִין דָּגִים חֲגָבִים שְׁקָצִים

וּרְמָשִׂים. אִם יֵשׁ עִמָּהֶן דָּם טְמֵיאָה. וְאִם לָאו טְהוֹרָה. וְתַטִּיל לְפוֹשְׁרִין. הָדָא יָלְפָה מִן הַהִיא וְהַהִיא יָלְפָה מִן הָדָא. הָדָא יָלְפָה מִן הַהִיא. שֶׁאִם נִמְחוּ טְמֵיאָה וְאִם לָאו טְהוֹרָה. וְהַהִיא יָלְפָה מִן הָדָא. שֶׁאִם יֵשׁ עִמָּהֶן דָּם טְמֵיאָה. וְאִם לָאו טְהוֹרָה. וְתַטִּיל לְפוֹשְׁרִין.

Halakhah 2: If a woman miscarried in the form of a lump,[16] etc. Rebbi Ḥanina[17] in the name of Rebbi Simeon ben Laqish: She has to soak it in lukewarm water[18]. But did we not state: "If a woman miscarried in the form of fishes, grasshoppers, abominable or crawling things; if this was accompanied by bleeding she is impure, otherwise pure." Can she not put it in lukewarm water[19]? The second learns from the first and the first learns from the second. The second learns from the first, that if they dissolved she is impure, if not, she is pure[20]. The first leans from the second, if this was accompanied by bleeding she is impure, otherwise pure, and she has to soak it in lukewarm water.

16 Obviously a misquote, from Mishnah 1.

17 This must be R. Ḥinena, the student, not R. Ḥanina, the teacher of R. Simeon ben Laqish.

18 Quoted also in the Babli, 22b.

19 Since the Sages at the end state that the event cannot be considered a birth.

20 There is an alternative way of checking: if the discharge was without blood, the woman would nevertheless be impure if the discharged material dissolved in water.

21 In case of a discharge that looked like peel or hair, if it was accompanied by bleeding, the woman is impure even without dissolving the object in water.

(50c line 17) תַּמָּן תַּנִּינָן. וְכַמָּה הִיא שְׁרִיָּיתָן. בְּפוֹשְׁרִין מֵעֵת לְעֵת. יְהוּדָה בֶּן נְקוֹסָה אוֹמֵר. צְרִיכִין שֶׁיְּהוּ פוֹשְׁרִין מֵעֵת לְעֵת. כֵּיצַד הוּא עוֹשֶׂה. נוֹתְנָן בְּרֶמֶץ אוֹ נוֹתֵן לְתוֹכָן חַמִּין כָּל־שֶׁהֵן.

There, we have stated[22]: How long does it have to be soaked? In lukewarm water, 24 hours." [23] "Jehudah ben Neqosa says, if has to be lukewarm for 24 hours"[24]. How does one proceed? One puts it into hot ashes or adds any amount of hot water.

22 Mishnah 7:1, speaking of body fluids other than blood, which transmit impurity only if moist, not when dry. There it is stated that dry matter becomes a carrier of prior impurity if it becomes moist after 24 hours of soaking in lukewarm water.

23 By analogy, that is the time of soaking in lukewarm water accepted here and in the Babli, 22b.

24 Before being used; Tosephta 6:11.

(50c line 20) הַמַּפֶּלֶת דָּם יָבֵשׁ. רַבִּי לָעֲזָר אוֹמֵר. טְמֵיאָה. רַבִּי יוֹסֵי בֶּן חֲנִינָה אָמַר. טְהוֹרָה. מַתְנִיתָא פְּלִיגָא עַל רַבִּי יוֹסֵי בֶּן חֲנִינָה. דַּם הַנִּידָה וּבְשַׂר הַמֵּת מְטַמִּין לַחִין וּמְטַמְאִין יְבֵשִׁין. פָּתַר לָהּ בִּשֶׁהָיוּ לַחִין וְיָבְשׁוּ. מַתְנִיתָא פְּלִיגָא עַל רַבִּי לָעֲזָר. הַמַּפֶּלֶת כְּמִין חֲתִיכָה כְּמִין שַׂעֲרָה כְּמִין עָפָר כְּמִין יַבְחוּשִׁין אֲדוּמִין תַּטִיל לַמַּיִם. וְאִם נִימֹחוּ טְמֵיאָה. פָּתַר לָהּ מִשּׁוּם בְּרִיָּיה. אָמַר רַבִּי זְעִירָה. וַאֲפִילוּ הֵתִיב עָפָר. עָפָר מִשּׁוּם בְּרִיָּיה. אָמַר רַבִּי בָּא. וַאֲפִילוּ תֵימַר עָפָר אִיתְּתָא עֲבְרָת וְקָמַת מִשּׁוּם בְּרִיָּיה. מַתְנִיתָא פְּלִיגָא עַל רַבִּי יוֹסֵי בֶּן חֲנִינָה. מַעֲשֶׂה בְּאִשָׁה אַחַת שֶׁהָיְתָה מַפֶּלֶת כְּמִין קְלִיפִּין אֲדוּמוֹת. וּבָא מַעֲשֶׂה לִפְנֵי חֲכָמִים וְשָׁלְחוּ וְקָרְאוּ לָרוֹפְאִין וְאָמְרוּ לָהֶן. מַכָּה יֵשׁ לָהּ מִבִּפְנִים. שׁוּב מַעֲשֶׂה בְּאִשָׁה אַחַת שֶׁהָיְתָה מְשָׁרֶת כְּמִין שְׂעָרוֹת אֲדוּמוֹת. וּבָא מַעֲשֶׂה לִפְנֵי חֲכָמִים וְשָׁלְחוּ וְקָרְאוּ לָרוֹפְאִין וְאָמְרוּ לָהֶן. שׁוּמָא יֵשׁ לָהּ בִּפְנִים. מִפְּנֵי שֶׁיֵּשׁ בָּהּ שׁוּמָא וּמִפְּנֵי שֶׁיֵּשׁ בָּהּ מַכָּה. הָא אֵין בָּהּ שׁוּמָא וְאֵין בָּהּ מַכָּה לֹא בְדָא. פְּלִיגִין עֲלֵיהּ וְלֵית לָהּ קִיּוּם.

If a woman miscarried dry blood, Rebbi Eleazar says, she is impure; Rebbi Yose ben Ḥanina said, she is pure[25]. A Mishnah disagrees with Rebbi Yose ben Ḥanina: "Menstrual blood and flesh from a corpse make impure moist and dry.[26]" He explains it that it was moist and then became dry[27]. A Mishnah disagrees with Rebbi Eleazar: "If a woman had a miscarriage in the form of a lump[28], a hair, dust, or red mosquitoes, it should be soaked in water; if it dissolves she is impure." He explains it, because of a creature[29]. Rebbi Ze'ira said, even there you can object about dust. Is dust a creature? Rebbi Abba said, You even may mention dust. The dust from a pregnant woman exists as a creature[30]. A *baraita* disagrees with Rebbi Yose ben Ḥanina[31]: "It happened that a woman miscarried with a kind of red membranes[32]. The case came before the Sages who sent and called the doctors who told them, she has an internal wound[33]. Also it happened that a woman miscarried with a kind of red hairs. The case came before the Sages who sent and called the doctors who told them, she has an internal wart[33]." Only because of a wart and a wound. Therefore, if there is no wart or no wound, it does not apply[34]. This disagrees with him and [his opinion] cannot be upheld.

25 In the Babli, 22a/b, this is formulated as a discussion between R. Yose ben Ḥanina and R. Eleazar, with only R. Eleazar's position fully articulated.

26 Mishnah 7:1. Blood contrasts with all other body fluids which are carriers of impurity only when moist.

27 Blood keeps its impurity once it has acquired it. This implies nothing for blood which never was moist when it left the body. The same answer is given in the Babli, 22a.

28 Since one speaks of a lump of dry blood, this probably is an intentional misquote of the Mishnah, instead of "membrane".

29 The reference is to the part of the Mishnah which was not quoted: "If it does not dissolve, she is pure." Then something had grown in her body, but since it is not human, it cannot make her impure, following the Sages at the end of the Mishnah. (Rashi on 22b).

30 The Mishnah does not say "dust" but "in the form of dust"; this can

HALAKHAH 2

represent microscopic creatures.
31 In a different formulation this is Tosephta 4:3-4, quoted in the Babli, 22b.
32 Rashi explains as scar tissue.
33 There cannot be any question of menstrual blood; the woman is pure.
34 In the absence of a sufficient medical reason, the woman has to be declared impure.

(50c line 34) אָמַר רִבִּי יוֹחָנָן. הַלֵּידָה הַזֹּאת כְּכָל־הַלֵּידוֹת שֶׁבַּתּוֹרָה. מַה הַלֵּידוֹת שֶׁבַּתּוֹרָה עַד שֶׁיֵּצֵא רֹאשׁוֹ וְרוּבּוֹ. וְזוֹ עַד שֶׁיֵּצֵא רֹאשׁוֹ וְרוּבּוֹ. רִבִּי שִׁמְעוֹן בֶּן לָקִישׁ אָמַר. מְשׁוּנָּה הִיא הַלֵּידָה הַזֹּאת מִכָּל־הַלֵּידוֹת שֶׁבַּתּוֹרָה. כָּל־הַלֵּידוֹת שֶׁבַּתּוֹרָה עַד שֶׁיֵּצֵא רֹאשׁוֹ וְרוּבּוֹ. וְזוֹ עַד שֶׁתֵּצֵא הַכָּרַת פָּנָיו. מַה נָּפִיק מִבֵּינֵיהוֹן. יָצָא מְחוּתָּךְ אוֹ מְסוּרָס. עַל דַּעְתֵּיהּ דְּרִבִּי יוֹחָנָן. עַד שֶׁיֵּצֵא רֹאשׁוֹ וְרוּבּוֹ. עַל דַּעְתֵּיהּ דְּרִבִּי שִׁמְעוֹן בֶּן לָקִישׁ. עַד שֶׁתֵּצֵא הַכָּרַת פָּנָיו.

[35]Rebbi Johanan said, this birth is like all other births mentioned in the Torah. Just as all other births mentioned in the Torah [are counted] from the appearance of either head or most of the body[36], this also [is counted] from the appearance of either head or most of the body. Rebbi Simeon ben Laqish said, this birth is different from all other births mentioned in the Torah. All other births mentioned in the Torah [are counted] from the appearance of either head or most of the body, this one once the face is recognized[37]. What is the difference between them? If he came cut or stunted. In the opinion of Rebbi Johanan, until the appearance of either head or most of the body. In the opinion of Rebbi Simeon ben Laqish, until the face is recognized[38].

35 Here starts the discussion of the positions of R. Meïr, who declares that a still-birth of an animal-shaped body is counted as a human birth, and the Sages who deny this. In a later paragraph, R. Johanan defines the human or animal character of a chimera or hybrid by its human or animal face.
36 Mishnah *Ahilot* 7:7: "If a woman

has difficulty giving birth, one dissects the fetus in her womb and removes it in pieces because her life has precedence over his life. If the greater part of his body came out one may not touch him since one does not choose between lives." Commentary of Maimonides: This is obvious and true and does not need a commentary. Similarly, the impurity of birth starts with the appearance of the forehead (head first) or most of the body (feet first).

37   Since the face of a chimera defines its human charater, there can be no recognition of human birth before that character is recognizable.

38   There is no human birth if there is no face even if there is a forehead and a body.

(50c line 40) וְאֵין יָדוּעַ. תֵּשֵׁב לַזָּכָר וְלַנְּקֵיבָה. דִּבְרֵי רִבִּי מֵאִיר. וַחֲכָמִים אוֹמְרִים. כָּל־שֶׁאֵין בּוֹ מִצּוּרַת הָאָדָם אֵינוֹ וָלָד. כָּל־הֵן דְּתַנִּינָן. תֵּשֵׁב לַזָּכָר וְלַנְּקֵיבָה. יד טְמֵאִין וכ״ו טְהוֹרִין. נוֹתְנִין עָלֶיהָ חוֹמְרֵי זָכָר וְחוֹמְרֵי נְקֵיבָה. הֲדָא דְתֵימַר. לְבֵיתָהּ. אֲבָל לִטְהָרוֹת תֵּשֵׁב לַנְּקֵיבָה.

"If it cannot be determined then she shall observe for both male and female, the words of Rebbi Meïr. But the Sages say, anything which has no human form is no child." Everywhere we stated "she shall observe for male and female, fourteen [days] impure and 26 pure[14]; one puts upon her the restrictions of the male and of the female. That means, for her house[39]. But for pure food, she shall observe for a female [birth].

39   The 26 days of purity are applicable only to her relations with her husband. For preparations of pure food, she can consider the full 66 days of a female birth as pure.

(50c line 44) אָמַר רִבִּי חֲנִינָה בְּרֵיהּ דְּרִבִּי אַבָּהוּ. טַעֲמָא דְּרִבִּי מֵאִיר. מִפְּנֵי שֶׁכָּתוּב בָּהֶן יְצִירָה כָּאָדָם. וַיִּיצֶר י״י אֱלֹהִים אֶת הָאָדָם עָפָר מִן הָאֲדָמָה. רִבִּי אַמִּי בָּעֵי. מִפְּנֵי שֶׁכָּתוּב בָּהֶן יְצִירָה כַּבְּהֵמָה. וַיִּיצֶר י״י אֱלֹהִים מִן הָאֲדָמָה כָּל־חַיַּת הַשָּׂדֶה וְכָל־עוֹף הַשָּׁמָיִם. וְהָא כְּתִיב כִּי הִנֵּה יוֹצֵר הָרִים וּבוֹרֵא רוּחַ.

מֵעַתָּה הַפִּילָה דְּמוּת הַר תְּהֵא טְמֵיאָה לֵידָה. שְׁנִיָּיא הִיא. שֶׁאֵין כָּתוּב בָּהֶן יְצִירָה מִתְּחִילַת בְּרִיָּיתוֹ שֶׁל עוֹלָם. רִבִּי יָסָא בְשֵׁם רִבִּי יוֹחָנָן. מִפְּנֵי שֶׁסּוֹקְרִין לִפְנֵיהֶן כְּאָדָם. אַבָּא בַּר בַּר חָנָה בְשֵׁם רִבִּי יוֹחָנָן. מִפְּנֵי שֶׁמְּהַלְכִין לִפְנֵיהֶן כְּאָדָם. הָתִיב רִבִּי בּוּן בַּר חִייָה. וְהָתַנִּינָן. שֶׁגַּלְגַּל עֵינוֹ עָגוּל כְּשֶׁלְּאָדָם. הֲוֵי מוּם הוּא. אָמַר רִבִּי יוֹסֵי. מַה תַּנִּינָן. סוֹקְרִין. מְהַלְכִין. מַאי כְדוֹן. גַּלְגְּלֵי אָדָם עֲגוּלִין וְגַלְגְּלֵי בְהֵמָה אֲרוּכִין. אָמַר רִבִּי יוֹסֵי בֵּירִבִּי בּוּן. בָּאָדָם לָבָן רָבָה עַל הַשָּׁחוֹר וּבַבְּהֵמָה שָׁחוֹר רָבָה עַל הַלָּבָן.

Rebbi Ḥanina the son of Rebbi Abbahu said, Rebbi Meïr's reason is that "shaping" is written for them as for humans[40]. "The Eternal God shaped man as dust from the earth.[41]" Rebbi Immi asked, because "shaping" is written for them as for animals, "the Eternal God shaped from the earth all animals of the field and the birds of the sky[42]"? But is it not written "for behold the Shaper of mountains and Creator of wind[43]"? Then, if she has a miscarriage in the shape of a mountain, she should be impure because of birth! There is a difference, for shaping is not written for them in the Creation story. Rebbi Yasa in the name of Rebbi Johanan: Because they look forward as humans do. Abba bar bar Hana said in the name of Rebbi Johanan: Because they walk forward as humans do[44]. Rebbi Abun bar Ḥiyya objected: Did we not state, "if his eyeball is round like that of a human," is that not a defect[45]? Rebbi Yose said, did we not state, look forward; did we not state, walk[46]? What about it[47]? Human eyeballs are round, animal eyeballs are elongated. Rebbi Yose ben Rebbi Abun said, human eyes have more white than black, animal eyes have more black than white.

40   In the Babli, 22b, this is attributed to Rav Jehudah in the name of Samuel.

41   *Gen.* 2:7.

42 *Gen.* 2:19. The masoretic text is slightly different from the text quoted.

43 *Am.* 4:13. The same question is asked in the Babli, 23a.

44 In the Babli, 23a, Rabba bar bar Hana in the name of R. Joḥanan gives the explanation attributed here to R. Yasa.

45 Mishnah *Bekhorot* 6:8. A firstling whose eyes look human is not acceptable as sacrifice.

46 R. Joḥanan only spoke about functions, not about looks. (But human eyes are forward looking as eyes of predators; the eyes of kosher animals are sideways looking eyes of prey. In the Babli, 23a, Abbai restricts the rule of R. Meïr about birds to owls who have forward-looking quasi-human eyes.)

47 Which features make animal eyes a bodily defect by being like human eyes?

(50c line 56) רִבִּי חַגַּי אָמַר רִבִּי חֲנִינָה. חֲבֵרִין דְּרַבָּנִין מַקְשֵׁי לָהּ עַל דְּרִבִּי מֵאִיר. הִפִּילָה דְּמוּת עוֹרֵב עוֹמֵד בְּרֹאשׁ הַדֶּקֶל. וְאוֹמֵר לוֹ. בּוֹא וַחֲלוֹץ אוֹ יַבֵּם. אָמַר לֵיהּ רִבִּי מָנָא. עַד דְּאַתְּ מַקְשֵׁי לָהּ עַל דְּרִבִּי מֵאִיר קְשִׁיתָהּ עַל דְּרַבָּנָן. דָּמַר רִבִּי יָסָא בְּשֵׁם רִבִּי יוֹחָנָן. כּוּלוֹ אָדָם וּפָנָיו בְּהֵמָה אֵינוֹ וְלָד. כּוּלוֹ בְּהֵמָה וּפָנָיו אָדָם וְלָד הוּא. כּוּלוֹ אָדָם וּפָנָיו בְּהֵמָה עוֹמֵד וְקוֹרֵא בַּתּוֹרָה. וְאוֹמֵר לוֹ. בּוֹא לְשָׁחֳטָךְ. כּוּלוֹ בְּהֵמָה וּפָנָיו אָדָם עוֹמֵד וְחוֹרֵשׁ בַּשָּׂדֶה. וְאוֹמֵר לוֹ. בּוֹא וַחֲלוֹץ אוֹ יַבֵּם.

Rebbi Ḥaggai said in the name of Rebbi Ḥanina: A colleague of the rabbis objected to the position of Rebbi Meïr: If she miscarried the likeness of a raven[48] and he stands on the top of a tree, can one say to him, come and give *ḥaliṣah* or marry in levirate? Rebbi Mana told him, instead of objecting to Rebbi Meïr, object to the rabbis[49]! Since Rebbi Yasa said in the name of Rebbi Joḥanan[50], if his entire body is human and only his face is animal, he is not counted as a child. If his entire body is animal and only his face is human, he is counted as a child. If his entire body is human and only his face is animal, when he is standing reading the

Torah one may tell him, come to be slaughtered[51]. If his entire body is animal and only his face is human, when he is ploughing the field[52] one may tell him, come and give *ḥaliṣah* or marry in levirate!

48   The *hiph'il* of the root נפל means "to miscarry, to abort (actively or passively)". נֵפֶל is the stillborn. The questioner here presumes that if a woman can give birth to a stillborn chimera. she can also give birth to a live chimera. Then R. Meïr must hold that there are animals which are counted as human, with paradoxical consequences.

49   Since the Sages disagree with R. Meïr only in the definition of what makes a woman impure as consequence of a birth, if R. Meïr accepts living chimeras so do the Sages. The implied conclusion is that the language of the Mishnah, the term "miscarried", was chosen judiciously to teach that chimeras by their nature are stillborn. The cases constructed here cannot happen; a conclusion stated explicitly in the Babli, 23a.

50   In the Babli, 23b, a statement of Rav Jeremiah bar Abba in the name of Rav.

51   If his face is that of a kosher animal.

52   An ox harnessed to the plough.

(50c line 64) וְאָמַר רְבִּי יָסָא בְּשֵׁם רְבִּי יוֹחָנָן. לֹא סוֹף דָּבָר כָּל־הַסִּימָנִין אֶלָּא אֲפִילוּ אֶחָד מִן הַסִּימָנִין. וְאֵילוּ הֵן הַסִּימָנִין. הַמֵּצַח וְהַגְּבִינִין וְהָעַיִן וְהָאוֹזֶן וְהַלֶּסֶת וְהַחוֹטֶם וְהַזָּקָן וְגוּמַת הַזָּקָן. אָמַר רְבִּי יָסָא בְּשֵׁם רְבִּי יוֹחָנָן. לֹא סוֹף דָּבָר כָּל־הַסִּימָנִין אֶלָּא אֲפִילוּ אֶחָד מִן הַסִּימָנִין. רְבִּי בָּא רְבִּי יִרְמְיָה בְּשֵׁם רַב. דִּבְרֵי רְבִּי. עַד שֶׁיְּהוּ כָּל־הַפָּנִים דּוֹמִין לְאָדָם. וְדִבְרֵי חֲכָמִים. אֲפִילוּ אֶחָד מִן הַסִּימָנִין. וְדִבְרֵי רְבִּי שִׁמְעוֹן בֶּן יוֹחַי. אֲפִילוּ צִפָּרְנָיו. רְבִּי פִּינְחָס בָּעֵי. מַחְלְפָה שִׁיטָתֵיהּ דְּרְבִּי שִׁמְעוֹן בֶּן יוֹחַי. תַּמָּן הוּא אוֹמֵר. עַד שֶׁיְּהוּ רֹאשׁוֹ וְרוּבּוֹ דּוֹמִין לְאִמּוֹ. וְהָכָא הוּא אָמַר הָכֵין. כָּאן בְּאָדָם כָּאן בַּבְּהֵמָה. אָמַר רְבִּי בָּא. רְבִּי חִייָה רוּבָּה אֲזַל לִדְרוֹמָה. שָׁאֲלוֹן לֵיהּ רְבִּי חָמָא אֲבוֹי דְּרְבִּי הוֹשַׁעְיָה וּבַר קַפָּרָא. כּוּלּוֹ אָדָם וּפָנָיו בִּבְהֵמָה מָהוּ. אֲתָא וְשָׁאַל לְרְבִּי. אָמַר לֵיהּ. צֵא וּכְתוֹב לָהֶן. אֵינוֹ וְלָד. אָמַר רְבִּי יִרְמְיָה. נְפַק זוּגָא לְבַר. שָׁאֲלוֹן לֵיהּ רְבִּי חָמָא אֲבוֹי דְּרְבִּי

הוֹשַׁעְיָה וּבַר קַפָּרָא. שְׁתֵּי עֵינָיו טוּחוֹת מָהוּ. אֲתָא וּשְׁאִיל לְרַבִּי. אָמַר לֵיהּ.
צֵא וּכְתוֹב לָהֶן. אֵינוֹ וָלָד. אָמַר רִבִּי יוֹסִי בֵּירְבִּי בּוּן. רִבִּי כְדַעְתֵּיהּ. דְּרִבִּי
אָמַר. עַד שֶׁיְּהוּ כָל־הַפָּנִים דּוֹמִין לְאָדָם. פָּנָיו מְמוּסְמָסוֹת מָהוּ. רִבִּי יָסָא אָמַר.
אִתְפַּלְּגוּן רִבִּי יוֹחָנָן וְרִבִּי שִׁמְעוֹן בֶּן לָקִישׁ. רִבִּי יוֹחָנָן אָמַר. אֵינוֹ וָלָד. רִבִּי
שִׁמְעוֹן בֶּן לָקִישׁ אָמַר. וָלָד הוּא. אָמַר רִבִּי זְעוּרָה. לֹא דְּרִבִּי יוֹחָנָן אָמַר. אֵינוֹ
וָלָד כָּל־דָּכֵן. אֶלָּא אֵינוֹ וָלָד לְהוֹשִׁיב אֶת אִמּוֹ יְמֵי טוֹהַר. אֲבָל וָלָד הוּא
לְהוֹשִׁיב אֶת אִמּוֹ יְמֵי לֵידָה. רִבִּי יוֹחָנָן אָמַר בְּשֵׁם רִבִּי יַנַּאי. וְיַרְכָתוֹ אֲטוּמָה
אֵינוֹ וָלָד. רִבִּי יוֹחָנָן בְּשֵׁם רִבִּי יוֹסֵי בֵּירְבִּי יְהוֹשֻׁעַ. טִיבּוּרוֹ אָטוּם אֵינוֹ וָלָד.
רִבִּי יוֹחָנָן בְּשֵׁם רִבִּי זַכַּאי. נְקוּבָתוֹ אֲטוּמָה אֵינוֹ וָלָד. רִבִּי זְעִירָה בְּשֵׁם גִּידוּל.
גּוּלְגּוֹלְתּוֹ אֲטוּמָה אֵינוֹ וָלָד.

And Rebbi Yasa said in the name of Rebbi Joḥanan: Not all the criteria together but only one criterion. The following are the criteria: The forehead, the eyebrows, the eye, the ear, the mandible, the nose, the beard, and the dimple. And Rebbi Yasa said in the name of Rebbi Joḥanan: Not all the criteria together but only one criterion. Rebbi Abba, Rav Jeremiah in the name of Rav: The words of Rebbi: Only if the entire face has human traits; but the words of the rabbis: Even one of the criteria[53]; and the words of Rebbi Simeon ben Ioḥai: Even its fingernails. Rebbi Phineas asked: Are not the statements of Rebbi Simeon bar Ioḥai inverted? There[54], he says, "only if its head and most of its body are like its mother," and here, he says so? Here about humans, there about animals[55]. Rebbi Abba said, the Elder Rebbi Ḥiyya went South. Rebbi Ḥama the father of Rebbi Hoshaia and bar Qappara asked him: What is the rule if its entire body is human and only its face is animal? He returned and asked Rebbi, who told him, go and write to them, it is no birth. Rebbi Jeremiah said, Zeugos went out, Rebbi Ḥama the father of Rebbi Hoshaia and bar

Qappara asked him: What is the rule if its eyes are shapeless[56]? He returned and asked Rebbi, who told him, go and write to them, there is no child. Rebbi Yose ben Rebbi Abun said, Rebbi follows his own opinion since Rebbi says, only if the entire face has human traits. What if its face was crushed[57]? Rebbi Yasa said, Rebbi Joḥanan and Rebbi Simeon ben Laqish differ. Rebbi Joḥanan says, it is no child; Rebbi Simeon ben Laqish says, it is a child. Rebbi Ze'ira said, not that Rebbi Joḥanan said it is no child in every respect but it is no child to provide the mother with days of purity; it is a child to require the mother to observe the days of birth[58]. Rebbi Joḥanan in the name of Rebbi Yannai: If its hip is unformed[59], it is not a child. Rebbi Joḥanan in the name of Rebbi Yose ben Rebbi Joshua: If the navel is unformed[60], it is no child. Rebbi Joḥanan in the name of Rebbi Zakkai: If its holes are unformed[61], it is no child. Rebbi Ze'ira[62] in the name of Gidul: If its skull is unformed there is no child.

53   In the Babli, 23b, one *baraita* states that one criterion is sufficient except for the ear but all Amoraim hold that all criteria together have to be fulfilled for a human birth.

54   Tosephta *Bekhorot* 1:9: "R. Simeon says, why does the verse say 'camel, camel' two times (*Lev.* 11:4, *Deut.* 14:7) to add a camel born from a cow as if it were born from a she-camel but if its head and most of its body are similar to its mother it is permitted as food. But the Sages say that what comes from an impure animal is impure, from a pure animal is pure, since no pure animal can be impregnated from an impure animal and vice versa, nor cattle from sheep and goats and vice versa, nor a human from an animal and vice versa." Here R. Simeon requires that most of the animal be similar to its mother to accept it as animal birth.

55   In *Sifra Šemini Pereq* 4(6), the fact that a camel is not kosher is brought as proof that one criterion for a kosher animal is not sufficient; all criteria must be satisfied. Since that statement is obvious from the verses, one may see in it a veiled attack on the

690   NIDDAH CHAPTER THREE

position that one criterion is sufficient to determine a human birth.

56   According to Rashi in the Babli, 24a, the skull has no sign of indenture where the eyes should be. In the Babli, R. Hiyya's sons were asked and gave the wrong answer.

57   The face is barely recognizable (Rashi in Babli 24a).

58   14 days of impurity for a female birth (Rashi in Babli 24a).

59   A stillbirth whose legs are not movable. This is a birth defect which is not mentioned in the Babli.

60   Since the navel is the point where the fetus is connected to the placenta, an absence of an indication of the place of the navel is proof that there is no human fetus. The Babli agrees, 24a.

61   Neither bladder nor intestines have an outlet. The Babli agrees, 24a.

62   In the Babli, 24a: R. Joḥanan.

(fol. 50b) **משנה ג:** הַמַּפֶּלֶת שְׁפִיר מָלֵא מַיִם מָלֵא דָם מָלֵא גְנִינִים אֵינָהּ חוֹשֶׁשֶׁת לַוָּלָד. וְאִם הָיָה מְרוּקָּם תֵּשֵׁב לְזָכָר וְלַנְּקֵיבָה.

Mishnah 3: If a woman miscarried an amnion full of water, or blood, or flakes[63], she does not have to consider this as a child. But if it showed tissue[64] she has to observe for male and female birth[14].

63   It looks like flakes of flesh but no body is formed.

64   If inside the amnion a form is seen but it is not recognizable what it is.

(50d line 9) **הלכה ג:** הַמַּפֶּלֶת שְׁפִיר מָלֵא מַיִם כול'. תַּנֵּי. מָלֵא מַיִם טְמֵיאָה לֵידָה. מָלֵא דָם טְמֵיאָה נִידָּה. מָלֵא בָשָׂר טְמֵיאָה נִידָּה. וְהָא תַּנִּינָן. הַמַּפֶּלֶת שְׁפִיר מָלֵא מַיִם מָלֵא דָם מָלֵא גְנִינִים אֵינָהּ חוֹשֶׁשֶׁת לַוָּלָד. רִבִּי בֵּיבַי בְּשֵׁם רִבִּי שִׁמְעוֹן בֶּן לָקִישׁ. מַתְנִיתָא בִּצְלוּלִין. בָּרַייתָא בַּעֲכוּרִין. רִבִּי סִימוֹן בְּשֵׁם רִבִּי יְהוֹשֻׁעַ בֶּן לֵוִי. וַאֲפִילוּ צְלוּלִין. שֶׁאֵין שְׁפִיר אֶלָּא בְּאָדָם בִּלְבַד. הָדָא הִיא

דִּכְתִיב בְּשׂוּמִי עָנָן לְבוּשׁוֹ וַעֲרָפֶל חֲתוּלָתוֹ. לְבוּשׁוֹ זֶה הַשָּׁפִיר. וַעֲרָפֶל חֲתוּלָתוֹ זוֹ הַשִּׁילְיָא.

Halakhah 3: "If a woman miscarried an amnion full of water," etc. It was stated[65]: Full of water[66], she is impure for a birth; full of blood, she is impure as menstruating; full of flesh[67], she is impure as menstruating. But did we not state: "If a woman miscarried an amnion full of water, or blood, or flakes, she does not have to consider this as a child"? Rebbi Bevai in the name of Rebbi Simeon ben Laqish: The Mishnah if [the contents are] clear; the *baraita* if [the contents are] turbid. Rebbi Simon in the name of R. Joshua ben Levi: Even if all was clear, since only humans have an amnion[68]! That is what is written[69]: "When I gave clouds as his garment and fog as his diapers." "His garment" is the amnion, "and fog his diapers" that is the placenta.

---

65 A similar but different *baraita* is quoted in the Babli, 25a.

66 This *baraita* holds that there is no amniotic fluid without a fetus.

67 Since there is no shape, there can be no birth; pieces of flesh contain blood and make the woman impure.

68 In the Babli, 25a, these statements refer to another *baraita*, (close to Tosephta 4:12): "If a woman gives birth to an amnion which does not contain tissue, R. Joshua says it is a birth but the Sages say it is no birth".

R. Simeon ben Laqish said in the name of R. Oshaia (= Hoshaia): They quarrel if it is turbid, but if the contents are clear everybody says that it is no birth, but R. Joshua ben Levi said, their quarrel is if the contents are clear.

In the end, Samuel declares in the Babli that an amnion is not a sign of birth only if it is transparent. This might agree with the Yerushalmi.

69 *Job* 38:9. The verse, which describes the creation of the world, is interpreted as describing human birth.

(50d line 16) שָׁפִיר שֶׁנִּתְקַלְקְלָה צוּרָתוֹ מָהוּ. רִבִּי יוֹחָנָן אָמַר. וְלָד. רִבִּי שִׁמְעוֹן בֶּן לָקִישׁ אָמַר. אֵינוֹ וְלָד. מְתִיב רִבִּי שִׁמְעוֹן בֶּן לָקִישׁ קוֹמֵי רִבִּי יוֹחָנָן. מַה בֵּינוֹ לְבֵין הַמֵּת שֶׁנִּסְרַח וְאֵין שִׁלְדּוֹ קַייֶמֶת. אָמַר לֵיהּ. תַּמָּן בְּדִין הָיָה אֲפִילוּ שִׁלְדּוֹ קַייֶמֶת יְהֵא טָהוֹר. וְלָמָּה אָמְרוּ. טָמֵא. מִפְּנֵי כְבוֹדוֹ. בְּרַם הָכָא וְלָד הוּא.

[70]If an amnion's shape was spoiled, what is the rule? Rebbi Johanan said, it is a child; Rebbi Simeon ben Laqish said, it is not a child. Rebbi Simeon ben Laqish objected before Rebbi Johanan: What is the difference between this and a rotting corpse without a spine[71]? He said to him, in the latter case it would have been correct that he should be pure even with his spine intact; why did they say, he is impure? That he should be treated with honor[72]. But in our case it is a birth.

70   Tosaphot *Niddah* 27b, s. v. מח has a different text: שָׁפִיר שֶׁנִּתְבַּלְבְּלָה צוּרָתוֹ מָהוּ. רִבִּי יוֹחָנָן אָמַר. טָמֵא. רִבִּי שִׁמְעוֹן בֶּן לָקִישׁ אָמַר. טָהוֹר. אִיתִיבֵי רִבִּי שִׁמְעוֹן בֶּן לָקִישׁ לְרִבִּי יוֹחָנָן מֵרְבִּי יִצְחָק מִגְדְלָאָה וּמְשַׁנֶּה. דְּבַר תּוֹרָה אֲפִילוּ שִׁלְדּוֹ קַייֶמֶת טְהוֹרָה. מִפְּנֵי מָה אָמְרוּ. טָמֵא. מִפְּנֵי כְבוֹדוֹ. "If an amnion's shape was *mixed up*, what is the rule? Rebbi Johanan said, it is *impure*; Rebbi Simeon ben Laqish said, it is *pure*. Rebbi Simeon ben Laqish objected[a] before Rebbi Johanan from the statement of R. Isaac from Magdala[b]. He said to him, biblical law even requires that he be pure even with his spine intact; why did they say, he is impure? That he should be treated with honor.

a   A Babylonian expression.

b   A statement in the Babli, 27b: "The corpse of a person who was burned is impure if the spine exists."

The quote of Tosaphot from "Yerushalmi" is probably from the Ashkenazic "Book Yerushalmi", containing Yerushalmi rules adapted to the Babli.

71   If the skeletal remains of a corpse are found and the spine is not complete, one does not have to worry that the earth below and around it is really decomposed flesh and should be impure. If the remains of the amnion are not recognizable as such, there

| seems to be no reason to treat it as impure. | 72   The impurity of the dead is a sign that the corpse needs burial. |

(50d line 20) אֵי זֶהוּ שָׁפִיר מְרוּקָם שֶׁאָמְרוּ. כָּל־שֶׁתְּחִילַת בְּרִייָתוֹ דוֹמֶה לְרָשׁוֹן. אֵין בּוֹדְקִין אוֹתוֹ בְּמַיִם מִפְּנֵי שֶׁהֵן עַזִּין וְעוֹכְרִין אוֹתוֹ. אֶלָּא בַשֶׁמֶן מִפְּנֵי שֶׁהוּא מָתוּן וּמְזַגְזֵג. וְאֵין בּוֹדְקִין אוֹתוֹ אֶלָּא בַחַמָּה.

What is the amnion containing tissue which they referred to? Any which initially looks like a *rāšôn*[73]. [74]One does not check it in water, for water is a solvent and destroys it, but only in oil which is neutral and clears up; also one checks only in sunlight.

| 73   In the Babli, *Ḥulin* 65a, *rāšôn* is identified as biblical סָלְעָם, a locust (*Lev.* 11:22). In the Tosephta (4:10) דושם in the Babli *Niddah* 25a *editio* | *princeps*, ראשו, reading of *'Arukh* רשון. 74   Tosephta 4:11 (there מזכזך for מזגזג); Babli 25a/b (מצחצח). |

(50d line 23) אַבָּא שָׁאוּל אוֹמֵר. מִטִּיבּוּרוֹ נוֹצָר אָדָם וּמְשַׁלֵּחַ שָׁרָשִׁין מִיכָּן וּמִיכָּן. תַּנֵּי. רוֹאִין שְׁתֵּי עֵינָיו כְּמִין שְׁתֵּי טִיפִּין שֶׁלַּזְּבוּב. שְׁנֵי נְקוּבֵי חוֹטְמוֹ כְּמִין שְׁתֵּי טִיפִּין שֶׁלַּזְּבוּב. פִּיו פָּתוּחַ כִּשְׂעוֹרָה. רוֹאִין שְׁתֵּי יָדָיו כְּמִין שְׁתֵּי טִיפִּין שֶׁלַּזְּבוּב. טִיבּוּרוֹ כְּמִין טִיפָּה שֶׁל זְבוּב. גְּוִייָתוֹ כְּמִין טִיפָּה שֶׁלַּזְּבוּב. וְאִם הָיְתָה נְקֵיבָה גְּוִייָתָהּ מָתוּחַ כִּשְׂעָרָה. תַּנֵּי. רִבִּי יוֹנָתָן אוֹמֵר. רוֹאִין שְׁתֵּי זְרוֹעוֹתָיו כְּמִין שְׁנֵי חוּטִין שֶׁל זְהוֹרִית וּשְׁאָר כָּל־אֵיבָרָיו כְּמִין גּוֹלֶם מְצוּמָּתִים. וּפִיתוּחַ יָדַיִם וְרַגְלַיִם אֵין לוֹ אֲדַיִין. וְעָלָיו הוּא מְפוֹרָשׁ בַּקַּבָּלָה גּוֹלְמִי רָאוּ עֵינֶיךָ וְעַל סִפְרְךָ כּוּלָּם יִכָּתֵבוּ יָמִים יוּצָרוּ וְלֹא אֶחָד בָּהֶם.

[75]"Abba Shaul said, a human is created from his navel; from there is spreads its roots in all directions. It was stated: One sees his two eyes like two fly-blows, his two nose holes like two fly-blows, his mouth opened like a barley grain. One sees his two hands like two fly-blows, his navel

like a fly-blow, his genital like a fly blow and if she is female, her genital spanned like a barley grain." It was stated: Rebbi Jonathan says, one sees his two arms like two threads of crimson wool and his other limbs like compressed unformed material; he has not yet developed hands and feet. On that it is explained in the Bible[76]: [77]"My unformed body was seen by Your eyes, in Your ledger they are all written down, the days bundled before one of them was."

75 Tosephta 4:10; Babli 25a; also *Soṭah* 45b, *Yoma* 85a.

76 קַבָּלָה "that which was received" denotes all parts of the Hebrew Bible other than the Torah.

77 *Ps.* 139:16. That Psalm, while ascribed to David, is generally interpreted to describe the experiences of Adam. Cf. H. Guggenheimer, *The Scholar's Haggadah* (Northvale 1995), p. 220.

(50d line 32) רַב יְהוּדָה שָׁאַל לִשְׁמוּאֵל. בְּגִין דַּאֲנָא חַכִּים מֵיחְמֵי סִימָנֵי שָׁפִיר. אָמַר לֵיהּ. רֵישֵׁיהּ דְּרֵישָׁךְ יְכַוֶה בְרוֹתְחִין. וְאַתָּה לֹא תִיכָוֶה אֲפִילוּ בְפוֹשְׁרִין. רִבִּי חִייָא בְשֵׁם רִבִּי יוֹחָנָן. אִילֵין נַשַׁיָּיא דְאָמְרָן. שֶׁכְּלוּלֵיהּ דָּכָר. שֶׁכְּלוּלָה נוּקְבָה. לֵית אֲנַן סָמְכִין עֲלֵיהוֹן. רִבִּי יַעֲקֹב בַּר זַבְדִּי רִבִּי אַבָּהוּ בְשֵׁם רִבִּי יוֹחָנָן. נֶאֱמֶנֶת אִשָּׁה לוֹמַר. יָלַדְתִּי וְלֹא יָלַדְתִּי. וְאֵינָהּ נֶאֱמֶנֶת לוֹמַר. דָּכָר הוּא. נוּקְבָה הִיא.

Rav Jehudah asked Samuel: Since I am learned, can I judge the signs of an amnion? He said to him, your head's head can be scalded by boiling water, you should not be scalded even by lukewarm water[78]. Rebbi Ḥiyya in the name of Rebbi Joḥanan, we do not rely on women who say, its completion[79] would have been male, its completion would have been female. Rebbi Jacon bar Zavdi, Rebbi Abbahu in the name of Rebbi Joḥanan: A woman is trustworthy if she said, I gave birth or I did not give birth. But she is not trustworthy if she says, it was male or it was female⁸⁰.

78   I, the medical authority and your teacher, can investigate the most difficult situations; you, a rabbi, should not give an opinion even in obvious cases. In the Babli, 25b, Samuel is reported to have told Rav Jehudah not to decide in cases in which there was a fetus with no hair on his skull.

79   *Editio princeps* reads שבלוליה "its snail" for שכלוליה "its completion".

80   This is quoted in *Or Zarua'* #340 (vol. 1, col. 90b), where the author, R. Isaac ben Moses of Vienna, notes that he does not understand why women should not be trusted in the matter of impurities and purity. But it seems that the students of R. Joḥanan only confirm the interpretation given to R. Joḥanan's position earlier, Note 58.

(fol. 50b) **משנה ד:** הַמַּפֶּלֶת סַנְדָּל אוֹ שִׁילְיָיא תֵּשֵׁב לַזָּכָר וְלַנְקֵיבָה. שִׁילְיָיא בַּבַּיִת הַבַּיִת טָמֵא. לֹא שֶׁהַשִּׁילְיָיא וְלָד אֶלָּא שֶׁאֵין שִׁילְיָיא בְּלֹא וְלָד. רַבִּי שִׁמְעוֹן אוֹמֵר. נִימּוֹק הַוְולָד עַד שֶׁלֹּא יָצָא.

Mishnah 4: If a woman miscarried a sole⁸¹ or a placenta⁸², she should observe for male and female birth¹⁴. A placenta in the house makes the house impure; not that the placenta is a child but there is no placenta without a child⁸³. Rebbi Simeon says, the child was dissolved before it came out⁸⁴.

81   Greek σάνδαλον "sandal; a flat fish (*solea*)". The object of the miscarriage was a flat piece, without recognizable face or limbs.

82   Without a body attached to it.

83   If there was a placenta, one may assume that it was accompanied by a small dead human embryo. Therefore, the house transmits the impurity of the dead as long as any tissue from this

birth is in the house.

84 While no placenta can be formed without a pregnancy, if no child was found at the moment of birth there is none and the house is pure. A stillbirth is not a source of impurity as long as it remains in the womb of a woman.

(50d line 38) **הלכה ד:** הַמַּפֶּלֶת סַנְדָּל אוֹ שִׁילְיָא כול׳. רִבִּי בָּא בְשֵׁם רַב יְהוּדָה. אֵין סַנְדָּל אֶלָּא שֶׁרְצָמוֹ חַי וְאֵינוֹ יוֹצֵא עִם הַחַי אֶלָּא עִם הַמֵּת. הָתִיב רִבִּי בּוּן בַּר חִייָה. וְהָא תַנִּינָן. הַמַּפֶּלֶת סַנְדָּל אוֹ שִׁילְיָא תֵּשֵׁב לַזָּכָר וְלַנְּקֵיבָה. הֲוֵי וְלָד הוּא. אָמַר רִבִּי הוּנָא. קַייָמְתָּהּ קוֹמֵי רִבִּי יִרְמְיָה. תִּיפְתָּר שֶׁיָּצָא הַוּוֹלָד דֶּרֶךְ הַדּוֹפָן וְסַנְדָּל דֶּרֶךְ הָרֶחֶם. וְלָד בְּתוֹךְ מְלֹאת. סַנְדָּל אַחַר מְלֹאת. וְלָד עַד שֶׁלֹּא נִתְגַּייְרָה. סַנְדָּל מִשֶּׁנִּתְגַּייְרָה. וְלָד. וַאֲפִילוּ תֵימַר. זֶה וְזֶה דֶּרֶךְ רֶחֶם. זֶה וְזֶה מִשֶּׁנִּתְגַּייְרָה. תִּיפְתָּר שֶׁיָּצָא הַוּוֹלָד תְּחִילָּה וְהִפְרִישָׁה לוֹ קָרְבָּן. לֹא הִסְפִּיקָה לְהָבִיא אוֹתוֹ הַקָּרְבָּן עַד שֶׁיָּצָא הַסַּנְדָּל וְנִדְחָה קָרְבָּן הָרִאשׁוֹן. וְנִמְצֵאת מְבִיאָה קָרְבָּן מַחְמַת הַסַּנְדָּל.

Halakhah 4: "If a woman miscarried a sole or a placenta," etc. Rebbi Abba in the name of Rav Jehudah: There only is a sole because it was weighed down by a living [fetus]; it comes out not with a living but with a dead [child][85]. Rebbi Abun bar Ḥiyya objected: did we not state, "if a woman miscarried a sole or a placenta, she should observe for male and female birth"? That means, it is a child[86]! Rebbi Huna said, I explained it before Rebbi Jeremiah. Explain it if the child was born through the wall of the womb[87] and the sole from the womb. The child within fulfilling, the sole after fulfilling[88]. The child before she converted, the sole after she converted[89]. But even you may say, both were born from the womb, both were born after she converted[90]. Explain that the child was born first and she designated a sacrifice for it. Before she could bring the sacrifice, the sole came out[91] and the first sacrifice was pushed away[92]. It turns out that she brings the sacrifice for the sole.

85 If one of a pair of twins kills its sibling in the womb, he himself will die in the womb.

86 It is stated in Mishnah *Keritut* 1:3 that a woman having a miscarriage of a sole or a placenta is obligated to bring a sacrifice (*Lev.* 12:6-8) which is eaten by the Temple priests. This implies that this miscarriage is a complete birth in the sense of the biblical text. But Rav Jehudah seems to imply that these miscarriages are always accompanied by a regular stillbirth, which requires a sacrifice by the simple wording of the text. It seems that the Mishnah in *Keritut* is superfluous. The Mishnah here can be justified as informing on the periods of impurity and purity which are changed from those induced by the stillbirth.

87 A delivery by caesarean section is not a birth; the mother is not impure for the birth and not required to bring a sacrifice (Mishnah *Niddah* 5:1). If one child is delivered by caesarean section and the other through the vagina, only the second is counted as birth for impurity and sacrifice.

88 "Fulfilling" refers to *Lev.* 12:6: "After *fulfilling* the days of her purity for son or daughter, she has to bring .." Immediately after the end of her period of purity, the obligation of a sacrifice starts. Any additional birth occuring between the first and the end of the period of purity does not create a new obligation of sacrifice, but any birth occuring when the mother already is obligated for a sacrifice creates a separate obligation after the observation of its periods of impurity and purity (Mishnah *Keritut* 2:4).

89 This is a different case. As a Gentile, the woman is not obligated for anything. If she converts before the miscarriage of the sole, she has to observe the rules of birth for the sole alone, even if it was accompanied by the birth of a recognizable child.

90 The constructions of R. Huna are unnecessary.

91 Within the days of "fulfilling", but after she had designated the sacrifice. She now has to bring one sacrifice dedicated to two births.

92 A purification sacrifice which cannot be used for its original purpose cannot be used for any other purpose. Therefore, a sacrifice dedicated to one birth cannot be used for two; the second miscarriage obligates the mother to dedicate a new sacrifice.

(50d line 47) אֵי זֶהוּ הַסַּנְדָּל שֶׁאָמְרוּ. כָּל־שֶׁהוּא דּוֹמֶה לְסַנְדָּל דָּג שֶׁבַּיָּם. רַבָּן שִׁמְעוֹן בֶּן גַּמְלִיאֵל אוֹמֵר. כָּל־שֶׁהוּא דּוֹמֶה לִלְשׁוֹנוֹ שֶׁל שׁוֹר. נִמְנוּ עָלָיו רַבּוֹתֵינוּ לוֹמַר. וְהוּא שֶׁיְּהֵא בּוֹ מְצוּרַת אָדָם. מָנוּ רַבּוֹתֵינוּ. רִבִּי יְהוּדָה הַנָּשִׂיא וּבֵית דִּינוֹ. בִּשְׁלשָׁה מְקוֹמוֹת נִקְרָא רִבִּי יְהוּדָה הַנָּשִׂיא רַבּוֹתֵינוּ. בְּגִיטִּין בַּשֶּׁמֶן וּבַסַּנְדָּל. סַנְדָּל. הָדָא דְאָמְרִינָן. בַּשֶּׁמֶן. כְּהַאי דְתַנִּינָן תַּמָּן. רִבִּי וּבֵית דִּינוֹ הִתִּירוּ בַשֶּׁמֶן. בְּגִיטִּין. כְּהִיא דְתַנִּינָן תַּמָּן. זֶה גִיטֵּיךְ אִם מֵתִי. זֶה גִיטֵּיךְ מֵחוֹלִי. זֶה גִיטֵּיךְ לְאַחַר מִיתָתִי. לֹא אָמַר כְּלוּם. וְרַבּוֹתֵינוּ אָמְרוּ. הֲרֵי זֶה גֵט. מָנוּ רַבּוֹתֵינוּ. רִבִּי יְהוּדָה הַנָּשִׂיא וּבֵית דִּינוֹ. וְיִקְרְאוּ לוֹ בֵּית דִּין שַׁרְיָיא. שֶׁכָּל־בֵּית דִּין שֶׁהוּא מַתִּיר שְׁלשָׁה דְבָרִים הוּא נִקְרָא בֵּית דִּין שַׁרְיָיא. אָמַר רִבִּי יוּדָן. בֵּית דִּינוֹ חָלוּק עָלָיו בְּגִיטִּין. רִבִּי יַנַּאי צָוַח. טִיהַרְתֶּם אַתֶּם אֶת הַיּוֹלְדוֹת. רִבִּי סִימוֹן בְּשֵׁם רִבִּי יְהוֹשֻׁעַ בֶּן לֵוִי. מֵעִידוּתוֹ שֶׁלְּרִבִּי חוֹנְיָיה מִבְּרַת חַוְרָן הִיא. כְּהָדָא רִבִּי זְעִירָא. אִם מֵעִידוּתוֹ שֶׁלְּרִבִּי חוֹנְיָיה מִבְּרַת חַוְרָן הִיא רִבִּי חֲנִינָה צָוַח. טִיהַרְתֶּם אֶת הַיּוֹלְדוֹת.

7 לא אמר כלום | ג אינו גט   הרי זה גט | ג בזה גט   8 ויקראו | ג וקראו   שרייא | ג שרייה   9 שכל בית דין - | ג . . . שרייא (entire sentence) | ג 10   בגיטין | ג בגטין   ינאי | ג ינייי   טיהרתם | ג טיהרתן (2 times)   11 היולדות | ג הילדות (2 times)   מעידותו | ג מעדותו   חונייה | ג חוניה (2 times)   12 כהדא ר' זעירא | ג ר' זעירה בעי   מברת חוורן | ג דברת חורן   היא | ג בזה

"What is the sole which they mentioned? Anything which looks like the sole, a sea fish. Rabban Simeon ben Gamliel says, anything which looks like an ox tongue. Our teachers voted about this to say, only if it exhibits human traits."[93] Who are "our teachers"? Rebbi Jehudah the Prince and his court[94]. At three places is Rebbi Jehudah the Prince called "our teachers", about bills of divorce, oil, and a sole. About a sole, as we just said. About oil, as we have stated: "Rebbi and his court permitted oil[94a]." About bills of divorce, as we have stated there[95]: "This is your bill of divorce if I die, this is your bill of divorce if [I die from this] sickness, this is your bill of divorce after my death; he did not say anything[96]." But our teachers said, this is a bill of divorce[97]. Who are "our teachers"? Rebbi Jehudah the Prince and his court. They should have called him "permissive court" since any court which permits three [previously forbidden] things is called "permissive court.[98]" Rebbi Yudan said, his court disagreed with him about the bills of divorce. Rebbi Yannai shouted, you purified the women giving birth[99]! Rebbi Simon in the name of Rebbi Joshua ben Levi: This is part of the testimony of Rebbi Onias from Hauran[100]; as from Rebbi Ze'ira: If this is part of the testimony of Rebbi Onias from Hauran then it was Rebbi Ḥanina[101] who shouted, you purified the women giving birth!

93   Tosephta 4:6, Babli 25b. The last sentence reads in the Babli: Our teachers testified that a sole [to be the source of birth impurity] needs the shape of a face.

94   *Šabbat* 1:1 (3d l.20), *Giṭṭin* 7:3 (48d l.17), *Avodah zarah* 2:8 (41d l.48); obliquely mentioned in the Babli *Giṭṭin* 72b, 76b; *Ketubot* 2b, *Avodah zarah* 37a.

94a   Mishnah *Avodah zarah* 2:9. The Mishnah has a list of foods that cannot be taken from Gentiles without kosher supervision since one cannot be sure that no forbidden ingredients were used but which are not forbidden for usufruct. A first group contains milk, bread, and olive oil, with a note that "our teachers permitted olive oil" [to be used without supervision.] In the Babli, this permission is attributed to Rebbi, not his grandson R. Jehudah the Prince. (The chronology of the House of Hillel in the third cent. and the attribution of decrees between Rabbis Jehudah I, II, and III is in dispute.)

95   Mishnah *Giṭṭin* 7:3. From here on there exists a Geniza text; its readings are given by א

96   After his death, no person can perform any legal action. Therefore, a bill of divorce which shall be valid only after the husband's death is invalid. If the husband is sick or goes on a trip overseas, and he wants to spare his wife (or prevent her from

contracting) a levirate marriage to his brother, he can give her a bill of divorce stating "if I die then this shall be your bill of divorce *valid from today*." But then he cannot live with her any longer without invalidating the divorce.

97   The Babli, *Gittin* 72b, reports the same but in 76b refers the decision to Mishnah 7:9: "If he says, this is your bill of divorce if I do not return within 12 months; if he dies in the meantime, the bill of divorce is void." In this case also, he did not specify *from today*. The Babli explains that in both cases they follow R. Yose who holds that "the date of a document is proof of its validity;" a bill of divorce executed before the husband's death is valid. The same explanation is tentatively accepted in the Yerushalmi, *Gittin* 7:3 (48d l. 25).

98   Mishnah *Idiut* 8:4, the oldest Mishnah on record.

99   By freeing all miscarriages without a recognizable fetus from the rules of birth impurity.

100   One should read חוֹנְיָה מִבֵּית חַוְרָן, cf. *Sevi'it* 1:7, Note 53.

101   Rebbi Onias's teacher.

(50d line 61) אֵי זוֹ הִיא שִׁלְיָיה שֶׁאָמְרוּ. כָּל־שֶׁהִיא דוֹמָה לְחוּט עָרֶב וְרֹאשָׁהּ תָּפוּחַ כְּתוּרְמוֹס. רַבָּן שִׁמְעוֹן בֶּן גַּמְלִיאֵל אוֹמֵר. כָּל־שֶׁהוּא דוֹמֶה לְדַקִּים שֶׁל תַּרְנְגוֹלִין וְרֹאשָׁהּ תָּפוּחַ כְּקַרְקְבָן וַחֲלוּלָה כַּחֲצוֹצֶרֶת. וְאֵין שִׁלְיָיה פְּחוּתָה מִטֶּפַח.

1 אי זו | ג איזה   שילייה | ג שיליה (2 times)   שהיא | ג שהוא   2 כתורמוס | ג כתורמוסים   דומה | ג -   לדקים | ג לדקין   3 כחצוצרת | ג כחצוצרות

¹⁰²"What is the placenta they mentioned? Anything looking like a thread of woof and its head is blown up like a lupine. Rabban Gamliel says, anything looking like chicken intestines and its head is blown up like a crop and it is hollow like a trumpet. No placenta is shorter than a handbreadth."

102   The Babylonian version has slightly different attributions: Babli 26a, Tosephta 4:9.

HALAKHAH 4 701

(50d line 65) רַב יְהוּדָה שָׁלַח שָׁאַל לְרִבִּי לֶעָזָר. שִׁילְיָה שֶׁיָּצְתָה מִקְצָתָהּ הַיּוֹם וּמִקְצָתָהּ לְמָחָר. אָמַר לֵיהּ. אִם לְדַם טוֹהַר מוֹנָה מִיּוֹם הָרִאשׁוֹן. וְאִם לְדַם טָמֵא מוֹנָה מִיּוֹם הַשֵּׁינִי. אָמַר רִבִּי מַתַּנְיָיה. הָדָא דְאַתְּ אָמַר בְּשֶׁלֹּא יָצָה עִמָּהּ וָלָד. אֲבָל אִם יָצָה עִמָּהּ וָלָד בֵּין לְדַם טוֹהַר בֵּין לְדַם טָמֵא אֵינָהּ מוֹנָה אֶלָּא מִשְׁעַת יְצִיאַת הַוָּלָד.

1 שיליה | ק שילייא   שיצתה | ק שיצאת ג שיצא   3 מונה | ג -   השיני | ק שיני מתנייה | ג מתניה   דאת אמר | קג דתימר   עמה ולד | ג עימה ולד   4 בין | ג ובין

[103]Rav Jehudah sent and asked Rebbi Eleazar: If a placenta came out partially today and partially tomorrow? He told him, for pure blood she counts from the first day, for impure blood she counts from the second day[104]. Rebbi Mattaniah said, this refers to the case that there was no child born with it. But if a child was born with it, then both for pure and for impure blood she counts only from the moment the child was born.

103   The same text is in *Qidduŝin* 1:4 (60b l. 43), ק. A different version is in the Babli, *Baba qama* 11a.

104   She has only 25 days of purity since the 14th day of her impurity is the 15th day of her count for purity. In the version of the Babli, during the first day she would make pure food impure but the count, including 26 days of purity, starts only on the second day.

(50d line 69) רִבִּי יוֹסֵי בֶּן שָׁאוּל בָּעָא קוֹמֵי רִבִּי. מַהוּ לִתְלוֹת שִׁילְיָיא בְּדָבָר שֶׁאֵינוֹ וָלָד. אָמַר לֵיהּ. אֵין תּוֹלִין שִׁילְיָיא בְּדָבָר שֶׁאֵינוֹ וָלָד. יָצָאת קְשׁוּרָה לוֹ מַהוּ. אָמַר לֵיהּ. אֵין שׁוֹנִין דָּבָר שֶׁאֵי אֶיפְשָׁר. תַּנָּא רִבִּי חָנִין דִּשְׁמוּאֵל. אֵין תּוֹלִין שִׁילְיָיא בְּדָבָר שֶׁאֵינוֹ וָלָד. יָצָאת קְשׁוּרָה לוֹ תּוֹלִין אוֹתוֹ בּוֹ. שְׁמוּאֵל שָׁאַל לְתַלְמִידוֹי דְרַב. מַהוּ לִתְלוֹת שִׁילְיָיא בִּנְפָלִים. אָמְרִין לֵיהּ. תּוֹלִין שִׁילְיָא בְּוָלָד וְתוֹלִין שִׁילְיָיא בִּנְפָלִים. וְקִלְסוֹן שְׁמוּאֵל. דְּאִינּוּן אָמְרִין שִׁיטָתֵיהּ דְּר' בּוֹן. תַּנָּא רִבִּי חָנִין דִּשְׁמוּאֵל. תּוֹלִין שִׁילְיָיא בְּוָלָד וְאֵין תּוֹלִין שִׁילְיָיא בִּנְפָלִים שֶׁאֵינָהּ פּוֹרֶשֶׁת מִמֶּנּוּ עַד שֶׁיִּגְמוֹר. רִבִּי זְעִירָא בְּשֵׁם דְּרַבָּנָן. הֵן דְּאַתְּ אָמְרַתְּ.

תּוֹלִין שִׁילְיָא בְּוָלָד שֶׁאֵין הָאִשָּׁה מִתְעַבֶּרֶת וְחוֹזֶרֶת וּמִתְעַבֶּרֶת. וְיִתְלוּ אוֹתוֹ בִּנְפָלִים שֶׁאֵין הָאִשָּׁה מַפֶּלֶת וְחוֹזֶרֶת וּמַפֶּלֶת. אֲנִי אוֹמֵר. עִבְּרָה תְאוֹמִים וְנִימוֹקָה שִׁילְיָיתוֹ שֶׁלְשְׁפִיר מִשְׁפִּיר שֶׁלְשְׁלִיָּיתָהּ. רִבִּי זְעִירָה רַב יְהוּדָה בְשֵׁם רַב. תּוֹלִין שִׁילְיָיא בְּוָלָד עַד שְׁלֹשָׁה יָמִים וְאֵין הַוָּלָד מִשְׁתָּהֵא לְאַחַר חֲבֵירוֹ שְׁלֹשָׁה יָמִים. אָמַר רִבִּי זְעִירָא. מָאן דָּמַר הָדָא אָמַר הָדָא וְאֵינוּן פְּלִיגִין הָדָא עַל הָדָא. אָמַר רִבִּי בָּא. אוּקְמָהּ רַב יְהוּדָה בְּשֵׁם רַב. הֵן דְּאַתְּ אָמַר. תּוֹלִין שִׁילְיָיה בְּוָלָד עַד שְׁלֹשָׁה יָמִים בְּשֶׁיָּצָא הַוָּלָד תְּחִילָּה. וְהֵן דְּאַתְּ אָמַר. אֵין הַוָּלָד מִשְׁתָּהֵא לְאַחַר חֲבֵירוֹ שְׁלֹשָׁה יָמִים כְּשֶׁיָּצָא הַסַּנְדָּל תְּחִילָּה. אָמַר רִבִּי מָנָא. וְיֵאוּת. אִילֵּין לַהֲטָיָיה נָפְקִין קַדְמָאֵי. אָמַר רִבִּי יוֹסֵי בֵּירְבִּי בּוּן. נִפְתַּח לְגָדוֹל נִפְתַּח לְקָטָן. נִפְתַּח לְקָטָן לֹא נִפְתַּח לְגָדוֹל.

1 יוסי | ג יוסה   שילייא | ג שיליה (all)   2 וולד | ג ולד (all)   3 ליה | ג לה   שאי אפשר | ג שאפשר   תנא | ג תנה (all)   דשמואל | ג ר' שמואל (all)   5 מהו | ג מהוא   שילייא | ג שילייה   אמרין ליה | ג א' לה   6 ותולין | ג ואינן תולין   שיטתיה דר' בון | ג שטתה דרבון   7 בנפילים | ג בנפלין (all)   8 שיגמור | ג שתיגמר   זעירא | ג זעורה   (all)   דרבנן | ג רבנין   דאת אמרת | ג דתמר   10 עיברה | ג שעיברה   11 שלשילייתה | ג על שילייה   12 בוולד | ג -   לאחר | ג על אתר   שלשה | ג אלא עד שלשה   13 מאן | ג מן   הדא | ג הדה (2 times)   ג הדה (2 times)   14 אוקמה | ג אקימה   רב יהודה | ג רב   דאת אמר | ג דתמר (2 times)   15 תחילה | ג תחלה   16 כשיצא | ג בשיצא   17 להטייא | ג להטיה   קדמאי | ג קדמיי   אמר ר' יוסי ביר' בון וכו' | ג כל זה חסר.

Rebbi Yose ben Shaul asked before Rebbi: Can one refer a placenta to something which is not a child[105]? He said to him, one does not refer a placenta to anything which is not a child. If it came out attached to it, what then? He said to him, one does not discuss anything impossible. Rebbi Ḥanin stated from Samuel[106]: One does not refer a placenta to something which is not a child, if [nevertheless] it came out attached to something else, one refers to it. Samuel asked the students of Rav: Can one refer a placenta to stillbirths? They said to him, one refers a placenta to a child and one [does not] refer(s) a placenta to stillbirths[107]. Samuel praised them because they follow the argument [of their teacher][108]. Rebbi Ḥanin stated from Samuel: One refers a placenta to a child but one does not refer a placenta to stillbirths since it does not separate until it [was completed][109]. Rebbi Ze'ira in the name of the rabbis: What you say, that one refers a placenta to a child, is because a pregnant woman does not become pregnant[110]. Why does one not refer it to stillbirth, can a woman not have a stillbirth followed by a stillbirth[111]? I say that she was pregnant with twins when the placenta of one amnion was crushed by the amnion of the other placenta. Rebbi Ze'ira, Rav Jehudah in the name of Rav: One refers a placenta to a child for up to three days[112], and no child remains after another child for three days. Rebbi Ze'ira said, he who said this also said the other, but they disagree with one another[113]! Rebbi Abba said, Rav Jehudah explained it following Rav: You say that one refers a placenta to a child for up to three days if the child was born first, and you say that no child remains after another child for three days if the sole appeared first. Rebbi Mana said, is that correct? The active ones come out first[114]. Rebbi Yose ben Rebbi Abun said, if [the womb] opened for the large, it opened for the small; if it opened for the small it did not open for the large[115].

105   If a woman is delivered of a placenta without a baby, does one have to assume that this represents a stillbirth or could she have developed a tumor in the form of a placenta which then was expelled from her body?

106   The reading of the Geniza: R. Ḥanina, R. Samuel, is preferable since R. Ḥanin was the student of R. Samuel bar Isaac.

107   After the birth of a live child, the placenta will be expelled separately; a placenta not followed by birth cannot be considered *placenta*

praevia of a stillbirth.

108   Translation of the Genizah text. Leiden ms: "The argument of Rebbi Abun" (who lived several generations after Rav and Samuel and is never mentioned in this connection.)

109   He holds that the stillbirth of an incomplete gestation is always expelled together with its placenta.

110   While pregnant (with one or several simultaneous children), a woman will not start a later pregnancy. This is asserted as certain truth in the Babli, 27a.

111   Can a woman not be pregnant with twins and lose them at different times?

112   After the birth of a child it can take up to three days before the placenta is expelled; the count of impurity starts with the birth of the child. If the placenta is expelled later that three days one considers this as a later stillbirth and starts the count of impurity for an indeterminate stillbirth from the later date. The same opinion in the Babli, 26b.

113   If twins can be born three days apart, then the placenta could be expelled after 6 days, not three as asserted in the first part of the statement.

114   He denies that in the case of twins a live birth can happen three days after a stillbirth.

115   A fetus whose development was arrested cannot stay in the womb after the birth of its live twin; the live child can stay in the womb after the dead was expelled. This sentence is missing in the Genizah text.

(51a line 15) אָמַר רִבִּי יוֹחָנָן. דְּרִבִּי שִׁמְעוֹן הִיא. דְּרִבִּי שִׁמְעוֹן אוֹמֵר. נִימוֹק הַוְולָד עַד שֶׁלֹּא יָצָא. אָמַר רִבִּי יוֹחָנָן. מוֹדֶה רִבִּי שִׁמְעוֹן שֶׁהוּא מוֹשִׁיב אֶת אִמּוֹ יְמֵי לֵידָה. מֵעַתָּה יְהֵא הַבַּיִת טָמֵא. אָמַר רִבִּי בּוּן בַּר חִייָה. תִּיפְתָּר שֶׁיָּצָא כָּל־שֶׁהוּא נִימוֹק. אָמַר לָהֶן רִבִּי שִׁמְעוֹן לַחֲכָמִים. אֵין אַתֶּם מוֹדִין לִי בְּמוֹצִיא אֶת הַסֶּפֶל מִבַּיִת הַפְּנִימִי לַחִיצוֹן שֶׁהוּא טָהוֹר. אָמְרוּ לוֹ. מִפְּנֵי שֶׁהוּא כְּטָרוּף. אָמַר לָהֶן. אַף זֶה כְּטָרוּף הוּא. כֵּלִים שֶׁהָיוּ שָׁם בְּשָׁעַת יְצִיאָה מָה הֵן. נִישְׁמְעִינָהּ מִן הָדָא דְּתַנִּינָן תַּמָּן. רִבִּי לִיעֶזֶר בֶּן יַעֲקֹב אוֹמֵר. בְּהֵמָה נֶפֶשׁ שֶׁשָּׁפְעָה חֲרֶרֶת דָּם הֲרֵי זֶה תִּיקָּבֵר וּפְטוּרָה מִן הַבְּכוֹרָה. וְתַנֵּי עֲלָהּ. אֵינָהּ מְטַמָּא בְמַשָּׂא. אָמַר רִבִּי יוֹחָנָן. רִבִּי שִׁמְעוֹן וְרִבִּי לִיעֶזֶר בֶּן יַעֲקֹב שְׁנֵיהֶן אָמְרוּ דָּבָר אֶחָד. הָדָא אָמְרָה. כֵּלִים שֶׁהָיוּ שָׁם בְּשָׁעַת יְצִיאָה טְהוֹרִין.

2 מודה | ג מודי   מושיב את | ג משיצאת   3 ימי | ג לימי   רבי | ג -   תיפתר | ג תפתר
4 כל שהוא | ג כל שהוא כל שהוא   נימוק | ג נמוק   לחכמים | ג -   מודין | ג מודים
6 אמ' להן | ג -   כלים | ג כלין (2 times)   7 ניישמעינה | ג נשמעינה   הדא | ג הדה (2
times)   7 ליעזר | ג לעזר   ששפאה ... הבכורה | ג שפשטה וג'   8 אינה | ג הרי זו
אינה   ליעזר | ג אליעזר   10 שם | ג -

Rebbi Joḥanan said, this[116] follows Rebbi Simeon, since Rebbi Simeon said, the child was dissolved before it came out. Rebbi Joḥanan said, Rebbi Simeon agrees that he causes his mother the days of birth[117]. Then the house should be impure[118]? Rebbi Abun bar Ḥiyya said, explain it if it came out partially dissolved[119]. Rebbi Simeon said to the Sages: Do you not agree with me that if the basin is carried from the inner to an outer room it is pure[120]? They said to him, because it becomes scrambled[121]. He said to them, this one is already scrambled. What is the rule about vessels which were there at the time of delivery? Let us hear from the following which we stated there[122]: "Rebbi Eliezer ben Jacob says, if a cow brought forth a cake of blood, that should be buried and she is freed from the rule of firstlings." It was stated on this: It does not bring impurity by being carried[123]. Rebbi Joḥanan said, Rebbi Simeon and Rebbi Eliezer ben Jacob said the same thing[124]. This implies that vessels which were there at the time of delivery are pure[125].

116 The entire Mishnah follows R. Simeon's reasoning that there must have been a fetus which failed to develop; the only difference between R. Simeon and the majority relates to the impurity of the dead. The same statement in the Babli, 27b.

117 R. Simeon agrees with the first statement in the Mishnah. The same statement in the Babli, 27b.

118 A complete human fetus (older than 40 days after conception) is a human corpse and causes the impurity of the dead, in particular the impurity of a "tent" which applies to all the vessels in the "tent" (*Num.* 19).

119 R. Simeon holds that a fetus whose existence can only be inferred from the existence of a placenta will never be born intact.

120 Tosephta 4:13. The Sages, who hold that the room in which the woman is delivered from the empty placenta becomes a "tent" containing human remains, will agree that, if the placenta and all that remains is carried out from there in a basin, the next room is no longer a "tent" and remains pure. The same argument in made the Babli, 27a.

121 By the delivery and the motion, the undeveloped fetus will no longer be complete in one piece.

122 Mishnah *Bekhorot* 3:1. If a cow is pregnant the first time and has a miscarriage, what she is delivered of is "opening of the womb" (*Ex.* 34:19) and must be treated as holy. While a calf born afterwards may be her firstling, it is no longer "opening the womb" and,

therefore, not a sacrifice.

123 If somebody carries the cadaver of a kosher animal (even without touching it), he and his clothing become impure (*Lev.* 11:40). If the stillbirth does not have any features which make it recognizable as an animal, it does not induce the impurity of cadavers.

124 The same statement is in the Babli, *Bekhorot* 22a.

125 For R. Simeon, the room in which the woman was delivered is not a "tent" transmitting the impurity of the dead. This argument also establishes that practice follows R. Simeon. In the Babli, 27a quoting Tosephta 4:13, this is clear since it identifies the anonymous Mishnah as R. Meïr's and states that R. Jehudah and R. Yose support R. Simeon. In the Babli, *Bekhorot* 21b, this is a *baraita* ascribed to R. Ḥiyya (the Elder.)

(fol. 50b) **משנה ח:** הַמַּפֶּלֶת טוּמְטוּם וְאַנְדְּרוֹגִינוֹס וְזָכָר תֵּשֵׁב לַזָּכָר וְלַנְּקֵיבָה. טוּמְטוּם וְזָכָר וְאַנְדְּרוֹגִינוֹס וְזָכָר תֵּשֵׁב לַזָּכָר וְלַנְּקֵיבָה. טוּמְטוּם וּנְקֵיבָה אַנְדְּרוֹגִינוֹס וּנְקֵיבָה תֵּשֵׁב לַנְּקֵיבָה בִּלְבַד. יָצָא מְחוּתָּךְ אוֹ מְסוֹרָס לִכְשֶׁיָּצָא רוּבּוֹ הֲרֵי הוּא כְיָלוּד. יָצָא כְדַרְכּוֹ עַד שֶׁיֵּצֵא רוֹב רֹאשׁוֹ. וְאֵי זֶה הוּא רוֹב רֹאשׁוֹ מִשֶּׁתֵּצֵא פַדַּחְתּוֹ.

Mishnah 5: If a woman miscarries[126] a sexless, or a hermaphrodite[127], and a male[128], she shall observe for a male and a female[129]. If it was a sexless and a male, or a hermaphrodite and a male, she shall observe for a male and a female[130]. A sexless and a female, or a hermaphrodite and a female, she shall observe for a female exclusively[131]. If it came out in pieces or defective, it is born as soon as most of its body came out[132]. If it was a regular birth, when most of its head came out. When is it most of its head? If the forehead came out[133].

משנה ו: הַמַּפֶּלֶת וְאֵין יָדוּעַ מַה הוּא תֵּשֵׁב לַזָּכָר וְלַנְּקֵיבָה. אֵין יָדוּעַ אִם וְלָד הָיָה תֵּשֵׁב לַזָּכָר וְלַנְּקֵיבָה וְלַנִּדָּה. הַמַּפֶּלֶת לְיוֹם אַרְבָּעִים אֵינָהּ חוֹשֶׁשֶׁת לְוָלָד. לְיוֹם אַרְבָּעִים וְאֶחָד תֵּשֵׁב לַזָּכָר וְלַנְּקֵבָה וְלַנִּדָּה. רְבִּי יִשְׁמָעֵאל אוֹמֵר יוֹם אַרְבָּעִים וְאֶחָד תֵּשֵׁב לַזָּכָר וְלַנִּדָּה יוֹם שְׁמוֹנִים וְאֶחָד תֵּשֵׁב לַזָּכָר וְלַנְּקֵיבָה וְלַנִּידָה שֶׁהַזָּכָר נִגְמַר לְאַרְבָּעִים וְאֶחָד וְהַנְּקֵיבָה לִשְׁמוֹנִים וְאֶחָד. וַחֲכָמִים אוֹמְרִים אֶחָד בְּרִיַּת הַזָּכָר וְאֶחָד בְּרִיאַת הַנְּקֵיבָה זֶה וָזֶה לְאַרְבָּעִים וְאֶחָד.

Mishnah 6: If a woman miscarries and it is not known what it was, she shall observe for a male and a female. If it is not known whether there was a fetus, she shall observe for a male, a female, and menstruation[134]. If she miscarries on the 40th day, she gives no thought to a child[135]. On the 41st day, she shall observe for a male, a female, and menstruation[136]. Rebbi Ismael says, on the 41st day, she shall observe for a male and menstruation, on the 81st day, she shall observe for a male, a female, and menstruation for the male is fully formed by the 41st day and the female by the 81st. But the Sages say, the creation of males and females is identical, both on the 41st.

---

126 The rules of this Mishnah are valid also for live births. It is formulated for a miscarriage since it is part of a series speaking mostly of

miscarriages.

127 A child without either male or female sex characteristics. The child could be either a male with an ingrown penis or an undeveloped female.

127 This word is missing in the Halakhah, the Babli, and the independent Mishnah mss.; it is a scribal error.

129 The restrictions for male and female, cf. Note 14.

130 Since the second child could be a female. While the mother of live twins, one a male and one a female, observes only the rules for a female, in this case the male is certain but the female uncertain. Therefore, the mother has to observe the rules for a male and only those rules of a female which are restrictive, not those which are permissive.

131 This is not different from the rules for twins of different sexes since the days of impurity and purity for a male are contained, respectively, in those for a female.

132 This is the point in time from which the impurity of birth is counted.

133 From this moment on, the child is a person in law and cannot be killed even if the birth endangers the life of the mother.

134 If there was no child, there are no days of purity. She is impure like a menstruating woman for 14 days. It is traditional that 11 days after the menstrual period, i. e., days 8 to 19 in the menstrual cycle, no menstruation can occur. Therefore, if the woman has a bloody discharge after day 8, she is impure in the impurity of flow (*Lev.* 15:25-30). For this, one follows the rules of the male, not the female.

135 The human character of a fetus starts at the end of the 40th day after conception. A termination of pregnancy before this time is no abortion.

136 Since so early in the pregnancy it falls under the rules of a miscarriage whose nature cannot be determined.

(51a line 26) **הלכה ח:** הַמַּפֶּלֶת טוּמְטוּם וְאַנְדְרוֹגִינוֹס כול׳. כָּל־הֵן דְּתַנִּינָן תֵּשֵׁב לַזָּכָר וְלַנְּקֵיבָה. יֹד טְמֵאִין וכֹו טְהוֹרִין. נוֹתְנִין עָלֶיהָ חוֹמְרֵי זָכָר וְחוֹמְרֵי נְקֵיבָה. הָדָא דְאַתְּ אָמַר. לְבִיתָהּ. אֲבָל לְטַהֲרוֹת תֵּשֵׁב לַנְּקֵיבָה. טוּמְטוּם וְזָכָר וְאַנְדְרוֹגִינוֹס וְזָכָר תֵּשֵׁב לַזָּכָר וְלַנְּקֵיבָה. וְחוֹשְׁשִׁין לְזָכָר. טוּמְטוּם וּנְקֵיבָה

אַנְדְּרוֹגִינוֹס וּנְקֵיבָה תֵּשֵׁב לַנְּקֵיבָה בִּלְבַד. וְאֵין חוֹשְׁשִׁין לְזָכָר. הָדָא אֲמְרָה. יָלְדָה זָכָר וּנְקֵיבָה אוֹ נְקֵיבָה וְזָכָר תֵּשֵׁב לִנְקֵיבָה.

1 כול׳ ‏| ג המפלת ואין ידוע   2 נקיבה | ג נקבה (in all occurrences)   יד | ג ארבעה עשר   וכו׳ | ג ועשרים וששה   טהורין | ג טהורים   3 נקיבה | ג הנקבה   דאת אמר | ג דתמר   וזכר | ג זכר (2 times)

Halakhah 5: "If a woman miscarries a sexless, or a hermaphrodite," etc. In all cases in which we have stated "she shall observe for a male and a female," it means 14 [days] impure and 26 pure; one puts on her the restrictions of both male and female[14]. That means, for her house[137]. But for pure food she observes the rules of a female [birth]. "If it was a sexless and a male, or a hermaphrodite and a male, she shall observe for a male and a female," one takes into account the possibility of a male[138]. "A sexless and a female, or a hermaphrodite and a female, she shall observe for a female exclusively," does one not take into account the possibility of a male? This implies that if she gave birth to a male and a female, or a female and a male[139], she observes the rules for a female[130].

137 For sexual relations with her husband; cf. Note 39.

138 The rules are restrictive since the sexless or the hermaphrodite might in reality be males. Therefore, the female influences only for impurity, not for purity.

139 The order in which the twins are born may be important for rules of inheritance; it is irrelevant for rules of purity and impurity.

(51a line 32) מְחוּתָּךְ שֶׁיָּצָא רֹאשׁוֹ מָהוּ. רִבִּי יָסָא אָמַר. אִתְפַּלְגוּן רִבִּי יוֹחָנָן וְרִבִּי לָעְזָר. רִבִּי יוֹחָנָן אָמַר. רֹאשׁוֹ כְּרוּבּוֹ. רִבִּי לָעְזָר אָמַר. רֹאשׁוֹ כְּאֶחָד מֵאֵיבָרָיו. מַתְנִיתָא פְּלִיגָא עַל רִבִּי יוֹחָנָן. יָצָא מְחוּתָּךְ אוֹ מְסוֹרָס מִשֶּׁיָּצָא רוּבּוֹ הֲרֵי הוּא כְּיָלוּד. פָּתַר לָהּ בְּשֶׁיָּצָא רֹאשׁוֹ. מַתְנִיתָא פְּלִיגָא עַל רִבִּי לָעְזָר. יָצָא

כְּדַרְכּוֹ עַד שֶׁיֵּצֵא רוֹב רֹאשׁוֹ. הָדָא קַדְמִיתָה אָמְרָה. רֹאשׁוֹ לֹא כְלוּם. פָּתַר לָהּ עַל מְסוּרָס. רִבִּי יוֹנָתָן וְרִבִּי שִׁמְעוֹן בֶּן לָקִישׁ. רִבִּי יוֹנָתָן כְּרִבִּי יוֹחָנָן. רִבִּי שִׁמְעוֹן בֶּן לָקִישׁ כְּרִבִּי לֶעְזָר. רִבִּי זְעִירָא מְחַוֵי לַחֲבֶרַיָּיא. פְּדַחְתּוֹ וְגוּלְגּוֹלְתּוֹ. חַד דְּבֵי נַמְלִיאֵל בֵּירְבִּי לֵיאָנִי בְּעָא קוֹמֵי רִבִּי מָנָא. מִכֵּיוָן דְּאַתְּ אָמַר. וְלָד הוּא. מֵעַתָּה הַבָּא אַחֲרָיו אֵינוֹ בְכוֹר לֹא לְנַחֲלָה וְלֹא לַכֹּהֵן. אָמַר לֵיהּ. תִּיפְתָּר שֶׁיָּצְאוּ מֵתִים.

1 מהו | ג מהוא   2 כרובו | ג ורובו   לעזר אמר | ג אלעזר   3 מאיבריו | ג מכל איבריו   4 הרי הוא כילוד | ג -   בשיצא | ג משיצא   5 הדא קדמיתא | ג הדה קדמייתה

If it was in pieces and the head came out, what is the rule? Rebbi Yasa said, Rebbi Joḥanan and Rebbi Eleazar disagree. Rebbi Joḥanan said, its head counts for most of it. Rebbi Eleazar said, its head is like any other of its limbs[140]. A Mishnah disagrees with Rebbi Joḥanan: "If it came out in pieces or defective, it is born as soon as most of its body came out." Explain it if its head came out[141]. A Mishnah disagrees with Rebbi Eleazar: "If it was a regular birth[142], when most of its head came out." Did not the first part say, the head is nothing?[143] Explain it[144] about the incomplete body. Rebbi Jonathan and Rebbi Simeon ben Laqish; Rebbi Jonathan agrees with Rebbi Joḥanan[145], Rebbi Simeon ben Laqish with Rebbi Eleazar. Rebbi Ze'ira showed the colleagues his forehead with the skull[146]. One of the house of Gamliel ben Rebbi Leani asked before Rebbi Mana: Since you say, it is a child, does this not imply that one who comes after him is firstborn neither for inheritance nor for the Cohen[147]. He said to him, explain it if both were stillborn[148].

140 Their disagreement is confirmed in the Babli, 29a.

141 The head is called "most of the body".

142 If the head appeared first, even if it was a stillbirth with an incomplete

body.

143 A "regular birth" must refer to a fully formed body since otherwise the first statement, that one needs most of the body, contradicts the second, that the skull with the forehead is enough. From the last statement of the Mishnah there is no objection to R. Eleazar since it does not speak of a defective fetus.

144 The first, but not the second statement of the second half of the Mishnah.

145 Here ends the Genizah fragment.

146 That a birth is counted only from the moment that the forehead with the greater part of the skull had appeared.

147 Mishnah *Bekhorot* 8:1 states that any child born after an initial miscarriage such as described in this Chapter is a firstborn for inheritance but not for redemption by a Cohen (*Ex.* 13:15).

148 Obviously any miscarriage produces a stillborn baby. The rules of the firstborn for inheritance have nothing to do with those of the firstborn for redemption. While the firstborn for inheritance must be born (*Deut* 21:15), he cannot have been delivered by caesarean section and he must be the father's first (*Deut* 21:17), but not necessarily the mother's. Since a miscarriage is not counted for the father, only for the mother, the next child still can claim the double part of the inheritance (*Sifry Deut.* 217).

(51a line 43) רִבִּי יִצְחָק בַּר נַחְמָן בְּשֵׁם רִבִּי לְעָזָר. גּוּלְגּוֹלֶת הָעוֹף בְּרוּבּוֹ. רִבִּי זְעִירָא בְּשֵׁם שְׁמוּאֵל. גַּרְגֶּרֶת הָעוֹף בְּרוּבּוֹ. אֲתָא עוֹבְדָא קוֹמֵי רִבִּי יוֹסֵי בְּאֶחָד שֶׁנִּיקֵב מְלֹא מַחַט. וְכִי אֵין אָנוּ יוֹדְעִין אֵי זֶה הוּא רוּבּוֹ.

Rebbi Isaac bar Naḥman in the name of Rebbi Eleazar: The head of a bird by most of it[149]. Rebbi Ze'ira in the name of Samuel: The throat of a bird by most of it. There came a case before Rebbi Yose about [a bird whose throat] was punctured by a needle's width. Do we not know what "most" means[150]?

149 This has nothing to do with the topics discussed before; it refers to the rules of kosher food. Since "you shall not eat meat from a torn animal" (*Ex.*

22:30), a four-legged animal whose membrane encasing the brain or esophagus is punctured by the most minute hole is unfit for consumption. It is asserted here that these strict rules do not apply for birds.

150   Certainly, a hole the width of a needle is not "most". In the Babli, *Ḥulin* 44a/b, the definition of "most of the throat" is in dispute.

בנות כותים פרק רביעי

(fol. 51b) **משנה א**: בְּנוֹת כּוּתִים נִידּוֹת מֵעֲרִיסָתָן. וְהַכּוּתִים מְטַמְּאִין מִשְׁכָּב תַּחְתּוֹן כָּעֶלְיוֹן מִפְּנֵי שֶׁהֵן בּוֹעֲלֵי נִידּוֹת וְהֵן יוֹשְׁבוֹת עַל כָּל דָּם. וְאֵין חַיָּיבִין עֲלֵיהֶן עַל בִּיאַת הַמִּקְדָּשׁ וְאֵין שׂוֹרְפִין עֲלֵיהֶן אֶת הַתְּרוּמָה מִפְּנֵי שֶׁטּוּמְאָתָן בְּסָפֵק.

Mishnah 1: The daughters of Samaritans are menstruating from their cribs[1], and Samaritan men make impure bottoms like uppers[2] because they sleep with menstruating woman since they sit for every blood[3]. But one is not guilty about them for entering the Temple and one does not burn heave because of them since their impurity is one of doubt[4].

1   It can happen that a newborn baby girl, under the influence of the activated sex hormones of the mother, shows a slight vaginal discharge. According to pharisaic tradition, such a baby girl has to be purified by immersion in a *miqweh*. The Samaritans, a Sadducee sect, apply the rules of menstruation only to girls from their puberty on. Therefore, a pre-puberty Samaritan girl might be impure by Pharisaic standards.

2   This is a technical term not easily translated. The sufferer from gonorrhea makes any textile on his couch severely impure; that textile has the ability to make humans and vessels impure. A garment worn by the sufferer from gonorrhea is also impure, but it makes only food and drink impure. The textile on the couch of a man who slept with a menstruating woman (the *bottom*) is impure in the impurity of a garment of the sufferer from gonorrhea (the *upper*).

3   Samaritans, like all Sadducees, are extremely careful not to sleep with menstruating women. They are treated

here as "sleepers with menstruating women" because they consider any vaginal discharge as menstrual; they do not recognize the different shades of blood at the core of pharisaic doctrine (Mishnah 2:5). If a woman has a discharge, she starts counting 7 days and then cleanses herself in a *miqweh*. But in pharisaic theory, she could have a pure discharge on the first day and an impure on the second or third; then the seventh day of her count would be only the sixth of fifth for a pharisaic woman. Therefore, a Samaritan woman might tell her husband that she was pure when in pharisaic theory she was still impure. (A pharisaic woman only has the choice either of showing her blood to a rabbi or to start counting from the last day of her period.)

The compliment was returned by the Sadducees who accused the Pharisees to "make the Temple impure because they do not separate themselves [from their wives] following the Torah and sleep with one who sees the blood of her discharge" (CD V:6).

4   Since it is very unlikely that a Samaritan girl or man really be impure when he or she say that they are pure, one cannot act on their impurity except of not using heave touched by a Samaritan.

הלכה א: בְּנוֹת כּוּתִים נִידּוֹת מֵעֲרִיסָתָן כול׳. דַּם נִידָּה זָהוּם דַּם (fol. 51b) בְּתוּלִים אֵינוֹ זָהוּם.   דַּם נִידָּה אָדוֹם דַּם בְּתוּלִים אֵינוֹ אָדוֹם.   דַּם נִידָּה מִן הַמָּקוֹר דַּם בְּתוּלִים אֵינוֹ מִן הַמָּקוֹר אֶלָּא מִן הַצַּד.

Halakhah 1: "The daughters of Samaritans are menstruating from their cribs," etc. [5]Menstrual blood is dirty, virginal blood is not dirty. Menstrual blood is red, virginal blood is not red. Menstrual blood is from the womb, virginal blood is not from the womb but from the side.

5   Also quoted in the Babli, 65b.

Indices

Index of Biblical Quotations

Gen. 1:22	10	22:24	197,269	21:20	548
1:28	10	34:19	706	25:13	64
2:3	10			27:6	76
2:7	685	Lev. 11:4	689	36:4	415
2:19	686	11:29	74,605		
12:17	369	12:1	601	Deut. 8:3	283
18:4	575	12:2	280	11:40	706
19:19	596	12:5	280	14:7	689
24:16	45	12:6	697	15:19	327
29:27	24	12:7	665	17:5	205
31:50	283	13:2	676	17:6	513,514
34:12	155	15:9	280	17:8	665
39:6	285	15:19	601,603,665,678	19:15	85,96,437
47:28	538			19:16	123
47:30	544	15:25	607,622,665	19:19	139
49:8	52	17:4	141	21:15	711
		18:8	283	21:16	471
Ex. 13:15	711	18:19	290,601	21:17	184,195,473
20:16	139	20:18	665	22:13	158,191
20:17	198	21:7	520	22:14	191,194
21:7	192	21:13	44	22:15	200
21:9	282,283,287	21:14	205,520	22:17	188,194
21:10	279	21:17	329	22:18	134,188,204
21:22	147	22:10	139	22:19	33,134,151,159,169,179,190
21:30	174	22:11	121,256,264		
21:32	171	22:14	139	22:21	169,189,190
21:35	77,483	24:21	135	22:22	160
22:2	171,195	25:14	509	22:23	160
22:8	379,438	27:8	518	22:24	168
22:9	99	27:11	394,509	22:26	170
22:15	33,48,127,149	27:12	510	22:28	127,149,166
22:16	151,153	27:22	518	22:29	132
22:16	129			22:29	33,127,129,152,153,157,159,170
22:30	712	Num. 3:47	33		

Deut. 23:3	520				
25:2	135	Ez. 36:24	544	Job 11:14	94
28:56	299	37:14	544	31:15	272
29:22	545	44:22	48	38:9	601
32:43	549				
		Hos. 4:11	298	Cant. 1:8	299
Jos. 34:33	402	Amos 4:13	686	Ruth 1:19	25
				4:2	24
Jud. 16:16	288			4:7	255
		Ps. 19:6	12	4:21	25
1K. 5:28	280	24:2	547		
22:20	546	62:1	17	Eccl. 7:6	340
		68:7	17	10:5	107
2K. 17:24	131	78:25	283		
		109:10	575	Dan. 9:27	545
Is. 41:19	369	116:9	544		
42:9	544	125:3	45	1Chr. 2:22	402
58:7	506	139:16	694	27:1	280
64:5	604	145:9	538		
Jer. 2:7	549	Prov. 3:9	216	Acts 9:36	631
20:6	545	17:5	120		
45:3	119	30:20	285		

Index of Talmudical Quotations

Babylonian Talmud

Berakhot 16b	631	21b	122	59b	43
				60b	48
Šabbat 14b	398	Ta'anit 25b	369	107a	30
32b	344			113a	38,40
		Mo'ed Qaṭan 18b	17		
Erubin 46a	634			Soṭah 2a	17
		Ḥagigah 14b	42	9b	288
Roš Haššanah 23a	369			13a	52
		Yebamot 24b	350		
Sukkah 37a	369	41b	262	Ketubot 2a	16
		46a	393	2b	699
Megillah 14a	676	59a	45	3a	15,16

INDEX OF TALMUDICAL QUOTATIONS 717

Ketubot 3b	13,15	42b	184		344
5a	16,23	43a	181,185,547	72b	342,345,354,
6b	11	43b	185,458		360
7a	16	44b	132,190,203	74b	356
7b	25	45b	205	75a	362,362
8b	13	46a	191,197	77a	364,365,367,
9a	20	47a	209		368
10a	30,599	47b	282	77b	369
10b	21,30,31	48a	277,282	78a	371,377
11b	42,46	49a	212	78b	376,377
12a	27,53	49b	213	79b	383,385
12b	57	50a	217	80a	386
13a	59	51b	226	81b	390
13b	62,63,64	52a	227	82a	390
14a	62,65	52b	228,229,319	82b	397
15a	62,68,69,74	53a	236,499	83a	403,404
16a	82,83	54a	156,500	83b	408
16b	82	55a	491	84a	382,422,447
18b	91	56a	244,250,251	84b	422,424
19b	94	57a	38,252,253	86b	427
20a	93,96	57b	257,258,264	87a	436
20b	96	58a	258,260	87b	439,440
21a	98	58b	494	88b	452
22a	105	59a	269	89a	456
23a	103,107	59b	274,393	90a	458
25a	109	60a	274,275,630	90b	465,467
25b	112	61a	273,277	91a	472
26a	109,110,114	61b	280	93a	480
26b	100,116	63a	285,287,289,	94a	485,486
27a	116,117,174		290	95a	404
27b	118	63b	290	96a	235,303,493,
28a	121	64a	286,290		494
28b	111,122	64b	292,298	96b	432,504
29a	167	65a	295,299	97a	501
29b	129,131	65b	297,493	97b	499
32b	133	66b	299	98a	509
33a	202	67a	309,314,474	100a	518
36a	49	68a	319	100b	519
36b	146	69b	321,323,324,	101a	348
38a	150		326	101b	291,527,598
38b	124,151	70a	331	102a	245,527
39a	154	71a	333,336	102b	531
40a	163,174	71b	337,338	103a	572
40b	167	72a	340,341,342,	104b	552

Ketubot 105a	556, 557	80b	588	136b	418
107a	559,561	87a	177	140a	529
107b	262,559,561	87b	178	144a	247
108b	581,584	90a	393	152a	497
109a	306,563,583, 586	107a	439		
		113a	18	Šebuot 40a	581
109b	587	114b	126	48b	439
110a	593	115a	433		
110b	596,598,599			Sanhedrin 6b	422
		Baba Meṣi'a 2a	476	8b	200
		2b	78	9b	198
Nedarim 39b	319	3a	80	22a	17
86b	393	3b	171	30b	100
88b	303	4b	80	66b	161,168
		5a	439	72a	195
Nazir 24b	493	10b	424	107a	288
		12b	30		
Giṭṭin 13a	497	13b	4684	Makkot 2b	198
25a	500	16a	269	7b	133
37b	456	17a	460	15a	159
40b	393	29b	432		
48b	446	36a	432	Abodah Zarah 37a	
72b	699,700	49b	494		699
77a	404	57a	509,510		
		67b	488	Bekhorot 21b	706
Qiddušin 9b	160, 161	98a	439	22a	706
				Keritut 17b	655
10b	35	Baba Batra 21a	398	24b	404
16b	181	31b	85		
19a	192	35b	488	Arakhin 5a	267
19b	292	43a	404	21b	517
23b	303	49a	404	22a	445,500
42b	197	51b	409		
45b	30	76a	497	Niddah 3a	606
		80b	369	4a	610
Baba Qama 11a	701	91a	25	4b	605
11b	433	93a	77,78	5a	615
35b	471	107a	414	6a	612,634
36a	133	111b	402	6b	649
40b	494	124a	480	9a	629,630
46a	78	129a	327	9b	610,630,634, 637,639
46b	80	131a	232		
71b	182	132a	251	10a	639
74b	174	136a	235		

Niddah 10b	636	20a	665,670,671,	26a	700
11a	622		674	27a	704,706
11b	659	20b	674,676	27b	692,705
12a	650	21a	673,678	29a	708
13a	648	21b	678	30b	663
13b	649	22a	682	35b	622
14b	652,655	22b	680,681,685	47a	174
15b	660	23a	686,687	54b	659
16b	659	23b	687,689	56a	606
17b	663	24a	690	60b	645
18a	74,663	25a	691,693	65a	642
19a	665	25b	695,699	65b	714
19b	668				

Jerusalem Talmud

Berakhot 1;1	611	Ta'aniot 4:9	17,556	4:4	619
7:1	131			9:13	22
9:5	595	Yebamot 1:1	48,60,	Nedarim 4:2	565
Peah 1:1	213,217		520	6:1	40
4:6	109,303	1:2	640	11:4	301
6:2	373	2:4	520	11:8	303
6:10	402	4:2	45,161	Nazir 2:1	267
Demay 2:2	342	4:3	387	8:5	407
3:4	131	4:4	396	Giṭṭin 1:1	513
Kilaim 2:5	588	4:11	625,633	3:4	117
Ševi'it 1:7	400	4:12	264	4:3	344
9:2	594	6:4	299	4:7	357
10:5	91	6:5	43	5:1	446
Terumot 7:1	133	7:16	131	5:3	215,445
Ma'serot 3:1		8:6	609	7:3	699
	331,561	9:4	521	8:1	404
Ma'aser Šeni 4:4	303	10:4	89	Qidduši̇n 1:1	45,161
Orlah 3:2	327	11:6	174	1:2	192
Bikkurim 1:5	48	12:7	193	1:3	426
1:6	382	13:15	50	1;4	432,701
3:4	91	15:3	217,380	2:5	354
		15:5	381	4:4	65
Šabbat 1	344,629	Soṭah 1:1			
Roš Haššanah 2:1	98		99,123,640	Baba Qama 4:1	482
Beṣah 5:2	17,18	1:3	119	4:7	174
Megillah 3:1	556	1:4	558	7:2	133
4:4	25,518	4:1	441	8:4	271

Baba Qama 8:6	216	8:8	292	7:7	440,449
Baba Meṣi'a 1:1	80	8:9	417,418	Sanhedrin 1:3	518
1:7	278,303	9:1	571	4:6	17
7:10	292	9:6	228	8:6	440
8:5	476	9:8	60	8:8	105
Baba Batra 3:4	85	10:2	80	Makkot 1:1	133
4:2	589	Šebuot 5:7	173	1:16	513
8:6	231,292,412, 414,491	6:3	580	Abodah Zarah 2:8	699
		7:1	445		

Mishnah and Related Texts

Berakhot 2:8	122	7:2	182	8:4	700
Peah 3:9	554	8:5	327	Abodah Zarah 2:9	
Terumot 6:1	135	8:6	231		699
Ḥallah 1:7	343	10:2	125	Abot 1:8	229
Orlah 3:3	327	Baba Meṣi'a 1:1	80,476		
		1:5	303	Keritut 1:3	697
Roš Haššanah 1:3	110	3:3	432	2:4	45,697
Šeqalim 4:3	555	4:9	509	Bekhorot 1:7	290, 193
Ta'anit 4:8	81	7:1	277		
		7:8	428	3:1	706
Yebamot 10:15	42	7:13	432	6:8	686
14:2	244	7:14	402	7:6	362,365
Soṭah 5:1	13	Baba Batra 1:10	511	8:1	711
Giṭṭin 4:1	63,67	4:2	589	8:7	33,35
4:4	65,108	8:5	402	Middot 3:4	667
4:7	356	10:2	80	Arakhin 6:1	516
5:1	184,554	Šebuot 6:3	576	6:2	393
5:2	446	6:6	279,380		
5:3	531	8:1	428	Ahilut 7:7	683
7:3	699,700	Sanhedrin 1:1	200, 201	Makhširim 6:5	666
Qiddušin 1:1	206			Niddah 5:4	40
1:5	582	1:2	200	9:11	28
2:6	246	7:15	168		
3:14	520	8:6	204	Semaḥot 1:13	631
		Idiut 2:2	618	14:7	249
Baba Qama 3:9	593	3:6	146		
4:1	483	5:7	618	Damascus Document	
5:1	77	8:2	116		343,506,714

Tosephta

Ševi'it 3:10	620	7:1	333,334	10:9	161
5:22	331	7:4	340	10:10	160
		7:6	341		
Yebamot 14:1	89	7:7	348,349	Arakhin 3:8	271
Ketubot 1:1	13,16,	7:8	354,356	Bekhorot 1:9	689
	23	7:9	360,362	6:17	480
1:3	38,40	7:10	364		
1:4	27,46	7:11	369	Tahorot 2:5	610
1:6	62,63	8:1	376,377	2:8	610
2:1	91,96	8:3	386	6:2	74
2:2	89	9:2	408	Niddah 1:1	605
2:3	108	10:1	463,464	1:3	609
3:1	109	10:5	598	1:8	637,638
3:3	120,124	11:1	504	1:9	610,634
3:4	146	11:3	516	1:10	623
3:7	159	12:3	551,552,553	2:1	629
3:8	167	12:4	561,583,584	2:3	275,630
4:2	209	12:5	596	2:5	274
4:5	227,228	12:6	33,598	2:8	648
4:7	254	13:4	306	3:8	614,659
4:8	212	Nedarim 6:7	269	3:11	670,671,673
4:9	217	Qiddušin 1:7	497	4:3	683
4:14	251	5:2	65	4:6	699
4:17	235			4:9	700
5:1	257,260,264	Baba Qama 4:7	174	4:10	693,694
5:4	273	9:8	177	4:11	693
5:6	280,190	9:9	178	4:12	691
5:7	289	Baba Meṣi'a 1:10	171	4:13	706
5:8	298	3:1	432	4:17	663
6:3	318,319	Baba Batra 8:4	417,	9:5	612
6:7	315		418	9:7	642
6:9	321	Sanhedrin 6:5	91	9:8	642,643
6:10	324	10:8	168		

Midrashim

Gen. rabba 45, 283,284,287,341,369,5 06,558,596
Lev. rabba 17,506

Ruth rabba 24,25
Threni rabbati 556
Eccl. rabba 52
Midraš Samuel 620

Šoḥer Tob 52
Mekhilta dR. Ismael,
Mišpaṭim 132
150,152,174,195,282,3

Mekhilta 79, 438,599	174,195,269,282,438	150,152,158,160,191,1
	Sifra 181,678,689	92,195,197,205,382
Mekhilta dR. Simeon bar Ioḥai, Mišpaṭim 150,	Sifry Num. 52,402, 711	Pirqe R. Eliezer 24
	Sifry Deut.	Tanna dbe Eliahu 506

Rabbinic Literature

Arukh 228,693	423,433,482,499	11,187, 246
Or Zarua 695	Šulḥan Arukh Even Ha'ezer	Yalqut Šim'oni 24,52, 506
Otzar he-Geonim 65		
Sefer Ha'iṭṭur 96,126		

Index of Greek, Latin, and Hebrew Words

ἀναφορά	487	παράφερνα	290	χαράκωμα	115
		πίστις	94		
διατάγματα	451	πλατεῖα	71	annona	487
		πολύπους	367		
ἐπίτροπος	62,427	πρόθυρος	661	capillamentum	345
ἐτόλμησεν	369	πρόσοδος	661	capillitium	345
εὐθέως	651	πύξινον	369		
				svetum	604
ἡγεμών	52	ῥέω	369		
				חופה	11
θεμελίωσις	247	σάνδαλον	695	חלט	552
θησαυριστής	506	στατήρ	286		
		στρατιώτης	52	כתובה	1
καθέδρα	272	σῶμα	369		
κασαυρεῖον	103			עונה	282
κῆρυξ	451	τρικλίνιον	211		
κοιτών	216	τροπαϊκόν	286	פרא	319
κρήνη	68	τρυγητής	28		
				קצצה	312
λῃστής	116	ὑμέναια	22		
				ריטל	295
μάγειρος	52	φερνή	239,304		
		φιάλη	673	שאר	282
ὁμολογία	455	φόρημα	22	שוחרא	479
				שקיעין	487

Author Index

Abramson, S.	350	
Alfassi	248,274,308,347, 348,351,357,385,417,421, 476,511,514,591	
Asaph, S.	351	
Ashkenazy, B.	366,435	
Aumann, R.J.	476	
Balinski, M.	476	
Crescas, H.	30	
Epstein. J. N.	250,313, 318,337,371,446,449,641	
Feldman, A. L.	30	
Finkelstein, L.	195	
Fleischer H.L.	631	
Fraenckel, D.	48,178,179	
Francus, I.	423,476	
Fränkel-Teomim, B.	188	
Friedman, M. A.	291,309, 312,314,419,440,470	
Gerondi, Nissim	30, 239, 347,357,511,533,591	
Gordianus III	363	
Grätz, H.	369	
Guggenheimer, E.	319,604, 631	
Guggenheimer, H.	25,71,313, 319,604,622,631,665,694	
Ḥabiba, Y.	351	
Herschler, M.	308	
Iehiel b. Asher, Rosh	237,238,292,408,412,422, 423,529,562	
Josephus	299
Justinian	483
Katzenellenbogen, M.H.	476
Lieberman, S.	13,39,52, 91,210,254,295,312,313, 374,487,519
Longworth, Ph.	622
Maimonides	188,318, 338,365,382,406,562,597, 684
Margalit, M.	39,312,468 516,608,609
Maschler, M.	476
Menaḥem b. Aaron	254
Musaphia, B.	94,117,506
Naḥmanides	24,188, 348,417,511,562
Petaḥia of Regensburg	254
Qimḥi, D.	604
Rabbinovicz, R.	418
Rashba	394
Rashi	393,421,514,517, 531,604,671,682,690
Rosanes, J.	406
Saadya Gaon	475
Schepansky, I.	14,292
Sforno, O.	22
Slucker, J. D.	394
Sperber, D.	35,363,502
Taubenschlag, R.	2,224,451
Weill, N.	238
Ziani, E.R.	292

Subject Index

Abortion	708	By possession	265	*Antoninianus*	363
Absent payor	449	Adolescent	127	*Asmakhta*	269
Acquisition	423	Adult	20	Assigned bride	192
Act of	255	Agent for sin	197		
By heirs	471	Aging	363	Bankruptcy	6,

INDICES

	462,475, 583	Courtyard, common			699,700
Classes	462,463		344	Forced	
Compromises	488	Criminal, underage		244,279,292,334,336,337,	
Bastard	60		203		523
marriage	129			For infidelity	291,350
Bet se'ah	511	Damage claims, inherited		Irrevocable	357
Birds, kosher	712		183	Undocumented	102
Birth, extended	701,704	Damages, assessment		*Dotalicium*	244
multiple	708,709		164,165	Double punishment	
Blood virgin	620	by animals	77,483		135,137,140,200
Blood, impure	664	For underage children		Doubt, single or double	
Book Yerushalmi	692		178,179		14
Burden of proof		Mutual	593	Dough widow	65
	21,54,56,60,77,586	Payment		Dowry	305
Burial costs	209,436		171,175,203	Claim of	
		Danger, time of	13		235,245,248
Calumniator	188	Daughter's earnings		Credit for	307,310
Cancellation of debts			183	Inflated value	309
	184	rights	181	In kind	307
Ceasarean section		renunciation		Of daughters	321
	697		236	Of orphan girl	315,316
Chattel mortgage	394	sustenance	570	Real estate	310
Child support	213	privileged		Recommended	230
Child, as person	708		573,574	Dowry, Return of	419
Child, illegitimate		Daughters' dowry,			
	112,114	limitations	277	"Eating"	285
Chimera	687	Dead-end street	344	Emancipation by marriage	
Claims, admitted partially		Deaf-mute	38		186
	576,581	Dedications	393	Equal cut	151,157
Consolidated	581	Conditions	267	Error, reversible	422
Inherited	184	Of futures	266	Esaw	52
Real estate	582	Of slaves	271	Estate, appraisal	572
Unenforceable	589	Redemption	393,510	Value	573
Clipping	124	Defects, disqualifying		Eulogies	120
Coins, *seqel*	33		352,360,364,366	Evidence, *prima facie*	
Tyrian	33	Definiteness, principle			62,68,353
Concubine	254		622		
Confession, civil	171	Denar, gold and silver		False oath, sacrifice for	
criminal	171,173		475,502		173
Cooling-off period		Discharge, not menstrual		Fate	546
	333		613	Father's rights	177
Court session, on Friday		Divorce settlement, wife's		Fetus, human character	
	18	fault	348		705,708
Court summons	451	Divorce, after death		Field of pieces	120

Field, access lost 586,587	Hermaphrodite 609,709	Intercalation, in Babylonia
Field, flood damaged	Herod 65	107
21,353	Hippos, city of 97	Investment power 410
Firstborn, Claim of	House of Hille, chronology	Journeymen's contract
235	699	277,281
inheritance 184	Husband, as administrator	Jubilee 467
Firstborn, for inheritance	208	
711	Rights and duties	*Ketubah* 1,32
Firstling, wool of 327	206,561	Additions 242
Flogging 159	duties, refused 329	Annulment 59
Food, Kosher 699		Biblical 599
Prepared in purity	Impurity, body fluids	By minor 461
610	681	Claim for partial
Sanctified 108	Bottom and Top	payment 437
Futures 269	713	Claim for payment
	By moving 613	420,441,448
Garden plot 511	In private domain	Claim limitation
Genital discharge,	605	550
Babylonian doctrine, 607	In public domain	Currency of payment
Sadducee doctrine	614	597
607	Of blood 682	Dating of 468
Pure 607	Of cadaver 706	Enforceable partially
Gibeonites 130,520	Of hands 399	532
Gift, testamentary	Of Gentiles 632	Enforcement 215
328	Of glass vessels	Foreclosure for payment
To the unborn 232	399	438
Gifts to daughters	Of menstruation	Immoral 225
562	603	Liquidation
Girl, pre-pubescent	Of metal 399	498,501,507
639	Of seat 613	Minimal 251,252
Good deed, indemnity for	Of stillbirth 696	Oath required 485
565	Preparation for 666	Of male children
Good-faith document	Retroactive 603,610	229,465,466, 470,472
94	Incest, rabbinical 520	Of minor 457
	Inheritance, from childless	Payment conventions
Hadrianic decrees	wife 314	474
453	From wife	Payment of
Ḥazaqah 265	314,382,383,402,415	235,312,314
Heave 260	Levir's 390,395	Rabbinic 35,233
Impure retroactively	Of daughters 321	Sale of 503
612	Of firstborn 469,473	Stipulations 224,241
Hebrew slave, female	Sale of future 417	Kidnap victim, priestly
166,167	Institutions of Usha	226,228
Heirs, intestate 76	214	Ransom 226,227

Land of Israel, preference 597	*Me'ilah* 393	
Coins of 599	Mina, Babylonian 21	*Qab* 292
Larceny, of Temple property 510	Greek 21	
	Minor girl, biblical marriage 347	Rape victim, fatherless 132
Law, Egyptian 2	Non-biblical marriage 347	Status of 70 ff.,89
Hellenic 2		Rape, fine for 128,147,148,161
Lessee, responsibility of 432	Minors, Acts to detriment of 307	Payment for suffering 154
Levirate 261,262	MMT text 611	
Liability, degrees of 428,433	Money in dispute 80	Statutory 14,48,169,170
Living with a snake 342.427	Negative proof, impossible 618	Rapist's fine collection of 164
Loan, not mortgaged 225	Nursing baby 275	Real estate, acquisition 246
	Oath, biblical 80,99	Claims 380
Manumission 174	Of heirs 442,444	Quality 446
Marital duties 279,284	Of partial claim 439	Restriction, Superimposed 265
Refusal of 285,290,330	Rabbinical 439,441	Resurrection 535,536,544
Marriage, Cohen's 265	Obligation towards minors 526	*Rotl* 259
Conditional 359,360	on third part 583	Rules, biblical 287,292
Contractual 224,584	Orphan girl, marriage 519	Sabbath boundary 120
Definitive 11,211	Overcharge 509,514	
Gift, informal 245,247,249	Parcels, minimal 511	Sacrifice, expiation 645
Made in Heaven 17	Perjurer 194,200	purification 645
Multiple simultaneous 246,264	Perjury, punishment 123	Sales between spouses 409
Of virgin 642	*Peruṭah* 245,246	Samaritans 131,713
On Sabbath 10	Place of residence 594,595	Schooling, mandatory 398
Preliminary 14	Plural 665	Seas of the Land 548
Prohibitions, general 520	Practice 62	Second mortgage 490
priestly 520	Presumptive state 46,265	Seduction, fine for 128
secondary 347	Priest, in rebuilt Temple 109	Separation of properties 331,401,403, 404,405
Termination of 291	*Prozbol* 453	Inheritance 414
Time of 256	Public sale 514,516	*Šeqel*, biblical 33
Martha bat Boethos 297	Public use of private land 587	
Medical expenses 227		

Sex act, definition 45
Sexless 609,709
She-ram 347,520
Signatures, certified 89,91,92,93,95
Slave girl, marriage 129,130
Slave, Canaanite 303
  Hebrew 303
Slaves, sexual relations 32
Soil, virgin 620
Spinning flax 278
Squatter's right 84,122
Stipulation, against biblical laws 402
  Money matters 412
  Of wives 404
Stipulation, for rape victim 155
  for seduced woman 155,156
Stipulations, implicit 531
Stoning, place of 205
Support, of daughter 235
  Of parents 214
  Of widow 214
Sustenance 529
  Oath of 560
Swarming bees 125
Sycamore, virgin 620
Syria 110

Tabitha Dorkas 631

Testimony, contradictory 85
  Negative 103
  Of adult about his youth 121,123,125
  Of minor 120,634
  Spontaneous 118
  Unchangeable 91,585
  Uncorroborated 83,105
  Validity 513
  Weight of 98
Thief, fine of 182
Tithes, levitic 110
Title guarantee 531
Tree sap 618

Underage sex 41
Unruly son 204

Violation, prosecutable 198
Vows, annulation 274

Water, purifying 611
Wedding feast 16
Welfare limits 315
Weregilt 174
Widow's dwelling 238
  Support 240,414,492
Wife's Acquisitions 303
  Duties 272,277,278,296
  Earnings 300
  New garments 283

Paraphernalia 384,385,388,406,418
Property 370,378
  husband's administration 374,381
  husband's interest 371,377
Provisions 294
Social standing 277
Support 301
  after divorce 305
Twice married 457,460
Vows 354,374
Wine 298
Wife, husband's agent 427,428,433,436
Husband's executor 435
Lying 343
Unsupported 446,452
Wills, 231,232,251,563
  Beneficiaries 327
  Executors 324
  Formulas of 326
  Multigenerational 418
Witness, disqualified 89
  Single 437
Witnesses, warning of 202
Woman Lecturer 254
Woman's anatomy 661

Zavah 622

www.ingramcontent.com/pod-product-compliance
Lightning Source LLC
Chambersburg PA
CBHW031841220426
43663CB00006B/460